James Orchard Halliwell-Phillipps, Charles Knight

The Complete Works of Shakespeare

From the original text: carefully collated and compared with the editions of

Halliwell, Knight, and Colloer: with historical and critical introductions, and notes to

each play; and a life of the great dramatist

James Orchard Halliwell-Phillipps, Charles Knight

The Complete Works of Shakespeare
From the original text: carefully collated and compared with the editions of Halliwell, Knight, and Colloer: with historical and critical introductions, and notes to each play; and a life of the great dramatist

ISBN/EAN: 9783337067298

Printed in Europe, USA, Canada, Australia, Japan

Cover: Foto ©Thomas Meinert / pixelio.de

More available books at **www.hansebooks.com**

THE

COMPLETE WORKS

OF

SHAKESPEARE,

FROM THE ORIGINAL TEXT:

CAREFULLY COLLATED AND COMPARED WITH THE EDITIONS OF

HALLIWELL, KNIGHT, AND COLLIER:

WITH HISTORICAL AND CRITICAL INTRODUCTIONS, AND NOTES TO EACH PLAY;

AND

A LIFE OF THE GREAT DRAMATIST,

BY CHARLES KNIGHT.

Illustrated

WITH NEW AND FINELY EXECUTED STEEL ENGRAVINGS CHIEFLY PORTRAITS
IN CHARACTER OF CELEBRATED AMERICAN ACTORS, DRAWN
FROM LIFE, EXPRESSLY FOR THIS EDITION.

HISTORICAL PLAYS.

NEW YORK:
JOHNSON, WILSON AND COMPANY,
27 BEEKMAN STREET.

CONTENTS.

𝔥istorical 𝔭lays.

General Introduction

TO THE

Historical Plays of Shakespeare.

BY JAMES ORCHARD HALLIWELL.

THE historical dramas of Shakespeare, although separately they are examples of his high dramatic art, are so connected with one another, it appeared preferable to unite our observations upon them into one Introduction, rather than make discursive notes upon each; and, by this arrangement, we shall be better enabled to place the poet's continuity of design in a clearer point of view. It is obvious that the subject will readily admit of unnatural expansion, and, indeed, scarcely a single Editor escapes falling into the temptation of mixing historical discussion with his observations on these plays; but this is unquestionably a course that may be better dispensed with; for Shakespeare merely adopted the statements of the English chronicles without any hesitation, or, if differing from them, only in cases where tradition or popular sources had furnished him with other versions, in the same way that, in his Comedies, he availed himself of contemporary novels. The object was to turn these chronicles into regular historical dramas. It is, therefore, quite idle to refer to the authentic data of history in opposition to the pictures of the times recorded by the great dramatist.

The first in order of the historical plays, *King John*, was founded on an earlier drama called "The first and second part of the troublesome Reign of John, King of England," which was first published in 1591. Shakespeare probably wrote his play shortly after that year, but no quarto edition of it is known to exist, and it is first mentioned by Meres in the year 1598. It is worthy of remark, that much of the ridicule against the monks and nuns in the older play has been altogether omitted by Shakespeare, who has, in fact, generally improved the incidents; but no comparison can be instituted between the two pieces.

King John was not printed till the folio of 1623 made its appearance. The next play in order, *Richard the Second*, was printed no less than four times during the author's life; first in 1597, under the title of, "The Tragedie of King Richard the Second, as it hath beene publikely acted by the Right Honourable the Lorde Chamberlaine his servants: London, Printed by Valentine Simmes for Andrew Wise, and are to be sold at his shop in Paules Church-yard at the signe of the Angel." This edition does not contain that portion of the fourth act in which Richard is introduced to make the surrender of his crown, which first appeared in the quarto of 1608, which is entitled, "The Tragedie of King

623

Richard the Second, *with new additions of the Parliament sceene, and the Deposing of King Richard,* as it hath been lately acted by the Kinges Majesties servantes at the Globe.' Mr. Knight seems to be of opinion that there are sufficient similarities between the story of *Richard the Second,* as related in Daniel's 'Civil Warres,' 1595, and Shakespeare's plays, to warrant the belief either that the poem of Daniel was known to Shakespeare, or that the play of Shakespeare was known to Daniel; but the coincidences he has pointed out are scarcely strong enough to warrant such a conclusion.

The next plays in order, the two parts of *Henry IV.,* are unquestionably the most original of Shakespeare's historical dramas; or, in other words, to avoid ambiguity, he was not so deeply indebted in those two plays to the labours of previous dramatists. We recognise in them the forms only of the old compositions; and they have undergone so complete a transformation, in passing through his hands, that little else than the title and general character can be traced. These still remain in an old play entitled "The famous victories of King Henry the Fifth," which has been satisfactorily proved to have been written before the year 1588. The connexion which exists between a character in that production, Sir John Oldcastle, and Shakespeare's ever-famous fat knight, is a subject to which I wish to draw the particular attention of the reader. I propose to discuss, and I hope I shall be able satisfactorily to set at rest a question which has arisen, grounded on a tradition of no earlier date than the commencement of the eighteenth century, whether Shakespeare in the first instance borrowed the name as well as amplified the character of the above-mentioned nobleman, who is so highly distinguished in the history of the reformed religion. This question does not in any way affect the fame of Shakespeare. It may be good policy to premise this, for I observe with regret that there are many readers of our immortal poet's works who, without a knowledge of the subject, despise the literature and criticism which have set the emanations of his genius in their true historical light, and who are also greatly averse to the idea of accusing Shakespeare of being indebted to previous writers for any portion of the material on which he has founded his dramas. I am now alluding to the general reader, and not to those who, with a competent knowledge of contemporary literature, have made it a matter of study. Among the numerous readers of Shakespeare with whom I have had the fortune to converse, I have never yet found one who did not consider him, in the words of an author who ought to have known better, as "the great poet whom nature framed to disregard the wretched models that were set before him, and to create a drama from his own native and original stores." The real fact is, that no dramatist ever made a freer use of those "wretched models" than Shakespeare. It may safely be said that not a single plot of any of his dramas is entirely his own. It is true that the sources of some of his plays have not yet been discovered, but they are those that we know he would not have invented, leaving the capability of doing so out of the question. There can, at any rate, be no doubt that all the historical plays which are ascribed to Shakespeare were on the stage before his time, and that he was employed by the managers to remodel and repair them, taking due care to retain the names of the characters, and preserve the most popular incidents. In two parts of *Henry IV.,* as I have observed above, he has so completely repaired the old model, that they may almost be considered in the light of original dramas. I can scarcely imagine a more interesting subject for literary enquiry than the tracing out the originals of these plays, and the examination of the particular *loci* where the master-hand of Shakespeare has commenced his own labours; yet it is a study so inadequately encouraged, and so little valued, that few have the courage to enlist in its cause. The public appear to consider it an obstacle, rather than otherwise, to the free reading of his works, and wonder more especially what possible connexion there can be between literary history and romantic dramas. It was but recently that one of our most learned and acute critics in this way was pronounced a perfect barbarian—a savage without a poetical soul, because he fixed by historic wand the scene of Prospero's enchantments. The master-stroke of the photogenic art was thought unfavourable to the interests of true poetry, and a "local habitation and a name" incompatible with the nature of the theme. Surely, in common fairness, the "still-vex'd Bermoothes" ought to be expunged, and all the earthly concomitants deposited, like Lampedusa, in ethereal uncertainty.

But do we, as Mr. Hunter asks, by researches such as these, lose any particle of the admiration in which we hold Shakespeare? If the positive be maintained, there is at least a satisfaction in knowing what is the real fact; and there is a love of truth, as well as a love of Shakespeare, and a homage due

624

to both. A careful historian would pause, no matter how strong the evidence was, before he would attribute to any genius, however vast, the mighty revolutions in poetry or science which are vulgarly ascribed to Shakespeare. The labours of successive, or more rarely, combined minds, alone are able to accomplish such things. When Pope said—

> Nature and Nature's laws lay hid in night :
> God said, "Let Newton be," and all was light !

he expressed himself very eloquently ; and the opinion implied in the couplet has become a popular dogma. But Newton owed as much to Kepler as Shakespeare did to Marlowe ; and Coleridge could not have been far wrong when he extended the weight of those obligations even beyond the boundary usually adopted by professed critics. In plain words, Shakespeare did not invent—he perfected a drama already ennobled by the labours of others ; and the history of that drama forms a very curious and important epoch in our vernacular literature.

Plays were ascribed to Plautus, if we may believe Aulus Gellius, which he only retouched and polished. They were, to use his own expression, *retractatæ et expolitæ*. It was so also with Shakespeare ; but few now would be guilty of ascribing that "drum and trumpet" thing, called the "First Part of Henry VI., to his pen, written doubtlessly before he entered the arena of dramatic competition, though it may have been afterwards slightly revised by him. I can see little evidence or reason for including it in his works, but as it is inserted as a genuine play, I will take it as a document in the history of his historical dramas, rather than consider it to have any necessary connexion with them. To tax Shakespeare with the character of Fastolf, as exhibited in that play, is an absolute libel on his genius. Who indeed can reasonably accuse him of introducing the same character in *Henry VI.*, whose death he had described in *Henry V.* in a manner so remarkable ? There is not, in fact, any ground for believing that the characters of Fastolf and Falstaff have any connexion whatever with each other. I much doubt whether Shakespeare even had the former in his memory, when he changed the name, as I shall afterwards show, of Oldcastle to Falstaff ; and I think it extremely probable that the latter name might have been inserted merely for the purpose of marking one of the principal traits in his character.

Yet we find historians and journalists constantly giving countenance to this vulgar error, and Fastolf is mentioned as the prototype of Falstaff with as much positiveness as though he were an actual original of a genuine historical character. Mr. Beltz, in his recent work on the Order of the Garter, and a reviewer of that book in a literary journal of high pretensions, have fallen into the same error. The point is of importance, because it affects a good deal of our reasoning on the sources of Shakespeare's most celebrated historical plays ; and we are surprised to find so many writers of reputation giving their authority to the common mistake.

This leads us to old Fuller, who was one of the earliest delinquents. In speaking of Sir John Fastolf, he says :

To avouch him by many arguments valiant, is to maintain that the sun is bright, though since the stage hath been overbold with his memory, making him a *thrasonical puff*, and emblem of mock valour.

True it is, Sir John Oldcastle did first bear the brunt of the one, being made the make-sport in all plays for a coward. It is easily known out of what purse this black penny came ; the Papists railing on him for a heretick, and therefore he must also be a coward, though indeed he was a man of arms, every inch of him, and as valiant as any in his age.

Now as I am glad that Sir John Oldcastle is put out, so I am sorry that Sir John Fastolfe is put in, to relieve his memory in this base service, to be the anvil for every dull wit to strike upon. Nor is our comedian excusable by some alteration of his name, writing him Sir John Falstafe, and making him the property of pleasure for King Henry the Fifth to abuse, seeing the vicinity of sounds intrench on the memory of that worthy knight—and few do heed the inconsiderable difference in spelling of their names.

This extract from Fuller, a very credible writer, will of itself go a considerable way towards establishing the truth of Rowe's tradition ; but I have other and more important documents to introduce to the notice of the reader, by means of which I hope to be enabled to prove—

1. That the stage was in the possession of a rude outline of Falstaff before Shakespeare wrote either part of *Henry IV.*, under the name of Sir John Oldcastle.

2. That the name of Oldcastle was retained for a time in Shakespeare's *Henry IV.*, but changed to Falstaff before the play was printed.

3. That, in all probability, some of the theatres, in acting *Henry IV.*, retained the name of Oldcastle after the author had made the alteration.

4. That Shakespeare probably made the change before the year 1593.

I must leave the consideration of the first of these propositions, until I have examined the second, because in this case the similarity consists rather in the adoption of the same *dramatis personæ* and subject by Shakespeare and his predecessors, than in the manner in which they are treated. My first witness for the truth of the second problem, which, with the others, I hope to transform into theorems, is one whose veracity is unimpeachable, because he could have had no possible object in publishing an untruth—I mean Dr. Richard James, librarian to Sir Robert Cotton, a contemporary of Shakespeare, and an intimate friend of "rare" Ben Jonson. He may thus, through the latter dramatist, have had access to the very best sources of information for the account which he gives in the following dedicatory epistle, prefixed to his work entitled 'The Legend and Defence of the Noble Knight and Martyr, Sir John Oldcastle,' never published, but preserved with his other manuscripts in the Bodleian Library, and which undoubtedly is a most valuable independent testimony in favour of the truth of Rowe's tradition.

To my noble friend Sir Henrye Bourchier.

Sir Harrie Bourchier, you are descended of Noble Ancestrie, and in the dutie of a good man, love to heare and see faire reputation preserved from slander and oblivion. Wherefore to you I dedicate this edition of Ocleve, where sir John Oldcastell appeeres to have binne a man of valour and vertue, and onely lost in his own times because he would not cowe under the foule superstition of Papistrie, from whence in so great light of Gosple and learning that there is not yet a more universall departure is to me the greatest scorne of men. But of this more in another place, and in preface will you please to heare me that which follows. A young Gentle Ladie of your acquaintance, having read the works of Shakespeare, made me this question: How Sir John Falstaffe, or Fastolf, as it is written in the statute book of Maudlin Colledge in Oxford, where everye daye that societie were bound to make memories of his soule, could be dead in Harrie the Fift's time and againe live in the time of Harrie the Sixt to be banisht for cowardize? Whereto I made answere that this was one of those humours and mistakes for which Plato banisht all Poets out of his commonwealth, that sir John Falstaffe was in those times a noble valiant soldier, as apeeres by a book in the Herald's office dedicated vnto him by a herald who had binne with him if I well remember for the space of twenty-five yeeres in the French wars; that he seemes allso to have binne a man of learning because in a librarie of Oxford I finde a book of dedicating churches sent from him for a present vnto Bishop Wainflete and inscribed with his owne hand. That in Shakespeare's first show of Harrie the Fifth, the person with which he undertook to playe a buffone was not Falstaffe, but Sir John Oldcastle, and that offence beinge worthily taken by personages descended from his title, as peradventure by manie others also who ought to have him in honourable memorie, the poet was putt to make an ignorant shifts of abusing Sir John Falstophe, a man not inferior of virtue though not so famous in pietie as the other, who gave witnesse vnto the trust of our reformation with a constant and resolute martyrdom, vnto which he was pursued by the Priests, Bishops, Monks, and Friers of those dayes. Noble sir, this is all my preface. God keepe you, and me, and all Christian people from the bloodie designes of that cruel religion.

Yours in all observance

RICH. JAMES.

With respect to this important letter, it will be observed that, by the "first showe of Harrie the Fifth," James unquestionably means Shakespeare's *Henry IV.* He could not have confused Shakespeare's play with "The Famous Victories," for in the latter drama the *nomen* of the character of Oldcastle had not been altered. The "young gentle ladie" had read the *works* of Shakespeare, most probably the folio edition, and it is not at all likely she would have alluded to a play which had then been entirely superseded. James and his lady friend also confuse the characters of Fastolf and Falstaff, another example of the unfortunate circumstance of the poet choosing a name so similar to that of the real hero.

Dr. James died at the close of the year 1638, and consequently the work, from which I have quoted the letter given above, must have been composed either in Shakespeare's life-time, or shortly after his death. On a careful comparison of the handwriting with other of his papers which are dated, I came to the conclusion that 1625 was the year in which the manuscript was written. This, however, must not by any means be considered conclusive; but a few years either way are not of great consequence. I have not succeeded in discovering the date of Bourchier's death, the person to whom the dedicatory epistle is addressed, or I might perhaps have been enabled to compress the uncertain date within even narrower limits. I have said that Dr. James, whom Wood calls "a humourous person," was intimate with Ben Jonson. I derive my knowledge of this fact from the papers of the former in the Bodleian Library, but I was disappointed in my expectation of finding notices of other dramatists. Jonson is frequently spoken of in high terms, and in one letter particularly he receives the greatest compliment from James that one scholar could pay to another:—"*Jam partres illi libenter spectarent ingenium fœcundissimi Benjamini Jonsoni, quem, et Thuanus de Petro Ronsardo, censeo cum omni antiquitate comparandum, si compta et plena sensibus poemata ejus et scenica septemus.*" When Jonson's "Staple of News" was produced in 1625, the Doctor addressed him poetically in the following lines, which are here given from the same collection of manuscripts:—

To Mr. Benj. Johnson, on his Staple of Newes first presented.

Sir, if my robe and garbe were richly worth
The darlinge of a statutes comming forth,
Were I a man of law or law-maker,
Or man of courte to be an undertaker,
For judgment would I then comme in and say
The manye honours of your *staple* play:
But being nothing so, I dare not hide
The mightie floates of ignorance, who saile
With winde and tide,—their Sires, as stories tell,
In our eighth Harrie's time crown'd Skelton's Nell,
And the soule Bess of Whittington with greene
Bayes, which on living tronkes are rarelye seene,
Soone sprung, soone fading, but deserving verse,
Must take more lasting glorie from the herse;
When vulgars loose their sight, and sacred peeres
Of poetrie conspire to make your yeeres
Of memorie eternall, then you shal be read
By all our race of Thespians, board and bed,
And banke and boure, vallie and mountaine will
Rejoice to knowe somme pieces of your skill!
Your rich Mossaique workes, indeed by arte
And curious industry with everie parte
And choice of all the ancients, so I write,
Though for your sake I dare not say and fighte.

This brief digression from our immediate argument is not without its use, because it satisfactorily shows that Dr. James was acquainted with one of the leading men in the drama of the time, and of course renders his testimony on such a subject of more than ordinary value. I will now proceed to give other, though less important, authorities for the truth of my second proposition; and joined with those already placed before the reader's notice, they will be found, I think, sufficient to place that conclusion beyond a doubt.

My first extract is from a tract entitled "The Meeting of Gallants at an Ordinarie, or the Walkes in Powles," 4to. London, 1604. The only known copy of this work is in Malone's collection in the Bodleian Library; some gallants are "entering into the ordinarie," when the following dialogue takes place between one of them and the "fatte hoste:"—

Host. What, Gallants, are you come! are you come! welcome, gentlemen; I have newes enough for ye all; welcome againe; and againe: I am so fatte and pursie, I cannot speake loude enough, but I am sure you heare mee, or you shall heare me: Welcome, welcome, Gentlemen! I haue Tales, and Quailes for you; seate yourselues, Gallantes; enter Boyes and Beardes, with dishes and Platters; I will be with you againe in a trice ere you looke for me.

Sig. Shuttlecocke. Now, Signiors, how like you mine Host? did I not tell you he was a madde round knaue, and a merrie one too : and if you chaunce to talke of fatte Sir John Old-castle, he will tell you he was his great grandfather, and not much vnlike him in Paunch, if you marke him well by all descriptions ; and see where hee appeares againe. Hee told you he would not be longe from you; let this humour haue scope enough, I pray, and there is no doubt but his Tales will make vs laugh ere we be out of our Porridge.

This merely shows that Sir John Oldcastle had been represented somewhere or other as a fat man, but I know of no existing account of any such representation, unless the supposition of the identity between Falstaff and Oldcastle be correct. My next extract is to the same effect, and is taken from a pamphlet entitled "The Wandering Jew telling Fortunes to Englishmen," 4to. Lond. 1640, p. 38, which was certainly written before the year 1630. The character Glutton is speaking :—

A chaire, a chaire, sweet master Jew, a chaire. All that I say is this,—I 'm a fat man. It has been a West Indian voyage for me to come reeking hither. A kitchen-stuffe wench might pick up a living by following me for the fat which I loose in stradling. I doe not live by the sweat of my browe, but am almost dead with sweating. I eate much, but can talke little. Sir John Oldcastle was my great-grandfather's father's uncle,—I come of a huge kindred! And of you desire to learne whether my fortune be to die a yeare or two hence, or to grow bigger, if I continue as I doe in feeding, for my victuals I cannot leave. Say, say, merciful Jew, what shall become of me !

Again I have recourse to Fuller, who, in another work, repeats what he said before, but asserting more distinctly that the character of Falstaff was *substituted* for that of Oldcastle :—

Stage poets haue themselues been very bold with, and others very merry at, the memory of Sir John Oldcastle, whom the haue fancied a boon companion, a jovial royster, and yet a coward to boot contrary to the credit of all chronicles, owning him a martial man of merit. The best is Sir John Falstaffe hath relieved the memory of Sir John Oldcastle, and of late is substituted buffone in his place, but it matters as little what petulant poets as what mallcious Papists haue written against him.

In 'Amends for Ladies,' 4to. Lond. 1639, a play by Nathaniel Field, which according to Mr. Collier, could not have been written before 1611, Falstaff's description of honour is mentioned by a citizen of London as if it had been delivered by Sir John Oldcastle :—

————I doe heare
Your Lordship this faire morning is to fight,
And for your honour. Did you never see
The play wheere the fat knight, hight Oldcastle,
Did tell you truely what this honour was ?

This single passage will alone render my third proposition highly probable, *viz.*, that some of the theatres, in acting *Henry IV.*, retained the name of Oldcastle after the author had altered it to that of Falstaff.

Early in the year 1600 appeared 'The first part of the true and honourable history of the Life of Sir John Oldcastle, the good Lord Cobham, as it hath bene lately acted by the Right Honourable the Earle of Nottingham Lord High Admiral of England, his servants. Written by William Shakespeare,' 4to. Lond. The name of the author is supposititious, and now it is a matter of wonder how so glaring an imposition could have been suffered to pass unpunished, and even unnoticed. Such works were then of much less moment than they are now. Bodley, who was then forming his collection, classes plays under the head of " riffe raffes," and declares "they shall never come into mie librarie." It is possible, however, that Shakespeare may have edited this play, but, if he allowed his name to be put on the title-page, it shows a carelessness for his own reputation, of which there are but too many instances. The speech of Lord Cobham (Sir John Oldcastle) to the King, at p. 27, may confirm my conjecture.

My gracious lord, unto your majesty,
Next nnto my God, I owe my life ;
And what is mine, either by nature's gift,
Or fortune's bounty, all is at your service ;

> But for obedience to the pope of Rome,
> I owe him none; nor shall his shaveling priests
> That are in England, alter my belief.
> If out of Holy Scripture they can prove
> That I am in error, I will yield,
> And gladly take instruction at their hands :
> But otherwise, I do beseech your Grace
> My conscience may not be encroach'd upon.

These, I think, are the only lines in the whole play which could with any probability be ascribed to Shakespeare, and even they possess but slender claims. The prologue contains an argument for two of the propositions I have been endeavouring to establish. It is as follows :—

> The doubtful title (Gentlemen) prefixt
> Upon the argument we haue in hand,
> May breed suspense, and wrongfully disturbe
> The peacefull quiet of your settled thoughts :
> To stop which scruple, let this breefe suffice.
> It is no pamper'd glutton we present,
> Nor aged Councellour to youthfull sinne :
> But one, whose vertue shone aboue the rest,
> A valiant Martyr, and a vertuous Peere,
> In whose true faith and loyalty exprest
> Unto his Soueraigne, and his countries weale
> We strive to pay that tribute of our loue
> Your fauours merit : Let faire Truth be grac'd,
> Since forg'd inuention former time defac'd.

If we now turn to the following scene in the same play, we shall find that the change in the name of Shakespeare's knight must have been made about the same time. The king in disguise has just met with Sir John, the thieving parson of Wrotham, when this dialogue takes place :—

Priest. Stand, true man, says a thief.

King. Stand, thief, says a true man. How, if a thief?

Priest. Stand, thief, too.

King. Then, thief or true man, I must stand, I see. However the world wags, the trade of thieving yet will never down. What art thou?

Priest. A good fellow.

King. So am I too ; I see thou dost know me.

Priest. If thou be a good fellow, play the good fellow's part. Deliver thy purse without more ado.

King. I have no money.

Priest. I must make you find some before we part. If you have no money, you shall have ware, as many sound blows as your skin can carry.

King. Is that the plain truth?

Priest. Sirrah, no more ado. Come, come, give me money you have. Dispatch, I cannot stand all day.

King. Well, if thou wilt needs have it, there it is. Just the proverb, one thief robs another. Where the devil are all my old thieves? Falstaffe, that villaine, is so fat, he cannot get on 's horse ; but methinks I'oins and I'vto should be stirring herebouts.

Priest. How much is there on 't, of thy word?

King. A hundred pound in angels, on my word : the time has been I would have done as much for thee, if thou hadst past this way as I have now.

Priest. Sirrah, what art thou? Thou seemst a gentleman.

King. I am no less ; yet a poor one now, for thou hast all my money.

Priest. From whence camst thou?

King. From the court at Eltham.

Priest. Art thou one of the king's servants?

King. Yes, that I am, and one of his chamber.

Priest. I am glad thou'rt no worse. Thou mayst the better spare thy money ; and think thou mightst get a poor thief his pardon, if he should have need?

King. Yes, that I can.

Priest. Wilt thou do so much for me, when I shall have occasion?

King. Yes, faith, will I, so it be for no murder.

Priest. Nay, I am a pitiful thief. All the hurt I do a man, I take but his purse. I 'll kill no man.

King. Then of my word I 'll do it.

Priest. Give me thy hand of the same.

King. There 't is.

Priest. Methinks the king should be good to thieves, because he has been a thief himself, although I think now he be turn'd a true man.

King. Faith, I have heard he has had an ill name that way in 's youth ; but how canst thou tell that so has been thief?

Priest. How? Because he once robb'd me before I fell to the trade myself, when that villanous gate that led him to all that roguery was in 's company there, that Falstaff.

I next consider the internal evidence in Shakespeare's plays themselves that Oldcastle once supplied the place of Falstaff. Every one will remember the rout of Falstaff and his companions by the Prince and Poins, near Gadshill, when Henry triumphantly exclaims:—

> Got with much ease. Now merrily to horse.
> The thieves are scatter'd, and possess'd with fear
> So strongly, that they dare not meet each other ;
> Each takes his fellow for an officer.
> *Away, good Ned ; Falstaff sweats to death,*
> And lards the lean earth as he walks along.
> Were 't not for laughing, I should pity him.

It will be seen that in the fifth line a foot is actually deficient, and *Oldcastle*, instead of *Falstaff*, would perfectly complete the metre. It is true that some other explanation might be offered, perhaps equally plausible ; but it is at any rate a singular coincidence, that in the very first place where the name Falstaff occurs in the text, an additional syllable should be required.

In the second scene of the first act, Falstaff asks the Prince, " Is not my hostess of the tavern a most sweet wench ?" Prince Henry answers, " As the honey of Hybla, my *old lad of the castle*." I consider this to be a pun, in the original play as first written, on the name of *Sir John Oldcastle*. The commentators say this passage was transferred from the old play ; but, as Master Ford observes, " I cannot put off my opinion so easily." I am confirmed in my conjecture by a passage in the play of ' Sir John Oldcastle,' where there is a similar play upon words :—

> There 's one, they call him sir John Oldcastle,
> He has not his name for nought ; for like a castle
> Doth he encompass them within his walls.
> But till that castle be subverted quite,
> We ne'er shall be at quiet in the realm.

I now beg to call the reader's particular attention to a passage in Part 2. Act iii., scene 2, which affords undeniable proof that the name of Oldcastle once occupied the place which Falstaff now holds. Shallow is recalling reminiscences of his younger days, and he brings Falstaff in among other wild companions :

Then was Jack Falstaff, now sir John, a boy, and *page to Thomas Mowbray, duke of Norfolk.*

It was Sir John Oldcastle, and not Falstaff, who was page to that nobleman. Shakespeare could not have fallen into an error by following the older play, because the circumstance is not there mentioned ; and it would be arming oneself against the force of evidence, which already is so overpowering on the opposite side, to class this among Shakespeare's historical blunders. I do not consider it necessary in this place to multiply references to the old chroniclers, in support of my assertion, that the historical fact, to which Shakespeare alludes in this passage, applies to Oldcastle, and not to Falstaff. One will be sufficient, and I have selected the following extract from Weever's ' Poetical Life of Oldcastle.' 12mo., Lond. 1601, where he is introduced speaking in his own person :—

> Within the spring-tide of my flowing youth,
> He (the father) stept into the winter of his age ;
> Made meanes (Mercurius thus begins the truth)
> That I was made Sir Thomas Mowbrai's page.

Perhaps, however, the conclusion of the epilogue to the two plays furnishes us with the most decisive evidence that Shakespeare had delineated a character under the name of Oldcastle, which had given offence, confirming the tradition handed down to us by Rowe, and the relation given by Dr. James :—

One word more, I beseech you. If you be not too much cloyed with fat meat, our humble author will continue the story with Sir John in it, and make you merry with fair Katherine of France: where, for anything I know, Falstaff shall die of a sweat, unless already he be killed with your hard opinions; for Oldcastle died a martyr, and this is not the man.

It is unnecessary to pursue this subject further. The other notices I have collected are mere repetitions of what are given above, and add little weight to the general evidence. I have now only my fourth position to defend, for I shall pass over my first proposition, as a point already decided, with a reference to Mr. Collier's work on the English stage, who gives it as his opinion that Shakespeare was indebted for the "bare hint" of the delightful creation of Falstaff to the old play of "The Famous Victories," and nothing more.

There must of course be great uncertainty in fixing the precise date when Shakespeare made the alteration in the name of the character of his fat knight; and my conjecture on this point depends entirely upon my opinion on the date of the composition of another play—the *Merry Wives of Windsor*. Believing the first sketch of that play to have been written in the year 1593, the name of Oldcastle must have been changed to Falstaff before that sketch was written. Everything tends to prove this. For instance, the first metrical piece which occurs in it could not have been written with the former name:—

> And I to Ford will likewise tell
> How Falstaff, varlet vile,
> Would haue her love, his dove would prove,
> And eke his bed defile.

It may be objected that, as the *Merry Wives* has little or no necessary connexion with the historical plays—as we have no certain evidence to show whether it was written before or after the two parts of *Henry IV.*, the settlement of the question of names, if I may so express myself, in the former, is no guide whatever to the period at which the change was made in the other plays. In reply, I must confess this position is hypothetical, unless my readers agree with me in believing the *Merry Wives* to have been written after the Second Part of *Henry IV.*, and before *Henry V.*, a subject which it would be irrelevant to discuss in this place.

The First Part of *Henry IV.* was entered at Stationers' Hall on Feb. 25th, 1597-8, under the title of, "A booke intitled the Historye of Henry the iiijth, with his battaile at Shrewsburye against Henry Hottspure of the Northe, with the conceipted mirth of Sir John Falstaffe." Falstaff was the name, then, at least as early as the year 1597. After this period we have frequent allusions to the character. Ben Jonson, in the epilogue to "Every Man out of his Humour," acted in 1599, thus alludes to the "thrasonical puff:"—

> Marry, I will not do as Plautus in his *Amphytrio*, for all this; "*Summum Jovis causa plaudite*, beg a plaudite, for God's sake; but if you, out of the bounty of your good-liking, will bestow it, why you may in time make lean *Macilente as fat as Sir John Falstaff*.

I will give one more example of the Knight's popularity from Roger Sharpe's "More Fooles Yet," 4to., Lond. 1610 :—

> *In Virosum.*
> How Falstaffe like doth swell Virosus looke,
> As though his paunch did foster every sinne;
> And sweares he is injured by this booke,—
> His worth is taxt, he hath abused hym :
> Swell still, Virosus, burst with emulation,
> I neither taxe thy vice nor reputation.

It would not be difficult to multiply similar extracts. Mr. Collier has printed a document which shows how Falstaff was probably attired for the stage at this early period, which is attested by the creditable name of Inigo Jones. A character is to be dressed "*like* a Sir John Falstaff, in a roabe or russett, quite low, with a great belley, like a swolen man, long moustacheos, the shoows shorte, and out of them great toes, like naked feete: buskins to sheaw a great swolen leg." Thus it would seem that size has always been the prevailing characteristic of Falstaff's theatrical appearance. This consideration leads me to remark that the character of Oldcastle, as exhibited in "The Famous Victories," could not by itself have developed so popular and general a notion of "hugeness," as that suggested in the extracts I have given relative to him or Falstaff. On the whole, then, independently of the entire evidence being in its favour, I think the account given by Dr. James would be the most plausible conjecture we could form, were we without the aid of that evidence.

The only objection, as far as I can see, which can be raised against the veracity of Dr. James's account, is the slight discrepancy I have previously mentioned. My own faith is not at all shaken by this circumstance, because he was repeating from memory the doubts of another, as he had heard them in conversation, and was probably more solicitous of placing the question in a position to enable him to defend his hero Oldcastle, than of giving a correct version of what he considered an error in Shakespeare. I cannot think that he would have introduced Shakespeare in the manner in which he has, if he had not been pretty certain of the truth of the anecdote. Fastolf, too, was an Oxford man, and he resents his supposed degradation under the title of Falstaff. His successors were apparently impressed with the same notion. Warton tells us that the "magnificent knight, Sir John Falstaff, bequeathed estates to Magdalen College, part of which were appropriated to buy liveries for some of the senior scholars; but the benefactions in time yielding no more than a penny a week to the scholars who received the liveries, they were called, by way of contempt, *Falstaff's Buckram men.*" An anonymous and inedited poet of the early part of the seventeenth century, whose MS. works were formerly in the possession of Oldys, and are now in the valuable library of my friend, the Rev. Thomas Corser, complains sadly of Shakespeare for a similar reason:—

> Here to evince that scandal has been thrown
> Upon a name of honour, charactred
> From a wrong person, coward and buffoon;
> Call in your easy faiths, from what you've read
> To laugh at Falstaffe; as a humour fram'd
> To grace the stage, to please the age, misnam'd.
>
> No longer please yourselves to injure names
> Who lived to honour: if, as who dare breathe
> A syllable from Harry's choice, the fames,
> Conferr'd by princes, may redeem from death?
> Live Fastolfe then; whose trust and courage once
> Merited the first government in France.

Henry IV. was an extremely popular play from its first appearance, no less than five editions of it having been printed during the author's lifetime; and the only contemporary manuscript of any of Shakespeare's plays known to exist is a condensation of the two parts of *Henry IV.* made into one drama, for the convenience of representation before a private audience. This very curious relic was found in the archives of Sir Edward Dering, Bart., by the Rev. L. B. Larking, and Sir Edward very kindly lent it to me for several weeks. It contains very few readings of great importance, but as an unique Shakespearian relic it cannot be too highly estimated.

Henry V. was first surreptitiously published in the year 1600, under the title of, "The Chronicle History of Henry the Fift, with his battell fought at Agin Court in France: togither with Auntient Pistoll: as it hath been sundry times playd by the Right Honorable the Lord Chamberlaine his servants: London, Printed by Thomas Creede for Tho. Millington and John Busby." The author's name is not given, and Mr. Collier is of opinion that all the early editions in quarto were published entirely without the author's consent. They are very imperfect, compared with the amended play in the folio: but there can be little doubt that Shakespeare corrected and altered it, after its first composition. Mr. Collier considers that it was first produced in its original form in 1599, and that it was enlarged and amended in the form in which it is now read, shortly before 1605, early in which year it was performed before the court at Whitehall.

The first part of *Henry VI.* is generally considered to be only partially the work of Shakespeare, and I have previously avowed my disbelief of the right attribution of it to him as an entire work. It appears in the first folio, but beyond this circumstance, we can only judge of the matter by internal evidence. The second and third parts are found in their primitive form in an old play in two parts, called, "The Contention of the two famous houses of York and Lancaster," entered on the books of the Stationers' Company in 1602, as the 2nd and 3rd parts of *Henry VI.*, which is a mistake for the first and second parts of the "Contention;" and we accordingly find that when Blount and Jaggard, in 1623, inserted a list of Shakespeare's plays "as are not formerly entered to other men" they omitted the first and second parts of *Henry VI.*, and only inserted "The Thirde Parte of Henry the Sixt." In the same way, we find they did not insert "King John" in the same list, although there is no reason to suppose that any copy of that play in its present form had previously been entered. The probable inference is, that the list was hastily compiled from the previous entries Millington, it appears, kept possession of the "Whole Contention," as Pavier afterwards called it, till 1602. There seems something mysterious in the words, "*salvo juris cujuscumque*," which occur in the entry above mentioned; and it may be asked why Pavier kept them so long without a republication, as they were not reprinted till 1619. The entry is, however, important, for it clearly shows that, as early as 1602, the present title of "Henry VI." had superseded the older one. These two plays are, I believe, the *First Sketches* of the Second and Third Parts of *Henry VI.*; but it is a question with the critics whether Shakespeare was their author, or whether he merely borrowed from some older dramatist.

The external evidence is in favour of Malone's theory, that Shakespeare was *not* the author of them. They appear to have been, as I have said, in the hands of Millington till 1602, and they were then transferred to Pavier, who retained them till 1626. Millington and Pavier managed between them to monopolize nearly the whole of Shakespeare's disputed plays. Thus Millington had the "First Part of the Contention," the "Chronicle History," and the "True Tragedie," which he transferred to Pavier in 1600 and 1602. In addition to these, Pavier also had "Sir John Oldcastle," "Titus Andronicus," "The Yorkshire Tragedy," "The Puritan," and "Pericles," all of which seem to be suspicious plays, to say the least of them. Again: Millington, who published these plays in 1594, 1595, and 1600, did not put the name of Shakespeare to them, though it would have been for his advantage to have done so. After the year 1598, none of the undisputed plays of Shakespeare were published without having his name conspicuously inserted on the title, and only three were ever published without his name, two in 1597, and one in 1598, although, between the years 1598 and 1655, forty-four quarto editions appeared with the authorship clearly announced. In 1600, when Millington published the two parts of the "Contention" without Shakespeare's name, six undisputed plays were published with his name, and seven disputed plays without; but Pavier was afterwards bolder, and out of the twenty-four editions of the disputed plays published between the years 1591 and 1635, we find eight with Shakespeare's name. This, however, was after 1609. The probability, therefore, is, that the first part of the "Contention," and the "True Tragedy," were published piratically, and altogether without Shakespeare's authority, if he had any share in them. In 1626, Pavier assigned to Edward Brewster and Robert Bird his right in the disputed plays, and we hear again of the two parts of the "Contention," for the last time, on November 8th, 1630, as "Yorke and Lancaster," when they were assigned to Richard Cotes by Mr. Bird and consent of a full court.

The first edition of the "True Tragedy of Richard Duke of York," as the second part of the "Contention" was originally called, does not appear to have been entered at Stationers' Hall, and it is probable that there is a secret history attached to its publication that remains to be unravelled. The first thing that strikes us is its title, and the reason why it was not published as the "Second Part of the Contention" till 1619. The title-page affirms it to contain "the *whole* Contention." Could this have been done for the purpose of deception? We may, however, infer that the amended plays appeared after 1595, and before 1602, or it is probable that the old titles would not have been retained. Perhaps, however, the same argument holds with respect to the edition of 1600, and this would place the date of the amended plays within a very narrow compass. There are some reasons for thinking that the Third Part of *Henry VI.*, in the form in which we now have it, was written before 1598, as, in one of the stage directions in the first folio, we have Gabriel, an actor, introduced, who, according to Mr. Collier, was killed by Ben Jonson in the September of that year. The Third Part of *Henry VI.* also introduces Sinklo, another actor, in a similar manner, who performed in Tarlton's play of the "Seven Deadly Sins," and who probably, therefore, did not survive the year 1598. It is reasonable to suppose that the editors of the first folio used copies transcribed when those actors performed.

The constant offences against grammar which occur in these early copies may perhaps be another proof that they were not published by authority, and, indeed, very little doubt can be entertained of the fact that Pavier's copies of the older plays were piratically published, and Shakespeare's name was *for the first time* appended to them in 1619, and not in 1600, probably because the poet was not alive to protect his interests, and in the latter case because he did not acknowledge them for his own.

I will now place before the reader certain evidences before unnoticed, which lead me to think that neither Malone, nor Knight, nor Collier, are exactly right in the results to which they have arrived concerning the authorship of the Second and Third Parts of *Henry VI.*

In a literary point of view, the first edition of the "First Part of the Contention" is far more valuable than the first edition of the "True Tragedy;" and considering that both are in the same library, it seems rather strange that Mr. Knight should have collated the Second Part, and left the more valuable copy. Perhaps, however, this remark is not necessary; nor should I have alluded to the circumstance, had not Mr. Knight written so extensively concerning these plays, that a reasonable doubt might be raised as to where new evidences, properly so called, could exist. To proceed. In the two first editions of "The First Part of the Contention," 1594 and 1600, act i., scene 2, we read :—

> This night when I was laid in bed, I dreampt that
> This, my staff, mine office-badge in court,
> Was broke in two, and on the ends were plac'd
> The heads of the Cardinal of Winchester,
> And William de la Poole, first duke of Suffolk.

This speech, in the edition of 1619, the only one used by Mr. Knight, stands thus :—

> This night, when I was laid in bed, I dreamt
> That this my staff, mine office-badge in court,
> Was broke in *twain ; by whom*, I cannot guess :
> *But, as I think, by the cardinal. What it* bodes
> *God knows ;* and on the ends were plac'd
> The heads of *Edmund duke of Somerset*,
> And William de la Poole, first duke of Suffolk.

Now let the reader carefully compare these different texts with the passage as corrected in the amended play :—

> Methought this staff, mine office-badge in court,
> Was broke in twain; by whom I have forgot,
> But as I think, it was by the cardinal ;
> And on the pieces of the broken wand,
> Were plac'd the heads of Edmund duke of Somerset,
> And William de la Poole, first duke of Suffolk.
> This was my dream : what it doth bode, God knows.

The words in italics in the second quotation are those which are common to the editions of **1619** and **1623**, but are not found in the earlier impressions of 1594 and 1600.

We have thus *an intermediate composition* between the edition of 1594 and the amended play. It will be at once seen that these differences cannot be the result of emendation, in the way that we account for the differences of the second folio. I will produce another and a stronger instance. In act i., sc. 2, the edition of 1594 has these two lines,

> But ere it be long, I'll go before them all,
> Despite of all that seek to cross me thus.

Instead of these two lines, we have a different speech, an elaboration of the other two :—

> I'll come after you, for I cannot go before,
> As long as *Gloster bears this base and humble mind :*
> *Were I a man,* and Protector, as he is,
> I'd reach to the crown, or make some hop headless.
> *And being but a woman, I'll not (be) behind*
> For playing of *my part,* in spite of all
> That seek to cross me thus.

Again, compare these versions with the amended play :—

> Follow I must : I cannot go before
> While Gloster bears this base and humble mind
> Were I a man, a duke, and next of blood,
> I would remove these tedious stumbling blocks,
> And smooth my way upon their headless necks :
> And, being a woman, I will not be slack
> To play my part in fortune's pageant.

Here perhaps is a still stronger evidence of an intermediate composition, and others of like importance may be seen from the notes. But more than this, the genealogy in act ii., sc. 2, in the edition of 1594, is entirely different from that given in the edition of 1619, and this latter very nearly corresponds with the amended play. It seems from these instances, that it will be a difficult matter to ascertain what really belongs to the first original play. I am inclined to think that there is a good deal of what may be termed the amended play in the two parts of the " Contention," and, although the evidence to my mind is so strong that Shakespeare was not the author of the whole of these plays, yet it seems little less than absurd to form an arithmetical computation of what was written by Shakespeare, and what was the work of the author of the original dramas.

There are so many passages in the two parts of the Contention that seem almost beyond the power of any of Shakespeare's predecessors or contemporaries, perhaps even not excepting Marlowe, that as one method of explaining away the difficulties which attend a belief in Malone's theory, my conjecture that when these plays were printed in 1594 and 1595, *they included the first additions which Shakespeare made to the originals,* does not seem impossible, borne out as it is by an examination of the early editions. If I am so far correct, we have yet to discover the originals of the two parts of the " Contention," as well as that of 1 *Henry VI.*

The well known passage in Greene's " Groat's-worth of Wit" proves that Shakespeare was the author of the line—

> O! tiger's heart, wrapp'd in a woman's hide,

before September 3rd, 1592, and the angry allusion to the " upstart crow, beautified with our feathers," may be best explained by supposing that Shakespeare had then superseded the older play, in which perhaps Greene may have had some very small share. The attempt to generalize this passage fails, for Greene is speaking of Shakespeare as a writer, not as an actor, a point which Mr. Knight does not sufficiently consider. But that Greene " parodies a line of his own," as the other critics tell us, is assuming a power in Greene of penning the speech in which that line occurs ; and it is only necessary to compare that speech with others in Greene's acknowledged plays, to be convinced that he was not equal to anything of the kind.

When Greene calls our great dramatist "in his own conceit the only Shake-scene in a country," it is scarcely possible that he could allude to Shakespeare's power of dramatic arrangement; yet the words imply something of the kind, and we may wish to believe they really do. The notice just quoted is the earliest introduction of Shakespeare in the printed literature of this country, and so valuable an authority is it, that it is unfortunate any dispute or doubt should arise relative to its meaning. That the address in which it is inserted excited much attention at the time, is told by more than one authority; and it probably proved a source of considerable vexation to Shakespeare himself, for shortly after its publication we find Chettle, who edited Greene's tract, apologizing for the insertion of the offensive passage. Nash also calls it "a scald, trivial, lying pamphlet," but there is no reason for supposing that the last epithet was applied to the part now under consideration. Chettle is enthusiastic. We may believe that he became acquainted with Shakespeare after the publication of Greene's work, and before the appearance of "Kind-Hart's Dreame." He tells us that Shakespeare was "excellent in the quality he professes," that is, as an actor; and had, moreover, a "facetious grace in writing that approves his art." This was in November or December, 1592. Shakespeare probably had written part of the "True Tragedy," before that time.

There is another passage in "Kind-Hart's Dreame," which seems rather at variance with the one just quoted. Chettle, speaking of Greene, says, " of whom, *however some suppose themselves injured,* I have learned to speak, considering he is dead, *nil nisi necessarium.* He was of singular pleasure, *the very supporter, and, to no man's disgrace be this intended,* the only comedian of a vulgar writer in this country." Chettle here seems to recollect the offence that the "address" had given; he exclaims to " *no man's disgrace be this* intended," he was not wronging Shakespeare in calling Greene "the *only* comedian of a vulgar writer in this country." Chettle professes to say nothing more of Greene than is requisite; this testimony to his merits is given, notwithstanding his alleged friendliness to Shakespeare. He probably alludes to Shakespeare, when he says, " however some suppose themselves injured." Mr. Collier thinks Chettle implies that Shakespeare had acquired no reputation as an *original* dramatic poet in 1592: and it certainly goes far to prove that his *comic* pieces had not then appeared, or, if they had, had obtained little applause. Our business is now with the histories; and the "First Part of the Contention," and the "True Tragedy," may have been *rifacimenti* by Shakespeare as early as 1592.

When Greene parodied the lines in "The True Tragedy," and alluded to the crow "beautified with *our* feathers," it is probable he meant to insinuate that he himself had some share in the composition of the play, which, in one state of its reconstruction or amendment by Shakespeare, fell under his satire. This probability is considerably strengthened by the following passage in "Greene's Funeralls," by R. B., gent., 4to., Lond. 1594, a rare tract of twelve leaves, preserved in the Bodleian library:

> Greene is the pleasing obiect of an eie;
> Greene pleasde the eies of all that lookt vppon him;
> Greene is the ground of euerie Painters die;
> Greene gaue the ground to all that wrote vpon him;
> Nay more, the men that so eclipst his fame,
> Purloynde his Plumes, can they deny the same?

This is "Sonnet IX," in this rare little volume, which contains the term "sugred sonnets," afterwards appropriated by Meres to Shakespeare. R. B., whoever he was, may write somewhat in partisanship, but how Nash's indignant rejection of the authorship of the other tract can be held a sufficient reply to this plain statement, seems mysterious. Yet so Mr. Knight would tell us, and adds that no "great author appeared in the world who was not reputed in the outset of his career to be a plagiarist." Was not Harriot held as plagiarist, when he promulgated his original theories? Was not his adoption of Vieta's notions discovered afterwards? The cases are nearly parallel, though there was no Vieta alive to claim the groundwork. We may not care to know who laid the foundation, but surely Greene's words are not to be altogether divested of any intelligible meaning.

The "True Tragedy," as originally composed, was, as we learn from the title page, played by the Earl of Pembrooke's servants, for whom Greene was in the habit of writing. None of Shakespeare's undisputed plays were played by this company. "Titus Andronicus," an earlier drama, also has this external evidence against its authenticity. Mr. Collier, indeed, tells us that *before* 1592, " a popular play written for one company, and perhaps acted by that company as it was written, might be surreptitiously obtained by another, having been at best taken down from the mouths of the original performers ; from the second company it might be procured by a third, and, after a succession of changes, corruptions, and omissions, it might find its way at last to the press." This, as Mr. Knight thinks, entirely overthrows Malone's argument on the point ; but the " True Tragedy" was not printed till 1595, and, according to Mr. Collier, this system probably concluded two years previously. Besides, the title-page would probably exhibit the name of the original company. If Malone is not right, it is very singular that the suspicious accounts should only appear on the titles of two suspicious dramas. Passing over Malone's conclusions from inaccuracies and anachronisms, which can hardly be considered safe guides, when we reflect how numerous they are throughout Shakespeare's plays, there is yet one other circumstance worthy of notice, that indirectly associates the name of Greene with the older dramas. In "The First Part of the Contention," mention is made of "Abradas, *the great Macedonian pirate.*" Who Abradas was, does not any where appear, and the only other mention of him that has been discovered is in "Penelope's Web," 4to., Lond., 1588, a tract written by Greene. " I remember Ismena, that Epicurus measured every man's dyet by his own principles, and Abradas, the great Macedonian pirate, thought every one had a letter of mart that bare sayles in the ocean." These coincidences are perhaps more curious than important, but still appear worth notice. It may likewise be mentioned, as a confirmatory circumstance, that Nash, in his " Apologie," 1593, mentions Greene "being chiefe agent for the companie, for hee writ more than foure other, how well I will not say." If, therefore, Greene was so intimately connected with the earl of Pembrook's servants, and Shakespeare not at all, the external evidence, as far as this goes, is strongly in favour of Greene's having had some share in the composition of the " True Tragedy," and, as a matter of course, " The First Part of the Contention."

I have followed Mr. Hunter in saying that the allusion to Shakespeare in the "Groatsworth of Wit," entered at Stationers' Hall September 20, 1592, is the earliest production of our great dramatic poet in the printed literature of this country. If, however, the opinion of Chalmers may be relied on, Gabriel Harvey, in his " Four Letters especially touching Robert Greene, and other parties by him abused," 1592, alludes to Shakespeare in the third letter, dated September 9th, 1592, wherein he says :—" I speak generally to every springing wit, but more especially to a few : and, at this instant, *singularly,* to *one,* whom I salute with a hundred blessings." These notices of Shakespeare are, however, digressions in this place, even if they prove that Shakespeare was not popularly known as a dramatic writer before 1592. Chettle's evidence in the same year is almost conclusive with respect to the histrionic powers of Shakespeare ; and it would be a curious addition to our poet's history to ascertain whether he performed in the two latter parts of *Henry VI.,* after they had been altered and amended. There is a well-known epigram by Davies, in his " Scourge of Folly," 1611, p. 76, that has some theatrical anecdote connected with it, now perhaps for ever lost, but which implies that Rowe was not exactly right when he stated that " the top of his performance was the ghost of *Hamlet.*" Another evidence may be adduced from Davies' " Humours Heav'n on Earth," 8vo., Lond., 1609, p. 208, which has not been yet quoted :—

> Some followed her (Fortune) by acting all men's parts,
> These on a stage she rais'd, in scorn to fall,
> And made them mirrors by their acting arts,
> Wherein men saw their faults, though ne'er so small :
> Yet some she guerdon'd not to their deserts ;
> But othersome were but ill-action all,
> Who, while they acted ill, ill stay'd behind,
> By custom of their manners, in their minds.

This alludes to Shakespeare and Burbage, as appears from the marginal note ; but the inference to be drawn from it is in favour of Shakespeare's capabilities as an actor. Davies is often rather unintelligible, and the allusion—

> Some say, good Will, which I, in sport, do sing,
> Hadst thou not play'd some kingly parts in sport,
> Thou hadst been a companion for a king,
> And been a king among the meaner sort—

remains to be unravelled. It clearly alludes to some circumstance which took place after the accession of James I.

This digression is not without its use, because it shows that as we have good grounds for believing Chettle's testimony to Shakespeare's histrionic merits, we can the more readily give credence to his assertion that our dramatist possessed a "facetious grace in writing, that approves his art." If the other passage just quoted, which alludes to Greene, proves that Shakespeare was not known as a comic writer as early as 1591, it by no means sufficiently outweighs Chettle's first testimony to make us doubt that Shakespeare had then largely contributed to the two parts of the "Contention." Mr. Knight tells us repeatedly, that if Malone's theory be adopted, Shakespeare was the most unblushing plagiarist that ever put pen to paper. Why so? Did Shakespeare adopt the labours of others as his own? If he had done so, why was his name effaced from the title-page of "Sir John Oldcastle?" and why was it not inserted on the early editions of the present plays? He would have been essentially a dishonest plagiarist, says Mr. Knight. But it was the common custom of the time for dramatists to be engaged to remodel and amplify the productions of others. A reference to Henslowe's Diary will at once establish this fact. In 1601, Decker was paid thirty shillings "for *altering* of Fayton," and, in the following year, we find Ben Jonson paid £10 on account, "in earnest of a boocke called Richard Crookebacke, and for *new adycions* for Jeronimo." According to Mr. Knight's theory, Decker, Jonson, and every unfortunate playwright who complied with the custom of the time, were "unblushing plagiarists." The great probability is, that the company for which Shakespeare wrote had become proprietors of the older plays, and that he made alterations, and added to them when necessary. There was no plagiarism in the case; and perhaps some day it will be discovered that little of the original dramas now remains in the Second and Third Parts of *Henry VI.*

From Henslowe's Diary it appears that a play called *Henry VI.* was acted thirteen times in the spring of 1592, by Lord Strange's players, who, be it remembered, never performed any of Shakespeare's plays. This is conjectured, with great probability, to be the First Part of *Henry VI.* in some state or other of its composition, and the play whose power "embalmed" the bones of "brave Talbot" with the tears of ten thousand spectators. The death scene of Talbot is, perhaps, the most powerfully constructed part of the play; our national sympathies have been awakened in his favour, and we pity his woeful end; but Nash gives like praise to the contemptible "Famous Victories." Mr. Knight places great reliance on the unity of action in the First Part of the "Contention" and the First Part of *Henry VI.*, to prove that they were both written by one and the same person; but surely these two plays have neither unity of characterisation, nor unity of style; and the want of these outweighs the unity of action. That there is considerable unity of action, I admit. In some cases, nearly the same expressions occur. Thus in 1 *Henry VI.*, act iv, sc. 1, King Henry says:—

> Cousin of York, we institute your grace
> To be our regent in these parts of France.

And in the First Part of the "Contention," act i., sc. 1, he says:—

> Cousin of York, we here discharge your grace
> From being regent in these parts of France.

But I suspect these coincidences, and the evidences of the unity of action, as well as those scenes which a cursory reader might suppose to have been written for the purpose of continuation, may be attributed to the writer having adopted his incidents out of the old chronicles, where such matters are placed in not very strict chronological arrangement. Thus, in *Richard III.*, the incident of the king sending the Bishop of Ely for strawberries is isolated, adopted in order with the other scenes from the chronicles, probably Holinshed, and useless for the purposes of continuation. With a discussion on the supposed onity of style I will not occupy these pages. Opinion in this matter is sufficient, for the plays are accessible. Mr. Hallam thinks the First Part of *Henry VI.* might have been written by Greene, and the very opening of the play is in the bombastic style of the older dramatists. Again, with respect to the characterization, is the Margaret of *I. Henry VI.* the Margaret of the First Part of the "Contention?" Perhaps her character is not sufficiently developed in the first of these to enable us to judge; but, in regard to the characters that are common to both, we may safely decide that not one characteristic of importance is to be found in *I. Henry VI.* not immediately derived from the chroniclers. Are we to suppose that Suffolk's instantaneous love was corresponded to by Margaret, or was she only haughty and not passionate when she quietly answers Suffolk in the speech in which she is introduced? I do not mean to assert that there is any inconsistency in her being represented merely haughty in one play, and passionate in the other, for different circumstances would render this very possible; but it is not easy to infer the strict unity of characterization that is attempted to be established.

If the First Part of *Henry VI.* were originally written by Shakespeare, and with all these scenes for the purposes of continuation, as Mr. Knight would have us believe, how does that writer account for the appearance of the Second Part of *Henry VI.* under the title of the First Part of the "Contention?" This is a point to which no attention has been given. Two editions of the First Part of the "Contention" were published in 1600 under the old title, but we find that in 1602, their later appellations as parts of *Henry VI.* had been given them. It seems reasonable to infer that, when Shakespeare remodelled the old plays, and formed the two parts of the "Contention," he had had nothing to do with the old play of "Henry VI." mentioned by Henslowe, and had intended the play now called the Second Part of *Henry VI.* to be the first of his own series. Afterwards, he might have been employed to make "new adjcyons" to the old play of "Henry VI.," and then the three plays may have been amalgamated into a series, and the old play rendered uniform by scenes written for continuations previously made. Take the First Part of *Henry VI.* away, and the concluding chorus to *Henry V.* remains equally intelligible. The "True Tragedy" may also have been called "Edward IV.," and so more naturally the series would have continued with *Richard III.* In vain have I looked for any identity of manner in the scene between Suffolk and Margaret in the First Part of *Henry VI.* and the similar scene in the First Part of the "Contention." But so much stress has been laid on this point, that I beg the reader will here carefully compare them together.

First Part of the Contention, Act iii. Sc. 2.

Queen. Sweet Suffolk, hie thee hence to France,
For if the king do come, thou sure must die.
Suf. And if I go I cannot live: but here to die,
What were it else,
But like a pleasant slumber in thy lap?
Here could I breathe my soul into the air,
As mild and gentle as the new-born babe,
That dies with mother's dug between his lips.
Where from thy sight I should be raging mad,
And call for thee to close mine eyes,
Or with thy lips to stop my dying soul,
That I might breathe it so into thy body,
And then it liv'd in sweet Elysium.
By thee to die, were torment more than death.
Oh, let me stay, befal what may befal.
    Queen. Oh might'st thou stay with safety of thy life,
Then should'st thou stay; but heavens deny it,
And therefore go, but hope ere long to be repeal'd.
    Suf. I go.
    Queen. And take my heart with thee.   [*She kisses him.*
    Suf. A jewel lock'd into the wofull'st cask,
That ever yet contain'd a thing of worth.
Thus, like a splitted bark, so sunder we;
This way fall I to death.   [*Exit* SUFFOLK.

Queen. This way for me.   [*Exit* QUEEN

First Part of Henry VI., Act v. Sc. 3.

Suf. Be what thou wilt, thou art my prisoner.
                            [*Gazes on her*
O fairest beauty, do not fear, nor fly;
For I will touch these but with reverent hands.
I kiss these fingers [*kissing her hand*] for eternal peace,
And lay them gently on thy tender side.
Who art thou? say, that I may honour thee.
    Mar. Margaret my name, and daughter to a king,
The king of Naples; whoso'er thou art.
    Suf. An earl I am, and Suffolk am I call'd.
Be not offended, nature's miracle,
Thou art allotted to be ta'en by me:
So doth the swan her downy cygnets save,
Keeping them prisoner underneath her wings.
Yet if this servile usage once offend,
Go, and be free again, as Suffolk's friend.
                    [*She turns away as going*
O, stay!—I have no power to let her pass;
My hand would free her, but my heart says,—no.
As plays the sun upon the glassy streams,
Twinkling another counterfeited beam,
So seems this gorgeous beauty to mine eyes.

Mr. Dyce could not have been far wrong, when he excluded the first of these plays from his chronology, as "exhibiting no traces of Shakespeare's peculiar style, and being altogether in the manner of an older school."

This judicious writer thinks that it may be attributed either to Marlowe or Kyd, and we are occasionally reminded of the former author. Henslowe's "Diary" lets us a good deal into the prison-house secrets of the relative position between author and manager in those days; we there find that sometimes four writers were occasionally employed on one play; and there seems to be strong internal evidence that the First Part of *Henry VI.* was not wholly the work of one hand.

Capell, struck with the power of the death-scene in *Henry VI.*, long since decided that it was unquestionably the work of Shakespeare. It is, indeed, a composition in Shakespeare's peculiar style; and it occurs in the "True Tragedy," with only a few verbal alterations, and the omission of five unimportant lines at the commencement. In the same way, the speech beginning—

I will go clad my body in gay ornaments,

is equal, if not superior, in smoothness and power, to a like speech in *Richard III.* How can Mr. Collier find it in his heart to deprive Shakespeare of these? There is nothing equal to them in the First Part of *Henry VI.*, and little superior to them in the other historical plays. It is, however, worthy of remark, that Meres in 1598 does not mention either "Henry VI." or the "Contention," which would seem to show that they were not highly estimated even in Shakespeare's own time.

Gildon tells us of a tradition, that Shakespeare, in a conversation with Ben Jonson, said, that, "finding the nation generally very ignorant of history, he wrote plays in order to instruct the people in that particular." This is absurd. "Plays," says Heywood in 1612, "have made the ignorant more apprehensive, taught the unlearned the knowledge of many famous histories, instructed such as cannot read in the discovery of all our English chronicles; and what man have you now of that weak capacity, that cannot discourse of any notable thing recorded even from William the Conqueror, nay, from the landing of Brute, until this day?" Henslowe mentions a play on the subject of William the Conqueror, and there can be little doubt that a complete series once existed, even up to Henry VIII., and perhaps even later. There was little authentic history in those days, and the researches of Cotton and Hayward were not popularly known. Most were content to take the "depraved lies" of the playwrights for truth, and, like the simpleton mentioned by Ben Jonson, prefer them to the sage chroniclers:—

No, I confess I have it from the play-books,
And think they are more authentic.

It is ridiculous to talk of Shakespeare having invented an historical drama, that had been gradually growing towards the perfection it reached in his hands from the middle of the sixteenth century. Let, therefore, Gildon's tradition be distributed with the other myths that the commencement of the seventeenth century interwove with the little that was then known of Shakespeare's authentic history.

There are other opinions that require notice in this place. It has been conjectured that the "First Part of the Contention" and the "True Tragedy" were not written by the same sort of person, because the account of Clifford's death at the conclusion of the former play varies with that given of the same occurrence at the commencement of the other. On the same principle we might conclude that the Second Parts of *Henry IV.* and *Henry VI.* are not by the same hand, because the story of Althea is erroneously told in the first of these plays, and rightly in the second. It is difficult to account for these inconsistencies, and it seems paradoxical that Shakespeare should at one time remember a well-known classical story, and forget it at another; but it is undoubtedly dangerous to build theories on such circumstances.

Dr. Johnson, who often speaks at random in these matters, asserts that the Second and Third Parts of *Henry VI.* were not written without a *dependance* on the first. Malone has answered him satisfactorily by saying, "the old play of Henry VI. had been exhibited before these were written in any form;" but it does not follow from this concession, either that the "Contention" was written by the author of the former play, or that Shakespeare was the author of these two pieces, as *originally composed*. This is exactly the point to which I would draw the reader's attention. I will leave the unity of action out of the question, because we are not dealing with works of imagination, and this can be accounted for, as I have previously contended, in the sources from which the incidents are derived. Had there been two Parts to the *Tempest*, and the same kind of unity of action, and similar instances of scenes written for the purposes of continuation, the argument would hold in that case, unless it could be shown that these were also to be found in the original romance or drama upon which it was founded. Here there is nothing of the kind. I believe that, with the present evidence, it is impossible to ascertain the exact portions of the two Parts of the "Contention," which were not written by Shakespeare, and belong to the older drama. There is nothing Shakespearian in this :—

> These gifts ere long will make me mighty rich.
> The duchess she thinks now that all is well,
> But I have gold comes from another place,
> From one that hired me to set her on,
> To plot these treasons gainst the king and peers ;
> And that is the mighty duke of Suffolk.
> For he it is, but I must not say so,
> That by my means must work the duchess' fall,
> Who now by conjuration thinks to rise.

This is one of the most favourable specimens of the rejections. Mr. Knight would have us believe that Shakespeare wrote the following speech, and put it into the mouth of Richard, after he had slain Somerset :—

> So lie thou there, and tumble in thy blood,
> What's here, the sign of the Castle ?
> Then the prophecy is come to pass,
> For Somerset was forewarn'd of castles,
> The which he always did observe,
> And now behold, under a paltry ale-house sign,
> The Castle in St. Alban's, Somerset
> Hath made the wizard famous by his death."

Is there in this one single characteristic of the language which *Shakespeare* gives to Richard ? Is there identity of manner ? Is not the style comparatively puerile ? Let this and similar passages be given to the author or authors of the original play, but let us retain for Shakespeare the parts that we may fairly judge from comparison to have been beyond the power of those of his contemporaries, whose works have descended to our times.

The following play, in point of time, is *Richard III.*, which was considerably more popular than either the two parts of the "Contention," or any of the three parts of *Henry VI.* There had been an older play on the same subject, alluded to by Harrington in 1591 as having been acted at St. John's College, Cambridge, but this was in Latin. An English play, entitled, "The True Tragedie of Richard the Third, wherein is showne the death of Edward the Fourth, with the smothering of the two yong Princes in the Tower, with a lamentable ende of Shore's wife, an example for all wicked women, and lastly, the conjunction and joyning of the two noble houses, Lancaster and Yorke," appeared in 1594, but there are no strong grounds for believing it to have been used or even read by Shakespeare.

The series of the historical plays concludes with *Henry VIII.*, which was first published in the folio of 1623. This drama was produced after the accession of the first James, there being an evident allusion to him in the well known lines, commencing, "Nor shall this peace sleep with her." It was entered on the registers of the Stationers' Company, early in 1605, to N. Butter, "yf he get good allowance for the Enterlude of K. Henry 8th. before he begyn to print it, and then procure the warden's hands to yt for the entrance of yt, he is to have the same for his copy ;" but no edition in quarto, or of that date, is known to exist. It seems to have been popular, and, according to Stowe, though his authority on this point has been questioned, the Globe Theatre was ignited at the fire in 1613 during the performance of this play. Sir H. Wotton, however, asserts that the play acted on that lamentable occurrence, was called, "All is True;" and the most evident solution of the discrepancy, though i cannot bring myself to consider it the true one, is that *Henry VIII.* had a double title, and was sometimes known under the denomination cited by Wotton.

King John.

THE plays of Shakespeare which he has founded upon English history, have seized so strongly on the national mind, that they are received not as dramas only but as history; but our poet did not invariably follow historic truth so closely as he might have done, nor are events always related with regard to their order in point of time. He seized the most dramatic incidents of a reign, and crowded them rapidly one upon another, drawing them within a narrow circle, and seeking for unity of dramatic interest, not unfrequently passed over some of the important events, in reference to the political and social state of the people. In *King John* no allusion is made to what every Englishman must regard as the great event of that reign, the wringing from the reluctant tyrant, at Runnymede, the great basis of our national liberties—the MAGNA CHARTA. In *Henry the Eighth*, also, the poet has, with great art, forborne to touch upon any of the numerous dark spots of that monarch's character, while the great event of that reign—the REFORMATION—remains, partially perhaps from the nature of the subject, untouched.

John ascended the throne in 1199, in his thirty-second year; Shakespeare's play commences shortly after, and embraces the whole of his reign, a period of seventeen years. The first two acts of the play carry us only through the first year of John's reign, up to 1200, when he gave his niece Blanch, of Castile, in marriage to Lewis, the eldest son of Philip of France. John's divorce of his first wife, and his marriage with Isabella, the daughter of the Count of Angouleme, together with the consequent revolts of many of his barons, are passed over in silence. The death of Arthur, the young duke of Brittany, which occurred in 1203, is not related in the manner in which it is now supposed it took place, although, as the event is shrouded in mystery, it is possible Shakespeare's account may be the correct one. Arthur was not a child, but rising to manhood, and had sought safety from his uncle by a coalition with Philip, the powerful king of France, to whose daughter he was affianced. Animated by a love of military fame, the young prince had broken into Poictou, at the head of a small army, and hearing that his grandmother, Queen Eleanor, who had always been his enemy, was residing at Mirabeau, he determined to take that fortress, and obtain possession of her person; in attempting this, he was himself captured, fell into the hands of his uncle John, and was committed to the custody of Hubert de Bourg. Hubert saved the prince from an assassin sent to destroy him, and spread a report of his death; but it excited such indignation in the revolted barons, that he thought it prudent to reveal the truth. This sealed the doom of the young prince; not long after he disappeared, and was never heard of again. Most accounts, however, represent the tyrant as murdering his nephew with his own hands. This deed of guilt was supposed to have taken place at Rouen; Shakespeare represents Arthur to have met his death by attempting to escape from the castle of Northampton. Of the prisoners taken by John with the prince, twenty-two noblemen are said to have been starved to death in Corfe Castle.

A lapse of ten years occurs between the fourth and fifth acts of Shakespeare's tragedy, during which the famous dispute between John and the astute and subtle pontiff, Innocent III., took place respecting the right of appointing the archbishop of Canterbury. After the pope had fulminated the sentences of excommunication and deposition against John, and had roused France to execute the latter decree, the feeble and vacillating monarch humbly submitted himself, and took an oath of fealty to Rome. He had previously, with flashing eyes and lips livid with anger, thundered out to his trembling prelates these haughty words:—"By God's teeth, if you, or any of your body, dare to lay my states under interdict, I will send you and all your clergy to Rome, and confiscate your property. As for the Roman shavelings, if I find any in my dominions, I will tear out their eyes and cut off their noses, and so send them to the pope, that the nations may witness their infamy." Had not John's weakness and timidity been equal to his ferocity, he might have been the scourge of Rome and the terror of Europe.

On the memorable 15th of June, 1215, John signed the Great Charter at Runnymede, having not long before said:—"And why do they not demand my crown, also? By God's teeth, I will not grant them liberties which will make me a slave!" After signing this memorable deed, John was plunged in despair, and is said to have acted with the furious imbecility of a madman; he blasphemed, raved, gnashed his teeth, and gnawed sticks and straws, in the intensity of his impotent passion. He soon repented of the liberty which he had granted to his barons and his people, and made war upon them to regain it. He surrounded himself with a host of savage foreign mercenaries, the chiefs of whom were called "Mauleon, the bloody;" "Falco, without bowels;" "Walter Buch, the murderer;" "Sottim, the merciless;" and "Godeschall, the iron-hearted." These ruffians gave every village they passed to the flames, and put John's English subjects to horrible tortures, to compel them to confess where they had concealed their wealth.

But the hand of heaven arrested the progress of this incarnate fiend; John died in the October of the year following that in which he had placed his hand to the charter. He breathed his last at the castle of Newark, on the Trent, and not at Swinsted (or Swineshead) Abbey. It is possible that he might have been poisoned, but that story is not told by any writer of the time, and is a tradition on which we cannot place much reliance. The most probable account is, that he ate gluttonously of some peaches, and immediately after drank a quantity of new cider. This, in his distempered state, was cause enough to produce the fever which destroyed him. The last acts of John's life, as represented by the iron pen of history, excite alternately the strongest feelings of indignation and disgust; but the death of John, as depicted by Shakespeare, wins our pity for the expiring tyrant. Even during his life, the poet represents him as not devoid of a certain princely courage and dignity.

A play, entitled *The Troublesome Reigne of John King of England, &c.*, in two parts, was printed in 1591, without the name of its author. Mr. Malone supposes it to have been written by Robert Greene, or George Peele and that it certainly preceded Shakespeare's play, which is supposed to have been written in 1596.

644

PERSONS REPRESENTED

KING JOHN.
Appears, Act I. sc. 1. Act II. sc. 1; sc. 2. Act III. sc. 1, sc. 2; sc. 3. Act IV. sc. 2. Act V. sc. 1; sc. 3; sc. 7.

PRINCE HENRY, *his Son ; afterwards* King Henry the Third.
Appears, Act V. sc. 7.

ARTHUR, *Duke of Bretagne ; Son of Geffrey, late Duke of Bretagne, and Elder Brother of* King John.
Appears, Act II. sc. 1. Act III. sc. 1; sc. 2; sc. 3. Act IV. sc. 1; sc. 3.

WILLIAM MARESHALL, *Earl of* Pembroke.
Appears, Act I. sc. 1. Act II. sc. 1. Act IV. sc. 2; sc. 3. Act V. sc. 2; sc. 4; sc. 7.

GEFFREY FITZ-PETER, *Earl of Essex, Chief Justiciary of England.*
Appears, Act I. sc. 1.

WILLIAM LONGSWORD, *Earl of* Salisbury.
Appears, Act I. sc. 1. Act III. sc. 1. Act IV. sc. 2; sc. 3. Act V. sc. 2; sc. 4; sc. 7.

ROBERT BIGOT, *Earl of* Norfolk.
Appears, Act IV. sc. 3. Act V. sc. 2; sc. 4; sc. 7.

HUBERT DE BURGH, *Chamberlain to the King.*
Appears, Act III. sc. 2; sc. 3. Act IV. sc. 1; sc. 2; sc. 3. Act V. sc. 3; sc. 6.

ROBERT FAULCONBRIDGE, *Son of Sir* Robert Faulconbridge.
Appears, Act I. sc. 1.

PHILIP FAULCONBRIDGE, *his Half-brother, Bastard Son to King* Richard the First.
Appears, Act I. sc. 1. Act II. sc. 1; sc. 2. Act III. sc. 1; sc. 2; sc. 3. Act IV. sc. 2; sc. 3. Act V. sc. 1; sc. 2; sc. 6, sc. 7.

JAMES GURNEY, *Servant to* Lady Faulconbridge.
Appears, Act I. sc. 1.

PETER OF POMFRET, *a Prophet.*
Appears, Act IV. sc. 2.

PHILIP, *King of* France.
Appears, Act II. sc. 1; sc. 2. Act III. sc. 1; sc. 4.

LEWIS, *the Dauphin.*
Appears, Act II. sc. 1; sc. 2. Act III. sc. 1; sc. 4. Act V. sc. 2; sc. 5.

ARCH-DUKE OF AUSTRIA.
Appears, Act II. sc. 1; sc. 2. Act III. sc. 1.

CARDINAL PANDULPH, *the Pope's Legate.*
Appears, Act III. sc. 1; sc. 4. Act V. sc. 1; sc. 2.

MELUN, *a French Lord.*
Appears, Act V. sc. 2; sc. 4.

CHATILLON, *Ambassador from* France *to King* John.
Appears, Act I. sc. 1. Act II. sc. 1.

ELINOR, *the Widow of King* Henry the Second, *and Mother of King* John.
Appears, Act I. sc. 1. Act II. sc. 1; sc. 2. Act III. sc. 1; sc. 3.

CONSTANCE, *Mother to* Arthur.
Appears, Act II. sc. 1. Act III. sc. 1; sc. 4.

BLANCH, *Daughter to* Alphonso, *King of* Castile, *and Niece to King* John.
Appears, Act II. sc. 1; sc. 2. Act III. sc. 1.

LADY FAULCONBRIDGE, *Mother to the* Bastard *and* Robert Faulconbridge.
Appears, Act I. sc. 1.

Lords, Ladies, Citizens of Angiers, *Sheriff, Heralds, Officers, Soldiers, Messengers, and other Attendants.*

SCENE,—*Sometimes in* ENGLAND, *and sometimes in* FRANCE.

645

King John.

ACT I.

SCENE I.—Northampton. *A Room of State in the Palace.*

Enter KING JOHN, QUEEN ELINOR, PEMBROKE, ESSEX, SALISBURY, *and* Others, *with* CHATILLON.

K. John. Now, say, Chatillon, what would France
   with us?

Chat. Thus, after greeting, speaks the king of
   France,
In my behaviour, to the majesty,
The borrow'd majesty of England here.

Eli. A strange beginning:—borrow'd majesty!

K. John. Silence, good mother; hear the embassy.

Chat. Philip of France, in right and true behalf
Of thy deceased brother Geffrey's son,
Arthur Plantagenet, lays most lawful claim
To this fair island, and the territories;
To Ireland, Poictiers, Anjou, Touraine, Maine;
Desiring thee to lay aside the sword,
Which sways usurpingly these several titles;
And put the same into young Arthur's hand,
Thy nephew, and right royal sovereign.

K. John. What follows, if we disallow of this?

Chat. The proud control of fierce and bloody
   war,
To enforce these rights so forcibly withheld.

K. John. Here have we war for war, and blood
   for blood,
Controlment for controlment: so answer France.

Chat. Then take my king's defiance from my
   mouth,
The furthest limit of my embassy.

646

K. John. Bear mine to him, and so depart in
   peace;
Be thou as lightning in the eyes of France;
For ere thou canst report I will be there.
The thunder of my cannon shall be heard:
So, hence! Be thou the trumpet of our wrath,
And sullen presage of your own decay.—
An honourable conduct let him have:—
Pembroke, look to 't: Farewell, Chatillon.

            [*Exeunt* CHAT. *and* PEM.

Eli. What now, my son? have I not ever said,
How that ambitious Constance would not cease,
Till she had kindled France, and all the world,
Upon the right and party of her son?
This might have been prevented, and made whole,
With very easy arguments of love;
Which now the manage of two kingdoms must
With fearful bloody issue arbitrate.

K. John. Our strong possession, and our right,
   for us.

Eli. Your strong possession, much more than
   your right;
Or else it must go wrong with you, and me;
So much my conscience whispers in your ear;
Which none but heaven, and you, and I, shall hear.

Enter the SHERIFF OF NORTHAMPTONSHIRE, *who whispers* ESSEX.

Essex. My liege, here is the strangest contro-
   versy,
Come from the country to be judg'd by you,
That e'er I heard: Shall I produce the men?

K. John. Let them approach.—   [*Exit* Sheriff
Our abbies, and our priories, shall pay

Re-enter SHERIFF, *with* ROBERT FAULCONBRIDGE, *and* PHILIP, *his bastard Brother.*

This expedition's charge.—What men are you?

Bast. Your faithful subject I, a gentleman,
Born in Northamptonshire; and eldest son,
As I suppose, to Robert Faulconbridge;
A soldier, by the honour-giving hand
Of Cœur-de-lion knighted in the field.

K. John. What art thou?

Rob. The son and heir to that same Faulconbridge.

K. John. Is that the elder, and art thou the heir?
You came not of one mother then, it seems.

Bast. Most certain of one mother, mighty king,
That is well known; and, as I think, one father;
But, for the certain knowledge of that truth,
I put you o'er to heaven, and to my mother;
Of that I doubt, as all men's children may.

Eli. Out on thee, rude man! thou dost shame
　　　　　thy mother,
And wound her honour with this diffidence.

Bast. I, madam? no, I have no reason for it;
That is my brother's plea, and none of mine;
The which if he can prove, 'a pops me out
At least from fair five hundred pound a year:
Heaven guard my mother's honour, and my land!

K. John. A good blunt fellow:—Why, being
　　　　　younger born,
Doth he lay claim to thine inheritance?

Bast. I know not why, except to get the land.
But once he slander'd me with bastardy;
But who'r I be as true begot, or no,
That still I lay upon my mother's head;
But, that I am as well begot, my liege,
(Fair fall the bones that took the pains for me!)
Compare our faces, and be judge yourself.
If old sir Robert did beget us both,
And were our father, and this son like him;—
O, old sir Robert, father, on my knee
I give heaven thanks, I was not like to thee.

K. John. Why, what a madcap hath heaven
　　　　　lent us here!

Eli. He hath a trick of Cœur-de-lion's face,
The accent of his tongue affecteth him:
Do you not read some tokens of my son
In the large composition of this man?

K. John. Mine eye hath well examined his parts,
And finds them perfect Richard.——Sirrah, speak,
What doth move you to claim your brother's land?

Bast. Because he hath a half-face, like my father;
With that half-face would he have all my land:
A half-faced groat five hundred pound a year!

Rob. My gracious liege, when that my father liv'd,
Your brother did employ my father much;——

Bast. Well, sir, by this you cannot get my land:
Your tale must be, how he employ'd my mother.

Rob. And once despatch'd him in an embassy
To Germany, there, with the emperor,
To treat of high affairs touching that time:
The advantage of his absence took the king.
And in the mean time sojourn'd at my father's;
Where how he did prevail, I shame to speak:
But truth is truth; large lengths of seas and shores
Between my father and my mother lay,
(As I have heard my father speak himself,)
When this same lusty gentleman was got.
Upon his death-bed he by will bequeath'd
His lands to me; and took it, on his death,
That this, my mother's son, was none of his;
And, if he were, he came into the world
Full fourteen weeks before the course of time.
Then, good my liege, let me have what is mine,
My father's land, as was my father's will.

K. John. Sirrah, your brother is legitimate;
Your father's wife did after wedlock bear him;
And, if she did play false, the fault was hers;
Which fault lies on the hazards of all husbands
That marry wives. Tell me, how if my brother,
Who, as you say, took pains to get this son,
Had of your father claim'd this son for his?
In sooth, good friend, your father might have kept
This calf, bred from his cow, from all the world;
In sooth, he might: then, if he were my brother's,
My brother might not claim him; nor your father,
Being none of his, refuse him: This concludes,—
My mother's son did get your father's heir;
Your father's heir must have your father's land.

Rob. Shall then my father's will be of no force,
To dispossess that child which is not his?

Bast. Of no more force to dispossess me, sir,
Than was his will to get me, as I think.

Eli. Whether hadst thou rather,—be a Faulcon-
　　　　　bridge,
And like thy brother, to enjoy thy land;
Or the reputed son of Cœur-de-lion,
Lord of thy presence, and no land beside?

Bast. Madam, an if my brother had my shape,
And I had his, sir Robert his, like him;
And if my legs were two such riding-rods,
My arms such eel-skins stuff'd; my face so thin,
That in mine ear I durst not stick a rose,
Lest men should say, Look, where three-farthings
　　　　　goes!
And, to his shape, were heir to all this land,

'Would I might never stir from off this place,
I'd give it every foot to have this face;
I would not be sir Nob in any case.'

　Eli. I like thee well: Wilt thou forsake thy fortune,
Bequeath thy land to him, and follow me?
I am a soldier, and now bound to France.

　Bast. Brother, take you my land, I'll take my chance:
Your face hath got five hundred pounds a year;
Yet sell your face for five-pence, and 't is dear.—
Madam, I'll follow you unto the death.

　Eli. Nay, I would have you go before me thither.

　Bast. Our country manners give our betters way.

　K. John. What is thy name?

　Bast. Philip, my liege; so is my name begun;
Philip, good old sir Robert's wife's eldest son.

　K. John. From henceforth bear his name whose form thou bear'st:
Kneel thou down Philip, but arise more great;
Arise sir Richard, and Plantagenet.

　Bast. Brother, by the mother's side, give me your hand;
My father gave me honour, yours gave land:—
Now blessed be the hour, by night or day,
When I was got, sir Robert was away.

　Eli. The very spirit of Plantagenet!—
I am thy grandame, Richard; call me so.

　Bast. Madam, by chance, but not by truth:
What though?
Something about, a little from the right,
In at the window, or else o'er the hatch
Who dares not stir by day, must walk by night;
And have is have, however men do catch;
Near or far off, well won is still well shot;
And I am I, howe'er I was begot.

　K. John. Go, Faulconbridge; now hast thou thy desire,
A landless knight makes thee a landed 'squire.—
Come, madam, and come, Richard; we must speed
For France, for France; for it is more than need.

　Bast. Brother, adieu: Good fortune come to thee!
For thou wast got i' the way of honesty.

　　　　　　　　　[Exeunt all but the Bastard.

A foot of honour better than I was;
But many a many foot of land the worse.
Well, now can I make any Joan a lady:——
"Good den, sir Richard,—God-a-mercy, fellow;"—
And if his name be George, I'll call him Peter:
For new-made honour doth forget men's names;
'T is too respective, and too sociable,
For your conversion. Now your traveller,—
613

He and his tooth-pick at my worship's mess;
And when my knightly stomach is suffic'd,
Why then I suck my teeth, and catechise
My picked man of countries:—"My dear sir,"
(Thus, leaning on mine elbow, I begin,)
"I shall beseech you"—That is question now;
And then comes answer like an ABC-book:—
"O sir," says answer, "at your best command;
At your employment; at your service, sir:"—
"No, sir," says question, "I, sweet sir, at yours:"
And so, ere answer knows what question would,
(Saving in dialogue of compliment;
And talking of the Alps, and Apennines,
The Pyrenean, and the river Po,)
It draws toward supper in conclusion so.
But this is worshipful society,
And fits the mounting spirit, like myself:
For he is but a bastard to the time,
That doth not smack of observation;
(And so am I, whether I smack, or no;)
And not alone in habit and device,
Exterior form, outward accoutrement;
But from the inward motion to deliver
Sweet, sweet, sweet poison for the age's tooth:
Which, though I will not practise to deceive,
Yet, to avoid deceit, I mean to learn;
For it shall strew the footsteps of my rising.—
But who comes in such haste, in riding robes?
What woman-post is this? hath she no husband,
That will take pains to blow a horn before her?

Enter LADY FAULCONBRIDGE *and* JAMES GURNEY.

O me! it is my mother:—How now, good lady?
What brings you here to court so hastily?

　Lady F. Where is that slave, thy brother? where is he
That holds in chase mine honour up and down?

　Bast. My brother Robert? old sir Robert's son?
Colbrand the giant, that same mighty man?
Is it sir Robert's son, that you seek so?

　Lady F. Sir Robert's son! Ay, thou unreverend boy,
Sir Robert's son: Why scorn'st thou at sir Robert?
He is sir Robert's son; and so art thou.

　Bast. James Gurney, wilt thou give us leave a while?

　Gur. Good leave, good Philip.

　Bast. Philip?—sparrow!—James,
There's toys abroad; anon I'll tell thee more.
　　　　　　　　　　　　　　　　[Exit Gur.
Madam, I was not old sir Robert's son;
Sir Robert might have eat his part in me

Upon Good-Friday, and ne'er broke his fast:
Sir Robert could do well; Marry, (to confess!)
Could he get me? Sir Robert could not do it;
We know his handy-work:—Therefore, good mo-
    ther,
To whom am I beholden for these limbs?
Sir Robert never help to make this leg.

   Lady F. Hast thou conspired with thy brother too,
That for thine own gain should'st defend mine
    honour?
What means this scorn, thou most untoward knave?

   Bast. Knight, knight, good mother,—Basilisco-
    like:—
What! I am dubb'd; I have it on my shoulder.
But, mother, I am not sir Robert's son;
I have disclaim'd sir Robert, and my land;
Legitimation, name, and all is gone:
Then, good my mother, let me know my father;
Some proper man, I hope: Who was it, mother?

   Lady F. Hast thou denied thyself a Faulcon-
    bridge?

   Bast. As faithfully as I deny the devil.

   Lady F. King Richard Cœur-de-lion was thy
    father;

By long and vehement suit I was seduc'd
To make room for him in my husband's bed:——
Heaven lay not my transgression to my charge!—
Thou art the issue of my dear offence,
Which was so strongly urg'd, past my defence.

   Bast. Now, by this light, were I to get again,
Madam, I would not wish a better father.
Some sins do bear their privilege on earth,
And so doth yours; your fault was not your folly,
Needs must you lay your heart at his dispose,—
Subjected tribute to commanding love,—
Against whose fury and unmatched force
The awless lion could not wage the fight,
Nor keep his princely heart from Richard's hand.
He, that perforce robs lions of their hearts,
May easily win a woman's. Ay, my mother,
With all my heart I thank thee for my father!
Who lives and dares but say, thou didst not well
When I was got, I 'll send his soul to hell.
Come, lady, I will show thee to my kin;
   And they shall say, when Richard me begot,
If thou hadst said him nay, it had been sin:
   Who says it was, he lies; I say, 'twas not.

                     [*Exeunt.*

ACT II.

SCENE I.—France. *Before the Walls of Angiers.*

Enter, on one side, the Archduke of Austria, *and
Forces; on the other,* PHILIP, *King of* France,
and Forces; LEWIS, CONSTANCE, ARTHUR, *and
Attendants.*

   Lew. Before Angiers well met, brave Austria.—
Arthur, that great forerunner of thy blood,
Richard, that robb'd the lion of his heart,
And fought the holy wars in Palestine,
By this brave duke came early to his grave:
And, for amends to his posterity,
At our importance hither is he come,
To spread his colours, boy, in thy behalf;
And to rebuke the usurpation
Of thy unnatural uncle, English John:
Embrace him, love him, give him welcome hither.

   Arth. God shall forgive you Cœur-de-lion's death,
The rather, that you give his offspring life,
Shadowing their right under your wings of war:
I give you welcome with a powerless hand,
But with a heart full of unstained love:

Welcome before the gates of Angiers, duke.

   Lew. A noble boy! Who would not do thee right?

   Aust. Upon thy cheek lay I this zealous kiss,
As seal to this indenture of my love;
That to my home I will no more return,
Till Angiers, and the right thou hast in France,
Together with that pale, that white-fac'd shore,
Whose foot spurns back the ocean's roaring tides,
And coops from other lands her islanders,
Even till that England, hedg'd in with the main,
That water-walled bulwark, still secure
And confident from foreign purposes,
Even till that utmost corner of the west
Salute thee for her king: till then, fair boy,
Will I not think of home, but follow arms.

   Const. O, take his mother's thanks, a widow's
    thanks,
Till your strong hand shall help to give him
    strength,
To make a more requital to your love.

   Aust. The peace of heaven is theirs, that lift
    their swords

In such a just and charitable war.

K. Phi. Well then, to work; our cannon shall
　　　be bent
Against the brows of this resisting town.——
Call for our chiefest men of discipline,
To cull the plots of best advantages:—
We'll lay before this town our royal bones,
Wade to the market-place in Frenchmen's blood,
But we will make it subject to this boy.

Const. Stay for an answer to your embassy,
Lest unadvis'd you stain your swords with blood:
My lord Chatillon may from England bring
That right in peace, which here we urge in war;
And then we shall repent each drop of blood,
That hot rash haste so indiscreetly shed.

Enter CHATILLON.

K. Phi. A wonder, lady!—lo, upon thy wish,
Our messenger Chatillon is arriv'd.—
What England says, say briefly, gentle lord,
We coldly pause for thee; Chatillon, speak.

Chat. Then turn your forces from this paltry
　　　siege,
And stir them up against a mightier task.
England, impatient of your just demands,
Hath put himself in arms; the adverse winds,
Whose leisure I have staid, have given him time
To land his legions all as soon as I:
His marches are expedient to this town,
His forces strong, his soldiers confident.
With him along is come the mother-queen,
An Até, stirring him to blood and strife;
With her her niece, the lady Blanch of Spain;
With them a bastard of the king deceas'd:
And all the unsettled humors of the land,—
Rash, inconsiderate, fiery voluntaries,
With ladies' faces, and fierce dragons' spleens,—
Have sold their fortunes at their native homes,
Bearing their birthrights proudly on their backs,
To make a hazard of new fortunes here.
In brief, a braver choice of dauntless spirits,
Than now the English bottoms have waft o'er,
Did never float upon the swelling tide,
To do offence and scath in Christendom.
The interruption of their churlish drums
　　　　　　　　　　　　[*Drums beat.*
Cuts off more circumstance: they are at hand,
To parley, or to fight; therefore, prepare.

K. Phi. How much unlook'd for is this expedi-
　　　tion!

Aust. By how much unexpected, by so much
We must awake endeavour for defence;

For courage mounteth with occasion:
Let them be welcome then, we are prepar'd.

Enter KING JOHN, ELINOR, BLANCH, *the Bastard,*
　　PEMBROKE, *and Forces.*

K. John. Peace be to France; if France in peace
　　　permit
Our just and lineal entrance to our own!
If not; bleed France, and peace ascend to heaven!
Whiles we, God's wrathful agent, do correct
Their proud contempt that beat his peace to heaven.

K. Phi. Peace be to England; if that war return
From France to England, there to live in peace!
England we love; and, for that England's sake
With burden of our armour here we sweat:
This toil of ours should be a work of thine;
But thou from loving England art so far,
That thou hast under-wrought his lawful king,
Cut off the sequence of posterity,
Outfaced infant state, and done a rape
Upon the maiden virtue of the crown.
Look here upon thy brother Geffrey's face;—
These eyes, these brows, were moulded out of his;
This little abstract doth contain that large,
Which died in Geffrey; and the hand of time
Shall draw this brief into as large a volume.
That Geffrey was thy elder brother born,
And this his son; England was Geffrey's right,
And this is Geffrey's: In the name of God,
How comes it then, that thou art call'd a king,
When living blood doth in these temples beat,
Which owe the crown that thou o'ermasterest?

K. John. From whom hast thou this great com-
　　mission, France,
To draw my answer from thy articles?

K. Phi. From that supernal judge, that stirs
　　good thoughts
In any breast of strong authority,
To look into the blots and stains of right.
That judge hath made me guardian to this boy:
Under whose warrant, I impeach thy wrong;
And, by whose help, I mean to chastise it.

K. John. Alack, thou dost usurp authority.

K. Phi. Excuse; it is to beat usurping down.

Eli. Who is it, thou dost call usurper, France?

Const. Let me make answer;—thy usurping
　　son.

Eli. Out, insolent! thy bastard shall be king;
That thou may'st be a queen, and check the world!

Const. My bed was ever to thy son as true,
As thine was to thy husband: and this boy
Liker in feature to his father Geffrey,

Than thou and John in manners; being as like,
As rain to water, or devil to his dam.
My boy a bastard! By my soul, I think,
His father never was so true begot;
It cannot be, an if thou wert his mother.⁹

   Eli. There's a good mother, boy, that blots thy
father.

   Const. There's a good grandam, boy, that would
blot thee.

   Aust. Peace!

   Bast.   Hear the crier.

   Aust.   What the devil art thou?

   Bast. One that will play the devil, sir with
you,
An 'a may catch your hide and you alone.
You are the hare of whom the proverb goes,
Whose valour plucks dead lions by the beard;
I'll smoke your skin-coat, an I catch you right;
Sirrah, look to 't; i' faith, I will, i' faith.

   Blanch. O, well did he become that lion's robe,
That did disrobe the lion of that robe!

   Bast. It lies as sightly on the back of him,
As great Alcides' shoes upon an ass:—
But, ass, I'll take that burden from your back;
Or lay on that, shall make your shoulders crack.

   Aust. What cracker is this same, that deafs our
ears
With this abundance of superfluous breath?

   K. Phi. Lewis, determine what we shall do
straight.

   Lew. Women and fools, break off your con-
ference.—
King John, this is the very sum of all,—
England, and Ireland, Anjou, Touraine, Maine,
In right of Arthur do I claim of thee:
Wilt thou resign them, and lay down thy arms?

   K. John. My life as soon:—I do defy thee,
France.
Arthur of Bretagne, yield thee to my hand;
And, out of my dear love, I'll give thee more
Than e'er the coward hand of France can win:
Submit thee, boy.

   Eli.   Come to thy grandam, child.

   Const. Do, child, go to it' grandam, child;
Give grandam kingdom, and it' grandam will
Give it a plum, a cherry, and a fig:
There's a good grandam.

   Arth.   Good my mother, peace!
I would, that I were low laid in my grave;
I am not worth this coil that's made for me.

   Eli. His mother shames him so, poor boy, he
weeps.

   Const. Now shame upon you, whe'r she does
or no.
His grandam's wrongs, and not his mother's shames,
Draw those heaven-moving pearls from his poor eyes,
Which heaven shall take in nature of a fee;
Ay, with these crystal beads heaven shall be brib'd
To do him justice, and revenge on you.

   Eli. Thou monstrous slanderer of heaven and
earth!

   Const. Thou monstrous injurer of heaven and
earth!
Call not me slanderer; thou, and thine, usurp
The dominations, royalties, and rights,
Of this oppressed boy: This is thy eldest son's son,
Infortunate in nothing but in thee;
Thy sins are visited in this poor child;
The canon of the law is laid on him,
Being but the second generation
Removed from thy sin-conceiving womb.

   K. John. Bedlam, have done.

   Const.   I have but this to say,—
That he's not only plagued for her sin,
But God hath made her sin and her the plague
On this removed issue, plagu'd for her,
And with her plague, her sin; his injury
Her injury,—the beadle to her sin;
All punish'd in the person of this child,
And all for her: A plague upon her!

   Eli. Thou unadvised scold, I can produce
A will, that bars the title of thy son.

   Const. Ay, who doubts that? a will! a wicked
will;
A woman's will; a canker'd grandam's will!

   K. Phi. Peace, lady; pause, or be more tempe-
rate:
It ill beseems this presence, to cry aim¹²
To these ill-tuned repetitions.—
Some trumpet summon hither to the walls,
These men of Angiers; let us hear them speak,
Whose title they admit, Arthur's or John's.

Trumpets sound.   Enter Citizens upon the walls.

   1st Cit. Who is it, that hath warn'd us to the
walls?

   K. Phi. 'Tis France, for England.

   K. John.   England, for itself:
You men of Angiers, and my loving subjects,——

   K. Phi. You loving men of Angiers, Arthur's
subjects,
Our trumpet call'd you to this gentle parle.

   K. John. For our advantage;—Therefore, hear
us first.——

651

These flags of France, that are advanced here
Before the eye and prospect of your town,
Have hither march'd to your endamagement;
The cannons have their bowels full of wrath;
And ready mounted are they, to spit forth
Their iron indignation 'gainst your walls:
All preparation for a bloody siege,
And merciless proceeding by these French,
Confront your city's eyes, your winking gates;
And, but for our approach, those sleeping stones
That as a waist do girdle you about,
By the compulsion of their ordnance
By this time from their fixed beds of lime
Had been dishabited, and wide havoc made
For bloody power to rush upon your peace.
But, on the sight of us, your lawful king,——
Who painfully, with much expedient march,
Have brought a countercheck before your gates,
To save unscratch'd your city's threaten'd cheeks,—
Behold, the French, amaz'd, vouchsafe a parle:
And now, instead of bullets wrapp'd in fire,
To make a shaking fever in your walls,
They shoot but calm words, folded up in smoke,
To make a faithless error in your ears:
Which trust accordingly, kind citizens,
And let us in. Your king, whose labour'd spirits,
Forewearied in this action of swift speed,
Craves harbourage within your city walls.

   K. Phi. When I have said, make answer to us
both.
Lo, in this right hand, whose protection
Is most divinely vow'd upon the right
Of him it holds, stands young Plantagenet;
Son to the elder brother of this man,
And king o'er him, and all that he enjoys;
For this down-trodden equity, we tread
In warlike march these greens before your town,
Being no further enemy to you,
Than the constraint of hospitable zeal,
In the relief of this oppressed child,
Religiously provokes. Be pleased then
To pay that duty, which you truly owe,
To him that owes it; namely, this young prince;
And then our arms, like to a muzzled bear,
Save in aspect, have all offence seal'd up;
Our cannons' malice vainly shall be spent
Against the invulnerable clouds of heaven;
And, with a blessed and unvex'd retire,
With unhack'd swords, and helmets all unbruis'd,
We will bear home that lusty blood again,
Which here we came to spout against your town,
And leave your children, wives, and you, in peace.

652

But if you fondly pass our proffer'd offer,
'Tis not the roundure of your old-fac'd walls
Can hide you from our messengers of war;
Though all these English, and their discipline,
Were harbour'd in their rude circumference.
Then, tell us, shall your city call us lord,
In that behalf which we have challeng'd it?
Or shall we give the signal to our rage,
And stalk in blood to our possession?

   1st Cit. In brief, we are the king of England's
subjects;
For him, and in his right, we hold this town.

   K. John. Acknowledge then the king, and let
me in.

   1st Cit. That can we not: but he that proves
the king,
To him will we prove loyal; till that time,
Have we ramm'd up our gates against the world.

   K. John. Doth not the crown of England prove
the king?
And, if not that, I bring you witnesses,
Twice fifteen thousand hearts of England's breed,—

   Bast. Bastards, and else.

   K. John. To verify our title with their lives,

   K. Phi. As many, and as well-born bloods as
those,——

   Bast. Some bastards too.

   K. Phi. Stand in his face, to contradict his
claim.

   1st Cit. Till you compound whose right is worthiest,
We for the worthiest, hold the right from both.

   K. John. Then God forgive the sin of all those
souls,
That to their everlasting residence,
Before the dew of evening fall, shall fleet,
In dreadful trial of our kingdom's king!

   K. Phi. Amen, amen :—Mount, chevaliers! to
arms!

   Bast. St. George,—that swing'd the dragon, and
e'er since
Sits on his horseback at mine hostess' door,
Teach us some fence!—Sirrah, were I at home,
At your den, sirrah, [*To* Aust.] with your lioness,
I'd set an ox-head to your lion's hide,
And make a monster of you.

   Aust.   Peace; no more.

   Bast. O, tremble; for you hear the lion roar.

   K. John. Up higher to the plain; where we'll
set forth,
In best appointment, all our regiments.

   Bast. Speed then, to take advantage of the field,

K. Phi. It shall be so;—[*To* Lew.] and at the
　　　other hill
Command the rest to stand,—God, and our right!
　　　　　　　　　　　　　　　　[*Exeunt.*

SCENE II.—*The Same.*

*Alarums and Excursions; then a Retreat. Enter
a French Herald, with trumpets, to the gates.*

F. Her. You men of Angiers, open wide your
　　　gates,
And let young Arthur, duke of Bretagne, in;
Who, by the hand of France, this day hath made
Much work for tears in many an English mother,
Whose sons lie scatter'd on the bleeding ground:
Many a widow's husband grovelling lies,
Coldly embracing the discolour'd earth;
And victory, with little loss, doth play
Upon the dancing banners of the French
Who are at hand, triumphantly display'd,
To enter conquerors, and to proclaim
Arthur of Bretagne, England's king, and yours.

Enter an English Herald, with trumpets.

E. Her. Rejoice, you men of Angiers, ring your
　　　bells;
King John, your king and England's, doth ap-
　　　proach
Commander of this hot malicious day!
Their armours, that march'd hence so silver-bright,
Hither return all gilt with Frenchmen's blood;
There stuck no plume in any English crest,
That is removed by a staff of France;
Our colours do return in those same hands
That did display them when we first march'd
　　　forth;
And, like a jolly troop of huntsmen, come
Our lusty English, all with purpled hands,
Died in the dying slaughter of their foes:
Open your gates, and give the victors way.
　　Cit. Heralds, from off our towers we might
　　　behold,
From first to last, the onset and retire
Of both your armies; whose equality
By our best eyes cannot be censured:
Blood hath bought blood, and blows have answer'd
　　　blows;
Strength match'd with strength, and power con-
　　　fronted power:
Both are alike; and both alike we like.
One must prove greatest: while they weigh so even
We hold our town for neither; yet for both.

Enter, at one side, King John, *with his power*,
Elinor, Blanch, *and the Bastard; at the other,*
King Philip, Lewis, Austria, *and Forces*

K. John. France, hast thou yet more blood to
　　　cast away?
Say, shall the current of our right run on?
Whose passage, vex'd with thy impediment,
Shall leave his native channel, and o'er-swell
With course disturb'd even thy confining shores;
Unless thou let his silver water keep
A peaceful progress to the ocean.
　　K. Phi. England, thou hast not sav'd one drop
　　　of blood,
In this hot trial, more than we of France;
Rather, lost more: And by this hand I swear,
That sways the earth this climate overlooks,—
Before we will lay down our just-borne arms,
We'll put thee down, 'gainst whom these arms we
　　　bear,
Or add a royal number to the dead;
Gracing the scroll, that tells of this war's loss,
With slaughter coupled to the name of kings.
　　Bast. Ha, majesty! how high thy glory towers,
When the rich blood of kings is set on fire!
O, now doth death line his dead chaps with steel;
The swords of soldiers are his teeth, his fangs;
And now he feasts, mouthing the flesh of men,
In undetermin'd differences of kings,—
Why stand these royal fronts amazed thus?
Cry, havoc, kings! back to the stained field,
You equal potents, fiery-kindled spirits!
Then let confusion of one part confirm
The other's peace; till then, blows, blood, and
　　　death!
　　K. John. Whose party do the townsmen yet
　　　admit?
　　K. Phi. Speak, citizens, for England; who's
　　　your king?
　　1st Cit. The king of England, when we know
　　　the king.
　　K. Phi. Know him in us, that here hold up his
　　　right.
　　K. John. In us, that are our own great deputy,
And bear possession of our person here;
Lord of our presence, Angiers, and of you.
　　1st Cit. A greater power than we, denies all
　　　this:
And, till it be undoubted, we do lock
Our former scruple in our strong-barr'd gates;
King'd of our fears; until our fears, resolv'd,
Be by some certain king purg'd and depos'd.

Bast. By heaven, these scroyles of Angiers[14] flout
　　you, kings;
And stand securely on their battlements,
As in a theatre, whence they gape and point
At your industrious scenes and acts of death.
Your royal presences be rul'd by me;
Do like the mutines of Jerusalem,[15]
Be friends a while, and both conjointly bend
Your sharpest deeds of malice on this town:
By east and west let France and England mount
Their battering cannon, charged to the mouths;
Till their soul-fearing clamours have brawl'd down
The flinty ribs of this contemptuous city:
I'd play incessantly upon these jades,
Even till unfenced desolation
Leave them as naked as the vulgar air.
That done, dissever your united strengths,
And part your mingled colours once again;
Turn face to face, and bloody point to point:
Then, in a moment, fortune shall call forth
Out of one side her happy minion;
To whom in favour she shall give the day,
And kiss him with a glorious victory.
How like you this wild counsel, mighty states?
Smacks it not something of the policy?

　K. John. Now, by the sky that hangs above our
　　heads,
I like it well;—France, shall we knit our powers,
And lay this Angiers even with the ground;
Then, after, fight who shall be king of it?

　Bast. An if thou hast the mettle of a king,—
Being wrong'd, as we are, by this peevish town,—
Turn thou the mouth of thy artillery,
As we will ours, against these saucy walls:
And when that we have dash'd them to the ground,
Why, then defy each other; and, pell-mell,
Make work upon ourselves, for heaven, or hell.

　K. Phi. Let it be so:—Say, where will you
　　assault?

　K. John. We from the west will send destruction
Into this city's bosom.

　Aust. I from the north.

　K. Phi. 　　　　Our thunder from the south,
Shall rain their drift of bullets on this town.

　Bast. O prudent discipline! From north to south:
Austria and France shoot in each other's mouth;
　　　　　　　　　　　　　　　　[*Aside.*
I'll stir them to it:—Come, away, away!

　1st Cit. Hear us, great kings: vouchsafe a while
　　to stay,
And I shall show you peace, and fair-faced league;
Win you this city without stroke, or wound;

Rescue those breathing lives to die in beds,
That here come sacrifices for the field:
Persévere not, but hear me, mighty kings.

　K. John. Speak on, with favour; we are bent
　　to hear.

　1st Cit. That daughter there of Spain, the lady
　　Blanch,
Is near to England: Look upon the years
Of Lewis the Dauphin, and that lovely maid:
If lusty love should go in quest of beauty,
Where should he find it fairer than in Blanch?
If zealous love should go in search of virtue,
Where should he find it purer than in Blanch?
If love ambitious sought a match of birth,
Whose veins bound richer blood than lady Blanch?
Such as she is, in beauty, virtue, birth,
Is the young Dauphin every way complete;
If not complete, O say, he is not she;
And she again wants nothing, to name want,
If want it be not, that she is not he:
He is the half part of a blessed man,
Left to be finished by such as she;
And she a fair divided excellence,
Whose fulness of perfection lies in him.
O, two such silver currents, when they join,
Do glorify the banks that bound them in:
And two such shores to two such streams made one,
Two such controlling bounds shall you be, kings,
To these two princes, if you marry them.
This union shall do more than battery can,
To our fast-closed gates; for, at this match,
With swifter spleen than powder can enforce,
The mouth of passage shall we fling wide ope,
And give you entrance; but, without this match,
The sea enraged is not half so deaf,
Lions more confident, mountains and rocks
More free from motion; no, not death herself
In mortal fury half so peremptory,
As we to keep this city.

　Bast. 　　　　Here's a stay,
That shakes the rotten carcase of old death
Out of his rags! Here's a large mouth, indeed,
That spits forth death, and mountains, rocks, and
　　seas;
Talks as familiarly of roaring lions,
As maids of thirteen do of puppy-dogs!
What cannoneer begot this lusty blood?
He speaks plain cannon, fire, and smoke, and
　　bounce;
He gives the bastinado with his tongue;
Our ears are cudgel'd; not a word of his,
But buffets better than a fist of France:

Zounds! I was never so bethump'd with words,
Since I first call'd my brother's father, dad.

Eli. Son, list to this conjunction, make this
 match;
Give with our niece a dowry large enough:
For by this knot thou shalt so surely tie
Thy now unsur'd assurance to the crown,
That yon green boy shall have no sun to ripe
The bloom that promiseth a mighty fruit.
I see a yielding in the looks of France;
Mark, how they whisper; urge them, while their
 souls
Are capable of this ambition:
Lest zeal, now melted, by the windy breath
Of soft petitions, pity, and remorse,
Cool and congeal again to what it was.

1st Cit. Why answer not the double majesties
This friendly treaty of our threaten'd town?

K. Phi. Speak England first, that hath been
 forward first
To speak unto this city: What say you?

K. John. If that the Dauphin there, thy
 princely son,
Can in this book of beauty read, I love,
Her dowry shall weigh equal with the queen:
For Anjou, and fair Touraine, Maine, Poictiers,
And all that we upon this side the sea
(Except this city now by us besieg'd,)
Find liable to our crown and dignity,
Shall gild her bridal bed; and make her rich
In titles, honours, and promotions,
As she in beauty, education, blood,
Holds hand with any princess of the world.

K. Phi. What say'st thou, boy? look in the
 lady's face.

Lew. I do, my lord, and in her eye I find
A wonder, or a wondrous miracle,
The shadow of myself form'd in her eye;
Which, being but the shadow of your son,
Becomes a sun, and makes your son a shadow:
I do protest, I never lov'd myself,
Till now infixed I beheld myself,
Drawn in the flattering table of her eye.
 [*Whispers with* BLANCH.

Bast. Drawn in the flattering table of her
 eye!—
Hang'd in the frowning wrinkle of her
 brow!—
And quarter'd in her heart!—he doth espy
 Himself love's traitor: This is pity now,
That hang'd, and drawn, and quarter'd, there
 should be,

In such a love, so vile a lout as he.

Blanch. My uncle's will, in this respect, is mine:
If he see aught in you, that makes him like,
That any thing he sees, which moves his liking,
I can with ease translate it to my will;
Or, if you will, (to speak more properly)
I will enforce it easily to my love.
Further I will not flatter you, my lord,
That all I see in you is worthy love,
Than this,—that nothing do I see in you,
(Though churlish thoughts themselves should be
 your judge,)
That I can find should merit any hate.

K. John. What say these young ones? What
 say you, my niece?

Blanch. That she is bound in honour still to do
What you in wisdom shall vouchsafe to say.

K. John. Speak then, prince Dauphin; can you
 love this lady?

Lew. Nay, ask me if I can refrain from love;
For I do love her most unfeignedly.

K. John. Then I do give Volquessen,[16] Touraine,
 Maine,
Poictiers, and Anjou, these five provinces,
With her to thee; and this addition more,
Full thirty thousand marks of English coin.—
Philip of France, if thou be pleas'd withal,
Command thy son and daughter to join hands.

K. Phi. It likes us well;—Young princes,
 close your hands.

Aust. And your lips too; for, I am well assur'd,
That I did so, when I was first assur'd.

K. Phi. Now, citizens of Angiers, ope your
 gates,
Let in that amity which you have made;
For at saint Mary's chapel, presently,
The rites of marriage shall be solemniz'd.—
Is not the lady Constance in this troop?—
I know, she is not; for this match, made up,
Her presence would have interrupted much:—
Where is she and her son? tell me, who knows.

Lew. She is sad and passionate at your highness' tent.

K. Phi. And, by my faith, this league, that
 we have made,
Will give her sadness very little cure.—
Brother of England, how may we content
This widow lady? In her right we came;
Which we, God knows, have turn'd another way
To our own vantage.

K. John.   We will heal up all,
For we'll create young Arthur duke of Bretagne,

And earl of Richmond ; and this rich fair town
We make him lord of.—Call the lady Constance ;
Some speedy messenger bid her repair
To our solemnity :—I trust we shall,
If not fill up the measure of her will,
Yet in some measure satisfy her so,
That we shall stop her exclamation.
Go we, as well as haste will suffer us,
To this unlook'd for unprepared pomp.

　　[*Exeunt all but the* Bast.—*The* Citizens
　　　　retire from the walls.

Bast. Mad world ! mad kings ! mad composition !
John, to stop Arthur's title in the whole,
Hath willingly departed with a part :
And France, (whose armour conscience buckled on ;
Whom zeal and charity brought to the field,
As God's own soldier,) rounded in the ear
With that same purpose-changer, that sly devil ;
That broker, that still breaks the pate of faith ;
That daily break-vow ; he that wins of all,
Of kings, of beggars, old men, young man,
　　maids ;—
Who having no external thing to lose
But the word maid,—cheats the poor maid of that ;
That smooth-faced gentleman, tickling commo-
　　dity,—

Commodity, the bias of the world ;
The world, who of itself is pois'd well,
Made to run even, upon even ground :
Till this advantage, this vile drawing bias,
This sway of motion, this commodity,
Makes it take head from all indifferency,
From all direction, purpose, course, intent :
And this same bias, this commodity,
This bawd, this broker, this all-changing word,
Clapp'd on the outward eye of fickle France,
Hath drawn him from his own determin'd aim,
From a resolv'd and honourable war,
To a most base and vile-concluded peace.—
And why rail I on this commodity ?
But for because he hath not woo'd me yet :
Not that I have not power to clutch my hand,
When his fair angels would salute my palm ;
But for my hand, as unattempted yet,
Like a poor beggar, raileth on the rich.
Well, whiles I am a beggar, I will rail,
And say,—there is no sin, but to be rich ;
And being rich, my virtue then shall be,
To say,—there is no vice, but beggary :
Since kings break faith upon commodity,
Gain, be my lord ! for I will worship thee !

　　　　　　　　　　　　　　　　　　[*Exit*

ACT III.

SCENE I.—*The Same.　The* French King's *Tent.*

Enter Constance, Arthur, *and* Salisbury.

Const. Gone to be married ! gone to swear a
　　peace !
False blood to false blood join'd ! Gone to be
　　friends !
Shall Lewis have Blanch ? and Blanch those pro-
　　vinces ?
It is not so ; thou hast misspoke, misheard ;
Be well advis'd, tell o'er thy tale again :
It cannot be ; thou dost but say, 't is so :
I trust, I may not trust thee ; for thy word
Is but the vain breath of a common man :
Believe me, I do not believe thee, man ;
I have a king's oath to the contrary.
Thou shalt be punish'd for thus frighting me,
For I am sick, and capable of fears ;
Oppress'd with wrongs, and therefore full of fears ;

A widow, husbandless, subject to fears ;
A woman, naturally born to fears ;
And though thou now confess, thou didst but jest,
With my vex'd spirits I cannot take a truce,
But they will quake and tremble all this day.
What dost thou mean by shaking of thy head ?
Why dost thou look so sadly on my son ?
What means that hand upon that breast of thine ?
Why holds thine eye that lamentable rheum,
Like a proud river peering o'er his bounds ?
Be these sad signs confirmers of thy words ?
Then speak again ; not all thy former tale,
But this one word, whether thy tale be true.
　　Sal. As true, as, I believe, you think them false
That give you cause to prove my saying true.
　　Const. O, if thou teach me to believe this sor-
　　row,
Teach thou this sorrow how to make me die ;
And let belief and life encounter so,

SS. MM. D. Pedro e D. Luiz Dom Luiz

As doth the fury of two desperate men,
Which, in the very meeting, fall, and die.—
Lewis marry Blanch! O, boy, then where art thou?
France friend with England! what becomes of me?
Fellow, be gone; I cannot brook thy sight;
This news hath made thee a most ugly man.

Sai. What other harm have I, good lady, done,
But spoke the harm that is by others done?

Const. Which harm within itself so heinous is,
As it makes harmful all that speak of it.

Arth. I do beseech you, madam, be content.

Const. If thou, that bidd'st me be content, wert grim,
Ugly, and sland'rous to thy mother's womb,
Full of unpleasing blots, and sightless stains,
Lame, foolish, crooked, swart, prodigious,
Patch'd with foul moles, and eye-offending marks,
I would not care, I then would be content;
For then I should not love thee; no, nor thou
Become thy great birth, nor deserve a crown.
But thou art fair; and at thy birth, dear boy!
Nature and fortune join'd to make thee great:
Of nature's gifts thou may'st with lilies boast,
And with the half-blown rose: but fortune, O!
She is corrupted, chang'd, and won from thee;
She adulterates hourly with thine uncle John;
And with her golden hand hath pluck'd on France
To tread down fair respect of sovereignty,
And made his majesty the bawd to theirs.
France is a bawd to fortune, and king John;
That strumpet fortune, that usurping John:—
Tell me, thou fellow, is not France forsworn?
Envenom him with words; or get thee gone,
And leave those woes alone, which I alone,
Am bound to under-bear.

Sal.   Pardon me, madam,
I may not go without you to the kings.

Const. Thou may'st, thou shalt, I will not go with thee:
I will instruct my sorrows to be proud;
For grief is proud, and makes his owner stout.
To me, and to the state of my great grief,
Let kings assemble; for my grief's so great,
That no supporter but the huge firm earth
Can hold it up: here I and sorrow sit;
Here is my throne, bid kings come bow to it.
(She throws herself on the ground.

Enter KING JOHN, KING PHILIP, LEWIS, BLANCH,
ELINOR, *Bastard,* AUSTRIA, *and Attendants.*

K. Phi. 'Tis true, fair daughter; and this blessed day,

Ever in France shall be kept festival:
To solemnize this day, the glorious sun
Stays in his course, and plays the alchemist;
Turning, with splendour of his precious eye,
The meagre cloddy earth to glittering gold:
The yearly course, that brings this day about,
Shall never see it but a holiday.

Const. A wicked day, and not a holiday.——
[Rising.
What hath this day deserv'd? what hath it done;
That it in golden letters should be set,
Among the high tides in the calendar?
Nay, rather, turn this day out of the week;
This day of shame, oppression, perjury:
Or, if it must stand still, let wives with child
Pray, that their burdens may not fall this day,
Lest that their hopes prodigiously be cross'd:
But on this day, let seamen fear no wreck;
No bargains break, that are not this day made:"
This day, all things begun come to ill end,
Yea, faith itself to hollow falsehood change!

K. Phi. By heaven, lady, you shall have no cause
To curse the fair proceedings of this day:
Have I not pawn'd to you my majesty?

Const. You have beguil'd me with a counterfeit,
Resembling majesty; which, being touch'd, and tried,
Proves valueless: You are forsworn, forsworn;
You came in arms to spill mine enemies' blood,
But now in arms you strengthen it with yours:
The grappling vigour and rough frown of war,
Is cold in amity and painted peace,
And our oppression hath made up this league:—
Arm, arm, you heavens, against these perjur'd kings!
A widow cries; be husband to me, heavens!
Let not the hours of this ungodly day
Wear out the day in peace; but, ere sunset,
Set armed discord 'twixt these perjur'd kings!
Hear me, O, hear me!

Aust.   Lady Constance, peace.

Const. War! war! no peace! peace is to me a war.
O Lymoges! O Austria! thou dost shame
That bloody spoil: Thou slave, thou wretch, thou coward;
Thou little valiant, great in villany!
Thou ever strong upon the stronger side!
Thou fortune's champion, that dost never fight
But when her humorous ladyship is by
To teach thee safety! thou art perjur'd too,

And sooth'st up greatness. What a fool art thou,
A ramping fool; to brag, and stamp, and swear,
Upon my party! Thou cold-blooded slave,
Hast thou not spoke like thunder on my side?
Been sworn my soldier! bidding me depend
Upon thy stars, thy fortune, and thy strength?
And dost thou now fall over to my foes?
Thou wear a lion's hide! doff it for shame,
And hang a calf's-skin on those recreant limbs.

　Aust. O, that a man should speak those words
　　to me!
　Bast. And hang a calf's-skin on those recreant
　　limbs.
　Aust. Thou dar'st not say so, villain, for thy life.
　Bast. And hang a calf's-skin on those recreant
　　limbs.
　K. John. We like not this; thou dost forget
　　thyself.

Enter PANDULPH.

　K. Phi. Here comes the holy legate of the pope.
　Pand. Hail, you anointed deputies of hea-
　　ven!—
To thee, king John, my holy errand is.
I Pandulph, of fair Milan cardinal,
And from pope Innocent the legate here,
Do, in his name, religiously demand,
Why thou against the church, our holy mother,
So wilfully dost spurn; and, force perforce,
Keep Stephen Langton, chosen archbishop
Of Canterbury, from that holy see?
This, in our 'foresaid holy father's name,
Pope Innocent, I do demand of thee.
　K. John. What earthly name to interrogatories,
Can task the free breath of a sacred king!
Thou canst not, cardinal, devise a name
So slight, unworthy, and ridiculous,
To charge me to an answer, as the pope.
Tell him this tale; and from the mouth of Eng-
　　land,
Add thus much more,—That no Italian priest
Shall tithe or toll in our dominions;
But as we under God are supreme head,
So, under him, that great supremacy,
Where we do reign, we will alone uphold,
Without the assistance of a mortal hand:
So tell the pope; all reverence set apart,
To him, and his usurp'd authority.
　K. Phi. Brother of England, you blaspheme
　　in this.
　K. John. Though you, and all the kings of
　　Christendom,
658

Are led so grossly by this meddling priest,
Dreading the curse that money may buy out;
And, by the merit of vile gold, dross, dust,
Purchase corrupted pardon of a man,
Who, in that sale, sells pardon from himself:
Though you, and all the rest, so grossly led,
This juggling witchcraft with revenue cherish;
Yet I, alone, alone do me oppose
Against the pope, and count his friends my foes.
　Pand. Then, by the lawful power that I have,
Thou shalt stand curs'd, and excommunicate:
And blessed shall he be, that doth revolt
From his allegiance to an heretic;
And meritorious shall that hand be call'd,
Canonized, and worshipp'd as a saint,
That takes away by any secret course
Thy hateful life.
　Const. 　　　O, lawful let it be,
That I have room with Rome to curse a while!
Good father cardinal, cry thou, amen,
To my keen curses; for, without my wrong,
There is no tongue hath power to curse him right.
　Pand. There's law and warrant, lady, for my
　　curse.
　Const. And for mine too; when law can do no
　　right,
Let it be lawful, that law bar no wrong:
Law cannot give my child his kingdom here,
For he, that holds his kingdom, holds the law:
Therefore, since law itself is perfect wrong,
How can the law forbid my tongue to curse?
　Pand. Philip of France, on peril of a curse,
Let go the hand of that arch-heretic;
And raise the power of France upon his head,
Unless he do submit himself to Rome.
　Eli. Look'st thou pale, France? do not let go
　　thy hand.
　Const. Look to that, devil! lest that France
　　repent,
And, by disjoining hands, hell lose a soul.
　Aust. King Philip, listen to the cardinal.
　Bast. And hang a calf's-skin on his recreant
　　limbs.
　Aust. Well, ruffian, I must pocket up these
　　wrongs,
Because——
　Bast. 　Your breeches best may carry them.
　K. John. Philip, what say'st thou to the cardi-
　　nal?
　Const. What should he say, but as the cardi-
　　nal?
　Lew. Bethink you, father; for the difference

Is, purchase of a heavy curse from Rome,
Or the light loss of England for a friend :
Forego the easier.

   Blanch.   That's the curse of Rome.

   Const. O Lewis, stand fast; the devil tempts
      thee here,
In likeness of a new untrimmed bride.

   Blanch. The lady Constance speaks not from
      her faith,
But from her need.

   Const.   O, if thou grant my need,
Which only lives but by the death of faith,
That need must needs infer this principle,——
That faith would live again by death of need;
O, then, tread down my need, and faith mounts
      up;
Keep my need up, and faith is trodden down.

   K. John. The king is moved, and answers not
      to this.

   Const. O, be remov'd from him, and answer
      well.

   Aust. Do so, king Philip; hang no more in
      doubt.

   Bast. Hang nothing but a calf's-skin, most sweet
      lout.

   K. Phi. I am perplex'd, and know not what to
      say.

   Pand. What can'st thou say, but will perplex
      thee more,
If thou stand excommunicate, and curs'd ?

   K. Phi. Good reverend father, make my person
      yours,
And tell me how you would bestow yourself.
This royal hand and mine are newly knit
And the conjunction of our inward souls
Married in league, coupled and link'd together
With all religious strength of sacred vows;
The latest breath that gave the sound of words
Was deep-sworn faith, peace, amity, true love,
Between our kingdoms, and our royal selves;
And even before this truce, but new before,——
No longer than we well could wash our hands,
To clap this royal bargain up of peace,——
Heaven knows, they were besmear'd and over-
      stain'd
With slaughter's pencil ! where revenge did paint
The fearful difference of incensed kings;
And shall these hands, so lately purg'd of blood,
So newly join'd in love, so strong in both,
Unyoke this seizure, and this kind regreet
Play fast and loose with faith ? so jest with heaven
Make such inconstant children of ourselves,

As now again to snatch our palm from palm ;
Unswear faith sworn ; and on the marriage bed
Of smiling peace to march a bloody host,
And make a riot on the gentle brow
Of true sincerity ? O holy sir,
My reverend father, let it not be so :
Out of your grace, devise, ordain, impose
Some gentle order; and then we shall be bless'd
To do your pleasure, and continue friends.

   Pand. All form is formless, order orderless,
Save what is opposite to England's love.
Therefore, to arms ! be champion of our church !
Or let the church, our mother, breathe her curse,
A mother's curse, on her revolting son.
France, thou may'st hold a serpent by the tongue,
A cased lion by the mortal paw,
A fasting tiger safer by the tooth,
Than keep in peace that hand which thou dost
      hold.

   K. Phi. I may disjoin my hand, but not my
      faith.

   Pand. So mak'st thou faith an enemy to faith
And, like a civil war, sett'st oath to oath,
Thy tongue against thy tongue. O, let thy vow
First made to heaven, first be to heaven per-
      form'd ;
That is, to be the champion of our church !
What since thou swor'st, is sworn against thyself,
And may not be performed by thyself:
For that, which thou hast sworn to do amiss,
Is not amiss when it is truly done;"
And being not done, where doing tends to ill,
The truth is then most done not doing it;
The better act of purposes mistook
Is, to mistake again ; though indirect,
Yet indirection thereby grows direct.
And falsehood falsehood cures ; as fire cools fire,
Within the scorched veins of one new burn'd.
It is religion, that doth make vows kept;
But thou hast sworn against religion ;
By what thou swear'st, against the thing thou
      swear'st;
And mak'st an oath the surety for thy truth
Against an oath : The truth thou art unsure
To swear, swear only not to be forsworn ;
Else, what a mockery should it be to swear ?
But thou dost swear only to be forsworn ;
And most forsworn, to keep what thou dost
      swear.
Therefore, thy latter vows, against thy first,
Is in thyself rebellion to thyself:
And better conquest never canst thou make,

Than arm thy constant and thy nobler parts
Against those giddy loose suggestions:
Upon which better part our prayers come in,
If thou vouchsafe them : but, if not, then know,
The peril of our curses light on thee;
So heavy, as thou shalt not shake them off,
But, in despair, die under their black weight.

Aust. Rebellion, flat rebellion!

Bast.　　　　　　　　　　Will 't not be?
Will not a calf's-skin stop that mouth of thine?

Lew. Father, to arms.

Blanch.　　　　　Upon thy wedding day?
Against the blood that thou hast married?
What, shall our feast be kept with slaughter'd
　　men?
Shall braying trumpets, and loud churlish drums—
Clamours of hell,—be measures to our pomp?
O husband, hear me!—ah, alack, how new
Is husband in my mouth!—even for that name,
Which till this time my tongue did ne'er pro-
　　nounce,
Upon my knee I beg, go not to arms
Against mine uncle.

Const.　　　　　O, upon my knee,
Made hard with kneeling, I do pray to thee,
Thou virtuous dauphin, alter not the doom
Fore-thought by heaven.

Blanch. Now shall I see thy love: What mo-
　　tive may
Be stronger with thee than the name of wife?

Const. That which upholdeth him that thee
　　upholds,
His honour: O, thine honour, Lewis, thine
　　honour!

Lew. I muse, your majesty doth seem so cold,
When such profound respects do pull you on.

Pand. I will denounce a curse upon his head.

K. Phi. Thou shalt not need:—England, I 'll
　　fall from thee.

Const. O fair return of banish'd majesty!

Eli. O foul revolt of French inconstancy!

K. John. France, thou shalt rue this hour
　　within this hour.

Bast. Old time the clock-setter, that bald sexton
　　time,
Is it as he will? well then, France shall rue.

Blanch. The sun 's o'ercast with blood: Fair
　　day, adieu!
Which is the side that I must go withal?
I am with both : each army hath a hand;
And, in their rage, I having hold of both,
They whirl asunder, and dismember me.

660

Husband, I cannot pray that thou may'st win;
Uncle, I needs must pray that thou may'st lose;
Father, I may not wish the fortune thine;
Grandam, I will not wish thy wishes thrive:
Whoever wins, on that side shall I lose;
Assured loss, before the match be play'd.

Lew. Lady, with me; with me thy fortune lies.

Blanch. There where my fortune lives, there my
　　life dies.

K. John. Cousin, go draw our puissance toge-
　　ther.—　　　　　　　　　　[*Exit* Bast.
France, I am burned up with inflaming wrath;
A rage, whose heat hath this condition,
That nothing can allay, nothing but blood,
The blood, and dearest-valu'd blood of France.

K. Phi. Thy rage shall burn thee up, and thou
　　shalt turn
To ashes, ere our blood shall quench that fire:
Look to thyself, thou art in jeopardy.

K. John. No more than he that threats.—To
　　arms let 's hie!　　　　　　　　[*Exeunt.*

SCENE II.—*The Same.　Plains near Angiers.*

Alarums, Excursions.　Enter the Bastard, *with*
Austria's *Head.*

Bast. Now, by my life, this day grows wondrous
　　hot;
Some airy devil hovers in the sky,
And pours down mischief.　Austria's head lie there;
While Philip breathes.

Enter King John, Arthur, *and* Hubert.

K. John. Hubert, keep this boy:—Philip,
　　make up:
My mother is assailed in our tent,
And ta'en, I fear.

Bast.　　　　My lord, I rescu'd her;
Her highness is in safety, fear you not:
But on, my liege; for very little pains
Will bring this labour to an happy end.　[*Exeunt.*

SCENE III.—*The Same.*

Alarums; Excursions; Retreat.　Enter King
John, Elinor, Arthur, *the* Bastard, Hubert
and Lords.

K. John. So shall it be: your grace shall stay
　　behind,　　　　　　　　　[*To* Eli
So strongly guarded.—Cousin, look not sad:
　　　　　　　　　　　　　　[*To* Arth
Thy grandam loves thee; and thy uncle will

As dear be to thee as thy father was.

Arth. O, this will make my mother die with grief.

K. John. Cousin, [*To the* BAST.] away for Eng-
land; haste before:
And, ere our coming, see thou shake the bags
Of hoarding abbots; angels imprisoned
Set thou at liberty: the fat ribs of peace
Must by the hungry now be fed upon:
Use our commission in his utmost force.

Bast. Bell, book, and candle shall not drive me
back,
When gold and silver becks me to come on.
I leave your highness:—Grandam, I will pray
(If ever I remember to be holy,)
For your fair safety: so I kiss your hand.

Eli. Farewell, my gentle cousin.

K. John. Coz, farewell.

                         [*Exit* BAST.

Eli. Come hither, little kinsman; hark, a word.

                [*She takes* ARTH. *aside.*

K. John. Come hither, Hubert. O my gentle
Hubert,
We owe thee much; within this wall of flesh
There is a soul, counts thee her creditor,
And with advantage means to pay thy love;
And, my good friend, thy voluntary oath
Lives in this bosom, dearly cherished.
Give me thy hand. I had a thing to say,—
But I will fit it with some better time.
By heaven, Hubert, I am almost asham'd
To say what good respect I have of thee.

Hub. I am much bounden to your majesty.

K. John. Good friend, thou hast no cause to say
so yet:
But thou shalt have; and creep time ne'er so slow,
Yet it shall come, for me to do thee good.
I had a thing to say,—But let it go:
The sun is in the heaven, and the proud day,
Attended with the pleasures of the world,
Is all too wanton, and too full of gawds,
To give me audience:—If the midnight bell
Did, with his iron tongue and brazen mouth,
Sound one unto the drowsy race of night;
If this same were a church-yard where we stand,
And thou possessed with a thousand wrongs;
Or if that surly spirit, melancholy,
Had bak'd thy blood, and made it heavy, thick;
(Which, else, runs tickling up and down the veins,
Making that idiot, laughter, keep men's eyes,
And strain their cheeks to idle merriment,
A passion hateful to my purposes;)
Or if that thou could'st see me without eyes,

Hear me without thine ears, and make reply
Without a tongue, using conceit alone,
Without eyes, ears, and harmful sound of words,
Then, in despite of broad-eyed watchful day,
I would into thy bosom pour my thoughts;
But ah, I will not:—Yet I love thee well;
And, by my troth, I think, thou lov'st me well.

Hub. So well, that what you bid me undertake,
Though that my death were adjunct to my act,
By heaven, I'd do 't.

K. John. Do not I know, thou would'st?
Good Hubert, Hubert, Hubert, throw thine eye
On yon young boy: I 'll tell thee what, my friend,
He is a very serpent in my way;
And, wheresoe'er this foot of mine doth tread,
He lies before me: Dost thou understand me?
Thou art his keeper.

Hub. And I will keep him so,
That he shall not offend your majesty.

K. John. Death.

Hub. My lord.

K. John. A grave.

Hub. He shall not live.

K. John. Enough
I could be merry now: Hubert, I love thee;
Well, I 'll not say what I intend for thee:
Remember.——Madam, fare you well:
I 'll send those powers o'er to your majesty.

Eli. My blessing go with thee!

K. John. For England, cousin
Hubert shall be your man, attend on you
With all true duty.—On toward Calais, ho!

                        [*Exeunt*

SCENE IV.—*The Same. The* French King's *Tent.*

Enter KING PHILIP, LEWIS, PANDULPH, *and*
Attendants.

K. Phi. So, by a roaring tempest on the flood,
A whole armado of convented sail
Is scatter'd and disjoin'd from fellowship.

Pand. Courage and comfort! all shall yet go
well.

K. Phi. What can go well, when we have run
so ill?
Are we not beaten? Is not Angiers lost?
Arthur ta'en prisoner? divers dear friends slain?
And bloody England into England gone,
O'erbearing interruption, spite of France?

Lew. What he hath won, that hath he fortified
So hot a speed with such advice dispos'd,
Such temperate order in so fierce a cause,

Doth want example: Who hath read, or heard,
Of any kindred action like to this?

   K. Phi. Well could I bear that England had
      this praise,
So we could find some pattern of our shame.

Enter CONSTANCE.

Look, who comes here! a grave unto a soul;
Holding the eternal spirit, against her will,
In the vile prison of afflicted breath:—
I pr'ythee, lady, go away with me.

   Const. Lo, now! now see the issue of your
      peace!

   K. Phi. Patience, good lady! comfort, gentle
      Constance!

   Const. No, I defy all counsel, all redress,
But that which ends all counsel, true redress,
Death, death:—O amiable lovely death!
Thou odoriferous stench! sound rottenness!
Arise forth from the couch of lasting night,
Thou hate and terror to prosperity,
And I will kiss thy detestable bones;
And put my eye-balls in thy vaulty brows;
And ring these fingers with thy household worms;
And stop this gap of breath with fulsome dust,
And be a carrion monster like thyself:
Come, grin on me; and I will think thou smil'st,
And buss thee as thy wife! Misery's love,
O, come to me!

   K. Phi.   O fair affliction, peace.

   Const. No, no, I will not, having breath to
      cry:—
O, that my tongue were in the thunder's mouth!
Then with a passion would I shake the world;
And rouse from sleep that fell anatomy,
Which cannot hear a lady's feeble voice,
Which scorns a modern invocation.

   Pand. Lady, you utter madness, and not sorrow.

   Const. Thou art not holy to belie me so;
I am not mad: this hair I tear, is mine;
My name is Constance; I was Geffrey's wife;
Young Arthur is my son, and he is lost:
I am not mad;—I would to heaven I were,
For then, 't is like I should forget myself:
O, if I could, what grief should I forget!
Preach some philosophy to make me mad,
And thou shalt be canoniz'd, cardinal;
For, being not mad, but sensible of grief,
My reasonable part produces reason
How I may be deliver'd of these woes,
And teaches me to kill or hang myself;
If I were mad, I should forget my son;

   662

Or madly think, a babe of clouts were he.
I am not mad; too well, too well I feel
The different plague of each calamity.

   K. Phi. Bind up those tresses: O, what love I
      note
In the fair multitude of those her hairs!
Where but by chance a silver drop hath fallen,
Even to that drop ten thousand wiry friends
Do glew themselves in sociable grief;
Like true, inseparable, faithful loves,
Sticking together in calamity.

   Const. To England, if you will.

   K. Phi.   Bind up your hairs.

   Const. Yes, that I will: And wherefore will I
      do it?
I tore them from their bonds; and cried aloud,
"O that these hands could so redeem my son,
As they have given these hairs their liberty!"
But now I envy at their liberty,
And will again commit them to their bonds,
Because my poor child is a prisoner.——
And, father cardinal, I have heard you say,
That we shall see and know our friends in heaven:
If that be true, I shall see my boy again;
For, since the birth of Cain, the first male child,
To him that did but yesterday suspire,
There was not such a gracious creature born.
But now will canker sorrow eat my bud,
And chase the native beauty from his cheek,
And he will look as hollow as a ghost;
As dim and meagre as an ague's fit;
And so he 'll die; and, rising so again,
When I shall meet him in the court of heaven
I shall not know him: therefore never, never
Must I behold my pretty Arthur more.

   Pand. You hold too heinous a respect of grief.

   Const. He talks to me, that never had a son.

   K. Phi. You are as fond of grief, as of your
      child.

   Const. Grief fills the room up of my absent
      child,
Lies in his bed, walks up and down with me,
Puts on his pretty looks, repeats his words,
Remembers me of all his gracious parts,
Stuffs out his vacant garments with his form;
Then, have I reason to be fond of grief.
Fare you well: had you such a loss as I,
I could give better comfort than you do.—
I will not keep this form upon my head,

       [*Tearing off her head-dress*
When there is such disorder in my wit.
O lord! my boy, my Arthur, my fair son!

My life, my joy, my food, my all the world!
My widow-comfort, and my sorrows' cure! [*Exit.*
  K. Phi. I fear some outrage, and I 'll follow
  her.   [*Exit.*
  Lew. There 's nothing in this world can make
    me joy:
Life is as tedious as a twice-told tale,
Vexing the dull ear of a drowsy man;
And bitter shame hath spoil'd the sweet world's
    taste,
That it yields naught, but shame and bitterness.
  Pand. Before the curing of a strong disease,
Even in the instant of repair and health,
The fit is strongest; evils, that take leave,
On their departure most of all show evil:
What have you lost by losing of this day?
  Lew. All days of glory, joy, and happiness.
  Pand. If you have won it, certainly, you had.
No, no; when fortune means to men most good,
She looks upon them with a threatening eye.
'Tis strange, to think how much king John hath lost
In this which he accounts so clearly won:
Are not you griev'd, that Arthur is his prisoner?
  Lew. As heartily, as he is glad he hath him.
  Pand. Your mind is all as youthful as your
    blood.
Now hear me speak, with a prophetic spirit;
For even the breath of what I mean to speak
Shall blow each dust, each straw, each little rub,
Out of the path which shall directly lead
Thy foot to England's throne; and, therefore,
    mark.
John hath seiz'd Arthur; and it cannot be,
That, whiles warm life plays in that infant's veins,
The mis-plac'd John should entertain an hour,
One minute, nay, one quiet breath of rest:
A sceptre, snatch'd with an unruly hand,
Must be as boisterously maintain'd as gain'd:
And he, that stands upon a slippery place,
Makes nice of no vile hold to stay him up:
That John may stand, then Arthur needs must fall;
So be it, for it cannot be but so.
  Lew. But what shall I gain by young Arthur's
    fall?
  Pand. You, in the right of lady Blanch your
    wife,

May then make all the claim that Arthur did.
  Lew. And lose it, life and all, as Arthur did.
  Pand. How green are you, and fresh in this old
    world!
John lays you plots; the times conspire with you
For he, that steeps his safety in true blood,
Shall find but bloody safety, and untrue.
This act, so evilly born, shall cool the hearts
Of all his people, and freeze up their zeal;
That none so small advantage shall step forth,
To check his reign, but they will cherish it:
No natural exhalation in the sky,
No scape of nature, no distemper'd day,
No common wind, no customed event,
But they will pluck away his natural cause,
And call them meteors, prodigies, and signs,
Abortives, présages, and tongues of heaven,
Plainly denouncing vengeance upon John.
  Lew. May be, he will not touch young Arthur's
    life,
But hold himself safe in his prisonment.
  Pand. O, sir, when he shall hear of your
    approach,
If that young Arthur be not gone already
E'en at that news he dies: and then the hearts
Of all his people shall revolt from him,
And kiss the lips of unacquainted change;
And pick strong matter of revolt, and wrath,
Out of the bloody fingers' ends of John.
Methinks, I see this hurly all on foot:
And, O, what better matter breeds for you,
Than I have nam'd!—The bastard Faulconbridge
Is now in England, ransacking the church,
Offending charity: If but a dozen French
Were there in arms, they would be as a call
To train ten thousand English to their side;
Or, as a little snow, tumbled about,
Anon becomes a mountain. O noble Dauphin,
Go with me to the king: 'T is wonderful,
What may be wrought out of their discontent:
Now that their souls are topfull of offence,
For England go; I will whet on the king.
  Lew. Strong reasons make strong actions: Let
    us go;
If you say, ay, the king will not say, no.
                        [*Exeunt*

ACT IV.

SCENE I.—Northampton.[2] *A Room in the Castle.*

Enter HUBERT *and Two* Attendants.

Hub. Heat me these irons hot; and, look thou stand

Within the arras; when I strike my foot

Upon the bosom of the ground, rush forth:

And bind the boy, which you shall find with me,

Fast to the chair: be heedful: hence, and watch.

1st Attend. I hope, your warrant will bear out the deed.

Hub. Uncleanly scruples! Fear not you: look to 't.—   [*Exeunt* Attend.

Young lad, come forth; I have to say with you.

Enter ARTHUR.

Arth. Good morrow, Hubert.

Hub.   Good morrow, little prince.

Arth. As little prince (having so great a title

To be more prince.) as may be.—You are sad.

Hub. Indeed, I have been merrier.

Arth.   Mercy on me!

Methinks, nobody should be sad but I:

Yet, I remember, when I was in France,

Young gentlemen would be as sad as night,

Only for wantonness. By my christendom,

So I were out of prison, and kept sheep,

I should be as merry as the day is long:

And so I would be here, but that I doubt

My uncle practises more harm to me:

He is afraid of me, and I of him:

Is it my fault that I was Geffrey's son?

No, indeed, is 't not: And I would to heaven,

I were your son, so you would love me, Hubert.

Hub. If I talk to him, with his innocent prate

He will awake my mercy, which lies dead:

Therefore I will be sudden, and despatch. [*Aside.*

Arth. Are you sick, Hubert? you look pale to-day:

In sooth, I would you were a little sick;

That I might sit all night, and watch with you:

I warrant, I love you more than you do me.

Hub. His words do take possession of my bosom.—

Read here, young Arthur.   [*Showing a Paper.*

How now, foolish rheum!   [*Aside.*

Turning dispiteous torture out of door!

I must be brief; lest resolution drop

Out at mine eyes, in tender womanish tears.——

Can you not read it? is it not fair writ?

Arth. Too fairly, Hubert, for so foul effect:

Must you with hot irons burn out both mine eyes?

Hub. Young boy, I must.

Arth.   And will you?

Hub.   And I will.

Arth. Have you the heart? When your head did but ache,

I knit my handkerchief about your brows,

(The best I had, a princess wrought it me.)

And I did never ask it you again:

And with my hand at midnight held your head;

And, like the watchful minutes to the hour,

Still and anon cheer'd up the heavy time;

Saying, What lack you? and, Where lies your grief?

Or, What good love may I perform for you?

Many a poor man's son would have lain still,

And ne'er have spoke a loving word to you;

But you at your sick service had a prince.

Nay, you may think my love was crafty love,

And call it, cunning: Do, an if you will:

If heaven be pleas'd that you must use me ill,

Why, then you must.—Will you put out mine eyes?

These eyes, that never did, nor never shall,

So much as frown on you?

Hub.   I have sworn to do it;

And with hot irons must I burn them out.

Arth. Ah, none, but in this iron age, would do it.

The iron of itself, though heat red-hot,

Approaching near these eyes, would drink my tears,

And quench his fiery indignation,

Even in the matter of mine innocence:

Nay, after that, consume away in rust,

But for containing fire to harm mine eye.

Are you more stubborn-hard than hammer'd iron?

An if an angel should have come to me,

And told me Hubert should put out mine eyes,

I would not have believ'd no tongue but Hubert's.

Hub. Come forth.   [*Stamps*

Re-enter Attendants, *with Cord, Irons, &c.*

Do as I bid you do.

Arth. O save me, Hubert, save me! my eyes are out.

664

Even with the fierce looks of these bloody men.

Hub. Give me the iron, I say, and bind him here.

Arth. Alas, what need you be so boist'rous-rough?
I will not struggle, I will stand stone-still.
For heaven's sake, Hubert, let me not be bound!
Nay, hear me, Hubert! drive these men away,
And I will sit as quiet as a lamb:
I will not stir, nor wince, nor speak a word,
Nor look upon the iron angerly:
Thrust but these men away, and I 'll forgive you,
Whatever torment you do put me to.

Hub. Go, stand within; let me alone with him.

1st Attend. I am best pleas'd to be from such a deed.   [*Exeunt* Attend.

Arth. Alas! I then have chid away my friend;
He hath a stern look, but a gentle heart:—
Let him come back, that his compassion may
Give life to yours.

Hub.   Come, boy, prepare yourself.

Arth. Is there no remedy?

Hub.   None, but to lose your eyes.

Arth. O heaven!—that there were but a mote in yours,
A grain, a dust, a gnat, a wand'ring hair,
Any annoyance in that precious sense!
Then, feeling what small things are boist'rous there,
Your vile intent must needs seem horrible.

Hub. Is this your promise? go to, hold your tongue.

Arth. Hubert, the utterance of a brace of tongues
Must needs want pleading for a pair of eyes:
Let me not hold my tongue; let me not, Hubert!
Or, Hubert, if you will, cut out my tongue,
So I may keep mine eyes; O, spare mine eyes;
Though to no use, but still to look on you!
Lo, by my troth, the instrument is cold,
And would not harm me.

Hub.   I can heat it, boy.

Arth. No, in good sooth; the fire is dead with grief,
Being create for comfort, to be us'd
In undeserved extremes: See else yourself;
There is no malice in this burning coal;
The breath of heaven hath blown his spirit out,
And strewed repentant ashes on his head.

Hub. But with my breath I can revive it, boy.

Arth. And if you do, you will but make it blush,

And glow with shame of your proceedings, Hubert:
Nay, it, perchance, will sparkle in your eyes;
And, like a dog that is compell'd to fight,
Snatch at his master that doth tarre him on.
All things, that you should use to do me wrong
Deny their office: only you do lack
That mercy which fierce fire, and iron, extends,
Creatures of note, for mercy-lacking uses.

Hub. Well, see to live; I will not touch thine eyes
For all the treasure that thine uncle owes:
Yet am I sworn, and I did purpose, boy,
With this same very iron to burn them out.

Arth. O, now you look like Hubert! all this while
You were disguised.

Hub.   Peace: no more. Adieu;
Your uncle must not know but you are dead:
I 'll fill these dogged spies with false reports.
And, pretty child, sleep doubtless, and secure,
That Hubert, for the wealth of all the world,
Will not offend thee.

Arth.   O heaven!—I thank you, Hubert.

Hub. Silence; no more: Go closely in with me;
Much danger do I undergo for thee.   [*Exeunt*

SCENE II.—*The Same.* A *Room of State in the Palace.*

Enter KING JOHN, *crowned;* PEMBROKE, SALISBURY, *and other Lords.* The *King takes his State.*

K. John. Here once again we sit, once again crown'd,[14]
And look'd upon, I hope, with cheerful eyes.

Pem. This once again, but that your highness pleas'd,
Was once superfluous: you were crown'd before,
And that high royalty was ne'er pluck'd off;
The faiths of men ne'er stained with revolt;
Fresh expectation troubled not the land,
With any long'd-for change, or better state.

Sal. Therefore, to be possess'd with double pomp,
To guard a title that was rich before,
To gild refined gold, to paint the lily,
To throw a perfume on the violet,
To smooth the ice, or add another hue
Unto the rainbow, or with taper-light
To seek the beauteous eye of heaven to garnish,
Is wasteful and ridiculous excess.

Pem. But that your royal pleasure must be done,
This act is as an ancient tale new told;
And, in the last repeating, troublesome,
Being urged at a time unseasonable.

Sal. In this, the antique and well-noted face
Of plain old form is much disfigured:
And, like a shifted wind unto a sail,
It makes the course of thoughts to fetch about;
Startles and frights consideration;
Makes sound opinion sick, and truth suspected,
For putting on so new a fashion'd robe.

Pem. When workmen strive to do better than well,
They do confound their skill in covetousness:
And, oftentimes, excusing of a fault,
Doth make the fault the worse by the excuse;
As patches, set upon a little breach,
Discredit more in hiding of the fault,
Than did the fault before it was so patch'd.

Sal. To this effect, before you were new-crown'd,
We breath'd our counsel: but it pleas'd your highness
To overbear it; and we are all well pleas'd;
Since all and every part of what we would,
Doth make a stand at what your highness will.

K. John. Some reasons of this double coronation
I have possess'd you with, and think them strong;
And more, more strong, (when lesser is my fear,)
I shall indue you with: Mean time, but ask
What you would have reform'd, that is not well;
And well shall you perceive, how willingly
I will both hear and grant you your requests.

Pem. Then I, (as one that am the tongue of these,
To sound the purposes of all their hearts,)
Both for myself and them, (but chief of all,
Your safety, for the which myself and them
Bend their best studies,) heartily request
The enfranchisement of Arthur; whose restraint
Doth move the murmuring lips of discontent
To break into this dangerous argument,—
If, what in rest you have, in right you hold,
Why should your fears, (which, as they say, attend
The steps of wrong,) then move you to mew up
Your tender kinsman, and to choke his days
With barbarous ignorance, and deny his youth
The rich advantage of good exercise?
That the time's enemies may not have this

To grace occasions, let it be our suit,
That you have bid us ask his liberty;
Which for our goods we do no further ask,
That whereupon our weal, on you depending,
Counts it your weal, he have his liberty.

K. John. Let it be so; I do commit his youth

Enter HUBERT.

To your direction.—Hubert, what news with you?

Pem. This is the man should do the bloody deed;
He show'd his warrant to a friend of mine:
The image of a wicked, heinous fault
Lives in his eye; that close aspect of his
Does show the mood of a much-troubled breast,
And I do fearfully believe, 'tis done,
What we so fear'd he had a charge to do.

Sal. The colour of the king doth come and go,
Between his purpose and his conscience,
Like heralds 'twixt two dreadful battles set;
His passion is so ripe, it needs must break.

Pem. And when it breaks, I fear, will issue thence
The foul corruption of a sweet child's death.

K. John. We cannot hold mortality's strong hand:—
Good lords, although my will to give is living,
The suit which you demand is gone and dead;
He tells us, Arthur is deceas'd to-night.

Sal. Indeed, we fear'd his sickness was past cure.

Pem. Indeed, we heard how near his death he was,
Before the child himself felt he was sick:
This must be answer'd, either here or hence.

K. John. Why do you bend such solemn brows on me?
Think you, I bear the shears of destiny?
Have I commandment on the pulse of life?

Sal. It is apparent foul play; and 'tis shame,
That greatness should so grossly offer it:
So thrive it in your game! and so farewell.

Pem. Stay yet, lord Salisbury; I'll go with thee,
And find the inheritance of this poor child,
His little kingdom of a forced grave.
That blood, which ow'd the breadth of all this isle,
Three foot of it doth hold: Bad world the while!
This must not be thus borne: this will break out
To all our sorrows, and ere long, I doubt.

[*Exeunt* Lords

K. John. They burn in indignation; I repent;

There is no sure foundation set on blood ;
No certain life achiev'd by others' death.——

Enter a Messenger.

A fearful eye thou hast : Where is that blood,
That I have seen inhabit in those cheeks ?
So foul a sky clears not without a storm :
Pour down thy weather :—How goes all in France ?

Mess. From France to England.—Never such a
　　　　power
For any foreign preparation,
Was levied in the body of a land !
The copy of your speed is learn'd by them ;
For, when you should be told they do prepare,
The tidings come, that they are all arriv'd.

K. John. O, where hath our intelligence been
　　　　drunk ?
Where hath it slept ? Where is my mother's care ?
That such an army could be drawn in France,
And she not hear of it ?

Mess.　　　　　　My liege, her ear
Is stopp'd with dust ; the first of April, died
Your noble mother : And, as I hear, my lord,
The lady Constance in a frenzy died
Three days before : but this from rumor's tongue
I idly heard ; if true or false, I know not.

K. John. Withhold thy speed, dreadful occasion !
O, make a league with me, till I have pleas'd
My discontented peers !—What ! mother dead !
How wildly then walks my estate in France !—
Under whose conduct came those powers of France,
That thou for truth giv'st out, are landed here ?

Mess. Under the Dauphin.

Enter the BASTARD *and* PETER OF POMFRET.

K. John.　　　　Thou hast made me giddy
With these ill tidings.—Now, what says the world
To your proceedings ? do not seek to stuff
My head with more ill news, for it is full.

Bast. But if you be afeard to hear the worst,
Then let the worst, unheard, fall on your head.

K. John. Bear with me, cousin ; for I was amaz'd
Under the tide : but now I breathe again
Aloft the flood ; and can give audience
To any tongue, speak it of what it will.

Bast. How I have sped among the clergymen,
The sums I have collected shall express.
But, as I travelled hither through the land,
I find the people strangely fantasied ;
Possess'd with rumors, full of idle dreams ;
Not knowing what they fear, but full of fear :
And here 's a prophet[b] that I brought with me

From forth the streets of Pomfret, whom I found
With many hundreds treading on his heels ;
To whom he sung, in rude harsh-sounding rhymes,
That, ere the next Ascension-day at noon,
Your highness should deliver up your crown.

K. John. Thou idle dreamer, wherefore didst
　　　　thou so ?

Peter. Foreknowing that the truth will fall out
　　　　so.

K. John. Hubert, away with him ; imprison him ·
And on that day, at noon, whereon, he says,
I shall yield up my crown, let him be hang'd :
Deliver him to safety, and return,
For I must use thee.—O my gentle cousin,
　　　　　　　　[*Exit* HUB. *with* PETER.
Hear'st thou the news abroad, who are arriv'd ?

Bast. The French, my lord ; men's mouths are
　　　　full of it :
Besides, I met lord Bigot, and lord Salisbury,
(With eyes as red as new-enkindled fire,)
And others more, going to seek the grave
Of Arthur, who, they say, is kill'd to-night
On your suggestion.

K. John.　　　　Gentle kinsman, go,
And thrust thyself into their companies :
I have a way to win their loves again ;
Bring them before me.

Bast.　　　　I will seek them out.

K. John. Nay, but make haste : the better
　　　　foot before.——
O, let me have no subject enemies,
When adverse foreigners affright my towns
With dreadful pomp of stout invasion !—
Be Mercury, set feathers to thy heels ;
And fly, like thought, from them to me again.

Bast. The spirit of the time shall teach me
　　　　speed.　　　　　　　　[*Exit.*

K. John. Spoke like a spriteful noble gentle-
　　　　man.—
Go after him ; for he, perhaps, shall need
Some messenger betwixt me and the peers ;
And be thou he.

Mess.　　　With all my heart, my liege. [*Exit.*

K. John. My mother dead !

Re-enter HUBERT.

Hub. My lord, they say, five moons were seen
　　　　to-night :
Four fixed ; and the fifth did whirl about
The other four, in wond'rous motion.

K. John. Five moons ?

Hub.　　　Old men, and beldams, in the streets
667

Do prophesy upon it dangerously:
Young Arthur's death is common in their mouths:
And when they talk of him, they shake their heads,
And whisper one another in the ear;
And he that speaks doth gripe the hearer's wrist;
Whilst he that hears makes fearful action,
With wrinkled brows, with nods, with rolling eyes.
I saw a smith stand with his hammer, thus,
And whilst his iron did on the anvil cool,
With open mouth swallowing a tailor's news;
Who, with his shears and measure in his hand,
Standing on slippers, (which his nimble haste
Had falsely thrust upon contrary feet,)
Told of a many thousand warlike French,
That were embatteled and rank'd in Kent:
Another lean unwash'd artificer
Cuts off his tale, and talks of Arthur's death.

    K. John. Why seek'st thou to possess me with
these fears?
Why urgest thou so oft young Arthur's death?
Thy hand hath murder'd him: I had mighty cause
To wish him dead, but thou hadst none to kill him.

    Hub. Had none, my lord! why, did you not
        provoke me?

    K. John. It is the curse of kings, to be attended
By slaves, that take their humors for a warrant
To break within the bloody house of life:
And, on the winking of authority,
To understand a law; to know the meaning
Of dangerous majesty, when, perchance, it frowns
More upon humor than advis'd respect.

    Hub. Here is your hand and seal for what I did.

    K. John. O, when the last account 'twixt
        heaven and earth
Is to be made, then shall this hand and seal
Witness against us to damnation!
How oft the sight of means to do ill deeds,
Makes ill deeds done! Hadest not thou been by,
A fellow by the hand of nature mark'd,
Quoted, and sign'd, to do a deed of shame,
This murder had not come into my mind;
But, taking note of thy abhorr'd aspect,
Finding thee fit for bloody villainy,
Apt, liable, to be employ'd in danger,
I faintly broke with thee of Arthur's death;
And thou, to be endeared to a king,
Made it no conscience to destroy a prince.

    Hub. My lord.——

    K. John. Hadst thou but shook thy head, or
        made a pause,
When I spake darkly what I purposed;
Or turn'd an eye of doubt upon my face,

As bid me tell my tale in express words;
Deep shame had struck me dumb, made me
    break off,
And those thy fears might have wrought fears
    in me:
But thou didst understand me by my signs,
And didst in signs again parley with sin,
Yea, without stop, didst let thy heart consent,
And, consequently, thy rude hand to act
The deed, which both our tongues held vile to
    name.—
Out of my sight, and never see me more!
My nobles leave me; and my state is brav'd,
Even at my gates, with ranks of foreign powers:
Nay, in the body of this fleshly land,
This kingdom, this confine of blood and breath,
Hostility and civil tumult reigns
Between my conscience, and my cousin's death.

    Hub. Arm you against your other enemies,
I'll make a peace between your soul and you.
Young Arthur is alive: This hand of mine
Is yet a maiden and an innocent hand,
Not painted with the crimson spots of blood.
Within this bosom never enter'd yet
The dreadful motion of a murd'rous thought;
And you have slander'd nature in my form;
Which, howsoever rude exteriorly,
Is yet the cover of a fairer mind
Than to be butcher of an innocent child.

    K. John. Doth Arthur live? O, haste thee to
    the peers,
Throw this report on their incensed rage,
And make them tame to their obedience!
Forgive the comment that my passion made
Upon thy feature; for my rage was blind,
And foul imaginary eyes of blood
Presented thee more hideous than thou art.
O, answer not; but to my closet bring
The angry lords, with all expedient haste:
I conjure thee but slowly; run more fast.
                      [*Exeunt.*

    SCENE III.—*The Same. Before the Castle.*

      Enter ARTHUR, *on the Walls.*

    Arth. The wall is high; and yet will I leap
    down:—
Good ground, be pitiful, and hurt me not!—
There's few, or none, do know me; if they did,
This ship-boy's semblance hath disguis'd me quite.
I am afraid; and yet I'll venture it.
If I get down, and do not break my limbs,

I 'll find a thousand shifts to get away:
As good to die, and go, as die, and stay.
                         [*Leaps down.*
O me! my uncle's spirit is in these stones:—
Heaven take my soul, and England keep my
    bones!   [*Dies.*

Enter PEMBROKE, SALISBURY, *and* BIGOT.

   Sal. Lords, I will meet him at saint Edmund's-
Bury;
It is our safety, and we must embrace
This gentle offer of the perilous time.
   Pem. Who brought that letter from the cardinal?
   Sal. The count Melun, a noble lord of France;
Whose private with me, of the Dauphin's love,
Is much more general than these lines import."
   Big. To-morrow morning let us meet him then.
   Sal. Or, rather then set forward: for 't will be
Two long days' journey, lords, or e'er we met.

Enter the BASTARD.

   Bast. Once more to-day well met, distemper'd
   lords!
The king, by me, requests your presence straight.
   Sal. The king hath dispossess'd himself of us;
We will not line his sin bestained cloak
With our pure honours, nor attend the foot
That leaves the print of blood where-e'er it walks;
Return, and tell him so; we know the worst.
   Bast. Whate'er you think, good words, I think,
were best.
   Sal. Our griefs, and not our manners, reason
now.
   Bast. But there is little reason in your grief;
Therefore, 't were reason, you had manners now.
   Pem. Sir, sir, impatience hath this privilege.
   Bast. 'Tis true; to hurt his master, no man else.
   Sal. This is the prison: What is he lies here?
                         [*Seeing* ARTH.
   Pem. O death, made proud with pure and
princely beauty!
The earth had not a hole to hide this deed.
   Sal. Murder, as hating what himself hath done,
Doth lay it open, to urge on revenge.
   Big. Or, when he doom'd this beauty to a grave,
Found it too precious-princely for a grave.
   Sal. Sir Richard, what think you? Have you
beheld,
Or have you read, or heard? or could you think?
Or do you almost think, although you see,
That you do see? could thought, without this
object,

Form such another? This is the very top,
The height, the crest, or crest unto the crest,
Of murder's arms: this is the bloodiest shame,
The wildest savag'ry, the vilest stroke,
That ever wall-ey'd wrath, or staring rage,
Presented to the tears of soft remorse.
   Pem. All murders past do stand excus'd in this;
And this, so sole, and so unmatchable,
Shall give a holiness, a purity,
To the yet-unbegotten sin of time;
And prove a deadly bloodshed but a jest,
Exampled by this heinous spectacle.
   Bast. It is a damned and a bloody work;
The graceless action of a heavy hand,
If that it be the work of any hand.
   Sal. If that it be the work of any hand?—
We had a kind of light, what would ensue:
It is the shameful work of Hubert's hand;
The practice, and the purpose, of the king:—
From whose obedience I forbid my soul,
Kneeling before this ruin of sweet life,
And breathing to his breathless excellence
The incense of a vow, a holy vow;
Never to taste the pleasures of the world,
Never to be infected with delight,
Nor conversant with ease and idleness,
Till I have set a glory to this hand,
By giving it the worship of revenge.
   Pem. Big. Our souls religiously confirm thy
words.

Enter HUBERT.

   Hub. Lords, I am hot with haste in seeking you;
Arthur doth live; the king hath sent for you.
   Sal. O, he is bold, and blushes not at death:—
Avaunt, thou hateful villain, get thee gone!
   Hub. I am no villain.
   Sal.   Must I rob the law?
                         [*Drawing his sword.*
   Bast. Your sword is bright, sir; put it up again.
   Sal. Not till I sheath it in a murderer's skin.
   Hub. Stand back, lord Salisbury, stand back, I
say;
By heaven, I think, my sword 's as sharp as yours,
I would not have you, lord, forget yourself,
Nor tempt the danger of my true defence;"
Lest I, by marking of your rage, forget
Your worth, your greatness, and nobility.
   Big. Out, dunghill! dar'st thou brave a noble
man?
   Hub. Not for my life: but yet I dare defend
My innocent life against an emperor.

Sal. Thou art a murderer.

Hub.   Do not prove me so;

Yet, I am none :^h Whose tongue soe'er speaks false,

Not truly speaks; who speaks not truly, lies.

Pem. Cut him to pieces.

Bast.   Keep the peace, I say.

Sal. Stand by, or I shall gall you, Faulconbridge.

Bast. Thou wert better gall the devil, Salisbury :

If thou but frown on me, or stir thy foot,

Or teach thy hasty spleen to do me shame,

I 'll strike thee dead. Put up thy sword betime;

Or I 'll so maul you and your toasting-iron,

That you shall think the devil is come from hell.

Big. What wilt thou do, renowned Faulconbridge ?

Second a villain, and a murderer ?

Hub. Lord Bigot, I am none.

Big.   Who kill'd this prince ?

Hub. 'T is not an hour since I left him well :

I honour'd him, I lov'd him ; and will weep

My date of life out, for his sweet life's loss.

Sal. Trust not those cunning waters of his eyes,

For villainy is not without such rheum ;

And he, long traded in it, makes it seem

Like rivers of remorse and innocency.

Away, with me, all you whose souls abhor

The uncleanly savours of a slaughter-house;

For I am stifled with this smell of sin.

Big. Away, toward Bury, to the Dauphin there !

Pem. There, tell the king, he may inquire us out.
         [*Exeunt* Lords.

Bast. Here 's a good world !—Knew you of this
 fair work ?

Beyond the infinite and boundless reach

Of mercy, if thou didst this deed of death,

Art thou damn'd, Hubert.

Hub.   Do but hear me, sir.

Bast. Ha ! I 'll tell thee what;

Thou art damn'd as black—nay, nothing is so
 black ;

670

Thou art more deep damn'd than prince Lucifer:

There is not yet so ugly a fiend of hell

As thou shalt be, if thou didst kill this child.³²

Hub. Upon my soul,——

Bast.   If thou didst but consent

To this most cruel act, do but despair,

And, if thou want'st a cord, the smallest thread

That ever spider twisted from her womb,

Will serve to strangle thee ; a rush will be

A beam to hang thee on ; or would'st thou drown
 thyself,

Put but a little water in a spoon,

And it shall be as all the ocean,

Enough to stifle such a villain up.——

I do suspect thee very grievously.

Hub. If I in act, consent, or sin of thought

Be guilty of the stealing that sweet breath

Which was embounded in this beauteous clay

Let hell want pains enough to torture me !

I left him well.

Bast.   Go, bear him in thine arms.—

I am amaz'd, methinks ; and lose my way

Among the thorns and dangers of this world.—

How easy dost thou take all England up !

From forth this morsel of dead royalty,

The life, the right, and truth of all this realm

Is fled to heaven ; and England now is left

To tug and scramble, and to part by the teeth

The unowed interest of proud-swelling state.

Now, for the bare-pick'd bone of majesty,

Doth dogged war bristle his angry crest,

And snarleth in the gentle eyes of peace :

Now powers from home, and discontents at home,

Meet in one line ; and vast confusion waits

(As doth a raven on a sick-fallen beast,)

The imminent decay of wrested pomp.

Now happy he, whose cloak and cincture can

Hold out this tempest. Bear away that child,

And follow me with speed ; I 'll to the king :

A thousand businesses are brief in hand,

And heaven itself doth frown upon the land.
         [*Exeunt*

ACT V.

SCENE I.—*The Same.　A Room in the Palace.*

Enter KING JOHN, PANDULPH *with the Crown, and Attendants.*

K. John. Thus have I yielded up into your hand
The circle of my glory.

Pand.　　　　Take again
　　　　　　　　　[*Giving* JOHN *the Crown.*
From this my hand, as holding of the pope,
Your sovereign greatness and authority:

K. John. Now keep your holy word: go meet
　　　the French;
And from his holiness use all your power
To stop their marches, 'fore we are inflam'd.
Our discontented counties do revolt;
Our people quarrel with obedience;
Swearing allegiance, and the love of soul,
To stranger blood, to foreign royalty.
This inundation of mistemper'd humour
Rests by you only to be qualified.
Then pause not; for the present time's so sick,
That present medicine must be minister'd,
Or overthrow incurable ensues.

Pand. It was my breath that blew this tempest
　　　up,
Upon your stubborn usage of the pope;
But, since you are a gentle convertite,
My tongue shall hush again this storm of war,
And make fair weather in your blustering land.
On this Ascension-day, remember well,
Upon your oath of service to the pope,
Go I to make the French lay down their arms.
　　　　　　　　　　　　　　[*Exit.*

K. John. Is this Ascension-day? Did not the
　　　prophet
Say, that, before Ascension-day at noon,
My crown I should give off? Even so I have:
I did suppose, it should be on constraint;
But, heaven be thank'd, it is but voluntary.

Enter the Bastard.

Bast. All Kent hath yielded; nothing there
　　　holds out,
But Dover castle: London hath receiv'd,
Like a kind host, the Dauphin and his powers:
Your nobles will not hear you, but are gone
To offer service to your enemy;

And wild amazement hurries up and down
The little number of your doubtful friends.

K. John. Would not my lords return to me
　　　again,
After they heard young Arthur was alive?

Bast. They found him dead, and cast into the
　　　streets;
An empty casket, where the jewel of life
By some damn'd hand was robb'd and ta'en away.

K. John. That villain Hubert told me he did live.

Bast. So, on my soul, he did, for aught he knew.
But wherefore do you droop? why look you sad?
Be great in act, as you have been in thought;
Let not the world see fear, and sad distrust,
Govern the motion of a kingly eye:
Be stirring as the time; be fire with fire;
Threaten the threat'ner, and outface the brow
Of bragging horror: so shall inferior eyes,
That borrow their behaviours from the great,
Grow great by your example, and put on
The dauntless spirit of resolution.
Away; and glister like the god of war,
When he intendeth to become the field:
Show boldness, and aspiring confidence.
What, shall they seek the lion in his den,
And fright him there? and make him tremble
　　　there?
O, let it not be said!—Courage, and run
To meet displeasure further from the doors;
And grapple with him, ere he come so nigh.

K. John. The legate of the pope hath been with
　　　me,
And I have made a happy peace with him;
And he hath promis'd to dismiss the powers
Led by the Dauphin.

Bast.　　　　O inglorious league!
Shall we, upon the footing of our land,
Send fair-play offers, and make compromise,
Insinuation, parley, and base truce,
To arms invasive? shall a beardless boy,
A cocker'd silken wanton brave our fields,
And flesh his spirit in a warlike soil,
Mocking the air with colours idly spread,
And find no check? Let us, my liege, to arms:
Perchance, the cardinal cannot make your peace
Or if he do, let it at least be said,
They saw we had a purpose of defence.
　　　　　　　　　　　　　　　61

K. John. Have thou the ordering of this present
    time.
Bast. Away then, with good courage; yet, I
    know,
Our party may well meet a prouder foe. [*Exeunt.*

SCENE II.—*A Plain, near St. Edmund's-Bury.*

    Enter, in arms, LEWIS, SALISBURY, MELUN,
      PEMBROKE, BIGOT, *and Soldiers.*

Lew. My lord Melun, let this be copied out,
And keep it safe for our remembrance;
Return the precedent to these lords again;
That, having our fair order written down,
Both they, and we, perusing o'er these notes,
May know wherefore we took the sacrament,
And keep our faiths firm and inviolable.
    Sal. Upon our sides it never shall be broken.
And, noble Dauphin, albeit we swear
A voluntary zeal, and unurg'd faith,
To your proceedings; yet, believe me, prince,
I am not glad that such a sore of time
Should seek a plaster by contemn'd revolt,
And heal the inveterate canker of one wound,
By making many; O, it grieves my soul,
That I must draw this metal from my side
To be a widow-maker; O, and there,
Where honourable rescue, and defence,
Cries out upon the name of Salisbury:
But such is the infection of the time,
That, for the health and physic of our right,
We cannot deal but with the very hand
Of stern injustice and confused wrong.—
And is't not pity, O my grieved friends!
That we, the sons and children of this isle,
Were born to see so sad an hour as this:
Wherein we step after a stranger march
Upon her gentle bosom, and fill up
Her enemies' ranks, (I must withdraw and weep
Upon the spot of this enforced cause,)
To grace the gentry of a land remote,
And follow unacquainted colours here?
What, here?—O nation, that thou could'st remove!
That Neptune's arms, who clippeth thee about,
Would bear thee from the knowledge of thyself,
And grapple thee unto a pagan shore;
Where these two Christian armies might combine
The blood of malice in a vein of league,
And not to spend it so unneighbourly!
    Lew. A noble temper dost thou show in this;
And great affections, wrestling in thy bosom,
Do make an earthquake of nobility.

O, what a noble combat hast thou fought,
Between compulsion and a brave respect!
Let me wipe off this honourable dew,
That silverly doth progress on thy cheeks:
My heart hath melted at a lady's tears,
Being an ordinary inundation:
But this effusion of such manly drops,
This shower, blown up by tempest of the soul,
Startles mine eyes, and makes me more amaz'd
Than had I seen the vaulty top of heaven
Figur'd quite o'er with burning meteors.
Lift up thy brow, renowned Salisbury,
And with a great heart heave away this storm:
Commend these waters to those baby eyes,
That never saw the giant world enrag'd;
Nor met with fortune other than at feasts,
Full warm of blood, of mirth, of gossiping.
Come, come; for thou shalt thrust thy hand as
    deep
Into the purse of rich prosperity,
As Lewis himself:—so, nobles, shall you all,
That knit your sinews to the strength of mine.

    Enter PANDULPH, *attended.*

And even there, methinks, an angel spake:
Look, where the holy legate comes apace,
To give us warrant from the hand of heaven,
And on our actions set the name of right,
With holy breath.
    Pand.   Hail, noble prince of France
The next is this,—king John hath reconcil'd
Himself to Rome; his spirit is come in,
That so stood out against the holy church,
The great metropolis and see of Rome:
Therefore thy threat'ning colours now wind up,
And tame the savage spirit of wild war;
That, like a lion foster'd up at hand,
It may lie gently at the foot of peace,
And be no further harmful than in show.
    Lew. Your grace shall pardon me, I will not
    back;
I am too high-born to be propertied,
To be a secondary at control,
Or useful serving-man, and instrument,
To any sovereign state throughout the world.
Your breath first kindled the dead coal of wars
Between this chastis'd kingdom and myself,
And brought in matter that should feed this fire
And now 'tis far too huge to be blown out
With that same weak wind which enkindled it.
You taught me how to know the face of right,
Acquainted me with interest to this land,

Yea, thrust this enterprise into my heart;
And come you now to tell me, John hath made
His peace with Rome? What is that peace to me?
I, by the honour of my marriage-bed,
After young Arthur, claim this land for mine
And, now it is half-conquer'd, must I back,
Because that John hath made his peace with
　　　Rome?
Am I Rome's slave? What penny hath Rome
　　　borne,
What men provided, what munition sent,
To underprop this action? is 't not I,
That undergo this charge? who else but I,
And such as to my claim are liable,
Sweat in this business, and maintain this war?
Have I not heard these islanders shout out,
" Vive le Roy!" as I have bank'd their towns?
Have I not here the best cards for the game,
To win this easy match play'd for a crown?
And shall I now give o'er the yielded set?
No, on my soul, it never shall be said.

　　Pand. You look but on the outside of this work.

　　Lew. Outside or inside, I will not return
Till my attempt so much be glorified
As to my ample hope was promised
Before I drew this gallant head of war,
And cull'd these fiery spirits from the world,
To outlook conquest, and to win renown
Even in the jaws of danger and of death.—

　　　　　　　　　　　　[Trumpet sounds.
What lusty trumpet thus doth summon us?

　　　　Enter the BASTARD, attended.

　　Bast. According to the fair play of the world,
Let me have audience; I am sent to speak:—
My holy lord of Milan, from the king
I come, to learn how you have dealt for him;
And as you answer, I do know the scope
And warrant limited unto my tongue.

　　Pand. The Dauphin is too wilful-opposite,
And will not temporise with my entreaties;
He flatly says, he 'll not lay down his arms.

　　Bast. By all the blood that ever fury breath'd,
The youth says well:—Now hear our English king;
For thus his royalty doth speak in me.
He is prepar'd; and reason too, he should:
This apish and unmannerly approach,
This harness'd masque, and unadvised revel,
This unhair'd sauciness, and boyish troops,"
The king doth smile at: and is well prepar'd
To whip this dwarfish war, these pigmy arms,
From out the circle of his territories.

That hand, which had the strength, even at your
　　　door,
To cudgel you, and make you take the hatch,"
To dive, like buckets, in concealed wells;
To crouch in litter of your stable planks;
To lie, like pawns, lock'd up in chests and trunks;
To hug with swine; to seek sweet safety out
In vaults and prisons; and to thrill, and shake,
Even at the crowing of your nation's cock,
Thinking his voice an armed Englishman;—
Shall that victorious hand be feebled here,
That in your chambers gave you chastisement?
No: Know, the gallant monarch is in arms;
And like an eagle o'er his aëry towers,
To souse annoyance that comes near his nest.—
And you degenerate, you ingrate revolts,
You bloody Neroes, ripping up the womb
Of your dear mother England, blush for shame:
For your own ladies, and pale-visag'd maids,
Like Amazons, come tripping after drums,
Their thimbles into armed gauntlets change,
Their needles to lances, and their gentle hearts
To fierce and bloody inclination.

　　Lew. There end thy brave, and turn thy face in
　　　peace;
We grant, thou canst outscold us: fare thee well
We hold our time too precious to be spent
With such a brabbler.

　　Pand.　　　　　Give me leave to speak.

　　Bast. No, I will speak.

　　Lew.　　　　We will attend to neither:—
Strike up the drums; and let the tongue of war
Plead for our interest, and our being here.

　　Bast. Indeed, your drums, being beaten, will cry
　　　out;
And so shall you, being beaten: Do but start
An echo with the clamour of thy drum,
And even at hand a drum is ready brac'd,
That shall reverberate all as loud as thine;
Sound but another, and another shall,
As loud as thine, rattle the welkin's ear,
And mock the deep-mouth'd thunder: for at
　　　hand
(Not trusting to this halting legate here,
Whom he hath us'd rather for sport than need,)
Is warlike John; and in his forehead sits
A bare-ribb'd death, whose office is this day
To feast upon whole thousands of the French.

　　Lew. Strike up our drums, to find this danger
　　　out.

　　Bast. And thou shalt find it, Dauphin, do not
　　　doubt.　　　　　　　　　　　　*[Exeunt.*

SCENE III.—*The Same. A Field of Battle.
Alarums.*

Enter KING JOHN *and* HUBERT.

K. John. How goes the day with us? O, tell me,
   Hubert.
Hub. Badly, I fear: How fares your majesty?
K. John. This fever, that hath troubled me so
   long,
Lies heavy on me; O, my heart is sick!

Enter a Messenger.

Mess. My lord, your valiant kinsman, Faulcon-
   bridge,
Desires your majesty to leave the field;
And send him word by me, which way you go.
   K. John. Tell him, toward Swinstead, to the
   abbey there.
Mess. Be of good comfort; for the great supply,
That was expected by the Dauphin here,
Are wreck'd three nights ago on Goodwin sands.
This news was brought to Richard but even now;
The French fight coldly, and retire themselves.
   K. John. Ah me! this tyrant fever burns me up,
And will not let me welcome this good news.——
Set on toward Swinstead: to my litter straight;
Weakness possesseth me, and I am faint. [*Exeunt.*

SCENE IV.—*The Same. Another Part of the
Same.*

Enter SALISBURY, PEMBROKE, BIGOT, *and Others.*

Sal. I did not think the king so stor'd with
   friends.
Pem. Up once again; put spirit in the French;
If they miscarry, we miscarry too.
Sal. That misbegotten devil, Faulconbridge,
In spite of spite, alone upholds the day.
Pem. They say, king John, sore sick, hath left
   the field.

Enter MELUN *wounded, and led by Soldiers.*

Mel. Lead me to the revolts of England here.
Sal. When we were happy, we had other names.
Pem. It is the count Melun.
Sal.   Wounded to death.
Mel. Fly, noble English, you are bought and
   sold;
Untread the road-way of rebellion,
And welcome home again discarded faith.
Seek out king John, and fall before his feet;
For, if the French be lords of this loud day,
674

He means to recompense the pains you take
By cutting off your heads: Thus hath he sworn,
And I with him, and many more with me,
Upon the altar at St. Edmund's-Bury:
Even on that altar, where we swore to you
Dear amity and everlasting love.
   Sal. May this be possible? may this be true?
   Mel. Have I not hideous death within my
   view,
Retaining but a quantity of life;
Which bleeds away, even as a form of wax
Resolveth from his figure 'gainst the fire?
What in the world should make me now deceive,
Since I must lose the use of all deceit?
Why should I then be false? since it is true
That I must die here, and live hence by truth!
I say again, if Lewis do win the day,
He is forsworn, if e'er those eyes of yours
Behold another day break in the east:
But even this night,—whose black contagious
   breath
Already smokes about the burning crest
Of the old, feeble, and day-wearied sun,—
Even this ill night, your breathing shall expire:
Paying the fine of rated treachery,
Even with a treacherous fine of all your lives,
If Lewis by your assistance win the day.
Commend me to one Hubert, with your king;
The love of him,—and this respect besides,
For that my grandsire was an Englishman,—
Awakes my conscience to confess all this.
In lieu whereof, I pray you, bear me hence
From forth the noise and rumour of the field;
Where I may think the remnant of my thoughts
In peace, and part this body and my soul
With contemplation and devout desires.
   Sal. We do believe thee,—And beshrew my
   soul,
But I do love the favour and the form
Of this most fair occasion, by the which
We will untread the steps of damned flight;
And, like a bated and retired flood,
Leaving our rankness and irregular course,
Stoop low within those bounds we have o'erlook'd,
And calmly run on in obedience
Even to our ocean, to our great king John.——
My arm shall give thee help to bear thee hence;
For I do see the cruel pangs of death
Right in thine eye.—Away, my friends! New
   flight;
And happy newness, that intends old right.
             [*Exeunt, leading off* MEL.

SCENE V.—*The Same.*   *The French Camp.*

Enter LEWIS *and his Train.*

Lew. The sun of heaven, methought, was loath
     to set ;
But stay'd, and made the western welkin blush,
When the English measur'd backward their own
     ground,
In faint retire : O, bravely came we off,
When with a volley of our needless shot,
After such bloody toil, we bid good night ;
And wound our tatter'd colours clearly up,
Last in the field, and almost lords of it !

Enter a Messenger.

Mess. Where is my prince, the Dauphin ?
Lew.   Here :—What news ?
Mess. The count Melun is slain ; the English
   lords,
By his persuasion, are again fallen off :
And your supply, which you have wish'd so long,
Are cast away, and sunk, on Goodwin sands.
Lew. Ah, foul shrewd news !—Beshrew thy very
   heart !
I did not think to be so sad to-night,
As this hath made me.—Who was he, that said,
King John did fly, an hour or two before
The stumbling night did part our weary powers ?
Mess. Whoever spoke it, it is true, my lord.
Lew. Well ; keep good quarter, and good care
     to-night ;
The day shall not be up so soon as I,
To try the fair adventure of to-morrow.   [*Exeunt.*

SCENE VI.—*An open Place in the Neighbour-*
hood of Swinstead Abbey.

Enter the BASTARD *and* HUBERT, *meeting.*

Hub. Who 's there ? speak, ho ! speak quickly,
   or I shoot.
Bast. A friend :—What art thou ?
Hub.   Of the part of England.
Bast. Whither dost thou go ?
Hub. What 's that to thee ?   Why may not I
   demand
Of thine affairs, as well as thou of mine ?
Bast. Hubert, I think.
Hub.   Thou hast a perfect thought ;
I will, upon all hazards, well believe
Thou art my friend, that know'st my tongue so well :
Who art thou ?
Bast.   Who thou wilt : an if thou please,

Thou may'st befriend me so much, as to think
I come one way of the Plantagenets.
Hub. Unkind remembrance ! thou, and endless
   night,
Have done me shame :—Brave soldier, pardon me,
That any accent, breaking from thy tongue,
Should 'scape the true acquaintance of mine ear.
Bast. Come, come ; sans compliment, what
   news abroad ?
Hub. Why, here walk I, in the black brow of
   night,
To find you out.
Bast.   Brief, then ; and what 's the news ?
Hub. O, my sweet sir, news fitting to the night,
Black, fearful, comfortless, and horrible.
Bast. Show me the very wound of this ill news ;
I am no woman, I 'll not swoon at it.
Hub. The king, I fear, is poison'd by a monk :[22]
I left him almost speechless, and broke out
To acquaint you with this evil ; that you might
The better arm you to the sudden time,
Than if you had at leisure known of this.
Bast. How did he take it ? who did taste to
   him ?
Hub. A monk, I tell you ; a resolved villain,
Whose bowels suddenly burst out : the king
Yet speaks, and, peradventure, may recover.
Bast. Who didst thou leave to tend his majesty ?
Hub. Why, know you not ? the lords are all
   come back,
And brought prince Henry in their company ;
At whose request the king hath pardon'd them,
And they are all about his majesty.
Bast. Withhold thine indignation, mighty
   heaven,
And tempt us not to bear above our power !—
I 'll tell thee, Hubert, half my power this night,
Passing these flats, are taken by the tide,
These Lincoln washes have devoured them ;
Myself, well-mounted, hardly have escap'd.
Away, before ! conduct me to the king ;
I doubt, he will be dead, or ere I come.   [*Exeunt.*

SCENE VII.—*The Orchard of Swinstead Abbey.*

Enter PRINCE HENRY,[23] SALISBURY, *and* BIGOT.

P. Hen. It is too late ; the life of all his blood
Is touch'd corruptibly ; and his pure brain
(Which some suppose the soul's frail dwelling-
   house,)
Doth, by the idle comments that it makes,
Foretell the ending of mortality.

Enter PEMBROKE.

Pem. His highness yet doth speak; and holds
    belief,
That, being brought into the open air,
It would allay the burning quality
Of that fell poison which assaileth him.

    P. Hen. Let him be brought into the orchard
       here.—
Doth he still rage?—   [*Exit* BIG.

    Pem.   He is more patient
Than when you left him; even now he sung.

    P. Hen. O vanity of sickness! fierce extremes,
In their continuance, will not feel themselves.
Death, having prey'd upon the outward parts,
Leaves them invisible; and his siege is now
Against the mind, the which he pricks and wounds
With many legions of strange fantasies;
Which, in their throng and press to that last
    hold,
Confound themselves. 'T is strange, that death
       should sing.——
I am the cygnet to this pale faint swan,
Who chants a doleful hymn to his own death,
And, from the organ-pipe of frailty, sings
His soul and body to their lasting rest.

    Sal. Be of good comfort, prince; for you are
    born
To set a form upon that indigest
Which he hath left so shapeless and so rude.

Re-enter BIGOT *and Attendants, who bring in*
    KING JOHN *in a Chair.*

    K. John. Ay, marry, now my soul hath elbow-
      room;
It would not out at windows, nor at doors.
There is so hot a summer in my bosom,
That all my bowels crumble up to dust:
I am a scribbled form, drawn with a pen
Upon a parchment; and against this fire
Do I shrink up.

    P. Hen.   How fares your majesty?

    K. John. Poison'd,—ill-fare;—dead, forsook,
    cast off:
And none of you will bid the winter come,
To thrust his icy fingers in my maw;
Nor let my kingdom's rivers take their course
Through my burn'd bosom; nor entreat the north
To make his bleak winds kiss my parched lips,
And comfort me with cold:—I do not ask you
    much.
I beg cold comfort; and you are so strait,
And so ingrateful, you deny me that.

676

    P. Hen. O, that there were some virtue in my
    tears,
That might relieve you!

    K. John.   The salt in them is hot.—
Within me is a hell; and there the poison
Is, as a fiend, confin'd to tyrannize
On unreprievable condemned blood.

Enter the BASTARD.

    Bast. O, I am scalded with my violent motion,
And spleen of speed to see your majesty.

    K. John. O cousin, thou art come to set mine
    eye:
The tackle of my heart is crack'd and burn'd;
And all the shrouds, wherewith my life should sail,
Are turned to one thread, one little hair:
My heart hath one poor string to stay it by,
Which holds but till thy news be uttered;
And then all this thou seest, is but a clod,
And module of confounded royalty."

    Bast. The Dauphin is preparing hitherward,
Where, heaven he knows, how we shall answer
    him:
For, in a night, the best part of my power,
As I upon advantage did remove,
Were in the washes, all unwarily,
Devoured by the unexpected flood.   [*The King dies.*

    Sal. You breathe these dead news in as dead
    an ear.—
My liege! my lord!—But now a king.—now thus.

    P. Hen. Even so must I run on, and even so stop.
What surety of the world, what hope, what stay,
When this was now a king, and now is clay!

    Bast. Art thou gone so? I do but stay behind,
To do the office for thee of revenge;
And then my soul shall wait on thee to heaven,
As it on earth hath been thy servant still.——
Now, now, you stars, that move in your right
    spheres,
Where be your powers? Show now your mended
    faiths;
And instantly return with me again,
To push destruction, and perpetual shame.
Out of the weak door of our fainting land.
Straight let us seek, or straight we shall be sought
The Dauphin rages at our very heels.

    Sal. It seems, you know not then so much
    as we;
The cardinal Pandulph is within at rest,
Who half an hour since came from the Dauphin;
And brings from him such offers of our peace

As we with honour and respect may take,
With purpose presently to leave this war.

Bast. He will the rather do it, when he sees
Ourselves well sinewed to our defence.

Sal. Nay, it is in a manner done already;
For many carriages he hath despatch'd
To the sea-side, and put his cause and quarrel
To the disposing of the cardinal:
With whom yourself, myself, and other lords,
If you think meet, this afternoon will post
To consummate this business happily.

Bast. Let it be so:—And you, my noble
         prince,
With other princes that may best be spar'd,
Shall wait upon your father's funeral.

P. Hen. At Worcester must his body be interr'd;
For so he will'd it.

Bast.   Thither shall it then.
And happily may your sweet self put on

The lineal state and glory of the land!
To whom, with all submission, on my knee,
I do bequeath my faithful services
And true subjection everlastingly.

Sal. And the like tender of our love we make
To rest without a spot for evermore.

P. Hen. I have a kind soul, that would give
        you thanks,
And knows not how to do it, but with tears.

Bast. O, let us pay the time but needful woe,
Since it hath been beforehand with our griefs.—
This England never did, (nor never shall,)
Lie at the proud foot of a conqueror,
But when it first did help to wound itself.
Now these her princes are come home again,
Come the three corners of the world in arms,
And we shall shock them: Nought shall make
        us rue,
If England to itself do rest but true.   [*Exeunt.*

677

NOTES TO KING JOHN.

---

¹ *Look, where three-farthings goes.*

An allusion to a coin of Queen Elizabeth, a three-farthing piece, one side of which bore the im-sculpture of a rose. Faulconbridge means that his brother Robert durst not put a rose in his ear lest it should induce people to compare him to one of those little thin coins. Shakespeare anticipates the existence of this coin, as a three-farthing piece was not issued until the reign of Elizabeth. It was at this period a fashion to wear a rose in the ear or hair.

² *I would not be sir Nob in any case.*

Sir Nob is a contemptuous term for sir Robert. The meaning of Faulconbridge is,—If to inherit my father's land I must also inherit such features as yours, I disclaim my title to it. In no case would I have it.

³ *My picked man of countries.*

That is, a fashionable or foppish traveller. One of the butterflies of good society, of whom our poet frequently expresses his contempt.

⁴ *Like an ABC-book.*

An ABC-book, says Dr. Johnson, or as they spelt and wrote it, an absey-book, is a catechism.

⁵ *Colbrand the giant.*

An allusion to the story of Colbrand the Danish giant, whom Guy of Warwick killed in the presence of king Athelstan.

⁶ *There 's toys abroad*, i. e. rumours, suspicions.

⁷ *Knight, knight, good mother,—Basilisco-like.*

Mr. Theobald tells us that this line is a satirical allusion to a stupid drama of that age, called *Soliman and Persida*. In it there is a bragging cowardly knight, called Basilisco, whose pretensions being discovered by Piston, a buffoon servant in the play, the latter compels him to swear according to his dictation, when the following dialogue occurs:—

Bas. O, I swear, I swear.
Pist. By the contents of this blade,—
Bas. By the contents of this blade,—
Pist. I, the aforesaid Basilisco,—
Bas. I, the aforesaid Basilisco,—knight, good fellow, knight,
Pist. Knave, good fellow, knave, knave.

678

In Shakespeare's time the play was no doubt fresh in the minds of the audience, and the allusion understood.

**⁸ *The awless lion could not wage the fight,*
*Nor keep his princely heart from Richard's hand.***

An allusion to a tradition respecting Richard the First that he acquired his surname of *Cœur-de-lion* from having plucked out the heart of a lion to whose fury he was exposed by the Duke of Austria.

**⁹ *His father never was so true begot;*
*It cannot be, an' if thou wert his mother.***

Elinor had been divorced from her first husband, Lewis the Seventh of France, to whom she had been married sixteen years, and whom she accompanied on a crusade to the Holy Land, because he suspected her of an intrigue with a handsome Saracen named Saladin.

¹⁰ *To cry aim*, i. e. to encourage, to urge on.

¹¹ *'Tis not the roundure.*

Roundure has the same meaning as the French word *rondeur*, i. e. the circle. So in *All's Lost by Lust*, a tragedy: Rowley, 1633—

—— Will she meet our arms
With an alternate *roundure*?

**¹² *And, like a jolly troop of huntsmen, come*
*Our lusty English, all with purpled hands.***

It was customary amongst huntsmen to stain their hands in the blood of the dying deer, as a trophy of their success. This habit is alluded to in *Julius Cæsar*, where the conspirators kneel and bathe their hands in the blood of the slain dictator.

**¹³ *—— whose equality*
*By our best eyes cannot be censured.***

That is, the equality in prowess of your armies cannot be reproached or denied. No superiority is to be discerned on either side.

¹⁴ *These scroyles of Angiers.*

Scroyle is a term of contempt, meaning a low, mean fellow. It is sometimes used to signify a person of a scrofulous habit; a leper.

15 *Do like the mutines of Jerusalem.*

Shakespeare appears to have alluded to an incident in a book current in his time, called:—*A compendious and most marvellous History of the latter times of the Jews' Common-weale, &c.* The people in Jerusalem were divided into three parties, who carried on a fierce civil war each upon the others. At the same time they were besieged by the Romans; leaving, therefore, their mutual hatred, they joined their powers, and setting open their gates, fell upon the Romans with such fury that the latter fled before them.

16 *Volquessen.*

The ancient name for the country now called *the Vexin*; in Latin, *Pagus Velocassinus.* That part of it called the Norman Vexin was in dispute between Philip and John.

17 *That smooth-faced gentleman, tickling commodity.*

Commodity, is interest or selfishness. The meaning of the passage is;—interested motives govern all mankind, and lure us from our good intentions.

18 *But on this day, let seamen fear no wreck;*
No bargains break, that are not this day made.

But on this day, means except on this day; let neither shipwreck nor any other evil be feared, except on this ominous day.

19 *For that, which thou hast sworn to do amiss,*
Is not amiss when it is truly done.

This is an apparent contradiction; Warburton would read,—Is *yet* amiss; and Sir T. Hanmer, *most* amiss. Some critics have imagined that by being truly done, the Cardinal means being omitted. That is, by the omission of evil, truth is most done; but this construction is a very hard and forced one.

20 *Philip.*

Here the King, who knighted Faulconbridge by the name of Sir *Richard,* calls him by his former name.

21 *To England, if you will.*

Neither the King nor the Cardinal had alluded to England since the entrance of Constance. Mr. Malone points out that perhaps she is, in despair, addressing the absent John:—"Take my son to England, if you will;" now that he is in your power, I have no prospect of seeing him again. It is, therefore, of no consequence to me where he is.

22 *John lays you plots.*

That is, John lays plots which must be serviceable to you. He is unwittingly forwarding your interest.

23 *Northampton.*

It has been stated in the introduction to this play, that Arthur did not perish in England, but at Rouen, in Normandy.

24 *Here once again we sit, once again crown'd.*

John's second coronation was at Canterbury, in the year 1201. He was crowned a third time at the same place, after the murder of Arthur, as if to confirm his title now that his competitor was removed.

25 *And here's a prophet.*

Peter, the hermit of Pomfret; this man was in great repute among the common people. John was much disturbed by the prediction, thinking that it betokened his death. Notwithstanding that the event came to pass, the tyrant ordered Peter and his son to be dragged at the tails of horses through the streets of Warham, and afterwards hanged. The prophecy, as it is called, was made only three days before the event predicted. A shrewd man might have guessed the result, and an enthusiast believed that to be derived from inspiration which proceeded only from calculation and foresight. The unhappy man paid a fearful penalty either for fraud or delusion.

26 *Advis'd respect,* i. e. deliberate consideration.

27 *Within this bosom never enter'd yet*
The dreadful motion of a murd'rous thought.

This assertion of Hubert's is a direct falsehood; he had not only premeditated the murder of Arthur, but was with great difficulty restrained by the tears and vehement entreaties of the unhappy prince, from carrying his diabolical idea into execution. He is willing to take credit for a more generous and merciful nature than he possessed, and as he had repented of his revolting intention, perhaps he also persuaded himself that he never really intended its commission. It is but just to state that the Hubert of history was a very different character from the one delineated by the pen of Shakespeare; in the next reign he played a very conspicuous part, and is described by Hume as "the ablest and most virtuous minister that Henry ever possessed, a man who had been steady to the crown in the most difficult and dangerous times, and who yet showed no disposition, in the height of his power, to enslave or oppress the people." He married the eldest sister of the king of Scots, was created Earl of Kent, and made Chief Justiciary of England for life, though he afterwards lost the favour of the fickle king.

28 *The wall is high; and yet I will leap down.*

Shakespeare has here followed the old play. The exact method of Arthur's death has not been ascertained; the greatest credence is placed in the relation of Ralph, Abbot of Coggeshall, who tells us that the young prince having been removed from Falaise to Rouen, was one night startled from his sleep and desired to descend to the foot of the tower, which was washed by the waters of the Seine. At the portal was a boat containing his uncle John, and Peter de Maulac, the esquire of the tyrant. The dark looks of these men, the gloom and silence of the spot, told the unhappy youth that his last hour was at hand. Falling on his knees, he implored John to save his life, but the merciless tyrant gave the signal, and De Maulac struck the fatal blow. Some say that this man shrunk from the deed, and that John himself, seizing his nephew by the hair, stabbed him to the heart, and then hurled the body into the river. Hemingford and Knyghton, however, who wrote near the time, say that De Maulac was the executioner, which is likely, as John afterwards bestowed upon this ruffian the heiress of the barony of Mulgrave in marriage, probably as the reward of this savage act. That the prince was murdered either by the hand of John or at his dictation all historians are agreed.

⁷⁹ *Whose private with me of the Dauphin's love,*
Is much more general than these lines import.

That is, his oral communication of the esteem in which the Dauphin holds us, is much more ample than the letter.

⁸⁰ *Of my true defence.*

Honest defence; defence in a good cause.

⁸¹ —————— *Do not prove me so ;*
Yet I am none.

That is, do not make me a murderer by compelling me to kill you in defending myself. I am not a murderer as yet—not hitherto one.

⁸² *There is not yet so ugly a fiend of hell*
As thou shalt be, if thou didst kill this child.

"I remember once," says Mr. Steevens, "to have met with a book, printed in the time of Henry the Eighth (which Shakespeare, possibly, might have seen), where we are told that the deformity of the condemned in the other world, is exactly in proportion to the degrees of their guilt. The author of it observes how difficult it would be, on this account, to distinguish between Belzebub and Judas Iscariot."

⁸³ *This unhair'd sauciness, and boyish troops.*

The printed copies read *unheard*, but that is a word of little force, and not very applicable to the sense of the line. It is *unhaired*, youthful, beardless. Hair was formerly written *heir*; hence the error. Faulconbridge has previously exclaimed,

Shall a *beardless* boy,
A cocker'd silken wanton, brave our fields ?

680

⁸⁴ *And make you take the hatch.*

That is, to leap the hatch in fear. To take a hedge or ditch is the hunter's phrase.

⁸⁵ *The king, I fear, is poison'd by a monk.*

We have spoken of this tradition in the introduction to this play. None of the historians who wrote within sixty years after the death of John, allude to this improbable story. Thomas Wykes is the first who relates it, in his *Chronicle*, as a *report*. Death produced by a violent poison would have been as rapid as the poet represented it, but John's illness lasted nearly three days, and he had for some time previously been much harassed in body and distressed in mind. Notwithstanding that his life had been passed in avowed irreligion, the terror-stricken tyrant breathed almost his last words into the ears of a priest. The Abbot of Croxton asked him where he would be buried ! With a faint groan John answered, "I commend my soul to God, and my body to St. Wulstan."

⁸⁶ *Enter Prince Henry.*

This prince was but nine years old when his father died. He reigned over England during a period of fifty-six years, but the Earl of Pembroke was regent until the death of that nobleman.

⁸⁷ *And module of confounded royalty.*

Module and *model* had, in Shakespeare's time, the same meaning, or were different modes of spelling the same word.

H. T

King Richard the Second.

BETWEEN the death of John and the commencement of this play four kings had successively worn the crown of England, and a period of nearly two centuries had elapsed; but this and the seven plays which follow are one continuous history. A certain connexion is kept up between them, and they may be termed one perfect historical romance, of which the different plays constitute the books, and the acts and scenes the chapters. These historic dramas must be regarded as lofty fictions, fiction teaching truth; great political parables, based on facts, but rearing their high and graceful pinnacles into the realms of imagination. But if they are pronounced to be strict literal history, then must we say that much of history is merely what Napoleon declared it to be—"a fiction agreed upon."

Richard ascended the throne in 1377, when but in his eleventh year; but notwithstanding his youth he was respected as the son of Edward the famous Black Prince, the darling of the people and as the grandson of the powerful and popular monarch Edward the Third. Shakespeare in this drama passes over one-and-twenty turbulent years of Richard's reign, and confines himself to the incidents of the two last; commencing with the accusation by Bolingbroke of the Duke of Norfolk of treason. Richard committed a great error in banishing these noblemen; during his whole reign he had been oppressed by the power of his uncles and others of his great nobility. His policy should have been to let them quarrel and fight among themselves, and thus have rendered each a counterpoise to the power of the rest. To banish Hereford was both unjust and impolitic, but to seize his estates on the death of his father, John of Gaunt, was grossly dishonest. This arbitrary act tore the crown from Richard's temples, and paved the gloomy road to his murder-tainted cell at Pomfret. It brought the banished duke to England, ostensibly to obtain his paternal estates, but in reality to seize the crown. Encouraged by his own popularity in England, by Richard's absence, and the general discontent of both nobles and people, the crafty Bolingbroke returned and landed at Ravenspur with but sixty attendants; but he had chosen his time wisely, and was soon at the head of an army of sixty thousand men.

Weak, dissipated, and frivolous as Richard was, he gave, on some few occasions, evidences of great courage and promptitude of character. His conduct on the death of the rebel Tyler at Smithfield, when he disarmed the fury of the populace by riding boldly up to them, and exclaiming, "What are ye doing, my people? Tyler was a traitor—I am your king, and I will be your captain and guide," was courageous and decisive. Such heroism in a boy of fifteen, promised great talents in his maturity. The spirit of his father seemed to animate him on that occasion. Of a similar character was his conduct to his tyrannical uncle Gloucester, whose ambitious schemes had robbed the young king of all real power, and left him but the shadow of a sceptre, by placing the government in the hands of a commission of the nobles. In a full council, Richard, suddenly addressing his uncle, said, "How old do you think I am?" "Your highness," replied the duke, "is in your twenty-second year." "Then," continued the king, "I am surely of age to manage my own affairs. I have been longer under the control of guardians than any ward in my dominions. I thank ye, my lords, for your past services, but I want them no longer." And he thereupon dissolved the commission, and resumed the exercise of his royal authority. But his mind appears to have been swayed by no just principles, and if for a time he won the esteem of his nobles or his people, he soon contrived by some selfish or tyrannical act to erase the favourable impression he had made.

Had he possessed a just and firm mind, he might have become the most popular and absolute monarch this country had yet acknowledged. The great insurrection of the peasantry was an incident he could have turned to his own advantage; had he kept faith with these ignorant and misguided people, he would have reigned their sovereign indeed, enthroned in their rude affections, kinged in their hearts. How he did keep his word with them, the headsman and the hangman best could tell. Promise-breaking and perfidy appear to have been vices of royalty, and they are vices behind which ever stalks the grim and gaunt avenger; treachery always calls down upon itself its own punishment. It led the vacillating Richard to a horrible death in Pomfret Castle, and in later times it brought another English monarch (whose character bore many points of resemblance to that of Richard) to perish on the scaffold, in the capital of his own land, and surrounded by his own people.

It is doubtful whether Shakespeare is correct in his account of the murder of the deposed monarch: it was long believed that he was dispatched by Sir Piers Exton and others of his guards, but it is now generally supposed that he was starved to death in prison; and it is added that the wretched captive lived a fortnight after all food was denied him. History is little more than a fearful record of crimes, at the bare relation of which humanity shudders; and in these barbarous times almost all men appear to have been either oppressors or oppressed.

This drama was first entered at Stationers' Hall by Andrew Wise, August 29, 1597, and is supposed to have been written in the same year. There was a play upon this subject in existence before Shakespeare's, but it appears to have been laid aside on the production of his drama, and has since perished.

682

PERSONS REPRESENTED

KING RICHARD THE SECOND.
Appears, Act I. sc. 1; sc. 3; sc. 4. Act II. sc. 1. Act III. sc. 2; sc. 3. Act IV. sc. 1. Act V. sc. 1; sc. 5.

EDMUND OF LANGLEY, *Duke of York, and Uncle to the King.*
Appears, Ac. II. sc. 1; sc. 2; sc. 3. Act III. sc. 1; sc. 3. Act V. sc. 1. Act V. sc. 2; sc. 3; sc. 6.

JOHN OF GAUNT, *Duke of Lancaster, and Uncle to the King.*
Appears, Act I. sc. 1; sc. 2; sc. 3. Act II. sc. 1.

HENRY, *surnamed* Bolingbroke, *Duke of* Hereford, *Son to* John of Gaunt; *afterwards* King Henry the Fourth.
Appears, Act I. sc. 1; sc. 3. Act II. sc. 3. Act III. sc. 1; sc. 3. Act IV. sc. 1. Act V. sc. 3; sc. 6.

DUKE OF AUMERLE, *Son to the Duke of* York.
Appears, Act I. sc. 3; sc. 4. Act II. sc. 1. Act III. sc. 2; sc. 3. Act IV. sc. 1. Act V. sc. 2; sc. 3.

MOWBRAY, *Duke of Norfolk.*
Appears, Act I. sc. 1; sc. 3.

DUKE OF SURREY.
Appears, Act IV. sc. 1.

EARL OF SALISBURY.
Appears, Act II. sc. 4. Act III. sc. 2; sc. 3.

EARL BERKLEY.
Appears, Act II. sc. 3.

EARL OF NORTHUMBERLAND.
Appears, Act II. sc. 1; sc. 3. Act III. sc. 1; sc. 3. Act IV. sc. 1. Act V. sc. 1; sc. 6.

HENRY PERCY, *his Son.*
Appears, Act II. sc. 3. Act III. sc. 1; sc. 3. Act IV. sc. 1. Act V. sc. 3; sc. 6.

LORD ROSS,
LORD WILLOUGHBY,
Appear, Act II. sc. 1; sc. 3. Act III. sc. 1.

LORD FITZWATER.
Appears, Act IV. sc. 1. Act V. sc. 6.

BISHOP OF CARLISLE.
Appears, Act III. sc. 2; sc. 3. Act IV. sc. 1. Act V. sc. 6.

ABBOT OF WESTMINSTER.
Appears, Act IV. sc. 1.

LORD MARSHAL.
Appears, Act I. sc. 3.

BUSHY, } *Favourites of the King.*
GREEN, }
Appear, Act I. sc. 4. Act II. sc. 1; sc. 2. Act III. sc. 1.

BAGOT, *also a Favourite of the King.*
Appears, Act I. sc. 4. Act II. sc. 1; sc. 2. Act IV. sc. 1.

SIR STEPHEN SCROOP.
Appears, Act III. sc. 2; sc. 3.

SIR PIERCE OF EXTON.
Appears, Act V. sc. 4; sc. 5; sc. 6.

CAPTAIN *of a Band of Welchmen.*
Appears, Act II. sc. 4.

A GARDENER.
Appears, Act III. sc. 4.

A GROOM.
Appears, Act V. sc. 5.

QUEEN *to King Richard.*
Appears, Act II. sc. 1; sc. 2. Act III. sc. 4. Act V. sc. 1.

DUCHESS OF GLOUCESTER.
Appears, Act I. sc. 2.

DUCHESS OF YORK.
Appears, Act V. sc. 2; sc. 3.

LADIES *attending on the* Queen.
Appear, Act III. sc. 4. Act V. sc. 1.

Lords, Heralds, Officers, Soldiers, Messengers, Keeper, and other Attendants.

SCENE,—*Dispersedly in* ENGLAND *and* WALES.

683

THE LIFE AND DEATH OF

King Richard the Second.

ACT I.

SCENE I.—London. *A Room in the Palace.*

Enter KING RICHARD, *attended;* JOHN OF GAUNT, *and other Nobles, with him.*

K. Rich. Old John of Gaunt, time-honour'd
    Lancaster,
Hast thou, according to thy oath and band,
Brought hither Henry Hereford thy bold son;
Here to make good the boisterous late appeal,
Which then our leisure would not let us hear,
Against the duke of Norfolk, Thomas Mowbray?
Gaunt. I have, my liege.
    K. Rich. Tell me moreover, hast thou sounded
    him,
If he appeal the duke on ancient malice;
Or worthily as a good subject should,
On some known ground of treachery in him?
    Gaunt. As near as I could sift him on that
    argument,—
On some apparent danger seen in him,
Aim'd at your highness, no inveterate malice.
    K. Rich. Then call them to our presence; face
    to face,
And frowning brow to brow, ourselves will hear
The accuser, and the accused, freely speak:—
              [*Exeunt some* Attends.
High-stomach'd are they both, and full of ire,
In rage deaf as the sea, hasty as fire.

Re-enter Attendants, *with* BOLINGBROKE *and*
NORFOLK.

Boling. Full many years of happy days befal
My gracious sovereign, my most loving liege!
    Nor. Each day still better other's happiness;

Until the heavens, envying earth's good hap,
Add an immortal title to your crown!
    K. Rich. We thank you both: yet one but
    flatters us,
As well appeareth by the cause you come;
Namely, to appeal each other of high treason.—
Cousin of Hereford, what dost thou object
Against the duke of Norfolk, Thomas Mowbray?
    Boling. First, (heaven be the record to my
    speech!)
In the devotion of a subject's love,
Tendering the precious safety of my prince,
And free from wrath or misbegotten hate,
Come I appellant to this princely presence.—
Now, Thomas Mowbray, do I turn to thee,
And mark my greeting well; for what I speak,
My body shall make good upon this earth,
Or my divine soul answer it in heaven.
Thou art a traitor, and a miscreant;
Too good to be so, and too bad to live;
Since, the more fair and crystal is the sky,
The uglier seem the clouds that in it fly.
Once more, the more to aggravate the note,
With a foul traitor's name stuff I thy throat;
And wish, (so please my sovereign,) ere I move,
What my tongue speaks, my right-drawn sword
    may prove.
    Nor. Let not my cold words here accuse my
    zeal:
'Tis not the trial of a woman's war,
The bitter clamour of two eager tongues,
Can arbitrate this cause betwixt us twain:
The blood is hot, that must be cool'd for this
Yet can I not of such tame patience boast,

As to be hush'd, and naught at all to say:
First, the fair reverence of your highness curbs me
From giving reins and spurs to my free speech;
Which else would post, until it had return'd
These terms of treason doubled down his throat.
Setting aside his high blood's royalty,
And let him be no kinsman to my liege,
I do defy him, and I spit at him;
Call him—a slanderous coward, and a villain:
Which to maintain, I would allow him odds;
And meet him, were I tied to run a-foot
Even to the frozen ridges of the Alps,
Or any other ground inhabitable,
Where ever Englishman durst set his foot.
Mean time, let this defend my loyalty,—
By all my hopes, most falsely doth he lie.

Boling. Pale trembling coward, there I throw
    my gage,
Disclaiming here the kindred of a king,
And lay aside my high blood's royalty,
Which fear, not reverence, makes thee to except:
If guilty dread hath left thee so much strength,
As to take up mine honour's pawn, then stoop;
By that, and all the rights of knighthood else,
Will I make good against thee, arm to arm,
What I have spoke, or thou canst worse devise.

Nor. I take it up; and, by that sword I swear,
Which gently lay'd my knighthood on my
    shoulder,
I'll answer thee in any fair degree,
Or chivalrous design of knightly trial:
And, when I mount, alive may I not light,
If I be traitor, or unjustly fight!

K. Rich. What doth our cousin lay to Mow-
    bray's charge?
It must be great, that can inherit us
So much as of a thought of ill in him.

Boling. Look, what I speak my life shall prove
    it true;—
That Mowbray hath receiv'd eight thousand nobles,
In name of lendings for your highness' soldiers;
The which he hath detain'd for lewd employments,
Like a false traitor, and injurious villain.
Besides I say, and will in battle prove,—
Or here, or elsewhere, to the furthest verge
That ever was survey'd by English eye,—
That all the treasons, for these eighteen years
Complotted and contrived in this land,
Fetch from false Mowbray their first head and
    spring.
Further I say,—and further will maintain
Upon his bad life, to make all this good,—

That he did plot the duke of Gloster's death;
Suggest his soon-believing adversaries;
And, consequently, like a traitor coward,
Sluic'd out his innocent soul through streams of
    blood:
Which blood, like sacrificing Abel's, cries,
Even from the tongueless caverns of the earth,
To me, for justice, and rough chastisement;
And, by the glorious worth of my descent,
This arm shall do it, or this life be spent.

K. Rich. How high a pitch his resolution
    soars!—
Thomas of Norfolk, what say'st thou to this?

Nor. O, let my sovereign turn away his face,
And bid his ears a little while be deaf,
Till I have told this slander of his blood,
How God, and good men, hate so foul a liar.

K. Rich. Mowbray, impartial are our eyes and
    ears:
Were he my brother, nay, my kingdom's heir,
(As he is but my father's brother's son,)
Now by my sceptre's awe I make a vow,
Such neighbour nearness to our sacred blood
Should nothing privilege him, nor partialize
The unstooping firmness of my upright soul;
He is our subject, Mowbray, so art thou;
Free speech, and fearless, I to thee allow.

Nor. Then, Bolingbroke, as low as to thy
    heart,
Through the false passage of thy throat, thou liest.
Three parts of that receipt I had for Calais,
Disburs'd I duly to his highness' soldiers;
The other part reserv'd I by consent;
For that my sovereign liege was in my debt,
Upon remainder of a clear account,
Since last I went to France to fetch his queen:
Now swallow down that lie.————For Gloster's
    death,——
I slew him not; but to my own disgrace,
Neglected my sworn duty in that case.—
For you, my noble lord of Lancaster,
The honourable father to my foe,
Once did I lay an ambush for your life,
A trespass that doth vex my grieved soul:
But, ere I last receiv'd the sacrament,
I did confess it; and exactly begg'd
Your grace's pardon, and I hope, I had it.
This is my fault: As for the rest appeal'd,
It issues from the rancour of a villain,
A recreant and most degenerate traitor:
Which in myself I boldly will defend;
And interchangeably hurl down my gage

Upon this overweening traitor's foot,
To prove myself a loyal gentleman
Even in the best blood chamber'd in his bosom:
In haste whereof, most heartily I pray
Your highness to assign our trial day.

   K. Rich. Wrath-kindled gentlemen, be rul'd
by me;
Let's purge this choler without letting blood:
This we prescribe though no physician;
Deep malice makes too deep incision:
Forget, forgive; conclude, and be agreed;
Our doctors say, this is no time to bleed.—
Good uncle, let this end where it begun;
We'll calm the duke of Norfolk, you your son.

   Gaunt. To be a make-peace shall become my
age:—
Throw down, my son, the duke of Norfolk's gage.

   K. Rich. And, Norfolk, throw down his.

   Gaunt. When, Harry? when?
Obedience bids, I should not bid again.

   K. Rich. Norfolk, throw down; we bid; there
is no boot.

   Nor. Myself I throw, dread sovereign, at thy
foot:
My life thou shalt command, but not my shame:
The one my duty owes; but my fair name,
(Despite of death, that lives upon my grave,)
To dark dishonour's use thou shalt not have.
I am disgrac'd, impeach'd, and baffled here;
Pierc'd to the soul with slander's venom'd spear:
The which no balm can cure, but his heart-blood
Which breath'd this poison.

   K. Rich. Rage must be withstood:
Give me his gage:—Lions make leopards tame.

   Nor. Yea, but not change their spots: take
but my shame,
And I resign my gage. My dear, dear lord,
The purest treasure mortal times afford,
Is—spotless reputation; that away,
Men are but gilded loam, or painted clay.
A jewel in a ten-times-barr'd-up chest
Is—a bold spirit in a loyal breast.
Mine honour is my life; both grow in one;
Take honour from me, and my life is done;
Then, dear my liege, mine honour let me try;
In that I live, and for that will I die.

   K. Rich. Cousin, throw down your gage; do
you begin.

   Boling. O, God defend my soul from such foul
sin!
Shall I seem crest-fallen in my father's sight?
Or with pale beggar fear impeach my height

686

Before this outdar'd dastard? Ere my tongue
Shall wound mine honour with such feeble wrong,
Or sound so base a parle, my teeth shall tear
The slavish motive of recanting fear;
And spit it bleeding in his high disgrace,
Where shame doth harbour, even in Mowbray's
face.   [*Exit* GAUNT.

   K. Rich. We were not born to sue, but to
command:
Which since we cannot do to make you friends,
Be ready, as your lives shall answer it,
At Coventry, upon Saint Lambert's day;
There shall your swords and lances arbitrate
The swelling difference of your settled hate;
Since we cannot atone you, we shall see
Justice design the victor's chivalry.—
Marshal, command our officers at arms
Be ready to direct these home-alarms. [*Exeunt.*

SCENE II.—*The Same. A Room in the Duke of
Lancaster's Palace.*

Enter GAUNT, *and* DUCHESS OF GLOSTER.

   Gaunt. Alas! the part I had in Gloster's blood
Doth more solicit me, than your exclaims,
To stir against the butchers of his life.
But since correction lieth in those hands,
Which made the fault that we cannot correct,
Put we our quarrel to the will of heaven;
Who when he sees the hours ripe on earth,
Will rain hot vengeance on offenders' heads.

   Duch. Finds brotherhood in thee no sharper
spur?
Hath love in thy old blood no living fire?
Edward's seven sons, whereof thyself art one,
Were as seven phials of his sacred blood,
Or seven fair branches springing from one root:
Some of those seven are dried by nature's course,
Some of those branches by the destinies cut;
But Thomas, my dear lord, my life, my Gloster,—
One phial full of Edward's sacred blood,
One flourishing branch of his most royal root,—
Is crack'd, and all the precious liquor spilt;
Is hack'd down, and his summer leaves all faded,
By envy's hand, and murder's bloody axe.
Ah, Gaunt! his blood was thine; that bed, that
womb,
That mettle, that self-mould, that fashion'd thee,
Made him a man; and though thou liv'st, and
breath'st,
Yet art thou slain in him: thou dost consent
In some large measure to thy father's death,

Mr. C. Pitchman, as King Richard

In that thou seest thy wretched brother die,
Who was the model of thy father's life.
Call it not patience, Gaunt, it is despair:
In suffering thus thy brother to be slaughter'd,
Thou show'st the naked pathway to thy life,
Teaching stern murder how to butcher thee:
That which in mean men we entitle—patience,
Is pale cold cowardice in noble breasts.
What shall I say? to safeguard thine own life,
The best way is—to 'venge my Gloster's death.
   Gaunt. Heaven's is the quarrel; for heaven's
       substitute,
His deputy anointed in his sight,
Hath caus'd his death: the which if wrongfully,
Let heaven revenge; for I may never lift
An angry arm against his minister.
   Duch. Where then, alas! may I complain
myself?
   Gaunt. To heaven, the widow's champion and
defence.
   Duch. Why then, I will. Farewell, old Gaunt.
Thou go'st to Coventry, there to behold
Our cousin Hereford and fell Mowbray fight:
O, sit my husband's wrongs on Hereford's spear,
That it may enter butcher Mowbray's breast!
Or, if misfortune miss the first career,
Be Mowbray's sins so heavy in his bosom,
That they may break his foaming courser's back,
And throw the rider headlong in the lists,
A caitiff recreant to my cousin Hereford!
Farewell, old Gaunt; thy sometimes brother's
    wife,
With her companion grief must end her life.
   Gaunt. Sister, farewell: I must to Coventry:
As much good stay with thee, as go with me!
   Duch. Yet one word more;—Grief boundeth
where it falls,
Not with the empty hollowness, but weight:
I take my leave before I have begun;
For sorrow ends not when it seemeth done.
Commend me to my brother, Edmund York.
Lo, this is all:—Nay, yet depart not so;
Though this be all, do not so quickly go;
I shall remember more. Bid him—O, what?—
With all good speed at Plashy visit me.
Alack, and what shall good old York there see,
But empty lodgings and unfurnish'd walls,
Unpeopled offices, untrodden stones?
And what cheer there for welcome, but my groans?
Therefore commend me; let him not come there,
To seek out sorrow that dwells every where:
Desolate, desolate, will I hence, and die;

The last leave of thee takes my weeping eye.
                  [Exeunt

SCENE III.—*Gosford Green, near Coventry.
Lists set out, and a Throne. Heralds, &c.,
attending.*

     Enter the LORD MARSHAL, *and* AUMERLE.

   Mar. My lord Aumerle, is Harry Hereford
arm'd?
   Aum. Yea, at all points; and longs to enter in.
   Mar. The duke of Norfolk, sprightfully and
bold,
Stays but the summons of the appellant's trumpet.
   Aum. Why then, the champions are prepar'd,
and stay
For nothing but his majesty's approach.

Flourish of Trumpets. Enter KING RICHARD,
who takes his seat on his Throne; GAUNT, *and
several Noblemen, who take their places. A
Trumpet is sounded, and answered by another
Trumpet within. Then enter* NORFOLK *in armour, preceded by a Herald.*

   K. Rich. Marshal, demand of yonder champion
The cause of his arrival here in arms:
Ask him his name; and orderly proceed
To swear him in the justice of his cause.
   Mar. In God's name, and the king's, say who
thou art,
And why thou com'st, thus knightly clad in arms:
Against what man thou com'st, and what thy
quarrel:
Speak truly, on thy knighthood, and thy oath;
And so defend thee heaven, and thy valour!
   Nor. My name is Thomas Mowbray, duke of
Norfolk;
Who hither come engaged by my oath,
(Which, heaven defend, a knight should violate!)
Both to defend my loyalty and truth,
To God, my king, and my succeeding issue,
Against the duke of Hereford that appeals me;
And, by the grace of God, and this mine arm,
To prove him, in defending of myself,
A traitor to my God, my king, and me:
And, as I truly fight, defend me heaven!
                  [He takes his seat.

Trumpet sounds. Enter BOLINGBROKE, *in armour; preceded by a Herald.*

   K. Rich. Marshal, ask yonder knight in arms,
Both who he is, and why he cometh hither

Thus plated in habiliments of war;
And formally according to our law
Depose him in the justice of his cause.

  Mar. What is thy name? and wherefore com'st
    thou hither,
Before king Richard, in his royal lists?
Against whom comest thou? and what's thy
    quarrel?
Speak like a true knight, so defend thee heaven!

  Boling. Harry of Hereford, Lancaster, and
    Derby,
Am I; who ready here do stand in arms,
To prove, by heaven's grace, and my body's valour,
In lists, on Thomas Mowbray duke of Norfolk,
That he's a traitor, foul and dangerous,
To God of heaven, king Richard, and to me;
And, as I truly fight, defend me heaven!

  Mar. On pain of death, no person be so bold,
Or daring-hardy, as to touch the lists;
Except the marshal, and such officers
Appointed to direct these fair designs.

  Boling. Lord marshal, let me kiss my sovereign's
    hand,
And bow my knee before his majesty:
For Mowbray, and myself, are like two men
That vow a long and weary pilgrimage;
Then let us take a ceremonious leave,
And loving farewell, of our several friends.

  Mar. The appellant in all duty greets your
    highness,
And craves to kiss your hand, and take his leave.

  K. Rich. We will descend, and fold him in our
    arms.
Cousin of Hereford, as thy cause is right,
So be thy fortune in this royal fight!
Farewell, my blood; which if to-day thou shed,
Lament we may, but not revenge thee dead.

  Boling. O, let no noble eye profane a tear
For me, if I be gor'd with Mowbray's spear;
As confident, as is the falcon's flight
Against a bird, do I with Mowbray fight.——
My loving lord, [*To* Lord Mar.] I take my leave
    of you;—
Of you, my noble cousin, lord Aumerle:—
Not sick, although I have to do with death;
But lusty, young, and cheerly drawing breath.——
Lo, as at English feasts, so I regreet
The daintiest last, to make the end most sweet;
O thou, the earthly author of my blood,—
             [*To* Gaunt.
Whose youthful spirit, in me regenerate,
Doth with a two-fold vigour lift me up

To reach at victory above my head,—
Add proof unto mine armour with thy prayers;
And with thy blessings steel my lance's point,
That it may enter Mowbray's waxen coat,
And furbish new the name of John of Gaunt,
Even in the lusty 'haviour of his son.

  Gaunt. Heaven in thy good cause make thee
    prosperous!
Be swift like lightning in the execution;
And let thy blows, doubly redoubled,
Fall like amazing thunder on the casque
Of thy adverse pernicious enemy:
Rouse up thy youthful blood, be valiant and
    live.

  Boling. Mine innocency, and Saint George to
    thrive!   [*He takes his seat.*

  Nor. [*Rising.*] However heaven, or fortune, cast
    my lot,
There lives or dies, true to king Richard's throne,
A loyal, just, and upright gentleman:
Never did captive with a freer heart
Cast off his chains of bondage, and embrace
His golden uncontroll'd enfranchisement,
More than my dancing soul doth celebrate
This feast of battle with mine adversary.—
Most mighty liege,—and my companion peers,—
Take from my mouth the wish of happy years:
As gentle and as jocund, as to jest,
Go I to fight: Truth hath a quiet breast.

  K. Rich. Farewell, my lord: securely I espy
Virtue with valour couched in thine eye.——
Order the trial, marshal, and begin.
    [*The* King *and the Lords return to their seats*

  Mar. Harry of Hereford, Lancaster, and Derby
Receive thy lance; and God defend the right!

  Boling. [*Rising.*] Strong as a tower in hope, I
    cry—amen.

  Mar. Go bear this lance [*To an Officer*] to
    Thomas duke of Norfolk.

  1st Her. Harry of Hereford, Lancaster, and
    Derby,
Stands here for God, his sovereign, and himself,
On pain to be found false and recreant,
To prove the duke of Norfolk, Thomas Mowbray,
A traitor to his God, his king, and him,
And dares him to set forward to the fight.

  2nd Her. Here standeth Thomas Mowbray
    duke of Norfolk,
On pain to be found false and recreant,
Both to defend himself, and to approve
Henry of Hereford, Lancaster, and Derby,
To God, his sovereign, and to him, disloys.·

Courageously, and with a free desire,
Attending but the signal to begin.
   Mor. Sound, trumpets; and set forward, com-
     batants.   [*A Charge sounded.*
Stay, the king hath thrown his warder down.*
   K. Rich. Let them lay by their helmets and
     their spears,
And both return back to their chairs again :——
Withdraw with us :—and let the trumpets sound,
While we return these dukes what we decree.
                [*A long flourish.*
Draw near.   [*To the Combatants.*
And list, what with our council, we have done.
For that our kingdom's earth should not be soil'd
With that dear blood which it hath fostered ;
And for our eyes do hate the dire aspect
Of civil wounds plough'd up with neighbours'
     swords ;
[And for we think the eagle-winged pride
Of sky-aspiring and ambitious thoughts,
With rival-hating envy, set you on
To wake our peace, which in our country's cradle
Draws the sweet infant breath of gentle sleep ;]
Which so rous'd up with boisterous untun'd drums,
With harsh resounding trumpets' dreadful bray,
And grating shock of wrathful iron arms,
Might from our quiet confines fright fair peace,
And make us wade even in our kindred's blood ;—
Therefore, we banish you our territories :——
You, cousin Hereford, upon pain of death,
Till twice five summers have enrich'd our fields,
Shall not regreet our fair dominions,
But tread the stranger paths of banishment.
   Boling. Your will be done: This must my
     comfort be,——
That sun, that warms you here, shall shine on me ;
And those his golden beams, to you here lent,
Shall point on me, and gild my banishment.
   K. Rich. Norfolk, for thee remains a heavier
     doom,
Which I with some unwillingness pronounce :
The fly-slow hours shall not determinate
The dateless limit of thy dear exile ;—
The hopeless word of—never to return,
Breathe I against thee, upon pain of life.
   Nor. A heavy sentence, my most sovereign
     liege,
And all unlook'd for from your highness' mouth :
A dearer merit, not so deep a maim
As to be cast forth in the common air,
Have I deserved at your highness' hand.
The language I have learn'd these forty years,

My native English, now I must forego :
And now my tongue's use is to me no more
Than an unstringed viol or a harp ;
Or like a cunning instrument cas'd up,
Or, being open, put into his hands
That knows no touch to tune the harmony.
Within my mouth you have engaol'd my tongue,
Doubly portcullis'd, with my teeth, and lips ;
And dull, unfeeling, barren ignorance
Is made my gaoler to attend on me.
I am too old to fawn upon a nurse,
Too far in years to be a pupil now ;
What is thy sentence then, but speechless death,
Which robs my tongue from breathing native
     breath ?
   K. Rich. It boots thee not to be compas-
     sionate ;²
After our sentence, plaining comes too late.
   Nor. Then thus I turn me from my country's
     light,
To dwell in solemn shades of endless night.
                [*Retiring*
   K. Rich. Return again, and take an oath with
     thee.
Lay on our royal sword your banish'd hands ;
Swear by the duty that you owe to heaven,
(Our part therein we banish with yourselves,)
To keep the oath that we administer :—
You never shall (so help you truth and heaven!)
Embrace each other's love in banishment ;
Nor never look upon each other's face ;
Nor never write, regreet, nor reconcile
This lowering tempest of your home-bred hate ;
Nor never by advised purpose meet,
To plot, contrive, or complot any ill,
'Gainst us, our state, our subjects, or our land.
   Boling. I swear.
   Nor. And I, to keep all this.
   Boling. Norfolk, so far as to mine enemy ;—
By this time, had the king permitted us,
One of our souls had wander'd in the air,
Banish'd this frail sepulchre of our flesh,
As now our flesh is banish'd from this land :
Confess thy treasons, ere thou fly the realm ;
Since thou hast far to go, bear not along
The clogging burden of a guilty soul.
   Nor. No, Bolingbroke ; if ever I were traitor,
My name be blotted from the book of life,
And I from heaven banish'd, as from hence !
But what thou art, heaven, thou, and I do know ;
And all too soon, I fear, the king shall rue.—
Farewell, my liege :—Now no way can I stray ;

Save back to England, all the world 's my way.
                                    [*Exit.*
  K. Rich. Uncle even in the glasses of thine
eyes
I see thy grieved heart: thy sad aspéct
Hath from the number of his banish'd years
Pluck'd four away;—Six frozen winters spent,
Return [*To* BOLING.] with welcome home from
        banishment.
  Boling. How long a time lies in one little word!
Four lagging winters, and four wanton springs,
End in a word: Such is the breath of kings.
  Gaunt. I thank my liege, that, in regard of
        me,
He shortens four years of my son's exile:
But little vantage shall I reap thereby;
For, ere the six years, that he hath to spend,
Can change their moons, and bring their times
        about,
My oil-dried lamp, and time-bewasted light,
Shall be extinct with age, and endless night;
My inch of taper will be burnt and done,
And blindfold death not let me see my son.
  K. Rich. Why, uncle, thou hast many years to
live.
  Gaunt. But not a minute, king, that thou
        canst give:
Shorten my days thou canst with sullen sorrow,
And pluck nights from me, but not lend a morrow:
Thou canst help time to furrow me with age,
But stop no wrinkle in his pilgrimage;
Thy word is current with him for my death;
But, dead, thy kingdom cannot buy my breath.
  K. Rich. Thy son is banish'd upon good advice,
Whereto thy tongue a party-verdict gave;
Why at our justice seem'st thou then to lower?
  Gaunt. Things sweet to taste, prove in digestion
        sour.
You urg'd me as a judge; but I had rather,
You would have bid me argue like a father:—
O, had it been a stranger, not my child,
To smooth his fault I should have been more mild:
A partial slander sought I to avoid,
And in the sentence my own life destroy'd.
Alas, I look'd, when some of you should say,
I was too strict, to make mine own away;
But you gave leave to my unwilling tongue,
Against my will, to do myself this wrong.
  K. Rich. Cousin, farewell;—and, uncle, bid him
        so;
Six years we banish him, and he shall go.
                [*Flourish. Exeunt* K. RICH. *and Train.*
690

  Aum. Cousin, farewell: what presence must
        not know,
From where you do remain, let paper show.
  Mar. My lord, no leave take I; for I will ride,
As far as land will let me, by your side.
  Gaunt. O, to what purpose dost thou hoard thy
        words,
That thou return'st no greeting to thy friends?
  Boling. I have too few to take my leave of you,
When the tongue's office should be prodigal
To breathe the abundant dolour of the heart.
  Gaunt. Thy grief is but thy absence for a time.
  Boling. Joy absent, grief is present for that time.
  Gaunt. What is six winters? they are quickly
        gone.
  Boling. To men in joy; but grief makes one
        hour ten.
  Gaunt. Call it a travel that thou tak'st for plea-
        sure.
  Boling. My heart will sigh, when I miscall it so,
Which finds it an enforced pilgrimage.
  Gaunt. The sullen passage of thy weary steps
Esteem a foil, wherein thou art to set
The precious jewel of thy home-return.
  Boling. Nay, rather, every tedious stride I make
Will but remember me, what a deal of world
I wander from the jewels that I love.
Must I not serve a long apprenticehood
To foreign passages; and in the end,
Having my freedom, boast of nothing else,
But that I was a journeyman to grief?
  Gaunt. All places that the eye of heaven visits
Are to a wise man ports and happy havens:
Teach thy necessity to reason thus;
There is no virtue like necessity.
Think not, the king did banish thee;
But thou the king: Woe doth the heavier sit,
Where it perceives it is but faintly borne.
Go, say—I sent thee forth to purchase honor,
And not—the king exil'd thee: or suppose,
Devouring pestilence hangs in our air,
And thou art flying to a fresher clime.
Look, what thy soul holds dear, imagine it
To lie that way thou go'st, not whence thou com'st:
Suppose the singing birds, musicians;
The grass whereon thou tread'st, the presence
        strew'd;
The flowers, fair ladies; and thy steps, no more
Than a delightful measure, or a dance:
For gnarling sorrow hath less power to bite
The man that mocks at it, and sets it light.
  Boling. O, who can hold a fire in his hand,

By thinking on the frosty Caucasus?
Or cloy the hungry edge of appetite,
By bare imagination of a feast?
Or wallow naked in December snow,
By thinking on fantastic summer's heat?
O, no! the apprehension of the good,
Gives but the greater feeling to the worse:
Fell sorrow's tooth doth never rankle more,
Than when it bites, but lanceth not the sore.
   Gaunt. Come, come, my son, I'll bring thee on
     thy way:
Had I thy youth, and cause, I would not stay.
   Boling. Then, England's ground, farewell; sweet
     soil, adieu;
My mother, and my nurse, that bears me yet!
Where-e'er I wander, boast of this I can,——
Though banish'd, yet a trueborn Englishman.
                 [*Exeunt.*

SCENE IV.—*The Same.   A Room in the* King's
Castle.

Enter KING RICHARD, BAGOT, *and* GREEN;
AUMERLE *following.*

   K. Rich. We did observe.—Cousin Aumerle,
How far brought you high Hereford on his way?
   Aum. I brought high Hereford, if you call him
     so,
But to the next highway, and there I left him.
   K. Rich. And, say, what store of parting tears
     were shed?
   Aum. 'Faith none by me: except the north-east
     wind,
Which then blew bitterly against our faces,
Awak'd the sleeping rheum: and so, by chance,
Did grace our hollow parting with a tear.
   K. Rich. What said our cousin, when you parted
     with him?
   Aum. Farewell:
And, for my heart disdained that my tongue
Should so profane the word, that taught me craft
To counterfeit oppression of such grief,
That words seem'd buried in my sorrow's grave.
Marry, would the word farewell have lengthen'd
     hours,
And added years to his short banishment,
He should have had a volume of farewells;
But, since it would not, he had none of me.
   K. Rich. He is our cousin, cousin; but 't is
     doubt,
When time shall call him home from banishment,

Whether our kinsman come to see his friends.
Ourself, and Bushy, Bagot here, and Green,
Observ'd his courtship to the common people:—
How he did seem to dive into their hearts,
With humble and familiar courtesy;
What reverence he did throw away on slaves,
Wooing poor craftsmen, with the craft of smiles,
And patient underbearing of his fortune,
As 't were, to banish their affects with him.
Off goes his bonnet to an oyster-wench;
A brace of draymen bid—God speed him well,
And had the tribute of his supple knee,
With — "Thanks, my countrymen, my loving
     friends;"—
As were our England in reversion his,
And he our subjects' next degree in hope.
   Green. Well, he is gone; and with him go these
     thoughts.
Now for the rebels, which stand out in Ireland;—
Expedient manage must be made, my liege;
Ere further leisure yield them further means,
For their advantage, and your highness' loss.
   K. Rich. We will ourself in person to this war.
And, for our coffers—with too great a court,
And liberal largess,—are grown somewhat light,
We are enforc'd to farm our royal realm;
The revenue whereof shall furnish us
For our affairs in hand: If that come short,
Our substitutes at home shall have blank charters;
Whereto, when they shall know what men are
     rich,
They shall subscribe them for large sums of gold,
And send them after to supply our wants;
For we will make for Ireland presently.

Enter BUSHY.

Bushy, what news?
   Bush. Old John of Gaunt is grievous sick, my
     lord;
Suddenly taken; and hath sent post-haste,
To entreat your majesty to visit him.
   K. Rich. Where lies he?
   Bushy. At Ely-house.
   K. Rich. Now put it, heaven, in his physician's
     mind,
To help him to his grave immediately!
The lining of his coffers shall make coats
To deck our soldiers for these Irish wars.--
Come, gentlemen, let 's all go visit him:
Pray God, we may make haste, and come too
     late!   [*Exeunt*

ACT II.

SCENE I.—London. *A Room in Ely-house.*

Gaunt on a Couch; the Duke of York, and Others standing by him.

Gaunt. Will the king come? that I may breathe my last
In wholesome counsel to his unstaied youth.

York. Vex not yourself, nor strive not with your breath;
For all in vain comes counsel to his ear.

Gaunt. O, but they say, the tongues of dying men
Enforce attention, like deep harmony:
Where words are scarce, they are seldom spent in vain;
For they breathe truth, that breathe their words in pain.
He, that no more must say, is listen'd more
Than they whom youth and ease have taught to glose;
More are men's ends mark'd, than their lives before:
The setting sun, and music at the close,
As the last taste of sweets, is sweetest last;
Writ in remembrance, more than things long past:
Though Richard my life's counsel would not hear,
My death's sad tale may yet undeaf his ear.

York. No; it is stopp'd with other flattering sounds,
As, praises of his state; then, there are found
Lascivious metres; to whose venom sound
The open ear of youth doth always listen;
Report of fashions in proud Italy;
Whose manners still our tardy apish nation
Limps after, in base imitation.
Where doth the world thrust forth a vanity,
(So it be new, there's no respect how vile,)
That is not quickly buzz'd into his ears?
Then all too late comes counsel to be heard,
Where will doth mutiny with wit's regard.
Direct not him, whose way himself will choose
'T is breath thou lack'st, and that breath wilt thou lose.

Gaunt. Methinks, I am a prophet new inspir'd;
And thus, expiring, do foretell of him:
His rash fierce blaze of riot cannot last;

For violent fires soon burn out themselves,
Small showers last long, but sudden storms are short;
He tires betimes, that spurs too fast betimes;
With eager feeding, food doth choke the feeder:
Light vanity, insatiate cormorant,
Consuming means, soon preys upon itself.
This royal throne of kings, this scepter'd isle,
This earth of majesty, this seat of Mars,
This other Eden, demi-paradise;
This fortress, built by nature for herself,
Against infection, and the hand of war;
This happy breed of men, this little world;
This precious stone set in the silver sea,
Which serves it in the office of a wall,
Or as a moat defensive to a house,
Against the envy of less happier lands;
This blessed plot, this earth, this realm, this England,
This nurse, this teeming womb of royal kings,
Fear'd by their breed, and famous by their birth,
Renowned for their deeds as far from home,
(For Christian service, and true chivalry,)
As is the sepulchre in stubborn Jewry,
Of the world's ransom, blessed Mary's son;
This land of such dear souls, this dear, dear land,
Dear for her reputation through the world,
Is now leas'd out (I die pronouncing it,)
Like to a tenement, or pelting farm:
England, bound in with the triumphant sea,
Whose rocky shore beats back the envious siege
Of watery Neptune, is now bound in with shame,
With inky blots, and rotten parchment bonds;[10]
That England, that was wont to conquer others,
Hath made a shameful conquest of itself:
O, would the scandal vanish with my life,
How happy then were my ensuing death!

Enter King Richard, *and* Queen;[11] Aumerle, Bushy, Green, Bagot, Ross, *and* Willoughby.

York. The king is come: deal mildly with his youth;
For young hot colts, being rag'd, do rage the more.[12]

Queen. How fares our noble uncle, Lancaster?

892

K. Rich. What comfort, man ? How is 't with
    aged Gaunt ?

Gaunt. O, how that name befits my composi-
    tion !

Old Gaunt, indeed ; and gaunt in being old :
Within me grief hath kept a tedious fast ;
And who abstains from meat, that is not gaunt ?
For sleeping England long time have I watch'd ;
Watching breeds leanness, leanness is all gaunt ;
The pleasure, that some fathers feed upon,
Is my strict fast, I mean—my children's looks ;
And, therein fasting, hast thou made me gaunt :
Gaunt am I for the grave, gaunt as a grave,
Whose hollow womb inherits nought but bones.

    K. Rich. Can sick men play so nicely with their
      names ?

Gaunt. No, misery makes sport to mock itself :
Since thou dost seek to kill my name in me,
I mock my name, great king, to flatter thee.

    K. Rich. Should dying men flatter with those
      that live ?

Gaunt. No, no ; men living flatter those that
    die.

K. Rich. Thou, now a dying, say'st—thou flat-
    ter'st me.

Gaunt. Oh ! no ; thou diest, though I the sicker
    be.

K. Rich. I am in health, I breathe, and see thee
    ill.

Gaunt Now, He that made me, knows I see
    thee ill ;

Ill in myself to see, and in thee seeing ill.
Thy death-bed is no lesser than the land,
Wherein thou liest in reputation sick :
And thou, too careless patient as thou art,
Commit'st thy anointed body to the cure
Of those physicians that first wounded thee.
A thousand flatterers sit within thy crown,
Whose compass is no bigger than thy head ;
And yet, incaged in so small a verge,
The waste is no whit lesser than thy land.
O, had thy grandsire, with a prophet's eye,
Seen how his son's son should destroy his sons,
From forth thy reach he would have laid thy
    shame ;
Deposing thee before thou wert possess'd,
Which art possess'd now to depose thyself.
Why, cousin, wert thou regent of the world,
It were a shame, to let this land by lease :
But, for thy world, enjoying but this land,
Is it not more than shame, to shame it so ?
Landlord of England art thou now, not king :

Thy state of law is bondslave to the law ;
And thou——

    K. Rich. —— a lunatic lean-witted fool.
Presuming on an ague's privilege,
Dar'st with thy frozen admonition
Make pale our cheek ; chasing the royal blood,
With fury, from his native residence.
Now by my seat's right royal majesty,
Wert thou not brother to great Edward's son,
This tongue that runs so roundly in thy head,
Should run thy head from thy unreverend shoul-
    ders.

    Gaunt. O, spare me not, my brother Edward's
      son,
For that I was his father Edward's son ;
That blood already, like the pelican,
Hast thou tapp'd out, and drunkenly carous'd
My brother Gloster, plain well-meaning soul,
(Whom fair befal in heaven 'mongst happy souls !)
May be a precedent and witness good,
That thou respect'st not spilling Edward's blood
Join with the present sickness that I have ;
And thy unkindness be like crooked age,
To crop at once a too-long wither'd flower.
Live in thy shame, but die not shame with thee !—
These words hereafter thy tormenters be !—
Convey me to my bed, then to my grave :
Love they to live, that love and honour have.

          [*Exit, borne out by his* Attend

    K. Rich. And let them die, that age and sul-
      lens have ;
For both hast thou, and both become the grave.

    York. Beseech your majesty, impute his words
To wayward sickliness and age in him :
He loves you, on my life, and holds you dear,
As Harry duke of Hereford, were he here.

    K. Rich. Right ; you say true : as Hereford's
      love, so his :
As theirs, so mine ; and all be as it is.

Enter NORTHUMBERLAND.

    North. My liege, old Gaunt commends him to
      your majesty.

    K. Rich. What says he now ?

    North.   Nay, nothing ; all is said :
His tongue is now a stringless instrument ;
Words, life, and all, old Lancaster hath spent.

    York. Be York the next that must be bank-
      rupt so !
Though death be poor, it ends a mortal woe.

    K. Rich. The ripest fruit first falls, and so
    doth he ;

His time is spent, our pilgrimage must be;
So much for that.——Now for our Irish wars:
We must supplant those rough rug-headed kerns;
Which live like venom, where no venom else,
But only they, hath privilege to live.[15]
And for these great affairs do ask some charge,
Towards our assistance, we do seize to us
The plate, coin, revenues, and moveables,
Whereof our uncle Gaunt did stand possess'd.

   York. How long shall I be patient? Ah, how
     long
Shall tender duty make me suffer wrong?
Not Gloster's death, nor Hereford's banishment,
Not Gaunt's rebukes, nor England's private
    wrongs,
Nor the prevention of poor Bolingbroke
About his marriage,[16] nor my own disgrace,
Have ever made me sour my patient cheek,
Or bend one wrinkle on my sovereign's face.—
I am the last of noble Edward's sons,
Of whom thy father, prince of Wales, was first;
In war, was never lion rag'd more fierce,
In peace was never gentle lamb more mild,
Than was that young and princely gentleman:
His face thou hast, for even so look'd he,
Accomplish'd with the number of thy hours;[15]
But, when he frown'd, it was against the French,
And not against his friends: his noble hand
Did win what he did spend, and spent not that
Which his triumphant father's hand had won;
His hands were guilty of no kindred's blood,
But bloody with the enemies of his kin.
O, Richard! York is too far gone with grief,
Or else he never would compare between.

   K. Rich. Why, uncle, what 's the matter?
   York.   O, my liege,
Pardon me, if you please; if not, I pleas'd
Not to be pardon'd, am content withal.
Seek you to seize, and gripe into your hands,
The royalties and rights of banish'd Hereford?
Is not Gaunt dead? and doth not Hereford live?
Was not Gaunt just? and is not Harry true?
Did not the one deserve to have an heir?
Is not his heir a well-deserving son?
Take Hereford's rights away, and take from time
His charters, and his customary rights;
Let not to-morrow then ensue to-day;
Be not thyself, for how art thou a king,
But by fair sequence and succession?
Now, afore God (God forbid, I say true!)
If you do wrongfully seize Hereford's rights,
Call in the letters patents that he hath
694

By his attornies-general to sue
His livery and deny his offer'd homage,
You pluck a thousand dangers on your head,
You lose a thousand well-disposed hearts,
And prick my tender patience to those thoughts
Which honour and allegiance cannot think.

   K. Rich. Think what you will; we seize into
    our hands
His plate, his goods, his money, and his lands.

   York. I'll not be by, the while: My liege, fare-
    well:
What will ensue hereof, there 's none can tell;
But by bad courses may be understood,
That their events can never fall out good. [*Exit.*

   K. Rich. Go, Bushy, to the earl of Wiltshire
    straight;
Bid him repair to us to Ely-house,
To see this business: To-morrow next
We will for Ireland; and 't is time, I trow;
And we create, in absence of ourself,
Our uncle York lord governor of England,
For he is just, and always lov'd us well.—
Come on, our queen: to-morrow must we part,
Be merry, for our time of stay is short. [*Flourish*
   [*Exeunt* KING, QUEEN, BUSHY, AUM.
    GREEN, *and* BAGOT.

   North. Well, lords, the duke of Lancaster is
    dead.

   Ross. And living too; for now his son is duke.

   Willo. Barely in title, not in revenue.

   North. Richly in both, if justice had her right.

   Ross. My heart is great; but it must break with
    silence,
Ere 't be disburden'd with a liberal tongue.

   North. Nay, speak thy mind; and let him ne'er
    speak more,
That speaks thy words again, to do thee harm!

   Willo. Tends that thou'dst speak, to the duke
    of Hereford?
If it be so, out with it boldly, man;
Quick is mine ear, to hear of good towards him.

   Ross. No good at all, that I can do for him;
Unless you call it good, to pity him,
Bereft and gelded of his patrimony.

   North. Now, afore heaven, 't is shame such
    wrongs are borne,
In him a royal prince, and many more
Of noble blood in this declining land.
The king is not himself, but basely led
By flatterers; and what they will inform,
Merely in hate, 'gainst any of us all,
That will the king severely prosecute

'Gainst us, our lives, our children, and our heirs.

Ross. The commons hath he pill'd with grievous
　taxes,
And lost their hearts : the nobles hath he fin'd
For ancient quarrels, and quite lost their hearts.

Willo. And daily new exactions are devis'd ;
As blanks, benevolences, and I wot not what :
But what, o' God's name, doth become of this ?

North. Wars have not wasted it, for warr'd he
　hath not,
But basely yielded upon compromise
That which his ancestors achiev'd with blows :
More hath he spent in peace, than they in wars.

Ross. The earl of Wiltshire hath the realm in
　farm.

Willo. The king's grown bankrupt, like a bro-
　ken man.

North. Reproach, and dissolution, hangeth over
　him.

Ross. He hath not money for these Irish wars,
His burdenous taxations notwithstanding,
But by the robbing of the banish'd duke.

North. His noble kinsman : most degenerate
　king !
But, lords, we hear this fearful tempest sing,
Yet seek no shelter to avoid the storm :
We see the wind sit sore upon our sails,
And yet we strike not, but securely perish.[16]

Ross. We see the very wreck that we must suffer ;
And unavoided is the danger now,
For suffering so the causes of our wreck.

North. Not so ; even through the hollow eyes
　of death,
I spy life peering ; but I dare not say
How near the tidings of our comfort is.

Willo. Nay, let us share thy thoughts, as thou
　dost ours.

Ross. Be confident to speak, Northumberland :
We three are but thyself ; and, speaking so,
Thy words are but as thoughts ; therefore, be bold.

North. Then thus :—I have from Port le Blanc,
　a bay
In Brittany, receiv'd intelligence,
That Harry Hereford, Reignold lord Cobham,
[The son of Richard Earl of Arundel,]
That late broke from the duke of Exeter,
His brother, archbishop late of Canterbury,
Sir Thomas Erpingham, sir John Ramston,
Sir John Norbery, sir Robert Waterton, and Fran-
　cis Quoint,——
All these well furnish'd by the duke of Bretagne,
With eight tall ships, three thousand men of war,

Are making hither with all due expedience,
And shortly mean to touch our northern shore ;
Perhaps, they had ere this ; but that they stay
The first departing of the king for Ireland.
If then we shall shake off our slavish yoke,
Imp out our drooping country's broken wing,[b]
Redeem from broking pawn the blemish'd crown,
Wipe off the dust that hides our sceptre's guilt,
And make high majesty look like itself,
Away, with me, in post to Ravenspurg :
But if you faint, as fearing to do so,
Stay, and be secret, and myself will go.

Ross. To horse, to horse ! urge doubts to them
　that fear.

Willo. Hold out my horse, and I will first be
　there.　　　　　　　　　　　　　　[*Exeunt.*

SCENE II.—*The Same. A Room in the Palace.*

Enter QUEEN, BUSHY, *and* BAGOT.

Bushy. Madam, your majesty is too much sad :
You promis'd, when you parted with the king,
To lay aside life-harming heaviness,
And entertain a cheerful disposition.

Queen. To please the king, I did ; to please my-
　self,
I cannot do it ; yet I know no cause
Why I should welcome such a guest as grief,
Save bidding farewell to so sweet a guest
As my sweet Richard : Yet, again, methinks,
Some unborn sorrow, ripe in fortune's womb,
Is coming towards me ; and my inward soul
With nothing trembles : at something it grieves,
More than with parting from my lord the king.

Bushy. Each substance of a grief hath twenty
　shadows,
Which show like grief itself, but are not so :
For sorrow's eye, glazed with blinding tears,
Divides one thing entire to many objects ;
Like perspectives, which, rightly gaz'd upon,
Show nothing but confusion ; ey'd awry,
Distinguish form :[19] so your sweet majesty,
Looking awry upon your lord's departure,
Finds shapes of grief, more than himself, to wail ;
Which, look'd on as it is, is nought but shadows
Of what it is not. Then, thrice-gracious queen,
More than your lord's departure weep not ; more[c]
　not seen :
Or if it be, 't is with false sorrow's eye,
Which, for things true, weeps things imaginary.

Queen. It may be so ; but yet my inward soul
Persuades me, it is otherwise : Howe'er it be,

I cannot but be sad ; so heavy sad,
As,—though, in thinking, on no thought I think,—
Makes me with heavy nothing faint and shrink,"
  Bushy. 'T is nothing but conceit, my gracious
    lady.
  Queen. 'T is nothing less : conceit is still deriv'd
From some fore-father grief; mine is not so ;
For nothing hath begot my something grief:
Or something hath the nothing that I grieve :
'T is in reversion that I do possess ;
But what it is, that is not yet known ; what
I cannot name ; 't is nameless woe, I wot.

Enter GREEN.

  Green. God save your majesty !—and well met,
    gentlemen :—
I hope, the king is not yet shipp'd for Ireland.
  Queen. Why hop'st thou so ? 't is better hope,
    he is ;
For his designs crave haste, his haste good hope ;
Then wherefore dost thou hope, he is not shipp'd ?
  Green. That he, our hope, might have retir'd
    his power,
And driven into despair an enemy's hope,
Who strongly hath set footing in this land ;
The banish'd Bolingbroke repeals himself,
And with uplifted arms is safe arriv'd
At Ravenspurg.
  Queen.   Now God in heaven forbid !
  Green. O, madam, 't is too true : and that is
    worse,—
The lord Northumberland, his young son Henry
    Percy,
The lords of Ross, Beaumond, and Willoughby,
With all their powerful friends, are fled to him.
  Bushy. Why have you not proclaim'd Northum-
    berland,
And all the rest of the revolting faction
Traitors ?
  Green. We have : whereon the earl of Wor-
    cester
Hath broke his staff, resign'd his stewardship,
And all the household servants fled with him
To Bolingbroke.
  Queen. So, Green, thou art the midwife to my
    woe,
And Bolingbroke my sorrow's dismal heir :
Now hath my soul brought forth her prodigy ;
And I, a gasping new-deliver'd mother,
Have woe to woe, sorrow to sorrow join'd.
  Bushy. Despair not, madam.
  Queen.   Who shall hinder me !
696

I will despair, and be at enmity
With cozening hope ; he is a flatterer,
A parasite, a keeper-back of death,
Who gently would dissolve the bands of life,
Which false hope lingers in extremity.

Enter YORK.

  Green. Here comes the duke of York.
  Queen. With signs of war about his aged neck
O, full of careful business are his looks !——
Uncle,
For heaven's sake, speak comfortable words.
  York. Should I do so, I should belie my
    thoughts :
Comfort 's in heaven ; and we are on the earth,
Where nothing lives but crosses, care, and grief.
Your husband he is gone to save far off,
Whilst others come to make him lose at home :
Here am I left to underprop his land ;
Who, weak with age, cannot support myself :——
Now comes the sick hour that his surfeit made ;
Now shall he try his friends that flatter'd him.

Enter a Servant.

  Serv. My lord, your son was gone before I came
  York. He was !—Why, so !—go all which way
    it will !——
The nobles they are fled, the commons cold,
And will, I fear, revolt on Hereford's side.
Sirrah,
Get thee to Plashy, to my sister Gloster ;
Bid her send me presently a thousand pound :—
Hold, take my ring.
  Serv. My lord, I had forgot to tell your lordship :
To-day, as I came by, I called there ;—
But I shall grieve you to report the rest.
  York. What is it, knave ?
  Serv. An hour before I came, the duchess died.
  York. God for his mercy ! what a tide of woes
Comes rushing on this woeful land at once !
I know not what to do :—I would to God,
(So my untruth had not provok'd him to it,)
The king had cut off my head with my broth-
    er's.——
What, are there posts despatch'd for Ireland ?
How shall we do for money for these wars ?—
Come, sister,—cousin, I would say : pray, pardon
    me.——
Go, fellow, [*To the Servant,*] get thee home, pro-
    vide some carts,
And bring away the armour that is there,—
                                [*Exit Serv*

Gentlemen, will you go muster men? if I know
How, or which way, to order these affairs,
Thus thrust disorderly into my hands,
Never believe me. Both are my kinsmen;—
The one's my sovereign, whom both my oath
And duty bids defend; the other again,
Is my kinsman, whom the king hath wronged;
Whom conscience and my kindred bids to right.
Well, somewhat we must do.—Come, cousin, I'll
Dispose of you:—Go, muster up your men,
And meet me presently at Berkley-castle.
I should to Plashy too:——
But time will not permit:—All is uneven,
And every thing is left at six and seven.

          [*Exeunt* YORK *and* QUEEN.

  Bushy. The wind sits fair for news to go to
Ireland,
But none returns. For us to levy power,
Proportionable to the enemy,
Is all impossible.

  Green. Besides, our nearness to the king in
love,
Is near the hate of those love not the king.

  Bagot. And that's the wavering commons: for
their love
Lies in their purses; and whoso empties them,
By so much fills their hearts with deadly hate.

  Bushy. Wherein the king stands generally
condemn'd.

  Bagot. If judgment lie in them, then so do we,
Because we ever have been near the king.

  Green. Well, I'll for refuge straight to Bristol
castle;
The earl of Wiltshire is already there.

  Bushy. Thither will I with you: for little office
The hateful commons will perform for us;
Except like curs to tear us all to pieces.—
Will you go along with us?

  Bagot. No; I'll to Ireland to his majesty.
Farewell: if heart's presages be not vain,
We three here part, that ne'er shall meet again.

  Bushy. That's as York thrives to beat back
Bolingbroke.

  Green. Alas, poor duke! the task he under-
takes
Is—numb'ring sands, and drinking oceans dry;
Where one on his side fights, thousands will fly.

  Bushy. Farewell at once; for once, for all, and
ever.

  Green. Well, we may meet again.

  Bagot.   I fear me, never.

                          [*Exeunt.*

SCENE III.—*The Wilds in* Glostershire.

Enter BOLINGBROKE *and* NORTHUMBERLAND, *with*
Forces.

  Boling. How far is it, my lord, to Berkley now?

  North. Believe me, noble lord,
I am a stranger here in Glostershire
These high wild hills, and rough uneven ways,
Draw out our miles, and make them wearisome;
And yet your fair discourse hath been as sugar,
Making the hard way sweet and delectable.
But, I bethink me, what a weary way
From Ravenspurg to Cotswold, will be found
In Ross and Willoughby, wanting your company;
Which, I protest, hath very much beguil'd
The tediousness and process of my travel:
But theirs is sweeten'd with the hope to have
The present benefit which I possess:
And hope to joy, is little less in joy,
Than hope enjoy'd: by this the weary lords
Shall make their way seem short; as mine hath
done
By sight of what I have, your noble company.

  Boling. Of much less value is my company,
Than your good words. But who comes here?

Enter HARRY PERCY.

  North. It is my son, young Harry Percy,
Sent from my brother Worcester, whencesoever.—
Harry, how fares your uncle?

  Percy. I had thought, my lord, to have learn'd
his health of you.

  North. Why, is he not with the queen?

  Percy. No, my good lord; he hath forsook the
court,
Broken his staff of office, and dispers'd
The household of the king.

  North.   What was his reason?
He was not so resolv'd, when last we spake together.

  Percy. Because your lordship was proclaimed
traitor.
But he, my lord, is gone to Ravenspurg,
To offer service to the duke of Hereford,
And sent me o'er by Berkley, to discover
What power the duke of York had levied there;
Then with direction to repair to Ravenspurg.

  North. Have you forgot the duke of Hereford,
boy?

  Percy. No, my good lord; for that is not forgot,
Which ne'er I did remember: to my knowledge,
I never in my life did look on him.

North. Then learn to know him now; this is the duke.

Percy. My gracious lord, I tender you my service,
Such as it is, being tender, raw, and young;
Which elder days shall ripen, and confirm
To more approved service and desert.

Boling. I thank thee, gentle Percy; and be sure,
I count myself in nothing else so happy,
As in a soul rememb'ring my good friends;
And, as my fortune ripens with thy love,
It shall be still thy true love's recompense:
My heart this covenant makes, my hand thus seals it.

North. How far is it to Berkley? And what stir
Keeps good old York there, with his men of war?

Percy. There stands the castle, by you tuft of trees,
Mann'd with three hundred men, as I have heard;
And in it are the lords of York, Berkley, and Seymour;
None else of name, and noble estimate.

Enter ROSS *and* WILLOUGHBY.

North. Here come the lords of Ross and Willoughby,
Bloody with spurring, fiery-red with haste.

Boling. Welcome, my lords: I wot, your love pursues
A banish'd traitor; all my treasury
Is yet but unfelt thanks, which, more enrich'd
Shall be your love and labour's recompense.

Ross. Your presence makes us rich, most noble lord.

Willo. And far surmounts our labour to attain it.

Boling. Evermore thanks, the exchequer of the poor;
Which, till my infant fortune comes to years,
Stands for my bounty. But who comes here?

Enter BERKLEY.

North. It is my lord of Berkley, as I guess.

Berk. My lord of Hereford, my message is to you.

Boling. My lord, my answer is—to Lancaster;
And I am come to seek that name in England;
And I must find that title in your tongue,
Before I make reply to aught you say.

Berk. Mistake me not, my lord; 't is not my meaning,
To raze one title of your honour out;—

698

To you, my lord, I come, (what lord you will,)
From the most glorious regent of this land,
The duke of York; to know, what pricks you on
To take advantage of the absent time,"
And fright our native peace with self borne arms.

Enter YORK, *attended.*

Boling. I shall not need transport my words by you;
Here comes his grace in person.—My noble uncle!
[*Kneels.*

York. Show me thy humble heart, and not thy knee,
Whose duty is deceivable and false.

Boling. My gracious uncle!—

York. Tut, tut!
Grace me no grace, nor uncle me no uncle:
I am no traitor's uncle; and that word—grace,
In an ungracious mouth, is but profane.
Why have those banish'd and forbidden legs
Dar'd once to touch a dust of England's ground?
But then more why;——Why have they dar'd to march
So many miles upon her peaceful bosom;
Frighting her pale-fac'd villages with war,
And ostentation of despised arms?"
Com'st thou because the anointed king is hence?
Why, foolish boy, the king is left behind,
And in my loyal bosom lies his power.
Were I but now the lord of such hot youth,
As when brave Gaunt, thy father, and myself,
Rescued the Black Prince, that young Mars of men,
From forth the rank of many thousand French;
O, then, how quickly should this arm of mine,
Now prisoner to the palsy, chastise thee,
And minister correction to thy fault!

Boling. My gracious uncle, let me know my fault!
On what condition stands it, and wherein?

York. Even in condition of the worst degree—
In gross rebellion, and detested treason:
Thou art a banish'd man, and here art come,
Before the expiration of thy time,
In braving arms against thy sovereign.

Boling. As I was banish'd, I was banish'd Hereford;
But as I come, I come for Lancaster.
And, noble uncle, I beseech your grace,
Look on my wrongs with an indifferent eye:"
You are my father, for, methinks, in you
I see old Gaunt alive; O, then, my father!
Will you permit that I shall stand condemn'd

A wand'ring vagabond; my rights and royalties
Pluck'd from my arms perforce, and given away
To upstart unthrifts? Wherefore was I born?
If that my cousin king be king of England,
It must be granted, I am duke of Lancaster.
You have a son, Aumerle, my noble kinsman;
Had you first died, and he been thus trod down,
He should have found his uncle Gaunt a father,
To rouse his wrongs, and chase them to the bay.
I am denied to sue my livery here,
And yet my letters-patent give me leave:
My father's goods are all distrain'd, and sold;
And these, and all, are all amiss employ'd.
What would you have me do? I am a subject,
And challenge law: Attornies are denied me:
And therefore personally I lay my claim
To my inheritance of free descent.

　　North. The noble duke hath been too much
　　　　abus'd.
　　Ross. It stands your grace upon, to do him
　　　　right.
　　Willo. Base men by his endowments are made
　　　　great.
　　York. My lords of England, let me tell you
　　　　this,—
I have had feeling of my cousin's wrongs,
And labour'd all I could to do him right:
But in this kind to come, in braving arms,
Be his own carver, and cut out his way,
To find out right with wrong,—it may not be;
And you, that do abet him in this kind,
Cherish rebellion, and are rebels all.

　　North. The noble duke hath sworn, his com-
　　　　ing is
But for his own: and, for the right of that,
We all have strongly sworn to give him aid:
And let him ne'er see joy, that breaks that oath.

　　York. Well, well, I see the issue of these arms:
I cannot mend it, I must needs confess,
Because my power is weak, and all ill left:
But, if I could, by him that gave me life,
I would attach you all, and make you stoop
Unto the sovereign mercy of the king;
But, since I cannot, be it known to you,
I do remain as neuter. So, fare you well;—
Unless you please to enter in the castle,

And there repose you for this night.

　　Boling. An offer, uncle, that we will accept.
But we must win your grace, to go with us
To Bristol castle; which, they say, is held
By Bushy, Bagot, and their complices,
The caterpillars of the commonwealth,
Which I have sworn to weed, and pluck away.

　　York. It may be, I will go with you:—but yet
　　　　I'll pause;
For I am loath to break our country's laws.
Nor friends, nor foes, to me welcome you are:
Things past redress, are now with me past care.
　　　　　　　　　　　　　　　　　　[*Exeunt.*

SCENE IV.—*A Camp in* Wales.

Enter SALISBURY, *and a* Captain.

　　Cap. My lord of Salisbury, we have staid ten
　　　　days,
And hardly kept our countrymen together,
And yet we hear no tidings from the king;
Therefore we will disperse ourselves: farewell.

　　Sal. Stay yet another day, thou trusty Welsh-
　　　　man;
The king reposeth all his confidence
In thee.

　　Cap. 'Tis thought, the king is dead; we will
　　　　not stay.
The bay-trees in our country are all wither'd,
And meteors fright the fixed stars of heaven;
The pale-fac'd moon looks bloody on the earth,
And lean-look'd prophets whisper fearful change;
Rich men look sad, and ruffians dance and leap,—
The one, in fear to lose what they enjoy,
The other, to enjoy by rage and war;
These signs forerun the death or fall of kings.—
Farewell; our countrymen are gone and fled.
As well assur'd, Richard their king is dead. [*Exit.*

　　Sal. Ah, Richard! with the eyes of heavy
　　　　mind,
I see thy glory, like a shooting star,
Fall to the base earth from the firmament.
Thy sun sets weeping in the lowly west,
Witnessing storms to come, woe, and unrest:
Thy friends are fled, to wait upon thy foes;
And crossly to thy good all fortune goes. [*Exit.*

ACT III.

SCENE I.—Bolingbroke's *Camp at* Bristol.

Enter BOLINGBROKE, YORK, NORTHUMBERLAND,
PERCY, WILLOUGHBY, ROSS: Officers *behind
with* BUSHY *and* GREEN, *prisoners.*

Boling. Bring forth these men.—
Bushy, and Green, I will not vex your souls
(Since presently your souls must part your bodies,)
With too much urging your pernicious lives,
For 't were no charity: yet, to wash your blood
From off my hands, here, in the view of men,
I will unfold some causes of your death.
You have misled a prince, a royal king,
A happy gentleman in blood and lineaments,
By you unhappied and disfigur'd clean.
You have, in manner, with your sinful hours,
Made a divorce betwixt his queen and him;
Broke the possession of a royal bed,
And stain'd the beauty of a fair queen's cheeks
With tears drawn from her eyes by your foul wrongs.
Myself—a prince, by fortune of my birth;
Near to the king in blood; and near in love,
Till you did make him misinterpret me,—
Have stoop'd my neck under your injuries,
And sigh'd my English breath in foreign clouds,
Eating the bitter bread of banishment:
Whilst you have fed upon my signories,
Dispark'd my parks, and fell'd my forest woods,
From my own windows torn my household coat,"
Raz'd out my imprese, leaving me no sign,—
Save men's opinions, and my living blood,—
To show the world I am a gentleman.
This, and much more, much more than twice all
    this,
Condemns you to the death:—See them deliver'd
    over
To execution and the hand of death.
    Bushy. More welcome is the stroke of death
        to me,
Than Bolingbroke to England.—Lords, farewell.
    Green. My comfort is,—that heaven will take
        our souls,
And plague injustice with the pains of hell.
    Boling. My lord Northumberland, see them
        dispatch'd.
    [*Exeunt* NORTH. *and Others with Prisoners.*
    700

Uncle, you say, the queen is at your house
For heaven's sake, fairly let her be entreated:
Tell her, I send to her my kind commends;
Take special care my greetings be deliver'd.
    York. A gentleman of mine I have despatch'd
With letters of your love to her at large.
    Boling. Thanks, gentle uncle.—Come, lords,
        away;
To fight with Glendower and his complices."
Awhile to work, and, after, holiday.   [*Exeunt.*

SCENE II.—*The Coast of Wales.   A Castle in
    view.*

Flourish: Drums and Trumpets.   Enter KING
    RICHARD, BISHOP OF CARLISLE, AUMERLE, *and*
    Soldiers.

    K. Rich. Barkloughly castle call you this at
        hand?
    Aum. Yea, my lord: How brooks your grace
        the air,
After late tossing on the breaking seas?
    K. Rich. Needs must I like it well; I weep
        for joy,
To stand upon my kingdom once again.——
Dear earth, I do salute thee with my hand,
Though rebels wound thee with their horses' hoofs
As a long parted mother, with her child
Plays fondly with her tears and smiles, in meeting
So, weeping, smiling, greet I thee, my earth,
And do thee favour with my royal hands.
Feed not thy sovereign's foe, my gentle earth,
Nor with thy sweets comfort his rav'nous sense:
But let thy spiders, that suck up thy venom,
And heavy-gaited toads, lie in their way;
Doing annoyance to the treacherous feet,
Which with usurping steps do trample thee.
Yield stinging nettles to mine enemies:
And when they from thy bosom pluck a flower,
Guard it, I pray thee, with a lurking adder;
Whose double tongue may with a mortal touch
Throw death upon thy sovereign's enemies.—
Mock not my senseless conjuration, lords;
This earth shall have a feeling, and these stones
Prove armed soldiers, ere her native king
Shall falter under foul rebellious arms

Bishop. Fear not, my lord; that Power, that made you king,
Hath power to keep you king, in spite of all.
The means that heaven yields must be embrac'd,
And not neglected; else, if heaven would,
And we will not, heaven's offer we refuse;
The proffer'd means of succour and redress.

　Aum. He means, my lord, that we are too remiss;
Whilst Bolingbroke, through our security,
Grows strong and great, in substance, and in friends.

　K. Rich. Discomfortable cousin! know'st thou not,
That when the searching eye of heaven is hid
Behind the globe, and lights the lower world,
Then thieves and robbers range abroad unseen,
In murders, and in outrage, boldly here;
But when, from under this terrestrial ball,
He fires the proud tops of the eastern pines,
And darts his light through every guilty hole,
Then murders, treasons, and detested sins,
The cloak of night being pluck'd from off their backs,
Stand bare and naked, trembling at themselves?
So when this thief, this traitor, Bolingbroke,—
Who all this while hath revell'd in the night,
Whilst we were wand'ring with the antipodes,—
Shall see us rising in our throne the east,
His treasons will sit blushing in his face,
Not able to endure the sight of day,
But, self-affrighted, tremble at his sin.
Not all the water in the rough rude sea
Can wash the balm from an anointed king:
The breath of worldly men cannot depose
The deputy elected by the Lord:*
For every man that Bolingbroke hath press'd,
To lift shrewd steel against our golden crown,
God for his Richard hath in heavenly pay
A glorious angel: then, if angels fight,
Weak men must fall; for heaven still guards the right.

Enter SALISBURY.

Welcome, my lord: How far off lies your power?

　Sal. Nor near, nor further off, my gracious lord,
Than this weak arm: Discomfort guides my tongue,
And bids me speak of nothing but despair.
One day too late, I fear, my noble lord,
Hath clouded all thy happy days on earth:
O, call back yesterday, bid time return,

And thou shalt have twelve thousand fighting men!
To-day, to-day, unhappy day, too late,
O'erthrows thy joys, friends, fortune, and thy state
For all the Welshmen, hearing thou wert dead,
Are gone to Bolingbroke, dispers'd, and fled.

　Aum. Comfort, my liege: why looks your grace so pale?

　K. Rich. But now, the blood of twenty thousand men
Did triumph in my face, and they are fled;
And, till so much blood thither come again,
Have I not reason to look pale and dead?
All souls that will be safe, fly from my side;
For time hath set a blot upon my pride.

　Aum. Comfort, my liege; remember who you are.

　K. Rich. I had forgot myself: Am I not king?
Awake, thou sluggard majesty! thou sleep'st.
Is not the king's name forty thousand names?
Arm, arm, my name! a puny subject strikes
At thy great glory.—Look not to the ground,
Ye favourites of a king: Are we not high?
High be our thoughts: I know, my uncle York
Hath power enough to serve our turn.　But who
Comes here?

Enter SCROOP.

　Scroop. More health and happiness betide my liege,
Than can my care-tun'd tongue deliver him.

　K. Rich. Mine ear is open, and my heart prepar'd;
The worst is worldly loss, thou canst unfold.
Say, is my kingdom lost? why, 't was my care;
And what loss is it, to be rid of care?
Strives Bolingbroke to be as great as we?
Greater he shall not be; if he serve God,
We'll serve him too, and be his fellow so:
Revolt our subjects? that we cannot mend;
They break their faith to God, as well as us:
Cry, woe, destruction, ruin, loss, decay;
The worst is—death, and death will have his day.

　Scroop. Glad am I, that your highness is so arm'd
To bear the tidings of calamity.
Like an unseasonable stormy day,
Which makes the silver rivers drown their shores
As if the world were all dissolv'd to tears;
So high above his limits swells the rage
Of Bolingbroke, covering your fearful land

With hard bright steel, and hearts harder than
  steel.
White-beards have arm'd their thin and hairless
  scalps
Against thy majesty; boys, with women's voices,
Strive to speak big, and clap their female joints
In stiff unwieldy arms against thy crown:
Thy very beadsmen learn to bend their bows
Of double-fatal yew against thy state;
Yea, distaff-women manage rusty bills
Against thy seat: both young and old rebel,
And all goes worse than I have power to tell.

  K. Rich. Too well, too well, thou tell'st a tale
  so ill.
Where is the earl of Wiltshire? where is Bagot?
What is become of Bushy? where is Green?
That they have let the dangerous enemy
Measure our confines with such peaceful steps?
If we prevail, their heads shall pay for it.
  warrant, they have made peace with Bolingbroke.

  Scroop. Peace have they made with him, indeed,
  my lord.

  K. Rich. O villains, vipers, damn'd without
  redemption!
Dogs, easily won to fawn on any man!
Snakes, in my heart-blood warm'd, that sting my
  heart!
Three Judases, each one thrice worse than Judas!
Would they make peace? terrible hell make war
Upon their spotted souls for this offence!

  Scroop. Sweet love, I see, changing his property,
Turns to the sourest and most deadly hate:—
Again uncurse their souls; their peace is made
With heads, and not with hands: those whom
  you curse,
Have felt the worst of death's destroying wound,
And lie full low, grav'd in the hollow ground.

  Aum. Is Bushy, Green, and the earl of Wiltshire, dead?

  Scroop. Yea, all of them at Bristol lost their
  heads.

  Aum. Where is the duke my father with his
  power?

  K. Rich. No matter where; of comfort no man
  speak:
Let's talk of graves, of worms, and epitaphs;
Make dust our paper, and with rainy eyes
Write sorrow on the bosom of the earth.
Let's choose executors, and talk of wills:
And yet not so,—for what can we bequeath,
Save our deposed bodies to the ground?
Our lands, our lives, and all are Bolingbroke's,
  702

And nothing can we call our own, but death;
And that small model of the barren earth,
Which serves as paste and cover to our bones.
For heaven's sake, let us sit upon the ground,
And tell sad stories of the death of kings:—
How some have been depos'd, some slain in war;
Some haunted by the ghosts they have depos'd;
Some poison'd by their wives, some sleeping kill'd;
All murder'd:—For within the hollow crown,
That rounds the mortal temples of a king,
Keeps death his court: and there the antic sits,
Scoffing his state, and grinning at his pomp;
Allowing him a breath, a little scene
To monarchize, be fear'd, and kill with looks:
Infusing him with self and vain conceit,—
As if this flesh, which walls about our life,
Were brass impregnable; and, humour'd thus,
Comes at the last, and with a little pin
Bores through his castle wall, and—farewell king!
Cover your heads, and mock not flesh and blood
With solemn reverence; throw away respect,
Tradition, form, and ceremonious duty,
For you have but mistook me all this while:
I live with bread like you, feel want, taste grief,
Need friends:—Subjected thus,
How can you say to me—I am a king?

  Car. My lord, wise men ne'er wail their present
  woes,
But presently prevent the ways to wail.
To fear the foe, since fear oppresseth strength,
Gives, in your weakness, strength unto your foe,
And so your follies fight against yourself.
Fear, and be slain; no worse can come, to fight;
And fight and die, is death destroying death;
Where fearing dying, pays death servile breath.

  Aum. My father hath a power, enquire of him,
And learn to make a body of a limb.

  K. Rich. Thou chid'st me well:—Proud Bol-
  ingbroke, I come,
To change blows with thee for our day of doom,
This ague-fit of fear is over-blown;
An easy task it is, to win our own.——
Say, Scroop, where lies our uncle with his power?
Speak sweetly, man, although thy looks be sour.

  Scroop. Men judge by the complexion of the
  sky
The state and inclination of the day:
So may you by my dull and heavy eye,
My tongue hath but a heavier tale to say.
I play the torturer, by small and small,
To lengthen out the worst that must be spoken:—
Your uncle York hath join'd with Bolingbroke.

And all your northern castles yielded up,
And all your southern gentlemen in arms
Upon his party.

    K. Rich.   Thou hast said enough.——
Beshrew thee, cousin, which didst lead me forth
                      [*To* AUM.
Of that sweet way I was in to despair!
What say you now? What comfort have we now?
By heaven, I'll hate him everlastingly,
That bids me be of comfort any more.
Go, to Flint castle; there I'll pine away;
A king, woe's slave, shall kingly woe obey.
That power I have, discharge; and let them go
To ear the land that hath some hope to grow,
For I have none:—Let no man speak again
To alter this, for council is but vain.

    Aum. My liege, one word.

    K. Rich.   He does me double wrong,
That wounds me with the flatteries of his tongue.
Discharge my followers, let them hence;—Away,
From Richard's night, to Bolingbroke's fair day.
                      [*Exeunt.*

SCENE III.—Wales. *Before* Flint *Castle.*

Enter, with Drum and Colours, BOLINGBROKE *and*
Forces; YORK, NORTHUMBERLAND, *and others.*

    Boling. So that by this intelligence we learn,
The Welshmen are dispers'd; and Salisbury
Is gone to meet the king, who lately landed,
With some few private friends, upon this coast.

    North. The news is very fair and good, my lord;
Richard, not far from hence, hath hid his head.

    York. It would beseem the lord Northumber-
        land,
To say—king Richard:—Alack the heavy day,
When such a sacred king should hide his head!

    North. Your grace mistakes me; only to be
        brief,
Left I his title out.

    York.   The time hath been,
Would you have been so brief with him, he would
Have been so brief with you, to shorten you,
For taking so the head,* your whole head's length.

    Boling. Mistake not, uncle, further than you
        should.

    York. Take not, good cousin, further than you
        should,
Lest you mistake: The heavens are o'er your
        head.

    Boling. I know it, uncle: and oppose not
Myself against their will.—But who comes here?

Enter PERCY.

    Well, Harry; what, will not this castle yield?

    Percy. The castle royally is mann'd, my lord,
Against thy entrance.

    Boling. Royally!
Why, it contains no king?

    Percy.   Yes, my good lord,
It doth contain a king; king Richard lies
Within the limits of yon lime and stone;
And with him are the lord Aumerle, lord Salisbury,
Sir Stephen Scroop: besides a clergyman
Of holy reverence, who, I cannot learn.

    North. Belike, it is the bishop of Carlisle.

    Boling. Noble lord,   [*To* NORTH.
Go to the rude ribs of that ancient castle;
Through brazen trumpet send the breath of parle
Into his ruin'd ears, and thus deliver.
Harry Bolingbroke
On both his knees doth kiss king Richard's hand;
And sends allegiance, and true faith of heart,
To his most royal person: hither come
Even at his feet to lay my arms and power;
Provided that, my banishment repeal'd,
And lands restor'd again, be freely granted:
If not, I'll use the advantage of my power,
And lay the summer's dust with showers of blood,
Rain'd from the wounds of slaughter'd English-
        men:
The which, how far off from the mind of Boling-
        broke
It is, such crimson tempest should bedrench
The fresh green lap of fair king Richard's land,
My stooping duty tenderly shall show.
Go, signify as much; while here we march
Upon the grassy carpet of this plain.—
         [NORTH. *advances to the Castle, with a Trumpet.*
Let's march without the noise of threat'ning
        drum,
That from the castle's totter'd battlements
Our fair appointments may be well perus'd.
Methinks, king Richard and myself should meet
With no less terror than the elements
Of fire and water, when their thund'ring shock
At meeting tears the cloudy cheeks of heaven.
Be he the fire, I'll be the yielding water:
The rage be his, while on the earth I rain
My waters; on the earth, and not on him.
March on, and mark king Richard how he looks.

A parle sounded, and answered by another Trum-
pet within. Flourish. Enter on the walls,
                        703

KING RICHARD, *the* BISHOP OF CARLISLE, AUMERLE, SCROOP, *and* SALISBURY.

York. See, see, king Richard doth himself appear.

As doth the blushing discontented sun
From out the fiery portal of the east;
When he perceives the envious clouds are bent
To dim his glory, and to stain the track
Of his bright passage to the occident.
Yet looks he like a king; behold, his eye,
As bright as is the eagle's, lightens forth
Controlling majesty: Alack, alack, for woe,
That any arm should stain so fair a show!

   K. Rich. We are amaz'd; and thus long have
       we stood
To watch the fearful bending of thy knee,
                  [*To* NORTH.
Because we thought ourself thy lawful king:
And if we be, how dare thy joints forget
To pay their awful duty to our presence?
If we be not, show us the hand of God
That hath dismiss'd us from our stewardship;
For well we know, no hand of blood and bone
Can gripe the sacred handle of our sceptre,
Unless he do profane, steal, or usurp.
And though you think, that all, as you have done,
Have torn their souls, by turning them from us,
And we are barren, and bereft of friends;——
Yet know,—my master, God omnipotent,
Is must'ring in his clouds, on our behalf,
Armies of pestilence; and they shall strike
Your children yet unborn, and unbegot,
That lift your vassal hands against my head,
And threat the glory of my precious crown.
Tell Bolingbroke, (for yona', methinks, he is,)
That every stride he makes upon my land,
Is dangerous treason: he is come to ope
The purple testament of bleeding war;
But ere the crown he looks for live in peace,
Ten thousand bloody crowns of mothers' sons
Shall ill become the flower of England's face;
Change the complexion of her maid-pale peace
To scarlet indignation, and bedew
Her pastures' grass with faithful English blood.

   North. The king of heaven forbid, our lord the
       king
Should so with civil and uncivil arms
Be rush'd upon! Thy thrice-noble cousin,
Harry Bolingbroke, doth humbly kiss thy hand;
And by the honourable tomb he swears,
That stands upon thy royal grandsire's bones,
And by the royalties of both your bloods,

Currents that spring from one most gracious head
And by the buried hand of warlike Gaunt;
And by the worth and honour of himself,
Comprising all that may be sworn or said,—
His coming hither hath no further scope,
Than for his lineal royalties, and to beg
Enfranchisement immediate on his knees:
Which on thy royal party granted once,
His glittering arms he will commend to rust,
His barbed steeds to stables, and his heart
To faithful service of your majesty.
This swears he, as he is a prince, is just;
And, as I am a gentleman, I credit him.

   K. Rich. Northumberland, say,—thus the king
       returns;——
His noble cousin is right welcome hither;
And all the number of his fair demands
Shall be accomplish'd without contradiction:
With all the gracious utterance thou hast,
Speak to his gentle hearing kind commends.—
We do debase ourself, cousin, do we not,
                  [*To* AUM.
To look so poorly, and to speak so fair?
Shall we call back Northumberland, and send
Defiance to the traitor, and so die?

   Aum. No, good my lord; let's fight with gentle
       words,
Till time lend friends, and friends their helpful
       swords.

   K. Rich. O God! O God! that ere this tongue
       of mine,
That laid the sentence of dread banishment
On yon proud man, should take it off again
With words of sooth! O, that I were as great
As is my grief, or lesser than my name!
Or that I could forget what I have been!
Or not remember what I must be now!
Swell'st thou, proud heart? I'll give thee scope
       to beat,
Since foes have scope to beat both thee and me.

   Aum. Northumberland comes back from Boling-
      broke.

   K. Rich. What must the king do now? Must
      he submit?
The king shall do it. Must he be depos'd?
The king shall be contented: Must he lose
The name of king? o' God's name, let it go:
I'll give my jewels, for a set of beads;
My gorgeous palace, for a hermitage;
My gay apparel, for an alms-man's gown;
My figur'd goblets, for a dish of wood;
My sceptre, for a palmer's walking-staff;

My subjects, for a pair of carved saints;
And my large kingdom for a little grave,
A little, little grave, an obscure grave:—
Or I 'll be buried in the king's highway,
Some way of common trade, where subjects' feet
May hourly trample on their sovereign's head:
For on my heart they tread, now whilst I live;
And, buried once, why not upon my head?——
Aumerle, thou weep'st; My tender-hearted cou-
    sin!—
We 'll make foul weather with despised tears;
Our sighs, and they, shall lodge the summer corn,
And make a dearth in this revolting land.
Or shall we play the wantons with our woes,
And make some pretty match with shedding tears?
As thus;—To drop them still upon one place,
Till they have fretted us a pair of graves
Within the earth; and, therein laid,—"There lies
Two kinsmen, digg'd their graves with weeping
    eyes!"
Would not this ill do well?—Well, well, I see
I talk but idly, and you mock at me.—
Most mighty prince, my lord Northumberland,
What says king Bolingbroke? will his majesty
Give Richard leave to live till Richard die?
You make a leg, and Bolingbroke says—ay.
  North. My lord, in the base court he doth attend
To speak with you; may 't please you to come
    down?
  K. Rich. Down, down, I come; like glistering
    Phaeton,
Wanting the manage of unruly jades.
             [*North. retires to* BOLING.
In the base court? Base court, where kings grow
    base,
To come at traitors' calls, and do them grace.
In the base court? Come down? Down, court!
    down king!
For night-owls shriek, where mounting larks
    should sing.   [*Exeunt, from above.*
  Boling. What says his majesty?
  North.   Sorrow and grief of heart
Makes him speak fondly, like a frantic man:
Yet he is come.

Enter KING RICHARD, *and his* Attendants, *below.*

  Boling. Stand all apart,
And show fair duty to his majesty.——
My gracious lord,—   [*Kneeling.*
  K. Rich. Fair cousin, you debase your princely
    knee,
To make the base earth proud with kissing it;

Me rather had, my heart might feel your love,
Than my unpleas'd eye see your courtesy.
Up, cousin, up; your heart is up, I know.
Thus high at least, [*Touching his own head,*] al
    though your knee be low.
  Boling. My gracious lord, I come but for mine
    own.
  K. Rich. Your own is yours, and I am yours,
    and all.
  Boling. So far be mine, my most redoubted lord,
As my true service shall deserve your love.
  K. Rich. Well you deserve:—They well deserve
    to have,
That know the strong'st and surest way to get.—
Uncle, give me your hand: nay, dry your eyes;
Tears show their love, but want their remedies.—
Cousin, I am too young to be your father,
Though you are old enough to be my heir.
What you will have, I 'll give, and willing too,
For do we must, what force will have us do.—
Set on towards London:—Cousin, is it so?
  Boling. Yea, my good lord.
  K. Rich.   Then I must not say, no.
                [*Flourish. Exeunt*

SCENE IV.—Langley. *The Duke of York's
    Garden.*

Enter the QUEEN, *and two* Ladies.

  Queen. What sport shall we devise here in this
    garden,
To drive away the heavy thought of care?
  1st Lady. Madam, we 'll play at bowls.
  Queen.   'T will make me think,
The world is full of rubs, and that my fortune
Runs 'gainst the bias.
  1st Lady.   Madam, we will dance.
  Queen. My legs can keep no measure in delight,
When my poor heart no measure keeps in grief:
Therefore, no dancing, girl; some other sport.
  1st Lady. Madam, we 'll tell tales.
  Queen.   Of sorrow, or of joy
  1st Lady. Of either, madam.
  Queen.   Of neither, girl:
For if of joy, being altogether wanting,
It doth remember me the more of sorrow;
Or if of grief, being altogether had,
It adds more sorrow to my want of joy:
For what I have, I need not to repeat;
And what I want, it boots not to complain.
  1st Lady. Madam, I 'll sing.
  Queen.   'T is well, that thou hast cause

But thou should'st please me better, would'st thou
   weep.
   1st Lady. I could weep, madam, would it do
   you good.
   Queen. And I could weep, would weeping do
   me good,
And never borrow any tear of thee.
But stay, here come the gardeners:
Let 's step into the shadow of these trees.—

    Enter a Gardener, *and Two* Servants.

My wretchedness unto a row of pins,
They 'll talk of state; for every one doth so
Against a change: Woe is forerun with woe.
                [QUEEN *and* LADIES *retire.*
   Gard. Go, bind thou up yon' dangling apricocks,
Which, like unruly children, make their sire
Stoop with oppression of their prodigal weight:
Give some supportance to the bending twigs.—
Go thou, and like an executioner,
Cut off the heads of too-fast-growing sprays,
That look too lofty in our commonwealth:
All must be even in our government.——
You thus employ'd, I will go root away
The noisome weeds, that without profit suck
The soil's fertility from wholesome flowers.
   1st Serv. Why should we, in the compass of
   a pale,
Keep law, and form, and due proportion,
Showing, as in a model, our firm estate?
When our sea-walled garden, the whole land,
Is full of weeds; her fairest flowers chok'd up,
Her fruit trees all unprun'd, her hedges ruin'd,
Her knots disorder'd, and her wholesome herbs
Swarming with caterpillars?
   Gard.   Hold thy peace:—
He that hath suffer'd this disorder'd spring,
Hath now himself met with the fall of leaf:
The weeds, that his broad-spreading leaves did
   shelter,
That seem'd in eating him to hold him up,
Are pluck'd up, root and all, by Bolingbroke;
I mean, the earl of Wiltshire, Bushy, and Green.
   1st Serv. What, are they dead?
   Gard.   They are; and Bolingbroke
Hath seiz'd the wasteful king.—Oh! what pity
   is it,
That he had not so trimm'd and dress'd his land,
As we this garden! We at time of year
Do wound the bark, the skin of our fruit-trees;
Lest, being over-proud with sap and blood,
With too much riches it confound itself:
   706

Had he done so to great and growing men,
They might have liv'd to bear, and he to taste
Their fruits of duty. All superfluous branches
We lop away, that bearing boughs may live:
Had he done so, himself had borne the crown,
Which waste of idle hours hath quite thrown
   down.
   1st Serv. What, think you then, the king shall
   be depos'd?
   Gard. Depress'd he is already; and depos'd,
'T is doubt, he will be: Letters came last night
To a dear friend of the good duke of York's,
That tell black tidings.
   Queen.   O, I am press'd to death,
Through want of speaking!—Thou, old Adam's
   likeness,
           [*Coming from her concealment.*
Set to dress this garden, how dares
Thy harsh-rude tongue sound this unpleasing
   news?
What Eve, what serpent hath suggested thee
To make a second fall of cursed man?
Why dost thou say, king Richard is depos'd?
Dar'st thou, thou little better thing than earth,
Divine his downfall! Say, where, when, and
   how,
Cam'st thou by these ill tidings? speak, thou
   wretch.
   Gard. Pardon me, madam: little joy have I
To breathe this news; yet, what I say, is true.
King Richard, he is in the mighty hold
Of Bolingbroke; their fortunes both are weigh'd:
In your lord's scale is nothing but himself,
And some few vanities that make him light;
But in the balance of great Bolingbroke,
Besides himself, are all the English peers,
And with that odds he weighs king Richard
   down.
Post you to London, and you 'll find it so;
I speak no more than every one doth know.
   Queen. Nimble mischance, that art so light of
   foot,
Doth not thy embassage belong to me,
And am I last that knows it? O, thou think'st
To serve me last, that I may longest keep
Thy sorrow in my breast.—Come, ladies, go,
To meet at London London's king in woe.—
What, was I born to this! that my sad look
Should grace the triumph of great Bolingbroke?—
Gardener, for telling me this news of woe,
I would, the plants thou graft'st, may never grow
           [*Exeunt* QUEEN *and* LADIES

Gard. Poor queen! so that thy state might be
　　no worse,
I would my skill were subject to thy curse.—
Here did she drop a tear; here, in this place,

I 'll set a bank of rue, sour herb of grace:
Rue, even for ruth, here shortly shall be seen,
In the remembrance of a weeping queen.

[*Exeunt.*

ACT IV.

SCENE I.—London.　Westminster *Hall.*-

The Lords spiritual on the right side of the Throne; the Lords temporal on the left; the Commons below. Enter BOLINGBROKE, AU-
MERLE, SURREY, NORTHUMBERLAND, PERCY,
FITZWATER, *another Lord,* BISHOP OF CARLISLE,
ABBOT OF WESTMINSTER, *and Attendants.
Officers behind with* BAGOT.

Boling. Call forth Bagot:——
Now Bagot, freely speak thy mind;
What thou dost know of noble Gloster's death;
Who wrought it with the king, and who perform'd
The bloody office of his timeless end.

Bagot. Then set before my face the lord Aumerle.
Boling. Cousin, stand forth, and look upon that
　　man.
Bagot. My lord Aumerle, I know your daring
　　tongue
Scorns to unsay what once it hath deliver'd.
In that dead time when Gloster's death was plotted,
I heard you say,—"Is not my arm of length,
That reacheth from the restful English court
As far as Calais, to my uncle's head?"
Amongst much other talk, that very time,
I heard you say, that you had rather refuse
The offer of an hundred thousand crowns,
Than Bolingbroke's return to England;
Adding withal, how blest this land would be,
In this your cousin's death.
Aum.　　　　　　Princes, and noble lords,
What answer shall I make to this base man?
Shall I so much dishonour my fair stars,
On equal terms to give him chastisement?
Either I must, or have mine honour soil'd
With the attainder of his sland'rous lips.——
There is my gage, the manual seal of death,
That marks thee out for hell: I say, thou liest,
And will maintain, what thou hast said, is false,
In thy heart-blood, though being all too base

To stain the temper of my knightly sword.
Boling. Bagot, forbear, thou shalt not take it up.
Aum. Excepting one, I would he were the best
In all this presence, that hath mov'd me so.
Fitz. If that thy valour stand on sympathies,
There is my gage, Aumerle, in gage to thine:
By that fair sun that shows me where thou stand'st.
I heard thee say, and vauntingly thou spak'st it,
That thou wert cause of noble Gloster's death.
If thou deny'st it, twenty times thou liest;
And I will turn thy falsehood to thy heart,
Where it was forged, with my rapier's point.
Aum. Thou dar'st not, coward, live to see that
　　day.
Fitz. Now, by my soul, I would it were this
　　hour.
Aum. Fitzwater, thou art damn'd to hell for this
Percy. Aumerle, thou liest; his honour is as
　　true,
In this appeal, as thou art all unjust:
And, that thou art so, there I throw my gage,
To prove it on thee to the extremest point
Of mortal breathing; seize it, if thou dar'st.
Aum. And if I do not, may my hands rot off,
And never brandish more revengeful steel
Over the glittering helmet of my foe!
Lord. I take the earth to the like, forsworn
　　Aumerle;-
And spur thee on with full as many lies
As may be holla'd in thy treacherous ear
From sun to sun: there is my honour's pawn;
Engage it to the trial, if thou dar'st.
Aum. Who sets me else? by heaven, I 'll throw
　　at all:
I have a thousand spirits in one breast,
To answer twenty thousand such as you.
Surrey. My lord Fitzwater, I do remember well
The very time Aumerle and you did talk.
Fitz. My lord, 't is true: you were in presence
　　then;

707

And you can witness with me, this is true.

   Surrey. As false, by heaven, as heaven itself is
true.

   Fitz. Surrey, thou liest.

   Surrey.   Dishonourable boy!
That lie shall lie so heavy on my sword,
That it shall render vengeance and revenge,
Till thou the lie-giver, and that lie, do lie
In earth as quiet as thy father's skull.
In proof whereof, there is my honour's pawn;
Engage it to the trial, if thou dar'st.

   Fitz. How fondly dost thou spur a forward horse.
If I dare eat, or drink, or breathe, or live,
I dare meet Surrey in a wilderness,
And spit upon him, whilst I say, he lies,
And lies, and lies; there is my bond of faith,
To tie thee to my strong correction.—
As I intend to thrive in this new world,[13]
Aumerle is guilty of my true appeal:
Besides, I heard the banish'd Norfolk say,
That thou, Aumerle, didst send two of thy men
To execute the noble duke at Calais.

   Aum. Some honest Christian trust me with a
gage,
That Norfolk lies: here do I throw down this,[14]
If he may be repeal'd to try his honour.

   Boling. These differences shall all rest under
gage,
Till Norfolk be repeal'd: repeal'd he shall be,
And, though mine enemy, restor'd again
To all his land and signories; when he 's return'd,
Against Aumerle we will enforce his trial.

   Car. That honourable day shall ne'er be seen.—
Many a time hath banish'd Norfolk fought
For Jesu Christ; in glorious Christian field
Streaming the ensign of the Christian cross,
Against black pagans, Turks, and Saracens:
And, toil'd with works of war, retir'd himself
To Italy; and there, at Venice, gave
His body to that pleasant country's earth,
And his pure soul unto his captain Christ,
Under whose colours he had fought so long.

   Boling. Why, bishop, is Norfolk dead?

   Car. As sure as I live, my lord.

   Boling. Sweet peace conduct his sweet soul to
the bosom
Of good old Abraham!—Lords appellants,
Your differences shall all rest under gage,
Till we assign you to your days of trial.

       Enter YORK, *attended.*

   York. Great duke of Lancaster I come to thee
From plume-pluck'd Richard; who with willing
soul
Adopts thee heir, and his high sceptre yields
To the possession of thy royal hand:
Ascend his throne, descending now from him,—
And long live Henry, of that name the fourth!

   Boling. In God's name, I 'll ascend the regal
throne.

   Car. Marry, God forbid!—
Worst in this royal presence may I speak,
Yet best beseeming me to speak the truth,
Would God, that any in this noble presence
Were enough noble to be upright judge
Of noble Richard; then true nobless would
Learn him forbearance from so foul a wrong.
What subject can give sentence on his king?
And who sits here, that is not Richard's subject?
Thieves are not judg'd, but they are by to hear,
Although apparent guilt be seen in them:
And shall the figure of God's majesty,
His captain, steward, deputy elect,
Anointed, crowned, planted many years,
Be judg'd by subject and inferior breath,
And he himself not present? O, forbid it, God,
That, in a Christian climate, souls refin'd
Should show so heinous, black, obscene a deed!
I speak to subjects, and a subject speaks,
Stirr'd up by heaven thus boldly for his king.
My lord of Hereford here, whom you call king,
Is a foul traitor to proud Hereford's king:
And if you crown him, let me prophesy,—
The blood of English shall manure the ground,
And future ages groan for this foul act:
Peace shall go sleep with Turks and infidels,
And, in this seat of peace, tumultuous wars
Shall kin with kin, and kind with kind confound
Disorder, horror, fear, and mutiny,
Shall here inhabit, and this land be call'd
The field of Golgotha, and dead men's skulls.
O, if you rear this house against this house.
It will the woefullest division prove,
That ever fell upon this cursed earth;
Prevent, resist it, let it not be so,
Lest child, child's children, cry against you—
woe!

   North. Well have you argu'd, sir; and, for
your pains,
Of capital treason we arrest you here:—
My lord of Westminster, be it your charge
To keep him safely till his day of trial.—
May 't please you, lords, to grant the commons'
suit.

Boling. Fetch hither Richard, that in common
    view
He may surrender, so we shall proceed
Without suspicion.
    York.   I will be his conduct. [*Exit.*
    Boling. Lords, you that are here under our
    arrest,
Procure your sureties for your days of answer:—
Little are we beholden to your love,   [*To* Car.
And little look'd for at your helping hands.

Re-enter York, *with* King Richard, *and* Officers
bearing the Crown, &c.

    K. Rich. Alack, why am I sent for to a king,
Before I have shook off the regal thoughts
Wherewith I reign'd? I hardly yet have learn'd
To insinuate, flatter, bow, and bend my knee:—
Give sorrow leave a while to tutor me
To this submission.   Yet I well remember
The favours of these men? Were they not mine?
Did they not sometime cry, all hail! to me?
So Judas did to Christ: but he, in twelve,
Found truth in all, but one; I, in twelve thousand,
    none.
God save the king!—Will no man say, amen?
Am I both priest and clerk? well then, amen.
God save the king! although I be not he;
And yet, amen, if heaven do think him me.—
To do what service am I sent for hither?
    York. To do that office, of thine own good will,
Which tired majesty did make thee offer,——
The resignation of thy state and crown
To Henry Bolingbroke.
    K. Rich. Give me the crown:—Here, cousin,
    seize the crown;
Here, on this side, my hand; on that side, thine.
Now is this golden crown like a deep well,
That owes two buckets filling one another;
The emptier ever dancing in the air,
The other down, unseen, and full of water:
That bucket down, and full of tears, am I,
Drinking my griefs, whilst you mount up on high.
    Boling. I thought you had been willing to
    resign.
    K. Rich. My crown, I am; but still my griefs
    are mine;
You may my glories and my state depose,
But not my griefs; still am I king of those.
    Boling. Part of your cares you give me with
    your crown.
    K. Rich. Your cares set up, do not pluck my
    cares down.

My care is—loss of care, by old care done;
Your care is—gain of care by new care won:
The cares I give, I have, though given away;
They tend the crown, yet still with me they stay.
    Boling. Are you contented to resign the crown?
    K. Rich. Ay, no;—no, ay;—for I must noth
    ing be;
Therefore no no, for I resign to thee.
Now mark me how I will undo myself:—
I give this heavy weight from off my head,
And this unwieldy sceptre from my hand,
The pride of kingly sway from out my heart;
With mine own tears I wash away my balm,
With mine own hands I give away my crown,
With mine own tongue deny my sacred state,
With mine own breath release all duteous oaths
All pomp and majesty I do forswear;
My manors, rents, revenues, I forego;
My acts, decrees, and statutes, I deny:
God pardon all oaths, that are broke to me!
God keep all vows unbroke, are made to thee!
Make me, that nothing have, with nothing
    griev'd;
And thou with all pleas'd, that hast all achiev'd!
Long may'st thou live in Richard's seat to sit,
And soon lie Richard in an earthy pit!
God save king Henry, unking'd Richard says,
And send him many years of sunshine days!—
What more remains?
    North.   No more, but that you read
    [*Offering a paper.*
These accusations, and these grievous crimes,
Committed by your person, and your followers,
Against the state and profit of this land;
That by confessing them, the souls of men
May deem that you are worthily depos'd.
    K. Rich. Must I do so? and must I ravel out
My weav'd-up follies? Gentle Northumberland,
If thy offences were upon record,
Would it not shame thee in so fair a troop,
To read a lecture of them? If thou would'st,
There should'st thou find one heinous article,—
Containing the deposing of a king,
And cracking the strong warrant of an oath.—
Mark'd with a blot, damn'd in the book of
    heaven:—
Nay, all of you, that stand and look upon me,
Whilst that my wretchedness doth bait myself,—
Though some of you, with Pilate, wash your hands
Showing an outward pity; yet you Pilates
Have here deliver'd me to my sour cross,
And water cannot wash away your sin.
    709

North. My lord, despatch; read o'er these
articles.

K. Rich. Mine eyes are full of tears, I cannot
see:
And yet salt water blinds them not so much,
But they can see a sort of traitors here.
Nay, if I turn mine eyes upon myself,
I find myself a traitor with the rest:
For I have given here my soul's consent,
To undeck the pompous body of a king;
Make glory base; and sovereignty, a slave;
Proud majesty, a subject; state, a peasant.

North. My lord,——

K. Rich. No lord of thine, thou haught, insult-
ing man,
Nor no man's lord; I have no name, no title,—
No, not that name was given me at the font,—
But 't is usurp'd:—Alack the heavy day
That I have worn so many winters out,
And know not now what name to call myself!
O, that I were a mockery king of snow,
Standing before the sun of Bolingbroke,
To melt myself away in water-drops!—
Good king,—great king,—(and yet not greatly
good,)
An if my word be sterling yet in England,
Let it command a mirror hither straight;
That it may show me what a face I have,
Since it is bankrupt of his majesty.

Boling. Go some of you, and fetch a looking-
glass.　　　　　　　　[*Exit an Attend.*

North. Read o'er this paper, while the glass
doth come.

K. Rich. Fiend! thou torment'st me ere I come
to hell.

Boling. Urge it no more, my lord Northumberland.

North. The commons will not then be satisfied.

K. Rich. They shall be satisfied: I'll read
enough,
When I do see the very book indeed
Where all my sins are writ, and that's—myself.

Re-enter Attendant, *with a Glass.*

Give me that glass, and therein will I read.—
No deeper wrinkles yet? Hath sorrow struck
So many blows upon this face of mine,
And made no deeper wounds?—O, flattering glass,
Like to my followers in prosperity,
Thou dost beguile me! Was this face the face,
That every day under his household roof
Did keep ten thousand men? Was this the face,

710

That, like the sun, did make beholders wink?
Was this the face, that fac'd so many follies,
And was at last out-fac'd by Bolingbroke?
A brittle glory shineth in this face:
As brittle as the glory is the face;
[*Dashes the Glass against the ground*
For there it is, crack'd in a hundred shivers.—
Mark, silent king, the moral of this sport,—
How soon my sorrow hath destroy'd my face.

Boling. The shadow of your sorrow hath destroy'd
The shadow of your face.

K. Rich.　　　　　　Say that again.
The shadow of my sorrow? Ha! let's see;—
'T is very true, my grief lies all within;
And these external manners of lament
Are merely shadows to the unseen grief,
That swells with silence in the tortur'd soul;
There lies the substance; and I thank thee, king,
For thy great bounty, that not only giv'st
Me cause to wail, but teachest me the way
How to lament the cause. I'll beg one boon,
And then be gone, and trouble you no more.
Shall I obtain it?

Boling.　　　　　　Name it, fair cousin.

K. Rich. Fair cousin? Why, I am greater than
a king:
For, when I was a king, my flatterers
Were then but subjects; being now a subject,
I have a king here to my flatterer.
Being so great, I have no need to beg.

Boling. Yet ask.

K. Rich. And shall I have?

Boling. You shall.

K. Rich. Then give me leave to go.

Boling. Whither?

K. Rich. Whither you will, so I were from
your sights.

Boling. Go, some of you, convey him to the
Tower.

K. Rich. O, good! Convey?—Conveyers are
you all,
That rise thus nimbly by a true king's fall.
[*Exeunt K. Rich., some Lords, and a Guard*

Boling. On Wednesday next, we solemnly set
down
Our coronation: lords, prepare yourselves.
[*Exeunt all but the Abbot, Car., and Aum.*

Abbot. A woeful pageant have we here beheld.

Car. The woe's to come; the children yet
unborn
Shall feel this day as sharp to them as thorn.

Abm. You holy clergymen, is there no plot
To rid the realm of this pernicious blot?
    Abbot. Before I freely speak my mind herein,
You shall not only take the sacrament
To bury mine intents, but to effect

Whatever I shall happen to devise:—
I see your brows are full of discontent,
Your hearts of sorrow, and your eyes of tears;
Come home with me to supper; I will lay
A plot, shall show us all a merry day.   [*Exeunt*

ACT V.

SCENE I.—London. *A Street leading to the
Tower.*

Enter QUEEN *and Ladies.*

    Queen. This way the king will come; this is
        the way
To Julius Cæsar's ill-erected tower,"
To whose flint bosom my condemned lord
Is doom'd a prisoner by proud Bolingbroke:
Here let us rest, if this rebellious earth
Have any resting for her true king's queen.

Enter KING RICHARD, *and Guards.*

But soft, but see, or rather do not see,
My fair rose wither: Yet look up; behold;
That you in pity may dissolve to dew,
And wash him fresh again with true-love tears.—
Ah, thou, the model where old Troy did stand;
Thou map of honour; thou king Richard's tomb,
And not king Richard; thou most beauteous inn,
Why should hard-favour'd grief be lodged in thee,
When triumph is become an ale-house guest?
    K. Rich. Join not with grief, fair woman, do
        not so,
To make my end too sudden: learn, good soul,
To think our former state a happy dream;
From which awak'd, the truth of what we are
Shows us but this: I am sworn brother, sweet,
To grim necessity; and he and I
Will keep a league till death. Hie thee to France,
And cloister thee in some religious house:
Our holy lives must win a new world's crown,
Which our profane hours here have stricken down.
    Queen. What, is my Richard both in shape and
        mind
Transform'd, and weaken'd? Hath Bolingbroke
Depos'd thine intellect? hath he been in thy
        heart?
The lion, dying, thrusteth forth his paw,

And wounds the earth, if nothing else, with rage
To be o'erpower'd; and wilt thou, pupil-like,
Take thy correction mildly? kiss the rod;
And fawn on rage with base humility,
Which art a lion, and a king of beasts?
    K. Rich. A king of beasts, indeed; if aught
        but beasts,
I had been still a happy king of men.
Good sometime queen, prepare thee hence for
        France:
Think, I am dead; and that even here thou
        tak'st,
As from my death-bed, my last living leave.
In winter's tedious nights, sit by the fire
With good old folks; and let them tell thee tales
Of woeful ages, long ago betid:
And, ere thou bid good night, to quit their grief,
Tell thou the lamentable fall of me,
And send the hearers weeping to their beds.
For why, the senseless brands will sympathize
The heavy accent of thy moving tongue,
And, in compassion, weep the fire out:
And some will mourn in ashes, some coal-black,
For the deposing of a rightful king.

Enter NORTHUMBERLAND, *attended.*

    North. My lord, the mind of Bolingbroke is
        chang'd:
You must to Pomfret, not unto the Tower.——
And, madam, there is order ta'en for you;
With all swift speed you must away to France.
    K. Rich. Northumberland, thou ladder where-
        withal
The mounting Bolingbroke ascends my throne,—
The time shall not be many hours of age
More than it is, ere foul sin, gathering head,
Shall break into corruption: thou shalt think,
Though he divide the realm, and give thee half,
It is too little, helping him to all;

And he shall think, that thou, which know'st the way
To plant unrightful kings, wilt know again,
Being ne'er so little urg'd, another way
To pluck him headlong from the usurped throne.
The love of wicked friends converts to fear;
That fear, to hate; and hate turns one, or both,
To worthy danger, and deserved death.

　　North. My guilt be on my head, and there an
　　　　end.
Take leave, and part; for you must part forthwith.

　　K. Rich. Doubly divore'd?—Bad men, ye vi-
　　　　olate
A twofold marriage: 'twixt my crown and me;
And then, betwixt me and my married wife.—
Let me unkiss the oath 'twixt thee and me;
And yet not so, for with a kiss 't was made.—
Part us, Northumberland; I towards the north,
Where shivering cold and sickness pines the clime:
My wife to France; from whence, set forth in pomp,
She came adorned hither like sweet May,
Sent back like Hallowmas, or short'st of day.

　　Queen. And must we be divided? must we part?

　　K. Rich. Ay, hand from hand, my love, and
　　　　heart from heart.

　　Queen. Banish us both, and send the king with
　　　　me.

　　North. That were some love, but little policy.

　　Queen. Then whither he goes, thither let me go.

　　K. Rich. So two, together weeping, make one
　　　　woe.
Weep thou for me in France, I for thee here;
Better far off, than—near, be ne'er the near.
Go, count thy way with sighs; I, mine with groans.

　　Queen. So longest way shall have the longest
　　　　moans.

　　K. Rich. Twice for one step I'll groan, the way
　　　　being short,
And piece the way out with a heavy heart.
Come, come, in wooing sorrow let's be brief,
Since, wedding it, there is such length in grief.
One kiss shall stop our mouths, and dumbly part;
Thus give I mine, and thus I take thy heart.
　　　　　　　　　　　　　[*They kiss.*

　　Queen. Give me mine own again; 't were no
　　　　good part,
To take on me to keep, and kill thy heart.
　　　　　　　　　　　　　[*Kiss again.*
So, now I have mine own again, begone,
That I may strive to kill it with a groan.

　　K. Rich. We make woe wanton with this fond
　　　　delay:
712

Once more, adieu; the rest let sorrow say.
　　　　　　　　　　　　　[*Exeunt.*

SCENE II.—*The Same. A Room in the Duke of
York's Palace.*

Enter YORK, and his DUCHESS.

　　Duch. My lord, you told me, you would tell the
　　　　rest,
When weeping made you break the story off
Of our two cousins coming into London.

　　York. Where did I leave?

　　Duch. 　　　　At that sad stop, my lord,
Where rude misgovern'd hands, from window's
　　　　tops,
Threw dust and rubbish on king Richard's head.

　　York. Then, as I said, the duke, great Boling-
　　　　broke,—
Mounted upon a hot and fiery steed,
Which his aspiring rider seem'd to know,—
With slow, but stately pace, kept on his course,
While all tongues cried—God save thee, Boling-
　　　　broke!
You would have thought the very windows spake,
So many greedy looks of young and old
Through casements darted their desiring eyes
Upon his visage; and that all the walls,
With painted imag'ry, had said at once,—
Jesu preserve thee! welcome, Bolingbroke!
Whilst he, from one side to the other turning,
Bare-headed, lower than his proud steed's neck,
Bespake them thus,—I thank you, countrymen:
And thus still doing, thus he pass'd along.

　　Duch. Alas, poor Richard! where rides he the
　　　　while?

　　York. As in a theatre, the eyes of men,
After a well-grac'd actor leaves the stage,
Are idly bent on him that enters next,
Thinking his prattle to be tedious:
Even so, or with much more contempt, men's eyes
Did scowl on Richard; no man cried, God save
　　　　him;
No joyful tongue gave him his welcome home:
But dust was thrown upon his sacred head;
Which with such gentle sorrow he shook off,—
His face still combating with tears and smiles,
The badges of his grief and patience,—
That had not God, for some strong purpose, steel'd
The hearts of men, they must perforce have melted,
And barbarism itself have pitied him.
But heaven hath a hand in these events;
To whose high will we bound our calm contents.

To Bolingbroke are we sworn subjects now,
Whose state and honour I for aye allow.

Enter AUMERLE.

Duch. Here comes my son Aumerle.
York.   Aumerle that was;
But that is lost, for being Richard's friend,
And, madam, you must call him Rutland now:
I am in parliament pledge for his truth,
And lasting fealty to the new-made king.
Duch. Welcome, my son: Who are the violets now,
That strew the green lap of the new-come spring?
Aum. Madam, I know not, nor I greatly care not:
God knows, I had as lief be none, as one.
York. Well, bear you well in this new spring of time,
Lest you be cropp'd before you come to prime.
What news from Oxford? hold those justs and triumphs?
Aum. For aught I know, my lord, they do.
York. You will be there, I know.
Aum. If God prevent it not; I purpose so.
York. What seal is that, that hangs without thy bosom?"
Yea, look'st thou pale? let me see the writing.
Aum. My lord, 't is nothing.
York.   No matter then who sees it:
I will be satisfied, let me see the writing.
Aum. I do beseech your grace to pardon me;
It is a matter of small consequence,
Which for some reasons I would not have seen.
York. Which for some reasons, sir, I mean to see.
I fear, I fear.——
Duch.   What should you fear?
'T is nothing but some bond that he is enter'd into
For gay apparel, 'gainst the triumph day.
York. Bound to himself? what doth he with a bond
That he is bound to? Wife, thou art a fool.—
Boy, let me see the writing.
Aum. I do beseech you, pardon me; I may not shew it.
York. I will be satisfied; let me see it, I say.
                              [*Snatches it, and reads.*
Treason! foul treason!—villain! traitor! slave!
Duch. What is the matter, my lord?
York. Ho! who is within there?

Enter a Servant.

Saddle my horse.

God for his mercy! what treachery is here!
Duch. Why, what is it, my lord?
York. Give me my boots, I say; saddle my horse;
Now by mine honour, by my life, my troth,
I will appeach the villain.   [*Exit* Serv.
Duch.   What 's the matter!
York. Peace, foolish woman.
Duch. I will not peace:—What is the matter, son?
Aum. Good mother, be content: it is no more
Than my poor life must answer.
Duch.   Thy life answer!

Re-enter Servant, *with Boots.*

York. Bring me my boots, I will unto the king
Duch. Strike him, Aumerle.—Poor boy, thou art amaz'd;
Hence, villain; never more come in my sight.—
                              [*To the* Serv.
York. Give me my boots, I say.
Duch. Why, York, what wilt thou do?
Wilt thou not hide the trespass of thine own?
Have we more sons? or are we like to have?
Is not my teeming date drunk up with time?
And wilt thou pluck my fair son from mine age,
And rob me of a happy mother's name?
Is he not like thee? Is he not thine own?
York. Thou fond mad woman,
Wilt thou conceal this dark conspiracy?
A dozen of them here have ta'en the sacrament,
And interchangeably set down their hands,
To kill the king at Oxford.
Duch.   He shall be none;
We'll keep him here: Then what is that to him?
York. Away,
Fond woman! were he twenty times my son,
I would appeach him.
Duch.   Hadst thou groan'd for him,
As I have done, thou'dst be more pitiful.
But now I know thy mind; thou dost suspect,
That I have been disloyal to thy bed,
And that he is a bastard, not thy son:
Sweet York, sweet husband, be not of that mind.
He is as like thee as a man may be.
Not like to me, or any of my kin,
And yet I love him.
York.   Make way, unruly woman.   [*Exit.*
Duch. After, Aumerle; mount thee upon his horse;
Spur, post; and get before him to the king,
And beg thy pardon ere he do accuse thee.

I 'll not be long behind; though I be old,
I doubt not but to ride as fast as York:
And never will I rise up from the ground,
Till Bolingbroke have pardon'd thee: Away;
Begone.   [*Exeunt.*

SCENE III.—Windsor. *A Room in the Castle.*

Enter BOLINGBROKE *as king;* PERCY, *and other Lords.*

Boling. Can no man tell of my unthrifty son?
'T is full three months, since I did see him last:—
If any plague hang over us, 't is he.
I would to God, my lords, he might be found:
Inquire at London, 'mongst the taverns there,
For there, they say, he daily doth frequent,
With unrestrained loose companions:
Even such, they say, as stand in narrow lanes,
And beat our watch, and rob our passengers;
While he, young, wanton, and effeminate boy,
Takes on the point of honour, to support
So dissolute a crew.

Percy. My lord, some two days since I saw the prince;
And told him of these triumphs held at Oxford.
Boling. And what said the gallant?
Percy. His answer was,—he would unto the stews;
And from the commonest creature pluck a glove,
And wear it as a favour; and with that
He would unhorse the lustiest challenger.

Boling. As dissolute, as desperate: yet, through both
I see some sparkles of a better hope,
Which elder days may happily bring forth.
But who comes here?

Enter AUMERLE, *hastily.*

Aum.   Where is the king?
Boling.   What means
Our cousin, that he stares and looks so wildly?
Aum. God save your grace. I do beseech your majesty,
To have some conference with your grace alone.
Boling. Withdraw yourselves, and leave us here alone.—   [*Exeunt* PERCY *and Lords.*
What is the matter with our cousin now?
Aum. For ever may my knees grow to the earth,   [*Kneels.*
My tongue cleave to my roof within my mouth,
Unless a pardon, ere I rise, or speak.
Boling. Intended, or committed, was this fault?

If but the first, how heinous e'er it be,
To win thy after-love, I pardon thee.
Aum. Then give me leave that I may turn the key,
That no man enter till my tale be done.
Boling. Have thy desire. [*Aum. locks the door.*
York. [*Within.*] My liege, beware; look to thyself;
Thou hast a traitor in thy presence there.
Boling. Villain, I 'll make thee safe. [*Drawing.*
Aum. Stay thy revengeful hand;
Thou hast no cause to fear.
York. [*Within.*] Open the door, secure, fool-hardy king:
Shall I, for love, speak treason to thy face?
Open the door, or I will break it open.
              [BOLING. *opens the door*

Enter YORK.

Boling. What is the matter, uncle? speak,
Recover breath; tell us how near is danger,
That we may arm us to encounter it.
York. Peruse this writing here, and thou shalt know
The treason that my haste forbids me show.
Aum. Remember, as thou read'st, thy promise past:
I do repent me; read not my name there,
My heart is not confederate with my hand.
York. 'T was, villain, ere thy hand did set it down.—
I tore it from the traitor's bosom, king;
Fear, and not love, begets his penitence:
Forget to pity him, lest thy pity prove
A serpent that will sting thee to the heart.
Boling. O heinous, strong, and bold conspiracy!
O loyal father of a treacherous son!
Thou sheer, immaculate, and silver fountain,
From whence this stream through muddy passages
Hath held his current, and defil'd himself!
Thy overflow of good converts to bad;
And thy abundant goodness shall excuse
This deadly blot in thy digressing son.
York. So shall my virtue be his vice's bawd;
And he shall spend mine honour with his shame,
As thriftless sons their scraping fathers' gold.
Mine honour lives when his dishonour dies,
Or my sham'd life in his dishonour lies:
Thou kill'st me in his life; giving him breath,
The traitor lives, the true man 's put to death.
Duch. [*Within.*] What ho, my liege! for God's sake let me in

Boling. What shrill-voic'd suppliant makes this
    eager cry?
Duch. A woman, and thine aunt, great king;
    't is I.
Speak with me, pity me, open the door:
A beggar begs, that never begg'd before.
    Boling. Our scene is alter'd,—from a serious
      thing,
And now chang'd to "The Beggar and the
    King."—
My dangerous cousin, let your mother in;
I know, she's come to pray for your foul sin.
    York. If thou do pardon, whosoever pray,
More sins, for this forgiveness, prosper may.
This fester'd joint cut off, the rest rests sound;
This, let alone, will all the rest confound.

Enter Duchess.

    Duch. O king, believe not this hard-hearted
      man;
Love, loving not itself, none other can.
    York. Thou frantic woman, what dost thou
      make here?
Shall thy old dugs once more a traitor rear?
    Duch. Sweet York, be patient: Hear me, gentle
      liege.   [*Kneels.*
    Boling. Rise up, good aunt.
    Duch.   Not yet, I thee beseech:
For ever will I kneel upon my knees,
And never see day that the happy sees,
Till thou give joy; until thou bid me joy,
By pardoning Rutland, my transgressing boy.
    Aum. Unto my mother's prayers, I bend my
      knee.   [*Kneels.*
    York. Against them both, my true joints
      bended be.   [*Kneels.*
Ill may'st thou thrive, if thou grant any grace!
    Duch. Pleads he in earnest? look upon his
      face;
His eyes do drop no tears, his prayers are in jest;
His words come from his mouth, ours from our
    breast:
He prays but faintly, and would be denied;
We pray with heart, and soul, and all beside:
His weary joints would gladly rise, I know;
Our knees shall kneel till to the ground they
    grow:
His prayers are full of false hypocrisy;
Ours, of true zeal and deep integrity.
Our prayers do out-pray his; then let them have
That mercy, which true prayers ought to have.
    Boling. Good aunt, stand up.

    Duch.   Nay, do not say—stand up:
But, pardon, first; and afterwards, stand up.
An if I were thy nurse, thy tongue to teach,
Pardon—should be the first word of thy speech.
I never long'd to hear a word till now;
Say—pardon, king; let pity teach thee how:
The word is short, but not so short as sweet;
No word like, pardon, for kings' mouths so meet.
    York. Speak it in French, king; say, "*par-
    donnez moy.*"
    Duch. Dost thou teach pardon pardon to de-
    stroy?
Ah, my sour husband, my hard-hearted lord,
That sett'st the word itself against the word!—
Speak, pardon, as 't is current in our land;
The chopping French we do not understand.
Thine eye begins to speak, set thy tongue there:
Or, in thy piteous heart plant thou thine ear:
That, hearing how our plants and prayers do pierce,
Pity may move thee, pardon to rehearse.
    Boling. Good aunt, stand up.
    Duch.   I do not sue to stand,
Pardon is all the suit I have in hand.
    Boling. I pardon him, as God shall pardon me.
    Duch. O happy vantage of a kneeling knee!
Yet am I sick for fear: speak it again;
Twice saying pardon, doth not pardon twain,
But makes one pardon strong.
    Boling.   With all my heart
I pardon him.
    Duch.   A god on earth thou art.
    Boling. But for our trusty brother-in-law,—
    and the abbot,
With all the rest of that consorted crew,—
Destruction straight shall dog them at the heels.—
Good uncle, help to order several powers
To Oxford, or where'er these traitors are:
They shall not live within this world, I swear,
But I will have them, if I once know where.
Uncle, farewell,—and cousin too, adieu:
Your mother well hath pray'd, and prove you
    true.
    Duch. Come, my old son;—I pray God make
    thee new.   [*Exeunt.*

SCENE IV.

Enter Exton, *and a Servant.*

    Exton. Didst thou not mark the king, what
    words he spake?
"Have I no friend will rid me of this living fear?"
Was it not so?

Serv. Those were his very words.
Exton. "Have I no friend?" quoth he: he spake
it twice,
And urg'd it twice together; did he not?
Serv. He did.
Exton. And, speaking it, he wistfully look'd
on me!
As who should say,—I would, thou wert the man
That would divorce this terror from my heart;
Meaning, the king at Pomfret. Come, let's go;
I am the king's friend, and will rid his foe.

           [*Exeunt.*

SCENE V.—Pomfret. *The Dungeon of the Castle.*

Enter KING RICHARD.

K. Rich. I have been studying how I may
compare
This prison, where I live, unto the world:
And, for because the world is populous,
And here is not a creature but myself,
I cannot do it;—Yet I'll hammer it out.
My brain I'll prove the female to my soul;
My soul, the father: and these two beget
A generation of still-breeding thoughts,
And these same thoughts people this little world;
In humours, like the people of this world,
For no thought is contented. The better sort,—
As thoughts of things divine,—are intermix'd
With scruples, and do set the word itself
Against the word:
As thus,—"Come, little ones;" and then again,—
"It is as hard to come, as for a camel
To thread the postern of a needle's eye."
Thoughts tending to ambition, they do plot
Unlikely wonders: how these vain weak nails
May tear a passage through the flinty ribs
Of this hard world, my ragged prison walls;
And, for they cannot, die in their own pride.
Thoughts tending to content, flatter themselves,—
That they are not the first of fortune's slaves,
Nor shall not be the last; like silly beggars,
Who, sitting in the stocks refuge their shame,—
That many have, and others must sit there:
And in this thought they find a kind of ease,
Bearing their own misfortune on the back
Of such as have before endur'd the like.
Thus play I, in one person, many people,
And none contented: Sometimes am I king;
Then treason makes me wish myself a beggar,
And so I am: Then crushing penury
Persuades me I was better when a king;

716

Then am I king'd again: and, by-and-by,
Think that I am unking'd by Bolingbroke,
And straight am nothing:—But, whate'er I am,
Nor I, nor any man, that but man is,
With nothing shall be pleas'd, till he be eas'd
With being nothing.—Music do I hear? [*Music*
Ha, ha! keep time:—How sour sweet music is,
When time is broke, and no proportion kept!
So is it in the music of men's lives,
And here have I the daintiness of ear,
To check time broke in a disorder'd string;
But, for the concord of my state and time,
Had not an ear to hear my true time broke.
I wasted time, and now doth time waste me.
For now hath time made me his numb'ring clock:
My thoughts are minutes; and, with sighs, they
     jar
Their watches on to mine eyes, the outward watch
Whereto my finger, like a dial's point,
Is pointing still, in cleansing them from tears.
Now, sir, the sound, that tells what hour it is,
Are clamorous groans, that strike upon my heart,
Which is the bell: So sighs, and tears, and groans
Show minutes, times, and hours:—but my time
Runs posting on in Bolingbroke's proud joy,
While I stand fooling here, his Jack o' the clock.
This music mads me, let it sound no more;
For, though it have holpe madmen to their wits,
In me, it seems it will make wise men mad.
Yet blessing on his heart that gives it me!
For 't is a sign of love; and love to Richard
Is a strange brooch in this all-hating world.

Enter GROOM.

Groom. Hail, royal prince!
K. Rich. Thanks, noble peer
The cheapest of us is ten groats too dear.
What art thou? and how comest thou hither,
Where no man never comes, but that sad dog
That brings me food, to make misfortune live?
Groom. I was a poor groom of thy stable, king
When thou wert king; who, travelling towards
     York,
With much ado, at length have gotten leave
To look upon my sometime master's face.
O, how it yern'd my heart, when I beheld,
In London streets, that coronation day,
When Bolingbroke rode on roan Barbary!
That horse, that thou so often hast bestrid!
That horse, that I so carefully have dress'd!
K. Rich. Rode he on Barbary? Tell me, gentle
friend,

How went he under him?

Groom. So proudly, as if he disdain'd the
ground.

K. Rich. So proud that Bolingbroke was on
his back!
That jade hath eat bread from my royal hand;
This hand hath made him proud with clapping
him.
Would he not stumble? Would he not fall down,
(Since pride must have a fall,) and break the neck
Of that proud man that did usurp his back?
Forgiveness, horse! why do I rail on thee,
Since thou, created to be aw'd by man,
Wast born to bear? I was not made a horse;
And yet I bear a burden like an ass,
Spur-gall'd, and tir'd, by jauncing Bolingbroke.

Enter Keeper, with a Dish.

Keep. Fellow, give place; here is no longer stay.
               [*To the Groom.*

K. Rich. If thou love me, 'tis time thou wert
away.

Groom. What my tongue dares not, that my
heart shall say.   [*Exit.*

Keep. My lord, will 't please you to fall to?

K. Rich. Taste of it first, as thou art wont to do.

Keep. My lord, I dare not; Sir Pierce of Exton,
who
lately came from the king, commands the contrary.

K. Rich. The devil take Henry of Lancaster,
and thee!
Patience is stale, and I am weary of it.
             [*Beats the Keeper.*

Keep. Help, help, help.

Enter Exton, and Servants, armed.

K. Rich. How now! what means death in this
rude assault?
Villain, thy own hand yields thy death's instrument.
      [*Snatching a weapon, and killing one.*
Go thou, and fill another room in hell.
     [*He kills another, then Exton strikes him down.*
That hand shall burn in never-quenching fire,
That staggers thus my person.—Exton, thy fierce
hand
Hath with the king's blood stain'd the king's own
land.
Mount, mount, my soul! thy seat is up on high;
Whilst my gross flesh sinks downward, here to
die."   [*Dies.*

Exton. As full of valour, as of royal blood:
Both have I spilt; O, would the deed were good!

For now the devil, that told me—I did well,
Says, that this deed is chronicled in hell.
This dead king to the living king I'll bear;
Take hence the rest, and give them burial here.
            [*Exeunt.*

SCENE VI.—*Windsor. A Room in the Castle.*
Flourish.

Enter Bolingbroke, *and* York, *with Lords and*
Attendants.

Boling. Kind uncle York, the latest news we
hear,
Is—that the rebels have consum'd with fire
Our town of Cicester in Glostershire;
But whether they be ta'en, or slain, we hear not.

Enter Northumberland.

Welcome, my lord! What is the news?

North. First, to thy sacred state wish I all hap-
piness.
The next news is,—I have to London sent
The heads of Salisbury, Spencer, Blunt, and Kent:
The manner of their taking may appear
At large discoursed in this paper here.
          [*Presenting a Paper.*

Boling. We thank thee, gentle Percy, for thy
pains;
And to thy worth will add right worthy gains.

Enter Fitzwater.

Fitz. My lord, I have from Oxford sent to Lon-
don
The heads of Brocas, and Sir Bennet Seely;
Two of the dangerous consorted traitors,
That sought at Oxford thy dire overthrow.

Boling. Thy pains, Fitzwater, shall not be
forgot;
Right noble is thy merit, well I wot.

Enter Percy, *with the* Bishop of Carlisle.

Percy. The grand conspirator, abbot of West-
minster,
With clog of conscience, and sour melancholy,
Hath yielded up his body to the grave;
But here is Carlisle living, to abide
Thy kingly doom, and sentence of his pride.

Boling. Carlisle, this is your doom:—
Choose out some secret place, some reverend room,
More than thou hast, and with it joy thy life;
So, as thou liv'st in peace, die free from strife:
For though mine enemy thou hast ever been,

High sparks of honour in thee have I seen.

Enter EXTON, *with* Attendants *bearing a Coffin.*

Exton. Great king, within this coffin I present
Thy buried fear; herein all breathless lies
The mightiest of thy greatest enemies,
Richard of Bourdeaux, by me hither brought.

Boling. Exton, I thank thee not; for thou hast
　wrought
A deed of slander, with thy fatal hand,
Upon my head, and all this famous land.

Exton. From your own mouth, my lord, did I
　this deed.

Boling. They love not poison that do poison
　need,

Nor do I thee; though I did wish him dead,
I hate the murderer, love him murdered.
The guilt of conscience take thou for thy labour,
But neither my good word, nor princely favour:
With Cain go wander through the shade of night,
And never show thy head by day nor light.——
Lords, I protest, my soul is full of woe,
That blood should sprinkle me, to make me
　grow:
Come, mourn with me for what I do lament
And put on sullen black incontinent;
I'll make a voyage to the Holy Land,
To wash this blood off from my guilty hand:—
March sadly after; grace my mournings here,
In weeping after this untimely bier.　*[Exeunt.*

NOTES TO KING RICHARD THE SECOND.

Inhabitable, i. e. not habitable, uninhabitable.

> *It must be great that can inherit us*
> *So much as of a thought of ill in him.*

To *inherit us* is to possess us with; though this is an uncommon use of the word.

> *Till I have told this slander of his blood.*

Bolingbroke was the king's cousin; Mowbray having accused him of falsehood, calls him a slander to the blood of majesty, a disgrace to his royal relative.

> *There is no boot.*

That is, there is no advantage in delay or refusal.

> *The slavish motive.*

His tongue; *motive* is used as instrument.

> *Alas! the part I had in Gloster's blood.*

That is, the nearness of my relationship to Gloucester. The Duke of Gloucester was the younger brother of John of Lancaster.

> *Aumerle.*

Richard Duke of Aumerle. He was the eldest son of Edward Langley Duke of York, fifth son of King Edward the Third. He officiated at the lists at Coventry, as High Constable of England.

> *Stay, the king hath thrown his warder down.*

A *warder* appears to have been a kind of truncheon carried by the person who presided at these combats.

> *Compassionate* is used for plaintive.

> *—————— bound in with shame,*
> *With inky blots, and rotten parchment bonds.*

Gaunt is alluding to the king's having farmed out the country to his favourite the earl of Wiltshire. Mr. Steevens says he suspects that the poet wrote inky *bolts,* that is, written restrictions, as blots cannot bind anything, and bolts correspond much better to the word *bonds.*

> *Queen.*

The introduction of the queen is an historical error.

Richard had married Ann, sister to the emperor Wenceslaus, king of Bohemia, but she was dead before the commencement of the play. Richard was afterwards affianced to Isabella, daughter of the king of France, but this young princess was but a child at his death.

> *For hot young colts, being rag'd, do rage the more.*

Mr. Ritson would read—being rein'd do rage the more. Certainly more elegant, and probably the poet's own word.

> *Which live like venom, where no venom else,*
> *But only they have privilege to live.*

This alludes to the popular tradition that St. Patrick drove every kind of venomous reptile out of Ireland.

> *Nor the prevention of poor Bolingbroke*
> *About his marriage.*

Bolingbroke was honourably entertained at the French court, and would have been married to the only daughter of the Duke of Berry, uncle to the French king, had not Richard interfered and prevented the match.

> *Accomplish'd with the number of thy hours.*

That is, when he was of thy age.

> *And yet we strike not, but securely perish.*

To strike the sails, is to contract them when there is too much wind. Northumberland uses the word equivocally to mean we see our danger, and do not arm and strike the man who threatens.

> *Imp out our drooping country's broken wing.*

When a hawk lost some of its wing feathers by any accident, it was usual to supply as many as were deficient. This operation was called to *imp* a hawk.

> *Like perspectives, which, rightly gaz'd upon,*
> *Show nothing but confusion; ey'd awry,*
> *Distinguish form.*

This is an allusion to an optical toy, in which a figure is represented wherein all the rules of perspective are inverted, so that if held in the same position with those pictures which are drawn according to the rules of perspective, it presents nothing but confusion; but looked upon from a contrary position, or "ey'd awry," 't is seen in regular and due proportion.

719

As,—though in thinking, on no thought I think,
Makes me with heavy nothing faint and shrink.

The meaning is, though I have no distinct idea of calamity, yet some undefined shadowy dread fills me with apprehension. Every one has sometimes felt this involuntary and unaccountable depression of mind.

The king had cut my head off with my brother's.

No brother of the Duke of York was beheaded; he alludes to the fate of Gloucester, who, after a life spent in opposing and oppressing his nephew, was at length arrested and secretly murdered by his orders at Calais. The duke was smothered with a pillow, while in bed, and it was reported that he had died of apoplexy, but the circumstances all transpired in the next reign.

To take advantage of the absent time.

That is, the time of the king's absence.

And ostentation of despised arms.

Warburton says the ostentation of *despised* arms would not fright any one, and suggests that we should read *disposed* arms, i. e. forces in battle array. Dr. Johnson says, " perhaps the old duke means to treat him with contempt, as well as with severity, and to insinuate that he despises his power, as being able to master it." But this cannot be, because York presently admits that his weakness alone prevents his opposing them.

Look on my wrongs with an indifferent eye.

Indifferent does not here mean inattentive, but impartial.

From my own windows torn my household coat.

That is, took out the coloured glass on which the arms of the family was displayed.

To fight with Glendower and his complices.

Theobald thinks this line an interpolation, and for reasons which from their probability I will quote entire. " Were we to acknowledge the line to be genuine, it must argue the poet guilty of forgetfulness and inattention to history. Bolingbroke is, as it were, but just arrived; he is now at Bristol, weak in his numbers; has had no meeting with a parliament; nor is so far assured of the succession, as to think of going to suppress insurrections before he is planted on the throne. Besides, we find the opposition of Glendower begins the first part of *King Henry IV.*, and Mortimer's defeat by that hardy Welshman is the tidings of the first scene of that play. Again, though Glendower, in the very first year of Henry IV. began to be troublesome, put in for the supremacy of Wales, and imprisoned Mortimer; yet it was not till the succeeding year that the king employed any force against him."

The breath of worldly men cannot depose
The deputy elected by the Lord.

The doctrine of the divine right of kings, and the passive obedience of subjects, is here strongly laid down. The poet, however, puts this language in the mouth of a king.

Thy very beadsmen learn to bend their bows
Of double-fatal yew.

The king's beadsmen were his priests; but beadsman

720

might also mean any man maintained by charity to pray for his benefactor. The yew is, perhaps, called *double-fatal* because its leaves are poison, and the wood is used for instruments of death.

For taking so the head.

To take the *head*, is to act without restraint; to take undue liberties.

Her knots disorder'd.

The comparison is of the kingdom to a garden, and knots are figures planted in box, the lines of which frequently intersect each other.

——— *O, I am press'd to death,*
Through want of speaking.

Nearly strangled by her emotions; but the poet probably alludes to the ancient punishment called *peine forte et dure*, which was inflicted on those persons who, being arraigned, refused to plead, and remained obstinately silent. They were pressed to death by a heavy weight being laid upon the chest.

Westminster Hall.

Westminster Hall was built by Richard, and the first meeting of parliament in it was for the purpose of deposing him.

I take the earth to the like, forsworn Aumerle.

This is an obscure line, which none of the editors satisfactorily explain. Dr. Johnson says—" For *the earth*, I suppose we should read *thy oath*."

As I intend to thrive in this new world.

In this world which is new to me, in which I have just begun to be an actor.

Here do I throw down this.

Holinshed says that on this occasion he threw down a *hood* that he had borrowed.

With my own tears I wash away my balm.

That is, the oil of consecration.

That every day under his household roof
Did keep ten thousand men.

It does not appear that this enormous number of retainers absolutely lived under Richard's roof, but the old chronicles say " that to his household came every day, to meate, ten thousand men." He had three hundred domestics in his kitchen, and there is no doubt but that this prodigality was the source of much exaction, and a great cause of the discontent of the people.

To Julius Cæsar's ill-erected tower.

The Tower of London is traditionally said to be the work of Julius Cæsar. *Ill-erected* means erected for evil purposes.

Sent back like Hallowmas.

All-hallows, or *All-hallowtide*, is the feast of November. The meaning is, the queen came from France with the gladness of spring, but that she returned with the gloom of winter.

" Better far off, than near, be ne'er the near.

They may as well be far apart as near, but not permitted to enjoy each other's society. To be *never the nigher* is an expression common in the midland counties.

" With painted imag'ry, had said at once.

It is difficult to understand how the painted imagery could have spoken; but, perhaps, Shakespeare was thinking of the painted cloths, in which the figures sometimes had labels issuing from their mouths.

" What seal is that which hangs without thy bosom?

The seals of deeds were formerly impressed on slips or labels of parchment, appendent to them.

" But for our trusty brother-in-law.

This was John Duke of Exeter and Earl of Huntingdon (own brother to Richard the Second), and who married with the Lady Elizabeth, sister of Bolingbroke.

91

" His Jack of the clock.

The little figure on some clocks, which is made to strike the hour.

" Whilst my gross flesh sinks downward, here to die.

There has been much controversy respecting the death of Richard, but the following quotation from the manifesto which the Percy family published against Henry the Fourth, in the third year of his reign, is decisive. They charge him with having "carried his sovereign lord traitorously within the castell of Pomfret, without the consent or the judgement of the lords of the realm, by the space of fifteen daies and so many nightes (which is horrible among Christian people to be heard), with *hunger, thirst, and cold, to perish.*" Had the story of Sir Pierce of Exton been true, the Percy family must have known it. Many of the old writers represent Richard as voluntarily abstaining from food, and dying of hunger and a broken heart.

" Carlisle, this is your doom.

The bishop was committed to the tower, but afterwards permitted to change his prison for Westminster Abbey. He was deprived of his see, and eventually retired to a rectory in Gloucestershire.

721

FIRST PART OF

King Henry the Fourth.

HENRY ascended the throne in 1399, and reigned for a period of fourteen years; he died on the 20th of March, 1413, at the age of forty-seven. His usurpation had been successful, his predecessor had perished unpitied and in obscurity, he had attained the rank of king, had suppressed all insurrections, and triumphed over every enemy; but when he had thus reached the summit of his ambition, and stood firm and unassailable upon the dazzling pinnacle of royalty, then, when every aspiration of his ambitious heart was gratified, his overtasked mind reacted upon his naturally iron frame; his early cheerfulness and attractive qualities forsook him, he became solitary in his habits, suspicious and gloomy in his nature, his strength left him—he was prematurely old; he became a bigot in religion, and persecuted heretics with extreme severity; and finally, subject to epileptic fits and afflicted with a cutaneous disorder, which some have said to be leprosy, he sunk into the grave, not past the fulness of maturity, and scarcely regretted by his subjects; a melancholy instance that wealth and power too often fail to confer happiness upon their envied possessor. If the spirit of the broken-hearted and murdered Richard could have gazed upon the last hours of Henry in the Jerusalem chamber, it might have rested satisfied and appeased.

Sensible that a drama embracing only a series of intrigues and acts of tergiversation, of insurrections and civil wars, and of struggles for supremacy between parties who are neither of them entitled to much sympathy or respect, would possess little interest, Shakespeare has introduced into this play, and its companion one, the richest and most brilliant comedy that ever rose even in the cheerful chambers of his sunny soul. It is the first of those dramas which are, strictly speaking, neither tragedy, comedy, nor history, but a happy mingling of all three; a kind of drama peculiar to Shakespeare, and singularly adapted to his comprehensive and variable muse.

The first part of *Henry the Fourth* commences with news of the victory of his troops under young Percy at Homildon Hill, in the September of 1402, and concludes with the defeat of Hotspur at Shrewsbury, on the 21st of July, 1403, which latter event may be said to have placed Henry firmly in the regal chair. The time comprised in this play is therefore less than a year. We should be inclined to view the struggles of Henry and Northumberland with indignation and disgust, were it not that their cold and crafty policy is redeemed by the graceful profligacy and generous courage of the Prince of Wales, and the blunt fiery nature of the noble but unfortunate Hotspur But the latter, though brave and chivalric, is too much the warrior; his manners are rough, self-willed, impetuous, and unconciliating. Haughty and ambitious to excess, he would break all things to his will; he laughs at the small gentle courtesies and elegances of life—for them he has no time. He is abrupt, if not unkind, to his wife, who is too gentle to need correction or reproof; impatient and defiant to Glendower; for his behaviour to whom his uncle gently chides him, for—

Defect of manners, want of government,
Pride, haughtiness, opinion, and disdain.

But we forget his faults in his misfortunes; he expiates all errors upon the blood-stained field of

Shrewsbury. The Prince is equally fearless, but more gentle; we like him the better even for his dissipation; his gaiety and good-humour contrast well with the stern military habits of Hotspur. Sir Richard Vernon gives a spirited description of the Prince mounting his war-steed, and armed for the encounter :—

> I saw young Harry, with his beaver on,
> His cuisses on his thighs, gallantly armed,
> Rise from the ground like feathered Mercury,
> And vaulted with such ease into his seat,
> As if an angel had dropped down from the clouds
> To turn and wind a fiery Pegasus,
> And witch the world with noble horsemanship.

Out of the early dissipation of Prince Henry,—a dissipation to which it is supposed that he abandoned himself in consequence of the jealousy entertained of his growing popularity by the king his father,—arises, in a very natural and easy manner, the comedy of the play. And what comedy it is! how hearty, rollicking, brilliant, and abandoned! what glimpses it gives us of low life in that remote time! it is a social revelation of the buried past.

Falstaff is the very midsummer of mirth, the broadest and most intensely humorous production ever delineated by the pen of the dramatist; not only a "tun of man," but a tun of wit. With his first introduction we are at home with him; he talks like an old acquaintance, and though he at once professes himself a thief, we are not repelled and disgusted, but feel a certain liking and respect for him. Such is the force of wit and intellect; for he is a shrewd man, and worldly wisdom appears in every speech he utters, heightened by irrepressible humour. Take as one instance among many, his exquisite soliloquy on honour. "Is it insensible, then? Yea, to the dead. But will it not live with the living? No. Why? Detraction will not suffer it." Plato could not have divulged a sounder philosophy. Falstaff is a genius in sensuality; he presents none of the disgusting or repulsive features of such a character; glutton, drunkard, thief, liar, slanderer, coward, as he must be confessed, he still palliates all these vices by his wit and good-humour. One reason why he is so universal a favourite is the utter absence of malice in his nature; he will gratify himself at any cost, but he has no desire to injure others; when he does so it is accidental. Shakespeare has invested him with a certain attractiveness of manner and charm of conversation; the prince can never long be angry with him for his abuse or slanders, and all his associates are attached to him.

Depraved as Falstaff is in principle, he is not offensive in his epicurism; the prince, while drawing an abusive character of him, says—"Wherein is he good but to taste sack and drink it? wherein neat and cleanly, but to carve a capon and eat it?" which implies that he was gentlemanly and agreeable at table. He is never without a plausible reason or apology when detected in any slander or cowardice; his reply when the prince reproaches him for running away at Gadshill—"By the Lord, I knew ye as well as he that made ye," is unanswerable. He was a coward upon instinct, and would not touch the true prince. There is also a delicate covert flattery concealed in this excuse. But his answer, when the prince detects his falsehood about the contents of his pocket, is better still. "Dost thou hear, Hal? thou knowest in the state of innocency Adam fell; and what should poor Jack Falstaff do in the days of villany? Thou seest I have more flesh than another man, and therefore more frailty." The cause of morality is in no degree injured by this exhibition of a man at once so attractive and vicious; with most authors Falstaff would have been a dangerous experiment; they would have made a libidinous satyr, ten times more repulsive than Silenus, a personification of depravity, a devil of lust and drunkenness, seen only to be despised and abhorred. Not so with our poet, for although Shakespeare makes us like the man, he never palliates his misdeeds; he renders Falstaff attractive, but never captivates us with lying, theft, or debauchery. These vices stand forth reprehensible in themselves and fatal in their results. The Prince is not depraved in heart; his errors are but the rude excrescences of an untamed and fugitive genius; he rises on the pinions of resolution from the corrupt and stagnant sea of sensuality, and throwing off the vices incidental to and natural in youth (especially where great animal spirits are united to a bold heart and able mind), stands erect in the stern dignity of a just and sovereign authority. But in Falstaff the moral principle is dead; for him there is no reformation, no change, and he dies in his depravity, a poor, discarded, broken-hearted man. Most of his companions also perish in poverty and infamy. Here lies the poet's moral, and I cannot think it a feeble one.

Falstaff is surrounded by a group of eccentricities, who are all laughable enough; but he is never eclipsed by them. They are satellites which never rise into rivalry with that great orb of mirth. In this play we have Bardolph, whose fiery carbuncled nose serves as a butt for the jests of his companions, though this character of course tells better on the stage than in the study. Then we have the voluble rogue Gadshill, Francis the valiant drawer with his pennyworth of sugar, comfortable Mrs. Quickly, the hostess, and in the second play the noisy braggart Pistol, the sharp-witted little page, the lean garrulous Justice Shallow, his cousin Silence, and his man Davy; together with that famous company of recruits, Mouldy, Shadow, Wart, Feeble, and Bullcalf; but still Sir John is the master-spirit of the scene.

The introduction of the two carriers, also, is exceedingly humorous; they are by no means simple people, nor do they attempt to amuse by saying smart things; they are portraits, blunt, rude, unsophisticated, and natural. They have evidently a suspicion of Gadshill; they dislike his appearance, and, perhaps, give a shrewd guess at his occupation. The care they take of their own property is very amusing. "Lend me thy lantern, quoth a'? marry, I'll see thee hanged first." These flea-bitten rustics are conservatives, too, in their way; they lament past times; in their estimation, nothing is so orderly or prosperous as it used to be: and the second carrier exclaims, with regret, "This house is turned upside down, since Robin ostler died." Such is the nature of the uncultivated mind; it always looks back with longing to the past, without reference to the character of that past; and, perhaps, with most of us, the memory dwells chiefly on the sunniest spots of life, and remains oblivious to its privations and terrors. We talk of the golden days of old England, but we forget the tyranny of its monarchs, the oppression of the people by the great nobles, the insurrections and civil wars, the ruined towns, the blazing farm-houses, the fields of downtrodden or smouldering corn, the violated virgins and slaughtered youth, the homes left ever desolate, the thriving farmer made a wandering beggar by fierce contentions in which he took no interest and no part; and, finally, the gibbet and attendant executioner, with the dresser on which to embowel the victims of political wrath, and the kindled fire ready to consume the heart of the living criminal who gazed upon it, sustained in those last dreadful moments by the courage of despair. Scenes like these were but too frequent in the golden days of old England.

It is to be regretted that the number of characters which Shakespeare has introduced into this play, prevented his giving more than a mere sketch of the Welsh patriot, Owen Glendower, though, certainly, that sketch is exceedingly bold and effective. He was a brave, but superstitious man, whose constant success in warfare convinced both himself and his enemies that he possessed a control over the services of evil spirits. Some supposed him a necromancer; others, in their ignorant dread, imagined him to be an embodiment of Satan himself. Owen thrice drove the king out of Wales, but he was finally overpowered by Prince Henry, who, in the mountains and morasses of that wild and picturesque country, fighting against a hardy and cunning adversary, acquired that knowledge of warfare which in after years rendered him so successful on the shores of France. Glendower being unfortunate, and, consequently, forsaken, wandered about for a time disguised as a shepherd; but, recovering his spirit, he again took up arms, and died, at last, a free man, amidst the mountains of that beloved country which he had so long sought to enfranchise from the power of England.

The little dialogue between Mortimer and his wife is exceedingly sweet and poetical; amidst scenes of angry disputation and the storm of war, it is like soft music in a summer's night stealing through garden groves and over beds of flowers, soothing and enchanting the senses, compared to the harsh braying of trumpets and the startling clang of cymbals on the marshy and blood-soaked field of war. Indeed, throughout the play, many startling and grand passages occur, alternating with exquisite poetry and irresistible drollery.

This drama was entered at Stationers' Hall, October 20th, 1597, and printed in that year, it and the second part of *Henry the Fourth*, were probably both produced in 1596.

PERSONS REPRESENTED.

KING HENRY THE FOURTH.
*Appears, Act I. sc. 1; sc. 3. Act III. sc. 2. Act V. sc. 1;
sc. 4; sc. 5.*

HENRY, *Prince of Wales, Eldest Son to the King.*
*Appears, Act I. sc. 2. Act II. sc. 2; sc. 4. Act III. sc. 2;
sc. 3. Act IV. sc. 2. Act V. sc. 1; sc. 3; sc. 4; sc. 5.*

PRINCE JOHN OF LANCASTER, *Son to the King.*
Appears, Act V. sc. 1; sc. 4; sc. 5.

EARL OF WESTMORELAND, *Friend to the King.*
Appears, Act I. sc. 1. Act IV. sc. 2. Act V. sc. 4; sc. 5.

SIR WALTER BLUNT, *Friend to the King.*
*Appears, Act I. sc. 1; sc. 3. Act III. sc. 2. Act IV. sc. 3.
Act V. sc. 1; sc. 3.*

THOMAS PERCY, *Earl of Worcester.*
*Appears, Act I. sc. 3. Act III. sc. 1. Act IV. sc. 1; sc. 3.
Act V. sc. 1; sc. 2; sc. 5.*

HENRY PERCY, *Earl of Northumberland.*
Appears, Act I. sc. 3.

HENRY PERCY, *surnamed* Hotspur, *his Son.*
*Appears, Act I. sc. 3. Act II. sc. 3. Act III. sc. 1. Act
IV. sc. 1; sc. 3. Act V. sc. 2; sc. 3; sc. 4.*

EDMUND MORTIMER, *Earl of* March
Appears, Act III. sc. 1.

SCROOP, *Archbishop of* York.
Appears, Act IV. sc. 4.

ARCHIBALD, *Earl of* Douglas.
Appears, Act IV. sc. 1; sc. 3. Act V. sc. 2; sc. 3 sc. 4.
726

OWEN GLENDOWER.
Appears, Act III. sc. 1.

SIR RICHARD VERNON.
Appears, Act IV. sc. 1; sc. 3. Act V. sc. 1; sc. 2; sc. 5.

SIR JOHN FALSTAFF.
*Appears, Act I. sc. 2. Act II. sc. 2; sc. 4. Act III. sc. 3.
Act IV. sc. 2. Act V. sc. 1; sc. 3; sc. 4.*

POINS.
Appears, Act I. sc. 2. Act II. sc. 2; sc. 4. Act III. sc. 3.

GADSHILL.
Appears, Act II. sc. 1; sc. 2; sc. 4.

PETO.
Appears, Act II. sc. 2; sc. 4.

BARDOLPH.
Appears, Act II. sc. 2; sc. 4. Act III. sc. 3. Act IV. sc. 2.

LADY PERCY, *Wife to* Hotspur, *and Sister to*
Mortimer.
Appears, Act II. sc. 3. Act III. sc. 1.

LADY MORTIMER, *Daughter to* Glendower, *and
Wife to* Mortimer.
Appears, Act III. sc. 1.

MRS. QUICKLY, *Hostess of a Tavern in* Eastcheap.
Appears, Act II. sc. 4. Act III. sc. 3.

*Lords, Officers, Sheriff, Vintner, Chamberlain,
Drawers, Two Carriers, Travellers, and
Attendants.*

SCENE,—ENGLAND.

FIRST PART OF

King Henry the Fourth.

ACT I.

SCENE I.—London.   *A Room in the Palace.*

Enter KING HENRY, WESTMORELAND, SIR WALTER
BLUNT, *and Others.*

K. Hen. So shaken as we are, so wan with care,
Find we a time for frighted peace to pant,
And breathe short-winded accents of new broils
To be commenc'd in strands afar remote.
No more the thirsty entrails of this soil
Shall daub her lips with her own children's blood ;
No more shall trenching war channel her fields,
Nor bruise her flow'rets with the armed hoofs
Of hostile paces : those opposed eyes,
Which,—like the meteors of a troubled heaven,
All of one nature, of one substance bred,—
Did lately meet in the intestine shock
And furious close of civil butchery,
Shall now, in mutual, well-beseeming ranks,
March all one way ; and be no more oppos'd
Against acquaintance, kindred, and allies :
The edge of war, like an ill-sheathed knife,
No more shall cut his master.   Therefore, friends,
As far as to the sepulchre of Christ,
(Whose soldier now, under whose blessed cross
We are impressed and engag'd to fight,)
Forthwith a power of English shall we levy ;
Whose arms were moulded in their mother's womb
To chase these pagans, in those holy fields,
Over whose acres walk'd those blessed feet,
Which, fourteen hundred years ago, were nail'd
For our advantage, on the bitter cross.
But this our purpose is a twelve-month old,
And bootless 't is to tell you—we will go ;
Therefore we meet not now :—Then let me hear

Of you, my gentle cousin Westmoreland,
What yesternight our council did decree,
In forwarding this dear expedience.
West. My liege, this haste was hot in question
And many limits of the charge' set down
But yesternight : when, all athwart, there came
A post from Wales, loaden with heavy news ;
Whose worst was,—that the noble Mortimer,
Leading the men of Herefordshire to fight
Against the irregular and wild Glendower,
Was by the rude hands of that Welshman taken,
And a thousand of his people butchered ;
Upon whose dead corps there was such misuse,
Such beastly, shameless transformation,
By those Welshwomen done, as may not be,
Without much shame, re-told or spoken of.
K. Hen. It seems then, that the tidings of this
broil
Brake off our business for the Holy Land.
West. This, match'd with other, did, my gra-
cious lord ;
For more uneven and unwelcome news
Came from the north, and thus it did import.
On Holy-rood day, the gallant Hotspur there,
Young Harry Percy, and brave Archibald,
That ever-valiant and approved Scot,
At Holmedon met,
Where they did spend a sad and bloody hour ;
As by discharge of their artillery,
And shape of likelihood, the news was told ;
For he that brought them, in the very heat
And pride of their contention did take horse,
Uncertain of the issue any way.
K. Hen. Here is a dear and true-industrious friend,

Sir Walter Blunt, new lighted from his horse,
Stain'd with the variation of each soil
Betwixt that Holmedon and this seat of ours;
And he hath brought us smooth and welcome
   news.
The earl of Douglas is discomfited;
Ten thousand bold Scots, two - and - twenty
   knights,
Balk'd in their own blood, did sir Walter see
On Holmedon's plains: Of prisoners, Hotspur
   took
Mordake the earl of Fife, and eldest son
To beaten Douglas; and the earls of Athol,
Of Murray, Angus, and Menteith.
And is not this an honourable spoil?
A gallant prize? ha, cousin, is it not?

West. Faith 't is a conquest for a prince to
   boast of.

   K. Hen. Yea, there thou mak'st me sad, and
   mak'st me sin
In envy that my lord Northumberland
Should be the father of so blest a son;
A son, who is the theme of honour's tongue;
Amongst a grove, the very straightest plant;
Who is sweet fortune's minion, and her pride;
Whilst I, by looking on the praise of him,
See riot and dishonour stain the brow
Of my young Harry. O, that it could be prov'd,
That some night-tripping fairy had exchang'd
In cradle-clothes our children where they lay,
And call'd mine—Percy, his—Plantagenet!
Then would I have his Harry, and he mine.
But let him from my thoughts:—What think
   you, coz',
Of this young Percy's pride? the prisoners,
Which he in this adventure hath surpris'd,
To his own use he keeps; and sends me word,
I shall have none but Mordake, earl of Fife.

West. This is his uncle's teaching, this is Wor-
   cester,
Malevolent to you in all aspects;
Which makes him prune himself, and bristle up
The crest of youth against your dignity.

   K. Hen. But I have sent for him to answer this;
And, for this cause, awhile we must neglect
Our holy purpose to Jerusalem.
Cousin, on Wednesday next our council we
Will hold at Windsor, so inform the lords:
But come yourself with speed to us again;
For more is to be said, and to be done,
Than out of anger can be uttered.

   West. I will, my liege.   [*Exeunt.*
   728

SCENE II.—*The Same. Another Room in the
Palace.*

Enter HENRY *Prince of Wales, and* FALSTAFF.

Fal. Now, Hal, what time of day is it, lad?

P. Henry. Thou art so fat-witted, with drinking
of old sack, and unbuttoning thee after supper, and
sleeping upon benches after noon, that thou hast
forgotten to demand that truly which thou would'st
truly know. What a devil hast thou to do with
the time of the day? unless hours were cups of
sack, and minutes capons, and clocks the tongues
of bawds, and dials the signs of leaping-houses, and
the blessed sun himself a fair hot wench in flame-
colour'd taffata; I see no reason, why thou should'st
be so superfluous to demand the time of the day.

Fal. Indeed, you come near me, now, Hal: for
we, that take purses, go by the moon and seven
stars; and not by Phœbus,—he, "that wandering
knight so fair." And I pray thee, sweet wag,
when thou art king,—as, God save thy grace,
(majesty, I should say; for grace thou wilt have
none,)——

P. Hen. What! none?

Fal. No, by my troth; not so much as will
serve to be prologue to an egg and butter.

P. Hen. Well, how then? come, roundly, roundly

Fal. Marry, then, sweet wag, when thou art
king, let not us, that are squires of the night's
body, be called thieves of the day's beauty: let
us be—Diana's foresters, gentlemen of the shade,
minions of the moon: And let men say, we be
men of good government; being governed as the
sea is, by our noble and chaste mistress the moon,
under whose countenance we—steal.

P. Hen. Thou say'st well; and it holds well too:
for the fortune of us, that are the moon's men,
doth ebb and flow like the sea; being governed as
the sea is, by the moon. As, for proof, now: A
purse of gold most resolutely snatched on Monday
night, and most dissolutely spent on Tuesday morning; got with swearing—lay by; and spent with
crying—bring in; now, in as low an ebb as the
foot of the ladder; and, by and by, in as high a
flow as the ridge of the gallows.

Fal. By the Lord, thou say'st true, lad. And
is not my hostess of the tavern a most sweet
wench?

P. Hen. As the honey of Hybla, my old lad of
the castle. And is not a buff jerkin a most sweet
robe of durance?

Fal. How now, how now, mad wag? what, in

thy quips, and thy quiddities? what a plague have I to do with a buff jerkin?

P. Hen. Why, what a pox have I to do with my hostess of the tavern?

Fal. Well, thou hast called her to a reckoning, many a time and oft.

P. Hen. Did I ever call for thee to pay thy part?

Fal. No; I'll give thee thy due, thou hast paid all there.

P. Hen. Yea, and elsewhere, so far as my coin would stretch; and, where it would not, I have used my credit.

Fal. Yea, and so used it, that were it not here apparent that thou ar their apparent,—But, I pr'ythee, sweet wag, shall there be gallows standing in England when thou art king? and resolution thus fobbed as it is, with the rusty curb of old father antic the law? Do not thou, when thou art king, hang a thief.

P. Hen. No; thou shalt.

Fal. Shall I? O rare! By the Lord, I'll be a brave judge.

P. Hen. Thou judgest false already; I mean, thou shalt have the hanging of the thieves, and so become a rare hangman.

Fal. Well, Hal, well; and in some sort it jumps with my humour, as well as waiting in the court, I can tell you.

P. Hen. For obtaining of suits?

Fal. Yea, for obtaining of suits: whereof the hangman hath no lean wardrobe. 'Sblood, I am as melancholy as a gib cat, or a lugged bear.

P. Hen. Or an old lion; or a lover's lute.

Fal. Yea, or the drone of a Lincolnshire bag-pipe.

P. Hen. What sayest thou to a hare, or the melancholy of Moor-ditch?

Fal. Thou hast the most unsavoury similes; and art, indeed, the most comparative, rascalliest,—sweet young prince,—But, Hal, I pr'ythee, trouble me no more with vanity. I would to God, thou and I knew where a commodity of good names were to be bought: An old lord of the council rated me the other day in the street about you, sir; but I marked him not: and yet he talked very wisely; but I regarded him not: and yet he talked wisely, and in the street too.

P. Hen. Thou did'st well; for wisdom cries out in the streets, and no man regards it.

Fal. O thou hast damnable iteration; and art, indeed, able to corrupt a saint. Thou hast done

much harm upon me, Hal,—God forgive thee for it! Before I knew thee, Hal, I knew nothing; and now am I, if a man should speak truly, little better than one of the wicked. I must give over this life, and I will give it over; by the Lord, an I do not, I am a villain; I'll be damned for never a king's son in Christendom.

P. Hen. Where shall we take a purse to-morrow, Jack?

Fal. Where thou wilt, lad, I'll make one; an I do not, call me villain, and baffle me.

P. Hen. I see a good amendment of life in thee; from praying, to purse-taking.

Enter POINS, *at a distance.*

Fal. Why, Hal, 't is my vocation, Hal; 't is no sin for a man to labour in his vocation. Poins!—Now shall we know if Gadshill have set a match. O, if men were to be saved by merit, what hole in hell were hot enough for him? This is the most omnipotent villain, that ever cried, Stand, to a true man.

P. Hen. Good morrow, Ned.

Poins. Good morrow, sweet Hal.—What says monsieur Remorse? What says sir John Sack-and-Sugar? Jack, how agrees the devil and thee about thy soul, that thou soldest him on Good-Friday last, for a cup of Madeira, and a cold capon's leg?

P. Hen. Sir John stands to his word, the devil shall have his bargain; for he was never yet a breaker of proverbs, he will give the devil his due.

Poins. Then art thou damned for keeping thy word with the devil.

P. Hen. Else he had been damned for cozening the devil.

Poins. But, my lads, my lads, to-morrow morning, by four o'clock, early at Gadshill: There are pilgrims going to Canterbury with rich offerings, and traders riding to London with fat purses: I have visors for you all, you have horses for yourselves; Gadshill lies to-night in Rochester: I have bespoke supper to-morrow night in East-cheap; we may do it as secure as sleep: If you will go, I will stuff your purses full of crowns: if you will not, tarry at home, and be hanged.

Fal. Hear me, Yedward, if I tarry at home, and go not, I'll hang you for going.

Poins. You will, chops?

Fal. Hal, wilt thou make one?

P. Hen. Who, I rob? I a thief? not I, by my faith.

Fal. There's neither honesty, manhood, nor good fellowship in thee, nor thou camest not of the blood royal, if thou darest not stand for ten shillings.[11]

P. Hen. Well, then once in my days I'll be a mad-cap.

Fal. Why, that's well said.

P. Hen. Well, come what will, I'll tarry at home.

Fal. By the Lord, I'll be a traitor then, when thou art king.

P. Hen. I care not.

Poins. Sir John, I pr'ythee, leave the prince and me alone; I will lay him down such reasons for this adventure, that he shall go.

Fal. Well, may'st thou have the spirit of persuasion, and he the ears of profiting, that what thou speakest may move, and what he hears may be believed, that the true prince may (for recreation sake,) prove a false thief; for the poor abuses of the time want countenance. Farewell: You shall find me in Eastcheap.

P. Hen. Farewell, thou latter spring! Farewell, All-hallown summer![12]   [*Exit* Fal.

Poins. Now, my good sweet-honey lord, ride with us to-morrow; I have a jest to execute, that I cannot manage alone. Falstaff, Bardolph, Peto, and Gadshill, shall rob those men that we have already way-laid; yourself, and I, will not be there; and when they have the booty, if you and I do not rob them, cut this head from my shoulders.

P. Hen. But how shall we part with them in setting forth?

Poins. Why, we will set forth before or after them, and appoint them a place of meeting, wherein it is at our pleasure to fail; and then will they adventure upon the exploit themselves: which they shall have no sooner achieved, but we'll set upon them.

P. Hen. Ay, but, 't is like, that they will know us, by our horses, by our habits, and by every other appointment, to be ourselves.

Poins. Tut! our horses they shall not see, I'll tie them in the wood; our visors we will change, after we leave them; and, sirrah,[13] I have cases of buckram for the nonce, to immask our noted outward garments.

P. Hen. But I doubt, they will be too hard for us.

Poins. Well, for two of them, I know them to be as true-bred cowards as ever turned back; and

for the third, if he fight longer than he sees reason, I'll forswear arms. The virtue of this jest will be, the incomprehensible lies that this same fat rogue will tell us, when we meet at supper: how thirty, at least, he fought with; what wards, what blows, what extremities he endured; and, in the reproof of this, lies the jest.

P. Hen. Well, I'll go with thee; provide us all things necessary, and meet me to-morrow night[14] in Eastcheap, there I'll sup. Farewell.

Poins. Farewell, my lord.   [*Exit* Poins.

P. Hen. I know you all, and will a while uphold
The unyok'd humour of your idleness:
Yet herein will I imitate the sun;
Who doth permit the base contagious clouds
To smother up his beauty from the world,
That, when he please again to be himself,
Being wanted, he may be more wonder'd at.
By breaking through the foul and ugly mists
Of vapours, that did seem to strangle him.
If all the year were playing holidays,
To sport would be as tedious as to work;
But, when they seldom come, they wish'd-for come,
And nothing pleaseth but rare accidents.
So, when this loose behaviour I throw off,
And pay the debt I never promised,
By how much better than my word I am,
By so much shall I falsify men's hopes;
And, like bright metal on a sullen ground,
My reformation, glittering o'er my fault,
Shall show more goodly, and attract more eyes,
Than that which hath no foil to set it off.
I'll so offend, to make offence a skill;
Redeeming time, when men think least I will.
[*Exit.*

SCENE III.—*The Same.   Another Room in the Palace.*

Enter KING HENRY, NORTHUMBERLAND, WORCESTER, HOTSPUR, SIR WALTER BLUNT, *and Others.*

K. Hen. My blood hath been too cold and temperate,
Unapt to stir at these indignities,
And you have found me; for, accordingly,
You tread upon my patience: but, be sure,
I will from henceforth rather be myself,
Mighty, and to be fear'd, than my condition;
Which hath been smooth as oil, soft as young down,
And therefore lost that title of respect,
Which the proud soul ne'er pays, but to the proud.

Wor. Our house, my sovereign liege, little de-
serves
The scourge of greatness to be used on it ;
And that same greatness too which our own hands
Have holp to make so portly.

North. My lord,——

K. Hen. Worcester, get thee gone, for I see
danger
And disobedience in thine eye : O, sir,
Your presence is too bold and peremptory,
And majesty might never yet endure
The moody frontier of a servant brow.
You have good leave to leave us ; when we need
Your use and counsel, we shall send for you.—
                                            [*Exit* Wor.
You were about to speak.   [*To* North.

North.   Yea, my good lord.
Those prisoners in your highness' name demanded,
Which Harry Percy here at Holmedon took,
Were, as he says, not with such strength denied
As is deliver'd to your majesty :
Either envy, therefore, or misprision
Is guilty of this fault, and not my son.

Hot. My liege, I did deny no prisoners.
But, I remember, when the fight was done,
When I was dry with rage, and extreme toil,
Breathless and faint, leaning upon my sword,
Came there a certain lord, neat, trimly dress'd,
Fresh as a bridegroom ; and his chin, new reap'd,
Show'd like a stubble-land at harvest-home ;
He was perfumed like a milliner ;
And 'twixt his finger and his thumb he held
A pouncet-box, which ever and anon
He gave his nose, and took 't away again ;——
Who, therewith angry, when it next came there,
Took it in snuff :—and still he smil'd, and talk'd ;
And, as the soldiers bore dead bodies by,
He call'd them—untaught knaves, unmannerly,
To bring a slovenly unhandsome corse
Betwixt the wind and his nobility.
With many holiday and lady terms
He question'd me ; among the rest demanded
My prisoners, in your majesty's behalf.
I then, all smarting with my wounds being cold,
To be so pester'd with a popinjay,
Out of my grief and my impatience,
Answer'd neglectingly, I know not what ;
He should, or he should not ;—for he made me mad,
To see him shine so brisk, and smell so sweet,
And talk so like a waiting-gentlewoman,
Of guns, and drums, and wounds, (God save the
mark !)

And telling me, the sovereign'st thing on earth
Was parmaceti, for an inward bruise ;
And that it was great pity, so it was,
That villanous salt-petre should be digg'd
Out of the bowels of the harmless earth,
Which many a good tall fellow had destroy'd
So cowardly ; and, but for these vile guns,
He would himself have been a soldier.
This bald unjointed chat of his, my lord,
I answer'd indirectly, as I said ;
And, I beseech you, let not his report
Come current for an accusation,
Betwixt my love and your high majesty.

Blunt. The circumstance consider'd, good my
lord,
Whatever Harry Percy then had said,
To such a person, and in such a place,
At such a time, with all the rest re-told,
May reasonably die, and never rise
To do him wrong, or any way impeach
What then he said, so he unsay it now.

K. Hen. Why, yet he doth deny his prisoners ;
But with proviso, and exception,—
That we, at our own charge, shall ransom straight
His brother-in-law, the foolish Mortimer ;[15]
Who, on my soul, hath wilfully betray'd
The lives of those that he did lead to fight
Against the great magician, damn'd Glendower ;
Whose daughter, as we hear, the earl of March
Hath lately married.   Shall our coffers then
Be emptied, to redeem a traitor home ?
Shall we buy treason ? and indent with fears,
When they have lost and forfeited themselves ?
No, on the barren mountains let him starve ;
For I shall never hold that man my friend,
Whose tongue shall ask me for one penny cost
To ransom home revolted Mortimer.

Hot. Revolted Mortimer !
He never did fall off, my sovereign liege,
But by the chance of war ;—To prove that true,
Needs no more but one tongue for all those wounds,
Those mouthed wounds, which valiantly he took,
When on the gentle Severn's sedgy bank,
In single opposition, hand to hand,
He did confound the best part of an hour   .
In changing hardiment with great Glendower :
Three times they breath'd, and three times did
they drink,
Upon agreement, of swift Severn's flood ;
Who then, affrighted with their bloody looks,
Ran fearfully among the trembling reeds,
And hid his crisp head in the hollow bank,

Blood-stained with these valiant combatants.
Never did bare and rotten policy
Colour her working with such deadly wounds,
Nor never could the noble Mortimer
Receive so many, and all willingly ;
Then let him not be slander'd with revolt.

　K. Hen. Thou dost belie him, Percy, thou dost
　　belie him,
He never did encounter with Glendower ;
I tell thee,
He durst as well have met the devil alone,
As Owen Glendower for an enemy.
Art not ashamed ?　But, sirrah, henceforth
Let me not hear you speak of Mortimer :
Send me your prisoners with the speediest means,
Or you shall hear in such a kind from me
As will displease you.—My lord Northumberland,
We license your departure with your son :—
Send us your prisoners, or you 'll hear of it.
　　　　　[*Exeunt K. Hen., Blunt, and Train.*

　Hot. And if the devil come and roar for them,
I will not send them :—I will after straight,
And tell him so ; for I will ease my heart,
Although it be with hazard of my head.

　North. What, drunk with choler ? stay, and
　　pause awhile ;
Here comes your uncle.

　　　　　Re-enter Worcester.

　Hot.　　　　　　Speak of Mortimer ?
'Zounds, I will speak of him ; and let my soul
Want mercy, if I do not join with him :
Yea, on his part, I 'll empty all these veins,
And shed my dear blood drop by drop i' the dust,
But I will lift the down-trod Mortimer
As high i' the air as this unthankful king,
As this ingrate and canker'd Bolingbroke.

　North. Brother, the king hath made your
　　nephew mad.　　　　　　[*To Wor.*

　Wor. Who struck this heat up, after I was gone ?

　Hot. He will, forsooth, have all my prisoners ;
And when I urg'd the ransom once again
Of my wife's brother, then his cheek look'd pale ;
And on my face he turn'd an eye of death,
Trembling even at the name of Mortimer.[16]

　Wor. I cannot blame him : Was he not pro-
　　claim'd,
By Richard that dead is, the next of blood ?

　North. He was : I heard the proclamation :
And then it was, when the unhappy king
(Whose wrongs in us God pardon !) did set forth
Upon his Irish expedition ;

From whence he, intercepted, did return
To be depos'd, and shortly, murdered.

　Wor. And for whose death, we in the world's
　　wide mouth
Live scandaliz'd, and foully spoken of.

　Hot. But, soft, I pray you : Did king Richard
　　then
Proclaim my brother Edmund Mortimer
Heir to the crown ?

　North.　　　He did ; myself did hear it.

　Hot. Nay, then I cannot blame his cousin king
That wish'd him on the barren mountains starv'd.
But shall it be, that you,—that set the crown
Upon the head of this forgetful man ;
And, for his sake, wear the detested blot
Of murd'rous subornation,—shall it be,
That you a world of curses undergo ;
Being the agents, or base second means,
The cords, the ladder, or the hangman rather ?—
O, pardon me, that I descend so low,
To show the line, and the predicament,
Wherein you range under this subtle king.—
Shall it, for shame, be spoken in these days,
Or fill up chronicles in time to come,
That men of your nobility and power,
Did gage them both in an unjust behalf,—
As both of you, God pardon it ! have done,—
To put down Richard, that sweet lovely rose.
And plant this thorn, this canker, Bolingbroke ?
And shall it, in more shame, be further spoken,
That you are fool'd, discarded, and shook off
By him, for whom these shames ye underwent ?
No ; yet time serves, wherein you may redeem
Your banish'd honours, and restore yourselves
Into the good thoughts of the world again :
Revenge the jeering, and disdain'd contempt.
Of this proud king ; who studies, day and night.
To answer all the debt he owes to you,
Even with the bloody payment of your deaths.
Therefore, I say,——

　Wor.　　　　Peace, cousin, say no more :
And now I will unclasp a secret book,
And to your quick-conceiving discontents
I 'll read you matter deep and dangerous ;
As full of peril and advent'rous spirit,
As to o'er-walk a current, roaring loud,
On the unsteadiest footing of a spear.

　Hot. If he fall in, good night :—or sink or
　　swim :—
Send danger from the east unto the west,
So honour cross it from the north to south,
And let them grapple ;—O ! the blood more stirs.

To rouse a lion, than to start a hare.

North. Imagination of some great exploit
Drives him beyond the bounds of patience.

Hot. By heaven, methinks, it were an easy
leap,
To pluck bright honour from the pale-fac'd moon;
Or dive into the bottom of the deep,
Where fathom-line could never touch the ground,
And pluck up drowned honour by the locks;
So he, that doth redeem her thence, might wear,
Without corrival, all her dignities:
But out upon this half-fac'd fellowship!

Wor. He apprehends a world of figures here,
But not the form of what he should attend.—
Good cousin, give me audience for a while.

Hot. I cry you mercy.

Wor.   Those same noble Scots,
That are your prisoners,——

Hot.   I'll keep them all;
By heaven, he shall not have a Scot of them:
No, if a Scot would save his soul, he shal! not:
I'll keep them, by this hand.

Wor.   You start away,
And lend no ear unto my purposes.—
Those prisoners you shall keep.

Hot.   Nay, I will; that's flat:—
He said, he would not ransom Mortimer;
Forbad my tongue to speak of Mortimer;
But I will find him when he lies asleep,
And in his ear I'll holla—Mortimer!
Nay,
I'll have a starling shall be taught to speak
Nothing but Mortimer, and give it him,
To keep his anger still in motion.

Wor.   Hear you,
Cousin; a word.

Hot. All studies here I solemnly defy,
Save how to gall and pinch this Bolingbroke:
And that same sword-and-buckler prince of
Wales,"
But that I think his father loves him not,
And would be glad he met with some mischance,
I'd have him poison'd with a pot of ale.

Wor. Farewell, kinsman! I will talk to you,
When you are better temper'd to attend.

North. Why, what a wasp-stung and impatient
fool
Art thou, to break into this woman's mood;
Tying thine ear to no tongue but thine own?

Hot. Why, look you, I am whipp'd and scourg'd
with rods,
Nettled, and stung with pismires, when I hear

Of this vile politician, Bolingbroke.
In Richard's time,—What do you call the place?—
A plague upon't!—it is in Gloucestershire;—
'Twas where the mad-cap duke his uncle kept;
His uncle York:—where I first bow'd my knee
Unto this king of smiles, this Bolingbroke,
When you and he came back from Ravenspurg.

North. At Berkley castle.

Hot. You say true:——
Why, what a candy deal of courtesy
This fawning greyhound then did proffer me!
Look,—"when his infant fortune came to age,"
And,—"gentle Harry Percy,"—and, "kind cou-
sin,"—
O, the devil take such cozeners!——God forgive
me!—
Good uncle, tell your tale, for I have done.

Wor. Nay, if you have not, to't again;
We'll stay your leisure.

Hot.   I have done, i' faith.

Wor. Then once more to your Scottish prisoners.
Deliver them up without their ransom straight,
And make the Douglas' son your only mean
For powers in Scotland; which,—for divers rea-
sons,
Which I shall send you written,—be assur'd,
Will easily be granted.—You, my lord,—
                              [*To* NORTH.
Your son in Scotland being thus employ'd,—
Shall secretly into the bosom creep
Of that same noble prelate, well belov'd,
The archbishop.

Hot. Of York, is't not?

Wor. True; who bears hard
His brother's death at Bristol, the lord Scroop.
I speak not this in estimation,
As what I think might be, but what I know
Is ruminated, plotted, and set down;
And only stays but to behold the face
Of that occasion that shall bring it on.

Hot. I smell it; upon my life, it will do well.

North. Before the game's a-foot, thou still lett'st
slip.

Hot. Why, it cannot choose but be a noble
plot:—
And then the power of Scotland, and of York,—
To join with Mortimer, ha?

Wor.   And so they shall.

Hot. In faith, it is exceedingly well aim'd.

Wor. And 't is no little reason bids us speed,
To save our heads by raising of a head:
For, bear ourselves as even as we can,

The king will always think him in our debt;
And think we think ourselves unsatisfied,
Till he hath found a time to pay us home.
And see already, how he doth begin
To make us strangers to his looks of love.

   Hot. He does, he does; we'll be reveng'd on
him.

   Wor. Cousin, farewell:—No further go in this,
Than I by letters shall direct your course.
When time is ripe, (which will be suddenly,)

I'll steal to Glendower, and lord Mortimer;
Where you and Douglas, and our powers at once,
(As I will fashion it,) shall happily meet,
To bear our fortunes in our own strong arms,
Which now we hold at much uncertainty.

   North. Farewell, good brother; we shall thrive
     I trust.

   Hot. Uncle, adieu:—O, let the hours be short,
Till fields, and blows, and groans applaud our
    sport!   [*Exeunt.*

ACT II.

SCENE I.—Rochester. *An Inn Yard.*

Enter a Carrier, with a Lantern in his hand.

   1st Car. Heigh ho! An't be not four by the
day, I'll be hang'd: Charles' wain is over the
new chimney, and yet our horse not packed.
What, ostler!

   Ost. [*Within.*] Anon, anon.

   1st Car. I pr'ythee, Tom, beat Cut's saddle, put
a few flocks in the point; the poor jade is wrung
in the withers out of all cess.

Enter another Carrier.

   2nd Car. Pease and beans are as dank here as
a dog, and that is the next way to give poor jades
the bots: this house is turned upside down, since
Robin ostler died.

   1st Car. Poor fellow! never joyed since the price
of oats rose; it was the death of him.

   2nd Car. I think, this be the most villanous
house in all London road for fleas: I am stung
like a tench.

   1st Car. Like a tench! by the mass, there is
ne'er a king in Christendom could be better bit
than I have been since the first cock.

   2nd Car. Why, they will allow us ne'er a jor-
den, and then we leak in your chimney; and your
chamber-lie breeds fleas like a loach.

   1st Car. What, ostler! come away and be
hanged, come away.

   2nd Car. I have a gammon of bacon, and two
razes of ginger, to be delivered as far as Charing-
cross.

   1st Car. 'Odsbody! the turkeys in my pannier
are quite starved.—What, ostler!—A plague on
thee! hast thou never an eye in thy head? canst
not hear? An't were not as good a deed as
drink, to break the pate of thee, I am a very
villain.—Come, and be hanged:—Hast no faith
in thee?

Enter GADSHILL.

   Gads. Good morrow, carriers. What's
o'clock?

   1st Car. I think it be two o'clock.

   Gads. I pr'ythee, lend me thy lantern, to see
my gelding in the stable.

   1st Car. Nay, soft, I pray ye; I know a trick
worth two of that, i' faith.

   Gads. I pr'ythee, lend me thine.

   2nd Car. Ay, when? canst tell?—Lend me thy
lantern, quoth a'?—marry, I'll see thee hanged
first.

   Gads. Sirrah carrier, what time do you mean
to come to London?

   2nd Car. Time enough to go to bed with a
candle. I warrant thee.—Come, neighbour Mugs,
we'll call up the gentlemen; they will along with
company, for they have great charge.

              [*Exeunt Carriers.*

   Gads. What, ho! chamberlain!

   Cham. [*Within.*] At hand, quoth pick-purse.

   Gads. That's even as fair as—at hand, quoth
the chamberlain: for thou variest no more from
picking of purses, than giving direction doth from
labouring; thou lay'st the plot how.

Enter Chamberlain.

Cham. Good morrow, master Gadshill. It holds current, that I told you yesternight: There's a franklin[31] in the wild of Kent, hath brought three hundred marks with him in gold: I heard him tell it to one of his company, last night at supper; a kind of auditor; one that hath abundance of charge too, God knows what. They are up already, and call for eggs and butter: They will away presently.

Gads. Sirrah, if they meet not with saint Nicholas' clerks,[32] I'll give thee this neck.

Cham. No, I'll none of it: I pr'ythee, keep that for the hangman; for, I know, thou worshipp'st saint Nicholas as truly as a man of falsehood may.

Gads. What talkest thou to me of the hangman? if I hang, I'll make a fat pair of gallows: for, if I hang, old sir John hangs with me; and, thou knowest, he's no starveling. Tut! there are other Trojans[35] that thou dreamest not of, the which, for sport sake, are content to do the profession some grace; that would, if matters should be looked into, for their own credit sake, make all whole. I am joined with no foot land-rakers, no long-staff, sixpenny strikers; none of these mad, mustachio purple-hued malt-worms;[37] but with nobility, and tranquillity; burgomasters, and great oneyers;[38] such as can hold in; such as will strike sooner than speak, and speak sooner than drink, and drink sooner than pray: And yet I lie; for they pray continually to their saint, the commonwealth: or, rather, not pray to her, put prey on her; for they ride up and down on her, and make her their boots.

Cham. What, the commonwealth their boots? will she hold out water in foul way?

Gads. She will, she will; justice hath liquored her. We steal as in a castle, cock-sure: we have the receipt of fern-seed, we walk invisible.[39]

Cham. Nay, by my faith; I think you are more beholden to the night, than to fern-seed, for your walking invisible.

Gads. Give me thy hand: thou shalt have a share in our purchase, as I am a true man.

Cham. Nay, rather let me have it, as you are a false thief.

Gads. Go to; *Homo* is a common name to all men. Bid the ostler bring my gelding out of the stable. Farewell, you muddy knave.

[*Exeunt.*

SCENE II.—*The Road by* Gadshill.

Enter PRINCE HENRY, *and* POINS; BARDOLPH *and* PETO, *at some distance.*

Poins. Come, shelter, shelter; I have removed Falstaff's horse, and he frets like a gummed velvet.

P. Hen. Stand close.

Enter FALSTAFF.

Fal. Poins! Poins and be hanged! Poins!

P. Hen. Peace, ye fat-kidneyed rascal: What a brawling dost thou keep!

Fal. Where's Poins, Hal?

P. Hen. He is walked up to the top of the hill; I'll go seek him.　　[*Pretends to seek* POINS.

Fal. I am accursed to rob in that thief's company: the rascal hath removed my horse, and tied him I know not where. If I travel but four foot by the squire further afoot, I shall break my wind. Well, I doubt not but to die a fair death for all this, if I 'scape hanging for killing that rogue. I have forsworn his company hourly any time this two-and-twenty years, and yet I am bewitched with the rogue's company. If the rascal have not given me medicines to make me love him, I'll be hanged; it could not be else; I have drank medicines.—Poins!—Hal!—a plague upon you both!—Bardolph!—Peto!—I'll starve, ere I'll rob a foot further. An 't were not as good a deed as drink, to turn true man, and leave these rogues, I am the veriest varlet that ever chewed with a tooth. Eight yards of uneven ground, is threescore and ten miles afoot with me; and the stony-hearted villains know it well enough: A plague upon 't, when thieves cannot be true to one another! [*They whistle.*] Whew!—A plague upon you all! Give me my horse, you rogues; give me my horse, and be hanged.

P. Hen. Peace, ye fat-guts! lie down; lay thine ear close to the ground, and list if thou canst hear the tread of travellers.

Fal. Have you any levers to lift me up again, being down? 'Sblood, I'll not bear mine own flesh so far afoot again, for all the coin in thy father's exchequer. What a plague mean ye to colt me thus?[40]

P. Hen. Thou liest, thou art not colted, thou art uncolted.

Fal. I pr'ythee, good prince Hal, help me to my horse; good king's son.

P. Hen. Out, you rogue! shall I be your ostler?

Fal. Go, hang thyself in thy own heir-apparent

735

garters! If I be ta'en, I'll peach for this. An I have not ballads made on you all, and sung to filthy tunes, let a cup of sack be my poison: When a jest is so forward, and afoot too,—I hate it.

Enter GADSHILL.

Gads. Stand.

Fal. So I do, against my will.

Poins. O, 't is our setter: I know his voice.

Enter BARDOLPH.

Bard. What news?

Gads. Case ye, case ye; on with your visors; there 's money of the king's coming down the hill; 't is going to the king's exchequer.

Fal. You lie, you rogue; 't is going to the king's tavern.

Gads. There 's enough to make us all.

Fal. To be hanged.

P. Hen. Sirs, you four shall front them in the narrow lane; Ned Poins and I will walk lower: if they 'scape from your encounter, then they light on us.

Peto. How many be there of them?

Gads. Some eight, or ten.

Fal. Zounds! will they not rob us?

P. Hen. What, a coward, sir John Paunch!

Fal. Indeed, I am not John of Gaunt, your grandfather; but yet no coward, Hal.

P. Hen. Well, we leave that to the proof.

Poins. Sirrah Jack, thy horse stands behind the hedge; when thou needest him, there thou shalt find him. Farewell, and stand fast.

Fal. Now cannot I strike him, if I should be hanged.

P. Hen. Ned, where are our disguises?

Poins. Here, hard by; stand close.

[*Exeunt* P. HEN. *and* POINS.

Fal. Now, my masters, happy man be his dole, say I; every man to his business.

Enter Travellers.

1st Trav. Come, neighbour; the boy shall lead our horses down the hill: we 'll walk afoot a while, and ease our legs.

Thieves. Stand.

Trav. Jesu bless us!

Fal. Strike; down with them; cut the villains' throats: Ah! whorson caterpillars! bacon-fed knaves! they hate us youth: down with them; fleece them.

1st Trav. O, we are undone, both we and ours, for ever.

Fal. Hang ye, gorbellied knaves: Are ye undone? No, ye fat chuffs; I would, your store were here! On, bacons, on! What, ye knaves? young men must live: You are grand-jurors are ye? We 'll jure ye, i' faith.

[*Exeunt* FAL. &c., *driving the Trav. out.*

Re-enter PRINCE HENRY *and* POINS.

P. Hen. The thieves have bound the true men: Now could thou and I rob the thieves, and go merrily to London, it would be argument for a week, laughter for a month, and a good jest for ever.

Poins. Stand close, I hear them coming.

Re-enter Thieves.

Fal. Come, my masters, let us share, and then to horse before day. An the prince and Poins be not two arrant cowards, there 's no equity stirring: there 's no more valour in that Poins, than in a wild duck.

P. Henry. Your money.

[*Rushing out upon them.*

Poins. Villains.

[*As they are sharing, the Prince and* POINS *set upon them.* FALSTAFF, *after a blow or two, and the rest, run away, leaving their booty behind them.*]

P. Hen. Got with much ease. Now merrily to horse:

The thieves are scatter'd, and possess'd with fear So strongly, that they dare not meet each other; Each takes his fellow for an officer.

Away, good Ned. Falstaff sweats to death, And lards the lean earth as he walks along: Wer 't not for laughing, I should pity him.

Poins. How the rogue roar'd! [*Exeunt.*

SCENE III.—Warkworth. *A Room in the Castle.*

Enter HOTSPUR, *reading a Letter.*

——"But, for mine own part, my lord, I could be well contented to be there, in respect of the love I bear your house."—He could be contented, —Why is he not then? In respect of the love he bears our house:—he shows in this, he loves his own barn better than he loves our house. Let me see some more. "The purpose you undertake is dangerous;"—Why, that 's certain; 't is dangerous to take a cold, to sleep, to drink: but I tell you, my lord fool, out of this nettle, danger, we pluck this flower, safety "The purpose you undertake.

is dangerous; the friends you have named, uncertain; the time itself unsorted; and your whole plot too light, for the counterpoise of so great an opposition."—Say you so, say you so? I say unto you again, you are a shallow, cowardly hind, and you lie. What a lack-brain is this? By the Lord, our plot is a good plot as ever was laid; our friends true and constant: a good plot, good friends, and full of expectation: an excellent plot, very good friends. What a frosty-spirited rogue is this? Why, my lord of York commends the plot, and the general course of the action. 'Zounds, an I were now by this rascal, I could brain him with his lady's fan. Is there not my father, my uncle, and myself? lord Edmund Mortimer, my lord of York, and Owen Glendower? Is there not, besides, the Douglas? Have I not all their letters, to meet me in arms by the ninth of the next month? and are they not, some of them, set forward already? What a pagan rascal is this? an infidel? Ha! you shall see now, in very sincerity of fear and cold heart, will he to the king, and lay open all our proceedings. O, I could divide myself, and go to buffets, for moving such a dish of skimmed milk with so honourable an action! Hang him! let him tell the king: We are prepared: I will set forward to-night.

Enter LADY PERCY.

How now, Kate? I must leave you within these
two hours.

Lady. O my good lord, why are you thus alone?
For what offence have I, this fortnight, been
A banish'd woman from my Harry's bed?
Tell me, sweet lord, what is 't that takes from thee
Thy stomach, pleasure, and thy golden sleep?
Why dost thou bend thine eyes upon the earth;
And start so often when thou sitt'st alone?
Why hast thou lost the fresh blood in thy cheeks;
And given my treasures, and my rights of thee,
To thick-ey'd musing, and curs'd melancholy?
In thy faint slumbers, I by thee have watch'd,
And heard thee murmur tales of iron wars:
Speak terms of manage to thy bounding steed;
Cry, "Courage!—to the field!" And thou hast
talk'd
Of sallies, and retires; of trenches, tents,
Of palisadoes, frontiers, parapets;
Of basilisks, of cannon, culverin;
Of prisoners' ransom, and of soldiers slain,
And all the 'currents of a heady fight.
Thy spirit within thee hath been so at war,

And thus hath so bestirr'd thee in thy sleep,
That beads of sweat have stood upon thy brow,
Like bubbles in a late-disturbed stream;
And in thy face strange motions have appear'd,
Such as we see when men restrain their breath
On some great sudden haste. O, what portents
are these?
Some heavy business hath my lord in hand,
And I must know it, else he loves me not.
  Hot. What, ho! is Gilliams with the packet
gone?

Enter Servant.

Serv. He is, my lord, an hour ago.
  Hot. Hath Butler brought those horses from
the sheriff?
  Serv. One horse, my lord, he brought even now.
  Hot. What horse? a roan, a crop-ear, is it
not?
  Serv. It is, my lord.
  Hot.   That roan shall be my throne.
Well, I will back him straight: O *esperance!*—
Bid Butler lead him forth into the park.
                                    [*Exit* Serv

  Lady. But hear you, my lord.
  Hot.   What say'st, my lady?
  Lady. What is it carries you away?
  Hot.   My horse,
My love, my horse.
  Lady.   Out, you mad-headed ape!
A weasel hath not such a deal of spleen,
As you are toss'd with. In faith,
I'll know your business, Harry, that I will.
I fear, my brother Mortimer doth stir
About his title; and hath sent for you,
To line his enterprise: But if you go—
  Hot. So far afoot, I shall be weary, love.
  Lady. Come, come, you paraquito, answer me
Directly to this question that I ask.
In faith, I'll break thy little finger, Harry,
An if thou wilt not tell me all things true.
  Hot. Away,
Away, you trifler!—Love!—I love thee not,
I care not for thee, Kate: this is no world,
To play with mammets, and to tilt with lips:
We must have bloody noses, and crack'd crowns,
And pass them current too.—Gods me, my
horse!—
What say'st thou, Kate? what would'st thou have
with me?
  Lady. Do you not love me? do you not, indeed?
Well, do not then; for, since you love me not,

I will not love myself. Do you not love me?
Nay, tell me, if you speak in jest, or no.

Hot. Come, wilt thou see me ride?
And when I am o' horse-back, I will swear
love thee infinitely. But hark you, Kate;
I must not have you henceforth question me
Whither I go, nor reason whereabout:
Whither I must, I must; and, to conclude,
This evening must I leave you, gentle Kate.
I know you wise; but yet no further wise,
Than Harry Percy's wife: constant you are;
But yet a woman: and for secrecy,
No lady closer; for I well believe,
Thou wilt not utter what thou dost not know;
And so far will I trust thee, gentle Kate!

Lady. How! so far?

Hot. Not an inch farther. But hark you,
Kate!
Whither I go, thither shall you go too;
To-day will I set forth, to-morrow you.—
Will this content you, Kate?

Lady.   It must, of force.
[*Exeunt.*

SCENE IV.—Eastcheap. *A Room in the* Boar's
Head *Tavern.*

Enter PRINCE HENRY *and* POINS.

P. Hen. Ned, pr'ythee, come out of that fat
room, and lend me thy hand to laugh a little.

Poins. Where hast been, Hal?

P. Hen. With three or four loggerheads,
amongst three or four score hogsheads. I have
sounded the very bass-string of humility. Sirrah,
I am sworn brother to a leash of drawers; and
can call them all by their Christian names, as—
Tom, Dick, and Francis. They take it already
upon their salvation, that, though I be but prince
of Wales, yet I am the king of courtesy; and tell
me flatly I am no proud Jack, like Falstaff; but
a Corinthian, a lad of mettle, a good boy,—by the
Lord, so they call me; and when I am king of
England, I shall command all the good lads in
Eastcheap. They call—drinking deep, dying
scarlet; and when you breathe in your watering,
they cry—hem! and bid you play it off.—To
conclude, I am so good a proficient in one quarter
of an hour, that I can drink with any tinker in
his own language during my life. I tell thee,
Ned, thou hast lost much honour, that thou wert
not with me in this action. But, sweet Ned,—to
sweeten which name of Ned, I give thee this pen-

758

nyworth of sugar, clapped even now in my hand
by an under-skinker; one that never spake other
English in his life, than—"Eight shillings and
sixpence," and—"You are welcome;" with this
shrill addition,—"Anon, anon, sir! Score a pint
of bastard in the Half-moon," or so. But, Ned,
to drive away the time till Falstaff come, I pr'y-
thee, do thou stand in some by-room, while I
question my puny drawer, to what end he gave me
the sugar; and do thou never leave calling—
Francis, that his tale to me may be nothing but—
anon. Step aside, and I'll show thee a precedent.

Poins. Francis!

P. Hen. Thou art perfect.

Poins. Francis!   [*Exit* POINS.

Enter FRANCIS.

Fran. Anon, anon, sir.—Look down into the
Pomegranate, Ralph.

P. Hen. Come hither, Francis.

Fran. My lord.

P. Hen. How long hast thou to serve, Francis?

Fran. Forsooth, five year, and as much as to—

Poins. [*Within.*] Francis!

Fran. Anon, anon, sir.

P. Hen. Five years! by'rlady, a long lease for
the clinking of pewter. But, Francis, darest thou
be so valiant, as to play the coward with thy
indenture, and to shew it a fair pair of heels, and
run from it?

Fran. O lord, sir! I'll be sworn upon all the
books in England, I could find in my heart—

Poins. [*Within.*] Francis!

Fran. Anon, anon, sir.

P. Hen. How old art thou, Francis?

Fran. Let me see,—About Michaelmas next I
shall be—

Poins. [*Within.*] Francis!

Fran. Anon, sir.—Pray you, stay a little, my
lord.

P. Hen. Nay, but hark you, Francis: For the
sugar thou gavest me,—'t was a pennyworth, was 't
not?

Fran. O lord, sir! I would, it had been two.

P. Hen. I will give thee for it a thousand pound:
ask me when thou wilt, and thou shalt have it.

Poins. [*Within.*] Francis!

Fran. Anon, anon.

P. Hen. Anon, Francis? No, Francis: but to-
morrow, Francis; or, Francis, on Thursday; or
indeed, Francis, when thou wilt. But, Francis,—

Fran. My lord?

P. Hen. Wilt thou rob this leathern-jerkin, crystal-button, nott-pated, agate-ring, puke-stocking, caddis-garter,[23] smooth-tongue, Spanish-pouch,—

Fran. O lord, sir, who do you mean?

P. Hen. Why then, your brown bastard[24] is your only drink: for, look you, Francis, your white canvas doublet will sully: in Barbary, sir, it cannot come to so much.

Fran. What, sir?

Poins. [*Within.*] Francis!

P. Hen. Away, you rogue: Dost thou not hear them call?

[*Here they both call him; the Drawer stands amazed, not knowing which way to go.*]

Enter Vintner.

Vint. What! stand'st thou still, and hear'st such a calling? Look to the guests within. [*Exit* Fran.] My lord, old sir John, with half a dozen more, are at the door: Shall I let them in?

P. Hen. Let them alone awhile, and then open the door. [*Exit Vint.*] Poins!

Re-enter Poins.

Poins. Anon, anon, sir.

P. Hen. Sirrah, Falstaff and the rest of the thieves are at the door: Shall we be merry?

Poins. As merry as crickets, my lad. But hark ye: What cunning match have you made with this jest of the drawer? come, what's the issue?

P. Hen. I am now of all humours, that have show'd themselves humours, since the old days of goodman Adam, to the pupil age of this present twelve o'clock at midnight. [*Re-enter* Fran. *with Wine.*] What's o'clock, Francis?

Fran. Anon, anon, sir.

P. Hen. That ever this fellow should have fewer words than a parrot, and yet the son of a woman!— His industry is—up-stairs, and down-stairs; his eloquence, the parcel of a reckoning. I am not yet of Percy's mind, the Hotspur of the north; he that kills me some six or seven dozen of Scots at a breakfast, washes his hands, and says to his wife,—"Fye upon this quiet life! I want work." "O my sweet Harry," says she, "how many hast thou killed to-day?" "Give my roan horse a drench," says he; and answers, "Some fourteen," an hour after; "a trifle, a trifle." I pr'ythee, call in Falstaff; I'll play Percy, and that damned brawn shall play dame Mortimer his wife. "Rivo," says the drunkard.[25] Call in ribs, call in tallow.

Enter Falstaff, Gadshill, Bardolph, *and* Peto.

Poins. Welcome, Jack. Where hast thou been?

Fal. A plague of all cowards, I say, and a vengeance too! marry, and amen!—Give me a cup of sack, boy.—Ere I lead this life long, I'll sew nether-stocks, and mend them, and foot them too. A plague of all cowards!—Give me a cup of sack, rogue.—Is there no virtue extant? [*He drinks.*]

P. Hen. Didst thou never see Titan kiss a dish of butter? pitiful-hearted Titan, that melted at the sweet tale of the sun?[26] if thou didst, then behold that compound.

Fal. You rogue, here's lime in this sack too: There is nothing but roguery to be found in villanous man: Yet a coward is worse than a cup of sack with lime in it; a villanous coward.—Go thy ways, old Jack; die when thou wilt, if manhood, good manhood, be not forgot upon the face of the earth, then am I a shotten herring. There live not three good men unhanged in England; and one of them is fat, and grows old: God help the while! a bad world, I say! I would, I were a weaver; I could sing psalms or any thing.[27] A plague of all cowards, I say still.

P. Hen. How now, wool-sack? what mutter you?

Fal. A king's son! If I do not beat thee out of thy kingdom with a dagger of lath, and drive all thy subjects afore thee like a flock of wild geese, I'll never wear hair on my face more. You prince of Wales?

P. Hen. Why, you whoreson round man! what's the matter?

Fal. Are you not a coward? answer me to that; and Poins there?

Poins. 'Zounds, ye fat paunch, and ye call me coward, I'll stab thee.

Fal. I call thee coward! I'll see thee damned ere I call thee coward: but I would give a thousand pound, I could run as fast as thou canst. You are straight enough in the shoulders, you care not who sees your back: Call you that backing of your friends? A plague upon such backing! give me them that will face me.—Give me a cup of sack:—I am a rogue, if I drunk to-day.

P. Hen. O villain! thy lips are scarce wiped since thou drunk'st last.

Fal. All's one for that. A plague of all cowards, still say I. [*He drinks.*]

P. Hen. What's the matter?

Fal. What's the matter? there be four of us here have ta'en a thousand pounds this morning.

P. Hen. Where is it, Jack? where is it?

Fal. Where is it? taken from us it is: a hundred upon poor four us.

P. Hen. What, a hundred, man?

Fal. I am a rogue, if I were not at half-sword with a dozen of them two hours together. I have scap'd by miracle. I am eight times thrust through the doublet; four, through the hose; my buckler cut through and through; my sword hacked like a hand-saw, *ecce signum.* I never dealt better since I was a man: all would not do. A plague of all cowards!—Let them speak: if they speak more or less than truth, they are villains, and the sons of darkness.

P. Hen. Speak, sirs; how was it?

Gads. We four set upon some dozen,——

Fal. Sixteen, at least, my lord.

Gads. And bound them.

Peto. No, no, they were not bound.

Fal. You rogue, they were bound, every man of them; or I am a Jew else, an Ebrew Jew.

Gads. As we were sharing, some six or seven fresh men set upon us,——

Fal. And unbound the rest, and then come in the other.

P. Hen. What, fought ye with them all?

Fal. All? I know not what ye call, all; but if I fought not with fifty of them, I am a bunch of radish: if there were not two or three and fifty upon poor old Jack, then am I no two-legged creature.

Poins. Pray God, you have not murdered some of them.

Fal. Nay, that's past praying for: for I have peppered two of them: two, I am sure, I have paid; two rogues in buckram suits. I tell thee what, Hal,—if I tell thee a lie, spit in my face, call me horse. Thou knowest my old ward;—here I lay, and thus I bore my point. Four rogues in buckram let drive at me,——

P. Hen. What, four? thou said'st but two, even now.

Fal. Four, Hal; I told thee four.

Poins. Ay, ay, he said four.

Fal. These four came all a-front, and mainly thrust at me. I made me no more ado, but took all their seven points in my target, thus.

P. Hen. Seven? why, there were but four even now.

Fal. In buckram?

Poins. Ay, four, in buckram suits.

Fal. Seven, by these hilts, or I am a villain else.

P. Hen. Pr'ythee, let him alone; we shall have more anon.

Fal. Dost thou hear me, Hal?

P. Hen. Ay, and mark thee too, Jack.

Fal. Do so, for it is worth the listening to. These nine in buckram, that I told thee of,——

P. Hen. So, two more already.

Fal. Their points being broken,——

Poins. Down fell their hose.

Fal. Began to give me ground: but I followed me close, came in foot and hand; and, with a thought, seven of the eleven I paid.

P. Hen. O monstrous! eleven buckram men grown out of two!

Fal. But, as the devil would have it, three misbegotten knaves, in Kendal green, came at my back, and let drive at me;—for it was so dark, Hal, that thou coul'st not see thy hand.

P. Hen. These lies are like the father that begets them; gross as a mountain, open, palpable. Why, thou clay-brained guts; thou knotty-pated fool; thou whoreson, obscene, greasy tallow keech,"——

Fal. What, art thou mad? art thou mad? is not the truth, the truth?

P. Hen. Why, how could'st thou know these men in Kendal green, when it was so dark thou could'st not see thy hand? come tell us your reason: What sayest thou to this?

Poins. Come, your reason, Jack, your reason.

Fal. What, upon compulsion? No; were I at the strappado, or all the racks in the world, I would not tell you on compulsion. Give you a reason on compulsion! if reasons were as plenty as blackberries, I would give no man a reason upon compulsion, I.

P. Hen. I'll be no longer guilty of this sin, this sanguine coward, this bed-presser, this horse-back-breaker, this huge hill of flesh;——

Fal. Away, you starveling, you elf-skin," you dried neats-tongue, bull's pizzle, you stock-fish,—O, for breath to utter what is like thee!—you tailor's yard, you sheath, you bow-case, you vile standing tuck;——

P. Hen. Well, breathe awhile, and then to it again: and when thou hast tired thyself in base comparisons, hear me speak but this.

Poins. Mark, Jack.

P. Hen. We two saw you four set on four

you bound them, and were masters of their wealth.——Mark now, how plain a tale shall put you down.——Then did we two set on you four: and, with a word out-faced you from your prize, and have it; yea, and can show it you here in the house:—and, Falstaff, you carried your guts away as nimbly, with as quick dexterity, and roared for mercy, and still ran and roared, as ever I heard bull-calf. What a slave art thou, to hack thy sword as thou hast done; and then say, it was in fight! What trick, what device, what starting-hole, canst thou now find out, to hide thee from this open and apparent shame?

Poins. Come, let's hear, Jack: What trick hast thou now?

Fal. By the Lord, I knew ye, as well as he that made ye. Why, hear ye, my masters: Was it for me to kill the heir apparent? Should I turn upon the true prince? Why, thou knowest, I am as valiant as Hercules: but beware instinct; the lion will not touch the true prince. Instinct is a great matter; I was a coward on instinct. I shall think the better of myself and thee, during my life; I, for a valiant lion, and thou for a true prince. But, by the Lord, lads, I am glad you have the money.——Hostess, clap to the doors; watch to-night, pray to-morrow.—Gallants, lads, boys, hearts of gold, All the titles of good fellowship come to you! What, shall we be merry? shall we have a play extempore?

P. Hen. Content;—and the argument shall be, thy running away.

Fal. Ah! no more of that, Hal, an thou lovest me.

Enter Hostess.

Host. My lord the prince,——

P. Hen. How now, my lady the hostess? what say'st thou to me?

Host. Marry, my lord, there is a nobleman of the court at door, would speak with you: he says, he comes from your father.

P. Hen. Give him as much as will make him a royal man," and send him back again to my mother.

Fal. What manner of man is he?

Host. An old man.

Fal. What doth gravity out of his bed at midnight?—Shall I give him his answer?

P. Hen. Pr'ythee, do, Jack.

Fal. 'Faith, and I'll send him packing. [*Exit.*

P. Hen. Now, sirs; by'r lady, you fought fair;

—so did you, Peto;—so did you, Bardolph: you are lions too, you ran away upon instinct, you will not touch the true prince; no,—fie!

Bard. 'Faith, I ran when I saw others run.

P. Hen. Tell me now in earnest, How came Falstaff's sword so hacked?

Peto. Why, he hacked it with his dagger; and said, he would swear truth out of England, but he would make you believe it was done in fight; and persuaded us to do the like.

Bard. Yea, and to tickle our noses with spear-grass, to make them bleed; and then to beslubber our garments with it, and to swear it was the blood of true men. I did that I did not this seven year before, I blushed to hear his monstrous devices.

P. Hen. O villain, thou stolest a cup of sack eighteen years ago, and wert taken with the manner, and ever since thou hast blushed extempore: Thou hadst fire and sword on thy side, and yet thou ran'st away: What instinct hadst thou for it?

Bard. My lord, do you see these meteors? do you behold these exhalations?

P. Hen. I do.

Bard. What think you they portend?

P. Hen. Hot livers and cold purses.

Bard. Choler, my lord, if rightly taken.

P. Hen. No, if rightly taken, halter.

Re-enter FALSTAFF.

Here comes lean Jack, here comes bare-bone How now, my sweet creature of bombast! How long is't ago, Jack, since thou sawest thine own knee?

Fal. My own knee? when I was about thy years, Hal, I was not an eagle's talon in the waist; I could have crept into any alderman's thumb-ring. A plague of sighing and grief! it blows a man up like a bladder. There's villanous news abroad: here was sir John Bracy from your father; you must to the court in the morning. That same mad fellow of the north, Percy; and he of Wales, that gave Amaimon the bastinado, and made Lucifer cuckold, and swore the devil his true liegeman upon the cross of a Welsh hook,"—What, a plague, call you him?——

Poins. O, Glendower.

Fal. Owen, Owen; the same;—and his son-in-law, Mortimer; and old Northumberland; and that sprightly Scot of Scots, Douglas, that runs o' horse-back up a hill perpendicular.

P. Hen. He that rides at high speed, and with his pistol kills a sparrow flying.

Fal. You have hit it.

P. Hen. So did he never the sparrow.

Fal. Well, that rascal hath good mettle in him; he will not run.

P. Hen. Why, what a rascal art thou then, to praise him so for running?

Fal. O' horseback, ye cuckoo! but, afoot, he will not budge a foot.

P. Hen. Yes, Jack, upon instinct.

Fal. I grant ye, upon instinct. Well, he is there too, and one Mordake, and a thousand blue-caps more; Worcester is stolen away to-night; thy father's beard is turned white with the news; you may buy land now as cheap as stinking mackerel.

P. Hen. Why then, 't is like, if there come a hot June, and this civil buffeting hold, we shall buy maidenheads as they buy hob-nails, by the hundreds.

Fal. By the mass, lad, thou sayest true; it is like, we shall have good trading that way.—But, tell me, Hal, art thou not horribly afeard? thou being heir apparent, could the world pick thee out three such enemies again, as that fiend Douglas, that spirit Percy, and that devil Glendower? Art thou not horribly afraid? doth not thy blood thrill at it?

P. Hen. Not a whit, i' faith; I lack some of thy instinct.

Fal. Well, thou wilt be horribly chid to-morrow, when thou comest to thy father: if thou love me, practise an answer.

P. Hen. Do thou stand for my father, and examine me upon the particulars of my life.

Fal. Shall I! content:—This chair shall be my state, this dagger my sceptre, and this cushion my crown.

P. Hen. Thy state is taken for a joint-stool, thy golden sceptre for a leaden dagger, and thy precious rich crown, for a pitiful bald crown!

Fal. Well, an the fire of grace be not quite out of thee, now shalt thou be moved.—Give me a cup of sack, to make mine eyes look red, that it may be thought I have wept; for I must speak in passion, and I will do it in king Cambyses' vein.

P. Hen. Well, here is my leg.[42]

Fal. And here is my speech:—Stand aside, nobility.

Host. This is excellent sport, i' faith.

Fal. Weep not, sweet queen, for trickling tears are vain.

742

Host. O, the father, how he holds his countenance!

Fal. For God's sake, lords, convey my tristful queen,

For tears do stop the flood-gates of her eyes.

Host. O rare! he doth it as like one of these harlotry players, as I ever see.

Fal. Peace, good pint-pot; peace, good tickle-brain.—Harry, I do not only marvel where thou spendest thy time, but also how thou art accompanied: for though the camomile, the more it is trodden on, the faster it grows, yet youth, the more it is wasted, the sooner it wears. That thou art my son, I have partly thy mother's word, partly my own opinion; but chiefly, a villanous trick of thine eye, and a foolish hanging of thy nether lip, that doth warrant me. If then thou be son to me, here lies the point;—Why, being son to me, art thou so pointed at? Shall the blessed sun of heaven prove a micher, and eat black berries?[43] a question not to be asked. Shall the son of England prove a thief, and take purses? a question to be asked. There is a thing, Harry, which thou hast often heard of, and it is known to many in our land by the name of pitch: this pitch, as ancient writers do report, doth defile: so doth the company thou keepest; for, Harry, now I do not speak to thee in drink, but in tears; not in pleasure, but in passion; not in words only, but in woes also;—And yet there is a virtuous man, whom I have often noted in thy company, but I know not his name.

P. Hen. What manner of man, an it like your majesty?

Fal. A good portly man, i' faith, and a corpulent; of a cheerful look, a pleasing eye, and a most noble carriage; and, as I think, his age some fifty, or, by'r-lady, inclining to threescore; and now I remember me, his name is Falstaff: if that man should be lewdly given, he deceiveth me; for, Harry, I see virtue in his looks. If then the tree may be known by the fruit, as the fruit by the tree, then, peremptorily I speak it, there is virtue in that Falstaff: him keep with, the rest banish. And tell me now, thou naughty varlet, tell me, where hast thou been this month?

P. Hen. Dost thou speak like a king? Do thou stand for me, and I'll play my father.

Fal. Depose me? if thou dost it half so gravely, so majestically, both in word and matter, hang me up by the heels for a rabbit-sucker, or a poulter's hare.[44]

P. Hen. Well, here I am set.

Fal. And here I stand :—judge, my masters.

P. Hen. Now, Harry ; whence come you ?

Fal. My noble lord, from Eastcheap.

P. Hen. The complaints I hear of thee are grievous.

Fal. 'Sblood, my lord, they are false :—nay, I 'll tickle ye for a young prince, i' faith.

P. Hen. Swearest thou, ungracious boy ? henceforth ne'er look on me. Thou art violently carried away from grace : there is a devil haunts thee in the likeness of a fat old man : a tun of man is thy companion. Why dost thou converse with that trunk of humours, that bolting-hutch⁴⁵ of beastliness, that swoln parcel of dropsies, that huge bombard of sack, that stuffed cloak-bag of guts, that roasted Manningtree ox⁴⁶ with the pudding in his belly, that reverend vice, that grey iniquity, that father ruffian, that vanity in years ? Wherein is he good, but to taste sack and drink it ? wherein neat and cleanly, but to carve a capon and eat it ? wherein cunning, but in craft ? wherein crafty, but in villany ? wherein villanous, but in all things ? wherein worthy, but in nothing ?

Fal. I would, your grace would take me with you : Whom means your grace ?

P. Hen. That villanous abominable misleader of youth, Falstaff, that old white-bearded Satan.

Fal. My lord, the man I know.

P. Hen. I know thou dost.

Fal. But to say, I know more harm in him than in myself, were to say more than I know. That he is old, (the more the pity,) his white hairs do witness it ; but that he is (saving your reverence,) a whoremaster, that I utterly deny. If sack and sugar be a fault, God help the wicked ! If to be old and merry be a sin, then many an old host that I know, is damned : if to be fat be to be hated, then Pharaoh's lean kine are to be loved. No, my good lord ; banish Peto, banish Bardolph, banish Poins : but for sweet Jack Falstaff, kind Jack Falstaff, true Jack Falstaff, valiant Jack Falstaff, and therefore more valiant, being as he is, old Jack Fal-staff, banish not him thy Harry's company ; banish not him thy Harry's company ; banish plump Jack, and banish all the world.

P. Hen. I do, I will.　　[*A knocking heard.*

[*Exeunt Hostess, Fran., and Bard.*

Re-enter BARDOLPH, *running.*

Bard. O, my lord, my lord ; the sheriff, with a most monstrous watch, is at the door.

Fal. Out, you rogue : play out the play : I have much to say in the behalf of that Falstaff.

Re-enter Hostess, hastily.

Host. O Jesu, my lord, my lord !——

Fal. Heigh, heigh ! the devil rides upon a fiddle-stick : What 's the matter ?

Host. The sheriff and all the watch are at the door : they are come to search the house : Shall I let them in ?

Fal. Dost thou hear, Hal ? never call a true piece of gold, a counterfeit ; thou art essentially mad, without seeming so.

P. Hen. And thou a natural coward, without instinct.

Fal. I deny your *major*: if you will deny the sheriff, so ; if not, let him enter : if I become not a cart as well as another man, a plague on my bringing up ! I hope, I shall as soon be strangled with a halter, as another.

P. Hen. Go, hide thee behind the arras ;—the rest walk up above. Now, my masters, for a true face, and good conscience.

Fal. Both which I have had : but their date is out, and therefore I 'll hide me.

[*Exeunt all but the* PRINCE *and* POINS

P. Hen. Call in the sheriff.——

Enter Sheriff and Carrier.

Now, master sheriff ; what 's your will with me ?

Sher. First, pardon me, my lord. A hue and cry

Hath follow'd certain men unto this house.

P. Hen. What men ?

Sher. One of them is well known, my gracious lord ;

A gross fat man.

Car.　　　　As fat as butter.

P. Hen. The man, I do assure you, is not here

For I myself at this time have employ'd him.

And, sheriff, I will engage my word to thee,

That I will, by to-morrow dinner-time,

Send him to answer thee, or any man,

For any thing he shall be charg'd withal :

And so let me entreat you leave the house.

Sher. I will, my lord : There are two gentlemen

Have in this robbery lost three hundred marks.

P. Hen. It may be so : if he have robb'd these men,

He shall be answerable ; and so, farewell.

Sher. Good night, my noble lord.

P. Hen. I think it is good morrow : Is it not ?

743

Sher. Indeed, my lord, I think it be two o'clock.
[*Exeunt Sher. and Car.*
P. Hen. This oily rascal is known as well as
Paul's. Go, call him forth.
Poins. Falstaff!—fast asleep behind the arras,
and snorting like a horse.
P. Hen. Hark, how hard he fetches breath:
Search his pockets. [*Poins searches.*] What hast
thou found?
Poins. Nothing but papers, my lord.
P. Hen. Let's see what they be: read them.
Poins. Item, A capon, 2*s.* 2*d.*
Item, Sauce, 4*d.*
Item, Sack, two gallons, 5*s.* 8*d.*

Item, Anchovies, and sack after supper, 2*s.* 6*d.*
Item, Bread, a halfpenny.
P. Hen. O monstrous! but one half-pennyworth
of bread to this intolerable deal of sack!—What
there is else, keep close; we'll read it at more
advantage: there let him sleep till day. I'll to
the court in the morning: we must all to the wars,
and thy place shall be honourable. I'll procure
this fat rogue a charge of foot; and, I know, his
death will be a march of twelve-score. The money
shall be paid back again with advantage. Be
with me betimes in the morning; and so good
morrow, Poins.
Poins. Good morrow, good my lord. [*Exeunt.*

ACT III.

SCENE I.—Bangor. *A Room in the Archdeacon's
House.*

Enter HOTSPUR, WORCESTER, MORTIMER, *and*
GLENDOWER.

Mort. These promises are fair, the parties sure,
And our induction full of prosperous hope.
Hot. Lord Mortimer,—and cousin Glendower,—
Will you sit down?——
And, uncle Worcester:—A plague upon it!
I have forgot the map.
Glend.   No, here it is.
Sit, cousin Percy; sit, good cousin Hotspur:
For by that name as oft as Lancaster
Doth speak of you, his cheek looks pale; and,
with
A rising sigh, he wisheth you in heaven.
Hot. And you in hell, as often as he hears
Owen Glendower spoken of.
Glend. I cannot blame him: at my nativity,
The front of heaven was full of fiery shapes,
Of burning cressets; and, at my birth,
The frame and huge foundation of the earth
Shak'd like a coward.
Hot.   Why, so it would have done
At the same season, if your mother's cat had
But kitten'd, though yourself had ne'er been born.
Glend. I say, the earth did shake when I was
born.
Hot. And I say, the earth was not of my mind,

If you suppose, as fearing you it shook.
Glend. The heavens were all on fire, the earth
did tremble.
Hot. O, then the earth shook to see the heavens
on fire,
And not in fear of your nativity.
Diseased nature oftentimes breaks forth
In strange eruptions: oft the teeming earth
Is with a kind of colic pinch'd and vex'd
By the imprisoning of unruly wind
Within her womb; which for enlargement striving,
Shakes the old beldame earth, and topples down
Steeples, and moss-grown towers. At your birth,
Our grandam earth, having this distemperature,
In passion shook.
Glend.   Cousin, of many men
I do not bear these crossings. Give me leave
To tell you once again,—that at my birth,
The front of heaven was full of fiery shapes,
The goats ran from the mountains, and the herds
Were strangely clamorous to the frighted fields.
These signs have mark'd me extraordinary;
And all the courses of my life do show,
I am not in the roll of common men.
Where is he living,—clipp'd in with the sea
That chides the banks of England, Scotland,
Wales,——
Which calls me pupil, or hath read to me?
And bring him out, that is but woman's son,
Can trace me in the tedious ways of art,

744

And hold me pace in deep experiments.

Hot. I think, there is no man speaks better
Welsh :——

I will to dinner.

Mort. Peace, cousin Percy; you will make him
mad.

Glend. I can call spirits from the vasty deep.

Hot. Why, so can I; or so can any man :
But will they come, when you do call for them ?

Glend. Why, I can teach you, cousin, to command
The devil.

Hot. And I can teach thee, coz, to shame the
devil,
By telling truth : Tell truth, and shame the
devil.——
If thou have power to raise him, bring him hither,
And I 'll be sworn, I have power to shame him
hence.
O, while you live, tell truth, and shame the devil.

Mort. Come, come,
No more of this unprofitable chat.

Glend. Three times hath Henry Bolingbroke
made head
Against my power : thrice from the banks of Wye,
And sandy-bottom'd Severn, have I sent him,
Bootless home, and weather-beaten back.

Hot. Home without boots, and in foul weather
too !
How 'scapes he agues, in the devil's name ?

Glend. Come, here 's the map: Shall we divide
our right,
According to our three-fold order ta'en ?

Mort. The archdeacon hath divided it
Into three limits, very equally :
England, from Trent and Severn hitherto,
By south and east, is to my part assign'd :
All westward, Wales beyond the Severn shore,
And all the fertile land within that bound,
To Owen Glendower :—and, dear coz, to you
The remnant northward, lying off from Trent.
And our indentures tripartite are drawn :
Which being sealed interchangeably,
(A business that this night may execute,)
To-morrow, cousin Percy, you, and I,
And my good lord of Worcester, will set forth,
To meet your father, and the Scottish power,
As is appointed us, at Shrewsbury.
My father Glendower is not ready yet,
Nor shall we need his help these fourteen days :—
Within that space, [*To* GLEND.] you may have
drawn together

Your tenants, friends, and neighbouring gentlemen.

Glend. A shorter time shall send me to you,
lords,
And in my conduct shall your ladies come,
From whom you now must steal, and take no
leave ;
For there will be a world of water shed,
Upon the parting of your wives and you.

Hot. Methinks, my moiety, north from Burton
here,
In quantity equals not one of yours :
See, how this river comes me cranking in,
And cuts me, from the best of all my land,
A huge half moon, a monstrous cantle out.
I 'll have the current in this place damm'd up;
And here the smug and silver Trent shall run,
In a new channel, fair and evenly :
It shall not wind with such a deep indent,
To rob me of so rich a bottom here.

Glend. Not wind ? it shall, it must; you see,
it doth.

Mort. Yea,
But mark, how he bears his course, and runs me up
With like advantage on the other side ;
Gelding the opposed continent as much,
As on the other side it takes from you.

Wor. Yea, but a little charge will trench him
here,
And on this north side win this cape of land ;
And then he runs all straight and evenly.

Hot. I 'll have it so ; a little charge will do it.

Glend. I will not have it alter'd.

Hot.　　　　　　Will not you ?

Glend. No, nor you shall not.

Hot.　　　　　Who shall say me nay ?

Glend. Why, that will I.

Hot.　　　　Let me not understand you then,
Speak it in Welsh.

Glend. I can speak English, lord, as well as
you ;
For I was train'd up in the English court :
Where, being but young, I framed to the harp
Many an English ditty, lovely well,　·
And gave the tongue a helpful ornament ;
A virtue that was never seen in you.

Hot. Marry, and I'm glad of it with all my heart
I had rather be a kitten, and cry—mew,
Than one of these same metre ballad-mongers ;
I had rather hear a brazen canstick turn'd,
Or a dry wheel grate on an axle-tree;
And that would set my teeth nothing on edge,

Nothing so much as mincing poetry;
'T is like the forc'd gait of a shuffling nag.

Glend. Come, you shall have Trent turn'd.

Hot. I do not care: I 'll give thrice so much
　　land
To any well-deserving friend;
But, in the way of bargain, mark ye me,
I 'll cavil on the ninth part of a hair.
Are the indentures drawn? shall we be gone?

Glend. The moon shines fair, you may away
　　by night:
I 'll haste the writer,⁹ and, withal,
Break with your wives of your departure hence:
I am afraid, my daughter will run mad,
So much she doteth on her Mortimer.　[*Exit.*

Mort. Fye, cousin Percy! how you cross my
　　father!

Hot. I cannot choose: sometimes he angers me,
With telling me of the moldwarp and the ant,¹⁰
Of the dreamer Merlin and his prophecies;
And of a dragon and a finless fish,
A clip-wing'd griffin, and a moulten raven,
A couching lion, and a ramping cat,
And such a deal of skimble-skamble stuff
As puts me from my faith. I tell you what,—
He held me, but last night, at least nine hours,
In reckoning up the several devils' names,
That were his lackeys: I cried, humph,—and
　　well,—go to,—
But mark'd him not a word. O, he 's as tedious
As is a tired horse, a railing wife;
Worse than a smoky house:—I had rather live
With cheese and garlic, in a windmill, far,
Than feed on cates, and have him talk to me,
In any summer house in Christendom.

Mort. In faith, he is a worthy gentleman;
Exceedingly well read, and profited
In strange concealments; valiant as a lion,
And wond'rous affable; and as bountiful
As mines of India. Shall I tell you, cousin?
He holds your temper in a high respect,
And curbs himself even of his natural scope,
When you do cross his humour; 'faith, he does:
I warrant you, that man is not alive,
Might so have tempted him as you have done,
Without the taste of danger and reproof;
But do not use it oft, let me entreat you.

Wor. In faith, my lord, you are too wilful-
　　blame;¹¹
And since your coming hither have done enough
To put him quite beside his patience.
You must needs learn, lord, to amend this fault:

Though sometimes it shows greatness, courage,
　　blood,
(And that 's the dearest grace it renders you,)
Yet oftentimes it doth present harsh rage,
Defect of manners, want of government,
Pride, haughtiness, opinion, and disdain:
The least of which, haunting a nobleman,
Loseth men's hearts; and leaves behind a stain
Upon the beauty of all parts besides,
Beguiling them of commendation.

Hot. Well, I am school'd; good manners be
　　your speed!
Here come our wives, and let us take our leave.

Re-enter GLENDOWER, *with the Ladies.*

Mort. This is the deadly spite that angers me,—
My wife can speak no English, I no Welsh.

Glend. My daughter weeps; she will not part
　　with you,
She 'll be a soldier too, she 'll to the wars.

Mort. Good father, tell her,—that she, and my
　　aunt Percy,
Shall follow in your conduct speedily.

　　[GLEND. *speaks to his daughter in Welsh, and
　　she answers him in the same.*

Glend. She 's desperate here; a peevish self-
　　will'd harlotry,
One no persuasion can do good upon.

　　[LADY M. *speaks to* MORT. *in Welsh.*

Mort. I understand thy looks: that pretty Welsh
Which thou pourest down from these welling
　　heavens,
I am too perfect in; and, but for shame,
In such a parley would I answer thee.

　　[LADY M. *speaks.*

I understand thy kisses, and thou mine,
And that 's a feeling disputation:
But I will never be a truant, love,
Till I have learn'd thy language; for thy tongue
Makes Welsh as sweet as ditties highly penn'd,
Sung by a fair queen in a summer's bower,
With ravishing division, to her lute.

Glend. Nay, if you melt, then will she run mad.

　　[LADY M. *speaks again.*

Mort. O, I am ignorance itself in this.

Glend. She bids you
Upon the wanton rushes lay you down,¹²
And rest your gentle head upon her lap,
And she will sing the song that pleaseth you,
And on your eye-lids crown the god of sleep,
Charming your blood with pleasing heaviness;
Making such difference 'twixt wake and sleep,

As is the difference betwixt day and night,
The hour before the heavenly-harness'd team
Begins his golden progress in the east.
Mort. With all my heart I 'll sit, and hear her
   sing:
By that time will our book, I think, be drawn.
Glend. Do so;
And those musicians that shall play to you,
Hang in the air a thousand leagues from hence;
Yet straight they shall be here: sit, and attend.
Hot. Come, Kate, thou art perfect in lying
down: Come, quick, quick; that I may lay my
head in thy lap.
Lady P. Go, ye giddy goose.

GLENDOWER *speaks some Welsh words, and then*
the Music plays.

Hot. Now I perceive, the devil understands
   Welsh;
And 't is no marvel, he 's so humorous.
By 'r-lady, he 's a good musician.
Lady P. Then should you be nothing but mu-
sical; for you are altogether governed by humours.
Lie still, ye thief, and hear the lady sing in Welsh.
Hot. I had rather hear "Lady," my brach,
howl in Irish.
Lady P. Would'st thou have thy head broken?
Hot. No.
Lady P. Then be still.
Hot. Neither; 't is a woman's fault.
Lady P. Now God help thee!
Hot. To the Welsh lady's bed.
Lady P. What 's that?
Hot. Peace! she sings.

A Welsh Song sung by LADY M.

Hot. Come, Kate, I 'll have your song too.
Lady P. Not mine, in good sooth.
Hot. Not yours, in good sooth! 'Heart, you
wear like a comfit-maker's wife! Not you, in
good sooth; and, As true as I live; and, As God
shall mend me; and, As sure as day:
And giv'st such sarcenet surety for thy oaths,
As if thou never walk'dst further than Finsbury.
Swear me, Kate, like a lady, as thou art,
A good mouth-filling oath; and leave in sooth,
And such protest of pepper-gingerbread,
To velvet-guards, and Sunday-citizens.
Come, sing.
Lady P. I will not sing.
Hot. 'T is the next way to turn tailor, or be
redbreast teacher." An the indentures be drawn.

I 'll away within these two hours; and so come
in when ye will. [*Exit.*
Glend. Come, come, lord Mortimer; you are
   as slow,
As hot lord Percy is on fire to go.
By this our book 's drawn; we 'll but seal, and then
To horse immediately.
Mort. With all my heart. [*Exeunt.*

SCENE II. London. *A Room in the Palace.*

Enter KING HENRY, PRINCE OF WALES, *and*
Lords.

K. Hen. Lords, give us leave; the Prince of
   Wales and I,
Must have some conference: But be near at hand,
For we shall presently have need of you.—
   [*Exeunt Lords.*
I know not whether God will have it so,
For some displeasing service I have done,
That in his secret doom, out of my blood
He 'll breed revengement and a scourge for me;
But thou dost, in thy passages of life,
Make me believe,—that thou art only mark'd
For the hot vengeance and the rod of heaven,
To punish my mis-treadings. Tell me else,
Could such inordinate, and low desires,
Such poor, such bare, such lewd, such mean at-
   tempts,
Such barren pleasures, rude society,
As thou art match'd withal, and grafted to,
Accompany the greatness of thy blood,
And hold their level with thy princely heart!
P. Hen. So please your majesty, I would, I could
Quit all offences with as clear excuse,
As well as, I am doubtless, I can purge
Myself of many I am charg'd withal:
Yet such extenuation let me beg,
As, in reproof of many tales devis'd,—
Which oft the ear of greatness needs must hear,—
By smiling pick-thanks and base newsmongers,
I may, for some things true, wherein my youth
Hath faulty wander'd and irregular,
Find pardon on my true submission.
K. Hen. God pardon thee!—yet let me wonder,
   Harry,
At thy affections, which do hold a wing
Quite from the flight of all thy ancestors.
Thy place in council thou hast rudely lost,
Which by thy younger brother is supplied;
And art almost an alien to the hearts
Of all the court and princes of my blood:

The hope and expectation of thy time
Is ruin'd; and the soul of every man
Prophetically does fore-think thy fall.
Had I so lavish of my presence been,
So common-hackney'd in the eyes of men,
So stale and cheap to vulgar company;
Opinion, that did help me to the crown,
Had still kept loyal to possession;
And left me in reputeless banishment,
A fellow of no mark, nor likelihood.
By being seldom seen, I could not stir,
But, like a comet, I was wonder'd at:
That men would tell their children, "This is he;"
Others would say,—"Where? which is Boling-
broke?"
And then I stole all courtesy from heaven,
And dress'd myself in such humility,
That I did pluck allegiance from men's hearts,
Loud shouts and salutations from their mouths,
Even in the presence of the crowned king.
Thus did I keep my person fresh, and new;
My presence, like a robe pontifical,
Never seen, but wonder'd at: and so my state,
Seldom, but sumptuous, showed like a feast;
And won, by rareness, such solemnity.
The skipping king, he ambled up and down
With shallow jesters, and rash bavin wits,
Soon kindled, and soon burn'd: carded his state;
Mingled his royalty with capering fools,
Had his great name profaned with their scorns;
And gave his countenance, against his name,
To laugh at gibing boys, and stand the push
Of every beardless vain comparative:
Grew a companion to the common streets,
Enfeoff'd himself to popularity:
That being daily swallow'd by men's eyes,
They surfeited with honey; and began
To loathe the taste of sweetness, whereof a little
More than a little is by much too much.
So, when he had occasion to be seen,
He was but as the cuckoo is in June,
Heard, not regarded; seen, but with such eyes,
As, sick and blunted with community,
Afford no extraordinary gaze,
Such as is bent on sun-like majesty
When it shines seldom in admiring eyes:
But rather drows'd, and hung their eye-lids down,
Slept in his face, and render'd such aspect
As cloudy men use to their adversaries;
Being with his presence glutted, gorg'd, and full.
And in that very line, Harry, stand'st thou:
For thou hast lost thy princely privilege,
748

With vile participation; not an eye
But is a-weary of thy common sight,
Save mine, which hath desir'd to see thee more,
Which now doth that I would not have it do,
Make blind itself with foolish tenderness.

P. Hen. I shall hereafter, my thrice-gracious
lord,
Be more myself.

K. Hen.   For all the world,
As thou art to this hour, was Richard then
When I from France set foot at Ravenspurg;
And even as I was then, is Percy now.
Now by my sceptre, and my soul to boot,
He hath more worthy interest to the state,
Than thou, the shadow of succession:
For, of no right, nor colour like to right,
He doth fill fields with harness in the realm;
Turns head against the lion's armed jaws;
And, being no more in debt to years than thou,
Leads ancient lords and reverend bishops on,
To bloody battles, and to bruising arms.
What never-dying honour hath he got
Against renowned Douglas; whose high deeds,
Whose hot incursions, and great name in arms,
Holds from all soldiers chief majority,
And military title capital,
Through all the kingdoms that acknowledge
Christ?
Thrice hath this Hotspur Mars in swathing
clothes,
This infant warrior, in his enterprises
Discomfited great Douglas: ta'en him once,
Enlarged him, and made a friend of him,
To fill the mouth of deep defiance up,
And shake the peace and safety of our throne.
And what say you to this? Percy, Northumber-
land,
The archbishop's grace of York, Douglas, Morti-
mer,
Capitulate against us, and are up.
But wherefore do I tell these news to thee?
Why, Harry, do I tell thee of my foes,
Which art my near'st and dearest enemy?
Thou that art like enough,—through vassal fear,
Base inclination, and the start of spleen,——
To fight against me under Percy's pay,
To dog his heels, and court'sy at his frowns,
To show how much degenerate thou art.

P. Hen. Do not think so, you shall not find
it so;
And God forgive them, that have so much sway'd
Your majesty's good thoughts away from me!

I will redeem all this on Percy's head,
And, in the closing of some glorious day,
Be bold to tell you, that I am your son;
When I will wear a garment all of blood,
And stain my favours in a bloody mask,
Which, wash'd away, shall scour my shame with it.
And that shall be the day, whene'er it lights,
That this same child of honour and renown,
This gallant Hotspur, this all-praised knight,
And your unthought-of Harry, chance to meet:
For every honour sitting on his helm,
'Would they were multitudes; and on my head
My shames redoubled! for the time will come,
That I shall make this northern youth exchange
His glorious deeds for my indignities.
Percy is but my factor, good my lord,
To engross up glorious deeds on my behalf;
And I will call him to so strict account,
That he shall render every glory up,
Yea, even the slightest worship of his time,
Or I will tear the reckoning from his heart.
This, in the name of God, I promise here:
The which if he be pleas'd I shall perform,
I do beseech your majesty, may salve
The long-grown wounds of my intemperance:
If not, the end of life cancels all bands:
And I will die a hundred thousand deaths,
Ere break the smallest parcel of this vow.

K. Hen. A hundred thousand rebels die in
    this:—
Thou shalt have charge, and sovereign trust,
    herein.

Enter BLUNT.

How now, good Blunt? thy looks are full of speed.
    Blunt. So hath the business that I come to
    speak of.
Lord Mortimer of Scotland hath sent word,"
That Douglas, and the English rebels, met,
The eleventh of this month, at Shrewsbury:
A mighty and a fearful head they are,
If promises be kept on every hand,
As ever offer'd foul play in a state.

K. Hen. The earl of Westmoreland set forth
    to-day;
With him my son, lord John of Lancaster;
For this advertisement is five days old:—
On Wednesday next, Harry, you shall set
Forward; on Thursday, we ourselves will march:
Our meeting is Bridgnorth: and, Harry, you
Shall march through Glostershire; by which
    account,

Our business valued, some twelve days hence
Our general forces at Bridgnorth shall meet.
Our hands are full of business: let 's away;
Advantage feeds him fat, while men delay.

                    [Exeunt.

SCENE III.—Eastcheap.   *A Room in the Boar's
                  Head Tavern.*

Enter FALSTAFF *and* BARDOLPH.

Fal. Bardolph, am I not fallen away vilely
since this last action? do I not bate? do I not
dwindle? Why, my skin hangs about me like
an old lady's loose gown; I am wither'd like an
old apple-John. Well, I 'll repent, and that suddenly, while I am in some liking; I shall be out
of heart shortly, and then I shall have no strength
to repent. An I have not forgotten what the inside of a church is made of, I am a pepper-corn,
a brewer's horse: the inside of a church! Company, villanous company, hath been the spoil
of me.

Bard. Sir John, you are so fretful, you cannot
live long.

Fal. Why, there is it:—come, sing me a bawdy
song; make me merry. I was as virtuously given,
as a gentleman need to be; virtuous enough:
swore little; diced, not above seven times a week;
went to a bawdy-house, not above once in a quarter—of an hour: paid money that I borrowed,
three or four times; lived well, and in good compass: and now I live out of all order, out of all
compass.

Bard. Why, you are so fat, sir John, that you
must needs be out of all compass; out of all reasonable compass, sir John.

Fal. Do thou amend thy face, and I 'll amend
my life: Thou art our admiral, thou bearest the
lantern in the poop,—but 't is in the nose of thee;
thou art the knight of the burning lamp.

Bard. Why, sir John, my face does you no
harm.

Fal. No, I 'll be sworn; I make as good use of
it as many a man doth of a death's head, or a
memento mori: I never see thy face, but I think
upon hell-fire, and Dives that lived in purple; for
there he is in his robes, burning, burning. If
thou wert any way given to virtue, I would swear
by thy face; my oath should be, By this fire; but
thou art altogether given over; and wert indeed,
but for the light in thy face, the son of utter darkness. When thou ran'st up Gads-hill in the night

to catch my horse, if I did not think thou hadst been an *ignis fatuus*, or a ball of wildfire, there's no purchase in money. O, thou art a perpetual triumph, an everlasting bonfire-light! Thou hast saved me a thousand marks in links and torches, walking with thee in the night betwixt tavern and tavern: but the sack that thou hast drunk me, would have bought me lights as good cheap, at the dearest chandler's in Europe. I have maintained that salamander of yours with fire, any time this two-and-thirty years: Heaven reward me for it!

Bard. 'Sblood, I would my face were in your belly!

Fal. God-a-mercy! so should I be sure to be heart-burned.

Enter Hostess.

How now, dame Partlet the hen? have you inquired yet, who picked my pocket?

Host. Why, sir John! what do you think, sir John? Do you think I keep thieves in my house? I have searched, I have inquired, so has my husband, man by man, boy by boy, servant by servant: the tithe of a hair was never lost in my house before.

Fal. You lie, hostess; Bardolph was shaved, and lost many a hair: and I'll be sworn, my pocket was picked: Go to, you are a woman, go.

Host. Who I? I defy thee: I was never called so in mine own house before.

Fal. Go to, I know you well enough.

Host. No, sir John; you do not know me, sir John: I know you, sir John: you owe me money, sir John, and now you pick a quarrel to beguile me of it: I bought you a dozen of shirts to your back.

Fal. Dowlas, filthy dowlas: I have given them away to bakers' wives, and they have made bolters of them.

Host. Now, as I am a true woman, holland of eight shillings an ell. You owe money here besides, sir John, for your diet, and by-drinkings, and money lent you, four-and-twenty pound.

Fal. He had his part of it; let him pay.

Host. He? alas, he is poor; he hath nothing.

Fal. How! poor? look upon his face: What call you rich? let them coin his nose, let them coin his cheeks; I'll not pay a denier. What, will you make a younker of me? shall I not take mine ease in mine inn, but I shall have my pocket picked? I have lost a seal-ring of my grandfather's, worth forty mark.

750

Host. O Jesu! I have heard the prince tell him, I know not how oft, that that ring was copper.

Fal. How! the prince is a Jack, a sneak-cup; and, if he were here, I would cudgel him like a dog, if he would say so.

Enter PRINCE HENRY *and* POINS, *marching.* FALSTAFF *meets the Prince, playing on his truncheon, like a fife.*

Fal. How now, lad? is the wind in that door, i' faith? must we all march?

Bard. Yea, two and two, Newgate-fashion.

Host. My lord, I pray you, hear me.

P. Hen. What sayest thou, mistress Quickly? How does thy husband? I love him well, he is an honest man.

Host. Good my lord, hear me.

Fal. Pr'ythee, let her alone, and list to me.

P. Hen. What sayest thou, Jack?

Fal. The other night I fell asleep here behind the arras, and had my pocket picked: this house is turned bawdy-house, they pick pockets.

P. Hen. What didst thou lose, Jack?

Fal. Wilt thou believe me, Hal? three or four bonds of forty pound a-piece, and a seal-ring of my grandfather's.

P. Hen. A trifle, some eight-penny matter.

Host. So I told him, my lord; and I said, I heard your grace say so: And, my lord, he speaks most vilely of you, like a foul-mouthed man as he is; and said, he would cudgel you.

P. Hen. What! he did not?

Host. There's neither faith, truth, nor womanhood in me else.

Fal. There's no more faith in thee than in a stewed prune; nor no more truth in thee, than in a drawn fox; and for womanhood, maid Marian may be the deputy's wife of the ward to thee. Go, you thing, go.

Host. Say, what thing? what thing?

Fal. What thing? why, a thing to thank God on.

Host. I am no thing to thank God on, I would thou should'st know it: I am an honest man's wife: and, setting thy knighthood aside, thou art a knave to call me so.

Fal. Setting thy womanhood aside, thou art a beast to say otherwise.

Host. Say, what beast, thou knave thou?

Fal. What beast? why an otter.

P. Hen. An otter, sir John! why an otter?

Fal. Why! she's neither fish, nor flesh; a man knows not where to have her.

Host. Thou art an unjust man in saying so; thou or any man knows where to have me, thou knave thou!

P. Hen. Thou sayest true, hostess; and he slanders thee most grossly.

Host. So he doth you, my lord; and said this other day, you ought him a thousand pound.

P. Hen. Sirrah, do I owe you a thousand pound?

Fal. A thousand pound, Hal? a million: thy love is worth a million; thou owest me thy love.

Host. Nay, my lord, he called you Jack, and said, he would cudgel you.

Fal. Did I, Bardolph?

Bard. Indeed, sir John, you said so.

Fal. Yea; if he said, my ring was copper.

P. Hen. I say, 't is copper: Darest thou be as good as thy word now?

Fal. Why, Hal, thou knowest, as thou art but man, I dare: but, as thou art prince, I fear thee, as I fear the roaring of the lion's whelp.

P. Hen. And why not, as the lion?

Fal. The king himself is to be feared as the lion: Dost thou think, I'll fear thee as I fear thy father? nay, an I do, I pray God, my girdle break!

P. Hen. O, if it should, how would thy guts fall about thy knees! But, sirrah, there's no room for faith, truth, nor honesty, in this bosom of thine; it is filled up with guts, and midriff. Charge an honest woman with picking thy pocket! Why, thou whoreson, impudent, embossed rascal, if there were any thing in thy pocket but tavern-reckonings, memorandums of bawdy-houses, and one poor pennyworth of sugar-candy to make thee long-winded; if thy pocket were enriched with any other injuries but these, I am a villain. And yet you will stand to it; you will not pocket up wrong: Art thou not ashamed?

Fal. Dost thou hear, Hal? thou knowest, in the state of innocency, Adam fell; and what should poor Jack Falstaff do, in the days of villany? Thou seest, I have more flesh than another man; and therefore more frailty.——You confess then, you icked my pocket?

P. Hen. It appears so by the story.

Fal. Hostess, I forgive thee: Go, make ready breakfast; love thy husband, look to thy servants, cherish thy guests: thou shalt find me tractable to any honest reason: thou seest, I am pacified.—Still!—Nay, pr'ythee, be gone. [*Exit Hostess.*] Now, Hal, to the news at court: for the robbery, lad,—How is that answered?

P. Hen. O, my sweet beef, I must still be good angel to thee:—The money is paid back again.

Fal. O, I do not like that paying back, 't is a double labour.

P. Hen. I am good friends with my father, and may do any thing.

Fal. Rob me the exchequer the first thing thou doest, and do it with unwashed hands too.

Bard. Do, my lord.

P. Hen. I have procured thee, Jack, a charge of foot.

Fal. I would, it had been of horse. Where shall I find one that can steal well? O for a fine thief, of the age of two-and-twenty, or thereabouts! I am heinously unprovided. Well, God be thanked for these rebels, they offend none but the virtuous; I laud them, I praise them.

P. Hen. Bardolph——

Bard. My lord.

P. Hen. Go bear this letter to lord John of Lancaster,

My brother John; this to my lord of Westmoreland.—

Go, Poins, to horse, to horse; for thou, and I,

Have thirty miles to ride yet ere dinner time.——Jack,

Meet me to-morrow i' the Temple-hall

At two o'clock i' the afternoon:

There shalt thou know thy charge; and there receive

Money, and order for their furniture.

The land is burning; Percy stands on high;

And either they, or we, must lower lie.

[*Exeunt Prince, Poins, and Bard.*

Fal. Rare words! brave world!——Hostess, my breakfast; come:——

O, I could wish, this tavern were my drum. [*Exit*

ACT IV.

SCENE I.—*The Rebel Camp near* Shrewsbury.

Enter HOTSPUR, WORCESTER, *and* DOUGLAS.

Hot. Well said, my noble Scot: If speaking truth,
In this fine age, were not thought flattery,
Such attribution should the Douglas have,
As not a soldier of this season's stamp
Should go so general current through the world.
By heaven, I cannot flatter; I defy
The tongues of soothers; but a braver place
In my heart's love, hath no man than yourself:
Nay, task me to the word; approve me, lord.
Doug. Thou art the king of honour:
No man so potent breathes upon the ground,
But I will beard him.
Hot.   Do so, and 't is well:—

Enter a Messenger, *with Letters.*

What letters hast thou there?—I can but thank you.
Mess. These letters come from your father,—
Hot. Letters from him! why comes he not himself?
Mess. He cannot come, my lord; he's grievous sick.
Hot. 'Zounds! how has he the leisure to be sick,
In such a justling time? Who leads his power?
Under whose government come they along?
Mess. His letters bear his mind, not I, my lord.
Wor. I pr'ythee, tell me, doth he keep his bed?
Mess. He did, my lord, four days ere I set forth;
And at the time of my departure thence,
He was much fear'd by his physicians.
Wor. I would, the state of time had first been whole,
Ere he by sickness had been visited;
His health was never better worth than now.
Hot. Sick now! droop now! this sickness doth infect
The very life-blood of our enterprise:
'T is catching hither, even to our camp.
He writes me here,—that inward sickness—
And that his friends by deputation could not
So soon be drawn, nor did he think it meet,

752

To lay so dangerous and dear a trust
On any soul remov'd, but on his own.
Yet doth he give us bold advertisement,—
That with our small conjunction, we should on,
To see how fortune is dispos'd to us:
For, as he writes, there is no quailing now;
Because the king is certainly possess'd
Of all our purposes. What say you to it?
Wor. Your father's sickness is a maim to us.
Hot. A perilous gash, a very limb lopp'd off:—
And yet, in faith, 't is not; his present want
Seems more than we shall find it:—Were it good,
To set the exact wealth of all our states
All at one cast? to set so rich a main
On the nice hazard of one doubtful hour?
It were not good: for therein should we read
The very bottom and the soul of hope;
The very list, the very utmost bound
Of all our fortunes.
Doug.   'Faith, and so we should;
Where now remains a sweet reversion:
We may boldly spend upon the hope of what
Is to come in:
A comfort of retirement[0] lives in this.
Hot. A rendezvous, a home to fly unto,
If that the devil and mischance look big
Upon the maidenhead of our affairs.
Wor. But yet, I would your father had been here.
The quality and hair of our attempt[1]
Brooks no division: It will be thought
By some, that know not why he is away,
That wisdom, loyalty, and mere dislike
Of our proceedings, kept the earl from hence:
And think, how such an apprehension
May turn the tide of fearful faction,
And breed a kind of question in our cause:
For, well you know, we of the offering side
Must keep aloof from strict arbitrement;
And stop all sight holes, every loop, from whence
The eye of reason may pry in upon us:
This absence of your father's draws a curtain,
That shows the ignorant a kind of fear
Before not dreamt of.
Hot.   You strain too far.
I, rather, of his absence make this use;—

It lends a lustre, and more great opinion,
A larger dare to our great enterprise,
Than if the earl were here: for men must think,
If we, without his help, can make a head
To push against the kingdom; with his help,
We shall o'erturn it topsy-turvy down.—
Yet all goes well, yet all our joints are whole.

Doug. As heart can think: there is not such a
    word
Spoke of in Scotland, as this term of fear.

Enter SIR RICHARD VERNON.

Hot. My cousin Vernon! welcome, by my soul.
Ver. Pray God, my news be worth a welcome,
    lord.
The earl of Westmoreland, seven thousand strong,
Is marching hitherwards; with him, prince John.
Hot. No harm: what more?
Ver.   And further, I have learn'd,—
The king himself in person is set forth,
Or hitherwards intended speedily,
With strong and mighty preparation.
Hot. He shall be welcome too. Where is his
    son?
The nimble-footed mad-cap prince of Wales,
And his comrades, that daff'd the world aside,
And bid it pass?
Ver.   All furnish'd, all in arms,
All plum'd like estridges that wing the wind;
Bated like eagles having lately bath'd;
Glittering in golden coats, like images;
As full of spirit as the month of May,
And gorgeous as the sun at midsummer;
Wanton as youthful goats, wild as young bulls.
I saw young Harry,—with his beaver on,
His cuisses on his thighs, gallantly arm'd,—
Rise from the ground like feather'd Mercury,
And vaulted with such ease into his seat,
As if an angel dropp'd down from the clouds,
To turn and wind a fiery Pegasus,
And witch the world with noble horsemanship.
Hot. No more, no more; worse than the sun
    in March,
This praise doth nourish agues. Let them come;
They come like sacrifices in their trim,
And to the fire-ey'd maid of smoky war,
All hot, and bleeding, will we offer them:
The mailed Mars shall on his altar sit,
Up to the ears in blood. I am on fire,
To hear this rich reprisal is so nigh,
And yet not ours:—Come, let me take my horse,
Who is to bear me, like a thunderbolt,

Against the bosom of the prince of Wales:
Harry to Harry shall, hot horse to horse,
Meet, and ne'er part, till one drop down a corse.—
O, that Glendower were come!
Ver.   There is more news:
I learn'd in Worcester, as I rode along,
He cannot draw his power this fourteen days.
Doug. That's the worst tidings that I hear of
    yet.
Wor. Ay, by my faith, that bears a frosty sound.
Hot. What may the king's whole battle reach
    unto?
Ver. To thirty thousand.
Hot.   Forty let it be;
My father and Glendower being both away,
The powers of us may serve so great a day.
Come, let us make a muster speedily:
Doomsday is near; die all, die merrily.
Doug. Talk not of dying; I am out of fear
Of death, or death's hand, for this one half-year.
                                [*Exeunt.*

SCENE II.—*A public Road near* Coventry.

Enter FALSTAFF *and* BARDOLPH.

Fal. Bardolph, get thee before to Coventry,
fill me a bottle of sack; our soldiers shall march
through; we'll to Sutton-Colfield to-night.
Bard. Will you give me money, captain?
Fal. Lay out, lay out.
Bard. This bottle makes an angel.
Fal. An if it do, take it for thy labour; and if
it make twenty, take them all, I'll answer the
coinage. Bid my lieutenant Peto meet me at the
town's end.
Bard. I will, captain: farewell.   [*Exit.*
Fal. If I be not ashamed of my soldiers, I am
a soused gurnet. I have misused the king's press
damnably. I have got, in exchange of a hundred
and fifty soldiers, three hundred and odd pounds.
I press me none but good householders, yeomen's
sons; inquire me out contracted bachelors, such
as had been asked twice on the bans; such a
commodity of warm slaves, as had as lief hear
the devil as a drum; such as fear the report of a
caliver, worse than a struck fowl, or a hurt wild-
duck. I pressed me none but such toasts and
butter, with hearts in their bellies no bigger than
pins' heads, and they have bought out their services; and now my whole charge consists of ancients, corporals, lieutenants, gentlemen of companies, slaves as ragged as Lazarus in the painted

cloth, where the glutton's dogs licked his sores: and such as, indeed, were never soldiers; but discarded unjust serving men, younger sons to younger brothers, revolted tapsters, and ostlers trade-fallen; the cankers of a calm world, and a long peace; ten times more dishonourable ragged than an old faced ancient:[13] and such have I, to fill up the rooms of them that have bought out their services, that you would think, that I had a hundred and fifty tattered prodigals, lately come from swine-keeping, from eating draff and husks. A mad fellow met me on the way, and told me, I had unloaded all the gibbets, and pressed the dead bodies. No eye hath seen such scare-crows. I 'll not march through Coventry with them, that 's flat :—Nay, and the villains march wide betwixt the legs, as if they had gyves on; for, indeed, I had the most of them out of prison. There 's but a shirt and a half in all my company: and the half-shirt is two napkins, tacked together, and thrown over the shoulders like a herald's coat without sleeves; and the shirt, to say the truth, stolen from my host at Saint Albans, or the red-nose innkeeper of Daintry.[14] But that 's all one; they 'll find linen enough on every hedge.

Enter PRINCE HENRY *and* WESTMORELAND.

P. Hen. How now, blown Jack? how now, quilt?

Fal. What, Hal? How now, mad wag? what a devil dost thou in Warwickshire?—My good lord of Westmoreland, I cry you mercy; I thought, your honour had already been at Shrewsbury.

West. 'Faith, sir John, 't is more than time that I were there, and you too; but my powers are there already: The king, I can tell you, looks for us all; we must away all night.

Fal. Tut, never fear me; I am as vigilant as a cat to steal cream.

P. Hen. I think, to steal cream indeed; for thy theft hath already made thee butter. But tell me, Jack; Whose fellows are those that come after?

Fal. Mine, Hal, mine.

P. Hen. I did never see such pitiful rascals.

Fal. Tut, tut; good enough to toss; food for powder, food for powder; they 'll fill a pit, as well as better: tush, man, mortal men, mortal men.

West. Ay, but, sir John, methinks they are exceeding poor and bare; too beggarly.

Fal. 'Faith, for their poverty,—I know not where they had that; and for their bareness,—I am sure, they never learned that of me.

754

P. Hen. No, I 'll be sworn; unless you call three fingers on the ribs, bare. But, sirrah, make haste; Percy is already in the field.

Fal. What, is the king encamped?

West. He is, sir John; I fear, we shall stay too long.

Fal. Well,
To the latter end of a fray, and the beginning of
    a feast,
Fits a dull fighter, and a keen guest.   [*Exeunt.*

SCENE III.—*The Rebel Camp near* Shrewsbury.

Enter HOTSPUR, WORCESTER, DOUGLAS, *and*
        VERNON.

Hot. We 'll fight with him to-night.

Wor.   It may not be.

Doug. You give him then advantage.

Ver.   Not a whit.

Hot. Why say you so? looks he not for supply?

Ver. So do we.

Hot.   His is certain, ours is doubtful.

Wor. Good cousin, be advis'd; stir not to-
    night.

Ver. Do not, my lord.

Doug.   You do not counsel well
You speak it out of fear, and cold heart.

Ver. Do me no slander, Douglas: by my life,
(And I dare well maintain it with my life,)
If well-respected honour bid me on,
I hold as little counsel with weak fear,
As you, my lord, or any Scot that lives :—
Let it be seen to-morrow in the battle,
Which of us fears.

Doug.   Yea, or to-night.

Ver.   Content.

Hot. To-night, say I.

Ver.   Come, come, it may not be.
I wonder much, being men of such great leading,
That you foresee not what impediments
Drag back our expedition: Certain horse
Of my cousin Vernon's are not yet come up:
Your uncle Worcester's horse came but to-day;
And now their pride and mettle is a-sleep,
Their courage with hard labour tame and dull,
That not a horse is half the half himself.

Hot. So are the horses of the enemy
In general, journey-bated and brought low;
The better part of ours is full of rest.

Wor. The number of the king exceedeth ours:
For God's sake, cousin, stay, till all come in.
          [*The Trumpet sounds a parley.*

Enter SIR WALTER BLUNT.

Blunt. I come with gracious offers from the
king,
If you vouchsafe me hearing, and respect.

Hot. Welcome, sir Walter Blunt; and 'would
to God,
You were of our determination!
Some of us love you well: and even those some
Envy your great deserving, and good name;
Because you are not of our quality,
But stand against us like an enemy.

Blunt. And God defend, but still I should
stand so,
So long as, out of limit, and true rule,
You stand against anointed majesty!
But, to my charge.—The king hath sent to know
The nature of your griefs; and whereupon
You conjure from the breast of civil peace
Such bold hostility, teaching his duteous land
Audacious cruelty: If that the king
Have any way your good deserts forgot,—
Which he confesseth to be manifold,—
He bids you name your griefs; and, with all speed,
You shall have your desires, with interest;
And pardon absolute for yourself, and these,
Herein misled by your suggestion.

Hot. The king is kind; and well we know, the
king
Knows at what time to promise, when to pay.
My father, and my uncle, and myself,
Did give him that same royalty he wears;
And,—when he was not six-and-twenty strong,
Sick in the world's regard, wretched and low,
A poor unminded outlaw sneaking home,—
My father gave him welcome to the shore:
And,—when he heard him swear, and vow to God,
He came but to be duke of Lancaster,
To sue his livery,[4] and beg his peace;
With tears of innocency, and terms of zeal,—
My father, in kind heart and pity mov'd,
Swore him assistance, and perform'd it too.
Now, when the lords, and barons of the realm,
Perceiv'd Northumberland did lean to him,
The more and less came in with cap and knee;
Met him in boroughs, cities, villages;
Attended him on bridges, stood in lanes,
Laid gifts before him, proffer'd him their oaths,
Gave him their heirs; as pages follow'd him,
Even at the heels, in golden multitudes.
He presently,—as greatness knows itself,—
Steps me a little higher than his vow
Made to my father, while his blood was poor

Upon the naked shore at Ravenspurg:
And now, forsooth, takes on him to reform
Some certain edicts, and some strait decrees,
That lie too heavy on the commonwealth:
Cries out upon abuses, seems to weep
Over his country's wrongs: and, by this face,
This seeming brow of justice, did he win
The hearts of all that he did angle for;
Proceeded further; cut me off the heads
Of all the favourites, that the absent king
In deputation left behind him here,
When he was personal in the Irish war.

Blunt. Tut, I came not to hear this.

Hot. Then, to the point.—
In short time after, he depos'd the king;
Soon after that, depriv'd him of his life:
And, in the neck of that, task'd the whole state
To make that worse, suffer'd his kinsman March
(Who is, if every owner were well plac'd,
Indeed his king.) to be engag'd in Wales,
There without ransom to lie forfeited;
Disgrac'd me in my happy victories;
Sought to entrap me by intelligence;
Rated my uncle from the council-board;
In rage dismiss'd my father from the court;
Broke oath on oath, committed wrong on wrong:
And, in conclusion, drove us to seek out
This head of safety; and, withal to pry
Into his title, the which we find
Too indirect for long continuance.

Blunt. Shall I return this answer to the king?

Hot. Not so, sir Walter: we'll withdraw awhile.
Go to the king; and let there be impawn'd
Some surety for a safe return again,
And in the morning early shall mine uncle
Bring him our purposes: and so farewell.

Blunt. I would, you would accept of grace and
love.

Hot. And, may be, so we shall.

Blunt. Pray heaven, you do! [*Exeunt.*

SCENE IV.—York. *A Room in the* Archbishop's
House.

Enter the ARCHBISHOP OF YORK, *and a Gentleman.*

Arch. Hie, good sir Michael; bear this sealed
brief,
With winged haste, to the lord marshal;
This to my cousin Scroop; and all the rest
To whom they are directed: if you knew
How much they do import, you would make haste

Gent. My good lord,

I guess their tenor.

Arch.   Like enough you do.
To-morrow, good sir Michael, is a day,
Wherein the fortune of ten thousand men
Must 'bide the touch: For, sir, at Shrewsbury,
As I am truly given to understand,
The king, with mighty and quick-raised power,
Meets with lord Harry: and I fear, sir Michael,—
What with the sickness of Northumberland,
(Whose power was in the first proportion,)
And what with Owen Glendower's absence, thence,
(Who with them was a rated sinew too,
And comes not in, o'er-ruled by prophecies,)—
I fear the power of Percy is too weak
To wage an instant trial with the king.

Gent. Why, good my lord, you need not fear;
                    there's Douglas,
And Mortimer.

Arch.   No, Mortimer's not there.

Gent. But there is Mordake, Vernon, lord Harry
          Percy,

And there's my lord of Worcester: and a head
Of gallant warriors, noble gentlemen.

Arch. And so there is: but yet the king hath
                    drawn
The special head of all the land together;—
The prince of Wales, lord John of Lancaster,
The noble Westmoreland, and warlike Blunt;
And many more co-rivals, and dear men
Of estimation and command in arms.

Gent. Doubt not, my lord, they shall be well
                    oppos'd.

Arch. I hope no less, yet needful 't is to fear;
And, to prevent the worst, sir Michael, speed;
For, if lord Percy thrive not, ere the king
Dismiss his power, he means to visit us,—
For he hath heard of our confederacy,
And 't is but wisdom to make strong against him
Therefore, make haste: I must go write again
To other friends; and so farewell, sir Michael.
                    [*Exeunt severally.*

ACT V.

SCENE I.—*The* King's Camp *near* Shrewsbury.

Enter KING HENRY, PRINCE HENRY, PRINCE
JOHN OF LANCASTER, SIR WALTER BLUNT, *and*
SIR JOHN FALSTAFF.

K. Hen. How bloodily the sun begins to peer
Above yon busky hill! the day looks pale
At his distemperature.

P. Hen.   The southern wind
Doth play the trumpet to his purposes;
And, by his hollow whistling in the leaves,
Foretels a tempest, and a blustering day.

K. Hen. Then with the losers let it sympa-
                    thize;
For nothing can seem foul to those that win.—

Trumpet. Enter WORCESTER *and* VERNON.

How now, my lord of Worcester? 't is not well,
That you and I should meet upon such terms
As now we meet: You have deceiv'd our trust;
And made us doff our easy robes of peace,
To crush our old limbs in ungentle steel:
This is not well, my lord, this is not well.
What say you to 't? will you again unknit
This churlish knot of all-abhorred war?

And move in that obedient orb again,
Where you did give a fair and natural light;
And be no more an exhal'd meteor,
A prodigy of fear, and a portent
Of broached mischief to the unborn times?

Wor. Hear me, my liege:
For mine own part, I could be well content
To entertain the lag-end of my life
With quiet hours; for, I do protest,
I have not sought the day of this dislike.

K. Hen. You have not sought for it! how comes
                    it then?

Fal. Rebellion lay in his way, and he found it.

P. Hen. Peace, chewet, peace.[46]

Wor. It pleas'd your majesty, to turn your looks
Of favour, from myself, and all our house;
And yet I must remember you, my lord,
We were the first and dearest of your friends.
For you, my staff of office did I break
In Richard's time: and posted day and night
To meet you on the way, and kiss your hand,
When yet you were in place and in account
Nothing so strong and fortunate as I.
It was myself, my brother, and his son,
That brought you home, and boldly did outdare

The dangers of the time : You swore to us,—
And you did swear that oath at Doncaster,—
That you did nothing purpose 'gainst the state ;
Nor claim no further than your new-fall'n right,
The seat of Gaunt, dukedom of Lancaster :
To this we swore our aid. But, in short space.
It rain'd down fortune showering on your head ;
And such a flood of greatness fell on you,—
What with our help ; what with the absent king ;
What with the injuries of a wanton time ;
The seeming sufferances that you had borne ;
And the contrarious winds, that held the king
So long in his unlucky Irish wars,
That all in England did repute him dead,—
And, from this swarm of fair advantages,
You took occasion to be quickly woo'd
To gripe the general sway into your hand :
Forgot your oath to us at Doncaster ;
And, being fed by us, you us'd us so
As that ungentle gull, the cuckoo's bird,
Useth the sparrow : did oppress our nest :
Grew by our feeding to so great a bulk,
That even our love durst not come near your sight,
For fear of swallowing ; but with nimble wing
We were enforc'd, for safety sake, to fly
Out of your sight, and raise this present head :
Whereby we stand opposed by such means
As you yourself have forg'd against yourself,
By unkind usage, dangerous countenance,
And violation of all faith and troth
Sworn to us in your younger enterprise.

    K. Hen. These things, indeed, you have artic-
        ulated,
Proclaim'd at market-crosses, read in churches ;
To face the garment of rebellion
With some fine color, that may please the eye
Of fickle changelings, and poor discontents,
Which gape, and rub the elbow, at the news
Of hurlyburly innovation :
And never yet did insurrection want
Such water-colours, to impaint his cause ;
Nor moody beggars, starving for a time
Of pellmell havoc and confusion.

    P. Hen. In both our armies, there is many a soul
Shall pay full dearly for this encounter,
If once they join in trial. Tell your nephew,
The prince of Wales doth join with all the world
In praise of Henry Percy : By my hopes,—
This present enterprise set off his head,—
I do not think, a braver gentleman,
More active valiant, or more valiant-young,
More daring, or more bold, is now alive,

To grace this latter age with noble deeds.
For my part, I may speak it to my shame,
I have a truant been to chivalry :
And so, I hear, he doth account me too :
Yet this before my father's majesty,——
I am content, that he shall take the odds
Of his great name and estimation ;
And will, to save the blood on either side,
Try fortune with him in a single fight.

    K. Hen. And, prince of Wales, so dare we ven-
        ture thee,
Albeit, considerations infinite
Do make against it :—No, good Worcester, no,
We love our people well ; even those we love,
That are misled upon your cousin's part :
And, will they take the offer of our grace,
Both he, and they, and you, yea, every man
Shall be my friend again, and I 'll be his :
So tell your cousin, and bring me word
What he will do :—But if he will not yield,
Rebuke and dread correction wait on us,
And they shall do their office. So, be gone ;
We will not now be troubled with reply :
We offer fair, take it advisedly.

        [*Exeunt* WOR. *and* VERN

    P. Hen. It will not be accepted, on my life :
The Douglas and the Hotspur both together
Are confident against the world in arms.

    K. Hen. Hence, therefore, every leader to his
        charge ;
For, on their answer, will we set on them :
And God befriend us, as our cause is just !

        [*Exeunt* KING, BLUNT, *and* P. JOHN.]

    Fal. Hal, if thou see me down in the battle,
and bestride me, so ; 't is a point of friendship.

    P. Hen. Nothing but a colossus can do thee
that friendship. Say thy prayers, and farewell.

    Fal. I would it were bed-time, Hal, and all well.

    P. Hen. Why, thou owest God a death. [*Exit.*

    Fal. 'T is not due yet ; I would be loath to pay
him before his day. What need I be so forward
with him that calls not on me ? Well, 't is no matter : Honour pricks me on ? Yea, but how if honour prick me off when I come on ? how then ? Can
honour set to a leg ? No. Or an arm ? No. Or
take away the grief of a wound ? No. Honour
hath no skill in surgery then ? No. What is honour ?
A word. What is in that word, honour ? What
is that honour ? Air. A trim reckoning !—Who
hath it ? He that died o' Wednesday. Doth he feel
it ? No. Doth he hear it ? No. Is it insensible
then ? Yea, to the dead. But will it not live with

the living? No. Why? Detraction will not suffer
it:—therefore I'll none of it: Honour is a mere
scutcheon, and so ends my catechism. 　　[*Exit.*

SCENE II.—*The Rebel Camp.*

Enter WORCESTER *and* VERNON.

Wor. O, no, my nephew must not know, sir
　Richard,
The liberal kind offer of the king.

Ver. 'T were best, he did.

Wor. 　　　　　Then are we all undone.
It is not possible, it cannot be.
The king should keep his word in loving us;
He will suspect us still, and find a time
To punish this offence in other faults:
Suspicion shall be all stuck full of eyes:
For treason is but trusted like the fox;
Who, ne'er so tame, so cherish'd, and lock'd up,
Will have a wild trick of his ancestors.
Look how we can, or sad, or merrily,
Interpretation will misquote our looks;
And we shall feed like oxen at a stall,
The better cherish'd, still the nearer death.
My nephew's trespass may be well forgot,
It hath the excuse of youth, and heat of blood;
And an adopted name of privilege,—
A hare-brain'd Hotspur, govern'd by a spleen:
All his offences live upon my head,
And on his father's:—we did train him on;
And, his corruption being ta'en from us,
We, as the spring of all, shall pay for all.
Therefore, good cousin, let not Harry know,
In any case, the offer of the king.

Ver. Deliver what you will, I 'll say, 't is so.
Here comes your cousin.

Enter HOTSPUR *and* DOUGLAS; *and* Officers *and*
Soldiers, *behind.*

Hot. My uncle is return'd:—Deliver up
My lord of Westmoreland.—Uncle, what news?

Wor. The king will bid you battle presently.

Doug. Defy him by the lord of Westmoreland.

Hot. Lord Douglas, go you and tell him so.

Doug. Marry, and shall, and very willingly.
　　　　　　　　　　　　[*Exit.*

Wor. There is no seeming mercy in the king.

Hot. Did you beg any? God forbid!

Wor. I told him gently of our grievances,
Of his oath-breaking; which he mended thus,—
By now forswearing that he is forsworn:

He calls us rebels, traitors; and will scourge
With haughty arms this hateful name in us.

Re-enter DOUGLAS.

Doug. Arm, gentlemen; to arms! for I have
　thrown
A brave defiance in King Henry's teeth,
And Westmoreland, that was engag'd, did bear it;
Which cannot choose but bring him quickly on.

Wor. The prince of Wales stepp'd forth before
　the king,
And, nephew, challeng'd you to single fight.

Hot. O, 'would the quarrel lay upon our heads;
And that no man might draw short breath to-day,
But I, and Harry Monmouth! Tell me, tell me,
How show'd his tasking? seem'd it in contempt?

Ver. No, by my soul; I never in my life
Did hear a challenge urg'd more modestly,
Unless a brother should a brother dare
To gentle exercise and proof of arms.
He gave you all the duties of a man;
Trimm'd up your praises with a princely tongue;
Spoke your deservings like a chronicle;
Making you ever better than his praise,
By still dispraising praise, valued with you:
And, which became him like a prince indeed,
He made a blushing cital of himself;
And chid his truant youth with such a grace,
As if he master'd there a double spirit,
Of teaching, and of learning, instantly.
There did he pause: But let me tell the world,—
If he outlive the envy of this day,
England did never owe so sweet a hope,
So much misconstrued in his wantonness.

Hot. Cousin, I think, thou art enamoured
Upon his follies: never did I hear
Of any prince, so wild, at liberty:—
But, be he as he will, yet once ere night
I will embrace him with a soldier's arm,
That he shall shrink under my courtesy.——
Arm, arm, with speed:——And, fellows, soldiers,
　friends,
Better consider what you have to do,
Than I, that have not well the gift of tongue,
Can lift your blood up with persuasion.

Enter a Messenger.

Mess. My lord, here are letters for you.

Hot. I cannot read them now.—
O gentlemen, the time of life is short;
To spend that shortness basely, were too long,
If life did ride upon a dial's point,

Still ending at the arrival of an hour.
An if we live, we live to tread on kings;
If die, brave death, when princes die with us!
Now for our conscience,—the arms are fair,
When the intent of bearing them is just.

Enter another Messenger.

Mess. My lord, prepare; the king comes on
    apace.
Hot. I thank him, that he cuts me from my tale.
For I profess not talking: Only this—
Let each man do his best: and here draw I
A sword, whose temper I intend to stain
With the best blood that I can meet withal
In the adventure of this perilous day.
Now,—Esperance!—Percy!—and set on.—
Sound all the lofty instruments of war,
And by that music let us all embrace:
For, heaven to earth, some of us never shall
A second time do such a courtesy.

    [*The Trumpets sound. They embrace, and
    exeunt.*

SCENE III.—*Plain near Shrewsbury.*

*Excursions, and Parties fighting. Alarum to the
Battle. Then enter* DOUGLAS *and* BLUNT,
meeting.

Blunt. What is thy name, that in the battle thus
Thou crossest me? what honour dost thou seek
Upon my head?
Doug.   Know then, my name is Douglas;
And I do haunt thee in the battle thus,
Because some tell me that thou art a king.
Blunt. They tell thee true.
Doug. The lord of Stafford dear to-day hath
    bought
Thy likeness; for, instead of thee, king Harry,
This sword hath ended him: so shall it thee,
Unless thou yield thee as my prisoner.
Blunt. I was not born a yielder, thou proud
    Scot;
And thou shalt find a king that will revenge
Lord Stafford's death.

    [*They fight, and* BLUNT *is slain.*

Enter HOTSPUR.

Hot. O Douglas, hadst thou fought at Holme-
    don thus,
I never had triumph'd upon a Scot.
Doug. All's done, all's won; here breathless
    lies the king.

Hot. Where?
Doug. Here.
Hot. This, Douglas? no, I know this face full
    well:
A gallant knight he was, his name was Blunt;
Semblably furnish'd like the king himself.
Doug. A fool go with thy soul, whither it
    goes!
A borrow'd title hast thou bought too dear.
Why didst thou tell me that thou wert a king?
Hot. The king hath many marching in his
    coats.
Doug. Now, by my sword, I will kill all his
    coats;
I'll murder all his wardrobe, piece by piece,
Until I meet the king.
Hot.   Up, and away;
Our soldiers stand full fairly for the day. [*Exeunt.*

Other Alarums. Enter FALSTAFF.

Fal. Though I could 'scape shot-free at London
I fear the shot here; here's no scoring, but upon
the pate.—Soft! who art thou? Sir Walter Blunt
—there's honour for you: Here's no vanity!
—I am as hot as molten lead, and as heavy too:
God keep lead out of me! I need no more weight
than mine own bowels.—I have led my ragga-
muffins where they are peppered: there's but
three of my hundred and fifty left alive; and they
are for the town's end, to beg during life. But
who comes here?

Enter PRINCE HENRY.

P. Hen. What, stand'st thou idle here? lend
    me thy sword:
Many a nobleman lies stark and stiff
Under the hoofs of vaunting enemies,
Whose deaths are unreveng'd: Pr'ythee, lend thy
    sword.
Fal. O Hal, I pr'ythee, give me leave to
breathe awhile.—Turk Gregory never did such
deeds in arms, as I have done this day. I have
paid Percy, I have made him sure.
P. Hen. He is, indeed; and living to kill thee.
Lend me thy sword, I pr'ythee.
Fal. Nay, before God, Hal, if Percy be alive,
thou gett'st not my sword; but take my pistol, if
thou wilt.
P. Hen. Give it me: What, is it in the case?
Fal. Ay, Hal; 't is hot, 't is hot; there's that
will sack a city.

    [*The Prince draws out a bottle of sack.*

P. Hen. What, is 't a time to jest and dally now?   [*Throws it at him, and exit.*

Fal. Well, if Percy be alive, I 'll pierce him. If he do come in my way, so: if he do not, if I come in his, willingly, let him make a carbonado of me. I like not such grinning honour as sir Walter hath: Give me life: which if I can save, so; if not, honour comes unlooked for, and there 's an end.   [*Exit.*

SCENE IV.—*Another Part of the Field.*

Alarums. Excursions. Enter the KING, PRINCE HENRY, PRINCE JOHN, *and* WESTMORELAND.

K. Hen. I pr'ythee,
Harry, withdraw thyself; thou bleed'st too much :—
Lord John of Lancaster, go you with him.

P. John. Not I, my lord, unless I did bleed too.

P. Hen. I do beseech your majesty, make up, Lest your retirement do amaze your friends.

K. Hen. I will do so :—
My lord of Westmoreland, lead him to his tent.

West. Come, my lord, I will lead you to your tent.

P. Hen. Lead me, my lord? I do not need your help:
And heaven forbid, a shallow scratch should drive The prince of Wales from such a field as this; Where stain'd nobility lies trodden on, And rebels' arms triumph in massacres.

P. John. We breathe too long:—Come, cousin Westmoreland,
Our duty this way lies; for God's sake, come.
                    [*Exeunt* P. JOHN *and* WEST.

P. Hen. By heaven, thou hast deceiv'd me, Lancaster,
I did not think thee lord of such a spirit: Before, I lov'd thee as a brother, John; But now, I do respect thee as my soul.

K. Hen. I saw him hold lord Percy at the point, With lustier maintenance than I did look for Of such an ungrown warrior.

P. Hen.   O, this boy Lends mettle to us all!   [*Exit.*

Alarums. Enter DOUGLAS.

Doug. Another king! they grow like Hydra's heads :
I am the Douglas, fatal to all those That wear those colours on them.—What art thou,
760

That counterfeit'st the person of a king?

K. Hen. The king himself; who, Douglas, grieves at heart,
So many of his shadows thou hast met, And not the very king. I have two boys, Seek Percy, and thyself, about the field: But, seeing thou fall'st on me so luckily, I will assay thee; so defend thyself.

Doug. I fear, thou art another counterfeit; And yet, in faith, thou bear'st thee like a king: But mine, I am sure, thou art, whoe'er thou be, And thus I win thee.

                [*They fight; the King being in danger, enter* PRINCE HENRY.

P. Hen. Hold up thy head, vile Scot, or thou art like
Never to hold it up again! the spirits Of Shirley, Stafford, Blunt, are in my arms: It is the prince of Wales, that threatens thee; Who never promiseth, but he means to pay.—
                    [*They fight; Doug. flies.*
Cheerly, my lord: How fares your grace?— Sir Nicholas Gawsey hath for succour sent. And so hath Clifton; I 'll to Clifton straight.

K. Hen. Stay, and breathe a while :— Thou hast redeem'd thy lost opinion; And show'd, thou mak'st some tender of my life, In this fair rescue thou hast brought to me.

P. Hen. O heaven! they did me too much injury,
That ever said, I hearken'd for your death. If it were so, I might have let alone The insulting hand of Douglas over you; Which would have been as speedy in your end, As all the poisonous potions in the world, And sav'd the treacherous labour of your son.

K. Hen. Make up to Clifton, I 'll to sir Nicholas Gawsey.   [*Exit* K. HEN.

Enter HOTSPUR.

Hot. If I mistake not, thou art Harry Monmouth.

P. Hen. Thou speak'st as if I would deny my name.

Hot. My name is Harry Percy.

P. Hen.   Why, then I see A very valiant rebel of the name.
I am the prince of Wales; and think not, Percy, To share with me in glory any more: Two stars keep not their motion in one sphere; Nor can one England brook a double reign, Of Harry Percy, and the prince of Wales.

Hot. Nor shall it, Harry, for the hour is come
To end the one of us; and 'would to God,
Thy name in arms were now as great as mine!

P. Hen. I 'll make it greater, ere I part from
thee ·
And all the building honours on thy crest
I 'll crop, to make a garland for my head.

Hot. I can no longer brook thy vanities.
                                        [*They fight.*

Enter FALSTAFF.

Fal. Well said, Hal! to it, Hal!—Nay, you
shall find no boy's play here, I can tell you.

Enter DOUGLAS; *he fights with* FALSTAFF, *who
falls down as if he were dead, and exit* DOUG-
LAS. HOTSPUR *is wounded, and falls.*

Hot. O, Harry, thou hast robb'd me of my
youth.[31]
I better brook the loss of brittle life,
Than those proud titles thou hast won of me;
They wound my thoughts, worse than thy sword
my flesh:—
But thought 's the slave of life, and life time's fool;
And time, that takes survey of all the world,
Must have a stop. O, I could prophesy,
But that the earthy and cold hand of death
Lies on my tongue:—No, Percy, thou art dust,
And food for——   [*Dies.*

P. Hen. For worms, brave Percy: Fare thee
well, great heart!—
Ill-weav'd ambition, how much art thou shrunk!
When that this body did contain a spirit,
A kingdom for it was too small a bound;
But now, two paces of the vilest earth
Is room enough:—This earth, that bears thee
dead,
Bears not alive so stout a gentleman.
If thou wert sensible of courtesy,
I should not make so dear a show of zeal:—
But let my favours hide thy mangled face;[32]
And, even in thy behalf, I 'll thank myself
For doing these fair rites of tenderness.
Adieu, and take thy praise with thee to heaven!
Thy ignomy sleep with thee in the grave,
But not remember'd in thy epitaph!—
                            [*He sees* FAL. *on the ground.*
What! old acquaintance! could not all this flesh
Keep in a little life? Poor Jack, farewell!
I could have better spared a better man.
O, I should have a heavy miss of thee,
If I were much in love with vanity.

Death hath not struck so fat a deer to-day,
Though many dearer, in this bloody fray:—
Embowell'd will I see thee by and by;
Till then, in blood by noble Percy lie.   [*Exit*

Fal. [*Rising slowly.*] Embowelled! if thou
embowel me to-day, I 'll give you leave to powder
me, and eat me too, to-morrow. 'Sblood, 't was
time to counterfeit, or that hot termagant Scot
had paid me scot and lot too. Counterfeit? I
lie. I am no counterfeit: To die, is to be a counterfeit; for he is but the counterfeit of a man,
who hath not the life of a man: but to counterfeit dying, when a man thereby liveth, is to be no
counterfeit, but the true and perfect image of life
indeed. The better part of valour is—discretion;
in the which better part, I have saved my life.
'Zounds, I am afraid of this gunpowder Percy,
though he be dead: How, if he should counterfeit too, and rise? I am afraid, he would prove
the better counterfeit. Therefore I 'll make him
sure; yea, and I 'll swear I killed him. Why
may not he rise, as well as I? Nothing confutes
me but eyes, and nobody sees me. Therefore,
sirrah, [*Stabbing him,*] with a new wound in
your thigh, come you along with me.
                            [*Takes* HOT. *on his back.*

Re-enter PRINCE HENRY *and* PRINCE JOHN.

P. Hen. Come, brother John, full bravely hast
thou flesh'd
Thy maiden sword.

P. John.   But, soft! whom have we here?
Did you not tell me, this fat man was dead?

P. Hen. I did; I saw him dead, breathless and
bleeding
Upon the ground.——
Art thou alive? or is it phantasy
That plays upon our eyesight? I pr'ythee, speak:
We will not trust our eyes, without our ears:—
Thou art not what thou seem'st.

Fal. No, that 's certain; I am not a double
man: but if I be not Jack Falstaff, then am I a
Jack. There is Percy: [*Throwing the body down.*]
if your father will do me any honour, so; if not,
let him kill the next Percy himself. I look to be
either earl or duke, I can assure you.

P. Hen. Why, Percy I killed myself, and saw
thee dead.

Fal. Didst thou?—Lord, lord, how this world
is given to lying!—I grant you I was down, and
out of breath; and so was he: but we rose both
at an instant, and fought a long hour by Shrews-
                                                    761

bury clock. If I may be believed, so; if not, let them, that should reward valour, bear the sin upon their own heads. I 'll take it upon my death, I gave him this wound in the thigh: if the man were alive, and would deny it, I would make him eat a piece of my sword.

P. John. This is the strangest tale that e'er I heard.

P. Hen. This is the strangest fellow, brother John.——

Come, bring your luggage nobly on your back: For my part, if a lie may do thee grace, I 'll gild it with the happiest terms I have.

[*A retreat is sounded.*

The trumpet sounds retreat, the day is ours. Come, brother, let 's to the highest of the field, To see what friends are living, who are dead.

[*Exeunt* P. HEN. *and* P. JOHN.

Ful. I 'll follow, as they say, for reward. He that rewards me, God reward him! If I do grow great, I 'll grow less; for I 'll purge, and leave sack, and live cleanly, as a nobleman should do.

[*Exit, bearing off the Body.*

SCENE V.—*Another part of the Field.*

The Trumpets sound.   Enter KING HENRY, PRINCE HENRY, PRINCE JOHN, WESTMORE-LAND, *and Others, with* WORCESTER *and* VER-NON, *prisoners.*

K. Hen. Thus ever did rebellion find rebuke,— Ill-spirited Worcester! did we not send grace, Pardon, and terms of love to all of you? And would'st thou turn our offers contrary? Misuse the tenor of thy kinsman's trust? Three knights upon our party slain to-day, A noble earl, and many a creature else, Had been alive this hour, If, like a Christian, thou hadst truly borne Betwixt our armies true intelligence.

752

Wor. What I have done, my safety urg'd me to; And I embrace this fortune patiently, Since not to be avoided it falls on me.

K. Hen. Bear Worcester to the death, and Ver-non too: Other offenders we will pause upon.—

[*Exeunt* WOR. *and* VERN., *guarded*

How goes the field?

P. Hen. The noble Scot, lord Douglas, when he saw The fortune of the day quite turn'd from him, The noble Percy slain, and all his men Upon the foot of fear,—fled with the rest: And, falling from a hill, he was so bruis'd, That the pursuers took him.   At my tent The Douglas is; and I beseech your grace, I may dispose of him.

K. Hen.   With all my heart.

P. Hen. Then, brother John of Lancaster to you This honourable bounty shall belong: Go to the Douglas, and deliver him Up to his pleasure, ransomless, and free: His valour, shown upon our crests to-day, Hath taught us how to cherish such high deeds, Even in the bosom of our adversaries.

K. Hen. Then this remains,—that we divide our power.—

You, son John, and my cousin Westmoreland, Towards York shall bend you, with your dearest speed, To meet Northumberland, and the prelate Scroop, Who, as we hear, are busily in arms: Myself,—and you, son Harry,— will towards Wales, To fight with Glendower, and the earl of March. Rebellion in this land shall lose his sway Meeting the check of such another day: And since this business so fair is done, Let us not leave till all our own be won.   *Exeunt*

NOTES TO KING HENRY THE FOURTH.

(PART THE FIRST.)

---

¹ No more the thirsty entrails of this soil
Shall daub her lips with her own children's blood.

There has been much debate respecting this passage, some reading the thirsty *Erinnys*, meaning the fury of discord. The poet appears to personify the earth, representing it as a mother, and its parched cracks, or furrows, as the lips by which it drank the blood of its own children.

² And many limits of the charge.

That is, calculations, or estimates of the expense.

³ Mordake the Earl of Fife, and eldest son
To beaten Douglas.

Shakespeare here represents the Earl of Fife as the eldest son of Douglas; this is an error. The account stands thus in Holinshed:—"and of prisoners, Mordacke earl of Fife, son to the governour Archembald carle Douglas," &c. The want of a comma after *governour*, makes these words appear to be the description of one and the same person, and in this sense Shakespeare understood them; but by putting a stop after the word *governour*, it will be evident that the first prisoner was Mordake, who was the son of the governor of Scotland, and Douglas was the second.

⁴ The prisoners.

Percy had by the law of arms an exclusive right to these prisoners; every soldier who had taken any captive whose redemption did not exceed ten thousand crowns, had him for himself, either to free or ransom as he pleased. Though Percy could not keep the Earl of Fife, as being a prince of royal blood, Henry might claim him by his acknowledged military prerogative.

⁵ Another room in the palace.

There must be some error in this description of the scene. The Prince and Falstaff would scarcely carry on their revels in a room of the king's palace. Such a resort would not be safe for Falstaff, and the Prince is described as absent from the court. It is not the tavern in Eastcheap, as Falstaff appoints to meet the Prince there; possibly it is the lodgings of the latter, or some tavern which they occasionally frequented.

⁶ Phœbus,—he, that wandering knight so fair.

Falstaff starts the idea of *Phœbus*, i. e., the sun; but runs off to an allusion to *El Donsel del Febo*, the knight of the sun in a Spanish romance, translated into English in the age of Shakespeare. Perhaps the words "that wandering knight so fair," are part of some forgotten ballad on the adventures of this hero.

⁷ Let not us that are squires of the night's body be called thieves of the day's beauty.

Theobald would read—of the day's *booty*, and the meaning then would be:—Let us not be called thieves, robbers of that which to its lawful owners was booty derivable by honest industry by day. Mr. Steevens thinks no alteration necessary, but says—" I believe our poet, by the expression, *thieves of the day's beauty*, meant only, let not us who are body squires to the night, i.e. adorn the night be called a disgrace to the day. To take away the beauty of the day, may probably mean, to disgrace it."

⁸ As the honey of Hybla, my old lad of the castle.

It has been said that this passage countenances a tradition that the part of Falstaff was originally written under the name of Oldcastle,—old *lad of the castle* according to refer to Oldcastle. The opinion that Falstaff was intended to ridicule Sir John Oldcastle is met and denied by the poet in the epilogue to the second part of *Henry IV.*, where he says, "for Oldcastle died a martyr, and this is not the man." In an old play on the subject of *Henry the Fifth*, Sir John, Oldcastle plays a similar part to that of Falstaff, and appears to have suggested the latter character to Shakespeare. Oldcastle was the companion and friend of Prince Henry in his youth; but although he might have been a boon companion, he was a brave and conscientious man: he became the leader of an insurrection of the Lollards, and was hanged, and afterwards burned on the gibbet. His character, at the suggestion of his Catholic persecutors, was exposed to ridicule and infamy on the stage; but it is a libel on the humanity of Shakespeare to suppose him guilty of heaping scorn upon the grave of a brave and noble-minded man, who by a number of people was esteemed a martyr. Dr. Farmer says, old *lad of the castle* is the same with old *lad of Castile*, a Castilian—probably a cant phrase of the day.

⁹ I am as melancholy as a gib cat.

A *gib cat* is probably a gelded cat; all animals so mutilated are said to lose their spirit, and grow tame and dull.

763

¹⁰ *What sayest thou to a hare, or the melancholy of Moor-ditch.*

The flesh of the hare was supposed to generate melancholy in those who partook of it. In Webster's *Vittoria Corombona*, 1612, we have the following allusion to the supposed dejection of this animal:—

——— Like your melancholy hare,
Feed after midnight.

Again, in Drayton's *Polyolbion*, song the second—

The melancholy hare is form'd in brakes and briars.

In Stowe's *Survey*, it appears that a broad and stagnant ditch formerly parted the hospital from Moorfields. That it might well be called an "unsavoury" object for a simile may be gathered from *News from Hell, brought by the Devil's Carrier*, 1606:— "As touching the river, looke how Moor-ditch shews when the water is three-quarters drayned out, and by reason the stomacke of it is overladen, is ready to fall to casting. So does that; it stinks almost worse, is almost as poysonous, altogether so muddy, altogether so black."

¹¹ *Thou camest not of the blood royal if thou darest not stand for ten shillings.*

Here is a poor jest which time has obscured. The real or royal was of the value of ten shillings. Falstaff means the prince is not royal (or a royal) if he will not stand (pass) for ten shillings.

¹² *Farewell, all-hallown summer.*

That is, thou cold or dead summer. *All-hallown* is *All-hallown tide*, or *All-Saints' Day*, which is the first of November.

¹³ *Sirrah.*

It has created surprise that Poins should use this abrupt term to the prince, but Mr. Malone tells us that in Shakespeare's time it was not invariably used as a term of disrespect.

¹⁴ *Meet me to-morrow night.*

Shakespeare is frequently careless with respect to time; we should read *to-night*, for the robbery was to be committed at four o'clock the next morning.

¹⁵ *His brother-in-law, the foolish Mortimer.*

Percy was not the brother-in-law of Mortimer, the Earl of March; it appears from Dugdale's and Sandford's account of the Mortimer family, that there were two Edmunds, each of whom was taken prisoner at different times by Glendower. Edmund the Earl of March, the Mortimer of this play, was nephew to Lady Percy, the other, Sir Edmund Mortimer, was uncle to the former, and brother to Lady Percy.

¹⁶ *And on my face he turn'd an eye of death, Trembling even at the name of Mortimer.*

An eye of death, says Dr. Johnson, is an eye menacing death; the king is trembling with rage rather than with fear; for this the critic is taken to task by Mr. M. Mason, who thinks he had more reason to *fear* the man who had a better title to the crown than himself. It is evident that if Henry felt fear he was not the man to reveal it; he

764

would have disguised it in anger; while the tenor of the whole scene shows that it was anger and not fear that influenced him.

¹⁷ *And that same sword-and-buckler Prince of Wales.*

The sword and buckler were weapons worn by servants and by low fellows. Thus, in Florio's *First Frutes*, 1578:— "What weapons bear they?—Some sword and dagger, some sword and buckler.—What weapon is that buckler?—A clownish, dastardly weapon, and not fit for a gentleman."

¹⁸ *Cousin, farewell.*

In Shakespeare's time, cousin was a common address to nephews, nieces, and grandchildren, and was, indeed, frequently applied to a relative of any kind. Hotspur was Worcester's nephew.

¹⁹ *Charles' wain.*

This is a vulgar name given to the constellation called the Bear.

²⁰ *Out of all cess*, i. e. out of all measure.

²¹ *The bots*, i. e. worms in the stomach of a horse.

²² *Breeds fleas like a loach.*

A *loach* is a small fish, and exceedingly prolific. The carrier therefore means to say, that "your chamber-lie breeds fleas as fast as the loach" breeds,—not fleas, but loaches.

²³ *I think it be two o'clock.*

It is evident that the carrier suspects Gadshill, and endeavours to mislead him as to the hour, because he has just said that it was *four* o'clock.

²⁴ *A franklin*, i. e. a landed gentleman.

²⁵ *Saint Nicholas' clerks.*

A cant name for thieves or highwaymen. St. Nicholas was the patron saint of scholars, who were therefore called St. Nicholas's clerks. Hence, by a quibble between Nicholas and Old Nick, the name has has been extended to highwaymen.

²⁶ *Other Trojans.*

A *Trojan* appears to be a cant name for swindler or thief.

²⁷ *I am joined with no foot land-rakers, no long-staff, six-penny strikers; none of these mad, mustachio purple-hued malt-worms.*

A *foot land-raker* was a foot-pad or wandering thief; a *sixpenny striker*, a paltry, brutal depredator, who would commit assault and robbery, even for the sake of sixpence; and a *purple-hued malt-worm*, a red or purple-faced drunkard who got intoxicated upon ale.

²⁸ *Burgomasters, and great oneyers.*

Probably *moneyers*, monied men, or bankers. A *moneyer* is an officer of the mint who makes coin and delivers out the king's money.

We have the receipt of fern-seed, we walk invisible.

The seed of the fern is contained in the back of the leaf, and is so small as to escape the sight; but as the fern was propagated by semination, it was commonly supposed that it possessed an invisible seed, and at length, a property of communicating the power of invisibility was attributed to it.

What a plague mean ye to colt me thus?

That is, to fool or trick me; but the prince, taking it in another sense, opposes it by uncolt, i. e. unhorse.

Enter Hotspur, reading a letter.

This letter was from George Dunbar, Earl of March, in Scotland.

Esperance.

This was the motto of the Percy family.

Will thou rob this leathern-jerkin, crystal-button, nott-pated, agate-ring, puke-stocking, caddis-garter.

The prince asks the drawer if he will rob his master, whom he denotes by the above contemptuous expressions. It is said that a leather jerkin with crystal buttons, was the dress of a pawnbroker, and probably, therefore, that of a tavern-keeper. A person was said to be nott-pated, when the hair was cut short and round. Ray says the word is still used in Essex for polled or shorn. Puke-stockings, are supposed to be stockings of a russet-black, and of a coarse material, worn by persons of inferior condition as a matter of economy. Caddis was probably a kind of coarse ferret. In our poet's time the garters were worn in sight, and, consequently, were often very costly. Servants and others, who were common ones, were sometimes called by the contemptuous name of caddis-garters.

Why then your brown bastard.

Bastard was a kind of sweet wine. "The prince," says Dr. Johnson, ' finding the waiter not able, or not willing, to understand his instigation, puzzles him with unconnected prattle, and drives him away."

Rivo, says the drunkard.

Rivo was a cant word among roysterers, probably meaning be merry. Thus Marston,—

If thou art sad at other's fate,
Rivo drink deep, give care the mate.

Didst thou never see Titan kiss a dish of butter? pitiful-hearted Titan, that melted at the sweet tale of the son.

This is a very obscure passage, and much controversy has been expended on it. The folio has son; but that reading has been rejected by most editors. Mr. Steevens says:—"Our author might have written pitiful-hearted Titan, who melted at the sweet tale of his son, i. e. of Phaëton, who by a plausible story, won on the easy nature of his father so far, as to obtain from him the guidance of his chariot for a day." Mr. Malone tells us,—" The prince, undoubtedly, by the words, 'Didst thou never see Titan kiss a dish of butter!' alludes to Falstaff's entering in a great heat, his fat dripping with the violence of his motion, as butter does with the heat of th sun. Our author here, as in many other places, having started an idea, leaves it, and goes to another that has but a very slight connexion

with the former. Thus the idea of butter melted by Titan or the sun, suggests to him the idea of Titan's being melted or softened by the tale of his son Phaëton."

I would I were a weaver; I could sing psalms or any thing.

Weavers were long distinguished for their love of psalmody and other music. In the persecution of the Protestants in Flanders, under Philip II., those who came over to England on that occasion brought with them the woollen manufactory. They were Calvinists, and much attached to sacred music. Falstaff wishes that he could be a weaver and sing like them, to divert his mind.

Tallow-keech.

A keech of tallow is the fat of an ox rolled up in a round lump, in order to be sent to the melters.

Away, you starveling, you elf-skin.

Many of the commentators would read eel-skin, as being more applicable than elf-skin; the skin of an imp or fairy bearing no resemblance to the prince, while a tall thin man may very fairly be humorously likened to a stuffed eel-skin. Shakespeare had historical authority for the leanness of the prince. Stowe says, "he exceeded the mean stature of men, his neck long, body slender and lean, and his bones small," &c.

Give him as much as will make him a royal man.

The prince intends a pun upon the words noble and royal. The value of the noble was 6s. 8d.; that of the royal, 10s. "This," says Mr. Tollet, "seems to allude to a jest of queen Elizabeth. Mr. John Blower, in a sermon before her majesty, said, ' My royal queen;' and a little after, ' My noble queen.' Upon which the queen exclaimed:—' What! am I ten groats worse than I was?'"

A Welsh hook.

An offensive instrument, pointed like a spear, to push or thrust with; and which below had a hook to seize the enemy if he should attempt to escape by flight.

Well, here is my leg.

That is, my obeisance to my father.

Prove a micher, and eat blackberries.

A micher is a truant; to mich is to lurk out of sight. The allusion is to a truant boy, who, unwilling to go to school, and afraid to go home, lurks in the fields, and picks wild fruit.

Hang me up by the heels for a rabbit-sucker, or a poulter's hare.

Dr. Johnson thinks rabbit sucker meant sucking rabbit; but it was more probably a weasel. Falstaff is comparing himself to something thin and little. A poulterer was formerly written a poulter.

Bolting-hutch, i. e. the wooden receptacle into which the meal is bolted.

That roasted Manningtree ox.

Manningtree, in Essex, was famous for the richness of

its surrounding pastures. Fairs were held there, at which moralities and other entertainments were represented, and it appears to have been customary on these occasions to roast an ox entire.

Methinks, my moiety, north from Burton here.

They had, in anticipation of victory, divided the land into three portions, over which Mortimer, Glendower, and Hotspur were to rule. A moiety was frequently used in Shakespeare's time as a portion of anything not divided into two parts

A brazen canstick turn'd.

A canstick is merely an abbreviation of candlestick, the latter word being too long for the line. Heywood, and several of the old writers, constantly use the word canstick in this sense.

I'll have the writer, i. e. the writer of the indentures just alluded to.

With telling me of the mould-warp and the ant.

This alludes to an old prophecy which influenced Glendower in taking up arms against the king. The mouldwarp, it is said, was to be subdued by a wolf, a dragon, and a lion. The mouldwarp was interpreted to be Henry, and the confederated nobles were the wolf, dragon, and lion. The mould-warp is the mole.

You are too wilful-blame.

"This," says Dr. Johnson, "is a mode of speech with which I am not acquainted. Perhaps it might be read—*too wilful blunt,* or, *too wilful bent;* or thus:—

"Indeed, my lord, you are to blame, too wilful."

Upon the wanton rushes lay you down.

It was long the custom of our ancestors to strew their floors with rushes, as we now cover them with carpets.

'Tis the next way to turn tailor, or be red-breast teacher.

The *next* way, is the *nearest* way. Tailors seem to have been almost as remarkable for singing as weavers; thus Beaumont and Fletcher.—"Never trust a tailor that does not sing at his work; his mind is on nothing but filching." Hotspur implies that singing is a mean employment, and that those who practise it are on the road to turn tailors or teachers of birds.

Rash bavin wits.

Bavin is brushwood, which when lighted burns fiercely, but is soon out; it was used in the poet's time for kindling fires. The king means thoughtless fiery talkers, reckless companions.

Carded his state.

A metaphor probably taken from the practice of mingling coarse wool with fine, and carding them together, by which means the value of the latter is diminished. But Mr. Ritson says, that by carding his state, the king means that Richard set his state to hazard, and played it away, as a man loses a fortune at cards.

Of every beardless vain comparative.

That is, of every boy whose vanity incited him to try his wit against the king.

766

Lord Mortimer of Scotland hath sent word.

There was no Lord Mortimer of Scotland; the person alluded to is the Lord March of Scotland. Shakespeare had a recollection that there was a Scottish lord on the side of Henry, who bore the same title with the English family on the rebel side, (one being the Earl of March in England, and the other the Earl of March in Scotland,) but his memory deceived him with respect to the name. He took it to be *Mortimer,* instead of *March.*

How now, Dame Partlet the hen.

Dame Partlet is the name of the hen in the old story-book of *Reynard the Fox;* and in Chaucer's tale of *The Cock and the Fox,* the favourite hen is called dame *Pertelote.*

There's no more faith in thee, than in a stewed prune; nor no more truth in thee, than in a drawn fox.

Stewed prunes were sold in brothels, and were considered not only as a provocative, but also as a remedy against infection. Their practical want of success in this direction, may have brought them into an ill name. Therefore Falstaff says, "there 's no more faith in thee than in a stewed prune." A *drawn fox* may be an embowelled fox, having the form without the life of one; or, as Mr. Heath observes, "a fox drawn over the ground to leave a scent, and exercise the hounds, may be said to have no truth in it, because it deceives the hounds, who run with the same eagerness as if they were in pursuit of a real fox."

And as for womanhood, Maid Marian may be the deputy's wife of the ward to thee.

In the ancient songs of Robin Hood, frequent mention is made of *Maid Marian,* who appears to have been his concubine. She was a character introduced into the old English morris-dances, and usually personated by a man dressed as a woman. Mr. Douce, in his interesting remarks on *The Ancient English Morris Dance,* says,—"Falstaff tells the hostess, that *for womanhood* Maid Marian may be the deputy's wife of the ward to her; meaning perhaps, that she was as masculine in her appearance as the country clown who personated Maid Marian; and in Fletcher's *Monsieur Thomas,* Dorothea desires her brother to conduct himself with more gentleness towards his mistress, unless he would choose to marry Mall-ye the May lady."

A comfort of retirement, i. e. a support to which we may resort.

The quality and hair of our attempt.

That is, the nature and complexion of it. *Hair* appears to have been sometimes used to denote character or manner. We still say something is *against the hair,* or *against the grain,* that is, against the natural tendency.

Ten times more dishonourable ragged than an old-faced ancient.

An old-faced ancient is an old standard patched to hide its dilapidations. To *face* a gown is to trim it. Shakespeare, however, uses the word *ancient* to imply either a standard or a standard-bearer.

Daintry, i. e. Daventry.

To see his livery.

"During the existence of the feudal tenures," says Mr

Mason, "on the death of any of the king's tenants, an inquest of office, called *inquisitio post mortem*, was held, to inquire of what lands he died seized, who was his heir, of what age he was, &c.; and in those cases where the heir was a minor, he became the ward of the crown; the land was seized by its officers, and continued in its possession, or that of the person to whom the crown granted it, till the heir came of age, and *sued out his livery*, or *ousterlemaine; that is, the delivery of his land out of his guardian's hands."

" *Peace, chewet, peace.*

A *chewet*, or *chuet*, is a noisy chattering bird; a pie. Falstaff's ill-timed jest deserves this rebuke.

" ———— *No, good Worcester, no,*
We love our people well.

There appears to be no reason for the introduction of these negatives into this sentence. Mr. M. Mason judiciously proposes that we should read—*Know, good Worcester, know*, &c.

" ———— *Deliver up*
My lord of Westmoreland.

He was "impawned as a surety for the safe return" of Worcester.

" *There's honour for you; here's no vanity.*

Here is no vain semblance of honour, but a reality of it;

though Warburton thinks the negative is used ironically and that Falstaff means, here is an excess of vanity, an excess through which Sir Walter has lost his life.

" *Turk Gregory never did such deeds in arms.*

Gregory the Seventh, called Hildebrand, a man who by his wonderful energy of character and recklessness of principle, raised himself from the humble station of a carpenter of Tuscany to the rank of Pontiff. Fox has represented him in so odious a light, that he was probably popularly known in England as *Turk Gregory*, thus uniting in himself the attributes of the two great enemies of liberty, the Turk and the Pope.

" *O, Harry, thou hast robb'd me of my youth.*

Shakespeare has here violated historic truth for the sake of dramatic effect; Hotspur did not fall by the hands of the prince, but he was struck by an arrow from an unknown hand; the barb entered his brain, and the brave Percy fell dead upon the field.

" *But let my favours hide thy mangled face.*

We must suppose that the prince covers the face of his noble foe with his own scarf, to hide the ghastliness of death.

H. T.

767

SECOND PART OF

King Henry the Fourth.

THIS play occupies a period of about nine years : it commences immediately after the defeat of the
rebels at Shrewsbury in 1403, and terminates with the death of Henry IV. and the coronation of
his son Henry V. It takes up the history precisely where the first play left it, and, in the language
of Dr. Johnson, the two parts will appear to every reader "to be so connected, that the second is
merely a sequel to the first ; to be two only because they are too long to be one."

The opening of this drama is remarkably fine ; the various rumours of the result of the battle at
Shrewsbury, which reach the Earl of Northumberland in his " worm-eaten hold of ragged stone," at
Warkworth ; his parental agony on learning the death of his brave son Hotspur, and the defeat of his
party, are vigorously and touchingly drawn. Cibber has transferred several passages of this powerful
scene to his hash of our poet's tragedy on the life of the third Richard. In Morton's speech,
Shakspeare reveals his knowledge of the necessary constituents of a successful revolution, the Archbishop of York having taken up arms, "turns insurrection to religion." Superstition has ever entered
largely into the conduct of every successful national change. But notwithstanding this aid, we plainly
foresee the defeat of Northumberland's party ; the want of capacity and unanimity in its leaders, and
the evident hollowness of their professions, prove them much too weak for the great task they have
undertaken. The insincerity of their pretensions was too glaring to deceive any except the most ignorant ; they had all assisted in the deposition of King Richard, and let his death pass unquestioned ;
yet they pretend to avenge his fate and to war against his murderer. Northumberland indeed had
been the chief persecutor of the wretched King, and this pretended compassion for his fate is either
rank hypocrisy or self-delusion. Time is the sure avenger of injustice, and the powerful noble who
triumphed over the humiliated monarch is now bowed down to the earth by the man whom he himself had placed in the regal chair.

Falstaff continues his vagaries, and is not a whit less amusing in this drama than in the first ;
his interview with the Lord Chief Justice bubbles over with fun, sparkles with wit, and is unctuous
with humour. Nothing can make the knight long serious ; life is with him one continued jest. His
assumed deafness, and his assertion that he is young, are eminently characteristic. "The truth is, I
am only old in judgment and understanding ; and he that will caper with me for a thousand marks, let
him lend me the money, and have at him." Very natural, too, is the description of age by the Justice ; he sees through Falstaff, has a just estimate of his abandoned character, and yet is softened by
the conversational powers of the fat knight. The scene of the arrest of the latter at the suit of the
hostess for a hundred marks, gives an excellent instance of his persuasiveness ; but like Milton's
Belial—

———— All was false and hollow ; though his tongue
Dropt manna, and could make the worse appear
The better reason.

He pacifies the enraged Mrs. Quickly, and induces her to pawn her plate and tapestries to add another loan to what he already owes her. He possesses the chief end of oratory in no mean degree,
and never fails in winning the good graces of those whom he desires to please. The speech of the

2ᵍ

hostess, in which she reminds Sir John of his promise to marry her, when he was sitting in her "Dolphin-chamber, at the round table by a sea-coal fire, upon Wednesday in Whitsun-week," &c., has been often quoted for its humour and natural quaintness of description.

The wit of the Prince is frequently forced,—it consists of rough practical jests; he is altogether deficient of that spontaneous humour which dwells in Falstaff. His wit is chiefly derived from association with the fat knight; when he is with Poins only he is perpetually recurring to his rank, and condescends to jest. "What a disgrace is it in me to remember thy name," he exclaims to his humble companion, who with the spirit of a parasite pockets up the affront. For the true display of wit there must be freedom of speech and equality of position; it never flashes in fetters or steps gracefully on stilts. A king cannot jest with his courtiers, for his tongue is bridled, and his limbs swathed round with the frigid etiquette of royalty; and although Prince Henry strives to divest himself of all the usual conventionalities of his rank, and put on "the cunning of a carper," still a consciousness of his position will peep through the disguise, and the wit frequently disappears in the heir-apparent to the throne. He talks at random, and banters drawers, and such poor rogues as have neither wit nor courage to reply. He provokes retorts from Falstaff, and answers them by abuse and threats of personal violence. He would make the knight his humble dependent and jocular parasite; but the facetious old reveller has sufficient address to place his companionship with the Prince on terms of equality. As the death of his father approaches, we see him gradually assuming his state: he becomes less familiar with his associates; sometimes he is sarcastic, and then turning moralist, exclaims: "Well, thus we play the fool with the time: and the spirits of the wise sit in the clouds and mock us:"—a reflection which is true enough, but one that does not come gracefully from his lips. His final abrupt dismission of Falstaff with reproach and disgrace, though it was expedient, was the more harsh from the fact that the knight had not made that pecuniary use of him that he might have done. Falstaff seems to have been really attached to his royal and profligate pupil, and depraved as the old rogue was, he still possessed so much of the spirit of a gentleman, as restrained him from making a purse out of the liberality or vanity of the Prince. He appears to gain nothing from the latter but the settlement of a few tavern bills,—no very imperial recompense, even for a court jester.

Although this play is certainly deficient in female interest, still the introduction of Lady Percy, the widow of the unfortunate Hotspur, is very touching; her devotion to the memory of her brave husband, places her in an exceedingly interesting and amiable light. The poet was always just to the character of woman, and threw around her a winning charm of tenderness and purity which fascinates and attracts all hearts. Even the ignorant and degraded Mrs. Quickly is redeemed from offending by her generous good-nature and clearness from vicious intentions.

The third act introduces the sick and worn-out King, with his beautiful apostrophe to sleep; illness and rebellion keep him waking; the "rank diseases" of his kingdom have infected him, and his retrospect of life is sad and solemn. If, he exclaims, we could see into the future—

> The happiest youth, viewing his progress through,
> What perils past, what crosses to ensue,
> Would shut the book, and sit him down and die.

The scene where Prince Henry takes away the crown from the pillow of his apparently lifeless father, the anguish of the dying monarch on this discovery of what he deems to be his son's anxiety for his death, and the latter's vindication of his conduct, are in Shakespeare's most powerful style. The sovereign disappears in the father, and we feel an active sympathy for this usually iron and cold-hearted man. We see that his race is run, the flame of life flickers in the socket, the chilled blood flows languidly from the heart, and we are prepared to hear in the next act that "he 's walked the way of nature."

The shameful treachery of Westmoreland and Prince John ought not to pass unnoticed; this act is without parallel, even in those barbarous days when people were accustomed to look with leaden eyes on deeds of violence and blood. Our poet, deviating from his usual mode, utters no condemnation of this atrocious act, a circumstance which has brought upon him the censure of the critics; for the poet should always be the friend of virtue, although he may have to be the historian of villany. Mowbray, Hastings, and the Archbishop, are lured into a trap by Prince John, and then murdered by the axe of the executioner. It is an historical fact that Scroop was the first prelate of his rank that had been publicly executed in England. Bishops had been imprisoned, and secretly starved or tortured, but had never before suffered death on the scaffold. But Henry was stern and pitiless; rebellion had been the spectre that had ever haunted him, and distilled bitterness into his cup of triumph, and he was resolved to crush it with an iron grasp. Usurpation is a gate through which a swollen flood of evils rush into the state; not only did it plunge England, during Henry's life, into civil war, but to conciliate the clergy and reconcile them to his usurpation, he passed the horrible statute for the burning of heretics; and in his reign men were first consumed at the stake in this country for exercising their own judgment on religious subjects. William Sawtre, who had been rector of Lynn, was condemned for heresy, and the first who perished in the flames at Smithfield. This tragedy took place in March, 1401, and was the beginning of a long series of horrors, the bare contemplation of which creates sensations of terror and disgust.

Great variety is made in this play by the introduction of the scenes at Justice Shallow's, in Gloucestershire, the lean bragging septuagenarian who talks of the wildness of his youth, and of his doings at Clement's Inn, Turnbull Street, and Mile-end Green. His reminiscences respecting John Doit of Staffordshire, black George Bare, Francis Pickbone, and Will Squell the Cotswold man; "you had not four such swinge-bucklers in all the inns of court again;" and of Jane Nightwork who was a "bona roba" fifty-five years ago, are highly natural and amusing. With what glee does he refer to his fight with one Sampson Stockfish behind Gray's Inn. His confusion of ideas is a satire on the sort of men who too often occupied the seat of justice in our poet's time; with the same breath he laments the death of old Double the archer, and asks the market price of a score of ewes. And with the forgetfulness and mental wandering of age, he unites a moral reflection on the certainty of death with the price of "a good yoke of bullocks at Stamford Fair."

What a foil is this garrulous old squire, this "man made after supper of a cheese-paring," to the robust hearty old knight. Falstaff and Shallow! what ludicrous contrasts, the representatives of plenty and famine, wit and senility; but our merry poet went further in his gleanings for mirth, and threw cousin Silence into the scale; cousin Silence whom it "well befits to be of the peace," who scarcely utters a word when he is sober, but will let no one else talk when he is drunk.

What a rare group of oddities, too, are thrust upon us in the recruiting scene; ragged abortions of humanity such as Shakespeare had perhaps sometimes seen at a fair or market day at Stratford-on-Avon. They are not however altogether mere caricatures, such as Ben Jonson too often drew—they had a spirit of vitality; we laugh heartily at the poor fellows, but we feel for them nevertheless, and wish them well home again from their encounter with the rebels. They are like some of the sketches of that great genius of the pencil, Hogarth; which, though struck off by a few masterly touches, yet seem to reveal a whole history.

In the concluding scene Prince Henry enters as king, disclaims his previous follies, confirms in authority the Lord Chief Justice who had committed him to prison, and dismisses Falstaff with reproof and contumely. We see the last of this cheerful votary of roguery and pleasure; the unlooked-for ingratitude of his "royal Hal" breaks his heart; early in the next play we hear of his death; and the drama terminates with an intimation that the King and his court will shortly bear their "civil swords and native fire as far as France."

PERSONS REPRESENTED.

KING HENRY THE FOURTH.
Appears, Act III. sc. 1. Act IV. sc. 4.

HENRY, *Prince of Wales, afterwards* King Henry the Fifth.
Appears, Act II. sc. 2; sc. 4. Act IV. sc. 4. Act V. sc. 2; sc. 5.

THOMAS, *Duke of* Clarence.
Appears, Act IV. sc. 4. Act V. sc. 2.

PRINCE JOHN OF LANCASTER, *afterwards Duke of* Bedford.
Appears, Act IV. sc. 2; sc. 3; sc. 4. Act V. sc. 2; sc. 5.

PRINCE HUMPHREY OF GLOUCESTER, *afterwards Duke of* Gloucester.
Appears, Act IV. sc. 4. Act V. sc. 2.

EARL OF WARWICK, *of the King's party.*
Appears, Act III. sc. 1. Act IV. sc. 4. Act V. sc. 2.

EARL OF WESTMORELAND, *of the King's party.*
Appears, Act IV. sc. 1; sc. 2; sc. 3; sc. 4. Act V. sc. 2.

GOWER, *a Gentleman of the King's party.*
Appears, Act II. sc. 1.

HARCOURT, *a Gentleman of the King's party.*
Appears, Act IV. sc. 4.

LORD CHIEF JUSTICE *of the King's Bench.*
Appears, Act I. sc. 2. Act II. sc. 1. Act V. sc. 2; sc. 5.

A GENTLEMAN, *attending on the Lord Chief Justice.*
Appears, Act I. sc. 2.

EARL OF NORTHUMBERLAND, *an Enemy to the King.*
Appears, Act I. sc. 1. Act II. sc. 3.

SCROOP, *Archbishop of York; an Enemy to the King.*
Appears, Act I. sc. 3. Act IV. sc. 1; sc. 2.

LORD MOWBRAY, } *Enemies to the King.*
LORD HASTINGS, }
Appear, Act I. sc. 3. Act IV. sc. 1; sc. 2.

LORD BARDOLPH, *an Enemy to the King.*
Appears, Act I. sc. 1; sc. 3.

SIR JOHN COLEVILLE, *an Enemy to the King.*
Appears, Act IV. sc. 3.

TRAVERS, } *Servants of* Northumberland.
MORTON, }
Appear, Act I. sc. 1.

SIR JOHN FALSTAFF.
Appears, Act I. sc. 2. Act II. sc. 1; sc. 4. Act III. sc. 2. Act IV. sc. 3. Act V. sc. 1; sc. 3; sc. 5.

BARDOLPH.
Appears, Act II. sc. 1; sc. 2; sc. 4. Act III. sc. 2. Act IV. sc. 3. Act V. sc. 1; sc. 3; sc. 5.

PISTOL.
Appears, Act II. sc. 4. Act V. sc. 3; sc. 5.

PAGE to Sir John Falstaff.
Appears, Act I. sc. 2. Act II. sc. 1; sc. 2. Act V. sc. 1; sc. 3; sc. 5.

POINS.
Appears, Act II. sc. 2; sc. 4.

PETO.
Appears, Act II. sc. 4.

SHALLOW, *a Country Justice.*
Appears, Act III. sc. 2. Act V. sc. 1; sc. 3; sc. 5.

SILENCE, *also a Country Justice.*
Appears, Act III. sc. 2; sc. 3.

DAVY, *Servant to* Shallow.
Appears, Act V. sc. 1; sc. 3

MOULDY, }
SHADOW, }
WART, } *Recruits.*
FEEBLE, }
BULLCALF, }
Appear, Act III. sc. 2.

FANG, } *Sheriff's Officers.*
SNARE, }
Appear, Act II. sc. 1.

A PORTER.
Appears, Act I. sc. 1.

RUMOUR.
Appears, before Act I.

A Dancer, *Speaker of the Epilogue.*

LADY NORTHUMBERLAND *and* LADY PERCY
Appear, Act II. sc. 3.

MRS. QUICKLY.
Appears, Act II. sc. 1; sc. 4. Act V. sc. 4.

DOLL TEARSHEET.
Appears, Act II. sc. 4. Act V. sc. 4.

Lords, and other Attendants; Officers, Soldiers, Messengers, Drawers, Beadle, Grooms, &c.

SCENE,—ENGLAND.

772

SECOND PART OF

King Henry the Fourth

INDUCTION.

Warkworth. *Before* Northumberland's *Castle.*

Enter Rumour, *painted full of Tongues.*

Rum. Open your ears; For which of you will
    stop
The vent of hearing, when loud Rumour speaks?
I, from the orient to the drooping west,
Making the wind my post-horse, still unfold
The acts commenced on this ball of earth:
Upon my tongues continual slanders ride;
The which in every language I pronounce,
Stuffing the ears of men with false reports.
I speak of peace, while covert enmity,
Under the smile of safety, wounds the world:
And who but Rumour, who but only I,
Make fearful musters, and prepar'd defence;
Whilst the big year, swoll'n with some other grief,
Is thought with child by the stern tyrant war,
And no such matter? Rumour is a pipe
Blown by surmises, jealousies, conjectures;
And of so easy and so plain a stop,
That the blunt monster with uncounted heads,
The still discordant wavering multitude,
Can play upon it. But what need I thus
My well-known body to anatomize
Among my household! Why is Rumour here?
I run before king Harry's victory;
Who, in a bloody field by Shrewsbury,
Hath beaten down young Hotspur, and his troops
Quenching the flame of bold rebellion
Even with the rebels' blood. But what mean I
To speak so true at first? my office is
To noise abroad,—that Harry Monmouth fell
Under the wrath of noble Hotspur's sword;
And that the king before the Douglas' rage
Stoop'd his anointed head as low as death.
This have I rumour'd through the peasant towns
Between that royal field of Shrewsbury
And this worm-eaten hold of ragged stone,
Where Hotspur's father, old Northumberland,
Lies crafty-sick: the posts come tiring on,
And not a man of them brings other news,
Than they have learn'd of me: From Rumour's
    tongues
They bring smooth comforts false, worse than
    true wrongs.   [*Exit.*

ACT I.

SCENE I.—*The Same.*

The Porter before the Gate; Enter Lord Bardolph.

Bard. Who keeps the gate here, ho?—Where
    is the earl?
Port. What shall I say you are?

Bard.   Tell thou the earl,
That the lord Bardolph doth attend him here.
Port. His lordship is walk'd forth into the or-
    chard;
Please it your honour, knock but at the gate,
And he himself will answer.

773

Enter NORTHUMBERLAND.

Bard.   Here comes the earl.

North. What news, lord Bardolph? every mi-
nute now
Should be the father of some stratagem:
The times are wild; contention, like a horse
Full of high feeding, madly hath broke loose,
And bears down all before him.

Bard.   Noble earl,
I bring you certain news from Shrewsbury.

North. Good, an heaven will!

Bard.   As good as heart can wish:—
The king is almost wounded to the death;
And, in the fortune of my lord your son,
Prince Harry slain outright; and both the Blunts
Kill'd by the hand of Douglas: young prince John,
And Westmoreland, and Stafford, fled the field;
And Harry Monmouth's brawn, the hulk sir John,
Is prisoner to your son: O, such a day,
So fought, so follow'd, and so fairly won,
Came not, till now, to dignify the times,
Since Cæsar's fortunes!

North.   How is this deriv'd?
Saw you the field? came you from Shrewsbury?

Bard. I spake with one, my lord, that came
from thence;
A gentleman well bred, and of good name,
That freely render'd me these news for true.

North. Here comes my servant, Travers, whom
I sent
On Tuesday last to listen after news.

Bard. My lord, I over-rode him on the way;
And he is furnish'd with no certainties,
More than he haply may retail from me.

Enter TRAVERS.

North. Now, Travers, what good tidings come
with you?

Tra. My lord, sir John Umfrevile turn'd me
back
With joyful tidings; and, being better hors'd,
Out-rode me. After him, came, spurring hard,
A gentleman, almost forspent with speed,
That stopp'd by me to breathe his bloodied horse:
He ask'd the way to Chester; and of him
I did demand, what news from Shrewsbury.
He told me, that rebellion had bad luck,
And that young Harry Percy's spur was cold:
With that, he gave his able horse the head,
And, bending forward, struck his armed heels
Against the panting sides of his poor jade
Up to the rowel-head: and, starting so,

774

He seem'd in running to devour the way,
Staying no longer question.

North.   Ha!——Again.
Said he, young Harry Percy's spur was cold?
Of Hotspur, coldspur? that rebellion
Had met ill luck?

Bard.   My lord, I 'll tell you what;—
If my young lord your son have not the day,
Upon mine honour, for a silken point
I 'll give my barony: never talk of it.

North. Why should the gentleman, that rode
by Travers,
Give him such instances of loss?

Bard.   Who, he?
He was some hilding fellow, that had stol'n
The horse he rode on; and, upon my life,
Spoke at a venture. Look, here comes more news.

Enter MORTON.

North. Yea, this man's brow, like to a title-leaf,
Foretels the nature of a tragic volume:
So looks the strand, whereon the imperious flood
Hath left a witness'd usurpation.——
Say, Morton, didst thou come from Shrewsbury?

Mor. I ran from Shrewsbury, my noble lord,
Where hateful death put on his ugliest mask,
To fright our party.

North.   How doth my son, and brother?
Thou tremblest; and the whiteness in thy cheek
Is apter than thy tongue to tell thy errand.
Even such a man, so faint, so spiritless,
So dull, so dead in look, so woe-begone,
Drew Priam's curtain in the dead of night,
And would have told him, half his Troy was burn'd:
But Priam found the fire, ere he his tongue,
And I my Percy's death, ere thou report'st it.
This thou would'st say,—Your son did thus, and
thus;
Your brother, thus; so fought the noble Douglas;
Stopping my greedy ear with their bold deeds:
But in the end, to stop mine ear indeed,
Thou hast a sigh to blow away this praise,
Ending with—brother, son, and all are dead.

Mor. Douglas is living, and your brother, yet:
But, for my lord your son——

North.   Why, he is dead.
See, what a ready tongue suspicion hath!
He, that but fears the thing he would not know,
Hath, by instinct, knowledge from others' eyes,
That what he fear'd is chanced. Yet speak, Morton
Tell thou thy earl, his divination lies;
And I will take it as a sweet disgrace,

And make thee rich for doing me such wrong.

Mor. You are too great to be by me gainsaid:
Your spirit is too true, your fears too certain.

North. Yet, for all this, say not that Percy's
dead.
I see a strange confession in thine eye:
Thou shak'st thy head; and hold'st it fear, or sin,
To speak a truth. If he be slain, say so: ·
The tongue offends not, that reports his death:
And he doth sin, that doth belie the dead;
Not he, which says the dead is not alive.
Yet the first bringer of unwelcome news
Hath but a losing office; and his tongue
Sounds ever after as a sullen bell,
Remember'd knolling a departing friend.

Bard. I cannot think, my lord, your son is
dead.

Mor. I am sorry, I should force you to believe
That, which I would to heaven I had not seen:
But these mine eyes saw him in bloody state,
Rend'ring faint quittance, wearied and out-
breath'd.
To Harry Monmouth; whose swift wrath beat down
The never-daunted Percy to the earth,
From whence with life he never more sprung up.
In few, his death (whose spirit lent a fire
Even to the dullest peasant in his camp,)
Being bruited once, took fire and heat away
From the best temper'd courage in his troops:
For from his metal was his party steel'd;
Which once in him abated, all the rest
Turn'd on themselves, like dull and heavy lead.
And as the thing that's heavy in itself,
Upon enforcement, flies with greatest speed;
So did our men, heavy in Hotspur's loss,
Lend to this weight such lightness with their fear,
That arrows fled not swifter toward their aim,
Than did our soldiers, aiming at their safety,
Fly from the field: Then was that noble Worcester
Too soon ta'en prisoner: and that furious Scot,
The bloody Douglas, whose well-labouring sword
Had three times slain the appearance of the king,
'Gan vail his stomach, and did grace the shame
Of those that turn'd their backs; and in his flight,
Stumbling in fear, was took. The sum of all
Is,—that the king hath won; and hath sent out
A speedy power, to encounter you, my lord,
Under the conduct of young Lancaster,
And Westmoreland: this is the news at full.

North. For this I shall have time enough to
mourn.
In poison there is physic; and these news,

Having been well, that would have made me sick,
Being sick, have in some measure made me well:
And as the wretch, whose fever-weaken'd joints,
Like strengthless hinges, buckle under life,
Impatient of his fit, breaks like a fire,
Out of his keeper's arms; even so my limbs,
Weaken'd with grief, being now enrag'd with grief,
Are thrice themselves: hence, therefore, thou nice
crutch;
A scaly gauntlet now, with joints of steel,
Must glove this hand: and hence, thou sickly quoif;
Thou art a guard too wanton for the head,
Which princes, flesh'd with conquest, aim to hit.
Now bind my brows with iron; and approach
The ragged'st hour that time and spite dare bring
To frown upon the enrag'd Northumberland!
Let heaven kiss earth! Now let not nature's hand
Keep the wild flood confin'd! let order die,
And let this world no longer be a stage,
To feed contention in a lingering act;
But let one spirit of the first-born Cain
Reign in all bosoms, that, each heart being set
On bloody courses, the rude scene may end,
And darkness be the burier of the dead!

Tra. This strain'd passion doth you wrong,
my lord.

Bard. Sweet earl, divorce not wisdom from
your honour.

Mor. The lives of all your loving complices,
Lean on your health; the which, if you give o'er
To stormy passion, must perforce decay.
You cast the event of war, my noble lord,
And summ'd the account of chance, before you
said,—
Let us make head. It was your presurmise,
That in the dole of blows your son might drop:
You knew, he walk'd o'er perils, on an edge,
More likely to fall in, than to get o'er:
You were advis'd, his flesh was capable
Of wounds, and scars; and that his forward spirit
Would lift him where most trade of danger rang'd;
Yet did you say,—Go forth; and none of this,
Though strongly apprehended, could restrain
The stiff-borne action: What hath then befallen,
Or what hath this bold enterprise brought forth,
More than that being which was like to be?

Bard. We all, that are engag'd to this loss,
Knew that we ventur'd on such dangerous seas,
That, if we wrought out life, 'twas ten to one:
And yet we ventur'd, for the gain proposed
Chok'd the respect of likely peril fear'd;
And, since we are o'erset, venture again.

Come, we will all put forth; body and goods.

Mor. 'T is more than time : And, my most noble
　　　lord,
I hear for certain, and do speak the truth,—
The gentle archbishop of York is up,
With well-appointed powers; he is a man,
Who with a double surety binds his followers:
My lord your son had only but the corps,
But shadows, and the shows of men, to fight :
For that same word, rebellion, did divide
The action of their bodies from their souls ;
And they did fight with queasiness, constrain'd,
As men drink potions ; that their weapons only
Seem'd on our side, but, for their spirits and souls,
This word, rebellion, it had froze them up,
As fish are in a pond : But now the bishop
Turns insurrection to religion :
Suppos'd sincere and holy in his thoughts,
He 's follow'd both with body and with mind ;
And doth enlarge his rising with the blood
Of fair king Richard, scrap'd from Pomfret stones :
Derives from heaven his quarrel, and his cause ;
Tells them, he doth bestride a bleeding land,
Gasping for life under great Bolingbroke ;
And more, and less, do flock to follow him.

North. I knew of this before ; but, to speak truth,
This present grief had wip'd it from my mind.
Go in with me ; and counsel every man
The aptest way for safety, and revenge :
Get posts, and letters, and make friends with speed ;
Never so few, and never yet more need. [*Exeunt.*

SCENE II.—London. *A Street.*

Enter Sir John Falstaff, *with his Page bearing
his Sword and Buckler.*

Fal. Sirrah, you giant, what says the doctor to
my water?

Page. He said, sir, the water itself was a good
healthy water : but, for the party that owed it, he
might have more diseases than he knew for.

Fal. Men of all sorts take a pride to gird at
me : The brain of this foolish-compounded clay,
man, is not able to vent any thing that tends to
laughter, more than I invent, or is invented on me :
I am not only witty in myself, but the cause that
wit is in other men. I do here walk before thee,
like a sow, that hath overwhelmed all her litter but
one. If the prince put thee into my service for
any other reason than to set me off, why then I have
no judgment. Thou whoreson mandrake, thou art
fitter to be worn in my cap, than to wait at my heels.

I was never manned with an agate till now : but I
will set you neither in gold nor silver, but in vile
apparel, and send you back again to your master,
for a jewel ; the juvenal, the prince your master,
whose chin is not yet fledged. I will sooner have
a beard grow in the palm of my hand, than he shall
get one on his cheek ; and yet he will not stick to
say, his face is a face-royal : God may finish it when
he will, it is not a hair amiss yet : he may keep it
still as a face-royal, for a barber shall never earn
sixpence out of it ; and yet he will be crowing, as
if he had writ man ever since his father was a
bachelor. He may keep his own grace, but he is
almost out of mine, I can assure him.—What
said master Dumbleton about the satin for my
short cloak, and slops ?

Page. He said, sir, you should procure him
better assurance than Bardolph : he would not take
his bond and yours ; he liked not the security.

Fal. Let him be damned like the glutton ! may
his tongue be hotter !—A whoreson Achitophel !
a rascally yea-forsooth knave ! to bear a gentleman
in hand, and then stand upon security !—The
whoreson smooth-pates do now wear nothing but
high shoes, and bunches of keys at their girdles ;
and if a man is thorough with them in honest
taking up, then they must stand upon—security.
I had as lief they would put ratsbane in my mouth,
as offer to stop it with security. I looked he
should have sent me two-and-twenty yards of satin,
as I am a true knight, and he sends me security.
Well, he may sleep in security ; for he hath the
horn of abundance, and the lightness of his wife
shines through it ; and yet cannot he see, though
he have his own lantern to light him.—Where 's
Bardolph ?

Page. He 's gone into Smithfield, to buy your
worship a horse.

Fal. I bought him in Paul's, and he 'll buy me
a horse in Smithfield : an I could get me but a wife
in the stews, I were manned, horsed, and wived.

Enter the Lord Chief Justice, *and an Attendant.*

Page. Sir, here comes the nobleman that committed the prince for striking him about Bardolph.

Fal. Wait close, I will not see him.

Ch. Just. What 's he that goes there ?

Atten. Falstaff, an 't please your lordship.

Ch. Just. He that was in question for the robbery ?

Atten. He, my lord : but he hath since done
good service at Shrewsbury ; and, as I hear, is now

going with some charge to the lord John of Lancaster.

Ch. Just. What, to York ? Call him back again.

Atten. Sir John Falstaff!

Fal. Boy, tell him I am deaf.

Page. You must speak louder, my master is deaf.

Ch. Just. I am sure he is, to the hearing of any thing good.—Go, pluck him by the elbow; I must speak with him

Atten. Sir John,——

Fal. What! a young knave, and beg ! Is there not wars ? is there not employment ? Doth not the king lack subjects ? do not the rebels need soldiers ? Though it be a shame to be on any side but one, it is worse shame to beg than to be on the worst side, were it worse than the name of rebellion can tell how to make it.

Atten. You mistake me, sir.

Fal. Why, sir, did I say you were an honest man ? setting my knighthood and my soldiership aside, I had lied in my throat if I had said so.

Atten. I pray you, sir, then set your knighthood and your soldiership aside; and give me leave to tell you, you lie in your throat, if you say I am any other than an honest man.

Fal. I give thee leave to tell me so ! I lay aside that which grows to me ! If thou gett'st any leave of me, hang me ; if thou takest leave, thou wert better be hanged : You hunt-counter, hence ! avaunt !

Atten. Sir, my lord would speak with you.

Ch. Just. Sir John Falstaff, a word with you.

Fal. My good lord !—God give your lordship good time of day. I am glad to see your lordship abroad : I heard say, your lordship was sick : I hope, your lordship goes abroad by advice. Your lordship, though not clean past your youth, hath yet some smack of age in you, some relish of the saltness of time ; and I most humbly beseech your lordship, to have a reverend care of your health.

Ch. Just. Sir John, I sent for you before your expedition to Shrewsbury.

Fal. An 't please your lordship, I hear his majesty is returned with some discomfort from Wales.

Ch. Just. I talk not of his majesty :—You would not come when I sent for you.

Fal. And I hear moreover, his highness is fallen into this same whoreson apoplexy.

Ch. Just. Well, heaven mend him ! I pray, let me speak with you.

Fal. This apoplexy is, as I take it, a kind of lethargy, an 't please your lordship; a kind of sleeping in the blood, a whoreson tingling.

Ch. Just. What tell you me of it ? be it as it is.

Fal. It hath its original from much grief ; from study, and perturbation of the brain : I have read the cause of his effects in Galen ; it is a kind of deafness.

Ch. Just. I think, you are fallen into the disease ; for you hear not what I say to you.

Fal. Very well, my lord, very well : rather, an 't please you, it is the disease of not listening, the malady of not marking, that I am troubled withal.

Ch. Just. To punish you by the heels, would amend the attention of your ears ; and I care not, if I do become your physician.

Fal. I am as poor as Job, my lord ; but not so patient : your lordship may minister the potion of imprisonment to me, in respect of poverty ; but how I should be your patient to follow your prescriptions, the wise may make some dram of a scruple, or, indeed, a scruple itself.

Ch. Just. I sent for you, when there were matters against you for your life, to come speak with me.

Fal. As I was then advised by my learned counsel in the laws of this land-service, I did not come.

Ch. Just. Well, the truth is, sir John, you live in great infamy.

Fal. He that buckles him in my belt, cannot live in less.

Ch. Just. Your means are very slender, and your waste is great.

Fal. I would it were otherwise ; I would my means were greater, and my waist slenderer.

Ch. Just. You have misled the youthful prince.

Fal. The young prince hath misled me : I am the fellow with the great belly, and he my dog.

Ch. Just. Well, I am loath to gall a new-healed wound ; your day's service at Shrewsbury hath a little gilded over your night's exploit on Gad's-hill : you may thank the unquiet time for your quiet o'erposting that action.

Fal. My lord ?

Ch. Just. But since all is well, keep it so : wake not a sleeping wolf.

Fal. To wake a wolf, is as bad as to smell a fox.

Ch. Just. What ! you are as a candle, the better part burnt out.

Fal. A wassel candle, my lord ; all tallow : if I did say of wax, my growth would approve the truth.

Ch. Just. There is not a white hair on your face, but should have his effect of gravity

Fal. His effect of gravy, gravy, gravy.

Ch. Just. You follow the young prince up and down, like his ill angel.

Fal. Not so, my lord; your ill angel is light; but, I hope, he that looks upon me, will take me without weighing: and yet, in some respects, I grant, I cannot go, I cannot tell:? Virtue is of so little regard in these costermonger times, that true valour is turned bear-herd: Pregnancy is made a tapster, and hath his quick wit wasted in giving reckonings: all the other gifts appertinent to man, as the malice of this age shapes them, are not worth a gooseberry. You, that are old, consider not the capacities of us that are young: you measure the heat of our livers with the bitterness of your galls: and we that are in the vaward of our youth, I must confess, are wags too.

Ch. Just. Do you set down your name in the scroll of youth, that are written down old with all the characters of age? Have you not a moist eye? a dry hand? a yellow cheek? a white beard? a decreasing leg? an increasing belly? Is not your voice broken? your wind short? your chin double? your wit single? and every part about you blasted with antiquity? and will you yet call yourself young? Fye, fye, fye, sir John!

Fal. My lord, I was born about three of the clock in the afternoon, with a white head, and something a round belly. For my voice,—I have lost it with holloing, and singing of anthems. To approve my youth further, I will not: the truth is, I am only old in judgment and understanding; and he that will caper with me for a thousand marks, let him lend me the money, and have at him. For the box o' the ear that the prince gave you,—he gave it like a rude prince, and you took it like a sensible lord. I have checked him for it; and the young lion repents: marry, not in ashes, and sackcloth; but in new silk, and old sack.

Ch. Just. Well, heaven send the prince a better companion!

Fal. Heaven send the companion a better prince! I cannot rid my hands of him.

Ch. Just. Well, the king hath severed you and prince Harry: I hear, you are going with lord John of Lancaster, against the archbishop, and the earl of Northumberland.

Fal. Yea; I thank your pretty sweet wit for it. But look you pray, all you that kiss my lady peace at home, that our armies join not in a hot day! for, by the Lord, I take but two shirts out with me, and I mean not to sweat extraordinarily: if it be a hot day, an I brandish any thing but my bottle, I would I might never spit white again. There is not a dangerous action can peep out his head, but I am thrust upon it: Well, I cannot last ever: But it was always yet the trick of our English nation, if they have a good thing, to make it too common. If you will needs say, I am an old man, you should give me rest. I would to God, my name were not so terrible to the enemy as it is. I were better to be eaten to death with rust, than to be scoured to nothing with perpetual motion.

Ch. Just. Well, be honest, be honest; and God bless your expedition!

Fal. Will your lordship lend me a thousand pound, to furnish me forth?

Ch. Just. Not a penny, not a penny; you are too impatient to bear crosses. Fare you well: Commend me to my cousin Westmoreland.

[*Exeunt* Ch. Just. *and* Atten.

Fal. If I do, fillip me with a three-man beetle. —A man can no more separate age and covetousness, than he can part young limbs and lechery: but the gout galls the one, and the pox pinches the other; and so both the diseases prevent my curses. —Boy!

Page. Sir?

Fal. What money is in my purse?

Page. Seven groats and two-pence.

Fal. I can get no remedy against this consumption of the purse: borrowing only lingers and lingers it out, but the disease is incurable.—Go bear this letter to my lord of Lancaster; this to the prince; this to the earl of Westmoreland; and this to old mistress Ursula, whom I have weekly sworn to marry since I perceived the first white hair on my chin: About it; you know where to find me. [*Exit Page.*] A pox of this gout! or, a gout of this pox! for the one, or the other, plays the rogue with my great toe. It is no matter, if I do halt; I have the wars for my colour, and my pension shall seem the more reasonable: A good wit will make use of any thing; I will turn diseases to commodity. [*Exit.*

SCENE III.—*York. A Room in the Archbishop's Palace.*

Enter the Archbishop of York, *the Lords* Hastings, Mowbray, *and* Bardolph.

Arch. Thus have you heard our cause, and known our means;

775

And, my most noble friends, I pray you all,
Speak plainly your opinions of our hopes:—
And first, lord marshal, what say you to it?

Mowb. I well allow the occasion of our arms;
But gladly would be better satisfied,
How, in our means, we should advance ourselves
To look with forehead bold and big enough
Upon the power and puissance of the king.

Hast. Our present musters grow upon the file
To five and twenty thousand men of choice;
And our supplies live largely in the hope
Of great Northumberland, whose bosom burns
With an incensed fire of injuries.

Bard. The question then, lord Hastings, standeth
    thus:—
Whether our present five and twenty thousand
May hold up head without Northumberland.

Hast. With him, we may.

Bard.   Ay, marry, there's the point;
But if without him we be thought too feeble,
My judgment is, we should not step too far
Till he had his assistance by the hand:
For, in a theme so bloody-fac'd as this,
Conjecture, expectation, and surmise
Of aids uncertain, should not be admitted.

Arch. 'Tis very true, lord Bardolph; for, indeed,
It was young Hotspur's case at Shrewsbury.

Bard. It was, my lord; who lin'd himself with
    hope,
Eating the air on promise of supply,
Flattering himself with project of a power
Much smaller than the smallest of his thoughts;
And so, with great imagination,
Proper to madmen, led his powers to death,
And, winking, leap'd into destruction.

Hast. But, by your leave, it never yet did hurt,
To lay down likelihoods, and forms of hope.

Bard. Yes, in this present quality of war;—
Indeed the instant action, (a cause on foot,)
Lives so in hope, as in an early spring
We see the appearing buds; which, to prove fruit,
Hope gives not so much warrant, as despair,
That frosts will bite them. When we mean to
    build,
We first survey the plot, then draw the model;
And when we see the figure of the house,
Then must we rate the cost of the erection:
Which if we find outweighs ability,
What do we then, but draw anew the model
In fewer offices; or, at least, desist
To build at all? Much more, in this great work,
(Which is, almost, to pluck a kingdom down,

And set another up,) should we survey
The plot of situation, and the model;
Consent upon a sure foundation;
Question surveyors; know our own estate,
How able such a work to undergo,
To weigh against his opposite; or else,
We fortify in paper, and in figures,
Using the names of men, instead of men:
Like one that draws the model of a house
Beyond his power to build it; who, half through,
Gives o'er, and leaves his part-created cost
A naked subject to the weeping clouds,
And waste for churlish winter's tyranny.

Hast. Grant, that our hopes (yet likely of fair
    birth,)
Should be still-born, and that we now possess'd
The utmost man of expectation;
I think, we are a body strong enough,
Even as we are, to equal with the king.

Bard. What! is the king but five and twenty
    thousand?

Hast. To us, no more; nay, not so much, lord
    Bardolph.
For his divisions, as the times do brawl,
Are in three heads: one power against the French,
And one against Glendower; perforce, a third
Must take up us: So is the unfirm king
In three divided; and his coffers found
With hollow poverty and emptiness.

Arch. That he should draw his several strengths
    together,
And come against us in full puissance,
Need not be dreaded.

Hast.   If he should do so,
He leaves his back unarm'd, the French and Welsh
Baying him at the heels: never fear that.

Bard. Who, is it like, should lead his forces
    hither?

Hast. The duke of Lancaster, and Westmore-
    land:
Against the Welsh, himself, and Harry Monmouth:
But who is substituted 'gainst the French,
I have no certain notice.

Arch.   Let us on;
And publish the occasion of our arms.
The commonwealth is sick of their own choice,
Their over-greedy love hath surfeited:—
An habitation giddy and unsure
Hath he, that buildeth on the vulgar heart.
O thou fond many! with what loud applause
Didst thou beat heaven with blessing Bolingbroke,
Before he was what thou would'st have him be!

779

And being now trimm'd in thine own desires,
Thou, beastly feeder, art so full of him,
That thou provok'st thyself to cast him up.
So, so, thou common dog, didst thou disgorge
Thy glutton bosom of the royal Richard;
And now thou would'st eat thy dead vomit up,
And howl'st to find it. What trust is in these
　　times?
They that, when Richard liv'd, would have him die,
Are now become enamour'd on his grave:
Thou, that threw'st dust upon his goodly head,

When through proud London he came sighing on
After the admired heels of Bolingbroke,
Cry'st now, " O earth, yield us that king again,
And take thou this!" O thoughts of men accurst!
Past, and to come, seem best; things present,
　　worst.

Mowb. Shall we go draw our numbers, and set
　　on?

Hast. We are time's subjects, and time bids be
　　gone. 　　　　　　　　　　 [*Exeunt.*

ACT II.

SCENE I.—London. *A Street.*

Enter Hostess; Fang, *and his Boy, with her; and*
Snare *following.*

Host. Master Fang, have you entered the action?

Fang. It is entered.

Host. Where is your yeoman? Is it a lusty
yeoman? will a' stand to 't?

Fang. Sirrah, where 's Snare?

Host. O lord, ay: good master Snare.

Snare. Here, here.

Fang. Snare, we must arrest sir John Falstaff.

Host. Yea, good master Snare; I have entered
him and all.

Snare. It may chance cost some of us our lives,
for he will stab.

Host. Alas the day! take heed of him; he stabbed
me in mine own house, and that most beastly: in
good faith, a' cares not what mischief he doth, if
his weapon be out: he will foin like any devil; he
will spare neither man, woman, nor child.

Fang. If I can close with him, I care not for his
thrust.

Host. No, nor I neither; I 'll be at your elbow.

Fang. An I but fist him once; an a' come but
within my vice;—

Host. I am undone by his going; I warrant you,
he 's an infinitive thing upon my score:—Good
master Fang, hold him sure:—good master Snare,
let him not 'scape. He comes continuantly to
Pie-corner, (saving your manhoods,) to buy a saddle; and he 's indited to dinner to the Lubbar's
Head'' in Lumbert-street, to master Smooth's the

silkman: I pray ye, since my exion is entered, and
my case so openly known to the world, let him be
brought in to his answer. A hundred mark is a
long score for a poor lone woman to bear: and I
have borne, and borne, and borne; and have been
fubbed off, and fubbed off, and fubbed off, from
this day to that day, that it is a shame to be
thought on. There is no honesty in such dealing;
unless a woman should be made an ass, and a
beast, to bear every knave's wrong.——

Enter Sir John Falstaff, Page, *and* Bardolph.

Yonder he comes; and that arrant malmsey-nose
knave, Bardolph, with him. Do your offices, do
your offices, master Fang, and master Snare; do
me, do me, do me your offices.

Fal. How now? whose mare 's dead? what 's
the matter?

Fang. Sir John, I arrest you at the suit of mistress Quickly.

Fal. Away, varlets!—Draw, Bardolph; cut me
off the villain's head; throw the quean in the
channel.

Host. Throw me in the channel? I 'll throw
thee in the channel. Wilt thou? wilt thou? thou
bastardly rogue!—Murder, murder! O thou
honey-suckle villain! wilt thou kill God's officers,
and the king's? O thou honey-seed rogue!" thou
art a honey-seed; a man-queller, and a woman-
queller.

Fal. Keep them off, Bardolph.

Fang. A rescue! a rescue!

Host. Good people, bring a rescue or two.—

Thou wo't, wo't thou? thou wo't, wo't thou? do,
do, thou rogue! do, thou hemp-seed!

Fal. Away, you scullion! you rampallian! you
fustilarian! I'll tickle your catastrophe.

Enter the LORD CHIEF JUSTICE, *attended.*

Ch. Just. What's the matter? keep the peace
here, ho!

Host. Good my lord, be good to me! I beseech
you, stand to me!

Ch. Just. How now, sir John? what, are you
brawling here?
Doth this become your place, your time, and business?
You should have been well on your way to York.—
Stand from him, fellow: Wherefore hang'st thou
on him?

Host. O my most worshipful lord, an't please
your grace, I am a poor widow of Eastcheap, and
he is arrested at my suit.

Ch. Just. For what sum?

Host. It is more than for some, my lord; it is
for all, all I have: he hath eaten me out of house
and home; he hath put all my substance into that
fat belly of his:—but I will have some of it out
again, or I'll ride thee o' nights, like the mare.

Fal. I think, I am as like to ride the mare, if I
have any vantage of ground to get up.

Ch. Just. How comes this, sir John? Fie! what
man of good temper would endure this tempest
of exclamation? Are you not ashamed, to enforce a
poor widow to so rough a course to come by her
own?

Fal. What is the gross sum that I owe thee?

Host. Marry, if thou wert an honest man, thyself, and the money too. Thou didst swear to me
upon a parcel-gilt goblet, sitting in my Dolphin-
chamber, at the round table, by a sea-coal fire, upon
Wednesday in Whitsun-week, when the prince
broke thy head for liking his father to a singing-
man of Windsor, thou didst swear to me then,
as I was washing thy wound, to marry me, and
make me my lady thy wife. Canst thou deny it?
Did not goodwife Keech, the butcher's wife, come
in then, and call me gossip Quickly? coming in to
borrow a mess of vinegar; telling us, she had a
good dish of prawns; whereby thou didst desire to
eat some; whereby I told thee, they were ill for a
green wound? And didst thou not, when she was
gone down stairs, desire me to be no more so familiarity with such poor people; saying, that ere long
they should call me madam? And didst thou not

kiss me, and bid me fetch thee thirty shillings?
I put thee now to thy book-oath; deny it, if thou
canst.

Fal. My lord, this is a poor mad soul: and she
says, up and down the town, that her eldest son is
like you: she hath been in good case, and the truth
is, poverty hath distracted her. But for these foolish
officers, I beseech you, I may have redress against
them.

Ch. Just. Sir John, sir John, I am well acquainted with your manner of wrenching the true
cause the false way. It is not a confident brow, nor
the throng of words that come with such more than
impudent sauciness from you, can thrust me from
a level consideration; you have, as it appears to
me, practised upon the easy-yielding spirit of this
woman, and made her serve your uses both in
purse and person.

Host. Yea, in troth, my lord.

Ch. Just. Pr'ythee, peace:—Pay her the debt
you owe her, and unpay the villany you have done
with her; the one you may do with sterling money,
and the other with current repentance.

Fal. My lord, I will not undergo this sneap[14]
without reply. You call honourable boldness, impudent sauciness: if a man will make court'sy, and
say nothing, he is virtuous: No, my lord, my humble duty remembered, I will not be your suitor; I
say to you, I do desire deliverance from these officers, being upon hasty employment in the king's
affairs.

Ch. Just. You speak as having power to do
wrong; but answer in the effect of your reputation,[14]
and satisfy the poor woman.

Fal. Come hither, hostess.   *[Taking her aside.*

Enter GOWER.

Ch. Just. Now, master Gower: What news?

Gow. The king, my lord, and Harry prince of
Wales
Are near at hand: the rest the paper tells.

Fal. As I am a gentleman;——

Host. Nay, you said so before.

Fal. As I am a gentleman;——Come, no more
words of it.

Host. By this heavenly ground I tread on, I
must be fain to pawn both my plate, and the ta-
pestry of my dining-chambers.

Fal. Glasses, glasses, is the only drinking: and
for thy walls,—a pretty slight drollery, or the story
of the prodigal, or the German hunting in water
work, is worth a thousand of these bed-hangings

and these fly-bitten tapestries. Let it be ten pound, if thou canst. Come, an it were not for thy humours, there is not a better wench in England. Go, wash thy face, and draw thy action: Come, thou must not be in this humour with me; dost not know me? Come, come, I know thou wast set on to this.

Host. Pray thee, sir John, let it be but twenty nobles; i'faith I am loath to pawn my plate, in good earnest, la.

Fal. Let it alone; I'll make other shift; you'll be a fool still.

Host. Well, you shall have it, though I pawn my gown. I hope, you'll come to supper: You'll pay me all together?

Fal. Will I live?—Go, with her, with her; [*To Bard.*] Hook on, hook on.

Host. Will you have Doll Tear-sheet meet you at supper?

Fal. No more words; let's have her.

[*Exeunt Host., Bard., Officers, and Page.*

Ch. Just. I have heard better news.

Fal. What's the news, my good lord?

Ch. Just. Where lay the king last night?

Gow. At Basingstoke, my lord.

Fal. I hope, my lord, all's well: What's the news, my lord?

Ch. Just. Come all his forces back?

Gow. No; fifteen hundred foot, five hundred horse,
Are march'd up to my lord of Lancaster,
Against Northumberland, and the archbishop.

Fal. Comes the king back from Wales, my noble lord?

Ch. Just. You shall have letters of me presently: Come, go along with me, good master Gower.

Fal. My lord!

Ch. Just. What's the matter?

Fal. Master Gower, shall I entreat you with me to dinner?

Gow. I must wait upon my good lord here: I thank you, good sir John.

Ch. Just. Sir John, you loiter here too long, being you are to take soldiers up in counties as you go.

Fal. Will you sup with me, master Gower?

Ch. Just. What foolish master taught you these manners, sir John?

Fal. Master Gower, if they become me not, he was a fool that taught them me.—This is the right fencing grace, my lord; tap for tap, and so part fair.

758

Ch. Just. Now the Lord lighten thee! thou art a great fool.　　　　　　[*Exeunt*

SCENE II.—*The Same. Another Street.*

Enter PRINCE HENRY *and* POINS.

P. Hen. Trust me, I am exceeding weary.

Poins. Is it come to that? I had thought, weariness durst not have attached one of so high blood.

P. Hen. 'Faith, it does me, though it discolours the complexion of my greatness to acknowledge it. Doth it not show vilely in me, to desire small beer?

Poins. Why, a prince should not be so loosely studied, as to remember so weak a composition.

P. Hen. Belike then, my appetite was not princely got: for, by my troth, I do now remember the poor creature, small beer. But, indeed, these humble considerations make me out of love with my greatness. What a disgrace is it to me, to remember thy name? or to know thy face to morrow? or to take note how many pair of silk stockings thou hast; viz. these, and those that were the peach-colour'd ones? or to bear the inventory of thy shirts; as, one for superfluity, and one other for use?—but that, the tennis-court keeper knows better than I; for it is a low ebb of linen with thee, when thou keepest not racket there; as thou hast not done a great while, because the rest of thy low-countries have made a shift to eat up thy holland: and God knows, whether those that bawl out the ruins of thy linen, shall inherit his kingdom: but the midwives say, the children are not in the fault; whereupon the world increases, and kindreds are mightily strengthened.

Poins. How ill it follows, after you have laboured so hard, you should talk so idly! Tell me, how many good young princes would do so, their fathers being so sick as yours at this time is?

P. Hen. Shall I tell thee one thing, Poins?

Poins. Yes; and let it be an excellent good thing.

P. Hen. It shall serve among wits of no higher breeding than thine.

Poins. Go to; I stand the push of your one thing that you will tell.

P. Hen. Why, I tell thee,—it is not meet that I should be sad, now my father is sick: albeit I could tell to thee, (as to one it pleases me, for fault of a better, to call my friend,) I could be sad, and sad indeed too.

Poins. Very hardly, upon such a subject.

P. Hen. By this hand, thou think'st me as far 'n the devil's book, as thou, and Falstaff, for obduracy and persistency : Let the end try the man. But I tell thee,—my heart bleeds inwardly, that my father is so sick : and keeping such vile company as thou art, hath in reason taken from me all ostentation of sorrow.

Poins. The reason !

P. Hen. What would'st thou think of me, if I should weep !

Poins. I would think thee a most princely hypocrite.

P. Hen. It would be every man's thought : and thou art a blessed fellow, to think as every man thinks ; never a man's thought in the world keeps the road-way better than thine : every man would think me an hypocrite indeed. And what incites your most worshipful thought, to think so !

Poins. Why, because you have been so lewd, and so much engrafted to Falstaff.

P. Hen. And to thee.

Poins. By this light, I am well spoken of, I can hear it with my own ears : the worst that they can say of me is, that I am a second brother, and that I am a proper fellow of my hands ; and those two things, I confess, I cannot help. By the mass, here comes Bardolph.

P. Hen. And the boy that I gave Falstaff: he had him from me christian ; and look, if the fat villain have not transformed him ape.

Enter BARDOLPH *and* Page.

Bard. 'Save your grace.

P. Hen. And yours, most noble Bardolph !

Bard. Come, you virtuous ass, [*To the Page.*] you bashful fool, must you be blushing ? wherefore blush you now ? What a maidenly-man-at-arms are you become ! Is it such a matter, to get a pottle-pot's maidenhead !

Page. He called me even now, my lord, through a red lattice," and I could discern no part of his face from the window : at last, I spied his eyes ; and, methought, he had made two holes in the ale-wife's new petticoat, and peeped through.

P. Hen. Hath not the boy profited !

Bard. Away, you whoreson upright rabbit, away !

Page. Away, you rascally Althea's dream, away !

P. Hen. Instruct us, boy : What dream, boy !

Page. Marry, my lord, Althea dreamed she was delivered of a fire-brand ; and therefore I call him her dream.

P. Hen. A crown's worth of good interpretation.—There it is, boy.   [*Gives him money.*

Poins. O, that this good blossom could be kept from cankers !—Well, there is sixpence to preserve thee.

Bard. And you do not make him be hanged among you, the gallows shall have wrong.

P. Hen. And how doth thy master, Bardolph !

Bard. Well, my lord. He heard of your grace's coming to town ; there 's a letter for you.

Poins. Delivered with good respect.—And how doth the martlemas, your master !

Bard. In bodily health, sir.

Poins. Marry, the immortal part needs a physician : but that moves not him ; though that be sick, it dies not.

P. Hen. I do allow this wen to be as familiar with me as my dog : and he holds his place ; for, look you, how he writes.

Poins. [*Reads.*] "John Falstaff, knight,"—— Every man must know that, as oft as he has occasion to name himself. Even like those that are kin to the king : for they never prick their finger, but they say, "There is some of the king's blood spilt : How comes that !" says he, that takes upon him not to conceive : the answer is as ready as a borrower's cap ; "I am the king's poor cousin, sir."

P. Hen. Nay, they will be kin to us, or they will fetch it from Japhet. But the letter :—

Poins. "Sir John Falstaff, knight, to the son of the king, nearest his father, Harry prince of Wales, greeting."—Why, this is a certificate.

P. Hen. Peace !

Poins. "I will imitate the honourable Roman in brevity :"—he sure means brevity in breath ; short-winded.—

"I commend me to thee, I commend thee, and I leave thee. Be not too familiar with Poins ; for he misuses thy favours so much, that he swears, thou art to marry his sister Nell. Repent at idle times as thou may'st, and so farewell.

"Thine, by yea and no, (which is as much as to say, as thou usest him,) JACK FALSTAFF, with my familiars ; John, with my brothers and sisters ; and sir John with all Europe."

My lord, I will steep this letter in sack, and make him eat it.

P. Hen. That 's to make him eat twenty of his words. But do you use me thus, Ned ? must I marry your sister !

782

Poins. May the wench have no worse fortune!
but I never said so.

P. Hen. Well, thus we play the fools with the
time; and the spirits of the wise sit in the clouds,
and mock us.—Is your master here in London?

Bard. Yes, my lord.

P. Hen. Where sups he? doth the old boar
feed in the old frank?[18]

Bard. At the old place, my lord; in Eastcheap.

P. Hen. What company?

Page. Ephesians, my lord;[19] of the old church.

P. Hen. Sup any women with him?

Page. None, my lord, but old mistress Quickly,
and mistress Doll Tear-sheet.

P. Hen. What pagan may that be?

Page. A proper gentlewoman, sir, and a kins-
woman of my master's.

P. Hen. Even such kin, as the parish heifers
are to the town bull.—Shall we steal upon them,
Ned, at supper?

Poins. I am your shadow, my lord; I'll follow
you.

P. Hen. Sirrah, you boy,—and Bardolph;—no
word to your master, that I am yet come to town:
There's for your silence.

Bard. I have no tongue, sir.

Page. And for mine, sir,—I will govern it.

P. Hen. Fare ye well; go. [*Exeunt* BARD. *and*
Page.]—This Doll Tear-sheet should be some
road.

Poins. I warrant you, as common as the way
between Saint Alban's and London.

P. Hen. How might we see Falstaff bestow
himself to-night in his true colours, and not ourselves be seen?

Poins. Put on two leather jerkins, and aprons,
and wait upon him at his table as drawers.

P. Hen. From a god to a bull! a heavy de-
scension! it was Jove's case. From a prince to
a prentice? a low transformation! that shall
be mine: for, in every thing, the purpose must
weigh with the folly. Follow me, Ned.

[*Exeunt.*

SCENE III.—Warkworth. *Before the Castle.*

Enter NORTHUMBERLAND, LADY NORTHUMBER-
LAND, *and* LADY PERCY.

North. I pray thee, loving wife, and gentle
daughter,
Give even way unto my rough affairs:
Put not you on the visage of the times,

And be, like them, to Percy troublesome.

Lady N. I have given over, I will speak no
more:
Do what you will; your wisdom be your guide.

North. Alas, sweet wife, my honour's at
pawn;
And, but my going, nothing can redeem it.

Lady P. O, yet, for God's sake, go not to these
wars:
The time was, father, that you broke your word,
When you were more endear'd to it than now;
When your own Percy, when my heart's dear
Harry,
Threw many a northward look, to see his father
Bring up his powers; but he did long in vain.
Who then persuaded you to stay at home?
There were two honours lost; yours, and your son's.
For yours,—may heavenly glory brighten it!
For his,—it struck upon him, as the sun
In the grey vault of heaven: and, by his light,
Did all the chivalry of England move
To do brave acts; he was, indeed, the glass
Wherein the noble youth did dress themselves.
He had no legs, that practis'd not his gait:
And speaking thick, which nature made his
blemish,
Became the accents of the valiant;
For those that could speak low, and tardily,
Would turn their own perfection to abuse,
To seem like him: So that, in speech, in gait,
In diet, in affections of delight,
In military rules, humours of blood,
He was the mark and glass, copy and book,
That fashion'd others. And him,—O wondrous
him!
O miracle of men!—him did you leave,
(Second to none, unseconded by you,)
To look upon the hideous god of war
In disadvantage; to abide a field,
Where nothing but the sound of Hotspur's name
Did seem defensible:—so you left him:
Never, O never, do his ghost the wrong,
To hold your honour more precise and nice
With others, than with him; let them alone;
The marshal, and the archbishop, are strong:
Had my sweet Harry had but half their numbers,
To-day might I, hanging on Hotspur's neck,
Have talk'd of Monmouth's grave.

North.   Beshrew your heart,
Fair daughter! you do draw my spirits from me
With new lamenting ancient oversights.
But I must go, and meet with danger there;

Or it will seek me in another place,
And find me worse provided.

    Lady N.   O, fly to Scotland,
Till that the nobles, and the armed commons,
Have of their puissance made a little taste.

    Lady P. If they get ground and vantage of the
                 king,
Then join you with them, like a rib of steel,
To make strength stronger; but, for all our loves,
First let them try themselves: So did your son;
He was so suffer'd; so came I a widow;
And never shall have length of life enough,
To rain upon remembrance with mine eyes,
That it may grow and sprout as high as heaven,
For recordation to my noble husband.

    North. Come, come, go in with me: 't is with
       my mind,
As with the tide swell'd up unto its height,
That makes a still-stand, running neither way.
Fain would I go to meet the archbishop,
But many thousand reasons hold me back:——
I will resolve for Scotland; there am I,
Till time and vantage crave my company.

                     [*Exeunt.*

SCENE IV.—London. *A Room in the* Boar's
Head *Tavern, in* Eastcheap.

    Enter Two Drawers.

    1st Draw. What the devil hast thou brought
there? apple-Johns? thou know'st, sir John cannot endure an apple-John.

    2nd Draw. Mass, thou sayest true: The
prince once set a dish of apple-Johns before him,
and told him, there were five more sir Johns:
and, putting off his hat, said, "I will now take
my leave of these six dry, round, old, withered
knights." It angered him to the heart; but he
hath forgot that.

    1st Draw. Why then, cover, and set them
down: And see if thou canst find out Sneak's
noise; mistress Tear-sheet would fain hear
some music. Despatch:—The room where they
supped is too hot; they'll come in straight.

    2nd Draw. Sirrah, here will be the prince,
and master Poins anon: and they will put on
two of our jerkins and aprons; and sir John must
not know of it: Bardolph hath brought word.

    1st Draw. By the mass, here will be old
utis: It will be an excellent stratagem.

    2nd Draw. I'll see, if I can find out Sneak.

                     [*Exit.*

    Enter Hostess *and* Doll Tear-sheet.

    Host. I' faith, sweet heart, methinks now you
are in an excellent good temperality: your pulsidge
beats as extraordinarily as heart would desire; and
your colour, I warrant you, is as red as any rose:
But, i' faith, you have drunk too much canaries;
and that 's a marvellous searching wine, and it
perfumes the blood ere one can say,—What 's
this? How do you now?

    Dol. Better than I was. Hem.

    Host. Why, that 's well said; a good heart 's
worth gold. Look, here comes sir John.

    Enter Falstaff, *singing.*

    Fal. "When Arthur first in court"—Empty
the jordan.—"And was a worthy king:" [*Exit
Drawer.*] How now, mistress Doll?

    Host. Sick of a calm: yea, good sooth.

    Fal. So is all her sect; an they be once in a
calm, they are sick.

    Dol. You muddy rascal, is that all the comfort
you give me?

    Fal. You make fat rascals, mistress Doll.

    Dol. I make them! gluttony and diseases
make them; I make them not.

    Fal. If the cook help to make the gluttony,
you help to make the diseases, Doll: we catch
of you, Doll, we catch of you; grant that, my
pure virtue, grant that.

    Dol. Ay, marry; our chains, and our jewels.

    Fal. "Your brooches, pearls, and owches;"
for to serve bravely, is to come halting off, you
know: To come off the breach with his pike
bent bravely, and to surgery bravely; to venture upon the charged chambers bravely:——

    Dol. Hang yourself, you muddy conger, hang
yourself!

    Host. By my troth, this is the old fashion; you
two never meet but you fall to some discord: you
are both, in good troth, as rheumatic as two dry
toasts: you cannot one bear with another's con-
firmities. What the good-year! one must bear,
and that must be you: [*To* Doll.] you are the
weaker vessel, as they say, the emptier vessel.

    Dol. Can a weak empty vessel bear such a
huge full hogshead? there's a whole merchant's
venture of Bordeaux stuff in him; you have not
seen a hulk better stuffed in the hold.—Come,
I'll be friends with thee, Jack: thou art going
to the wars; and whether I shall ever see thee
again, or no, there is nobody cares.

Re-enter Drawer.

Draw. Sir, ancient Pistol's below, and would speak with you.

Dol. Hang him, swaggering rascal! let him not come hither: it is the foul-mouth'dst rogue in England.

Host. If he swagger, let him not come here: no, by my faith; I must live amongst my neighbours; I'll no swaggerers: I am in good name and fame with the very best:—Shut the door:—there comes no swaggerers here: I have not lived all this while, to have swaggering now:—shut the door, I pray you.

Fal. Dost thou hear, hostess?—

Host. Pray you, pacify yourself, sir John; there comes no swaggerers here.

Fal. Dost thou hear? it is mine ancient.

Host. Tilly-fally, sir John, never tell me; your ancient swaggerer comes not in my doors. I was before master Tisick, the deputy, the other day; and, as he said to me,—it was no longer ago than Wednesday last.—"Neighbour Quickly," says he;—master Dumb, our minister, was by then;—"Neighbour Quickly," says he, "receive those that are civil; for," said he, "you are in an ill name;"—now he said so, I can tell whereupon; "for," says he, "you are an honest woman, and well thought on; therefore take heed what guests you receive: Receive," says he, "no swaggering companions."——There comes none here:—you would bless you to hear what he said:—no, I'll no swaggerers.

Fal. He's no swaggerer, hostess; a tame cheater, he; you may stroke him as gently as a puppy-greyhound: he will not swagger with a Barbary hen, if her feathers turn back in any show of resistance.—Call him up, drawer.

Host. Cheater, call you him? I will bar no honest man my house, nor no cheater: But I do not love swaggering; by my troth, I am the worse, when one says—swagger: feel, masters, how I shake; look you, I warrant you.

Dol. So you do, hostess.

Host. Do I? yea, in very truth, do I, an't were an aspen leaf: I cannot abide swaggerers.

Enter PISTOL, BARDOLPH, *and* Page.

Pist. 'Save you, sir John!

Fal. Welcome, ancient Pistol. Here, Pistol, I charge you with a cup of sack: do you discharge upon mine hostess.

Pist. I will discharge upon her, sir John, with two bullets.

Fal. She is pistol-proof, sir; you shall hardly offend her.

Host. Come, I'll drink no proofs, nor no bullets: I'll drink no more than will do me good, for no man's pleasure, I.

Pist. Then to you, mistress Dorothy; I will charge you.

Dol. Charge me? I scorn you, scurvy companion. What! you poor, base, rascally, cheating lack-linen mate! Away, you mouldy rogue, away! I am meet for your master.

Pist. I know you, mistress Dorothy.

Dol. Away, you cut-purse rascal! you filthy bung, away! by this wine, I'll thrust my knife in your mouldy chaps, an you play the saucy cuttle with me. Away, you bottle-ale rascal! you basket-hilt stale juggler, you!—Since when, I pray you, sir?—What, with two points on your shoulder? much?[?]

Pist. I will murder your ruff for this.

Fal. No more, Pistol; I would not have you go off here: discharge yourself of our company, Pistol.

Host. No, good captain Pistol; not here, sweet captain.

Dol. Captain! thou abominable damned cheater, art thou not ashamed to be called—captain? If captains were of my mind, they would truncheon you out, for taking their names upon you before you have earned them. You a captain, you slave! for what? for tearing a poor whore's ruff in a bawdy-house?—He a captain! Hang him, rogue! He lives upon mouldy stewed prunes, and dried cakes. A captain! these villains will make the word captain as odious as the word occupy;[?] which was an excellent good word before it was ill sorted: therefore captains had need look to it.

Bard. Pray thee, go down, good ancient.

Fal. Hark thee hither, mistress Doll.

Pist. Not I: tell thee what, corporal Bardolph;—I could tear her:—I'll be revenged on her.

Page. Pray thee, go down.

Pist. I'll see her damned first;—to Pluto's damned lake, to the infernal deep, with Erebus and tortures vile also. Hold hook and line, say I. Down! down, dogs! down faitors! Have we not Hiren here?[?]

Host. Good captain Peesel, be quiet; it is very late, i' faith: I beseek you now aggravate your choler.

Pist. These be good humours, indeed! Shall
    packhorses,
And hollow pamper'd jades of Asia,
Which cannot go but thirty miles a day,
Compare with Cæsars, and with Cannibals,[18]
And Trojan Greeks? nay, rather damn them with
King Cerberus; and let the welkin roar.
Shall we fall foul for toys?

Host. By my troth, captain, these are very bitter words.

Bard. Be gone, good ancient: this will grow to a brawl anon.

Pist. Die men, like dogs; give crowns like pins: Have we not Hiren here?

Host. O' my word, captain, there 's none such here. What the good-year! do you think, I would deny her? for God's sake, be quiet.

Pist. Then, feed, and be fat, my fair Calipolis:[19]
Come, give 's some sack.

  Si fortuna me tormenta, sperato me contenta.—
Fear we broad-sides? no, let the fiend give fire:
Give me some sack;—and, sweetheart, lie thou
    there.   [*Laying down his sword.*
Come we to full points here; and are *et cetera's*
    nothing?

Fal. Pistol, I would be quiet.

Pist. Sweet knight, I kiss thy neif:[20] What! we have seen the seven stars.

Dol. Thrust him down stairs: I cannot endure such a fustian rascal.

Pist. Thrust him down stairs! know we not Galloway nags?[21]

Fal. Quoit him down, Bardolph, like a shove-groat shilling: nay, if he do nothing but speak nothing, he shall be nothing here.

Bard. Come, get you down stairs.

Pist. What! shall we have incision? shall we imbrue!—   [*Snatching up his sword.*
Then death rock me asleep, abridge my doleful
    days!
Why then, let grievous, ghastly, gaping wounds
Untwine the sisters three! Come, Atropos, I say!

Host. Here 's goodly stuff toward!

Fal. Give me my rapier, boy.

Dol. I pray thee, Jack, I pray thee, do not draw.

Fal. Get you down stairs.
    [*Drawing, and driving* Pist. *out.*

Host. Here 's a goodly tumult! I 'll forswear keeping house, afore I 'll be in these territs and frights. So; murder, I warrant now.——Alas, alas! put up your naked weapons, put up your naked weapons.   [*Exeunt* Pist. *and* Bard.

Dol. I pray thee, Jack, be quiet; the rascal is gone. Ah, you whoreson little valiant villain, you.

Host. Are you not hurt i' the groin? methought, he made a shrewd thrust at your belly.

Re-enter Bardolph.

Fal. Have you turned him out of doors?

Bard. Yes, sir. The rascal 's drunk; you have hurt him, sir, in the shoulder.

Fal. A rascal! to brave me!

Dol. Ah, you sweet little rogue, you! Alas, poor ape, how thou sweat'st! Come, let me wipe thy face;—come on, you whoreson chops:—Ah, rogue! i' faith, I love thee. Thou art as valorous as Hector of Troy, worth five of Agamemnon, and ten times better than the nine worthies. Ah, villain!

Fal. A rascally slave! I will toss the rogue in a blanket.

Dol. Do, if thou darest for thy heart: if thou dost, I 'll canvass thee between a pair of sheets.

Enter Music.

Page. The music is come, sir.

Fal. Let them play;—Play, sirs.—Sit on my knee, Doll. A rascal bragging slave! the rogue fled from me like quicksilver.

Dol. i' faith, and thou followedst him like a church. Thou whoreson little tidy Bartholomew boar-pig, when wilt thou leave fighting o' days, and foining o' nights, and begin to patch up thine old body for heaven?

Enter behind, Prince Henry *and* Poins, *disguised like Drawers.*

Fal. Peace, good Doll! do not speak like a death's head: do not bid me remember mine end.

Dol. Sirrah, what humour is the prince of?

Fal. A good shallow young fellow: he would have made a good pantler, he would have chipped bread well.

Dol. They say, Poins has a good wit.

Fal. He a good wit! hang him, baboon! his wit is as thick as Tewksbury mustard; there is no more conceit in him, than is in a mallet.

Dol. Why does the prince love him so then?

Fal. Because their legs are both of a bigness; and he plays at quoits well; and eats conger and fennel; and drinks off candles' ends for flap-dragons; and rides the wild mare with the boys; and jumps upon joint-stools; and swears with a good grace; and wears his boot very smooth, like unto the sign of the leg; and breeds no bate with telling of discreet stories; and such other gambol faculties he hath, that show a weak mind and an able body, for the which the prince admits him: for the prince himself is such another; the weight of a hair will turn the scales between their avoirdupois.

P. Hen. Would not this nave of a wheel have his ears cut off?

Poins. Let 's beat him before his whore.

P. Hen. Look, if the withered elder hath not his poll clawed like a parrot.

Poins. Is it not strange, that desire should so many years outlive performance?

Fal. Kiss me, Doll.

P. Hen. Saturn and Venus this year in conjunction! what says the almanac to that?

Poins. And, look, whether the fiery Trigon, his man, be not lisping to his master's old tables,²⁰ his note-book, his counsel-keeper.

Fal. Thou dost give me flattering busses.

Dol. Nay, truly; I kiss thee with a most constant heart.

Fal. I am old, I am old.

Dol. I love thee better than I love e'er a scurvy young boy of them all.

Fal. What stuff wilt have a kirtle of? I shall receive money on Thursday: thou shalt have a cap to-morrow. A merry song, come: it grows late, we 'll to bed. Thou 'lt forget me, when I am gone.

Dol. By my troth thou 'lt set me a weeping, an thou sayest so: prove that ever I dress myself handsome till thy return. —— Well, hearken the end.

Fal. Some sack, Francis.

P. Hen. Poins. Anon, anon, sir. [*Advancing.*

Fal. Ha! a bastard son of the king's?—And art not thou Poins his brother?

P. Hen. Why, thou globe of sinful continents, what a life dost thou lead?

Fal. A better than thou; I am a gentleman, thou art a drawer.

P. Hen. Very true, sir; and I come to draw you out by the ears.

Host. O, the Lord preserve thy good grace! by my troth, welcome to London.—Now the Lord bless that sweet face of thine! O Jesu, are you come from Wales?

Fal. Thou whoreson mad compound of majesty,—by this light flesh and corrupt blood, thou art welcome. [*Leaning his hand upon Dol.*

788

Dol. How! you fat fool, I scorn you.

Poins. My lord, he will drive you out of your revenge, and turn all to a merriment, if you take not the heat.

P. Hen. You whoreson candle-mine, you, how vilely did you speak of me even now, before this honest, virtuous, civil gentlewoman?

Host. 'Blessing o' your good heart! and so she is, by my troth.

Fal. Didst thou hear me?

P. Hen. Yes; and you knew me, as you did when you ran away by Gads-hill: you knew, I was at your back; and spoke it on purpose, to try my patience.

Fal. No, no, no; not so; I did not think, thou wast within hearing.

P. Hen. I shall drive you then to confess the wilful abuse; and then I know how to handle you.

Fal. No abuse, Hal, on mine honour; no abuse.

P. Hen. Not! to dispraise me; and call me—pantler, and bread-chipper, and I know not what?

Fal. No abuse, Hal.

Poins. No abuse?

Fal. No abuse, Ned, in the world; honest Ned, none. I dispraised him before the wicked, that the wicked might not fall in love with him; —in which doing, I have done the part of a careful friend, and a true subject, and thy father is to give me thanks for it. No abuse, Hal;—none, Ned, none;—no, boys, none.

P. Hen. See now, whether pure fear, and entire cowardice, doth not make thee wrong this virtuous gentlewoman to close with us? Is she of the wicked? Is thine hostess here of the wicked? Or is the boy of the wicked? Or honest Bardolph, whose zeal burns in his nose, of the wicked?

Poins. Answer, thou dead elm, answer.

Fal. The fiend hath pricked down Bardolph irrecoverable; and his face is Lucifer's privy-kitchen, where he doth nothing but roast malt worms. For the boy,—there is a good angel about him; but the devil outbids him too.

P. Hen. For the women,——

Fal. For one of them,—she is in hell already, and burns, poor soul! For the other,—I owe her money; and whether she be damned for that, I know not.

Host. No, I warrant you.

Fal. No, I think thou art not; I think, thou

art quit for that: Marry, there is another indictment upon thee, for suffering flesh to be eaten in
thy house, contrary to the law; for the which, I
think, thou wilt howl.

Host. All victuallers do so: What 's a joint of
mutton or two in a whole Lent?

P. Hen. You, gentlewoman.——

Dol. What says your grace?

Fal. His grace says that which his flesh rebels
against.

Host. Who knocks so loud at door? look to
the door there, Francis.

Enter PETO.

P. Hen. Peto, how now? what news?

Peto. The king your father is at Westminster;
And there are twenty weak and wearied posts,
Come from the north: and, as I came along,
I met, and overtook, a dozen captains,
Bare-headed, sweating, knocking at the taverns,
And asking every one for sir John Falstaff.

P. Hen. By heaven, Poins, I feel me much to
blame,
So idly to profane the precious time;
When tempest of commotion, like the south
Borne with black vapour, doth begin to melt,
And drop upon our bare unarmed heads.
Give me my sword, and cloak:—Falstaff, good
night.

[*Exeunt* P. HEN., POINS, PETO, *and* BARD.

Fal. Now comes in the sweetest morsel of the
night, and we must hence, and leave it unpicked.
[*Knocking heard.*] More knocking at the door?

Re-enter BARDOLPH.

How now? what 's the matter?

Bard. You must away to court, sir, presently;
a dozen captains stay at door for you.

Fal. Pay the musicians, sirrah. [*To the Page.*]
—Farewell, hostess;—farewell, Doll.—You see,
my good wenches, how men of merit are sought
after: the undeserver may sleep, when the man of
action is called on. Farewell, good wenches: If
I be not sent away post, I will see you again ere
I go.

Dol. I cannot speak;—If my heart be not
ready to burst:—Well, sweet Jack, have a care of
thyself.

Fal. Farewell, farewell.

[*Exeunt* FAL. *and* BARD

Host. Well, fare thee well: I have known thee
these twenty-nine years, come peascod-time; but
an honester, and truer-hearted man.—Well, fare
thee well.

Bard. [*Within.*] Mistress Tear-sheet,——

Host. What 's the matter?

Bard. [*Within.*] Bid mistress Tear-sheet come
to my master.

Host. O run, Doll, run; run, good Doll.

[*Exeunt*

ACT III.

SCENE I.—*A Room in the Palace.*

Enter KING HENRY *in his Nightgown, with a Page.*

K. Hen. Go, call the earls of Surrey and of
Warwick;
But, ere they come, bid them o'er-read these letters,
And well consider of them: Make good speed.——

[*Exit Page.*

How many thousand of my poorest subjects
Are at this hour asleep!—Sleep, gentle sleep,
Nature's soft nurse, how have I frighted thee,
That thou no more wilt weigh my eyelids down,
And steep my senses in forgetfulness?

Why rather, sleep, liest thou in smoky cribs,
Upon uneasy pallets stretching thee,
And hush'd with buzzing night-flies to thy slumber
Than in the perfumed chambers of the great,
Under the canopies of costly state,
And lull'd with sounds of sweetest melody?
O thou dull god, why liest thou with the vile,
In loathsome beds; and leav'st the kingly couch
A watch-case, or a common 'larum bell?
Wilt thou upon the high and giddy mast
Seal up the ship-boy's eyes, and rock his brains
In cradle of the rude imperious surge;
And in the visitation of the winds,

759

Who take the ruffian billows by the top,
Curling their monstrous heads, and hanging them
With deaf'ning clamours in the slippery clouds,
That, with the hurly, death itself awakes?
Can'st thou, O partial sleep! give thy repose
To the wet sea-boy in an hour so rude;
And, in the calmest and most stillest night,
With all appliances and means to boot,
Deny it to a king? Then, happy low, lie down!
Uneasy lies the head that wears a crown.

Enter WARWICK *and* SURREY.

War. Many good morrows to your majesty!
K. Hen. Is it good morrow, lords?
War. T is one o'clock, and past.
K. Hen. Why then, good morrow to you all,
　　my lords.
Have you read o'er the letters that I sent you?
War. We have, my liege.
K. Hen. Then you perceive, the body of our
　　kingdom
How foul it is; what rank diseases grow,
And with what danger, near the heart of it.
War. It is but as a body, yet, distemper'd;
Which to his former strength may be restor'd,
With good advice, and little medicine:——
My lord Northumberland will soon be cool'd.
K. Hen. O heaven! that one might read the
　　book of fate:
And see the revolution of the times
Make mountains level, and the continent
(Weary of solid firmness,) melt itself
Into the sea! and, other times, to see
The beachy girdle of the ocean
Too wide for Neptune's hips; how chances mock,
And changes fill the cup of alteration
With divers liquors! O, if this were seen,
The happiest youth,—viewing his progress through,
What perils past, what crosses to ensue,—
Would shut the book, and sit him down and die.
T is not ten years gone,
Since Richard, and Northumberland, great friends,
Did feast together, and, in two years after,
Were they at wars: It is but eight years, since
This Percy was the man nearest my soul;
Who like a brother toil'd in my affairs,
And laid his love and life under my foot;
Yea, for my sake, even to the eyes of Richard,
Gave him defiance. But which of you was by,
(You, cousin Nevil, as I may remember,)
　　　　　　　　　　　　　　　[*To* WAR.
When Richard,—with his eye brimful of tears,

Then check'd and rated by Northumberland,—
Did speak these words, now prov'd a prophecy?
"Northumberland, thou ladder, by the which
My cousin Bolingbroke ascends my throne;"—
Though then, heaven knows, I had no such intent.
But that necessity so bow'd the state,
That I and greatness were compell'd to kiss:——
"The time shall come," thus did he follow it,
"The time will come, that foul sin, gathering head
Shall break into corruption:"—so went on,
Foretelling this same time's condition,
And the division of our amity.
War. There is a history in all men's lives,
Figuring the nature of the times deceas'd:
The which observ'd, a man may prophesy,
With a near aim, of the main chance of things
As yet not come to life; which in their seeds,
And weak beginnings, lie intreasured.
Such things become the hatch and brood of time
And, by the necessary form of this,
King Richard might create a perfect guess,
That great Northumberland, then false to him,
Would, of that seed, grow to a greater falseness;
Which should not find a ground to root upon.
Unless on you.
K. Hen. Are these things then necessities?
Then let us meet them like necessities:—
And that same word even now cries out on us;
They say, the bishop and Northumberland
Are fifty thousand strong.
War. 　　　　　　It cannot be, my lord;
Rumour doth double, like the voice and echo,
The numbers of the fear'd:—Please it your grace,
To go to bed; upon my life, my lord,
The powers that you already have sent forth,
Shall bring this prize in very easily.
To comfort you the more, I have receiv'd
A certain instance, that Glendower is dead."
Your majesty hath been this fortnight ill;
And these unseason'd hours, perforce, must add
Unto your sickness.
K. Hen. 　　　　I will take your counsel:
And, were these inward wars once out of hand,
We would, dear lords, unto the Holy Land.
　　　　　　　　　　　　　　　[*Exeunt.*

SCENE II.—*Court before* Justice Shallow's *House
in Gloucestershire.*

Enter SHALLOW, *and* SILENCE, *meeting;* MOULDY,
SHADOW, WART, FEEBLE, BULLCALF, *and Servants, behind.*

Shal. Come on, come on, come on; give me

your hand, sir, give me your hand, sir: an early stirrer by the rood." And how doth my good cousin Silence?

Sil. Good morrow, good cousin Shallow.

Shal. And how doth my cousin, your bed-fellow? and your fairest daughter, and mine, my god-daughter Ellen?

Sil. Alas, a black ouzel, cousin Shallow.

Shal. By yea and nay, sir, I dare say, my cousin William is become a good scholar: He is at Oxford, still, is he not?

Sil. Indeed, sir; to my cost.

Shal. He must then to the inns of court shortly: I was once of Clement's-inn; where, I think, they will talk of mad Shallow yet.

Sil. You were called—lusty Shallow, then, cousin.

Shal. By the mass, I was called any thing; and I would have done any thing, indeed, and roundly too. There was I, and little John Doit of Staffordshire, and black George Bare, and Francis Pickbone, and Will Squele a Cotswold man,—you had not four such swinge-bucklers in all the inns of court again: and, I may say to you, we knew where the bona-robas² were; and had the best of them all at commandment. Then was Jack Falstaff, now sir John, a boy; and page to Thomas Mowbray, duke of Norfolk.

Sil. This sir John, cousin, that comes hither anon about soldiers?

Shal. The same sir John, the very same. I saw him break Skogan's head¹⁴ at the court gate, when he was a crack, not thus high: and the very same day did I fight with one Sampson Stockfish, a fruiterer, behind Gray's-inn. O, the mad days that I have spent! and to see how many of mine old acquaintance are dead!

Sil. We shall all follow, cousin.

Shal. Certain, 't is certain; very sure, very sure: death, as the Psalmist saith, is certain to all; all shall die. How a good yoke of bullocks at Stamford fair?

Sil. Truly, cousin, I was not there.

Shal. Death is certain.—Is old Double of your town living yet?

Sil. Dead, sir.

Shal. Dead!—see, see!—he drew a good bow;—And dead!—he shot a fine shoot:—John of Gaunt loved him well, and betted much money on his head. Dead!—he would have clapped i' the clout²⁸ at twelve score; and carried you a forehand shaft a fourteen and fourteen and-a-half,

that it would have done a man's heart good to see.——How a score of ewes now?

Sil. Thereafter as they be: a score of good ewes may be worth ten pounds.

Shal. And is old Double dead!

Enter BARDOLPH, *and one with him.*

Sil. Here come two of sir John Falstaff's men, as I think.

Bard. Good morrow, honest gentlemen: I beseech you, which is justice Shallow?

Shal. I am Robert Shallow, sir; a poor esquire of this county, and one of the king's justices o' the peace: What is your good pleasure with me?

Bard. My captain, sir, commends him to you: my captain, sir John Falstaff: a tall gentleman, by heaven, and a most gallant leader.

Shal. He greets me well, sir; I knew him a good backsword man: How doth the good knight? may I ask, how my lady his wife doth?

Bard. Sir, pardon; a soldier is better accommodated, than with a wife.

Shal. It is well said, in faith, sir; and it is well said indeed too. Better accommodated!—it is good; yea, indeed, it is: good phrases are surely, and ever were, very commendable. Accommodated!—it comes from *accommodo:* very good; a good phrase.

Bard. Pardon me, sir; I have heard the word. Phrase, call you it? By this good day, I know not the phrase: but I will maintain the word with my sword to be a soldier-like word, and a word of exceeding good command. Accommodated! That is, when a man is, as they say, accommodated: or, when a man is,—being,—whereby,—he may be thought to be accommodated; which is an excellent thing.

Enter FALSTAFF.

Shal. It is very just:—Look, here comes good sir John.—Give me your good hand, give me your worship's good hand: By my troth, you look well, and bear your years very well: welcome, good sir John.

Fal. I am glad to see you well, good master Robert Shallow:—Master Sure-card, as I think.

Shal. No, sir John; it is my cousin Silence, in commission with me.

Fal. Good master Silence, it well befits you should be of the peace.

Sil. Your good worship is welcome.

Fal. Fye! this is hot weather.—Gentlemen,

have you provided me here half a dozen sufficient men?

Shal. Marry, have we, sir. Will you sit?

Fal. Let me see them, I beseech you.

Shal. Where's the roll? where's the roll? where's the roll?—Let me see, let me see. So, so, so, so: Yea, marry, sir:—Ralph Mouldy:—let them appear as I call; let them do so, let them do so.——Let me see: Where is Mouldy?

Moul. Here, an't please you.

Shal. What think you, sir John? a good limbed fellow: young, strong, and of good friends.

Fal. Is thy name Mouldy?

Moul. Yea, an't please you.

Fal. 'T is the more time thou wert used.

Shal. Ha, ha, ha! most excellent, i' faith! things, that are mouldy, lack use: Very singular good!—In faith, well said, sir John; very well said.

Fal. Prick him. [*To* SHAL.

Moul. I was pricked well enough before, an you could have let me alone: my old dame will be undone now, for one to do her husbandry, and her drudgery: you need not to have pricked me; there are other men fitter to go out than I.

Fal. Go to; peace, Mouldy, you shall go. Mouldy, it is time you were spent.

Moul. Spent!

Shal. Peace, fellow, peace; stand aside: Know you where you are?—For the other, sir John:—let me see;—Simon Shadow!

Fal. Ay marry, let me have him to sit under: he's like to be a cold soldier.

Shal. Where's Shadow?

Shad. Here, sir.

Fal. Shadow, whose son art thou?

Shad. My mother's son, sir.

Fal. Thy mother's son! like enough; and thy father's shadow: so the son of the female is the shadow of the male: It is often so, indeed; but not much of the father's substance.

Shal. Do you like him, sir John?

Fal. Shadow will serve for summer,—prick him;—for we have a number of shadows to fill up the muster-book.

Shal. Thomas Wart.

Fal. Where's he?

Wart. Here, sir.

Fal. Is thy name Wart?

Wart. Yea, sir.

Fal. Thou art a very ragged wart.

Shal. Shall I prick him, sir John?

Fal. It were superfluous; for his apparel is built upon his back, and the whole frame stands upon pins: prick him no more.

Shal. Ha, ha, ha!—you can do it, sir; you can do it: I commend you well.—Francis Feeble!

Fee. Here, sir.

Fal. What trade art thou, Feeble?

Fee. A woman's tailor, sir.

Shal. Shall I prick him, sir?

Fal. You may: but if he had been a man tailor, he would have pricked you.—Wilt thou make as many holes in an enemy's battle, as thou hast done in a woman's petticoat?

Fee. I will do my good will, sir; you can have no more.

Fal. Well said, good woman's tailor! well said, courageous Feeble! Thou wilt be as valiant as the wrathful dove, or most magnanimous mouse.—Prick the woman's tailor well, master Shallow; deep, master Shallow.

Fee. I would, Wart might have gone, sir.

Fal. I would, thou wert a man's tailor; that thou might'st mend him, and make him fit to go. I cannot put him to a private soldier, that is the leader of so many thousands: Let that suffice, most forcible Feeble.

Fee. It shall suffice, sir.

Fal. I am bound to thee, reverend Feeble.—Who is next?

Shal. Peter Bull-calf of the green!

Fal. Yea, marry, let us see Bull-calf.

Bull. Here, sir.

Fal. 'Fore God, a likely fellow!—Come, prick me Bull-calf till he roar again.

Bull. O lord! good my lord captain,—

Fal. What, dost thou roar before thou art pricked?

Bull. O lord, sir! I am a diseased man.

Fal. What disease hast thou?

Bull. A whoreson cold, sir; a cough, sir; which I caught with ringing in the king's affairs, upon his coronation day, sir.

Fal. Come, thou shalt go to the wars in a gown; we will have away thy cold; and I will take such order, that thy friends shall ring for thee.—Is here all?

Shal. Here is two more called than your number; you must have but four here, sir;—and so, I pray you, go in with me to dinner.

Fal. Come, I will go drink with you, but I cannot tarry dinner. I am glad to see you, in good troth, master Shallow.

Shal. O, sir John, do you remember since we lay all night in the windmill in Saint George's fields?

Fal. No more of that, good master Shallow, no more of that.

Shal. Ha, it was a merry night. And is Jane Night-work alive?

Fal. She lives, master Shallow.

Shal. She never could away with me.

Fal. Never, never: she would always say, she could not abide master Shallow.

Shal. By the mass, I could anger her to the heart. She was then a bona-roba. Doth she hold her own well?

Fal. Old, old, master Shallow.

Shal. Nay, she must be old: she cannot choose but be old; certain, she 's old; and had Robin Night-work by old Night-work, before I came to Clement's-inn.

Sil. That 's fifty-five year ago.

Shal. Ha, cousin Silence, that thou hadst seen that that this knight and I have seen!—Ha, sir John, said I well?

Fal. We have heard the chimes at midnight, master Shallow.

Shal. That we have, that we have, that we have; in faith, sir John, we have; our watch-word was, "Hem, boys!"—Come, let 's to dinner; come, let 's to dinner:—O, the days that we have seen!—Come, come.

[*Exeunt* FAL., SHAL., *and* SIL.

Bull. Good master corporate Bardolph, stand my friend; and here is four Harry ten shillings in French crowns for you. In very truth, sir, I had as lief be hanged, sir, as go: and yet, for mine own part, sir, I do not care; but, rather, because I am unwilling, and, for mine own part, have a desire to stay with my friends; else, sir, I did not care, for mine own part, so much.

Bard. Go to; stand aside.

Moul. And good master corporal captain, for my old dame's sake, stand my friend: she has nobody to do anything about her, when I am gone; and she is old, and cannot help herself: you shall have forty, sir.

Bard. Go to; stand aside.

Fee. By my troth I care not;—a man can die but once;—we owe God a death;—I 'll ne'er bear a base mind:—an 't be my destiny, so; an 't be not, so: No man 's too good to serve his prince; and, let it go which way it will, he that dies this year, is quit for the next.

100

Bard. Well said; thou 'rt a good fellow.

Fee. 'Faith, I 'll bear no base mind.

Re-enter FALSTAFF, *and Justices.*

Fal. Come, sir, which men shall I have?

Shal. Four, of which you please.

Bard. Sir, a word with you:—I have three pound to free Mouldy and Bull-calf.

Fal. Go to; well.

Shal. Come, sir John, which four will you have?

Fal. Do you choose for me.

Shal. Marry then,—Mouldy, Bull-calf, Feeble, and Shadow.

Fal. Mouldy, and Bull-calf:—For you, Mouldy, stay at home still; you are past service:—and, for your part, Bull-calf,—grow till you come unto it; I will none of you.

Shal. Sir John, sir John, do not yourself wrong; they are your likeliest men, and I would have you served with the best.

Fal. Will you tell me, master Shallow, how to choose a man? Care I for the limb, the thewes, the stature, bulk, and big assemblance of a man! Give me the spirit, master Shallow.—Here 's Wart;—you see what a ragged appearance it is; he shall charge you, and discharge you, with the motion of a pewterer's hammer; come off, and on, swifter than he that gibbets-on the brewer's bucket. And this same half-faced fellow, Shadow —give me this man; he presents no mark to the enemy; the foeman may with as great aim level at the edge of a penknife: And, for a retreat, —how swiftly with this Feeble, the woman's tailor, run off? O, give me the spare men, and spare me the great ones.—Put me a caliver⁶⁴ into Wart's hand, Bardolph.

Bard. Hold, Wart, traverse; thus, thus, thus.

Fal. Come, manage me your caliver. So:— very well:—go to:—very good:—exceeding good. O, give me always a little, lean, old, chopped, bald shot.—Well said, i' faith, Wart; thou 'rt a good scab: hold, there 's a tester for thee.

Shal. He is not his craft's master, he doth not do it right. I remember at Mile-end green, (when I lay at Clement's-inn I was then sir Dagonet in Arthur's show,) there was a little quiver fellow, and 'a would manage you his piece thus; and 'a would about, and about, and come you in, and come you in: "rah, tah, tah," would 'a say; "bounce," would 'a say; and away again would 'a go, and again would 'a come:—I shall never see such a fellow.

705

Fal. These fellows will do well, master Shallow.
—God keep you, master Silence; I will not use
many words with you:—Fare you well, gentlemen
both: I thank you; I must a dozen mile to-night.
—Bardolph, give the soldiers coats.

Shal. Sir John, heaven bless you, and prosper
your affairs and send us peace! As you return,
visit my house; let our old acquaintance be re-
newed: peradventure, I will with you to the court.

Fal. I would you would, master Shallow.

Shal. Go to; I have spoke, at a word. Fare
you well.   [*Exeunt* SHAL. *and* SIL.

Fal. Fare you well, gentle gentlemen. On,
Bardolph; lead the men away. [*Exeunt* BAR-
DOLPH, *Recruits, &c.*] As I return, I will fetch
off these justices: I do see the bottom of justice
Shallow. Lord, Lord, how subject we old men are
to this vice of lying! This same starved justice
hath done nothing but prate to me of the wildness of his youth, and the feats he hath done
about Turnbull-street;[?] and every third word a
lie, duer paid to the hearer than the Turk's tribute.
I do remember him at Clement's-inn, like a man
made after supper of a cheese-paring: when he
was naked, he was, for all the world, like a forked
radish, with a head fantastically carved upon it
with a knife: he was so forlorn, that his dimen-
sions to any thick sight were invisible: he was
the very Genius of famine; yet lecherous as a
monkey, and the whores called him—mandrake:
he came ever in the rear-ward of the fashion; and
sung those tunes to the over-scutched huswives
that he heard the carmen whistle, and sware—
they were his fancies, or his good-nights. And
now is this Vice's dagger become a squire; and
talks as familiarly of John of Gaunt, as if he had
been sworn brother to him: and I'll be sworn he
never saw him but once in the Tilt-yard; and
then he burst his head, for crowding among the
marshal's men. I saw it; and told John of Gaunt,
he beat his own name: for you might have trussed
him, and all his apparel, into an eel-skin: the
case of a treble hautboy was a mansion for him,
a court; and now has he lands and beeves. Well;
I will be acquainted with him, if I return: and
it shall go hard, but I will make him a philoso-
pher's two stones to me: If the young dace be a
bait for the old pike, I see no reason, in the law
of nature, but I may snap at him. Let time
shape, and there an end.   [*Exit.*

ACT IV.

SCENE I.—*A Forest in Yorkshire.*

Enter the ARCHBISHOP OF YORK, MOWBRAY,
HASTINGS, *and Others.*

Arch. What is this forest call'd?

Hast. 'T is Gaultree forest, an 't shall please
your grace.

Arch. Here stand, my lords; and send dis-
coverers forth,
To know the numbers of our enemies.

Hast. We have sent forth already.

Arch.   'T is well done.
My friends, and brethren in these great affairs,
I must acquaint you that I have receiv'd
New-dated letters from Northumberland;
Their cold intent, tenor and substance, thus:—
Here doth he wish his person, with such powers
As might hold sortance with his quality,

The which he could not levy; whereupon
He is retir'd, to ripe his growing fortunes,
To Scotland: and concludes in hearty prayers,
That your attempts may overlive the hazard,
And fearful meeting of their opposite.

Mowb. Thus do the hopes we have in him touch
ground,
And dash themselves to pieces.

Enter a Messenger.

Hast.   Now, what news?

Mess. West of this forest, scarcely off a mile,
In goodly form comes on the enemy:
And, by the ground they hide, I judge their number
Upon, or near, the rate of thirty thousand.

Mowb. The just proportion that we gave them
out.
Let us sway on, as I face them in the field.

Enter WESTMORELAND.

Arch. What well-appointed leader fronts us
here?

Mowb. I think, it is my lord of Westmoreland.

West. Health and fair greeting from our general,
The prince, lord John and duke of Lancaster.

Arch. Say on, my lord of Westmoreland, in
peace;
What doth concern your coming?

West.   Then, my lord,
Unto your grace do I in chief address
The substance of my speech. If that rebellion
Came like itself, in base and abject routs,
Led on by bloody youth, guarded with rags,
And countenanc'd by boys, and beggary;
I say, if damn'd commotion so appear'd,
In his true, native, and most proper shape,
You, reverend father, and these noble lords,
Had not been here, to dress the ugly form
Of base and bloody insurrection
With your fair honours. You, lord archbishop,—
Whose see is by a civil peace maintained;
Whose beard the silver hand of peace hath touch'd;
Whose learning and good letters peace hath tutor'd;
Whose white investments figure innocence,
The dove and very blessed spirit of peace,—
Wherefore do you so ill translate yourself,
Out of the speech of peace, that bears such grace,
Into the harsh and boist'rous tongue of war?
Turning your books to graves, your ink to blood,
Your pens to lances; and your tongue divine
To a loud trumpet, and a point of war?

Arch. Wherefore do I this?—so the question
stands.
Briefly to this end:—We are all diseas'd;
And, with our surfeiting, and wanton hours,
Have brought ourselves into a burning fever,
And we must bleed for it: of which disease
Our late king, Richard, being infected, died.
But, my most noble lord of Westmoreland,
I take not on me here as a physician;
Nor do I, as an enemy to peace,
Troop in the throngs of military men:
But, rather show a while like fearful war,
To diet rank minds, sick of happiness;
And purge the obstructions, which begin to stop
Our very veins of life. Hear me more plainly.
I have in equal balance justly weigh'd
What wrongs our arms may do, what wrongs we
suffer,
And find our griefs heavier than our offences.

We see which way the stream of time doth run,
And are enforc'd from our most quiet sphere
By the rough torrent of occasion:
And have the summary of all our griefs,
When time shall serve, to show in articles;
Which, long ere this, we offer'd to the king,
And might by no suit gain our audience:
When we are wrong'd, and would unfold our griefs,
We are denied access unto his person,
Even by those men that most have done us wrong
The dangers of the days but newly gone,
(Whose memory is written on the earth
With yet-appearing blood,) and the examples
Of every minute's instance, (present now,)
Have put us in these ill-beseeming arms:
Not to break peace, or any branch of it;
But to establish here a peace indeed,
Concurring both in name and quality.

West. When ever yet was your appeal denied?
Wherein have you been galled by the king?
What peer hath been suborn'd to grate on you?
That you should seal this lawless bloody book
Of forg'd rebellion with a seal divine,
And consecrate commotion's bitter edge?

Arch. My brother, general! the commonwealth,
To brother born an household cruelty,
I make my quarrel in particular.

West. There is no need of any such redress;
Or, if there were, it not belongs to you.

Mowb. Why not to him, in part; and to us all,
That feel the bruises of the days before;
And suffer the condition of these times
To lay a heavy and unequal hand
Upon our honours?

West.   O my good lord Mowbray,
Construe the times to their necessities,
And you shall say indeed,—it is the time,
And not the king, that doth you injuries.
Yet, for your part, it not appears to me,
Either from the king, or in the present time,
That you should have an inch of any ground
To build a grief on: Were you not restor'd
To all the duke of Norfolk's signiories,
Your noble and right-well-remember'd father's?

Mowb. What thing, in honour, had my father
lost,
That need to be reviv'd, and breath'd in me?
The king, that lov'd him, as the state stood then,
Was, force perforce, compell'd to banish him:
And then, when Harry Bolingbroke, and he,—
Being mounted, and both roused in their seats,
Their neighing coursers daring of the spur

795

Their armed staves in charge, their beavers down,
Their eyes of fire sparkling through sights of steel,
And the loud trumpet blowing them together ;
Then, then, when there was nothing could have
    staid
My father from the breast of Bolingbroke.
O, when the king did throw his warder down,
His own life hung upon the staff he threw ;
Then threw he down himself ; and all their lives,
That, by indictment, and by dint of sword,
Have since miscarried under Bolingbroke.

West. You speak, lord Mowbray, now you know
    not what :
The earl of Hereford was reputed then
In England the most valiant gentleman ;
Who knows, on whom fortune would then have
    smil'd ?
But, if your father had been victor there,
He ne'er had borne it out of Coventry :
For all the country, in a general voice,
Cried hate upon him ; and all their prayers, and
    love,
Were set on Hereford, whom they doted on,
And bless'd, and grac'd indeed, more than the king.
But this is mere digression from my purpose.—
Here come I from our princely general,
To know your griefs ; to tell you from his grace,
That he will give you audience : and wherein
It shall appear that your demands are just,
You shall enjoy them ; every thing set off,
That might so much as think you enemies.

Mowb. But he hath forc'd us to compel this
    offer ;
And it proceeds from policy, not love.

West. Mowbray, you overween, to take it so ;
This offer comes from mercy, not from fear :
For, lo ! within a ken, our army lies ;
Upon mine honour, all too confident
To give admittance to a thought of fear.
Our battle is more full of names than yours,
Our men more perfect in the use of arms,
Our armour all as strong, our cause the best ;
Then reason wills, our hearts should be as good :—
Say you not then, our offer is compell'd.

Mowb. Well, by my will, we shall admit no
    parley.

West. That argues but the shame of your
    offence :
A rotten case abides no handling.

Hast. Hath the prince John a full commission,
In very ample virtue of his father,
To hear, and absolutely to determine

Of what conditions we shall stand upon ?

West. That is intended in the general's name :
I muse, you make so slight a question.

Arch. Then take, my lord of Westmoreland,
    this schedule ;
For this contains our general grievances :—
Each several article herein redress'd ;
All members of our cause, both here and hence,
That are insinew'd to this action,
Acquitted by a true substantial form ;
And present execution of our wills
To us, and to our purposes, consign'd :
We come within our awful banks again,
And knit our powers to the arm of peace.

West. This will I show the general. Please
    you, lords,
In sight of both our battles we may meet :
And either end in peace, which heaven so frame !
Or to the place of difference call the swords
Which must decide it.

Arch.   My lord, we will do so.
                   [*Exit* WEST.

Mowb. There is a thing within my bosom, tells
    me,
That no conditions of our peace can stand.

Hast. Fear you not that : if we can make our
    peace
Upon such large terms, and so absolute,
As our conditions shall consist upon,
Our peace shall stand as firm as rocky mountains.

Mowb. Ay, but our valuation shall be such,
That every slight and false-derived cause,
Yea, every idle, nice, and wanton reason,
Shall, to the king, taste of this action :
That, were our royal faiths martyrs in love,
We shall be winnow'd with so rough a wind,
That even our corn shall seem as light as chaff,
And good from bad find no partition.

Arch. No, no, my lord : Note this,—the king
    is weary
Of dainty and such picking grievances :
For he hath found,—to end one doubt by death,
Revives two greater in the heirs of life.
And therefore will he wipe his tables clean ;
And keep no tell-tale to his memory,
That may repeat and history his loss
To new remembrance : For full well he knows,
He cannot so precisely weed this land,
As his misdoubts present occasion :
His foes are so enrooted with his friends,
That, plucking to unfix an enemy,
He doth unfasten so, and shake a friend.

So that this land, like an offensive wife,
That hath enrag'd him on to offer strokes;
As he is striking, holds his infant up,
And hangs resolv'd correction in the arm
That was uprear'd to execution.

Hast. Besides, the king hath wasted all his rods
On late offenders, that he now doth lack
The very instruments of chastisement:
So that his power, like to a fangless lion,
May offer, but not hold.

Arch.   'T is very true:—
And therefore be assur'd, my good lord marshal,
If we do now make our atonement well,
Our peace will, like a broken limb united,
Grow stronger for the breaking.

Mowb.   Be it so.
Here is return'd my lord of Westmoreland.

Re-enter WESTMORELAND.

West. The prince is here at hand: Pleaseth
        your lordship,
To meet his grace just distance 'tween our armies?

Mowb. Your grace of York, in God's name then
        set forward.

Arch. Before, and greet his grace:—my lord,
        we come.   [*Exeunt.*

SCENE II.—*Another Part of the Forest.*

*Enter, from one side, MOWBRAY, the ARCHBISHOP,
HASTINGS, and Others: from the other side,
PRINCE JOHN OF LANCASTER, WESTMORELAND,
Officers, and Attendants.*

P. John. You are well encounter'd here, my
        cousin Mowbray:—
Good day to you, gentle lord archbishop:—
And so to you, lord Hastings,—and to all.—
My lord of York, it better show'd with you,
When that your flock, assembled by the bell,
Encircled you, to hear with reverence
Your exposition on the holy text:
Than now to see you here an iron man,
Cheering a rout of rebels with your drum,
Turning the word to sword, and life to death.
That man, that sits within a monarch's heart,
And ripens in the sunshine of his favour,
Would he abuse the countenance of the king,
Alack, what mischiefs might he set abroach,
In shadow of such greatness! With you, lord
        bishop,
It is even so:—Who hath not heard it spoken,
How deep you were within the books of God?

To us, the speaker in his parliament;
To us, the imagin'd voice of God himself;
The very opener, and intelligencer,
Between the grace, the sanctities of heaven,
And our dull workings: O, who shall believe,
But you misuse the reverence of your place;
Employ the countenance and grace of heaven,
As a false favourite doth his prince's name,
In deeds dishonourable? You have taken up,
Under the counterfeited zeal of God,
The subjects of his substitute, my father;
And, both against the peace of heaven and him,
Have here up-swarm'd them.

Arch.   Good my lord of Lancaster,
I am not here against your father's peace:
But, as I told my lord of Westmoreland,
The time misorder'd doth, in common sense,
Crowd us, and crush us, to this monstrous form,
To hold our safety up. I sent your grace
The parcels and particulars of our grief;
The which hath been with scorn shov'd from the
        court,
Whereon this Hydra son of war is born:
Whose dangerous eyes may well be charm'd
        asleep,
With grant of our most just and right desires;
And true obedience of this madness cur'd,
Stoop tamely to the foot of majesty.

Mowb. If not, we ready are to try our fortunes
To the last man.

Hast.   And though we here fall down,
We have supplies to second our attempt;
If they miscarry, theirs shall second them:
And so, success of mischief shall be born;
And heir from heir shall hold this quarrel up,
Whiles England shall have generation.

P. John. You are too shallow, Hastings, much
        too shallow,
To sound the bottom of the after-times.

West. Pleaseth your grace, to answer them
        directly,
How far-forth you do like their articles?

P. John. I like them all, and do allow them,
        well:
And swear here by the honour of my blood,
My father's purposes have been mistook:
And some about him have too lavishly
Wrested his meaning, and authority.—
My lord, these griefs shall be with speed redress'd;
Upon my soul, they shall. If this may please you,
Discharge your powers unto their several counties,
As we will ours: and here, between the armies,

Let's drink together friendly, and embrace;
That all their eyes may bear those tokens home,
Of our restored love, and amity.

   Arch. I take your princely word for these re-
    dresses.

   P. John. I give it you, and will maintain my
    word:
And thereupon I drink unto your grace.

   Host. Go, captain, [*To an* Officer.] and deliver
    to the army
This news of peace; let them have pay, and part:
I know, it will well please them; Hie thee, captain.
                [*Exit* Officer.

   Arch. To you, my noble lord of Westmore-
    land.

   West. I pledge your grace: And, if you knew
    what pains
I have bestow'd, to breed this present peace,
You would drink freely; but my love to you
Shall show itself more openly hereafter.

   Arch. I do not doubt you.

   West.   I am glad of it,—
Health to my lord, and gentle cousin, Mowbray.

   Mowb. You wish me health in very happy
    season;
For I am, on the sudden, something ill.

   Arch. Against ill chances, men are ever merry;
But heaviness foreruns the good event.

   West. Therefore be merry, coz; since sudden
    sorrow
Serves to say thus,—Some good thing comes to-
    morrow.

   Arch. Believe me, I am passing light in spirit.

   Mowb. So much the worse, if your own rule be
    true.   [*Shouts within.*

   P. John. The word of peace is render'd: Hark,
    how they shout!

   Mowb. This had been cheerful, after victory.

   Arch. A peace is of the nature of a conquest;
For then both parties nobly are subdued,
And neither party loser.

   P. John.   Go, my lord,
And let our army be discharged too.—
                [*Exit* West.
And, good my lord, so please you, let our trains
March by us; that we may peruse the men
We should have cop'd withal.

   Arch.   Go, good lord Hastings,
And, ere they be dismiss'd, let them march by.
                [*Exit* Hast.

   P. John. I trust, my lords, we shall lie to-night
    together.—

798

          Re-enter Westmoreland.

Now, cousin, wherefore stands our army still?

   West. The leaders, having charge from you to
    stand,
Will not go off until they hear you speak.

   P. John. They know their duties.

          Re-enter Hastings.

   Host. My lord, our army is dispers'd already:
Like youthful steers unyok'd, they take their
    courses
East, west, north, south; or, like a school broke up,
Each hurries toward his home, and sporting-place.

   West. Good tidings, my lord Hastings; for the
    which
I do arrest thee, traitor, of high treason:—
And you, lord Archbishop,—and you, lord Mow-
    bray,
Of capital treason I attach you both.

   Mowb. Is this proceeding just and honourable?

   West. Is your assembly so?

   Arch. Will you thus break your faith?

   P. John.   I pawn'd thee none:
I promis'd you redress of these same grievances,
Whereof you did complain; which, by mine
    honour,
I will perform with a most christian care.
But, for you, rebels,—look to taste the due
Meet for rebellion, and such acts as yours.
Most shallowly did you these arms commence,
Fondly brought here, and foolishly sent hence.—
Strike up our drums, pursue the scatter'd stray;
Heaven, and not we, hath safely fought to-day.—
Some guard these traitors to the block of death;
Treason's true bed, and yielder up of breath.
                [*Exeunt.*

SCENE III.—*Another Part of the Forest.*

Alarums: Excursions. Enter Falstaff *and*
    Colevile, *meeting.*

   Fal. What's your name, sir? of what condition
are you; and of what place, I pray?

   Cole. I am a knight, sir: and my name is—
Colevile of the dale.

   Fal. Well then, Colevile is your name; a knight
is your degree; and your place, the dale: Colevile
shall still be your name; a traitor your degree;
and the dungeon your place,—a place deep enough;
so shall you still be Colevile of the dale.

   Cole. Are not you sir John Falstaff?

Fal. As good a man as he, sir, whoe'er I am. Do ye yield, sir? or shall I sweat for you? If I do sweat, they are drops of thy lovers, and they weep for thy death: therefore rouse up fear and trembling, and do observance to my mercy.

Cole. I think, you are sir John Falstaff; and, in that thought, yield me.

Fal. I have a whole school of tongues in this belly of mine; and not a tongue of them all speaks any other word but my name. An I had but a belly of any indifferency, I were simply the most active fellow in Europe: My womb, my womb, my womb undoes me.—Here comes our general.

Enter PRINCE JOHN OF LANCASTER, WESTMORE-LAND, *and Others.*

P. John. The heat is past, follow no further now ;—
Call in the powers, good cousin Westmoreland.—
　　　　　　　　　　　　　　　[*Exit* WEST.
Now, Falstaff, where have you been all this while?
When every thing is ended, then you come:
These tardy tricks of yours will, on my life,
One time or other break some gallows' back.

Fal. I would be sorry, my lord, but it should be thus; I never knew yet, but rebuke and check was the reward of valour. Do you think me a swallow, an arrow, or a bullet? have I, in my poor and old motion, the expedition of thought? I have speeded hither with the very extremest inch of possibility; I have foundered nine-score and odd posts: and here, travel-tainted as I am, have, in my pure and immaculate valour, taken sir John Colevile of the dale, a most furious knight, and valorous enemy: But what of that? he saw me, and yielded; that I may justly say with the hook-nosed fellow of Rome,——I came, saw, and overcame.

P. John. It was more of his courtesy than your deserving.

Fal. I know not; here he is, and here I yield him: and I beseech your grace, let it be booked with the rest of this day's deeds; or, by the lord, I will have it in a particular ballad else, with mine own picture on the top of it, Colevile kissing my foot: To the which course if I be enforced, if you do not all show like gilt two-pences to me; and I, in the clear sky of fame, o'ershine you as much as the full moon doth the cinders of the element, which show like pins' heads to her; believe not

the word of the noble: Therefore let me have right, and let desert mount.

P. John. Thine's too heavy to mount.

Fal. Let it shine then.

P. John. Thine 's too thick to shine.

Fal. Let it do something, my good lord, that may do me good, and call it what you will.

P. John. Is thy name Colevile?

Cole. It is, my lord.

P. John. A famous rebel art thou, Colevile.

Fal. And a famous true subject took him.

Cole. I am, my lord, but as my betters are,
That led me hither; had they been rul'd by me,
You should have won them dearer than you have.

Fal. I know not how they sold themselves: but thou, like a kind fellow, gavest thyself away; and I thank thee for thee.

Re-enter WESTMORELAND.

P. John. Now, have you left pursuit?

West. Retreat is made, and execution stay'd.

P. John. Send Colevile, with his confederates,
To York, to present execution:—
Blunt, lead him hence; and see you guard him sure.
　　　　　　　　　　　[*Exeunt some with* COLE.
And now despatch we toward the court, my lord-:
I hear, the king my father is sore sick:
Our news shall go before us to his majesty,—
Which, cousin, you shall bear,—to comfort him,
And we with sober speed will follow you.

Fal. My lord, I beseech you, give me leave to go through Glostershire: and, when you come to court, stand my good lord, 'pray, in your good report.

P. John. Fare you well, Falstaff; I, in my condition,
Shall better speak of you than you deserve. [*Exit.*

Fal. I would, you had but the wit; 't were better than your dukedom.—Good faith, this same young sober-blooded boy doth not love me; nor a man cannot make him laugh:—but that 's no marvel, he drinks no wine. There 's never any of these demure boys come to any proof: for thin drink doth so over-cool their blood, and making many fish-meals, that they fall into a kind of male green-sickness; and then, when they marry, they get wenches: they are generally fools and cowards ;—which some of us should be too, but for inflammation. A good sherris-sack hath a two-fold operation in it. It ascends me into the brain; dries me there all the foolish, and dull, and crudy vapours which environ it; makes it apprehensive, quick, forgetive," full of nimble, fiery, and delectable shapes; which deliver'd o'er to the voice, (the tongue,) which is the birth, becomes excellent wit. The second property of your excellent sherris is,—the warming of the blood; which, before cold and settled, left the liver white and pale, which is the badge of pusillanimity and cowardice: but the sherris warms it, and makes it course from the inwards to the parts extreme. It illumineth the face; which, as a beacon, gives warning to all the rest of this little kingdom, man, to arm: and then the vital commoners, and inland petty spirits, muster me all to their captain, the heart; who, great, and puffed up with this retinue, doth any deed of courage; and this valour comes of sherris: So that skill in the weapon is nothing, without sack; for that sets it a-work: and learning, a mere hoard of gold kept by a devil;" till sack commences it, and sets it in act and use. Hereof comes it, that prince Harry is valiant: for the cold blood he did naturally inherit of his father, he hath, like lean, sterile, and bare land, manured, husbanded, and tilled, with excellent endeavour of drinking good, and good store of fertile sherris; that he is become very hot and valiant. If I had a thousand sons, the first human principle I would teach them, should be,—to forswear thin potations, and addict themselves to sack.

Enter BARDOLPH.

How now, Bardolph?

Bard. The army is discharged all, and gone.

Fal. Let them go. I'll through Glostershire; and there will I visit master Robert Shallow, esquire: I have him already tempering between my finger and my thumb, and shortly will I seal with him. Come away.   [*Exeunt.*

SCENE IV.—*Westminster. A Room in the Palace.*

Enter KING HENRY, CLARENCE, PRINCE HUMPHREY, WARWICK, *and Others.*

K. Hen. Now, lords, if heaven doth give successful end
To this debate that bleedeth at our doors,
We will our youth lead on to higher fields,
And draw no swords but what are sanctified.
Our navy is address'd, our power collected,
Our substitutes in absence well invested,
And every thing lies level to our wish:
Only, we want a little personal strength;
And pause us, till these rebels, now afoot,

Come underneath the yoke of government.

War. Both which, we doubt not but your majesty
Shall soon enjoy.

K. Hen.   Humphrey, my son of Gloster,
Where is the prince your brother?

P. Humph. I think he's gone to hunt, my lord, at Windsor.

K. Hen. And how accompanied?

P. Humph.   I do not know, my lord.

K. Hen. Is not his brother, Thomas of Clarence, with him?

P. Humph. No, my good lord; he is in presence here.

Cla. What would my lord and father?

K. Hen. Nothing but well to thee, Thomas of Clarence.
How chance, thou art not with the prince thy brother?
He loves thee, and thou dost neglect him, Thomas.
Thou hast a better place in his affection,
Than all thy brothers: cherish it, my boy;
And noble offices thou may'st effect
Of mediation, after I am dead,
Between his greatness and thy other brethren:—
Therefore, omit him not; blunt not his love:
Nor loose the good advantage of his grace,
By seeming cold, or careless of his will.
For he is gracious, if he be observ'd;
He hath a tear for pity, and a hand
Open as day for melting charity;
Yet notwithstanding, being incens'd, he's flint;
As humorous as winter, and as sudden
As flaws congealed in the spring of day.
His temper, therefore, must be well observ'd:
Chide him for faults, and do it reverently,
When you perceive his blood inclin'd to mirth;
But, being moody, give him line and scope;
Till that his passions, like a whale on ground,
Confound themselves with working. Learn this, Thomas,
And thou shalt prove a shelter to thy friends;
A hoop of gold, to bind thy brothers in;
That the united vessel of their blood,
Mingled with venom of suggestion,
(As, force perforce, the age will pour it in,)
Shall never leak, though it do work as strong
As aconitum, or rash gunpowder.

Cla. I shall observe him with all care and love.

K. Hen. Why art thou not at Windsor with him, Thomas?

Cla. He is not there to-day; he dines in London.

K. Hen. And how accompanied? can'st thou
tell that?

Cla. With Poins, and other his continual followers.

K. Hen. Most subject is the fattest soil to weeds;
And he, the noble image of my youth,
Is overspread with them: Therefore my grief
Stretches itself beyond the hour of death;
The blood weeps from my heart, when I do shape,
In forms imaginary, the unguided days,
And rotten times, that you shall look upon
When I am sleeping with my ancestors.
For when his headstrong riot hath no curb,
When rage and hot blood are his counsellors,
When means and lavish manners meet together,
O, with what wings shall his affections fly
Towards fronting peril and oppos'd decay!

War. My gracious lord, you look beyond him
quite:
The prince but studies his companions,
Like a strange tongue: wherein, to gain the lan-,
guage,
'T is needful, that the most immodest word
Be look'd upon, and learn'd: which once attain'd,
Your highness knows, comes to no further use,
But to be known, and hated. So, like gross terms,
The prince will, in the perfectness of time,
Cast off his followers: and their memory
Shall as a pattern or a measure live,
By which his grace must mete the lives of others;
Turning past evils to advantages.

K. Hen. 'T is seldom, when the bee doth leave
her comb
In the dead carrion.—Who 's here? Westmoreland?

Enter WESTMORELAND.

West. Health to my sovereign! and new happi-
ness
Added to that that I am to deliver!
Prince John, your son, doth kiss your grace's hand:
Mowbray, the bishop Scroop, Hastings, and all,
Are brought to the correction of your law;
There is not now a rebel's sword unsheath'd,
But peace puts forth her olive every where.
The manner how this action hath been borne,
Here at more leisure may your highness read;
With every course, in his particular.

K. Hen. O Westmoreland, thou art a summer
bird,
Which ever in the haunch of winter sings
The lifting up of day. Look! here 's more news.

101

Enter HARCOURT.

Har. From enemies heaven keep your majesty;
And, when they stand against you, may they fall
As those that I am come to tell you of!
The earl Northumberland, and the lord Bardolph,
With a great power of English, and of Scots,
Are by the sheriff of Yorkshire overthrown:
The manner and true order of the fight,
This packet, please it you, contains at large.

K. Hen. And wherefore should these good news
make me sick?
Will fortune never come with both hands full,
But write her fair words still in foulest letters?
She either gives a stomach, and no food,—
Such are the poor, in health; or else a feast,
And takes away the stomach,—such are the rich,
That have abundance, and enjoy it not.
I should rejoice now at this happy news;
And now my sight fails, and my brain is giddy:—
O me! come near me, now I am much ill. [*Swoons*
P. Humph. Comfort, your majesty!
Cla.   O my royal father!
West. My sovereign lord, cheer up yourself;
look up!
War. Be patient, princes; you do know, these
fits
Are with his highness very ordinary.
Stand from him, give him air; he 'll straight be
well.
Cla. No, no; he cannot long hold out these
pangs;
The incessant care and labour of his mind
Hath wrought the mure, that should confine it in,"
So thin, that life looks through, and will break out.
P. Humph. The people fear me; for they do
observe
Unfather'd heirs," and loathly births of nature:
The seasons change their manners, as the year
Had found some months asleep, and leap'd them
over.
Cla. The river hath thrice flow'd, no ebb be-
tween:
And the old folk, time's doting chronicles,
Say, it did so, a little time before
That our great grandsire, Edward, sick'd and died.
War. Speak lower, princes, for the king re-
covers.
P. Humph. This apoplex will, certain, be his
end.
K. Hen. I pray you, take me up, and bear me
hence

Into some other chamber: softly, 'pray.

[They convey the King into an inner part of
the Room, and place him on a Bed.

Let there be no noise made, my gentle friends;
Unless some dull and favourable hand
Will whisper music to my weary spirit.

War. Call for the music in the other room.

K. Hen. Set me the crown upon my pillow
here.

Cla. His eye is hollow, and he changes much.

War. Less noise, less noise.

Enter PRINCE HENRY.

P. Hen.　　　Who saw the duke of Clarence?

Cla. I am here, brother, full of heaviness.

P. Hen. How now! rain within doors, and none
abroad!
How doth the king?

P. Humph. Exceeding ill.

P. Hen.　　　Heard he the good news yet?
Tell it him.

P. Humph. He alter'd much upon the hearing it.

P. Hen. If he be sick
With joy, he will recover without physic.

War. Not so much noise, my lords:—sweet
prince, speak low;
The king your father is dispos'd to sleep.

Cla. Let us withdraw into the other room.

War. Will 't please your grace to go along
with us?

P. Hen. No; I will sit and watch here by the
king.　　　*[Exeunt all but P. HENRY.*
Why doth the crown lie there upon his pillow,
Being so troublesome a bedfellow?
O polish'd perturbation! golden care!
That keep'st the ports of slumber open wide
To many a watchful night!—sleep with it now!
Yet not so sound, and half so deeply sweet,
As he, whose brow, with homely biggin bound,
Snores out the watch of night. O majesty!
When thou dost pinch thy bearer, thou dost sit
Like a rich armour worn in heat of day,
That scalds with safety. By his gates of breath
There lies a downy feather, which stirs not;
Did he suspire, that light and weightless down
Perforce must move.—My gracious lord! my
father!—
This sleep is sound indeed; this is a sleep,
That from this golden rigol hath divorc'd
So many English kings. Thy due, from me,
Is tears, and heavy sorrows of the blood;
Which nature, love, and filial tenderness,

802

Shall, O dear father, pay thee plenteously:
My due, from thee, is this imperial crown;
Which, as immediate from thy place and blood,
Derives itself to me. Lo, here it sits,—

[Putting it on his head.

Which heaven shall guard: and put the world's
whole strength
Into one giant arm, it shall not force
This lineal honour from me: This from thee
Will I to mine leave, as 't is left to me.　*[Exit.*

K. Hen. Warwick! Gloster! Clarence!

Re-enter WARWICK, *and the rest.*

Cla.　　　　　Doth the king call?

War. What would your majesty? How fares
your grace?

K. Hen. Why did you leave me here alone,
my lords?

Cla. We left the prince my brother here, my
liege,
Who undertook to sit and watch by you.

K. Hen. The prince of Wales? Where is he?
let me see him:
He is not here.

War. This door is open; he is gone this way.

P. Humph. He came not through the chamber
where we stay'd.

K. Hen. Where is the crown? who took it from
my pillow?

War. When we withdrew, my liege, we left it
here.

K. Hen. The prince hath ta'en it hence:—go
seek him out.
Is he so hasty, that he doth suppose
My sleep my death?——
Find him, my lord of Warwick; chide him hither.

[Exit WAR.

This part of his conjoins with my disease,
And helps to end me.—See, sons, what things
you are!
How quickly nature falls into revolt,
When gold becomes her object!
For this the foolish over-careful fathers
Have broke their sleep with thoughts, their brains
with care,
Their bones with industry;
For this they have engrossed and pil'd up
The canker'd heaps of strange-achieved gold;
For this they have been thoughtful to invest
Their sons with arts, and martial exercises:
When, like the bee, tolling from every flower
The virtuous sweets:

Our thighs pack'd with wax, our mouths with
			honey,
We bring it to the hive ; and, like the bees,
Are murder'd for our pains. This bitter taste
Yield his engrossments to the ending father.—

Re-enter WARWICK.

Now, where is he that will not stay so long
Till his friend sickness hath determin'd me ?
  War. My lord, I found the prince in the next
			room,
Washing with kindly tears his gentle cheeks ;
With such a deep demeanour in great sorrow,
That tyranny, which never quaff'd but blood,
Would, by beholding him, have wash'd his knife
With gentle eye-drops. He is coming hither.
  K. Hen. But wherefore did he take away the
			crown ?

Re-enter PRINCE HENRY.

Lo, where he comes.—Come hither to me, Harry :—
Depart the chamber, leave us here alone.
			[*Exeunt* CLAR., P. HUMPH., Lords, &c.
  P. Hen. I never thought to hear you speak
			again.
  K. Hen. Thy wish was father, Harry, to that
			thought :
I stay too long by thee, I weary thee.
Dost thou so hunger for my empty chair,
That thou wilt needs invest thee with mine honours
Before thy hour be ripe ? O foolish youth !
Thou seek'st the greatness that will overwhelm thee.
Stay but a little ; for my cloud of dignity
Is held from falling with so weak a wind,
That it will quickly drop : my day is dim.
Thou hast stol'n that, which, after some few hours,
Were thine without offence ; and, at my death,
Thou hast seal'd up my expectation :
Thy life did manifest, thou lov'dst me not,
And thou wilt have me die assured of it.
Thou hid'st a thousand daggers in thy thoughts,
Which thou hast whetted on thy stony heart,
To stab at half an hour of my life.
What ! canst thou not forbear me half an hour ?
Then get thee gone ; and dig my grave thyself ;
And bid the merry bells ring to thine ear,
That thou art crowned, not that I am dead.
Let all the tears that should bedew my hearse,
Be drops of balm, to sanctify thy head :
Only compound me with forgotten dust ;
Give that, which gave thee life, unto the worms.
Pluck down my officers, break my decrees ;

For now a time is come to mock at form.
Harry the Fifth is crown'd :—Up, vanity !
Down, royal state ! all you sage counsellors, hence !
And to the English court assemble now,
From every region, apes of idleness !
Now, neighbour confines, purge you of your scum :
Have you a ruffian, that will swear, drink, dance,
Revel the night ; rob, murder, and commit
The oldest sins the newest kind of ways !
Be happy, he will trouble you no more :
England shall double gild his treble guilt ;
England shall give him office, honour, might .
For the fifth Harry from curl'd licence plucks
The muzzle of restraint, and the wild dog
Shall flesh his tooth in every innocent.
O my poor kingdom, sick with civil blows !
When that my care could not withhold thy riots,
What wilt thou do, when riot is thy care ?
O, thou wilt be a wilderness again,
Peopled with wolves, thy old inhabitants !
  P. Hen. O, pardon me, my liege ! but for my
			tears,			[*Kneeling*
The moist impediments unto my speech,
I had forestall'd this dear and deep rebuke,
Ere you with grief had spoke, and I had heard
The course of it so far. There is your crown ;
And He that wears the crown immortally,
Long guard it yours ! If I affect it more,
Than as your honour, and as your renown,
Let me no more from this obedience rise,
(Which my most true and inward-duteous spirit
Teacheth,) this prostrate and exterior bending !
Heaven witness with me, when I here came in,
And found no course of breath within your majesty,
How cold it struck my heart ! If I do feign,
O, let me in my present wildness die ;
And never live to show the incredulous world
The noble change that I have purposed !
Coming to look on you, thinking you dead,
(And dead almost, my liege, to think you were,)
I spake unto the crown, as having sense,
And thus upbraided it : "The care on thee de-
			pending,
Hath fed upon the body of my father ;
Therefore, thou, best of gold, art worst of gold.
Other, less fine in carat, is more precious,
Preserving life in med'cine potable :"
But thou, most fine, most honour'd, most renown'd,
Hast eat thy bearer up." Thus, my most royal
			liege,
Accusing it, I put it on my head ;
To try with it,—as with an enemy,

803

That had before my face murder'd my father,—
The quarrel of a true inheritor.
But if it did infect my blood with joy,
Or swell my thoughts to any strain of pride;
If any rebel or vain spirit of mine
Did, with the least affection of a welcome,
Give entertainment to the might of it,
Let God for ever keep it from my head!
And make me as the poorest vassal is,
That doth with awe and terror kneel to it!

    K. Hen. O my son!
Heaven put it in thy mind, to take it hence,
That thou might'st win the more thy father's
        love,
Pleading so wisely in excuse of it.
Come hither, Harry, sit thou by my bed;
And hear, I think, the very latest counsel
That ever I shall breathe. Heaven knows, my son,
By what by-paths, and indirect crook'd ways,
I met this crown; and I myself know well,
How troublesome it sat upon my head:
To thee it shall descend with better quiet,
Better opinion, better confirmation;
For all the soil of the achievement goes
With me into the earth. It seem'd in me,
But as an honour snatch'd with boisterous hand;
And I had many, living, to upbraid
My gain of it by their assistances;
Which daily grew to quarrel, and to bloodshed,
Wounding supposed peace: all these bold fears,
Thou see'st, with peril I have answered:
For all my reign hath been but as a scene
Acting that argument; and now my death
Changes the mode; for what in me was purchas'd,
Falls upon thee in a more fairer sort;
So thou the garland wear'st successively.
Yet, though thou stand'st more sure than I
      could do,
Thou art not firm enough, since griefs are green;
And all my friends, which thou must make thy
      friends,
Have but their stings and teeth newly ta'en out;
By whose fell working I was first advanc'd,

And by whose power I well might lodge a fear
To be again displac'd: which to avoid,
I cut some off; and had a purpose now
To lead out many to the Holy Land;
Lest rest, and lying still, might make them look
Too near unto my state. Therefore, my Harry,
Be it thy course, to busy giddy minds
With foreign quarrels: that action, hence borne
    out,
May waste the memory of the former days.
More would I, but my lungs are wasted so,
That strength of speech is utterly denied me.
How I came by the crown, O God, forgive!
And grant it may with thee in true peace live!

    P. Hen. My gracious liege,
You won it, wore it, kept it, gave it me:
Then plain, and right, must my possession be:
Which I, with more than with a common pain,
'Gainst all the world will rightfully maintain.

Enter PRINCE JOHN OF LANCASTER, WARWICK,
    Lords, and Others.

    K. Hen. Look, look, here comes my John of
      Lancaster.
    P. John. Health, peace, and happiness, to my
      royal father!
    K. Hen. Thou bring'st me happiness, and peace,
      son John;
But health, alack, with youthful wings is flown
From this bare, wither'd trunk: upon thy sight,
My worldly business makes a period.——
Where is my lord of Warwick?
    P. Hen.   My lord of Warwick!
    K. Hen. Doth any name particular belong
Unto the lodging where I first did swoon?
    War. 'Tis call'd Jerusalem, my noble lord.
    K. Hen. Laud be to God!—even there my life
      must end.
It hath been prophesied to me many years,
I should not die but in Jerusalem;
Which vainly I suppos'd, the Holy Land;—
But, bear me to that chamber; there I'll lie;
In that Jerusalem shall Harry die.   [*Exeunt*

ACT V.

SCENE I.—Glostershire. *A Hall in* SHALLOW'S
House.

Enter SHALLOW, FALSTAFF, BARDOLPH, *and* PAGE.

Shal. By cock and pye," sir, you shall not
away to-night.——What, Davy, I say!

Fal. You must excuse me, master Robert Shallow.

Shal. I will not excuse you; you shall not be
excused; excuses shall not be admitted; there is
no excuse shall serve; you shall not be excused.—
Why, Davy!

Enter DAVY.

Davy. Here, sir.

Shal. Davy, Davy, Davy,—let me see, Davy;
let me see:—yea, marry, William cook, bid him
come hither.—Sir John, you shall not be excused.

Davy. Marry, sir, thus:—those precepts cannot
be served;" and, again, sir,—Shall we sow the
headland with wheat?

Shal. With red wheat, Davy. But for William cook;——Are there no young pigeons?

Davy. Yes, sir.——Here is now the smith's note,
for shoeing, and plough-irons.

Shal. Let it be cast, and paid:—sir John, you
shall not be excused.

Davy. Now, sir, a new link to the bucket must
needs be had:—And, sir, do you mean to stop
any of William's wages, about the sack he lost
the other day at Hinckley fair?

Shal. He shall answer it:——Some pigeons,
Davy; a couple of short-legged hens; a joint of
mutton; and any pretty little tiny kickshaws, tell
William cook.

Davy. Doth the man of war stay all night, sir?

Shal. Yes, Davy. I will use him well: A friend
i' the court is better than a penny in purse. Use
his men well, Davy; for they are arrant knaves,
and will backbite.

Davy. No worse than they are back-bitten, sir;
for they have marvellous foul linen.

Shal. Well conceited, Davy. About thy business, Davy.

Davy. I beseech you, sir, to countenance William
Visor of Wincot against Clement Perkes of the hill.

Shal. There are many complaints, Davy, against
that Visor; that Visor is an arrant knave, on my
knowledge.

Davy. I grant your worship, that he is a knave,
sir: but yet, God forbid, sir, but a knave should
have some countenance at his friend's request. An
honest man, sir, is able to speak for himself, when
a knave is not. I have served your worship truly,
sir, this eight years; and if I cannot once or twice
in a quarter bear out a knave against an honest
man, I have but a very little credit with your worship. The knave is mine honest friend, sir; therefore, I beseech your worship, let him be counte-
nanced.

Shal. Go to; I say, he shall have no wrong.
Look about, Davy. [*Exit* DAVY.] Where are you,
sir John? Come, off with your boots.—Give me
your hand, master Bardolph.

Bard. I am glad to see your worship.

Shal. I thank thee with all my heart, kind
master Bardolph:—and welcome, my tall fellow
[*To the* Page.] Come, sir John. [*Exit* SHAL.

Fal. I'll follow you, good master Robert Shallow. Bardolph, look to our horses. [*Exeunt* BARD.
and Page.] If I were sawed into quantities, I
should make four dozen of such bearded hermit's-
staves as master Shallow. It is a wonderful thing
to see the semblable coherence of his men's spirits
and his: They, by observing him, do bear themselves like foolish justices; he, by conversing with
them, is turned into a justice-like serving-man;
their spirits are so married in conjunction with
the participation of society, that they flock together in consent, like so many wild-geese. If I
had a suit to master Shallow, I would humour his
men, with the imputation of being near their
master: if to his men, I would curry with master
Shallow, that no man could better command his
servants. It is certain, that either wise bearing,
or ignorant carriage, is caught, as men take diseases, one of another: therefore, let men take heed
of their company. I will devise matter enough
out of this Shallow, to keep prince Harry in continual laughter, the wearing-out of six fashions,
(which is four terms, or two actions,) and he shall
laugh without *intervallums*. O, it is much, that

a lie, with a slight oath, and a jest, with a sad
brow, will do with a fellow that never had the
ache in his shoulders! O, you shall see him
laugh, till his face be like a wet cloak ill laid up.

Shal. [*Within.*] Sir John!

Fal. I come, master Shallow; I come, master
Shallow.   [*Exit* FAL.

SCENE II.—Westminster. *A Room in the Palace.*

Enter WARWICK, *and the* LORD CHIEF JUSTICE.

War. How now, my lord chief justice? whither
away?

Ch. Just. How doth the king?

War. Exceeding well; his cares are now all ended.

Ch. Just. I hope, not dead.

War.   He's walk'd the way of nature;
And, to our purposes, he lives no more.

Ch. Just. I would, his majesty had call'd me
with him:
The service that I truly did his life,
Hath left me open to all injuries.

War. Indeed, I think, the young king loves
you not.

Ch. Just. I know, he doth not; and do arm
myself,
To welcome the condition of the time;
Which cannot look more hideously upon me
Than I have drawn it in my fantasy.

Enter PRINCE JOHN, PRINCE HUMPHREY, CLA-
RENCE, WESTMORELAND, *and Others.*

War. Here come the heavy issue of dead Harry:
O, that the living Harry had the temper
Of him, the worst of these three gentlemen!
How many nobles then should hold their places,
That must strike sail to spirits of vile sort!

Ch. Just. Alas! I fear, all will be overturn'd.

P. John. Good morrow, cousin Warwick.

P. Humph., Cla. Good morrow, cousin.

P. John. We meet like men that had forgot to
speak.

War. We do remember; but our argument
Is all too heavy to admit much talk.

P. John. Well, peace be with him that hath
made us heavy!

Ch. Just. Peace be with us, lest we be heavier!

P. Humph. O, good my lord, you have lost a
friend, indeed:
And I dare swear, you borrow not that face
Of seeming sorrow; it is, sure, your own.

P. John. Though no man be assur'd what grace
to find,
You stand in coldest expectation:
I am the sorrier; 'would, 't were otherwise.

Cla. Well, you must now speak sir John Falstaff fair;
Which swims against your stream of quality.

Ch. Just. Sweet princes, what I did, I did in
honour,
Led by the impartial conduct of my soul;
And never shall you see, that I will beg
A ragged and forestall'd remission.—
If truth and upright innocency fail me,
I'll to the king my master that is dead,
And tell him who hath sent me after him.

War. Here comes the prince.

Enter KING HENRY V.

Ch. Just. Good morrow; and heaven save your
majesty!

King. This new and gorgeous garment, majesty,
Sits not so easy on me as you think.—
Brothers, you mix your sadness with some fear;
This is the English, not the Turkish court;
Not Amurath an Amurath succeeds,
But Harry, Harry; Yet be sad, good brothers,
For, to speak truth, it very well becomes you;
Sorrow so royally in you appears,
That I will deeply put the fashion on,
And wear it in my heart. Why then, be sad:
But entertain no more of it, good brothers,
Than a joint burden laid upon us all.
For me, by heaven, I bid you be assur'd,
I'll be your father and your brother too;
Let me but bear your love, I'll bear your cares.
Yet weep, that Harry's dead; and so will I:
But Harry lives, that shall convert those tears,
By number, into hours of happiness.

P. John, &c. We hope no other from your majesty.

King. You all look strangely on me:—and you
most: [*To the* CH. JUST.
You are, I think, assur'd I love you not.

Ch. Just. I am assur'd, if I be measur'd rightly,
Your majesty hath no just cause to hate me.

King. No!
How might a prince of my great hopes forget
So great indignities you laid upon me?
What! rate, rebuke, and roughly send to prison
The immediate heir of England! Was this easy?
May this be wash'd in Lethe, and forgotten?

Ch. Just. I then did use the person of your
  father;
The image of his power lay then in me:
And, in the administration of his law,
Whiles I was busy for the commonwealth,
Your highness pleased to forget my place,
The majesty and power of law and justice,
The image of the king whom I presented,
And struck me in my very seat of judgment;
Whereon, as an offender to your father,
I gave bold way to my authority,
And did commit you. If the deed were ill,
Be you contented, wearing now the garland,
To have a son set your decrees at nought;
To pluck down justice from your awful bench;
To trip the course of law, and blunt the sword
That guards the peace and safety of your person:
Nay, more; to spurn at your most royal image,
And mock your workings in a second body.
Question your royal thoughts, make the case yours;
Be now the father, and propose a son:
Hear your own dignity so much profan'd,
See your most dreadful laws so loosely slighted,
Behold yourself so by a son disdain'd;
And then imagine me taking your part,
And, in your power, soft silencing your son;
After this cold considerance, sentence me;
And, as you are a king, speak in your state,—
What I have done, that misbecame my place,
My person, or my liege's sovereignty.

 King. You are right, justice; and you weigh
   this well;
Therefore still bear the balance, and the sword:
And I do wish your honours may increase,
Till you do live to see a son of mine
Offend you, and obey you, as I did.
So shall I live to speak my father's words;—
"Happy am I, that have a man so bold,
That dares do justice on my proper son:
And not less happy, having such a son,
That would deliver up his greatness so
Into the hands of justice."—You did commit me;
For which, I do commit into your hand
The unstained sword that you have us'd to bear;
With this remembrance,—That you use the same
With the like bold, just, and impartial spirit,
As you have done 'gainst me. There is my hand;
You shall be as a father to my youth:
My voice shall sound as you do prompt mine ear;
And I will stoop and humble my intents
To your well-practis'd, wise directions.——
And, princes all, believe me, I beseech you;—

My father is gone wild into his grave,
For in his tomb lie my affections;
And with his spirit sadly I survive,
To mock the expectation of the world;
To frustrate prophecies; and to raze out
Rotten opinion, who hath writ me down
After my seeming. The tide of blood in me
Hath proudly flow'd in vanity, till now:
Now doth it turn, and ebb back to the sea;
Where it shall mingle with the state of floods,
And flow henceforth in formal majesty.
Now call we our high court of parliament:
And let us choose such limbs of noble counsel,
That the great body of our state may go
In equal rank with the best govern'd nation;
That war, or peace, or both at once, may be
As things acquainted and familiar to us:——
In which you, father, shall have foremost hand.—
        [*To the* Ch. Just.
Our coronation done, we will accite,
As I before remember'd, all our state:
And (God consigning to my good intents,)
No prince, nor peer, shall have just cause to say,—
Heaven shorten Harry's happy life one day.
          [*Exeunt*

SCENE III.—Glostershire. *The Garden of*
    Shallow's *House.*

Enter FALSTAFF, SHALLOW, SILENCE, BARDOLPH,
   the Page, *and* DAVY.

 Shal. Nay, you shall see mine orchard: where,
in an arbour, we will eat a last year's pippin of my
own graffing, with a dish of carraways, and so
forth;—come, cousin Silence; and then to bed.

 Fal. 'Fore God, you have here a goodly dwelling, and a rich.

 Shal. Barren, barren, barren; beggars all, beggars all, sir John:—marry, good air.—Spread,
Davy; spread, Davy; well said, Davy.

 Fal. This Davy serves you for good uses; he is
your serving-man, and your husbandman.

 Shal. A good varlet, a good varlet, a very good
varlet, sir John.—By the mass, I have drunk too
much sack at supper;—A good varlet. Now sit
down, now sit down:—come, cousin.

 Sil. Ah, sirrah! quoth a,—we shall

Do nothing but eat, and make good cheer, [*Singing*
 And praise heaven for the merry year;
 When flesh is cheap and females dear,
 And lusty lads roam here and there,
  So merrily,
 And ever among so merrily.

Fal. There 's a merry heart!—Good master Silence, I 'll give you a health for that anon.

Shal. Give master Bardolph some wine, Davy.

Davy. Sweet sir, sit; [*Seating* BARD. *and the Page at another table.*] I 'll be with you anon :—most sweet sir, sit.——Master page, good master page, sit : proface!" What you want in meat, we 'll have in drink. But you must bear : The heart 's all.   [*Exit.*

Shal. Be merry, master Bardolph ;—and my little soldier there, be merry.

Sil. Be merry, be merry, my wife 's as all ;" [*Sing.*
For women are shrews, both short and tall :
'T is merry in hall, when beards wag all,
And welcome merry shrove-tide,
Be merry, be merry, &c.

Fal. I did not think, master Silence had been a man of this mettle.

Sil. Who I? I have been merry twice and once, ere now.

Re-enter DAVY.

Davy. There is a dish of leather-coats for you.
[*Setting them before* BARD.

Shal. Davy,—

Davy. Your worship?—I 'll be with you straight.
[*To* BARD.]—A cup of wine, sir !

Sil. A cup of wine, that 's brisk and fine, [*Singing.*
And drink unto the leman mine ;
And a merry heart lives long-a.

Fal. Well said, master Silence.

Sil. And we shall be merry ;—now comes in the sweet of the night.

Fal. Health and long life to you, master Silence.

Sil. Fill the cup, and let it come ;
I 'll pledge you a mile to the bottom.

Shal. Honest Bardolph, welcome : If thou wantest any thing, and wilt not call, beshrew thy heart.—Welcome, my little tiny thief ; [*To the Page.*] and welcome, indeed, too.—I 'll drink to master Bardolph, and to all the cavaleroes about London.

Davy. I hope to see London once ere I die.

Bard. An I might see you there, Davy,—

Shal. By the mass, you 'll crack a quart together. Ha ! will you not, master Bardolph ?

Bard. Yes, sir, in a pottle pot.

Shal. I thank thee :—The knave will stick by thee. I can assure thee that : he will not out ; he is true bred.

Bard. And I 'll stick by him, sir.

Shal. Why, there spoke a king. Lack noth-

ing : be merry. [*Knocking heard.*] Look who 's at door there : Ho ! who knocks ?   [*Exit* DAVY.

Fal. Why, now you have done me right.
[*To* SIL., *who drinks a bumper*

Sil.   Do me right,   [*Singing*
And dub me knight :
Samingo.

Is 't not so ?

Fal. 'T is so.

Sil. Is 't so ? Why, then say, an old man can do somewhat.

Re-enter DAVY.

Davy. An it please your worship, there 's one Pistol come from the court with news.

Fal. From the court, let him come in.—

Enter PISTOL.

How now, Pistol ?

Pist. God save you, sir John !

Fal. What wind blew you hither, Pistol ?

Pist. Not the ill wind which blows no man to good.—Sweet knight, thou art now one of the greatest men in the realm.

Sil. By 'r lady, I think 'a be ; but goodman Puff of Barson.

Pist. Puff ?

Puff in thy teeth, most recreant coward base !—
Sir John, I am thy Pistol, and thy friend,
And helter-skelter have I rode to thee ;
And tidings do I bring, and lucky joys,
And golden times, and happy news of price.

Fal. I pr'ythee now, deliver them like a man of this world.

Pist. A foutra for the world, and worldings base !
I speak of Africa, and golden joys.

Fal. O base Assyrian knight, what is thy news ?
Let king Cophetua know the truth thereof.

Sil. And Robin Hood, Scarlet, and John. [*Sings.*

Pist. Shall dunghill curs confront the Helicons ?
And shall good news be baffled ?
Then, Pistol, lay thy head in Furies' lap.

Shal. Honest gentleman, I know not your breeding.

Pist. Why then, lament therefore.

Shal. Give me pardon, sir ;—if, sir, you come with news from the court, I take it, there is but two ways ; either to utter them, or to conceal them. I am, sir, under the king, in some authority

Pist. Under which king, Bezonian ? speak or die.

Shal. Under king Harry

Pist. Harry the fourth? or fifth?

Shal. Harry the fourth.

Pist. A foutra for thine office!—
Sir John, thy tender lambkin now is king;
Harry the fifth 's the man. I speak the truth:
When Pistol lies, do this; and fig me, like
The bragging Spaniard.

Fal. What! is the old king dead?

Pist. As nail in door: the things I speak, are
just.

Fal. Away, Bardolph; saddle my horse.—
Master Robert Shallow, choose what office thou
wilt in the land, 't is thine.—Pistol, I will double-
charge thee with dignities.

Bard. O joyful day!—I would not take a
knighthood for my fortune.

Pist. What? I do bring good news?

Fal. Carry master Silence to bed.—Master
Shallow, my lord Shallow, be what thou wilt, I
am fortune's steward. Get on thy boots; we 'll
ride all night:—O, sweet Pistol:—Away, Bardolph. [*Exit Bard.*]—Come, Pistol, utter more to
me: and, withal, devise something, to do thyself
good.—Boot, boot, master Shallow; I know, the
young king is sick for me. Let us take any man's
horses; the laws of England are at my commandment. Happy are they which have been my
friends; and woe to my lord chief justice!

Pist. Let vultures vile seize on his lungs also!
"Where is the life that late I led," say they:
Why, here it is: Welcome these pleasant days.
[*Exeunt.*]

SCENE IV.—London. *A Street.*

Enter Beadles, *dragging in Hostess* Quickly, *and*
Doll Tear-sheet.

Host. No, thou arrant knave; I would I might
die, that I might have thee hanged: thou hast
drawn my shoulder out of joint.

1st Bead. The constables have delivered her
over to me; and she shall have whipping-cheer
enough, I warrant her: There hath been a man or
two lately killed about her.

Doll. Nut-hook, nut-hook, you lie. Come on;
I 'll tell thee what, thou damned tripe-visaged
rascal; an the child I now go with, do miscarry,
thou hadst better thou hadst struck thy mother,
thou paper-faced villain.

Host. O the Lord, that sir John were come!
he would make this a bloody day to somebody.
But I pray God the fruit of her womb miscarry!

192

1st Bead. If it do, you shall have a dozen of
cushions again; you have but eleven now." Come,
I charge you both go with me; for the man is
dead, that you and Pistol beat among you.

Doll. I 'll tell thee what, thou thin man in a
censer! I will have you as soundly swinged for
this, you blue-bottle rogue! you filthy famished
correctioner! if you be not swinged, I 'll forswear
half-kirtles.

1st Bead. Come, come, you she knight-errant,
come.

Host. O, that right should thus overcome
might! Well; of sufferance comes ease.

Doll. Come, you rogue, come; bring me to a
justice.

Host. Ay; come, you starved blood-hound.

Doll. Goodman death! goodman bones!

Host. Thou atomy thou!

Doll. Come, you thin thing; come, you rascal!

1st Bead. Very well. [*Exeunt.*]

SCENE V.—*A public Place near* Westminster
Abbey.

Enter Two Grooms, *strewing Rushes.*

1st Groom. More rushes, more rushes.

2nd Groom. The trumpets have sounded twice.

1st Groom. It will be two o'clock ere they come
from the coronation: Despatch, despatch.
[*Exeunt Grooms.*]

Enter Falstaff, Shallow, Pistol, Bardolph,
and the Page.

Fal. Stand here by me, master Robert Shallow; I will make the king do you grace: I will
leer upon him, as 'a comes by; and do but mark
the countenance that he will give me.

Pist. God bless thy lungs, good knight.

Fal. Come here, Pistol; stand behind me.—
O, if I had had time to have made new liveries,
I would have bestowed the thousand pound I borrowed of you. [*To* Shal.] But 't is no matter;
this poor show doth better: this doth infer the
zeal I had to see him.

Shal. It doth so.

Fal. It shows my earnestness of affection.

Shal. It doth so.

Fal. My devotion.

Shal. It doth, it doth, it doth.

Fal. As it were, to ride day and night: and
not to deliberate, not to remember, not to have
patience to shift me.

Shal. It is most certain.

Fal. But to stand stained with travel, and sweating with desire to see him : thinking of nothing else ; putting all affairs else in oblivion ; as if there were nothing else to be done, but to see him.

Pist. 'T is *semper idem, for absque hoc nihil est;* 'T is all in every part.

Shal. 'T is so, indeed.

Pist. My knight, I will inflame thy noble liver,
And make thee rage.
Thy Doll, and Helen of thy noble thoughts,
Is in base durance, and contagious prison ;
Haul'd thither
By most mechanical and dirty hand :—
Rouse up revenge from ebon den with fell Alecto's
snake,
For Doll is in ; Pistol speaks nought but truth.

Fal. I will deliver her.

    [*Shouts within, and the Trumpets sound.*

Pist. There roar'd the sea, and trumpet-clanger
sounds.

Enter the KING *and his* Train, *the* CHIEF JUSTICE
among them.

Fal. God save thy grace, king Hal! my royal
Hal!

Pist. The heavens thee guard and keep, most
royal imp of fame !

Fal. God save thee, my sweet boy !

King. My lord chief justice, speak to that vain
man.

Ch. Just. Have you your wits ? know you what
't is you speak ?

Fal. My king ! my Jove ! I speak to thee, my
heart !

King. I know thee not, old man : Fall to thy
prayers ;
How ill white hairs become a fool, and jester!
I have long dream'd of such a kind of man,
So surfeit-swell'd, so old, and so profane ;
But, being awake, I do despise my dream.
Make less thy body, hence, and more thy grace ;
Leave gormandizing ; know, the grave doth gape
For thee thrice wider than for other men :—
Reply not to me with a fool-born jest ;
Presume not, that I am the thing I was :
For heaven doth know, so shall the world perceive,
That I have turn'd away my former self ;
So will I those that kept me company.
When thou dost hear I am as I have been,
Approach me ; and thou shalt be as thou wast,
The tutor and the feeder of my riots :

Till then, I banish thee, on pain of death,—
As I have done the rest of my misleaders,—
Not to come near our person by ten mile.
For competence of life, I will allow you ;
That lack of means enforce you not to evil :
And, as we hear you do reform yourselves,
We will,—according to your strength, and quali-
ties,—
Give you advancement.—Be it your charge, my
lord,
To see perform'd the tenor of our word.—
Set on.   [*Exeunt* KING, *and his* Train.

Fal. Master Shallow, I owe you a thousand
pound.

Shal. Ay, marry, sir John : which I beseech
you to let me have home with me.

Fal. That can hardly be, master Shallow. Do
not you grieve at this ; I shall be sent for in private to him : look you, he must seem thus to the
world. Fear not your advancement ; I will be the
man yet, that shall make you great.

Shal. I cannot perceive how ; unless you give
me your doublet, and stuff me out with straw. I
beseech you, good sir John, let me have five hundred of my thousand.

Fal. Sir, I will be as good as my word ; this
that you heard, was but a colour.

Shal. A colour, I fear, that you will die in, sir
John.

Fal. Fear no colours ; go with me to dinner.
Come, lieutenant Pistol ;—come, Bardolph :—I
Shall be sent for soon at night.

Re-enter PRINCE JOHN, *the* CHIEF JUSTICE, *Officers, &c.*

Ch. Just. Go, carry sir John Falstaff to the
Fleet : Take all his company along with him.

Fal. My lord, my lord,——

Ch. Just. I cannot now speak ; I will hear you
soon. Take them away.

Pist. Si fortuna me tormenta, spero me contenta.
    [*Exeunt* FAL., SHAL., PIST., BARD., Page
and Officers.

P. John. I like this fair proceeding of the king's
He hath intent, his wonted followers
Shall all be very well provided for ;
But all are banish'd, till their conversations
Appear more wise and modest to the world.

Ch. Just. And so they are.

P. John. The king hath call'd his parliament,
my lord.

Ch. Just. He hath.

P. John. I will lay odds,—that, ere this year
          expire,
We bear our civil swords, and native fire,

As far as France; I heard a bird so sing,
Whose music, to my thinking, pleas'd the king.
Come, will you hence?   [*Exeunt.*

EPILOGUE.—(Spoken by a Dancer.)

First, my fear; then, my court'sy; last, my speech. My fear is, your displeasure; my court'sy, my duty; and my speech, to beg your pardons. If you look for a good speech now, you undo me: for what I have to say, is of my own making; and what, indeed, I should say, will, I doubt, prove mine own marring. But to the purpose, and so to the venture.—Be it known to you, (as it is very well,) I was lately here in the end of a displeasing play, to pray your patience for it, and to promise you a better. I did mean, indeed, to pay you with this; which, if, like an ill venture, it come unluckily home, I break, and you, my gentle creditors, lose. Here, I promised you, I would be, and here I commit my body to your mercies: bate me some, and I will pay you some, and, as most debtors do, promise you infinitely.

If my tongue cannot entreat you to acquit me, will you command me to use my legs? and yet that were but light payment,—to dance out of your debt. But a good conscience will make any possible satisfaction, and so will I. All the gentlewomen here have forgiven me; if the gentlemen will not, then the gentlemen do not agree with the gentlewomen, which was never seen before in such an assembly.

One word more, I beseech you. If you be not too much cloyed with fat meat, our humble author will continue the story, with sir John in it, and make you merry with fair Katharine of France: where, for any thing I know, Falstaff shall die of a sweat, unless already he be killed with your hard opinions; for Oldcastle died a martyr, and this is not the man.[12] My tongue is weary; when my legs are too, I will bid you good night: and so kneel down before you;—but, indeed, to pray for the queen.[13]

811

NOTES TO KING HENRY THE FOURTH.

(PART THE SECOND.)

---

[1] *And hold'st it fear or sin.*

Fear is used as *danger*. You hold it dangerous or sinful to tell me at once of the death of my son.

[2] *Read'ring faint quittance.*

Quittance is return; giving a faint return of the blows of his adversary.

[3] *'Gan vail his stomach.*

To lose heart: to let his spirits sink under the pressure of calamity.

[4] *What says the doctor to my water?*

An allusion to the method of ascertaining diseases by an inspection of the urine of the patient; a custom in fashion long after the time of Shakespeare.

[5] *I never was manned with an agate till now.*

An *agate* appears to have been an expression to signify anything diminutive, though I cannot say for what reason. See note 67 to *Much Ado About Nothing*. Falstaff's meaning is, I never had so small an attendant before.

He may keep it still as a face-royal, for a barber shall never earn sixpence out of it.

Mr. Steevens tells us—"Perhaps this quibbling allusion is to the English *real*, *rial*, or *royal*. The poet seems to mean that a barber can no more earn sixpence by his *face-royal*, than by the face stamped on the coin called a *royal*; the one requiring as little shaving as the other."

[7] *To bear a gentleman in hand.*

To *bear in hand* is to keep in expectation.

[8] *I bought him in Paul's.*

St. Paul's was at that time the common resort of unemployed, idle, or dissolute people. It possessed a great advantage for this class of people, as it partook so far of the nature of a sanctuary that no debtor could be arrested within its precincts. In an old *Collection of Proverbs* there is the following:—"Who goes to Westminster for a wife, to St. Paul's for a man, and to Smithfield for a horse, may meet with a whore, a knave, and a jade."

[9] *And yet, in some respects, I grant, I cannot go, I cannot tell.*

That is, in some respects I cannot pass current, am objected to, and unappreciated.

[10] *You are too impatient to bear crosses.*

The justice appears to be quibbling here; there is a coin called a *cross*. Falstaff had asked for the loan of a thousand pounds, and the reply indicates that he is too impetuous to bear reverses, or, in its pecuniary sense, to be trusted with money.

[11] *If I do, fillip me with a three-man beetle.*

To *fillip* is to strike a smart sudden blow; a *three-man beetle* is a kind of huge mallet, with three handles, which was used in driving piles.

[12] *To dinner at the Lubbar's head.*

A colloquial corruption of the Libbard's head, or more probably of the Lombard's head.

[13] *O thou honey-suckle villain! wilt thou kill God's officers, and the king's? O thou honey-seed rogue!*

Honey-suckle and *honey-seed* are Mrs. Quickly's corruptions of homicidal and homicide.

[14] *Sneap,* i. e. a reprimand, a check.

[15] *Answer in the effect of your reputation.*

That is, answer in a manner becoming your reputation and position in society.

[16] *Those that bawl out the ruins of thy linen.*

An elliptical phrase, implying—those that bawl out of the ruins of thy linen; i. e. thy illegitimate children wrapt up in thy old shirts.

[17] *He called me even now, my lord, through a red lattice.*

Red lattice at the doors and windows were formerly the signs of an ale-house. Hence the present *chequers*. Bardolph had called the page from an ale-house window.

⁵ Frank, i. e. a sty.

¹⁶ Ephesians, my lord.

An *Ephesian* was a cant term which Dr. Johnson thinks may have meant toper. Might it not signify the same as Corinthian? i. e. a frequenter of brothels. The Page might have heard the associates of Falstaff called Ephesians, and have repeated the word without understanding its meaning.

¹⁸ See if thou canst find out Sneak's noise.

Sneak was a street musician, and the drawer requests his companion to go out and listen if he can hear him in the neighbourhood. A company of musicians was anciently called a noise of musicians.

¹⁹ By the mass, here will be old utis.

Utis or utas, is an old word, which Pope says was still in use in some counties in his time, signifying a merry festival. Thus, in *A Contention between Liberality and Prodigality*, a comedy, 1602 :—

Then if you please, with some roysting harmony,
Let us begin the utas of our jollitie.

²¹ You are both in good truth as rheumatic.

Possibly Mrs. Quickly means epilenetic, though Mr. Steevens contends that rheumatic, in the cant language of the time, signified capricious, humorsome.

²² What, with two points on your shoulder? much!

The two points on his shoulder were a mark of his commission; Doll means that she would not associate with one of his humble grade. Much was a common expression of contempt at that period, implying, is it likely?

²⁴ These villains will make the word captain as odious as the word occupy.

Occupant seems to have been a term for a woman of the town, as occupier was for a wencher. Thus, in Marston's *Satires*, 1599 :—

———— He with his occupant
Are cling'd so close, like dew-worms in the morne,
That he 'll not stir.

This word is used with different senses in the following jest from *Wits, Fits, and Fancies*, 1614 :—"One threw stones at an yll-favor'd old woman's owle, and the old woman said : Faith (sir knave) you are well occupy'd, to throw stones at my poore owle, that doth you no harme. Yea marie (answered the wag) so would you be better occupy'd too (I wisse) if you were young again and had a better face."

²⁵ Have we not Hiren here?

The language of Pistol appears to be made up of allusions to, and passages from many plays which were then, doubtless, familiar to the play-goer, but are now chiefly either lost or forgotten. The line above is probably a quotation from Peele's play, which has now perished, called *The Turkish Mahomet, and Hyren the fair Greek*. Mr. Tollet observes, that in Adam's *Spiritual Navigator*, &c., 1615, there is the following passage: "There be sirens in the sea of the world. Syrens? Hirens, as they are now

called. What a number of these syrens, hirens, cocka-trices, courteghians,—in plain English, harlots,—swimme amongst us!"

²⁶ Compare with Cæsars and with Cannibals.

Pistol used Cannibals as a blunder for Hannibals. The preceding lines are a burlesque quotation from Marlow's play of *Tamerlane's Conquests; or the Scythian Shepherds*

²⁷ Feed, and be fat, my fair Calipolis.

This is a burlesque on a line in an old play, entitled *The Battel of Alcazar*, &c., in which Muley Mahomet enters to his wife with lion's flesh on his sword, and exclaims :—

Feed then, and faint not, my faire Calypolis.

²⁸ Neif, i. e. fist.

²⁹ Know we not Galloway nags.

Common hacks. Pistol means, I know you for common hacks; you have not strength or courage to execute your threat.

³⁰ And, look, whether the fiery Trigon, his man, be not lisping to his master's old tables.

Trigonum igneum, is the astronomical term when the upper planets meet in a fiery sign. Warburton would read, clasping to his master's old tables; i. e. kissing Falstaff's cast off mistress. But lisping may be right; Bardolph was probably drunk, and might lisp a little in his courtship. The old table-book was a counsel-keeper, a preserver of secrets, and so also was Mrs. Quickly.

³¹ Glendower is dead.

Glendower did not die until after Henry the Fourth, but the date and place of his death have not been correctly ascertained. It is traditionally stated that he was buried in the Cathedral of Bangor, where a grave, under the great window in the south aisle wall, is still pointed out as the place of his interment.

³² By the rood, i. e. the image of Christ on the rood.

³³ Bona-robas, i. e. ladies of pleasure.

³⁴ I saw him break Skogan's head.

In Ben Jonson's masque, *The Fortunate Isles*, is the following account of this Skogan :—

———— Scogan? what was he?
Oh, a fine gentleman, and a master of arts
Of *Henry the Fourth's times*, that made disguises
For the king's sons, and writ in ballad royal
Daintily well.

³⁵ Clapped i' the clout, i. e. hit the white mark.

³⁶ A collier.

A collier was smaller and lighter than a musket. Sir John means, that although Wart, as a feeble undersized man, is unfit for a musketeer, yet, armed with a lighter weapon, he may do good service.

813

" I was then Sir Dagonet in Arthur's show.

It is doubted whether Shakespeare means the justice to say that he performed the part of Sir Dagonet, the fool, in the interlude of *King Arthur*; or whether he represented Sir Dagonet in a show of archery which was given, not at Clement's Inn, but at Mile-End Green. A society of archers calling themselves *Arthur's Knights*, existed in Shakespeare's time, who used to give exhibitions of archery, and Master Shallow might have been a member, and the representative of Sir Dagonet. Mr. Douce says,—" We see, therefore, that Shakespeare, having *left these shows* in his recollection, has made Shallow, a talkative simpleton, refer to them indistinctly, and that probably by design, and with a due attention to the nature of his character."

" And the feats he hath done about Turnbull-street.

Turnbull-street was notorious for houses of ill-fame. Nash, in *Pierce l'ennilesse, his Supplication*, &c., commends the sisters of Turnbull-street to the patronage of the Devil. And in Beaumont and Fletcher's *Scornful Lady :*—" Here has been such a hurry, such a din, such dismal drinking, swearing, &c., we have all lived in a perpetual *Turnbull-street.*"

" Over-scutched huswives.

Dr. Johnson thinks that *over-scutched* means dirty or grimed. That Shallow visited mean houses, and boasted his accomplishments to dirty women. Ray, however, among his north-country works, says that *over-scutched huswife* means a strumpet.

" They were his fancies, or his good-nights.

Fancies and *good-nights* were the titles of little poems, songs, or epigrams.

" Makes it apprehensive, quick, forgetive.

Apprehensive, is quick of understanding ; *forge-tive*, a word made from *forge* ; to devise ; inventive, imaginative.

" A mere hoard of gold kept by a devil.

Falstaff alludes to an ancient superstition, that all mines of gold and jewels were guarded by evil spirits. In a book by Edward Fenton, entitled, *Certaine Secrete Wonders of Nature, &c.,* 1569 :—" There appeare at this day many strange visions and wicked spirites in the metal-mines of the Greate Turke."—" In the mine at Annenberg was a metall sprite which killed twelve workmen ; the same causing the rest to forsake the myne, albeit it was very riche."

" Hath wrought the mure that should confine it in.

Mure is the wall ; the agitation of his mind had wrought or worn out the head that contained it. The same thought is more clearly expressed in Daniel's *Civil Wars, &c.,* Book IV.—

As that the walls worn thin, permit the mind
To look out thorow, and his frailtie find.

*" The people fear me ; for they do observe
Unfather'd heirs, &c.*

To fear me is used for make me afraid. I fear the peo-

ple, for they observe unfathered heirs, i. e. equivocal births, productions not brought forth according to the known laws of nature. It was thought that great changes or disasters in a kingdom were usually preceded by prodigies and unnatural events.

" Golden rigol, i. e. golden circle.

" Preserving life in med'cine potable.

An opinion anciently prevailed that the incorruptibility of gold might be communicated to the body impregnated with it.

" By cock and pye.

Cock is a corruption of the sacred name ; thus in the old interludes we have *cock's-bones, cock's-wounds, cock's-body, cock's-passion,* by *cock's-mother,* &c. The *pie* is a table or rule in the old Roman offices, showing how to find out the service which is to be read upon each day.

" Those precepts cannot be served.

A *precept* is a justice's warrant.

" Proface, i. e. Italian from profaccio ; much good may it do you.

" Be merry, be merry, my wife 's as all.

That is, as all women are, she is a shrew like the rest of them ; according to this not very gallant ballad.

" If it do you shall have a dozen of cushions again ; you have but eleven now.

The beadle means that Doll had taken one of the cushions to stuff out her figure, that she might counterfeit pregnancy.

" For Oldcastle died a martyr, and this is not the man.

I have already alluded in note 8, first part of *Henry IV.,* to the opinion entertained by some critics that Falstaff was originally called Oldcastle. "Shakespeare, I think," says Mr. Malone, " meant only to say, that 'Falstaff may perhaps die of his débaucheries in France,' (having mentioned Falstaff's *death,* he then, with his usual licence, uses the word in a metaphorical sense, adding,) ' unless he be already killed by the hard and unjust opinions of those who imagined that the knight's character (like his predecessor in the old play) was intended as a ridicule on Sir John Oldcastle, the *good* Lord Cobham. This our author disclaims, reminding the audience that there can be no ground for such a supposition. I call them (says he) hard and *unjust opinions,* ' for Sir John Oldcastle was no debauchee, but a protestant martyr, and our Falstaff *is not the man ;'* i. e. is no representation of him, has no allusion whatever to him."

" I will bid you good night ; and so kneel down before you but, indeed, to pray for the queen.

It was anciently a custom for the actors at the end of the performance to pray for their patrons, and most of the old interludes terminate with a prayer for the king, queen, house of commons, &c.

King Henry the Fifth.

IN the construction of this play Shakespeare appears to have felt himself more than usually confined and fettered by the smallness of the theatres, and the rude state of dramatic art in his age. Participating largely in the affection borne by the English nation to the memory of Henry the Fifth, the poet deeply regretted the poor and bare nature of that medium through which his drama was to be made known to his countrymen. Although it does not rank among his best and most powerful plays, he has evidently bestowed great care upon it; he was desirous that the memory of his favourite king should be gilded by the brightest coruscations of his genius, and be embalmed in the glorious robes of imperishable poetry. Anxious to do every justice to the subject, Shakespeare, contrary to his usual custom, has adopted a Chorus to prepare the minds of the spectators, to solicit indulgence for unavoidable imperfections in representation, and to explain what is supposed to pass between the acts of the drama. Of this innovation on the established usage of the English drama, Dr. Johnson has said, "The lines given to the Chorus have many admirers; but the truth is, that in them a little may be praised, and much must be forgiven; nor can it be easily discovered why the intelligence given by the Chorus is more necessary in this play than in many others where it is omitted."

If we were to transpose Johnson's judgment on the beauty of the speeches given to the Chorus, and say, in them much must be praised and a little forgiven, we should be nearer the truth. Some explanatory matter spoken occasionally between the acts, would doubtless be an improvement to most of Shakespeare's historical plays, as it would remove that fragmentary appearance which some of them possess, and render them more valuable as mediums of historical instruction. To the reader fresh from the perusal of actual history, the incidents in our poet's plays appear crushed and jambed together, and to follow one another with a supernatural rapidity, like the line of visionary kings the witches exhibited to Macbeth. A little explanation between the acts or scenes would remove this, and the necessary links of connexion would be restored. But because the poet has not given us information when it has been necessary elsewhere, that furnishes no reason for his omission of it here. This play being chiefly the record of a single battle, a subject in itself more epic than dramatic, Shakespeare employed the former style to convey by description that which could not be condensed into representation. This play would be absolutely unintelligible, without the accompaniment of a descriptive Chorus. For instance, two years elapse between the fourth and fifth acts, that is, between Henry's return to England after the victory at Agincourt, and his second expedition to France; still, the fourth act terminates in France, and the fifth commences there, which would give rise to error and confusion, if the Chorus did not play "the interim, by remembering you—'t is past."

It is not an uncommon event, even in the present day, for authors to attach to their dramas an introductory preface reciting what is supposed to have occurred before the commencement of the action. Dr. Johnson, though he was an acute critic, and, notwithstanding his occasional ill-temper with our poet, generally an appreciative one, has much underrated these speeches of the Chorus. They are interesting, vigorous, and poetical; the first eight lines of the introduction grand and picturesque, the comparison of "warlike Harry," prepared for conquest, to Mars, with Famine, Sword,

815

and Fire, leashed in like hounds, and crouching at his feet for employment, is a very martial and spirit-stirring metaphor; a blast on war's brazen trumpet, admirably calculated to prepare the mind for the chivalric display about to be presented.

The poet has carefully elaborated the character of Henry; he introduces him into three dramas, carries him uncontaminated through scenes of riot and dissipation, represents him repenting his lost hours with tears of shame and affection, at the feet of his father, and, on his accession to the "golden rigol," after winning the good graces of prelates, nobility, and people, and passing undaunted through a fearful ordeal, such as would have overwhelmed many a stout heart, leaves him on a summit of military glory more brilliant than had been achieved even by his brave and illustrious ancestors. The fine description by the Archbishop of Canterbury of the King's reformation, and the sudden blaze of those virtues and accomplishments which he was not suspected to have possessed, has been aptly applied to Shakespeare himself. Like Henry, the wildness of his youth promised not the brilliant performances of his manhood. With the poet, as with the prince—

> Consideration like an angel came,
> And whipp'd the offending Adam out of him;
> Leaving his body as a paradise,
> To envelop and contain celestial spirits.

The introductory dialogue between the two bishops, independent of its exquisite beauty, easily and naturally prepares us for the change of the frolicsome idle prince to the serious and majestic king.

The mirthful and early pranks of Henry are not forgotten in this play; his acceptance of the glove of the soldier as a challenge, and bestowal of it upon Fluellen, show that his sportive disposition is not extinguished, but tempered by rank and responsibility of station. Still he turns moralist in his extremity, and exclaims to his brother—

> There is some soul of goodness in things evil,
> Would men observingly distil it out.

Henry's claim upon France was politic but ungenerous, for that unhappy country was distracted by internal broils, possessed a lunatic for a king, and was laid waste by the furious contentions of its own nobles. So far from his having any title to the crown of France, his right to the sovereignty of his own country would not bear examination; and it was to evade inquiry, and that his nobility might not have leisure to conspire against him in England, that he led them to war against France; and the archbishop encourages and justifies the design, that Henry may not pry too closely into the vast possessions of the church. Such are the secret springs of war and conquest.

In this play we hear the last of Falstaff; his death is related by Mrs. Quickly. We cannot help feeling sad for the poor old knight, dying in an inn, surrounded only by rude dependents, and the faithful hostess, whom we respect for her kind attachment to him to the last. No wife or child is near; no gentle kindred hand to do kind offices in the hour of weakness and despondency. In his half-delirious moments his last joke was made upon the flea on Bardolph's nose, which he said "was a black soul burning in hell-fire." The scene between the Welsh, Irish, and Scotch captains, each speaking in his peculiar *patois*, is very humorous, but these three do not amount to one Falstaff. The episode between Pistol and the French soldier, whom, by his fierce looks, he frightens into paying a good ransom for his life, is much richer; but the crown of mirth in this play is where the Welshman cudgels Pistol, and makes him eat his leek for having mocked him respecting it. All the group that surrounded Falstaff are here disposed of; Bardolph and Nym are hanged, the boy is killed by the flying French soldiers after the battle, Mrs. Quickly dies in the hospital, and Pistol sneaks home to disgrace and obscurity.

Although there is tragic matter enough in this play, it ends like a comedy—with a marriage of convenience. Henry espoused the princess Katharine, on the 2nd of June, 1418, in the church of St. John, at Troyes. The next day, after he had given a splendid banquet, it was proposed by the French that the event should be honoured by a series of tournaments and public rejoicings. This Henry would not sanction. "I pray," said he to the French monarch, "my lord the king to permit, and I command his servants and mine to be all ready to-morrow morning to go and lay siege to Seus, wherein are our enemies: there every man may have jousting and tourneying enough, and may give proof of his prowess; *for there is no finer prowess than that of doing justice on the wicked, in order that the poor people may breathe and live.*" In the exhibition of this courage, activity, and feeling for the lower orders, lay the secret of Henry's popularity. He lived four years after his marriage a period which Shakespeare has left unrecorded; but the death of this heroic king was a scene for the poet. Still only in his thirty-fourth year, a conqueror in the full blaze of military glory, a king beloved by his people almost to idolatry, the husband of a young, beautiful, and accomplished wife, and the father of an infant son, this world was to him a demi-paradise, an earthly Eden; still he breathed his last without one complaint, and was himself calm and resigned, though all around wept as they promised to protect his wife and child. The solemn pomp displayed at his funeral was extraordinary; no such procession had hitherto attended the remains of any English king. His funeral car was preceded and flanked by a crowd of heralds, banner-bearers, and priests clothed in white and carrying lighted torches, and it was followed by some hundreds of knights and esquires in black armour and plumes, with their lances reversed in token of mourning; while, far in the rear, travelled the young widow, with a gorgeous and numerous retinue. She, however, does not appear to have been inconsolable, for she was married again shortly after Henry's death, to a Welsh gentleman, Sir Owen Tudor, one of the handsomest men of his time. She brought him two sons, of whom the eldest, Edmund, was created earl of Richmond, and his son afterwards ascended the English throne, under the title of Henry the Seventh.

Henry the Fifth was produced in 1599; it was entered on the Stationers' books, August 14th, 1600; and printed in the same year.

PERSONS REPRESENTED.

KING HENRY THE FIFTH.
Appears, Act I. sc. 2. Act II. sc. 2. Act III. sc. 1; sc. 3; sc. 6. Act IV. sc. 1; sc. 3; sc. 6; sc. 7; sc. 8. Act V. sc. 2.

DUKE OF GLOUCESTER, *Brother to the King.*
Appears, Act I. sc. 2. Act III. sc. 1; sc. 6. Act IV. sc. 1; sc. 3; sc. 7; sc. 8. Act V. sc. 2.

DUKE OF BEDFORD, *Brother to the King.*
Appears, Act I. sc. 2. Act II. sc. 2. Act III. sc. 1. Act IV. sc. 1; sc. 3. Act V. sc. 2.

DUKE OF EXETER, *Uncle to the King.*
Appears, Act I. sc. 2. Act II. sc. 2; sc. 4. Act III. sc. 1. Act IV. sc. 3; sc. 6; sc. 7; sc. 8. Act V. sc. 2.

DUKE OF YORK, *Cousin to the King.*
Appears, Act IV. sc. 3.

EARL OF SALISBURY.
Appears, Act IV. sc. 3.

EARL OF WESTMORELAND.
Appears, Act I. sc. 2. Act II. sc. 2. Act IV. sc. 3. Act V. sc. 2.

EARL OF WARWICK.
Appears, Act I. sc. 2. Act IV. sc. 7; sc. 8. Act V. sc. 2.

ARCHBISHOP OF CANTERBURY.
BISHOP OF ELY.
Appear, Act I. sc. 1; sc. 2.

EARL OF CAMBRIDGE,
LORD SCROOP, } *Conspirators against the King.*
SIR THOMAS GREY,
Appear, Act II. sc. 2.

SIR THOMAS ERPINGHAM.
Appears, Act IV. sc. 1.

GOWER, *an Officer in King Henry's army.*
FLUELLEN, *a Welsh Officer.*
Appear, Act III. sc. 2; sc. 6. Act IV. sc. 1; sc. 7; sc. 8. Act V. sc. 1.

MACMORRIS, *an Irish Officer.*
JAMY, *a Scotch Officer.*
Appear, Act III. sc. 2.

WILLIAMS, *a Soldier.*
Appears, Act IV. sc. 1; sc. 7; sc. 8.

BATES,
COURT, } *Soldiers.*
Appear, Act IV. sc. 1.

NYM.
BARDOLPH.
Appear, Act II. sc. 1; sc. 3. Act III. sc. 2.

818

PISTOL.
Appears, Act II. sc. 1; sc. 3. Act III. sc. 2; sc. 6. Act IV. sc. 1; sc. 4. Act V. sc. 1.

BOY, *attending on Nym, Bardolph, and Pistol.*
Appears, Act II. sc. 1; sc. 3. Act III. sc. 2. Act IV. sc. 4.

AN ENGLISH HERALD.
Appears, Act IV. sc. 8.

CHARLES THE SIXTH, *King of France.*
Appears, Act II. sc. 4. Act III. sc. 5. Act V. sc. 2.

LEWIS, *the Dauphin.*
Appears, Act II. sc. 4. Act III. sc. 5; sc. 7. Act IV. sc. 2; sc. 5.

DUKE OF BURGUNDY.
Appears, Act II. sc. 4. Act V. sc. 2.

DUKE OF ORLEANS.
Appears, Act III. sc. 7. Act IV. sc. 2; sc. 5.

DUKE OF BOURBON.
Appears, Act III. sc. 5. Act IV. sc. 5.

THE CONSTABLE OF FRANCE.
Appears, Act II. sc. 4. Act III. sc. 5; sc. 7. Act IV. sc. 2; sc. 5.

LORD RAMBURES.
Appears, Act III. sc. 3. Act IV. sc. 2; sc. 5.

LORD GRANDPREE.
Appears, Act IV. sc. 2.

GOVERNOR OF HARFLEUR.
Appears, Act III. sc. 3.

MONTJOY, *a French Herald.*
Appears, Act III. sc. 6. Act IV. sc. 3; sc. 7.

AMBASSADORS FROM FRANCE.
Appear, Act I. sc. 2.

CHORUS.
Enters before each Act, and at the conclusion of the Play.

ISABEL, *Queen of France.*
Appears, Act V. sc. 2.

KATHERINE, *Daughter of Charles and Isabel.*
ALICE, *a Lady attending on the Princess Katherine.*
Appear, Act III. sc. 4. Act V. sc. 2.

HOSTESS, *now married to Pistol.*
Appears, Act II. sc. 1; sc. 3.

Lords, Ladies, Officers, French and English Soldiers, Messengers, and Attendants.

SCENE,—*At the beginning of the Play lies in* ENGLAND: *but afterwards wholly in* FRANCE.

King Henry the Fifth.

CHORUS.

Enter Chorus.

O, for a muse of fire, that would ascend
The brightest heaven of invention!
A kingdom for a stage, princes to act,
And monarchs to behold the swelling scene!
Then should the warlike Harry, like himself,
Assume the port of Mars; and, at his heels,
Leash'd in like hounds, should famine, sword, and
    fire,
Crouch for employment. But pardon, gentles all,
The flat unraised spirit, that hath dar'd,
On this unworthy scaffold, to bring forth
So great an object: Can this cockpit hold
The vasty fields of France? or may we cram
Within this wooden O, the very casques,
That did affright the air at Agincourt?
O, pardon! since a crooked figure may
Attest, in little place, a million;

And let us, ciphers to this great accompt,
On your imaginary forces work:
Suppose, within the girdle of these walls
Are now confin'd two mighty monarchies,
Whose high upreared and abutting fronts
The perilous, narrow ocean parts asunder.
Piece out our imperfections with your thoughts;
Into a thousand parts divide one man,
And make imaginary puissance
Think, when we talk of horses, that you see them
Printing their proud hoofs i' the receiving earth:
For 't is your thoughts that now must deck our
    kings,
Carry them here and there; jumping o'er times;
Turning the accomplishment of many years
Into an hour-glass: For the which supply,
Admit me chorus to this history;
Who, prologue-like, your humble patience pray
Gently to hear, kindly to judge, our play

ACT I.

SCENE I.—London. *An Ante-chamber in the*
    King's Palace.

Enter the Archbishop of Canterbury *and* Bishop
    of Ely.

Cant. My lord, I 'll tell you,—that self bill is
    urg'd,[2]
Which, in the eleventh year o' the last king's reign
Was like, and had indeed against us pass'd,

But that the scambling and unquiet time
Did push it out of further question.
    Ely. But how, my lord, shall we resist it now!
    Cant. It must be thought on. If it pass
        against us,
We lose the better half of our possession:
For all the temporal lands, which men devout
By testament have given to the church,
Would they strip from us; being valued thus,—

819

As much as would maintain, to the king's honour,
Full fifteen earls, and fifteen hundred knights;
Six thousand and two hundred good esquires;
And, to relief of lazars, and weak age,
Of indigent faint souls, past corporal toil,
A hundred alms-houses, right well supplied;
And to the coffers of the king beside.
A thousand pounds by the year: Thus runs the bill.

   Ely. This would drink deep.
   Cant.   'T would drink the cup and all.
   Ely. But what prevention?
   Cant. The king is full of grace, and fair regard.
   Ely. And a true lover of the holy church.
   Cant. The courses of his youth promis'd it not.
The breath no sooner left his father's body,
But that his wildness, mortified in him,
Seem'd to die too: yea, at that very moment,
Consideration like an angel came,
And whipp'd the offending Adam out of him,
Leaving his body as a paradise,
To envelop and contain celestial spirits.
Never was such a sudden scholar made:
Never came reformation in a flood,
With such a heady current, scouring faults;
Nor never Hydra-headed wilfulness
So soon did lose his seat, and all at once,
As in this king.

   Ely.   We are blessed in the change.
   Cant. Hear him but reason in divinity,
And, all-admiring, with an inward wish
You would desire, the king were made a prelate:
Hear him debate of commonwealth affairs,
You would say,—it hath been all-in-all his study:
List his discourse of war, and you shall hear
A fearful battle render'd you in music:
Turn him to any cause of policy,
The Gordian knot of it he will unloose,
Familiar as his garter; that, when he speaks,
The air, a charter'd libertine, is still,
And the mute wonder lurketh in men's ears,
To steal his sweet and honeyed sentences;
So that the art and practic part of life
Must be the mistress to this theoric:
Which is a wonder, how his grace should glean it,
Since his addiction was to courses vain:
His companies unletter'd, rude, and shallow;
His hours fill'd up with riots, banquets, sports;
And never noted in him any study,
Any retirement, any sequestration
From open haunts and popularity.

   Ely. The strawberry grows underneath the nettle,
And wholesome berries thrive and ripen best,

Neighbour'd by fruit of baser quality;
And so the prince obscur'd his contemplation
Under the veil of wildness; which, no doubt,
Grew like the summer grass, fastest by night,
Unseen, yet crescive' in his faculty.

   Cant. It must be so: for miracles are ceas'd;
And therefore we must needs admit the means,
How things are perfected.

   Ely.   But, my good lord,
How now for mitigation of this bill
Urg'd by the commons? Doth his majesty
Incline to it, or no?

   Cant.   He seems indifferent,
Or, rather, swaying more upon our part,
Than cherishing the exhibiters against us:
For I have made an offer to his majesty,—
Upon our spiritual convocation;
And in regard of causes now in hand,
Which I have open'd to his grace at large,
As touching France,—to give a greater sum
Than ever at one time the clergy yet
Did to his predecessors part withal.

   Ely. How did this offer seem receiv'd, my lord?
   Cant. With good acceptance of his majesty;
Save, that there was not time enough to hear
(As, I perceiv'd, his grace would fain have done,)
The severals, and unhidden passages,
Of his true titles to some certain dukedoms:
And, generally, to the crown and seat of France,
Deriv'd from Edward, his great grandfather.

   Ely. What was the impediment that broke
      this off?

   Cant. The French ambassador, upon that instant,
Crav'd audience: and the hour, I think, is come,
To give him hearing: Is it four o'clock?

   Ely.   It is.
   Cant. Then go we in, to know his embassy:
Which I could, with a ready guess, declare,
Before the Frenchman speak a word of it.

   Ely. I'll wait upon you; and I long to hear it
                    [*Exeunt.*

SCENE II.—*The same. A Room of State in the
      same.*

Enter KING HENRY, GLOSTER, BEDFORD, EXE-
TER, WARWICK, WESTMORELAND, *and* Attendants.

   K. Hen. Where is my gracious lord of Canter
      bury?
   Exe. Not here in presence.
   K. Hen. Send for him, good uncle.

West. Shall we call in the ambassador, my
    liege?

K. Hen. Not yet, my cousin; we would be re-
    solv'd,
Before we hear him, of some things of weight,
That task our thoughts, concerning us and France

    Enter the ARCHBISHOP OF CANTERBURY, *and*
      BISHOP OF ELY.

    Cant. God, and his angels, guard your sacred
      throne,
And make you long become it!

    K. Hen.   Sure, we thank you.
My learned lord, we pray you to proceed;
And justly and religiously unfold,
Why the law Salique, that they have in France,
Or should, or should not, bar us in our claim.
And God forbid, my dear and faithful lord,
That you should fashion, wrest, or bow your read-
    ing,
Or nicely charge your understanding soul
With opening titles miscreate, whose right
Suits not in native colours with the truth:
For God doth know, how many, now in health,
Shall drop their blood in approbation
Of what your reverence shall incite us to:
Therefore take heed how you impawn our person,
How you awake the sleeping sword of war;
We charge you in the name of God, take heed:
For never two such kingdoms did contend,
Without much fall of blood; whose guiltless drops
Are every one a woe, a sore complaint,
'Gainst him, whose wrongs give edge unto the
    swords
That make such waste in brief mortality.
Under this conjuration, speak, my lord:
And we will hear, note, and believe in heart,
That what you speak is in your conscience wash'd
As pure as sin with baptism.

    Cant. Then hear me, gracious sovereign,—and
      you peers,
That owe your lives, your faith, and services,
To this imperial throne;—There is no bar
To make against your highness' claim to France,
But this, which they produce from Pharamond,—
In terram Salicam mulieres ne succedant,
"No woman shall succeed in Salique land:"
Which Salique land the French unjustly gloze
To be the realm of France, and Pharamond
The founder of this law and female bar.
Yet their own authors faithfully affirm,
That the land Salique lies in Germany,

Between the floods of Sala and of Elbe:
Where Charles the Great, having subdued the
    Saxons,
There left behind and settled certain French;
Who, holding in disdain the German women,
For some dishonest manners of their life,
Establish'd there this law,—to wit, no female
Should be inheritrix in Salique land;
Which Salique, as I said, 'twixt Elbe and Sala,
Is at this day in Germany call'd—Meisen.
Thus doth it well appear, the Salique law
Was not devised for the realm of France:
Nor did the French possess the Salique land
Until four hundred one and twenty years
After defunction of king Pharamond,
Idly suppos'd the founder of this law;
Who died within the year of our redemption
Four hundred twenty-six; and Charles the Great
Subdued the Saxons, and did seat the French
Beyond the river Sala, in the year
Eight hundred five. Besides, their writers say,
King Pepin, which deposed Childerick,
Did, as heir general, being descended
Of Blithild, which was daughter to king Clothair,
Make claim and title to the crown of France.
Hugh Capet also,—that usurp'd the crown
Of Charles the duke of Lorain, sole heir male
Of the true line and stock of Charles the Great,—
To fine his title with some show of truth,
(Though, in pure truth, it was corrupt and naught,)
Convey'd himself as heir to the lady Lingare,
Daughter to Charlemain, who was the son
To Lewis the emperor, and Lewis the son
Of Charles the Great. Also king Lewis the tenth,
Who was sole heir to the usurper Capet,
Could not keep quiet in his conscience,
Wearing the crown of France, till satisfied
That fair queen Isabel, his grandmother,
Was lineal of the lady Ermengare,
Daughter to Charles the foresaid duke of Lorain:
By the which marriage, the line of Charles the Great
Was re-united to the crown of France.
So that, as clear as is the summer's sun,
King Pepin's title, and Hugh Capet's claim,
King Lewis his satisfaction, all appear
To hold in right and title of the female;
So do the kings of France unto this day;
Howbeit they would hold up this Salique law,
To bar your highness claiming from the female;
And rather choose to hide them in a net,
Than amply to imbare their crooked titles
Usurp'd from you and your progenitors.

K. Hen. May I, with right and conscience, make
this claim?

Cant. The sin upon my head, dread sovereign;
For in the book of Numbers is it writ,—
When the son dies, let the inheritance
Descend unto the daughter. Gracious lord,
Stand for your own: unwind your bloody flag;
Look back unto your mighty ancestors:
Go, my dread lord, to your great grandsire's tomb,
From whom you claim; invoke his warlike spirit,
And your great uncle's, Edward the Black Prince,
Who on the French ground play'd a tragedy,
Making defeat on the full power of France;
Whiles his most mighty father on a hill
Stood smiling, to behold his lion's whelp
Forage in blood of French nobility.
O noble English, that could entertain
With half their forces the full pride of France;
And let another half stand laughing by,
All out of work, and cold for action!

Ely. Awake remembrance of these valiant dead,
And with your puissant arm renew their feats:
You are their heir, you sit upon their throne;
The blood and courage, that renowned them,
Runs in your veins; and my thrice-puissant liege
Is in the very May-morn of his youth,
Ripe for exploits and mighty enterprizes.

Exe. Your brother kings and monarchs of the earth
Do all expect that you should rouse yourself,
As did the former lions of your blood.

West. They know, your grace hath cause, and means, and might;
So hath your highness; never king of England
Had nobles richer, and more loyal subjects,
Whose hearts have left their bodies here in England,
And lie pavilion'd in the fields of France.

Cant. O, let their bodies follow, my dear liege,
With blood, and sword, and fire, to win your right:
In aid whereof, we of the spirituralty
Will raise your highness such a mighty sum,
As never did the clergy at one time
Bring in to any of your ancestors.

K. Hen. We must not only arm to invade the French,
But lay down our proportions to defend
Against the Scot, who will make road upon us
With all advantages.

Cant. They of those marches, gracious sovereign,
Shall be a wall sufficient to defend
Our inland from the pilfering borderers.

K. Hen. We do not mean the coursing snatchers only,
But fear the main intendment of the Scot,
Who hath been still a giddy neighbour to us;
For you shall read, that my great grandfather
Never went with his forces into France,
But that the Scot on his unfurnish'd kingdom
Came pouring, like the tide into a breach,
With ample and brim fulness of his force;
Galling the gleaned land with hot essays;
Girding with grievous siege, castles and towns;
That England, being empty of defence,
Hath shook, and trembled at the ill neighbourhood.

Cant. She hath been then more fear'd than harm'd, my liege:
For hear her but exampled by herself,—
When all her chivalry hath been in France,
And she a mourning widow of her nobles,
She hath herself not only well defended,
But taken, and impounded as a stray,
The king of Scots; whom she did send to France
To fill king Edward's fame with prisoner kings;
And make your chronicle as rich with praise,
As is the ooze and bottom of the sea
With sunken wreck and sumless treasuries.

West. But there's a saying, very old and true,—
"If that you will France win,
Then with Scotland first begin:"
For once the eagle England being in prey,
To her unguarded nest the weasel Scot
Comes sneaking, and so sucks her princely eggs,
Playing the mouse, in absence of the cat,
To spoil and havoc more than she can eat.

Exe. It follows then, the cat must stay at home:
Yet that is but a curs'd necessity;
Since we have locks to safeguard necessaries,
And pretty traps to catch the petty thieves,
While that the armed hand doth fight abroad,
The advised head defends itself at home:
For government, though high, and low, and lower,
Put into parts, doth keep in one consent,
Congruing in a full and natural close,
Like music.

Cant. True: therefore doth heaven divide
The state of man in divers functions,
Setting endeavour in continual motion;
To which is fixed, as an aim or butt,
Obedience: for so work the honey bees;
Creatures, that, by a rule in nature, teach
The act of order to a peopled kingdom.

822

They have a king, and officers of sorts:
Where some, like magistrates, correct at home;
Others, like merchants, venture trade abroad;
Others, like soldiers, armed in their stings,
Make boot upon the summer's velvet buds;
Which pillage they with merry march bring home
To the tent-royal of their emperor:
Who, busied in his majesty, surveys
The singing masons building roofs of gold;
The civil citizens kneading up the honey;
The poor mechanic porters crowding in
Their heavy burdens at his narrow gate;
The sad-ey'd justice, with his surly hum,
Delivering o'er to executors pale
The lazy yawning drone. 'I this infer,—
That many things, having full reference
To one concent, may work contrariously;
As many arrows, loosed several ways,
Fly to one mark;
As many several ways meet in one town;
As many fresh streams run in one self sea;
As many lines close in the dial's centre;
So may a thousand actions, once afoot,
End in one purpose, and be all well borne
Without defeat. Therefore to France, my liege.
Divide your happy England into four;
Whereof take you one quarter into France,
And you withal shall make all Gallia shake.
If we, with thrice that power left us at home,
Cannot defend our own door from the dog,
Let us be worried; and our nation lose
The name of hardiness, and policy.

    K. Hen. Call in the messengers sent from the
Dauphin.

[*Exit an* Attend. *The* KING *ascends his Throne.*
Now are we well resolv'd: and, by God's help;
And yours, the noble sinews of our power,—
France being ours, we 'll bend it to our awe,
Or break it all to pieces: Or there we 'll sit,
Ruling, in large and ample empery,
O'er France, and all her almost kingly dukedoms;
Or lay these bones in an unworthy urn,
Tombless, with no remembrance over them:
Either our history shall, with full mouth,
Speak freely of our acts; or else our grave,
Like Turkish mute, shall have a tongueless mouth,
Not worshipp'd with a waxen epitaph.

Enter Ambassadors *of France.*

    Now are we well prepared to know the pleasure
Of our fair cousin Dauphin; for, we hear,
Your greeting is from him, not from the king.

    Amb. May it please your majesty, to give us
leave
Freely to render what we have in charge;
Or shall we sparingly show you far off
The Dauphin's meaning, and our embassy?

    K. Hen. We are no tyrant, but a Christian king
Unto whose grace our passion is as subject,
As are our wretches fetter'd in our prisons:
Therefore, with frank and with uncurbed plain
ness,
Tell us the Dauphin's mind.

    Amb.   Thus then, in few.
Your highness, lately sending into France,
Did claim some certain dukedoms, in the right
Of your great predecessor, king Edward the Third.
In answer of which claim, the prince our master
Says,—that you savour too much of your youth;
And bids you be advis'd, there 's nought in France,
That can be with a nimble galliard won;
You cannot revel into dukedoms there:
He therefore sends you, meeter for your spirit,
This tun of treasure; and, in lieu of this,
Desires you, let the dukedoms, that you claim,
Hear no more of you. This the Dauphin speaks.

    K. Hen. What treasure, uncle!

    Exe.   Tennis-balls, my liege.

    K. Hen. We are glad, the Dauphin is so pleasant
with us;
His present, and your pains, we thank you for:
When we have match'd our rackets to these balls,
We will, in France, by God's grace, play a set,
Shall strike his father's crown into the hazard:
Tell him, he hath made a match with such a
wrangler,
That all the courts of France will be disturb'd
With chaces.' And we understand him well,
How he comes o'er us with our wilder days,
Not measuring what use we made of them.
We never valu'd this poor seat of England;
And therefore, living hence, did give ourself
To barbarous licence: As 't is ever common,
That men are merriest when they are from home:
But tell the Dauphin,—I will keep my state;
Be like a king, and show my soul of greatness,
When I do rouse me in my throne of France:
For that I have laid by my majesty,
And plodded like a man for working-days;
But I will rise there with so full a glory,
That I will dazzle all the eyes of France,
Yea, strike the Dauphin blind to look on us.
And tell the pleasant prince,—this mock of his
Hath turn'd his balls to gun-stones;' and his soul,

Shall stand sore charged for the wasteful vengeance
That shall fly with them: for many a thousand
    widows
Shall this his mock mock out of their dear hus-
    bands;
Mock mothers from their sons, mock castles down;
And some are yet ungotten, and unborn,
That shall have cause to curse the Dauphin's scorn.
But this lies all within the will of God,
To whom I do appeal: And in whose name,
Tell you the Dauphin, I am coming on,
To venge me as I may, and to put forth
My rightful hand in a well-hallow'd cause.
So, get you hence in peace; and tell the Dauphin,
His jest will savour but of shallow wit,
When thousands weep, more than did laugh at
    it.—

Convey them with safe conduct.—Fare you well.
                                [Exeunt Amb
Exe. This was a merry message.
K. Hen. We hope to make the sender blush at it.
                            [Descends from his Throne.
Therefore, my lords, omit no happy hour,
That may give furtherance to our expedition
For we have now no thought in us but France;
Save those to God, that run before our business.
Therefore, let our proportions for these wars
Be soon collected; and all things thought upon,
That may, with reasonable swiftness, add
More feathers to our wings; for, God before,
We'll chide this Dauphin at his father's door.
Therefore, let every man now task his thought,
That this fair action may on foot be brought.
                                        [Exeunt.

ACT II.

Enter CHORUS.

Chor. Now all the youth of England are on fire,
And silken dalliance in the wardrobe lies;
Now thrive the armourers, and honour's thought
Reigns solely in the breast of every man:
They sell the pasture now, to buy the horse;
Following the mirror of all Christian kings,
With winged heels, as English Mercuries.
For now sits expectation in the air;
And hides a sword, from hilts unto the point,
With crowns imperial, crowns, and coronets,
Promis'd to Harry, and his followers.
The French, advis'd by good intelligence
Of this most dreadful preparation,
Shake in their fear; and with pale policy
Seek to divert the English purposes.
O England!—model to thy inward greatness,
Like little body with a mighty heart,—
What might'st thou do, that honour would thee do,
Were all thy children kind and natural!
But see thy fault! France hath in thee found out
A nest of hollow bosoms, which he fills
With treacherous crowns: and three corrupted
    men,—
One, Richard earl of Cambridge; and the second,
Henry lord Scroop of Masham; and the third,

Sir Thomas Grey, knight of Northumberland,—
Have, for the gilt of France, (O guilt, indeed!)
Confirm'd conspiracy with fearful France;
And by their hands this grace of kings must die
(If hell and treason hold their promises,)
Ere he take ship for France, and in Southampton.
Linger your patience on; and well digest
The abuse of distance, while we force a play.
The sum is paid; the traitors are agreed;
The king is set from London; and the scene
Is now transported, gentles, to Southampton:
There is the playhouse now, there must you sit
And thence to France shall we convey you safe
And bring you back, charming the narrow seas
To give you gentle pass; for, if we may,
We'll not offend one stomach with our play
But, till the king come forth, and not till then,
Unto Southampton do we shift our scene. [Exit

SCENE I.—*The Same.* Eastcheap.

Enter NYM *and* BARDOLPH.

Bard. Well met, corporal Nym.
Nym. Good morrow, lieutenant Bardolph.
Bard. What, are ancient Pistol and you friends
yet?
Nym. For my part, I care not: I say little; but

when time shall serve, there shall be smiles;—
but that shall be as it may. I dare not fight;
but I will wink, and hold out mine iron: It is a
simple one; but what though? it will toast cheese,
and it will endure cold as another man's sword
will: and there's the humour of it.

Bard. I will bestow a breakfast, to make you
friends; and we'll be all three sworn brothers to
France;" let it be so, good corporal Nym.

Nym. 'Faith, I will live so long as I may, that's
tho certain of it; and when I cannot live any
longer, I will do as I may; that is my rest, that
is the rendezvous of it.

Bard. It is certain, corporal, that he is married
to Nell Quickly: and, certainly, she did you wrong;
for you were troth-plight to her.

Nym. I cannot tell; things must be as they
may: men may sleep, and they may have their
throats about them at that time; and, some say,
knives have edges. It must be as it may; though
patience be a tired mare, yet she will plod. There
must be conclusions. Well, I cannot tell.

Enter PISTOL and MRS. QUICKLY.

Bard. Here comes ancient Pistol, and his wife:
—good corporal, be patient here.—How now,
mine host Pistol?

Pist. Base tike, call'st thou me—host?
Now, by this hand I swear, I scorn the term;
Nor shall my Nell keep lodgers.

Quick. No, by my troth, not long: for we cannot lodge and board a dozen or fourteen gentlewomen, that live honestly by the prick of their
needles, but it will be thought we keep a bawdy-
house straight. [NYM *draws his sword.*] O well-a-
day, Lady, if he be not drawn now! O Lord!
here's corporal Nym's—now shall we have wilful adultery and murder committed. Good lieutenant Bardolph—good corporal, offer nothing
here.

Nym. Pish!

Pist. Pish for thee, Iceland dog! thou prick-
eared cur of Iceland!

Quick. Good corporal Nym, show the valour
of a man, and put up thy sword.

Nym. Will you shog off?" I would have you
solus. [*Sheathing his sword.*]

Pist. Solus, egregious dog! O viper vile!
The *solus* in thy most marvellous face;
The *solus* in thy teeth, and in thy throat,
And in thy hateful lungs, yea, in thy maw, perdy;
And, which is worse, within thy nasty mouth!

I do retort the *solus* in thy bowels:
For I can take, and Pistol's cock is up,
And flashing fire will follow.

Nym. I am not Barbason; you cannot conjure
me." I have an humour to knock you indif
ferently well: If you grow foul with me, Pistol, I
will scour you with my rapier, as I may, in fair
terms: if you would walk off, I would prick your
guts a little, in good terms, as I may; and that's
the humour of it.

Pist. O braggard vile, and damned furious
wight!
The grave doth gape, and doting death is near;
Therefore exhale. [PIST. *and* NYM. *draw.*

Bard. Hear me, hear me what I say:—he that
strikes the first stroke, I'll run him up to the
hilts, as I am a soldier. [*Draws.*

Pist. An oath of mickle might; and fury shall
abate.
Give me thy fist, thy fore-foot to me give;
Thy spirits are most tall.

Nym. I will cut thy throat, one time or other,
in fair terms; that is the humour of it.

Pist. Coupe le gorge, that's the word?—I thee
defy again
O hound of Crete, think'st thou my spouse to get?
No; to the spital go,
And from the powdering tub of infamy
Fetch forth the lazar kite of Cressid's kind,
Doll Tear-sheet she by name, and her espouse;
I have, and I will hold, the *quondam* Quickly
For the only she; and—*Pauca*, there's enough.

Enter the Boy.

Boy. Mine host Pistol, you must come to my
master.—and you, hostess;—he is very sick, and
would to bed.—Good Bardolph, put thy nose between his sheets, and do the office of a warming-
pan: 'faith, he's very ill.

Bard. Away, you rogue.

Quick. By my troth, he'll yield the crow a
pudding one of these days: the king has killed
his heart.—Good husband, come home presently.
[*Exeunt* MRS. QUICKLY *and* Boy

Bard. Come, shall I make you two friends?
We must to France together: Why, the devil,
should we keep knives to cut one another's throats?

Pist. Let floods o'erswell, and fiends for food
howl on!

Nym. You'll pay me the eight shillings I won
of you at betting!

Pist. Base is the slave that pays.

Nym. That now I will have; that's the humour of it.

Pist. As manhood shall compound: Push home.

Bard. By this sword, he that makes the first thrust, I 'll kill him; by this sword, I will.

Pist. Sword is an oath, and oaths must have their course.

Bard. Corporal Nym, an thou wilt be friends, be friends: an thou wilt not, why then be enemies with me too. Pr'ythee, put up.

Nym. I shall have my eight shillings, I won of you at betting?

Pist. A noble shalt thou have, and present pay; And liquor likewise will I give to thee, And friendship shall combine, and brotherhood: I 'll live by Nym, and Nym shall live by me;— Is not this just?—for I shall sutler be Unto the camp, and profits will accrue. Give me thy hand.

Nym. I shall have my noble?

Pist. In cash most justly paid.

Nym. Well then, that 's the humour of it.

Re-enter MRS. QUICKLY.

Quick. As ever you came of women, come in quickly to sir John: Ah, poor heart! he is so shaked of a burning quotidian tertian, that it is most lamentable to behold. Sweet men, come to him.

Nym. The king hath run bad humours on the knight, that 's the even of it.

Pist. Nym, thou hast spoke the right; His heart is fracted, and corroborate.

Nym. The king is a good king: but it must be as it may; he passes some humours, and careers.

Pist. Let us condole the knight; for, lambkins, we will live.   [*Exeunt.*

SCENE II.—Southampton. *A Council-Chamber.*

Enter EXETER, BEDFORD, *and* WESTMORELAND.

Bed. 'Fore God, his grace is bold, to trust these traitors.

Exe. They shall be apprehended by and by.

West. How smooth and even they do bear themselves! As if allegiance in their bosom sat, Crowned with faith, and constant loyalty.

Bed. The king hath note of all that they intend, By interception which they dream not of.

Exe. Nay, but the man that was his bedfellow,

Whom he hath cloy'd and grac'd with princely favours,— That he should, for a foreign purse, so sell His sovereign's life to death and treachery!

Trumpet sounds. Enter KING HENRY, SCROOP, CAMBRIDGE, GREY, Lords, *and* Attendants.

K. Hen. Now sits the wind fair, and we will aboard. My lord of Cambridge,—and my kind lord of Masham,— And you, my gentle knight,——give me your thoughts: Think you not, that the powers we bear with us Will cut their passage through the force of France, Doing the execution, and the act, For which we have in head assembled them?

Scroop. No doubt, my liege, if each man do his best.

K. Hen. I doubt not that: since we are well persuaded, We carry not a heart with us from hence, That grows not in a fair consent with ours; Nor leave not one behind, that doth not wish Success and conquest to attend on us.

Cam. Never was monarch better fear'd and lov'd, Than is your majesty: there 's not, I think, a subject, That sits in heart-grief and uneasiness Under the sweet shade of your government.

Grey. Even those, that were your father's enemies, Have steep'd their galls in honey; and do serve you With hearts create of duty and of zeal.

K. Hen. We therefore have great cause of thankfulness; And shall forget the office of our hand, Sooner than quittance of desert and merit, According to the weight and worthiness.

Scroop. So service shall with steeled sinews toil, And labour shall refresh itself with hope, To do your grace incessant services.

K. Hen. We judge no less.—Uncle of Exeter, Enlarge the man committed yesterday, That rail'd against our person: we consider, It was excess of wine that set him on; And, on his more advice, we pardon him.

Scroop. That 's mercy, but too much security: Let him be punish'd, sovereign; lest example Breed, by his sufferance, more of such a kind.

K. Hen. O, let us yet be merciful.

Cam. So may your highness, and yet punish too.

Grey. Sir, you show great mercy, if you give
him life,
After the taste of much correction.

K. Hen. Alas, your too much love and care
of me
Are heavy orisons 'gainst this poor wretch.
If little faults, proceeding on distemper,
Shall not be wink'd at, how shall we stretch our
eye,
When capital crimes, chew'd, swallow'd, and di-
gested,
Appear before us?—We 'll yet enlarge that man,
Though Cambridge, Scroop, and Grey,—in their
dear care,
And tender preservation of our person.—
Would have him punish'd. And now to our
French causes;
Who are the late commissioners?

Cam. I one, my lord;
Your highness bade me ask for it to-day.

Scroop. So did you me, my liege.

Grey. And me, my royal sovereign.

K. Hen. Then, Richard, earl of Cambridge, there
is yours;—
There yours, lord Scroop of Masham;—and, sir
knight,
Grey of Northumberland, this same is yours:—
Read them; and know, I know your worthiness.—
My lord of Westmorland,—and uncle Exeter,—
We will aboard to-night.—Why, how now, gentle-
men?
What see you in those papers, that you lose
So much complexion?—look ye, how they change!
Their cheeks are paper.—Why, what read you
there,
That hath so cowarded and chas'd your blood
Out of appearance?

Cam.   I do confess my fault;
And do submit me to your highness' mercy.

Grey. Scroop. To which we all appeal.

K. Hen. The mercy, that was quick in us but
late,
By your own counsel is suppress'd and kill'd;
You must not dare, for shame, to talk of mercy;
For your own reasons turn into your bosoms,
As dogs upon their masters, worrying them.—
See you, my princes, and my noble peers,
These English monsters! My lord of Cambridge
here,—
You know, how apt our love was, to accord

To furnish him with all appertinents
Belonging to his honour; and this man
Hath, for a few light crowns, lightly conspir'd,
And sworn unto the practices of France,
To kill us here in Hampton: to the which,
This knight, no less for bounty bound to us
Than Cambridge is,—hath likewise sworn.—
But O!
What shall I say to thee, lord Scroop: thou cruel
Ingrateful, savage, and inhuman creature!
Thou, that didst bear the key of all my counsels,
That knew'st the very bottom of my soul,
That almost might'st have coin'd me into gold,
Would'st thou have practis'd on me for thy use!
May it be possible, that foreign hire
Could out of thee extract one spark of evil,
That might annoy my finger? 't is so strange,
That, though the truth of it stands off as gross
As black from white, my eye will scarcely see it.
Treason, and murder, ever kept together,
As two yoke-devils sworn to either's purpose,
Working so grossly in a natural cause,
That admiration did not whoop at them;
But thou, 'gainst all proportion, didst bring in
Wonder, to wait on treason, and on murder:
And whatsoever cunning fiend it was,
That wrought upon thee so preposterously,
H'ath got the voice in hell for excellence:
And other devils, that suggest by treasons,
Do botch and bungle up damnation
With patches, colours, and with forms being fetch'd
From glistering semblances of piety;
But he, that temper'd thee, bade thee stand up,
Gave thee no instance why thou should'st do
treason,
Unless to dub thee with the name of traitor.
If that same dæmon, that hath gull'd thee thus,
Should with his lion gait walk the whole world,
He might return to vasty Tartar back,
And tell the legions—I can never win
A soul so easy as that Englishman's.
O, how hast thou with jealousy infected
The sweetness of affiance! Show men dutiful?
Why, so didst thou: Seem they grave and learned?
Why, so didst thou: Come they of noble family?
Why, so didst thou: Seem they religious?
Why, so didst thou: Or are they spare in diet;
Free from gross passion, or of mirth, or anger;
Constant in spirit, not swerving with the blood;
Garnish'd and deck'd in modest complement;
Not working with the eye, without the ear,
And, but in purged judgment, trusting neither?

827

Such, and so finely bolted, didst thou seem:
And thus thy fall hath left a kind of blot,
To mark the full-fraught man, and best endued,
With some suspicion. I will weep for thee;
For this revolt of thine, methinks, is like
Another fall of man.—Their faults are open,
Arrest them to the answer of the law;—
And God acquit them of their practices!

Exe. I arrest thee of high treason, by the name
of Richard earl of Cambridge.

I arrest thee of high treason, by the name of
Henry lord Scroop of Masham.

I arrest thee of high treason, by the name of
Thomas Grey, knight of Northumberland.

Scroop. Our purposes God justly hath discover'd;
And I repent my fault, more than my death;
Which I beseech your highness to forgive,
Although my body pay the price of it.

Cam. For me,—the gold of France did not seduce;

Although I did admit it as a motive,
The sooner to effect what I intended;
But God be thanked for prevention;
Which I in sufferance heartily will rejoice,
Beseeching God, and you, to pardon me.

Grey. Never did faithful subject more rejoice
At the discovery of most dangerous treason,
Than I do at this hour joy o'er myself,
Prevented from a damned enterprise:
My fault, but not my body, pardon, sovereign.

K. Hen. God quit you in his mercy! Hear
your sentence.

You have conspir'd against our royal person,
Join'd with an enemy proclaim'd, and from his
coffers

Receiv'd the golden earnest of our death;
Wherein you would have sold your king to
slaughter,

His princes and his peers to servitude,
His subjects to oppression and contempt,
And his whole kingdom unto desolation.
Touching our person, seek we no revenge;
But we our kingdom's safety must so tender,
Whose ruin you three sought, that to her laws
We do deliver you. Get you therefore hence,
Poor miserable wretches, to your death:
The taste whereof, God, of his mercy, give you
Patience to endure, and true repentance
Of all your dear offences!—Bear them hence.

[*Exeunt Conspirators, guarded.*

Now, lords, for France; the enterprise whereof
Shall be to you, as us, like glorious.

828

We doubt not of a fair and lucky war;
Since God so graciously hath brought to light
This dangerous treason, lurking in our way,
To hinder our beginnings, we doubt not now,
But every rub is smoothed on our way.
Then, forth, dear countrymen; let us deliver
Our puissance into the hand of God,
Putting it straight in expedition.
Cheerly to sea; the signs of war advance:
No king of England, if not king of France. [*Exeunt*

SCENE III.—London. Mrs. Quickly's *House in*
Eastcheap.

Enter PISTOL, MRS. QUICKLY, NYM, BARDOLPH,
and BOY.

Quick. Pr'ythee, honey-sweet husband, let me
bring thee to Staines.

Pist. No; for my manly heart doth yearn.—
Bardolph, be blithe;—Nym, rouse thy vaunting
veins;

Boy, bristle thy courage up; for Falstaff he is dead
And we must yearn therefore.

Bard. 'Would, I were with him, wheresome'er
he is, either in heaven, or in hell!

Quick. Nay, sure, he's not in hell; he is in
Arthur's bosom, if ever man went to Arthur's
bosom. 'A made a finer end, and went away,
an it had been any christom child; 'a parted even
just between twelve and one, e'en at turning o'
the tide; for after I saw him fumble with the
sheets, and play with flowers, and smile upon his
fingers' ends, I knew there was but one way; for
his nose was as sharp as a pen, and 'a babbled
of green fields. How now, sir John? quoth I:
what, man! be of good cheer. So 'a cried out—
God, God, God! three or four times: now I, to
comfort him, bid him, 'a should not think of God;
I hoped, there was no need to trouble himself
with any such thoughts yet: So, 'a bade me lay
more clothes on his feet: I put my hand into the
bed, and felt them, and they were as cold as any
stone; then I felt to his knees, and so upward,
and upward, and all was as cold as any stone.

Nym. They say, he cried out of sack.

Quick. Ay, that 'a did.

Bard. And of women.

Quick. Nay, that 'a did not.

Boy. Yes, that 'a did; and said, they were
devils incarnate.

Quick. 'A could never abide carnation; 'twas
a colour he never liked.

Boy. 'A said once, the devil would have him about women.

Quick. A did in some sort, indeed, handle women: but then he was rheumatic;" and talked of the whore of Babylon.

Boy. Do you not remember, 'a saw a flea stick upon Bardolph's nose; and 'a said, it was a black soul burning in hell-fire!

Bard. Well, the fuel is gone, that maintained that fire: that 's all the riches I got in his service.

Nym. Shall we shog off? the king will be gone from Southampton.

Pist. Come, let 's away.—My love, give me thy lips.
Look to my chattels, and my moveables:
Let senses rule; the word is, " Pitch and pay;"
Trust none;
For oaths are straws, men's faiths are wafer-cakes,
And hold-fast is the only dog, my duck;
Therefore, *caveto* be thy counsellor.
Go, clear thy crystals.—Yoke-fellows in arms,
Let us to France! like horse-leeches, my boys;
To suck, to suck, the very blood to suck!

Boy. And that is but unwholesome food, they say.

Pist. Touch her soft mouth, and march.

Bard. Farewell, hostess. [*Kissing her.*

Nym. I cannot kiss, that is the humour of it; but adieu.

Pist. Let housewifery appear; keep close, I thee command.

Quick. Farewell; adieu. [*Exeunt.*

SCENE IV.—France. *A Room in the* French King's *Palace.*

Enter the FRENCH KING *attended; the* DAUPHIN, *the* DUKE OF BURGUNDY, *the* CONSTABLE, *and Others.*

Fr. King. Thus come the English with full power upon us;
And more than carefully it us concerns,
To answer royally in our defences.
Therefore the dukes of Berry, and of Bretagne,
Of Brabant, and of Orleans, shall make forth,—
And you, prince Dauphin,—with all swift despatch,
To line, and new repair, our towns of war,
With men of courage, and with means defendant:
For England his approaches makes as fierce,
As waters to the sucking of a gulph.
It fits us then, to be as provident
As fear may teach us, out of late examples
Left by the fatal and neglected English
Upon our fields.

Dau. My most redoubted father,
It is most meet we arm us 'gainst the foe:
For peace itself should not so dull a kingdom,
(Though war, nor no known quarrel, were it question,)
But that defences, musters, preparations,
Should be maintain'd, assembled, and collected,
As were a war in expectation.
Therefore, I say, 't is meet we all go forth,
To view the sick and feeble parts of France:
And let us do it with no show of fear;
No, with no more, than if we heard that England
Were busied with a Whitsun morris-dance:
For, my good liege, she is so idly king'd,
Her sceptre so fantastically borne
By a vain, giddy, shallow, humorous youth,
That fear attends her not.

Con. O peace, prince Dauphin!
You are too much mistaken in this king:
Question your grace the late ambassadors,—
With what great state he heard their embassy,
How well supplied with noble counsellors,
How modest in exception, and, withal,
How terrible in constant resolution,—
And you shall find, his vanities fore-spent
Were but the outside of the Roman Brutus,
Covering discretion with a coat of folly;
As gardeners do with ordure hide those roots
That shall first spring, and be most delicate.

Dau. Well, 't is not so, my lord high constable,
But though we think it so, it is no matter:
In cases of defence, 't is best to weigh
The enemy more mighty than he seems,
So the proportions of defence are fill'd;
Which, of a weak and niggardly projection,"
Doth, like a miser, spoil his coat, with scanting
A little cloth.

Fr. King. Think we king Harry strong;
And, princes, look, you strongly arm to meet him.
The kindred of him hath been flesh'd upon us:
And he is bred out of that bloody strain,
That haunted us in our familiar paths:
Witness our too much memorable shame,
When Cressy battle fatally was struck,
And all our princes captiv'd, by the hand
Of that black name, Edward Black Prince of Wales;
Whiles that his mountain sire,—on mountain standing,
Up in the air, crown'd with the golden sun,—

Saw his heroical seed, and smil'd to see him
Mangle the work of nature, and deface
The patterns that by God and by French fathers
Had twenty years been made.   This is a stem
Of that victorious stock; and let us fear
The native mightiness and fate of him.

Enter a Messenger.

Mess. Ambassadors from Henry King of England
Do crave admittance to your majesty.

Fr. King. We'll give them present audience.
Go, and bring them.

    [*Exeunt Mess. and certain Lords.*
You see, this chase is hotly follow'd, friends.

Dau. Turn head, and stop pursuit: for coward
   dogs
Most spend their mouths, when what they seem
   to threaten,
Runs far before them.   Good my sovereign,
Take up the English short; and let them know
Of what a monarchy you are the head:
Self-love, my liege, is not so vile a sin
As self-neglecting.

Re-enter Lords *with* Exeter *and Train.*

Fr. King.   From our brother England?

Exe. From him; and thus he greets your ma-
   jesty.
He wills you, in the name of God Almighty,
That you divest yourself, and lay apart
The borrow'd glories, that, by gift of heaven,
By law of nature, and of nations, 'long
To him, and to his heirs; namely, the crown,
And all wide-stretched honours that pertain,
By custom and the ordinance of times,
Unto the crown of France.   That you may know,
'T is no sinister, nor no awkward claim,
Pick'd from the worm-holes of long-vanish'd days,
Nor from the dust of old oblivion rak'd,
He sends you this most memorable line.
    [*Gives a paper.*
In every branch truly demonstrative:
Willing you, overlook this pedigree:
And, when you find him evenly deriv'd
From his most fam'd of famous ancestors,
Edward the Third, he bids you then resign
Your crown and kingdom, indirectly held
From him the native and true challenger.

Fr. King. Or else what follows?

Exe. Bloody constraint; for if you hide the crown
Even in your hearts, there will he rake for it:
And therefore in fierce tempest is he coming,

In thunder, and in earthquake, like a Jove;
(That, if requiring fail, he will compel;)
And bids you, in the bowels of the Lord,
Deliver up the crown; and to take mercy
On the poor souls, for whom this hungry war
Opens his vasty jaws: and on your head
Turns he the widows' tears, the orphans' cries,
The dead men's blood, the pining maidens' groans
For husbands, fathers, and betrothed lovers,
That shall be swallow'd in this controversy.
This is his claim, his threat'ning, and my message
Unless the Dauphin be in presence here,
To whom expressly I bring greeting too.

Fr. King. For us, we will consider of this fur-
    ther:
To-morrow shall you bear our full intent
Back to our brother England.

Dau.   For the Dauphin,
I stand here for him: What to him from England?

Exe. Scorn, and defiance; slight regard, contempt,
And any thing that may not misbecome
The mighty sender, doth he prize you at.
Thus says my king: and, if your father's highness
Do not, in grant of all demands at large,
Sweeten the bitter mock you sent his majesty,
He'll call you to so hot an answer for it,
That caves and womby vaultages of France
Shall chide your trespass, and return your mock
In second accent of his ordinance.

Dau. Say, if my father render fair reply,
It is against my will: for I desire
Nothing but odds with England; to that end,
As matching to his youth and vanity,
I did present him with those Paris balls.

Exe. He'll make your Paris Louvre shake for it,
Were it the mistress court of mighty Europe:
And, be assur'd, you'll find a difference,
(As we, his subjects, have in wonder found,)
Between the promise of his greener days,
And these he masters now; now he weighs time,
Even to the utmost grain; which you shall read
In your own losses, if he stay in France.

Fr. King. To-morrow shall you know our mind
    at full.

Exe. Despatch us with all speed, lest that our
    king
Come here himself to question our delay;
For he is footed in this land already.

Fr. King. You shall be soon despatch'd with fair
    conditions:
A night is but small breath, and little pause,
To answer matters of this consequence.   [*Exeunt.*

ACT III.

Enter CHORUS.

Chor. Thus with imagin'd wing our swift scene
    flies,
In motion of no less celerity
Than that of thought. Suppose, that you have seen
The well-appointed king at Hampton pier
Embark his royalty; and his brave fleet
With silken streamers the young Phœbus fanning.
Play with your fancies; and in them behold,
Upon the hempen tackle, ship-boys climbing:
Hear the shrill whistle, which doth order give
To sounds confus'd: behold the threaden sails,
Borne with the invisible and creeping wind,
Draw the huge bottoms through the furrow'd sea,
Breasting the lofty surge: O, do but think,
You stand upon the rivage, and behold
A city on the inconstant billows dancing;
For so appears this fleet majestical,
Holding due course to Harfleur. Follow, follow!
Grapple your minds to sternage of this navy;
And leave your England, as dead midnight, still,
Guarded with grandsires, babies, and old women,
Either past, or not arriv'd to, pith and puissance:
For who is he, whose chin is but enrich'd
With one appearing hair, that will not follow
These cull'd and choice-drawn cavaliers to France?
Work, work your thoughts, and therein see a siege;
Behold the ordnance on their carriages,
With fatal mouths gaping on girded Harfleur.
Suppose, the ambassador from the French comes
    back;
Tells Harry—that the king doth offer him
Katharine his daughter; and with her, to dowry,
Some petty and unprofitable dukedoms.
The offer likes not: and the nimble gunner
With linstock now the devilish cannon touches,
    [*Alarum; and Chambers go off.*
And down goes all before them. Still be kind,
And eke out our performance with your mind.
    [*Exit.*

SCENE I.—*The Same. Before Harfleur.*

Alarums. Enter KING HENRY, EXETER, BEDFORD,
GLOSTER, *and Soldiers, with Scaling Ladders.*

K. Hen. Once more unto the breach, dear
    friends, once more;

Or close the wall up with our English dead!
In peace, there's nothing so becomes a man,
As modest stillness, and humility:
But when the blast of war blows in our ears,
Then imitate the action of the tiger;
Stiffen the sinews, summon up the blood,
Disguise fair nature with hard-favour'd rage:
Then lend the eye a terrible aspect;
Let it pry through the portage of the head,
Like the brass cannon; let the brow o'erwhelm it,
As fearfully, as doth a galled rock
O'erhang and jutty his confounded base,
Swill'd with the wild and wasteful ocean.
Now set the teeth, and stretch the nostril wide;
Hold hard the breath, and bend up every spirit
To his full height!—On, on, you noblest English!
Whose blood is fet from fathers of war-proof!
Fathers, that, like so many Alexanders,
Have, in these parts, from morn till even fought,
And sheath'd their swords for lack of argument,
Dishonour not your mothers; now attest,
That those, whom you call'd fathers, did beget you!
Be copy now to men of grosser blood,
And teach them how to war!—And you, good
    yeomen,
Whose limbs were made in England, show us here
The mettle of your pasture; let us swear
That you are worth your breeding: which I doubt
    not;
For there is none of you so mean and base,
That hath not noble lustre in your eyes.
I see you stand like greyhounds in the slips,
Straining upon the start. The game's afoot;
Follow your spirit: and, upon this charge,
Cry—God for Harry! England! and Saint George!
    [*Exeunt. Alarum, and Chambers go off.*

SCENE II.—*The Same.*

Forces pass over; then enter NYM, BARDOLPH,
PISTOL, *and* BOY.

Bard. On, on, on, on, on! to the breach, to the
    breach!

Nym. 'Pray thee, corporal, stay; the knocks
are too hot; and, for mine own part, I have not a
case of lives: the humour of it is too hot, that is
the very plain-song of it.

Pist. The plain-song is most just; for humours
          do abound;
   Knocks go and come to all and some;
   God's vassals feel the same.
          And sword and shield,
          In bloody field,
   Doth win immortal fame.

Boy. Would I were in an alehouse in London!
I would give all my fame for a pot of ale and safety.

Pist. And I:
       If wishes would prevail with me,
       My purpose should not fail with me,
       But thither would I hie.

Boy. As duly, but not as truly,
       As bird doth sing on bough.

Enter FLUELLEN.

Flu. God's plood!—Up to the preaches, you
rascals! will you not up to the preaches?
                    [*Driving them forward.*

Pist. Be merciful, great duke, to men of mould!
Abate thy rage, abate thy manly rage!
Abate thy rage, great duke!
Good bawcock, bate thy rage! use lenity, sweet
     chuck!

Nym. These be good humours!—your honour
wins bad humours.
     [*Exeunt* NYM., PIST., *and* BAR., *followed by* FLU.

Boy. As young as I am, I have observed these
three swashers. I am boy to them all three: but
all they three, though they would serve me, could
not be man to me; for, indeed, three such antics
do not amount to a man. For Bardolph,—he is
white-livered, and red-faced; by the means whereof, 'a faces it out, but fights not. For Pistol,—he
hath a killing tongue, and a quiet sword; by the
means whereof 'a breaks words, and keeps whole
weapons. For Nym,—he hath heard, that men
of few words are the best men; and therefore he
scorns to say his prayers, lest 'a should be thought
a coward; but his few bad words are match'd
with as few good deeds; for 'a never broke any
man's head but his own; and that was against a
post, when he was drunk. They will steal any
thing, and call it,—purchase. Bardolph stole a
lute case; bore it twelve leagues, and sold it for
three halfpence. Nym, and Bardolph, are sworn
brothers in filching; and in Calais they stole a
fire-shovel: I knew, by that piece of service, the
men would carry coals. They would have me
as familiar with men's pockets, as their gloves or
their handkerchiefs: which makes much against

my manhood, if I should take from another's
pocket, to put into mine; for it is plain pocketing
up of wrongs. I must leave them, and seek some
better service: their villany goes against my weak
stomach, and therefore I must cast it up.
                              [*Exit Boy.*

Re-enter FLUELLEN, GOWER *following.*

Gow. Captain Fluellen, you must come presently to the mines; the duke of Gloster would speak
with you.

Flu. To the mines! tell you the duke, it is not
so good to come to the mines: For, look you, the
mines is not according to the disciplines of the
war; the concavities of it is not sufficient; for,
look you, th' athversary (you may discuss unto
the duke, look you,) is dight himself four yards
under the countermines: by Cheshu, I think, 'a
will plow up all, if there is not better directions.

Gow. The duke of Gloster, to whom the order
of the siege is given, is altogether directed by an
Irishman; a very valiant gentleman, i' faith.

Flu. It is captain Macmorris, is it not?

Gow. I think, it be.

Flu. By Cheshu, he is an ass, as in the 'orld
I will verify as much in his peard: he has no
more directions in the true disciplines of the wars,
look you, of the Roman disciplines, than is a
puppy-dog.

Enter MACMORRIS and JAMY, at a distance.

Gow. Here 'a comes; and the Scots captain,
captain Jamy, with him.

Flu. Captain Jamy is a marvellous falorous
gentleman, that is certain; and of great expedition, and knowledge, in the ancient wars, upon
my particular knowledge of his directions: by
Cheshu, he will maintain his argument as well as
any military man in the 'orld, in the disciplines
of the pristine wars of the Romans.

Jamy. I say, gud-day, captain Fluellen.

Flu. God-den to your worship, goot captain
Jamy.

Gow. How now, captain Macmorris? have you
quit the mines? have the pioneers given o'er?

Mac. By Crish la, tish ill done; the work ish
give over, the trumpet sound the retreat. By my
hand, I swear, and by my father's soul, the work
ish ill done; it ish give over: I would have blow
ed up the town, so Crish save me, la, in an hour.
O, tish ill done, ish ill done; by my hand, tish
ill done!

Flu. Captain Macmorris, I peseech you now, will you voutsafe me, look you, a few disputations with you, as partly touching or concerning the disciplines of the war, the Roman wars, in the way of argument, look you, and friendly communication; partly, to satisfy my opinion, and partly, for the satisfaction, look you, of my mind, as touching the direction of the military discipline; that is the point.

Jamy. It sall be very gud, gud feith, gud captains bath; and I sall quit you with gud leve, as I may pick occasion; that sall I, marry.

Mac. It is no time to discourse, so Crish save me, the day is hot, and the weather, and the wars, and the king, and the dukes; it is no time to discourse. The town is beseeched, and the trumpet calls us to the breach; and we talk, and, by Crish, do nothing; 't is shame for us all: so God sa' me, 't is shame to stand still; it is shame, by my hand: and there is throats to be cut, and works to be done; and there ish nothing done, so Crish sa' me, la.

Jamy. By the mess, ere theise eyes of mine take themselves to slumber, aile do gude service, or aile ligge i' the grund for it; ay, or go to death; and aile pay it as valorously as I may, that sal I surely do, that is the breff and the long: Mary, I wad full fain heard some question 'tween you 'tway.

Flu. Captain Macmorris, I think, look you, under your correction, there is not many of your nation——

Mac. Of my nation? What ish my nation? What ish my nation? Who talks of my nation ish a villain, and a bastard, and a knave, and a rascal.

Flu. Look you, if you take the matter otherwise than is meant, captain Macmorris, peradventure, I shall think you do not use me with that affability as in discretion you ought to use me, look you; being as goot a man as yourself, both in the disciplines of wars, and in the derivation of my birth, and in other particularities.

Mac. I do not know you so good a man as myself: so Crish save me, I will cut off your head.

Gow. Gentlemen both, you will mistake each other.

Jamy. Au! that 's a foul fault.
              [*A Parley sounded.*

Gow. The town sounds a parley.

Flu. Captain Macmorris, when there is more better opportunity to be required, look you, I will

be so bold as to tell you, I knew the disciplines of war; and there is an end.   [*Exeunt*

SCENE III.—*The same. Before the Gates of Harfleur.*

The Governor and some Citizens on the Walls; the English Forces below. Enter KING HENRY, *and his Train.*

K. Hen. How yet resolves the governor of the town?
This is the latest parle we will admit:
Therefore, to our best mercy give yourselves;
Or, like to men proud of destruction,
Defy us to our worst: for, as I am a soldier,
(A name, that, in my thoughts, becomes me best,)
If I begin the battery once again,
I will not leave the half-achieved Harfleur,
Till in her ashes she lie buried.
The gates of mercy shall be all shut up;
And the flesh'd soldier—rough and hard of heart—
In liberty of bloody hand, shall range
With conscience wide as hell; mowing like grass
Your fresh-fair virgins, and your flowering infants
What is it then to me, if impious war,—
Array'd in flames, like to the prince of fiends,—
Do, with his smirch'd complexion, all fell feats
Enlink'd to waste and desolation?
What is 't to me, when you yourselves are cause
If your pure maidens fall into the hand
Of hot and forcing violation?
What rein can hold licentious wickedness,
When down the hill he holds his fierce career?
We may as bootless spend our vain command
Upon the enraged soldiers in their spoil,
As send precepts to the Leviathan
To come ashore. Therefore, you men of Harfleur,
Take pity of your town, and of your people,
Whiles yet my soldiers are in my command;
Whiles yet the cool and temperate wind of grace
O'erblows the filthy and contagious clouds
Of deadly murder, spoil, and villany.
If not, why, in a moment, look to see
The blind and bloody soldier with foul hand
Defile the locks of your shrill-shrieking daughters:
Your fathers taken by the silver beards,
And their most reverend heads dash'd to the walls;
Your naked infants spitted upon pikes;
Whiles the mad mothers with their howls confus'd
Do break the clouds, as did the wives of Jewry
At Herod's bloody-hunting slaughtermen.

What say you ? will you yield, and this avoid ?
Or, guilty in defence, be thus destroy'd ?

Gov. Our expectation hath this day an end :
The Dauphin, whom of succour we entreated,
Returns us—that his powers are not yet ready
To raise so great a siege. Therefore, dread king,
We yield our town, and lives, to thy soft mercy :
Enter our gates ; dispose of us, and ours ;
For we no longer are defensible.

K. Hen. Open your gates.—Come, uncle Exeter,
Go you and enter Harfleur ; there remain,
And fortify it strongly 'gainst the French :
Use mercy to them all. For us, dear uncle,—
The winter coming on, and sickness growing
Upon our soldiers,—we 'll retire to Calais.
To-night in Harfleur will we be your guest ;
To-morrow for the march are we addrest.

[*Flourish. The* KING, *&c., enter the Town.*

SCENE IV.—*Roüen. A Room in the Palace.*

Enter KATHARINE *and* ALICE.

Kath. Alice, tu as esté en Angleterre, et tu
parles bien le language.

Alice. En peu, madame.

Kath. Je te prie, m'enseignez ; il faut que
j'apprenne à parler. Comment appellez vous la
main, en Anglois ?

Alice. La main ? elle est appellée, de hand.

Kath. De hand. Et les doigts ?

Alice. Les doigts ? may foy, je oublie les doigts;
mais je me souviendray. Les doigts ? je pense,
qu'ils sont appellé de fingres; ouy, de fingres.

Kath. La main, de hand ; les doigts, de fingres.
Je pense, que je suis le bon escolier. J'ay gagné
deux mots d'Anglois vistement. Comment appellez
vous les ongles ?

Alice. Les ongles ? les appellons, de nails.

Kath. De nails. Escoutez ; dites moy, si je
parle bien : de hand, de fingres, de nails.

Alice. C'est bien dit, madame ; il est fort bon
Anglois.

Kath. Dites moy en Anglois le bras.

Alice. De arm, madame.

Kath. Et le coude.

Alice. De elbow.

Kath. De elbow. Je m'en faitz la repetition de
tous les mots, que vous m'avez appris dès à present.

Alice. Il est trop difficile, madame, comme je
pense.

Kath. Excusez moy, Alice ; escoutez : De hand,
de fingre, de nails, de arm, de bilbow.

Alice. De elbow, madame.

Kath. O Seigneur Dieu! je m'en oublie : De
elbow. Comment appellez vous le col ?

Alice. De neck, madame.

Kath. De neck : Et le menton ?

Alice. De chin.

Kath. De sin. Le col, de neck : le menton, de sin.

Alice. Ouy. Sauf vostre honneur ; en verité,
vous prononcez les mots aussi droict que les natifs
d'Angleterre.

Kath. Je ne doute point d'apprendre par la
grace de Dieu ; et en peu de temps.

Alice. N'avez vous pas deja oublié ce que je
vous ay enseigné ?

Kath. Non, je reciteray à vous promptement.
De hand, de fingre, de mails,—

Alice. De nails, madame.

Kath. De nails, de arme, de ilbow.

Alice. Souf vostre honneur, de elbow.

Kath. Ainsi dis je ; de elbow, de neck, et de
sin : Comment appellez vous le pieds et la robe?

Alice. De foot, madame ; et de con.

Kath. De foot, et de con ? O Seigneur Dieu!
ces sont mots de son mauvais, corruptible, grosse, et
impudique, et non pour les dames d'honneur d'user :
Je ne voudrois prononcer ces mots devant les Sei
gneurs de France, pour tout le monde. Il faut de
foot, et de con, neant-moins. Je reciterai une
autre fois ma leçon ensemble : De hand, de fingre,
de nails, de arm, de elbow, de neck, de sin, de foot,
de con.

Alice. Excellent, madame !

Kath. C'est assez pour une fois ; allons vous à
disner.   [*Exeunt.*

SCENE V.—*The Same. Another Room in the
same.*

Enter the FRENCH KING, *the* DAUPHIN, DUKE OF
BOURBON, *the* CONSTABLE OF FRANCE, *and
Others.*

Fr. King. 'T is certain, he hath pass'd the river
Somme.

Con. And if he be not fought withal, my lord,
Let us not live in France ; let us quit all,
And give our vineyards to a barbarous people.

Dau. O Dieu vivant ! shall a few sprays
of us,—
The emptying of our fathers' luxury,
Our scions, put in wild and savage stock,
Spirt up so suddenly into the clouds,
And overlook their grafters ?

Bour. Normans, but bastard Normans, Norman
bastards!
Mort de ma vie! if they march along
Unfought withal, but I will sell my dukedom,
To buy a slobbery and a dirty farm
In that nook-shotten isle of Albion."
  Con. Dieu de battailes! where have they this
mettle?
Is not their climate foggy, raw, and dull?
On whom, as in despite, the sun looks pale,
Killing their fruit with frowns? Can sodden water,
A drench for sur-rein'd jades, their barley broth,
Decoct their cold blood to such valiant heat?
And shall our quick blood, spirited with wine,
Seem frosty? O, for honour of our land,
Let us not hang like roping icicles
Upon our houses' thatch, whiles a more frosty
people
Sweat drops of gallant youth in our rich fields,
Poor—we may call them, in their native lords.
  Dau. By faith and honour,
Our madams mock at us; and plainly say,
Our mettle is bred out; and they will give
Their bodies to the lust of English youth,
To new-store France with bastard warriors.
  Bour. They bid us—to the English dancing-
schools,
And teach lavoltas high, and swift corantos;
Saying, our grace is only in our heels,
And that we are most lofty runaways.
  Fr. King. Where is Montjoy, the herald? speed
him hence;
Let him greet England with our sharp defiance.—
Up, princes; and, with spirit of honour edg'd,
More sharper than your swords, hie to the field:
Charles De-la-bret, high constable of France;
You dukes of Orleans, Bourbon, and of Berry,
Alençon, Brabant, Bar, and Burgundy;
Jaques Chatillion, Rambures, Vaudemont,
Beaumont, Grandpré, Roussi, and Fauconberg,
Foix, Lestrale, Bouciqualt, and Charolois;
High dukes, great princes, barons, lords, and
knights,
For your great seats, now quit you of great shames.
Bar Harry England, that sweeps through our land
With pennons painted in the blood of Harfleur:
Rush on his host, as doth the melted snow
Upon the valleys; whose low vassal seat
The Alps doth spit and void his rheum upon:
Go down upon him,—you have power enough,—
And in a captive chariot, into Rouen
Bring him our prisoner.

  Con.   This becomes the great.
Sorry are I, his numbers are so few,
His soldiers sick, and famish'd in their march;
For, I am sure, when he shall see our army,
He'll drop his heart into the sink of fear,
And .or achievement, offer us his ransom.
  Fr. King. Therefore, lord constable, haste on
Montjoy;
And let him say to England, that we send
To know what willing ransom he will give.——
Prince Dauphin, you shall stay with us in Rouen.
  Dau. Not so, I do beseech your majesty.
  Fr. King. Be patient, for you shall remain
with us.—
Now, forth, lord constable, and princes all;
And quickly bring us word of England's fall.
                                    [*Exeunt.*

SCENE VI.—*The* English *Camp in* Picardy.

Enter GOWER *and* FLUELLEN.

  Gow. How now, captain Fluellen? come you
from the bridge?
  Flu. I assure you, there is very excellent service committed at the pridge.
  Gow. Is the duke of Exeter safe?
  Flu. The duke of Exeter is as magnanimous as
Agamemnon; and a man that I love and honour
with my soul, and my heart, and my duty, and my
life, and my livings, and my uttermost powers; he
is not, (God be praised, and blessed!) any hurt in
the 'orld; but keeps the pridge most valiantly,
with excellent discipline. There is an ensign there
at the pridge,—I think, in my very conscience, he
is as valiant as Mark Antony; and he is a man
of no estimation in the 'orld: but I did see him
do gallant service.
  Gow. What do you call him?
  Flu. He is called—ancient Pistol.
  Gow. I know him not.

Enter PISTOL.

  Flu. Do you not know him? Here comes the
man.
  Pist. Captain, I thee beseech to do me favours:
The duke of Exeter doth love thee well.
  Flu. Ay, I praise Got; and I have merited
some love at his hands.
  Pist. Bardolph, a soldier, firm and sound of
heart,
Of buxom valour, hath,—by cruel fate,
And giddy fortune's furious fickle wheel,

That goddess blind,
That stands upon the rolling restless stone,—

Flu. By your patience, ancient Pistol. Fortune is painted blind, with a muffler before her eyes, to signify to you, that fortune is blind: And she is painted also with a wheel; to signify to you, which is the moral of it, that she is turning, and inconstant, and variations, and mutabilities: and her foot, look you, is fixed upon a spherical stone, which rolls, and rolls, and rolls:—In good truth, the poet is make a most excellent description of fortune: fortune, look you, is an excellent moral.

Pist. Fortune is Bardolph's foe, and frowns on him;
For he has stol'n a *pix*, and hanged must 'a be."
A damned death!
Let gallows gape for dog, let man go free,
And let not hemp his wind-pipe suffocate:
But Exeter hath given the doom of death,
For *pix* of little price.
Therefore, go speak, the duke will hear thy voice;
And let not Bardolph's vital thread be cut:
With edge of penny cord, and vile reproach:
Speak, captain, for his life, and I will thee requite.

Flu. Ancient Pistol, I do partly understand your meaning.

Pist. Why then rejoice therefore.

Flu. Certainly, ancient, it is not a thing to rejoice at: for if, look you, he were my brother, I would desire the duke to use his good pleasure, and put him to executions; for disciplines ought to be used.

Pist. Die and be damn'd; and *figo* for thy friendship!

Flu. It is well.

Pist. The fig of Spain! [*Exit* Pist.

Flu. Very good.

Gow. Why, this is an arrant counterfeit rascal; I remember him now; a cutpurse.

Flu. I'll assure you, 'a utter'd as prave 'ords at the pridge, as you shall see in a summer's day: But it is very well; what he has spoke to me, that is well, I warrant you, when time is serve.

Gow. Why, 't is a gull, a fool, a rogue; that now and then goes to the wars, to grace himself, at his return into London, under the form of a soldier. And such fellows are perfect in great commanders' names: and they will learn you by rote, where services were done;—at such and such a sconce, at such a breach, at such a convoy; who came off bravely, who was shot, who disgraced, what terms the enemy stood on; and this they

con perfectly in the phrase of war, which they trick up with new-coined oaths: And what a beard of the general's cut," and a horrid suit of the camp, will do among foaming bottles, and ale-washed wits, is wonderful to be thought on! but you must learn to know such slanders of the age, or else you may be marvellous mistook.

Flu. I tell you what, captain Gower;—I do perceive, he is not the man that he would gladly make show to the 'orld he is; if I find a hole in his coat, I will tell him my mind. [*Drum heard.*] Hark you, the king is coming; and I must speak with him from the pridge.

Enter King Henry, Gloster, *and* Soldiers.

Flu. Got pless your majesty.

K. Hen. How now, Fluellen? camest thou from the bridge?

Flu. Ay, so please your majesty. The duke of Exeter has very gallantly maintained the pridge: the French is gone off, look you; and there is gallant and most prave passages: Marry, th' athversary was have possession of the pridge; but he is enforced to retire, and the duke of Exeter is master of the pridge: I can tell your majesty, the duke is a prave man.

K. Hen. What men have you lost, Fluellen?

Flu. The perdition of th' athversary hath been very great, very reasonable great: marry, for my part, I think the duke hath lost never a man, but one that is like to be executed for robbing a church, one Bardolph, if your majesty know the man; his face is all bubukles, and whelks, and knobs, and flames of fire; and his lips plows at his nose, and it is like a coal of fire, sometimes plue, and sometimes red; but his nose is executed, and his fire 's out.

K. Hen. We would have all such offenders so cut off:—and we give express charge, that, in our marches through the country, there be nothing compelled from the villages, nothing taken but paid for; none of the French upbraided, or abused in disdainful language: For when lenity and cruelty play for a kingdom, the gentler gamester is the soonest winner.

Tucket sounds. Enter Montjoy.

Mont. You know me by my habit.

K. Hen. Well then, I know thee; What shall I know of thee?

Mont. My master's mind.

K. Hen. Unfold it.

Mont. Thus says my king:—Say thou to Harry
of England, Though we seemed dead, we did but
sleep: Advantage is a better soldier, than rashness. Tell him, we could have rebuked him at
Harfleur; but that we thought not good to bruise
an injury, till it were full ripe:—now we speak
upon our cue, and our voice is imperial: England
shall repent his folly, see his weakness, and ad-
mire our sufferance. Bid him, therefore, consider
of his ransom; which must proportion the losses
we have borne, the subjects we have lost, the disgrace we have digested; which, in weight to re-
answer, his pettiness would bow under. For our
losses, his exchequer is too poor; for the effusion
of our blood, the muster of his kingdom too faint
a number; and for our disgrace, his own person,
kneeling at our feet, but a weak and worthless
satisfaction. To this add—defiance: and tell him,
for conclusion, he hath betrayed his followers,
whose condemnation is pronounced. So far my
king and master; so much my office.

K. Hen. What is thy name? I know thy
quality.

Mont. Montjoy.

K. Hen. Thou dost thy office fairly. Turn thee
back,
And tell thy king,—I do not seek him now:
But could be willing to march on to Calais
Without impeachment: for, to say the sooth,
(Though 't is no wisdom to confess so much
Unto an enemy of craft and vantage,)
My people are with sickness much enfeebled;
My numbers lessen'd; and those few I have,
Almost no better than so many French;
Who when they were in health, I tell thee, herald,
I thought, upon one pair of English legs
Did march three Frenchmen.—Yet, forgive me,
God,
That I do brag thus! this your air of France
Hath blown that vice in me; I must repent.
Go, therefore, tell thy master, here I am;
My ransom, is this frail and worthless trunk;
My army, but a weak and sickly guard;
Yet, God before, tell him we will come on,
Though France himself, and such another neigh-
bour,
Stand in our way. There 's for thy labour, Montjoy.
Go, bid thy master well advise himself:
If we may pass, we will; if we be hinder'd,
We shall your tawny ground with your red blood
Discolour: and so, Montjoy, fare you well.
The sum of all our answer is but this:

We would not seek a battle, as we are;
Nor, as we are, we say, we will not shun it;
So tell your master.

Mont. I shall deliver so. Thanks to your highness.   [*Exit* MONT.

Glo. I hope, they will not come upon us now.

K. Hen. We are in God's hand, brother, not
in theirs.
March to the bridge; it now draws toward night:—
Beyond the river we 'll encamp ourselves;
And on to-morrow bid them march away. [*Exeunt.*

SCENE VII.—*The* French Camp, *near* Agincourt.

Enter the CONSTABLE OF FRANCE, *the* LORD RAM-
BURES, *the* DUKE OF ORLEANS, DAUPHIN, *and
Others.*

Con. Tut! I have the best armour of the world
—'Would, it were day!

Orl. You have an excellent armour; but let
my horse have his due.

Con. It is the best horse of Europe.

Orl. Will it never be morning?

Dau. My lord of Orleans, and my lord high
Constable, you talk of horse and armour,—

Orl. You are as well provided of both, as any
prince in the world.

Dau. What a long night is this!——I will not
change my horse with any that treads but on four
pasterns. *Ça, ha!* He bounds from the earth, as
if his entrails were hairs; *le cheval volant,* the
Pegasus, *que a les narines de feu!* When I bestride him, I soar, I am a hawk: he trots the air;
the earth sings when he touches it; the basest
horn of his hoof is more musical than the pipe of
Hermes.

Orl. He 's of the colour of the nutmeg.

Dau. And of the heat of the ginger. It is a
beast for Perseus: he is pure air and fire; and
the dull elements of earth and water never appear
in him, but only in patient stillness, while his
rider mounts him; he is, indeed, a horse; and all
other jades you may call—beasts.

Con. Indeed, my lord, it is a most absolute and
excellent horse.

Dau. It is the prince of palfreys: his neigh is
like the bidding of a monarch, and his countenance
enforces homage.

Orl. No more, cousin.

Dau. Nay, the man hath no wit, that cannot,
from the rising of the lark to the lodging of the
lamb, vary deserved praise on my palfrey: it is a

637

theme as fluent as the sea; turn the sands into eloquent tongues, and my horse is argument for them all: 't is a subject for a sovereign to reason on, and for a sovereign's sovereign to ride on; and for the world (familiar to us, and unknown,) to lay apart their particular functions, and wonder at him. I once writ a sonnet in his praise, and began thus: "Wonder of nature,"—

Orl. I have heard a sonnet begin so to one's mistress.

Dau. Then did they imitate that which I composed to my courser; for my horse is my mistress.

Orl. Your mistress bears well.

Dau. Me well; which is the prescript praise and perfection of a good and particular mistress.

Con. Ma foy! the other day, methought, your mistress shrewdly shook your back.

Dau. So, perhaps, did yours.

Con. Mine was not bridled.

Dau. O! then, belike, she was old and gentle; and you rode, like a Kerne of Ireland, your French hose off, and in your straight trossers.⁸

Con. You have good judgment in horseman-hip.

Dau. Be warned by me then: they that ride so, and ride not warily, fall into foul bogs; I had rather have my horse to my mistress.

Con. I had as lief have my mistress a jade.

Dau. I tell thee, constable, my mistress wears her own hair.

Con. I could make as true a boast as that, if I had a sow to my mistress.

Dau. Le chien est retourné à son propre vomissement, et la truie lavée au bourbier: thou makest use of any thing.

Con. Yet do I not use my horse for my mistress; or any such proverb, so little kin to the purpose.

Ram. My lord constable, the armour that I saw in your tent to-night, are those stars, or suns, upon it?

Con. Stars, my lord.

Dau. Some of them will fall to-morrow, I hope.

Con. And yet my sky shall not want.

Dau. That may be, for you bear a many superfluously; and 't were more honour, some were away.

Con. Even as your horse bears your praises; who would trot as well, were some of your brags dismounted.

Dau. 'Would, I were able to load him with his desert! Will it never be day? I will trot to-morrow a mile, and my way shall be paved with English faces.

838

Con. I will not say so, for fear I should be faced out of my way: but I would it were morning, for I would fain be about the ears of the English.

Ram. Who will go to hazard with me for twenty English prisoners?

Con. You must first go yourself to hazard, ere you have them.

Dau. 'T is midnight, I 'll go arm myself. [*Exit.*

Orl. The Dauphin longs for morning.

Ram. He longs to eat the English.

Con. I think, he will eat all he kills.

Orl. By the white hand of my lady, he 's a gallant prince.

Con. Swear by her foot, that she may tread out the oath.

Orl. He is, simply, the most active gentleman of France.

Con. Doing is activity: and he will still be doing.

Orl. He never did harm, that I heard of.

Con. Nor will do none to-morrow; he will keep that good name still.

Orl. I know him to be valiant.

Con. I was told that, by one that knows him better than you.

Orl. What 's he?

Con. Marry, he told me so himself; and he said, he cared not who knew it.

Orl. He needs not, it is no hidden virtue in him.

Con. By my faith, sir, but it is; never any body saw it, but his lackey: 't is a hooded valour; and, when it appears, it will bate.

Orl. Ill will never said well.

Con. I will cap that proverb with—There is flattery in friendship.

Orl. And I will take up that with—Give the devil his due.

Con. Well placed; there stands your friend for the devil: have at the very eye of that proverb, with—A pox of the devil.

Orl. You are the better at proverbs, by how much—A fool's bolt is soon shot.

Con. You have shot over.

Orl. 'T is not the first time you were overshot.

Enter a Messenger.

Mess. My lord high Constable, the English lie within fifteen hundred paces of your tent.

Con. Who hath measured the ground?

Mess. The lord Grandpré.

Con. A valiant and most expert gentleman.—

Would it were day!—Alas, poor Harry of England! he longs not for the dawning, as we do.

Orl. What a wretched and peevish fellow is this king of England, to mope with his fat-brained followers so far out of his knowledge!

Con. If the English had any apprehension, they would run away.

Orl. That they lack; for if their heads had any intellectual armour, they could never wear such heavy head-pieces.

Ram. That island of England breeds very valiant creatures: their mastiffs are of unmatchable courage.

Orl. Foolish curs! that run winking into the mouth of a Russian bear, and have their heads crushed like rotten apples: You may as well say,

—that's a valiant flea, that dare eat his breakfast on the lip of a lion.

Con. Just, just; and the men do sympathise with the mastiffs, in robustious and rough coming on, leaving their wits with their wives: and then give them great meals of beef, and iron and steel, they will eat like wolves, and fight like devils.

Orl. Ay, but these English are shrewdly out of beef.

Con. Then we shall find to-morrow—they have only stomachs to eat, and none to fight. Now is it time to arm: Come, shall we about it?

Orl. It is now two o'clock: but, let me see,— by ten,

We shall have each a hundred Englishmen.

[*Exeunt.*

ACT IV.

Enter Chorus.

Chor. Now entertain conjecture of a time,
When creeping murmur, and the poring dark,
Fills the wide vessel of the universe.
From camp to camp, through the foul womb of night,
The hum of either army stilly sounds,
That the fix'd sentinels almost receive
The secret whispers of each other's watch:
Fire answers fire; and through their paly flames
Each battle sees the other's umber'd face:
Steed threatens steed, in high and boastful neighs,
Piercing the night's dull ear; and from the tents,
The armourers, accomplishing the knights,
With busy hammers closing rivets up,
Give dreadful note of preparation.
The country cocks do crow, the clocks do toll,
And the third hour of drowsy morning name.
Proud of their numbers, and secure in soul,
The confident and over-lusty French
Do the low-rated English play at dice;"
And chide the cripple tardy-gaited night,
Who, like a foul and ugly witch, doth limp
So tediously away. The poor condemned English,
Like sacrifices, by their watchful fires
Sit patiently, and inly ruminate

The morning's danger; and their gesture sad,
Investing lank-lean cheeks, and war-worn coats,
Presenteth them unto the gazing moon
So many horrid ghosts. O, now, who will behold
The royal captain of this ruin'd band,
Walking from watch to watch, from tent to tent,
Let him cry—Praise and glory on his head!
For forth he goes, and visits all his host;
Bids them good-morrow, with a modest smile;
And calls them—brothers, friends, and country men.
Upon his royal face there is no note,
How dread an army hath enrounded him;
Nor doth he dedicate one jot of colour
Unto the weary and all-watched night:
But freshly looks, and over-bears attaint,
With cheerful semblance, and sweet majesty;
That every wretch, pining and pale before,
Beholding him, plucks comfort from his looks:
A largess universal, like the sun,
His liberal eye doth give to every one,
Thawing cold fear. Then, mean and gentle all,
Behold, as may unworthiness define,
A little touch of Harry in the night:
And so our scene must to the battle fly:
Where (O for pity!) we shall much disgrace—
With four or five most vile and ragged foils,

839

Right ill-disposed, in brawl ridiculous,—
The name of Agincourt: Yet, sit and see;
Minding true things, by what their mockeries be.
  [*Exit.*

SCENE I.—*The* English *Camp at Agincourt.*

Enter KING HENRY, BEDFORD, *and* GLOSTER.

K. Hen. Gloster, 't is true, that we are in great
  danger;
The greater therefore should our courage be.—
Good morrow, brother Bedford.—God Almighty!
There is some soul of goodness in things evil,
Would men observingly distil it out;
For our bad neighbour makes us early stirrers,
Which is both healthful, and good husbandry:
Besides, they are our outward consciences,
And preachers to us all; admonishing,
That we should dress us fairly for our end.²²
Thus may we gather honey from the weed,
And make a moral of the devil himself.

Enter ERPINGHAM.

Good morrow, old sir Thomas Erpingham:
A good soft pillow for that good white head
Were better than a churlish turf of France.
  Erp. Not so, my liege; this lodging likes me
    better,
Since I may say—now lie I like a king.
  K. Hen. 'T is good for men to love their present
    pains,
Upon example; so the spirit is eased:
And, when the mind is quicken'd, out of doubt,
The organs, though defunct and dead before,
Break up their drowsy grave, and newly move
With casted slough and fresh legerity.³⁴
Lend me thy cloak, sir Thomas.—Brothers both,
Commend me to the princes in our camp;
Do my good morrow to them; and, anon,
Desire them all to my pavilion.
  Glo. We shall, my liege. [*Exeunt* GLO. *and* BED.
  Erp. Shall I attend your grace?
  K. Hen.   No, my good knight;
Go with my brothers to my lords of England:
I and my bosom must debate a while,
And then I would no other company.
  Erp. The Lord in heaven bless thee, noble
    Harry! [*Exit* ERP.
  K. Hen. God-a-mercy, old heart! thou speakest
    cheerfully.

Enter PISTOL.

Pist. Qui va là?
840

K. Hen. A friend.
Pist. Discuss unto me: Art thou officer?
Or art thou base, common, and popular?
K. Hen. I am a gentleman of a company.
Pist. Trailest thou the puissant pike?
K. Hen. Even so: What are you?
Pist. As good a gentleman as the emperor.
K. Hen. Then you are a better than the king.
Pist. The king's a bawcock, and a heart of
  gold,
A lad of life, an imp of fame;
Of parents good, of fist most valiant:
I kiss his dirty shoe, and from my heart-strings
I love the lovely bully. What's thy name?
K. Hen. Harry *le Roy*.
Pist. Le Roy! a Cornish name: art thou of
  Cornish crew?
K. Hen. No, I am a Welshman.
Pist. Knowest thou Fluellen?
K. Hen. Yes.
Pist. Tell him, I'll knock his leek about his
  pate,
Upon Saint Davy's day.
K. Hen. Do not you wear your dagger in your
cap that day, lest he knock that about yours.
Pist. Art thou his friend?
K. Hen. And his kinsman too.
Pist. The *figo* for thee then!
K. Hen. I thank you: God be with you!
Pist. My name is Pistol called. [*Exit.*
K. Hen. It sorts well with your fierceness.

Enter FLUELLEN *and* GOWER, *severally.*

Gow. Captain Fluellen!
Flu. So! in the name of Cheshu Christ, speak
lower. It is the greatest admiration in the universal 'orld, when the true and aunceint preroga-
tifes and laws of the wars is not kept: if you would
take the pains but to examine the wars of Pompey the Great, you shall find, I warrant you, that
there is no tiddle taddle, or pibble pabble, in Pompey's camp; I warrant you, you shall find the
ceremonies of the wars, and the cares of it, and
the forms of it, and the sobriety of it, and the
modesty of it, to be otherwise.
Gow. Why, the enemy is loud; you heard
him all night.
Flu. If the enemy is an ass and a fool, and a
prating coxcomb, is it meet, think you, that we
should also, look you, be an ass, and a fool, and a
prating coxcomb; in your own conscience now?
Gow. I will speak lower.

Flu. I pray you, and beseech you, that you will. [*Exeunt Gow. and Flu.*

K. Hen. Though it appear a little out of fashion, There is much care and valour in this Welshman.

Enter BATES, COURT, *and* WILLIAMS.

Court. Brother John Bates, is not that the morning which breaks yonder?

Bates. I think it be: but we have no great cause to desire the approach of day.

Will. We see yonder the beginning of the day, but, I think, we shall never see the end of it.— Who goes there?

K. Hen. A friend.

Will. Under what captain serve you?

K. Hen. Under sir Thomas Erpingham.

Will. A good old commander, and a most kind gentleman: I pray you, what thinks he of our estate?

K. Hen. Even as men wrecked upon a sand, that look to be washed off the next tide.

Bates. He hath not told his thought to the king?

K. Hen. No; nor it is not meet he should. For, though I speak it to you, I think, the king is but a man, as I am: the violet smells to him, as it doth to me; the element shows to him, as it doth to me; all his senses have but human conditions; his ceremonies laid by, in his nakedness he appears but a man; and though his affections are higher mounted than ours, yet, when they stoop, they stoop with the like wing; therefore when he sees reason of fears, as we do, his fears, out of doubt, be of the same relish as ours are: Yet, in reason, no man should possess him with any appearance of fear, lest he, by showing it, should dishearten his army.

Bates. He may show what outward courage he will: but, I believe, as cold a night as 't is, he could wish himself in the Thames up to the neck; and so I would he were, and I by him, at all adventures, so we were quit here.

K. Hen. By my troth, I will speak my conscience of the king; I think, he would not wish himself any where but where he is.

Bates. Then, 'would he were here alone; so should he be sure to be ransomed, and a many poor men's lives saved.

K. Hen. I dare say, you love him not so ill, to wish him here alone; howsoever you speak this, to feel other men's minds: Methinks, I could not die any where so contented, as in the king's company; his cause being just, and his quarrel honourable.

Will. That 's more than we know.

Bates. Ay, or more than we should seek after; for we know enough, if we know we are the king's subjects; if his cause be wrong, our obedience to the king wipes the crime of it out of us.

Will. But, if the cause be not good, the king himself hath a heavy reckoning to make; when all those legs, and arms, and heads, chopped off in a battle, shall join together at the latter day, and cry all—We died at such a place; some swearing; some, crying for a surgeon; some, upon their wives left poor behind them; some, upon the debts they owe; some, upon their children rawly left. I am afeard there are few die well, that die in battle; for how can they charitably dispose of any thing, when blood is their argument? Now, if these men do not die well, it will be a black matter for the king that led them to it; whom to disobey, were against all proportion of subjection.

K. Hen. So, if a son, that is by his father sent about merchandise, do sinfully miscarry upon the sea, the imputation of his wickedness, by your rule, should be imposed upon his father that sent him: or if a servant, under his master's command transporting a sum of money, be assailed by robbers, and die in many irreconciled iniquities, you may call the business of the master the author of the servant's damnation:—But this is not so; the king is not bound to answer the particular endings of his soldiers, the father of his son, nor the master of his servant; for they purpose not their death, when they purpose their services. Besides, there is no king, be his cause never so spotless, if it come to the arbitrement of swords, can try it out with all unspotted soldiers. Some, peradventure, have on them the guilt of premeditated and contrived murder; some, of beguiling virgins with the broken seals of perjury; some, making the wars their bulwark, that have before gored the gentle bosom of peace with pillage and robbery. Now, if these men have defeated the law, and outrun native punishment, though they can outstrip men, they have no wings to fly from God: war is his beadle, war is his vengeance; so that here men are punished, for before-breach of the king's laws, in now the king's quarrel: where they feared the death, they have borne life away; and where they would be safe, they perish: Then if they die unprovided, no more is the king guilty of their damnation than he was before guilty of those impieties for the which they are now visited. Every subject's duty is the king's; but every subject's soul is his own. Therefore should every soldier in the wars do as every sick man in his bed, wash every mote out of his conscience: and dying so, death is to him advantage; or not dying, the time was blessedly lost, wherein such preparation was gained: and, in him that escapes, it were not sin to think, that making God so free an offer, he let him outlive that day to see his greatness, and to teach others how they should prepare.

Will. 'T is certain, every man that dies ill, the ill is upon his own head, the king is not to answer for it.

Bates. I do not desire he should answer for me; and yet I determine to fight lustily for him.

K. Hen. I myself heard the king say, he would not be ransomed.

Will. Ay, he said so, to make us fight cheerfully: but, when our throats are cut, he may be ransomed, and we ne'er the wiser.

K. Hen. If I live to see it, I will never trust his word after.

Will. 'Mass, you 'll pay him then!'' That 's a perilous shot out of an elder gun, that a poor and private displeasure can do against a monarch! you may as well go about to turn the sun to ice, with fanning in his face with a peacock's feather. You 'll never trust his word after! come, 't is a foolish saying.

K. Hen. Your reproof is something too round; I should be angry with you, if the time were convenient.

Will. Let it be a quarrel between us, if you live.

K. Hen. I embrace it.

Will. How shall I know thee again?

K. Hen. Give me any gage of thine, and I will wear it in my bonnet: then, if ever thou darest acknowledge it, I will make it my quarrel.

Will. Here 's my glove; give me another of thine.

K. Hen. There.

Will. This will I also wear in my cap: if ever thou come to me and say, after to-morrow, " This is my glove," by this hand, I will take thee a box on the ear.

K. Hen. If ever I live to see it, I will challenge it.

Will. Thou darest as well be hanged.

K. Hen. Well, I will do it, though I take thee in the king's company.

848

Will. Keep thy word; fare thee well.

Bates. Be friends, you English fools, be friends; we have French quarrels enough, if you could tell how to reckon.

K. Hen. Indeed, the French may lay twenty French crowns to one, they will beat us; for they bear them on their shoulders: But it is no English treason, to cut French crowns; and, to-morrow, the king himself will be a clipper.

[*Exeunt* Soldiers.

Upon the king! let us our lives, our souls,
Our debts, our careful wives, our children, and
Our sins, lay on the king;—we must bear all.
O hard condition! twin-born with greatness,
Subjected to the breath of every fool,
Whose sense no more can feel but his own wring-
　　ing!
What infinite heart's ease must kings neglect,
That private men enjoy!
And what have kings, that privates have not too,
Save ceremony, save general ceremony?
And what art thou, thou idol ceremony?
What kind of god art thou, that suffer'st more
Of mortal griefs, than do thy worshippers?
What are thy rents? what are thy comings-in?
O ceremony, show me but thy worth!
What is the soul of adoration?
Art thou aught else but place, degree, and form,
Creating awe and fear in other men?
Wherein thou art less happy being fear'd
Than they in fearing.
What drink'st thou oft, instead of homage sweet,
But poison'd flattery? O, be sick, great greatness,
And bid thy ceremony give thee cure!
Think'st thou, the fiery fever will go out
With titles blown from adulation?
Will it give place to flexure and low bending?
Canst thou, when thou command'st the beggar's
　　knee,
Command the health of it? No, thou proud dream,
That play'st so subtly with a king's repose;
I am a king, that find thee; and I know,
'T is not the balm, the sceptre, and the ball,
The sword, the mace, the crown imperial,
The enter-tissued robe of gold and pearl,
The farced title running 'fore the king,
The throne he sits on, nor the tide of pomp
That beats upon the high shore of this world,
No, not all these, thrice-gorgeous ceremony,
Not all these, laid in bed majestical,
Can sleep so soundly as the wretched slave;
Who, with a body fill'd, and vacant mind,

Gets him to rest, cramm'd with distressful bread;
Never sees horrid night, the child of hell;
But, like a lackey, from the rise to set,
Sweats in the eye of Phœbus, and all night
Sleeps in Elysium; next day, after dawn,
Doth rise, and help Hyperion to his horse;
And follow so the ever-running year
With profitable labour, to his grave:
And, but for ceremony, such a wretch,
Winding up days with toil, and nights with sleep,
Had the fore-hand and vantage of a king.
The slave, a member of the country's peace,
Enjoys it; but in gross brains little wots,
What watch the king keeps to maintain the
        peace,
Whose hours the peasant best advantages.

Enter ERPINGHAM.

Erp. My lord, your nobles, jealous of your ab-
sence,
Seek through your camp to find you.
K. Hen.   Good old knight,
Collect them all together at my tent:
I'll be before thee.
Erp.   I shall do't, my lord.   [*Exit.*
K. Hen. O God of battles! steel my soldiers'
        hearts!
Possess them not with fear; take from them now
The sense of reckoning, if the opposed numbers
Pluck their hearts from them!—Not to-day, O
        Lord,
O not to-day, think not upon the fault
My father made in compassing the crown!
I Richard's body have interred new;
And on it have bestow'd more contrite tears,
Than from it issued forced drops of blood.
Five hundred poor I have in yearly pay,
Who twice a day their wither'd hands hold up
Toward heaven, to pardon blood; and I have
        built
Two chantries, where the sad and solemn priests
Sing still for Richard's soul.   More will I do:
Though all that I can do, is nothing worth;
Since that my penitence comes after all,
Imploring pardon.

Enter GLOSTER.

Glo. My liege!
K. Hen.   My brother Gloster's voice?—Ay;
I know thy errand, I will go with thee:—
The day, my friends, and all things stay for me.
                                    [*Exeunt.*

SCENE II.—*The* French *Camp.*

Enter DAUPHIN, ORLEANS, RAMBURES, *and Others.*

Orl. The sun doth gild our armour; up, my
        lords.
Dau. Montez à cheval:—My horse! *va'et! lee-
        quay!* ha!
Orl. O brave spirit!
Dau. Via!—les eaux et la terre——
Orl. Rien puis? l'air et le feu——
Dau. Ciel! cousin Orleans.——

Enter CONSTABLE.

Now, my lord Constable!
Con. Hark, how our steeds for present service
        neigh.
Dau. Mount them, and make incision in their
        hides;
That their hot blood may spin in English eyes,
And dout them with superfluous courage: Ha!
Ram. What, will you have them weep our
        horses' blood?
How shall we then behold their natural tears?

Enter a Messenger.

Mess. The English are embattled, you French
        peers.
Con. To horse, you gallant princes! straight to
        horse!
Do but behold yon poor and starved band,
And your fair show shall suck away their souls,
Leaving them but the shales and husks of men.
There is not work enough for all our hands;
Scarce blood enough in all their sickly veins,
To give each naked curtle-axe a stain,
That our French gallants shall to-day draw out,
And sheath for lack of sport: let us but blow on
        them,
The vapour of our valour will o'erturn them.
'Tis positive 'gainst all exceptions, lords,
That our superfluous lackeys, and our peasants,—
Who, in unnecessary action, swarm
About our squares of battle,—were enough
To purge this field of such a hilding foe;
Though we, upon this mountain's basis by
Took stand for idle speculation:
But that our honours must not.   What's to say
A very little little let us do,
And all is done.   Then let the trumpets sound
The tucket-sonance,[33] and the note to mount;
For our approach shall so much dare the field,

That England shall couch down in fear, and
　　yield.

Enter GRANDPREE.

G·nd. Why do you stay so long, my lords of
　France?
Yon island carrions, desperate of their bones,
Ill-favour'dly become the morning field:
Their ragged curtains poorly are let loose,
And our air shakes them passing scornfully.
Big Mars seems bankrupt in their beggar'd host,
And faintly through a rusty beaver peeps.
Their horsemen sit like fixed candlesticks,
With torch-staves in each hand: and their poor
　jades
Lob down their heads, dropping the hides and
　lips;
The gum down-roping from their pale-dead eyes;
And in their pale dull mouths the gimmal bit
Lies foul with chew'd grass, still and motionless;
And their executors, the knavish crows,
Fly o'er them all, impatient for their hour.
Description cannot suit itself in words,
To demonstrate the life of such a battle
In life so lifeless as it shows itself.

Con. They have said their prayers, and they
　stay for death.

Dau. Shall we go send them dinners, and fresh
　suits,
And give their fasting horses provender,
And after fight with them?

Con. I stay but for my guard: On, to the field:
I will the banner from a trumpet take,
And use it for my haste. Come, come away!
The sun is high, and we outwear the day.

　　　　　　　　　　　　　　　[*Exeunt.*

SCENE III.—*The English Camp.*

Enter the English Host; GLOSTER, BEDFORD,
EXETER, SALISBURY, *and* WESTMORELAND.

Glo. Where is the king?

Bed. The king himself is rode to view their
　battle.

West. Of fighting men they have full threescore
　thousand.

Exe. There's five to one; besides, they all are
　fresh.

Sal. God's arm strike with us! 'tis a fearful
　odds.
God be wi' you, princes all; I'll to my charge:
If we no more meet, till we meet in heaven,

Then, joyfully,—my noble lord of Bedford,—
My dear lord Gloster,—and my good lord Exeter,—
And my kind kinsman,—warriors all, adieu.

Bed. Farewell, good Salisbury; and good luck
　go with thee!

Exe. Farewell, kind lord; fight valiantly to-day:
And yet I do thee wrong, to mind thee of it,
For thou art fram'd of the firm truth of valour.

　　　　　　　　　　　　　　　[*Exit* SAL.

Bed. He is as full of valour, as of kindness;
Princely in both.

West. 　　　　　O that we had now here

Enter KING HENRY.

But one ten thousand of those men in England,
That do no work to-day!

K. Hen. 　　　　　What's he, that wishes so?
My cousin Westmoreland?—No, my fair cousin:
If we are mark'd to die, we are enough
To do our country loss; and if to live,
The fewer men, the greater share of honour.
God's will! I pray thee, wish not one man more
By Jove, I am not covetous for gold;
Nor care I, who doth feed upon my cost;
It yearns me not, if men my garments wear;
Such outward things dwell not in my desires:
But, if it be a sin to covet honour,
I am the most offending soul alive.
No, 'faith, my coz, wish not a man from England:
God's peace! I would not lose so great an honour,
As one man more, methinks, would share from me,
For the best hope I have. O, do not wish one
　more:
Rather proclaim it, Westmoreland, through my host,
That he, which hath no stomach to this fight,
Let him depart; his passport shall be made,
And crowns for convoy put into his purse:
We would not die in that man's company,
That fears his fellowship to die with us.
This day is call'd—the feast of Crispian:
He, that outlives this day, and comes safe home,
Will stand a tip-toe when this day is nam'd,
And rouse him at the name of Crispian.
He, that shall live this day, and see old age,
Will yearly on the vigil feast his friends,
And say—to-morrow is Saint Crispian:
Then will he strip his sleeve, and show his scars.
And say, these wounds I had on Crispin's day,
Old men forget; yet all shall be forgot,
But he'll remember, with advantages.
What feats he did that day: Then shall our names
Familiar in their mouths as household words,—

Harry the king, Bedford, and Exeter,
Warwick and Talbot, Salisbury and Gloster,—
Be in their flowing cups freshly remember'd :
This story shall the good man teach his son ;
And Crispin Crispian shall ne'er go by,
From this day to the ending of the world,
But we in it shall be remembered :
We few, we happy few, we band of brothers ;
For he, to-day that sheds his blood with me,
Shall be my brother ; be he ne'er so vile,
This day shall gentle his condition :
And gentlemen in England, now a-bed,
Shall think themselves accurs'd, they were not
    here ;
And hold their manhoods cheap, while any speaks,
That fought with us upon Saint Crispin's day.

Enter SALISBURY.

Sal. My sovereign lord, bestow yourself with
    speed :
The French are bravely in their battles set,
And will with all expedience charge on us.
    K. Hen. All things are ready, if our minds be so.
    West. Perish the man whose mind is backward
        now !
    K. Hen. Thou dost not wish more help from
        England, cousin ?
    West. God's will, my liege, 'would you and I
        alone,
Without more help, might fight this battle out !
    K. Hen. Why, now thou hast unwish'd five
        thousand men ;
Which likes me better, than to wish us one.—
You know your places : God be with you all !

Tucket. Enter MONTJOY.

    Mont. Once more I come to know of thee, king
        Harry,
If for thy ransom thou wilt now compound,
Before thy most assured overthrow ;
For, certainly, thou art so near the gulf,
Thou needs must be englutted. Besides, in mercy,
The Constable desires thee—thou wilt mind
Thy followers of repentance ; that their souls
May make a peaceful and a sweet retire
From off these fields, where (wretches) their poor
    bodies
Must lie and fester.
    K. Hen.   Who hath sent thee now ?
    Mont. The Constable of France.
    K. Hen. I pray thee, bear my former answer
        back ;

Bid them achieve me, and then sell my bones.
Good God ! why should they mock poor fellows
    thus ?
The man, that once did sell the lion's skin
While the beast lived, was kill'd with hunting
    him.
A many of our bodies shall, no doubt,
Find native graves ; upon the which, I trust,
Shall witness live in brass of this day's work :
And those that leave their valiant bones in France,
Dying like men, though buried in your dunghills,
They shall be fam'd ; for there the sun shall greet
    them,
And draw their honours reeking up to heaven ;
Leaving their earthly parts to choke your clime,
The smell whereof shall breed a plague in France.
Mark then a bounding valour in our English ;
That, being dead, like to the bullet's grazing,
Break out into a second course of mischief,
Killing in relapse of mortality.
Let me speak proudly :—Tell the Constable,
We are but warriors for the working day :
Our gayness, and our gilt, are all besmirch'd
With rainy marching in the painful field ;
There 's not a piece of feather in our host,
(Good argument, I hope, we shall not fly.)
And time hath worn us into slovenry :
But, by the mass, our hearts are in the trim :
And my poor soldiers tell me—yet ere night
They 'll be in fresher robes ; or they will pluck
The gay new coats o'er the French soldiers'
    heads,
And turn them out of service. If they do this,
(As, if God please, they shall,) my ransom then
Will soon be levied. Herald, save thou thy labour ;
Come thou no more for ransom, gentle herald ;
They shall have none, I swear, but these my joints ;
Which if they have as I will leave 'em to them,
Shall yield them little, tell the Constable.
    Mont. I shall, king Harry. And so fare thee
        well :
Thou never shalt hear herald any more.   [*Exit.*
    K. Hen. I fear, thou 'lt once more come again
        for ransom.

Enter the DUKE OF YORK.[11]

    York. My lord, most humbly on my knee I beg
The leading of the vaward.
    K. Hen. Take it, brave York.—Now, soldiers,
        march away :—
And how thou pleasest, God, dispose the day !
                                        [*Exeunt.*

                                            845

SCENE IV.—*The Field of Battle.*

Alarums: Excursions. Enter French Soldier, Pistol, *and* Boy.

Pist. Yield, cur.

Fr. Sol. Je pense, que vous estes le gentilhomme de bonne qualité.

Pist. Quality, call you me?—Construe me, art thou a gentleman? What is thy name? discuss.

Fr. Sol. O seigneur Dieu!

Pist. O, signieur Dew should be a gentleman:—
Perpend my words, O signieur Dew, and mark;—
O signieur Dew, thou diest on point of fox,[32]
Except, O signieur, thou do give to me
Egregious ransom.

Fr. Sol. O, prennez miséricorde! ayez pitié de moy!

Pist. Moy shall not serve, I will have forty moys;
For I will fetch thy rim out at thy throat,[33]
In drops of crimson blood.

Fr. Sol. Est il impossible d'eschapper la force de ton bras?

Pist. Brass, cur!
Thou damned and luxurious mountain goat,
Offer'st me brass?

Fr. Sol. O pardonnez moy!

Pist. Say'st thou me so? is that a ton of moys?[34]—
Come hither, boy; Ask me this slave in French,
What is his name.

Boy. Escoutez; Comment estes vous appellé?

Fr. Sol. Monsieur le Fer.

Boy. He says, his name is—master Fer.

Pist. Master Fer! I'll fer him, and firk him, and ferret him:—discuss the same in French unto him.

Boy. I do not know the French for fer, and ferret, and firk.

Pist. Bid him prepare, for I will cut his throat.

Fr. Sol. Que dit-il, monsieur?

Boy. Il me commande de vous dire que vous faites vous prest; car ce soldat icy est disposé tout à cette heure de couper vostre gorge.

Pist. Ouy, couper gorge, par ma foy, pesant,
Unless thou give me crowns, brave crowns;
Or mangled shalt thou be by this my sword.

Fr. Sol. O, je vous supplie pour l'amour de Dieu, me pardonner! Je suis gentilhomme de bonne maison; gardez ma vie, et je vous donneray deux cents escus.

846

Pist. What are his words?

Boy. He prays you to save his life: he is a gentleman of a good house: and, for his ransom, he will give you two hundred crowns.

Pist. Tell him.—my fury shall abate, and I
The crowns will take.

Fr. Sol. Petit monsieur, que dit-il?

Boy. Encore qu'il est contre son jurement, de pardonner aucun prisonnier; neantmoins, pour les escus que vous l'avez promis, il est content de vous donner la liberté, le franchisement.

Fr. Sol. Sur mes genoux, je vous donne mille remerciemens: et je m'estime heureux que je suis tombé entre les mains d'un chevalier, je pense, le plus brave, valiant, et tres distingué seigneur d'Angleterre.

Pist. Expound unto me, boy.

Boy. He gives you, upon his knees, a thousand thanks: and he esteems himself happy that he hath fallen into the hands of (as he thinks) the most brave, valorous, and thrice-worthy signieur of England.

Pist. As I suck blood, I will some mercy show.—
Follow me, cur.   [*Exit* Pist.

Boy. Suivez vous le grand capitaine.
             [*Exit* Fr. Sol.
I did never know so full a voice issue from so empty a heart; but the saying is true,—The empty vessel makes the greatest sound.—Bardolph, and Nym, had ten times more valour than this roaring devil i' the old play,[35] that every one may pare his nails with a wooden dagger; and they are both hanged; and so would this be, if he durst steal any thing adventurously. I must stay with the lackeys, with the luggage of our camp: the French might have a good prey of us, if he knew of it; for there is none to guard it, but boys.   [*Exit*

SCENE V.—*Another Part of the Field of Battle.*

Alarums. Enter Dauphin, Orleans, Bourbon, Constable, Rambures, *and* Others.

Con. O diable!

Orl. O seigneur!—le jour est perdu, tout est perdu!

Dau. Mort de ma vie! all is confounded, all!
Reproach and everlasting shame
Sits mocking in our plumes.—O meschante fortune!—
Do not run away.   [*A short Alarum.*

Con.   Why, all our ranks are broke.
Dau. O perdurable shame!—let 's stab our-
selves.
Be these the wretches that we play'd at dice for?
Orl. Is this the king we sent to for his ransom?
Bour. Shame, and eternal shame, nothing but
shame!
Let us die instant: Once more back again;
And he that will not follow Bourbon now,
Let him go hence, and, with his cap in hand,
Like a base pander, hold the chamber-door,
Whilst by a slave, no gentler than my dog,
His fairest daughter is contaminate.
    Con. Disorder, that hath spoil'd us, friend us
                                                          now!
Let us, in heaps, go offer up our lives
Unto these English, or else die with fame.
    Orl. We are enough yet living in the field,
To smother up the English in our throngs,
If any order might be thought upon.
    Bour. The devil take order now! I 'll to the
                                                          throng;
Let life be short; else, shame will be too long.
                                                          [*Exeunt.*

SCENE VI.—*Another Part of the Field.*

Alarums. Enter KING HENRY *and Forces; Ex-*
ETER, and Others.

    K. Hen. Well have we done, thrice-valiant coun-
                                                          trymen;
But all 's not done, yet keep the French the field.
    Exe. The duke of York commends him to your
                                                          majesty.
    K. Hen. Lives he, good uncle? thrice within
                                                          this hour,
I saw him down; thrice up again, and fighting;
From helmet to the spur, all blood he was.
    Exe. In which array, (brave soldier,) doth he lie,
Larding the plain: and by his bloody side,
(Yoke-fellow to his honour-owing wounds,)
The noble earl of Suffolk also lies.
Suffolk first died: and York, all haggled over,
Comes to him, where in gore he lay insteep'd,
And takes him by the beard; kisses the gashes,
That bloodily did yawn upon his face;
And cries aloud,—"Tarry, dear cousin Suffolk!
My soul shall thine keep company to heaven:
Tarry, sweet soul, for mine, then fly a-breast;
As, in this glorious and well-foughten field,
We kept together in our chivalry!"
Upon these words I came, and cheer'd him up:

He smil'd me in the face, raught me his hand,
And, with a feeble gripe, says,—"Dear my lord,
Commend my service to my sovereign."
So did he turn, and over Suffolk's neck
He threw his wounded arm, and kiss'd his lips;
And so, espous'd to death, with blood he seal'd
A testament of noble-ending love.
The pretty and sweet manner of it forc'd
These waters from me, which I would have stopp'd;
But I had not so much of man in me,
But all my mother came into mine eyes,
And gave me up to tears.
    K. Hen.   I blame you not;
For, hearing this, I must perforce compound
With mistful eyes, or they will issue too. [*Alarum.*
But, hark! what new alarum is this same!
The French have reinforced their scatter'd men:—
Then every soldier kill his prisoners;
Give the word through.   [*Exeunt.*

SCENE VII.—*Another Part of the Field.*

Alarums. Enter FLUELLEN *and* GOWER.

    Flu. Kill the poys and the luggage! 't is ex-
pressly against the law of arms; 't is as arrant a
piece of knavery, mark you now, as can be offered,
in the 'orld: In your conscience now, is it not?
    Gow. 'T is certain, there 's not a boy left alive
and the cowardly rascals, that ran from the battle, have done this slaughter: besides, they have
burned and carried away all that was in the king's
tent; wherefore the king, most worthily, hath
caused every soldier to cut his prisoner's throat.
O, 't is a gallant king!
    Flu. Ay, he was porn at Monmouth, captain
Gower: What call you the town's name, where
Alexander the pig was born?
    Gow. Alexander the Great.
    Flu. Why, I pray you, is not pig, great? The
pig, or the great, or the mighty, or the huge, or
the magnanimous, are all one reckonings, save the
phrase is a little variations.
    Gow. I think, Alexander the Great was born
in Macedon; his father was called—Philip of Macedon, as I take it.
    Flu. I think, it is in Macedon, where Alexander
is porn. I tell you, captain,—If you look in the
maps of the 'orld, I warrant, you shall find, in the
comparisons between Macedon and Monmouth,
that the situations, look you, is both alike. There
is a river in Macedon; and there is also moreover
a river at Monmouth: it is called Wye, at Mon-
                                                          617

mouth: but it is out of my prains, what is the name of the other river; but 't is all one, 't is so like as my fingers is to my fingers, and there is salmons in both. If you mark Alexander's life well, Harry of Monmouth's life is come after it indifferent well; for there is figures in all things. Alexander (God knows, and you know,) in his rages, and his furies, and his wraths, and his cholers, and his moods, and his displeasures, and his indignations, and also being a little intoxicates in his prains, did, in his ales and his angers, look you, kill his pest friend, Clytus.

Gow. Our king is not like him in that; he never killed any of his friends.

Flu. It is not well done, mark you know, to take tales out of my mouth, ere it is made an end and finished. I speak but in the figures and comparisons of it: As Alexander is kill his friend Clytus, being in his ales and his cups; so also Harry Monmouth, being in his right wits and his goot judgments, is turn away the fat knight with the great pelly-doublet: he was full of jests, and gipes, and knaveries, and mocks; I am forget his name.

Gow. Sir John Falstaff.

Flu. That is he: I can tell you, there is goot men born at Monmouth.

Gow. Here comes his majesty.

Alarum. Enter KING HENRY, *with a Part of the English Forces;* WARWICK, GLOSTER, EXETER, *and Others.*

K. Hen. I was not angry since I came to France Until this instant.—Take a trumpet, herald;
Ride thou unto the horsemen on yon hill;
If they will fight with us, bid them come down,
Or void the field; they do offend our sight:
If they 'll do neither, we will come to them;
And make them skirr away, as swift as stones
Enforced from the old Assyrian slings;
Besides, we 'll cut the throats of those we have;
And not a man of them, that we shall take,
Shall taste our mercy:—Go, and tell them so.

Enter MONTJOY.

Exe. Here comes the herald of the French, my liege.

Glo. His eyes are humbler than they us'd to be.

K. Hen. How now! what means this, herald? know'st thou not,
That I have fin'd these bones of mine for ransom?
Com'st thou again for ransom?

Mont.   No, great king:

I come to thee for charitable license,
That we may wander o'er this bloody field,
To book our dead, and then to bury them;
To sort our nobles from our common men;
For many of our princes (woe the while!)
Lie drown'd and soak'd in mercenary blood;
(So do our vulgar drench their peasant limbs
In blood of princes;) and their wounded steeds
Fret fetlock deep in gore, and, with wild rage,
Yerk out their armed heels at their dead masters,
Killing them twice. O, give us leave, great king,
To view the field in safety, and dispose
Of their dead bodies.

K. Hen.   I tell thee truly, herald,
I know not, if the day be ours, or no;
For yet a many of your horsemen peer,
And gallop o'er the field.

Mont.   The day is yours.

K. Hen. Praised be God, and not our strength, for it!—
What is this castle call'd, that stands hard by?

Mont. They call it—Agincourt.

K. Hen. Then call we this—the field of Agincourt,
Fought on the day of Crispin Crispianus.

Flu. Your grandfather of famous memory, an 't please your majesty, and your great-uncle Edward the plack prince of Wales, as I have read in the chronicles, fought a most prave pattle here in France.

K. Hen. They did, Fluellen.

Flu. Your majesty says very true: If your majesty is remembered of it, the Welshman did goot service in a garden where leeks did grow, wearing leeks in their Monmouth caps; which, your majesty knows, to this hour is an honourable padge of the service; and, I do believe, your majesty takes no scorn to wear the leek upon Saint Tavy's day.

K. Hen. I wear it for a memorable honour: For I am Welsh, you know, good countryman.

Flu. All the water in Wye cannot wash your majesty's Welsh plood out of your pody, I can tell you that: Got pless it and preserve it, as long as it pleases his grace, and his majesty too!

K. Hen. Thanks, good my countryman.

Flu. By Cheshu, I am your majesty's country man, I care not who know it; I will confess it to all the 'orld; I need not to be ashamed of your majesty, praised be God, so long as your majesty is an honest man.

K. Hen. God keep me so!—Our heralds go with him;

Bring me just notice of the numbers dead
On both our parts.—Call yonder fellow hither.

[Points to WILL. *Exeunt* MONT. *and Others.*

Exe. Soldier, you must come to the king.

K. Hen. Soldier, why wear'st thou that glove
in thy cap?

Will. An 't please your majesty, 't is the gage
of one that I should fight withal, if he be alive.

K. Hen. An Englishman?

Will. An 't please your majesty, a rascal, that
swaggered with me last night: who, if 'a live, and
ever dare to challenge this glove, I have sworn to
take him a box o' the ear: or, if I can see my glove
in his cap, (which he swore, as he was a soldier, he
would wear, if alive,) I will strike it out soundly.

K. Hen. What think you, captain Fluellen? is
it fit this soldier keep his oath?

Flu. He is a craven and a villain else, an 't
please your majesty, in my conscience.

K. Hen. It may be, his enemy is a gentleman
of great sort, quite from the answer of his degree.

Flu. Though he be as goot a gentleman as the
tevil is, as Lucifer and Belzebub himself, it is necessary, look your grace, that he keep his vow
and his oath: if he be perjured, see you now, his
reputation is as arrant a villain, and a Jack-
sauce, as ever his black shoe trod upon Got's
ground and his earth, in my conscience la.

K. Hen. Then keep thy vow, sirrah, when thou
meet'st the fellow.

Will. So I will, my liege, as I live.

K. Hen. Who servest thou under?

Will. Under captain Gower, my liege.

Flu. Gower is a goot captain; and is good
knowledge and literature in the wars.

K. Hen. Call him hither to me, soldier.

Will. I will, my liege.   *[Exit.*

K. Hen. Here, Fluellen; wear thou this favour
for me, and stick it in thy cap: When Alençon
and myself were down together, I plucked this
glove from his helm: if any man challenge this,
he is a friend to Alençon and an enemy to our
person; if thou encounter any such, apprehend
him, an thou dost love me.

Flu. Your grace does me as great honours, as
can be desired in the hearts of his subjects: I
would fain see the man, that has but two legs,
that shall find himself aggrieved at this glove, that
is all; but I would fain see it once; an please
Got of his grace, that I might see it.

K. Hen. Knowest thou Gower?

Flu. He is my dear friend, an please you.

K. Hen. Pray thee, go seek him, and bring him
to my tent.

Flu. I will fetch him.   *[Exit.*

K. Hen. My lord of Warwick,—and my brother
Gloster,
Follow Fluellen closely at the heels:
The glove, which I have given him for a favour,
May, haply, purchase him a box o' the ear;
It is the soldier's; I, by bargain, should
Wear it myself.   Follow, good cousin War-
wick:
If that the soldier strike him, (as, I judge
By his blunt bearing, he will keep his word,)
Some sudden mischief may arise of it;
For I do know Fluellen valiant,
And, touch'd with choler, hot as gunpowder,
And quickly will return an injury:
Follow, and see there be no harm between them.—
Go you with me, uncle of Exeter.   *[Exeunt.*

SCENE VIII.—*Before King Henry's Pavilion.*

Enter GOWER *and* WILLIAMS.

Will. I warrant, it is to knight you, captain.

Enter FLUELLEN

Flu. Got's will and his pleasure, captain, I beseech you now, come apace to the king: there is
more goot toward you, peradventure than is in
your knowledge to dream of.

Will. Sir, know you this glove?

Flu. Know the glove? I know, the glove is a
glove.

Will. I know this; and thus I challenge it.

[Strikes him.

Flu. 'Sblud, an arrant traitor, as any 's in the
universal 'orld, or in France, or in England.

Gow. How now, sir? you villain!

Will. Do you think I 'll be forsworn?

Flu. Stand away, captain Gower; I will give
treason his payment into plows, I warrant you.

Will. I am no traitor.

Flu. That 's a lie in thy throat.—I charge you
in his majesty's name, apprehend him; he 's a
friend of the duke Alençon's.

Enter WARWICK *and* GLOSTER.

War. How now, how now! what 's the matter?

Flu. My lord of Warwick, here is (praised be
Got for it!) a most contagious treason come to
light, look you, as you shall desire in a summer's
day. Here is his majesty.

107   849

Enter King Henry *and* Exeter.

K. Hen. How now, what 's the matter?

Flu. My liege, here is a villain, and a traitor, that, look your grace, has struck the glove which your majesty is take out of the helmet of Alençon.

Will. My liege, this was my glove; here is the fellow of it: and he, that I gave it to in change, promised to wear it in his cap; I promised to strike him, if he did: I met this man with my glove in his cap, and I have been as good as my word.

Flu. Your majesty hear now, (saving your majesty's manhood,) what an arrant, rascally, beggarly, lousy knave it is: I hope, your majesty is pear me testimony, and witness, and avouchments, that this is the glove of Alençon, that your majesty is give me, in your conscience now.

K. Hen. Give me thy glove, soldier: Look, here is the fellow of it. 'T was I, indeed, thou promisedst to strike; and thou hast given me most bitter terms.

Flu. An please your majesty, let his neck answer for it, if there is any martial law in the 'orld.

K. Hen. How canst thou make me satisfaction?

Will. All offences, my liege, come from the heart: never came any from mine, that might offend your majesty.

K. Hen. It was ourself thou didst abuse.

Will. Your majesty came not like yourself: you appeared to me but as a common man; witness the night, your garments, your lowliness; and what your highness suffered under that shape, I beseech you, take it for your own fault, and not mine: for had you been as I took you for, I made no offence; therefore, I beseech your highness, pardon me.

K. Hen. Here, uncle Exeter, fill this glove with crowns,

And give it to this fellow.—Keep it, fellow:
And wear it for an honour in thy cap,
Till I do challenge it.—Give him the crowns:—
And, captain, you must needs be friends with him.

Flu. By this day and this light, the fellow has mettle enough in his belly:—Hold, there is twelve pence for you, and I pray you to serve God, and keep you out of prawls, and prabbles, and quarrels, and dissensions, and, I warrant you, it is the petter for you.

Will. I will none of your money.

Flu. It is with a goot will; I can tell you, it

will serve you to mend your shoes: Come, wherefore should you be so pashful; your shoes is not so goot: 't is a goot silling, I warrant you, or I will change it.

Enter an English Herald.

K. Hen. Now, herald: are the dead number'd?

Her. Here is the number of the slaughter'd French. [*Delivers a Paper.*

K. Hen. What prisoners of good sort are taken, uncle?

Exe. Charles duke of Orleans, nephew to the king;
John duke of Bourbon, and lord Bouciqualt:
Of other lords, and barons, knights, and 'squires,
Full fifteen hundred, besides common men.

K. Hen. This note doth tell me of ten thousand French,
That in the field lie slain: of princes, in this number,
And nobles bearing banners, there lie dead
One hundred twenty-six: added to these,
Of knights, esquires, and gallant gentlemen,
Eight thousand and four hundred; of the which,
Five hundred were but yesterday dubb'd knights:
So that, in these ten thousand they have lost,
There are but sixteen hundred mercenaries;
The rest are—princes, barons, lords, knights, 'squires,
And gentlemen of blood and quality.
The names of those their nobles that lie dead,
Charles De-la-Bret, high constable of France;
Jaques of Chatillon, admiral of France;
The master of the cross-bows, lord Rambures;
Great-master of France, the brave sir Guischard Dauphin;
John duke of Alençon; Antony duke of Brabant,
The brother to the duke of Burgundy;
And Edward duke of Bar: of lusty earls,
Grandpré, and Roussi, Fauconberg, and Foix,
Beaumont, and Marle, Vaudemont, and Lestrale.
Here was a royal fellowship of death!——
Where is the number of our English dead?
[*Herald presents another Paper.*
Edward the duke of York, the earl of Suffolk,
Sir Richard Ketly, Davy Gam, esquire:[9]
None else of name; and, of all other men,
But five and twenty. O God, thy arm was here,
And not to us, but to thy arm alone,
Ascribe we all.—When, without stratagem,
But in plain shock, and even play of battle,
Was ever known so great and little loss,

On one part and on the other!—Take it, God,
For it is only thine!
 Exe.   'T is wonderful!
 K. Hen. Come, go we in procession to the
  village:
And be it death proclaimed through our host,
To boast of this, or take that praise from God,
Which is his only.
 Flu. Is it not lawful, an please your majesty, to
tell how many is killed?

K. Hen. Yes, captain; but with this acknow-
 ledgment,
That God fought for us.
 Flu. Yes, my conscience, he did us great goot.
 K. Hen. Do we all holy rites;"
Let there be sung *Non nobis*, and *Te Deum*.
The dead with charity enclos'd in clay,
We 'll then to Calais; and to England then;
Where ne'er from France arriv'd more happy men.
         [*Exeunt.*

ACT V.

Enter Chorus.

 Chor. Vouchsafe to those that have not read
  the story,
That I may prompt them: and of such as have,
I humbly pray them to admit the excuse
Of time, of numbers, and due course of things,
Which cannot in their huge and proper life
Be here presented. Now we bear the king
Toward Calais: grant him there: there seen,
Heave him away upon your winged thoughts,
Athwart the sea: Behold, the English beach
Pales in the flood with men, with wives, and boys,
Whose shouts and claps out-voice the deep-mouth'd
  sea,
Which, like a mighty whiffler 'fore the king,
Seems to prepare his way: so let him land;
And, solemnly, see him set on to London.
So swift a pace hath thought, that even now
You may imagine him upon Blackheath:
Where that his lords desire him, to have borne
His bruised helmet, and his bended sword,
Before him, through the city: he forbids it,
Being free from vainness and self-glorious pride;
Giving full trophy, signal, and ostent,
Quite from himself, to God. But now behold,
In the quick forge and workinghouse of thought,
How London doth pour out her citizens!
The mayor, and all his brethren, in best sort,—
Like to the senators of the antique Rome,
With the plebeians swarming at their heels,—
Go forth, and fetch their conquering Cæsar in:
As, by a lower but by loving likelihood,

Were now the general of our gracious empress"
(As, in good time, he may,) from Ireland coming,
Bringing rebellion broached on his sword,
How many would the peaceful city quit,
To welcome him? much more, and much more
  cause,
Did they this Harry. Now in London place
 him;
(As yet the lamentation of the French
Invites the king of England's stay at home:
The emperor 's coming in behalf of France,
To order peace between them;) and omit
All the occurrences, whatever chanc'd,
Till Harry's back-return again to France;
There must we bring him; and myself have play'd
The interim, by remembering you—'t is past.
Then brook abridgment; and your eyes advance
After your thoughts, straight back again to
 France.   [*Exit.*

SCENE I.—France. *An English Court of Guard.*

Enter Fluellen *and* Gower.

 Gow. Nay, that 's right: but why wear you
your leek to-day? Saint Davy's day is past.
 Flu. There is occasions and causes why and
wherefore in all things: I will tell you, as my
friend, captain Gower: The rascally, scald, beggarly, lousy, pragging knave, Pistol,—which you
and yourself, and all the 'orld, know to be no
petter than a fellow, look you now, of no merits,
—he is come to me, and prings me pread and salt
yesterday, look you, and bid me eat my leek: it

was in a place where I could not breed no con-
entions with him; but I will be so bold as to
wear it in my cap till I see him once again, and
then I will tell him a little piece of my desires.

Enter PISTOL.

Gow. Why, here he comes, swelling like a tur-
key-cock.

Flu. 'T is no matter for his swellings, nor his
turkey-cocks.—Got pless you, ancient Pistol! you
scurvy, lousy knave, Got pless you!

Pist. Ha! art thou Bedlam? dost thou thirst,
base Trojan,
To have me fold up Parca's fatal web?
Hence! I am qualmish at the smell of leek.

Flu. I peseech you heartily, scurvy lousy knave,
at my desires, and my requests, and my petitions,
to eat, look you, this leek; because, look you, you
do not love it, nor your affections, and your appe-
tites, and your digestions, does not agree with it,
I would desire you to eat it.

Pist. Not for Cadwallader, and all his goats.

Flu. There is one goat for you.   [*Strikes him.*]
Will you be so goot, scald knave, as eat it?

Pist. Base Trojan, thou shalt die.

Flu. You say very true, scald knave, when
Got's will is: I will desire you to live in the
mean time, and eat your victuals; come, there is
sauce for it.   [*Striking him again.*]   You called
me yesterday, mountain-squire; but I will make
you to-day a squire of low degree.   I pray you,
fall to: if you can mock a leek, you can eat a
leek.

Gow. Enough, captain: you have astonish'd him.

Flu. I say, i will make him eat some part of
my leek, or I will peat his pate four days:—Pite,
I pray you; it is goot for your green wound, and
your ploody coxcomb.

Pist. Must I bite?

Flu. Yes, certainly; and out of doubt, and out
of questions too, and ambiguities.

Pist. By this leek, I will most horribly revenge:
I eat, and eke I swear—

Flu. Eat, I pray you: Will you have some
more sauce to your leek? there is not enough leek
to swear by.

Pist. Quiet thy cudgel; thou dost see, I eat.

Flu. Much goot do you, scald knave, heartily.
Nay, 'pray you, throw none away; the skin is
goot for your proken coxcomb.   When you take
occasions to see leeks hereafter, I pray you, mock
at them; that is all.

852

Pist. Good.

Flu. Ay, leeks is goot:—Hold you, there is a
groat to heal your pate.

Pist. Me a groat!

Flu. Yes, verily, and in truth, you shall take
it; or I have another leek in my pocket, which
you shall eat.

Pist. I take thy groat, in earnest of revenge.

Flu. If I owe you any thing, I will pay you in
cudgels; you shall be a woodmonger, and buy
nothing of me but cudgels.   God be wi' you, and
keep you, and heal your pate.   [*Exit.*

Pist. All hell shall stir for this.

Gow. Go, go; you are a counterfeit cowardly
knave.   Will you mock at an ancient tradition,—
begun upon an honourable respect, and worn as a
memorable trophy of predeceased valour,—and
dare not avouch in your deeds any of your words?
I have seen you glecking and galling at this gentleman twice or thrice.   You thought, because he
could not speak English in the native garb, he
could not therefore handle an English cudgel:
you find it otherwise; and, henceforth, let a Welsh
correction teach you a good English condition.
Fare ye well.   [*Exit.*

Pist. Doth fortune play the huswife with me
now?
News have I, that my Nell is dead i' the spital
Of malady of France;
And there my rendezvous is quite cut off.
Old I do wax; and from my weary limbs
Honour is cudgell'd.   Well, bawd will I turn,
And something lean to cutpurse of quick hand.
To England will I steal, and there I 'll steal:
And patches will I get unto these scars,
And swear, I got them in the Gallia wars.   [*Exit.*

SCENE II.—*Troyes in Champagne.   An Apartment in the French King's Palace.*

Enter, at one Door, KING HENRY, BEDFORD,
GLOSTER, EXETER, WARWICK, WESTMORELAND,
and other Lords; at another, the FRENCH KING,
QUEEN ISABEL, *the* PRINCESS KATHARINE, *Lords,
Ladies, &c., the* DUKE OF BURGUNDY, *and his*
Train.

K. Hen. Peace to this meeting, wherefore we
are met!
Unto our brother France,—and to our sister,
Health and fair time of day:—joy and good
wishes
To our most fair and princely cousin Katharine,

And (as a branch and member of this royalty,
By whom this great assembly is contriv'd,)
We do salute you, duke of Burgundy:—
And, princes French, and peers, health to you all!

Fr. King. Right joyous are we to behold your
face,
Most worthy brother England; fairly met:—
So are you, princes English, every one.

Q. Isa. So happy be the issue, brother England,
Of this good day, and of this gracious meeting,
As we are now glad to behold your eyes,
Your eyes, which hitherto have borne in them
Against the French, that met them in their bent,
The fatal balls of murdering basilisks:
The venom of such looks, we fairly hope,
Have lost their quality; and that this day
Shall change all griefs, and quarrels, into love.

K. Hen. To cry amen to that, thus we appear.

Q. Isa. You English princes all, I do salute you.

Bur. My duty to you both, on equal love,
Great kings of France and England! That I have
labour'd
With all my wits, my pains, and strong en-
deavours,
To bring your most imperial majesties
Unto this bar and royal interview,
Your mightiness on both parts best can witness.
Since then my office hath so far prevail'd,
That, face to face, and royal eye to eye,
You have congreeted; let it not disgrace me,
If I demand, before this royal view,
What rub, or what impediment, there is,
Why that the naked, poor, and mangled peace,
Dear nurse of arts, plenties, and joyful births,
Should not, in this best garden of the world,
Our fertile France, put up her lovely visage?
Alas! she hath from France too long been chas'd;
And all her husbandry doth lie on heaps,
Corrupting in its own fertility.
Her vine, the merry cheerer of the heart,
Unpruned dies: her hedges even-pleach'd,—
Like prisoners wildly over-grown with hair,
Put forth disorder'd twigs: her fallow leas
The darnel, hemlock, and rank fumitory,
Doth root upon; while that the coulter rusts,
That should deracinate such savagery:
The even mead, that erst brought sweetly forth
The freckled cowslip, burnet, and green clover,
Wanting the scythe, all uncorrected, rank,
Conceives by idleness; and nothing teems,
But hateful docks, rough thistles, keeksies, burs,
Losing both beauty and utility.

And as our vineyards, fallows, meads, and hedges,
Defective in their natures, grow to wildness;
Even so our houses, and ourselves, and children
Have lost, or do not learn, for want of time,
The sciences that should become our country;
But grow, like savages,—as soldiers will,
That nothing do but meditate on blood,—
To swearing, and stern looks, diffus'd attire,
And every thing that seems unnatural.
Which to reduce into our former favour,
You are assembled: and my speech entreats,
That I may know the let, why gentle peace
Should not expel these inconveniences,
And bless us with her former qualities.

K. Hen. If, duke of Burgundy, you would the
peace,
Whose want gives growth to the imperfections
Which you have cited, you must buy that peace
With full accord to all our just demands;
Whose tenors and particular effects
You have, enscheduled briefly, in your hands.

Bur. The king hath heard them; to the which,
as yet,
There is no answer made.

K. Hen.   Well then, the peace,
Which you before so urg'd, lies in his answer.

Fr. King. I have but with a cursorary eye
O'er-glanc'd the articles: pleaseth your grace
To appoint some of your council presently
To sit with us once more, with better heed
To re-survey them, we will, suddenly,
Pass or accept, and peremptory answer.

K. Hen. Brother, we shall.—Go, uncle Exeter,—
And brother Clarence,—and you, brother Glos-
ter,—
Warwick,—and Huntingdon,—go with the king
And take with you free power, to ratify,
Augment, or alter, as your wisdoms best
Shall see advantageable for our dignity,
Any thing in, or out of, our demands;
And we'll consign thereto.—Will you, fair sister,
Go with the princes, or stay here with us?

Q. Isa. Our gracious brother, I will go with
them;
Haply, a woman's voice may do some good,
When articles, too nicely urg'd, be stood on.

K. Hen. Yet leave our cousin Katharine here
with us;
She is our capital demand, compris'd
Within the fore-rank of our articles.

Q. Isa. She hath good leave.

[*Exeunt all but* HEN.. KATH., *and her gentlewoman*

K. Hen.   Fair Katharine, and most fair!
Will you vouchsafe to teach a soldier terms,
Such as will enter at a lady's ear,
And plead his love-suit to her gentle heart?

Kath. Your majesty shall mock at me; I cannot speak your England.

K. Hen. O fair Katharine, if you will love me soundly with your French heart, I will be glad to hear you confess it brokenly with your English tongue. Do you like me, Kate?

Kath. Pardonnez moy, I cannot tell vat is—like me.

K. Hen. An angel is like you, Kate; and you are like an angel.

Kath. Que dit-il? que je suis semblable à les anges?

Alice. Ouy, vrayment, (sauf vostre grace) ainsi dit il.

K. Hen. I said so, dear Katharine; and I must not blush to affirm it.

Kath. O bon Dieu! les langues des hommes sont pleines des tromperies.

K. Hen. What says she, fair one? that the tongues of men are full of deceits?

Alice. Ouy; dat de tongues of de mans is so full of deceits: dat is de princess.

K. Hen. The princess is the better Englishwoman. I' faith, Kate, my wooing is fit for thy understanding: I am glad thou canst speak no better English; for, if thou couldst, thou wouldst find me such a plain king, that thou wouldst think, I had sold my farm to buy my crown. I know no ways to mince it in love, but directly to say—I love you: then, if you urge me farther than to say—Do you in faith? I wear out my suit. Give me your answer; i' faith, do; and so clap hands, and a bargain: How say you, lady?

Kath. Sauf vostre honneur, me understand well.

K. Hen. Marry, if you would put me to verses, or to dance for your sake, Kate, why you undid me: for the one, I have neither words nor measure; and for the other, I have no strength in measure, yet a reasonable measure in strength. If I could win a lady at leap-frog, or by vaulting into my saddle with my armour on my back, under the correction of bragging be it spoken, I should quickly leap into a wife. Or, if I might buffet for my love, or bound my horse for her favours, I could lay on like a butcher, and sit like a jack-an-apes, never off: but, before God, I cannot look greenly, nor gasp out my eloquence, no,

I have no cunning in protestation; only downright oaths, which I never use till urged, nor never break for urging. If thou canst love a fellow of this temper, Kate, whose face is not worth sunburning, that never looks in his glass for love of any thing he sees there, let thine eye by thy cook. I speak to thee plain soldier: if thou canst love me for this, take me; if not, to say to thee—that I shall die, is true; but—for thy love, by the Lord, no; yet I love thee too. And while thou livest, dear Kate, take a fellow of plain and uncoined constancy; for he perforce must do thee right, because he hath not the gift to woo in other places: for these fellows of infinite tongue, that can rhyme themselves into ladies' favours,—they do always reason themselves out again. What! a speaker is but a prater; a rhyme is but a ballad. A good leg will fall; a straight back will stoop; a black beard will turn white; a curled pate will grow bald; a fair face will wither; a full eye will wax hollow: but a good heart, Kate, is the sun and moon; or, rather the sun, and not the moon; for it shines bright, and never changes, but keeps his course truly. If thou would have such a one, take me: And take me, take a soldier; take a soldier, take a king: And what sayest thou then to my love? speak, my fair, and fairly, I pray thee.

Kath. Is it possible dat I should love de enemy of France?

K. Hen. No; it is not possible, you should love the enemy of France, Kate; but, in loving me, you should love the friend of France; for I love France so well, that I will not part with a village of it; I will have it all mine: and, Kate, when France is mine, and I am yours, then yours is France, and you are mine.

Kath. I cannot tell vat is dat.

K. Hen. No, Kate? I will tell thee in French; which, I am sure, will hang upon my tongue, like a new-married wife about her husband's neck, hardly to be shook off. *Quand j'ay possession de France, et quand vous avez le possession de moi,* (let me see, what then? Saint Dennis be my speed!)—*donc vostre est France, et vous estes mienne.* It is as easy for me, Kate, to conquer the kingdom, as to speak so much more French: I shall never move thee in French, unless it be to laugh at me.

Kath. Sauf vostre honneur, le François que vous parlez, est meilleur que l'Anglois lequel je parle.

K. Hen. No, 'faith, is 't not, Kate: but thy speaking of my tongue, and I thine, most truly falsely, must needs be granted to be much at one. But, Kate, dost thou understand thus much English? Canst thou love me?

Kath. I cannot tell.

K. Hen. Can any of your neighbours tell, Kate? I 'll ask them. Come, I know, thou lovest me: and at night when you come into your closet, you 'll question this gentlewoman about me; and I know, Kate, you will, to her, dispraise those parts in me, that you love with your heart: but, good Kate, mock me mercifully; the rather, gentle princess, because I love thee cruelly. If ever thou be'st mine, Kate, (as I have a saving faith within me, tells me,—thou shalt.) I get thee with scambling, and thou must therefore needs prove a good soldier-breeder: Shall not thou and I, between Saint Dennis and Saint George, compound a boy, half French, half English, that shall go to Constantinople, and take the Turk by the beard? shall we not? what sayest thou, my fair flower-de-luce?

Kath. I do not know dat.

K. Hen. No; 't is hereafter to know, but now to promise: do but now promise, Kate, you will endeavour for your French part of such a boy; and, for my English moiety, take the word of a king and a bachelor. How answer you, *la plus belle Katharine du monde, mon tres chere et divine dæsse?*

Kath. Your *majesté 'ave fausse* French enough to deceive the most *sage damoiselle* dat is en *France.*

K. Hen. Now, fye upon my false French! By mine honour, in true English, I love thee, Kate: by which honour I dare not swear, thou lovest me, yet my blood begins to flatter me that thou dost, notwithstanding the poor and untempering effect of my visage. Now beshrew my father's ambition! he was thinking of civil wars when he got me; therefore was I created with a stubborn outside, with an aspect of iron, that, when I come to woo ladies, I fright them. But, in faith, Kate, the elder I wax, the better I shall appear: my comfort is, that old age, that ill layer up of beauty, can do no more spoil upon my face; thou hast me, if thou hast me, at the worst; and thou shalt wear me, if thou wear me, better and better: And therefore tell me, most fair Katharine, will you have me? Put off your maiden blushes; avouch the thoughts of your heart with the looks of an

empress; take me by the hand, and say—Harry of England, I am thine: which word thou shalt no sooner bless mine ear withal, but I will tell thee aloud—England is thine, Ireland is thine, France is thine, and Henry Plantagenet is thine; who, though I speak it before his face, if he be not fellow with the best king, thou shalt find the best king of good fellows. Come, your answer in broken music; for thy voice is music, and thy English broken: therefore, queen of all, Katharine, break thy mind to me in broken English, Wilt thou have me?

Kath. Dat is, as it shall please de *roy mon pere.*

K. Hen. Nay, it will please him well, Kate; it shall please him, Kate.

Kath. Den it shall also content me.

K. Hen. Upon that I will kiss your hand, and I call you—my queen.

Kath. Laissez, mon seigneur, laissez, laissez: ma foy, je ne veux point que vous abbaissez votre grandeur, en baisant la main d'une vostre indigne serviteure; excusez moy, je vous supplie, mon tres puissant seigneur.

K. Hen. Then I will kiss your lips, Kate.

Kath. Les dames et damoiselles, pour estre baisées devant leur nopces, il n'est pas le coûtume de France.

K. Hen. Madam my interpreter, what says she?

Alice. Dat it is not be de fashion *pour les la-* dies of France,—I cannot tell what is, *baiser, en* English.

K. Hen. To kiss.

Alice. Your majesty *entendre* better *que moy.*

K. Hen. It is not the fashion for the maids in France to kiss before they are married, would she say?

Alice. Oui, vrayment.

K. Hen. O, Kate, nice customs curt'sy to great kings. Dear Kate, you and I cannot be confined within the weak list of a country's fashion: we are the makers of manners, Kate; and the liberty that follows our places, stops the mouths of all find-faults; as I will do yours, for upholding the nice fashion of your country, in denying me a kiss: therefore, patiently, and yielding. [*Kissing her.*] You have witchcraft in your lips, Kate: there is more eloquence in a sugar touch of them, than in the tongues of the French council; and they should sooner persuade Harry of England, than a general petition of monarchs. Here comes your father.

Enter the FRENCH KING *and* QUEEN, BURGUNDY,
BEDFORD, GLOSTER, EXETER, WESTMORELAND,
and other French and English Lords.

Bur. God save your majesty! my royal cousin,
teach you our princess English?

K. Hen. I would have her learn, my fair cousin, how perfectly I love her; and that is good English.

Bur. Is she not apt?

K. Hen. Our tongue is rough, coz; and my condition is not smooth; so that, having neither the
voice nor the heart of flattery about me, I cannot
so conjure up the spirit of love in her, that he will
appear in his true likeness.

Bur. Pardon the frankness of my mirth, if I
answer you for that. If you would conjure in her,
you must make a circle: if conjure up love in her
in his true likeness, he must appear naked, and
blind: Can you blame her then, being a maid yet
rosed over with the virgin crimson of modesty, if
she deny the appearance of a naked blind boy in
her naked seeing self? It were, my lord, a hard
condition for a maid to consign to.

K. Hen. Yet they do wink, and yield; as love
is blind, and enforces.

Bur. They are then excused, my lord, when
they see not what they do.

K. Hen. Then, good my lord, teach your cousin
to consent to winking.

Bur. I will wink on her to consent, my lord, if
you will teach her to know my meaning: for
maids, well summered and warm kept, are like flies
at Bartholomew-tide, blind, though they have
their eyes; and then they will endure handling,
which before would not abide looking on.

K. Hen. This moral ties me over to time, and
a hot summer; and so I will catch the fly, your
cousin, in the latter end, and she must be blind too.

Bur. As love is, my lord, before it loves.

K. Hen. It is so: and you may, some of you,
thank love for my blindness; who cannot see
many a fair French city, for one fair French maid
that stands in my way.

Fr. King. Yes, my lord, you see them perspec-
tively, the cities turned into a maid; for they are
all girdled with maiden walls, that war hath never
entered.

K. Hen. Shall Kate be my wife?

Fr. King. So please you.

K. Hen. I am content; so the maiden cities you
talk of, may wait on her: so the maid that stood

in the way of my wish, shall show me the way to
my will.

Fr. King. We have consented to all terms of
reason.

K. Hen. Is 't so, my lords of England?

West. The king hath granted every article:
His daughter, first; and then, in sequel, all,
According to their firm proposed natures.

Exe. Only, he hath not yet subscribed this:—
Where your majesty demands,—That the king of
France, having any occasion to write for matter of
grant, shall name your highness in this form, and
with this addition, in French,—*Notre tres cher fils
Henry roy d'Angleterre, heretier de France;* and
thus in Latin,—*Præclarissimus filius noster Hen-
ricus, rex Angliæ, et hæres Franciæ.*

Fr. King. Not this I have not, brother, so denied,
But your request shall make me let it pass.

K. Hen. I pray you then, in love and dear
alliance,
Let that one article rank with the rest:
And, thereupon, give me your daughter.

Fr. King. Take her, fair son; and from her
blood raise up
Issue to me: that the contending kingdoms
Of France and England, whose very shores look
pale
With envy of each other's happiness,
May cease their hatred; and this dear conjunction
Plant neighbourhood and christian-like accord
In their sweet bosoms, that never war advance
His bleeding sword 'twixt England and fair France.

All. Amen!

K. Hen. Now welcome, Kate:—and bear me
witness all,
That here I kiss her as my sovereign queen.
　　　　　　　　　　　　　　　　　[*Flourish.*

Q. Isa. God, the best maker of all marriages,
Combine your hearts in one, your realms in one!
As man and wife, being two, are one in love,
So be there 'twixt your kingdoms such a spousal,
That never may ill office, or fell jealousy,
Which troubles oft the bed of blessed marriage,
Thrust in between the paction of these kingdoms,
To make divorce of their incorporate league;
That English may as French, French Englishmen,
Receive each other!—God speak this amen!

All. Amen!

K. Hen. Prepare we for our marriage:—on
which day,
My lord of Burgundy, we 'll take your oath,
And all the peers', for surety of our leagues.—

856

Then shall I swear to Kate, and you to me;
And may your oaths well kept and prosp'rous be!
　　　　　　　　　　　　　　　[Exeunt.

Enter Chorus.

Thus far, with rough, and all unable pen,
　Our bending author hath pursued the story;
In little room confining mighty men,
　Mangling by starts the full course of their glory.
Small time; but, in that small, most greatly liv'd

This star of England: fortune made his sword!
By which the world's best garden he achiev'd,
　And of it left his son imperial lord.
Henry the Sixth, in infant bands crown'd king
　Of France and England, did this king succeed;
Whose state so many had the managing,
　That they lost France, and made his England
　　　bleed:
Which oft our stage hath shown; and, for their sake,
In your fair minds let this acceptance take. [Exit.

NOTES TO KING HENRY THE FIFTH.

¹ *On your imaginary forces work.*

Imaginary is used for *imaginative*.

² *My lord, I'll tell you,—that self bill is urg'd.*

The archbishop refers to a bill which was proposed by the commons, when applied to by Henry IV., to grant supplies. It enacted that the king should be authorized to seize all the temporalities of the church, and employ them as a perpetual fund for the service of the state. They estimated the ecclesiastical revenues at 485,000 marks a year, and as being derived from 18,400 ploughs of land. They proposed to divide this property among fifteen new earls, 1,500 knights, 6,000 esquires, and 100 hospitals; which still left a surplus of £20,000 a-year, which the king might apply to his own purposes. The clerical functions they said would be better performed by 15,000 parish priests with a salary each of seven marks a-year. The clergy were greatly alarmed at this proposed aggression, and made an appeal to the king, who thought it prudent to discountenance the scheme, and reprehend the projectors of it.

Crescive, i. e., constantly increasing.

³ *They know your grace hath cause, and means, and might; So hath your highness.*

The meaning of this passage is rendered clear by placing an emphasis on the last *hath*; i. e., 'your highness hath also what they think and know you to have.'

⁴ *They of those marches.*

The *marches* are the borders, the limits or confines. Hence the *Lords Marchers,* i. e., the lords presidents of the marches.

Doth keep in one concent.

Concent is connected harmony in general, and not confined to any specific consonance.

That all the courts of France will be disturb'd with chaces.

A *chace* at tennis is that spot where a ball falls, beyond which the adversary must strike his ball to gain a point or *chace*. The king probably quibbles on the word, its secondary meaning being that he will play such a game in France that the whole country will be disturbed by the flight and chasing of armies.

⁸ *We never valued this poor seat of England.*

The *seat* is the throne; we never, says the prince, aspired to royal state and honours, and therefore lived from the court in "barbarous license;" but since this honour has fallen on me, I will act like a king.

⁹ *Hath turn'd his balls to gun-stones.*

When ordnance was first used, they discharged balls not of iron, but of stone. So Holinshed—"About seaven of the clocke marched forward the light pieces of ordnance, with stone and powder."

¹⁰ *While we force a play.*

To *force a play,* is to produce a play by bringing many incidents into a narrow compass. Heaping events closely together.

¹¹ *We'll not offend one stomach.*

You shall pass the sea in imagination only, therefore your stomachs will be undisturbed by the qualms of sea-sickness.

¹² *We'll be all three sworn brothers to France.*

That is, *in* France. In France they will live in communion as brothers.

¹³ *Will you shog off?*

A cant phrase, meaning will you go. In Beaumont and Fletcher's *Coxcomb*—

Come, pr'ythee, let us *shog* off.

¹⁴ *I am not Barbason; you cannot conjure me.*

Barbason is the name of a demon mentioned in *The Merry Wives of Windsor.* See note 110 to that play. The high-sounding nonsense of Pistol's speech reminds Nym of the obscure and extravagant language of conjurers.

¹⁵ *And on his more advice we pardon him.*

More advice is better reflection on ————————

¹⁶ *Who are the late commissioners?*

This is a loose sentence, ———————— ing to be, who are the persons lately appointed commissioners.

¹⁷ *He might return to vasty Tartar.*

That is, *Tartarus,* the fabled place of ——————

"A parted even just between twelve and one, e'en at turning o' the tide.

It is a very old superstition, and is at this day common in some seaport towns and villages near the coast, that dying people usually breathe their last at the ebb of the tide.

But then he was rheumatic.

Shakespeare sometimes uses this word for peevish or splenetic, but Mrs. Quickley doubtless means *lunatic*.

Which of a weak and niggardly projection.

We should, I think, read *oft* for *of*; the sense would then be clear. Projection is used as *preparation*.

The rivage, i. e., the bank or shore.

O'erhand and jutty his confounded base.

To *o'erhand and jutty* is to overhang and jut out from; the rock is described as projecting into the sea; *his confounded base* is his worn or wasted base.

I have not a case of lives.

That is, a pair of lives; as we say a *case* of pistols, a brace or pair.

I knew, by that piece of service, the men would carry coals.

That is, put up with insults. See note 2, to *Romeo and Juliet.*

Is dight himself four yards under the counter-mines.

Fluellen means that the enemy had dug counter-mines four yards under the mines.

In that nook-shotten isle of Albion.

A *nook-shotten* country is a country that shoots out promontories and nooks of land into the sea. The coast-line of England is very irregular.

But keeps the bridge most valiantly.

In Henry's return to Calais, after he had passed the river Soane, the French endeavoured to intercept him by attempting to break down the only bridge there was over the deep and rapid river of Ternois. But Henry having notice of their design, sent a body of troops in advance, who drove away the French, and preserved the bridge till the whole of the army arrived and passed over it.

For he hath stolen a pix, and hanged must 'a be.

A *pix* is a small chest in which the consecrated host was kept. Hall says—" A foolish soldier stole a pix out of a church, and unreverently did eat the holy hostes within the same contained."

And what a beard of the general's cut.

Our ancestors were very particular respecting the fashion of their beards, and a certain cut was appropriated to the soldier, the bishop, the judge, &c. The following extract from an old ballad, inserted in a miscellany, entitled *Le Prince d'Amour*, 8vo, 1660, gives some curious information upon this subject:—

> Now of beards there be
> Such a companie,
> Of fashions such a throng,

That it is very hard
To treat of the beard,
Though it be ne'er so long.

* * * *

The *stiletto* beard,
O, it makes me afeard,
It is so sharp beneath ;
For he that doth place
A dagger in his face,
What wears he in his sheeth ?

* * * *

The *soldier's* beard
Doth match in this herd,
In figure like a *spade* ;
With which he will make
His enemies quake,
To think their grave is made, &c.

You rode like a kerne of Ireland, your French hose off, and in your strait trousers.

Trousers are a kind of breeches made to fit close to the body; it is said the kerns of Ireland wore no breeches, any more than the Scotch highlanders; therefore *strait trousers* probably means in their naked skin, which sits close to them. In this sense the Dauphin evidently uses the word.

Do the low-rated English play at dice.

That is, not play with them, but play at dice for them.

That we should dress us fairly for our end.

Dress, for *address*. That we should prepare our minds for death, our souls for heaven.

Legerity, i. e., lightness, nimbleness.

Mess, you'll pay him then.

That is, bring him to account, punish him; though *pay*, in old language, usually meant to beat or thrash.

The tucket-sonnance.

That is, an introductory flourish on the trumpet; he speaks as in contempt of the easiness of the conquest.

The gimmal bit.

Gimmal is, in the western counties, a ring; a *gimmal bit* is, therefore, a bit of which the parts played one within another. *Gimmal* or *gimmal'd* mail, means armour composed of links like those of a chain, which by its flexibility fitted better to the shape of the body than any other kind of defensive contrivance.

The feast of Crispian.

The battle of Agincourt was fought upon the 25th of October, 1415, St. Crispin's day. The legend upon which this is founded is as follows :—" Crispinus and Crispianus were brethren born at Rome ; from whence they travelled to Soissons, in France, about the year 303, to propagate the Christian religion ; but because they would not be changeable to others for their maintenance, they exercised the trade of shoemakers: but the governor of the town discovering them to be Christians, ordered them to be beheaded. From which time the shoemakers made choice of them for their tutelar saints."

The Duke of York.

This is the same person who appears in Richard the Second by the title of Duke of Aumerle. After a life of intrigue, and having been in danger of losing his head on the scaffold, he at length perishes on the field of battle.

" Thou diest on point of fox.

Fox is an old cant word for sword. Thus, in *The Devil's Charter*, 1607 :—

> And by this awful cross upon my blade,
> And by this *fox* which stinks of Pagan blood.

" For I will fetch thy rim out at thy throat.

The word *rim* has given rise to much conjecture; Warburton would read,—

> Or, I will fetch thy *ransome* out of thy throat.

But although this restores sense, it destroys the metre, and Shakespeare was not likely to have written so unmusical a line. Mr. Steevens says.—"It appears from Sir Arthur Gorge's translation of *Lucan*, 1614, that some part of the intestines was anciently called the *rim.—Lucan*, B. i.

> The slender *rimmer* too weake to part
> The boyling liver from the heart.

I believe it is now called the *diaphragm*, in human creatures, and the skirt or midriff in beasts; but still, in some places, the rim."

" Is that a ton of moys?

Moy is a piece of money; whence *moi d'or*, or *moi* of gold.

880

" Thou this roaring devil of the old play.

The boy compares Pistol to the devil in the old moralities, because he is as noisy, turbulent, and vain-glorious.

" Davy Gam, esquire.

This was a brave Welsh gentleman who saved the King's life on the field. Being sent by Henry before the battle to reconnoitre the enemy and attempt to discover their numbers, he returned with this report:—"May it please you, my liege, there are enough to be killed, enough to be taken prisoners, and enough to run away."

" Do we all holy rites.

According to Hollinshed,—The King, when he saw no appearance of enemies, caused the retreat to be blown, and gathering his army together, gave thanks to Almighty God for so happy a victory, causing his prelates and chaplains to sing this psalme, *In exitu Israel de Egypto*; and commanding every man to kneele downe on the grounde, at this verse, *Non nobis, Domine, non nobis, sed nomini tuo da gloriam*; which done, he caused *Te Deum* and certain anthems to be sung, giving laud and praise to God, and not boasting of his own force, or any humaine power."

" Were now the general of our gracious empress.

The Earl of Essex, in the reign of Elizabeth.

King Henry the Sixth.

(PART THE FIRST.)

THE question of the authorship of this play has been previously considered. Whoever was its author, the earlier scenes of this drama are most artistically adapted to introduce the misrule and dark and bloody struggles of the turbulent reign of Henry. The iron hand of the hero of Agincourt being laid in the grave, and the enthusiastic patriotism, which was warmed into active existence by his gorgeous and triumphant career, having subsided into the calm stream of common life, the elements of discord break forth. The fierce contentions of Beaufort and Gloucester show the disordered state of the kingdom consequent upon the supremacy of a child, and are a natural prelude to the savage contests which afterwards took place under the name of the Wars of the Roses.

Talbot is a boldly drawn character; he resembles a grim armed giant, whose presence everywhere causes terror and flight, yet he is thoroughly English in his nature—that is, he possesses all those qualities which were prominent in the most just and patriotic warriors of this country in the fifteenth century. Terrible to his enemies, fierce and savage in war, he is yet mild and genial to his associates, while on his tenderness as a father the great interest of his character depends. The scene between him and the Countess of Auvergne is an admirable episode, full of life and vigour, and written by the pen of genius; if, according to the conjecture of Mr. Malone, either Greene or Peele was the author of this play, it is to be regretted that they have not left more such scenes for the admiration of posterity. The generosity of Talbot to the crafty but outwitted Frenchwoman, is the result of a noble spirit; a meaner general would probably have razed her castle to its foundations, or left it in flames, as a punishment for her perfidious abuse of the sacred laws of hospitality.

The brave Talbot is at last sacrificed through the dissensions and treachery of York and Somerset: each blames the other for neglect, but stands aloof himself; the intrepid general is surrounded without the walls of Bordeaux by forces immeasurably superior to his own, and, after performing prodigies of valour, is slain. Just before his death he has an interview with his son, whom after an absence of seven years he had sent for, to tutor in the strategies of war. The meeting is a melancholy one; certain death awaits them both, unless avoided by flight—the elder Talbot, grown grey in peril and in honour, counsels his son to escape, but will himself remain to meet his fate; the young hero will not stir from the side of his father, who eventually dies with the dead body of his son in his arms.

In the scene in the Temple Garden, the great Earl of Warwick is introduced—that Warwick whose after achievements gained for him the title of the "King-maker," and although he does not appear so prominently in this play, as in the two following ones, yet here we have the germs of his future character, and a very spirited and Shakesperian speech is uttered by him. Somerset and Plantagenet having disputed on some legal question, appeal to the Earl, who at first declines to side with either party, exclaiming,—

> Between two hawks, which flies the higher pitch,
> Between two dogs, which hath the deeper mouth,
> Between two blades, which bears the better temper,
> Between two horses, which doth bear him best,
> Between two girls, which hath the merriest eye,

> I have, perhaps, some shallow spirit of judgment:
> But in these nice sharp quillets of the law,
> Good faith, I am no wiser than a daw.

Something of the princely and chivalrous earl, whose hospitality was as royal and boundless as his wealth, and who kept so many retainers, that sometimes six oxen were eaten by them at a breakfast, is shadowed forth in this hearty and bounding speech. They who are conversant with the language of our poet, will need no argument to induce them to believe that it was the work of his pen. In this scene we have detailed the supposed origin of the two badges, the white rose and the red, afterwards worn by the rival houses of York and Lancaster.

The character of Joan la Pucelle, though it has not the finish of Shakespeare's later works, yet partakes of their strength. It is only to be regretted that he has attributed to satanic agency what was doubtless the result of pure patriotism and vivid religious enthusiasm; but the era of the poet was one of intense and obstinate superstition, when to express a disbelief in witchcraft was frequently deemed an act of impiety, and it is not to be expected that in his youth he should be emancipated from the errors of his time. But this unjust picture has given Schlegel occasion to say that "the wonderful saviour of her country, Joan of Arc, is portrayed by Shakespeare with an Englishman's prejudices." History has since done justice to her memory, and time has found the solution of her supposed miraculous influence. The inhabitants of the little hamlet where she was born were remarkable for their simplicity and their superstition; and the poor peasant girl, whom a pious education had ripened into a religious enthusiast, was led, while tending her flocks in solitude among the hills and pastures of a wild and picturesque country, to occupy herself with day-dreams concerning the ascetic and miraculous lives of the saints, and the wonderful heroism of the virgin martyrs. This sort of life led to its natural result in a fervent and susceptible mind; after a short time she was haunted by visions, and listened in ecstasy to the voices of spirits; angelic faces appeared to her surrounded by a halo of light and glory; amongst them were St. Catherine and St. Margaret, wearing crowns which glittered with celestial jewels, and these heavenly visitants spoke to her in voices which were sweeter than the softest music. They commanded her to deliver her country, and told her that she would be endowed with strength from heaven. The devoted enthusiast went to the king, declared her mission, liberated France, and was finally, with a cruelty at which humanity recoils, burnt at the stake for sorcery. It is to be wished that Shakespeare had taken a more lofty and generous view of her character. The family of this unhappy woman was ennobled by the monarch to whom she had rendered such important services, but he made no effort whatever to rescue from the hands of the English a heroine "to whom the more generous superstition of the ancients would have erected altars."

Viewed historically, there are some slight apologies to be made for the conduct of York in attempting to supplant Henry on the throne; but in the drama he stands convicted of complicated treachery and constant perjury. The feeble but generous king restores him to his rank and estates, which had been forfeited by the treason of his father, who was beheaded for a plot to assassinate Henry the Fifth. He promises eternal gratitude and allegiance, exclaiming—

> And so thrive Richard as thy foes may fall!
> And as my duty springs, so perish they
> That grudge one thought against your majesty!

Yet this very man, perceiving the imbecility of Henry, casts an evil eye unto the crown, and eventually he and his sons, after shedding the blood of nearly a hundred thousand Englishmen, exterminate the house of Lancaster, and place the sensual perjured Edward upon the throne.

In the early part of the play the young king does not appear, and when he does, it is only to make a miserable exhibition of his weakness and vacillation of mind; for, although contracted to another lady, he falls in love with Margaret merely from Suffolk's description of her personal charms, and thus becomes the dupe of that cunning courtier, who loves her himself. The play ends abruptly with Henry's dispatching Suffolk to France to woo Margaret for him, and the wily emissary speeds on his mission rejoicing in the probable success of his treachery. The date of this drama cannot be fixed with any degree of certainty, but it was probably one of the poet's earliest efforts.

PERSONS REPRESENTED.

KING HENRY THE SIXTH.
Appears, Act III. sc. 1, sc.4. Act IV. sc. 1. Act V. sc. 1; sc. 5.

DUKE OF GLOUCESTER, *Uncle to the King, and Protector.*
Appears, Act I. sc. 1; sc. 3. Act III. sc. 1; sc. 4. Act IV. sc. 1. Act V. sc. 1; sc. 5.

DUKE OF BEDFORD, *Uncle to the King, and Regent of France.*
Appears, Act I. sc. 1. Act II. sc. 1; sc. 2. Act III. sc. 2.

THOMAS BEAUFORT, *Duke of* Exeter, *Great-uncle to the King.*
Appears, Act I. sc. 1. Act III. sc. 1. Act IV. sc. 1. Act V. sc. 1; sc. 5.

HENRY BEAUFORT, *Great-uncle to the King, Bishop of* Winchester, *and afterwards Cardinal.*
Appears, Act I. sc. 1; sc. 3. Act III. sc. 1. Act IV. sc. 1. Act V. sc. 4.

RICHARD PLANTAGENET, *eldest Son of* Richard, *late Earl of Cambridge; afterwards Duke of York.*
Appears, Act II. sc. 4; sc. 5. Act III. sc. 1. Act IV. sc. 1; sc. 3. Act V. sc. 3; sc. 4.

EARL OF WARWICK.
Appears Act I. sc. 1. Act II. sc. 4. Act III. sc. 1. Act IV. sc. 1. Act V. sc. 4.

EARL OF SALISBURY.
Appears, Act I. sc. 4.

EARL OF SUFFOLK.
Appears, Act I. sc. 1. Act III. sc. 1. Act IV. sc. 1. Act V. sc. 1; sc. 5.

LORD TALBOT, *afterwards Earl of* Shrewsbury.
Appears, Act I. sc. 4; sc. 5. Act II. sc. 1; sc. 2; sc. 3. Act III. sc. 2; sc. 3; sc. 4. Act IV. sc. 1; sc. 2; sc. 5; sc. 6; sc. 7.

JOHN TALBOT, *his Son.*
Appears, Act IV. sc. 5; sc. 6; sc. 7.

EDMUND MORTIMER, *Earl of* March.
TWO OFFICERS OF THE TOWER, *his Keepers.*
Appear, Act II. sc. 5.

SIR JOHN FASTOLFE.
Appears, Act III. sc. 2. Act IV. sc. 1.

SIR WILLIAM LUCY.
Appears, Act IV. sc. 3; sc. 4; sc. 7.

SIR WILLIAM GLANSDALE.
SIR THOMAS GARGRAVE.
Appear, Act I. sc. 4.

MAYOR OF LONDON.
Appears, Act I. sc. 3. Act III. sc. 1.

WOODVILLE, *Lieutenant of the* Tower.
Appears, Act I. sc. 3.

VERNON, *of the White Rose or* York *faction.*
Appears, Act II. sc. 4. Act III. sc. 4. Act IV. sc. 1.

BASSET, *of the Red Rose or* Lancaster *faction.*
Appears, Act III. sc. 4. Act IV. sc. 1.

CHARLES, Dauphin, *and afterwards King of France.*
Appears, Act I. sc. 2; sc. 5; sc. 6. Act II. sc. 1. Act III. sc. 2; sc. 3. Act IV. sc. 7. Act V. sc. 2; sc. 4.

REIGNIER, *Duke of* Anjou, *and titular King of* Naples.
Appears, Act I. sc. 2; sc. 6. Act II. sc. 1. Act V. sc. 3; sc. 4.

DUKE OF BURGUNDY.
Appears, Act II. sc. 1; sc. 2. Act III. sc. 2; sc. 3. Act IV. sc. 7. Act V. sc. 2.

DUKE OF ALENÇON.
Appears, Act I. sc. 2; sc. 6. Act II. sc. 1. Act III. sc. 3; sc. 3. Act IV. sc. 7. Act V. sc. 2; sc. 4.

BASTARD OF ORLEANS.
Appears, Act I. sc. 2. Act III. sc. 2; sc. 3; sc. 7. Act V. sc. 4.

GOVERNOR OF PARIS.
Appears, Act IV. sc. 1.

MASTER GUNNER OF ORLEANS, *and his Son.*
Appear, Act I. sc. 4.

GENERAL OF THE FRENCH FORCES *in* Bordeaux.
Appears, Act IV. sc. 2.

A FRENCH SERGEANT *and* TWO SENTINELS.
Appear, Act II. sc. 1.

A PORTER.
Appears, Act II. sc. 2.

AN OLD SHEPHERD, *Father to* Joan la Pucelle.
Appears, Act V. sc. 4.

MARGARET, *Daughter to* Reignier; *afterwards married to King* Henry.
Appears, Act V. sc. 3.

COUNTESS OF AUVERGNE.
Appears, Act II. sc. 3.

JOAN LA PUCELLE, *commonly called* Joan of Arc.
Appears, Act I. sc. 2; sc. 5; sc. 6. Act II. sc. 1. Act III. sc. 2; sc. 3. Act IV. sc. 7. Act V. sc. 3; sc. 4.

Fiends appearing to La Pucelle, *Lords, Warders of the Tower, Heralds, Officers, Soldiers, Messengers, and several Attendants both of the* English *and* French.

SCENE,—*Sometimes in* ENGLAND, *and sometimes in* FRANCE.

ACT I.

SCENE I.—Westminster *Abbey.*

Dead march. Corpse of King Henry the Fifth discovered, lying in state; attended on by the DUKES OF BEDFORD, GLOSTER, *and* EXETER; *the* EARL OF WARWICK, *the* BISHOP OF WIN-CHESTER, Heralds, &c.

Bed. Hung be the heavens with black, yield day to night!
Comets, importing change of times and states,
Brandish your crystal tresses in the sky;
And with them scourge the bad revolting stars,
That have consented unto Henry's death!
Henry the Fifth, too famous to live long!
England ne'er lost a king of so much worth.

Glo. England ne'er had a king, until his time.
Virtue he had, deserving to command:
His brandish'd sword did blind men with his beams;
His arms spread wider than a dragon's wings;
His sparkling eyes replete with wrathful fire,
More dazzled and drove back his enemies,
Than mid-day sun, fierce bent against their faces.
What should I say? his deeds exceed all speech:
He ne'er lift up his hand, but conquered.

Exe. We mourn in black: Why mourn we not in blood?
Henry is dead, and never shall revive:
Upon a wooden coffin we attend;
And death's dishonourable victory
We with our stately presence glorify,
Like captives bound to a triumphant car.
What? shall we curse the planets of mishap,
That plotted thus our glory's overthrow?
Or shall we think the subtle-witted French
Conjurers and sorcerers, that, afraid of him,
By magic verses have contriv'd his end?

Win. He was a king bless'd of the King of kings.
Unto the French the dreadful judgment day
So dreadful will not be, as was his sight.
The battles of the Lord of hosts he fought:
The church's prayers made him so prosperous.

Glo. The church! where is it? Had not churchmen pray'd,
His thread of life had not so soon decay'd:
None do you like but an effeminate prince,
Whom, like a school-boy, you may over-awe.

Win. Gloster, whate'er we like, thou art protector;
And lookest to command the prince, and realm.
Thy wife is proud; she holdeth thee in awe,
More than God, or religious churchmen, may.

Glo. Name not religion, for thou lov'st the flesh;
And ne'er throughout the year to church thou go'st,
Except it be to pray against thy foes.

Bed. Cease, cease these jars, and rest your minds in peace!
Let 's to the altar:—Heralds, wait on us:—
Instead of gold, we 'll offer up our arms;
Since arms avail not, now that Henry's dead.—
Posterity, await for wretched years,
When at their mothers' moist eyes babes shall suck;
Our isle be made a nourish of salt tears,

And none but women left to wail the dead.—
Henry the Fifth! thy ghost I invocate;
Prosper this realm, keep it from civil broils!
Combat with adverse planets in the heavens!
A far more glorious star thy soul will make,
Than Julius Cæsar, or bright——

Enter a Messenger.

Mess. My honourable lords, health to you all!
Sad tidings bring I to you out of France,
Of loss, of slaughter, and discomfiture:
Guienne, Champaigne, Rheims, Orleans,
Paris, Guysors, Poictiers, are all quite lost.

Bed. What say'st thou, man, before dead Hen-
ry's corse?
Speak softly; or the loss of those great towns
Will make him burst his lead, and rise from death.

Glo. Is Paris lost? is Roüen yielded up?
If Henry were recall'd to life again,
These news would cause him once more yield the
ghost.

Exe. How were they lost? what treachery was
us'd?

Mess. No treachery; but want of men and
money.
Among the soldiers this is muttered,—
That here you maintain several factions;
And, whilst a field should be despatch'd and fought,
You are disputing of your generals.
One would have ling'ring wars, with little cost;
Another would fly swift, but wanteth wings;
A third man thinks, without expense at all,
By guileful fair words peace may be obtain'd.
Awake, awake, English nobility!
Let not sloth dim your honours, new-begot:
Cropp'd are the flower-de-luces in your arms;
Of England's coat one half is cut away.

Exe. Were our tears wanting to this funeral,
These tidings would call forth her flowing tides.

Bed. Me they concern; regent I am of France:—
Give me my steeled coat, I 'll fight for France.—
Away with these disgraceful wailing robes!
Wounds I will lend the French, instead of eyes,
To weep their intermissive miseries.

Enter another Messenger.

2nd Mess. Lords, view these letters, full of bad
mischance,
France is revolted from the English quite;
Except some petty towns of no import:
The Dauphin Charles is crowned king in Rheims;
The bastard of Orleans with him is join'd;

Reignier, duke of Anjou, doth take his part;
The duke of Alençon flieth to his side.

Exe. The Dauphin crowned king! all fly to
him!
O, whither shall we fly from this reproach?

Glo. We will not fly, but to our enemies'
throats:—
Bedford, if thou be slack, I 'll fight it out.

Bed. Gloster, why doubt'st thou of my forward-
ness?
An army have I muster'd in my thoughts,
Wherewith already France is over-run.

Enter a third Messenger.

3rd Mess. My gracious lords,—to add to your
laments,
Wherewith you now bedew king Henry's hearse,—
I must inform you of a dismal fight,
Betwixt the stout lord Talbot and the French.

Win. What! wherein Talbot overcame? is 't so?

3rd Mess. O, no; wherein lord Talbot was o'er-
thrown:
The circumstance I 'll tell you more at large.
The tenth of August last, this dreadful lord,
Retiring from the siege of Orleans,
Having full scarce six thousand in his troop,
By three and twenty thousand of the French
Was round encompassed and set upon:
No leisure had he to enrank his men;
He wanted pikes to set before his archers;
Instead whereof, sharp stakes, pluck'd out of hedges,
They pitched in the ground confusedly,
To keep the horsemen off from breaking in.
More than three hours the fight continued;
Where valiant Talbot, above human thought,
Enacted wonders with his sword and lance.
Hundreds he sent to hell, and none durst stand
him;
Here, there, and every where, enrag'd he slew:
The French exclaim'd, The devil was in arms;
All the whole army stood agaz'd on him:
His soldiers, spying his undaunted spirit,
A Talbot! a Talbot! cried out amain,
And rush'd into the bowels of the battle.
Here had the conquest fully been seal'd up,
If sir John Fastolfe had not play'd the coward;
He being in the vaward, (plac'd behind,
With purpose to relieve and follow them,)
Cowardly fled, not having struck one stroke.
Hence grew the general wreck and massacre:
Enclosed were they with their enemies:
A base Walloon, to win the Dauphin's grace,

Thrust Talbot with a spear into the back;
Whom all France, with their chief assembled
     strength,
Durst not presume to look once in the face.

Bed. Is Talbot slain? then I will slay myself,
For living idly here, in pomp and ease,
Whilst such a worthy leader, wanting aid,
Unto his dastard foe-men is betray'd.

3rd Mess. O no, he lives; but is took prisoner,
And lord Scales with him, and lord Hungerford:
Most of the rest slaughter'd, or took, likewise.

Bed. His ransom there is none but I shall pay:
I 'll hale the Dauphin headlong from his throne,
His crown shall be the ransom of my friend;
Four of their lords I 'll change for one of ours.—
Farewell, my masters; to my task will I;
Bonfires in France forthwith I am to make,
To keep our great Saint George's feast withal:
Ten thousand soldiers with me I will take,
Whose bloody deeds shall make all Europe quake.

3rd Mess. So you had need; for Orleans is be-
     sieg'd;
The English army is grown weak and faint;
The Earl of Salisbury craveth supply,
And hardly keeps his men from mutiny,
Since they, so few, watch such a multitude.

Exe. Remember, lords, your oaths to Henry
     sworn;
Either to quell the Dauphin utterly,
Or bring him in obedience to your yoke.

Bed. I do remember it; and here take leave,
To go about my preparation.   [*Exit.*

Glo. I 'll to the Tower, with all the haste I can,
To view the artillery and munition;
And then I will proclaim young Henry king. [*Exit.*

Exe. To Eltham will I, where the young king is,
Being ordain'd his special governor;
And for his safety there I 'll best devise.   [*Exit.*

Win. Each hath his place and function to at-
     tend:
I am left out; for me nothing remains.
But long I will not be Jack-out-of-office;
The king from Eltham I intend to send,
And sit at chiefest stern of public weal.
                              [*Exit. Scene closes.*

SCENE II.—France.   *Before Orleans.*

Enter CHARLES, *with his* Forces; ALENÇON,
     REIGNIER, *and* Others.

Char. Mars his true moving, even as in the
     heavens,
866

So in the earth, to this day is not known:
Late did he shine upon the English side;
Now we are victors, upon us he smiles.
What towns of any moment, but we have?
At pleasure here we lie, near Orleans;
Otherwhiles, the famish'd English, like pale ghosts
Faintly besiege us one hour in a month.

Alen. They want their porridge, and their fat
     bull-beeves:
Either they must be dieted like mules,
And have their provender tied to their mouths,
Or piteous they will look, like drowned mice.

Reig. Let 's raise the siege: Why live we idly
     here?
Talbot is taken, whom we wont to fear:
Remaineth none but mad-brain'd Salisbury;
And he may well in fretting spend his gall,
Nor men, nor money, hath he to make war.

Char. Sound, sound alarum; we will rush on
     them,
Now for the honour of the forlorn French:—
Him I forgive my death, that killeth me,
When he sees me go back one foot, or fly. [*Exeunt.*

Alarums; Excursions; afterwards a Retreat.

Re-enter CHARLES, ALENÇON, REIGNIER, *and*
     Others.

Char. Who ever saw the like? what men have
     I!—
Dogs! cowards! dastards!—I would ne'er have fled,
But that they left me 'midst my enemies.

Reig. Salisbury is a desperate homicide;
He fighteth as one weary of his life.
The other lords, like lions wanting food,
Do rush upon us as their hungry prey.

Alen. Froissard, a countryman of ours, records
England all Olivers and Rowlands bred,
During the time Edward the Third did reign.
More truly now may this be verified;
For none but Samsons, and Goliasses,
It sendeth forth to skirmish. One to ten!
Lean raw-bon'd rascals! who would e'er suppose
They had such courage and audacity?

Char. Let 's leave this town; for they are hair-
     brain'd slaves,
And hunger will enforce them to be more eager:
Of old I know them; rather with their teeth
The walls they 'll tear down, than forsake the siege.

Reig. I think, by some odd gimmals, or device,
Their arms are set, like clocks, still to strike on;
Else ne'er could they hold out so, as they do.

By my consent, we 'll e'en let them alone.

Alen. Be it so.

    Enter the BASTARD OF ORLEANS.

Bast. Where 's the prince Dauphin, I have news
    for him.

Char. Bastard of Orleans, thrice welcome to us.'

Bast. Methinks, your looks are sad, your cheer
    appall'd;

Hath the late overthrow wrought this offence?

Be not dismay'd, for succour is at hand:

A holy maid hither with me I bring,

Which, by a vision sent to her from heaven,

Ordained is to raise this tedious siege,

And drive the English forth the bounds of France.

The spirit of deep prophecy she hath,

Exceeding the nine sibyls of old Rome:'

What 's past, and what 's to come, she can descry.

Speak, shall I call her in? Believe my words,

For they are certain and unfallible.

    Char. Go, call her in: [*Exit* Bast.] But, first,
    to try her skill,

Reignier, stand thou as Dauphin in my place:

Question her proudly, let thy looks be stern:—

By this means shall we sound what skill she hath.
                        [*Retires.*

  Enter LA PUCELLE, BASTARD OF ORLEANS, *and
    Others.*

    Reig. Fair maid, is 't thou wilt do these wen-
    d'rous feats?

    Puc. Reignier, is 't thou that thinkest to be-
    guile me?—

Where is the Dauphin?—come, come from behind;

I know thee well, though never seen before.

Be not amaz'd, there 's nothing hid from me:

In private will I talk with thee apart;—

Stand back, you lords, and give us leave a while.

    Reig. She takes upon her bravely at first dash.

    Puc. Dauphin, I am by birth a shepherd's
    daughter,

My wit untrain'd in any kind of art.

Heaven, and our Lady gracious, hath it pleas'd

To shine on my contemptible estate:

Lo, whilst I waited on my tender lambs,

And to sun's parching heat display'd my cheeks,

God's mother deigned to appear to me;

And, in a vision full of majesty,

Will'd me to leave my base vocation,

And free my country from calamity:

Her aid she promis'd, and assur'd success:

In complete glory she reveal'd herself;

And, whereas I was black and swart before,

With those clear rays which she infus'd on me,

That beauty am I bless'd with, which you see.

Ask me what question thou canst possible,

And I will answer unpremeditated:

My courage try by combat, if thou dar'st,

And thou shalt find that I exceed my sex.

Resolve on this: Thou shalt be fortunate,

If thou receive me for thy warlike mate.

    Char. Thou hast astonish'd me with thy high
    terms:

Only this proof I 'll of thy valour make,—

In single combat thou shalt buckle with me;

And, if thou vanquishest, thy words are true;

Otherwise, I renounce all confidence.

    Puc. I am prepar'd: here is my keen-edg'd sword,

Deck'd with five flower-de-luces on each side;

The which at Touraine, in Saint Katharine's
    churchyard,

Out of a deal of old iron I chose forth.

    Char. Then come o' God's name, I fear no
    woman.

    Puc. And, while I live, I 'll ne'er fly from a man.
                       [*They fight.*

    Char. Stay, stay thy hands; thou art an
    Amazon,

And fightest with the sword of Deborah.

    Puc. Christ's mother helps me, else I were too
    weak.

    Char. Whoe'er helps thee, 't is thou that must
    help me:

Impatiently I burn with thy desire;

My heart and hands thou hast at once subdu'd.

Excellent Pucelle, if thy name be so,

Let me thy servant, and not sovereign, be;

'T is the French Dauphin sueth to thee thus.

    Puc. I must not yield to any rites of love,

For my profession 's sacred from above:

When I have chased all thy foes from hence,

Then will I think upon a recompense.

    Char. Mean time, look gracious on thy prostrate
    thrall.

    Reig. My lord, methinks, is very long in talk.

    Alen. Doubtless he shrives this woman to her
    smock;

Else ne'er could he so long protract his speech.

    Reig. Shall we disturb him, since he keeps no
    mean?

    Alen. He may mean more than we poor men
    do know:

These women are shrewd tempters with their
    tongues.

Reig. My lord, where are you? what devise
  you on?
Shall we give over Orleans, or no?
 Puc. Why, no, I say, distrustful recreants!
Fight till the last gasp; I will be your guard.
 Char. What she says, I'll confirm; we'll fight
  it out.
 Puc. Assign'd am I to be the English scourge.
This night the siege assuredly I'll raise:
Expect Saint Martin's summer, halcyon days,
Since I have entered into these wars.
Glory is like a circle in the water,
Which never ceaseth to enlarge itself,
Till, by broad spreading, it disperse to nought.
With Henry's death, the English circle ends;
Dispersed are the glories it included.
Now am I like that proud insulting ship,
Which Cæsar and his fortune bare at once.
 Char. Was Mahomet inspired with a dove?[10]
Thou with an eagle art inspired then.
Helen, the mother of great Constantine,
Nor yet Saint Philip's daughters, were like thee.[11]
Bright star of Venus, fall'n down on the earth,
How may I reverently worship thee enough!
 Alen. Leave off delays, and let us raise the
  siege.
 Reig. Woman, do what thou canst to save our
  honours;
Drive them from Orleans, and be immortaliz'd.
 Char. Presently we'll try:—Come, let's away
  about it:
No prophet will I trust, if she prove false.
          [*Exeunt.*

SCENE III.—London. *Hill before the Tower.*

*Enter, at the Gates, the DUKE OF GLOSTER, with
 his Serving-men, in blue coats.*

 Glo. I am come to survey the Tower this day:
Since Henry's death, I fear, there is conveyance.[12]
Where be these warders, that they wait not here?
Open the gates; Gloster it is that calls.
         [*Servants knock.*
 1st Ward. [*Within.*] Who is there that knocks
  so imperiously?
 1st Serv. It is the noble duke of Gloster.
 2nd Ward. [*Within.*] Whoe'er he be, you may
  not be let in.
 1st Serv. Answer you so the lord protector, villains?
 1st Ward. [*Within.*] The Lord protect him!
  so we answer him:
264

We do no otherwise than we are will'd.
 Glo. Who willed you? or whose will stands
  but mine?
There's none protector of the realm, but I.—
Break up the gates, I'll be your warrantize:
Shall I be flouted thus by dunghill grooms?
    *Servants rush at the Tower Gates. Enter, to the
    Gates, WOODVILLE, the Lieutenant.*
 Wood. [*Within.*] What noise is this? what
  traitors have we here?
 Glo. Lieutenant, is it you, whose voice I hear?
Open the gates; here's Gloster, that would enter.
 Wood. [*Within.*] Have patience, noble duke;
  I may not open:
The cardinal of Winchester forbids:
From him I have express commandment,
That thou, nor none of thine, shall be let in.
 Glo. Faint-hearted Woodville, prize-t him 'fore
  me?
Arrogant Winchester? that haughty prelate,
Whom Henry, our late sovereign, ne'er could
  brook?
Thou art no friend to God, or to the king:
Open the gates, or I'll shut thee out shortly.
 1st Serv. Open the gates unto the lord protector
Or we'll burst them open, if that you come not
  quickly.

*Enter WINCHESTER, attended by a Train of Ser-
 vants in tawny Coats.*

 Win. How now, ambitious Humphry? what
  means this?
 Glo. Piel'd priest,[13] dost thou command me to
  be shut out?
 Win. I do, thou most usurping proditor,
And not protector of the king or realm.
 Glo. Stand back, thou manifest conspirator;
Thou, that contriv'dst to murder our dead lord;
Thou, that giv'st whores indulgences to sin;[14]
I'll canvass thee in thy broad cardinal's hat,[15]
If thou proceed in this thy insolence.
 Win. Nay, stand thou back, I will not budge a
  foot;
This be Damascus, be thou cursed Cain,[16]
To slay thy brother Abel, if thou wilt.
 Glo. I will not slay thee, but I'll drive thee
  back:
Thy scarlet robes, as a child's bearing-cloth
I'll use, to carry thee out of this place.
 Win. Do what thou dar'st; I beard thee to thy
  face.

Glo. What? am I dar'd, and bearded to my
     face?
Draw, men, for all this privileged place;
Blue-coats to tawny-coats. Priest, beware your
     beard;
       [Glo. *and his* Men *attack the* Bishop.
I mean to tug it, and to cuff you soundly:
Under my feet I stamp thy cardinal's hat;
In spite of Pope or dignities of church,
Here by the cheeks I 'll drag thee up and down.
     Win. Gloster, thou 'lt answer this before the
     Pope.
     Glo. Winchester goose, I cry—a rope! a rope!—
Now beat them hence, Why do you let them stay?—
Thee I 'll chase hence, thou wolf in sheep's array.—
Out, tawny coats!—out, scarlet hypocrite!

*Here a great Tumult. In the midst of it, Enter
the* Mayor of London, *and* Officers.

     May. Fye, lords! that you, being supreme ma-
     gistrates,
Thus contumeliously should break the peace!
     Glo. Peace, mayor; thou know'st little of my
     wrongs;
Here 's Beaufort, that regards nor God nor king,
Hath here distrain'd the Tower to his use.
     Win. Here 's Gloster too, a foe to citizens;
One that still motions war, and never peace,
O'ercharging your free purses with large fines;
That seeks to overthrow religion,
Because he is protector of the realm;
And would have armour here out of the Tower,
To crown himself king, and suppress the prince.
     Glo. I will not answer thee with words, but
     blows.   [*Here they skirmish again.*
     May. Nought rests for me, in this tumultuous
     strife,
But to make open proclamation:—
Come, officer; as loud as e'er thou canst.
     Off. "All manner of men, assembled here in
arms this day, against God's peace and the king's,
we charge and command you, in his highness'
name, to repair to your several dwelling-places;
and not to wear, handle, or use, any sword,
weapon, or dagger, henceforward, upon pain of
death."
     Glo. Cardinal, I 'll be no breaker of the law:
But we shall meet, and break our minds at large.
     Win. Gloster, we 'll meet; to thy dear cost, be
     sure:
Thy heart-blood I will have, for this day's work.
     May. I 'll call for clubs, if you will not away:—

This cardinal is more haughty than the devil.
     Glo. Mayor, farewell: thou dost but what thou
     may'st.
     Win. Abominable Gloster! guard thy head;
For I intend to have it, ere long."   [*Exeunt.*
     May. See the coast clear'd, and then we will
     depart.—
Good God! that nobles should such stomachs
     bear!
I myself fight not once in forty year.   [*Exeunt.*

     SCENE IV.—France. *Before Orleans.*

Enter, on the Walls, the Master Gunner *and
his* Son.

     M. Gun. Sirrah, thou know'st how Orleans is
     besieg'd;
And how the English have the suburbs won.
     Son. Father, I know; and oft have shot at
     them,
Howe'er, unfortunate, I miss'd my aim.
     M. Gun. But now thou shalt not. Be thou
     rul'd by me:
Chief master-gunner am I of this town;
Something I must do, to procure me grace.
The prince's espials have informed me,
How the English, in the suburbs close intrench'd,
Wont, through a secret grate of iron bars
In yonder tower, to overpeer the city;
And thence discover, how, with most advantage,
They may vex us, with shot, or with assault.
To intercept this inconvenience,
A piece of ordnance 'gainst it I have plac'd;
And fully even these three days have I watch'd,
If I could see them. Now, boy, do thou watch,
For I can stay no longer.
If thou spy'st any, run and bring me word;
And thou shalt find me at the governor's. [*Exit.*
     Son. Father, I warrant you; take you no care;
I 'll never trouble you, if I may spy them.

Enter, in an upper Chamber of a Tower, the Lords
Salisbury *and* Talbot, Sir William Glansdale, Sir Thomas Gargrave, *and Others.*

     Sal. Talbot, my life, my joy, again return'd!
How wert thou handled, being prisoner?
Or by what means got'st thou to be releas'd?
Discourse, I pr'ythee, on this turret's top.
     Tal. The duke of Bedford had a prisoner,
Called—the brave lord Ponton de Santrailles
For him I was exchang'd and ransomed.
But with a baser man of arms by far,

Once, in contempt, they would have barter'd me:
Which I, disdaining, scorn'd; and craved death
Rather than I would be so pil'd esteem'd."
In fine, redeem'd I was as I desir'd.
But, O! the treacherous Fastolfe wounds my heart!
Whom with my bare fists I would execute,
If I now had him brought into my power.

   Sal. Yet tell'st thou not, how thou wert enter-
     tain'd.

   Tal. With scoffs, and scorns, and contumelious
    taunts.
In open market-place produc'd they me,
To be a public spectacle to all;
Here, said they, is the terror of the French,
The scare-crow that affrights our children so.
Then broke I from the officers that led me;
And with my nails digg'd stones out of the ground,
To hurl at the beholders of my shame.
My grisly countenance made others fly;
None durst come near for fear of sudden death.
In iron walls they deem'd me not secure;
So great fear of my name 'mongst them was
   spread,
That they suppos'd I could rend bars of steel,
And spurn in pieces posts of adamant:
Wherefore a guard of chosen shot I had,
That walk'd about me every minute-while;
And if I did but stir out of my bed,
Ready they were to shoot me to the heart.

   Sal. I grieve to hear what torments you en-
    dur'd;
But we will be reveng'd sufficiently.
Now it is supper-time in Orleans:
Here, thorough this grate, I count each one,
And view the Frenchmen how they fortify;
Let us look in, the sight will much delight thee.—
Sir Thomas Gargrave, and sir William Glansdale,
Let me have your express opinions,
Where is best place to make our battery next.

   Gar. I think, at the north gate; for there stand
    lords.

   Glan. And I, here, at the bulwark of the bridge.

   Tal. For aught I see, this city must be famish'd,
Or with light skirmishes enfeebled.

   [*Shot from the Town.* SAL. *and* GAR. *fall.*

   Sal. O Lord, have mercy on us, wretched
    sinners!

   Gar. O Lord, have mercy on me, woeful man!

   Tal. What chance is this, that suddenly hath
    cross'd us?—
Speak, Salisbury; at least, if thou canst speak;
How far'st thou, mirror of all martial men!

One of thy eyes, and thy cheek's side struck off!—
Accursed tower! accursed fatal hand,
That hath contriv'd this woeful tragedy!
In thirteen battles Salisbury o'ercame;
Henry the Fifth he first train'd to the wars;
Whilst any trump did sound, or drum struck up,
His sword did ne'er leave striking in the field.—
Yet liv'st thou, Salisbury? though thy speech doth
   fail,
One eye thou hast, to look to heaven for grace:
The sun with one eye vieweth all the world.—
Heaven, be thou gracious to none alive,
If Salisbury wants mercy at thy hands!—
Bear hence his body, I will help to bury it.—
Sir Thomas Gargrave, hast thou any life?
Speak unto Talbot; nay, look up to him.
Salisbury, cheer thy spirit with this comfort;
Thou shalt not die, whiles——
He beckons with his hand, and smiles on me;
As who should say, "When I am dead and gone,
Remember to avenge me on the French.—"
Plantagenet, I will; and Nero-like,
Play on the lute, beholding the towns burn:
Wretched shall France be only in my name.

   [*Thunder heard; afterwards an Alarum.*

What stir is this?　What tumult 's in the
   heavens?
Whence cometh this alarum, and the noise?

         Enter a Messenger.

   Mess. My lord, my lord, the French have
    gather'd head:
The Dauphin, with one Joan la Pucelle join'd,—
A holy prophetess, new risen up,—
Is come with a great power to raise the siege.

                 [SAL. *groans.*

   Tal. Hear, hear, how dying Salisbury doth
    groan!
It irks his heart, he cannot be reveng'd.—
Frenchmen, I 'll be a Salisbury to you:—
Pucelle or puzzel, dolphin or dogfish,
Your hearts I 'll stamp out with my horse's heels,
And make a quagmire of your mingled brains.—
Convey me Salisbury into his tent,
And then we 'll try what these dastard Frenchmen
   dare.　[*Exeunt, bearing out the Bodies.*

SCENE V.—*The Same.　Before one of the Gates.*
*Alarum.　Skirmishings.　*TALBOT *pursueth the*
DAUPHIN, and driveth him in: then enter JOAN
LA PUCELLE, *driving* Englishmen *before her.*
Then enter TALBOT.

Tal. Where is my strength, my valour, and my
    force ?
Our English troops retire, I cannot stay them ;
A woman, clad in armour, chaseth them.

        Enter LA PUCELLE.

Here, here she comes :——I 'll have a bout with
    thee ;
Devil, or devil's dam, I 'll conjure thee :
Blood will I draw on thee, thou art a witch,"
And straightway give thy soul to him thou serv'st.

    Puc. Come, come, 't is only I that must dis-
    grace thee.   [*They fight.*

    Tal. Heavens, can you suffer hell so to prevail !
My breast I 'll burst with straining of my courage,
And from my shoulders crack my arms asunder,
But I will chastise this high-minded strumpet.

    Puc. Talbot, farewell ; thy hour is not yet
    come :
I must go victual Orleans forthwith.
O'ertake me, if thou canst ; I scorn thy strength.
Go, go, cheer up thy hunger-starved men ;
Help Salisbury to make his testament :
This day is ours, as many more shall be.
        [*Puc. enters the Town, with Soldiers.*

    Tal. My thoughts are whirled like a potter's
    wheel ;
I know not where I am, nor what I do :
A witch, by fear, not force, like Hannibal,
Drives back our troops, and conquers as she lists :
So bees with smoke, and doves with noisome
    stench,
Are from their hives, and houses, driven away.
They call'd us, for our fierceness, English dogs ;
Now, like to whelps, we crying run away.
            [*A short Alarum.*

Hark, countrymen ! either renew the fight,
Or tear the lions out of England's coat ;
Renounce your soil, give sheep in lion's stead :
Sheep run not half so timorous from the wolf,
Or horse, or oxen, from the leopard,   · ,
As you fly from your oft-subdued slaves.
      [*Alarum.*   *Another skirmish.*

It will not be :——Retire into your trenches :
You all consented unto Salisbury's death,
For none would strike a stroke in his revenge.——

Pucelle is enter'd into Orleans,
In spite of us, or aught that we could do.
O, would I were to die with Salisbury !
The shame hereof will make me hide my head.
    [*Alarum. Retreat. Exeunt* TAL. *and his Forces, &c.*

        SCENE VI.—*The Same.*

Enter on the Walls, PUCELLE, CHARLES, REIG-
    NIER, ALENÇON, *and Soldiers.*

    Puc. Advance our waving colours on the walls ;
Rescu'd is Orleans from the English wolves :
Thus Joan la Pucelle hath perform'd her word.

    Char. Divinest creature, bright Astræa's daugh-
    ter,
How shall I honour thee for this success ?
Thy promises are like Adonis' gardens,
That one day bloom'd, and fruitful were the next.—
France, triumph in thy glorious prophetess !—
Recover'd is the town of Orleans :
More blessed hap did ne'er befal our state.

    Reig. Why ring not out the bells throughout
    the town ?
Dauphin, command the citizens make bonfires,
And feast and banquet in the open streets,
To celebrate the joy that God hath given us.

    Alen. All France will be replete with mirth
    and joy,
When they shall hear how we have play'd the men.

    Char. 'T is Joan, not we, by whom the day is
    won ;
For which, I will divide my crown with her :
And all the priests and friars in my realm
Shall, in procession, sing her endless praise.
A statelier pyramis to her I 'll rear,
Than Rhodope's, or Memphis', ever was :"
In memory of her, when she is dead,
Her ashes, in an urn more precious
Than the rich-jewel'd coffer of Darius,"
Transported shall be at high festivals
Before the kings and queens of France.
No longer on Saint Dennis will we cry,
But Joan la Pucelle shall be France's saint.
Come in ; and let us banquet royally,
After this golden day of victory.
        [*Flourish.*   *Exeunt.*

                   671

ACT II.

SCENE I.—The Same.

Enter to the Gates, a French Sergeant, and Two Sentinels.

Serg. Sirs, take your places, and be vigilant:
If any noise, or soldier, you perceive,
Near to the walls, by some apparent sign,
Let us have knowledge at the court of guard.

1st Sent. Sergeant, you shall. [*Exit Serg.*] Thus
   are poor servitors
(When others sleep upon their quiet beds.)
Constrain'd to watch in darkness, rain, and cold.

Enter TALBOT, BEDFORD, BURGUNDY, *and Forces,
with scaling Ladders ; their Drums beating a
dead March.*

Tal. Lord regent,—and redoubted Burgundy,—
By whose approach, the regions of Artois,
Walloon, and Picardy, are friends to us,—
This happy night the Frenchmen are secure,
Having all day carous'd and banqueted :
Embrace we then this opportunity ;
As fitting best to quittance their deceit,
Contriv'd by art, and baleful sorcery.

Bed. Coward of France !—how much he wrongs
   his fame,
Despairing of his own arm's fortitude,
To join with witches, and the help of hell.

Bur. Traitors have never other company.—
But what's that Pucelle, whom they term so pure?

Tal. A maid, they say.

Bed.   A maid! and be so martial!

Bur. Pray God, she prove not masculine ere
   long ;
If underneath the standard of the French,
She carry armour, as she hath begun.

Tal. Well, let them practise and converse with
   spirits :
God is our fortress ; in whose conquering name,
Let us resolve to scale their flinty bulwarks.

Bed. Ascend, brave Talbot ; we will follow
   thee.

Tal. Not all together : better far, I guess,
That we do make our entrance several ways ;
That, if it chance the one of us do fail,
The other yet may rise against their force.

Bed. Agreed ; I 'll to yon corner.

Bur.   And I to this.

Tal. And here will Talbot mount, or make his
   grave.—
Now, Salisbury ! for thee, and for the right
Of English Henry, shall this night appear
How much in duty I am bound to both.

[*The English scale the Walls, crying* St. George !
   A Talbot ! *and all enter by the Town.*

Sent. [*Within.*] Arm, arm ! the enemy doth
   make assault !

*The French leap over the Walls in their Shirts.
Enter, several ways,* BASTARD, ALENÇON, REIG-
NIER, *half ready, and half unready.*

Alen. How now, my lords ? what, all unready
   so !

Bast. Unready ? ay, and glad we 'scap'd so well.

Reig. 'T was time, I trow, to wake and leave
   our beds,
Hearing alarums at our chamber doors.

Alen. Of all exploits, since first I follow'd arms,
Ne'er heard I of a warlike enterprise
More venturous, or desperate than this.

Bast. I think, this Talbot be a fiend of hell.

Reig. If not of hell, the heavens, sure, favour
   him.

Alen. Here cometh Charles ; I marvel, how he
   sped.

Enter CHARLES *and* LA PUCELLE.

Bast. Tut ! holy Joan was his defensive guard.

Char. Is this thy cunning, thou deceitful dame ?
Didst thou at first, to flatter us withal,
Make us partakers of a little gain,
That now our loss might be ten times so much ?

Puc. Wherefore is Charles impatient with his
   friend ?
At all times will you have my power alike ?
Sleeping, or waking, must I still prevail,
Or will you blame and lay the fault on me ?—
Improvident soldiers ! had your watch been good,
This sudden mischief never could have fall'n.

Char. Duke of Alençon, this was your default,
That, being captain of the watch to-night,
Did look no better to that weighty charge.

Alen. Had all your quarters been as safely kept,
As that whereof I had the government,
We had not been thus shamefully surpris'd.

Bast. Mine was secure.

Reig.   And so was mine, my lord.

Char. And, for myself, most part of all this
     night,
Within her quarter, and mine own precinct,
I was employ'd in passing to and fro,
About relieving of the sentinels:
Then how, or which way, should they first
     break in?

Puc. Question, my lords, no further of the case,
How, or which way; 't is sure, they found some
     place
But weakly guarded, where the breach was made.
And now there rests no other shift but this,—
To gather our soldiers, scatter'd and dispers'd,
And lay new platforms to endamage them.

Alarum. Enter an English Soldier, *crying, A
Talbot! A Talbot! They fly, leaving their
Clothes behind.*

Sold. I 'll be so bold to take what they have
left.
The cry of Talbot serves me for a sword;
For I have loaden me with many spoils,
Using no other weapon but his name.   [*Exit.*

     SCENE II.—Orleans. *Within the Town.*

Enter TALBOT, BEDFORD, BURGUNDY, *a Captain,
and Others.*

Bed. The day begins to break, and night is fled,
Whose pitchy mantle over-veil'd the earth.
Here sound retreat, and cease our hot pursuit.
               [*Retreat sounded.*

Tal. Bring forth the body of old Salisbury;
And here advance it in the market-place,
The middle centre of this cursed town.—
Now have I paid my vow unto his soul;
For every drop of blood was drawn from him,
There hath at least five Frenchmen died to-night.
And, that hereafter ages may behold
What ruin happen'd in revenge of him,
Within their chiefest temple I 'll erect
A tomb, wherein his corpse shall be interr'd:
Upon the which, that every one may read,
Shall be engrav'd the sack of Orleans;
The treacherous manner of his mournful death,
And what a terror he had been to France.
But, lords, in all our bloody massacre,

I muse, we met not with the Dauphin's grace;
His new-come champion, virtuous Joan of Arc;
Nor any of his false confederates.

Bed. 'T is thought, lord Talbot, when the fight
     began,
Rous'd on the sudden from their drowsy beds,
They did, amongst the troops of armed men,
Leap o'er the walls for refuge in the field.

Bur. Myself (as far as I could well discern,
For smoke, and dusky vapours of the night,)
Am sure, I scar'd the Dauphin, and his trull;
When arm in arm they both came swiftly running,
Like to a pair of loving turtle-doves,
That could not live asunder day or night.
After that things are set in order here,
We 'll follow them with all the power we have.

       Enter a Messenger.

Mess. All hail, my lords! which of this princely
     train
Call ye the warlike Talbot, for his acts
So much applauded through the realm of France?

Tal. Here is the Talbot; who would speak with
     him?

Mess. The virtuous lady, countess of Auvergne,
With modesty admiring thy renown,
By me entreats, good lord, thou wouldst vouch-
     safe
To visit her poor castle where she lies:
That she may boast, she hath beheld the man
Whose glory fills the world with loud report.

Bur. Is it even so? Nay, then, I see, our wars
Will turn unto a peaceful comic sport,
When ladies crave to be encounter'd with.—
You may not, my lord, despise her gentle suit.

Tal. Ne'er trust me then; for, when a world of
     men
Could not prevail with all their oratory,
Yet hath a woman's kindness over-rul'd:—
And therefore tell her, I return great thanks;
And in submission will attend on her.—
Will not your honours bear me company?

Bed. No, truly; it is more than manners will:
And I have heard it said,—Unbidden guests
Are often welcomest when they are gone.

Tal. Well then, alone, since there 's no reme-
     dy,
I mean to prove this lady's courtesy.
Come hither, captain. [*Whispers.*]—You perceive
     my mind.

Capt. I do, my lord; and mean accordingly.
               [*Exeunt.*

SCENE III.—*Auvergne. Court of the Castle.*

Enter the COUNTESS *and her* PORTER.

Count. Porter, remember what I gave in charge;
And, when you have done so, bring the keys to me.
Port. Madam, I will.   [*Exit.*
Count. The plot is laid: if all things fall out right,
I shall as famous be by this exploit,
As Scythian Thomyris by Cyrus' death.
Great is the rumour of this dreadful knight,
And his achievements of no less account:
Fain would mine eyes be witness with mine ears,
To give their censure of these rare reports.

Enter Messenger *and* TALBOT.

Mess. Madam,
According as your ladyship desir'd,
By message crav'd, so is lord Talbot come.
Count. And he is welcome. What! is this the man?
Mess. Madam, it is.
Count.   Is this the scourge of France?
Is this the Talbot, so much fear'd abroad,
That with his name the mothers still their babes?
I see, report is fabulous and false:
I thought, I should have seen some Hercules,
A second Hector, for his grim aspéct,
And large proportion of his strong-knit limbs.
Alas! this is a child, a silly dwarf:
It cannot be, this weak and writhled shrimp
Should strike such terror to his enemies.
Tal. Madam, I have been bold to trouble you:
But, since your ladyship is not at leisure,
I'll sort some other time to visit you.
Count. What means he now?—Go ask him whither he goes.
Mess. Stay, my lord Talbot; for my lady craves
To know the cause of your abrupt departure.
Tal. Marry, for that she's in a wrong belief,
I go to certify her, Talbot's here.

Re-enter Porter, *with Keys.*

Count. If thou be he, then art thou prisoner.
Tal. Prisoner! to whom?
Count.   To me, blood-thirsty lord;
And for that cause I train'd thee to my house.
Long time thy shadow hath been thrall to me,
For in my gallery thy picture hangs:
But now the substance shall endure the like;
674

And I will chain these legs and arms of thine,
That hast by tyranny, these many years,
Wasted our country, slain our citizens,
And sent our sons and husbands captivate.
Tal. Ha, ha, ha!
Count. Laughest thou, wretch? thy mirth shall turn to moan.
Tal. I laugh to see your ladyship so fond,
To think that you have aught but Talbot's shadow,
Whereon to practise your severity.
Count. Why, art not thou the man?
Tal.   I am indeed.
Count. Then have I substance too.
Tal. No, no, I am but shadow of myself:
You are deceiv'd, my substance is not here;
For what you see, is but the smallest part
And least proportion of humanity:
I tell you, madam, were the whole frame here,
It is of such a spacious lofty pitch,
Your roof were not sufficient to contain it.
Count. This is a riddling merchant for the nonce;
He will be here, and yet he is not here:
How can these contrarieties agree?
Tal. That will I show you presently.

He winds a Horn. Drums heard; then a Peal of Ordnance. The Gates being forced, enter Soldiers.

How say you, madam? are you now persuaded,
That Talbot is but shadow of himself?
These are his substance, sinews, arms, and strength,
With which he yoketh your rebellious necks;
Razeth your cities, and subverts your towns,
And in a moment makes them desolate.
Count. Victorious Talbot! pardon my abuse:
I find, thou art no less than fame hath bruited,
And more than may be gather'd by thy shape.
Let my presumption not provoke thy wrath;
For I am sorry, that with reverence
I did not entertain thee as thou art.
Tal. Be not dismay'd, fair lady; nor misconstrue
The mind of Talbot, as you did mistake
The outward composition of his body.
What you have done, hath not offended me;
No other satisfaction do I crave,
But only (with your patience,) that we may
Taste of your wine, and see what cates you have;
For soldiers' stomachs always serve them well.
Count. With all my heart; and think me honoured
To feast so great a warrior in my house.
                              [*Exeunt.*

SCENE IV.—London. *The* Temple *Garden.*

Enter the EARLS OF SOMERSET, SUFFOLK, *and*
WARWICK; RICHARD PLANTAGENET, VERNON,
and another Lawyer.

  Plan. Great lords, and gentlemen, what means
    this silence?
Dare no man answer in a case of truth?
  Suf. Within the Temple hall we were too loud;
The garden here is more convenient.
  Plan. Then say at once, if I maintain'd the
    truth;
Or, else, was wrangling Somerset in the error?
  Suf. 'Faith, I have been a truant in the law;
And never yet could frame my will to it;
And, therefore, frame the law unto my will.
  Som. Judge you, my lord of Warwick, then be-
    tween us.
  War. Between two hawks, which flies the higher
    pitch,
Between two dogs, which hath the deeper mouth,
Between two blades, which bears the better temper,
Between two horses, which doth bear him best,
Between two girls, which hath the merriest eye,
I have, perhaps, some shallow spirit of judgment:
But in these nice sharp quillets of the law,
Good faith, I am no wiser than a daw.
  Plan. Tut, tut, here is a mannerly forbearance:
The truth appears so naked on my side,
That any purblind eye may find it out.
  Som. And on my side it is so well apparell'd,
So clear, so shining, and so evident,
That it will glimmer through a blind man's eye.
  Plan. Since you are tongue-ty'd, and so loath
    to speak,
In dumb significants proclaim your thoughts:
Let him, that is a true-born gentleman,
And stands upon the honour of his birth,
If he suppose that I have pleaded truth,
From off this brier pluck a white rose with me.
  Som. Let him that is no coward, nor no flatterer,
But dare maintain the party of the truth,
Pluck a red rose from off this thorn with me.
  War. I love no colours; and, without all colour
Of base insinuating flattery,
I pluck this white rose, with Plantagenet.
  Suf. I pluck this red rose, with young Somerset;
And say withal, I think he held the right.
  Ver. Stay, lords, and gentlemen; and pluck no
    more,
Till you conclude,—that he, upon whose side

The fewest roses are cropp'd from the tree,
Shall yield the other in the right opinion.
  Som. Good master Vernon, it s well objected;
If I have fewest, I subscribe in silence.
  Plan. And I.
  Ver. Then, for the truth and plainness of the
    case,
I pluck this pale, and maiden blossom here,
Giving my verdict on the white rose side.
  Som. Prick not your finger as you pluck it off,
Lest, bleeding, you do paint the white rose red,
And fall on my side so against your will.
  Ver. If I, my lord, for my opinion bleed,
Opinion shall be surgeon to my hurt,
And keep me on the side where still I am.
  Som. Well, well, come on: Who else?
  Law. Unless my study and my books be false,
The argument you held, was wrong in you;
                       [*To* SOM.
In sign whereof, I pluck a white rose too.
  Plan. Now, Somerset, where is your argument?
  Som. Here, in my scabbard; meditating that,
Shall dye your white rose in a bloody red.
  Plan. Mean time, your cheeks do counterfeit
    our roses;
For pale they look with fear, as witnessing
The truth on our side.
  Som.   No, Plantagenet,
'T is not for fear: but anger,—that thy cheeks
Blush for pure shame, to counterfeit our roses;
And yet thy tongue will not confess thy error.
  Plan. Hath not thy rose a canker, Somerset?
  Som. Hath not thy rose a thorn, Plantagenet?
  Plan. Ay, sharp and piercing, to maintain his
    truth;
Whiles thy consuming canker eats his falsehood.
  Som. Well, I 'll find friends to wear my bleeding
    roses,
That shall maintain what I have said is true,
Where false Plantagenet dare not be seen.
  Plan. Now, by this maiden blossom in my hand,
I scorn thee and thy fashion, peevish boy.
  Suf. Turn not thy scorns this way, Plantagenet.
  Plan. Proud Poole, I will; and scorn both him
    and thee.
  Suf. I 'll turn my part thereof into thy throat.
  Som. Away, away, good William De-la-Poole!
We grace the yeoman, by conversing with him.
  War. Now, by God's will, thou wrong'st him
    Somerset;
His grandfather was Lionel, duke of Clarence,
Third son to the third Edward king of England;
                           875

Spring crestless yeoman from so deep a root!

Plan. He bears him on the place's privilege,
Or durst not, for his craven heart, say thus.

Som. By him that made me, I'll maintain my
    words
On any plot of ground in Christendom:
Was not thy father, Richard, earl of Cambridge,
For treason executed in our late king's days?
And, by his treason, stand'st not thou attainted,
Corrupted, and exempt from ancient gentry?
His trespass yet lives guilty in thy blood;
And, till thou be restor'd, thou art a yeoman.

Plan. My father was attached, not attainted;
Condemn'd to die for treason, but no traitor;
And that I'll prove on better men than Somerset,
Were growing time once ripen'd to my will,
For your partaker Poole, and you yourself,
I'll note you in my book of memory,
To scourge you for this apprehension:
Look to it well; and say you are well warn'd.

Som. Ay, thou shalt find us ready for thee still;
And know us, by these colours, for thy foes:
For these my friends, in spite of thee, shall wear.

Plan. And, by my soul, this pale and angry rose,
As cognizance of my blood-drinking hate,
Will I for ever, and my faction, wear;
Until it wither with me to my grave,
Or flourish to the height of my degree.

Suf. Go forward, and be chok'd with thy ambi-
    tion!
And so farewell, until I meet thee next.   [*Exit.*

Som. Have with thee, Poole.—Farewell, ambi-
    tious Richard.   [*Exit.*

Plan. How I am brav'd, and must perforce en-
    dure it!

War. This blot, that they object against your
    house,
Shall be wip'd out in the next parliament,
Call'd for the truce of Winchester and Gloster;
And, if thou be not then created York,
I will not live to be accounted Warwick.
Mean time, in signal of my love to thee,
Against proud Somerset, and William Poole,
Will I upon thy party wear this rose:
And here I prophesy,—This brawl to-day,
Grown to this faction, in the Temple garden,
Shall send, between the red rose and the white,
A thousand souls to death and deadly night.

Plan. Good master Vernon, I am bound to you,
That you on my behalf would pluck a flower.

Ver. In your behalf still will I wear the same.

Law. And so will I.

876

Plan. Thanks, gentle sir.
Come, let us four to dinner: I dare say,
This quarrel will drink blood another day.
        [*Exeunt.*

SCENE V.—*The Same.—A Room in the Tower.*

Enter MORTIMER,[34] *brought in a Chair by Two
    Keepers.*

Mor. Kind keepers of my weak decaying age,
Let dying Mortimer here rest himself.—
Even like a man new haled from the rack,
So fare my limbs with long imprisonment:
And these grey locks, the pursuivants of death,
Nestor-like aged, in an age of care,
Argue the end of Edmund Mortimer.
These eyes,—like lamps whose wasting oil is
    spent,—
Wax dim, as drawing to their exigent:
Weak shoulders, overborne with burd'ning grief;
And pithless arms, like to a wither'd vine
That droops his sapless branches to the ground:—
Yet are these feet—whose strengthless stay is numb
Unable to support this lump of clay,—
Swift-winged with desire to get a grave,
As witting I no other comfort have.—
But tell me, keeper, will my nephew come?

1st Keep. Richard Plantagenet, my lord, will
    come:
We sent unto the Temple, to his chamber;
And answer was return'd that he will come.

Mor. Enough; my soul shall then be satisfied.—
Poor gentleman! his wrong doth equal mine.
Since Henry Monmouth first began to reign,
(Before whose glory I was great in arms,)
This loathsome sequestration have I had:
And even since then hath Richard been obscur'd,
Depriv'd of honour and inheritance:
But now, the arbitrator of despairs,
Just death, kind umpire of men's miseries,
With sweet enlargement doth dismiss me hence:
I would, his troubles likewise were expir'd,
That so he might recover what was lost.

Enter RICHARD PLANTAGENET.

1st Keep. My lord, your loving nephew now is
    come.

Mor. Richard Plantagenet, my friend? Is he
    come?

Plan. Ay, noble uncle, thus ignobly us'd,
Your nephew, late-despised Richard, comes.

Mor. Direct mine arms, I may embrace his neck,.

And in his bosom spend my latter gasp:
O, tell me, when my lips do touch his cheeks,
That I may kindly give one fainting kiss.—
And now declare, sweet stem from York's great
    stock,
Why didst thou say—of late thou wert despis'd ?
  Plan. First, lean thine aged back against mine
    arm ;
And, in that case, I 'll tell thee my disease.
This day, in argument upon a case,
Some words there grew 'twixt Somerset and me:
Among which terms he used his lavish tongue,
And did upbraid me with my father's death ;
Which obloquy set bars before my tongue,
Else with the like I had requited him:
Therefore, good uncle,—for my father's sake,
In honour of a true Plantagenet,
And for alliance sake,—declare the cause
My father, earl of Cambridge, lost his head.
  Mor. That cause, fair nephew, that imprison'd me,
And hath detain'd me, all my flow'ring youth,
Within a loathsome dungeon, there to pine,
Was cursed instrument of his decease.
  Plan. Discover more at large what cause that
    was ;
For I am ignorant, and cannot guess.
  Mor. I will; if that my fading breath permit,
And death approach not ere my tale be done.
Henry the Fourth, grandfather to this king,
Depos'd his nephew Richard ;[25] Edward's son,
The first-begotten, and the lawful heir
Of Edward king, the third of that descent:
During whose reign, the Percys of the north,
Finding his usurpation most unjust,
Endeavour'd my advancement to the throne:
The reason mov'd these warlike lords to this,
Was—for that (young king Richard thus remov'd,
Leaving no heir begotten of his body,)
I was the next by birth and parentage ;
For by my mother I derived am
From Lionel duke of Clarence, the third son
To king Edward the Third, whereas he,
From John of Gaunt doth bring his pedigree,
Being but fourth of that heroic line.
But mark ; as, in this haughty great attempt,
They laboured to plant the rightful heir,
I lost my liberty, and they their lives.
Long after this, when Henry the Fifth,—
Succeeding his father Bolingbroke,—did reign,
Thy father, earl of Cambridge,—then deriv'd
From famous Edmund Langley, duke of York,—

Marrying my sister, that thy mother was,
Again, in pity of my hard distress,
Levied an army ;[26] weening to redeem,
And have install'd me in the diadem :
But, as the rest, so fell that noble earl,
And was beheaded. Thus the Mortimers,
In whom the title rested, were suppress'd.
  Plan. Of which, my lord, your honour is the last.
  Mor. True ; and thou seest, that I no issue
    have ;
And that my fainting words do warrant death :
Thou art my heir ; the rest, I wish thee gather :
But yet be wary in thy studious care.
  Plan. Thy grave admonishments prevail with
    me:
But yet, methinks, my father's execution
Was nothing less than bloody tyranny.
  Mor. With silence, nephew, be thou politic ;
Strong-fixed is the house of Lancaster,
And, like a mountain, not to be remov'd.
But now thy uncle is removing hence ;
As princes do their courts, when they are cloy'd
With long continuance in a settled place.
  Plan. O, uncle, 'would some part of my young
    years
Might but redeem the passage of your age !
  Mor. Thou dost then wrong me ; as the slaugh-
    t'rer doth,
Which giveth many wounds, when one will kill.
Mourn not, except thou sorrow for my good ;
Only, give order for my funeral ;
And so farewell ; and fair be all thy hopes !
And prosperous be thy life, in peace, and war !
                                          [*Dies*

  Plan. And peace, no war, befal thy parting
    soul !
In prison hast thou spent a pilgrimage,
And like a hermit overpass'd thy days.—
Well, I will lock his counsel in my breast ;
And what I do imagine, let that rest.—
Keepers, convey him hence ; and I myself
Will see his burial better than his life.—
              [*Exeunt Keepers, bearing out Mor.*
Here dies the dusky torch of Mortimer,
Chok'd with ambition of the meaner sort :—
And, for those wrongs, those bitter injuries,
Which Somerset hath offer'd to my house,—
I doubt not, but with honour to redress ;
And therefore haste I to the parliament ;
Either to be restored to my blood,
Or make my ill the advantage of my good. [*Exit*

ACT III.

SCENE I.—*The Same. The Parliament-house.*

Flourish. Enter KING HENRY, EXETER, GLOSTER,
WARWICK, SOMERSET, *and* SUFFOLK; *the* BISHOP
OF WINCHESTER, RICHARD PLANTAGENET, *and
Others.* GLOSTER *offers to put up a Bill;* WIN-
CHESTER *snatches it, and tears it.*

Win. Com'st thou with deep premeditated
    lines,
With written pamphlets studiously devis'd,
Humphrey of Gloster? if thou canst accuse,
Or aught intend'st to lay unto my charge,
Do it without invention suddenly;
As I with sudden and extemporal speech
Purpose to answer what thou canst object.

Glo. Presumptuous priest! this place com-
    mands my patience,
Or thou should'st find thou hast dishonour'd me.
Think not, although in writing I preferr'd
The manner of thy vile outrageous crimes,
That therefore I have forg'd, or am not able
Verbatim to rehearse the method of my pen:
No, prelate; such is thy audacious wickedness,
Thy lewd, pestiferous, and dissentious pranks,
As very infants prattle of thy pride.
Thou art a most pernicious usurer:
Froward by nature, enemy to peace;
Lascivious, wanton, more than well beseems
A man of thy profession, and degree;
And for thy treachery, What 's more manifest?
In that thou laid'st a trap to take my life,
As well at London bridge, as at the Tower?
Beside, I fear me, if thy thoughts were sifted,
The king, thy sovereign, is not quite exempt
From envious malice of thy swelling heart.

Win. Gloster, I do defy thee.—Lords, vouch-
    safe
To give me hearing what I shall reply.
If I were covetous, ambitious, or perverse,
As he will have me, How am I so poor?
Or how haps it, I seek not to advance
Or raise myself, but keep my wonted calling?
And for dissension, Who preferreth peace
More than I do,—except I be provok'd?
No, my good lords, it is not that offends;
It is not that, that hath incens'd the duke:

278

It is, because no one should sway but he;
No one, but he, should be about the king;
And that engenders thunder in his breast,
And makes him roar these accusations forth.
But he shall know, I am as good——

Glo.   As good?
Thou bastard of my grandfather!"—

Win. Ay, lordly sir: For what are you, I
    pray,
But one imperious in another's throne?

Glo. Am I not the protector, saucy priest?

Win. And am I not a prelate of the church?

Glo. Yes, as an outlaw in a castle keeps,
And useth it to patronage his theft.

Win. Unreverent Gloster!

Glo.   Thou art reverent
Touching thy spiritual function, not thy life.

Win. This Rome shall remedy.

War.   Roam thither then.

Som. My lord, it were your duty to forbear.

War. Ay, see the bishop be not overborne.

Som. Methinks, my lord should be religious,
And know the office that belongs to such.

War. Methinks, his lordship should be hum-
    bler;
It fitteth not a prelate so to plead.

Som. Yes, when his holy state is touch'd so
    near.

War. State holy, or unhallow'd, what of that?
Is not his grace protector to the king?

Plan. Plantagenet, I see, must hold his tongue;
Lest it be said, "Speak, sirrah, when you should
Must your bold verdict enter talk with lords?"
Else would I have a fling at Winchester. [*Aside*

K. Hen. Uncles of Gloster, and of Winchester
The special watchmen of our English weal;
I would prevail, if prayers might prevail,
To join your hearts in love and amity,
O, what a scandal is it to our crown,
That two such noble peers as ye, should jar!
Believe me, lords, my tender years can tell,
Civil dissension is a viperous worm,
That gnaws the bowels of the commonwealth.—
    [*A Noise within;* "Down with the tawny coats!"
What tumult 's this?

War.   An uproar, I dare warrant,

Begun through malice of the bishop's men.
[*A Noise again;* "Stones! Stones!"]

Enter the MAYOR OF LONDON, *attended.*

May. O, my good lords,—and virtuous Hen-
ry,—
Pity the city of London, pity us!
The bishop and the duke of Gloster's men,
Forbidden late to carry any weapon,
Have fill'd their pockets full of pebble-stones;
And, banding themselves in contrary parts,
Do pelt so fast at one another's pate,
That many have their giddy brains knock'd out:
Our windows are broke down in every street,
And we, for fear, compell'd to shut our shops.

Enter, skirmishing, the Retainers *of* GLOSTER *and*
WINCHESTER, *with bloody pates.*

K. Hen. We charge you, on allegiance to our-
self,
To hold your slaught'ring hands, and keep the
peace.
Pray, uncle Gloster, mitigate this strife.
1st Serv. Nay, if we be
Forbidden stones, we'll fall to it with our teeth.
2nd Serv. Do what ye dare, we are as resolute.
[*Skirmish again.*
Glo. You of my household, leave this peevish
broil,
And set this unaccustom'd fight aside.
1st Serv. My lord, we know your grace to be
a man
Just and upright; and, for your royal birth,
Inferior to none, but his majesty:
And, ere that we will suffer such a prince,
So kind a father of the commonweal,
To be disgraced by an inkhorn mate,
We, and our wives, and children, all will fight,
And have our bodies slaughter'd by thy foes.
2nd Serv. Ay, and the very parings of our nails
Shall pitch a field, when we are dead.
[*Skirmish again.*
Glo.   Stay, stay, I say!
And, if you love me, as you say you do,
Let me persuade you to forbear a while.
K. Hen. O, how this discord doth afflict my
soul!—
Can you, my lord of Winchester, behold
My sighs and tears, and will not once relent?
Who should be pitiful, if you be not!
Or who should study to prefer a peace,
If holy churchmen take delight in broils?

War. My lord protector, yield;—yield, Win-
chester;—
Except you mean, with obstinate repulse,
To slay your sovereign, and destroy the realm,
You see what mischief, and what murder too,
Hath been enacted through your enmity;
Then be at peace, except ye thirst for blood.
Win. He shall submit, or I will never yield.
Glo. Compassion on the king commands me
stoop;
Or, I would see his heart out, ere the priest
Should ever get that privilege of me.
War. Behold, my lord of Winchester, the duke
Hath banish'd moody discontented fury,
As by his smoothed brows it doth appear:
Why look you still so stern, and tragical?
Glo. Here, Winchester, I offer thee my hand.
K. Hen. Fye, uncle Beaufort! I have heard
you preach,
That malice was a great and grievous sin:
And will not you maintain the thing you teach,
But prove a chief offender in the same?
War. Sweet king!—the bishop hath a kindly
gird.—
For shame, my lord of Winchester! relent;
What, shall a child instruct you what to do?
Win. Well, duke of Gloster, I will yield to
thee;
Love for thy love, and hand for hand I give.
Glo. Ay; but, I fear me, with a hollow heart.—
See here, my friends, and loving countrymen·
This token serveth for a flag of truce,
Betwixt ourselves, and all our followers:
So help me God, as I dissemble not!
Win. So help me God, as I intend it not!
[*Aside*
K. Hen. O loving uncle, kind duke of Gloster,
How joyful am I made by this contract!—
Away, my masters! trouble us no more;
But join in friendship, as your lords have done.
1st Serv. Content; I'll to the surgeon's.
2nd Serv.   And so will I.
3rd Serv. And I will see what physic the tavern
affords.   [*Exeunt* Servants, Mayor, &c.
War. Accept this scroll, most gracious sove-
reign; ·
Which in the right of Richard Plantagenet
We do exhibit to your majesty.
Glo. Well urg'd, my lord of Warwick;—for
sweet prince,
An if your grace mark every circumstance,
You have great reason to do Richard right:

Especially, for those occasions
At Eltham-place I told your majesty.

K. Hen. And those occasions, uncle, were of
　　force:
Therefore, my loving lords, our pleasure is,
That Richard be restored to his blood.

War. Let Richard be restored to his blood;
So shall his father's wrongs be recompens'd.

Win. As will the rest, so willeth Winchester.

K. Hen. If Richard will be true, not that alone,
But all the whole inheritance I give,
That doth belong unto the house of York,
From whence you spring by lineal descent.

Plan. Thy honour'd servant vows obedience,
And humble service, till the point of death.

K. Hen. Stoop then, and set your knee against
　　my foot;
And, in reguerdon of that duty done,
I girt thee with the valiant sword of York:
Rise, Richard, like a true Plantagenet;
And rise created princely duke of York.

Plan. And so thrive Richard, as thy foes may
　　fall!
And as my duty springs, so perish they
That grudge one thought against your majesty!

All. Welcome, high prince, the mighty duke
　　of York!

Som. Perish, base prince, ignoble duke of York.
　　　　　　　　　　　　　　　　[*Aside.*

Glo. Now will it best avail your majesty,
To cross the seas, and to be crown'd in France:
The presence of a king engenders love
Amongst his subjects, and his loyal friends;
As it disanimates his enemies.

K. Hen. When Gloster says the word, king
　　Henry goes;
For friendly counsel cuts off many foes.

Glo. Your ships already are in readiness.
　　　　　　　　　　　　[*Exeunt all but* EXE.

Exe. Ay, we may march in England, or in
　　France
Not seeing what is likely to ensue:
This late dissension, grown betwixt the peers,
Burns under feigned ashes of forg'd love,
And will at last break out into a flame:
As fester'd members rot but by degrees,
Till bones, and flesh, and sinews, fall away,
So will this base and envious discord breed.
And now I fear that fatal prophecy,
Which, in the time of Henry, nam'd the Fifth,
Was in the mouth of every sucking babe,—
That Henry, born at Monmouth, should win all;

And Henry, born at Windsor, should lose all:
Which is so plain, that Exeter doth wish
His days may finish ere that hapless time. [*Exit.*

SCENE II.—France.　*Before Rouen*

Enter LA PUCELLE *disguised, and Soldiers dressed
like Countrymen, with Sacks upon their Backs.*

Puc. These are the city gates, the gates of
　　Rouen,
Through which our policy must make a breach:
Take heed, be wary how you place your words;
Talk like the vulgar sort of market men,
That come to gather money for their corn.
If we have entrance, (as, I hope, we shall,)
And that we find the slothful watch but weak,
I'll by a sign give notice to our friends,
That Charles the Dauphin may encounter them.

1st Sold. Our sacks shall be a mean to sack the
　　city,
And we be lords and rulers over Rouen:
Therefore we'll knock.　　　　　[*Knocks.*

Guard. [*Within.*] Qui est là?

Puc. Paisans, pauvres gens de France:
Poor market-folks, that come to sell their corn.

Guard. Enter, go in; the market bell is rung.
　　　　　　　　　　　　[*Opens the Gates.*

Puc. Now, Rouen, I'll shake thy bulwarks to
　　the ground. [*Puc., &c., enter the City.*

Enter CHARLES, BASTARD OF ORLEANS, ALENÇON,
and Forces.

Char. Saint Dennis bless this happy stratagem!
And once again we'll sleep secure in Rouen.

Bast. Here enter'd Pucelle, and her practi-
　　sants;
Now she is there, how will she specify
Where is the best and safest passage in?

Alen. By thrusting out a torch from yonder
　　tower;
Which, once discern'd, shows, that her meaning
　　is,—
No way to that, for weakness, which she enter'd."

Enter LA PUCELLE *on a Battlement; holding out
a Torch burning.*

Puc. Behold, this is the happy wedding torch,
That joineth Rouen unto her countrymen;
But burning fatal to the Talbotites.

Bast. See, noble Charles! the beacon of our
　　friend,
The burning torch in yonder turret stands.

Char. Now shine it like a comet of revenge,
A prophet to the fall of all our foes !

Alen. Defer no time, Delays have dangerous
ends ;
Enter, and cry—"The Dauphin !"—presently,
And then do execution on the watch. [*They enter.*

[*Alarums. Enter* TALBOT, *and certain English.*

Tal. France, thou shalt rue this treason with thy
tears,
If Talbot but survive thy treachery.
Pucelle, that witch, that damned sorceress,
Hath wrought this hellish mischief unawares
That hardly we escap'd the pride of France.
[*Exeunt to the Town.*

Alarum: Excursions. Enter, from the Town,
BEDFORD, *brought in sick, in a Chair, with*
TALBOT, BURGUNDY, *and the English Forces.*
Then, enter on the Walls, LA PUCELLE, CHARLES,
BASTARD, ALENÇON, *and Others.*

Puc. Good morrow, gallants ! want ye corn for
bread ?
I think, the duke of Burgundy will fast,
Before he 'll buy again at such a rate :
'T was full of darnel : Do you like the taste ?

Bur. Scoff on, vile fiend, and shameless cour-
tezan !
I trust, ere long, to choke thee with thine own,
And make thee curse the harvest of that corn.

Char. Your grace may starve, perhaps, before
that time.

Bed. O, let no words, but deeds, revenge this
treason !

Puc. What will you do, good grey-beard ?
break a lance,
And run a tilt at death within a chair ?

Tal. Foul fiend of France, and hag of all de-
spite,
Encompass'd with thy lustful paramours !
Becomes it thee to taunt his valiant age,
And twit with cowardice a man half dead ?
Damsel, I 'll have a bout with you again.
Or else let Talbot perish with this shame.

Puc. Are you so hot, sir ?—Yet, Pucelle, hold
thy peace ;
If Talbot do but thunder, rain will follow—
[TAL. *and the rest, consult together.*
God speed the parliament ! who shall be the
speaker ?

Tal. Dare ye come forth, and meet us in the
field ?

Puc. Belike, your lordship takes us then for
fools,
To try if that our own be ours, or no.

Tal. I speak not to that railing Hécaté,
But unto thee, Alençon, and the rest ;
Will ye, like soldiers, come and fight it out ?

Alen. Signior, no.

Tal. Signior, hang !—base muleteers of France !
Like peasant foot-boys do they keep the walls,
And dare not take up arms like gentlemen.

Puc. Captains, away : let 's get us from the
walls ;
For Talbot means no goodness, by his looks.—
God be wi' you, my lord ! we came, sir, but to tell
you
That we are here.
[*Exeunt* LA PUC., &c., *from the Walls.*

Tal. And there will we be too, ere it be long,
Or else reproach be Talbot's greatest fame !—
Vow, Burgundy, by honour of thy house,
(Prick'd on by public wrongs, sustain'd in France,)
Either to get the town again, or die :
And I,—as sure as English Henry lives,
And as his father here was conqueror ;
As sure as in this late-betrayed town
Great Cœur-de-Lion's heart was buried ;
So sure I swear, to get the town, or die.

Bur. My vows are equal partners with thy
vows.

Tal. But, ere we go, regard this dying prince,
The valiant duke of Bedford :—Come, my lord,
We will bestow you in some better place,
Fitter for sickness, and for crazy age.

Bed. Lord Talbot, do not so dishonour me :
Here will I sit before the walls of Rouen,
And will be partner of your weal, or woe.

Bur. Courageous Bedford, let us now persuade
you.

Bed. Not to be gone from hence ; for once I
read,
That stout Pendragon, in his litter,[*] sick,
Came to the field, and vanquished his foes :
Methinks, I should revive the soldiers' hearts,
Because I ever found them as myself.

Tal. Undaunted spirit in a dying breast :—
Then be it so :—Heavens keep old Bedford
safe !—
And now no more ado, brave Burgundy,
But gather we our forces out of hand,
And set upon our boasting enemy.
[*Exeunt* BUR., TAL., *and Forces, leaving* BED.,
and Others.

III

Alarum: Excursions. Enter Sir JOHN FASTOLFE, *and a Captain.*

Cap. Whither away, sir John Fastolfe, in such haste?

Fast. Whither away? to save myself by flight;
We are like to have the overthrow again.

Cap. What! will you fly, and leave lord Talbot?

Fast.　　　　　　　　　　Ay,
All the Talbots in the world, to save my life.
　　　　　　　　　　　　　　　　　[*Exit.*

Cap. Cowardly knight! ill fortune follow thee!
　　　　　　　　　　　　　　　　　[*Exit.*

Retreat: Excursions. Enter, from the Town, LA PUCELLE, ALENÇON, CHARLES, *&c., and Excunt, flying.*

Bed. Now, quiet soul, depart when heaven please;
For I have seen our enemies' overthrow.
What is the trust or strength of foolish man?
They, that of late were daring with their scoffs,
Are glad and fain by flight to save themselves.
　　　　　　[*Dies, and is carried off in his Chair.*

Alarum: Enter TALBOT, BURGUNDY, *and Others.*

Tal. Lost, and recover'd in a day again!
This is a double honour, Burgundy:
Yet, heavens have glory for this victory!

Bur. Warlike and matchless Talbot, Burgundy
Enshrines thee in his heart; and there erects
Thy noble deeds, as valour's monument.

Tal. Thanks, gentle duke. But where is Pucelle now?
I think, her old familiar is asleep:
Now where 's the Bastard's braves, and Charles his glceks?
What, all a-mort? Rouen hangs her head for grief,
That such a valiant company are fled.
Now will we take some order in the town,
Placing therein some expert officers;
And then depart to Paris, to the king;
For there young Harry, with his nobles, lies.

Bur. What wills lord Talbot, pleaseth Burgundy.

Tal. But yet, before we go, let 's not forget
The noble duke of Bedford, late deceas'd
But see his exequies fulfill'd in Rouen;
A braver soldier never couched lance,
A gentler heart did never sway in court
852

But kings and mightiest potentates, must die
For that 's the end of human misery.　[*Exeunt.*

SCENE III.—*The Same. The Plains near the City.*

Enter CHARLES, *the* BASTARD, ALENÇON, LA PUCELLE, *and Forces.*

Puc. Dismay not, princes, at this accident,
Nor grieve that Rouen is so recover'd:
Care is no cure, but rather corrosive,
For things that are not to be remedied.
Let frantic Talbot triumph for a while,
And like a peacock sweep along his tail;
We 'll pull his plumes, and take away his train,
If Dauphin, and the rest, will be but rul'd.

Char. We have been guided by thee hitherto,
And of thy cunning had no diffidence;
One sudden foil shall never breed distrust.

Bast. Search out thy wit for secret policies,
And we will make thee famous through the world.

Alen. We 'll set thy statue in some holy place,
And have thee reverenc'd like a blessed saint;
Employ thee then, sweet virgin, for our good.

Puc. Then thus it must be; this doth Joan devise:
By fair persuasions, mix'd with sugar'd words,
We will entice the duke of Burgundy
To leave the Talbot, and to follow us.

Char. Ay, marry, sweeting, if we could do that,
France were no place for Henry's warriors;
Nor should that nation boast it so with us,
But be extirped from our provinces.

Alen. For ever should they be expuls'd from France,
And not have title to an earldom here.

Puc. Your honours shall perceive how I will work,
To bring this matter to the wished end.
　　　　　　　　　　　　　　　　　[*Drums heard.*
Hark! by the sound of drum, you may perceive
Their powers are marching unto Paris-ward.

An English March. Enter, and pass over at a distance, TALBOT *and his Forces.*

There goes the Talbot, with his colours spread,
And all the troops of English after him.

A French March. Enter the DUKE OF BURGUNDY *and Forces.*

Now, in the rearward, comes the duke, and his
Fortune, in favour, makes him lag behind.

Summon a parley, we will talk with him.
[*A Parley sounded.*
Char. A parley with the duke of Burgundy.
Bur. Who craves a parley with the Burgundy?
Puc. The princely Charles of France, thy coun-
    tryman.
Bur. What say'st thou, Charles? for I am
    marching hence.
Char. Speak, Pucelle; and enchant him with
    thy words.
Puc. Brave Burgundy, undoubted hope of
    France!
Stay, let thy humble handmaid speak to thee.
Bur. Speak on; but be not over-tedious.
Puc. Look on thy country, look on fertile
    France,
And see the cities and the towns defac'd
By wasting ruin of the cruel foe!
As looks the mother on her lovely babe,
When death doth close his tender dying eyes,
See, see, the pining malady of France;
Behold the wounds, the most unnatural wounds,
Which thou thyself hast given her woful breast!
O, turn thy edged sword another way;
Strike those that hurt, and hurt not those that
    help!
One drop of blood, drawn from thy country's
    bosom,
Should grieve thee more than streams of foreign
    gore;
Return thee, therefore, with a flood of tears,
And wash away thy country's stained spots!
Bur. Either she hath bewitch'd me with her
    words,
Or nature makes me suddenly relent.
Puc. Besides, all French and France exclaims
    on thee,
Doubting thy birth and lawful progeny.
Who join'st thou with, but with a lordly nation,
That will not trust thee, but for profit's sake?
When Talbot hath set footing once in France,
And fashion'd thee that instrument of ill,
Who then, but English Henry, will be lord,
And thou be thrust out, like a fugitive?
Call we to mind,—and mark but this, for proof;—
Was not the duke of Orleans thy foe?
And was he not in England prisoner?
But, when they heard he was thine enemy,
They set him free, without his ransom paid,
In spite of Burgundy, and all his friends.
See then! thou fight'st against thy countrymen,
And join'st with them will be thy slaughter-men.

Come, come, return; return, thou wand'ring lord;
Charles, and the rest, will take thee in their arms.
Bur. I am vanquished; these haughty words
    of hers
Have batter'd me like roaring cannon-shot,
And made me almost yield upon my knees.—
Forgive me, country, and sweet countrymen!
And, lords, accept this hearty kind embrace:
My forces and my power of men are yours;
So, farewell, Talbot; I'll no longer trust thee.
Puc. Done like a Frenchman; turn, and turn
    again!
Char. Welcome, brave duke! thy friendship
    makes us fresh.
Bast. And doth beget new courage in our
    breasts.
Alen. Pucelle hath bravely played her part in
    this,
And doth deserve a coronet of gold.
Char. Now let us on, my lords, and join our
    powers;
And seek how we may prejudice the foe. [*Exeunt.*

SCENE IV.—Paris. *A Room in the Palace.*

Enter KING HENRY, GLOSTER, *and other Lords,*
VERNON, BASSET, &c. *To them,* TALBOT, *and
some of his* Officers.

Tal. My gracious prince,—and honourable
    peers,—
Hearing of your arrival in this realm,
I have a while given truce unto my wars,
To do my duty to my sovereign:
In sign whereof, this arm—that hath reclaim'd
To your obedience fifty fortresses,
Twelve cities, and seven walled towns of strength,
Beside five hundred prisoners of esteem,—
Lets fall his sword before your highness' feet;
And, with submissive loyalty of heart,
Ascribes the glory of his conquest got,
First to my God, and next unto your grace.
K. Hen. Is this the lord Talbot, uncle Gloster,
That hath so long been resident in France?
Glo. Yes, if it please your majesty, my liege.
K. Hen. Welcome, brave captain, and victo-
    rious lord!
When I was young, (as yet I am not old,)
I do remember how my father said,
A stouter champion never handled sword.
Long since we were resolved of your truth,
Your faithful service, and your toil in war;
Yet never have you tasted our reward,

Or been reguerdon'd with so much as thanks,
Because till now we never saw your face:
Therefore, stand up; and, for these good deserts,
We here create you earl of Shrewsbury;
And in our coronation take your place.

[*Exeunt* K. HEN., GLO., TAL., *and* Nobles.

  Ver. Now, sir, to you, that were so hot at sea,
Disgracing of these colours that I wear
In honour of my noble lord of York,—
Dar'st thou maintain the former words thou
           spak'st?

  Bas. Yes, sir; as well as you dare patronage
The envious barking of your saucy tongue
Against my lord, the duke of Somerset.

  Ver. Sirrah, thy lord I honour as he is.

  Bas. Why, what is he? as good a man as
    York.

  Ver. Hark ye; not so: in witness, take ye
    that.   [*Strikes him.*

  Bas. Villain, thou know'st, the law of arms is
    such,
That, who so draws a sword, 't is present death;
Or else this blow should broach thy dearest blood.
But I 'll unto his majesty, and crave
I may have liberty to venge this wrong;
When thou shalt see, I 'll meet thee to thy cost.

  Ver. Well, miscreant, I 'll be there as soon as
    you;
And, after, meet you sooner than you would.
              [*Exeunt.*

ACT IV.

SCENE I.—*The Same. A Room of State.*

Enter KING HENRY, GLOSTER, EXETER, YORK,
SUFFOLK, SOMERSET, WINCHESTER, WARWICK,
TALBOT, *the* GOVERNOR OF PARIS, *and Others.*

  Glo. Lord bishop, set the crown upon his head.

  Win. God save king Henry, of that name the
    sixth!

  Glo. Now, governor of Paris, take your oath,—
              [Gov. *kneels.*
That you elect no other king but him:
Esteem none friends, but such as are his friends;
And none your foes, but such as shall pretend
Malicious practices against his state:
This shall ye do, so help you righteous God!
        [*Exeunt* Gov. *and his Train.*

Enter SIR JOHN FASTOLFE.

  Fast. My gracious sovereign, as I rode from
    Calais,
To haste unto your coronation,
A letter was deliver'd to my hands,
Writ to your grace from the duke of Burgundy.

  Tal. Shame to the duke of Burgundy, and thee!
I vow'd, base knight, when I did meet thee next,
To tear the garter from thy craven's leg.
           [*Plucking it off.*
(Which I have done) because unworthily

Thou wast installed in that high degree.—
Pardon me, princely Henry, and the rest:
This dastard, at the battle of Patay,
When but in all I was six thousand strong,
And that the French were almost ten to one,—
Before we met, or that a stroke was given,
Like to a trusty squire, did run away;
In which assault we lost twelve hundred men;
Myself, and divers gentlemen beside,
Were there surpris'd, and taken prisoners.
Then judge, great lords, if I have done amiss;
Or whether that such cowards ought to wear
This ornament of knighthood, yea, or no.

  Glo. To say the truth, this fact was infamous
And ill beseeming any common man;
Much more a knight, a captain, and a leader.

  Tal. When first this order was ordain'd, my
    lords,
Knights of the garter were of noble birth;
Valiant, and virtuous, full of haughty courage,
Such as were grown to credit by the wars;
Not fearing death, nor shrinking for distress,
But always resolute in worst extremes.
He then, that is not furnish'd in this sort,
Doth but usurp the sacred name of knight,
Profaning this most honourable order;
And should (if I were worthy to be judge,)
Be quite degraded, like a hedge-born swain

That doth presume to boast of gentle blood.

K. Hen. Stain to thy countrymen! thou hear'st
thy doom:
Be packing therefore, thou that wast a knight;
Henceforth we banish thee, on pain of death.—
              [*Exit* Fast.
And now, my lord protector, view the letter
Sent from our uncle duke of Burgundy.

Glo. What means his grace, that he hath
chang'd his style?
         [*Viewing the superscription.*
No more but, plain and bluntly,—" To the king!"
Hath he forgot, he is his sovereign?
Or doth this churlish superscription
Pretend some alteration in good will?
What 's here?——   [*Reads.*

   I have, upon especial cause,—
Mov'd with compassion of my country's wreck,
Together with the pitiful complaints
Of such as your oppression feeds upon,—
Forsaken your pernicious faction,
And join'd with Charles, the rightful king of France.

O monstrous treachery! Can this be so
That in alliance, amity, and oaths,
There should be found such false dissembling guile?

K. Hen. What! doth my uncle Burgundy revolt?

Glo. He doth, my lord; and is become your foe.

K. Hen. Is that the worst, this letter doth contain?

Glo. It is the worst, and all, my lord, he writes.

K. Hen. Why then, lord Talbot there shall talk
with him,
And give him chastisement for this abuse:—
My lord, how say you? are you not content?

Tal. Content, my liege? Yes; but that I am
prevented,
I should have begg'd I might have been employ'd.

K. Hen. Then gather strength, and march unto
him straight:
Let him perceive, how ill we brook his treason,
And what offence it is, to flout his friends.

Tal. I go, my lord; in heart desiring still,
You may behold confusion of your foes.   [*Exit.*

       Enter Vernon *and* Basset.

Ver. Grant me the combat, gracious sovereign!

Bass. And me, my lord, grant me the combat
too!

York. This is my servant: Hear him, noble
prince!

Som. And this is mine: Sweet Henry, favour
him!

K. Hen. Be patient, lords; and give them leave
to speak.—
Say, gentlemen, What makes you thus exclaim?
And wherefore crave you combat? or with whom?

Ver. With him, my lord; for he hath done me
wrong.

Bas. And I with him; for he hath done me
wrong.

K. Hen. What is that wrong whereof you both
complain?
First let me know, and then I 'll answer you.

Bas. Crossing the sea from England into
France,
This fellow here, with envious carping tongue,
Upbraided me about the rose I wear;
Saying,—the sanguine colour of the leaves
Did represent my master's blushing cheeks,
When stubbornly he did repugn the truth,
About a certain question in the law,
Argu'd betwixt the duke of York and him;
With other vile and ignominious terms:
In confutation of which rude reproach,
And in defence of my lord's worthiness,
I crave the benefit of law of arms.

Ver. And that is my petition, noble lord:
For though he seem, with forged quaint conceit,
To set a gloss upon his bold intent,
Yet know, my lord, I was provok'd by him;
And he first took exceptions at this badge,
Pronouncing—that the paleness of this flower
Bewray'd the faintness of my master's heart.

York. Will not this malice, Somerset, be left?

Som. Your private grudge, my lord of York,
will out,
Though ne'er so cunningly you smother it.

K. Hen. Good Lord! what madness rules in
brain-sick men;
When, for so slight and frivolous a cause,
Such factious emulations shall arise!
Good cousins both, of York and Somerset,
Quiet yourselves, I pray, and be at peace.

York. Let this dissension first be tried by fight,
And then your highness shall command a peace.

Som. The quarrel toucheth none but us alone;
Betwixt ourselves let us decide it then.

York. There is my pledge; accept it, Somerset.

Ver. Nay, let it rest where it began at first.

Bas. Confirm it so, mine honourable lord.

Glo. Confirm it so? Confounded be your strife
And perish ye, with your audacious prate!
Presumptuous vassals! are you not asham'd,
With this immodest clamorous outrage

To trou'le and disturb the king and us?
And you, my lords,—methinks, you do not well,
To bear with their perverse objections;
Much less, to take occasion from their mouths
To raise a mutiny betwixt yourselves;
Let me persuade you take a better course.

   Exe. It grieves his higness;—Good my lords;
be friends.

   K. Hen. Come hither, you that would be combatants:

Henceforth, I charge you, as you love our favour,
Quite to forget this quarrel, and the cause.—
And you, my lords,—remember where we are;
In France, amongst a fickle wavering nation:
If they perceive dissension in our looks,
And that within ourselves we disagree,
How will their grudging stomachs be provok'd
To wilful disobedience, and rebel!
Beside, What infamy will there arise,
When foreign princes shall be certified,
That, for a toy, a thing of no regard,
King Henry's peers, and chief nobility,
Destroy'd themselves, and lost the realm of France?
O, think upon the conquest of my father,
My tender years; and let us not forego
That for a trifle, that was bought with blood!
Let me be umpire in this doubtful strife.
I see no reason, if I wear this rose,

      [*Putting on a red Rose.*

That any one should therefore be suspicious
I more incline to Somerset, than York:
Both are my kinsmen, and I love them both:
As well they may upbraid me with my crown,
Because, forsooth, the king of Scots is crown'd.
But your discretions better can persuade,
Than I am able to instruct or teach:
And therefore, as we hither came in peace,
So let us still continue peace and love.—
Cousin of York, we institute your grace
To be our regent in these parts of France:—
And good my lord of Somerset, unite
Your troops of horsemen with his bands of foot;—
And, like true subjects, sons of your progenitors,
Go cheerfully together, and digest
Your angry choler on your enemies.
Ourself, my lord protector, and the rest,
After some respite, will return to Calais;
From thence to England; where I hope ere long
To be presented, by your victories,
With Charles, Alençon, and that traitorous rout.

    [*Flourish.   Exeunt K. HEN., GLO., SOM.,*
      WIN., SUF., *and* BAS.

   War. My lord of York, I promise you, the king
Prettily, methought, did play the orator.

   York. And so he did; but yet I like it not,
In that he wears the badge of Somerset.

   War. Tush! that was but his fancy, blame him
not;
I dare presume, sweet prince, he thought no harm.

   York. And, if I wist, he did,—But let it rest;
Other affairs must now be managed.

     [*Exeunt* YORK, WAR., *and* VER.

   Exe. Well didst thou, Richard, to suppress thy
voice:
For, had the passions of thy heart burst out,
I fear, we should have seen decipher'd there
More rancorous spite, more furious raging broils,
Than yet can be imagin'd or suppos'd.
But howsoe'er, no simple man that sees
This jarring discord of nobility,
This should'ring of each other in the court,
This factious bandying of their favourites,
But that it doth presage some ill event.
'Tis much, when sceptres are in children's hands;
But more, when envy breeds unkind division;
There comes the ruin, there begins confusion.

      [*Exit.*

SCENE II.—France.   *Before* Bourdeaux.

Enter TALBOT, *with his Forces.*

   Tal. Go to the gates of Bourdeaux, trumpeter,
Summon their general unto the wall.

*Trumpet sounds a Parley.   Enter, on the Walls,
the* GENERAL *of the French Forces, and Others.*

English John Talbot, captains, calls you forth,
Servant in arms to Harry king of England;
And thus he would,—Open your city gates,
Be humble to us; call my sovereign yours,
And do him homage as obedient subjects,
And I'll withdraw me and my bloody power:
But, if you frown upon this proffer'd peace,
You tempt the fury of my three attendants,
Lean famine, quartering steel, and climbing fire
Who, in a moment, even with the earth
Shall lay your stately and air-braving towers,
If you forsake the offer of their love.

   Gen. Thou ominous and fearful owl of death,
Our nation's terror, and their bloody scourge!
The period of thy tyranny approacheth.
On us thou canst not enter, but by death:
For, I protest, we are well fortified,
And strong enough to issue out and fight:

If thou retire, the Dauphin, well appointed,
Stands with the snares of war to tangle thee:
On either hand thee there are squadrons pitch'd,
To wall thee from the liberty of flight;
And no way canst thou turn thee for redress,
But death doth front thee with apparent spoil,
And pale destruction meets thee in the face.
Ten thousand French have ta'en the sacrament,
To rive their dangerous artillery
Upon no christian soul but English Talbot.
Lo! there thou stand'st, a breathing valiant man,
Of an invincible unconquer'd spirit:
This is the latest glory of thy praise,
That I, thy enemy, due thee withal;
For ere the glass, that now begins to run,
Finish the process of his sandy hour,
These eyes, that see thee now well coloured,
Shall see thee wither'd, bloody, pale, and dead.
　　　　　　　　　　　　　　[*Drum afar off.*
Hark! hark! the Dauphin's drum, a warning bell,
Sings heavy music to thy timorous soul;
And mine shall ring thy dire departure out.
　　　　　　[*Exeunt* GEN., *&c., from the Walls.*
Tal. He fables not, I hear the enemy;—
Out, some light horsemen, and peruse their wings.—
O, negligent and heedless discipline!
How are we park'd, and bounded in a pale;
A little herd of England's timorous deer,
Maz'd with a yelping kennel of French curs!
If we be English deer, be then in blood;
Not rascal-like, to fall down with a pinch;
But rather moody-mad, and desperate stags,
Turn on the bloody hounds with heads of steel,
And make the cowards stand aloof at bay:
Sell every man his life as dear as mine,
And they shall find dear deer of us, my friends.—
God, and Saint George! Talbot, and England's
　　　right!
Prosper our colours in this dangerous fight!
　　　　　　　　　　　　　　　　[*Exeunt.*

SCENE III.—*Plains in Gascony.*

Enter YORK, *with Forces; to him a Messenger.*

York. Are not the speedy scouts return'd again,
That dogg'd the mighty army of the Dauphin?
Mess. They are return'd, my lord; and give it
　　　out,
That he is march'd to Bourdeaux with his power,
To fight with Talbot: As he march'd along,
By your espial's were discovered
Two mightier troops than that the Dauphin led;

Which join'd with him, and made their march for
　　　Bourdeaux.
York. A plague upon that villain Somerset;
That thus delays my promised supply
Of horsemen, that were levied for this siege!
Renowned Talbot doth expect my aid;
And I am lowted by a traitor villain,[33]
And cannot help the noble chevalier:
God comfort him in this necessity!
If he miscarry, farewell wars in France.

Enter SIR WILLIAM LUCY.

Lucy. Thou princely leader of our English
　　　strength,
Never so needful on the earth of France,
Spur to the rescue of the noble Talbot;
Who now is girdled with a waist of iron,
And hemm'd about with grim destruction:
To Bourdeaux, warlike duke! to Bourdeaux, York!
Else, farewell Talbot, France, and England's hon-
　　　our.
York. O God! that Somerset—who in proud
　　　heart
Doth stop my cornets—were in Talbot's place!
So should we save a valiant gentleman,
By forfeiting a traitor and a coward.
Mad ire, and wrathful fury, makes me weep,
That thus we die, while remiss traitors sleep.
Lucy. O, send some succour to the distress'd
　　　lord!
York. He dies, we lose; I break my warlike word;
We mourn, France smiles; we lose, they daily get;
All 'long of this vile traitor Somerset.
Lucy. Then, God take mercy on brave Talbot's
　　　soul!
And on his son, young John; whom, two hours
　　　since,
I met in travel toward his warlike father!
This seven years did not Talbot see his son;
And now they meet where both their lives are done.
York. Alas! what joy shall noble Talbot have,
To bid his young son welcome to his grave!
Away! vexation almost stops my breath,
That sunder'd friends greet in the hour of death.—
Lucy, farewell: no more my fortune can,
But curse the cause I cannot aid the man.—
Maine, Blois, Poictiers, and Tours, are won away
'Long all of Somerset, and his delay.　　[*Exit.*
Lucy. Thus, while the vulture of sedition
Feeds in the bosom of such great commanders,
Sleeping neglection doth betray to loss
The conquest of our scarce-cold conqueror,

That ever-living man of memory,
Henry the Fifth :—Whiles they each other cross,
Lives, honours, lands, and all, hurry to loss. [*Exit.*

SCENE IV.—*Other Plains of Gascony.*

Enter SOMERSET, *with his Forces; an Officer of*
TALBOT'S *with him.*

Som. It is too late; I cannot send them now;
This expedition was by York, and Talbot,
Too rashly plotted; all our general force
Might with a sally of the very town
Be buckled with : the over-daring Talbot
Hath sullied all his gloss of former honour,
By this unheedful, desperate, wild adventure :
York set him on to fight, and die in shame,
That, Talbot dead, great York might bear the
    name.
Off. Here is sir William Lucy, who with me
Set from our o'er-match'd forces forth for aid.

Enter SIR WILLIAM LUCY.

Som. How now, sir William! whither were you
    sent ?
Lucy. Whither, my lord ? from bought and
    sold lord Talbot !
Who, ring'd about with bold adversity,
Cries out for noble York and Somerset,
To beat assailing death from his weak legions.
And whiles the honourable captain there
Drops bloody sweat from his war-wearied limbs,
And, in advantage ling'ring, looks for rescue,
You, his false hopes, the trust of England's
    honour,
Keep off aloof with worthless emulation.
Let not your private discord keep away
The levied succours that should lend him aid
While he, renowned noble gentleman,
Yields up his life unto a world of odds :
Orleans the Bastard, Charles, and Burgundy,
Alençon, Reignier, compass him about,
And Talbot perisheth by your default.
Som. York set him on, York should have sent
    him aid.
Lucy. And York as fast upon your grace ex-
    claims ;
Swearing that you withhold his levied host,
Collected for this expedition
Som. York lies ; he might have sent and had
    the horse :
I owe him little duty, and less love ;
And take foul scorn, to fawn on him by sending

Lucy. The fraud of England, not the force of
    France,
Hath now entrapp'd the noble-minded Talbot :
Never to England shall he bear his life ;
But dies, betray'd to fortune by your strife.
Som. Come, go ; I will despatch the horsemen
    straight :
Within six hours they will be at his aid.
Lucy. Too late comes rescue ; he is ta'en, or
    slain :
For fly he could not, if he would have fled ;
And fly would Talbot never, though he might.
Som. If he be dead, brave Talbot then adieu !
Lucy. His fame lives in the world, his shame
    in you.   [*Exeunt.*

SCENE V.—*The English Camp near* Bourdeaux.

Enter TALBOT *and* JOHN *his Son.*

Tal. O young John Talbot ! I did send for thee,
To tutor thee in stratagems of war ;
That Talbot's name might be in thee reviv'd,
When sapless age, and weak unable limbs,
Should bring thy father to his drooping chair.
But,—O malignant and ill-boding stars !—
Now thou art come unto a feast of death,
A terrible and unavoided danger :
Therefore, dear boy, mount on my swiftest horse,
And I'll direct thee how thou shalt escape
By sudden flight : come, dally not, be gone.
John. Is my name Talbot ? and am I your
    son ?
And shall I fly ? O, if you love my mother,
Dishonour not her honourable name,
To make a bastard, and a slave of me :
The world will say—He is not Talbot's blood,
That basely fled, when noble Talbot stood.
Tal. Fly, to revenge my death, if I be slain.
John. He, that flies so, will ne'er return again.
Tal. If we both stay, we both are sure to die.
John. Then let me stay ; and, father, do
    you fly :
Your loss is great, so your regard should be ;
My worth unknown, no loss is known in me.
Upon my death the French can little boast ;
In yours they will, in you all hopes are lost.
Flight cannot stain the honour you have won ;
But mine it will, that no exploit have done :
You fled for vantage every one will swear ;
But, if I bow, they'll say—it was for fear.
There is no hope that ever I will stay,
If, the first hour, I shrink, and run away.

Here, on my knee, I beg mortality,
Rather than life preserv'd with infamy.

Tal. Shall all thy mother's hopes lie in one
    tomb?

John. Ay, rather than I 'll shame my mother's
    womb.

Tal. Upon my blessing I command thee go.

John. To fight I will, but not to fly the foe.

Tal. Part of thy father may be sav'd in thee.

John. No part of him, but will be shame in me.

Tal. Thou never hadst renown, nor can'st not
    lose it.

John. Yes, your renowned name: Shall flight
    abuse it?

Tal. Thy father's charge shall clear thee from
    that stain.

John. You cannot witness for me, being slain.
If death be so apparent, then both fly.

Tal. And leave my followers here, to fight, and
    die?
My age was never tainted with such shame.

John. And shall my youth be guilty of such
    blame?
No more can I be sever'd from your side,
Than can yourself yourself in twain divide:
Stay, go, do what you will, the like do I;
For live I will not, if my father die.

Tal. Then here I take my leave of thee, fair
    son,
Born to eclipse thy life this afternoon.
Come, side by side together live and die;
And soul with soul from France to heaven fly.
                  [*Exeunt.*

SCENE VI.—*A Field of Battle.*

Alarum: Excursions, wherein TALBOT'S *Son is
hemmed about, and* TALBOT *rescues him.*

Tal. Saint George and victory! fight, soldiers,
    fight:
The regent hath with Talbot broke his word,
And left us to the rage of France his sword.
Where is John Talbot?—pause, and take thy
    breath;
I gave thee life, and rescu'd thee from death.

John. O twice my father! twice am I thy son:
The life, thou gav'st me first, was lost and done;
Till with thy warlike sword, despite of fate,
To my determin'd time thou gav'st new date.

Tal. When from the Dauphin's crest thy sword
    struck fire,
It warm'd thy father's heart with proud desire

Of bold fac'd victory. Then leaden age,
Quicken'd with youthful spleen, and warlike rage,
Beat down Alençon, Orleans, Burgundy,
And from the pride of Gallia rescu'd thee.
The ireful bastard Orleans—that drew blood
From thee, my boy; and had the maidenhood
Of thy first fight—I soon encountered;
And, interchanging blows, I quickly shed
Some of his bastard blood; and, in disgrace,
Bespoke him thus: "Contaminated, base,
And misbegotten blood I spill of thine,
Mean and right poor; for that pure blood of mine,
Which thou didst force from Talbot, my brave
    boy:"—
Here, purposing the Bastard to destroy,
Came in strong rescue. Speak, thy father's care;
Art not thou weary, John? How dost thou fare?
Wilt thou yet leave the battle, boy, and fly,
Now thou art seal'd the son of chivalry?
Fly, to revenge my death, when I am dead;
The help of one stands me in little stead.
O, too much folly is it, well I wot,
To hazard all our lives in one small boat.
If I to-day die not with Frenchmen's rage,
To-morrow I shall die with mickle age:
By me they nothing gain, an if I stay,
'T is but the short'ning of my life one day:
In thee thy mother dies, our household's name,
My death's revenge, thy youth, and England's
    fame:
All these, and more, we hazard by thy stay;
All these are sav'd, if thou wilt fly away.

John. The sword of Orleans hath not made me
    smart,
These words of yours draw life-blood from my
    heart:
On that advantage, bought with such a shame,
(To save a paltry life, and slay bright fame,)
Before young Talbot from old Talbot fly,
The coward horse, that bears me, fall and die!
And like me to the peasant boys of France;
To be shame's scorn, and subject of mischance!
Surely, by all the glory you have won,
An if I fly, I am not Talbot's son;
Then talk no more of flight, it is no boot;
If son to Talbot, die at Talbot's foot.

Tal. Then follow thou thy desperate sire of
    Crete,
Thou Icarus; thy life to me is sweet:
If thou wilt fight, fight by thy father's side;
And, commendable prov'd, let's die in pride.
                  [*Exeunt.*

SCENE VII.—*Another Part of the Same.*

Alarum: Excursions. Enter TALBOT *wounded, supported by a Servant.*

Tal. Where is my other life?—mine own is gone;—
O, where 's young Talbot? where is valiant John?—
Triumphant death, smear'd with captivity!
Young Talbot's valour makes me smile at thee:—
When he perceiv'd me shrink, and on my knee,
His bloody sword he brandish'd over me,
And, like a hungry lion, did commence
Rough deeds of rage, and stern impatience;
But when my angry guardant stood alone,
Tend'ring my ruin, and assail'd of none,
Dizzy-ey'd fury, and great rage of heart,
Suddenly made him from my side to start
Into the clust'ring battle of the French;
And in that sea of blood my boy did drench
His overmounting spirit; and there died
My Icarus, my blossom, in his pride.

Enter Soldiers, *bearing the Body of* JOHN TALBOT.

Serv. O my dear lord! lo, where your son is borne!
Tal. Thou antic death, which laugh'st us here to scorn,
Anon, from thy insulting tyranny,
Coupled in bonds of perpetuity,
Two Talbots, winged through the lither sky,[38]
In thy despite, shall 'scape mortality.—
O thou whose wounds become hard-favour'd death,
Speak to thy father, ere thou yield thy breath:
Brave death by speaking, whether he will, or no;
Imagine him a Frenchman, and thy foe.—
Poor boy! he smiles, methinks; as who should say—
Had death been French, then death had died today.
Come, come, and lay him in his father's arms;
My spirit can no longer bear these harms.
Soldiers, adieu! I have what I would have,
Now my old arms are young John Talbot's grave.
       [*Dies.*

Alarums. Exeunt Soldiers *and* Servant, *leaving the two Bodies. Enter* CHARLES, ALENÇON, BURGUNDY, BASTARD, LA PUCELLE, *and* Forces.

Char. Had York and Somerset brought rescue in,
We should have found a bloody day of this.

Bast. How the young whelp of Talbot's, raging-wood,
Did flesh his puny sword in Frenchmen's blood!
Puc. Once I encounter'd him, and thus I said,
"Thou maiden youth, be vanquish'd by a maid:"
But—with a proud, majestical high scorn,—
He answer'd thus: "Young Talbot was not born
To be the pillage of a giglot wench:"
So, rushing in the bowels of the French,
He left me proudly, as unworthy fight.
Bur. Doubtless, he would have made a noble knight;
See, where he lies inhersed in the arms
Of the most bloody nurser of his harms.
Bast. Hew them to pieces, hack their bones asunder;
Whose life was England's glory, Gallia's wonder.
Char. O, no; forbear: for that which we have fled
During the life, let us not wrong it dead.

Enter SIR WILLIAM LUCY, *attended; a French* Herald *preceding.*

Lucy. Herald,
Conduct me to the Dauphin's tent: to know
Who hath obtain'd the glory of the day.
Char. On what submissive message art thou sent?
Lucy. Submission, Dauphin? 't is a mere French word:
We English warriors wot not what it means,
I come to know what prisoners thou hast ta'en,
And to survey the bodies of the dead.
Char. For prisoners ask'st thou? hell our prison is.
But tell me whom thou seek'st.
Lucy. Where is the great Alcides of the field,
Valiant lord Talbot, earl of Shrewsbury?
Created for his rare success in arms,
Great earl of Washford,[39] Waterford, and Valence;
Lord Talbot of Goodrig and Urchinfield,
Lord Strange of Blackmere, lord Verdun of Alton,
Lord Cromwell of Wingfield, lord Furnival of Sheffield,
The thrice-victorious lord of Falconbridge;
Knight of the noble order of Saint George,
Worthy Saint Michael, and the Golden Fleece;
Great marshal to Henry the Sixth,
Of all his wars within the realm of France?
Puc. Here is a silly stately style indeed!
The Turk, that two-and-fifty kingdoms hath,
Writes not so tedious a style as this,—

Him, that thou magnifiest with all these titles,
Stinking, and fly-blown, lies here at our feet.
  Lucy. Is Talbot slain; the Frenchmen's only
    scourge,
Your kingdom's terror and black Nemesis?
O, were mine eye-balls into bullets turn'd,
That I, in rage, might shoot them at your faces!
O, that I could but call these dead to life!
It were enough to fright the realm of France:
Were but his picture left among you here,
It would amaze the proudest of you all.
Give me their bodies; that I may bear them
    hence,
And give them burial as beseems their worth.

  Puc. I think, this upstart is old Talbot's ghost,
He speaks with such a proud commanding spirit.
For God's sake, let him have 'em; to keep them
    here,
They would but stink, and putrefy the air.
  Char. Go, take their bodies hence.
  Lucy.   I 'll bear them hence:
But from their ashes shall be rear'd
A phœnix that shall make all France afeard.
  Char. So we be rid of them, do with 'em what
    thou wilt.
And now to Paris, in this conquering vein;
All will be ours, now bloody Talbot's slain.
                       [*Exeunt.*

ACT V.

SCENE I.—London.   *A Room in the Palace.*

Enter KING HENRY, GLOSTER, *and* EXETER.

  K. Hen. Have you perus'd the letters from the
    Pope,
The emperor, and the earl of Armagnac?
  Glo. I have, my lord; and their intent is this,—
They humbly sue unto your excellence,
To have a goodly peace concluded of,
Between the realms of England and of France.
  K. Hen. How doth your grace affect their mo-
    tion?
  Glo. Well, my good lord; and as the only
    means
To stop effusion of our Christian blood,
And 'stablish quietness on every side.
  K. Hen. Ay, marry, uncle; for I always
    thought,
It was both impious and unnatural,
That such immanity and bloody strife
Should reign among professors of one faith.
  Glo. Beside, my lord,—the sooner to effect,
And surer bind, this knot of amity,—
The earl of Armagnac—near kin to Charles,
A man of great authority in France,—
Proffers his only daughter to your grace
In marriage, with a large and sumptuous dowry.
  K. Hen. Marriage, uncle! alas! my years are
    young;

And fitter is my study and my books,
Than wanton dalliance with a paramour.
Yet, call the ambassadors; and, as you please,
So let them have their answers every one:
I shall be well content with any choice,
Tends to God's glory, and my country's weal.

Enter a Legate, and Two Ambassadors, with WIN-
CHESTER, *in a Cardinal's Habit.*

  Exe. What! is my lord of Winchester install'd,
And call'd unto a cardinal's degree!
Then, I perceive, that will be verified,
Henry the Fifth did sometime prophesy,
" If once he come to be a cardinal,
He 'll make his cap co-equal with the crown."
  K. Hen. My lords ambassadors, your several
    suits
Have been consider'd and debated on.
Your purpose is both good and reasonable:
And, therefore, are we certainly resolv'd
To draw conditions of a friendly peace;
Which, by my lord of Winchester, we mean
Shall be transported presently to France.
  Glo. And for the proffer of my lord your
    master,—
I have inform'd his highness so at large,
As—liking of the lady's virtuous gifts,
Her beauty, and the value of her dower,—
He doth intend she shall be England's queen.

K. Hen. In argument and proof of which con-
tract,
Bear her this jewel, [*To the Amb.*] pledge of my
affection.
And so, my Lord Protector, see them guarded,
And safely brought to Dover; where, inshipp'd,
Commit them to the fortune of the sea.

[*Exeunt* K. HEN. *and* Train; GLO., EXE., *and*
Amb.

Win. Stay, my lord legate; you shall first
receive
The sum of money, which I promised
Should be deliver'd to his holiness
For clothing me in these grave ornaments.

Leg. I will attend upon your lordship's leisure.

Win. Now, Winchester will not submit, I trow,
Or be inferior to the proudest peer.
Humphrey of Gloster, thou shalt well perceive,
That, neither in birth, or for authority,
The bishop will be overborne by thee:
I'll either make thee stoop, and bend thy knee,
Or sack this country with a mutiny.   [*Exeunt.*

SCENE II.—France. *Plains in Anjou.*

Enter CHARLES, BURGUNDY, ALENÇON, LA PU-
CELLE, *and Forces, marching.*

Char. These news, my lords, may cheer our
drooping spirits:
'T is said, the stout Parisians do revolt,
And turn again unto the warlike French.

Alen. Then march to Paris, royal Charles of
France,
And keep not back your powers in dalliance.

Puc. Peace be amongst them, if they turn to us;
Else, ruin combat with their palaces!

Enter a Messenger.

Mess. Success unto our valiant general,
And happiness to his accomplices!

Char. What tidings send our scouts? I pr'y-
thee, speak.

Mess. The English army, that divided was
Into two parts, is now conjoin'd in one;
And means to give you battle presently.

Char. Somewhat too sudden, sirs, the warning is;
But we will presently provide for them.

Bur. I trust, the ghost of Talbot is not there;
Now he is gone, my lord, you need not fear.

Puc. Of all base passions, fear is most accurs'd:—

832

Command the conquest, Charles, it shall be
thine;
Let Henry fret, and all the world repine.

Char. Then, on, my lords; and France be fortunate!   [*Exeunt*

SCENE III.— *The Same.* *Before Angiers.*

Alarums: Excursions. Enter LA PUCELLE.

Puc. The Regent conquers, and the French
men fly.—
Now help, ye charming spells, and periapts;
And ye choice spirits that admonish me,
And give me signs of future accidents! [*Thunder*
You speedy helpers, that are substitutes
Under the lordly monarch of the north,
Appear, and aid me in this enterprise!

Enter Fiends.

This speedy quick appearance argues proof
Of your accustom'd diligence to me.
Now, ye familiar spirits, that are cull'd
Out of the powerful regions under earth,
Help me this once, that France may get the field.
     [*They walk about, and speak not*
O, hold me not with silence over-long!
Where I was wont to feed you with my blood,
I'll lop a member off, and give it you,
In earnest of a farther benefit;
So you do condescend to help me now.
       [*They hang their heads.*
No hope to have redress?—My body shall
Pay recompense, if you will grant my suit.
       [*They shake their heads*
Cannot my body, nor blood-sacrifice,
Entreat you to your wonted furtherance?
Then take my soul; my body, soul, and all,
Before that England give the French the foil.
       [*They depart.*
See! they forsake me. Now the time is come,
That France must veil her lofty-plumed crest,
And let her head fall into England's lap.
My ancient incantations are too weak,
And hell too strong for me to buckle with:
Now, France, thy glory droopeth to the dust.
       [*Exit.*

Alarums. Enter French *and* English, *fighting.*
LA PUCELLE *and* YORK *fight hand to hand.* LA
PUCELLE *is taken. The* French *fly.*

York. Damsel of France, I think I have you
fast:

Unchain your spirits now with spelling charms,
And try if they can gain your liberty.—
A goodly prize, fit for the devil's grace!
See, how the ugly witch doth bend her brows,
As if, with Circe, she would change my shape.

    Puc. Chang'd to a worser shape thou canst
        not be.

    York. O, Charles the Dauphin is a proper
        man ;
No shape but his can please your dainty eye.

    Puc. A plaguing mischief light on Charles, and
        thee !
And may ye both be suddenly surpris'd
By bloody hands, in sleeping on your beds !

    York. Fell, banning hag ! enchantress, hold
        thy tongue.

    Puc. I prythee, give me leave to curse a while.

    York. Curse, miscreant, when thou comest to
        the stake.   [*Exeunt.*

Alarums. Enter SUFFOLK, *leading in* LADY
    MARGARET.

    Suf. Be what thou wilt, thou art my prisoner.
         [*Gazes on her.*
O fairest beauty, do not fear, nor fly ;
For I will touch thee but with reverent hands,
And lay them gently on thy tender side.
I kiss these fingers [*kissing her hand.*] for eternal
    peace :
Who art thou ? say, that I may honour thee.

    Mar. Margaret my name ; and daughter to a
        king,
The king of Naples, whosoe'er thou art.

    Suf. An earl I am, and Suffolk am I call'd.
Be not offended, nature's miracle.
Thou art allotted to be ta'en by me :
So doth the swan her downy cygnets save,
Keeping them prisoners underneath her wings.
Yet, if this servile usage once offend,
Go, and be free again as Suffolk's friend.
         [*She turns away as going.*
O, stay !—I have no power to let her pass ;
My hand would free her, but my heart says—no.
As plays the sun upon the glassy streams,
Twinkling another counterfeited beam,
So seems this gorgeous beauty to mine eyes.
Fain would I woo her, yet I dare not speak :
I 'll call for pen and ink, and write my mind :
Fie, De la Poole ! disable not thyself ;
Hast not a tongue ? is she not here thy prisoner ?
Wilt thou be daunted at a woman's sight ?
Ay ; beauty's princely majesty is such,

Confounds the tongue, and makes the senses
    rough.

    Mar. Say, earl of Suffolk,—if thy name be so,—
What ransom must I pay before I pass ?
For, I perceive, I am thy prisoner.

    Suf. How canst thou tell, she will deny thy
        suit.
Before thou make a trial of her love ?   [*Aside.*

    Mar. Why speak'st thou not ? what ransom
        must I pay ?

    Suf. She 's beautiful ; and therefore to be woo'd
She is a woman ; therefore to be won.   [*Aside*

    Mar. Wilt thou accept of ransom, yea, or no ?

    Suf. Fond man ! remember, that thou hast a
        wife ;
Then how can Margaret be thy paramour ? [*Aside*

    Mar. I were best leave him, for he will not hear.

    Suf. There all is marr'd ; there lies a cooling
        card.

    Mar. He talks at random ; sure, the man is
        mad.

    Suf. And yet a dispensation may be had.

    Mar. And yet I would that you would an-
        swer me.

    Suf. I 'll win this lady Margaret. For whom ?
Why, for my king : Tush ! that 's a wooden thing.

    Mar. He talks of wood : It is some carpenter.

    Suf. Yet so my fancy may be satisfied,
And peace established between these realms.
But there remains a scruple in that too :
For though her father be the king of Naples,
Duke of Anjou and Maine, yet is he poor,
And our nobility will scorn the match.   [*Aside.*

    Mar. Hear ye, captain ? Are you not at
        leisure ?

    Suf. It shall be so, disdain they ne'er so much :
Henry is youthful, and will quickly yield.—
Madam, I have a secret to reveal.

    Mar. What though I be enthrall'd ? he seems
        a knight,
And will not any way dishonour me.   [*Aside*

    Suf. Lady, vouchsafe to listen what I say.

    Mar. Perhaps, I shall be rescu'd by the French ;
And then I need not crave his courtesy.   [*Aside.*

    Suf. Sweet madam, give me hearing in a
        cause—

    Mar. Tush ! women have been captivate ere
        now.   [*Aside.*

    Suf. Lady, wherefore talk you so ?

    Mar. I cry you mercy, 't is but *quid* for *quo.*

    Suf. Say, gentle princess, would you not
        suppose

Your bondage happy, to be made a queen?

Mar. To be a queen in bondage, is more vile,
Than is a slave in base servility;
For princes should be free.

Suf.   And so shall you,
If happy England's royal king be free.

Mar. Why, what concerns his freedom unto me?

Suf. I'll undertake to make thee Henry's
        queen;
To put a golden sceptre in thy hand,
And set a precious crown upon thy head,
If thou wilt condescend to be my—

Mar.   What?

Suf. His love.

Mar. I am unworthy to be Henry's wife.

Suf. No, gentle madam; I unworthy am
To woo so fair a dame to be his wife,
And have no portion in the choice myself.
How say you, madam; are you so content?

Mar. An if my father please, I am content.

Suf. Then call our captains, and our colours,
        forth;
And, madam, at your father's castle walls
We'll crave a parley, to confer with him.

                    [*Troops come forward.*

A Parley sounded. Enter REIGNIER, *on the Walls.*

Suf. See, Reignier, see, thy daughter prisoner.

Reig. To whom?

Suf.   To me.

Reig.   Suffolk, what remedy?
I am a soldier; and unapt to weep,
Or to exclaim on fortune's fickleness.

Suf. Yes, there is remedy enough, my lord:
Consent, (and, for thy honour, give consent,)
Thy daughter shall be wedded to my king;
Whom I with pain have woo'd and won thereto;
And this her easy-held imprisonment
Hath gain'd thy daughter princely liberty.

Reig. Speaks Suffolk as he thinks?

Suf.   Fair Margaret knows,
That Suffolk doth not flatter, face, or feign.

Reig. Upon thy princely warrant, I descend,
To give thee answer of thy just demand.

                    [*Exit, from the Walls.*

Suf. And here I will expect thy coming.

Trumpets sounded. Enter REIGNIER, *below.*

Reig. Welcome, brave earl, into our territories;
Command in Anjou what your honour pleases.

Suf. Thanks, Reignier, happy for so sweet a
        child,

Fit to be made companion with a king:
What answer makes your grace unto my suit?

Reig. Since thou dost deign to woo her little
        worth,
To be the princely bride of such a lord;
Upon condition I may quietly
Enjoy mine own, the county Maine, and Anjou,
Free from oppression, or the stroke of war,
My daughter shall be Henry's, if he please.

Suf. That is her ransom, I deliver her;
And those two counties, I will undertake,
Your grace shall well and quietly enjoy.

Reig. And I again,—in Henry's royal name,
As deputy unto that gracious king,
Give thee her hand, for sign of plighted faith.

Suf. Reignier of France, I give thee kingly
        thanks,
Because this is in traffic of a king:
And yet, methinks, I could be well content
To be mine own attorney in this case.   [*Aside.*
I'll over then to England with this news,
And make this marriage to be solemniz'd;
So, farewell, Reignier! Set this diamond safe
In golden palaces, as it becomes.

Reig. I do embrace thee, as I would embrace
The Christian prince, king Henry, were he here.

Mar. Farewell, my lord! Good wishes, praise,
        and prayers,
Shall Suffolk ever have of Margaret.   [*Going.*

Suf. Farewell, sweet madam! But hark you,
        Margaret;
No princely commendations to my king?

Mar. Such commendations as become a maid,
A virgin, and his servant, say to him.

Suf. Words sweetly plac'd, and modestly di-
        rected.
But, madam, I must trouble you again,—
No loving token to his majesty?

Mar. Yes, my good lord; a pure unspotted
        heart,
Never yet taint with love, I send the king.

Suf. And this withal.   [*Kisses her.*

Mar. That for thyself;—I will not so presume,
To send such peevish tokens to a king.

                    [*Exeunt* REIG. *and* MAR.

Suf. O, wert thou for myself!—But, Suffolk,
        stay;
Thou may'st not wander in that labyrinth;
There Minotaurs, and ugly treasons, lurk.
Solicit Henry with her wond'rous praise:
Bethink thee on her virtues that surmount,
Mad natural graces that extinguish art;

Repeat their semblance often on the seas,
That, when thou com'st to kneel at Henry's feet,
Thou may'st bereave him of his wits with wonder.
                      [*Exit.*

SCENE IV.—*Camp of the* Duke of York, *in Anjou.*

    Enter YORK, WARWICK, *and Others.*

  York. Bring forth that sorceress, condemn'd to
    burn.

  Enter LA PUCELLE, *guarded, and a* Shepherd.

  Shep. Ah, Joan! this kills thy father's heart
    outright!
Have I sought every country far and near,
And, now it is my chance to find thee out,
Must I behold thy timeless cruel death?
Ah, Joan! sweet daughter Joan, I'll die with thee!
  Puc. Decrepit miser! base ignoble wretch!
I am descended of a gentler blood;
Thou art no father, nor no friend, of mine.
  Shep. Out, out!—My lords, an please you, 't is
    not so;
I did beget her, all the parish knows;
Her mother liveth yet, can testify,
She was the first fruit of my bachelorship.
  War. Graceless; wilt thou deny thy parentage?
  York. This argues what her kind of life hath
    been;
Wicked and vile; and so her death concludes.
  Shep. Fie, Joan! that thou wilt be so obstacle!
God knows, thou art a collop of my flesh;
And for thy sake have I shed many a tear:
Deny me not, I pr'ythee, gentle Joan.
  Puc. Peasant, avaunt!—You have suborn'd
    this man,
Of purpose to obscure my noble birth.
  Shep. 'T is true, I gave a noble to the priest,
The morn that I was wedded to her mother.—
Kneel down and take my blessing, good my girl.
Wilt thou not stoop? Now cursed be the time
Of thy nativity! I would, the milk
Thy mother gave thee, when thou suck'dst her
    breast,
Had been a little ratsbane for thy sake!
Or else, when thou didst keep my lambs-a-field,
I wish some ravenous wolf had eaten thee!
Dost thou deny thy father, cursed drab?
O, burn her, burn her; hanging is too good. [*Exit.*
  York. Take her away; for she hath liv'd too
    long,
To fill the world with vicious qualities.

  Puc. First, let me tell you whom you have con-
    demn'd:
Not me begotten of a shepherd swain,
But issu'd from the progeny of kings;
Virtuous, and holy; chosen from above,
By inspiration of celestial grace,
To work exceeding miracles on earth.
I never had to do with wicked spirits:
But you,—that are polluted with your lusts,
Stain'd with the guiltless blood of innocents,
Corrupt and tainted with a thousand vices,—
Because you want the grace that others have,
You judge it straight a thing impossible
To compass wonders, but by help of devils.
No, misconceived! Joan of Arc hath been
A virgin from her tender infancy,
Chaste and immaculate in every thought;
Whose maiden blood, thus rigorously effus'd,
Will cry for vengeance at the gates of heaven.
  York. Ay, ay;—away with her to execution.
  War. And hark ye, sirs; because she is a maid,
Spare for no fagots, let there be enough:
Place barrels of pitch upon the fatal stake,
That so her torture may be shortened.
  Puc. Will nothing turn your unrelenting
    hearts?—
Then, Joan, discover thine infirmity;
That warranteth by law to be thy privilege.—
I am with child, ye bloody homicides:
Murder not then the fruit within my womb,
Although ye hale me to a violent death.
  York. Now heaven forefend! the holy maid
    with child?
  War. The greatest miracle that e'er ye wrought:
Is all your strict preciseness come to this?
  York. She and the Dauphin have been juggling;
I did imagine what would be her refuge.
  War. Well, go to; we will have no bastards
    live;
Especially, since Charles must father it.
  Puc. You are deceiv'd; my child is none of his;
It was Alençon, that enjoy'd my love.
  York. Alençon! that notorious Machiavel!
It dies, an if it had a thousand lives.
  Puc. O, give me leave, I have deluded you;
'T was neither Charles, nor yet the duke I nam'd,
But Reignier, king of Naples, that prevail'd.
  War. A married man! that 's most intolerable.
  York. Why, here 's a girl! I think she knows
    not well,
There were so many, whom she may accuse.
  War. It 's sign, she hath been liberal and free.

York. And yet, forsooth, she is a virgin pure.—
Strumpet, thy words condemn thy brat, and thee:
Use no entreaty, for it is in vain.

Puc. Then lead me hence;—with whom I leave
　　my curse:
May never glorious sun reflex his beams
Upon the country where you make abode!
But darkness and the gloomy shade of death
Environ you; till mischief, and despair,
Drive you to break your necks, or hang yourselves!
　　　　　　　　　　　　　　[*Exit, guarded.*

York. Break thou in pieces, and consume to
　　ashes,
Thou foul accursed minister of hell!

Enter CARDINAL BEAUFORT, *attended.*

Car. Lord regent, I do greet your excellence
With letters of commission from the king.
For know, my lords, the states of Christendom,
Mov'd with remorse of these outrageous broils,
Have earnestly implor'd a general peace
Betwixt our nation and the aspiring French:
And here at hand the Dauphin, and his train,
Approacheth, to confer about some matter.

York. Is all our travail turn'd to this effect?
After the slaughter of so many peers,
So many captains, gentlemen, and soldiers,
That in this quarrel have been overthrown,
And sold their bodies for their country's benefit,
Shall we at last conclude effeminate peace?
Have we not lost most part of all the towns,
By treason, falsehood, and by treachery,
Our great progenitors had conquer'd?—
O, Warwick, Warwick! I foresee with grief
The utter loss of all the realm of France.

War. Be patient, York: if we conclude a peace,
It shall be with such strict and severe covenants,
As little shall the Frenchmen gain thereby.

Enter CHARLES, *attended;* ALENÇON, BASTARD,
REIGNIER, *and Others.*

Char. Since, lords of England, it is thus agreed,
That peaceful truce shall be proclaim'd in France,
We come to be informed by yourselves
What the conditions of that league must be.

York. Speak, Winchester; for boiling choler
　　chokes
The hollow passage of my poison'd voice,
By sight of these our baleful enemies.

Win. Charles, and the rest, it is enacted thus:
That—in regard king Henry gives consent,
Of mere compassion, and of lenity,

896

To ease your country of distressful war,
And suffer you to breathe in fruitful peace,—
You shall become true liegemen to his crown:
And, Charles, upon condition thou wilt swear
To pay him tribute, and submit thyself,
Thou shalt be plac'd as viceroy under him,
And still enjoy thy regal dignity.

Alen. Must he be then as shadow of himself?
Adorn his temples with a coronet;
And yet, in substance and authority,
Retain but privilege of a private man?
This proffer is absurd and reasonless.

Char. 'T is known, already, that I am possess'd
With more than half the Gallian territories,
And therein reverenc'd for their lawful king:
Shall I, for lucre of the rest unvanquish'd,
Detract so much from that prerogative,
As to be call'd but viceroy of the whole?
No, lord ambassador; I'll rather keep
That which I have, than, coveting for more,
Be cast from possibility of all.

York. Insulting Charles! hast thou by secret
　　means
Used intercession to obtain a league;
And, now the matter grows to compromise,
Stand'st thou aloof upon comparison?
Either accept the title thou usurp'st,
Of benefit proceeding from our king,
And not of any challenge of desert,
Or we will plague thee with incessant wars.

Reig. My lord, you do not well in obstinacy
To cavil in the course of this contract:
If once it be neglected, ten to one,
We shall not find like opportunity.

Alen. To say the truth, it is your policy,
To save your subjects from such massacre,
And ruthless slaughters, as are daily seen
By our proceeding in hostility:
And therefore take this compact of a truce,
Although you break it when your pleasure serves
　　　　　　　　　　　　　[*Aside, to* CHAR.

War. How say'st thou, Charles? shall our con-
　　dition stand?

Char. It shall:
Only reserv'd, you claim no interest
In any of our towns of garrison.

York. Then swear allegiance to his majesty.
As thou art knight, never to disobey,
Nor be rebellious to the crown of England,
Thou, nor thy nobles, to the crown of England.—
　　　[CHAR. *and the rest, give Tokens of fealty*
So, now dismiss your army when ye please:

Hang up your ensigns, let your drums be still,
For here we entertain a solemn peace.

                    [*Exeunt.*

SCENE V.—London.   *A Room in the Palace.*

Enter KING HENRY, *in conference with* SUFFOLK;
   GLOSTER *and* EXETER *following.*

  K. Hen. Your wond'rous rare description, noble
       earl,
Of beauteous Margaret hath astonish'd me:
Her virtues, graced with external gifts,
Do breed love's settled passions in my heart:
And like as rigour in tempestuous gusts
Provokes the mightiest hulk against the tide;
So am I driven, by breath of her renown,
Either to suffer shipwreck, or arrive
Where I may have fruition of her love.
  Suf. Tush! my good lord! this superficial tale
Is but a preface of her worthy praise;
The chief perfections of that lovely dame,
(Had I sufficient skill to utter them,)
Would make a volume of enticing lines,
Able to ravish any dull conceit.
And, which is more, she is not so divine,
So full replete with choice of all delights,
But, with as humble lowliness of mind,
She is content to be at your command;
Command, I mean, of virtuous chaste intents,
To love and honour Henry as her lord.
  K. Hen. And otherwise will Henry ne'er pre-
       sume.
Therefore, my lord protector, give consent,
That Margaret may be England's royal queen.
  Glo. So should I give consent to flatter sin.
You know, my lord, your highness is betroth'd
Unto another lady of esteem;
How shall we then dispense with that contract,
And not deface your honour with reproach?
  Suf. As doth a ruler with unlawful oaths;
Or one, that, at a triumph having vow'd
To try his strength, forsaketh yet the lists
By reason of his adversary's odds:
A poor earl's daughter is unequal odds,
And therefore may be broke without offence.
  Glo. Why, what, I pray, is Margaret more than
       that?
Her father is no better than an earl,
Although in glorious titles he excel.
  Suf. Yes, my good lord, her father is a king,
The king of Naples, and Jerusalem;
And of such great authority in France,

As his alliance will confirm our peace,
And keep the Frenchmen in allegiance.
  Glo. And so the earl of Armaguac may do,
Because he is near kinsman unto Charles.
  Exe. Beside, his wealth doth warrant liberal
       dower;
While Reignier sooner will receive, than give.
  Suf. A dower, my lords! disgrace not so your
       king,
That he should be so abject, base, and poor,
To choose for wealth, and not for perfect love.
Henry is able to enrich his queen,
And not to seek a queen to make him rich:
So worthless peasants bargain for their wives,
As market-men for oxen, sheep, or horse.
Marriage is a matter of more worth,
Than to be dealt in by attorneyship;
Not whom we will, but whom his grace affects,
Must be companion of his nuptial bed:
And therefore, lords, since he affects her most,
It most of all these reasons bindeth us,
In our opinions she should be preferr'd.
For what is wedlock forced, but a hell,
An age of discord and continual strife?
Whereas the contrary bringeth forth bliss,
And is a pattern of celestial peace.
Whom should we match, with Henry, being a
       king,
But Margaret, that is daughter to a king?
Her peerless feature, joined with her birth,
Approves her fit for none, but for a king:
Her valiant courage, and undaunted spirit,
(More than in women commonly is seen,)
Will answer our hope in issue of a king;
For Henry, son unto a conqueror,
Is likely to beget more conquerors,
If with a lady of so high resolve,
As is fair Margaret, he be link'd in love.
Then yield, my lords; and here conclude with me,
That Margaret shall be queen, and none but she.
  K. Hen. Whether it be through force of your
       report,
My noble lord of Suffolk; or for that
My tender youth was never yet attaint
With any passion of inflaming love,
I cannot tell; but this I am assur'd,
I feel such sharp dissension in my breast,
Such fierce alarums both of hope and fear,
As I am sick with working of my thoughts.
Take, therefore, shipping; post, my lord, to France;
Agree to any covenants; and procure
That lady Margaret do vouchsafe to come

To cross the seas to England, and be crown'd
King Henry's faithful and anointed queen:
For your expenses and sufficient charge,
Among the people gather up a tenth.
Be gone, I say; for, till you do return,—
I rest perplexed with a thousand cares.—
And you, good uncle, banish all offence:
If you do censure me by what you were,
Not what you are, I know it will excuse
This sudden execution of my will.
And so conduct me, where from company,

I may revolve and ruminate my grief.　　　[Exit.
Glo. Ay, grief, I fear me, both at first and last.
　　　　　　　　　[Exeunt Glo. and Exe.
Suf. Thus Suffolk hath prevail'd: and thus he
　　goes,
As did the youthful Paris once to Greece;
With hope to find the like event in love,
But prosper better than the Trojan did.
Margaret shall now be queen, and rule the king;
But I will rule both her, the king, and realm.
　　　　　　　　　　　　　　　　[Exit

NOTES TO KING HENRY THE SIXTH.

(PART THE FIRST.)

---

¹ *The Earl of Warwick.*

This nobleman is Richard Beauchamp, who is a character in Henry the Fifth. The earl who appears in the subsequent part of the play is Richard Nevil, the son of the Earl of Salisbury, who became possessed of the title in right of his wife, Anne, sister of Henry Beauchamp, Duke of Warwick, on the death of Anne, his only child, in 1449. Thus the second earl is son-in-law to the first. Mr. Ritson says there is no reason to think that the author meant to confound the two characters. What the poet meant to do, it is difficult to decide; but he has certainly not given us to understand that two distinct persons are referred to by the title of Earl of Warwick.

² *Hung be the heavens with black.*

When a tragedy was to be performed in our poet's time, the stage was hung with black, to prepare the spectators for a solemn exhibition.

**³ ———— The bad revolting stars,
That have consented unto Henry's death.***

Consented, or more properly, consenting, means, have disposed themselves into a malignant configuration, to promote the death of Henry.

⁴ *Our isle be made a nourish of salt tears.*

Pope reads, a marish of salt tears; marish being an old word for marsh or fen.

⁵ *Than Julius Cæsar, or bright ————*

This imperfect line probably arose from the compositor being unable to read the word, and so leaving it blank, in which state, by a negligence not uncommon in those days, it was printed. Dr. Johnson suggests that it should have read,—or bright Berenice.

⁶ *If Sir John Fastolfe.*

This Sir John must not be confounded with Shakespeare's fat and merry knight Falstaff. Fastolfe was an historical character, mention of whom may be found both in Hall and Holinshed; Falstaff was merely a creation of the poet's brain: though it is more than probable that the imputed cowardice of the former suggested to Shakespeare the name of the latter. Sir John Fastolfe, though degraded for cowardice, was afterwards restored to his knighthood, it being considered he was justified in his conduct. He is elsewhere described as a wise and valiant captain. In the eighteenth song of Drayton's *Polyolbion*, he is thus alluded to:—

Strong Fastolph with this man compare we justly may;
By Salsbury who oft being seriously imploy'd
In many a brave attempt the general foe annoy'd;
With excellent success in Main and Anjou fought,
And many a bulwark there into our keeping brought,
And chosen to go forth with Vadumont in warre,
Most resolutely tooke proud Renate, duke of Barre.

⁷ *England all Olivers and Rowlands bred.*

That is, England bred nothing but heroes; Oliver and Rowland being two of the most famous of Charlemagne's twelve peers.

⁸ *Bastard of Orleans, thrice welcome to us.*

In former times *bastard* was not a term of reproach; one of William the Conqueror's charters begins thus,— "*Ego Guillelmus cognomento Bastardus.*" The ancients also held illegitimate children in no disrepute; they would not brand the son for the error of the father.

⁹ *Exceeding the nine sibyls of old Rome.*

This is an error: he means the nine books of oracles which a sibyl brought and offered for a large sum to one of the Tarquins.

¹⁰ *Was Mahomet inspired with a dove?*

This extraordinary enthusiast or impostor had a dove which used at times to alight on his shoulder and put its bill in his ear, and the "prophet" persuaded the deluded people that it was the Holy Ghost, who in that form gave him advice. Others have said that he placed peas or wheat in his ear, and that the bird, when hungry, went there for a meal.

¹¹ *Nor yet Saint Philip's daughters were like thee.*

The daughters of Philip the Evangelist, mentioned in

Acts xxi., v. 9.—"And the same man had four daughters, virgins, which did prophesy."

¹³ Since Henry's death, I fear there is conveyance.

Conveyance, is theft; Gloucester doubts the honesty and fidelity of the governor.

¹³ Piel'd priest.

Piel'd was an ancient mode of spelling *peeled*. Peeled, alluding to his shaven crown.

¹⁴ Thou that gie'st whores indulgences to sin.

Brothels were anciently under the jurisdiction of the Bishop of Winchester; hence a strum[p]et was called a Winchester goose.

¹⁵ I'll canvas thee in thy broad cardinal's hat.

Mr. Steevens thinks that this means—I'll tumble thee into thy great hat, and shake thee, as bran and meal are shaken in a sieve. Gloucester, however, may mean that he will toss the priest in a sheet, even while he was invested with the peculiar badge of his ecclesiastical dignity. Coarse sheets were formerly termed *canvas sheets*. It should be observed that Winchester is not yet a cardinal; he does not appear as a cardinal until the fifth act of the play.

¹⁶ This is Damascus, be thou cursed Cain.

About four miles from Damascus is a lofty hill which a tradition avers to be the same on which Cain slew his brother Abel. Thus, in Sir John Mandeville's Travels: "And in that place where Damascus was founded, Kayne slaughe Abel his brother."

¹⁷ For I intend to have it, ere long.

This is a hard and unmusical line; the metre would be rendered perfect by reading,—yet ere long.

¹⁸ So pil'd esteem'd.

This phrase has no discernible meaning; some have conjectured that the author wrote *vile-esteemed*, and Mr. Steevens thinks it probable that we should read—*so Philistin'd*, i. e. treated with scorn and degradation, as Sampson was by the Philistines.

¹⁹ Blood will I draw on thee, thou art a witch.

It was a superstition of the poet's time that he who could shed the blood of a witch was free from her power.

²⁰ Than Rhodope's, or Memphis', ever was.

Rhodope was a celebrated courtezan who by her beauty and dissipation acquired immense riches. She was born at Thrace, and was a slave in the same house with Æ-op Ca Lamon fabulist. The brother of Sappho having fallen in love with her, purchased her freedom at a great price. She is said afterwards to have married Psammeticus, king of Egypt, and the smallest but most finished of the pyramids was built by her. Allusion is made to her in the play of *The Costly Whore*, 1633:—

—— A base *Rhodope*,
Whose body is as common as the sea
In the receipt of every lustful spring.

²¹ Than the rich-jewell'd coffer of Darius.

When Alexander the Great had taken Gaza, the metropolis of Syria, he found among the treasures of Darius contained in the city, a small chest or casket of great value and exquisite beauty of workmanship. All the generals who were around him having expressed their admiration of it, Alexander asked what they thought best fitted to be contained in it? After each had delivered his opinion, the conqueror said that he esteemed nothing so worthy to be preserved in it as Homer's *Iliad*. Pliny tells us that this casket, when found, was full of precious oils and was decorated with jewels of immense value.

²² Then say at once, if I maintain'd the truth; Or else was wrangling Somerset in the error?

This passage is confused; if Plantagenet was right, of course Somerset was wrong; we should read:—

Or else was wrangling Somerset i' th' right?

Or,—

And was not wrangling Somerset in the error?

²³ His grandfather was Lionel, duke of Clarence.

This statement is incorrect. Plantagenet's paternal grandfather was Edmund of Langley, duke of York. His maternal grandfather was Roger Mortimer, earl of March, who was the son of Philippa, the daughter of Lionel, duke of Clarence. The duke was therefore his maternal great-great-grandfather.

²⁴ Enter Mortimer.

Shakespeare has fallen into error by introducing Mortimer dying in confinement in the Tower. Edmund Mortimer served under Henry the Fifth, revealed to that king the plot to assassinate him formed by Cambridge, Scroop, and Grey, at Southampton, and followed the king in his expedition to France. At the coronation of Queen Katherine he attended and held the sceptre. Soon after the accession of Henry the Sixth, he was appointed chief governor of Ireland, and he finally died there in his castle at Trim, in January, 1424-5.

²⁵ Depos'd his nephew Richard.

Bolingbroke was Richard's cousin, not his nephew. In Shakespeare's time a nephew was sometimes called cousin; but it does not appear that a cousin was ever called a nephew.

²⁶ Levied an army.

This is another historical error. The earl of Cambridge did no such thing; he entered into a plot to assassinate Henry the Fifth, as correctly described in Act iii., sc. 2, of that play. The old play on which Shakespeare founded his Henry the Sixth, Part 1., contained these errors, and the poet negligently followed them. At that time he himself might have known no better, as Henry the Fifth was written at a later period, and when the poet had become familiar with the chronicles of Holinshed.

Thou bastard of my grandfather.

The bishop of Winchester was an illegitimate son of John of Gaunt, duke of Lancaster, by Katherine Swynford, whom the duke afterwards married.

The bishop hath a kindly gird.

A *kindly gird* is probably a gentle rebuke. Warwick means that the king had blamed the bishop with great gentleness.

No way to that for weakness which she enter'd.

That is, no way equal to that; no way so fit as that.

That stout Pendragon, in his litter.

Pendragon was the father of King Arthur, and esteemed a great hero. He caused himself to be carried with his army in a litter when he was too ill to fight; and his presence so encouraged his soldiers that they won the victory. Holinshed, however, attributes this exploit to his brother Aurelius.

Whither away, Sir John Fastolfe, in such haste?

"I have no doubt," says Mr. Malone, "that it was the exaggerated representation of Sir John Fastolfe's cowardice which the author of this play has given (i. e., the old play on which Shakespeare founded his) that induced Shakespeare to give the name of Falstaff to his knight. Sir John Fastolfe did indeed fly at the battle of Patay, in the year 1429; and is reproached by Talbot in a subsequent scene for his conduct on that occasion; but no historian has said that he fled before Rouen."

Dies, and is carried off in his chair.

The Duke of Bedford died at Rouen, but not in any action before the town. He was buried in the cathedral there. Mr. Hume says he was "a prince of great abilities, and of many virtues; and whose memory, except from the barbarous execution of the Maid of Orleans, was unsullied by any considerable blemish." He, however, is the Prince John, who, in the Second Part of *Henry the Fourth*, Act IV., so treacherously captures, and sends to the block, the Archbishop of York and the peers who were joined with him in his insurrection.

Done like a Frenchman; turn, and turn again.

This satire on the inconstancy of the French was, no doubt, much enjoyed by English audiences of the poet's time; but it appears very inconsistent to place it in the mouth of Joan, who would scarcely affront Burgundy to his face the moment she had won his alliance. Dr. Johnson says—"I have read a dissertation written to prove that the index of the wind upon our steeples was made in the form of a cock, to ridicule the French for their frequent changes."

I do remember how my father said.

This play abounds in historical errors. Henry the Sixth had never seen his father, who was in France when he was born, where he remained until his death, when the young Henry was but nine months old.

And I am louted by a traitor villain.

Louted is baffled and insulted; treated like a lowt, or low country fellow.

Winged through the lither sky.

Lither is the comparative of the adjective *lithe*, i. e., flexible, pliant, yielding.

A giglot wench.

A *giglot* is a light and wantonly disposed woman, or a strumpet.

Great earl of Washford.

Washford appears to be a corruption of *Wexford*.

But from their ashes shall be reared.

The defect in the metre argues that some word has been omitted in the line; probably *honour'd*. "But from their honour'd ashes," &c.

Immanity, i. e., barbarity, savageness.

Now help, ye charming spells, and periapts.

Periapts were amulets or charms carried about the person as preservatives against disease or mischief. Of these the first chapter of St. John's Gospel was considered the most efficacious.

Under the lordly monarch of the north.

"The monarch of the north," says Mr. Douce, "was Zimimar, one of the four principal devils invoked by witches. The others were Amaimon, king of the east; Gorson, king of the south; and Goap, king of the west. Under these devil kings were devil marquises, dukes, prelates, knights, presidents, and earls. They are all enumerated in Scott's *Discoverie of Witchcraft*."

Decrepit miser.

Miser here does not mean that he is avaricious, but is used in its obsolete sense of a wretched mean person.

Fie, Joan! that thou wilt be so obstacle.

Obstacle is a corruption of obstinate.

Not me begotten of a shepherd swain.

Probably the poet wrote, not *one*, &c.

Alençon! that notorious Machiavel.

Machiavel is mentioned somewhat before this time; but his character seems to have made so deep an impression on the dramatic writers of the Elizabethan age, that he is many times prematurely spoken of.

Of my poison'd voice.

Poison'd voice is not a very intelligible phrase. Pope reads *prisoned* voice. York's voice was choked with passion, prisoned in his throat.

*———— Accept the title thou usurp'st,
Of benefit proceeding from our king.*

That is, accept the title of king of France, as a vassal and dependent upon the sovereign of England.

King Henry the Sixth.

IN perusing this play we seem to be walking among covered pitfalls: the snares of treachery are spread in all directions; every noble is striving for supremacy, and each exclaiming on the ambition of the rest. The drama forms a dark and terrible picture of the wickedness of courts; for sophistry, perjury, and murder stain nearly every character except the weak king and the "good duke Humphrey." We recoil in disgust from this diabolical exhibition of state-craft: these wily courtiers play for the crown of the feeble Henry with all the recklessness of ruined gamblers: they stake body and soul upon the cast, or rather play as if they had no souls to lose. The poet with all the ingenuity of youth, scourges hypocrisy with unsparing vehemence, treachery is made transparent, and the great struggle for self rendered obvious and disgusting: he tears aside the disguises of patriotism and religion, and shows us the human fiends concealed beneath them.

This drama commences with the marriage of Henry, which took place in his twenty-fourth year; but the feebleness of infancy had not given way to the strength and vigour of manhood; and the son of that determined prince, who was regarded by the people with affectionate awe, was a gentle, weak, spiritless, and superstitious man. As a village priest, he would have proved a valuable member of society; happy would it have been for him and England had he been born to such a station; but as a king who had to govern a powerful and insolent nobility, and a semi-barbarous people, his very virtues were his chief defects. In those times a strong bad man, so that he had judgment enough not to stretch his prerogative too far, made a better sovereign than a weak good man. Where much power attaches to the crown, a feeble king is worse than no king; for the powers of government are wielded by any hand that is bold enough to seize them, and strong enough to guide them. Thus with Henry—Gloucester, Beaufort, Suffolk, Somerset, York, and Warwick, each in turn influence and coerce this phantom of a king. The mind of the unfortunate monarch was worse than feeble, it was diseased: he was several times seized with an extraordinary apathy and imbecility, which rendered him unfit for the commonest duties of life, and unconscious of the presence or inquiries of his friends; but Shakespeare has not alluded to this mental defect in his portraiture of the unhappy king.

Margaret of Anjou was selected by the cardinal and his compeers for Henry as a wife calculated to rouse him into greater activity, and to impart to him some of the decision of character and strength of mind that she possessed. Added to great personal beauty and remarkable vivacity, she had a courageous temper and masculine intellect, and was regarded as the most accomplished woman of her age. Her pride and vindictiveness of temper she had not yet revealed; no royal state or adverse fortune had called them into activity. The young beauty had lived in comparative seclusion, adding accomplishments to natural graces; and it was thought, with much probability, that when she shared the throne of Henry, she would increase its lustre, and elevate the character of its occupant. Had her husband possessed a sounder judgment, and a royalty of nature, she would doubtless have fulfilled these hopes respecting her; but Margaret had no one whose influence could restrain in her those arbitrary doctrines which she had learnt in France, and attempted to apply in England. She was distinguished by a haughtiness greater than had hitherto been assumed by any of our native kings, and she sank into unpopularity and dislike.

After Henry, the Duke of Gloster is the most amiable character, indeed almost the only one not stained with treachery and crime; but even he cannot refrain from constant and unseemly broils with the Cardinal Beaufort. The last surviving brother of Henry the Fifth, the duke was the idol of the people, and is painted by the poet as a wise and honest counsellor. He was a great patron of literature in those days; he gave a valuable library to the University of Oxford, and invited to England an Italian historian named Titus Livius Forojuliensis, whom he appointed his poet and orator. The incident where his vain and ambitious duchess engages the assistance of necromancers to prophesy the death of the king is rendered more dramatic than natural; in a play professing to treat of a comparatively modern period of history, satanic agency and the appearances of spirits are inconsistent with the actual events enacted. The guilt of the duchess consisted in her search for supernatural aid; and here perhaps Shakespeare, in his maturity, would have paused; but in his youth before he knew his own strength, and was content to rely entirely upon natural incidents for effect, he omitted no opportunity of giving to his play the character of a spectacle, and crowding into it every circumstance likely to be attractive to an audience.

The incidents in this drama are remarkably varied, and follow one another with great rapidity: there is no pause in the action; the attention is never suffered to flag; thus Hume, Bolingbroke, and Mother Jourdain, have no sooner been arrested for sorcery, than we are transported to St. Albans, and witness the mirth-moving miracle performed on the impostor Simpcox; the humour here is admirable—we recognise the hand that in after days drew the inimitable Falstaff. The characters of the whole group are well preserved in this scene; the pious and simple Henry has faith in the supposed miracle, and bids the fellow ever devoutly to remember what the Lord has done for him; but the more subtle courtiers doubt its authenticity, and question the knave, while Gloucester detects him by a very philosophical process. Had he been born blind, it would have been impossible for him to have distinguished colours immediately upon receiving his sight. Queen Margaret laughs at the discovery, but Henry mourns at the duplicity of man.

We have next the trial by combat between the armourer Horner and his 'prentice, Peter Thump. Duels of this character are of great antiquity, and in them the vanquished was considered to be the guilty party. Men of low condition were not permitted to fight with the sword or lance—these were honourable weapons, reserved for knights and nobles; therefore the common people in these trials fought with an ebon staff, at the end of which was fixed a bag crammed hard with sand, which made a more formidable weapon than might at first be conceived, and one with which a powerful man might easily strike his opponent dead. With this instrument the timorous Peter kills his master, the latter having drank so freely with his neighbours as to be incapable of defending himself.

We are next led to the bedside of the chief murderer of the unhappy duke; the great cardinal has been seized with a sudden sickness,—

> That makes him gasp, and stare, and catch the air,
> Blaspheming God, and cursing men on earth.

Henry approaches the dying wretch, who is perishing in the fearful recollection of his unrepented sins, and who, in his delirium, beholds the spirit of the murdered duke, whose sightless orbs are bent upon him, while his upright hair bespeaks his dying agony. The cardinal is convulsed with the pangs of death, and becomes speechless, when the king conjures him to give some sign of a hope of salvation. The turbulent and once haughty priest dies and makes no sign.

The mind is recalled from dwelling too seriously upon the terrible incidents just alluded to, by the introduction of Jack Cade and the Kentish rebels. Cade was not a native of Kent, but of Ireland, and had spent some time in France, either as a soldier or an outlaw; his great courage and hardihood admirably fitted him for the leader of a popular insurrection, and for some time he preserved great order among his rude followers, and punished them for theft or violence; but the passions of an excited crowd are not to be long restrained, and they soon broke out into furious excesses.

The insurrection of Cade and his followers, though extinguished, left the country in a state which enabled a few discontented nobles to plunge it into a savage civil war; thousands of discontented and unemployed peasants were ready to flock to any standard, and to fight for any cause. If peace would yield them nothing, they were willing to try what war could do. The poet truly represents the tragic results of such a rising among a rude and barbarous people; the murder of Lord Say is both affecting and horrible: he pleads for his life with a manly eloquence which would have won it from any but a people inured to acts of bloodshed. Cade, however, is distinguished from his followers by his great courage and consistency; and we pity the poor starving wretch when he is slain by Iden the Kentish esquire.

In the fifth act of this play, the storm which has been so long lowering at length breaks forth, ambition throws aside its thin disguise; the perfidious and ungrateful duke of York, forgetting that Henry has restored him to his honours and estates, defies his sovereign, and claims the crown. The banner of rebellion floats gaudily in the air, civil war commences in England, and the play terminates with the victory of York at St. Albans, and the flight of the Lancastrian party to London.

This and the following drama Mr. Malone believes to have been produced in their present form in the year 1591. The poet was then in his twenty-ninth year, the year to which Mr. Drake assigns the production of *Love's Labour's Lost*, certainly Shakespeare's most feeble comedy.

PERSONS REPRESENTED.

KING HENRY THE SIXTH.
Appears, Act I. sc. 1; sc. 3. Act II. sc. 1; sc. 3. Act III. sc. 1;
sc. 2; sc. 3. Act IV. sc. 4; sc. 9. Act V. sc. 1; sc. 2.

HUMPHREY, *Duke of* Gloster, *his Uncle.*
Appears, Act I. sc. 1; sc. 2; sc. 3. Act II. sc. 1; sc. 3; sc.
4. Act III. sc. 1.

CARDINAL BEAUFORT, *Bishop of* Winchester,
Great-Uncle to the King.
Appears, Act I. sc. 1; sc. 3. Act II. sc. 1. Act III. sc. 1;
sc. 2; sc. 3.

RICHARD PLANTAGENET, *Duke of* York.
Appears, Act I. sc. 1; sc. 3; sc. 4. Act II. sc. 2; sc. 3.
Act III. sc. 1. Act V. sc. 1; sc. 2; sc. 3.

EDWARD, *Son to the Duke of* York.
Appears, Act V. sc. 1.

RICHARD, *Son to the Duke of* York.
Appears, Act V. sc. 1; sc. 2; sc. 3.

DUKE OF SOMERSET, *of the* King's *Party.*
Appears, Act I. sc. 1; sc. 3. Act III. sc. 1; sc. 2. Act IV.
sc. 9. Act V. sc. 1; sc. 2.

DUKE OF SUFFOLK, *of the* King's *Party.*
Appears, Act I. sc. 1; sc. 3. Act II. sc. 1; sc. 3. Act III.
sc. 1; sc. 2. Act IV. sc. 1.

DUKE OF BUCKINGHAM, *of the* King's *Party.*
Appears, Act I. sc. 1; sc. 3; sc. 4. Act II. sc. 1. Act III. sc. 1.
Act IV. sc. 4; sc. 8; sc. 9. Act V. sc. 1.

LORD CLIFFORD, *of the* King's *Party.*
Appears, Act IV. sc. 8; sc. 9. Act V. sc. 1; sc. 2.

YOUNG CLIFFORD, *his Son.*
Appears, Act V. sc. 1; sc. 2.

EARL OF SALISBURY, *of the* York *Faction.*
Appears, Act I. sc. 1. Act II. sc. 2; sc. 3. Act III. sc. 2;
sc. 3. Act V. sc. 1; sc. 2.

EARL OF WARWICK, *his Son, also of the* York
Faction.
Appears, Act I. sc. 1. Act II. sc. 2. Act III. sc. 2;
sc. 3. Act V. sc. 1; sc. 2; sc. 3.

LORD SCALES, *Governor of the Tower.*
Appears, Act IV. sc. 5.

LORD SAY.
Appears, Act IV. sc. 4; sc. 7.

SIR HUMPHREY STAFFORD *and his* BROTHER.
Appear, Act IV. sc. 2; sc. 3.

SIR JOHN STANLEY.
Appears, Act II. sc. 4.

906

A SEA CAPTAIN, MASTER, MASTER'S MATE, *and*
WALTER WHITMORE.
Appear, Act IV. sc. 1.

TWO GENTLEMEN, *Prisoners with* Suffolk.
Appear, Act IV. sc. 1.

VAUX.
Appears, Act III. sc. 2.

HUME, *a Priest.*
Appears, Act I. sc. 2; sc. 4. Act II. sc. 3.

SOUTHWELL, *a Priest.*
BOLINGBROKE, *a Conjurer.*
Appear, Act I. sc. 4. Act II. sc. 3.

A SPIRIT *raised by them.*
Appears, Act I. sc. 4.

THOMAS HORNER, *an Armourer.*
PETER, *his Man.*
Appear, Act I. sc. 3. Act II. sc. 3.

CLERK OF CHATHAM.
Appears, Act IV. sc. 4.

MAYOR OF ST. ALBANS.
SIMPCOX, *an Impostor.*
Appear, Act II. sc. 1.

TWO MURDERERS.
Appear, Act III. sc. 2.

JACK CADE, *a Rebel.*
Appears, Act IV. sc. 2; sc. 3; sc. 6; sc. 7; sc. 8; sc. 10.

GEORGE BEVIS, JOHN HOLLAND, DICK *the Butcher*
SMITH *the Weaver,* MICHAEL, *and other Fol-*
lowers of Cade.
Appear, Act IV. sc. 2; sc. 3; sc. 6; sc. 7; sc. 8.

ALEXANDER IDEN, *a Kentish Gentleman.*
Appears, Act IV. sc. 10. Act V. sc. 1.

MARGARET, *Queen to King* HENRY.
Appears, Act I. sc. 1; sc. 3. Act II. sc. 1; sc. 3. Act III.
sc. 1; sc. 2. Act IV. sc. 4; sc. 9. Act V. sc. 1; sc. 2.

ELEANOR, *Duchess of* Gloster.
Appears, Act I. sc. 2; sc. 4. Act II. sc. 3; sc. 4.

MARGERY JOURDAIN, *a Witch.*
Appears, Act I. sc. 2. Act II. sc. 3.

WIFE TO SIMPCOX.
Appears, Act II. sc. 1.

Lords, Ladies, and Attendants ; Petitioners, Alder-
men, a Herald, a Beadle, Sheriff, and Officers ;
Citizens, Prentices, Falconers, Guards, Soldiers,
Messengers, &c.

SCENE,—*Dispersedly in various parts of* ENGLAND

SECOND PART OF

King Henry the Sixth.

ACT I.

SCENE I.—London.—*A Room of State in the Palace.*

Flourish of Trumpets: then Hautboys. Enter, on one side, KING HENRY, DUKE OF GLOSTER, SALISBURY, WARWICK, and CARDINAL BEAUFORT; on the other, QUEEN MARGARET, led in by SUFFOLK; YORK, SOMERSET, BUCKINGHAM, and Others, following.

Suf. As by your high imperial majesty
I had in charge at my depart for France,
As procurator to your excellence,
To marry princess Margaret for your grace;
So, in the famous ancient city, Tours,—
In presence of the kings of France and Sicil,
The dukes of Orleans, Calaber, Bretaigne, and
  Alençon,
Seven earls, twelve barons, twenty reverend bish-
  ops,—
I have perform'd my task, and was espous'd:
And humbly now upon my bended knee,
In sight of England and her lordly peers,
Deliver up my title in the queen
To your most gracious hands, that are the sub-
  stance
Of that great shadow I did represent;
The happiest gift that ever marquess gave,
The fairest queen that ever king receiv'd.

K. Hen. Suffolk, arise.—Welcome, queen Mar-
  garet:
I can express no kinder sign of love,
Than this kind kiss.—O Lord, that lends me life,
Lend me a heart replete with thankfulness!

For thou hast given me, in this beauteous face,
A world of earthly blessings to my soul,
If sympathy of love unite our thoughts.

Q. Mar. Great king of England, and my gra-
  cious lord;
The mutual conference that my mind hath had—
By day, by night; waking, and in my dreams;
In courtly company, or at my beads,—
With you mine alder-liefest sovereign,'
Makes me the bolder to salute my king
With ruder terms; such as my wit affords,
And over-joy of heart doth minister.

K. Hen. Her sight did ravish: but her grace
  in speech,
Her words y-clad with wisdom's majesty,
Makes me, from wondering fall to weeping joys;
Such is the fulness of my heart's content.—
Lords, with one cheerful voice welcome my love.

All. Long live queen Margaret, England's happiness!

Q. Mar. We thank you all. 			[*Flourish.*

Suf. My lord protector, so it please your
  grace,
Here are the articles of contracted peace,
Between our sovereign and the French king
  Charles,
For eighteen months concluded by consent.

Glo. [*Reads.*] *Imprimis, It is agreed between the French king, Charles, and William de la Poole, marquess of Suffolk, ambassador for Henry king of England,— that the said Henry shall espouse the lady Margaret, daughter unto Reignier king of Naples, Sicilia, and Jeru- salem, and crown her queen of England, ere the thirtieth of May next ensuing.——Item.—That the duchy of An-* [*jou*

947

and the county of Maine shall be released and delivered
to the king her father——

K. Hen. Uncle, how now?

Glo.   Pardon me, gracious lord;
Some sudden qualm hath struck me at the heart,
And dimm'd mine eyes, that I can read no further.

K. Hen. Uncle of Winchester, I pray, read on.

Win. *Item,*—It is further agreed between them,—that
the duchies of Anjou and Maine shall be released and delivered over to the king her father; and she sent over of
the king of England's own proper cost and charges, without having dowry.

K. Hen. They please us well.—Lord marquess,
      kneel down;
We here create thee the first duke of Suffolk,
And girt thee with the sword.—
Cousin of York, we here discharge your grace
From being regent in the parts of France,
Till term of eighteen months be full expir'd.—
Thanks, uncle Winchester, Gloster, York, and
      Buckingham,
Somerset, Salisbury, and Warwick;
We thank you all for this great favour done,
In entertainment to my princely queen.
Come, let us in; and with all speed provide
To see her coronation be perform'd.
      [*Exeunt* KING, QUEEN, *and* SUF.

Glo. Brave peers of England, pillars of the state,
To you duke Humphrey must unload his grief,
Your grief, the common grief of all the land.
What! did my brother Henry spend his youth,
His valour, coin, and people, in the wars?
Did he so often lodge in open field,
In winter's cold, and summer's parching heat,
To conquer France, his true inheritance?
And did my brother Bedford toil his wits,
To keep by policy what Henry got?
Have you yourselves, Somerset, Buckingham,
Brave York, Salisbury, and victorious Warwick,
Receiv'd deep scars in France and Normandy?
Or hath my uncle Beaufort, and myself,
With all the learned council of the realm,
Studied so long, sat in the council-house,
Early and late, debating to and fro
How France and Frenchmen might be kept in awe?
And hath his highness in his infancy
Been crown'd in Paris, in despite of foes?
And shall these labours and these honours die?
Shall Henry's conquest, Bedford's vigilance,
Your deeds of war, and all our counsel, die?
O peers of England, shameful is this league!
Fatal this marriage, cancelling your fame;

Blotting your names from books of memory;
Razing the characters of your renown;
Defacing monuments of conquer'd France;
Undoing all, as all had never been!

Car. Nephew, what means this passionate dis-
      course?
This peroration with such circumstance?
For France, 't is ours; and we will keep it still.

Glo. Ay, uncle, we will keep it, if we can;
But now it is impossible we should:
Suffolk, the new-made duke that rules the roast,
Hath given the duchies of Anjou and Maine
Unto the poor king Reignier, whose large style
Agrees not with the leanness of his purse.

Sal. Now, by the death of him that died for all,
These counties were the keys of Normandy;—
But, wherefore weeps Warwick, my valiant son?

War. For grief that they are past recovery:
For, were there hope to conquer them again,
My sword should shed hot blood, mine eyes no
      tears.
Anjou and Maine! myself did win them both;
Those provinces these arms of mine did conquer:
And are the cities, that I got with wounds,
Deliver'd up again with peaceful words?
Mort Dieu!

York. For Suffolk's duke—may he be suffocate,
That dims the honour of this warlike isle!
France should have torn and rent my very heart,
Before I would have yielded to this league.
I never read but England's kings have had
Large sums of gold, and dowries, with their wives:
And our king Henry gives away his own,
To match with her that brings no vantages.

Glo. A proper jest, and never heard before,
That Suffolk should demand a whole fifteenth,
For costs and charges in transporting her!
She should have staid in France, and starv'd in
      France,
Before——

Car. My lord of Gloster, now you grow too hot;
It was the pleasure of my lord the king.

Glo. My lord of Winchester, I know your mind;
'T is not my speeches that you do mislike,
But 't is my presence that doth trouble you.
Rancour will out: Proud prelate, in thy face
I see thy fury: if I longer stay,
We shall begin our ancient bickerings.—
Lordings, farewell; and say, when I am gone,
I prophesied—France will be lost ere long. [*Exit.*

Car. So, there goes our protector in a rage.
'T is known to you, he is mine enemy:

Nay, more, an enemy unto you all;
And no great friend, I fear me, to the king.
Consider, lords, he is the next of blood,
And heir apparent to the English crown;
Had Henry got an empire by his marriage,
And all the wealthy kingdoms of the west,
There's reason he should be displeased at it.
Look to it, lords; let not his smoothing words
Bewitch your hearts; be wise, and circumspect.
What though the common people favour him,
Calling him—"Humphrey, the good duke of
    Gloster;"
Clapping their hands, and crying with loud voice—
"Jesu maintain your royal excellence!"
With—"God preserve the good duke Humphrey!"
I fear me, lords, for all this flattering gloss,
He will be found a dangerous protector.

Buck. Why should he then protect our sovereign,
He being of age to govern of himself?—
Cousin of Somerset, join you with me,
And all together—with the duke of Suffolk,—
We'll quickly hoise duke Humphrey from his seat.

Car. This weighty business will not brook delay;
I'll to the duke of Suffolk presently. [*Exit.*

Som. Cousin of Buckingham, though Hum-
    phrey's pride,
And greatness of his place be grief to us,
Yet let us watch the haughty cardinal;
His insolence is more intolerable
Than all the princes in the land beside;
If Gloster be displaced, he'll be protector.

Buck. Or thou, or I, Somerset, will be protector.
Despite duke Humphrey, or the cardinal.

[*Exit* BUCK. *and* SOM.

Sal. Pride went before, ambition follows him.
While these do labour for their own preferment,
Behoves it us to labour for the realm.
I never saw but Humphrey duke of Gloster
Did bear him like a noble gentleman.
Oft have I seen the haughty cardinal,—
More like a soldier, than a man o' the church,
As stout, and proud, as he were lord of all,—
Swear like a ruffian, and demean himself
Unlike the ruler of a commonweal.—
Warwick, my son, the comfort of my age!
Thy deeds, thy plainness, and thy house-keeping,
Hath won the greatest favour of the commons,
Excepting none but good duke Humphrey.—
And, brother York, thy acts in Ireland,
In bringing them to civil discipline;
Thy late exploits done in the heart of France,
When thou wert regent for our sovereign,

Have made thee fear'd, and honour'd, of the peo-
    ple:—
Join we together, for the public good;
In what we can to bridle and suppress
The pride of Suffolk, and the cardinal,
With Somerset's and Buckingham's ambition;
And, as we may, cherish duke Humphrey's deeds,
While they do tend the profit of the land.

War. So God help Warwick, as he loves the land,
And common profit of his country!

York. And so says York, for he hath greatest
    cause.

Sal. Then let's make haste away, and look un-
    to the main.

War. Unto the main! O, father, Maine is lost;
That Maine, which by main force Warwick did win,
And would have kept, so long as breath did last:
Main chance, father, you meant; but I meant Maine,
Which I will win from France, or else be slain.

[*Exeunt* WAR. *and* SAL.

York. Anjou and Maine are given to the
    French;
Paris is lost; the state of Normandy
Stands on a tickle point, now they are gone:
Suffolk concluded on the articles;
The peers agreed, and Henry was well pleas'd,
To change two dukedoms for a duke's fair daughter.
I cannot blame them all: What is't to them?
'Tis thine they give away, and not their own.
Pirates may make cheap pennyworths of their
    pillage,
And purchase friends, and give to courtezans,
Still revelling, like lords, till all be gone:
While as the silly owner of the goods
Weeps over them, and wrings his hapless hands,
And shakes his head, and trembling stands aloof,
While all is shar'd, and all is borne away;
Ready to starve, and dare not touch his own.
So York must sit, and fret, and bite his tongue,
While his own lands are bargain'd for, and sold.
Methinks, the realms of England, France, and
    Ireland,
Bear that proportion to my flesh and blood,
As did the fatal brand Althea burn'd,
Unto the prince's heart of Calydon.
Anjou and Maine, both given unto the French!
Cold news for me; for I had hope of France,
Even as I have of fertile England's soil.
A day will come, when York shall claim his own;
And therefore I will take the Nevils' parts,
And make a show of love to proud duke Hum-
    phrey.

And, when I spy advantage, claim the crown,
For that 's the golden mark I seek to hit:
Nor shall proud Lancaster usurp my right,
Nor hold his sceptre in his childish fist,
Nor wear the diadem upon his head,
Whose church-like humours fit not for a crown.
Then, York, be still a while, till time do serve:
Watch thou, and wake, when others be asleep,
To pry into the secrets of the state;
Till Henry, surfeiting in joys of love,
With his new bride, and England's dear-bought
    queen,
And Humphrey with the peers be fall'n at jars:
Then will I raise aloft the milk-white rose,
With whose sweet smell the air shall be perfum'd;
And in my standard bear the arms of York,
To grapple with the house of Lancaster:
And, force perforce, I 'll make him yield the
    crown,
Whose bookish rule hath pull'd fair England down.
                                              [*Exit.*

SCENE II.—*The Same. A Room in the* Duke *of*
    Gloster's House.

Enter GLOSTER *and the* DUCHESS.

    Duch. Why droops my lord, like over-ripen'd
        corn,
Hanging the head at Ceres' plenteous load?
Why doth the great duke Humphrey knit his
        brows,
As frowning at the favours of the world?
Why are thine eyes fix'd to the sullen earth,
Gazing on that which seems to dim thy sight?
What see'st thou there? king Henry's diadem,
Enchas'd with all the honours of the world?
If so, gaze on, and grovel on thy face,
Until thy head be circled with the same.
Put forth thy hand, reach at the glorious gold:—
What, is 't too short? I 'll lengthen it with mine:
And, having both together heav'd it up,
We 'll both together lift our heads to heaven;
And never more abase our sight so low,
As to vouchsafe one glance unto the ground.
    Glo. O Nell, sweet Nell, if thou dost love thy
        lord,
Banish the canker of ambitious thoughts:
And may that thought, when I imagine ill
Against my king and nephew, virtuous Henry,
Be my last breathing in this mortal world!
My troublous dream this night doth make me sad.

    Duch. What dream'd my lord? tell me, and
        I 'll requite it
With sweet rehearsal of my morning's dream.
    Glo. Methought, this staff, mine office-badge in
        court,
Was broke in twain; by whom, I have forgot,
But, as I think, it was by the cardinal;
And on the pieces of the broken wand
Were plac'd the heads of Edmond duke of Som
        erset,
And William de la Poole first duke of Suffolk.
This was my dream; what it doth bode, God
        knows.
    Duch. Tut, this was nothing but an argument,
That he that breaks a stick of Gloster's grove,
Shall lose his head for his presumption.
But list to me, my Humphrey, my sweet duke:
Methought, I sat in seat of majesty,
In the cathedral church of Westminster,
And in that chair where kings and queens are
        crown'd;
Where Henry, and dame Margaret, kneel'd to me,
And on my head did set the diadem.
    Glo. Nay, Eleanor, then must I chide outright:
Presumptuous dame, ill-nurtur'd Eleanor!
Art thou not second woman in the realm;
And the protector's wife, belov'd of him?
Hast thou not worldly pleasure at command,
Above the reach or compass of thy thought?
And wilt thou still be hammering treachery,
To tumble down thy husband and thyself,
From top of honour to disgrace's feet?
Away from me, and let me hear no more.
    Duch. What, what, my lord! are you so cho
        leric
With Eleanor, for telling but her dream?
Next time, I 'll keep my dreams unto myself,
And not be check'd.
    Glo. Nay, be not angry, I am pleas'd again.

Enter a Messenger.

    Mess. My lord protector, 't is his highness
        pleasure,
You do prepare to ride unto Saint Albans,
Whereas the king and queen do mean to hawk.
    Glo. I go.—Come, Nell, thou wilt ride with us?
    Duch. Yes, good my lord, I 'll follow presently
                              [*Exeunt* GLO. *and* Mess.
Follow I must, I cannot go before,
While Gloster bears this base and humble mind:
Were I a man, a duke, and next of blood,
I would remove these tedious stumbling-blocks,

And smooth my way upon their headless necks;
And, being a woman, I will not be slack
To play my part in fortune's pageant.
Where are you there? Sir John?' nay, fear not, man,
We are alone; here 's none but thee, and I.

Enter HUME.

Hume. Jesu preserve your royal majesty!
Duch. What say'st thou, majesty! I am but grace.
Hume. But, by the grace of God, and Hume's advice,
Your grace's title shall be multiplied.
Duch. What say'st thou, man! hast thou as yet conferr'd
With Margery Jourdain, the cunning witch;
And Roger Bolingbroke, the conjurer?
And will they undertake to do me good?
Hume. This they have promised,—to show your highness
A spirit rais'd from depth of under ground,
That shall make answer to such questions,
As by your grace shall be propounded him.
Duch. It is enough; I'll think upon the questions:
When from Saint Albans we do make return,
We'll see these things effected to the full.
Here, Hume, take this reward: make merry, man,
With thy confederates in this weighty cause.
                                                [*Exit* Duch.
Hume. Hume must make merry with the duchess' gold;
Marry, and shall. But how now, Sir John Hume?
Seal up your lips, and give no words but—mum!
The business asketh silent secrecy.
Dame Eleanor gives gold, to bring the witch:
Gold cannot come amiss, were she a devil.
Yet have I gold, flies from another coast:
I dare not say, from the rich cardinal,
And from the great and new-made duke of Suffolk;
Yet I do find it so: for, to be plain,
They, knowing dame Eleanor's aspiring humour,
Have hired me to undermine the duchess,
And buzz these conjurations in her brain.
They say, A crafty knave does need no broker;
Yet am I Suffolk and the cardinal's broker.
Hume, if you take not heed, you shall go near
To call them both—a pair of crafty knaves.
Well, so it stands: And thus, I fear, at last,
Hume's knavery will be the duchess' wreck;

And her attainture will be Humphrey's fall:
Sort how it will, I shall have gold for all. [*Exit*

SCENE III.—*The Same. A Room in the Palace.*

Enter PETER, *and Others, with Petitions.*

1st Pet. My masters, let 's stand close; my lord protector will come this way by and by, and then we may deliver our supplications in the quill.'
2nd Pet. Marry, the Lord protect him, for he 's a good man! Jesu bless him!

Enter SUFFOLK, *and* QUEEN MARGARET.

1st Pet. Here 'a comes, methinks, and the queen with him: I'll be the first, sure.
2nd Pet. Come back, fool; this is the duke of Suffolk, and not my lord protector.
Suf. How now, fellow! would'st any thing with me?
1st Pet. I pray, my lord, pardon me! I took ye for my lord protector.
Q. Mar. [*Reading the superscription.*] "To my lord protector?" are your supplications to his lordship? Let me see them: What is thine?
1st Pet. Mine is, an 't please your grace, against John Goodman, my lord cardinal's man, for keeping my house, and lands, and wife and all, from me.
Suf. Thy wife too? that is some wrong, indeed.
— What 's yours?—What 's here! [*Reads.*] "Against the duke of Suffolk, for enclosing the commons of Melford."—How now, sir knave?
2nd Pet. Alas, sir, I am but a poor petitioner of our whole township.
Peter. [*Presenting his Petition.*] Against my master, Thomas Horner, for saying that the duke of York was rightful heir to the crown.
Q. Mar. What say'st thou? Did the duke of York say, he was rightful heir to the crown?
Peter. That my master was? No, forsooth. my master said, That he was; and that the king was an usurper.
Suf. Who is there? [*Enter Servants.*]—Take this fellow in, and send for his master with a pursuivant presently:—we'll hear more of your matter before the king. [*Exeunt Servants, with* PETER.
Q. Mar. And as for you, that love to be protected
Under the wings of our protector's grace,
Begin your suits anew, and sue to him.
                                          [*Tears the Petition.*
Away, base cullions —Suffolk, let them go.
All. Come, let 's be gone. [*Exeunt* Petitioners.

Q. Mar. My lord of Suffolk, say, is this the
    guise,
Is this the fashion in the court of England?
Is this the government of Britain's isle,
And this the royalty of Albion's king?
What, shall king Henry be a pupil still,
Under the surly Gloster's governance?
Am I a queen in title and in style,
And must be made a subject to a duke?
I tell thee, Poole, when in the city Tours
Thou ran'st a tilt in honour of my love,
And stol'st away the ladies' hearts of France;
I thought king Henry had resembled thee,
In courage, courtship, and proportion:
But all his mind is bent to holiness,
To number *Ave-Maries* on his beads:
His champions are—the prophets and apostles;
His weapons, holy saws of sacred writ;
His study is his tilt-yard, and his loves
Are brazen images of canoniz'd saints.
I would, the college of cardinals
Would choose him pope, and carry him to Rome,
And set the triple crown upon his head;
That were a state fit for his holiness.
    Suf. Madam, be patient; as I was cause
Your highness came to England, so will I
In England work your grace's full content.
    Q. Mar. Beside the haught protector, have we
    Beaufort,
The imperious churchman; Somerset, Bucking-
    ham,
And grumbling York: and not the least of these,
But can do more in England than the king.
    Suf. And he of these, that can do most of all,
Cannot do more in England than the Nevils:
Salisbury, and Warwick, are no simple peers.
    Q. Mar. Not all these lords do vex me half so
    much,
As that proud dame, the lord protector's wife.
She sweeps it through the court with troops of
    ladies,
More like an empress than duke Humphrey's
    wife;
Strangers in court do take her for the queen:
She bears a duke's revenues on her back,
And in her heart she scorns our poverty:
Shall I not live to be aveng'd on her?
Contemptuous base-born callat as she is,
She vaunted 'mong her minions t' other day,
The very train of her worst wearing-gown
Was better worth than all my father's lands,
Till Suffolk gave two dukedoms for his daughter.

Suf. Madam, myself have lim'd a bush for her;
And plac'd a quire of such enticing birds,
That she will light to listen to the lays,
And never mount to trouble you again.
So, let her rest: And, madam, list to me;
For I am bold to counsel you in this.
Although we fancy not the cardinal,
Yet must we join with him, and with the lords,
Till we have brought duke Humphrey in disgrace.
As for the duke of York,—this late complaint
Will make but little for his benefit:
So, one by one, we 'll weed them all at last,
And you yourself shall steer the happy helm.

Enter KING HENRY, YORK, *and* SOMERSET, *con-
    versing with him;* DUKE *and* DUCHESS OF GLOS-
    TER, CARDINAL BEAUFORT, BUCKINGHAM, SALIS-
    BURY, *and* WARWICK.

    K. Hen. For my part, noble lords, I care not
        which;
Or Somerset, or York, all 's one to me.
    York. If York have ill demean'd himself in
        France,
Then let him be denay'd the regentship.
    Som. If Somerset be unworthy of the place,
Let York be regent, I will yield to him.
    War. Whether your grace be worthy, yea, or
        no,
Dispute not that: York is the worthier.
    Car. Ambitious Warwick, let thy betters speak.
    War. The cardinal 's not my better in the field.
    Buck. All in this presence are thy betters,
        Warwick.
    War. Warwick may live to be the best of all.
    Sal. Peace, son;——and show some reason,
        Buckingham,
Why Somerset should be preferr'd in this.
    Q. Mar. Because the king, forsooth, will have
        it so.
    Glo. Madam, the king is old enough himself
To give his censure: these are no women's mat-
    ters.
    Q. Mar. If he be old enough, what needs your
        grace
To be protector of his excellence?
    Glo. Madam, I am protector of the realm;
And, at his pleasure, will resign my place.
    Suf. Resign it then, and leave thine insolence.
Since thou wert king, (as who is king, but thou?)
The commonwealth hath daily run to wreck:
The Dauphin hath prevail'd beyond the seas,
And all the peers and nobles of the realm

Have been as bondmen to thy sovereignty.

Car. The commons hast thou rack'd : the
clergy's bags
Are lank and lean with thy extortions.

Som. Thy sumptuous buildings, and thy wife's
attire,
Have cost a mass of public treasury.

Buck. Thy cruelty in execution,
Upon offenders, hath exceeded law,
And left thee to the mercy of the law.

Q. Mar. Thy sale of offices, and towns in
France,—
If they were known, as the suspect is great,—
Would make thee quickly hop without thy head.
[*Exit Glo. The* Queen *drops her Fan.*
Give me my fan : What, minion ! can you not?
[*Gives the* Duchess *a box on the Ear.*
I cry you mercy, madam : Was it you?

Duch. Was't I? yea, I it was, proud French-
woman :
Could I come near your beauty with my nails,
I'd set my ten commandments in your face.

K. Hen. Sweet aunt, be quiet; 't was against
her will.

Duch. Against her will! Good king, look to't
in time;
She'll hamper thee, and dandle thee like a baby :
Though in this place most master wear no breeches,
She shall not strike dame Eleanor unreveng'd.
[*Exit* Duch.

Buck. Lord cardinal, I will follow Eleanor,
And listen after Humphrey, how he proceeds :
She's tickled now ; her fume can need no spurs,
She'll gallop fast enough to her destruction.
[*Exit* Buck.

Re-enter Gloster.

Glo. Now, lords, my choler being over-blown,
With walking once about the quadrangle,
I come to talk of commonwealth affairs.
As for your spiteful false objections,
Prove them, and I lie open to the law :
But God in mercy so deal with my soul,
As I in duty love my king and country !
But, to the matter that we have in hand :—
I say, my sovereign, York is meetest man
To be your regent in the realm of France.

Suf. Before we make election, give me leave
To show some reason, of no little force,
That York is most unmeet of any man.

York. I'll tell thee, Suffolk, why I am unmeet.
First, for I cannot flatter thee in pride :

Next, if I be appointed for the place,
My lord of Somerset will keep me here,
Without discharge, money, or furniture,
Till France be won into the Dauphin's hands.
Last time, I danc'd attendance on his will,
Till Paris was besieg'd, famish'd, and lost.

War. That I can witness ; and a fouler fact
Did never traitor in the land commit.

Suf. Peace, head-strong Warwick !

War. Image of pride, why should I hold my
peace?

Enter Servants of Suffolk, *bringing in* Horner
and Peter.

Suf. Because here is a man accus'd of treason :
Pray God, the duke of York excuse himself !

York. Doth any one accuse York for a traitor !

K. Hen. What mean'st thou, Suffolk? tell me.
What are these?

Suf. Please it your majesty, this is the man
That doth accuse his master of high treason :
His words were these ;—that Richard, duke of
York,
Was rightful heir unto the English crown ;
And that your majesty was an usurper.

K. Hen. Say, man, were these thy words?

Hor. An't shall please your majesty, I never
said nor thought any such matter : God is my witness, I am falsely accused by the villain.

Pet. By these ten bones, my lords, [*Holding
up his Hands.*] he did speak them to me in the
garret one night, as we were scouring my lord of
York's armour.

York. Base dunghill villain, and mechanical,
I'll have thy head for this thy traitor's speech :—
I do beseech your royal majesty,
Let him have all the rigour of the law.

Hor. Alas, my lord, hang me, if ever I spake
the words. My accuser is my 'prentice ; and when
I did correct him for his fault the other day, he
did vow upon his knees he would be even with
me : I have good witness of this ; therefore, I beseech your majesty, do not cast away an honest
man for a villain's accusation.

K. Hen. Uncle, what shall we say to this in law?

Glo. This doom, my lord, if I may judge.
Let Somerset be regent o'er the French,
Because in York this breeds suspicion :
And let these have a day appointed them
For single combat in convenient place ;
For he hath witness of his servant's malice :
This is the law, and this duke Humphrey's doom.

K. Hen. Then be it so.   My lord of Somerset.
We make your grace lord regent o'er the French.

Som. I humbly thank your royal majesty.

Hor. And I accept the combat willingly.

Pet. Alas, my lord, I cannot fight; for God's
sake, pity my case! the spite of man prevaileth
against me. O, Lord have mercy upon me! I
shall never be able to fight a blow: O Lord, my
heart!

Glo. Sirrah, or you must fight, or else be hang'd.

K. Hen. Away with them to prison: and the day
Of combat shall be the last of the next month.—
Come, Somerset, we 'll see thee sent away. [*Exeunt.*

SCENE IV.— *The Same.   The* Duke of Gloster's
Garden.

Enter MARGERY JOURDAIN, HUME, SOUTHWELL,
and BOLINGBROKE.

Hume. Come, my masters; the duchess, I tell
you, expects performance of your promises.

Boling. Master Hume, we are therefore provided: Will her ladyship behold and hear our ex-
orcisms?

Hume. Ay: What else? fear you not her courage.

Boling. I have heard her reported to be a
woman of an invincible spirit: but it shall be
convenient, master Hume, that you be by her
aloft, while we be busy below; and so, I pray you,
go in God's name, and leave us. [*Exit* Hume.]
Mother Jourdain, be you prostrate, and grovel on
the earth;—John Southwell, read you; and let
us to our work.

Enter DUCHESS, *above.*

Duch. Well said, my masters; and welcome all.
To this gear; the sooner the better.

Boling. Patience, good lady; wizards know their
times:

Deep night, dark night, the silence of the night,
The time of night when Troy was set on fire;
The time when screech-owls cry, and ban-dogs
howl,
And spirits walk, and ghosts break up their graves,
That time best fits the work we have in hand.
Madam, sit you, and fear not; whom we raise,
We will make fast within a hallow'd verge.

[*Here they perform the Ceremonies appertaining,
and make the Circle;* BOLING., *or* SOUTH.,
reads, "Conjuro te," *&c.   It thunders and
lightens terribly; then the Spirit riseth.*
314

Spir. Adsum.

M. Jourd. Asmath,
By the eternal God, whose name and power
Thou tremblest at, answer that I shall ask;
For, till thou speak, thou shalt not pass from
hence.

Spir. Ask what thou wilt:—That I had said
and done!

Boling. "First, of the king.   What shall of him
become?"   [*Reading out of a Paper.*

Spir. The duke yet lives, that Henry shall depose;
But him outlive, and die a violent death.

[*As the Spirit speaks,* SOUTH. *writes the answer.*

Boling. "What fate awaits the duke of Suffolk?"

Spir. By water shall he die, and take his end.

Boling. "What shall befall the duke of Somerset?"

Spir. Let him shun castles;
Safer shall he be upon the sandy plains
Than where castles mounted stand.
Have done, for more I hardly can endure.

Boling. Descend to darkness, and the burning
lake:
False fiend, avoid!

[*Thunder and Lightning.* Spir. *descends.*

Enter YORK *and* BUCKINGHAM, *hastily, with their
Guards, and Others.*

York. Lay hands upon these traitors, and their
trash.
Beldame, I think we watch'd you at an inch.—
What, madam, are you there? the king and com-
monweal
Are deeply indebted for this piece of pains;
My lord protector will, I doubt it not,
See you well guerdon'd for these good deserts.

Duch. Not half so bad as thine to England's
king,
Injurious duke; that threat'st where is no cause.

Buck. True, madam, none at all.   What call
you this?   [*Showing her the papers.*
Away with them; let them be clapp'd up close,
And kept asunder:—You, madam, shall with us:—
Stafford, take her to thee,—

[*Exit* Duch. *from above.*
We 'll see your trinkets here all forth-coming;
All.—Away!

[*Exeunt Guards, with* SOUTH., BOLING., *&c.*

York. Lord Buckingham, methinks you watch'd
her well:

A pretty plot, well chosen to build upon!
Now, pray, my lord, let 's see the devil's writ.
What have we here?   [Reads.
"The duke yet lives, that Henry shall depose;
But him outlive, and die a violent death."
Why, this is just,
Aio te, Æacida, Romanos, vincere posse.
Well, to the rest:
"Tell me, what fate awaits the duke of Suffolk?"
"By water shall he die, and take his end."—
"What shall betide the duke of Somerset?"
"Let him shun castles;
Safer shall he be upon the sandy plains,
Than where castles mounted stand."
Come, come, my lords;
These oracles are hardily attain'd,

And hardily understood.
The king is now in progress toward Saint Albans.
With him, the husband of this lovely lady:
Thither go these news, as fast as horse can carry
them;
A sorry breakfast for my lord protector.

Buck. Your grace shall give me leave, my lord
of York,
To be the post, in hope of his reward.

York. At your pleasure, my good lord.—Who 's
within there, ho!

Enter a Servant.

Invite my lords of Salisbury, and Warwick,
To sup with me to-morrow night.—Away!
[Exeunt

ACT II.

SCENE I.—Saint Albans.

Enter KING HENRY, QUEEN MARGARET, GLOSTER,
CARDINAL, *and* SUFFOLK, *with* Falconers hol-
laing.

Q. Mar. Believe me, lords, for flying at the
brook,
I saw not better sport these seven years' day:
Yet, by your leave, the wind was very high;
And, ten to one, old Joan had not gone out.

K. Hen. But what a point, my lord, your falcon
made,
And what a pitch she flew above the rest!—
To see how God in all his creatures works!
Yea, man and birds, are fain of climbing high.

Suf. No marvel, an it like your majesty,
My lord protector's hawks do tower so well;
They know their master loves to be aloft,
And bears his thoughts above his falcon's pitch.

Glo. My lord, 't is but a base ignoble mind
That mounts no higher than a bird can soar.

Car. I thought as much; he 'd be above the
clouds.

Glo. Ay my lord cardinal: How think you by
that?
Were it not good, your grace could fly to heaven?

K. Hen. The treasury of everlasting joy!

Car. Thy heaven is on earth; thine eyes and
thoughts
Beat on a crown, the treasure of thy heart;
Pernicious protector, dangerous peer,
That smooth'st it so with king and commonweal.

Glo. What, cardinal, is your priesthood grown
peremptory?
Tantæne animis cœlestibus iræ?
Churchmen so hot? good uncle, hide such malice;
With such holiness can you do it?

Suf. No malice, sir; no more than well becomes
So good a quarrel, and so bad a peer.

Glo. As who, my lord?

Suf.   Why, as you, my lord;
An 't like your lordly lord-protectorship.

Glo. Why, Suffolk, England knows thine insolence.

Q. Mar. And thy ambition, Gloster.

K. Hen.   I pr'ythee, peace,
Good queen; and whet not on these furious peers,
For blessed are the peacemakers on earth.

Car. Let me be blessed for the peace I make,
Against this proud protector, with my sword!

Glo. 'Faith, holy uncle, 'would 't were come to
that!   [Aside to the CAR.

Car. Marry, when thou dar'st.   [Aside.

Glo. Make up no factious numbers for the
matter,
In thine own person answer thy abuse. [*Aside.*
  Car. Ay, where thou dar'st not peep: an if
thou dar'st,
This evening on the east side of the grove. [*Aside.*
  K. Hen. How now, my lords?
  Car.   Believe me, cousin Gloster.
Had not your man put up the fowl so suddenly,
We had had more sport.—Come with thy two-
      hand sword.   [*Aside to* Glo.
  Glo. True, uncle.
  Car. Are you advis'd?—the east side of the
      grove?
  Glo. Cardinal, I am with you.   [*Aside.*
  K. Hen.   Why, how now, uncle Gloster?
  Glo. Talking of hawking; nothing else, my
lord.—
Now, by God's mother, priest, I 'll shave your
      crown for this,
Or all my fence shall fail.   [*Aside.*
  Car. Medice teipsum;
Protector, see to 't well, protect yourself. [*Aside.*
  K. Hen. The winds grow high; so do your sto-
machs, lords.
How irksome is this music to my heart!
When such strings jar, what hope of harmony?
I pray, my lords, let me compound this strife.

Enter an Inhabitant *of Saint Albans, crying, "A
      Miracle."*[10]

  Glo. What means this noise?
Fellow, what miracle dost thou proclaim?
  Inhab. A miracle! a miracle!
  Suf. Come to the king, and tell him what mir-
acle.
  Inhab. Forsooth, a blind man at Saint Alban's
shrine,
Within this half hour, hath received his sight;
A man, that ne'er saw in his life before.
  K. Hen. Now, God be prais'd! that to believ-
ing souls
Gives light in darkness, comfort in despair!

Enter the Mayor of Saint Albans, *and his
Brethren; and* Simpcox, *borne between two persons in a Chair; his Wife and a great Multitude following.*

  Car. Here come the townsmen on procession,
To present your highness with the man.
  K. Hen. Great is his comfort in this earthly
vale,
916

Although by his sight his sin be multiplied.
  Glo. Stand by, my masters, bring him near the
king.
His highness' pleasure is to talk with him.
  K. Hen. Good fellow, tell us here the circum-
stance,
That we for thee may glorify the Lord.
What, hast thou been long blind, and now restor'd?
  Simp. Born blind, an 't please your grace.
  Wife. Ay, indeed, was he.
  Suf. What woman is this?
  Wife. His wife, an 't like your worship.
  Glo. Had'st thou been his mother, thou could'st
have better told.
  K. Hen. Where wert thou born?
  Simp. At Berwick in the north, an 't like your
grace.
  K. Hen. Poor soul! God's goodness hath been
great to thee:
Let never day nor night unhallow'd pass,
But still remember what the Lord hath done.
  Q. Mar. Tell me, good fellow, cam'st thou here
by chance,
Or of devotion, to this holy shrine?
  Simp. God knows, of pure devotion: being
call'd
A hundred times, and oftener, in my sleep
By good Saint Alban; who said,—"Simpcox,
come;
Come, offer at my shrine, and I will help thee."
  Wife. Most true, forsooth; and many time and
oft
Myself have heard a voice to call him so.
  Car. What, art thou lame?
  Simp.   Ay, God Almighty help me!
  Suf. How cam'st thou so?
  Simp.   A fall off of a tree.
  Wife. A plum-tree, master.
  Glo.   How long hast thou been blind?
  Simp. O, born so, master.
  Glo.   What, and would'st climb a tree?
  Simp. But that in all my life, when I was a
youth.
  Wife. Too true; and bought his climbing very
dear.
  Glo. 'Mass, thou lov'dst plums well that would'st
venture so.
  Simp. Alas, good master, my wife desir'd some
damsons,
And made me climb, with danger of my life.
  Glo. A subtle knave! but yet it shall not
serve.—

Let me see thine eyes:—wink now;—now open
　them:—
in my opinion yet thou see'st not well.

Simp. Yes, master, clear as day; I thank God,
　and Saint Alban.

Glo. Say'st thou me so? What colour is this
　cloak of?

Simp. Red, master; red as blood.

Glo. Why, that's well said: What colour is
　my gown of?

Simp. Black, forsooth; coal-black, as jet.

K. Hen. Why then, thou know'st what colour
　jet is of?

Suf. And yet, I think, jet did he never see.

Glo. But cloaks, and gowns, before this day, a
　many.

Wife. Never, before this day, in all his life.

Glo. Tell me, sirrah, what's my name?

Simp. Alas, master, I know not.

Glo. What's his name?

Simp. I know not.

Glo. Nor his?

Simp. No, indeed, master.

Glo. What's thine own name?

Simp. Saunder Simpcox, an if it please you,
master.

Glo. Then, Saunder, sit thou there, the lyingest
　knave
In Christendom. If thou hadst been born blind,
Thou might'st as well have known our names, as thus
To name the several colours we do wear.
Sight may distinguish of colours; but suddenly
To nominate them all, 's impossible.—
My lords, Saint Alban here hath done a miracle;
And would ye not think that cunning to be great,
That could restore this cripple to his legs?

Simp. O, master, that you could!

Glo. My masters of Saint Albans, have you not
beadles in your town, and things called whips?

May. Yes, my lord, if it please your grace.

Glo. Then send for one presently.

May. Sirrah, go fetch the beadle hither straight.
　　　　　　　　　　　　　[*Exit an* Attend.

Glo. Now fetch me a stool hither by and by. [*A
Stool brought out.*] Now, sirrah, if you mean to
save yourself from whipping, leap me over this
stool, and run away.

Simp. Alas, master, I am not able to stand
alone: You go about to torture me in vain.

　Re-enter Attendant, *with the* Beadle.

Glo. Well, sir, we must have you find your legs.

Sirrah Beadle, whip him till he leap over that same
stool.

Bead. I will, my lord.—Come on, sirrah; off
with your doublet quickly.

Simp. Alas, master, what shall I do? I am
not able to stand.

　[*After the* Beadle *hath hit him once, he leaps
　　over the Stool, and runs away; and the
　　People follow, and cry, A Miracle!*

K. Hen. O God, see'st thou this, and bear'st so
　long?

Q. Mar. It made me laugh, to see the villain
　run.

Glo. Follow the knave; and take this drab
　away.

Wife. Alas, sir, we did it for pure need.

Glo. Let them be whipped through every market
town, till they come to Berwick, whence they
came.　　　　　　　[*Exeunt* May., Bead., Wife, &c.

Car. Duke Humphrey has done a miracle to-
　day.

Suf. True; made the lame to leap, and fly away.

Glo. But you have done more miracles than I
You made, in a day, my lord, whole towns to fly.

　　　　　Enter BUCKINGHAM.

K. Hen. What tidings with our cousin Buck-
　ingham?

Buck. Such as my heart doth tremble to
　unfold.
A sort of naughty persons, lewdly bent,—
Under the countenance and confederacy
Of lady Eleanor, the protector's wife,
The ringleader and head of all this rout,—
Have practis'd dangerously against your state,
Dealing with witches, and with conjurers:
Whom we have apprehended in the fact;
Raising up wicked spirits from under ground,
Demanding of king Henry's life and death,
And other of your highness' privy council,
As more at large your grace shall understand.

Car. And so, my lord protector, by this means
Your lady is forthcoming yet at London.
This news, I think, hath turn'd your weapon's
　edge;
'T is like, my lord, you will not keep your hour.
　　　　　　　　　　　　　[*Aside to* Glo.

Glo. Ambitious churchman, leave to afflict my
　heart!
Sorrow and grief have vanquish'd all my powers
And, vanquish'd as I am, I yield to thee,
Or to the meanest groom.

　　　　　　　　　　　　　　　　　　317

K. Hen. O God, what mischiefs work the wicked
    ones;
Heaping confusion on their own heads thereby!
  Q. Mar. Gloster, see here the tainture of thy
    nest;
And, look, thyself be faultless, thou wert best.
  Glo. Madam, for myself, to heaven I do appeal,
How I have lov'd my king, and commonweal:
And, for my wife, I know not how it stands;
Sorry I am to hear what I have heard:
Noble she is; but if she have forgot
Honour and virtue, and convers'd with such
As, like to pitch, defile nobility,
I banish her, my bed, and company;
And give her, as a prey, to law, and shame,
That hath dishonour'd Gloster's honest name.
  K. Hen. Well, for this night, we will repose us
    here,
Tomorrow, toward London, back again,
To look into this business thoroughly,
And call these foul offenders to their answers;
And poise the cause in justice' equal scales,
Whose beam stands sure, whose rightful cause
    prevails.   [*Flourish. Exeunt.*

SCENE II.—London. *The Duke of York's
    Garden.*

Enter YORK, SALISBURY, *and* WARWICK.

  York. Now, my good lords of Salisbury and
    Warwick.
Our simple supper ended, give me leave,
In this close walk, to satisfy myself,
In craving your opinion of my title,
Which is infallible, to England's crown.
  Sal. My lord, I long to hear it at full.
  War. Sweet York, begin: and if thy claim be
    good,
The Nevils are thy subjects to command.
  York. Then thus:—
Edward the Third, my lords, had seven sons:
The first, Edward the Black Prince, Prince of
    Wales;
The second, William of Hatfield; and the third,
Lionel, duke of Clarence; next to whom,
Was John of Gaunt, the duke of Lancaster;
The fifth, was Edmund Langley, duke of York;
The sixth, was Thomas of Woodstock, duke of
    Gloster;
William of Windsor was the seventh, and last.
Edward, the Black Prince, died before his father,
And left behind him Richard, his only son,

Who, after Edward the Third's death, reign'd as
    king;
Till Henry Bolingbroke, duke of Lancaster,
The eldest son and heir of John of Gaunt,
Crown'd by the name of Henry the Fourth,
Seiz'd on the realm; deposed the rightful king;
Sent his poor queen to France, from whence she
    came,
And him to Pomfret; where, as all you know,
Harmless Richard was murder'd traitorously.
  War. Father, the duke hath told the truth;
Thus got the house of Lancaster the crown.
  York. Which now they hold by force, and not
    by right;
For Richard, the first son's heir, being dead,
The issue of the next son should have reign'd.
  Sal. But William of Hatfield died without an
    heir.
  York. The third son, duke of Clarence, (from
    whose line
I claim the crown,) had issue—Phillippe, a daugh-
    ter,
Who married Edmund Mortimer, earl of March;
Edmund had issue—Roger, earl of March;
Roger had issue—Edmund, Anne, and Eleanor.
  Sal. This Edmund, in the reign of Bolingbroke,
As I have read, laid claim unto the crown;
And, but for Owen Glendower, had been king,
Who kept him in captivity, till he died.
But, to the rest.
  York.   His eldest sister, Anne,
My mother, being heir unto the crown,
Married Richard, earl of Cambridge; who was son
To Edmund Langley, Edward the Third's fifth
    son.
By her I claim the kingdom; she was heir
To Roger, earl of March; who was the son
Of Edmund Mortimer; who married Phillippe,
Sole daughter unto Lionel, duke of Clarence:
So, if the issue of the elder son
Succeed before the younger, I am king.
  War. What plain proceedings are more plain
    than this?
Henry doth claim the crown from John of Gaunt,
The fourth son: York claims it from the third.
Till Lionel's issue fails, his should not reign:
It fails not yet; but flourishes in thee,
And in thy sons, fair slips of such a stock.—
Then, father Salisbury, kneel we both together;
And, in this private plot, be we the first,
That shall salute our rightful sovereign
With honour of his birthright to the crown.

Both. Long live our sovereign Richard, England's king!

York. We thank you, lords. But I am not your king
Till I be crown'd; and that my sword be stain'd
With heart-blood of the house of Lancaster:
And that 's not suddenly to be perform'd;
But with advice, and silent secrecy.
Do you, as I do, in these dangerous days,
Wink at the duke of Suffolk's insolence,
At Beaufort's pride, at Somerset's ambition,
At Buckingham, and all the crew of them,
Till they have snar'd the shepherd of the flock,
That virtuous prince, the good duke Humphrey:
'T is that they seek; and they, in seeking that,
Shall find their deaths, if York can prophesy.

Sal. My lord, break we off; we know your
mind at full.

War. My heart assures me, that the earl of
Warwick
Shall one day make the duke of York a king.

York. And, Nevil, this I do assure myself,
Richard shall live to make the earl of Warwick
The greatest man in England, but the king.
[*Exeunt.*

SCENE III.—*The Same.　A Hall of Justice.*

Trumpets sounded.　Enter KING HENRY, QUEEN
MARGARET, GLOSTER, YORK, SUFFOLK, *and*
SALISBURY; *the* DUCHESS OF GLOSTER, MAR-
GERY JOURDAIN, SOUTHWELL, HUME, *and* BO-
LINGBROKE, *under guard.*

K. Hen. Stand forth, dame Eleanor Cobham,
Gloster's wife:
In sight of God, and us, your guilt is great;
Receive the sentence of the law, for sins
Such as by God's book are adjudg'd to death.—
You four, from hence to prison back again;
[*To* JOURD., *&c.*
From thence, unto the place of execution:
The witch in Smithfield shall be burn'd to ashes,
And you three shall be strangled on the gallows.—
You, madam, for you are more nobly born,
Despoiled of your honour in your life,
Shall, after three days' open penance done,
Live in your country here, in banishment,
With sir John Stanley, in the Isle of Man.

Duch. Welcome is banishment, welcome were
my death.

Glo. Eleanor, the law, thou seest, hath judged
thee;

I cannot justify whom the law condemns.—
[*Exeunt the* DUCH., *and the other Prisoners
guarded.*
Mine eyes are full of tears, my heart of grief.
Ah, Humphrey, this dishonour in thine age
Will bring thy head with sorrow to the ground!
I beseech your majesty, give me leave to go;
Sorrow would solace, and mine age would ease.

K. Hen. Stay, Humphrey duke of Gloster: ere
thou go,
Give up thy staff; Henry will to himself
Protector be: and God shall be my hope,
My stay, my guide, and lantern to my feet.
And go in peace, Humphrey; no less belov'd,
Than when thou wert protector to thy king.

Q. Mar. I see no reason, why a king of years
Should be to be protected like a child.—
God and king Henry govern England's helm:
Give up your staff, sir, and the king his realm.

Glo. My staff?—here, noble Henry, is my
staff:
As willingly do I the same resign,
As e'er thy father Henry made it mine;
And even as willingly at thy feet I leave it,
As others would ambitiously receive it.
Farewell, good king: When I am dead and gone,
May honourable peace attend thy throne! [*Exit.*

Q. Mar. Why, now is Henry king, and Mar-
garet queen;
And Humphrey, duke of Gloster, scarce himself,
That bears so shrewd a maim; two pulls at
once,—
His lady banish'd, and a limb lopp'd off;
This staff of honour raught:—There let it stand,
Where it best fits to be, in Henry's hand.

Suf. Thus droops this lofty pine, and hangs his
sprays;
Thus Eleanor's pride dies in her proudest days.

York. Lords, let him go.—Please it your ma-
jesty,
This is the day appointed for the combat;
And ready are the appellant and defendant,
The armourer and his man, to enter the lists,
So please your highness to behold the fight.

Q. Mar. Ay, good my lord; for purposely
therefore
Left I the court, to see this quarrel tried.

K. Hen. O' God's name, see the lists and all
things fit;
Here let them end it, and God defend the
right!

York. I never saw a fellow worse bested.

Or more afraid to fight, than is the appellant,
The servant of this armourer, my lords.

Enter, on one side, HORNER, and his Neighbours,
drinking to him so much that he is drunk;
and he enters bearing his staff with a sand-
bag fastened to it; a drum before him: at
the other side, PETER, with a drum and a simi-
lar staff; accompanied by 'Prentices drinking
to him.

1st Neigh. Here, neighbour Horner, I drink to
you in a cup of sack: And fear not, neighbour,
you shall do well enough.

2nd Neigh. And here, neighbour, here's a cup
of charneco.

3rd Neigh. And here's a pot of good double
beer, neighbour: drink, and fear not your man.

Hor. Let it come, i' faith, and I'll pledge you
all: And a fig for Peter!

1st Pren. Here, Peter, I drink to thee; and be
not afraid.

2nd Pren. Be merry, Peter, and fear not thy
master; fight for credit of the 'prentices.

Peter. I thank you all: drink, and pray for
me, I pray you: for, I think, I have taken my
last draught in this world.—Here, Robin, an if I
die, I give thee my apron: and, Will, thou shalt
have my hammer:—and here, Tom, take all the
money that I have.—O Lord, bless me, I pray
God! for I am never able to deal with my master,
he hath learnt so much fence already.

Sal. Come, leave your drinking, and fall to
blows.—Sirrah, what's thy name?

Peter. Peter, forsooth.

Sal. Peter! what more?

Peter. Thump.

Sal. Thump? then see thou thump thy master
well.

Hor. Masters, I am come hither, as it were,
upon my man's instigation, to prove him a knave,
and myself an honest man: and touching the duke
of York,—will take my death, I never meant him
any ill, nor the king, nor the queen: And therefore, Peter, have at thee with a downright blow,
as Bevis of Southampton fell upon Ascapart.

York. Despatch:—this knave's tongue begins
to double.

Sound trumpets, alarum to the combatants.

[*Alarum. They fight, and PETER strikes*
down his master.

Hor. Hold, Peter, hold! I confess, I confess
treason.   [*Dies.*

920

York. Take away his weapon:—Fellow, thank
God, and the good wine in thy master's way.

Peter. O God! have I overcome mine enemies
in this presence? O Peter, thou hast prevail'd
in right!

K. Hen. Go, take hence that traitor from our
sight;

For, by his death, we do perceive his guilt:
And God, in justice, hath reveal'd to us
The truth and innocence of this poor fellow,
Which he had thought to have murder'd wrong-
fully.—
Come, fellow, follow us for thy reward. [*Exeunt*

SCENE IV.—*The Same. A Street.*

Enter GLOSTER and Servants, in mourning Cloaks.

Glo. Thus, sometimes, hath the brightest day
a cloud;

And, after summer, evermore succeeds
Barren winter, with his wrathful nipping cold:
So cares and joys abound, as seasons fleet.—
Sirs, what's o'clock?

Serv. Ten, my lord.

Glo. Ten is the hour that was appointed me,
To watch the coming of my punish'd duchess:
Uneath may she endure the flinty streets,
To tread them with her tender-feeling feet.
Sweet Nell, ill can thy noble mind abrook
The abject people, gazing on thy face,
With envious looks still laughing at thy shame,
That erst did follow thy proud chariot wheels,
When thou didst ride in triumph through the
streets.
But, soft! I think, she comes; and I'll prepare
My tear-stain'd eyes to see her miseries.

Enter the DUCHESS OF GLOSTER, in a white sheet,
with papers pinned upon her back, her feet bare,
and a taper burning in her hand; SIR JOHN
STANLEY, a Sheriff, and Officers.

Serv. So please your grace, we'll take her from
the sheriff.

Glo. No, stir not for your lives; let her
pass by.

Duch. Come you, my lord, to see my open
shame?
Now thou dost penance too. Look, how they
gaze!
See, how the giddy multitude do point,
And nod their heads, and throw their **eyes on**
thee!

Ah, Gloster, hide thee from their hateful looks;
And, in thy closet pent up, rue my shame,
And ban thine enemies, both mine and thine.

Glo. Be patient, gentle Nell; forget this grief.

Duch. Ah, Gloster, teach me to forget myself:
For, whilst I think I am thy married wife,
And thou a prince, protector of this land,
Methinks, I should not thus be led along,
Mail'd up in shame, with papers on my back;
And follow'd with a rabble, that rejoice
To see my tears, and hear my deep-fet groans.
The ruthless flint doth cut my tender feet;
And, when I start, the envious people laugh,
And bid me be advised how I tread.
Ah, Humphrey, can I bear this shameful yoke?
Trow'st thou, that e'er I 'll look upon the world;
Or count them happy, that enjoy the sun?
No; dark shall be my light, and night my day;
To think upon my pomp, shall be my hell.
Sometime I 'll say, I am duke Humphrey's wife;
And he a prince, and ruler of the land:
Yet so he rul'd, and such a prince he was,
As he stood by, whilst I, his forlorn duchess,
Was made a wonder, and a pointing-stock,
To every idle rascal follower.
But be thou mild, and blush not at my shame;
Nor stir at nothing, till the axe of death
Hang over thee, as, sure, it shortly will.
For Suffolk,—he that can do all in all
With her, that hateth thee, and hates us all,—
And York, and impious Beaufort, that false priest,
Have all lim'd bushes to betray thy wings,
And, fly thou how thou canst, they 'll tangle thee:
But fear not thou, until thy foot be snar'd,
Nor never seek prevention of thy foes.

Glo. Ah, Nell, forbear; thou aimest all awry;
I must offend, before I be attainted:
And had I twenty times so many foes,
And each of them had twenty times their power,
All these could not procure me any scathe,
So long as I am loyal, true, and crimeless.
Would'st have me rescue thee from this reproach?
Why, yet thy scandal were not wip'd away,
But I in danger for the breach of law.
Thy greatest help is quiet, gentle Nell:
I pray thee, sort thy heart to patience:
These few days' wonder will be quickly worn.

Enter a Herald.

Her. I summon your grace to his majesty's
parliament, holden at Bury the first of this next
month.

116

Glo. And my consent ne'er ask'd herein before.
This is close dealing.—Well, I will be there.

[Exit Her.

My Nell, I take my leave:—and, master sheriff,
Let not her penance exceed the king's commission.

Sher. An 't please your grace, here my com-
mission stays:
And sir John Stanley is appointed now
To take her with him to the Isle of Man.

Glo. Must you, sir John, protect my lady here?

Stan. So am I given in charge, may 't please
your grace.

Glo. Entreat her not the worse, in that I pray
You use her well: the world may laugh again;
And I may live to do you kindness, if
You do it her. And so, sir John, farewell.

Duch. What gone, my lord; and bid me not
farewell!

Glo. Witness my tears, I cannot stay to speak.

[Exeunt Glo., and Servants.

Duch. Art thou gone too! All comfort go
with thee!
For none abides with me: my joy is—death;
Death, at whose name I oft have been afear'd,
Because I wish'd this world's eternity.—
Stanley, I pr'ythee, go, and take me hence;
I care not whither, for I beg no favour,
Only convey me where thou art commanded.

Stan. Why, madam, that is to the Isle of Man;
There to be used according to your state.

Duch. That 's bad enough, for I am but reproach:
And shall I then be us'd reproachfully?

Stan. Like to a duchess, and duke Humphrey's
lady,
According to that state you shall be used.

Duch. Sheriff, farewell, and better than I fare;
Although thou hast been conduct of my shame!

Sher. It is my office; and, madam, pardon
me.

Duch. Ay, ay, farewell; thy office is discharg'd.—
Come, Stanley, shall we go?

Stan. Madam, your penance done, throw off
this sheet,
And go we to attire you for our journey.

Duch. My shame will not be shifted with my
sheet:
No, it will hang upon my richest robes,
And show itself, attire me how I can.
Go, lead the way; I long to see my prison.

[Exeunt.

991

ACT III.

SCENE I.—*The Abbey at* Bury.

Enter to the Parliament, KING HENRY, QUEEN
MARGARET, CARDINAL BEAUFORT, SUFFOLK,
YORK, BUCKINGHAM, *and Others.*

K. Hen. I muse, my lord of Gloster is not
come:
'T is not his wont to be the hindmost man,
Whate'er occasion keeps him from us now.

Q. Mar. Can you not see? or will you not ob-
serve
The strangeness of his alter'd countenance?
With what a majesty he bears himself;
How insolent of late he is become,
How proud, peremptory, and unlike himself?
We know the time, since he was mild and affable;
And, if we did but glance a far-off look,
Immediately he was upon his knee,
That all the court admir'd him for submission:
But meet him now, and, be it in the morn,
When every one will give the time of day,
He knits his brow, and shows an angry eye,
And passeth by with stiff unbowed knee,
Disdaining duty that to us belongs.
Small curs are not regarded, when they grin;
But great men tremble, when the lion roars;
And Humphrey is no little man in England.
First, note, that he is near you in descent;
And should you fall, he is the next will mount.
Me seemeth then, it is no policy,—
Respecting what a rancorous mind he bears,
And his advantage following your decease,—
That he should come about your royal person,
Or be admitted to your highness' council.
By flattery hath he won the commons' hearts;
And, when he please to make commotion,
'T is to be fear'd, they all will follow him.
Now 't is the spring, and weeds are shallow-
rooted;
Suffer them now, and they 'll o'ergrow the garden,
And choke the herbs for want of husbandry.
The reverent care, I bear unto my lord,
Made me collect these dangers in the duke.
If it be fond, call it a woman's fear;

Which fear if better reasons can supplant,
I will subscribe and say—I wrong'd the duke.
My lord of Suffolk,—Buckingham,—and York,—
Reprove my allegation, if you can:
Or else conclude my words effectual.

Suf. Well hath your highness seen into this
duke;
And, had I first been put to speak my mind,
I think, I should have told your grace's tale.
The duchess, by his subornation,
Upon my life, began her devilish practices·
Or if he were not privy to those faults,
Yet, by reputing of his high descent,
(As next the king, he was successive heir,)
And such high vaunts of his nobility,
Did instigate the bedlam brain-sick duchess,
By wicked means to frame our sovereign's fall.
Smooth runs the water, where the brook is deep;
And in his simple show he harbours treason.
The fox barks not, when he would steal the lamb.
No, no, my sovereign; Gloster is a man
Unsounded yet, and full of deep deceit.

Car. Did he not, contrary to form of law,
Devise strange deaths for small offences done?

York. And did he not, in his protectorship,
Levy great sums of money through the realm,
For soldiers' pay in France, and never sent it?
By means whereof, the towns each day revolted.

Buck. Tut! these are petty faults to faults un-
known,
Which time will bring to light in smooth duke
Humphrey.

K. Hen. My lords, at once: The care you have
of us,
To mow down thorns that would annoy our foot,
Is worthy praise: But shall I speak my conscience?
Our kinsman Gloster is as innocent
From meaning treason to our royal person,
As is the sucking lamb, or harmless dove:
The duke is virtuous, mild; and too well given,
To dream on evil, or to work my downfall.

Q. Mar. Ah, what 's more dangerous than this
fond alliance!
Seems he a dove? his feathers are but borrow'd,

For he 's disposed as the hateful raven.
Is he a lamb? his skin is surely lent him,
For he 's inclin'd as are the ravenous wolves.
Who cannot steal a shape, that means deceit?
Take heed, my lord; the welfare of us all
Hangs on the cutting short that fraudful man.

Enter SOMERSET.

Som. All health unto my gracious sovereign!
K. Hen. Welcome, lord Somerset. What news
    from France?
Som. That all your interest in those territories
Is utterly bereft you; all is lost.
K. Hen. Cold news, lord Somerset: but God's
    will be done!
York. Cold news for me; for I had hope of
    France,
As firmly as I hope for fertile England.
Thus are my blossoms blasted in the bud,
And caterpillars eat my leaves away:
But I will remedy this gear ere long,
Or sell my title for a glorious grave.   [*Aside.*

Enter GLOSTER.

Glo. All happiness unto my lord the king.
Pardon, my liege, that I have staid so long.
Suf. Nay, Gloster, know, that thou art come
    too soon,
Unless thou wert more loyal than thou art:
I do arrest thee of high treason here.
Glo. Well, Suffolk's duke, thou shalt not see
    me blush,
Nor change my countenance for this arrest;
A heart unspotted is not easily daunted.
The purest spring is not so free from mud,
As I am clear from treason to my sovereign:
Who can accuse me? wherein am I guilty?
York. 'T is thought, my lord, that you took
    bribes of France,
And, being protector, stayed the soldiers' pay;
By means whereof, his highness hath lost France.
Glo. Is it but thought so? What are they that
    think it?
I never robb'd the soldiers of their pay,
Nor ever had one penny bribe from France.
So help me God, as I have watch'd the night,—
Ay, night by night,—in studying good for Eng-
    land!
That doit that e'er I wrested from the king,
Or any groat I hoarded to my use,
Be brought against me at my trial day!
No! many a pound of mine own proper store,

Because I would not tax the needy commons,
Have I dispursed to the garrisons,
And never ask'd for restitution.
Car. It serves you well, my lord, to say so much.
Glo. I say no more than truth, so help me God!
York. In your protectorship, you did devise
Strange tortures for offenders, never heard of,
That England was defam'd by tyranny.
Glo. Why, 't is well known, that whiles I was
    protector,
Pity was all the fault that was in me;
For I should melt at an offender's tears,
And lowly words were ransom for their fault,
Unless it were a bloody murderer,
Or foul felonious thief that fleec'd poor passengers,
I never gave them condign punishment:
Murder, indeed, that bloody sin, I tortur'd
Above the felon, or what trespass else.
Suf. My lord, these faults are easy, quickly an-
    swer'd:
But mightier crimes are laid unto your charge,
Whereof you cannot easily purge yourself.
I do arrest you in his highness' name;
And here commit you to my lord cardinal
To keep, until your further time of trial.
K. Hen. My lord of Gloster, 't is my special
    hope,
That you will clear yourself from all suspects;
My conscience tells me, you are innocent.
Glo. Ah, gracious lord, these days are dange-
    ous!
Virtue is chok'd with foul ambition,
And charity chas'd hence by rancour's hand:
Foul subornation is predominant,
And equity exil'd your highness' land.
I know, their complot is to have my life;
And, if my death might make this island happy,
And prove the period of their tyranny,
I would expend it with all willingness;
But mine is made the prologue to their play;
For thousands more, that yet suspect no peril,
Will not conclude their plotted tragedy.
Beaufort's red sparkling eyes blab his heart's ma
    lice,
And Suffolk's cloudy brow his stormy hate;
Sharp Buckingham unburdens with his tongue
The envious load that lies upon his heart,
And dogged York, that reaches at the moon,
Whose overweening arm I have pluck'd back,
By false accuse doth level at my life:—
And you, my sovereign lady, with the rest,
Causeless have laid disgraces on my head;

923

And, with your best endeavour, have stirr'd up
My liefest liege to be mine enemy:—
Ay, all of you have laid your heads together:
Myself had notice of your conventicles.
I shall not want false witness to condemn me,
Nor store of treasons to augment my guilt;
The ancient proverb will be well affected,—
A staff is quickly found to beat a dog.

Car. My liege, his railing is intolerable:
If those that care to keep your royal person
From treason's secret knife, and traitors' rage,
Be thus upbraided, chid, and rated at,
And the offender granted scope of speech,
'T will make them cool in zeal unto your grace.

Suf. Hath he not twit our sovereign lady here,
With ignominious words, though clerkly conch'd,
As if she had suborned some to swear
False allegations to o'erthrow his state?

Q. Mar. But I can give the loser leave to chide.

Glo. Far truer spoke, than meant; I lose indeed:—
Beshrew the winners, for they play'd me false!
And well such losers may have leave to speak.

Buck. He 'll wrest the sense, and hold us here
  all day:—
Lord cardinal, he is your prisoner.

Car. Sirs, take away the duke, and guard him
  sure.

Glo. Ah, thus king Henry throws away his
  crutch,
Before his legs be firm to bear his body:
Thus is the shepherd beaten from thy side,
And wolves are gnarling who shall gnaw thee first.
Ah, that my fear were false! ah, that it were!
For, good king Henry, thy decay I fear.
      [*Exeunt* Attendants, *with* Glo.

K. Hen. My lords, what to your wisdoms seemeth best,
Do, or undo, as if ourself were here.

Q. Mar. What, will your highness leave the
  parliament?

K. Hen. Ay, Margaret; my heart is drown'd
  with grief,
Whose flood begins to flow within mine eyes;
My body round engirt with misery;
For what 's more miserable than discontent?—
Ah, uncle Humphrey! in thy face I see
The map of honour, truth, and loyalty;
And yet, good Humphrey, is the hour to come,
That e'er I prov'd thee false, or fear'd thy faith.
What low'ring star now envies thy estate,
That these great lords, and Margaret our queen,

Do seek subversion of thy harmless life?
Thou never didst them wrong, nor no man wrong:
And as the butcher takes away the calf,
And binds the wretch, and beats it when it strays,
Bearing it to the bloody slaughter-house;
Even so, remorseless, have they borne him hence;
And as the dam runs lowing up and down,
Looking the way her harmless young one went,
And can do nought but wail her darling's loss;
Even so myself bewails good Gloster's case,
With sad unhelpful tears; and with dimm'd eyes
Look after him, and cannot do him good;
So mighty are his vowed enemies.
His fortunes I will weep; and, 'twixt each groan,
Say,—" Who 's a traitor, Gloster he is none."
      [*Exit.*

Q. Mar. Free lords, cold snow melts with the
  sun's hot beams.
Henry my lord is cold in great affairs,
Too full of foolish pity: and Gloster's show
Beguiles him, as the mournful crocodile
With sorrow snares relenting passengers;
Or as the snake, roll'd in a flowering bank,
With shining checker'd slough, doth sting a child
That, for the beauty, thinks it excellent.
Believe me, lords, were none more wise than I,
(And yet, herein, I judge mine own wit good,)
This Gloster should be quickly rid the world,
To rid us from the fear we have of him.

Car. That he should die, is worthy policy;
But yet we want a colour for his death:
'T is meet, he be condemn'd by course of law.

Suf. But, in my mind, that were no policy:
The king will labour still to save his life,
The commons haply rise to save his life;
And yet we have but trivial argument,
More than mistrust, that shows him worthy death.

York. So that, by this, you would not have
  him die.

Suf. Ah, York, no man alive so fain as I.

York. 'T is York that hath more reason for his
  death.—
But, my lord cardinal, and you, my lord of
  Suffolk,—
Say as you think, and speak it from your souls,—
Wer 't not all one, an empty eagle were set
To guard the chicken from a hungry kite,
As place Duke Humphrey for the king's protector?

Q. Mar. So the poor chicken should be sure of
  death.

Suf. Madam, 't is true: And wer 't not madness then,

To make the fox surveyor of the fold ?
Who being accus'd a crafty murderer,
His guilt should be but idly posted over,
Because his purpose is not executed.
No; let him die, in that he is a fox,
By nature prov'd an enemy to the flock,
Before his chaps be stain'd with crimson blood;
As Humphrey, prov'd by reasons, to my liege.
And do not stand on quillets, how to slay him:
Be it by gins, by snares, by subtility,
Sleeping, or waking, 't is no matter how,
So he be dead; for that is good deceit
Which mates him first, that first intends deceit.

   Q. Mar. Thrice-noble Suffolk, 't is resolutely
     spoke.

   Suf. Not resolute, except so much were done;
For things are often spoke, and seldom meant:
But, that my heart accordeth with my tongue,—
Seeing the deed is meritorious,
And to preserve my sovereign from his foe,—
Say but the word, and I will be his priest.

   Car. But I would have him dead, my lord of
     Suffolk,
Ere you can take due orders for a priest:
Say, you consent, and censure well the deed,
And I 'll provide his executioner,
I tender so the safety of my liege.

   Suf. Here is my hand, the deed is worthy
     doing.

   Q. Mar. And so say I.

   York. And I: and now we three have spoke it,
It skills not greatly who impugns our doom.

       Enter a Messenger.

   Mess. Great lords, from Ireland am I come
     amain,
To signify—that rebels there are up,
And put the Englishmen unto the sword:
Send succours, lords, and stop the rage betime,
Before the wound do grow incurable;
For, being green, there is great hope of help.

   Car. A breach, that craves a quick expedient
     stop.
What counsel give you in this weighty cause?

   York. That Somerset be sent as regent thither:
'T is meet, that lucky ruler be employ'd;
Witness the fortune he hath had in France.

   Som. If York, with all his far-set policy,
Had been the regent there instead of me,
He never would have staid in France so long.

   York. No, not to lose it all, as thou hast
     done:

I rather would have lost my life betimes,
Than bring a burden of dishonour home,
By staying there so long, till all were lost.
Show me one scar character'd on thy skin:
Men's flesh preserved so whole, do seldom win.

   Q. Mar. Nay then, this spark will prove a
     raging fire,
If wind and fuel be brought to feed it with:
No more, good York;—sweet Somerset, be still;—
Thy fortune, York, hadst thou been regent there,
Might happily have prov'd far worse than his.

   York. What, worse than naught ? nay, then a
     shame take all !

   Som. And, in the number, thee, that wishes
     shame !

   Car. My lord of York, try what your fortune is.
The uncivil Kernes of Ireland are in arms,
And temper clay with blood of Englishmen:
To Ireland will you lead a band of men,
Collected choicely, from each county some,
And try your hap against the Irishmen ?

   York. I will, my lord, so please his majesty.

   Suf. Why, our authority is his consent;
And, what we do establish, he confirms:
Then, noble York, take thou this task in hand.

   York. I am content: Provide me soldiers,
     lords,
Whiles I take order for mine own affairs.

   Suf. A charge, lord York, that I will see per
     form'd.
But now return we to the false duke Humphrey.

   Car. No more of him; for I will deal with him
That, henceforth, he shall trouble us no more.
And so break off; the day is almost spent:
Lord Suffolk, you and I must talk of that event.

   York. My lord of Suffolk, within fourteen
     days,
At Bristol I expect my soldiers:
For there I 'll ship them all for Ireland.

   Suf. I 'll see it truly done, my lord of York.
            [*Exeunt all but York.*

   York. Now, York, or never, steel thy fearful
     thoughts,
And change misdoubt to resolution:
Be that thou hop'st to be; or what thou art
Resign to death, it is not worth the enjoying:
Let pale-fac'd fear keep with the mean-born man
And find no harbour in a royal heart.
Faster than spring-time showers, comes thought
     on thought;
And not a thought, but thinks on dignity.
My brain, more busy than the labouring spider,

Weaves tedious snares to trap mine enemies.
Well, nobles, well, 't is politicly done,
To send me packing with an host of men:
I fear me, you but warm the starved snake,
Who, cherish'd in your breasts, will sting your
    hearts.
'T was men I lack'd, and you will give them me:
I take it kindly; yet, be well assur'd
You put sharp weapons in a madman's hands.
Whiles I in Ireland nourish a mighty band,
I will stir up in England some black storm,
Shall blow ten thousand souls to heaven, or hell:
And this fell tempest shall not cease to rage
Until the golden circuit on my head,
Like to the glorious sun's transparent beams,
Do calm the fury of this mad-bred flaw.
And, for a minister of my intent,
I have seduc'd a headstrong Kentishman,
John Cade of Ashford,
To make commotion, as full well he can,
Under the title of John Mortimer.
In Ireland have I seen this stubborn Cade
Oppose himself against a troop of Kernes;
And fought so long, till that his thighs with
    darts
Were almost like a sharp-quill'd porcupine:
And, in the end being rescu'd, I have seen him
Caper upright like a wild Morisco,"
Shaking the bloody darts, as he his bells.
Full often, like a shag-hair'd crafty Kerne,
Hath he conversed with the enemy;
And undiscover'd come to me again,
And given me notice of their villanies.
This devil here shall be my substitute;
For that John Mortimer, which now is dead,
In face, in gait, in speech, he doth resemble:
By this I shall perceive the commons' mind,
How they affect the house and claim of York.
Say, he be taken, rack'd, and tortured;
I know, no pain, they can inflict upon him,
Will make him say—I mov'd him to those arms,
Say, that he thrive, (as 't is great like he will,)
Why, then from Ireland come I with my strength,
And reap the harvest which that rascal sow'd:
For, Humphrey being dead, as he shall be,
And Henry put apart, the next for me.   [Exit.

SCENE II.—Bury. A Room in the Palace.

Enter certain Murderers, hastily.

1st Mur. Run to my lord of Suffolk: let him
    know
926

We have despatch'd the duke, as he commanded.
2nd Mur. O, that it were to do!—What have
    we done?
Did'st ever hear a man so penitent?

Enter SUFFOLK.

1st Mur. Here comes my lord.
Suf.   Now, sirs, have you
Despatch'd this thing?
1st Mur.   Ay, my good lord, he's dead.
Suf. Why, that's well said. Go, get you to
    my house;
I will reward you for this venturous deed.
The king and all the peers are here at hand:—
Have you laid fair the bed? are all things well,
According as I gave directions?
1st Mur. 'T is, my good lord.
Suf. Away, be gone!   [Exeunt Murderers

Enter KING HENRY, QUEEN MARGARET, CARDINAL
BEAUFORT, SOMERSET, Lords, and Others.

K. Hen. Go, call our uncle to our presence
    straight:
Say, we intend to try his grace to-day,
If he be guilty, as 't is published.
Suf. I'll call him presently, my noble lord.
                      [Exit.
K. Hen. Lords, take your places;—And, I pray
    you all,
Proceed no straiter 'gainst our uncle Gloster,
Than from true evidence, of good esteem,
He be approv'd in practice culpable.
Q. Mar. God forbid any malice should prevail,
That faultless may condemn a nobleman!
Pray God, may acquit him of suspicion!
K. Hen. I thank thee, Margaret; these words
    content me much.—

Re-enter SUFFOLK.

How now? why look'st thou pale? why tremblest
    thou?
Where is our uncle? what is the matter, Suffolk?
Suf. Dead in his bed, my lord; Gloster is dead.
Q. Mar. Marry, God forefend!
Car. God's secret judgment:—I did dream to-
    night,
The duke was dumb, and could not speak a word.
                  [The KING swoons
Q. Mar. How fares my lord?—Help, lords! the
    king is dead.
Som. Rear up his body; wring him by the
    nose."

Q. Mar. Run, go, help, help!—O, Henry, ope
  thine eyes!
Suf. He doth revive again ;—Madam, be pa-
  tient.
K. Hen. O heavenly God!
Q. Mar. How fares my gracious lord?
Suf. Comfort, my sovereign! gracious Henry,
  comfort!
K. Hen. What, doth my lord of Suffolk com-
  fort me?
Came he right now to sing a raven's note,
Whose dismal tune bereft my vital powers ;
And thinks he, that the chirping of a wren,
By crying comfort from a hollow breast,
Can chase away the first-conceived sound?
Hide not thy poison with such sugar'd words,
Lay not thy hands on me ; forbear, I say ;
Their touch affrights me, as a serpent's sting.
Thou baleful messenger, out of my sight!
Upon thy eye-balls murderous tyranny
Sits in grim majesty, to fright the world.
Look not upon me, for thine eyes are wounding :—
Yet do not go away ;—Come, basilisk,
And kill the innocent gazer with thy sight :
For in the shade of death I shall find joy ;
In life, but double death, now Gloster 's dead.
  Q. Mar. Why do you rate my lord of Suffolk
    thus?
Although the duke was enemy to him,
Yet he, most christian-like, laments his death :
And for myself,—foe as he was to me,
Might liquid tears, or heart-offending groans,
Or blood-consuming sighs recal his life,
I would be blind with weeping, sick with groans,
Look pale as primrose, with blood-drinking sighs,
And all to have the noble duke alive.
What know I how the world may deem of me?
For it is known, we were but hollow friends ;
It may be judg'd, I made the duke away :
So shall my name with slander's tongue be
  wounded,
And princes' courts be fill'd with my reproach.
This get I by his death : Ah me, unhappy!
To be a queen, and crown'd with infamy!
  K. Hen. Ah, woe is me for Gloster, wretched
    man!
  Q. Mar. Be woe for me, more wretched than
    he is.
What, dost thou turn away, and hide thy face?
I am no loathsome leper, look on me.
What, art thou, like the adder, waxen deaf?
Be poisonous too, and kill thy forlorn queen.

Is all thy comfort shut in Gloster's tomb?
Why, then dame Margaret was ne'er thy joy :
Erect his statue then, and worship it,
And make my image but an alehouse sign.
Was I, for this, nigh wreck'd upon the sea ;
And twice by awkward wind from England's bank
Drove back again unto my native clime?
What boded this, but well-forewarning wind
Did seem to say,—Seek not a scorpion's nest,
Nor set no footing on this unkind shore?
What did I then, but curs'd the gentle gusts,
And he that loos'd them from their brazen caves ;
And bid them blow towards England's blessed
  shore,
Or turn our stern upon a dreadful rock?
Yet Æolus would not be a murderer,
But left that hateful office unto thee :
The pretty vaulting sea refus'd to drown me ;
Knowing, that thou would'st have me drown'd on
  shore,
With tears as salt as sea through thy unkindness
The splitting rocks cow'rd in the sinking sands,
And would not dash me with their ragged sides ;
Because thy flinty heart, more hard than they,
Might in thy palace perish Margaret.
As far as I could ken thy chalky cliffs,
When from the shore the tempest beat us back,
I stood upon the hatches in the storm :
And when the dusky sky began to rob
My earnest-gaping sight of thy land's view,
I took a costly jewel from my neck,—
A heart it was, bound in with diamonds,—
And threw it towards thy land ; the sea receiv'd
  it ;
And so, I wish'd, thy body might my heart :
And even with this, I lost fair England's view,
And bid mine eyes be packing with my heart :
And call'd them blind and dusky spectacles,
For losing ken of Albion's wished coast.
How often have I tempted Suffolk's tongue
(The agent of thy foul inconstancy,)
To sit and witch me, as Ascanius did,
When he to madding Dido would unfold
His father's acts, commenc'd in burning Troy?
Am I not witch'd like her? or thou not false like
  him?
Ah me, I can no more! Die, Margaret!
For Henry weeps, that thou dost live so long.

Noise within. Enter WARWICK *and* SALISBURY.
  The Commons press to the door.

  War. It is reported, mighty sovereign,

That good duke Humphrey traitorously is murder'd
By Suffolk and the cardinal Beaufort's means.
The commons, like an angry hive of bees,
That want their leader, scatter up and down,
And care not who they sting in his revenge.
Myself have calm'd their spleenful mutiny,
Until they hear the order of his death.

  K. Hen. That he is dead, good Warwick, 'tis
    too true;
But how he died, God knows, not Henry:
Enter his chamber, view his breathless corpse,
And comment then upon his sudden death.

  War. That I shall do, my liege:—Stay, Salis-
    bury,
With the rude multitude, till I return.

  [*War. goes into an inner Room, and Sal. retires.*

  K. Hen. O thou that judgest all things, stay
    my thoughts;
My thoughts, that labour to persuade my soul,
Some violent hands were laid on Humphrey's life!
If my suspect be false, forgive me, God;
For judgment only doth belong to thee!
Fain would I go to chase his paly lips
With twenty thousand kisses, and to drain
Upon his face an ocean of salt tears;
To tell my love unto his dumb deaf trunk,
And with my fingers feel his hand unfeeling.
But all in vain are these mean obsequies;
And, to survey his dead and earthly image,
What were it but to make my sorrow greater?

*The folding Doors of an inner Chamber are thrown
open, and* GLOSTER *is discovered dead in his bed:*
WARWICK *and others standing by it.*

  War. Come hither, gracious sovereign, view
    this body.

  K. Hen. That is to see how deep my grave is
    made;
For, with his soul, fled all my worldly solace;
For seeing him, I see my life in death.

  War. As surely as my soul intends to live
With that dread King that took our state upon
    him
To free us from his Father's wrathful curse,
I do believe that violent hands were laid
Upon the life of this thrice-famed duke.

  Suf. A dreadful oath, sworn with a solemn
    tongue!
What instance gives lord Warwick for his vow?

  War. See, how the blood is settled in his face!
I have seen a timely-parted ghost,
Of ashy semblance, meagre, pale, and bloodless,

Being all descended to the labouring heart:
Who, in the conflict that it holds with death,
Attracts the same for aidance 'gainst the enemy:
Which with the heart there cools and ne'er re-
    turneth
To blush and beautify the cheek again.
But, see, his face is black, and full of blood;
His eye-balls further out than when he liv'd,
Staring full ghastly like a strangled man:
His hair uprear'd, his nostrils stretch'd with strug-
    gling;
His hands abroad display'd, as one that grasp'd
And tugg'd for life, and was by strength subdu'd.
Look on the sheets, his hair, you see, is sticking;
His well-proportion'd beard made rough and
    rugged,
Like to the summer's corn by tempest lodg'd.
It cannot be, but he was murder'd here;
The least of all these signs were probable.

  Suf. Why, Warwick, who should do the duke
    to death?
Myself, and Beaufort, had him in protection;
And we, I hope, sir, are no murderers.

  War. But both of you were vow'd duke Hum-
    phrey's foes;
And you, forsooth, had the good duke to keep;
'Tis like, you would not feast him like a friend;
And 'tis well seen he found an enemy.

  Q. Mar. Then you, belike, suspect these noble-
    men
As guilty of duke Humphrey's timeless death.

  War. Who finds the heifer dead, and bleeding
    fresh,
And sees fast by a butcher with an axe,
But will suspect, 'twas he that made the slaughter?
Who finds the partridge in the puttock's nest,
But may imagine how the bird was dead,
Although the kite soar with unbloodied beak?
Even so suspicious is this tragedy.

  Q. Mar. Are you the butcher, Suffolk? where's
    your knife?
Is Beaufort term'd a kite? where are his talons?

  Suf. I wear no knife, to slaughter sleeping
    men;
But here's a vengeful sword, rusted with ease,
That shall be scoured in his rancorous heart,
That slanders me with murder's crimson badge:—
Say, if thou dar'st, proud lord of Warwickshire,
That I am faulty in duke Humphrey's death.

    [*Exeunt* Car., Som., *and Others.*

  War. What dares not Warwick, if false Suf-
    folk dare him?

Q. Mar. He dares not calm his contumelious
    spirit,
Nor cease to be an arrogant controller,
Though Suffolk dare him twenty thousand times.
  War. Madam, be still; with reverence may I
    say;
For every word, you speak in his behalf,
Is slander to your royal dignity.
  Suf. Blunt-witted lord, ignoble in demeanour!
If ever lady wrong'd her lord so much,
Thy mother took into her blameful bed
Some stern untutor'd churl, and noble stock
Was graft with crab-tree slip; whose fruit thou
    art,
And never of the Nevils' noble race.
  War. But that the guilt of murder bucklers
    thee,
And I should rob the deathsman of his fee,
Quitting thee thereby of ten thousand shames,
And that my sovereign's presence makes me mild,
I would, false murderous coward, on thy knee
Make thee beg pardon for thy passed speech,
And say—it was thy mother that thou meant'st,
That thou thyself wast born in bastardy:
And, after all this fearful homage done,
Give thee thy hire, and send thy soul to hell,
Pernicious bloodsucker of sleeping men!
  Suf. Thou shalt be waking, while I shed thy
    blood,
If from this presence thou dar'st go with me.
  War. Away even now, or I will drag thee
    hence:
Unworthy though thou art, I'll cope with thee,
And do some service to duke Humphrey's ghost.
         [*Exeunt Suf. and War.*
  K. Hen. What stronger breast-plate than a
    heart untainted?
Thrice is he arm'd, that hath his quarrel just;
And he but naked, though lock'd up in steel,
Whose conscience with injustice is corrupted.
         [*A Noise within.*
  Q. Mar. What noise is this?

Re-enter SUFFOLK *and* WARWICK, *with their
    Weapons drawn.*

  K. Hen. Why, how now, lords? your wrathful
    weapons drawn
Here in our presence? dare you be so bold?—
Why, what tumultuous clamour have we here?
  Suf. The traitorous Warwick, with the men of
    Bury,
Set all upon me, mighty sovereign.

Noise of a Crowd within.   Re-enter SALISBURY.

  Sal. Sirs, stand apart; the king shall know
    your mind.— [*Speaking to those within.*
Dread lord, the commons send you word by me,
Unless false Suffolk straight be done to death,
Or banished fair England's territories,
They will by violence tear him from your palace,
And torture him with grievous ling'ring death.
They say, by him the good duke Humphrey died;
They say, in him they fear your highness' death;
And mere instinct of love, and loyalty,—
Free from a stubborn opposite intent,
As being thought to contradict your liking,—
Makes them thus forward in his banishment.
They say, in care of your most royal person,
That, if your highness should intend to sleep,
And charge—that no man should disturb your rest
In pain of your dislike, or pain of death;
Yet notwithstanding such a strait edict,
Were there a serpent seen, with forked tongue,
That slily glided towards your majesty,
It were but necessary, you were wak'd;
Lest, being suffer'd in that harmful slumber,
The mortal worm might make the sleep eternal:
And therefore do they cry, though you forbid,
That they will guard you, whe'r you will, or no,
From such fell serpents as false Suffolk is;
With whose envenom'd and fatal sting.
Your loving uncle, twenty times his worth,
They say, is shamefully bereft of life.
  Commons. [*Within.*] An answer from the king,
    my lord of Salisbury.
  Suf. 'T is like, the commons, rude unpolish'd
    hinds,
Could send such message to their sovereign;
But you, my lord, were glad to be employ'd,
To show how quaint an orator you are:
But all the honour Salisbury hath won,
Is—that he was the lord ambassador,
Sent from a sort of tinkers to the king.
  Commons. [*Within.*] An answer from the king,
    or we'll all break in.
  K. Hen. Go, Salisbury, and tell them all from me,
I thank them for their tender loving care;
And had I not been 'cited so by them,
Yet did I purpose as they do entreat;
For sure, my thoughts do hourly prophesy
Mischance unto my state by Suffolk's means:
And therefore,—by His majesty I swear,
Whose far unworthy deputy I am,—
He shall not breathe infection in this air

But three days longer, on the pain of death.

[*Exit* Sal.

Q. Mar. O Henry, let me plead for gentle Suffolk!

K. Hen. Ungentle queen, to call him gentle
Suffolk.

No more, I say; if thou dost plead for him,
Thou wilt but add increase unto my wrath.
Had I but said, I would have kept my word;
But, when I swear, it is irrevocable:—
If, after three days' space, thou here be'st found
On any ground that I am ruler of,
The world shall not be ransom for thy life.—
Come, Warwick, come, good Warwick, go with
me;
I have great matters to impart to thee.

[*Exeunt* K. Hen., War., *Lords, &c.*

Q. Mar. Mischance, and sorrow, go along with
you!
Heart's discontent, and sour affliction,
Be playfellows to keep you company!
There's two of you; the devil make a third!
And threefold vengeance tend upon your steps!

Suf. Cease, gentle queen, these execrations,
And let thy Suffolk take his heavy leave.

Q. Mar. Fye, coward woman, and soft-hearted
wretch!
Hast thou not spirit to curse thine enemies?

Suf. A plague upon them! wherefore should I
curse them?
Would curses kill, as doth the mandrake's groan,
I would invent as bitter-searching terms,
As curst, as harsh, and horrible to hear,
Deliver'd strongly through my fixed teeth,
With full as many signs of deadly hate,
As lean-fac'd Envy in her loathsome cave:
My tongue should stumble in mine earnest words;
Mine eyes should sparkle like the beaten flint;
My hair be fix'd on end, as one distract;
Ay, every joint should seem to curse and ban:
And even now my burden'd heart would break,
Should I not curse them. Poison be their drink!
Gall, worse than gall, the daintiest that they taste!
Their sweetest shade, a grove of cypress trees!
Their chiefest prospect, murdering basilisks!
Their softest touch, as smart as lizards' stings!
Their music, frightful as the serpent's hiss;
And boding screech-owls make the concert full!
All the foul terrors in dark-seated hell——

Q. Mar. Enough, sweet Suffolk; thou torment'st thyself;
these dread curses—like the sun 'gainst glass,
320

Or like an overcharged gun,—recoil,—
And turn the force of them upon thyself.

Suf. You bade me ban, and will you bid me
leave
Now, by the ground that I am banish'd from,
Well could I curse away a winter's night,
Though standing naked on a mountain top,
Where biting cold would never let grass grow,
And think it but a minute spent in sport.

Q. Mar. O, let me entreat thee, cease. Give
me thy hand,
That I may dew it with my mournful tears;
Nor let the rain of heaven wet this place,
To wash away my woeful monuments.
O, could this kiss be printed in thy hand;

[*Kisses his hand.*

That thou might'st think upon these by the seal,
Through whom a thousand sighs are breath'd for
thee!
So, get thee gone, that I may know my grief;
'Tis but surmis'd whilst thou art standing by,
As one that surfeits thinking on a want.
I will repeal thee, or, be well assur'd,
Adventure to be banished myself:
And banished I am, if but from thee.
Go, speak not to me; even now be gone.—
O, go not yet:—Even thus two friends condemn'd
Embrace, and kiss, and take ten thousand leaves,
Loather a hundred times to part than die.
Yet now farewell; and farewell life with thee!

Suf. Thus is poor Suffolk ten times banished,
Once by the king, and three times thrice by thee.
'Tis not the land I care for, wert thou hence;
A wilderness is populous enough,
So Suffolk had thy heavenly company:
For where thou art, there is the world itself,
With every several pleasure in the world;
And where thou art not, desolation.
I can no more:—Live thou to joy thy life;
Myself to joy in nought, but that thou liv'st.

Enter Vaux.

Q. Mar. Whither goes Vaux so fast? what news
I pr'ythee?

Vaux. To signify unto his majesty,
That cardinal Beaufort is at point of death:
For suddenly a grievous sickness took him,
That makes him gasp, and stare, and catch the air,
Blaspheming God, and cursing men on earth.
Sometime, he talks as if duke Humphrey's ghost
Were by his side; sometime, he calls the king,
And whispers to his pillow, as to him,

The secrets of his overcharged soul:
And I am sent to tell his majesty,
That even now he cries aloud for him.

   Q. Mar. Go, tell this heavy message to the
    king.   [*Exit* VAUX.
Ah! me! what is this world! what news are
    these?
But wherefore grieve I at an hour's poor loss,
Omitting Suffolk's exile, my soul's treasure?
Why only, Suffolk, mourn I not for thee,
And with the southern clouds contend in tears;
Theirs for the earth's increase, mine for my sor-
    rows?
Now, get thee hence: The king, thou know'st, is
    coming;
If thou be found by me, thou art but dead.

   Suf. If I depart from thee, I cannot live:
And in thy sight to die, what were it else,
But like a pleasant slumber in thy lap?
Here could I breathe my soul into the air,
As mild and gentle as the cradle-babe,
Dying with mother's dug between its lips:
Where, from thy sight, I should be raging mad,
And cry out for thee to close up mine eyes,
To have thee with thy lips to stop my mouth;
So should'st thou either turn my flying soul,
Or I should breathe it so into thy body,
And then it liv'd in sweet Elysium.
To die by thee, were but to die in jest:
From thee to die, were torture more than death:
O, let me stay, befall what may befall.

   Q. Mar. Away! though parting be a fretful
    corrosive,
It is applied to a deathful wound.
To France, sweet Suffolk: Let me hear from
   thee;
For wheresoe'er thou art in this world's globe,
I'll have an Iris that shall find thee out."

   Suf. I go.
   Q. Mar.   And take my heart with thee.
   Suf. A jewel, lock'd into the woeful'st cask
That ever did contain a thing of worth.
Even as a splitted bark, so sunder we;
This way fall I to death.

   Q. Mar.   This way for me.
                  [*Exeunt, severally.*

SCENE III.—London.   *Cardinal* Beaufort's
                   Bed-chamber.

Enter KING HENRY, SALISBURY, WARWICK, *and
   Others. The* CARDINAL *in bed; Attendants
   with him.*

   K. Hen. How fares my lord? speak, Beaufort,
    to thy sovereign.
   Car. If thou best death, I'll give thee Eng-
    land's treasure,"
Enough to purchase such another island,
So thou wilt let me live, and feel no pain.

   K. Hen. Ah, what a sign it is of evil life,
When death's approach is seen so terrible!

   War. Beaufort, it is thy sovereign speaks to
    thee.
   Car. Bring me unto my trial when you will.
Died he not in his bed? where should he die?
Can I make men live, whe'r they will or no?
O! torture me no more, I will confess.—
Alive again? then show me where he is;
I'll give a thousand pound to look upon him.—
He hath no eyes, the dust hath blinded them.—
Comb down his hair; look! look! it stands up-
    right,
Like lime-twigs set to catch my winged soul!—
Give me some drink; and bid the apothecary
Bring the strong poison that I bought of him.

   K. Hen. O thou eternal Mover of the heavens,
Look with a gentle eye upon this wretch!
O, beat away the busy meddling fiend,
That lays strong siege unto this wretch's soul,
And from his bosom purge this black despair!

   War. See, how the pangs of death do make him
    grin.
   Sal. Disturb him not, let him pass peaceably.
   K. Hen. Peace to his soul, if God's good plea-
    sure be!
Lord cardinal, if thou think'st on heaven's bliss,
Hold up thy hand, make signal of thy hope.—
He dies, and makes no sign: O God, forgive him!

   War. So bad a death argues a monstrous life.
   K. Hen. Forbear to judge, for we are sinners
    all.—
Close up his eyes, and draw the curtains close;
And let us all to meditation.   [*Exeun*

ACT IV.

SCENE I.—Kent. *The Sea-shore near* Dover.

Firing heard at Sea.   Then enter from a Boat, a
Captain, *a* Master, *a* Master's-Mate, WALTER
WHITMORE, *and Others ; with them* SUFFOLK,
and other Gentlemen, prisoners.

Cap. The gaudy, blabbing, and remorseful day
Is crept into the bosom of the sea ;
And now loud-howling wolves arouse the jades
That drag the tragic melancholy night ;
Who with their drowsy, slow, and flagging wings
Clip dead men's graves, and from their misty jaws
Breathe foul contagious darkness in the air.
Therefore, bring forth the soldiers of our prize ;
For, whilst our pinnace anchors in the Downs,
Here shall they make their ransom on the sand,
Or with their blood stain this discolour'd shore.—
Master, this prisoner freely give I thee ;—
And thou that art his mate, make boot of this ;—
The other, [*Pointing to* SUF.] Walter Whitmore,
is thy share.

1st Gent. What is my ransom, master? let me
know.

Mast. A thousand crowns, or else lay down your
head.

Mate. And so much shall you give, or off goes
yours.

Cap. What, think you much to pay two thou-
sand crowns,
And bear the name and port of gentlemen ?—
Cut both the villains' throats ; for die you shall ;
Can lives of those which we have lost in fight,
Be counterpois'd with such a petty sum ?

1st Gent. I 'll give it, sir ; and therefore spare
my life.

2nd Gent. And so will I, and write home for it
straight.

Whit. I lost mine eye in laying the prize
aboard.
And therefore, to revenge it, shalt thou die ;
[*To* SUF.
And so should these, if I might have my will.

Cap. Be not so rash ; take ransom, let him live.

Suf. Look on my George, I am a gentleman ;
Rate me at what thou wilt, thou shalt be paid.

Whit. And so am I ; my name is—Walter
Whitmore.
How now ? why start'st thou? what, doth death
affright ?

Suf. Thy name affrights me, in whose sound is
death.
A cunning man did calculate my birth,
And told me that by "Water" I should die :
Yet let not this make thee be bloody minded ;
Thy name is—"Gualtier," being rightly sounded.

Whit. "Gualtier," or "Walter," which it is, I
care not ;
Ne'er yet did base dishonour blur our name,
But with our sword we wip'd away the blot ;
Therefore, when merchant-like I sell revenge,
Broke be my sword, my arms torn and defac'd,
And I proclaim'd a coward through the world !
[*Lays hold on* SUF.

Suf. Stay, Whitmore ; for thy prisoner is a
prince,
The duke of Suffolk, William de la Pole.

Whit. The duke of Suffolk, muffled up in rags?

Suf. Ay, but these rags are no part of the
duke ;
Jove sometime went disguis'd, And why not I ?

Cap. But Jove was never slain, as thou shalt be.

Suf. Obscure and lowly swain, king Henry's
blood,
The honourable blood of Lancaster,
Must not be shed by such a jaded groom.
Hast thou not kiss'd thy hand, and held my
stirrup ?
Bare-headed plodded by my foot-cloth mule,
And thought thee happy when I shook my head !
How often hast thou waited at my cup,
Fed from my trencher, kneel'd down at the board,
When I have feasted with queen Margaret ?
Remember it, and let it make thee crest-fall'n ;
Ay, and allay this thy abortive pride :
How in our voiding lobby hast thou stood,
And duly waited for my coming forth ?
This hand of mine hath writ in thy behalf,
And therefore shall it charm thy riotous tongue.

Whit. Speak, captain, shall I stab the forlorn
swain ?

Cap. First let my words stab him, as he hath me.

Suf. Base slave! thy words are blunt, and so
    art thou.

Cap. Convey him hence, and on our long-boat's
    side
Strike off his head.

Suf.   Thou dar'st not for thy own.

Cap. Yes, Poole.

Suf.   Poole!

Cap.   Poole? Sir Poole? lord?
Ay, kennel, puddle, sink; whose filth and dirt
Troubles the silver spring where England drinks.
Now will I dam up this thy yawning mouth,
For swallowing the treasure of the realm:
Thy lips, that kiss'd the queen, shall sweep the
    ground;
And thou, that smil'dst at good duke Humphrey's
    death,
Against the senseless winds shalt grin in vain,
Who, in contempt, shall hiss at thee again:
And wedded be thou to the hags of hell,
For daring to affy* a mighty lord
Unto the daughter of a worthless king,
Having neither subject, wealth, nor diadem.
By devilish policy art thou grown great,
And, like ambitious Sylla, overgorg'd
With gobbets of thy mother's bleeding heart.
By thee, Anjou and Maine were sold to France;
The false revolting Normans, through thee,
Disdain to call us lord; and Picardy
Hath slain their governors, surpris'd our forts,
And sent the ragged soldiers wounded home.
The princely Warwick, and the Nevils all,—
Whose dreadful swords were never drawn in
    vain,—
As hating thee, are rising up in arms:
And now the house of York—thrust from the
    crown,
By shameful murder of a guiltless king,
And lofty proud encroaching tyranny,—
Burns with revenging fire; whose hopeful colours
Advance our half-fac'd sun, striving to shine,
Under the which is writ—*Invitis nubibus*.
The commons here in Kent are up in arms:
And, to conclude, reproach, and beggary,
Is crept into the palace of our king.
And all by thee:—Away! convey him hence.

Suf. O that I were a god, to shoot forth
    thunder
Upon these paltry, servile, abject drudges!
Small things make base men proud: this villain
    here,

Being captain of a pinnace, threatens more
Than Bargulus the strong Illyrian pirate.
Drones suck not eagles' blood, but rob bee hives.
It is impossible, that I should die
By such a lowly vassal as thyself.
Thy words move rage, and not remorse, in me:
I go of message from the queen to France;
I charge thee, waft me safely cross the channel.

Cap. Walter,——

Whit. Come, Suffolk, I must waft thee to thy
    death.

Suf. Gelidus timor occupat artus:—'t is thee
    I fear.

Whit. Thou shalt have cause to fear, before I
    leave thee.

What, are ye daunted now? now will ye stoop?

1st Gent. My gracious lord, entreat him, speak
    him fair.

Suf. Suffolk's imperial tongue is stern and
    rough,
Us'd to command, untaught to plead for favour.
Far be it, we should honour such as these
With humble suit: no, rather let my head
Stoop to the block, than these knees bow to any,
Save to the God of heaven, and to my king;
And sooner dance upon a bloody pole,
Than stand uncover'd to the vulgar groom.
True nobility is exempt from fear:—
More can I bear, than you dare execute.

Cap. Hale him away, and let him talk no more.

Suf. Come, soldiers, show what cruelty ye can,
That this my death may never be forgot!—
Great men oft die by vile bezonians:
A Roman swordcr and banditto slave,
Murder'd sweet Tully; Brutus' bastard hand
Stabb'd Julius Cæsar; savage islanders,
Pompey the Great: and Suffolk dies by pirates.
    [*Exit SUF. with WHIT. and Others*

Cap. And as for these whose ransom we have
    set,
It is our pleasure, one of them depart:—
Therefore come you with us, and let him go.
    [*Exeunt all but the 1st Gent.*

Re-enter WHITMORE, with SUFFOLK's Body.

Whit. There let his head and lifeless body lie,
Until the queen his mistress bury it.   [*Exit*

1st Gent. O barbarous and bloody spectacle!
His body will I bear unto the king:
If he revenge it not, yet will his friends;
So will the queen, that living held him dear.
    [*Exit, with the Body*

SCENE II.—Blackheath.

Enter GEORGE BEVIS *and* JOHN HOLLAND.

Geo. Come, and get thee a sword, though made of a lath; they have been up these two days.

John. They have the more need to sleep now then.

Geo. I tell thee, Jack Cade the clothier means to dress the commonwealth, and turn it, and set a new nap upon it.

John. So he had need, for 't is threadbare. Well, I say, it was never merry world in England, since gentlemen came up.

Geo. O miserable age! Virtue is not regarded in handycrafts-men.

John. The nobility think scorn to go in leather aprons.

Geo. Nay more, the king's council are no good workmen.

John. True: And yet it is said,—Labour in thy vocation: which is as much to say, as,—let the magistrates be labouring men; and therefore should we be magistrates.

Geo. Thou hast hit it; for there's no better sign of a brave mind, than a hard hand.

John. I see them! I see them! There's Best's son, the tanner of Wingham:——

Geo. He shall have the skins of our enemies, to make dog's leather of.

John. And Dick the butcher,——

Geo. Then is sin struck down like an ox, and iniquity's throat cut like a calf.

John. And Smith the weaver:——

Geo. Argo, their thread of life is spun.

John. Come, come, let 's fall in with them.

Drum. Enter CADE, DICK *the Butcher*, SMITH *the Weaver, and Others in great number.*

Cade. We John Cade, so termed of our supposed father,——

Dick. Or rather, of stealing a cade of herrings.   [*Aside.*

Cade. —for our enemies shall fall before us, inspired with the spirit of putting down kings and princes,—Command silence.

Dick. Silence!

Cade. My father was a Mortimer,——

Dick. He was an honest man, and a good bricklayer.   [*Aside.*

Cade. My mother a Plantagenet,——

Dick. I knew her well, she was a midwife.   [*Aside.*

Cade. My wife descended of the Laces,—

Dick. She was, indeed, a pedlar's daughter, and sold many laces.   [*Aside.*

Smith. But, now of late, not able to travel with her furred pack, she washes bucks here at home.   [*Aside.*

Cade. Therefore am I of an honourable house.

Dick. Ay, by my faith, the field is honourable; and there was he born, under a hedge; for his father had never a house, but the cage.   [*Aside.*

Cade. Valiant I am.

Smith. 'A must needs; for beggary is valiant.   [*Aside.*

Cade. I am able to endure much.

Dick. No question of that; for I have seen him whipped three market days together.   [*Aside.*

Cade. I fear neither sword nor fire.

Smith. He need not fear the sword, for his coat is of proof.   [*Aside.*

Dick. But, methinks, he should stand in fear of fire, being burnt i' the hand for stealing of sheep.   [*Aside.*

Cade. Be brave then; for your captain is brave, and vows reformation. There shall be, in England, seven half-penny loaves sold for a penny: the three-hooped pot shall have ten hoops; and I will make it felony, to drink small beer: all the realm shall be in common, and in Cheapside shall my palfrey go to grass. And, when I am king, (as king I will be,)——

All. God save your majesty!

Cade. I thank you, good people:—there shall be no money; all shall eat and drink on my score; and I will apparel them all in one livery, that they may agree like brothers, and worship me their lord.

Dick. The first thing we do, let 's kill all the lawyers.

Cade. Nay, that I mean to do. Is not this a lamentable thing, that of the skin of an innocent lamb should be made parchment? that parchment, being scribbled o'er, should undo a man? Some say, the bee stings: but I say, 't is the bee's wax; for I did but seal once to a thing, and I was never mine own man since. How now! who 's there?

Enter some, bringing in the Clerk of Chatham.

Smith. The clerk of Chatham: he can write and read, and cast accompt.

Cade. O monstrous!

Smith. We took him setting of boys' copies.

Cade. Here 's a villain!

Smith. H'as a book in his pocket, with red letters in 't.

Cade. Nay, then he is a conjurer.

Dick. Nay, he can make obligations,² and write court-hand.

Cade. I am sorry for 't: the man is a proper man, on mine honour; unless I find him guilty, he shall not die,—Come hither, sirrah, I must examine thee; What is thy name?

Clerk. Emmanuel.

Dick. They use to write it on the top of letters;—'T will go hard with you.

Cade. Let me alone: Dost thou use to write thy name? or hast thou a mark to thyself, like an honest plain-dealing man?

Clerk. Sir, I thank God, I have been so well brought up, that I can write my name.

All. He hath confessed: away with him; he's a villain, and a traitor.

Cade. Away with him, I say: hang him with his pen and inkhorn about his neck.

[*Exeunt some with the Clerk.*

Enter MICHAEL.

Mich. Where's our general?

Cade. Here I am, thou particular fellow.

Mich. Fly, fly, fly! sir Humphrey Stafford and his brother are hard by, with the king's forces.

Cade. Stand, villain, stand, or I'll fell thee down: He shall be encountered with a man as good as himself: He is but a knight, is 'a?

Mich. No.

Cade. To equal him, I will make myself a knight presently: Rise up sir John Mortimer. Now have at him.

Enter SIR HUMPHREY STAFFORD, *and* WILLIAM *his Brother, with Drum and Forces.*

Staf. Rebellious hinds, the filth and scum of Kent,

Mark'd for the gallows,—lay your weapons down,
Home to your cottages, forsake this groom;—
The king is merciful, if you revolt.

W. Staf. But angry, wrathful, and inclin'd to blood,

If you go forward; therefore yield, or die.

Cade. As for these silken-coated slaves, I pass not;²

It is to you, good people, that I speak,
O'er whom, in time to come, I hope to reign;
For I am rightful heir unto the crown.

Staf. Villain, thy father was a plasterer;

And thou thyself, a shearman, Art thou not?

Cade. And Adam was a gardener.

W. Staf. And what of that?

Cade. Marry, this:—Edmund Mortimer, earl of March,

Married the duke of Clarence' daughter: Did he not?

Staf. Ay, sir.

Cade. By her, he had two children at one birth.

W. Staf. That's false.

Cade. Ay, there's the question; but, I say, 't is true:

The elder of them, being put to nurse,
Was by a beggar-woman stol'n away;
And ignorant of his birth and parentage,
Became a bricklayer, when he came to age:
His son am I; deny it, if you can.

Dick. Nay, 't is too true; therefore he shall be king.

Smith. Sir, he made a chimney in my father's house, and the bricks are alive at this day to testify it; therefore, deny it not.

Staf. And will you credit this base drudge's words,

That speaks he knows not what?

All. Ay, marry, will we; therefore get ye gone.

W. Staf. Jack Cade, the duke of York hath taught you this.

Cade. He lies, for I invented it myself. [*Aside.*] Go to, sirrah, Tell the king from me, that—for his father's sake, Henry the Fifth, in whose time boys went to span-counter for French crowns,—I am content he shall reign; but I'll be protector over him.

Dick. And, furthermore, we'll have the lord Say's head, for selling the dukedom of Maine.

Cade. And good reason; for thereby is England maimed, and fain to go with a staff, but that my puissance holds it up. Fellow kings, I tell you, that that lord Say hath gelded the commonwealth, and made it an eunuch: and more than that, he can speak French, and therefore he is a traitor.

Staf. O gross and miserable ignorance!

Cade. Nay, answer, if you can: The Frenchmen are our enemies: go to then, I ask but this: Can he, that speaks with the tongue of an enemy, be a good counsellor, or no?

All. No, no; and therefore we'll have his head.

W. Staf. Well, seeing gentle words will not prevail,

Assail them with the army of the king.

935

Staf. Herald, away: and, throughout every
town,
Proclaim them traitors that are up with Cade;
That those, which fly before the battle ends,
May, even in their wives' and children's sight,
Be hang'd up for example at their doors:—
And you, that be the king's friends, follow me.

[*Exeunt the Two* STAFFORDS *and Forces.*

Cade. And you, that love the commons, follow
me.—
Now show yourselves men, 't is for liberty.
We will not leave one lord, one gentleman:
Spare none, but such as go in clouted shoon;
For they are thrifty honest men, and such
As would I (but that they dare not,) take our parts.

Dick. They are all in order, and march toward us.

Cade. But then are we in order, when we are
most out of order. Come, march forward.

[*Exeunt.*

SCENE III.—*Another Part of* Blackheath.

*Alarums. The Two Parties enter, and fight, and
both the* STAFFORDS *are slain.*

Cade. Where 's Dick, the butcher of Ashford?

Dick. Here, sir.

Cade. They fell before thee like sheep and oxen,
and thou behavedst thyself as if thou hadst been
in thine own slaughter-house; therefore thus will
I reward thee,—The Lent shall be as long again
as it is; and thou shalt have a licence to kill for
a hundred lacking one.

Dick. I desire no more.

Cade. And, to speak truth, thou deservest no
less. This monument of the victory will I bear;
and the bodies shall be dragged at my horse' heels,
till I do come to London, where we will have the
mayor's sword borne before us.

Dick. If we mean to thrive and do good, break
open the gaols, and let out the prisoners.

Cade. Fear not that, I warrant thee. Come,
let 's march towards London.   [*Exeunt.*

SCENE IV.—London. *A Room in the Palace.*

Enter KING HENRY, *reading a Supplication; the*
DUKE OF BUCKINGHAM *and* LORD SAY *with him;*
at a distance, QUEEN MARGARET, *mourning over*
SUFFOLK'S *head.*

Q. Mar. Oft have I heard—that grief softens
the mind,
And makes it fearful and degenerate

Think therefore on revenge, and cease to weep.
But who can cease to weep, and look on this?
Here may his head lie on my throbbing breast:
But where 's the body that I should embrace?

Buck. What answer makes your grace to the
rebels' supplication?

K. Hen. I 'll send some holy bishop to entreat:
For God forbid, so many simple souls
Should perish by the sword! And I myself,
Rather than bloody war shall cut them short,
Will parley with Jack Cade their general.—
But stay, I 'll read it over once again.

Q. Mar. Ah, barbarous villains! hath this lovely
face
Rul'd, like a wandering planet, over me;
And could it not enforce them to relent,
That were unworthy to behold the same?

K. Hen. Lord Say, Jack Cade hath sworn to
have thy head.

Say. Ay, but I hope, your highness shall have
his.

K. Hen. How now, madam? Still
Lamenting, and mourning for Suffolk's death?
I fear, my love, if that I had been dead,
Thou wouldest not have mourn'd so much for me.

Q. Mar. No, my love, I should not mourn, but
die for thee.

Enter a Messenger.

K. Hen. How now, what news? why com'st
thou in such haste?

Mess. The rebels are in Southwark; Fly, my
lord!
Jack Cade proclaims himself lord Mortimer,
Descended from the duke of Clarence' house;
And calls your grace usurper, openly,
And vows to crown himself in Westminster.
His army is a ragged multitude
Of hinds and peasants, rude and merciless:
Sir Humphrey Stafford and his brother's death
Hath given them heart and courage to proceed:
All scholars, lawyers, courtiers, gentlemen,
They call—false caterpillars, and intend their
death.

K. Hen. O graceless men! they know not what
they do.

Buck. My gracious lord, retire to Kenelworth,
Until a power be rais'd to put them down.

Q. Mar. Ah! were the duke of Suffolk now
alive,
These Kentish rebels would be soon appeas'd.

K. Hen. Lord Say, the traitors hate thee.

Therefore away with us to Kenelworth.

Say. So might your grace's person be in danger;
The sight of me is odious in their eyes:
And therefore in this city will I stay,
And live alone as secret as I may.

Enter another Messenger.

2nd Mess. Jack Cade hath gotten London-bridge; the citizens
Fly and forsake their houses:
The rascal people, thirsting after prey,
Join with the traitor; and they jointly swear,
To spoil the city, and your royal court.

Buck. Then linger not, my lord; away, take horse.

K. Hen. Come, Margaret; God, our hope, will succour us.

Q. Mar. My hope is gone, now Suffolk is deceas'd.

K. Hen. Farewell, my lord; [*To* Say.] trust not the Kentish rebels.

Buck. Trust no body, for fear you be betray'd.

Say. The trust I have is in mine innocence,
And therefore am I bold and resolute. [*Exeunt.*

SCENE V.—*The Same. The Tower.*

Enter Lord Scales, *and Others, on the Walls. Then enter certain* Citizens, *below.*

Scales. How now? is Jack Cade slain?

1st Cit. No, my lord, nor likely to be slain; for they have won the bridge, killing all those that withstand them: The lord mayor craves aid of your honour from the Tower, to defend the city from the rebels.

Scales. Such aid as I can spare, you shall command;
But I am troubled here with them myself,
The rebels have assay'd to win the Tower.
But get you to Smithfield, and gather head,
And thither I will send you Matthew Gough:
Fight for your king, your country, and your lives;
And so farewell, for I must hence again. [*Exeunt.*

SCENE VI.—*The Same. Cannon Street.*

Enter Jack Cade, *and his Followers. He strikes his Staff on London-stone.*

Cade. Now is Mortimer lord of this city. And here, sitting upon London-stone, I charge and command, that, of the city's cost, the pissing-

conduit run nothing but claret wine this first year of our reign. And now, henceforward, it shall be treason for any that calls me other than—lord Mortimer.

Enter a Soldier, running.

Sold. Jack Cade! Jack Cade!

Cade. Knock him down there. [*They kill him.*

Smith. If this fellow be wise, he'll never call you Jack Cade more: I think, he hath a very fair warning.

Dick. My lord, there's an army gathered together in Smithfield.

Cade. Come then, let's go fight with them: But, first, go and set London-bridge on fire; and, if you can, burn down the Tower too. Come, let's away. [*Exeunt.*

SCENE VII.—*The Same. Smithfield.*

Alarum. Enter, on one side, Cade *and his Company; on the other, Citizens, and the King's Forces, headed by* Matthew Gough. *They fight, the Citizens are routed, and* Matthew Gough *is slain.*

Cade. So, sirs:—Now go some and pull down the Savoy; others to the inns of court; down with them all.

Dick. I have a suit unto your lordship.

Cade. Be it a lordship, thou shalt have it for that word.

Dick. Only, that the laws of England may come out of your mouth.

John. Mass, 't will be sore law then; for he was thrust in the mouth with a spear, and 't is not whole yet. [*Aside.*

Smith. Nay, John, it will be stinking law; for his breath stinks with eating toasted cheese. [*Aside.*

Cade. I have thought upon it, it shall be so. Away, burn all the records of the realm; my mouth shall be the parliament of England.

John. Then we are like to have biting statutes, unless his teeth be pulled out. [*Aside.*

Cade. And henceforward all things shall be in common.

Enter a Messenger.

Mess. My lord, a prize, a prize! here's the lord Say, which sold the towns in France; he that made us pay one-and-twenty fifteens, and one shilling to the pound, the last subsidy.

Enter GEORGE BEVIS, *with the* LORD SAY.

Cade. Well, he shall be beheaded for it ten times.—Ah, thou say, thou serge, nay, thou buckram lord!" now art thou within point blank of our jurisdiction regal. What canst thou answer to my majesty, for giving up of Normandy unto monsieur Basimecu, the dauphin of France? Be it known unto thee by these presence, even the presence of lord Mortimer, that I am the besom that must sweep the court clean of such filth as thou art. Thou hast most traitorously corrupted the youth of the realm, in erecting a grammar-school; and whereas, before, our fore-fathers had no other books but the score and the tally, thou hast caused printing to be used; and, contrary to the king, his crown, and dignity, thou hast built a paper-mill. It will be proved to thy face, that thou hast men about thee, that usually talk of a noun, and a verb; and such abominable words as no Christian ear can endure to hear. Thou hast appointed justices of peace, to call poor men before them about matters they were not able to answer. Moreover, thou hast put them in prison; and because they could not read, thou hast hanged them;" when, indeed, only for that cause they have been most worthy to live. Thou dost ride in a foot-cloth," dost thou not?

Say. What of that?

Cade. Marry, thou oughtest not to let thy horse wear a cloak, when honester men than thou go in their hose and doublets.

Dick. And work in their shirt too; as myself, for example, that am a butcher.

Say. You men of Kent,——

Dick. What say you of Kent?

Say. Nothing but this: 'T is *bona terra, mala gens.*

Cade. Away with him, away with him! he speaks Latin.

Say. Hear me but speak, and bear me where you will.

Kent, in the commentaries Cæsar writ,
Is term'd the civil'st place of all this isle.
Sweet is the country, because full of riches;
The people liberal, valiant, active, wealthy;
Which makes me hope you are not void of pity.
I sold not Maine, I lost not Normandy;
Yet, to recover them, would lose my life.
Justice with favour have I always done;
Prayers and tears have mov'd me, gifts could never.
258

When have I aught exacted at your hands,
Kent to maintain, the king, the realm, and you?
Large gifts have I bestow'd on learned clerks,
Because my book preferr'd me to the king:
And—seeing ignorance is the curse of God,
Knowledge the wing wherewith we fly to heaven,—
Unless you be possess'd with devilish spirits,
You cannot but forbear to murder me.
This tongue hath parley'd unto foreign kings
For your behoof.——

Cade. Tut! when struck'st thou one blow in the field?

Say. Great men have reaching hands: oft have I struck
Those that I never saw, and struck them dead.

Geo. O monstrous coward! what, to come behind folks?

Say. These cheeks are pale for watching for your good.

Cade. Give him a box o' the ear, and that will make 'em red again.

Say. Long sitting to determine poor men's causes
Hath made me full of sickness and diseases.

Cade. Ye shall have a hempen candle then, and the pap of a hatchet.

Dick. Why dost thou quiver, man?

Say. The palsy, and not fear, provoketh me.

Cade. Nay, he nods at us; as who should say, I'll be even with you. I'll see if his head will stand steadier on a pole, or no: Take him away, and behead him.

Say. Tell me, wherein I have offended most?
Have I affected wealth, or honour? speak:
Are my chests fill'd up with extorted gold?
Is my apparel sumptuous to behold?
Whom have I injur'd, that ye seek my death?
These hands are free from guiltless blood-shedding,
This breast from harbouring foul deceitful thoughts.
O, let me live!

Cade. I feel remorse in myself with his words; but I'll bridle it; he shall die, an it be but for pleading so well for his life. Away with him! he has a familiar under his tongue; he speaks not o' God's name. Go, take him away, I say, and strike off his head presently; and then break into his son in-law's house, Sir James Cromer, and strike off his head, and bring them both upon two poles hither.

All. It shall be done.

Say. Ah, countrymen! if when you make your
    prayers,
God should be so obdurate as yourselves,
How would it fare with your departed souls?
And therefore yet relent, and save my life.

Cade. Away with him, and do as I command
ye.   [*Exeunt some, with* SAY.
The proudest peer in the realm shall not wear a
head on his shoulders, unless he pay me tribute;
there shall not a maid be married, but she shall
pay to me her maidenhead ere they have it:
Men shall hold of me *in capite*; and we charge
and command, that their wives be as free as heart
can wish, or tongue can tell.

Dick. My lord, when shall we go to Cheapside,
and take up commodities upon our bills?

Cade. Marry, presently.

All. O brave!

Re-enter Rebels, *with the heads of* LORD SAY *and
his Son-in-law.*

Cade. But is not this braver?—Let them kiss
one another, for they loved well when they were
alive. Now part them again, lest they consult
about the giving up of some more towns in France.
Soldiers, defer the spoil of the city until night:
for with these borne before us, instead of maces,
will we ride through the streets; and, at every
corner, have them kiss.—Away!   [*Exeunt.*

SCENE VIII.—*Southwark.*

Alarum. Enter CADE, *and all his Rabblement.*

Cade. Up Fish-street! down Saint Magnus'
corner! kill and knock down! throw them into
Thames!—   [*A Parley sounded, then a Retreat.*]
What noise is this I hear? Dare any be so bold
to sound retreat or parley, when I command them
kill?

Enter BUCKINGHAM, *and Old* CLIFFORD, *with
Forces.*

Buck. Ay, here they be that dare and will dis-
turb thee:
Know, Cade, we come ambassadors from the king
Unto the commons whom thou hast misled;
And here pronounce free pardon to them all,
That will forsake thee, and go home in peace.

Clif. What say ye, countrymen! will ye relent,
And yield to mercy, whilst 't is offer'd you;
Or let a rabble lead you to your deaths?
Who loves the king, and will embrace his pardon,
Fling up his cap, and say —God save his majesty!
Who hateth him, and honours not his father,
Henry the Fifth, that made all France to quake,
Shake he his weapon at us, and pass by.

All. God save the king! God save the king!

Cade. What, Buckingham, and Clifford, are ye
so brave?—And you, base peasants, do ye believe
him? will you needs be hanged with your pardons about your necks? Hath my sword therefore broke through London Gates, that you should
leave me at the White Hart in Southwark? I
thought, you would never have given out these
arms, till you had recovered your ancient freedom:
but you are all recreants, and dastards; and delight to live in slavery to the nobility. Let them
break your backs with burdens, take your houses
over your heads, ravish your wives and daughters
before your faces: For me,—I will make shift for
one: and so—God's curse 'light upon you all.

All. We 'll follow Cade, we 'll follow Cade.

Clif. Is Cade the son of Henry the Fifth,
That thus you do exclaim—you 'll go with him?
Will he conduct you through the heart of France,
And make the meanest of you earls and dukes?
Alas, he hath no home, no place to fly to;
Nor knows he how to live, but by the spoil,
Unless by robbing of your friends, and us.
Were 't not a shame, that whilst you live at jar,
The fearful French, whom you late vanquished,
Should make a start o'er seas, and vanquish you?
Methinks already, in this civil broil,
I see them lording it in London streets,
Crying—*Villagois!* unto all they meet.
Better, ten thousand base-born Cades miscarry,
Than you should stoop unto a Frenchman's mercy.
To France, to France, and get what you have lost;
Spare England, for it is your native coast:
Henry hath money, you are strong and manly;
God on our side, doubt not of victory.

All. A Clifford! a Clifford! we 'll follow the
king, and Clifford.

Cade. Was ever feather so lightly blown to and
fro, as this multitude? the name of Henry the
Fifth hales them to an hundred mischiefs, and
makes them leave me desolate. I see them lay
their heads together, to surprise me: my sword
make way for me, for here 's no staying.—In despite of the devils and hell, have through the very
midst of you! and heavens and honour be witness, that no want of resolution in me, but only
my followers' base and ignominious treasons
makes me betake me to my heels.   [*Exit.*

Buck. What, is he fled? go some, and follow him:
And he, that brings his head unto the king,
Shall have a thousand crowns for his reward.—
                   [*Exeunt some of them.*
Follow me, soldiers; we 'll devise a mean
To reconcile you all unto the king.   [*Exeunt.*

SCENE IX.—Kenelworth Castle.

Enter KING HENRY, QUEEN MARGARET, *and*
SOMERSET, *on the Terrace of the Castle.*

  K. Hen. Was ever king that joy'd an earthly throne,
And could command no more content than I?
No sooner was I crept out of my cradle,
But I was made a king, at nine months old:
Was never subject long'd to be a king,
As I do long and wish to be a subject.

Enter BUCKINGHAM *and* CLIFFORD.

  Buck. Health, and glad tidings, to your majesty!
  K. Hen. Why, Buckingham, is the traitor, Cade, surpris'd?
Or is he but retir'd to make him strong?

Enter, below, a great number of CADE'S *Followers,*
with Halters about their Necks.

  Clif. He 's fled, my lord, and all his powers do yield;
And humbly thus, with halters on their necks,
Expect your highness' doom, of life, or death.
  K. Hen. Then, heaven, set ope thy everlasting gates,
To entertain my vows of thanks and praise!—
Soldiers, this day have you redeem'd your lives,
And show'd how well you love your prince and country:
Continue still in this so good a mind,
And Henry, though he be infortunate,
Assure yourselves, will never be unkind:
And so, with thanks, and pardon to you all,
I do dismiss you to your several countries.
  All. God save the king! God save the king!

Enter a Messenger.

  Mess. Please it your grace to be advertised,
The duke of York is newly come from Ireland:
And with a puissant and a mighty power,
Of Gallowglasses, and stout Kernes,
Is marching hitherward in proud array;

And still proclaimeth, as he comes along,
His arms are only to remove from thee
The duke of Somerset, whom he terms a traitor.
  K. Hen. Thus stands my state, 'twixt Cade and York distress'd:
Like to a ship, that, having scap'd a tempest,
Is straightway calm'd and boarded with a pirate:
But now is Cade driven back, his men dispers'd;
And now is York in arms to second him.—
I pray thee, Buckingham, go forth and meet him,
And ask him what 's the reason of these arms.
Tell him, I 'll send duke Edmund to the Tower;—
And, Somerset, we will commit thee thither,
Until his army be dismiss'd from him.
  Som. My lord,
I 'll yield myself to prison willingly,
Or unto death, to do my country good.
  K. Hen. In any case, be not too rough in terms.
For he is fierce, and cannot brook hard language.
  Buck. I will, my lord; and doubt not so to deal,
As all things shall redound unto your good.
  K. Hen. Come, wife, let 's in, and learn to govern better;
For yet may England curse my wretched reign.
                   [*Exeunt.*

SCENE X.—Kent. IDEN's Garden.

Enter CADE.

  Cade. Fie on ambition! fie on myself; that have a sword, and yet am ready to famish! These five days have I hid me in these woods; and durst not peep out, for all the country is lay'd for me; but now am I so hungry, that if I might have a lease of my life for a thousand years, I could stay no longer. Wherefore, on a brick-wall have I climbed into this garden; to see if I can eat grass, or pick a sallet another while, which is not amiss to cool a man's stomach this hot weather. And, I think, this word sallet was born to do me good: for, many a time, but for a sallet my brain-pan had been cleft with a brown bill; and, many a time, when I have been dry, and bravely marching, it hath served me instead of a quart-pot to drink in; and now the word sallet must serve me to feed on.

Enter IDEN, *with Servants.*

  Iden. Lord, who would live turmoiled in the court,
And may enjoy such quiet walks as these?

This small inheritance, my father left me,
Contenteth me, and is worth a monarchy.
I seek not to wax great by others' waning;
Or gather wealth, I care not with what envy;
Sufficeth, that I have maintains my state,
And sends the poor well pleased from my gate.

Cade. Here's the lord of the soil come to seize
me for a stray, for entering his fee-simple without
leave. Ah, villain, thou wilt betray me, and get
a thousand crowns of the king for carrying my
head to him; but I'll make thee eat iron like an
ostrich, and swallow my sword like a great pin,
ere thou and I part.

Iden. Why, rude companion, whatsoe'er thou be,
I know thee not: Why then should I betray thee?
Is 't not enough, to break into my garden,
And, like a thief, to come to rob my grounds,
Climbing my walls in spite of me the owner,
But thou wilt brave me with these saucy terms?

Cade. Brave thee? ay, by the best blood that
ever was broached, and beard thee too. Look on
me well: I have eat no meat these five days;
yet, come thou and thy five men, and if I do not
leave you all as dead as a door nail, I pray God,
I may never eat grass more.

Iden. Nay, it shall ne'er be said, while England
stands,
That Alexander Iden, an esquire of Kent,
Took odds to combat a poor famish'd man.
Oppose thy stedfast-gazing eyes to mine,
See if thou canst outface me with thy looks.
Set limb to limb, and thou art far the lesser;
Thy hand is but a finger to my fist;
Thy leg a stick, compared with this truncheon;
My foot shall fight with all the strength thou hast;
And if mine arm be heaved in the air,
Thy grave is digg'd already in the earth.

As for more words, whose greatness answers words,
Let this my sword report what speech forbears.

Cade. By my valour, the most complete champion that ever I heard.—Steel, if thou turn the
edge, or cut not out the burly-boned clown in
chines of beef ere thou sleep in thy sheath, I beseech God on my knees, thou mayest be turned
to hobnails. [*They fight. CADE falls.*] O, I
am slain! famine, and no other, hath slain me:
let ten thousand devils come against me, and give
me but the ten meals I have lost, and I'd defy
them all. Wither, garden; and be henceforth a
burying-place to all that do dwell in this house,
because the unconquered soul of Cade is fled.

Iden. Is 't Cade that I have slain, that mon-
strous traitor?
Sword, I will hallow thee for this thy deed,
And hang thee o'er my tomb, when I am dead:
Ne'er shall this blood be wiped from thy point;
But thou shalt wear it as a herald's coat,
To emblaze the honour that thy master got.

Cade. Iden, farewell; and be proud of thy victory: Tell Kent from me, she hath lost her best
man, and exhort all the world to be cowards: for
I, that never feared any, am vanquished by famine,
not by valour. [*Dies.*

Iden. How much thou wrong'st me, heaven be
my judge.
Die, damned wretch, the curse of her that bare thee!
And as I thrust thy body in with my sword,
So wish I, I might thrust thy soul to hell.
Hence will I drag thee headlong by the heels
Unto a dunghill, which shall be thy grave,
And there cut off thy most ungracious head;
Which I will bear in triumph to the king,
Leaving thy trunk for crows to feed upon.

[*Exit, dragging out the Body.*

ACT V.

SCENE I.—*The Same. Fields between* Dartford
and Blackheath.

*The King's Camp on one side. On the other, en-
ter* YORK, *attended, with Drum and Colours:
his Forces at some distance.*

York. From Ireland thus comes York, to claim
his right,

And pluck the crown from feeble Henry's head:
Ring, bells, aloud; burn, bonfires, clear and bright,
To entertain great England's lawful king.
Ah, *sancta majestas!* who would not buy thee
dear?
Let them obey, that know not how to rule;
This hand was made to handle nought but gold
I cannot give due action to my words,

Except a sword, or sceptre, balance it.
A sceptre shall it have, have I a soul;
On which I 'll toss the flower-de-luce of France.

   Enter BUCKINGHAM.

Whom have we here? Buckingham, to disturb
  me?
The king hath sent him, sure: I must dissemble.
  Buck. York, if thou meanest well, I greet thee
well.
  York. Humphrey of Buckingham, I accept thy
greeting.
Art thou a messenger, or come of pleasure?
  Buck. A messenger from Henry, our dread
liege,
To know the reason of these arms in peace;
Or why, thou—being a subject as I am—
Against thy oath and true allegiance sworn,
Should'st raise so great a power without his leave,
Or dare to bring thy force so near the court.
  York. Scarce can I speak, my choler is so
great.
O, I could hew up rocks, and fight with flint,
I am so angry at these abject terms;
And now, like Ajax Telamonius,
On sheep or oxen could I spend my fury!
I am far better born than is the king;
More like a king, more kingly in my thoughts:
But I must make fair weather yet a while,
Till Henry be more weak, and I more strong.—
          [*Aside.*
O Buckingham, I pr'ythee, pardon me,
That I have given no answer all this while;
My mind was troubled with deep melancholy.
The cause why I have brought this army hither,
Is—to remove proud Somerset from the king,
Seditious to his grace, and to the state.
  Buck. That is too much presumption on thy
part:
But if thy arms be to no other end,
The king hath yielded unto thy demand:
The duke of Somerset is in the Tower.
  York. Upon thine honour, is he prisoner?
  Buck. Upon mine honour, he is prisoner.
  York. Then, Buckingham, I do dismiss my
powers.—
Soldiers, I thank you all; disperse yourselves;
Meet me to-morrow in Saint George's field,
You shall have pay, and everything you wish.
And let my sovereign, virtuous Henry,
Command my eldest son,—nay, all my sons,
As pledges of my fealty and love.

I 'll send them all as willing as I live
Lands, goods, horse, armour, any thing I have,
Is his to use, so Somerset may die.
  Buck. York, I commend this kind submission
We twain will go into his highness' tent.

  Enter KING HENRY, *attended.*

  K. Hen. Buckingham, doth York intend no
harm to us,
That thus he marcheth with thee arm in arm?
  York. In all submission and humility,
York doth present himself unto your highness.
  K. Hen. Then what intend these forces thou
dost bring?
  York. To heave the traitor Somerset from
hence;
And fight against that monstrous rebel, Cade,
Who since I heard to be discomfited.

  Enter IDEN, *with* CADE'S *Head.*

  Iden. If one so rude, and of so mean condition,
May pass into the presence of a king,
Lo, I present your grace a traitor's head,
The head of Cade, whom I in combat slew.
  K. Hen. The head of Cade!—Great God, how
just art thou!—
O, let me view his visage being dead,
That living wrought me such exceeding trouble.
Tell me, my friend, art thou the man that slew
him?
  Iden. I was, an 't like your majesty.
  K. Hen. How art thou call'd? and what is thy
degree?
  Iden. Alexander Iden, that 's my name;
A poor esquire of Kent, that loves his king.
  Buck. So please it you, my lord, 't were not
amiss
He were created knight for his good service.
  K. Hen. Iden, kneel down: [*He kneels.*] Rise
up a knight.
We give thee for reward a thousand marks;
And will, that thou henceforth attend on us.
  Iden. May Iden live to merit such a bounty,
And never live but true unto his liege!
  K. Hen. See, Buckingham! Somerset comes
with the queen;
Go, bid her hide him quickly from the duke.

  Enter QUEEN MARGARET *and* SOMERSET.

  Q. Mar. For thousand Yorks he shall not hide
his head,
But boldly stand, and front him to his face.

York. How now! Is Somerset at liberty?
Then, York, unloose thy long-imprison'd thoughts,
And let thy tongue be equal with thy heart.
Shall I endure the sight of Somerset?—
False king! why hast thou broken faith with me,
Knowing how hardly I can brook abuse?
King did I call thee? no, thou art not king;
Not fit to govern and rule multitudes,
Which dar'st not, no, nor canst not rule a traitor.
That head of thine doth not become a crown;
Thy hand is made to grasp a palmer's staff,
And not to grace an awful princely sceptre.
That gold must round engirt these brows of mine;
Whose smile and frown, like to Achilles' spear,
Is able with the change to kill and cure.
Here is a hand to hold a sceptre up,
And with the same to act controlling laws.
Give place; by heaven, thou shalt rule no more
O'er him, whom heaven created for thy ruler.

Som. O monstrous traitor!—I arrest thee,
York,
Of capital treason 'gainst the king and crown:
Obey, audacious traitor; kneel for grace.

York. Would'st have me kneel? first let me
ask of these,
If they can brook I bow a knee to man.—
Sirrah, call in my sons to be my bail;
　　　　　　　　　　[*Exit an Attendant.*
I know, ere they will have me go to ward,
They 'll pawn their swords for their enfranchisement.

Q. Mar. Call hither Clifford; bid him come
amain,
To say, if that the bastard boys of York
Shall be the surety for their traitor father.

York. O blood-bespotted Neapolitan,
Outcast of Naples, England's bloody scourge!
The sons of York, thy betters in their birth,
Shall be their father's bail; and bane to those
That for my surety will refuse the boys.

Enter EDWARD *and* RICHARD PLANTAGENET, *with
Forces, at one side; at the other, with Forces
also, old* CLIFFORD *and his* SON.

See, where they come; I 'll warrant they 'll make
it good.

Q. Mar. And here comes Clifford, to deny their
bail.

Clif. Health and all happiness to my lord the
king!　　　　　　　　　　　　　[*Kneels.*

York. I thank thee, Clifford: Say, what news
with thee?
Nay, do not fright us with an angry look.

We are thy sovereign, Clifford, kneel again;
For thy mistaking so, we pardon thee.

Clif. This is my king, York, I do not mistake;
But thou mistak'st me much, to think I do:—
To Bedlam with him! is the man grown mad?

K. Hen. Ay, Clifford; a bedlam and ambitious
humour
Makes him oppose himself against his king.

Clif. He is a traitor; let him to the Tower,
And chop away that factious pate of his.

Q. Mar. He is arrested, but will not obey;
His sons, he says, shall give their words for him.

York. Will you not, sons?

Edw. Ay, noble father, if our words will serve.

Rich. And if words will not, then our weapons
shall.

Clif. Why, what a brood of traitors have we
here!

York. Look in a glass, and call thy image so;
I am thy king, and thou a false-hearted traitor.—
Call hither to the stake my two brave bears,"
That, with the very shaking of their chains,
They may astonish these fell lurking curs;
Bid Salisbury, and Warwick, come to me.

Drums.　Enter WARWICK *and* SALISBURY, *with
Forces.*

Clif. Are these thy bears? we 'll bait thy bears
to death,
And manacle the bear-ward in their chains,
If thou dar'st bring them to the baiting-place.

Rich. Oft have I seen a hot o'erweening cur
Run back and bite, because he was withheld;
Who, being suffer'd with the bear's fell paw,
Hath clapp'd his tail between his legs, and cry'd:
And such a piece of service will you do,
If you oppose yourselves to match lord Warwick.

Clif. Hence, heap of wrath, foul indigested
lump,
As crooked in thy manners as thy shape!

York. Nay, we shall heat you thoroughly anon.

Clif. Take heed, lest by your heat you burn
yourselves.

K. Hen. Why, Warwick, hath thy knee forgot
to bow?—
Old Salisbury,—shame to thy silver hair,
Thou mad misleader of thy brain-sick son!—
What, wilt thou on thy death-bed play the ruffian,
And seek for sorrow with thy spectacles?
O, where is faith? O, where is loyalty?
If it be banish'd from the frosty head,
Where shall it find a harbour in the earth?—

Wilt thou go dig a grave to find out war,
And shame thine honourable age with blood?
Why art thou old, and want'st experience?
Or wherefore dost abuse it, if thou hast it?
For shame! in duty bend thy knee to me,
That bows unto the grave with mickle age.

Sal. My lord, I have consider'd with myself
The title of this most renowned duke;
And in my conscience do repute his grace
The rightful heir to England's royal seat.

  K. Hen. Hast thou not sworn allegiance unto
    me?

  Sal. I have.

  K. Hen. Canst thou dispense with heaven for
    such an oath?

  Sal. It is great sin, to swear unto a sin;
But greater sin, to keep a sinful oath.
Who can be bound by any solemn vow
To do a murderous deed, to rob a man,
To force a spotless virgin's chastity,
To reave the orphan of his patrimony,
To wring the widow from her custom'd right;
And have no other reason for this wrong,
But that he was bound by a solemn oath?

  Q. Mar. A subtle traitor needs no sophister.

  K. Hen. Call Buckingham, and bid him arm
    himself.

  York. Call Buckingham, and all the friends
    thou hast,
I am resolv'd for death, or dignity.

  Clif. The first, I warrant thee, if dreams prove
    true.

  War. You were best to go to bed, and dream
    again,
To keep thee from the tempest of the field.

  Clif. I am resolv'd to bear a greater storm,
Than any thou canst conjure up to-day;
And that I 'll write upon thy burgonet,
Might I but know thee by thy household badge.

  War. Now, by my father's badge, old Nevil's
    crest,
The rampant bear chain'd to the ragged staff,
This day I 'll wear aloft my burgonet,
(As on a mountain-top the cedar shows,
That keeps his leaves in spite of any storm,)
Even to affright thee with the view thereof.

  Clif. And from thy burgonet I 'll rend thy
    bear,
And tread it under foot with all contempt,
Despite the bear-ward that protects the bear.

  Y. Clif. And so to arms, victorious father,
To quell the rebels, and their 'complices.

  Rich. Fye! charity, for shame! speak not in
    spite,
For you shall sup with *Jesu Christ* to-night.

  Y. Clif. Foul stigmatic, that 's more than thou
    canst tell.

  Rich. If not in heaven, you 'll surely sup in
    hell.   [*Exeunt severally*

SCENE II.—Saint Albans.

Alarums: Excursions. Enter WARWICK.

  War. Clifford of Cumberland, 't is Warwick
    calls!
And if thou dost not hide thee from the bear,
Now,—when the angry trumpet sounds alarm,
And dead men's cries do fill the empty air,—
Clifford, I say, come forth and fight with me!
Proud northern lord, Clifford of Cumberland,
Warwick is hoarse with calling thee to arms.

Enter YORK.

How now, my noble lord? what, all a-foot?

  York. The deadly-handed Clifford slew my
    steed,
But match to match I have encounter'd him,
And made a prey for carrion kites and crows
Even of the bonny beast he lov'd so well.

Enter CLIFFORD.

  War. Of one or both of us the time is come.

  York. Hold, Warwick, seek thee out some
    other chase,
For I myself must hunt this deer to death.

  War. Then, nobly, York; 't is for a crown
    thou fight'st.—
As I intend, Clifford, to thrive to-day,
It grieves my soul to leave thee unassail'd.
        [*Exit* WAR.

  Clif. What seest thou in me, York? why dost
    thou pause?

  York. With thy brave bearing should I be in
    love,
But that thou art so fast mine enemy.

  Clif. Nor should thy prowess want praise and
    esteem,
But that 't is shown ignobly, and in treason.

  York. So let it help me now against thy sword,
As I in justice and true right express it!

  Clif. My soul and body on the action both!—

  York. A dreadful lay?—address thee instantly.
        [*They fight, and* CLIF. *falls.*

  Clif. La fin couronne les œuvres.   [*Dies.*

York. Thus war hath given thee peace, for
    thou art still.
Peace with his soul, heaven, if it be thy will!
                          [*Exit.*

      Enter young CLIFFORD.

Y. Clif. Shame and confusion! all is on the
    rout;
Fear frames disorder, and disorder wounds
Where it should guard. O war, thou son of
    hell,
Whom angry heavens do make their minister,
Throw in the frozen bosoms of our part
Hot coals of vengeance!—Let no soldier fly:
He that is truly dedicate to war,
Hath no self-love; nor he, that loves himself,
Hath not essentially, but by circumstance,
The name of valour.—O, let the vile world end,
            [*Seeing his dead Father.*
And the premised flames of the last day
Knit earth and heaven together!
Now let the general trumpet blow his blast,
Particularities and petty sounds
To cease!—Wast thou ordain'd, dear father,
To lose thy youth in peace, and to achieve
The silver livery of advised age;
And, in thy reverence, and thy chair-days, thus
To die in ruffian battle?—Even at this sight,
My heart is turn'd to stone: and, while 't is
    mine,
It shall be stony. York not our old men spares;
No more will I their babes: tears virginal
Shall be to me even as the dew to fire;
And beauty, that the tyrant oft reclaims,
Shall to my flaming wrath be oil and flax.
Henceforth, I will not have to do with pity:
Meet I an infant of the house of York,
Into as many gobbets will I cut it,
As wild Medea young Absyrtus did;"
In cruelty will I seek out my fame.
Come, thou new ruin of old Clifford's house:
            [*Taking up the Body.*
As did Æneas old Anchises bear,
So bear I thee upon my manly shoulders;
But then Æneas bare a living load,
Nothing so heavy as these woes of mine. [*Exit.*

   Enter RICHARD PLANTAGENET *and* SOMERSET
     fighting, and SOMERSET *is killed.*

   Rich. So, lie thou there:—
For, underneath an alehouse' paltry sign,
The Castle in Saint Albans, Somerset

Hath made the wizard famous in his death.—
Sword, hold thy temper; heart, be wrathful still·
Priests pray for enemies, but princes kill. [*Exit.*

Alarums: Excursions. Enter KING HENRY,
   QUEEN MARGARET, *and others, retreating.*

   Q. Mar. Away, my lord! you are slow; for
    shame, away!
   K. Hen. Can we outrun the heavens? good
    Margaret, stay.
   Q. Mar. What are you made of? you 'll not
    fight, nor fly:
Now is it manhood, wisdom, and defence,
To give the enemy way; and to secure us
By what we can, which can no more but fly.
               [*Alarum afar off.*
If you be ta'en, we then should see the bottom
Of all our fortunes: but if we haply scape,
(As well we may, if not through your neglect,)
We shall to London get; where you are lov'd;
And where this breach, now in our fortunes
    made,
May readily be stopp'd.

      Enter young CLIFFORD.

   Y. Clif. But that my heart 's on future mis
    chief set,
I would speak blasphemy ere bid you fly;
But fly you must; uncurable discomfit
Reigns in the hearts of all our present friends.
Away, for your relief! and we will live
To see their day, and them our fortune give:
Away my lord, away!   [*Exeunt.*

   SCENE III.—*Fields near Saint Albans.*

Alarum: Retreat. Flourish; then enter YORK,
  RICHARD PLANTAGENET, WARWICK, *and Sol-*
  diers, with Drum and Colours.

   York. Old Salisbury, who can report of him;
That winter lion, who, in rage, forgets
Aged contusions and all brush of time;
And, like a gallant in the bloom of youth,
Repairs him with occasion? this happy day
Is not itself, nor have we won one foot,
If Salisbury be lost.
   Rich.   My noble father,
Three times to-day I holp him to his horse,
Three times bestrid him, thrice I led him off,
Persuaded him from any further act:
But still, where danger was, still there I met him
And like rich hangings in a homely house,

So was his will in his old feeble body.
But, noble as he is, look where he comes.

Enter SALISBURY.

Sal. Now, by my sword, well hast thou fought
     to-day;
By the mass, so did we all.—I thank you, Rich-
     ard:
God knows how long it is I have to live;
And it hath pleas'd him, that three times to-day
You have defended me from imminent death.—
Well, lords, we have not got that which we have:
'T is not enough our foes are this time fled,

Being opposites of such repairing nature.[e]
York. I know our safety is to follow them;
For, as I hear, the king is fled to London,
To call a present court of parliament.[d]
Let us pursue him, ere the writs go forth :—
What says lord Warwick! shall we after them !
War. After them! nay, before them, if we can
Now, by my faith, lords, 't was a glorious day:
Saint Albans' battle won by famous York,
Shall be eterniz'd in all age to come.—
Sound, drums and trumpets ;—and to London
     all :
And more such days as those to us befall ! [*Exeunt*

946

NOTES TO KING HENRY THE SIXTH.

(PART THE SECOND.)

' *Mine alder-liefest sovereign.*

Alder-liefest is a corruption of the German word *alder-liebst*, beloved above all things; dearest of all. It appears to have been adopted in the English language, as it is found in Chaucer, Marston, and others. Thus, in Marston—

—— Pretty sweetheart of mine alder-liefest affection.

Again, in Gascoigne:—

—— And to mine *alder-lievest* lord I must indite.

' *And all the wealthy kingdoms of the west.*

Probably Shakespeare wrote of the east.

' *And, brother York, thy acts in Ireland,*
In bringing them to civil discipline.

This is an anachronism. The present scene is in 1445; but Richard Duke of York was not viceroy of Ireland till 1449.

' *As did the fatal brand Althea burn'd,*
Unto the prince's heart of Calydon.

The prince of Calydon was Meleager, a celebrated hero of antiquity, son of Æneas, king of Ætolia, by Althea, daughter of Thestius. The Parcæ (i. e., the Fates) were present at his birth. Clotho said that he would be brave and courageous; Lachesis foretold his uncommon strength; and Atropos declared that he should live so long as a brand then on the fire remained unconsumed. The mother immediately snatched the log from the flames, and preserved it with the most jealous care. Meleager destroyed the famous wild boar which Diana had sent to punish the people of Calydon by laying waste the country; this monster, from its enormous size and fierceness, was the terror of the entire land; and many princes and chiefs assembled, each anxious to obtain the honour of killing it. Meleager having at length slain both his uncles in a quarrel, his mother, Althea, in a fit of grief and passion, threw the fatal log into the fire, and he died as soon as it was consumed. Althea was afterwards so grieved at her rash act, that she committed suicide in a paroxysm of despair.

' *Sir John.*

Sir, was a title commonly bestowed on the clergy; it is the designation of a bachelor of arts in the Universities of Cambridge and Dublin, but is there always annexed, not to the christian name, but to the surname. In consequence of this, however, all the inferior clergy in Eng and were distinguished by this title affixed to their christian names for many centuries. Thus we have *Sir Hugh*, in *The Merry Wives of Windsor*; *Sir Topas*, in *Twelfth Night*; *Sir Oliver*, in *As You Like It*, &c.

' *A crafty knave does need no broker.*

This is a proverbial sentence. See Ray's *Collection*.

' *We may deliver our supplications in the quill.*

Probably this means our *penned* or *written* supplications, as we now say a drawing *in chalk*, when we mean a drawing executed by the aid of chalk. Mr. Tollet, however, thinks that *in the quill* may mean, with great exactness and observance of form, or with the utmost punctilio of ceremony. The phrase, he thinks, was suggested by the quilted ruffs worn by our ancestors, and which were kept scrupulously neat, so that it might have become usual to say a thing was in the quill, when it was exact and ceremonious.

' *Though in this place most master wear no breeches.*

As it stands, this line has no sense. I have no doubt we should read,—*most master*, &c.; i. e., though the master of this place has no authority, yet the mistress of it shall not insult me with impunity.

' *For flying at the brook.*

Flying *at the brook* is *the falconer's term for* hawking at water fowl. Mr. Steevens tells us " that the terms belonging to this once popular amusement were in general settled with the utmost precision; and I may at least venture to declare, that a mistress might have been kept at a cheaper rate than a falcon. To compound a medicine to cure one of these birds of worms, it was necessary to destroy no fewer animals than a *lamb*, a *calves*, a *pigeon*, a *buck*, and a *cat*. I have this intelligence from the *Boole of Hawkinge*, &c., v. 1, no date. This work was written by Dame Julyana Berners, prioress of the nunnery of Sopwell near St. Albans (where Shakespeare has fixed the present scene), and one of the editions of it was *Printed at Westminster by Wynkyn de Worde*, 1496, together with an additional treatise on fishing."

947

[10] *A miracle.*

Mr. Malone tells us that "this scene is founded on a story which Sir Thomas More has related, and which he says was communicated to him by his father. The imposter's name is not mentioned, but he was detected by Humphrey Duke of Gloster, and in the manner here represented."

**[11] *But you have done more miracles than I;*
*You made, in a day, my lord, whole towns to fly.***

This is a satirical allusion to Suffolk's abandonment of Maine and Anjou to Reignier, the father of Queen Margaret.

[12] *Lords, let him go.*

Let him pass out of your thoughts. The duke had already left the stage.

[13] *I never saw a fellow worse bested.*

So deserted by his faculties, or in a less fit condition to cope with an adversary.

[14] *Here's a cup of charneco.*

Charneco is a sort of sweet wine named from a village near Lisbon, where it is made.

**[15] *Go, take hence that traitor from our sight;*
*For, by his death, we do perceive his guilt.***

According to the laws of these duels, the party who was defeated or slain was adjudged guilty of the crime imputed to him, and if not killed in the lists, was taken out of it and hanged or beheaded. Indeed, the dead body of the vanquished was equally condemned to the punishment of a convicted traitor, in order that his posterity might participate in his infamy. The real names of the combatants on this occasion were, William Catour, the armourer, and John Davy, his apprentice. The expenses attending this engagement have been preserved, and amounted to £10 18s. 9d. One of the items in the account is, "also paid for 1 pole and naylls, and for setting up of ye said mannys hed on London Bridge, v.d."

[16] *Ueath.*

That is, not easily. *Eath* is the ancient word for *ease* or *easy*. Thus, in Spenser's *Fairy Queen*, B. iv. c. 6:—

More *eath* was new impression to receive.

[17] *Caper upright, like a wild Morisco.*

Morisco is probably a term applied to any morris-dancer, though Dr. Johnson thinks it means a country fellow dressed as a Moor in these rustic dances.

[18] *Rear up his body; wring him by the nose.*

As neither Somerset nor the Cardinal speak again during this scene, and as nothing occurs to show that they continue in the presence of their sovereign, we must presume that they take advantage of Henry's fainting to slip away unnoticed. The next that we hear of the Cardinal is, that he is at the point of death.

[19] *Would curses kill, as doth the mandrake's groan.*

This line alludes to a superstition respecting the mandrake, which is thus related in Bulleine's *Bulwarke of*

948

Defence against Sickness, &c., 1579:—"They do affyrme that this herbe commeth of the seede of some convicted dead men; and also without the death of some lyvinge thinge it cannot be drawn out of the earth to man's use. Therefore they did tye some dogge or other lyvinge beast unto the roote thereof wyth a corde, and digged the earth in compasse round about, and in the meane tyme stopped their own eares for feare of the terrible shriek and cry of this mandrake. In whych cry it doth not only dye itselfe, but the feare thereof kylleth the dogge or beast which pulleth it out of the earth."

[20] *I'll have an Iris that shall find thee out.*

Iris was a messenger of the gods, but more particularly of Juno. She is identical with the rainbow, and is represented with wings possessing all its variegated and beautiful colours. She had also other offices, one of which was to cut the thread which seemed to detain the soul in the body of those that were dying, and the other to supply the clouds with water, that they might refresh the earth.

[21] *If thou be'st death, I'll give thee England's treasure, &c.*

This passage was suggested by the following account of the death of the cardinal in Hall's *Chronicle*:—" During these doynges, Henry Beauford, byshop of Winchester, and called the riche Cordynail, departed out of this worlde. This man was haut in stomach and hygh in countenance, ryche above measure of all men, and to fewe liberal; disdaynful to his kynne, and dreadful to his lovers. His covetous insaciable and hope of long lyfe made hym loth to forget God, his prynce, and himselfe, in his latter dayes: for Doctor John Baker, his pryvie counsailer and his chapellayn, wrote, that lying on his death-bed, he said these wordes:—' Why should I dye, having so moche riches? If the whole realme would save my life, I am able either by pollicie to get it, or by ryches to bye it. Fye, will not death be hyred, nor will money do nothynge? When my nephew of Bedford died, I thought myselfe halfe up the whele, but when I sawe myne other nephew of Gloucester disceased, then I thought myselfe able to be equal with kinges, and so thought to increase my treasure in hope to have worne a trypple crowne. But I se nowe the worlde fayleth me, and so I am decevyed; praying you all to pray for me.'"

[22] *To affy,* i. e., to betroth in marriage.

[23] *He can make obligations,* i. e., write bonds.

[24] *As for these silken-coated slaves, I pass not.*

That is, I pay them no regard. So, in Drayton's *Quest of Cynthia*:—

Transform me to what shape you can,
I pass not what it be.

[25] *The Lent shall be as long again as it is, and thou shalt have a licence to kill for a hundred lacking one.*

Butchers were formerly not permitted to sell meat during Lent; some, however, had the interest to obtain a special licence to kill a certain number per week in consideration of the sick and feeble; a monopoly that was doubtless highly profitable to them

⁸ This monument of the victory will I bear.

He alludes to Stafford's armour, which he stript from the body and put upon himself, and thus arrayed returned to London.

⁹ Queen Margaret, mourning over Suffolk's head.

The old play led Shakespeare into this disgusting and unnatural incident; a queen with the head of her murdered paramour hid in her bosom in the presence of her husband.

²⁰ But, first, go and set London-bridge on fire.

At that time London-bridge was made chiefly of wood; the houses upon it were burnt in this rebellion, and many of the inhabitants perished.

²¹ Matthew Gough is slain.

According to Holinshed, Gough was "a man of great wit and much experience in feats of chivalrie, the which in continuall warres had spent his time in serving of the king and his father."

²² He that made us pay one and twenty fifteens.

A *fifteenth* was the fifteenth part of all the movables or personal property of each subject.

²³ Ah, thou say, thou serge, nay, thou buckram lord!

Cade is quibbling upon the name of the unfortunate nobleman, *say* being an old term for silk; on this depends the series of degradation, from *say* to *serge*, from *serge* to *buckram.*

²⁴ And because they could not read thou hast hanged them.

That is, they were hanged for their offences because they could not claim the benefit of clergy.

²⁵ Thou dost ride on a foot-cloth.

A *footcloth* was a kind of robe which covered the horse and reached almost to the ground. It was frequently made of velvet, and trimmed with gold.

²⁶ When have I aught exacted at your hands,
Kent to maintain, the king, the realm, and you?

Dr. Johnson would read *but* to maintain ; the word Kent he thinks has crept into the text by a mistake of the printers ; as the passage stands, Lord Say implies that the men of Kent have been altogether exempt from taxes, which is evidently not his meaning. This alteration makes the line clear and intelligible.

²⁷ When shall we go to Cheapside, and take up commodities upon our bills?

This is an equivoque alluding to the brown bills, or halberds, with which the commons were anciently armed, and to a written paper representing money.

²⁸ No sooner was I crept out of my cradle,
But I was made a king, at nine months old.

This is correct, and yet in the First Part of Henry the Sixth, Act iii., sc. 4, Henry is made to remark—

I do remember how my father said,

which some critics think to be a conclusive proof that the whole of that play was not written by the same author as this. But as an argument this is worth nothing, for Shakespeare has frequently fallen into similar inconsistencies, by sometimes adhering to and sometimes departing from the old dramas which he selected to build his own upon.

²⁹ Many a time, but for a sallet, my brain-pan had been cleft with a brown bill.

Sallet was a common name for a helmet; thus in Sir Thomas North's translation of Plutarch—" One of the company seeing Brutus almost also, he ran to the river for water, and brought it in his *sallet.*" Again, in The longer thou livest the more Fool thou art, 1570—

This will beare away a good rappe,
As good as a *sallet* to me verilie.

³⁰ Call hither to the stake my two brave bears.

That is, the Earl of Warwick, and his father, the Earl of Salisbury ; a bear and ragged staff, were the arms of their family.

³¹ A dreadful lay, i. e., a fearful wager.

³² Dies.

Clifford did not fall by the hand of York ; his death is correctly described in the first scene of the Third part of Henry the Sixth, where it is stated that he fell by the swords of the common soldiers while charging the adverse ranks. Shakespeare not unfrequently departs from the truth of history to render his characters more considerable.

³³ As wild Medea young Absyrtus did.

Medea was a celebrated enchantress, and the daughter of Aetes, king of Colchis. Having become enamoured of Jason, she assisted him in obtaining the golden fleece, and fled with him to Greece. To stop the pursuit of her father, she killed and cut in pieces her brother Absyrtus, and left his mangled limbs in the way through which his father must pass. This savage act has by some been attributed to Jason, and not to her.

³⁴ Being opposites of such repairing nature.

That is, being enemies not likely to be utterly defeated by this action, likely soon to rally and recover themselves. Shakespeare often uses the word *repair* in the sense of *renewal.*

³⁵ For, as I hear, the king is fled to London,
To call a present court of parliament.

York could not have heard this, as Henry had but just left the stage to fly to London, and had not said a word of calling a parliament. In the old play the king does say he will call a parliament, but Shakespeare has omitted the line, and then afterwards forgetfully alludes to it. It must be borne in mind that the poet wrote these plays only to be acted, and in representation such errors could not readily be detected ; had he corrected the press himself, he would have erased this and similar inconsistencies. They were doubtless produced hastily, and the activity of his subsequent life probably prevented a return to them.

THIRD PART OF

King Henry the Sixth.

THIS tragedy includes a period of sixteen years, commencing immediately after the first battle of St. Albans, on May 23rd, 1455, and closing with the murder of Henry the Sixth, and the birth of Prince Edward, in 1471. In this division of his triune play, though Shakespeare certainly inclines to the Lancastrian interest, yet he does not greatly exhibit his disgust at the turbulence and treachery of the York faction. Every scene is filled with deeds of violence and murder; the story grows darker and more dark towards its close, and the crimes of the Yorkists are at length consummated by the murder of a pious and well-meaning king; yet the poet utters no condemnation of the promoters of this reign of terror, and the play terminates with Edward's triumph, and a picture of his domestic felicity. Shakespeare, contrary to his usual custom, does not—

> " Assert eternal Providence,
> And justify the ways of God to men."

Edward gains power by treachery, lives in luxury, and dies in peace; no poetical justice overtakes him, but the thunderbolt descends upon his children, who perish miserably by the murderous devices of their uncle Richard.

The reckless perjury of Edward is early shown in this play; in persuading his father to claim the crown, he exclaims—

> But, for a kingdom, any oath may be broken:
> I 'd break a thousand oaths, to reign one year.

Sunk and degraded indeed must be that father whom his son could think of thus addressing; such unblushing depravity is evidence of a very corrupt nature. It is difficult to say which is most offensive, the open recommendation of perjury by Edward, or the subtilty of Richard, his younger brother who urges that an oath, not taken before a lawful magistrate, cannot be binding. It is but proper to say that Richard was but eight years old at this period, and the part which he is made to play consequently proceeds entirely from the imagination of the poet.

The slaughter of young Rutland, though a barbarous action, may still admit of some excuse when we consider the provocation which Clifford has received; he is under a vow to revenge his father's death, and he does revenge it with "blood-thirsty filial love." The following scene, where Clifford and Queen Margaret take York prisoner, and after mocking and torturing him by placing a crown of paper upon his head, and presenting him with a handkerchief stained with the blood of his son, despatch him with their daggers, is a fearful instance of the insatiate fury of party strife and civil war. The bitterness of Margaret's character is here fully displayed; she seems an impersonation of Atè, revelling in butchery, and mad for blood, her eyes glaring with the intoxication of gratified vengeance. But we are not greatly touched by the sufferings of York; his ingratitude and perfidy are too recent to permit us to sympathize with him; we remember his promise of eternal loyalty and obedience to Henry, and the shameless manner in which he has broken all oaths and obligations, and we cannot grieve at his punishment. Savage as was this act of Margaret, much may be said in palliation of her misdeeds; like another striking creation of our poet's genius, she was

951

"more sinned against than sinning;" outrage drives her from a woman to a fury, but years of misfortune elevate and give a terrible sublimity to her character. Now she is impelled onward like a hunted and infuriate tigress; but as years roll on, a mystic dignity and equivocal inspiration hang around the character of Margaret the prophetess.

Shakespeare always prepares us for the subsequent deeds of any of his characters, though for some time they may be not much engaged in the action of the drama. Thus, when the news of the duke of York's death is brought to his two sons, Edward and Richard, the first shudderingly bids the messenger stop short in his tale—he cannot bear the relation of the circumstances of his father's death; not so Richard,—he too, is shocked (for Shakespeare attributes to him the one virtue of filial affection), but his iron nature is enraged, not softened, and he exclaims to the man, "Say how he died, for I will hear it all." In the third act Richard reveals his character to the reader; he unveils his innate love of villany, his resolute ambition; he revels in a dream of anticipated sovereignty, and familiarizes his mind with murder. But Richard's nature and conduct are easily accounted for; sprung from a strong-minded but treacherous race, he had been educated on the field of battle, and early familiarized with acts of cruelty and blood.

It is in this drama that the character of Henry most enlists our sympathy; in the two previous plays his apathy occasionally provokes our anger, but here we become convinced of his incapacity, and pity him. Peace is his longing, his idol; at any price, peace: and to all sides he turns a yielding and supplicating aspect, forgetful that peace may be bought too dearly, and when obtained, be but a hollow purchase; forgetful that in turbulent times the best mode of preventing war is to be prepared for it, and to offer the olive on the point of the sword. Men respect strength and decision, and will seldom provoke it; the house of York would have lived tranquilly enough under the rule of the heroic Henry the Fifth. The placid character of his son is finely portrayed when he sits upon a hill near the battle-field of Towton, and envies the condition of the homely shepherd, who is never disturbed by ambition or regal cares, but makes the welfare of his flock his only occupation. "Ah, what a life were this! how sweet! how lovely!" says the melancholy monarch. Here his meditations are interrupted by the horrors of civil war being brought home to his sight; a son enters, dragging in the body of his father, whom he had unknowingly slain in the heat of the battle; full of joy at his triumph, he proceeds to rifle the corpse, when he recognizes the being who had given him life. The agony and remorse attending such a terrible discovery, are painted with an unflinching pencil; but the picture of terror is not yet complete. A father enters with the body of his son, whom he had also killed unknowingly, in the fury of the action; and the wretched men mingle their groans and tears with those of their unhappy sovereign, who is an accidental witness of the misery of which he is an innocent cause.

When the "king-maker" restores the deposed Henry to the crown, the humility of this religious king is extremely touching; he yields the real burden of government to Warwick, because that leader is always fortunate in his deeds, and the latter chooses for his associate in the task, his son in-law, the duke of Clarence. Henry thus resigns his claims, and offers the remainder of his life to the service of heaven—

> I make you both protectors of this land;
> While I myself will lead a private life,
> And in devotion spend my later days,
> To sin's rebuke, and my Creator's praise.

But this tranquillity is of brief duration; the waves of contention are but lulled for a moment, and the storm again rages with all its former fierceness. Henry is a second time seized and deposed by Edward; the great Warwick, the master-spirit of the age, is slain in the battle at Barnet; Queen Margaret makes one last attempt to regain her lost power, at Tewkesbury, where her friends are dispersed, herself and son taken prisoners, and the brave young prince murdered by Edward and his triumphant associates. Then comes the gloomy catastrophe of this dark history, and the saintly Henry is murdered in the Tower by the fiendish Richard. The power of contrast can scarcely go further than in this scene; the principles of peace, piety, humility, and affection, are opposed to those of violence, hypocrisy, ambition, and hatred.

PERSONS REPRESENTED.

KING HENRY THE SIXTH.
appears Act I. sc. 1. Act II. sc. 2; sc. 5. Act III. sc. 1;
Act IV. sc. 6; sc. 8. Act V. sc. 6.

EDWARD, *Prince of Wales, his Son.*
Appears, Act I. sc. 1. Act II. sc. 2; sc. 5. Act III. sc. 3.
Act V. sc. 4; sc. 5.

LEWIS THE ELEVENTH, *King of France.*
Appears, Act III. sc. 3.

DUKE OF SOMERSET, *of King Henry's Party.*
Appears, Act IV. sc. 1; sc. 2; sc. 3; sc. 6. Act V. sc. 1;
sc. 2; sc. 4; sc. 5.

DUKE OF EXETER, *of King Henry's Party.*
Appears, Act I. sc. 1. Act II. sc. 5. Act IV. sc. 8.

EARL OF OXFORD, *of King Henry's Party.*
Appears, Act III. sc. 3. Act IV. sc. 3; sc. 6; sc. 8. Act V.
sc. 1; sc. 2; sc. 4, sc. 5.

EARL OF NORTHUMBERLAND, *of King Henry's
Party.*
Appears, Act I. sc. 1; sc. 4. Act II. sc. 2.

EARL OF WESTMORELAND, *of King Henry's Party.*
Appears, Act I. sc. 1.

LORD CLIFFORD, *of King Henry's Party.*
Appears, Act I. sc. 1; sc. 3; sc. 4. Act II. sc. 2; sc. 4; sc. 6.

RICHARD PLANTAGENET, *Duke of York.*
Appears, Act I. sc. 1; sc. 2; sc. 4.

EDWARD, *his Son, Earl of March, afterwards King
Edward the Fourth.*
Appears, Act I. sc. 1; sc. 2. Act II. sc. 1; sc. 2; sc. 3;
sc. 6. Act III. sc. 2. Act IV. sc. 1; sc. 3; sc. 5; sc. 7;
sc. 8. Act V. sc. 1; sc. 2; sc. 3; sc. 4; sc. 5.

EDMUND, *Son to the Duke of York, and Earl of
Rutland.*
Appears, Act I. sc. 3.

GEORGE, *Son to the Duke of York, and afterwards Duke of Clarence.*
Appears, Act II. sc. 2; sc. 3; sc. 6. Act III. sc. 2. Act IV.
sc. 1; sc. 2; sc. 3; sc. 6; sc. 8. Act V. sc. 1; sc. 3; sc. 4;
sc. 5; sc. 7.

RICHARD, *Son to the Duke of York, and afterwards Duke of Gloucester.*
Appears, Act I. sc. 1; sc. 2. Act II. sc. 1; sc. 2; sc. 3; sc. 4.
sc. 6. Act III. sc. 2. Act IV. sc. 1; sc. 3; sc. 5; sc. 7;
sc. 8. Act V. sc. 1; sc. 3; sc. 4; sc. 5; sc. 6; sc. 7.

DUKE OF NORFOLK, *of the Duke of York's Party.*
Appears, Act I. sc. 1. Act II. sc. 2.

MARQUIS OF MONTAGUE, *of the Duke of York's
Party.*
Appears, Act I. sc. 1; Act II. sc. 1; sc. 2; sc. 6. Act IV.
sc. 1; sc. 6; sc. 8. Act V. sc. 1

EARL OF WARWICK, *of the Duke of York's Party*
Appears, Act I. sc. 1. Act II. sc. 1; sc. 2; sc. 3; sc. 4.
sc. 6. Act III. sc. 3. Act IV. sc. 2; sc. 3; sc. 6; sc. 8
Act V. sc. 1; sc. 2.

LORD HASTINGS, *of the Duke of York's Party.*
Appears, Act IV. sc. 1; sc. 3; sc. 5; sc. 7. Act V. sc. 7

EARL OF PEMBROKE, } *of the Duke of York's
LORD STAFFORD,* } *Party.*
Appear, Act IV. sc. 1.

SIR JOHN MORTIMER, } *Uncles to the Duke of
SIR HUGH MORTIMER,* } *York.*
Appear, Act I. sc. 2.

HENRY, *Earl of Richmond, a Youth.*
Appears, Act IV. sc. 6.

LORD RIVERS, *Brother to Lady Grey.*
Appears, Act IV. sc. 4.

SIR WILLIAM STANLEY.
Appears, Act IV. sc. 5.

SIR JOHN MONTGOMERY.
Appears, Act IV. sc. 7.

SIR JOHN SOMERVILLE.
Appears, Act V. sc. 1.

TUTOR TO RUTLAND.
Appears, Act I. sc. 3.

MAYOR OF YORK.
Appears, Act IV. sc. 7.

LIEUTENANT OF THE TOWER.
Appears, Act IV. sc. 6. Act V. sc. 6.

A NOBLEMAN.
Appears, Act III. sc. 2.

TWO KEEPERS.
Appear, Act III. sc. 1.

A HUNTSMAN.
Appears, Act IV. sc. 5.

A SON *that has killed his Father,*
A FATHER *that has killed his Son.*
Appear, Act II. sc. 5.

THREE WATCHMEN.
Appear, Act IV. sc. 3.

QUEEN MARGARET.
Appears, Act I. sc. 1; sc. 4. Act II. sc. 2; sc. 5. Act III
sc. 3. Act V. sc. 4; sc. 5.

LADY GREY, *afterwards Queen to Edward the
Fourth.*
Appears, Act III. sc. 2. Act IV. sc. 1; sc. 4. Act V. sc. 7

BONA, *Sister to the French King.*
Appears, Act III. sc. 3.

*Soldiers, and other Attendants on King Henry
and King Edward, Messengers, &c.*

SCENE,—*During part of the Third Act in* FRANCE;
during all the rest of the play in ENGLAND.

THIRD PART OF

King Henry the Sixth.

ACT I.

SCENE I.—London. *The Parliament-House.*

Drums. Some Soldiers of York's party break in. Then, Enter the DUKE OF YORK, EDWARD, RICHARD, NORFOLK, MONTAGUE, WARWICK, *and Others, with White Roses in their Hats.*

War. I wonder how the king escap'd our hands.

York. While we pursu'd the horsemen of the north,
He slily stole away, and left his men :
Whereat the great lord of Northumberland,
Whose warlike ears could never brook retreat,
Cheer'd up the drooping army ; and himself,
Lord Clifford, and lord Stafford, all a-breast,
Charg'd our main battle's front, and, breaking in,
Were by the swords of common soldiers slain.

Edw. Lord Stafford's father, duke of Buckingham,
Is either slain, or wounded dangerously :
I cleft his beaver with a downright blow ;
That this is true, father, behold his blood.
[*Showing his bloody Sword.*

Mont. And, brother, here 's the earl of Wiltshire's blood, [*To York, showing his.*
Whom I encounter'd as the battles join'd.

Rich. Speak thou for me, and tell them what I did.[1]
[*Throwing down* SOMERSET'S *Head.*

York. Richard hath best deserv'd of all my sons.—
What, is your grace dead, my lord of Somerset ?

Norf. Such hope have all the line of John of Gaunt !

Rich. Thus do I hope to shake king Henry's head.

War. And so do I.—Victorious prince of York,
Before I see thee seated in that throne
Which now the house of Lancaster usurps,
I vow by heaven, these eyes shall never close.
This is the palace of the fearful king,
And this the regal seat : possess it, York ;
For this is thine, and not king Henry's heirs'.

York. Assist me then, sweet Warwick, and I will ;
For hither we have broken in by force.

Norf. We 'll all assist you ; he, that flies, shall die.

York. Thanks, gentle Norfolk,—Stay by me, my lords ;—
And, soldiers, stay, and lodge by me this night.

War. And, when the king comes, offer him no violence,
Unless he seek to thrust you out by force.
[*They retire.*

York. The queen, this day, here holds her parliament,
But little thinks we shall be of her council :
By words, or blows, here let us win our right.

Rich. Arm'd as we are, let 's stay within this house.

War. The bloody parliament shall this be call'd
Unless Plantagenet, duke of York, be king ;
And bashful Henry depos'd, whose cowardice
Hath made us by-words to our enemies.

854

York. Then leave me not, my lords; be reso-
    lute
I mean to take possession of my right.
    War. Neither the king, nor he that loves him
    best,
The proudest he that holds up Lancaster,
Dares stir a wing, if Warwick shake his bells.'
I 'll plant Plantagenet, root him up who dares:—
Resolve thee, Richard; claim the English crown.
    [WAR. *leads* YORK *to the Throne, who
    seats himself.*

Flourish. Enter KING HENRY, CLIFFORD, NOR-
THUMBERLAND, WESTMORELAND, EXETER, *and
Others, with red Roses in their Hats.*

    K. Hen. My lords, look where the sturdy rebel
    sits,
Even in the chair of state! belike, he means,
(Back'd by the power of Warwick, that false
    peer,)
To aspire unto the crown, and reign as king.—
Earl of Northumberland, he slew thy father;—
And thine, lord Clifford; and you both have vow'd
    revenge
On him, his sons, his favourites, and his friends.
    North. If I be not, heavens, be reveng'd on me!
    Clif. The hope thereof makes Clifford mourn in
    steel.
    West. What, shall we suffer this? let 's pluck
    him down:
My heart for anger burns, I cannot brook it.
    K. Hen. Be patient, gentle earl of Westmore-
    land.
    Clif. Patience is for poltroons, and such as he;
He durst not sit there had your father liv'd.
My gracious lord, here in the parliament
Let us assail the family of York.
    North. Well hast thou spoken, cousin; be it so.
    K. Hen. Ah, know you not, the city favours
    them,
And they have troops of soldiers at their beck?
    Exe. But when the duke is slain, they 'll quickly
    fly.
    K. Hen. Far be the thought of this from Hen-
    ry's heart,
To make a shambles of the parliament-house!
Cousin of Exeter, frowns, words, and threats,
Shall be the war that Henry means to use.—
    [*They advance to the Duke.*
Thou factious duke of York, descend my throne,
And kneel for grace and mercy at my feet;
I am thy sovereign.

    York.   Thou art deceiv'd, I am thine.
    Exe. For shame, come down; he made thee
    duke of York.
    York. 'T was my inheritance, as the earldom
    was.
    Exe. Thy father was a traitor to the crown.
    War. Exeter, thou art a traitor to the crown,
In following this usurping Henry.
    Clif. Whom should he follow, but his natural
    king?
    War. True, Clifford; and that 's Richard, duke
    of York.
    K. Hen. And shall I stand, and thou sit in my
    throne?
    York. It must and shall be so. Content thyself.
    War. Be duke of Lancaster, let him be king.
    West. He is both king and duke of Lancaster;
And that the lord of Westmoreland shall maintain.
    War. And Warwick shall disprove it. You
    forget,
That we are those, which chas'd you from the
    field,
And slew your fathers, and with colours spread
March'd through the city to the palace gates.
    North. Yes, Warwick, I remember it to my
    grief;
And, by his soul, thou and thy house shall rue it.
    West. Plantagenet, of thee, and these thy sons,
Thy kinsmen, and thy friends, I 'll have more
    lives,
Than drops of blood were in my father's veins.
    Clif. Urge it no more; lest that, instead of
    words,
I send thee, Warwick, such a messenger,
As shall revenge his death, before I stir.
    War. Poor Clifford! how I scorn his worthless
    threats!
    York. Will you, we show our title to the
    crown?
If not, our swords shall plead it in the field.
    K. Hen. What title hast thou, traitor, to the
    crown?
Thy father was, as thou art, duke of York;
Thy grandfather, Roger Mortimer, earl of March:
I am the son of Henry the Fifth,
Who made the Dauphin and the French to
    stoop,
And seiz'd upon their towns and provinces.
    War. Talk not of France, sith thou hast lost it
    all.
    K. Hen. The lord protector lost it, and not I;
When I was crown'd, I was but nine months old.

Rich. You are old enough now, and yet, methinks you lose :—
Father, tear the crown from the usurper's head.

Edw. Sweet father, do so ; set it on your head.

Mont. Good brother, [*To* YORK.] as thou lov'st
and honour'st arms,
Let 's fight it out, and not stand cavilling thus.

Rich. Sound drums and trumpets, and the king
will fly.

York. Sons, peace !

K. Hen. Peace thou ! and give king Henry
leave to speak.

War. Plantagenet shall speak first :—hear him,
lords ;
And be you silent and attentive too,
For he, that interrupts him, shall not live.

K. Hen. Think'st thou, that I will leave my
kingly throne,
Wherein my grandsire, and my father, sat ?
No : first shall war unpeople this my realm ;
Ay, and their colours—often borne in France ;
And now in England, to our heart's great sorrow,—
Shall be my winding-sheet.—Why faint you, lords ?
My title 's good, and better far than his.

War. But prove it, Henry, and thou shalt be
king.

K. Hen. Henry the Fourth by conquest got
the crown.

York. 'T was by rebellion against his king.

K. Hen. I know not what to say ; my title 's
weak.
Tell me, may not a king adopt an heir ?

York. What then ?

K. Hen. An if he may, then am I lawful king :
For Richard, in the view of many lords,
Resign'd the crown to Henry the Fourth ;
Whose heir my father was, and I am his.

York. He rose against him, being his sovereign,
And made him to resign his crown perforce.

War. Suppose, my lords, he did it uncon-
strain'd,
Think you, 't were prejudicial to his crown ?

Exe. No ; for he could not so resign his crown,
But that the next heir should succeed and reign.

K. Hen. Art thou against us, duke of Exeter ?

Exe. His is the right, and therefore pardon me.

York. Why whisper you, my lords, and answer
not ?

Exe. My conscience tells me he is lawful king.

K. Hen. All will revolt from me, and turn to
him.

North. Plantagenet, for all the claim thou lay'st,
956

Think not, that Henry shall be so depos'd.

War. Depos'd he shall be, in despite of all.

North. Thou art deceiv'd : 't is not thy southern
power,
Of Essex, Norfolk, Suffolk, nor of Kent,—
Which makes thee thus presumptuous and
proud,—
Can set the duke up, in despite of me.

Clif. King Henry, be thy title right or wrong,
Lord Clifford vows to fight in thy defence :
May that ground gape, and swallow me alive,
Where I shall kneel to him that slew my father !

K. Hen. O Clifford, how thy words revive my
heart !

York. Henry of Lancaster, resign thy crown :—
What mutter you, or what conspire you, lords ?

War. Do right unto this princely duke of York ;
Or I will fill the house with armed men,
And, o'er the chair of state, where now he sits,
Write up his title with usurping blood.
[*He stamps, and the Soldiers show themselves.*

K. Hen. My lord of Warwick, hear me but one
word :—
Let me, for this my life-time, reign as king.

York. Confirm the crown to me, and to mine
heirs,
And thou shalt reign in quiet while thou liv'st.

K. Hen. I am content : Richard Plantagenet,
Enjoy the kingdom after my decease.

Clif. What wrong is this unto the prince your
son !

War. What good is this to England, and himself !

West. Base, fearful, and despairing Henry !

Clif. How hast thou injur'd both thyself and us !

West. I cannot stay to hear these articles.

North. Nor I.

Clif. Come, cousin, let us tell the queen these
news.

West. Farewell, faint-hearted and degenerate
king,
In whose cold blood no spark of honour bides.

North. Be thou a prey unto the house of York,
And die in bands for this unmanly deed !

Clif. In dreadful war may'st thou be over-
come !
Or live in peace, abandon'd, and despis'd !
[*Exeunt* NORTH., CLIF., *and* WEST.

War. Turn this way, Henry, and regard them
not.

Exe. They seek revenge, and therefore will not
yield.

K. Hen. Ah, Exeter!

War. Why should you sigh, my lord?

K. Hen. Not for myself, lord Warwick, but my
    son,

Whom I unnaturally shall disinherit.
But, be it as it may :—I here entail
The crown to thee, and to thine heirs for ever;
Conditionally, that here thou take an oath
To cease this civil war, and, whilst I live,
To honour me as thy king and sovereign;
And neither by treason, nor hostility,
To seek to put me down, and reign thyself.

    York. This oath I willingly take, and will per-
       form.   [*Coming from the Throne.*

War. Long live king Henry!—Plantagenet,
    embrace him.

K. Hen. And long live thou, and these thy for-
    ward sons!

York. Now York and Lancaster are reconcil'd.

Exe. Accurs'd be he, that seeks to make them
    foes! [*Senet. The Lords come forward.*

York. Farewell, my gracious lord; I 'll to my
    castle.

War. And I 'll keep London, with my soldiers.

Norf. And I to Norfolk, with my followers.

Mont. And I unto the sea, from whence I came.
    [*Exeunt* York, *and his Sons,* War., Nor.,
      Mont., *Soldiers, and Attend.*

K. Hen. And I, with grief and sorrow, to the
    court.

Enter Queen Margaret *and the* Prince of
    Wales.

Exe. Here comes the queen, whose looks bewray her anger:
I 'll steal away.

    K. Hen. Exeter, so will I.   [*Going.*

Q. Mar. Nay, go not from me, I will follow
    thee.

K. Hen. Be patient, gentle queen, and I will
    stay.

Q. Mar. Who can be patient in such extremes?
Ah, wretched man! 'would I had died a maid,
And never seen thee, never borne thee son,
Seeing thou hast prov'd so unnatural a father!
Hath he deserv'd to lose his birthright thus?
Hadst thou but lov'd him half so well as I;
Or felt that pain which I did for him once;
Or nourish'd him, as I did with my blood;
Thou wouldst have left thy dearest heart-blood
    there,
Rather than made that savage duke thine heir,

And disinherited thine only son.

Prince. Father, you cannot disinherit me:
If you be king, why should not I succeed?

    K. Hen. Pardon me, Margaret;—pardon me,
      sweet son :—

The earl of Warwick, and the duke, enforc'd me.

Q. Mar. Enforc'd thee! art thou king, and
    wilt be forc'd?

I shame to hear thee speak. Ah, timorous wretch!
Thou hast undone thyself, thy son, and me;
And given unto the house of York such head,
As thou shalt reign but by their sufferance.
To entail him and his heirs unto the crown,
What is it, but to make thy sepulchre,
And creep into it far before thy time?
Warwick is chancellor, and the lord of Calais;
Stern Faulconbridge commands the narrow seas;
The duke is made protector of the realm;
And yet shalt thou be safe? such safety finds
The trembling lamb, environed with wolves.
Had I been there, which am a silly woman,
The soldiers should have toss'd me on their pikes,
Before I would have granted to that act.
But thou prefer'st thy life before thine honour:
And seeing thou dost, I here divorce myself,
Both from thy table, Henry, and thy bed,
Until that act of parliament be repeal'd,
Whereby my son is disinherited.
The northern lords, that have forsworn thy colours,
Will follow mine, if once they see them spread:
And spread they shall be; to thy foul disgrace,
And utter ruin of the house of York.
Thus do I leave thee;—Come, son, let 's away;
Our army 's ready; come, we 'll after them.

    K. Hen. Stay, gentle Margaret, and hear me
    speak.

Q. Mar. Thou hast spoke too much already;
    get thee gone.

K. Hen. Gentle son Edward, thou wilt stay
    with me?

Q. Mar. Ay, to be murder'd by his enemies.

Prince. When I return with victory from the
    field,

I 'll see your grace: till then, I 'll follow her.

Q. Mar. Come, son, away; we may not linger
    thus.

    [*Exeunt* Q. Mar., *and the Prince.*

K. Hen. Poor queen! how love to me, and to
    her son,

Hath made her break out into terms of rage!
Reveng'd may she be on that hateful duke;
Whose haughty spirit, winged with desire,

Will cost my crown, and, like an empty eagle,
Tire on the flesh of me, and of my son!
The loss of those three lords torments my heart;'
I 'll write unto them, and entreat them fair;—
Come, cousin, you shall be the messenger.

   Exe. And I, I hope, shall reconcile them all.
                        Exeunt.

SCENE II.—*A Room in* Sandal *Castle, near*
Wakefield, *in Yorkshire.*

Enter EDWARD, RICHARD, *and* MONTAGUE.

   Rich. Brother, though I be youngest, give me
     leave.
   Edw. No, I can better play the orator.
   Mont. But I have reasons strong and forcible.

Enter YORK.

   York. Why, how now, sons and brother,' at a
     strife?
What is your quarrel? how began it first?
   Edw. No quarrel, but a slight contention.
   York. About what?
   Rich. About that which concerns your grace,
     and us;
The crown of England, father, which is yours.
   York. Mine, boy? not till king Henry be dead.
   Rich. Your right depends not on his life, or
     death.
   Edw. Now you are heir, therefore enjoy it now:
By giving the house of Lancaster leave to breathe,
It will outrun you, father, in the end.
   York. I took an oath, that he should quietly
     reign.
   Edw. But, for a kingdom, any oath may be
     broken:
I 'll break a thousand oaths, to reign one year.
   Rich. No; God forbid your grace should be
     forsworn.
   York. I shall be, if I claim by open war.
   Rich. I 'll prove the contrary, if you 'll hear me
     speak.
   York. Thou canst not, son; it is impossible.
   Rich. An oath is of no moment, being not
     took
Before a true and lawful magistrate,
That hath authority over him that swears;
Henry had none, but did usurp the place;
Then, seeing 't was he that made you to depose,
Your oath, my lord, is vain and frivolous.
Therefore to arms. And, father, do but think,
How sweet a thing it is to wear a crown;

Within whose circuit is Elysium,
And all that poets feign of bliss and joy.
Why do we linger thus? I cannot rest,
Until the white rose, that I wear, be dyed
Even in the lukewarm blood of Henry's heart.
   York. Richard, enough; I will be king, or die—
Brother, thou shalt to London presently,
And whet on Warwick to this enterprise.—
Thou, Richard, shalt unto the duke of Norfolk,
And tell him privily of our intent.—
You, Edward, shall unto my lord Cobham,
With whom the Kentishmen will willingly rise:
In them I trust; for they are soldiers,
Witty and courteous, liberal, full of spirit.—
While you are thus employ'd, what resteth more,
But that I seek occasion how to rise;
And yet the king not privy to my drift,
Nor any of the house of Lancaster?

Enter a Messenger.

But, stay: What news? Why com'st thou in such
     post?
   Mess. The queen, with all the northern earls
     and lords,
Intend here to besiege you in your castle:
She is hard by with twenty thousand men;
And therefore fortify your hold, my lord.
   York. Ay, with my sword. What! think'st
     thou, that we fear them?
Edward and Richard, you shall stay with me;—
My brother Montague shall post to London:
Let noble Warwick, Cobham, and the rest,
Whom we have left protectors of the king,
With powerful policy strengthen themselves,
And trust not simple Henry, nor his oaths.
   Mont. Brother, I go; I 'll win them, fear it
     not:
And thus most humbly I do take my leave. [*Exit.*

Enter SIR JOHN *and* SIR HUGH MORTIMER.

   York. Sir John, and Sir Hugh Mortimer, mine
     uncles!
You are come to Sandal in a happy hour;
The army of the queen mean to besiege us.
   Sir John. She shall not need, we 'll meet her in
     the field.
   York. What, with five thousand men?
   Rich. Ay, with five hundred, father, for a need.
A woman 's general: What should we fear?
                   [*A March afar off.*
   Edw. I hear their drums; let 's set our men in
     order:

And issue forth, and bid them battle straight.

York. Five men to twenty!—though the odds be great,
I doubt not, uncle, of our victory.
Many a battle have I won in France,
When as the enemy hath been ten to one;
Why should I not now have the like success?
                       [*Alarum. Exeunt.*

SCENE III.—*Plains near Sandal Castle.*

Alarums: Excursions. Enter RUTLAND, *and his Tutor.*

Rut. Ah, whither shall I fly, to 'scape their hands!
Ah, tutor! look, where bloody Clifford comes!

Enter CLIFFORD, *and Soldiers.*

Clif. Chaplain, away! thy priesthood saves thy life.
As for the brat of this accursed duke,
Whose father slew my father,—he shall die.

Tut. And I, my lord, will bear him company.

Clif. Soldiers, away with him.

Tut. Ah, Clifford! murder not this innocent child,
Lest thou be hated both of God and man.
            [*Exit, forced off by Soldiers.*

Clif. How now! is he dead already? Or, is it fear,
That makes him close his eyes?—I'll open them.

Rut. So looks the pent-up lion o'er the wretch
That trembles under his devouring paws:
And so he walks, insulting o'er his prey;
And so he comes to rend his limbs asunder.
Ah, gentle Clifford, kill me with thy sword,
And not with such a cruel threat'ning look.
Sweet Clifford, hear me speak before I die:—
I am too mean a subject for thy wrath,
Be thou reveng'd on men, and let me live.

Clif. In vain thou speak'st, poor boy; my father's blood
Hath stopp'd the passage where thy words should enter.

Rut. Then let my father's blood open it again;
He is a man, and, Clifford, cope with him.

Clif. Had I thy brethren here, their lives, and thine,
Were not revenge sufficient for me;
No, if I digg'd up thy forefathers' graves,
And hung their rotten coffins up in chains,
It could not slake mine ire, nor ease my heart.

The sight of any of the house of York
Is as a fury to torment my soul;
And till I root out their accursed line,
And leave not one alive, I live in hell.
Therefore——   [*Lifting his Hand.*

Rut. O, let me pray before I take my death:—
To thee I pray: Sweet Clifford, pity me!

Clif. Such pity as my rapier's point affords.

Rut. I never did thee harm: Why wilt thou slay me?

Clif. Thy father hath.

Rut.   But 't was ere I was born?
Thou hast one son, for his sake pity me;
Lest, in revenge thereof,—sith God is just,—
He be as miserably slain as I.
Ah, let me live in prison all my days;
And when I give occasion of offence,
Then let me die, for now thou hast no cause.

Clif. No cause?
Thy father slew my father; therefore, die.
               [CLIF. *stabs him.*

Rut. Dii faciant, laudis summa sit ista tuæ!   [*Dies.*

Clif. Plantagenet! I come, Plantagenet!
And this thy son's blood cleaving to my blade,
Shall rust upon my weapon, till thy blood,
Congeal'd with this, do make me wipe off both.
                    [*Exit.*

SCENE IV.—*The Same.*

Alarum. Enter YORK.

York. The army of the queen hath got the field:
My uncles both are slain in rescuing me;
And all my followers to the eager foe
Turn back, and fly, like ships before the wind,
Or lambs pursu'd by hunger-starved wolves.
My sons—God knows, what hath bechanced them:
But this I know,—they have demean'd themselves
Like men born to renown, by life, or death.
Three times did Richard make a lane to me;
And thrice cried,—"Courage, father! fight it out!"
And full as oft came Edward to my side,
With purple faulchion, painted to the hilt
In blood of those that had encounter'd him:
And when the hardiest warriors did retire,
Richard cried,—"Charge! and give no foot of ground!"
And cried,—"A crown, or else a glorious tomb!
A sceptre, or an earthly sepulchre!"
With this, we charg'd again: but, out, alas!

We lodg'd again; as I have seen a swan
With bootless labour swim against the tide,
And spend her strength with over-matching waves.
　　　　　　　　　　[*A short Alarum within.*
Ah, hark! the fatal followers do pursue;
And I am faint, and cannot fly their fury:
And, were I strong, I would not shun their fury:
The sands are number'd that make up my life;
Here must I stay, and here my life must end.

Enter QUEEN MARGARET, CLIFFORD, NORTHUM-
　　　BERLAND, *and* Soldiers.

Come, bloody Clifford,—rough Northumberland,—
I dare your quenchless fury to more rage:
I am your butt, and I abide your shot.
　　North. Yield to our mercy, proud Plantagenet.
　　Clif. Ay, to such mercy, as his ruthless arm,
With downright payment, show'd unto my father.
Now Phaeton hath tumbled from his car,
And made an evening at the noontide prick.
　　York. My ashes, as the phoenix, may bring
　　　forth
A bird that will revenge upon you all:
And, in that hope, I throw mine eyes to heaven,
Scorning whate'er you can afflict me with.
Why come you not? what! multitudes, and fear?
　　Clif. So cowards fight, when they can fly no
　　　further;
So doves do peck the falcon's piercing talons;
So desperate thieves, all hopeless of their lives,
Breathe out invectives 'gainst the officers.
　　York. O, Clifford, but bethink thee once again,
And in thy thought o'er-run my former time:
And, if thou canst for blushing, view this face;
And bite thy tongue, that slanders him with cow-
　　ardice,
Whose frown hath made thee faint and fly ere this.
　　Clif. I will not bandy with thee word for word;
But buckle with thee blows, twice two for one.
　　　　　　　　　　[*Draws.*
　　Q. Mar. Hold, valiant Clifford! for a thousand
　　　causes,
I would prolong awhile the traitor's life:—
Wrath makes him deaf: speak thou, Northum-
　　berland.
　　North. Hold, Clifford; do not honour him so
　　　much,
To prick thy finger, though to wound his heart:
What valour were it, when a cur doth grin,
For one to thrust his hand between his teeth,
When he might spurn him with his foot away?
It is war's prize to take all vantages:
960

And ten to one is no impeach of valour.
　　　　　[*They lay hands on* YORK, *who struggles.*
　　Clif. Ay, ay, so strives the woodcock with the
　　　gin.
　　North. So doth the coney struggle in the net.
　　　　　　　　　　[*York is taken prisoner.*
　　York. So triumph thieves upon their conquer'd
　　　booty;
So true men yield, with robbers so o'er-match'd.
　　North. What would your grace have done unto
　　　him now?
　　Q. Mar. Brave warriors, Clifford, and North-
　　　umberland,
Come make him stand upon this molehill here;
That raught at mountains with outstretched arms,
Yet parted but the shadow with his hand.—
What! was it you, that would be England's king?
Was 't you that revell'd in our parliament,
And made a preachment of your high descent?
Where are your mess of sons to back you now?
The wanton Edward, and the lusty George?
And where's that valiant crook-back prodigy,
Dicky your boy, that, with his grumbling voice,
Was wont to cheer his dad in mutinies?
Or, with the rest, where is your darling Rutland?
Look, York; I stain'd this napkin with the blood
That valiant Clifford, with his rapier's point,
Made issue from the bosom of the boy;
And, if thine eyes can water for his death,
I give thee this to dry thy cheeks withal.
Alas, poor York! but that I hate thee deadly,
I should lament thy miserable state.
I pr'ythee, grieve, to make me merry, York;
Stamp, rave, and fret, that I may sing and dance.
What, hath thy fiery heart so parch'd thine en-
　　trails,
That not a tear can fall for Rutland's death?
Why art thou patient, man? thou shouldst be
　　mad;
And I, to make thee mad, do mock thee thus.
Thou would'st be fee'd, I see, to make me sport;
York cannot speak, unless he wear a crown.—
A crown for York;—and, lords, bow low to him.—
Hold you his hands, whilst I do set it on.—
　　　　　　　[*Putting a paper Crown on his Head.*
Ay, marry, sir, now looks he like a king!
Ay, this is he that took king Henry's chair;
And this is he was his adopted heir.—
But how is it that great Plantagenet
Is crown'd so soon, and broke his solemn oath?
As I bethink me, you should not be king,
Till our king Henry had shook hands with death.

And will you pale your head in Henry's glory,
And rob his temples of the diadem,
Now in his life, against your holy oath?
O, 'tis a fault, too, too unpardonable!—
Off with the crown; and, with the crown, his head;
And, whilst we breathe, take time to do him dead.
　Clif. That is my office, for my father's sake.
　Q. Mar. Nay, stay; let's hear the orisons he makes.
　York. She-wolf of France, but worse than wolves of France,
Whose tongue more poisons than the adder's tooth!
How ill-beseeming is it in thy sex,
To triumph like an Amazonian trull,
Upon their woes, whom fortune captivates!
But that thy face is, vizard-like, unchanging,
Made impudent with use of evil deeds,
I would essay, proud queen, to make thee blush:
To tell thee whence thou cam'st, of whom deriv'd,
Were shame enough to shame thee, wert thou not shameless.
Thy father bears the type of king of Naples,
Of both the Sicils, and Jerusalem;
Yet not so wealthy as an English yeoman.
Hath that poor monarch taught thee to insult?
It needs not, nor it boots thee not, proud queen;
Unless the adage must be verified,—
That beggars, mounted, run their horse to death.
'Tis beauty, that doth oft make women proud;
But, God he knows, thy share thereof is small:
'Tis virtue, that doth make them most admir'd;
The contrary doth make thee wonder'd at:
'Tis government, that makes them seem divine;
The want thereof makes thee abominable:
Thou art as opposite to every good,
As the Antipodes are unto us,
Or as the south to the septentrion.
O, tiger's heart, wrapp'd in a woman's hide!
How couldst thou drain the life-blood of the child,
To bid the father wipe his eyes withal,
And yet be seen to bear a woman's face?
Women are soft, mild, pitiful, and flexible;
Thou stern, obdurate, flinty, rough, remorseless.
Bid'st thou me rage? why, now thou hast thy wish:
Wouldst have me weep? why, now thou hast thy will:

For raging wind blows up incessant showers,
And, when the rage allays, the rain begins.
These tears are my sweet Rutland's obsequies:
And every drop cries vengeance for his death,—
'Gainst thee, fell Clifford,—and thee, false French woman.
　North. Beshrew me, but his passions move me so,
That hardly can I check mine eyes from tears.
　York. That face of his the hungry cannibals
Would not have touch'd, would not have stain'd with blood:
But you are more inhuman, more inexorable,—
O, ten times more,—than tigers of Hyrcania.
See, ruthless queen, a hapless father's tears:
This cloth thou dipp'dst in blood of my sweet boy,
And I with tears do wash the blood away,
Keep thou the napkin, and go boast of this:
　　　　[*He gives back the Handkerchief.*
And, if thou tell'st the heavy story right,
Upon my soul, the hearers will shed tears;
Yea, even my foes will shed fast-falling tears,
And say,—Alas, it was a piteous deed!—
There, take the crown, and, with the crown, my curse;
And, in thy need, such comfort come to thee,
As now I reap at thy too cruel hand!—
Hard-hearted Clifford, take me from the world;
My soul to heaven, my blood upon your heads.
　North. Had he been slaughter-man to all my kin,
I should not for my life but weep with him,
To see how inly sorrow gripes his soul.
　Q. Mar. What, weeping-ripe, my lord Northumberland?
Think but upon the wrong he did us all,
And that will quickly dry thy melting tears.
　Clif. Here's for my oath, here's for my father's death. [*Stabbing him.*
　Q. Mar. And here's to right our gentle-hearted king. [*Stabbing him.*
　York. Open thy gate of mercy, gracious God!
My soul flies through these wounds to seek out thee. [*Dies.*
　Q. Mar. Off with his head, and set it on York gates;
So York may overlook the town of York.
　　　　[*Exeunt.*

ACT II.

SCENE I.—*A Plain near* Mortimer's Cross *in Herefordshire.*

Drums. Enter EDWARD, *and* RICHARD, *with their Forces, marching.*

Edw. I wonder, how our princely father scap'd;
Or whether he be 'scap'd away, or no,
From Clifford's and Northumberland's pursuit;
Had he been ta'en, we should have heard the news;
Had he been slain, we should have heard the news;
Or, had he 'scap'd, methinks, we should have heard
The happy tidings of his good escape.—
How fares my brother? why is he so sad?

Rich. I cannot joy, until I be resolv'd
Where our right valiant father is become.
I saw him in the battle range about;
And watch'd him, how he singled Clifford forth.
Methought, he bore him in the thickest troop,
As doth a lion in a herd of neat:
Or as a bear, encompass'd round with dogs;
Who having pinch'd a few, and made them cry,
The rest stand all aloof, and bark at him.
So far'd our father with his enemies;
So fled his enemies my warlike father:
Methinks, 't is prize enough to be his son.
See, how the morning opes her golden gates,
And takes her farewell of the glorious sun!
How well resembles it the prime of youth,
Trimm'd like a younker, prancing to his love!

Edw. Dazzle mine eyes, or do I see three suns?

Rich. Three glorious suns, each one a perfect sun;
Not separated with the racking clouds,
But sever'd in a pale clear-shining sky.
See, see! they join, embrace, and seem to kiss,
As if they vow'd some league inviolable:
Now are they but one lamp, one light, one sun.
In this the heaven figures some event.

Edw. 'T is wondrous strange, the like yet never heard of.
I think, it cites us, brother, to the field;

That we, the sons of brave Plantagenet,
Each one already blazing by our meeds,
Should, notwithstanding, join our lights together,
And over-shine the earth, as this the world.
Whate'er it bodes, henceforward will I bear
Upon my target three fair shining suns.

Rich. Nay, bear three daughters;—by your leave I speak it,
You love the breeder better than the male.

Enter a Messenger.

But what art thou, whose heavy looks foretel
Some dreadful story hanging on thy tongue?

Mess. Ah, one that was a woful looker on,
When as the noble duke of York was slain,
Your princely father, and my loving lord.

Edw. O, speak no more! for I have heard too much.

Rich. Say how he died, for I will hear it all.

Mess. Environed he was with many foes;
And stood against them as the hope of Troy
Against the Greeks, that would have enter'd Troy.
But Hercules himself must yield to odds;
And many strokes, though with a little axe,
Hew down and fell the hardest-timber'd oak.
By many hands your father was subdu'd;
But only slaughter'd by the ireful arm
Of unrelenting Clifford, and the queen:
Who crown'd the gracious duke in high despite;
Laugh'd in his face; and, when with grief he wept,
The ruthless queen gave him, to dry his cheeks,
A napkin steeped in the harmless blood
Of sweet young Rutland, by rough Clifford slain:
And, after many scorns, many foul taunts,
They took his head, and on the gates of York,
They set the same; and there it doth remain,
The saddest spectacle that e'er I view'd.

Edw. Sweet duke of York, our prop to lean upon;
Now thou art gone, we have no staff, no stay!—
O Clifford, boist'rous Clifford, thou hast slain
The flower of Europe for his chivalry;
And treacherously hast thou vanquish'd him,

962

For, hand to hand, he would have vanquish'd
   thee!—
Now my soul's palace is become a prison:
Ah, would she break from hence! that this my
   body
Might in the ground be closed up in rest:
For never henceforth shall I joy again,
Never, O never, shall I see more joy.

   Rich. I cannot weep; for all my body's moist-
   ure
Scarce serves to quench my furnace-burning heart:
Nor can my tongue unload my heart's great bur-
   den;
For self-same wind, that I should speak withal,
Is kindling coals, that fire all my breast,
And burn me up with flames, that tears would
   quench.
To weep, is to make less the depth of grief:
Tears, then, for babes; blows, and revenge, for
   me!—
Richard, I bear thy name, I'll venge thy death,
Or die renowned by attempting it.

   Edw. His name that valiant duke hath left
   with thee;
His dukedom and his chair with me is left.

   Rich. Nay, if thou be that princely eagle's bird,
Show thy descent by gazing 'gainst the sun:
For chair and dukedom, throne and kingdom say;
Either that is thine, or else thou wert not his.

March.   *Enter* WARWICK *and* MONTAGUE, *with
   Forces.*

   War. How now, fair lords? What fare? what
   news abroad?

   Rich. Great lord of Warwick, if we should re-
   count
Our baleful news, and, at each word's deliverance,
Stab poniards in our flesh till all were told,
The words would add more anguish than the
   wounds.
O valiant lord, the duke of York is slain.

   Edw. O Warwick! Warwick! that Plantage-
   net,
Which held thee dearly, as his soul's redemption,
Is by the stern lord Clifford done to death.

   War. Ten days ago I drown'd these news in
   tears:
And now, to add more measure to your woes,
I come to tell you things since then befall'n.
After the bloody fray at Wakefield fought,
Where your brave father breath'd his latest gasp,
Tidings, as swiftly as the posts could run,

Were brought me of your loss, and his depart.
I then in London, keeper of the king,
Muster'd my soldiers, gather'd flocks of friends,
And very well appointed, as I thought,
March'd towards Saint Alban's to intercept the
   queen,
Bearing the king in my behalf along:
For by my scouts I was advértised,
That she was coming with a full intent
To dash our late decree in parliament,
Touching king Henry's oath, and your succession.
Short tale to make,—we at Saint Alban's met,
Our battles join'd, and both sides fiercely fought:
But, whether 't was the coldness of the king,
Who look'd full gently on his warlike queen,
That robb'd my soldiers of their hated spleen;
Or whether 't was report of her success;
Or more than common fear of Clifford's rigour,
Who thunders to his captives—blood and death,
I cannot judge: but, to conclude with truth,
Their weapons like to lightning came and went;
Our soldiers'—like the night-owl's lazy flight,
Or like a lazy thrasher with a flail,—
Fell gently down, as if they struck their friends.
I cheer'd them up with justice of our cause,
With promise of high pay, and great rewards:
But all in vain; they had no heart to fight,
And we, in them, no hope to win the day,
So that we fled; the king, unto the queen;
Lord George your brother, Norfolk, and myself,
In haste, post-haste, are come to join with you;
For in the marches here, we heard you were,
Making another head to fight again.

   Edw. Where is the duke of Norfolk, gentle
   Warwick?
And when came George from Burgundy to Eng-
   land?

   War. Some six miles off the duke is with the
   soldiers:
And for your brother,—he was lately sent
From your kind aunt, duchess of Burgundy,
With aid of soldiers to this needful war.

   Rich. 'T was odds, belike, when valiant Warwick
   fled:
Oft have I heard his praises in pursuit,
But ne'er, till now, his scandal of retire.

   War. Nor now my scandal, Richard, dost thou
   hear:
For thou shalt know, this strong right hand of
   mine
Can pluck the diadem from faint Henry's head,
And wring the awful sceptre from his fist;

Were he as famous and as bold in war,
As he is fam'd for mildness, peace, and prayer
 Rich. I know it well, lord Warwick: blame me
  not ;
'T is love, I bear thy glories, makes me speak.
But, in this troublous time, what's to be done ?
Shall we go throw away our coats of steel,
And wrap our bodies in black mourning gowns,
Numb'ring our Ave-Maries with our beads ?
Or shall we on the helmets of our foes
Tell our devotion with revengeful arms ?
If for the last, say—Ay, and to it, lords.
 War. Why, therefore Warwick came to seek
  you out ;
And therefore comes my brother Montague.
Attend me, lords. The proud insulting queen,
With Clifford, and the haught Northumberland,
And of their feather, many more proud birds,
Have wrought the easy-melting king like wax.
He swore consent to your succession,
His oath enrolled in the parliament ;
And now to London all the crew are gone,
To frustrate both his oath, and what beside
May make against the house of Lancaster.
Their power, I think, is thirty thousand strong ;
Now, if the help of Norfolk, and myself,
With all the friends that thou, brave earl of March,
Amongst the loving Welshmen canst procure,
Will but amount to five and twenty thousand,
Why, *Via !* to London will we march amain ;
And once again bestride our foaming steeds,
And once again cry—Charge upon our foes !
But never once again turn back, and fly.
 Rich. Ay, now, methinks, I hear great War-
  wick speak :
Ne'er may he live to see a sunshine day,
That cries—Retire, if Warwick bid him stay.
 Edw. Lord Warwick, on thy shoulder will I
  lean :
And when thou fall'st, (as God forbid the hour !)
Must Edward fall, which peril heaven forefend !
 War. No longer earl of March, but duke of York ;
The next degree is, England's royal throne ;
For king of England shalt thou be proclaim'd
In every borough as we pass along ;
And he that throws not up his cap for joy,
Shall for the fault make forfeit of his head.
King Edward,—valiant Richard,—Montague,—
Stay we no longer dreaming of renown,
But sound the trumpets, and about our task.
 Rich. Then, Clifford, were thy heart as hard as
  steel,
964

(As thou hast shown it flinty by thy deeds,)
I come to pierce it,—or to give thee mine.
 Edw. Then strike up, drums ;—God, and Saint
  George, for us !

   Enter a Messenger.

 War. How now ! what news !
 Mess. The duke of Norfolk sends you word by
  me,
The queen is coming with a puissant host ;
And craves your company for speedy counsel.
 War. Why then it sorts, brave warriors : Let's
  away.   [*Exeunt.*

   SCENE II.—*Before York.*

Enter KING HENRY, QUEEN MARGARET, *the*
PRINCE OF WALES, CLIFFORD, *and* NORTHUM-
BERLAND, *with Forces.*

 Q. Mar. Welcome, my lord, to this brave town
  of York.
Yonder 's the head of that arch enemy,
That sought to be encompass'd with your crown ?
Doth not the object cheer your heart, my lord ?
 K. Hen. Ay, as the rocks cheer them that fear
  their wreck ;—
To see this sight, it irks my very soul.—
Withhold revenge, dear God ! 't is not my fault,
Not wittingly have I infring'd my vow.
 Clif. My gracious liege, this too much lenity
And harmful pity, must be laid aside.
To whom do lions cast their gentle looks ?
Not to the beast that would usurp their den.
Whose hand is that the forest bear doth lick ?
Not his, that spoils her young before her face.
Who 'scapes the lurking serpent's mortal sting ?
Not he, that sets his foot upon her back.
The smallest worm will turn, being trodden on ;
And doves will peck, in safeguard of their brood
Ambitious York did level at thy crown,
Thou smiling, while he knit his angry brows :
He, but a duke, would have his son a king,
And raise his issue, like a loving sire ;
Thou, being a king, bless'd with a goodly son,
Didst yield consent to disinherit him,
Which argued thee a most unloving father.
Unreasonable creatures feed their young :
And though man's face be fearful to their eyes,
Yet, in protection of their tender ones,
Who hath not seen them (even with those wings
Which sometime they have us'd with fearful
  flight,)

Make war with him that climb'd unto their nest.
Offering their own lives in their young's defence?
For shame, my liege, make them your precedent!
Were it not pity that this goodly boy
Should lose his birthright by his father's fault;
And long hereafter say unto his child,—
"What my great-grandfather and grandsire got,
My careless father fondly gave away?"
Ah, what a shame were this! Look on the boy;
And let his manly face, which promiseth
Successful fortune, steel thy melting heart,
To hold thine own, and leave thine own with him.

K. Hen. Full well hath Clifford play'd the orator,
Inferring arguments of mighty force.
But, Clifford, tell me, didst thou never hear,—
That things ill got had ever bad success?
And happy always was it for that son,
Whose father for his hoarding went to hell.
I'd leave my son his virtuous deeds behind;
And 'would, my father had left me no more!
For all the rest is held at such a rate,
As brings a thousand-fold more care to keep,
Than in possession any jot of pleasure.
Ah, cousin York! 'would thy best friends did
    know,
How it doth grieve me that thy head is here!

Q. Mar. My lord, cheer up your spirits; our
    foes are nigh,
And this soft carriage makes your followers faint.
You promis'd knighthood to our forward son;
Unsheath your sword, and dub him presently.—
Edward, kneel down.

K. Hen. Edward Plantagenet, arise a knight;
And learn this lesson,—Draw thy sword in right.
Prince. My gracious father, by your kingly
    leave,
I'll draw it as apparent to the crown,
And in that quarrel use it to the death.
Clif. Why, that is spoken like a toward prince.

Enter a Messenger.

Mess. Royal commanders, be in readiness:
For, with a band of thirty thousand men,
Comes Warwick, backing of the duke of York!
And, in the towns as they do march along,
Proclaims him king, and many fly to him:
Darraign your battle, for they are at hand.
Clif. I would, your highness would depart the
    field;
The queen hath best success when you are absent.
Q. Mar. Ay, good my lord, and leave us to
    our fortune.

K. Hen. Why, that's my fortune too: there
    fore I'll stay.
North. Be it with resolution then to fight.
Prince. My royal father, cheer these noble
    lords,
And hearten those that fight in your defence:
Unsheath your sword, good father; cry—"Saint
    George!"

March. Enter EDWARD, GEORGE, RICHARD, WAR-
WICK, NORFOLK, MONTAGUE, *and Soldiers.*

Edw. Now, perjur'd Henry! wilt thou kneel for
    grace,
And set thy diadem upon my head;
Or bide the mortal fortune of the field?
Q. Mar. Go, rate thy minions, proud insulting
    boy!
Becomes it thee to be thus bold in terms,
Before thy sovereign, and thy lawful king?
Edw. I am his king, and he should bow his
    knee;
I was adopted heir by his consent:
Since when, his oath is broke; for, as I hear,
You—that are king, though he do wear the
    crown,—
Have caus'd him, by new act of parliament,
To blot me out, and put his own son in.
Clif. And reason too;
Who should succeed the father, but the son?
Rich. Are you there, butcher?—O, I cannot
    speak!
Clif. Ay, crook-back; here I stand, to answer
    thee,
Or any he the proudest of thy sort.
Rich. 'T was you that kill'd young Rutland, was
    it not?
Clif. Ay, and old York, and yet not satisfied.
Rich. For God's sake, lords, give signal to the
    fight.
War. What say'st thou, Henry, wilt thou yield
    the crown?
Q. Mar. Why, how now, long-tongu'd War-
    wick! dare you speak?
When you and I met at Saint Albans last,
Your legs did better service than your hands.
War. Then 't was my turn to fly, and now 't is
    thine.
Clif. You said so much before, and yet you fled.
War. 'T was not your valour, Clifford, drove
    me thence.
North. No, nor your manhood, that durst make
    you stay.

Rich. Northumberland, I hold thee reverent-
ly ;—
Break off the parle ; for scarce I can refrain
The execution of my big-swoln heart
Upon that Clifford, that cruel child-killer.

    Clif. I slew thy father: Call'st thou him a
child ?

    Rich. Ay, like a dastard, and a treacherous
coward,
As thou didst kill our tender brother Rutland ;
But, ere sun-set, I 'll make thee curse the deed.

    K. Hen. Have done with words, my lords, and
hear me speak.

    Q. Mar. Defy them then, or else hold close thy
lips.

    K. Hen. I pr'ythee, give no limits to my tongue;
I am a king, and privileg'd to speak.

    Clif. My liege, the wound, that bred this meet-
ing here,
Cannot be cur'd by words : therefore be still.

    Rich. Then, executioner, unsheath thy sword :
By Him that made us all, I am resolv'd,
That Clifford's manhood lies upon his tongue.

    Edw. Say, Henry, shall I have my right, or no?
A thousand men have broke their fasts to-day,
That ne'er shall dine, unless thou yield the crown.

    War. If thou deny, their blood upon thy head;
For York in justice puts his armour on.

    Prince. If that be right, which Warwick says
is right,
There is no wrong, but every thing is right.

    Rich. Whoever got thee, there thy mother
stands ;
For, well I wot, thou hast thy mother's tongue.

    Q. Mar. But thou art neither like thy sire, nor
dam ;
But like a foul mishapen stigmatic,[11]
Mark'd by the destinies to be avoided,
As venom toads, or lizards' dreadful stings.

    Rich. Iron of Naples, hid with English gilt,
Whose father bears the title of a king,
(As if a channel should be call'd the sea,)[12]
Sham'st thou not, knowing whence thou art ex-
traught,
To let thy tongue detect thy base-born heart ?

    Edw. A wisp of straw[13] were worth a thousand
crowns,
To make this shameless callet know herself,—
Helen of Greece was fairer far than thou,
Although thy husband may be Menelaus ;[14]
And ne'er was Agamemnon's brother wrong'd
By that false woman, as this king by thee.

His father revell'd in the heart of France,
And tam'd the king, and made the Dauphin
stoop ;
And, had he match'd according to his state,
He might have kept that glory to this day :
But, when he took a beggar to his bed,
And grac'd thy poor sire with his bridal day;
Even then that sunshine brew'd a shower for him,
That wash'd his father's fortunes forth of France,
And heap'd sedition on his crown at home.
For what hath broach'd this tumult, but thy pride !
Hadst thou been meek, our title still had slept ;
And we, in pity of the gentle king,
Had slipp'd our claim until another age.

    Geo. But, when we saw our sunshine made thy
spring,
And that thy summer bred us no increase,
We set the axe to thy usurping root :
And though the edge hath something hit our-
selves,
Yet, know thou, since we have begun to strike,
We 'll never leave, till we have hewn thee down,
Or bath'd thy growing with our heated bloods.

    Edw. And, in this resolution, I defy thee ;
Not willing any longer conference,
Since thou deny'st the gentle king to speak.—
Sound trumpets !—let our bloody colours wave !—
And either victory, or else a grave.

    Q. Mar. Stay, Edward.

    Edw. No, wrangling woman ; we 'll no longer
stay :—
These words will cost ten thousand lives to-day.
                       [*Exeunt.*

SCENE III.—*A Field of Battle between* Towton
and Saxton *in* Yorkshire.

Alarums: Excursions. Enter WARWICK.

    War. Forspent with toil, as runners with a
race,
I lay me down a little while to breathe :
For strokes receiv'd, and many blows repaid,
Have robb'd my strong-knit sinews of their
strength,
And, spite of spite, needs must I rest awhile.

Enter EDWARD, *running.*

    Edw. Smile, gentle heaven! or strike, ungentle
death !
For this world frowns, and Edward's sun is clouded.

    War. How now, my lord ! what hap ! what
hope of good ?

Enter GEORGE.

Geo. Our hap is loss, our hope but sad despair;
Our ranks are broke, and ruin follows us:
What counsel give you, whither shall we fly?

Edw. Bootless is flight, they follow us with
    wings;
And weak we are, and cannot shun pursuit.

Enter RICHARD.

Rich. Ah, Warwick, why hast thou withdrawn
    thyself?
Thy brother's blood the thirsty earth hath drunk,
Broach'd with the steely point of Clifford's lance:
And, in the very pangs of death, he cried,—
Like to a dismal clangor heard from far,—
" Warwick, revenge! brother, revenge my death!"
So underneath the belly of their steeds,
That stain'd their fetlocks in his smoking blood,
The noble gentleman gave up the ghost.

War. Then let the earth be drunken with our
    blood;
I 'd kill my horse, because I will not fly.
Why stand we like soft-hearted women here,
Wailing our losses, whiles the foe doth rage;
And look upon, as if the tragedy
Were play'd in jest by counterfeiting actors?
Here on my knee I vow to God above,
I 'll never pause again, never stand still,
Till either death hath clos'd these eyes of mine,
Or fortune given me measure of revenge.

Edw. O Warwick, I do bend my knee with
    thine;
And, in this vow, do chain my soul to thine.—
And, ere my knee rise from the earth's cold face,
I throw my hands, mine eyes, my heart to Thee,
Thou setter up and plucker down of kings!
Beseeching Thee,—if with Thy will it stands,
That to my foes this body must be prey,
Yet that Thy brazen gates of heaven may ope,
And give sweet passage to my sinful soul!—
Now, lords, take leave until we meet again,
Where-e'er it be, in heaven, or on earth.

Rich. Brother, give me thy hand;—and, gentle,
    Warwick,
Let me embrace thee in my weary arms;
I, that never did weep, now melt with woe,
That winter should cut off our spring-time so.

War. Away, away! Once more, sweet lords,
    farewell.

Geo. Yet let us all together to our troops,
And give them leave to fly that will not stay;

And call them pillars, that will stand to us;
And, if we thrive, promise them such rewards
As victors wear at the Olympian games:
This may plant courage in their quailing breasts:
For yet is hope of life, and victory.—
Fore-slow no longer, make we hence amain.
    [*Exeunt.*

SCENE IV.—*The Same. Another Part of the
    Field.*

Excursions. Enter RICHARD *and* CLIFFORD.

Rich. Now, Clifford, I have singled thee alone:
Suppose, this arm is for the duke of York,
And this for Rutland; both bound to revenge,
Wert thou environ'd with a brazen wall.

Clif. Now, Richard, I am with thee here alone:
This is the hand, that stabb'd thy father York;
And this the hand that slew thy brother Rutland;
And here's the heart, that triumphs in their death,
And cheers these hands, that slew thy sire and
    brother,
To execute the like upon thyself;
And so, have at thee.

    [*They fight.* WAR. *enters;* CLIF. *flies.*
Rich. Nay, Warwick, single out some other
    chase;
For I myself will hunt this wolf to death. [*Exeunt.*

SCENE V.—*Another Part of the Field.*

Alarum. Enter KING HENRY.

K. Hen. This battle fares like to the morning's
    war,
When dying clouds contend with growing light;
What time the shepherd, blowing of his nails,
Can neither call it perfect day, nor night.
Now sways it this way, like a mighty sea,
Forc'd by the tide to combat with the wind;
Now sways it that way, like the self-same sea
Forc'd to retire by fury of the wind:
Sometime, the flood prevails; and then, the wind
Now, one the better; then, another best;
Both tugging to be victors, breast to breast,
Yet neither conqueror, nor conquered:
So is the equal poise of this fell war.
Here on this molehill will I sit me down.
To whom God will, there be the victory!
For Margaret my queen, and Clifford too,
Have chid me from the battle; swearing both,
They prosper best of all when I am thence.
Would I were dead! if God's good will were so;

967

For what is in this world, but grief and woe?
O God! methinks, it were a happy life,
To be no better than a homely swain;
To sit upon a hill, as I do now,
To carve out dials quaintly, point by point,
Thereby to see the minutes how they run:
How many make the hour full complete,
How many hours bring about the day,
How many days will finish up the year,
How many years a mortal man may live.
When this is known, then to divide the times:
So many hours must I tend my flock;
So many hours must I take my rest;
So many hours must I contemplate;
So many hours must I sport myself;
So many days my ewes have been with young;
So many weeks ere the poor fools will yean;
So many years ere I shall shear the fleece;
So minutes, hours, days, weeks, months, and years,
Pass'd over to the end they were created,
Would bring white hairs unto a quiet grave.
Ah, what a life were this! how sweet! how lovely!
Gives not the hawthorn bush a sweeter shade
To shepherds, looking on their silly sheep,
Than doth a rich embroider'd canopy
To kings, that fear their subjects' treachery?
O, yes it doth; a thousand fold it doth.
And to conclude,—the shepherd's homely curds,
His cold thin drink out of his leather bottle,
His wonted sleep under a fresh tree's shade,
All which secure and sweetly he enjoys,
Is far beyond a prince's delicates,
His viands sparkling in a golden cup,
His body couched in a curious bed,
When care, mistrust, and treason wait on him.

*Alarum. Enter a Son that has killed his Father,
dragging in the dead Body.*

Son. Ill blows the wind, that profits no-body.—
This man, whom hand to hand I slew in fight,
May be possessed with some store of crowns:
And I, that haply take them from him now,
May yet ere night yield both my life and them
To some man else, as this dead man doth me.—
Who 's this?—O God! it is my father's face,
Whom in this conflict I unwares have kill'd.
O heavy times, begetting such events!
From London by the king was I press'd forth;
My father, being the earl of Warwick's man,
Came on the part of York, press'd by his master;
And I, who at his hands receiv'd my life,
Have by my hands of life bereaved him.—

Pardon me, God, I knew not what I did!
And pardon, father, for I knew not thee!—
My tears shall wipe away these bloody marks;
And no more words, till they have flow'd their fill.

K. Hen. O piteous spectacle! O bloody times!
Whilst lions war, and battle for their dens,
Poor harmless lambs abide their enmity.—
Weep, wretched man, I 'll aid thee tear for tear;
And let our hearts, and eyes, like civil war,
Be blind with tears, and break o'ercharg'd with
    grief.

*Enter a Father, who has killed his Son, with the
Body in his Arms.*

Fath. Thou that so stoutly hath resisted me,
Give me thy gold, if thou hast any gold;
For I have bought it with an hundred blows.—
But let me see:—is this our foeman's face?
Ah, no, no, no, it is mine only son!—
Ah, boy, if any life be left in thee,
Throw up thine eye; see, see, what showers arise,
Blown with the windy tempest of my heart,
Upon thy wounds, that kill mine eye and heart!—
O, pity, God, this miserable age!—
What stratagems, how fell, how butcherly,
Erroneous, mutinous, and unnatural,
This deadly quarrel daily doth beget!—
O boy, thy father gave thee life too soon,
And hath bereft thee of thy life too late!!!

K. Hen. Woe above woe! grief more than
    common grief!
O, that my death would stay these ruthful deeds!—
O pity, pity, gentle heaven, pity!—
The red rose and the white are on his face,
The fatal colours of our striving houses;
The one, his purple blood right well resembles;
The other, his pale cheeks, methinks, present;
Wither one rose, and let the other flourish!
If you contend, a thousand lives must wither.

Son. How will my mother, for a father's death,
Take on with me, and ne'er be satisfied!

Fath. How will my wife, for slaughter of my
    son,
Shed seas of tears, and ne'er be satisfied!

K. Hen. How will the country, for these woful
    chances,
Misthink the king, and not be satisfied!

Son. Was ever son, so ru'd a father's death?

Fath. Was ever father, so bemoan'd a son?

K. Hen. Was ever king, so griev'd for subjects'
    woe?
Much is your sorrow; mine, ten times so much.

Son. I'll bear thee hence, where I may weep
my fill.   [*Exit, with the Body.*
Fath. These arms of mine shall be thy wind-
ing-sheet;
My heart, sweet boy, shall be thy sepulchre!
For from my heart thine image ne'er shall go,
My sighing breast shall be thy funeral bell:
And so obsequious will thy father be,¹⁸
Sad for the loss of thee, having no more,
As Priam was for all his valiant sons.
I'll bear thee hence; and let them fight that will,
For I have murder'd where I should not kill.
       [*Exit, with the Body.*

K. Hen. Sad-hearted men, much overgone with
care,
Here sits a king more woful than you are.

Alarums : Excursions. Enter QUEEN MARGARET,
PRINCE OF WALES, *and* EXETER.

Prince. Fly, father, fly! for all your friends are
fled,
And Warwick rages like a chafed bull;
Away! for death doth hold us in pursuit.

Q. Mar. Mount you, my lord, towards Berwick
post amain:
Edward and Richard, like a brace of greyhounds
Having the fearful flying hare in sight,
With fiery eyes, sparkling for very wrath,
And bloody steel grasp'd in their ireful hands,
Are at our backs; and therefore hence amain.

Exe. Away! for vengeance comes along with
them:
Nay, stay not to expostulate, make speed;
Or else come after, I'll away before.

K. Hen. Nay, take me with thee, good sweet
Exeter:
Not that I fear to stay, but love to go
Whither the queen intends. Forward; away!
       [*Exeunt.*

SCENE VI.—*The Same.*

A loud Alarum. Enter CLIFFORD, *wounded.*

Clif. Here burns my candle out, ay, here it dies,
Which, while it lasted, gave king Henry light.
O, Lancaster! I fear thy overthrow,
More than my body's parting with my soul.
My love, and fear, glew'd many friends to thee;
And, now I fall, thy tough commixtures melt,
Impairing Henry, strength'ning mis-proud York,
The common people swarm like summer flies:
And whither fly the gnats, but to the sun?

And who shines now but Henry's enemies?
O Phœbus! hadst thou never given consent
That Phaeton should check thy fiery steeds,
Thy burning car never had scorch'd the earth:
And, Henry, had'st thou sway'd as kings should
do,
Or as thy father, and his father, did,
Giving no ground unto the house of York,
They never then had sprung like summer flies;
I, and ten thousand in this luckless realm,
Had left no mourning widows for our death,
And thou this day hadst kept thy chair in peace.
For what doth cherish weeds but gentle air?
And what makes robbers bold, but too much
lenity?
Bootless are plaints, and cureless are my wounds;
No way to fly, nor strength to hold out flight:
The foe is merciless, and will not pity;
For, at their hands, I have deserv'd no pity.
The air hath got into my deadly wounds,
And much effuse of blood doth make me faint:—
Come, York, and Richard, Warwick, and the rest;
I stabb'd your father's bosom, split my breast.
       [*He faints.*

Alarum and Retreat. Enter EDWARD, GEORGE,
RICHARD, MONTAGUE, WARWICK, *and* Soldiers.

Edw. Now, breathe we, lords; good fortune
bids us pause,
And smooth the frowns of war with peaceful
looks,—
Some troops pursue the bloody-minded queen;—
That led calm Henry, though he were a king,
As doth a sail, fill'd with a fretting gust,
Command an argosy to stem the waves.
But think you, lords, that Clifford fled with them?

War. No, 't is impossible he should escape:
For, though before his face I speak the words,
Your brother Richard mark'd him for the grave:
And, wheresoe'er he is, he's surely dead.
       [CLIF. *groans and dies.*

Edw. Whose soul is that which takes her heavy
leave?

Rich. A deadly groan, like life and death's departing.

Edw. See who it is: and, now the battle's
ended,
If friend, or foe, let him be gently us'd.

Rich. Revoke that doom of mercy, for 't is Clif-
ford;
Who not contented that he lopp'd the branch
In hewing Rutland when his leaves put forth,

But set his murdering knife unto the root
From whence that tender spray did sweetly spring;
I mean, our princely father, duke of York.

War. From off the gates of York fetch down
the head,
Your father's head, which Clifford placed there:
Instead whereof, let this supply the room;
Measure for measure must be answered.

Edw. Bring forth that fatal screech-owl to our
house,
That nothing sung but death to us and ours:
Now death shall stop his dismal threatening sound,
And his ill-boding tongue no more shall speak.

[*Attendants bring the Body forward.*

War. I think his understanding is bereft:—
Speak, Clifford, dost thou know who speaks to
thee?
Dark cloudy death o'ershades his beams of life,
And he nor sees, nor hears us what we say.

Rich. O, 'would he did! and so, perhaps, he doth:
'T is but his policy to counterfeit,
Because he would avoid such bitter taunts
Which in the time of death he gave our father.

Geo. If so thou think'st, vex him with eager
words.

Rich. Clifford, ask mercy, and obtain no grace.

Edw. Clifford, repent in bootless penitence.

War. Clifford, devise excuses for thy faults.

Geo. While we devise fell tortures for thy faults.

Rich. Thou didst love York, and I am son to
York.

Edw. Thou pitied'st Rutland, I will pity thee.

Geo. Where 's captain Margaret, to fence you
now?

War. They mock thee, Clifford! swear as thou
wast wont.

Rich. What, not an oath? nay, then the world
goes hard,

When Clifford cannot spare his friends an oath:—
I know by that, he 's dead; And, by my soul,
If this right hand would buy two hours' life,
That I in all despite might rail at him,
This hand should chop it off; and with the issuing
blood
Stifle the villain, whose unstanched thirst
York and young Rutland could not satisfy.

War. Ay, but he 's dead: Off with the traitor's
head,
And rear it in the place your father's stands,—
And now to London with triumphant march,
There to be crowned England's royal king.
From whence shall Warwick cut the sea to France,
And ask the lady Bona for thy queen:
So shalt thou sinew both these lands together;
And, having France thy friend, thou shalt not
dread
The scatter'd foe, that hopes to rise again;
For though they cannot greatly sting to hurt,
Yet look to have them buzz, to offend thine ears.
First, will I see the coronation;
And then to Brittany I 'll cross the sea,
To effect this marriage, so it please my lord.

Edw. Even as thou wilt, sweet Warwick, let
it be:
For on thy shoulder do I build my seat;
And never will I undertake the thing,
Wherein thy counsel and consent is wanting.—
Richard, I will create thee duke of Gloster;
And George, of Clarence;—Warwick, as ourself,
Shall do, and undo, as him pleaseth best.

Rich. Let me be duke of Clarence; George of
Gloster;
For Gloster's dukedom is too ominous.[19]

War. Tut, that 's a foolish observation.
Richard, be duke of Gloster: Now to London,
To see these honours in possession.   [*Exeunt*

ACT III.

SCENE I.— *A Chase in the North of* England.

*Enter Two Keepers, with Cross-bows in their
Hands.*

1st Keep. Under this thick-grown brake we 'll
shroud ourselves;

For through this laund[19] anon the deer will
come;
And in this covert will we make our stand,
Calling the principal of all the deer.

2nd Keep. I 'll stay above the hill, so both may
shoot.

1st Keep. That cannot be; the noise of thy
　cross-bow
Will scare the herd, and so my shoot is lost.
Here stand we both, and aim we at the best:
And, for the time shall not seem tedious,
I 'll tell thee what befell me on a day,
In this self-place where now we mean to stand.
　2nd Keep. Here comes a man, let 's stay till he
　be past.

Enter KING HENRY *disguised, with a Prayer-
　book.*

　K. Hen. From Scotland am I stol'n, even of
　pure love,
To greet mine own land with my wishful sight.
No, Harry, Harry, 't is no land of thine;
Thy place is fill'd, thy sceptre wrung from thee,
Thy balm wash'd off, wherewith thou wast
　anointed:
No bending knee will call thee Cæsar now,
No humble suitors press to speak for right,
No, not a man comes for redress of thee;
For how can I help them, and not myself?
　1st Keep. Ay, here 's a deer whose skin 's a
　keeper's fee:
This is the *quondam* king; let 's seize upon him.
　K. Hen. Let me embrace these four adver-
　sities;
For wise men say, it is the wisest course.
　2nd Keep. Why linger we? let us lay hands
　upon him.
　1st Keep. Forbear a while; we 'll hear a little
　more.
　K. Hen. My queen, and son, are gone to France
　for aid;
And, as I hear, the great commanding Warwick
Is thither gone, to crave the French king's sister
To wife for Edward: If this news be true,
Poor queen, and son, your labour is but lost;
For Warwick is a subtle orator,
And Lewis a prince soon won with moving words.
By this account, then, Margaret may win him;
For she 's a woman to be pitied much:
Her sighs will make a battery in his breast;
Her tears will pierce into a marble heart;
The tiger will be mild, while she doth mourn;
And Nero will be tainted with remorse,
To hear, and see, her plaints, her brinish tears.
Ay, but she 's come to beg; Warwick, to give:
She, on his left side, craving aid for Henry;
He, on his right, asking a wife for Edward.
She weeps, and says—her Henry is depos'd;

He smiles, and says—his Edward is install'd;
That she, poor wretch, for grief can speak no more
Whiles Warwick tells his title, smooths the wrong,
Inferreth arguments of mighty strength;
And, in conclusion, wins the king from her,
With promise of his sister, and what else,
To strengthen and support king Edward's place.
O Margaret, thus 't will be; and thou, poor soul,
Art then forsaken, as thou went'st forlorn.
　2nd Keep. Say, what art thou, that talk'st of
　kings and queens?
　K. Hen. More than I seem, and less than I was
　born to:
A man at least, for less I should not be;
And men may talk of kings, and why not I?
　2nd Keep. Ay, but thou talk'st as if thou wert
　a king.
　K. Hen. Why, so I am, in mind; and that 's
　enough.
　2nd Keep. But, if thou be a king, where is thy
　crown?
　K. Hen. My crown is in my heart, not on my
　head;
Not deck'd with diamonds, and Indian stones,
Nor to be seen: my crown is call'd, content;
A crown it is, that seldom kings enjoy.
　2nd Keep. Well, if you be a king crown'd with
　content,
Your crown content, and you, must be contented
To go along with us: for, as we think,
You are the king, king Edward hath depos'd;
And we his subjects, sworn in all allegiance,
Will apprehend you as his enemy.
　K. Hen. But did you never swear, and break
　an oath?
　2nd Keep. No, never such an oath, nor will not
　now.
　K. Hen. Where did you dwell, when I was king
　of England?
　2nd Keep. Here in this country, where we now
　remain.
　K. Hen. I was anointed king at nine months
　old;
My father and my grandfather, were kings;
And you were sworn true subjects unto me:
And, tell me then, have you not broke your oaths?
　1st Keep. No;
For we were subjects, but while you were king.
　K. Hen. Why, am I dead? do I not breathe a
　man?
Ah, simple men, you know not what you swear.
Look, as I blow this feather from my face,

And as the air blows it to me again,
Obeying with my wind when I do blow,
And yielding to another when it blows,
Commanded always by the greater gust;
Such is the lightness of you common men.
But do not break your oaths; for, of that sin
My mild entreaty shall not make you guilty.
Go where you will, the king shall be commanded;
And be you kings; command, and I'll obey.

1st Keep. We are true subjects to the king,
king Edward.

K. Hen. So would you be again to Henry,
If he were seated as king Edward is.

1st Keep. We charge you, in God's name, and
in the king's,
To go with us unto the officers.

K. Hen. In God's name, lead; your king's
name be obey'd:
And what God will, then let your king perform;
And what he will, I humbly yield unto. [*Exeunt.*

SCENE II.—London. *A Room in the Palace.*

Enter KING EDWARD, GLOSTER, CLARENCE, *and*
LADY GREY.

K. Edw. Brother of Gloster, at Saint Albans'
field
This lady's husband, sir John Grey, was slain,
His lands then seiz'd on by the conqueror:
Her suit is now, to repossess those lands;
Which we in justice cannot deny,
Because in quarrel of the house of York
The worthy gentleman did lose his life.

Glo. Your highness shall do well, to grant her
suit;
It were dishonour, to deny it her.

K. Edw. It were no less; but yet I'll make a
pause.

Glo. Yea! is it so?
I see, the lady hath a thing to grant,
Before the king will grant her humble suit.

Clar. He knows the game: How true he keeps
the wind! [*Aside.*

Glo. Silence! [*Aside.*

K. Edw. Widow, we will consider of your suit;
And come some other time, to know our mind.

L. Grey. Right gracious lord, I cannot brook
delay:
May it please your highness to resolve me now;
And what your pleasure is, shall satisfy me.

Glo. [*Aside.*] Ay, widow? then I'll warrant
you all your lands.
972

An if what pleases him, shall pleasure you.
Fight closer, or, good faith, you'll catch a blow.

Clar. I fear her not, unless she chance to fall.
[*Aside.*

Glo. God forbid that! for he'll take vantages.
[*Aside.*

K. Edw. How many children hast thou, widow? tell me.

Clar. I think, he means to beg a child of her.
[*Aside.*

Glo. Nay, whip me then; he'll rather give her
two. [*Aside.*

L. Grey. Three, my most gracious lord.

Glo. You shall have four, if you'll be rul'd by
him. [*Aside.*

K. Edw. 'T were pity they should lose their
father's land.

L. Grey. Be pitiful, dread lord, and grant it then.

K. Edw. Lords, give us leave; I'll try this
widow's wit.

Glo. Ay, good leave have you; for you will
have leave,
Till youth take leave, and leave you to the crutch.
[*Glo. and Clar. retire to the other side.*

K. Edw. Now, tell me, madam, do you love
your children?

L. Grey. Ay, full as deadly as I love myself.

K. Edw. And would you not do much, to do
them good?

L. Grey. To do them good, I would sustain
some harm.

K. Edw. Then get your husband's lands, to do
them good.

L. Grey. Therefore I came unto your majesty.

K. Edw. I'll tell you how these lands are to
be got.

L. Grey. So shall you bind me to your highness' service.

K. Edw. What service wilt thou do me, if I
give them?

L. Grey. What you command, that rests in me
to do.

K. Edw. But you will take exceptions to my
boon.

L. Grey. No, gracious lord, except I cannot
do it.

K. Edw. Ay, but thou canst do what I mean
to ask.

L. Grey. Why, then I will do what your grace
commands.

Glo. He plies her hard; and much rain wears
the marble. [*Aside.*

Clar. As red as fire! nay, then her wax must
　melt.　　　　　　　　　　　　　[*Aside.*
L. Grey. Why stops my lord? shall I not hear
　my task?
K. Edw. An easy task; 't is but to love a king.
L. Grey. That 's soon perform'd, because I am
　a subject.
K. Edw. Why then, thy husband's lands I
　freely give thee.
L. Grey. I take my leave with many thousand
　thanks.
Glo. The match is made; she seals it with a
　curt'sy.
K. Edw. But stay thee, 't is the fruits of love
　I mean.
L. Grey. The fruits of love I mean, my loving
　liege.
K. Edw. Ay, but, I fear me, in another sense.
What love, think'st thou, I sue so much to get?
L. Grey. My love till death, my humble thanks,
　my prayers;
That love, which virtue begs, and virtue grants.
K. Edw. No, by my troth, I did not mean such
　love.
L. Grey. Why, then you mean not as I thought
　you did.
K. Edw. But now you partly may perceive my
　mind.
L. Grey. My mind will never grant what I per-
　ceive
Your highness aims at, if I aim aright.
K. Edw. To tell thee plain, I aim to lie with
　thee.
L. Grey. To tell you plain, I had rather lie in
　prison.
K. Edw. Why, then thou shalt not have thy
　husband's lands.
L. Grey. Why, then mine honesty shall be my
　dower;
For by that loss I will not purchase them.
K. Edw. Therein thou wrong'st thy children
　mightily.
L. Grey. Herein your highness wrongs both
　them and me.
But, mighty lord, this merry inclination
Accords not with the sadness of my suit:
Please you dismiss me, either with ay, or no.
K. Edw. Ay; if thou wilt say ay, to my re-
　quest;
No; if thou dost say no, to my demand.
L. Grey. Then, no, my lord. My suit is at an
　end.

Glo. The widow likes him not, she knits her
　brows.　　　　　　　　　　　　[*Aside.*
Clar. He is the bluntest wooer in Christendom.
　　　　　　　　　　　　　　　[*Aside.*
K. Edw. [*Aside.*] Her looks do argue her re-
　plete with modesty;
Her words do show her wit incomparable;
All her perfections challenge sovereignty:
One way, or other, she is for a king;
And she shall be my love, or else my queen.—
Say, that king Edward take thee for his queen?
L. Grey. 'T is better said than done, my gra-
　cious lord:
I am a subject fit to jest withal,
But far unfit to be a sovereign.
K. Edw. Sweet widow, by my state I swear to
　thee,
I speak no more than what my soul intends;
And that is, to enjoy thee for my love.
L. Grey. And that is more than I will yield
　unto:
I know, I am too mean to be your queen;
And yet too good to be your concubine.
K. Edw. You cavil, widow; I did mean, my
　queen.
L. Grey. 'T will grieve your grace, my sons
　should call you—father.
K. Edw. No more, than when thy daughters
　call thee mother.
Thou art a widow, and thou hast some children;
And, by God's mother, I, being but a bachelor,
Have other some: why, 't is a happy thing
To be the father unto many sons.
Answer no more, for thou shalt be my queen.
Glo. The ghostly father now hath done his
　shrift.　　　　　　　　　　　　[*Aside.*
Clar. When he was made a shriver, 't was for
　shift.　　　　　　　　　　　　[*Aside.*
K. Edw. Brothers, you muse what chat we two
　have had.
Glo. The widow likes it not, for she looks sad.
K. Edw. You 'd think it strange if I should
　marry her.
Clar. To whom, my lord?
K. Edw.　　　　　Why, Clarence, to myself.
Glo. That would be ten days' wonder, at the
　least.
Clar. That 's a day longer than a wonder lasts.
Glo. By so much is the wonder in extremes.
K. Edw. Well, jest on, brothers: I can tell you
　both,
Her suit is granted for her husband's lands.

Enter a Nobleman.

Nob. My gracious lord, Henry your foe is taken,
And brought your prisoner to your palace gate.

K. Edw. See, that he be conveyed unto the Tower:—
And go we, brothers, to the man that took him,
To question of his apprehension.—
Widow, go you along;—Lords, use her honourable.

[*Exeunt* K. Edw., L. Grey, Clar., *and* Lord.

Glo. Ay, Edward will use women honourably.
'Would he were wasted, marrow, bones, and all,
That from his loins no hopeful branch may spring,
To cross me from the golden time I look for!
And yet, between my soul's desire, and me,
(The lustful Edward's title buried,)
Is Clarence, Henry, and his son young Edward,
And all the unlook'd-for issue of their bodies,
To take their rooms, ere I can place myself:
A cold premeditation for my purpose!
Why, then I do but dream on sovereignty;
Like one that stands upon a promontory,
And spies a far-off shore where he would tread,
Wishing his foot were equal with his eye;
And chides the sea that sunders him from thence,
Saying—he'll lade it dry to have his way;
So do I wish the crown, being so far off;
And so I chide the means that keep me from it;
And so I say—I'll cut the causes off,
Flattering me with impossibilities.—
My eye 's too quick, my heart o'erweens too much,
Unless my hand and strength could equal them.
Well, say there is no kingdom then for Richard;
What other pleasure can the world afford!
I 'd make my heaven in a lady's lap,
And deck my body in gay ornaments,
And witch sweet ladies with my words and looks.
O miserable thought! and more unlikely,
Than to accomplish twenty golden crowns!
Why, love forswore me in my mother's womb;
And, for I should not deal in her soft laws,
She did corrupt frail nature with some bribe
To shrink mine arm up like a wither'd shrub;
To make an envious mountain on my back,
Where sits deformity to mock my body;
To shape my legs of an unequal size;
To disproportion me in every part,
Like to a chaos, or an unlick'd bear-whelp,
That carries no impression like the dam.

274

And am I then a man to be belov'd?
O, monstrous fault, to harbour such a thought!
Then, since this earth affords no joy to me,
But to command, to check, to o'erbear such
As are of better person than myself,
I 'll make my heaven—to dream upon the crown
And, whiles I live, to account this world but hell
Until my misshap'd trunk that bears this head,
Be round impaled with a glorious crown.
And yet I know not how to get the crown,
For many lives stand between me and home:
And I,—like one lost in a thorny wood,
That rents the thorns, and is rent with the thorns,
Seeking a way, and straying from the way;
Not knowing how to find the open air,
But toiling desperately to find it out,—
Torment myself to catch the English crown:
And from that torment I will free myself,
Or hew my way out with a bloody axe.
Why, I can smile, and murder while I smile;
And cry, content, to that which grieves my heart;
And wet my cheeks with artificial tears,
And frame my face to all occasions.
I 'll drown more sailors than the mermaid shall;
I 'll slay more gazers than the basilisk;
I 'll play the orator as well as Nestor,
Deceive more slily than Ulysses could,
And, like a Sinon, take another Troy:
I can add colours to the chameleon;
Change shapes, with Proteus, for advantages,
And set the murd'rous Machiavel to school.
Can I do this, and cannot get a crown?
Tut! were it further off, I 'll pluck it down. [*Exit.*

SCENE III.—France. *A Room in the Palace.*

Flourish. Enter Lewis *the French King, and*
Lady Bona, *attended; the King takes his State.*
Then enter Queen Margaret, Prince Edward
her Son, and the Earl of Oxford.

K. Lew. Fair queen of England, worthy Margaret,
[*Rising.*
Sit down with us; it ill befits thy state,
And birth, that thou should'st stand, while Lewis doth sit.

Q. Mar. No, mighty king of France; now Margaret
Must strike her sail, and learn a while to serve,
Where kings command. I was, I must confess,
Great Albion's queen in former golden days:
But now mischance hath trod my title down,
And with dishonour laid me on the ground:

Where I must take like seat unto my fortune,
And to my humble seat conform myself.

K. Lew. Why, say, fair queen, whence springs
this deep despair?

Q. Mar. From such a cause as fills mine eyes
with tears,
And stops my tongue, while heart is drown'd in
cares.

K. Lew. Whate'er it be, be thou still like thyself,
And sit thee by our side: yield not thy neck
　　　　　　　　　　[*Seats her by him.*
To fortune's yoke, but let thy dauntless mind
Still ride in triumph over all mischance.
Be plain, queen Margaret, and tell thy grief;
It shall be eas'd, if France can yield relief.

Q. Mar. Those gracious words revive my droop-
ing thoughts,
And give my tongue-tied sorrows leave to speak.
Now, therefore, be it known to noble Lewis,—
That Henry, sole possessor of my love,
Is, of a king, become a banish'd man,
And forc'd to live in Scotland a forlorn;
While proud ambitious Edward, duke of York,
Usurps the regal title, and the seat
Of England's true-anointed lawful king.
This is the cause, that I, poor Margaret,—
With this my son, prince Edward, Henry's heir,—
Am come to crave thy just and lawful aid;
And, if thou fail us, all our hope is done:
Scotland hath will to help, but cannot help;
Our people and our peers are both misled,
Our treasures seiz'd, our soldiers put to flight,
And, as thou see'st, ourselves in heavy plight.

K. Lew. Renowned queen, with patience calm
the storm,
While we bethink a means to break it off.

Q. Mar. The more we stay, the stronger grows
our foe.

K. Lew. The more I stay, the more I'll succour thee.

Q. Mar. O, but impatience waiteth on true
sorrow;
And see, where comes the breeder of my sorrow.

Enter WARWICK, *attended.*[12]

K. Lew. What's he, approacheth boldly to
our presence?

Q. Mar. Our earl of Warwick, Edward's greatest friend.

K. Lew. Welcome, brave Warwick! What
brings thee to France?
　　　[*Descending from his state.* Q. MAR. *rises.*

Q. Mar. Ay, now begins a second storm to
rise;
For this is he, that moves both wind and tide.

War. From worthy Edward, king of Albion,
My lord and sovereign, and thy vowed friend,
I come,—in kindness, and unfeigned love,—
First, to do greetings to thy royal person;
And, then, to crave a league of amity;
And, lastly, to confirm that amity
With nuptial knot, if thou vouchsafe to grant
That virtuous lady Bona, thy fair sister,
To England's king in lawful marriage.

Q. Mar. If that go forward, Henry's hope is
done.

War. And, gracious madam, [*To* BONA.] in
our king's behalf,
I am commanded, with your leave and favour,
Humbly to kiss your hand, and with my tongue
To tell the passion of my sovereign's heart;
Where fame, late entering at his heedful ears,
Hath plac'd thy beauty's image, and thy virtue.

Q. Mar. King Lewis,—and lady Bona,—hear
me speak.
Before you answer Warwick. His demand
Springs not from Edward's well-meant honest love,
But from deceit, bred by necessity;
For how can tyrants safely govern home,
Unless abroad they purchase great alliance?
To prove him tyrant, this reason may suffice,—
That Henry liveth still: but were he dead,
Yet here prince Edward stands, king Henry's son.
Look therefore, Lewis, that by this league and
marriage
Thou draw not on thy danger and dishonour:
For though usurpers sway the rule a while,
Yet heavens are just, and time suppresseth wrongs.

War. Injurious Margaret!

Prince. 　　　　　And why not queen?

War. Because thy father Henry did usurp;
And thou no more art prince, than she is queen.

Oxf. Then Warwick disannuls great John of
Gaunt,
Which did subdue the greatest part of Spain;
And, after John of Gaunt, Henry the Fourth,
Whose wisdom was a mirror to the wisest;
And, after that wise prince, Henry the Fifth,
Who by his prowess conquered all France:
From these our Henry lineally descends.

War. Oxford, how haps it, in this smooth dis-
course,
You told not, how Henry the Sixth hath lost
All that which Henry the Fifth had gotten?

Methinks, these peers of France should smile at
  that.
But for the rest,—You tell a pedigree
Of threescore and two years; a silly time
To make prescription for a kingdom's worth.
  Oxf. Why, Warwick, canst thou speak against
     thy liege,
Whom thou obey'd'st thirty and six years,
And not bewray thy treason with a blush?
  War. Can Oxford, that did ever fence the
     right,
Now buckler falsehood with a pedigree?
For shame, leave Henry, and call Edward king.
  Oxf. Call him my king, by whose injurious
     doom
My elder brother, the lord Aubrey Vere,
Was done to death? and more than so, my
     father,
Even in the downfall of his mellow'd years,
When nature brought him to the door of death?
No, Warwick, no; while life upholds this arm,
This arm upholds the house of Lancaster.
  War. And I the house of York.
  K. Lew. Queen Margaret, prince Edward, and
     Oxford,
Vouchsafe, at our request, to stand aside,
While I use further conference with Warwick.
  Q. Mar. Heaven grant, that Warwick's words
     bewitch him not!
                    [*Retiring with the* Prince *and* Oxf.
  K. Lew. Now, Warwick, tell me, even upon thy
     conscience,
Is Edward your true king? for I were loath,
To link with him that were not lawful chosen.
  War. Thereon I pawn my credit and mine
     honour.
  K. Lew. But is he gracious in the people's eye?
  War. The more, that Henry was unfortunate.
  K. Lew. Then further,—all dissembling set
     aside,
Tell me for truth the measure of his love
Unto our sister Bona.
  War.   Such it seems,
As may beseem a monarch like himself.
Myself have often heard him say, and swear,—
That this his love was an eternal plant;
Whereof the root was fix'd in virtue's ground,
The leaves and fruit maintain'd with beauty's sun;
Exempt from envy, but not from disdain,
Unless the lady Bona quit his pain.
  K. Lew. Now, sister, let us hear your firm
     resolve.

v76

Bona. Your grant, or your denial, shall be
     mine :—
Yet I confess, [*To* War.] that often ere this day,
When I have heard your king's desert recounted,
Mine ear hath tempted judgment to desire.
  K. Lew. Then, Warwick, thus,—Our sister
     shall be Edward's;
And now forthwith shall articles be drawn
Touching the jointure that your king must make,
Which with her dowry shall be counterpoised :—
Draw near, queen Margaret ; and be a witness,
That Bona shall be wife to the English king.
  Prince. To Edward, but not to the English
     king.
  Q. Mar. Deceitful Warwick ! it was thy device
By this alliance to make void my suit ;
Before thy coming, Lewis was Henry's friend.
  K. Lew. And still is friend to him and Mar-
     garet :
But if your title to the crown be weak,—
As may appear by Edward's good success,—
Then 't is but reason, that I be released
From giving aid, which late I promised.
Yet shall you have all kindness at my hand,
That your estate requires, and mine can yield.
  War. Henry now lives in Scotland, at his ease ;
Where having nothing, nothing he can lose.
And as for you yourself, our *quondam* queen,—
You have a father able to maintain you ;
And better 't were, you troubled him than France.
  Q. Mar. Peace, impudent and shameless War-
     wick, peace :
Proud setter-up and puller-down of kings !
I will not hence, till with my talk and tears,
Both full of truth, I make king Lewis behold
Thy sly conveyance, and thy lord's false love ;
For both of you are birds of self-same feather.
                    [*A Horn sounded within.*
  K. Lew. Warwick, this is some post to us, or
     thee.

                Enter a Messenger.

  Mess. My lord ambassador, these letters are for
     you ;
Sent from your brother, marquis Montague.—
These from our king unto your majesty.—
And, madam, these for you ; from whom I know
     not.
                    [*To* Mar. *They all read their Letters.*
  Oxf. I like it well, that our fair queen and mis-
     tress
Smiles at her news, while Warwick frowns at his.

Prince. Nay, mark, how Lewis stamps as he
were nettled :
I hope, all 's for the best.

K. Lew. Warwick, what are thy news ? and
yours, fair queen ?

Q. Mar. Mine, such as fill my heart with un-
hop'd joys.

War. Mine, full of sorrow and heart's discontent.

K. Lew. What! has your king married the lady
Grey ?
And now, to sooth your forgery and his,
Sends me a paper to persuade me patience ?
Is this the alliance that he seeks with France ?
Dare he presume to scorn us in this manner ?

Q. Mar. I told your majesty as much before :
This proveth Edward's love, and Warwick's
honesty.

War. King Lewis, I here protest,—in sight of
heaven,
And by the hope I have of heavenly bliss,—
That I am clear from this misdeed of Edward's ;
No more my king, for he dishonours me ;
But most himself, if he could see his shame.—
Did I forget, that by the house of York
My father came untimely to his death ?
Did I let pass the abuse done to my niece ?
Did I impale him with the regal crown ?
Did I put Henry from his native right ?
And am I guerdon'd at the last with shame ?
Shame on himself ! for my desert is honour.
And, to repair my honour lost for him,
I here renounce him, and return to Henry :
My noble queen, let former grudges pass,
And henceforth I am thy true servitor ;
I will revenge his wrong to lady Bona,
And replant Henry in his former state.

Q. Mar. Warwick, these words have turn'd my
hate to love ;
And I forgive and quite forget old faults,
And joy that thou becom'st king Henry's friend.

War. So much his friend, ay, his unfeigned
friend,
That, if king Lewis vouchsafe to furnish us
With some few bands of chosen soldiers,
I 'll undertake to land them on our coast,
And force the tyrant from his seat by war.
T is not his new-made bride shall succour him :
And as for Clarence,—as my letters tell me,
He 's very likely now to fall 'rom him ;
For matching more for wanton lust than honour,
Or than for strength and safety of our country.

Bona. Dear brother, how shall Bona be reveng'd,
But by thy help to this distressed queen ?

Q. Mar. Renowned prince, how shall poor
Henry live,
Unless thou rescue him from foul despair ?

Bona. My quarrel, and this English queen's, are
one.

War. And mine, fair lady Bona, joins with
yours.

K. Lew. And mine, with hers, and thine, and
Margaret's.
Therefore, at last, I firmly am resolv'd,
You shall have aid.

Q. Mar. Let me give humble thanks for all at
once.

K. Lew. Then, England's messenger, return in
post ;
And tell false Edward, thy supposed king,—
That Lewis of France is sending over maskers,
To revel it with him and his new bride :
Thou seest what 's past, go fear thy king withal.

Bona. Tell him, In hope he 'll prove a widower
shortly,
I 'll wear the willow garland for his sake.

Q. Mar. Tell him, My mourning weeds are laid
aside,
And I am ready to put armour on.

War. Tell him from me, That he hath done me
wrong ;
And therefore I 'll uncrown him, ere 't be long.
There 's thy reward ; be gone. [*Exit* Mess

K. Lew. But, Warwick, thou
And Oxford, with five thousand men,
Shall cross the seas, and bid false Edward battle :
And, as occasion serves, this noble queen
And prince shall follow with a fresh supply,
Yet, ere thou go, but answer me one doubt ;—
What pledge have we of thy firm loyalty ?

War. This shall assure my constant loyalty :—
That if our queen and this young prince agree,
I 'll join mine eldest daughter, and my joy,
To him forthwith in holy wedlock bands.

Q. Mar. Yes, I agree, and thank you for your
motion :—
Son Edward, she is fair and virtuous,
Therefore delay not, give thy hand to Warwick,
And, with thy hand, thy faith irrevocable,
That only Warwick's daughter shall be thine.

Prince. Yes, I accept her, for she well deserves
it ;
And here, to pledge my vow, I give my hand.
[*He gives his hand to* WAR.

K. Lew. Why stay we now? These soldiers
   shall be levied,
And thou, lord Bourbon, our high admiral,
Shalt waft them over with our royal fleet.—
I long, till Edward fall by war's mischance,
For mocking marriage with a dame of France.
             [Exeunt all but WAR.

War. I came from Edward as ambassador,
But I return his sworn and mortal foe:

Matter of marriage was the charge he gave
   me,
But dreadful war shall answer his demand.
Had he none else to make a stale, but me?
Then none but I shall turn his jest to sorrow.
I was the chief that rais'd him to the crown,
And I'll be chief to bring him down again:
Not that I pity Henry's misery,
But seek revenge on Edward's mockery.   *[Exit.*

ACT IV.

SCENE I.—London.   *A Room in the Palace.*

Enter GLOSTER, CLARENCE, SOMERSET, MONTAGUE,
   and Others.

  Glo. Now tell me, brother Clarence, what think
     you
Of this new marriage with the lady Grey?
Hath not our brother made a worthy choice?
  Clar. Alas, you know, 't is far from hence to
    France;
How could he stay till Warwick made return?
  Som. My lords, forbear this talk; here comes
    the king.

Flourish. *Enter* KING EDWARD, *attended;* LADY
   GREY, *as Queen;* PEMBROKE, STAFFORD, HAST-
   INGS, *and Others.*

  Glo. And his well-chosen bride.
  Clar. I mind to tell him plainly what I think.
  K. Edw. Now, brother of Clarence, how like
    you our choice,
That you stand pensive, as half malcontent?
  Clar. As well as Lewis of France, or the earl of
    Warwick;
Which are so weak of courage, and in judgment,
That they'll take no offence at our abuse.
  K. Edw. Suppose, they take offence without a
    cause,
They are but Lewis and Warwick: I am Edward,
Your king and Warwick's, and must have my will.
  Glo. And you shall have your will, because our
    king:
Yet hasty marriage seldom proveth well.
    978

  K. Edw. Yea, brother Richard, are you offended
    too?
  Glo. Not I:
No; God forbid, that I should wish them sever'd
Whom God hath join'd together: ay, and 't were
    pity,
To sunder them that yoke so well together.
  K. Edw. Setting your scorns, and your mislike,
    aside,
Tell me some reason, why the lady Grey
Should not become my wife, and England's
    queen:—
And you too, Somerset, and Montague,
Speak freely what you think.
  Clar. Then this is my opinion,—that king Lewis
Becomes your enemy, for mocking him
About the marriage of the lady Bona.
  Glo. And Warwick, doing what you gave in
    charge,
Is now dishonoured by this new marriage.
  K. Edw. What, if both Lewis and Warwick be
    appeas'd,
By such invention as I can devise?
  Mont. Yet to have join'd with France in such
    alliance,
Would more have strengthen'd this our commen-
    wealth
'Gainst foreign storms, than any home-bred mar-
    riage.
  Hast. Why, knows not Montague, that of itself
England is safe, if true within itself?
  Mont. Yes; but the safer, when 't is back'd with
    France.

Hast. 'T is better using France, than trusting
　　France :
Let us be back'd with God, and with the seas,
Which he hath given for fence impregnable,
And with their helps only defend ourselves ;
lu them, and in ourselves, our safety lies.

　Clar. For this one speech, lord Hastings well
　　deserves
To have the heir of the lord Hungerford.

　K. Edw. Ay, what of that ? it was my will, and
　　grant ;
And, for this once, my will shall stand for law.

　Glo. And yet, methinks, your grace hath not
　　done well,
To give the heir and daughter of lord Scales
Unto the brother of your loving bride ;
She better would have fitted me, or Clarence :
But in your bride you bury brotherhood.

　Clar. Or else you would not have bestow'd the
　　heir
Of the lord Bonville on your new wife's son,
And leave your brothers to go speed elsewhere.

　K. Edw. Alas, poor Clarence ! is it for a wife
That thou art malcontent ? I will provide thee.

　Clar. In choosing for yourself, you show'd your
　　judgment ;
Which being shallow, you shall give me leave
To play the broker in mine own behalf ;
And, to that end, I shortly mind to leave you.

　K. Edw. Leave me, or tarry, Edward will be
　　king,
And not be tied unto his brother's will.

　Q. Eliz. My lords, before it pleas'd his majesty
To raise my state to title of a queen,
Do me but right, and you must all confess
That I was not ignoble of descent,²⁸
And meaner than myself have had like fortune.
But as this title honours me and mine,
So your dislikes, to whom I would be pleasing,
Do cloud my joys with danger and with sorrow.

　K. Edw. My love, forbear to fawn upon their
　　frowns :
What danger, or what sorrow can befall thee,
So long as Edward is thy constant friend,
And their true sovereign, whom they must
　　obey !
Nay, whom they shall obey, and love thee too,
Unless they seek for hatred at my hands :
Which if they do, yet will I keep thee safe,
And they shall feel the vengeance of my wrath.

　Glo. I hear, yet say not much, but think the
　　more.　　　　　　　　　　[*Aside.*

Enter a Messenger.

　K. Edw. Now, messenger, what letters, or what
　　news,
From France ?

　Mess. My sovereign liege, no letters ; and few
　　words,
But such as I, without your special pardon,
Dare not relate.

　K. Edw. Go to, we pardon thee ; therefore, in
　　brief,
Tell me their words as near as thou canst guess
　　them.
What answer makes king Lewis unto our letters ?

　Mess. At my depart, these were his very
　　words,
" Go tell false Edward, thy supposed king,—
That Lewis of France is sending over maskers,
To revel with him and his new bride."

　K. Edw. Is Lewis so brave ? belike, he thinks
　　me Henry.
But what said lady Bona to my marriage ?

　Mess. These were her words, utter'd with mild
　　disdain ;
" Tell him, in hope he 'll prove a widower shortly,
I 'll wear the willow garland for his sake."

　K. Edw. I blame not her, she could say little
　　less ;
She had the wrong. But what said Henry's queen ?
For I have heard, that she was there in place.

　Mess. " Tell him," quoth she, " my mourning
　　weeds are done,
And I am ready to put armour on."

　K. Edw. Belike, she minds to play the Amazon.
But what said Warwick to these injuries ?

　Mess. He, more incens'd against your majesty
Than all the rest, discharg'd me with these words ;
" Tell him from me, that he hath done me wrong,
And therefore I 'll uncrown him, ere 't be long."

　K. Edw. Ha ! durst the traitor breathe out so
　　proud words ?
Well, I will arm me, being thus forewarn'd :
They shall have wars, and pay for their pre-
　　sumption.
But say, is Warwick friends with Margaret ?

　Mess. Ay, gracious sovereign ; they are so link'd
　　in friendship,
That young prince Edward marries Warwick's
　　daughter.

　Clar. Belike, the elder ; Clarence will have the
　　younger.²⁹
Now, brother king, farewell, and sit you fast,

For I will hence to Warwick's other daughter;
That, though I want a kingdom, yet in marriage
I may not prove inferior to yourself.—
You, that love me and Warwick, follow me.

　　　　　　　　　[*Exit* CLAR., *and* SOM. *follows.*

Glo. Not I:
My thoughts aim at a further matter; I
Stay not for love of Edward, but the crown.

　　　　　　　　　　　　　　[*Aside.*

K. Edw. Clarence and Somerset both gone to
　　　Warwick!
Yet am I arm'd against the worst can happen;
And haste is needful in this desperate case.—
Pembroke, and Stafford, you in our behalf
Go levy men, and make prepare for war;
They are already, or quickly will be landed:
Myself in person will straight follow you.

　　　　　　　　　[*Exeunt* PEM. *and* STAF.

But, ere I go, Hastings,—and Montague,—
Resolve my doubt. You twain, of all the rest,
Are near to Warwick, by blood, and by alliance:
Tell me, if you love Warwick more than me?
If it be so, then both depart to him;
I rather wish you foes, than hollow friends;
But if you mind to hold your true obedience,
Give me assurance with some friendly vow,
That I may never have you in suspect.

Mont. So God help Montague, as he proves true!
Hast. And Hastings, as he favours Edward's
　　　cause!
K. Edw. Now, brother Richard, will you stand
　　　by us?
Glo. Ay, in despite of all that shall withstand
　　　you.
K. Edw. Why so; then am I sure of victory.
Now therefore let us hence; and lose no hour,
Till we meet Warwick with his foreign power.

　　　　　　　　　　　　[*Exeunt.*

SCENE II.—*A Plain in* Warwickshire.

Enter WARWICK *and* OXFORD, *with French and
other Forces.*

War. Trust me, my lord, all hitherto goes well;
The common people by numbers swarm to us.

Enter CLARENCE *and* SOMERSET.

But, see, where Somerset and Clarence come;—
Speak suddenly, my lords, are we all friends?
Clar. Fear not that, my lord.
War. Then, gentle Clarence, welcome unto
　　　Warwick;

And welcome, Somerset:—I hold it cowardice,
To rest mistrustful where a noble heart
Hath pawn'd an open hand in sign of love;
Else might I think, that Clarence, Edward's brother
Were but a feigned friend to our proceedings:
But welcome, Clarence; my daughter shall be thine.
And now what rests, but, in night's coverture,
Thy brother being carelessly encamp'd,
His soldiers lurking in the towns about,
And but attended by a simple guard,
We may surprise and take him at our pleasure?
Our scouts have found the adventure very easy:
That as Ulysses, and stout Diomede,
With sleight and manhood stole to Rhesus' tents,
And brought from thence the Thracian fatal
　　　steeds;
So we, well cover'd with the night's black mantle,
At unawares may beat down Edward's guard,
And seize himself; I say not,—slaughter him,
For I intend but only to surprise him.—
You, that will follow me to this attempt,
Applaud the name of Henry, with your leader.

　　　　　　　[*They all cry,* "Henry!"

Why, then, let 's on our way in silent sort:
For Warwick and his friends, God and Saint
　　　George!　　　　　　　　[*Exeunt.*

SCENE III.—Edward's *Camp, near* Warwick.

Enter certain Watchmen, to guard the King's *Tent.*

1st Watch. Come on, my masters, each man
　　　take his stand:
The king, by this, is set him down to sleep.
2nd Watch. What, will he not to bed?
1st Watch. Why, no: for he hath made a sol-
　　　emn vow
Never to lie and take his natural rest,
Till Warwick, or himself, be quite suppress'd.
2nd Watch. To-morrow then, belike, shall be
　　　the day,
If Warwick be so near as men report.
3rd Watch. But say, I pray, what nobleman is
　　　that,
That with the king here resteth in his tent?
1st Watch. 'T is the lord Hastings, the king's
　　　chiefest friend.
3rd Watch. O, is it so? But why commands the
　　　king,
That his chief followers lodge in towns about him,
While he himself keepeth in the cold field?
2nd Watch. 'T is the more honour, because
　　　more dangerous.

3rd Watch. Ay; but give me worship and qui-
etness,
I like it better than a dangerous honour.
If Warwick knew in what estate he stands,
'T is to be doubted, he would waken him.

1st Watch. Unless our halberds did shut up
his passage.

2nd Watch. Ay; wherefore else guard we his
royal tent,
But to defend his person from night-foes?

Enter WARWICK, CLARENCE, OXFORD, SOMERSET,
and Forces.

War. This is his tent; and see, where stand
his guard.
Courage, my masters! honour now, or never!
But follow me, and Edward shall be ours.

1st Watch. Who goes there?

2nd Watch. Stay, or thou diest.

[WAR. *and the rest, cry all—*"Warwick!
Warwick!" *and set upon the Guard; who
fly, crying—*"Arm! Arm!" WAR. *and
the rest, following them.*

*The Drum beating, and Trumpets sounding, Re-
enter* WARWICK, *and the rest, bringing the King
out in a Gown, sitting in a Chair:* GLOS. *and
HAST. fly.*

Som.   What are they that fly there?

War. Richard, and Hastings: let them go,
here 's the duke.

K. Edw. The duke! why, Warwick, when we
parted last,
Thou call'dst me king?

War.   Ay, but the case is alter'd:
When you disgrac'd me in my embassade,
Then I degraded you from being king,
And come now to create you duke of York.
Alas! how should you govern any kingdom,
That know not how to use ambassadors;
Nor how to be contented with one wife;
Nor how to use your brothers brotherly;
Nor how to study for the people's welfare;
Nor how to shroud yourself from enemies?

K. Edw. Yea, brother of Clarence, art thou
here too?
Nay, then I see, that Edward needs must down.—
Yet, Warwick, in despite of all mischance,
Of thee thyself, and all thy 'complices,
Edward will always bear himself as king:
Though fortune's malice overthrow my state,
My mind exceeds the compass of her wheel.

War. Then, for his mind, be Edward England's
king: [*Takes off his Crown.*
But Henry now shall wear the English crown,
And be true king indeed; thou but the shadow.—
My lord of Somerset, at my request,
See that forthwith duke Edward be convey'd
Unto my brother, archbishop of York.
When I have fought with Pembroke and his fel-
lows,
I 'll follow you, and tell what answer
Lewis, and the lady Bona, send to him:—
Now, for a while, farewell, good duke of York.

K. Edw. What fates impose, that men must
needs abide;
It boots not to resist both wind and tide.
[*Exit K. Edw., led out;* Som. *with him.*

Oxf. What now remains, my lords, for us to do,
But march to London with our soldiers?

War. Ay, that 's the first thing that we have
to do;
To free king Henry from imprisonment,
And see him seated in the regal throne. [*Exeunt.*

SCENE IV.—London. *A Room in the Palace.*

Enter QUEEN ELIZABETH *and* RIVERS.

Riv. Madam, what makes you in this sudden
change?

Q. Eliz. Why, brother Rivers, are you yet to
learn,
What late misfortune is befall'n king Edward?

Riv. What, loss of some pitch'd battle against
Warwick?

Q. Eliz. No, but the loss of his own royal person.

Riv. Then is my sovereign slain?

Q. Eliz. Ay, almost slain, for he is taken pri-
soner:
Either betray'd by falsehood of his guard,
Or by his foe surpris'd at unawares:
And, as I further have to understand,
Is now committed to the bishop of York,
Fell Warwick's brother, and by that our foe.

Riv. These news, I must confess, are full of
grief:
Yet, gracious madam, bear it as you may;
Warwick may lose, that now hath won the day.

Q. Eliz. Till then, fair hope must hinder life's
decay.
And I the rather wean me from despair,
For love of Edward's offspring in my womb:
This is it that makes me bridle passion,

And bear with mildness my misfortune's cross;
Ay, ay, for this I draw in many a tear,
And stop the rising of blood-sucking sighs,
Lest with my sighs or tears I blast or drown
King Edward's fruit, true heir to the English
    crown.
    Riv. But, madam, where is Warwick then be-
      come?
    Q. Eliz. I am informed, that he comes towards
      London,
To set the crown once more on Henry's head:
Guess thou the rest; king Edward's friends must
    down.
But, to prevent the tyrant's violence,
(For trust not him that hath once broken faith,)
I'll hence forthwith unto the sanctuary,
To save at least the heir of Edward's right;
There shall I rest secure from force, and fraud.
Come therefore, let us fly, while we may fly;
If Warwick take us, we are sure to die. [*Exeunt.*

SCENE V.—*A Park near* Middleham Castle, *in*
    Yorkshire.

Enter GLOSTER, HASTINGS, SIR WILLIAM STAN-
    LEY, *and Others.*

    Glo. Now, my lord Hastings, and sir William
    Stanley,
Leave off to wonder why I drew you hither,
Into this chiefest thicket of the park.
Thus stands the case: You know, our king, my
    brother,
Is prisoner to the bishop here, at whose hands
He hath good usage and great liberty;
And often, but attended with weak guard,
Comes hunting this way to disport himself.
I have advertis'd him by secret means,
That if about this hour, he make this way
Under the colour of his usual game,
He shall here find his friends, with horse and
    men,
To set him free from his captivity.

    Enter KING EDWARD, *and a* Huntsman.

    Hunt. This way, my lord; for this way lies the
    game.
    K. Edw. Nay, this way, man; see, where the
    huntsmen stand.—
Now, brother of Gloster, lord Hastings, and the
    rest,
Stand you thus close, to steal the bishop's deer?
378

    Glo. Brother, the time and case requireth haste
Your horse stands ready at the park corner.
    K. Edw. But whither shall we then?
    Hast. To Lynn, my lord; and ship from thence
    to Flanders.
    Glo. Well guess'd, believe me; for that was
    my meaning.
    K. Edw. Stanley, I will requite thy forwardness.
    Glo. But wherefore stay we? 't is no time to
    talk.
    K. Edw. Huntsman, what say'st thou? wilt
    thou go along?
    Hunt. Better do so, than tarry and be hang'd.
    Glo. Come then, away; let's have no more ado.
    K. Edw. Bishop, farewell: shield thee from
    Warwick's frown;
And pray that I may repossess the crown.
                       [*Exeunt*

SCENE VI.—*A Room in the Tower.*

Enter KING HENRY, CLARENCE, WARWICK, SO-
MERSET, *young* RICHMOND, OXFORD, MONTAGUE,
Lieutenant of the Tower, *and* Attendants.

    K. Hen. Master lieutenant, now that God and
    friends
Have shaken Edward from the regal seat;
And turn'd my captive state to liberty,
My fear to hope, my sorrows unto joys;
At our enlargement what are thy due fees?
    Lieu. Subjects may challenge nothing of their
    sovereigns;
But, if an humble prayer may prevail,
I then crave pardon of your majesty.
    K. Hen. For what, lieutenant? for well using
    me?
Nay, be thou sure, I'll well requite thy kindness,
For that it made my imprisonment a pleasure;
Ay, such a pleasure as incaged birds
Conceive, when, after many moody thoughts,
At last, by notes of household harmony,
They quite forget their loss of liberty.—
But, Warwick, after God, thou set'st me free,
And chiefly therefore I thank God, and thee;
He was the author, thou the instrument.
Therefore, that I may conquer fortune's spite,
By living low, where fortune cannot hurt me;
And that the people of this blessed land
May not be punish'd with my thwarting stars;
Warwick, although my head still wear the crown,
I here resign my government to thee
For thou art fortunate in all thy deeds.

War. Your grace hath still been fam'd for
    virtuous:
And now may seem as wise as virtuous,
By spying, and avoiding, fortune's malice,
For few men rightly temper with the stars;"
Yet in this one thing let me blame your grace,
For choosing me, when Clarence is in place.
  Clar. No, Warwick, thou art worthy of the
    sway,
To whom the heavens, in thy nativity,
Adjudg'd an olive branch, and laurel crown,
As likely to be blest in peace, and war;
And therefore I yield thee my free consent.
  War. And I choose Clarence only for protector.
  K. Hen. Warwick, and Clarence, give me both
    your hands;
Now join your hands, and, with your hands,
    your hearts,
That no dissension hinder government:
I make you both protectors of this land;
While I myself will lead a private life,
And in devotion spend my latter days,
To sin's rebuke, and my Creator's praise.
  War. What answers Clarence to his sovereign's
    will?
  Clar. That he consents, if Warwick yield con-
    sent;
For on thy fortune I repose myself.
  War. Why then, though loath, yet must I be
    content:
We 'll yoke together, like a double shadow
To Henry's body, and supply his place;
I mean, in bearing weight of government,
While he enjoys the honour, and his ease.
And, Clarence, now then it is more than needful,
Forthwith that Edward be pronounc'd a traitor,
And all his lands and goods be confiscate.
  Clar. What else? and that succession be de-
    termin'd.
  War. Ay, therein Clarence shall not want his
    part.
  K. Hen. But, with the first of all your chief
    affairs,
Let me entreat, (for I command no more,)
That Margaret your queen, and my son Edward,
Be sent for, to return from France with speed:
For, till I see them here, by doubtful fear
My joy of liberty is half eclips'd.
  Clar. It shall be done, my sovereign, with all
    speed.
  K. Hen. My lord of Somerset, what youth is
    that,

Of whom you seem to have so tender care?
  Som. My liege, it is young Henry, earl of Rich-
    mond.
  K. Hen. Come hither, England's hope: If se-
    cret powers
             [*Lays his Hand on his Head.*
Suggest but truth to my divining thoughts,
This pretty lad will prove our country's bliss.
His looks are full of peaceful majesty;
His head by nature fram'd to wear a crown,
His hand to wield a sceptre; and himself
Likely, in time, to bless a regal throne.
Make much of him, my lords; for this is he,
Must help you more than you are hurt by me.

Enter a Messenger.

  War. What news, my friend?
  Mess. That Edward is escaped from your
    brother,
And fled, as he hears since, to Burgundy.
  War. Unsavoury news: But how made he
    escape?
  Mess. He was convey'd by Richard duke of
    Gloster,
And the lord Hastings, who attended him
In secret ambush on the forest side,
And from the bishop's huntsmen rescued him;
For hunting was his daily exercise.
  War. My brother was too careless of his
    charge.—
But let us hence, my sovereign, to provide
A salve for any sore that may betide.
    [*Exeunt* K. HEN., WAR., CLAR., *Lieut., and
    Attendants.*
  Som. My lord, I like not of this flight of Ed-
    ward's;
For, doubtless, Burgundy will yield him help;
And we shall have more wars, before 't be long.
As Henry's late presaging prophecy
Did glad my heart, with hope of this young Rich-
    mond;
So doth my heart misgive me, in these conflicts,
What may befall him, to his harm, and ours:
Therefore, lord Oxford, to prevent the worst,
Forthwith we 'll send him hence to Brittany,
Till storms be past of civil enmity.
  Oxf. Ay; for, if Edward repossess the crown,
'T is like, that Richmond with the rest shall
    down.
  Som. It shall be so; he shall to Brittany.
Come, therefore, let 's about it speedily.
                [*Exeunt.*

SCENE VII.—*Before York.*

Enter King Edward, Gloster, Hastings, *and Forces.*

K. Edw. Now, brother Richard, lord Hastings,
    and the rest;
Yet thus far fortune maketh us amends,
And says—that once more I shall interchange
My waned state for Henry's regal crown.
Well have we pass'd, and now repass'd the seas,
And brought desir'd help from Burgundy:
What then remains, we being thus arriv'd
From Raven-spurg haven before the gates of
    York,
But that we enter, as into our dukedom?
    Glo. The gates made fast!—Brother, I like not
    this;
For many men, that stumble at the threshold,
Are well foretold—that danger lurks within.
    K. Edw. Tush, man! abodements must not
    now affright us:
By fair or foul means we must enter in,
For hither will our friends repair to us.
    Hast. My liege, I 'll knock once more, to sum-
mon them.

Enter, on the Walls, the Mayor of York, *and his Brethren.*

    May. My lords, we were forewarned of your
    coming,
And shut the gates for safety of ourselves;
For now we owe allegiance unto Henry.
    K. Edw. But, master mayor, if Henry be your
    king,
Yet Edward, at the least, is duke of York.
    May. True, my good lord; I know you for no
    less.
    K. Edw. Why, and I challenge nothing but
    my dukedom;
As being well content with that alone.
    Glo. But, when the fox hath once got in his
    nose,
He 'll soon find means to make the body follow.
                       [*Aside.*
    Hast. Why, master mayor, why stand you in
    a doubt?
Open the gates, we are king Henry's friends.
    May. Ay, say you so? the gates shall then be
    open'd.   [*Exeunt from above.*
    Glo. A wise stout captain, and persuaded
    soon!

    Hast. The good old man would fain that all
    were well,
So 't were not long of him: but, being enter'd,
I doubt not, I, but we shall soon persuade
Both him, and all his brothers, unto reason.

Re-enter the Mayor *and Two Aldermen, below.*

    K. Edw. So, master mayor: these gates must
    not be shut,
But in the night, or in the time of war.
What! fear not, man, but yield me up the keys;
                    [*Takes his Keys.*
For Edward will defend the town, and thee,
And all those friends that deign to follow me.

    Drum.   *Enter* Montgomery, *and Forces, marching.*

    Glo. Brother, this is sir John Montgomery,
Our trusty friend, unless I be deceiv'd.
    K. Edw. Welcome, sir John! But why come
    you in arms?
    Mont. To help king Edward in his time of
    storm,
As every loyal subject ought to do.
    K. Edw. Thanks, good Montgomery; But we
    now forget
Our title to the crown; and only claim
Our dukedom, till God please to send the rest.
    Mont. Then fare you well, for I will hence
    again;
I came to serve a king, and not a duke,—
Drummer, strike up, and let us march away.
                 [*A March begun.*
    K. Edw. Nay, stay, sir John, a while; and
    we 'll debate,
By what safe means the crown may be recover'd.
    Mont. What talk you of debating? in few words
If you 'll not here proclaim yourself our king,
I 'll leave you to your fortune; and be gone,
To keep them back that come to succour you:
Why should we fight, if you pretend no title?
    Glo. Why, brother, wherefore stand you on
    nice points?
    K. Edw. When we grow stronger, then we 'll
    make our claim:
Till then, 't is wisdom to conceal our meaning.
    Hast. Away with scrupulous wit! now arms
    must rule.
    Glo. And fearless minds climb soonest unto
    crowns.
Brother, we will proclaim you out of hand;
The bruit thereof will bring you many friends.

K. Edw. Then be it as you will; for 't is my
    right,
And Henry but usurps the diadem.
  Mont. Ay, now my sovereign speaketh like
    himself;
And now will I be Edward's champion.
  Hast. Sound, trumpet; Edward shall be here
    proclaim'd:—
Come, fellow-soldier, make thou proclamation.
             [*Gives him a Paper. Flourish.*

  Sold. [*Reads.*] Edward the Fourth, by the grace of
God, king of England and France, and lord of Ireland, &c.

  Mont. And whosoe'er gainsays king Edward's
    right,
By this I challenge him to single fight.
             [*Throws down a Gauntlet.*
  All. Long live Edward the Fourth!
  K. Edw. Thanks, brave Montgomery;—and
    thanks unto you all.
If fortune serve me, I 'll requite this kindness.
Now, for this night, let 's harbour here in York:
And, when the morning sun shall raise his car
Above the border of this horizon,
We 'll forward towards Warwick, and his mates;
For, well I wot, that Henry is no soldier.—
Ah, froward Clarence!—how evil it beseems thee,
To flatter Henry, and forsake thy brother!
Yet, as we may, we 'll meet both thee and War-
    wick.—
Come on, brave soldiers; doubt not of the day;
And, that once gotten, doubt not of large pay.
                   [*Exeunt.*

SCENE VIII.—London.   *A Room in the Palace.*

Enter KING HENRY, WARWICK, CLARENCE, MON-
TAGUE, EXETER, *and* OXFORD.

  War. What counsel, lords? Edward from
    Belgia,
With hasty Germans, and blunt Hollanders,
Hath pass'd in safety through the narrow seas,
And with his troops doth march amain to London;
And many giddy people flock to him.
  Oxf. Let 's levy men, and beat him back again.
  Clar. A little fire is quickly trodden out;
Which, being suffer'd, rivers cannot quench.
  War. In Warwickshire I have true-hearted
    friends,
Not mutinous in peace, yet bold in war;
Those will I muster up:—and thou, son Clarence,

Shalt stir, in Suffolk, Norfolk, and in Kent,
The knights and gentlemen to come with thee:—
Thou, brother Montague, in Buckingham,
Northampton, and in Leicestershire, shalt find
Men well inclin'd to hear what thou com
    mand'st:—
And thou, brave Oxford, wondrous well belov'd,
In Oxfordshire shalt muster up thy friends.—
My sovereign, with the loving citizens,—
Like to his island, girt in with the ocean,
Or modest Dian, circled with her nymphs,—
Shall rest in London, till we come to him.—
Fair lords, take leave, and stand not to reply.—
Farewell, my sovereign.
  K. Hen. Farewell, my Hector, and my Troy's
    true hope.
  Clar. In sign of truth, I kiss your highness'
    hand.
  K. Hen. Well-minded Clarence, be thou for-
    tunate!
  Mont. Comfort, my lord;—and so I take my
    leave.
  Oxf. And thus [*Kissing* HENRY'S *hand.*] I seal
    my truth, and bid adieu.
  K. Hen. Sweet Oxford, and my loving Mon-
    tague,
And all at once, once more a happy farewell.
  War. Farewell, sweet lords; let 's meet at
    Coventry.
        [*Exeunt* WAR., CLAR., OXF., *and* MONT.
  K. Hen. Here at the palace will I rest a while
Cousin of Exeter, what thinks your lordship?
Methinks, the power, that Edward hath in field,
Should not be able to encounter mine.
  Exe. The doubt is, that he will seduce the rest.
  K. Hen. That 's not my fear, my meed hath got
    me fame:
I have not stopp'd mine ears to their demands;
Nor posted off their suits with slow delays;
My pity hath been balm to heal their wounds,
My mildness hath allay'd their swelling griefs,
My mercy dry'd their bitter-flowing tears:
I have not been desirous of their wealth,
Nor much oppress'd them with great subsidies,
Nor forward of revenge, though they much err'd;
Then why should they love Edward more than me?
No, Exeter, these graces challenge grace:
And, when the lion fawns upon the lamb,
The lamb will never cease to follow him.
    [*Shout within.* "A Lancaster! A Lancaster!"
  Exe. Hark, hark, my lord! what shouts are
    these?

Enter KING EDWARD, GLOSTER, *and Soldiers.*

K. Edw. Seize on the shame-fac'd Henry, bear
    him hence,
And once again proclaim us king of England.—
You are the fount, that makes small brooks to
    flow;
Now stops thy spring; my sea shall suck them
    dry,
And swell so much the higher by their ebb.—

Hence with him to the Tower; let him not speak
                    [*Exeunt some with K.* Hen
And, lords, towards Coventry bend we our course;
Where peremptory Warwick now remains?"
The sun shines hot, and, if we use delay,
Cold-biting winter mars our hop'd for hay.
    Glo. Away betimes, before his forces join,
And take the great-grown traitor unawares:
Brave warriors, march amain towards Coventry.
                    [*Exeunt*

ACT V.

SCENE I.—Coventry.

Enter, upon the Walls, WARWICK, *the* MAYOR OF
COVENTRY, *Two Messengers, and Others.*

War. Where is the post, that came from valiant
    Oxford?
How far hence is thy lord, mine honest fellow?
    1st Mess. By this at Dunsmore, marching hither-
    ward.
    War. How far off is our brother Montague?—
Where is the post that came from Montague?
    2nd Mess. By this at Daintry, with a puissant
    troop.

Enter SIR JOHN SOMERVILLE.

    War. Say, Somerville, what says my loving son?
And, by thy guess, how nigh is Clarence now?
    Som. At Southam I did leave him with his
    forces,
And do expect him here some two hours hence.
                    [*Drum heard.*
    War. Then Clarence is at hand, I hear his drum.
    Som. It is not his, my lord; here Southam lies;
The drum your honour hears, marcheth from War-
    wick.
    War. Who should that be? belike, unlook'd-
    for friends.
    Som. They are at hand, and you shall quickly
    know.

Drums. Enter KING EDWARD, GLOSTER, *and
Forces, marching.*

    K. Edw. Go, trumpet, to the walls, and sound
    a parle.

Glo. See, how the surly Warwick mans the
    wall.
    War. O, unbid spite! is sportful Edward
    come?
Where slept our scouts, or how are they seduc'd,
That we could hear no news of his repair?
    K. Edw. Now, Warwick, wilt thou ope the
    city gates,
Speak gentle words, and humbly bend thy knee?—
Call Edward—king, and at his hands beg mercy,
And he shall pardon thee these outrages.
    War. Nay, rather, wilt thou draw thy forces
    hence,
Confess who set thee up, and pluck'd thee down?—
Call Warwick—patron, and be penitent,
And thou shalt still remain the duke of York.
    Glo. I thought, at least, he would have said—
    the king;
Or did he make the jest against his will?
    War. Is not a dukedom, sir, a goodly gift?
    Glo. Ay, by my faith, for a poor earl to
    give;
I'll do thee service for so good a gift.
    War. 'T was I, that gave the kingdom to thy
    brother.
    K. Edw. Why, then 't is mine, if but by War-
    wick's gift.
    War. Thou art no Atlas for so great a weight:
And, weakling, Warwick takes his gift again;
And Henry is my king, Warwick his subject.
    K. Edw. But Warwick's king is Edward's
    prisoner:
And, gallant Warwick, do but answer this,—
What is the body, when the head is off?

Glo. Alas, that Warwick had no more forecast,
But, whiles he thought to steal the single ten,
The king was slily finger'd from the deck!
You left poor Henry at the bishop's palace,
And, ten to one, you'll meet him in the Tower.

K. Edw. 'T is even so; yet you are Warwick
still.

Glo. Come, Warwick, take the time, kneel
down, kneel down :

Nay, when? strike now, or else the iron cools.

War. I had rather chop this hand off at a
blow,
And with the other fling it at thy face,
Than bear so low a sail, to strike to thee.

K. Edw. Sail how thou canst, have wind and
tide thy friend ;
This hand, fast wound about thy coal-black hair,
Shall, whiles the head is warm, and new cut off,
Write in the dust this sentence with thy blood,—
" Wind-changing Warwick now can change no
more."

Enter OXFORD, *with Drum and Colours.*

War. O cheerful colours! see, where Oxford
comes!

Oxf. Oxford, Oxford, for Lancaster!
        [OXF. *and his Forces enter the City.*

Glo. The gates are open, let us enter too.

K. Edw. So other foes may set upon our
backs,
Stand we in good array; for they, no doubt,
Will issue out again, and bid us battle;
If not, the city, being but of small defence,
We'll quickly rouse the traitors in the same.

War. O, welcome, Oxford! for we want thy
help.

Enter MONTAGUE, *with Drum and Colours.*

Mont. Montague, Montague, for Lancaster!
        [*He and his Forces enter the City.*

Glo. Thou and thy brother both shall buy this
treason
Even with the dearest blood your bodies bear.

K. Edw. The harder match'd, the greater victory;
My mind presageth happy gain, and conquest.

Enter SOMERSET, *with Drum and Colours.*

Som. Somerset, Somerset, for Lancaster!
        [*He and his Forces enter the City.*

Glo. Two of thy name, both dukes of Somerset,

Have sold their lives unto the house of York;
And thou shalt be the third, if this sword hold.

Enter CLARENCE, *with Drum and Colours.*

War. And lo, where George of Clarence sweeps
along,
Of force enough to bid his brother battle;
With whom an upright zeal to right prevails,
More than the nature of a brother's love :—
Come, Clarence, come; thou wilt, if Warwick
calls.

Clar. Father of Warwick, know you what this
means?
        [*Taking the red Rose out of his Cap.*
Look here, I throw my infamy at thee:
I will not ruinate my father's house,
Who gave his blood to lime the stones together,
And set up Lancaster.   Why, trow'st thou, War-
wick,
That Clarence is so harsh, so blunt, unnatural,
To bend the fatal instruments of war
Against his brother, and his lawful king?
Perhaps, thou wilt object my holy oath :
To keep that oath, were more impiety
Than Jephtha's, when he sacrific'd his daughter.
I am so sorry for my trespass made,
That, to deserve well at my brother's hands,
I here proclaim myself thy mortal foe ;
With resolution, wheresoe'er I meet thee,
(As I will meet thee, if thou stir abroad,)
To plague thee for thy foul misleading me.
And so, proud-hearted Warwick, I defy thee,
And to my brother turn my blushing cheeks.—
Pardon me, Edward, I will make amends ;
And, Richard, do not frown upon my faults,
For I will henceforth be no more unconstant.

K. Edw. Now welcome more, and ten times
more belov'd,
Than if thou never hadst deserv'd our hate.

Glo. Welcome, good Clarence; this is brother
like.

War. O passing traitor, perjur'd, and unjust!

K. Edw. What, Warwick, wilt thou leave the
town, and fight?
Or shall we beat the stones about thine ears?

War. Alas, I am not coop'd here for defence:
I will away towards Barnet presently,
And bid thee battle, Edward, if thou dar'st.

K. Edw. Yes, Warwick, Edward dares, and
leads the way :—
Lords, to the field; Saint George, and victory!
        [*March.   Exeunt.*

387

SCENE II.—*A Field of Battle near* Barnet.

Alarums, and Excursions. Enter KING EDWARD, *bringing in* WARWICK, *wounded.*

K. Edw. So, lie thou there: die thou, and die
   our fear;
For Warwick was a bug, that fear'd us all.—
Now, Montague, sit fast; I seek for thee,
That Warwick's bones may keep thine company.
                       [*Exit.*

War. Ah, who is nigh? come to me, friend, or
   foe,
And tell me, who is victor, York, or Warwick?
Why ask I that? my mangled body shows,
My blood, my want of strength, my sick heart
   shows,
That I must yield my body to the earth,
And, by my fall, the conquest to my foe.
Thus yields the cedar to the axe's edge,
Whose arms gave shelter to the princely eagle,
Under whose shade the ramping lion slept;
Whose top-branch overpeer'd Jove's spreading
   tree,
And kept low shrubs from winter's powerful wind.
These eyes, that now are dimm'd with death's
   black veil,
Have been as piercing as the mid-day sun,
To search the secret treasons of the world:
The wrinkles in my brows, now fill'd with blood,
Were liken'd oft to kingly sepulchres;
For who liv'd king, but I could dig his grave?
And who durst smile, when Warwick bent his
   brow?
Lo, now my glory smear'd in dust and blood!
My parks, my walks, my manors that I had,
Even now forsake me; and, of all my lands,
Is nothing left me, but my body's length!
Why, what is pomp, rule, reign, but earth and
   dust?
And, live we how we can, yet die we must.

Enter OXFORD *and* SOMERSET.

Som. Ah, Warwick, Warwick! wert thou as
   we are,
We might recover all our loss again!
The queen from France hath brought a puissant
   power;
Even now we heard the news: Ah, couldst thou
   fly!
War. Why, then I would not fly.—Ah, Montague,
488

If thou be there, sweet brother, take my hand,
And with thy lips keep in my soul a while!
Thou lov'st me not; for, brother, if thou didst,
Thy tears would wash this cold congealed blood
That glues my lips, and will not let me speak.
Come quickly, Montague, or I am dead.
   Som. Ah, Warwick, Montague hath breath'd
   his last;
And to the latest gasp, cried out for Warwick,
And said—Commend me to my valiant brother.
And more he would have said; and more he
   spoke,
Which sounded like a cannon in a vault,
That might not be distinguish'd; but, at last,
I well might hear deliver'd, with a groan,—
O, farewell, Warwick!
   War.   Sweet rest to his soul!—
Fly, lords, and save yourselves; for Warwick bids
You all farewell, to meet again in heaven. [*Dies.*
   Oxf. Away, away, to meet the queen's great
   power!
       [*Exeunt, bearing off* WAR.'s *Body.*

SCENE III.—*Another part of the Field.*

Flourish. Enter KING EDWARD, *in triumph; with* CLARENCE, GLOSTER, *and the rest.*

K. Edw. Thus far our fortune keeps an upward
   course,
And we are grac'd with wreaths of victory.
But, in the midst of this bright-shining day,
I spy a black, suspicious, threat'ning cloud,
That will encounter with our glorious sun,
Ere he attain his easeful western bed:
I mean, my lords,—those powers, that the queen
Hath rais'd in Gallia, have arriv'd our coast,
And, as we hear, march on to fight with us.
   Clar. A little gale will soon disperse that cloud,
And blow it to the source from whence it came:
Thy very beams will dry those vapours up;
For every cloud engenders not a storm.
   Glo. The queen is valued thirty thousand strong
And Somerset, with Oxford, fled to her;
If she have time to breathe, be well assur'd,
Her faction will be full as strong as ours.
   K. Edw. We are advertis'd by our loving
   friends,
That they do hold their course toward Tewkes-
   bury;
We having now the best at Barnet field,
Will thither straight, For willingness rids way;
And, as we march, our strength will be augmented

In every county as we go along.—
Strike up the drum; cry—Courage! and away.
[*Exeunt.*

SCENE IV.—*Plains near Tewkesbury.*

March. Enter QUEEN MARGARET, PRINCE ED-
WARD, SOMERSET, OXFORD, *and Soldiers.*

Q. Mar. Great lords, wise men ne'er sit and
wail their loss,
But cheerly seek how to redress their harms.
What though the mast be now blown over-board,
The cable broke, the holding anchor lost,
And half our sailors swallow'd in the flood?
Yet lives our pilot still: Is 't meet, that he
Should leave the helm, and, like a fearful lad,
With tearful eyes add water to the sea,
And give more strength to that which hath too
much ;
Whiles, in his moan, the ship splits on the rock,
Which industry and courage might have sav'd?
Ah, what a shame! ah, what a fault were this!
Say, Warwick was our anchor: What of that?
And Montague our top-mast: What of him?
Our slaughter'd friends the tackles: What of these?
Why, is not Oxford here another anchor?
And Somerset another goodly mast?
The friends of France our shrouds and tacklings?
And, though unskilful, why not Ned and I
For once allow'd the skilful pilot's charge?
We will not from the helm, to sit and weep;
But keep our course, though the rough wind say—
no,
From shelves and rocks that threaten us with wreck.
As good to chide the waves, as speak them fair.
And what is Edward, but a ruthless sea?
What Clarence, but a quicksand of deceit?
And Richard, but a ragged fatal rock?
All these the enemies to our poor bark.
Say, you can swim; alas, 't is but a while:
Tread on the sand; why, there you quickly sink:
Bestride the rock; the tide will wash you off,
Or else you famish, that 's a threefold death.
This speak I, lords, to let you understand,
In case some one of you would fly from us,
That there 's no hop'd-for mercy with the brothers,
More than with ruthless waves, with sands, and
rocks.
Why, courage, then! what cannot be avoided
'T were childish weakness to lament, or fear.

Prince. Methinks, a woman of this valiant spirit
Should, if a coward heard her speak these words,

Infuse his breast with magnanimity,
And make him, naked, foil a man at arms.
I speak not this, as doubting any here;
For, did I but suspect a fearful man,
He should have leave to go away betimes;
Lest, in our need, he might infect another,
And make him of like spirit to himself.
If any such be here, as God forbid!
Let him depart, before we need his help.

Oxf. Women and children of so high a courage!
And warriors faint! why, 't were perpetual
shame.—
O, brave young prince! thy famous grandfather
Doth live again in thee: Long may'st thou live,
To bear his image, and renew his glories!

Som. And he, that will not fight for such a
hope,
Go home to bed, and, like the owl by day,
If he arise, be mock'd and wonder'd at.

Q. Mar. Thanks, gentle Somerset ;—sweet Oxford, thanks.

Prince. And take his thanks, that yet hath
nothing else.

Enter a Messenger.

Mess. Prepare you, lords, for Edward is at
hand,
Ready to fight; therefore be resolute.

Oxf. I thought no less: it is his policy,
To haste thus fast, to find us unprovided.

Som. But he 's deceiv'd, we are in readiness.

Q. Mar. This cheers my heart, to see your for-
wardness.

Oxf. Here pitch our battle, hence we will not
budge.

March. Enter, at a distance, KING EDWARD,
CLARENCE, GLOSTER, *and Forces.*

K. Edw. Brave followers, yonder stands the
thorny wood,
Which, by the heavens' assistance, and your
strength,
Must by the roots be hewn up yet ere night.
I need not add more fuel to your fire,
For, well I wot, ye blaze to burn them out:
Give signal to the fight, and to it, lords.

Q. Mar. Lords, knights, and gentlemen, what
I should say,
My tears gainsay ; for every word I speak,
Ye see, I drink the water of mine eyes.
Therefore, no more but this :—Henry, your sove-
reign,

is prisoner to the foe; his state usurp'd,
His realm a slaughter-house, his subjects slain,
His statutes cancell'd, and his treasure spent;
And yonder is the wolf, that makes this spoil.
You fight in justice: then, in God's name, lords,
Be valiant, and give signal to the fight.

[*Exeunt both Armies.*

SCENE V.—*Another Part of the Same.*

*Alarums: Excursions: and afterwards a Retreat.
Then Enter* KING EDWARD, CLARENCE, GLOS-
TER, *and Forces; with* QUEEN MARGARET, OX-
FORD, *and* SOMERSET, *Prisoners.*

K. Edw. Now, here a period of tumultuous
broils.
Away with Oxford to Hammes' castle straight:
For Somerset, off with his guilty head.
Go, bear them hence; I will not hear them
speak.
Oxf. For my part, I 'll not trouble thee with
words.
Som. Nor I, but stoop with patience to my for-
tune. [*Exeunt Oxf. and Som. guarded.*
Q. Mar. So part we sadly in this troublous world,
To meet with joy in sweet Jerusalem.
K. Edw. Is proclamation made,—that, who
finds Edward,
Shall have a high reward, and he his life?
Glo. It is: and, lo, where youthful Edward
comes.

Enter Soldiers, with PRINCE EDWARD.

K. Edw. Bring forth the gallant, let us hear
him speak:
What! can so young a thorn begin to prick?
Edward, what satisfaction canst thou make,
For bearing arms, for stirring up my subjects,
And all the trouble thou hast turn'd me to?
Prince. Speak like a subject, proud ambitious
York!
Suppose, that I am now my father's mouth;
Resign thy chair, and, where I stand, kneel thou,
Whilst I propose the self-same words to thee,
Which, traitor, thou wouldst have me answer to.
Q. Mar. Ah, that thy father had been so re-
solv'd!
Glo. That you might still have worn the pet-
ticoat,
And ne'er have stol'n the breech from Lancaster.
Prince. Let Æsop fable in a winter's night;
His currish riddles sort not with this place.

Glo. By heaven, brat, I 'll plague you for that
word.
Q. Mar. Ay, thou wast born to be a plague to
men.
Glo. For God's sake, take away this captive
scold.
Prince. Nay, take away this scolding crook-
back rather.
K. Edw. Peace, wilful boy, or I will charm
your tongue.
Clar. Untutor'd lad, thou art too malapert.
Prince. I know my duty, you are all undutiful:
Lascivious Edward,—and thou perjur'd George,—
And thou misshapen Dick,—I tell ye all,
I am your better, traitors as ye are;—
And thou usurp'st my father's right and mine.
K. Edw. Take that, the likeness of this railer
here. [*Stabs him.*
Glo. Sprawl'st thou? take that to end thy
agony. [GLO. *stabs him.*
Clar. And there 's for twitting me with perjury.
[CLAR. *stabs him.*
Q. Mar. O, kill me too!
Glo. Marry, and shall. [*Offers to kill her.*
K. Edw. Hold, Richard, hold, for we have done
too much.
Glo. Why should she live, to fill the world with
words?
K. Edw. What! doth she swoon? use means
for her recovery.
Glo. Clarence, excuse me to the king my
brother;
I 'll hence to London on a serious matter:
Ere ye come there, be sure to hear some news.
Clar. What? what?
Glo. The Tower, the Tower! [*Exit.*
Q. Mar. O, Ned, sweet Ned! speak to thy
mother, boy!
Canst thou not speak?—O traitors! murderers!—
They, that stabb'd Cæsar, shed no blood at all,
Did not offend, nor were not worthy blame,
If this foul deed were by, to equal it.
He was a man; this, in respect, a child:
And men ne'er spend their fury on a child.
What 's worse than murderer, that I may name it?
No, no; my heart will burst, an if I speak:—
And I will speak, that so my heart may burst.—
Butchers and villains, bloody cannibals!
How sweet a plant have you untimely cropp'd!
You have no children, butchers! if you had,
The thought of them would have stirr'd up re-
morse:

But, if you ever chance to have a child,
Look in his youth to have him so cut off,*
As, deathsmen! you have rid this sweet young
prince!

K. Edw. Away with her; go, bear her hence
perforce.

Q. Mar. Nay, never bear me hence, despatch
me here;
Here sheath thy sword, I'll pardon thee my
death:
What! wilt thou not?—then, Clarence, do it thou.

Clar. By heaven, I will not do thee so much
ease.

Q. Mar. Good Clarence, do; sweet Clarence,
do thou do it.

Clar. Didst thou not hear me swear, I would
not do it.

Q. Mar. Ay, but thou usest to forswear thyself;
'T was sin before, but now 't is charity.
What! wilt thou not? where is that devil's
butcher,
Hard-favour'd Richard? Richard, where art thou?
Thou art not here: Murder is thy alms-deed;
Petitioners for blood thou ne'er put'st back.

K. Edw. Away, I say; I charge ye, bear her
hence.

Q. Mar. So come to you, and yours, as to this
prince! *[Exit, led out forcibly.*

K. Edw. Where's Richard gone?

Clar. To London, all in post; and, as I guess,
To make a bloody supper in the Tower.

K. Edw. He's sudden, if a thing comes in his
head.
Now march we hence: discharge the common sort
With pay and thanks, and let's away to London,
And see our gentle queen how well she fares;
By this, I hope, she hath a son for me. *[Exeunt.*

SCENE VI.—London. *A Room in the Tower.*

KING HENRY *is discovered sitting with a Book in
his hand, the* Lieutenant *attending. Enter*
GLOSTER.

Glo. Good day, my lord! What, at your book
so hard?

K. Hen. Ay, my good lord: My lord, I should
say rather;
'T is sin to flatter, good was little better:
Good Gloster, and good devil, were alike,
And both preposterous; therefore, not good lord.

Glo. Sirrah, leave us to ourselves: we must
confer. *[Exit Lieut.*

K. Hen. So flies the reckless shepherd from the
wolf;
So first the harmless sheep doth yield his fleece,
And next his throat unto the butcher's knife.—
What scene of death hath Roscius now to act?*

Glo. Suspicion always haunts the guilty mind.
The thief doth fear each bush an officer.

K. Hen. The bird, that hath been limed in a
bush,
With trembling wings misdoubteth every bush:
And I, the hapless male to one sweet bird,
Have now the fatal object in my eye,
Where my poor young was limed, was caught,
and kill'd.

Glo. Why, what a peevish fool was that of
Crete,
That taught his son the office of a fowl!
And yet, for all his wings, the fool was drown'd.

K. Hen. I, Dædalus, my poor boy, Icarus;
Thy father, Minos, that denied our course;
The sun, that sear'd the wings of my sweet boy,
Thy brother Edward; and thyself, the sea,
Whose envious gulf did swallow up his life.
Ah, kill me with thy weapon, not with words:
My breast can better brook thy dagger's point,
Than can my ears thy tragic history.—
But wherefore dost thou come? is 't for my life?

Glo. Think'st thou, I am an executioner?

K. Hen. A persecutor, I am sure, thou art;
If murdering innocents be executing,
Why, then thou art an executioner.

Glo. Thy son I kill'd for his presumption.

K. Hen. Hadst thou been kill'd, when first
thou didst presume,
Thou hadst not liv'd to kill a son of mine.
And thus I prophesy, that many a thousand,
Which now mistrust no parcel of my fear;
And many an old man's sigh, and many a
widow's,
And many an orphan's water-standing eye,—
Men for their sons, wives for their husbands'
fate,
And orphans for their parents' timeless death,—
Shall rue the hour that ever thou wast born.
The owl shriek'd at thy birth, an evil sign;
The night-crow cried, aboding luckless time;
Dogs howl'd, and hideous tempests shook down
trees;
The raven rook'd her on the chimney's top,*
And chattering pies in dismal discords sung.
Thy mother felt more than a mother's pain,
And yet brought forth less than a mother's hope

To wit,—an indigest deformed lump,
Not like the fruit of such a goodly tree.
Teeth hadst thou in thy head, when thou wast
    born,
To signify,—thou cam'st to bite the world:
And, if the rest be true which I have heard,
Thou cam'st——

   Glo. I 'll hear no more;—Die, prophet, in thy
    speech ;   [*Stabs him.*
For this, amongst the rest, was I ordain'd.

   K. Hen. Ay, and for much more slaughter after
    this.
O God! forgive my sins, and pardon thee! [*Dies.*

   Glo. What, will the aspiring blood of Lan-
    caster
Sink in the ground? I thought it would have
    mounted.
See, how my sword weeps for the poor king's
    death!
O, may such purple tears be always shed
From those that wish the downfal of our house!—
If any spark of life be yet remaining,
Down, down to hell; and say—I sent thee thither,
                     [*Stabs him again.*
I, that have neither pity, love, nor fear.—
Indeed, 't is true, that Henry told me of;
For I have often heard my mother say,
I came into the world with my legs forward:
Had I not reason, think ye, to make haste,
And seek their ruin that usurp'd our right?
The midwife wonder'd; and the women cried,
"O, Jesus bless us, he is born with teeth!"
And so I was; which plainly signified—
That I should snarl, and bite, and play the dog.
Then, since the heavens have shap'd my body so,
Let hell make crook'd my mind to answer it.
I have no brother, I am like no brother;
And this word—love, which greybeards call
    divine,
Be resident in men like one another,
And not in me; I am myself alone.—
Clarence, beware; thou keep'st me from the
    light;
But I will sort a pitchy day for thee:
For I will buzz abroad such prophecies,
That Edward shall be fearful of his life;
And then, to purge his fear, I 'll be thy death.
King Henry, and the prince his son, are gone:
Clarence, thy turn is next, and then the rest;
Counting myself but bad, till I be best.—
I 'll throw thy body in another room,
And triumph, Henry, in thy day of doom. [*Exit.*
992

SCENE VII.—*The Same. A Room in the Palace*

KING EDWARD *is discovered sitting on his Throne,*
QUEEN ELIZABETH *with the infant Prince,*
CLARENCE, GLOSTER, HASTINGS, *and Others,*
near him.

   K. Edw. Once more we sit in England's royal
    throne,
Re-purchas'd with the blood of enemies.
What valiant foemen, like to autumn's corn,
Have we mow'd down, in tops of all their pride?
Three dukes of Somerset, threefold renown'd
For hardy and undoubted champions:
Two Cliffords, as the father and the son,
And two Northumberlands; two braver men
Ne'er spurr'd their coursers at the trumpets
    sound:
With them, the two brave bears, Warwick and
    Montague,
That in their chains fetter'd the kingly lion,
And made the forest tremble when they roar'd.
Thus have we swept suspicion from our seat,
And made our footstool of security.—
Come hither, Bess, and let me kiss my boy:—
Young Ned, for thee, thine uncles, and myself,
Have in our armours watch'd the winter's night;
Went all a-foot in summer's scalding heat,
That thou might'st repossess the crown in peace;
And of our labours thou shalt reap the gain.

   Glo. I 'll blast his harvest, if your head were
    laid;
For yet I am not look'd on in the world.
This shoulder was ordain'd so thick, to heave;
And heave it shall some weight, or break my
    back :—
Work thou the way,—and thou shalt execute."
                        [*Aside.*

   K. Edw. Clarence, and Gloster, love my lovely
    queen;
And kiss your princely nephew, brothers both.

   Clar. The duty, that I owe unto your majesty,
I seal upon the lips of this sweet babe.

   K. Edw. Thanks, noble Clarence; worthy bro-
    ther, thanks.

   Glo. And, that I love the tree from whence
    thou sprang'st,
Witness the loving kiss I give the fruit:—
To say the truth, so Judas kiss'd his ⎱
    master;   ⎰ *Aside.*
And cried—all hail! when as he meant ⎰
    —all harm.

K. Edw. Now am I seated as my soul delights,
Having my country's peace, and brothers' loves.
    Clar. What will your grace have done with
      Margaret?
Reignier, her father, to the king of France
Hath pawn'd the Sicils and Jerusalem,
And hither have they sent it for her ransom.

125

K. Edw. Away with her, and waft her hence
    to France.
And now what rests, but that we spend the time
With stately triumphs, mirthful comic shows,
Such as befit the pleasures of the court?
Sound, drums and trumpets!—farewell, sour annoy!
For here, I hope, begins our lasting joy. [*Exeunt.*

293

NOTES TO KING HENRY THE SIXTH.

(PART THE THIRD.)

Speak thou for me, and tell them what I did.

There are doubts as to the exact time when Richard was born; but this is evidently an anachronism. Mr. Elderton supposes him to have been born at Fotheringay castle, on the 21st of October, 1454. Assuming this calculation to be correct, he would have been but one year old at the time of the first battle of St. Albans; and in the fifth act of this play, where he is represented as stabbing king Henry in the Tower, not more than sixteen years and eight months. By other historians it is supposed that his birth occurred about two years earlier.

Dare stir a wing if Warwick shakes his bells.

That is, if Warwick arms himself for opposition; the metaphor is borrowed from falconry. The hawks sometimes had little bells hung upon them, perhaps to terrify the birds, and prevent them from rising.

The loss of those three lords torments my heart.

He alludes to Northumberland, Westmoreland, and Clifford, who had left him from disgust at his weakness.

Why, how now, sons and brother.

Montague was a brother of Warwick, and not of York; Mr. Steevens, therefore, thinks we should read *cousin* instead of *brother*, which was the relationship between them. York may, however, apply the word as a term of affection—meaning brother in arms.

But 't was ere I was born.

This is an error; according to Hall, the historian, Rutland was twelve years old when he was killed by Clifford. The battle of St. Albans, in which old Clifford was slain, happened in 1455; that of Wakefield in 1460; Rutland was therefore seven years old at the death of the father of his destroyer.

My uncles both are slain in rescuing me.

These were two bastard uncles by the mother's side, Sir John and Sir Hugh Mortimer.

We body'd again.

Body'd probably means boggled, we made unskilful and bungling work of it; but some commentators would read *budged*, i. e., fled. Thus in *Coriolanus*—
394

The mouse ne'er shunn'd the cat, as they did *budge*
From rascals worse than they.

Or as the south to the septentrion.

The *septentrion* is the north. The same word is used by Milton as an adjective—

——— Cold *septentrion* blasts.

Dazzle mine eyes, or do I see three suns?

This singular phenomenon is thus described by Holinshed :—" At which tyme the sun (as some write) appeared to the earle of March like three sunnes, and sodainely ioyned altogether in one, uppon whiche sight hee tooke such courage, that he fiercely setting on his enemys, put them to flight; and for this cause menne ymagined that he gaue the sun in his full brightnesse for his badge or cognisaunce." The reader will see that the old chronicler does not appear to place any great faith in this supernatural appearance. At this time, he says, the sun, *as some write*, &c.; he does not assert the truth of it himself.

And happy always was it for that son,
Whose father for his hoarding went to hell.

Henry means, that it was well for the son that the father should be punished for his sins in his own person, instead of their being visited upon his children.

Darraign your battle.

That is, range your troops; put them in fighting order.

I would your highness would depart the field;
The queen hath best success when you are absent.

Henry was so spiritless, and invariably unfortunate, that it at length grew into a belief that his presence in the field of battle was an evil omen auguring defeat. This superstition is thus alluded to by Drayton, in *The Miseries of Queen Margaret*:—

Some think that Warwick had not lost the day,
But that the king into the field he brought;
For with the worse that side went still away
Which had king Henry with them when they fought:
Upon his birth so sad a curse there lay,
As that he never prospered in aught.
The queen won too, among the loss of many,
Her husband absent; present, never any.

¹³ *But like a foul misshapen stigmatic.*

A *stigmatic* denoted a criminal who had been branded or stigmatized with a hot iron as a token of punishment. It is applied to Richard in allusion to his deformity, meaning that he is branded by nature as a man to be avoided.

¹⁴ *As if a channel should be call'd the sea.*

A *channel* in Shakespeare's time signified what we now call a *kennel*. Thus in Stowe's *Chronicle*, 1605, "such a storme of raine happened at London, as the like of long time could not be remembered; whereupon the *channels* of the citie su ddenly rising," &c.

¹⁵ *A wisp of straw.*

It would appear that a wisp of straw, twisted into the form of a crown or head-dress, was sometimes placed upon termagant women as a disgrace. Thus, in *A Dialogue between John and Joan, striving who shall wear the Breeches.—Pleasures of Poetry*, no date—

   Good gentle Jone, with-holde thy hands,
     This once let me entreat thee,
   And make me promise, never more
     That thou shalt mind to beat me.
   For feare thou weare the wispe, good wife,
     And make our neighbours ride.

¹⁶ *Although thy husband may be Menelaus.*

That is, may be a cuckold.

¹⁷ *O boy, thy father gave thee life too soon,*
And hath bereft thee of thy life too late.

The meaning of this obscure passage appears to be, thy father gave thee life too soon; for hadst thou been born later, thou hadst been yet a boy, and therefore not engaged in this fearful battle. And he hath bereft thee of thy life too late; for it would have been better that thou hadst perished in infancy than have lived to be killed by thy father in early manhood.

¹⁸ *And so obsequious shall thy father be.*

Obsequious is here, careful of obsequies, or funeral rites.

¹⁹ *For Gloster's dukedom is too ominous.*

Richard is alluding to Thomas of Woodstock and Humphrey, the two previous dukes of Gloster, who were both murdered. The author probably had in his mind the following passage from Hall's *Chronicle*:—"It seemeth in many men that the name and title of Gloucester hath bene unfortunate and unluckie to diverse, whiche for their honour have bene erected by creation of princes to that stile and dignitie; as Hugh Spencer, Thomas of Woodstocke, (who was killed at Bury;) whiche three persons by miserable death finished their daies; and after them king Richard the III. also duke of Gloucester, in civil warre was slain and confounded; so that this name of Gloucester is taken for an unhappie and unfortunate stile, as the proverbe speaketh of Sejanus horse, whoso ryde was ever unluckye, and whose possessor was ever brought to misery."

²⁰ *Laund,* i. e., lawn, a plain extended between two woods.

²¹ *Because in quarrel of the house of York,*
The worthy gentleman did lose his life.

This is an error; Sir John Grey was killed at the second battle of St. Albans, fighting on the side of king Henry; and his estate was seized, not by Margaret, but by Edward.

²² *Or an unlick'd bear-whelp.*

An opinion anciently prevailed that the bear brings forth only shapeless lumps of animated flesh, which she licks into the form of bears; and to this absurdity Richard alludes. Ross, in his *Arcana microcosmi*, states that it is true that bears bring forth their young apparently deformed and misshapen, as the cubs are born wrapped up in a thick membrane, which is covered with a mucilaginous matter, and thus gives them the appearance of misshapen lumps. The mucilage is licked away by the dam, and the membrane broken, when the cub appears in its natural shape.

²³ *Enter Warwick, attended.*

Mr. Ritson says,—"There needs no other proof how little our common histories are to be depended upon, than this fabulous story of Warwick and the Lady Bona. The king was privately married to Lady Elizabeth Woodville, in 1463, and in February, 1465, Warwick actually stood sponsor to the Princess Elizabeth, their first child. What severely displeased him was:—first, the king's marrying one of the queen's sisters to the Duke of Buckingham; secondly, his conferring the office of lord treasurer (which he had taken from Lord Montjoy,) upon Lord Rivers, the queen's brother; thirdly,—his making a match between the son and heir of Lord Herbert and another of the queen's sisters; and between that nobleman's daughter and the young Lord Lisle; and creating young Herbert knight and Lord of Dunster; fourthly,—his making a match between Sir Thomas Grey, the queen's son, and Lady Ann, daughter and heiress of the Duke of Exeter, the king's niece, who had been talked of as a wife for the Earl of Northumberland, Warwick's brother.—See *Wm. of Wyrcester Annales*, which are unfortunately defective from the beginning of November, 1468, at which time no open rupture had taken place between the king and Warwick, who, for anything that appears to the contrary, were, at least, upon speaking terms."

²⁴ *Did I let pass the abuse done to my niece?*

It is supposed, that before the rupture between Warwick and Edward, the latter repaid the services of that great earl by an attempt to violate his niece or daughter. Holinshed thus refers to this singular and ungrateful outrage:—"King Edward did attempt a thing once in the earle's house, which was much against the earle's honestie (whether he would have deflowered his daughter or his neice, the certaintie was not for both their honours revealed), for surely such a thing was attempted by King Edward."

²⁵ *I'll o join mine eldest daughter.*

This is an error; Margaret's son, Edward, was married to Warwick's youngest daughter, the Lady Anne.

²⁶ *I was not ignoble of descent.*

Her mother was Jaquelin, the widow of the celebrated Duke of Bedford, regent of France, and brother of Henry the Fifth. Her father was Sir Richard Woodville, who had tee; previously a private gentleman, but, after his daughter's marriage with Edward, was raised to the rank of Earl Rivers.

Es'de, the elder ; Clarence will have the younger.

This error I have before noticed; Clarence was engaged to, and eventually married, the Lady Isabella, Warwick's eldest daughter.

With sleight and manhood stole to Rhesus' tents,
And brought from thence the Thracian fatal steeds.

Rhesus was a warlike king of Thrace, who assisted Priam in the defence of Troy against the Greeks. An ancient oracle had declared that Troy should never be taken while the horses of Rhesus drank the waters of the Xanthus, and fed upon the grass of the Trojan plains. The Greeks being acquainted with this prophecy, deputed two of their bravest generals, Diomedes and Ulysses, to capture these horses either by craft or force. They accordingly stole to the tent of Rhesus in the night, and having killed him, carried away his horses to their camp.

For few men rightly temper with the stars.

That is, adapt themselves to their own talents and destiny ; Warwick is commending Henry's wisdom in giving into stronger hands a government which he found himself unable to conduct.

My meed hath got me fame.

Meed here means not reward or recompense, but merit. Henry's reputation for meekness and sanctity had procured him fame ; men having got over their disappointment in not finding him a hero, were pleased to discover him to be a saint.

A Lancaster ! A Lancaster !

As Edward and his party are here the invaders, the shouts should be, A York! a York! unless we suppose them to come from Henry's guard, on the sudden appearance of their adversaries.

And, lords, towards Coventry bend we our course,
Where peremptory Warwick now remains.

Warwick has but just left the stage, declaring his inten-

tion to go to Coventry ; he could not yet have arrived there, nor could Edward have been acquainted with his intention. Shakespeare was led into this impropriety by the old play, and copied the error without examination.

But, whiles he thought to steal the single ten,
The king was slily finger'd from the deck !

That is, from the pack ; a pack of cards was anciently called a deck of cards.

To Hammes' castle straight.

This was a castle in Picardy, where Oxford was confined for many years.

Take that, the likeness of this railer here.

That is, thou that art the likeness of this railer here, i. e. his mother, Queen Margaret.

But, if you ever chance to have a child,
Look in his youth to have him so cut off.

This warning by Margaret is prophetic ; Edward's children were cut off by violence.

What scene of death hath Roscius now to act.

Roscius, the famous Roman actor, was a comedian ; but Shakespeare, wishing to compare Richard to some player about to represent a scene of murder, took the first or only name of antiquity that occurred to him, without being very particular about its propriety.

The raven rook'd her on the chimney's top.

To rook, or rather, to ruck, is a north-country word, meaning to squat down or lodge on anything.

Work thou the way,—and thou shalt execute.

I think we should read,—and this shalt execute.

Thanks, noble Clarence ; worthy brother, thanks.

The first and second folios have, by mistake, given this line to Clarence. Mr. Steevens tells us, that in his copy of the second folio, which had belonged to Charles the First, the king had erased Cla., and written King in its stead. The catalogue of the restorers of Shakespeare therefore includes a royal name.

LIFE AND DEATH OF

King Richard the Third.

———

THIS remarkable tragedy is properly the conclusion of the three parts of Henry the Sixth, and with it terminates Shakespeare's unbroken series of dramas on English history. The battle of Bosworth Field was the last war of the Roses; and the conflicting claims of the houses of York and Lancaster were united and buried in the person of Henry the Seventh.

This play, though called *The Life and Death of King Richard the Third*, is in reality the history only of Richard's intrigues for the throne, and of his brief reign, which lasted but for two years and two months. But Shakespeare was never particular about chronological propriety; and although this play, strictly speaking, comprises but a period of seven years, for it commences with the arrest of Clarence, which happened in the beginning of 1478, and terminates with the death of Richard at the battle of Bosworth, which was fought on the 22nd of August, 1485; yet the second scene carries us back a period of seven years more, to the funeral of the unhappy Henry the Sixth, which took place in May, 1471; so that the events of fourteen years are irregularly contained in it.

Richard and Margaret stand out prominently from the drama, two dark and awful creations; the one a subtle fiend, covering a satanic spirit with a mask of meekness; the other an avenging being, threatening God's wrath upon the destroyers of her family and party. Years of suffering seem to have elevated the active and intellectual Margaret into something above humanity: sorrow is the school of inspiration, and long watching had taught her to look with an understanding eye into the ghostly future. Her first entrance is grand and startling; she is like one resuscitated from the dead to denounce the sins of the living, and her imprecations upon the blood-stained members of the court of Edward are fearfully awful and harrowing. In her curses and prophecies are to be found the germ of the action; she addresses herself to each one that had been instrumental in the destruction of her family, and reveals the wrath in store for them: the queen, she prophesies, shall, like her, "die neither mother, wife, nor England's queen." She prays God that Rivers, Dorset, and Hastings may be suddenly cut off by violence as a punishment for their participation in the death of her son Edward. To Richard she foretells his brief career of terror, and infers his death; and she warns Buckingham, who scorns her counsel, that he will remember it another day, when Richard shall split his very heart with sorrow. Crying out, in the bitterness of her soul, on the treachery of the house of York, she appeals to heaven, and vehemently exclaims—

> O God, that seest it, do not suffer it;
> As it was won with blood, lost be it so!

The poet represents the eternal Providence as listening to and granting this fearful prayer, and the action of the tragedy is the realization of Margaret's prophetic maledictions. Steevens objects to this scene, and says—"Margaret, bullying the court of England in the royal palace, is a circumstance as absurd as the courtship of Gloster in a public street." It may be so, but the tragic grandeur of the incident more than outweighs its improbability. Whilst criticism requires likelihood and consistency

997

with truth from an author, it must not become too literal and exacting; if so, it breaks the poet's wing, and dooms him for ever to grovel on the ground.

Richard is brave and haughty; a polished courtier, a crafty statesman, and a perfect hypocrite. He is fond of deceiving under the form of religion, and "seems a saint when most he plays the devil;" yet, although he tramples upon its principles in every act of his life, he does not appear to reject and disbelieve them. He has a touch of superstitious awe respecting futurity; he does not deny immortality and hell, but is satisfied to risk eternal peril for present gratification. When visited by his awful dream on the eve of battle, he calls on the sacred name for mercy; like the devils, he believes and trembles. Though he resembles Iago in many points, he differs from him in this: Iago has no conscience, is never touched by compunction or repentance, and is utterly indifferent respecting a future state, the existence of which he does not appear to credit. Iago regards futurity as a fable, but Richard believes and defies it. Richard is witty and satirical, exceedingly proud of his eloquence and cunning; he triumphs in his success in winning Lady Anne's consent to become his wife, and in talking over the queen dowager to woo her daughter for him. These scenes have both been censured as unnatural; but it may be observed that the eloquence of princes seldom fails of success. Edward's widow was a vain intriguing woman, who was determined to have her daughter a queen if possible; she was in reality ready enough to marry her to Richard, and when that design failed, she, with equal readiness, contracted her to Richmond.

Richard's remarkable energy, and intellectual power, bear him undaunted through his career of violence; Margaret's imprecations, or his mother's curse when she takes her eternal leave of him, never for a moment appal his heart, or turn him from his purposes; his firm and resolute mind commands our respect, if not our admiration. He is a striking instance of great intellect allied to an utter want of principle or heart; he seems rather above than deficient in human affections. His mind is further embittered by his personal deformity; he laments that Nature has robbed him of the love of woman, therefore he will renounce love, and seek for happiness alone in regal power. He is terrible in the intensity of his selfishness, and possessed of a gigantic egotism, which induces him to regard even murder as an insignificant matter in comparison with the realization of his ambition. He will not recognize affinity of blood, but exclaims:—

I have no brother, I am like no brother;
And this word—love, which greybeards call divine,
Be resident in men, like one another,
And not in me; I am myself alone.

He lives to himself, and requires no sympathy from others; but, in the latter part of the tragedy, he is oppressed by the multitude of opposing circumstances—treachery and desertion environ him, doubt and feverish excitement weaken his strong mind; he gives contradictory orders, and on the eve of battle complains of the loss of his ordinary cheerfulness and alacrity. Then in his sleep he is visited by a long train of spectres; the spirits of those whom he had slain encourage his rival, and bid him despair. This vision lifts the veil which hides the future from us, and indicates the eternal doom of the tyrant. The poet thought that it was not sufficient that so great a villain should die upon the field of battle, but he shows him on the verge of the pit of eternal darkness and lamentation.

If we except the two young princes in the Tower, the victims of Richard's cruelty do not excite our commiseration at their fate; Clarence deserved his death for repeated treacheries; we cannot pity Hastings, for he triumphs in the unjust execution of his adversaries, when, though unknowingly within an hour of his own doom; and we experience a satisfaction in the execution of Buckingham, who in villany is only second to Richard himself; while poor Queen Anne is so feeble and inconsistent a character that she is forgotten in the long list of sufferers.

The murder of Clarence is traced with a vivid pencil; his dream previous to that event is a fearful picture of the terrors of conscience; the poet justly represents him suffering in this manner, for his whole life had been a scene of selfishness and treachery. Indeed the house of York cannot boast one virtuous and noble member; the curse of innocent blood seems to have rested upon it, for king Edward was the only one of that turbulent family who did not die by violence, though I may also except Cicely, the aged dowager duchess of York, who lived to see her husband, children, and grand-children perish successively on the battle-field, the public scaffold, or in the secret dungeon.

The dialogue between the two ruffians who murder Clarence is very fine; one of those remarkable episodes seldom found but in the pages of Shakespeare. Savage as is their nature, they are human in comparison with the master-spirit of this tragedy; they hesitate on the threshold of murder, and talk merely to delay an act which they fear to commit. Like Hamlet, when reasoning on suicide, they almost argue themselves out of their evil resolution. The accidental mention of the word judgment breeds remorse in one of the assassins; the terrors of the great day of judgment present themselves in a misty but appalling form to his mind, and he determines that the duke shall live. But the other suggests the reward, and the villain is steel again.

Shakespeare gave additional exaltation to the Earl of Richmond, by making him slay Richard with his own hand. This was not the case; Richard's eagle eye having caught sight of his adversary surrounded by a staff of officers, he thought to end the battle by a single blow, and therefore spurred furiously towards him, killing two gentlemen of distinction who opposed his impetuous charge, but immediately afterwards was himself surrounded and slain. The few adherents who remained faithful to Richard seem to have shared his fate. Norfolk and Ratcliffe were found dead upon the field, and Catesby was executed by Richmond immediately after the battle. Considering the interests involved in this action, it was not conducted on a very extensive scale; both armies did not amount to more than eighteen thousand men, and of these scarcely three thousand perished. The fate of a great kingdom was, perhaps, never before decided by so small a power.

This tragedy was first entered at Stationers' Hall, October 20, 1597, and is supposed by Mr. Malone to have been written in the same year.

909

PERSONS REPRESENTED.

KING EDWARD THE FOURTH.
Appears, Act II. sc. 1.

EDWARD, *Prince of Wales, Son to the King, afterwards* King Edward the Fifth.
Appears, Act III. sc. 1.

RICHARD, *Duke of York, Son to the King.*
Appears, Act II. sc. 4. Act III. sc. 1.

GEORGE, *Duke of Clarence, Brother to the King.*
Appears, Act I. sc. 1; sc. 4.

RICHARD, *Duke of Gloucester, Brother to the King, and afterwards* King Richard the Third.
Appears, Act I. sc. 1; sc. 2; sc. 3. Act II. sc. 1; sc. 2.
Act III. sc. 1; sc. 4; sc. 5; sc. 7. Act IV. sc. 2; sc. 3.
sc. 4. Act V. sc. 3; sc. 4.

A YOUNG SON OF CLARENCE.
Appears, Act II. sc. 2.

HENRY, *Earl of* Richmond, *afterwards* King Henry the Seventh.
Appears, Act V. sc. 2; sc. 3; sc. 4.

CARDINAL BOURCHIER, *Archbishop of* Canterbury.
Appears, Act III. sc. 1.

THOMAS ROTHERAM, *Archbishop of* York.
Appears, Act II. sc. 4.

JOHN MORTON, *Bishop of* Ely.
Appears, Act III. sc. 4.

DUKE OF BUCKINGHAM.
Appears, Act I. sc. 3. Act II. sc. 1; sc. 2. Act III. sc. 1;
sc. 2; sc. 4; sc. 5; sc. 7. Act IV. sc. 2. Act V. sc. 1.

DUKE OF NORFOLK.
Appears, Act V. sc. 3; sc. 4.

EARL OF SURREY, *his Son.*
Appears, Act V. sc. 3.

EARL RIVERS, *Brother to* King Edward's Queen.
Appears, Act I. sc. 3. Act II. sc. 1; sc. 2. Act III. sc. 3.

MARQUIS OF DORSET, *Son to* Queen Elizabeth.
Appears, Act I. sc. 3. Act II. sc. 1; sc. 2. Act IV. sc. 1.

LORD GREY, *Son to* Queen Elizabeth.
Appears Act I. sc. 3. Act II. sc. 1. Act III. sc. 3.

EARL OF OXFORD.
Appears, Act V. sc. 2; sc. 3.

LORD HASTINGS.
Appears, Act I. sc. 1; sc. 3. Act II. sc. 1; sc. 2. Act III.
sc. 1; sc. 2; sc. 4.

LORD STANLEY.
Appears, Act I. sc. 3. Act II. sc. 1. Act III. sc. 2; sc. 4.
Act IV. sc. 1; sc. 2; sc. 4; sc. 5. Act V. sc. 3; sc. 4.

LORD LOVEL.
Appears, Act III. sc. 4; sc. 5.
1000

SIR THOMAS VAUGHAN.
Appears, Act III. sc. 3.

SIR RICHARD RATCLIFFE.
Appears, Act II. sc. 2. Act III. sc. 3; sc. 5. Act IV. sc. 4
Act V. sc. 3.

SIR WILLIAM CATESBY.
Appears, Act I. sc. 3. Act III. sc. 1; sc. 2; sc. 4; sc. 5
sc. 7. Act IV. sc. 2; sc. 3; sc. 4. Act V. sc. 3. sc. 4.

SIR JAMES TYRREL.
Appears, Act IV. sc. 2; sc. 3.

SIR JAMES BLUNT.
SIR WALTER HERBERT.
Appear, Act V. sc. 2; sc. 3.

SIR ROBERT BRAKENBURY, *Lieutenant of the* Tower.
Appears, Act I. sc. 1; sc. 4. Act IV. sc. 1.

CHRISTOPHER URSWICK, *a Priest.*
Appears, Act IV. sc. 5.

ANOTHER PRIEST.
A PURSUIVANT.
Appear, Act III. sc. 2.

LORD MAYOR OF LONDON.
Appears, Act III. sc. 1; sc. 5; sc. 7.

SHERIFF OF WILTSHIRE.
Appears, Act V. sc. 1.

TWO MURDERERS.
Appear, Act I. sc. 3; sc. 4.

A SCRIVENER.
Appears, Act III. sc. 6.

ELIZABETH, *Queen of* Edward the Fourth.
Appears, Act I. sc. 3. Act II. sc. 1; sc. 2; sc. 4. Act IV
sc. 1; sc. 4.

MARGARET, *Widow of* King Henry the Sixth.
Appears, Act I. sc. 3. Act IV. sc. 4.

DUCHESS OF YORK, *Mother to* King Edward the Fourth, Clarence, *and* Gloucester.
Appears, Act II. sc. 2; sc. 4. Act IV. sc. 1; sc. 4.

LADY ANNE, *Widow of* Edward, *Prince of* Wales, Son to King Henry the Sixth, *afterwards married to the* Duke *of* Gloucester.
Appears, Act I. sc. 2. Act IV. sc. 1.

A YOUNG DAUGHTER OF CLARENCE.
Appears, Act II. sc. 2. Act IV. sc. 1.

Lords, Gentlemen, Attendants, Citizens, Messengers, Ghosts, Soldiers, &c.

SCENE,—ENGLAND.

LIFE AND DEATH OF

King Richard the Third.

ACT I.

SCENE I.—London. *A Street.*

Enter GLOSTER.

Glo. Now is the winter of our discontent
Made glorious summer by this sun of York;
And all the clouds, that lower'd upon our house,
In the deep bosom of the ocean buried.
Now are our brows bound with victorious wreaths;
Our bruised arms hung up for monuments;
Our stern alarums chang'd to merry meetings,
Our dreadful marches to delightful measures.
Grim-visag'd war hath smooth'd his wrinkled
    front;
And now,—instead of mounting barbed steeds,
To fright the souls of fearful adversaries,—
He capers nimbly in a lady's chamber,
To the lascivious pleasing of a lute.
But I,—that am not shap'd for sportive tricks,
Nor made to court an amorous looking-glass;
I, that am rudely stamped, and want love's majesty,
To strut before a wanton ambling nymph;
I, that am curtail'd of this fair proportion,
Cheated of feature by dissembling nature,
Deform'd, unfinish'd, sent before my time
Into this breathing world, scarce half made up,
And that so lamely and unfashionable,
That dogs bark at me, as I halt by them;—
Why I, in this weak piping time of peace,
Have no delight to pass away the time;
Unless to spy my shadow in the sun,
And descant on mine own deformity;
And therefore,—since I cannot prove a lover,
To entertain these fair well-spoken days,—

I am determined to prove a villain,
And hate the idle pleasures of these days.
Plots have I laid, inductions dangerous,
By drunken prophecies, libels, and dreams,
To set my brother Clarence, and the king,
In deadly hate the one against the other:
And, if king Edward be as true and just,
As I am subtle, false, and treacherous,
This day should Clarence closely be mew'd up:
About a prophecy, which says—that G
Of Edward's heirs the murderer shall be.
Dive, thoughts, down to my soul! here Clarence
    comes.

Enter CLARENCE, *guarded, and* BRAKENBURY.

Brother, good day: What means this armed guard,
That waits upon your grace?
    Clar.   His majesty,
Tendering my person's safety, hath appointed
This conduct to convey me to the Tower.
    Glo. Upon what cause?
    Clar.   Because my name is—George.
    Glo. Alack, my lord, that fault is none of
    yours:
He should, for that, commit your godfathers:——
O, belike, his majesty hath some intent,
That you shall be new christen'd in the Tower.
But what's the matter, Clarence? may I know?
    Clar. Yea, Richard, when I know; for, I
    protest,
As yet I do not: But, as I can learn,
He hearkens after prophecies, and dreams;
And from the cross-row plucks the letter G,

And says—a wizard told him, that by G
His issue disinherited should be;
And, for my name of George begins with G,
It follows in his thought, that I am he:
These, as I learn, and such like toys as these,
Have mov'd his highness to commit me now.

  Glo. Why, this it is, when men are rul'd by
         women:—
'T is not the king, that sends you to the Tower;
My lady Grey, his wife, Clarence, 't is she,
That tempers him to this extremity.
Was it not she, and that good man of worship,
Antony Woodeville, her brother there,
That made him send lord Hastings to the Tower,
From whence this present day he is deliver'd?
We are not safe, Clarence, we are not safe.

  Clar. By heaven, I think, there is no man
         secure,
But the queen's kindred, and night-walking heralds
That trudge betwixt the king and mistress Shore.
Heard you not, what an humble suppliant
Lord Hastings was to her for his delivery?

  Glo. Humbly complaining to her deity
Got my lord chamberlain his liberty.
I 'll tell you what,—I think, it is our way,
If we will keep in favour with the king,
To be her men, and wear her livery:
The jealous o'er-worn widow, and herself,
Since that our brother dubb'd them gentlewomen,
Are mighty gossips in this monarchy.

  Brak. I beseech your graces both to pardon me;
His majesty hath straitly given in charge,
That no man shall have private conference,
Of what degree so ever, with his brother.

  Glo. Even so? an please your worship, Braken-
         bury,
You may partake of any thing we say:
We speak no treason, man;—We say, the king
Is wise, and virtuous; and his noble queen
Well struck in years; fair, and not jealous:—
We say, that Shore's wife hath a pretty foot,
A cherry lip,
A bonny eye, a passing pleasing tongue;
And the queen's kindred are made gentlefolks:
How say you, sir? can you deny all this?

  Brak. With this, my lord, myself have nought
         to do.

  Glo. Nought to do with mistress Shore? I tell
         thee, fellow,
He that doth naught with her, excepting one,
Were best to do it secretly, alone.

  Brak. What one, my lord?
1902

  Glo. Her husband, knave:—Would'st thou
         betray me?

  Brak. I beseech your grace to pardon me;
         and, withal,
Forbear your conference with the noble duke.

  Clar. We know thy charge, Brakenbury, and
         will obey.

  Glo. We are the queen's abjects, and must
         obey.
Brother, farewell: I will unto the king;
And whatsoever you will employ me in,—
Were it, to call king Edward's widow—sister,—
I will perform it to enfranchise you.
Mean time, this deep disgrace in brotherhood,
Touches me deeper than you can imagine.

  Clar. I know it pleaseth neither of us well.

  Glo. Well, your imprisonment shall not be long;
I will deliver you, or else lie for you:
Mean time, have patience.

  Clar.   I must perforce; farewell.
         [*Exeunt* CLAR., BRAK., *and* Guard.

  Glo. Go, tread the path that thou shalt ne'er
         return,
Simple, plain Clarence!—I do love thee so,
That I will shortly send thy soul to heaven,
If heaven will take the present at our hands.
But who comes here? the new-deliver'd Hastings?

Enter HASTINGS.

  Hast. Good time of day unto my gracious lord!

  Glo. As much unto my good lord chamberlain!
Well are you welcome to this open air.
How hath your lordship brook'd imprisonment?

  Hast. With patience, noble lord, as prisoners
         must:
But I shall live, my lord, to give them thanks,
That were the cause of my imprisonment.

  Glo. No doubt, no doubt; and so shall Clar-
         ence too;
For they, that were your enemies, are his,
And have prevail'd as much on him, as you.

  Hast. More pity, that the eagle should be
         mew'd,
While kites and buzzards prey at liberty.

  Glo. What news abroad?

  Hast. No news so bad abroad, as this at
         home;—
The king is sickly, weak, and melancholy,
And his physicians fear him mightily.

  Glo. Now, by Saint Paul, this news is bad in-
         deed.
O, he hath kept an evil diet long,

And over much consum'd his royal person;
'T is very grievous to be thought upon.
What, is he in his bed?
  Hast.   He is.
  Glo. Go you before, and I will follow you.
                                         [*Exit* HAST.
He cannot live, I hope; and must not die,
Till George be pack'd with posthaste up to heaven.
I 'll in, to urge his hatred more to Clarence,
With lies well steel'd with weighty arguments;
And, if I fail not in my deep intent,
Clarence hath not another day to live:
Which done, God take king Edward to his mercy,
And leave the world for me to bustle in!
For then I 'll marry Warwick's youngest daughter:
What though I kill'd her husband, and her father?
The readiest way to make the wench amends,
Is—to become her husband, and her father:
The which will I; not all so much for love,
As for another secret close intent,
By marrying her, which I must reach unto.
But yet I run before my horse to market:
Clarence still breathes; Edward still lives, and
  reigns;
When they are gone, then must I count my gains.
                                         [*Exit.*

  SCENE II.—*The same. Another Street.*

Enter the Corpse of King Henry the Sixth, *borne
in an open Coffin, Gentlemen bearing Halberds,
to guard it; and* LADY ANNE *as Mourner.*

  Anne. Set down, set down your honourable
  load,—
If honour may be shrouded in a hearse,—
Whilst I a while obsequiously lament
The untimely fall of virtuous Lancaster.—
Poor key-cold figure of a holy king!
Pale ashes of the house of Lancaster!
Thou bloodless remnant of that royal blood!
Be it lawful that I invocate thy ghost,
To hear the lamentations of poor Anne,
Wife to thy Edward, to thy slaughter'd son,
Stabb'd by the self-same hand that made these
  wounds!
Lo, in these windows, that let forth thy life,
I pour the helpless balm of my poor eyes:—
O, cursed be the hand that made these holes!
Cursed the heart, that had the heart to do it!
Cursed the blood, that let this blood from hence!
More direful hap betide that hated wretch,
That makes us wretched by the death of thee,

Than I can wish to adders, spiders, toads,
Or any creeping venom'd thing that lives!
If ever he have child, abortive be it,
Prodigious, and untimely brought to light,
Whose ugly and unnatural aspéct
May fright the hopeful mother at the view;
And that be heir to his unhappiness!
If ever he have wife, let her be made
More miserable by the death of him,
Than I am made by my young lord, and thee —
Come, now, toward Chertsey with your holy load,
Taken from Paul's to be interred there;
And, still as you are weary of the weight,
Rest you, whiles I lament king Henry's corse.
         [*The Bearers take up the Corpse, and advance*

              Enter GLOSTER.

  Glo. Stay you, that bear the corse, and set it
  down.
  Anne. What black magician conjures up this
  fiend,
To stop devoted charitable deeds?
  Glo. Villains, set down the corse; or, by Saint
  Paul,
I 'll make a corse of him that disobeys.
  1st Gent. My lord, stand back, and let the coffin
  pass.
  Glo. Unmanner'd dog! stand thou when I
  command:
Advance thy halberd higher than my breast,
Or, by Saint Paul, I 'll strike thee to my foot,
And spurn upon thee, beggar, for thy boldness.
              [*The bearers set down the Coffin.*
  Anne. What, do you tremble? are you all
  afraid?
Alas, I blame you not; for you are mortal,
And mortal eyes cannot endure the devil.—
Avaunt, thou dreadful minister of hell!
Thou had'st but power over his mortal body,
His soul thou canst not have; therefore, be gone.
  Glo. Sweet saint, for charity, be not so curst.
  Anne. Foul devil, for God's sake, hence, and
  trouble us not;
For thou hast made the happy earth thy hell,
Fill'd it with cursing cries, and deep exclaims.
If thou delight to view thy heinous deeds,
Behold this pattern of thy butcheries:—
O, gentlemen, see, see! dead Henry's wounds
Open their congeal'd mouths, and bleed afresh!—
Blush, blush, thou lump of foul deformity;
For 't is thy presence that exhales this blood
From cold and empty veins, where no blood dwells;

Thy deed, inhuman and unnatural,
Provokes this deluge most unnatural.——
O God, which this blood mad'st, revenge his
    death !
O earth, which this blood drink'st, revenge his
    death !
Either, heaven, with lightning strike the mur-
    derer dead,
Or, earth, gape open wide, and eat him quick ;
As thou dost swallow up this good king's blood,
Which his hell-govern'd arm hath butchered !
    Glo. Lady, you know no rules of charity,
Which renders good for bad, blessings for curses.
    Anne. Villain, thou know'st no law of God nor
    man ;
No beast so fierce, but knows some touch of pity.
    Glo. But I know none, and therefore am no
    beast.
    Anne. O wonderful, when devils tell the truth !
    Glo. More wonderful, when angels are so an-
    gry.—
Vouchsafe, divine perfection of a woman,
Of these supposed evils, to give me leave,
By circumstance but to acquit myself.
    Anne. Vouchsafe, diffus'd infection of a man,
For these known evils, but to give me leave,
By circumstance, to curse thy cursed self.
    Glo. Fairer than tongue can name thee, let me
    have
Some patient leisure to excuse myself.
    Anne. Fouler than heart can think thee, thou
    canst make
No excuse current, but to hang thyself.
    Glo. By such despair, I should accuse myself.
    Anne. And, by despairing, shalt thou stand ex-
    cused ;
For doing worthy vengeance on thyself,
That didst unworthy slaughter upon others.
    Glo. Say, that I slew them not?
    Anne.   Why then, they are not dead:
But dead they are, and, devilish slave, by thee.
    Glo. I did not kill your husband.
    Anne.   Why, then he is alive.
    Glo. Nay, he is dead; and slain by Edward's
    hand.
    Anne. In thy soul's throat thou liest; queen
    Margaret saw
Thy murderous faulchion smoking in his blood;
The which thou once didst bend against her breast,
But that thy brothers beat aside the point.
    Glo. I was provoked by her slanderous tongue,
That laid their guilt upon my guiltless shoulders.

1004

    Anne. Thou wast provoked by thy bloody mind,
That never dreamt on aught but butcheries :
Didst thou not kill this king ?
    Glo.   I grant ye.
    Anne. Dost grant me, hedge-hog? then, God
    grant me too,
Thou may'st be damned for that wicked deed !
O, he was gentle, mild, and virtuous.
    Glo. The fitter for the king of heaven that hath
    him.
    Anne. He is in heaven, where thou shalt never
    come.
    Glo. Let him thank me, that help to send him
    thither;
For he was fitter for that place, than earth.
    Anne. And thou unfit for any place but hell.
    Glo. Yes, one place else, if you will hear me
    name it.
    Anne. Some dungeon.
    Glo.   Your bed-chamber.
    Anne. Ill rest betide the chamber where thou
    liest !
    Glo. So will it, madam, till I lie with you.
    Anne. I hope so.
    Glo.   I know so.—But, gentle lady Anne,—
To leave this keen encounter of our wits,
And fall somewhat into a slower method ;—
Is not the causer of the timeless deaths
Of these Plantagenets, Henry, and Edward,
As blameful as the executioner ?
    Anne. Thou wast the cause, and most accurs d
    effect.
    Glo. Your beauty was the cause of that effect ;
Your beauty, which did haunt me in my sleep,
To undertake the death of all the world,
So I might live one hour in your sweet bosom.
    Anne. If I thought that, I tell thee, homicide,
These nails should rend that beauty from my
    cheeks.
    Glo. These eyes could not endure that beauty's
    wreck.
You should not blemish it, if I stood by :
As all the world is cheered by the sun,
So I by that; it is my day, my life.
    Anne. Black night o'ershade thy day, and death
    thy life !
    Glo. Curse not thyself, fair creature ; thou art
    both.
    Anne. I would I were, to be reveng'd on thee
    Glo. It is a quarrel most unnatural,
To be reveng'd on him that loveth thee.
    Anne. It is a quarrel just and reasonable.

To be reveng'd on him that kill'd my husband.

Glo. He that bereft thee, lady, of thy husband,
Did it to help thee to a better husband.

Anne. His better doth not breathe upon the
earth.

Glo. He lives, that loves you better than he
could.

Anne. Name him.

Glo.   Plantagenet.

Anne.   Why, that was he.

Glo. The self-same name, but one of better nature.

Anne. Where is he?

Glo.   Here: [*She spits at him.*] Why
dost thou spit at me?

Anne. 'Would it were mortal poison for thy
sake!

Glo. Never came poison from so sweet a place.

Anne. Never hung poison on a fouler toad.
Out of my sight! thou dost infect mine eyes.

Glo. Thine eyes, sweet lady, have infected mine.

Anne. 'Would they were basilisks, to strike
thee dead!

Glo. I would they were, that I might die at
once,
For now they kill me with a living death.
Those eyes of thine from mine have drawn salt
tears,
Sham'd their aspects with store of childish drops:
These eyes, which never shed remorseful tear,—
No, when my father York and Edward wept,
To hear the piteous moan that Rutland made,
When black-fac'd Clifford shook his sword at him;
Nor when thy warlike father, like a child,
Told the sad story of my father's death;
And twenty times made pause, to sob, and weep,
That all the standers-by had wet their cheeks,
Like trees bedash'd with rain; in that sad time,
My manly eyes did scorn an humble tear;
And what these sorrows could not thence exhale,
Thy beauty hath, and made them blind with
weeping.
I never su'd to friend, nor enemy;
My tongue could never learn sweet soothing word;
But now thy beauty is propos'd my fee,
My proud heart sues, and prompts my tongue to
speak.   [*She looks scornfully at him.*]
Teach not thy lip such scorn; for it was made
For kissing, lady, not for such contempt.
If thy revengeful heart cannot forgive,
Lo! here I lend thee this sharp-pointed sword;
Which if thou please to hide in this true breast,

And let the soul forth that adoreth thee,
I lay it naked to the deadly stroke,
And humbly beg the death upon my knee.

          [*He lays his Breast open; she offers at it
          with his Sword.*]

Nay, do not pause; for I did kill king Henry;—
But 't was thy beauty that provoked me.
Nay, now despatch; 't was I that stabb'd young
Edward;—

          [*She again offers at his Breast.*]

But 't was thy heavenly face that set me on.

          [*She lets fall the Sword.*]

Take up the sword again, or take up me.

Anne. Arise, dissembler: though I wish thy
death,
I will not be thy executioner.

Glo. Then bid me kill myself, and I will do it.

Anne. I have already.

Glo.   That was in thy rage:
Speak it again, and, even with the word,
This hand, which, for thy love, did kill thy love,
Shall, for thy love, kill a far truer love;
To both their deaths shalt thou be accessary.

Anne. I would, I knew thy heart.

Glo.   'T is figur'd in
My tongue.

Anne.   I fear me, both are false.

Glo.   Then never man
Was never true.

Anne. Well, well, put up your sword.

Glo. Say then, my peace is made.

Anne.   That shall you know
Hereafter.

Glo. But shall I live in hope?

Anne.   All men,
I hope, live so.

Glo. Vouchsafe to wear this ring.

Anne. To take, is not to give.

          [*She puts on the Ring.*]

Glo. Look, how this ring encompasseth thy
finger,
Even so thy breast encloseth my poor heart;
Wear both of them, for both of them are thine.
And if thy poor devoted servant may
But beg one favour at thy gracious hand,
Thou dost confirm his happiness for ever.

Anne. What is it?

Glo. That it may please you leave these sad
designs
To him that hath more cause to be a mourner
And presently repair to Cro-by-place:
Where—after I have solemnly interr'd,

At Chertsey monast'ry, this noble king,
And wet his grave with my repentant tears,—
I will with all expedient duty see you:
For divers unknown reasons, I beseech you,
Grant me this boon.

Anne. With all my heart; and much it joys
me too,
To see you are become so penitent.—
Tressel, and Berkley, go along with me.

Glo. Bid me farewell.

Anne.   T is more than you deserve:
But, since you teach me how to flatter you,
Imagine I have said farewell already.

     [*Exeunt L.* ANNE, TRES., *and* BERK.

Glo. Take up the corse, sirs.

Gent.   Towards Chertsey, noble lord?

Glo. No, to White-Friars; there attend my
coming. [*Exeunt the rest, with the Corse.*
Was ever woman in this humour woo'd?
Was ever woman in this humour won?
I 'll have her,—but I will not keep her long.
What! I, that kill'd her husband, and his father,
To take her in her heart's extremest hate;
With curses in her mouth, tears in her eyes,
The bleeding witness of her hatred by;
With God, her conscience, and these bars against
me,
And I no friends to back my suit withal,
But the plain devil, and dissembling looks,
And yet to win her,—all the world to nothing!
Ha!
Hath she forgot already that brave prince,
Edward, her lord, whom I some three months
since,
Stabb'd in my angry mood at Tewkesbury?[11]
A sweeter and a lovelier gentleman,
Fram'd in the prodigality of nature,
Young, valiant, wise, and, no doubt, right royal,—
The spacious world cannot again afford:
And will she yet abase her eyes on me,
That cropp'd the golden prime of this sweet prince,
And made her widow to a woful bed?
On me, whose all not equals Edward's moiety!
On me, that halt, and am misshapen thus?
My dukedom to a beggarly denier,[12]
I do mistake my person all this while:
Upon my life, she finds, although I cannot,
Myself to be a marvellous proper man.
I 'll be at charges for a looking-glass;
And entertain a score or two of tailors,
To study fashions to adorn my body:
Since I am crept in favour with myself,

I will maintain it with some little cost.
But, first, I 'll turn yon' fellow in his grave ·
And then return lamenting to my love.——
Shine out, fair sun, till I have bought a glass,
That I may see my shadow as I pass.   [*Exit.*

SCENE III.—*The Same. A Room in the Palace.*

Enter QUEEN ELIZABETH, LORD RIVERS, *and*
LORD GREY.

Riv. Have patience, madam; there 's no doubt
his majesty
Will soon recover his accustom'd health.

Grey. In that you brook it ill, it makes him
worse:
Therefore, for God's sake, entertain good comfort,
And cheer his grace with quick and merry words.

Q. Eliz. If he were dead, what would betide of
me?

Grey. No other harm, but loss of such a lord.

Q. Eliz. The loss of such a lord includes all
harms.

Grey. The heavens have bless'd you with a
goodly son,
To be your comforter, when he is gone.

Q. Eliz. Ah, he is young; and his minority
Is put unto the trust of Richard Gloster,
A man that loves not me, nor none of you.

Riv. Is it concluded, he shall be protector?

Q. Eliz. It is determin'd, not concluded yet:
But so it must be, if the king miscarry.

Enter BUCKINGHAM *and* STANLEY.

Grey. Here come the lords of Buckingham
and Stanley.

Buck. Good time of day unto your royal
grace!

Stan. God make your majesty joyful as you
have been!

Q. Eliz. The countess Richmond,[13] good my
lord of Stanley,
To your good prayer will scarcely say—amen.
Yet, Stanley, notwithstanding she 's your wife,
And loves not me, be you, good lord, assur'd,
I hate not you for her proud arrogance.

Stan. I do beseech you, either not believe
The envious slanders of her false accusers;
Or, if she be accus'd on true report,
Bear with her weakness, which, I think, proceeds,
From wayward sickness, and no grounded malice.

Q. Eliz. Saw you the king to-day, my lord of
Stanley?

Stan. But now, the duke of Buckingham, and I,
Are come from visiting his majesty.

   Q. Eliz. What likelihood of his amendment,
      lords?

   Buck. Madam, good hope; his grace speaks
      cheerfully.

   Q. Eliz. God grant him health! did you confer
      with him?

   Buck. Ay, madam: he desires to make atone-
      ment
Between the duke of Gloster and your brothers,
And between them and my lord chamberlain;
And sent to warn them to his royal presence.

   Q. Eliz. 'Would all were well!—But that will
      never be;—
I fear, our happiness is at the height.

   Enter GLOSTER, HASTINGS, *and* DORSET.

   Glo. They do me wrong, and I will not endure
      it:—
Who are they, that complain unto the king
That I, forsooth, am stern, and love them not?
By holy Paul, they love his grace but lightly,
That fill his ears with such dissentious rumours.
Because I cannot flatter, and speak fair,
Smile in men's faces, smooth, deceive, and cog,
Duck with French nods and apish courtesy,
I must be held a rancorous enemy.
Cannot a plain man live, and think no harm,
But thus his simple truth must be abus'd
By silken, sly, insinuating Jacks?

   Grey. To whom in all this presence speaks
      your grace?

   Glo. To thee, that hast nor honesty, nor grace.
When have I injur'd thee? when done thee
      wrong?—
Or thee?—or thee?—or any of your faction?
A plague upon you all! His royal grace,—
Whom God preserve better than you would
      wish!—
Cannot be quiet scarce a breathing-while,
But you must trouble him with lewd complaints.

   Q. Eliz. Brother of Gloster, you mistake the
      matter:
The king, of his own royal disposition,
And not provok'd by any suitor else;
Aiming, belike, at your interior hatred,
That in your outward action shows itself,
Against my children, brothers, and myself,
Makes him to send; that thereby he may gather
The ground of your ill-will, and so remove it.

   Glo. I cannot tell;—The world is grown so bad,

That wrens may prey where eagles dare not perch:
Since every Jack became a gentleman,
There's many a gentle person made a Jack.

   Q. Eliz. Come, come, we know your meaning,
      brother Gloster;
You envy my advancement, and my friends';
God grant, we never may have need of you!

   Glo. Meantime, God grants that we have need
      of you:
Our brother is imprison'd by your means,
Myself disgrac'd, and the nobility
Held in contempt; while great promotions
Are daily given, to enoble those
That scarce, some two days since, were worth a
      noble.

   Q. Eliz. By Him, that rais'd me to this careful
      height
From that contented hap which I enjoy'd,
I never did incense his majesty
Against the duke of Clarence, but have been
An earnest advocate to plead for him.
My lord, you do me shameful injury,
Falsely to draw me in these vile suspects.

   Glo. You may deny that you were not the cause
Of my lord Hastings' late imprisonment.

   Riv. She may, my lord; for——

   Glo. She may, lord Rivers?—why, who knows
      not so?
She may do more, sir, than denying that:
She may help you to many fair preferments;
And then deny her aiding hand therein,
And lay those honours on your high desert.
What may she not? She may,—ay, marry, may
      she.—

   Riv. What, marry, may she?

   Glo. What, marry, may she! marry with a king,
A bachelor, a handsome stripling too:
I wis, your grandam had a worser match.

   Q. Eliz. My lord of Gloster, I have too long
      borne
Your blunt upbraidings, and your bitter scoffs:
By heaven, I will acquaint his majesty,
Of those gross taunts I often have endur'd.
I had rather be a country servant-maid,
Than a great queen, with this condition—
To be so baited, scorn'd, and stormed at:
Small joy have I in being England's queen.

   Enter QUEEN MARGARET, *behind.*

   Q. Mar. And lessen'd be that small, God, I be-
      seech thee!
Thy honour, state, and seat, is due to me.

Glo. What? threat you me with telling of the
　　king?
Tell him, and spare not look, what I have said
I will avouch, in presence of the king:
I dare adventure to be sent to the Tower.
'T is time to speak, my pains are quite forgot.
　Q. Mar. Out, devil! I remember them too well:
Thou kill'dst my husband Henry in the Tower,
And Edward, my poor son, at Tewkesbury.
　　Glo. Ere you were queen, ay, or your husband
　　　king,
I was a pack-horse in his great affairs,
A weeder-out of his proud adversaries,
A liberal rewarder of his friends;
To royalize his blood, I spilt mine own.
　　Q. Mar. Ay, and much better blood than his,
　　　or thine.
　　Glo. In all which time, you, and your husband
　　　Grey,
Were factions for the house of Lancaster;—
And, Rivers, so were you:—Was not your husband
In Margaret's battle at Saint Albans slain?
Let me put in your minds, if you forget,
What you have been ere now, and what you are;
Withal, what I have been, and what I am.
　　Q. Mar. A murd'rous villain, and so still thou
　　　art.
　　Glo. Poor Clarence did forsake his father War-
　　　wick,
Ay, and forswore himself,—which Jesu par-
　　don!—
　　Q. Mar. Which God revenge!
　　Glo. To fight on Edward's party, for the crown;
And, for his meed, poor lord, he is mew'd up:
I would to God, my heart were flint like Edward's,
Or Edward's soft and pitiful, like mine;
I am too childish-foolish for this world.
　　Q. Mar. Hie thee to hell for shame, and leave
　　　this world,
Thou cacodæmon! there thy kingdom is.
　　Riv. My lord of Gloster, in those busy days,
Which here you urge, to prove us enemies,
We follow'd then our lord, our lawful king;
So should we you, if you should be our king.
　　Glo. If I should be?—I had rather be a
　　　pedlar:
Far be it from my heart, the thought thereof!
　　Q. Eliz. As little joy, my lord, as you suppose
You should enjoy, were you this country's king;
As little joy you may suppose in me,
That I enjoy, being the queen thereof.
　　Q. Mar. A little joy enjoys the queen thereof;

For I am she, and altogether joyless.
I can no longer hold me patient.— [*Advancing.*
Hear me, you wrangling pirates, that fall out
In sharing that which you have pill'd from me:
Which of you trembles not, that looks on me?
If not, that, I being queen, you bow like subjects;
Yet that, by you depos'd, you quake like rebels:—
Ah, gentle villain, do not turn away!
　　Glo. Foul wrinkled witch, what mak'st thou in
　　　my sight?
　　Q. Mar. But repetition of what thou hast marr'd
That will I make, before I let thee go.
　　Glo. Wert thou not banished on pain of death?
　　Q. Mar. I was; but I do find more pain in
　　　banishment,
Than death can yield me here by my abode.
A husband, and a son, thou ow'st to me,—
And thou, a kingdom;—all of you, allegiance:
This sorrow that I have, by right is yours;
And all the pleasures you usurp, are mine.
　　Glo. The curse my noble father laid on thee,—
When thou didst crown his warlike brows with
　　paper,
And with thy scorns drew'st rivers from his eyes;
And then, to dry them, gav'st the duke a clout,
Steep'd in the faultless blood of pretty Rutland;—
His curses, then from bitterness of soul
Denounc'd against thee, are all fallen upon thee;
And God, not we, have plagu'd thy bloody deed.
　　Q. Eliz. So just is God, to right the innocent.
　　Hast. O, 't was the foulest deed to slay that
　　　babe,
And the most merciless, that e'er was heard of.
　　Riv. Tyrants themselves wept when it was re-
　　　ported.
　　Dors. No man but prophesied revenge for it.
　　Buck. Northumberland, then present, wept to
　　　see it.
　　Q. Mar. What! were you snarling all, before
　　　I came,
Ready to catch each other by the throat,
And turn you all your hatred now on me?
Did York's dread curse prevail so much with
　　heaven,
That Henry's death, my lovely Edward's death,
Their kingdom's loss, my woful banishment,
Could all but answer for that peevish brat?
Can curses pierce the clouds, and enter heaven?
Why, then give way, dull clouds, to my quick
　　curses!——
Though not by war, by surfeit die your king,
As ours by murder, to make him a king!

Edward, thy son, that now is prince of Wales,
For Edward, my son, that was prince of Wales,
Die in his youth, by like untimely violence!
Thyself a queen, for me that was a queen,
Outlive thy glory, like my wretched self!
Long may'st thou live, to wail thy children's loss,
And see another, as I see thee now,
Deck'd in thy rights, as thou art stall'd in mine!
Long die thy happy days before thy death;
And, after many lengthen'd hours of grief,
Die neither mother, wife, nor England's queen!—
Rivers,—and Dorset,—you were standers by,—
And so wast thou, lord Hastings,—when my son
Was stabb'd with bloody daggers; God, I pray
    him,
That none of you may live your natural age,
But by some unlook'd accident cut off!

   Glo. Have done thy charm, thou hateful wither'd
    hag.

   Q. Mar. And leave out thee? stay, dog, for
    thou shalt hear me.
If heaven have any grievous plague in store,
Exceeding those that I can wish upon thee,
O, let them keep it, till thy sins be ripe,
And then hurl down their indignation
On thee, the troubler of the poor world's peace!
The worm of conscience still be-gnaw thy soul!
Thy friends suspect for traitors while thou liv'st,
And take deep traitors for thy dearest friends!
No sleep close up that deadly eye of thine,
Unless it be while some tormenting dream
Affrights thee with a hell of ugly devils!
Thou elvish-mark'd, abortive, rooting hog!"
Thou that wast seal'd in thy nativity
The slave of nature, and the son of hell!
Thou slander of thy mother's heavy womb!
Thou loathed issue of thy father's loins!
Thou rag of honour! thou detested——
   Glo. Margaret.
   Q. Mar.   Richard!
   Glo.   Ha!
   Q. Mar.   I call thee not.
   Glo. I cry thee mercy then; for I did think,
That thou hadst call'd me all these bitter names.
   Q. Mar. Why, so I did; but look'd for no re-
    ply.
O, let me make the period to my curse.
   Glo. 'T is done by me: and ends in—Margaret.
   Q. Eliz. Thus have you breath'd your curse
    against yourself.
   Q. Mar. Poor painted queen, vain flourish of
    my fortune!

Why strew'st thou sugar on that bottle-spider,
Whose deadly web ensnareth thee about?
Fool, fool! thou whet'st a knife to kill thyself.
The day will come, that thou shalt wish for me
To help thee curse this pois'nous hunch-back'd
    toad.
   Hast. False-boding woman, end thy frantic
    curse;
Lest, to thy harm, thou move our patience.
   Q. Mar. Foul shame upon you! you have all
    mov'd mine.
   Riv. Were you well serv'd, you would be taught
    your duty.
   Q. Mar. To serve me well, you all should do
    me duty.
Teach me to be your queen, and you my subjects:
O, serve me well, and teach yourselves that duty.
   Dor. Dispute not with her, she is lunatic.
   Q. Mar. Peace, master marquis, you are mala-
    pert:
Your fire-new stamp of honour is scarce current:
O, that your young nobility could judge,
What 't were to lose it, and be miserable!
They that stand high, have many blasts to shake
    them;
And, if they fall, they dash themselves to pieces.
   Glo. Good counsel, marry;—learn it, learn it,
    marquis.
   Dor. It touches you, my lord, as much as me.
   Glo. Ay, and much more: But I was born so
    high,
Our aerie buildeth in the cedar's top,
And dallies with the wind, and scorns the sun.
   Q. Mar. And turns the sun to shade;—alas!
    alas!—
Witness my son, now in the shade of death;
Whose bright out-shining beams thy cloudy wrath
Hath in eternal darkness folded up.
Your aerie buildeth in our aerie's nest:—
O God, that seest it, do not suffer it;
As it was won with blood, lost be it so!
   Buck. Peace, peace, for shame, if not for charity.
   Q. Mar. Urge neither charity nor shame to
    me;
Uncharitably with me have you dealt,
And shamefully by you my hopes are butcher'd.
My charity is outrage, life my shame,—
And in my shame still live my sorrow's rage!
   Buck. Have done, have done.
   Q. Mar. O princely Buckingham, I kiss thy
    hand,
In sign of league and amity with thee:

Now fair befal thee, and thy noble house!
Thy garments are not spotted with our blood,
Nor thou within the compass of my curse.

Buck. Nor no one here; for curses never pass
The lips of those that breathe them in the air.

Q. Mar. I 'll not believe but they ascend the
sky,
And there awake God's gentle-sleeping peace.
O Buckingham, beware of yonder dog;
Look, when he fawns, he bites: and, when he
bites,
His venom tooth will rankle to the death:
Have not to do with him, beware of him;
Sin, death, and hell, have set their marks on him;
And all their ministers attend on him.

Glo. What doth she say, my lord of Buckingham?

Buck. Nothing that I respect, my gracious lord.

Q. Mar. What, dost thou scorn me for my
gentle counsel?
And sooth the devil that I warn thee from?
O, but remember this another day,
When he shall split thy very heart with sorrow;
And say, poor Margaret was a prophetess.—
Live each of you the subjects to his hate,
And he to yours, and all of you to God's! [*Exit.*

Hast. My hair doth stand on end to hear her
curses.

Riv. And so doth mine; I muse, why she 's at
liberty.

Glo. I cannot blame her, by God's holy mother;
She hath had too much wrong, and I repent
My part thereof, that I have done to her.

Q. Eliz. I never did her any, to my knowledge.

Glo. Yet you have all the vantage of her wrong.
I was too hot to do some body good,
That is too cold in thinking of it now.
Marry, as for Clarence, he is well repaid;
He is frank'd up to fatting for his pains;—
God pardon them that are the cause thereof!

Riv. A virtuous and a christian-like conclusion,
To pray for them that have done scath to us.

Glo. So do I ever, being well advis'd;—
For had I curs'd now, I had curs'd myself. [*Aside.*

Enter CATESBY.

Cates. Madam, his majesty doth call for you,—
And for your grace,—and you, my noble lords.

Q. Eliz. Catesby, I come:—Lords, will you go
with me?

Riv. Madam, we will attend upon your grace.
[*Exeunt all but* GLO.

1010

Glo. I do the wrong, and first begin to brawl.
The secret mischiefs that I set abroach,
I lay unto the grievous charge of others.
Clarence,—whom I, indeed, have laid in dark-
ness,—
I do beweep to many simple gulls;
Namely, to Stanley, Hastings, Buckingham;
And tell them—'t is the queen and her allies,
That stir the king against the duke my brother.
Now they believe it; and withal whet me
To be reveng'd on Rivers, Vaughan, Grey:
But then I sigh, and, with a piece of scripture,
Tell them—that God bids us do good for evil:
And thus I clothe my naked villany
With old odd ends, stol'n forth of holy writ;
And seem a saint, when most I play the devil.

Enter Two Murderers.

But soft, here come my executioners.—
How now, my hardy, stout resolved mates?
Are you now going to despatch this thing?

1st Murd. We are, my lord; and come to have
the warrant,
That we may be admitted where he is.

Glo. Well thought upon, I have it here about
me: [*Gives the Warrant.*
When you have done, repair to Crosby-place.
But, sirs, be sudden in the execution,
Withal obdurate, do not hear him plead;
For Clarence is well spoken, and, perhaps,
May move your hearts to pity, if you mark him.

1st Murd. Tut, tut, my lord, we will not stand
to prate.
Talkers are no good doers; be assur'd,
We go to use our hands, and not our tongues.

Glo. Your eyes drop mill-stones, when fools' eyes
drop tears:
I like you, lads;—about your business straight;
Go, go, despatch.

1st Murd.   We will, my noble lord. [*Exeunt.*

SCENE IV.—*The Same.   A Room in the Tower.*

Enter CLARENCE *and* BRAKENBURY.

Brak. Why looks your grace so heavily to-
day?

Clar. O, I have pass'd a miserable night,
So full of fearful dreams, of ugly sights,
That, as I am a christian faithful man,
I would not spend another such a night,
Though 't were to buy a world of happy days,
So full of dismal terror was the time.

Brak. What was your dream, my lord? I pray
    you, tell me.
Clar. Methought, that I had broken from the
    Tower,
And was embark'd to cross to Burgundy;
And, in my company, my brother Gloster:
Who from my cabin tempted me to walk
Upon the hatches; thence we look'd toward Eng-
    land,
And cited up a thousand heavy times,
During the wars of York and Lancaster
That had befall'n us. As we pac'd along
Upon the giddy footing of the hatches,
Methought, that Gloster stumbled; and, in falling,
Struck me, that thought to stay him, over board,
Into the tumbling billows of the main.
O Lord! methought, what pain it was to drown!
What dreadful noise of water in mine ears!
What sights of ugly death within mine eyes!
Methought, I saw a thousand fearful wrecks;
A thousand men, that fishes gnaw'd upon;
Wedges of gold, great anchors, heaps of pearl,
Inestimable stones, unvalued jewels,
All scatter'd in the bottom of the sea;
Some lay in dead men's sculls; and, in those holes
Where eyes did once inhabit, there were crept
(As 't were in scorn of eyes,) reflecting gems,
That woo'd the slimy bottom of the deep,
And mock'd the dead bones that lay scatter'd by.
    Brak. Had you such leisure in the time of
    death,
To gaze upon these secrets of the deep?
    Clar. Methought, I had: and often did I strive
To yield the ghost: but still the envious flood
Kept in my soul, and would not let it forth
To seek the empty, vast, and wand'ring air;
But smother'd it within my panting bulk,
Which almost burst to belch it in the sea.
    Brak. Awak'd you not with this sore agony?
    Clar. O, no, my dream was lengthen'd after
    life;
O, then began the tempest to my soul!
I pass'd, methought, the melancholy flood,
With that grim ferryman which poets write of,
Unto the kingdom of perpetual night.
The first that there did greet my stranger soul,
Was my great father-in-law, renowned Warwick;
Who cry'd aloud,—"What scourge for perjury
Can this dark monarchy afford false Clarence?"
And so he vanish'd: Then came wand'ring by
A shadow like an angel, with bright hair
Dabbled in blood; and he shriek'd out aloud,—

"Clarence is come,—false, fleeting, perjur'd Clar-
    ence,—
That stabb'd me in the field by Tewkesbury;—
Seize on him, furies, take him to your torments'—"
With that, methought, a legion of foul fiends
Environ'd me, and howled in mine ears
Such hideous cries, that, with the very noise,
I trembling wak'd, and, for a season after,
Could not believe but that I was in hell;
Such terrible impression made my dream.
    Brak. No marvel, lord, though it affrighted
    you:
I am afraid, methinks, to hear you tell it.
    Clar. O Brakenbury, I have done these
    things,—
That now give evidence against my soul,—
For Edward's sake; and, see, how he requites
    me!—
O God! if my deep prayers cannot appease thee,
But thou wilt be aveng'd on my misdeeds,
Yet execute thy wrath on me alone:
O, spare my guiltless wife, and my poor chil-
    dren!—
I pray thee, gentle keeper, stay by me;
My soul is heavy, and I fain would sleep.
    Brak. I will, my lord; God give your grace
    good rest!—
        [*Clar. reposes himself on a Chair.*
Sorrow breaks seasons, and reposing hours,
Makes the night morning, and the noon-tide
    night.
Princes have but their titles for their glories,
An outward honour for an inward toil;
And, for unfelt imaginations,
They often feel a world of restless cares:
So that, between their titles, and low name,
There 's nothing differs but the outward fame.

    Enter the Two Murderers.

    1st Murd. Ho! who 's here?
    Brak. What would'st thou, fellow? and how
    cam'st thou hither?
    1st Murd. I would speak with Clarence, and I
came hither on my legs.
    Brak. What, so brief?
    2nd Murd. O, sir, 't is better to be brief than
    tedious:—
Let him see our commission; talk no more.
    [*A Paper is delivered to Brak., who reads it*
    Brak. I am, in this, commanded to deliver
The noble duke of Clarence to your hands:—
I will not reason what is meant hereby,

Because I will be guilt'ess of the meaning.
Here are the keys;—there sits the duke asleep:
I'll to the king; and signify to him,
That thus I have resign'd to you my charge.

1st Murd. You may, sir: 't is a point of wisdom;
Fare you well.   [*Exit* Brak.

2nd Murd. What, shall we stab him as he
sleeps?

1st Murd. No; he 'll say, 't was done cowardly,
when he wakes.

2nd Murd. When he wakes! why, fool, he shall
never wake until the great judgment day.

1st Murd. Why, then he 'll say, we stabb'd him
sleeping.

2nd Murd. The urging of that word, judgment, hath bred a kind of remorse in me.

1st Murd. What? art thou afraid?

2nd Murd. Not to kill him, having a warrant
for it; but to be damn'd for killing him, from the
which no warrant can defend me.

1st Murd. I thought, thou had'st been resolute.

2nd Murd. So I am, to let him live.

1st Murd. I'll back to the duke of Gloster, and
tell him so.

2nd Murd. Nay, I pr'ythee, stay a little: I
hope, this holy humour of mine will change; it
was wont to hold me but while one would tell
twenty.

1st Murd. How dost thou feel thyself now?

2nd Murd. 'Faith, some certain dregs of conscience are yet within me.

1st Murd. Remember our reward, when the
deed 's done.

2nd Murd. Come, he dies; I had forgot the
reward.

1st Murd. Where 's thy conscience now?

2nd Murd. In the duke of Gloster's purse.

1st Murd. So, when he opens his purse to give
us our reward, thy conscience flies out.

2nd Murd. 'T is no matter; let it go; there 's
few, or none, will entertain it.

1st Murd. What, if it come to thee again?

2nd Murd. I'll not meddle with it, it is a dangerous thing, it makes a man a coward; a man
cannot steal, but it accuseth him; a man cannot
swear, but it checks him; a man cannot lie with
his neighbour's wife, but it detects him: 'T is a
blushing shame-faced spirit, that mutinies in a
man's bosom; it fills one full of obstacles: it
made me once restore a purse of gold, that by
chance I found; it beggars any man that keeps
it; it is turned out of all towns and cities for a

dangerous thing; and every man, that means to
live well, endeavours to trust to himself, and live
without it.

1st Murd. 'Zounds, it is even now at my elbow,
persuading me not to kill the duke.

2nd Murd. Take the devil in thy mind, and
believe him not: he would insinuate with thee,
but to make thee sigh.

1st Murd. I am strong-fram'd, he cannot prevail with me.

2nd Murd. Spoke like a tall fellow, that respects his reputation. Come, shall we fall to
work?

1st Murd. Take him over the costard with
the hilts of thy sword, and then throw him into
the malmsey-butt, in the next room.

2nd Murd. O excellent device! and make a
sop of him.

1st Murd. Soft! he wakes.

2nd Murd. Strike.

1st Murd. No, we 'll reason with him.

Clar. Where art thou, keeper? give me a cup
of wine.

1st Murd. You shall have wine enough, my
lord, anon.

Clar. In God's name, what art thou?

1st Murd. A man, as you are.

Clar. But not, as I am, royal.

1st Murd. Nor you, as we are, loyal.

Clar. Thy voice is thunder, but thy looks are
humble.

1st Murd. My voice is now the king's, my looks
mine own.

Clar. How darkly, and how deadly dost thou
speak!
Your eyes do menace me; why look you pale?
Who sent you hither? Wherefore do you come?

Both Murd. To, to, to,——

Clar. To murder me?

Both Murd. Ay, ay.

Clar. You scarcely have the hearts to tell me so,
And therefore cannot have the hearts to do it.
Wherein, my friends, have I offended you?

1st Murd. Offended us you have not, but the
king.

Clar. I shall be reconcil'd to him again.

2nd Murd. Never, my lord; therefore prepare
to die.

Clar. Are you call'd forth from out a world of
men,
To slay the innocent? What is my offence?
Where is the evidence that doth accuse me?

What lawful quest have given their verdict up
Unto the frowning judge? or who pronounc'd
The bitter sentence of poor Clarence' death?
Before I be convict by course of law,
To threaten me with death is most unlawful.
I charge you, as you hope for any goodness,
By Christ's dear blood, shed for our grievous sins,
That you depart, and lay no hands on me;
The deed you undertake is damnable.

    1st Murd. What we will do, we do upon command.

    2nd Murd. And he, that hath commanded, is our king.

    Clar. Erroneous vassal! the great King of kings
Hath in the table of his law commanded,
That thou shalt do no murder: Wilt thou then
Spurn at his edict, and fulfil a man's?
Take heed; for he holds vengeance in his hand,
To hurl upon their heads that break his law.

    2nd Murd. And that same vengeance doth he hurl on thee,
For false forswearing and for murder too:
Thou didst receive the sacrament, to fight
In quarrel of the house of Lancaster.

    1st Murd. And, like a traitor to the name of God,
Didst break that vow; and, with thy treacherous blade,
Unrip'dst the bowels of thy sovereign's son.

    2nd Murd. Whom thou wast sworn to cherish and defend.

    1st Murd. How canst thou urge God's dreadful law to us,
When thou hast broke it in such dear degree?

    Clar. Alas! for whose sake did I that ill deed?
For Edward, for my brother, for his sake:
He sends you not to murder me for this;
For in that sin he is as deep as I.
If God will be avenged for the deed,
O, know you, that he doth it publicly;
Take not the quarrel from his powerful arm;
He needs no indirect nor lawless course,
To cut off those that have offended him.

    1st Murd. Who made thee then a bloody minister,
When gallant-springing, brave Plantagenet,
That princely novice, was struck dead by thee?

    Clar. My brother's love, the devil, and my rage.

    1st Murd. Thy brother's love, our duty, and thy fault,
Provoke us hither now to slaughter thee.

    Clar. If you do love my brother, hate not me;
I am his brother, and I love him well.
If you are hir'd for meed, go back again,
And I will send you to my brother Gloster;
Who shall reward you better for my life,
Than Edward will for tidings of my death.

    2nd Murd. You are deceiv'd, your brother Gloster hates you.

    Clar. O, no; he loves me, and he holds me dear:
Go you to him from me.

    Both Murd.   Ay, so we will.

    Clar. Tell him, when that our princely father York
Bless'd his three sons with his victorious arm,
And charg'd us from his soul to love each other,
He little thought of this divided friendship:
Bid Gloster think on this, and he will weep.

    1st Murd. Ay, mill-stones; as he lesson'd us to weep.

    Clar. O, do not slander him, for he is kind.

    1st Murd. Right, as snow in harvest.—Come, you deceive yourself;
'T is he that sends us to destroy you here.

    Clar. It cannot be; for he bewept my fortune,
And hugg'd me in his arms, and swore, with sobs,
That he would labour my delivery.

    1st Murd. Why, so he doth, when he delivers you
From this earth's thraldom to the joys of heaven.

    2nd Murd. Make peace with God, for you must die, my lord.

    Clar. Hast thou that holy feeling in thy soul,
To counsel me to make my peace with God,
And art thou yet to thy own soul so blind,
That thou wilt war with God by murdering me?—
Ah, sirs, consider, he, that set you on
To do this deed, will hate you for the deed.

    2nd Murd. What shall we do?

    Clar.   Relent, and save your souls.

    1st Murd. Relent! 't is cowardly, and womanish.

    Clar. Not to relent, is beastly, savage, devilish.—
Which of you, if you were a prince's son,
Being pent from liberty, as I am now,—
If two such murderers as yourselves came to you,—
Would not entreat for life?—
My friend, I spy some pity in thy looks;
O, if thine eye be not a flatterer,
Come thou on my side, and entreat for me,
As you would beg, were you in my distress.
A begging prince what beggar pities not?

    2nd Murd. Look behind you, my lord.

1st Murd. Take that, and that; if all this will
not do,   [Stabs him.
I'll drown you in the malmsey-butt within.
                          [Exit, with the Body.
2nd Murd. A bloody deed, and desperately despatch'd!
How fain, like Pilate, would I wash my hands
Of this most grievous guilty murder done!

Re-enter first Murderer.

1st Murd. How now! what mean'st thou, that
thou help'st me not?

By heaven, the duke shall know how slack you
have been.
2nd Murd. I would he knew, that I had sav'd
his brother!
Take thou the fee, and tell him what I say ·
For I repent me that the duke is slain.   [Exit.
1st Murd. So do not I; go, coward, as thou
art.—
Well, I'll go hide the body in some hole,
Till that the duke give order for his burial:
And when I have my meed, I will away;
For this will out, and then I must not stay. [Exit

ACT II.

SCENE I.—The Same. A Room in the Palace.

Enter KING EDWARD, (led in sick,) QUEEN ELIZA-
BETH, DORSET, RIVERS, HASTINGS, BUCKING-
HAM, GREY, and Others.

K. Edw. Why, so:—now have I done a good
day's work:—
You, peers, continue this united league:
I every day expect an embassage
From my Redeemer to redeem me hence:
And more in peace my soul shall part to heaven,
Since I have made my friends at peace on earth,
Rivers, and Hastings, take each other's hand;
Dissemble not your hatred, swear your love.
Riv. By heaven, my soul is purg'd from grudg-
ing hate;
And with my hand I seal my true heart's love.
Hast. So thrive I, as I truly swear the like!
K. Edw. Take heed, you dally not before your
king;
Lest he, that is the supreme King of kings,
Confound your hidden falsehood, and award
Either of you to be the other's end.
Hast. So prosper I, as I swear perfect love!
Riv. And I, as I love Hastings with my heart!
K. Edw. Madam, yourself are not exempt in
this,—
Nor your son Dorset,—Buckingham, nor you;—
You have been factious one against the other.
Wife, love lord Hastings, let him kiss your hand;
And what you do, do it unfeignedly.
Q. Eliz. There, Hastings;—I will never more
remember

Our former hatred, So thrive I, and mine!
K. Edw. Dorset, embrace him,—Hastings, love
lord marquis.
Dor. This interchange of love, I here protest,
Upon my part shall be inviolable.
Hast. And so swear I.   [Embraces Dor.
K. Edw. Now, princely Buckingham, seal thou
this league
With thy embracements to my wife's allies,
And make me happy in your unity.
Buck. Whenever Buckingham doth turn his hate
Upon your grace, [To the Queen.] but with all
duteous love
Both cherish you, and yours, God punish me
With hate in those where I expect most love!
When I have most need to employ a friend,
And most assured that he is a friend,
Deep, hollow, treacherous, and full of guile,
Be he unto me! this do I beg of heaven,
When I am cold in love, to you, or yours.
                          [Embracing Riv., &c
K. Edw. A pleasing cordial, princely Bucking-
ham,
Is this thy vow unto my sickly heart.
There wanteth now our brother Gloster here,
To make the blessed period of this peace.
Buck. And, in good time, here comes the noble
duke.

Enter GLOSTER.

Glo. Good-morrow to my sovereign king, and
queen;
And, princely peers, a happy time of day!

K. Edw. Happy, indeed, as we have spent the day :—
Brother, we have done deeds of charity ;
Made peace of enmity, fair love of hate,
Between these swelling wrong-incensed peers.

Glo. A blessed labour, my most sovereign liege.—
Among this princely heap, if any here,
By false intelligence, or wrong surmise,
Hold me a foe ;
If I unwittingly, or in my rage,
Have aught committed that is hardly borne
By any in this presence, I desire
To reconcile me to his friendly peace :
'T is death to me, to be at enmity ;
I hate it, and desire all good men's love.---
First, madam, I entreat true peace of you,
Which I will purchase with my duteous service,—
Of you, my noble cousin Buckingham,
If ever any grudge were lodg'd between us ;
Of you, lord Rivers,—and, lord Grey, of you,—
That all without desert have frown'd on me ;—
Dukes, earls, lords, gentlemen ; indeed, of all.
I do not know that Englishman alive,
With whom my soul is any jot at odds,
More than the infant that is born to-night ;
I thank my God for my humility.

Q. Eliz. A holy-day shall this be kept hereafter :—
I would to God, all strifes were well compounded.—
My sovereign lord, I do beseech your highness
To take our brother Clarence to your grace.

Glo. Why, madam, have I offer'd love for this,
To be so flouted in this royal presence ?
Who knows not, that the gentle duke is dead ?
[*They all start.*
You do him injury, to scorn his corse.

K. Edw. Who knows not, he is dead ! who knows he is ?

Q. Eliz. All-seeing heaven, what a world is this !

Buck. Look I so pale, lord Dorset, as the rest ?

Dor. Ay, my good lord ; and no man in the presence,
But his red colour hath forsook his cheeks.

K. Edw. Is Clarence dead ? the order was revers'd.

Glo. But he, poor man, by your first order died ;
And that a winged Mercury did bear :
Some tardy cripple bore the countermand,
That came too lag to see him buried :—
God grant, that some, less noble, and less loyal,
Nearer in bloody thoughts, and not in blood,
Deserve not worse than wretched Clarence did,
And yet go current from suspicion !

Enter STANLEY.

Stan. A boon, my sovereign, for my service done !

K. Edw. I pr'ythee, peace ; my soul is full of sorrow.

Stan. I will not rise, unless your highness hear me.

K. Edw. Then say at once, what is it thou request'st.

Stan. The forfeit, sovereign, of my servant's life ;
Who slew to-day a riotous gentleman
Lately attendant on the duke of Norfolk.

K. Edw. Have I a tongue to doom my brother's death,
And shall that tongue give pardon to a slave ?
My brother kill'd no man, his fault was thought,
And yet his punishment was bitter death.
Who sued to me for him ? who, in my wrath,
Kneel'd at my feet, and bade me be advis'd ?
Who spoke of brotherhood ? who spoke of love ?
Who told me, how the poor soul did forsake
The mighty Warwick, and did fight for me ?
Who told me, in the field at Tewkesbury,
When Oxford had me down, he rescu'd me,
And said, "Dear brother, live, and be a king ?"
Who told me, when we both lay in the field,
Frozen almost to death, how he did lap me
Even in his garments ; and did give himself,
All thin and naked, to the numb-cold night ;
All this from my remembrance brutish wrath
Sinfully pluck'd, and not a man of you
Had so much grace to put it in my mind.
But, when your carters, or your waiting-vassals
Have done a drunken slaughter, and defac'd
The precious image of our dear Redeemer,
You straight are on your knees for pardon, pardon ;
And I, unjustly too, must grant it you :—
But for my brother, not a man would speak,—
Nor I (ungracious) speak unto myself
For him, poor soul.—The proudest of you all
Have been beholden to him in his life ;
Yet none of you would once plead for his life.—
O God ! I fear, thy justice will take hold
On me, and you, and mine, and yours, for this.--

Come, Hastings, help me to my closet. O,
Poor Clarence!

  [*Exeunt* KING, QUEEN, HAST., RIV., DOR.,
    and GREY.

  Glo. This is the fruit of rashness!—Mark'd
you not,
How that the guilty kindred of the queen
Look'd pale, when they did hear of Clarence'
death?
O! they did urge it still unto the king:
God will revenge it. Come, lords; will you go,
To comfort Edward with our company?

  Buck. We wait upon your grace.   [*Exeunt.*

SCENE II.—*The Same.*

Enter the DUCHESS OF YORK, *with a* SON *and*
DAUGHTER *of* CLARENCE.

  Son. Good grandam, tell us, is our father dead?
  Duch. No, boy.
  Daugh. Why do you weep so oft? and beat
your breast;
And cry—"O Clarence, my unhappy son!"
  Son. Why do you look on us, and shake your
head,
And call us—orphans, wretches, cast-aways,
If that our noble father be alive?
  Duch. My pretty cousins, you mistake me both;
I do lament the sickness of the king,
As loath to lose him, not your father's death;
It were lost sorrow, to wail one that 's lost.
  Son. Then, grandam, you conclude that he is
dead.
The king my uncle is to blame for this:
God will revenge it; whom I will importune
With earnest prayers all to that effect.
  Daugh. And so will I.
  Duch. Peace, children, peace! the king doth
love you well:
Incapable and shallow innocents,
You cannot guess who caus'd your father's death.
  Son. Grandam, we can: for my good uncle
Gloster
Told me, the king, provok'd to 't by the queen,
Devis'd impeachments to imprison him:
And when my uncle told me so, he wept,
And pitied me, and kindly kiss'd my cheek;
Bade me rely on him, as on my father,
And he would love me dearly as his child.
  Duch. Ah, that deceit should steal such gentle
shapes,
And with a virtuous visor hide deep vice!
1916

He is my son, ay, and therein my shame,
Yet from my dugs he drew not this deceit.
  Son. Think you my uncle did dissemble,
grandam?
  Duch. Ay, boy.
  Son. I cannot think it. Hark! what noise is
this?

Enter QUEEN ELIZABETH, *distractedly;* RIVERS
and DORSET, *following her.*

  Q. Eliz. Ah! who shall hinder me to wail and
weep?
To chide my fortune, and torment myself?
I 'll join with black despair against my soul,
And to myself become an enemy.
  Duch. What means this scene of rude impa-
tience?
  Q. Eliz. To make an act of tragic violence:—
Edward, my lord, thy son, our king, is dead.—
Why grow the branches, when the root is gone?
Why wither not the leaves, that want their
sap?—
If you will live, lament; if die, be brief;
That our swift-winged souls may catch the king's:
Or, like obedient subjects, follow him
To his new kingdom of perpetual rest.
  Duch. Ah, so much interest have I in thy
sorrow,
As I had title in thy noble husband!
I have bewept a worthy husband's death,
And liv'd by looking on his images:
But now, two mirrors of his princely semblance
Are crack'd in pieces by malignant death;
And I for comfort have but one false glass,
That grieves me when I see my shame in him.
Thou art a widow; yet thou art a mother,
And hast the comfort of thy children left thee:
But death hath snatch'd my husband from my
arms,
And pluck'd two crutches from my feeble hands,
Clarence, and Edward. O what cause have I,
(Thine being but a moiety of my grief,)
To overgo thy plaints, and drown thy cries?
  Son. Ah, aunt! you wept not for our father's
death;
How can we aid you with our kindred tears?
  Daugh. Our fatherless distress was left unmoan'd,
Your widow-dolour likewise be unwept!
  Q. Eliz. Give me no help in lamentation,
I am not barren to bring forth laments:
All springs reduce their currents to mine eyes,
That I, being govern'd by the wat'ry moon,

May send forth plenteous tears to drown the world!
Ah, for my husband, for my dear lord Edward!

  Chil. Ah, for our father, for our dear lord Clarence!

  Duch. Alas, for both, both mine, Edward and Clarence!

  Q. Eliz. What stay had I, but Edward? and he 's gone.

  Chil. What stay had we, but Clarence? and he 's gone.

  Duch. What stays had I, but they? and they are gone.

  Q. Eliz. Was never widow, had so dear a loss.

  Chil. Were never orphans, had so dear a loss.

  Duch. Was never mother had so dear a loss.
Alas! I am the mother of these griefs;
Their woes are parcell'd, mine are general.
She for an Edward weeps, and so do I;
I for a Clarence weep, so doth not she:
These babes for Clarence weep, and so do I;
I for an Edward weep, so do not they:—
Alas! you three, on me, threefold distress'd,
Pour all your tears, I am your sorrow's nurse,
And I will pamper it with lamentations.

  Dor. Comfort, dear mother; God is much displeas'd,
That you take with unthankfulness his doing;
In common worldly things, 't is call'd—ungrateful,
With dull unwillingness to repay a debt,
Which with a bounteous hand was kindly lent;
Much more to be thus opposite with heaven,
For it requires the royal debt it lent you.

  Riv. Madam, bethink you, like a careful mother,
Of the young prince, your son: send straight for him,
Let him be crown'd; in him your comfort lives:
Drown desperate sorrow in dead Edward's grave,
And plant your joys in living Edward's throne.

Enter GLOSTER, BUCKINGHAM, STANLEY, HASTINGS, RATCLIFFE, *and Others.*

  Glo. Sister, have comfort: all of us have cause
To wail the dimming of our shining star;
But none can cure their harms by wailing them.—
Madam, my mother, I do cry you mercy,
I did not see your grace:—Humbly on my knee
I crave your blessing.

  Duch. God bless thee; and put meekness in thy breast,
Love, charity, obedience, and true duty!

  Glo. Amen; and make me die a good old man!—

That is the butt-end of a mother's blessing; [*Aside*
I marvel, that her grace did leave it out.

  Buck. You cloudy princes, and heart-sorrowing peers,
That bear this mutual heavy load of moan.
Now cheer each other in each other's love:
Though we have spent our harvest of this king,
We are to reap the harvest of his son.
The broken rancour of your high-swoln hearts,
But lately splinter'd, knit, and join'd together,
Must gently be preserv'd, cherish'd, and kept:
Me seemeth good, that, with some little train,
Forthwith from Ludlow the young prince be fetch'd
Hither to London, to be crown'd our king.

  Riv. Why with some little train, my lord of Buckingham?

  Buck. Marry, my lord, lest, by a multitude,
The new-heal'd wound of malice should break out;
Which would be so much the more dangerous,
By how much the estate is green, and yet ungovern'd:
Where every horse bears his commanding rein,
And may direct his course as please himself,
As well the fear of harm, as harm apparent,
In my opinion, ought to be prevented.

  Glo. I hope, the king made peace with all of us;
And the compact is firm, and true, in me.

  Riv. And so in me; and so, I think, in all:
Yet, since it is but green, it should be put
To no apparent likelihood of breach,
Which, haply, by much company might be urg'd:
Therefore I say, with noble Buckingham,
That it is meet so few should fetch the prince.

  Hast. And so say I.

  Glo. Then be it so; and go we to determine
Who they shall be that straight shall post to Ludlow.
Madam,—and you, my mother, will you go
To give your censures in this weighty business?

[*Exeunt all but* BUCK. *and* GLO.

  Buck. My lord, whoever journeys to the prince,
For God's sake, let not us two stay at home;
For, by the way, I 'll sort occasion,
As index to the story we late talk'd of,
To part the queen's proud kindred from the prince.

  Glo. My other self, my counsel's consistory,
My oracle, my prophet!—My dear cousin,
I, as a child, will go by thy direction.
Towards Ludlow then, for we 'll not stay behind.

[*Exeunt*

SCENE III.—*The Same.   A Street.*

Enter Two Citizens, meeting.

1st Cit. Good morrow, neighbour: Whither
away so fast?

2nd Cit. I promise you, I scarcely know myself:
Hear you the news abroad?

1st Cit.   Yes: the king's dead.

2nd Cit. Ill news, by'r lady; seldom comes the
better:
I fear, I fear, 't will prove a giddy world.

Enter another Citizen.

3rd Cit. Neighbours, God speed!

1st Cit.   Give you good morrow, sir.

3rd Cit. Doth the news hold of good king Edward's death?

2nd Cit. Ay, sir, it is too true; God help, the
while!

3rd Cit. Then, masters, look to see a troublous
world.

1st Cit. No, no; by God's good grace, his son
shall reign.

3rd Cit. Woe to that land, that's governed by
a child!

2nd Cit. In him there is a hope of govern-
ment;
That, in his nonage, council under him,
And, in his full and ripen'd years, himself,
No doubt, shall then, and till then, govern well.

1st Cit. So stood the state, when Henry the
Sixth
Was crown'd in Paris but at nine months old.

3rd Cit. Stood the state so? no, no, good friends,
God wot;
For then this land was famously enrich'd
With politic grave counsel; then the king
Had virtuous uncles to protect his grace.

1st Cit. Why, so hath this, both by his father
and mother.

3rd Cit. Better it were, they all came by his
father;
Or, by his father, there were none at all:
For emulation now, who shall be nearest,
Will touch us all too near, if God prevent not.
O, full of danger is the duke of Gloster;
And the queen's sons, and brothers, haught and
proud;
And were they to be rul'd, and not to rule,
This sickly land might solace as before.

1st Cit. Come, come, we fear the worst; all will
be well.

1618

3rd Cit. When clouds are seen, wise men put
on their cloaks;
When great leaves fall, then winter is at hand;
When the sun sets, who doth not look for night
Untimely storms make men expect a dearth:
All may be well; but, if God sort it so.
'T is more than we deserve, or I expect.

2nd Cit. Truly, the hearts of men are full of fear:
You cannot reason almost with a man
That looks not heavily, and full of dread.

3rd Cit. Before the days of change, still is it so:
By a divine instinct, men's minds mistrust
Ensuing danger; as, by proof, we see
The water swell before a boist'rous storm.
But leave it all to God.   Whither away?

2nd Cit. Marry, we were sent for to the justices.

3rd Cit. And so was I; I'll bear you company.
                                    [*Exeunt.*

SCENE IV.—*The Same.   A Room in the Palace.*

Enter the ARCHBISHOP *of* YORK, *the young* DUKE
of YORK, QUEEN ELIZABETH, *and the* DUCHESS
of YORK.

Arch. Last night, I heard, they lay at Stony-
Stratford;
And at Northampton they do rest to-night;
To-morrow, or next day, they will be here.

Duch. I long with all my heart to see the prince;
I hope, he is much grown since last I saw him.

Q. Eliz. But I hear, no; they say, my son of
York
Hath almost overta'en him in his growth.

York. Ay, mother, but I would not have it so.

Duch. Why, my young cousin? it is good to
grow.

York. Grandam, one night, as we did sit at
supper,
My uncle Rivers talk'd how I did grow
More than my brother: "Ay," quoth my uncle
Gloster,
"Small herbs have grace, great weeds do grow
apace:"
And since, methinks, I would not grow so fast,
Because sweet flowers are slow, and weeds make
haste.

Duch. 'Good faith, 'good faith, the saying did
not hold
In him that did object the same to thee:
He was the wretched'st thing, when he was young,
So long a growing, and so leisurely,
That, if his rule were true, he should be gracious

Arch. And so, no doubt, he is, my gracious
    madam.
Duch. I hope, he is; but yet let mothers doubt.
York. Now, by my troth, if I had been re-
    member'd,
I could have given my uncle's grace a flout,
To touch his growth, nearer than he touch'd mine.
Duch. How, my young York! I pr'ythee let
    me hear it.
York. Marry, they say, my uncle grew so fast,
That he could gnaw a crust at two hours old;
'T was full two years ere I could get a tooth.
Grandam, this would have been a biting jest.
Duch. I pr'ythee, pretty York, who told thee
    this?
York. Grandam, his nurse.
Duch. His nurse! why, she was dead ere thou
    wast born.
York. If 't were not she, I cannot tell who told
    me.
Q. Eliz. A parlous boy: Go to, you are too
    shrewd.
Arch. Good madam, be not angry with the
    child.
Q. Eliz. Pitchers have ears.

Enter a Messenger.

Arch.   Here comes a messenger:
What news?
Mess.   Such news, my lord,
As grieves me to unfold.
Q. Eliz.   How doth the prince?
Mess. Well, madam, and in health.
Duch.   What is thy news?
Mess. Lord Rivers, and lord Grey, are sent to
    Pomfret,
With them sir Thomas Vaughan, prisoners.

Duch. Who hath committed them?
Mess.   The mighty dukes,
Gloster and Buckingham.
Q. Eliz.   For what offence?
Mess. The sum of all I can, I have disclos'd;
Why, or for what, the nobles were committed,
Is all unknown to me, my gracious lady.
Q. Eliz. Ah me, I see the ruin of my house!
The tiger now hath seiz'd the gentle hind;
Insulting tyranny begins to jet
Upon the innocent and awless throne:—
Welcome, destruction, blood, and massacre,
I see, as in a map, the end of all.
Duch. Accursed and unquiet wrangling days!
How many of you have mine eyes beheld?
My husband lost his life to get the crown;
And often up and down my sons were tost,
For me to joy, and weep, their gain, and loss;
And being seated, and domestic broils
Clean over-blown, themselves, the conquerors,
Make war upon themselves; brother to brother,
Blood to blood, self 'gainst self:—O, preposterous
And frantic outrage, end thy damned spleen;
Or let me die, to look on death no more!
Q. Eliz. Come, come, my boy, we will to sanc-
    tuary.—
Madam, farewell.
Duch.   Stay, I will go with you.
Q. Eliz. You have no cause.
Arch.   My gracious lady, go,
                    [*To the* QUEEN.
And thither bear your treasure and your goods.
For my part, I 'll resign unto your grace
The seal I keep: And so betide to me,
As well I tender you, and all of yours!
Come, I 'll conduct you to the sanctuary.
                              [*Exeunt.*

ACT III.

SCENE I.—*The Same. A Street.*

The Trumpets sound. Enter the PRINCE OF
    WALES, GLOSTER, BUCKINGHAM, CARDINAL
    BOURCHIER, *and Others.*

Buck. Welcome, sweet prince, to London, to
    your chamber.
Glo. Welcome, dear cousin, my thought's sove
    reign;
The weary way hath made you melancholy.
Prince. No, uncle; but our crosses on the
    way
Have made it tedious, wearisome, and heavy
I want more uncles here to welcome me.

Glo. Sweet prince, the untainted virtue of your
years
Hath not yet div'd into the world's deceit :
No more can you distinguish of a man,
Than of his outward show ; which, God he knows,
Seldom, or never, jumpeth with the heart.
Those uncles, which you want, were dangerous ;
Your grace attended to the sugar'd words,
But look'd not on the poison of their hearts :
God keep you from them, and from such false
friends !
   Prince. God keep me from false friends ! but
they were none.
   Glo. My lord, the Mayor of London comes to
greet you.

   Enter the LORD MAYOR, *and his* Train.

   May. God bless your grace with health and
happy days !
   Prince. I thank you, good my lord ;—and
thank you all.—   [*Exeunt* MAY., *&c.*
I thought my mother, and my brother York,
Would long ere this have met us on the way :
Fye, what a slug is Hastings ! that he comes not
To tell us, whether they will come, or no.

   Enter HASTINGS.

   Buck. And in good time, here comes the sweat-
ing lord.
   Prince. Welcome, my lord : What, will our
mother come !
   Hast. On what occasion, God he knows, not I,
The queen your mother, and your brother York,
Have taken sanctuary : The tender prince
Would fain have come with me to meet your
grace,
But by his mother was perforce withheld.
   Buck. Fye ! what an indirect and peevish course
Is this of hers ?—Lord Cardinal, will your grace
Persuade the queen to send the duke of York
Unto his princely brother presently !
If she deny,—lord Hastings, go with him,
And from her jealous arms pluck him perforce.
   Card. My lord of Buckingham, if my weak
oratory
Can from his mother win the duke of York,
Anon expect him here : But if she be obdurate
To mild entreaties, God in heaven forbid
We should infringe the holy privilege
Of blessed sanctuary ! not for all this land,
Would I be guilty of so deep a sin.
   Buck. You are too senseless-obstinate, my lord,
1020

Too ceremonious, and traditional :
Weigh it but with the grossness of this age,
You break not sanctuary in seizing him.
The benefit thereof is always granted
To those whose dealings have deserv'd the place,
And those who have the wit to claim the place :
This prince hath neither claim'd it, nor deserv'd
it ;
And therefore, in mine opinion, cannot have it :
Then, taking him from thence, that is not there,
You break no privilege nor charter there.
Oft have I heard of sanctuary men ;
But sanctuary children, ne'er till now.
   Card. My lord, you shall o'er-rule my mind for
once.—
Come on, lord Hastings, will you go with me !
   Hast. I go, my lord.
   Prince. Good lords, make all the speedy haste
you may.   [*Exeunt* CARD. *and* HAST.
Say, uncle Gloster, if our brother come,
Where shall we sojourn till our coronation ?
   Glo. Where it seems best unto your royal self.
If I may counsel you, some day, or two,
Your highness shall repose you at the Tower :
Then where you please, and shall be thought most
fit
For your best health and recreation.
   Prince. I do not like the Tower, of any place :—
Did Julius Cæsar build that place, my lord !
   Glo. He did, my gracious lord, begin that
place ;
Which, since, succeeding ages have re-edified.
   Prince. Is it upon record ? or else reported
Successively from age to age he built it !
   Buck. Upon record, my gracious lord.
   Prince. But say, my lord, it were not register'd ;
Methinks, the truth should live from age to age,
As 't were retail'd to all posterity,
Even to the general all-ending day.
   Glo. So wise so young, they say, do ne'er live
long.   [*Aside.*
   Prince. What say you, uncle !
   Glo. I say, without characters, fame lives long.
Thus, like the formal vice, Iniquity,   [*Aside.*
I moralize two meanings in one word.
   Prince. That Julius Cæsar was a famous man ;
With what his valour did enrich his wit,
His wit set down to make his valour live :
Death makes no conquest of this conqueror ;
For now he lives in fame, though not in life—
I 'll tell you what, my cousin Buckingham.
   Buck. What, my gracious lord ?

Prince. An if I live until I be a man,
I 'll win our ancient right in France again,
Or die a soldier, as I liv'd a king.
  Glo. Short summers lightly have a forward
          spring.   [*Aside.*

Enter YORK, HASTINGS, *and the* CARDINAL.

  Buck. Now, in good time, here comes the duke
      of York.
  Prince. Richard of York! how fares our loving
      brother?
  York. Well, my dread lord; so must I call
      you now.
  Prince. Ay, brother; to our grief, as it is yours:
Too late he died, that might have kept that title,
Which by his death hath lost much majesty.
  Glo. How fares our cousin, noble lord of York?
  York. I thank you, gentle uncle. O, my lord,
You said, that idle weeds are fast in growth:
The prince my brother hath outgrown me far.
  Glo. He hath, my lord.
  York.   And therefore is he idle?
  Glo. O, my fair cousin, I must not say so.
  York. Then is he more beholden to you than I?
  Glo. He may command me, as my sovereign;
But you have power in me, as in a kinsman.
  York. I pray you, uncle, then, give me this
      dagger.
  Glo. My dagger, little cousin? with all my heart.
  Prince. A beggar, brother?
  York. Of my kind uncle, that I know will give;
And, being but a toy, which is no grief to give.
  Glo. A greater gift than that I 'll give my
      cousin.
  York. A greater gift! O, that 's the sword to it?
  Glo. Ay, gentle cousin, were it light enough.
  York. O then, I see, you 'll part but with light
      gifts;
In weightier things you 'll say a beggar, nay.
  Glo. It is too weighty for your grace to wear.
  York. I weigh it lightly, were it heavier.
  Glo. What, would you have my weapon, little
      lord?
  York. I would, that I might thank you as you
      call me.
  Glo. How?
  York. Little.
  Prince. My lord of York will still be cross in
      talk;—
Uncle, your grace knows how to bear with him.
  York. You mean, to bear me, not to bear with
      me:—

Uncle, my brother mocks both you and me;
Because that I am little, like an ape,
He thinks that you should bear me on your shoul
      ders.
  Buck. With what a sharp provided wit he rea
      sons!
To mitigate the scorn he gives his uncle,
He prettily and aptly taunts himself:
So cunning, and so young, is wonderful.
  Glo. My gracious lord, will 't please you pass
      along?
Myself, and my good cousin Buckingham,
Will to your mother; to entreat of her,
To meet you at the Tower, and welcome you.
  York. What, will you go unto the Tower, my
      lord?
  Prince. My lord protector needs will have it so.
  York. I shall not sleep in quiet at the Tower.
  Glo. Why, sir, what should you fear?
  York. Marry, my uncle Clarence' angry ghost;
My grandam told me, he was murder'd there.
  Prince. I fear no uncles dead.
  Glo. Nor none that live, I hope.
  Prince. An if they live, I hope, I need not
      fear.
But come, my lord, and, with a heavy heart,
Thinking on them, go I unto the Tower.
                    [*Exeunt* PRINCE, YORK, HAST., CARD.,
                          and Attend.
  Buck. Think you, my lord, this little prating
      York
Was not incensed by his subtle mother,
To taunt and scorn you thus opprobriously?
  Glo. No doubt, no doubt: O, 't is a parlous
      boy;
Bold, quick, ingenious, forward, capable;
He 's all the mother's, from the top to toe.
  Buck. Well, let them rest.—
Come hither, gentle Catesby; thou art sworn
As deeply to effect what we intend,
As closely to conceal what we impart:
Thou know'st our reasons urg'd upon the way;—
What think'st thou? is it not an easy matter
To make William lord Hastings of our mind,
For the instalment of this noble duke
In the seat royal of this famous isle?
  Cate. He for his father's sake so loves the
      prince,
That he will not be won to aught against him.
  Buck. What think'st thou then of Stanley? will not he?
  Cate. He will do all in all as Hastings doth.
                                            102?

Buck. Well then, no more but this: Go, gentle Catesby,
And, as it were far off, sound thou lord Hastings,
How he doth stand affected to our purpose;
And summon him to-morrow to the Tower
To sit about the coronation.
If thou dost find him tractable to us,
Encourage him, and tell him all our reasons:
If he be leaden, icy, cold, unwilling,
Be thou so too; and so break off the talk,
And give us notice of his inclination:
For we to-morrow hold divided councils,³⁵
Wherein thyself shalt highly be employ'd.

Glo. Commend me to lord William: tell him, Catesby,
His ancient knot of dangerous adversaries
To-morrow are let blood at Pomfret-castle;
And bid my friend, for joy of this good news,
Give mistress Shore one gentle kiss the more.

Buck. Good Catesby, go, effect this business soundly.

Cate. My good lords both, with all the heed I can.

Glo. Shall we hear from you, Catesby, ere we sleep?

Cate. You shall, my lord.

Glo. At Crosby-place, there shall you find us both.   [*Exit* CATE.

Buck. Now, my lord, what shall we do if we perceive
Lord Hastings will not yield to our complots?

Glo. Chop off his head, man;—somewhat we will do:—
And, look, when I am king, claim thou of me
The earldom of Hereford, and all the movables
Whereof the king my brother was possess'd.

Buck. I'll claim that promise at your grace's hand.

Glo. And look to have it yielded with all kindness.
Come, let us sup betimes; that afterwards
We may digest our complots in some form.   [*Exeunt.*

SCENE II.—*Before* Lord Hastings' *House.*

Enter a Messenger.

Mess. My lord, my lord.—   [*Knocking.*
Hast. [*Within.*]   Who knocks?
Mess.   One from lord Stanley.
Hast. [*Within.*] What is't o'clock?
Mess. Upon the stroke of four.

1022

Enter HASTINGS.

Hast. Cannot thy master sleep the tedious nights?

Mess. So it should seem by that I have to say.
First, he commends him to your noble lordship.

Hast. And then,——

Mess. And then he sends you word, he dreamt
To-night the boar had rased off his helm:
Besides, he says, there are two councils held;
And that may be determin'd at the one,
Which may make you and him to rue at the other.
Therefore he sends to know your lordship's pleasure,
If presently, you will take horse with him,
And with all speed post with him toward the north,
To shun the danger that his soul divines.

Hast. Go, fellow, go, return unto thy lord;
Bid him not fear the separated councils:
His honour, and myself, are at the one;
And, at the other, is my good friend Catesby;
Where nothing can proceed, that toucheth us,
Whereof I shall not have intelligence.
Tell him, his fears are shallow, wanting instance:
And for his dreams—I wonder he's so fond
To trust the mockery of unquiet slumbers;
To fly the boar, before the boar pursues,
Were to incense the boar to follow us,
And make pursuit, where he did mean no chase.
Go, bid thy master rise and come to me;
And we will both together to the Tower,
Where, he shall see, the boar will use us kindly.

Mess. I'll go, my lord, and tell him what you say.   [*Exit.*

Enter CATESBY.

Cate. Many good morrows to my noble lord!

Hast. Good morrow, Catesby; you are early stirring:
What news, what news, in this our tottering state?

Cate. It is a reeling world, indeed, my lord;
And, I believe, will never stand upright,
Till Richard wear the garland of the realm.

Hast. How! wear the garland? dost thou mean the crown?

Cate. Ay, my good lord.

Hast. I'll have this crown of mine cut from my shoulders,
Before I'll see the crown so foul misplac'd.
But canst thou guess that he doth aim at it?

Cate. Ay, on my life; and hopes to find you forward
Upon his party, for the gain thereof:
And, thereupon, he sends you this good news,—
That, this same very day, your enemies,
The kindred of the queen, must die at Pomfret.

Hast. Indeed, I am no mourner for that news,
Because they have been still my adversaries:
But, that I'll give my voice on Richard's side,
To bar my master's heirs in true descent,
God knows, I will not do it, to the death.

Cate. God keep your lordship in that gracious mind!

Hast. But I shall laugh at this a twelve-month hence,—
That they, who brought me in my master's hate,
I live to look upon their tragedy.
Well, Catesby, ere a fortnight make me older,
I'll send some packing, that yet think not on 't.

Cate. 'T is a vile thing to die, my gracious lord,
When men are unprepar'd, and look not for it.

Hast. O monstrous, monstrous! and so falls it out
With Rivers, Vaughan, Grey: and so 't will do
With some men else, who think themselves as safe
As thou, and I; who, as thou know'st, are dear
To princely Richard, and to Buckingham.

Cate. The princes both make high account of you,—
For they account his head upon the bridge. [*Aside.*

Hast. I know, they do; and I have well deserv'd it.

Enter STANLEY.

Come on, come on, where is your boar-spear, man?
Fear you the boar, and go so unprovided?

Stan. My lord, good morrow; and good morrow, Catesby:—
You may jest on, but, by the holy rood,
I do not like these several councils, I.

Hast. My lord, I hold my life as dear as yours;
And never, in my life, I do protest,
Was it more precious to me than 't is now:
Think you, but that I know our state secure,
I would be so triumphant as I am?

Stan. The lords at Pomfret, when they rode from London,
Were jocund, and suppos'd their states were sure,
And they, indeed, had no cause to mistrust;

But yet, you see, how soon the day o'er-cast.
This sudden stab of rancour I misdoubt;
Pray God, I say, I prove a needless coward!
What, shall we toward the Tower? the day is spent.

Hast. Come, come, have with you.—Wot you what, my lord?
To-day, the lords you talk of are beheaded.

Stan. They, for their truth, might better wear their heads,
Than some, that have accus'd them, wear their hats.
But come, my lord, let 's away.

Enter a Pursuivant.

Hast. Go on before, I'll talk with this good fellow. [*Exeunt* STAN. *and* CATES.
How now, sirrah? how goes the world with thee?

Purs. The better, that your lordship please to ask.

Hast. I tell thee, man, 't is better with me now,
Than when thou met'st me last where now we meet:
Then was I going prisoner to the Tower,
By the suggestion of the queen's allies;
But now, I tell thee, (keep it to thyself,)
This day those enemies are put to death,
And I in better state than ere I was.

Purs. God hold it, to your honour's good content!

Hast. Gramercy, fellow: There, drink that for me. [*Throwing him his Purse.*

Purs. I thank your honour. [*Exit* Purs.

Enter a Priest.

Pr. Well met, my lord; I am glad to see your honour.

Hast. I thank thee, good sir John, with all my heart.
I am in your debt for your last exercise;
Come the next Sabbath, and I will content you.

Pr. I'll wait upon your lordship.

Enter BUCKINGHAM.

Buck. What, talking with a priest, lord chamberlain?
Your friends at Pomfret, they do need the priest,
Your honour hath no shriving work in hand.

Hast. Good faith, and when I met this holy man,
The men you talk of came into my mind.
What, go you toward the Tower?

1023

Buck. I do, my lord; but long I cannot stay
  there :
I shall return before your lordship thence.

Hast. Nay, like enough, for I stay dinner there.

Buck. And supper too, although thou know'st
  it not.   [*Aside.*
Come, will you go ?

Hast.   I 'll wait upon your lordship.
                                             [*Exeunt.*

SCENE III.—Pomfret. *Before the Castle.*

Enter RATCLIFF, *with a Guard, conducting* RIV-
ERS, GREY, *and* VAUGHAN, *to Execution.*

Rat. Come, bring forth the prisoners.

Riv. Sir Richard Ratcliff, let me tell thee this,—
To-day, shalt thou behold a subject die,
For truth, for duty, and for loyalty.

Grey. God keep the prince from all the pack
  of you !
A knot you are of damned blood-suckers.

Vaugh. You live, that shall cry woe for this
  hereafter.

Rat. Despatch ; the limit of your lives is out.

Riv. O Pomfret, Pomfret ! O thou bloody prison,
Fatal and ominous to noble peers !
Within the guilty 'closure of thy walls,
Richard the Second here was hack'd to death :
And, for more slander to thy dismal seat,
We give thee up our guiltless blood to drink.

Grey. Now Margaret's curse is fallen upon our
  heads,
When she exclaim'd on Hastings, you, and I,
For standing by when Richard stabb'd her son.

Riv. Then curs'd she Hastings, then curs'd she
  Buckingham,
Then curs'd she Richard :—O, remember, God,
To hear her prayers for them, as now for us !
And for my sister, and her princely sons,—
Be satisfied, dear God, with our true bloods,
Which, as thou know'st, unjustly must be spilt !

Rat. Make haste, the hour of death is expiate.

Riv. Come, Grey,—come, Vaughan,—let us
  here embrace :
Farewell, until we meet again in heaven. [*Exeunt.*

SCENE IV.—London. *A Room in the Tower.*

BUCKINGHAM, STANLEY, HASTINGS, *the* BISHOP OF
ELY, CATESBY, LOVEL, *and Others, sitting at a
Table : Officers of the Council attending.*

Hast. Now, noble peers, the cause why we are met
Is—to determine of the coronation :
In God's name, speak, when is the royal day ?

Buck. Are all things ready for that royal time ?

Stan. They are ; and wants but nomination.

Ely. To-morrow then I judge a happy day.

Buck. Who knows the lord protector's mind
  herein ?
Who is most inward with the noble duke ?

Ely. Your grace, we think, should soonest
  know his mind.

Buck. We know each other's faces : for our
  hearts,—
He knows no more of mine, than I of yours ;
Nor I, of his, my lord, than you of mine :—
Lord Hastings, you and he are near in love.

Hast. I thank his grace, I know he loves me
  well ;
But, for his purpose in the coronation,
I have not sounded him, nor he deliver'd
His gracious pleasure any way therein :
But you, my noble lord, may name the time ;
And in the duke's behalf I 'll give my voice,
Which, I presume, he 'll take in gentle part.

Enter GLOSTER.

Ely. In happy time, here comes the duke himself.

Glo. My noble lords and cousins, all, good
  morrow :
I have been long a sleeper ; but, I trust,
My absence doth neglect no great design,
Which by my presence might have been con-
  cluded.

Buck. Had you not come upon your cue, my
  lord,
William lord Hastings had pronounc'd your part,—
I mean, your voice,—for crowning of the king.

Glo. Than my lord Hastings, no man might be
  bolder ;
His lordship knows me well, and loves me well.—
My lord of Ely, when I was last in Holborn,
I saw good strawberries in your garden there ;
I do beseech you, send for some of them.

Ely. Marry, and will, my lord, with all my
  heart.   [*Exit* ELY.

Glo. Cousin of Buckingham, a word with you.
                                    [*Takes him aside*
Catesby hath sounded Hastings in our business ;
And finds the testy gentleman so hot,
That he will lose his head, ere give consent,
His master's child, as worshipfully he terms it,
Shall lose the royalty of England's throne.

1024

Buck. Withdraw yourself awhile, I 'll go with
you.　　　　　[*Exeunt* GLO. *and* BUCK.
Stan. We have not yet set down this day of
triumph.
To-morrow, in my judgment, is too sudden;
For I myself am not so well provided,
As else I would be, were the day prolong'd.

Re-enter BISHOP OF ELY.

Ely. Where is my lord protector? I have sent
For these strawberries.
Hast. His grace looks cheerfully and smooth
this morning;
There 's some conceit or other likes him well,
When he doth bid good morrow with such spirit.
I think, there 's ne'er a man in Christendom,
Can lesser hide his love, or hate, than he;
For by his face straight shall you know his heart.
Stan. What of his heart perceive you in his
face,
By any likelihood he show'd to-day?
Hast. Marry, that with no man here he is of-
fended;
For, were he, he had shown it in his looks.

Re-enter GLOSTER *and* BUCKINGHAM.

Glo. I pray you all, tell me what they deserve,
That do conspire my death with devilish plots
Of damned witchcraft; and that have prevail'd
Upon my body with their hellish charms?
Hast. The tender love I bear your grace, my
lord,
Makes me most forward in this noble presence
To doom the offenders: Whosoe'er they be,
I say, my lord, they have deserved death.
Glo. Then be your eyes the witness of their evil.
Look how I am bewitch'd; behold mine arm
Is, like a blasted sapling, wither'd up:
And this is Edward's wife, that monstrous witch,
Consorted with that harlot, strumpet Shore,
That by their witchcraft thus have marked me.
Hast. If they have done this deed, my noble
lord,——
Glo. If! thou protector of this damned strumpet,
Talk'st thou to me of ifs?—Thou art a traitor:—
Off with his head:—now, by Saint Paul I swear,
I will not dine until I see the same.—
Lovel, and Catesby, look, that it be done;
The rest, that love me, rise, and follow me.
　　　　　[*Exeunt* Council, *with* GLO. *and* BUCK.
Hast. Woe, woe, for England! not a whit for
me;

For I, too fond, might have prevented this ·
Stanley did dream, the boar did rase his helm:
But I disdain'd it, and did scorn to fly.
Three times to-day my foot-cloth horse did stum-
ble,[30]
And startled, when he look'd upon the Tower,
As loath to bear me to the slaughter-house.
O, now I want the priest that spake to me:
I now repent I told the pursuivant,
As too triumphing, how mine enemies,
To-day at Pomfret bloodily were butcher'd,
And I myself secure in grace and favour.
O, Margaret, Margaret, now thy heavy curse
Is lighted on poor Hastings' wretched head.
Cate. Despatch, my lord, the duke would be at
dinner;
Make a short shrift, he longs to see your head.
Hast. O momentary grace of mortal men,
Which we more hunt for than the grace of
God!
Who builds his hope in air of your fair looks,
Lives like a drunken sailor on a mast;
Ready, with every nod, to tumble down
Into the fatal bowels of the deep.
Lov. Come, come, despatch; 't is bootless to
exclaim.
Hast. O, bloody Richard!—miserable England;
I prophesy the fearful'st time to thee,
That ever wretched age hath look'd upon.—
Come, lead me to the block, bear him my head;
They smile at me, who shortly shall be dead.
　　　　　[*Exeunt.*

SCENE V.—*The Same. The Tower Walls.*

Enter GLOSTER *and* BUCKINGHAM, *in rusty armour, marvellous ill-favoured.*[31]

Glo. Come, cousin, canst thou quake, and change
thy colour?
Murder thy breath in middle of a word,—
And then again begin, and stop again,
As if thou wert distraught, and mad with terror?
Buck. Tut, I can counterfeit the deep tragedian;
Speak, and look back, and pry on every side,
Tremble and start at wagging of a straw,
Intending deep suspicion: ghastly looks
Are at my service, like enforced smiles;
And both are ready in their offices,
At any time, to grace my stratagems.
But what, is Catesby gone?
Glo. He is; and, see, he brings the mayor
along.

129

Enter the Lord Mayor *and* Catesby.

Buck. Let me alone to entertain him.—Lord
     mayor,——

Glo. Look to the draw-bridge there.

Buck.   Hark, hark! a drum.

Glo. Catesby, o'erlook the walls.

Buck. Lord mayor, the reason we have sent for
     you,——

Glo. Look back, defend thee, here are enemies.

Buck. God and our innocence defend and guard
     us!

Enter Lovel *and* Ratcliff, *with* Hastings'
Head.

Glo. Be patient, they are friends; Ratcliff, and
     Lovel.

Lov. Here is the head of that ignoble traitor,
The dangerous and unsuspected Hastings.

Glo. So dear I lov'd the man, that I must
     weep.
I took him for the plainest, harmles't creature,
That breath'd upon the earth a Christian:
Made him my book, wherein my soul recorded
The history of all her secret thoughts;
So smooth he daub'd his vice with show of virtue,
That his apparent open guilt omitted,—
I mean, his conversation with Shore's wife,"
He liv'd from all attainder of suspect.

Buck. Well, well, he was the covert'st shelter'd
     traitor
That ever liv'd.—Look you, my lord mayor,
Would you imagine, or almost believe,
(Were 't not, that by great preservation
We live to tell it you,) the subtle traitor
This day had plotted, in the council-house,
To murder me, and my good lord of Gloster?

May. What! had he so?

Glo. What! think you we are Turks, or in-
     fidels?
Or that we would, against the form of law,
Proceed thus rashly in the villain's death;
But that the extreme peril of the case,
The peace of England, and our persons' safety,
Enforc'd us to this execution?

May. Now, fair befal you, he deserv'd his death;
And your good graces both have well proceeded,
To warn false traitors from the like attempts.
I never look'd for better at his hands,
After he once fell in with mistress Shore.

Buck. Yet had we not determin'd he should
     die,
1894

Until your lordship came to see his end;
Which now the loving haste of these our friends,
Somewhat against our meaning, hath prevented:
Because, my lord, we would have had you heard
The traitor speak, and timorously confess
The manner and the purpose of his treasons;
That you might well have signified the same
Unto the citizens, who, haply, may
Misconstrue us in him, and wail his death.

May. But, my good lord, your grace's word
     shall serve,
As well as I had seen, and heard him speak;
And do not doubt, right noble princes both,
But I 'll acquaint our duteous citizens
With all your just proceedings in this case.

Glo. And to that end we wish'd your lordship
     here,
To avoid the censures of the carping world.

Buck. But since you came too late of our intent,
Yet witness what you hear we did intend:
And so, my good lord mayor, we bid farewell.
          [*Exit* May.

Glo. Go, after, after, cousin Buckingham.
The mayor towards Guildhall hies him in all
     post:—
There, at your meetest vantage of the time,
Infer the bastardy of Edward's children:
Tell them, how Edward put to death a citizen,
Only for saying—he would make his son
Heir to the crown;" meaning, indeed, his house,
Which, by the sign thereof, was termed so.
Moreover, urge his hateful luxury.
And bestial appetite in change of lust;
Which stretch'd unto their servants, daughters,
     wives,
Even where his raging eye, or savage heart,
Without control, listed to make his prey.
Nay, for a need, thus far come near my person:—
Tell them, when that my mother went with child
Of that insatiate Edward, noble York,
My princely father, then had wars in France;
And, by just computation of the time,
Found, that the issue was not his begot;
Which well appeared in his lineaments,
Being nothing like the noble duke my father:
Yet touch this sparingly, as 't were far off;
Because, my lord, you know, my mother lives.

Buck. Doubt not, my lord; I 'll play the orator
As if the golden fee, for which I plead,
Were for myself: and so, my lord, adieu.

Glo. If you thrive well, bring them to Baynard's
     castle;

Where you shall find me well accompanied,
With reverend fathers, and well-learned bishops.

Buck. I go; and, towards three or four o'clock,
Look for the news that the Guildhall affords.

[*Exit* BUCK.

Glo. Go, Lovel, with all speed to doctor
Shaw,—
Go thou [*To* CAT.] to friar Penker;—bid them
both
Meet me, within this hour, at Baynard's castle.

[*Exeunt* LOV. *and* CAT.

Now will I in, to take some privy order
To draw the brats of Clarence out of sight;[21]
And to give notice, that no manner of person
Have, any time, recourse unto the princes. [*Exit.*

SCENE VI.—*A Street.*

Enter a Scrivener.

Scriv. Here is the indictment of the good lord
Hastings;
Which in a set hand fairly is engross'd,
That it may be to-day read o'er in Paul's.
And mark how well the sequel hangs together:—
Eleven hours I have spent to write it over,
For yesternight by Catesby was it sent me;
The precedent was full as long a doing:
And yet within these five hours Hastings liv'd,
Untainted, unexamin'd, free, at liberty.
Here's a good world the while!—Who is so gross,
That cannot see this palpable device?
Yet who so bold, but says—he sees it not?
Bad is the world, and all will come to nought,
When such bad dealing must be seen in thought.

[*Exit.*

SCENE VII.—*The Same.   Court of* Baynard's
Castle.

Enter GLOSTER *and* BUCKINGHAM, *meeting.*

Glo. How now, how now? what say the
citizens?

Buck. Now by the holy mother of our Lord,
The citizens are mum, say not a word.

Glo. Touch'd you the bastardy of Edward's
children?

Buck. I did; with his contract with Lady
Lucy,[22]
And his contract by deputy in France:
The insatiate greediness of his desires,
And his enforcement of the city wives;
His tyranny for trifles; his own bastardy,—

As being got, your father then in France;
And his resemblance, being not like the duke.
Withal, I did infer your lineaments,—
Being the right idea of your father,
Both in your form and nobleness of mind:
Laid open all your victories in Scotland,
Your discipline in war, wisdom in peace,
Your bounty, virtue, fair humility;
Indeed, left nothing, fitting for your purpose,
Untouch'd, or slightly handled, in discourse.
And, when my oratory grew to an end,
I bade them, that did love their country's good,
Cry—"God save Richard, England's royal king!"

Glo. And did they so?

Buck. No, so God help me, they spake not a
word;
But, like dumb statuas, or breathless stones,
Star'd on each other, and look'd deadly pale.
Which when I saw, I reprehended them;
And ask'd the mayor, what meant this wilful
silence:—
His answer was,—the people were not us'd
To be spoke to, but by the recorder.
Then he was urg'd to tell my tale again;—
"Thus saith the duke, thus hath the duke inferr'd;"
But nothing spoke in warrant from himself.
When he had done, some followers of mine own,
At lower end o' the hall, hurl'd up their caps,
And some ten voices cried, "God save king
Richard!"
And thus I took the vantage of those few,
"Thanks, gentle citizens, and friends," quoth I;
"This general applause, and cheerful shout,
Argues your wisdom, and your love to Richard:"
And even here brake off, and came away.

Glo. What tongueless blocks were they! Would
they not speak?
Will not the mayor then, and his brethren, come?

Buck. The mayor is here at hand; intend some
fear;
Be not you spoke with, but by mighty suit:
And look you get a prayer-book in your hand,
And stand between two churchmen, good my
lord;
For on that ground I'll make a holy descant;
And be not easily won to our requests;
Play the maid's part, still answer nay, and take it.

Glo. I go: And if you plead as well for them,
As I can say nay to thee for myself,
No doubt we'll bring it to a happy issue.

Buck. Go, go, up to the leads; the lord mayor
knocks.   [*Exit* GLO.

Enter the LORD MAYOR, *Aldermen, and Citizens.*

Welcome, my lord: I dance attendance here;
I think, the duke will not be spoke withal.—

Enter, from the Castle, CATESBY.

Now, Catesby! what says your lord to my request?
    Cate. He doth entreat your grace, my noble
        lord,
To visit him to-morrow, or next day.
He is within, with two right reverend fathers,
Divinely bent to meditation;
And in no worldly suit would he be mov'd,
To draw him from his holy exercise.
    Buck. Return, good Catesby, to the gracious
        duke;
Tell him, myself, the mayor and aldermen,
In deep designs, in matter of great moment,
No less importing than our general good,
Are come to have some conference with his grace.
    Cate. I'll signify so much unto him straight.
                                        [*Exit.*
    Buck. Ah, ha, my lord, this prince is not an
        Edward!
He is not lolling on a lewd day-bed,
But on his knees at meditation;
Not dallying with a brace of courtezans,
But meditating with two deep divines;
Not sleeping, to engross his idle body,
But praying, to enrich his watchful soul:
Happy were England, would this virtuous prince
Take on himself the sovereignty thereof:
But, sore, I fear, we shall ne'er win him to it.
    May. Marry, God defend, his grace should say
        us nay!
    Buck. I fear, he will: Here Catesby comes
        again;—

Re-enter CATESBY.

Now, Catesby, what says his grace?
    Cate. He wonders to what end you have as-
        sembled
Such troops of citizens to come to him,
His grace not being warn'd thereof before.
He fears, my lord, you mean no good to him.
    Buck. Sorry I am, my noble cousin should
Suspect me, that I mean no good to him:
By heaven, we come to him in perfect love,
And so once more return and tell his grace.
                                    [*Exit* CATE.
When holy and devout religious men

Are at their beads, 't is hard to draw them thence:
So sweet is zealous contemplation.

Enter GLOSTER, *in a Gallery above, between Two*
        Bishops. CATESBY *returns.*

    May. See, where his grace stands 'tween two
        clergymen!
    Buck. Two props of virtue for a Christian prince,
To stay him from the fall of vanity:
And, see, a book of prayer in his hand;
True ornaments to know a holy man.—
Famous Plantagenet, most gracious prince,
Lend favourable ear to our requests;
And pardon us the interruption
Of thy devotion, and right Christian zeal.
    Glo. My lord, there needs no such apology;
I rather do beseech you pardon me,
Who, earnest in the service of my God,
Neglect the visitation of my friends.
But, leaving this, what is your grace's pleasure?
    Buck. Even that, I hope, which pleaseth God
        above,
And all good men of this ungovern'd isle.
    Glo. I do suspect, I have done some offence,
That seems disgracious in the city's eye;
And that you come to reprehend my ignorance.
    Buck. You have, my lord: Would it might
        please your grace,
On our entreaties to amend your fault!
    Glo. Else wherefore breathe I in a Christian
        land?
    Buck. Know, then, it is your fault, that you
        resign
The supreme seat, the throne majestical,
The sceptred office of your ancestors,
Your state of fortune, and your due of birth,
The lineal glory of your royal house,
To the corruption of a blemish'd stock:
Whilst, in the mildness of your sleepy thoughts
(Which here we waken to our country's good,)
The noble isle doth want her proper limbs;
Her face defac'd with scars of infamy,
Her royal stock graft with ignoble plants,
And almost shoulder'd in the swallowing gulf
Of dark forgetfulness and deep oblivion.
Which to recure, we heartily solicit
Your gracious self to take on you the charge
And kingly government of this your land:
Not as protector, steward, substitute,
Or lowly factor for another's gain;
But as successively, from blood to blood,
Your right of birth, your empery, your own.

For this, consorted with the citizens,
Your very worshipful and loving friends,
And by their vehement instigation,
In this just suit come I to move your grace.

Glo. I cannot tell, if to depart in silence,
Or bitterly to speak in your reproof,
Best fitteth my degree, or your condition:
If, not to answer,—you might haply think,
Tongue-tied ambition, not replying, yielded
To bear the golden yoke of sovereignty,
Which fondly you would here impose on me;
If to reprove you for this suit of yours,
So season'd with your faithful love to me,
Then, on the other side, I check'd my friends.
Therefore,—to speak, and to avoid the first,
And then, in speaking, not to incur the last,—
Definitively thus I answer you.
Your love deserves my thanks; but my desert
Unmeritable, shuns your high request.
First, if all obstacles were cut away,
And that my path were even to the crown,
As the ripe revenue and due of birth;
Yet so much is my poverty of spirit,
So mighty, and so many, my defects,
That I would rather hide me from my greatness,—
Being a bark to brook no mighty sea,—
Than in my greatness covet to be hid,
And in the vapour of my glory smother'd.
But, God be thank'd, there is no need of me;
(And much I need to help you, if need were:)
The royal tree hath left us royal fruit,
Which, mellow'd by the stealing hours of time,
Will well become the seat of majesty,
And make, no doubt, us happy by his reign.
On him I lay what you would lay on me,
The right and fortune of his happy stars,—
Which, God defend, that I should wring from him!

Buck. My lord, this argues conscience in your grace;
But the respects thereof are nice and trivial,
All circumstances well considered.
You say, that Edward is your brother's son;
So say we too, but not by Edward's wife:
For first he was contract to lady Lucy,
Your mother lives a witness to his vow;
And afterwards by substitute betroth'd
To Bona, sister to the king of France.
These both put by, a poor petitioner,
A care-craz'd mother to a many sons,
A beauty-waning and distressed widow,
Even in the afternoon of her best days,
Made prize and purchase of his wanton eye,

Seduc'd the pitch and height of all his thoughts
To base declension and loath'd bigamy:
By her, in his unlawful bed, he got
This Edward, whom our manners call—the prince.
More bitterly could I expostulate,
Save that, for reverence to some alive,
I give a sparing limit to my tongue.
Then, good my lord, take to your royal self
This proffer'd benefit of dignity:
If not to bless us and the land withal,
Yet to draw forth your noble ancestry
From the corruption of abusing time,
Unto a lineal true-derived course.

May. Do, good my lord; your citizens entreat you.

Buck. Refuse not, mighty lord, this proffer'd love.

Cate. O, make them joyful, grant their lawful suit.

Glo. Alas, why would you heap those cares on me?
I am unfit for state and majesty;—
I do beseech you, take it not amiss;
I cannot, nor I will not, yield to you.

Buck. If you refuse it,—as in love and zeal,
Loath to depose the child, your brother's son;
As well we know your tenderness of heart,
And gentle, kind, effeminate remorse,
Which we have noted in you to your kindred,
And equally, indeed, to all estates,—
Yet know, whe'r you accept our suit or no,
Your brother's son shall never reign our king;
But we will plant some other in your throne,
To the disgrace and downfal of your house:
And, in this resolution, here we leave you;—
Zounds, citizens, we will entreat no more.

Glo. O! do not swear, my lord of Buckingham.

[*Exeunt* BUCK. *and Citizens.*

Cate. Call them again, sweet prince, accept their suit;
If you deny them, all the land will rue it.

Glo. Will you enforce me to a world of cares?
Well, call them again; I am not made of stone,
But penetrable to your kind entreaties,

[*Exit* CATE

Albeit against my conscience and my soul.—

Re-enter BUCKINGHAM, *and the Rest.*

Cousin of Buckingham,—and sage, grave men,—
Since you will buckle fortune on my back,
To bear her burden, whe'r I will, or no,
I must have patience to endure the load

1929

But if black scandal, or foul-fac'd reproach,
Attend the sequel of your imposition,
Your mere enforcement shall acquittance me
From all the impure blots and stains thereof;
For God he knows, and you may partly see,
How far I am from the desire of this.

   May. God bless your grace! we see it, and will
    say it.
   Glo. In saying so, you shall but say the truth.
   Buck. Then I salute you with this royal
    title,—
Long live king Richard, England's worthy king!

   All. Amen.
   Buck. To-morrow may it please you to be
    crown'd?
   Glo. Even when you please, since you will have
    it so.
   Buck. To-morrow then we will attend your
    grace;
And so, most joyfully, we take our leave.
   Glo. Come, let us to our holy work again :—
                          [*To the Bishops*
Farewell, good cousin ;—farewell, gentle friends.
                          [*Exeunt*

ACT IV.

SCENE I.—*Before the Tower.*

Enter, on one side, QUEEN ELIZABETH, DUCHESS OF YORK, *and* MARQUIS OF DORSET; *on the other,* ANNE, DUCHESS OF GLOSTER, *leading* LADY MARGARET PLANTAGENET, *Clarence's young daughter.*

   Duch. Who meets us here?—my niece Plantagenet,
Led in the hand of her kind aunt of Gloster?
Now, for my life, she's wandering to the Tower,
On pure heart's love, to greet the tender prince.—
Daughter, well met.
   Anne.   God give your graces both
A happy and a joyful time of day!
   Q. Eliz. As much to you, good sister! Whither
    away?
   Anne. No further than the Tower; and, as I
    guess,
Upon the like devotion as yourselves,
To gratulate the gentle princes there.
   Q. Eliz. Kind sister, thanks; we'll enter all to-
    gether :

Enter BRAKENBURY.

And, in good time, here the lieutenant comes.—
Master lieutenant, pray you, by your leave,
How doth the prince, and my young son of York?
   Brak. Right well, dear madam : By your pa-
    tience,
I may not suffer you to visit them;
The king hath strictly charg'd the contrary.

   Q. Eliz. The king! who's that?
   Brak.   I mean, the lord protector.
   Q. Eliz. The Lord protect him from that kingly
    title !
Hath he set bounds between their love, and me?
I am their mother, who shall bar me from them?
   Duch. I am their father's mother, I will see
    them.
   Anne. Their aunt I am in law, in love their
    mother :
Then bring me to their sights ; I'll bear thy blame,
And take thy office from thee, on thy peril.
   Brak. No, madam, no, I may not leave it so;
I am bound by oath, and therefore pardon me.
                          [*Exit* BRAK.

Enter STANLEY.

   Stan. Let me but meet you, ladies, one hour
    hence,
And I'll salute your grace of York as mother,
And reverend looker-on of two fair queens.—
Come, madam, you must straight to Westminster,
                          [*To the Duch.*
There to be crowned Richard's royal queen.
   Q. Eliz. Ah, cut my lace asunder!
That my pent heart may have some scope to beat,
Or else I swoon with this dead-killing news.
   Anne. Despiteful tidings! O unpleasing news!
   Dor. Be of good cheer :—Mother, how fares
    your grace?
   Q. Eliz. O Dorset, speak not to me, get thee
    gone,

Death and destruction dog thee at the heels;
Thy mother's name is ominous to children;
If thou wilt outstrip death, go cross the seas,
And live with Richmond, from the reach of hell.
Go hie thee, hie thee, from this slaughter-house,
Lest thou increase the number of the dead;
And make me die the thrall of Margaret's curse,—
Nor mother, wife, nor England's counted queen.
   Stan. Full of wise care is this your counsel,
     madam :—
Take all the swift advantage of the hours;
You shall have letters from me to my son
In your behalf, to meet you on the way:
Be not ta'en tardy by unwise delay.
   Duch. O ill-dispersing wind of misery!—
O my accursed womb, the bed of death;
A cockatrice hast thou hatch'd to the world,
Whose unavoided eye is murderous!
   Stan. Come, madam, come; I in all haste was
     sent.
   Anne. And I with all unwillingness will go.—
O, would to God, that the inclusive verge
Of golden metal, that must round my brow,
Were red-hot steel, to sear me to the brain!"
Anointed let me be with deadly venom;
And die, ere men can say—God save the queen!
   Q. Eliz. Go, go, poor soul, I envy not thy
     glory;
To feed my humour, wish thyself no harm.
   Anne. No! why?—When he, that is my hus-
     band now,
Came to me, as I follow'd Henry's corse;
When scarce the blood was well wash'd from his
     hands,
Which issu'd from my other angel husband,
And that dead saint which then I weeping follow'd;
O, when, I say, I look'd on Richard's face,
This was my wish,—"Be thou," quoth I, "ac-
     curs'd,
For making me, so young, so old a widow!
And, when thou wed'st, let sorrow haunt thy bed;
And be thy wife (if any be so mad)
More miserable by the life of thee,
Than thou hast made me by my dear lord's death!
Lo, ere I can repeat this curse again,
Even in so short a space, my woman's heart
Grossly grew captive to his honey words,
And prov'd the subject of mine own soul's curse:
Which ever since hath held mine eyes from rest;
For never yet one hour in his bed
Did I enjoy the golden dew of sleep,
But with his timorous dreams was still awak'd.

Besides, he hates me for my father Warwick;
And will, no doubt, shortly be rid of me.
   Q. Eliz. Poor heart, adieu; I pity thy com-
     plaining.
   Anne. No more than with my soul I mourn for
     yours.
   Dor. Farewell, thou woeful welcomer of glory!
   Anne. Adieu, poor soul, that tak'st thy leave of
     it!
   Duch. Go thou to Richmond, and good fortune
     guide thee!—   [*To Dor.*
Go thou to Richard, and good angels tend thee!—
               [*To Anne*
Go thou to sanctuary, and good thoughts possess
     thee!   [*To Q. Eliz.*
I to my grave, where peace and rest lie with me!
Eighty odd years of sorrow have I seen,
And each hour's joy wreck'd with a week of teen."
   Q. Eliz. Stay yet; look back, with me, unto
     the Tower.—
Pity, you ancient stones, those tender babes,
Whom envy hath immur'd within your walls!
Rough cradle for such little pretty ones!
Rude ragged nurse! old sullen play-fellow
For tender princes, use my babies well!
So foolish sorrow bids your stones farewell.
               [*Exeunt*

SCENE II.—*A Room of State in the Palace*

Flourish of Trumpets. RICHARD, *as King upon
his Throne;* BUCKINGHAM, CATESBY, *a Page,
and Others.*

   K. Rich. Stand all apart.—Cousin of Bucking-
     ham,——
   Buck. My gracious sovereign.
   K. Rich. Give me thy hand. Thus high, by
     thy advice,
And thy assistance, is king Richard seated:—
But shall we wear these glories for a day?
Or shall they last, and we rejoice in them?
   Buck. Still live they, and for ever let them last!
   K. Rich. Ah, Buckingham, now do I play the
     touch,
To try if thou be current gold, indeed:—
Young Edward lives:—Think now what I would
     speak.
   Buck. Say on, my loving lord.
   K. Rich. Why, Buckingham, I say, I would be
     king.
   Buck. Why, so you are, my thrice-renowned
     liege.

K. Rich. Ha! am I king? 'T is so: but Edward lives.

Buck. True, noble prince.

K. Rich.   O bitter consequence,
That Edward still should live,—true, noble
        prince!—
Cousin, thou wast not wont to be so dull:—
Shall I be plain? I wish the bastards dead;
And I would have it suddenly perform'd.
What say'st thou now? speak suddenly, be brief.

Buck. Your grace may do your pleasure.

K. Rich. Tut, tut, thou art all ice, thy kindness
        freezes:
Say, have I thy consent, that they shall die?

Buck. Give me some breath, some little pause,
        dear lord,
Before I positively speak in this:
I will resolve your grace immediately. [*Exit* BUCK.

Cate. The king is angry; see, he gnaws his lip.
                                      [*Aside.*

K. Rich. I will converse with iron-witted fools,
                           [*Descends from his Throne.*
And unrespective boys; none are for me,
That look into me with considerate eyes:—
High-reaching Buckingham grows circumspect.—
Boy,——

Page. My lord.

K. Rich. Know'st thou not any, whom corrupting gold
Would tempt unto a close exploit of death?

Page. I know a discontented gentleman,
Whose humble means match not his haughty
        mind:
Gold were as good as twenty orators,
And will, no doubt, tempt him to any thing.

K. Rich. What is his name?

Page.   His name, my lord, is—Tyrrel.

K. Rich. I partly know the man: Go, call him
        hither, boy.——   [*Exit* Page.
The deep revolving witty Buckingham
No more shall be the neighbour to my counsels:
Hath he so long held out with me untir'd,
And stops he now for breath?—well, be it so.—

Enter STANLEY.

How now, lord Stanley! what 's the news?

Stan.   Know, my loving lord,
The marquis Dorset, as I hear, is fled
To Richmond, in the parts where he abides.

K. Rich. Come hither, Catesby: rumour it
        abroad,
That Anne, my wife, is very grievous sick:
1632

I will take order for her keeping close.
Inquire me out some mean-born gentleman,
Whom I will marry straight to Clarence' daughter:—
The boy is foolish,[20] and I fear not him.—
Look, how thou dream'st!—I say again, give out,
That Anne my queen is sick, and like to die:
About it; for it stands me much upon,
To stop all hopes, whose growth may damage
        me.—   [*Exit* CATE.
I must be married to my brother's daughter,
Or else my kingdom stands on brittle glass:—
Murder her brothers, and then marry her!
Uncertain way of gain! But I am in
So far in blood, that sin will pluck on sin.
Tear-falling pity dwells not in this eye.—

Re-enter Page, *with* TYRREL.

Is thy name—Tyrrel?

Tyr. James Tyrrel, and your most obedient
        subject.

K. Rich. Art thou, indeed?

Tyr.   Prove me, my gracious lord.

K. Rich. Dar'st thou resolve to kill a friend of
        mine?

Tyr. Please you; but I had rather kill two
        enemies.

K. Rich. Why, then thou hast it; two deep
        enemies,
Foes to my rest, and my sweet sleep's disturbers,
Are they that I would have thee deal upon:
Tyrrel, I mean those bastards in the Tower.

Tyr. Let me have open means to come to them,
And soon I 'll rid you from the fear of them.

K. Rich. Thou sing'st sweet music. Hark,
        come hither, Tyrrel;
Go, by this token:—Rise, and lend thine ear:
                                      [*Whispers*
There is no more but so:—Say, it is done,
And I will love thee, and prefer thee for it.

Tyr. I will despatch it straight.   [*Exit*

Re-enter BUCKINGHAM.

Buck. My lord, I have consider'd in my mind
The late demand that you did sound me in.

K. Rich. Well, let that rest. Dorset is fled to
        Richmond.

Buck. I hear the news, my lord.

K. Rich. Stanley, he is your wife's son:—Well,
        look to it.

Buck. My lord, I claim the gift, my due by
        promise.

For which your honour and your faith is pawn'd;
The earldom of Hereford, and the movables,
Which you have promised I shall possess.

K. Rich. Stanley, look to your wife; if she
    convey
Letters to Richmond, you shall answer it.

Buck. What says your highness to my just re-
    quest?

K. Rich. I do remember me,—Henry the Sixth
Did prophesy, that Richmond should be king,
When Richmond was a little peevish boy.
A king!—perhaps——

Buck. My lord,——

K. Rich. How chance, the prophet could not
    at that time,
Have told me, I being by, that I should kill him?

Buck. My lord, your promise for the earldom.—

K. Rich. Richmond!—When last I was at
Exeter,
The mayor in courtesy show'd me the castle,
And call'd it—Rouge-mont: at which name, I
    started;
Because a bard of Ireland told me once,
I should not live long after I saw Richmond.

Buck. My lord,——

K. Rich.   Ay, what 's o'clock?

Buck.   I am thus bold
To put your grace in mind of what you promis'd
    me.

K. Rich. Well, but what is 't o'clock?

Buck.   Upon the stroke
Of ten.

K. Rich. Well, let it strike.

Buck.   Why, let it strike?

K. Rich. Because that, like a Jack, thou keep'st
    the stroke
Betwixt thy begging and my meditation.
I am not in the giving vein to-day.

Buck. Why, then resolve me whe'r you will,
    or no.

K. Rich. Thou troublest me; I am not in the
    vein.   [*Exeunt K. Rich. and Train.*

Buck. And is it thus? repays he my deep service
With such contempt? made I him king for this?
O, let me think on Hastings; and be gone
To Brecknock," while my fearful head is on. [*Exit.*

SCENE III.—*The Same.*

Enter TYRREL.

Tyr. The tyrannous and bloody act is done;
The most arch deed of piteous massacre

That ever yet this land was guilty of.
Dighton, and Forrest, whom I did suborn
To do this piece of ruthless butchery,
Albeit they were flesh'd villains, bloody dogs,
Melting with tenderness and mild compassion,
Wept like two children, in their death's sad story
"O thus," quoth Dighton, "lay the gentle babes,—"
"Thus, thus," quoth Forrest, "girdling one another
Within their alabaster innocent arms:
Their lips were four red roses on a stalk,
Which in their summer beauty, kiss'd each other.
A book of prayers on their pillow lay;
Which once," quoth Forrest, "almost chang'd my
    mind;
But, O, the devil"—there the villain stopp'd;
When Dighton thus told on,—" we smothered
The most replenished sweet work of nature,
That, from the prime creation, e'er she fram'd.—"
Hence both are gone with conscience and remorse,
They could not speak; and so I left them both,
To bear this tidings to the bloody king.

Enter KING RICHARD.

And here he comes:—All health, my sovereign
    lord!

K. Rich. Kind Tyrrel! am I happy in thy
    news?

Tyr. If to have done the thing you gave in
    charge
Beget your happiness, be happy then,
For it is done.

K. Rich.   But didst thou see them dead?

Tyr. I did, my lord.

K. Rich.   And buried, gentle Tyrrel?

Tyr. The chaplain of the Tower hath buried
    them;
But where, to say the truth, I do not know.

K. Rich. Come to me, Tyrrel, soon, at after
    supper,
When thou shalt tell the process of their death.
Mean time, but think how I may do thee good,
And be inheritor of thy desire.
Farewell, till then.

Tyr.   I humbly take my leave. [*Exit.*

K. Rich. The son of Clarence have I pen'd up
    close;
His daughter meanly have I match'd in marriage;
The sons of Edward sleep in Abraham's bosom,
And Anne my wife hath bid the world good
    night.
Now, for I know the Bretagne Richmond aims
At young Elizabeth, my brother's daughter,

And, by that knot, looks proudly on the crown,
To her go I, a jolly thriving wooer.

Enter CATESBY.

Cate. My lord,——

K. Rich. Good news or bad, that thou com'st
in so bluntly?

Cate. Bad news, my lord: Morton is fled to
Richmond;
And Buckingham, back'd with the hardy Welsh-
men,
Is in the field, and still his power increaseth.

K. Rich. Ely with Richmond troubles me more
near,
Than Buckingham and his rash-levied strength.
Come,—I have learn'd, that fearful commenting
Is leaden servitor to dull delay;
Delay leads impotent and snail-pac'd beggary:
Then fiery expedition be my wing,
Jove's Mercury, and herald for a king!
Go, muster men: My counsel is my shield;
We must be brief, when traitors brave the field.
                                        [*Exeunt.*

SCENE IV.—*The Same.   Before the Palace.*

Enter QUEEN MARGARET.

Q. Mar. So, now prosperity begins to mellow,
And drop into the rotten mouth of death.
Here in these confines slily have I lurk'd,
To watch the waning of mine enemies.
A dire induction am I witness to,
And will to France; hoping, the consequence
Will prove as bitter, black, and tragical.
Withdraw thee, wretched Margaret! who comes
here?

Enter QUEEN ELIZABETH, *and the* DUCHESS OF
YORK.

Q. Eliz. Ah, my poor princes! ah, my tender
babes!
My unblown flowers, new-appearing sweets!
If yet your gentle souls fly in the air,
And be not fix'd in doom perpetual,
Hover about me with your airy wings,
And hear your mother's lamentation!

Q. Mar. Hover about her; say, that right for
right
Hath dimm'd your infant morn to aged night.

Duch. So many miseries have craz'd my voice,
That my woe-wearied tongue is still and mute,—
Edward Plantagenet, why art thou dead?
1684

Q. Mar. Plantagenet doth quit Plantagenet,
Edward for Edward pays a dying debt.

Q. Eliz. Wilt thou, O God, fly from such gentle lambs,
And throw them in the entrails of the wolf?
When didst thou sleep, when such a deed was
done?

Q. Mar. When holy Harry died, and my sweet
son.

Duch. Dead life, blind sight, poor mortal-living
ghost,
Woe's scene, world's shame, grave's due by life
usurp'd,
Brief abstract and record of tedious days,
Rest thy unrest on England's lawful earth,
                                    [*Sitting down.*
Unlawfully made drunk with innocent blood!

Q. Eliz. Ah, that thou would'st as soon afford a
grave,
As thou canst yield a melancholy seat:
Then would I hide my bones, not rest them here!
Ah, who hath any cause to mourn, but we?
                                [*Sitting down by her.*

Q. Mar. If ancient sorrow be most reverent,
Give mine the benefit of seniory,
And let my griefs frown on the upper hand.
If sorrow can admit society,
                            [*Sitting down with them.*
Tell o'er your woes again by viewing mine:—
I had an Edward, till a Richard kill'd him;
I had a husband, till a Richard kill'd him:
Thou hadst an Edward, till a Richard kill'd him;
Thou hadst a Richard, till a Richard kill'd him,

Duch. I had a Richard too, and thou didst kill
him:
I had a Rutland too, thou holp'st to kill him.

Q. Mar. Thou hadst a Clarence too, and Rich-
ard kill'd him.
From forth the kennel of thy womb hath crept
A hell-hound, that doth hunt us all to death:
That dog, that had his teeth before his eyes,
To worry lambs, and lap their gentle blood;
That foul defacer of God's handy-work;
That excellent grand tyrant of the earth,
That reigns in galled eyes of weeping souls,
Thy womb let loose, to chase us to our graves.—
O upright, just, and true-disposing God,
How do I thank thee, that this carnal cur
Preys on the issue of his mother's body,
And makes her pew-fellow with others' moan!

Duch. O, Harry's wife, triumph not in my woes;
God witness with me, I have wept for thine.

Q. Mar. Bear with me; I am hungry for revenge,
And now I cloy me with beholding it.
Thy Edward he is dead, that kill'd my Edward;
Thy other Edward dead, to quit my Edward;
Young York he is but boot, because both they
Match not the high perfection of my loss.
Thy Clarence he is dead, that stabb'd my Edward;
And the beholders of this tragic play,
The adulterate Hastings, Rivers, Vaughan, Grey,
Untimely smother'd in their dusky graves.
Richard yet lives, hell's black intelligencer;
Only reserv'd their factor, to buy souls,
And send them thither : But at hand, at hand,
Ensues his piteous and unpitied end :
Earth gapes, hell burns, fiends roar, saints pray,
To have him suddenly convey'd from hence :—
Cancel his bond of life, dear God, I pray,
That I may live to say, The dog is dead !
   Q. Eliz. O, thou didst prophesy the time would come,
That I should wish for thee to help me curse
That bottled spider, that foul bunch-back'd toad.
   Q. Mar. I call'd thee then, vain flourish of my fortune ;
I call'd thee then, poor shadow, painted queen ;
The presentation of but what I was,
The flattering index of a direful pageant,
One heav'd a high, to be hurl'd down below :
A mother only mock'd with two fair babes ;
A dream of what thou wast ; a garish flag,
To be the aim of every dangerous shot ;
A sign of dignity, a breath, a bubble ;
A queen in jest, only to fill the scene.
Where is thy husband now ? where be thy brothers ?
Where be thy two sons ? wherein dost thou joy ?
Who sues, and kneels, and says—God save the queen ?
Where be the bending peers that flatter'd thee ?
Where be the thronging troops that follow'd thee ?
Decline all this,⁴² and see what now thou art.
For happy wife, a most distressed widow ;
For joyful mother, one that wails the name :
For one being sued to, one that humbly sues !
For queen, a very caitiff crown'd with care :
For one that scorn'd at me, now scorn'd of me ;
For one being fear'd of all, now fearing one ;
For one commanding all, obey'd of none.
Thus hath the course of justice wheel'd about,
And left thee but a very prey to time ;
Having no more but thought of what thou wert,

To torture thee the more, being what thou art.
Thou didst usurp my place, And dost thou not
Usurp the just proportion of my sorrow ?
Now thy proud neck bears half my burden'd yoke ;
F'om which even here I slip my wearied head,
And leave the burden of it all on thee.
Farewell, York's wife,—and queen of sad mischance,—
These English woes shall make me smile in France.
   Q. Eliz. O thou well skill'd in curses, stay a while,
And teach me how to curse mine enemies.
   Q. Mar. Forbear to sleep the night, and fast the day ;
Compare dead happiness with living woe ;
Think that thy babes were fairer than they were,
And he, that slew them, fouler than he is :
Bettering thy loss makes the bad-causer worse ;
Revolving this will teach thee how to curse.
   Q. Eliz. My words are dull, O, quicken them with thine !
   Q. Mar. Thy woes will make them sharp, and pierce like mine.   [*Exit Q. Mar.*
   Duch. Why should calamity be full of words ?
   Q. Eliz. Windy attorneys to their client woes,
Airy succeeders of intestate joys,
Poor breathing orators of miseries !
Let them have scope : though what they do impart
Help nothing else, yet do they ease the heart.
   Duch. If so, then be not tongue-ty'd : go with me,
And in the breath of bitter words let 's smother
My damned son, that thy two sweet sons smother'd.
                 [*Drum, within.*
I hear his drum,—be copious in exclaims.

Enter KING RICHARD, *and his Train, marching.*

   K. Rich. Who intercepts me in my expedition ?
   Duch. O, she, that might have intercepted thee,
By strangling thee in her accursed womb,
From all the slaughters, wretch, that thou hast done.
   Q. Eliz. Hid'st thou that forehead with a golden crown,
Where should be branded, if that right were right,
The slaughter of the prince that ow'd that crown,
And the dire death of my poor sons, and brothers ?
Tell me, thou villain-slave, where are my children ?
   Duch. Thou toad, thou toad, where is thy brother Clarence ?
And little Ned Plantagenet, his son ?

Q. Eliz. Where is the gentle Rivers, Vaughan, Grey?

Duch. Where is kind Hastings!

K. Rich. A flourish, trumpets!—strike alarum, drums!

Let not the heavens hear these tell-tale women
Rail on the Lord's anointed: Strike, I say.—

　　　　　　　　[*Flourish. Alarums.*

Either be patient, and entreat me fair,
Or with the clamorous report of war
Thus will I drown your exclamations.

Duch. Art thou my son?

K. Rich. Ay; I thank God, my father, and
yourself.

Duch. Then patiently hear my impatience.

K. Rich. Madam, I have a touch of your condition,
That cannot brook the accent of reproof.

Duch. O, let me speak.

K. Rich. 　　　Do, then; but I 'll not hear.

Duch. I will be mild and gentle in my words.

K. Rich. And brief, good mother; for I am in
haste.

Duch. Art thou so hasty? I have staid for thee,
God knows, in torment and in agony.

K. Rich. And came I not at last to comfort
you?

Duch. No, by the holy rood, thou know'st it well,
Thou cam'st on earth to make the earth my hell.
A grievous burden was thy birth to me;
Tetchy and wayward was thy infancy;
Thy school-days, frightful, desperate, wild, and
furious;
Thy prime of manhood, daring, bold, and ven-
turous;
Thy age confirm'd, proud, subtle, sly, and bloody,
More mild, but yet more harmful, kind in hatred:
What comfortable hour canst thou name,
That ever grac'd me in thy company?

K. Rich. 'Faith, none but Humphrey Hour,"
that call'd your grace
To breakfast once, forth of my company.
If I be so disgracious in your sight,
Let me march on, and not offend you, madam.—
Strike up the drum.

Duch. 　　　　I pr'ythee, hear me speak.

K. Rich. You speak too bitterly.

Duch. 　　　　Hear me a word;
For I shall never speak to thee again.

K. Rich. So.

Duch. Either thou wilt die, by God's just ordinance,

1036

Ere from this war thou turn a conqueror;
Or I with grief and extreme age shall perish,
And never look upon thy face again.
Therefore, take with thee my most heavy curse;
Which, in the day of battle, tire thee more,
Than all the complete armour that thou wear'st!
My prayers on the adverse party fight;
And there the little souls of Edward's children
Whisper the spirits of thine enemies,
And promise them success and victory.
Bloody thou art, bloody will be thy end;
Shame serves thy life, and doth thy death attend.
　　　　　　　　[*Exit*

Q. Eliz. Though far more cause, yet much less
spirit to curse
Abides in me; I say amen to her. 　　[*Going.*

K. Rich. Stay, madam, I must speak a word
with you.

Q. Eliz. I have no more sons of the royal
blood.
For thee to murder: for my daughters, Richard,—
They shall be praying nuns, not weeping queens;
And therefore level not to hit their lives.

K. Rich. You have a daughter call'd—Elizabeth
Virtuous and fair, royal and gracious.

Q. Eliz. And must she die for this? O, let her
live,
And I 'll corrupt her manners, stain her beauty,
Slander myself, as false to Edward's bed
Throw over her the veil of infamy:
So she may live unscarr'd of bleeding slaughter,
I will confess she was not Edward's daughter.

K. Rich. Wrong not her birth, she is of royal
blood.

Q. Eliz. To save her life, I 'll say —she is not so

K. Rich. Her life is safest only in her birth.

Q. Eliz. And only in that safety died her
brothers.

K. Rich. Lo, at their births good stars were
opposite.

Q. Eliz. No, to their lives bad friends were
contrary.

K. Rich. All unavoided is the doom of destiny.

Q. Eliz. True, when avoided grace makes
destiny:
My babes were destin'd to a fairer death,
If grace had bless'd thee with a fairer life.

K. Rich. You speak, as if that I had slain my
cousins.

Q. Eliz. Cousins, indeed; and by their uncle
cozen'd
Of comfort, kingdom, kindred, freedom, life.

Whose hands soever lanc'd their tender hearts,
Thy head, all indirectly, gave direction:
No doubt the murderous knife was dull and blunt,
Till it was whetted on thy stone-hard heart,
To revel in the entrails of my lambs.
But that still use of grief makes wild grief tame,
My tongue should to thy ears not name my
          boys,
Till that my nails were anchor'd in thine eyes;
And I, in such a desperate bay of death,
Like a poor bark, of sails and tackling reft,
Rush all to pieces on thy rocky bosom.

   K. Rich. Madam, so thrive I in my enterprise,
And dangerous success of bloody wars,
As I intend more good to you and yours,
Than ever you or yours by me were harm'd!

   Q. Eliz. What good is cover'd with the face of
          heaven,
To be discover'd, that can do me good?

   K. Rich. The advancement of your children,
gentle lady.

   Q. Eliz. Up to some scaffold, there to lose their
heads?

   K. Rich. No, to the dignity and height of
fortune,
The high imperial type of this earth's glory.

   Q. Eliz. Flatter my sorrows with report of it;
Tell me, what state, what dignity, what honour,
Canst thou demise to any child of mine?

   K. Rich. Even all I have; ay, and myself
and all,
Will I withal endow a child of thine;
So in the Lethe of thy angry soul
Thou drown the sad remembrance of those wrongs,
Which, thou supposest, I have done to thee.

   Q. Eliz. Be brief, lest that the process of thy
kindness
Last longer telling than thy kindness' date.

   K. Rich. Then know, that from my soul, I love
thy daughter.

   Q. Eliz. My daughter's mother thinks it with
her soul.

   K. Rich. What do you think?

   Q. Eliz. That thou dost love my daughter,
from thy soul:
So, from thy soul's love, didst thou love her
brothers;
And, from my heart's love, I do thank thee for it.

   K. Rich. Be not so hasty to confound my
meaning:
I mean, that with my soul I love thy daughter,
And do intend to make her queen of England.

   Q. Eliz. Well then, who dost thou mean shall
be her king?

   K. Rich. Even he, that makes her queen: Who
else should be?

   Q. Eliz. What, thou?

   K. Rich.   Even so: What think you
of it, madam?

   Q. Eliz. How canst thou woo her?

   K. Rich.   That I would learn of you,
As one being best acquainted with her humour.

   Q. Eliz. And wilt thou learn of me?

   K. Rich.   Madam, with all my heart.

   Q. Eliz. Send to her, by the man that slew her
brothers,
A pair of bleeding hearts; thereon engrave,
Edward, and York; then, haply, will she weep:
Therefore present to her,—as sometime Margaret
Did to thy father, steep'd in Rutland's blood,—
A handkerchief; which, say to her, did drain
The purple sap from her sweet brother's body,
And bid her wipe her weeping eyes withal.
If this inducement move her not to love,
Send her a letter of thy noble deeds;
Tell her, thou mad'st away her uncle Clarence,
Her uncle Rivers; ay, and, for her sake,
Mad'st quick conveyance with her good aunt
Anne.

   K. Rich. You mock me, madam; this is not
the way
To win your daughter.

   Q. Eliz.   There is no other way;
Unless thou could'st put on some other shape,
And not be Richard that hath done all this.

   K. Rich. Say, that I did all this for love of her?

   Q. Eliz. Nay, then indeed, she cannot choose
but hate thee,
Having bought love with such a bloody spoil.

   K. Rich. Look, what is done cannot be now
amended:
Men shall deal unadvisedly sometimes,
Which after-hours give leisure to repent.
If I did take the kingdom from your sons,
To make amends, I 'll give it to your daughter.
If I have kill'd the issue of your womb,
To quicken your increase, I will beget
Mine issue of your blood upon your daughter.
A grandam's name is little less in love,
Than is the doting title of a mother;
They are as children, but one step below,
Even of your mettle, of your very blood;
Of all one pain,—save for a night of groans
Endur'd of her, for whom you bid like sorrow

Your children were vexation to your youth,
But mine shall be a comfort to your age.
The loss, you have, is but—a son being king,
And, by that loss, your daughter is made queen.
I cannot make you what amends I would,
Therefore accept such kindness as I can,
Dorset, your son, that, with a fearful soul,
Treads discontented steps in foreign soil,
This fair alliance quickly shall call home
To high promotions and great dignity:
The king, that calls your beauteous daughter—
    wife,
Familiarly shall call thy Dorset—brother;
Again shall you be mother to a king,
And all the ruins of distressful times
Repair'd with double riches of content.
What! we have many goodly days to see:
The liquid drops of tears that you have shed,
Shall come again, transform'd to orient pearl;
Advantaging their loan, with interest
Of ten-times double gain of happiness.
Go then, my mother, to thy daughter go;
Make bold her bashful years with your ex-
    perience;
Prepare her ears to hear a wooer's tale;
Put in her tender heart the aspiring flame
Of golden sov'reignty; acquaint the princess
With the sweet silent hours of marriage joys:
And when this arm of mine hath chastised
The petty rebel, dull-brain'd Buckingham,
Bound with triumphant garlands will I come,
And lead thy daughter to a conqueror's bed;
To whom I will retail my conquest won,
And she shall be sole victress, Cæsar's Cæsar.

    Q. Eliz. What were I best to say? her father's
      brother
Would be her lord? Or shall I say, her uncle?
Or, he that slew her brothers, and her uncles?
Under what title shall I woo for thee,
That God, the law, my honour, and her love,
Can make seem pleasing to her tender years?
    K. Rich. Infer fair England's peace by this
      alliance.
    Q. Eliz. Which she shall purchase with still
      lasting war.
    K. Rich. Tell her, the king, that may command,
      entreats.
    Q. Eliz. That at her hands, which the king's
      King forbids.
    K. Rich. Say, she shall be a high and mighty
      queen.
    Q. Eliz. To wail the title, as her mother doth.

    K. Rich. Say, I will love her everlastingly.
    Q. Eliz. But how long shall that title, ever,
      last?
    K. Rich. Sweetly in force unto her fair life's
      end.
    Q. Eliz. But how long fairly shall her sweet
      life last?
    K. Rich. As long as heaven, and nature, length-
      ens it.
    Q. Eliz. As long as hell, and Richard, likes of it,
    K. Rich. Say, I, her sov'reign, am her subject
      low.
    Q. Eliz. But she, your subject, loaths such
      sov'reignty,
    K. Rich. Be eloquent in my behalf to her.
    Q. Eliz. An honest tale speeds best, being
      plainly told.
    K. Rich. Then, in plain terms tell her my lov-
      ing tale.
    Q. Eliz. Plain, and not honest, is too harsh a
      style.
    K. Rich. Your reasons are too shallow and too
      quick.
    Q. Eliz. O, no, my reasons are too deep and
      dead;—
Too deep and dead, poor infants, in their *graves*.
    K. Rich. Harp not on that string, madam; that
      is past.
    Q. Eliz. Harp on it still shall I, till heart-
      strings break.
    K. Rich. Now, by my George, my garter, and
      my crown,—
    Q. Eliz. Profan'd, dishonour'd, and the third
      usurp'd.
    K. Rich. I swear.
    Q. Eliz.   By nothing; for this is no oath.
Thy George, profan'd, hath lost his holy honour;
Thy garter, blemish'd, pawn'd his knightly virtue;
Thy crown, usurp'd, disgrac'd his kingly glory:
If something thou would'st swear to be believ'd,
Swear then by something that thou hast not
    wrong'd.
    K. Rich. Now by the world,—
    Q. Eliz.   'T is full of thy foul wrongs.
    K. Rich. My father's death,—
    Q. Eliz.   Thy life hath that dishonour'd.
    K. Rich. Then, by myself,—
    Q. Eliz.   Thyself is self-misus'd.
    K. Rich. Why then, by God,—
    Q. Eliz.   God's wrong is most of all.
If thou hadst fear'd to break an oath by him,
The unity, the king thy brother made,

Had not been broken, nor my brother slain.
If thou had'st fear'd to break an oath by him,
The imperial metal, circling now thy head,
Had grac'd the tender temples of my child;
And both the princes had been breathing here,
Which now, two tender bed-fellows for dust,
Thy broken faith hath made a prey for worms.
What canst thou swear by now?

K. Rich. By the time to come.

Q. Eliz. That thou hast wrong'd in the time
o'er-past;
For I myself have many tears to wash
Hereafter time, for time past, wrong'd by thee.
The children live, whose parents thou hast slaugh-
ter'd,
Ungovern'd youth, to wail it in their age:
The parents live, whose children thou hast
butcher'd,
Old barren plants, to wail it with their age.
Swear not by time to come; for that thou hast
Miss'd ere us'd, by times ill-us'd o'er past.

K. Rich. As I intend to prosper, and repent!
So thrive I in my dangerous attempt
Of hostile arms! myself myself confound!
Heaven, and fortune, bar me happy hours!
Day, yield me not thy light! nor, night, thy
rest!
Be opposite all planets of good luck
To my proceeding, if, with pure heart's love,
Immaculate devotion, holy thoughts,
I tender not thy beauteous princely daughter!
In her consists my happiness, and thine;
Without her, follows to myself and thee,
Herself, the land, and many a Christian soul,
Death, desolation, ruin, and decay:
It cannot be avoided, but by this;
It will not be avoided, but by this.
Therefore, dear mother, (I must call you so,)
Be the attorney of my love to her.
Plead what I will be, not what I have been;
Not my deserts, but what I will deserve:
Urge the necessity and state of times,
And be not peevish found in great designs.

Q. Eliz. Shall I be tempted of the devil thus?

K. Rich. Ay, if the devil tempt thee to do
good.

Q. Eliz. Shall I forget myself, to be myself?

K. Rich. Ay, if your self's remembrance wrong
yourself.

Q. Eliz. But thou didst kill my children.

K. Rich. But in your daughter's womb I bury
them:

Where, in that nest of spicery, they shall breed
Selves of themselves, to your recomforture.

Q. Eliz. Shall I go win my daughter to thy
will?

K. Rich. And be a happy mother by the deed.

Q. Eliz. I go.—Write to me very shortly,
And you shall understand from me her mind.

K. Rich. Bear her my true love's kiss, and so
farewell. [*Kissing her. Exit Q. Eliz.*
Relenting fool, and shallow, changing—woman!"
How now? what news?

Enter Ratcliff; Catesby *following.*

Rat. Most mighty sovereign, on the western coast
Rideth a puissant navy; to the shore
Throng many doubtful hollow-hearted friends,
Unarm'd, and unresolv'd to beat them back:
'T is thought, that Richmond is their admiral;
And there they hull, expecting but the aid
Of Buckingham, to welcome them ashore.

K. Rich. Some light-foot friend post to the duke
of Norfolk:—
Ratcliff, thyself,—or Catesby; where is he?

Cate. Here, my good lord.

K. Rich. Catesby, fly to the duke.

Cate. I will, my lord, with all convenient haste

K. Rich. Ratcliff, come hither: Post to Salisbury;
When thou com'st thither,—Dull unmindful villain, [*To* Cate.
Why stay'st thou here, and go'st not to the duke?

Cate. First, mighty liege, tell me your highness
pleasure,
What from your grace I shall deliver to him.

K. Rich. O, true, good Catesby;—Bid him levy
straight
The greatest strength and power he can make,
And meet me suddenly at Salisbury.

Cate. I go. [*Exit.*

Rat. What, may it please you, shall I do at
Salisbury?

K. Rich. Why, what would'st thou do there,
before I go?

Rat. Your highness told me, I should post
before.

Enter Stanley.

K. Rich. My mind is chang'd.—Stanley, what
news with you?

Stan. None good, my liege, to please you with
the hearing;
Nor none so bad, but well may be reported

K. Rich. Heyday, a riddle! neither good nor
    bad!
What need'st thou run so many miles about,
When thou may'st tell thy tale the nearest way?
Once more, what news?
    Stan.   Richmond is on the seas.
    K. Rich. There let him sink, and be the seas
    on him!
White-liver'd runagate, what doth he there?
    Stan. I know not, mighty sovereign, but by
    guess.
    K. Rich. Well, as you guess?
    Stan. Stirr'd up by Dorset, Buckingham, and
    Morton,
He makes for England, here to claim the crown.
    K. Rich. Is the chair empty? is the sword
    unsway'd?
Is the king dead? the empire unpossess'd?
What heir of York is there alive, but we?
And who is England's king, but great York's
    heir?
Then, tell me, what makes he upon the seas?
    Stan. Unless for that, my liege, I cannot guess.
    K. Rich. Unless for that he comes to be your
    liege,
You cannot guess wherefore the Welshman comes.
Thou wilt revolt, and fly to him, I fear.
    Stan. No, mighty liege; therefore mistrust me
    not.
    K. Rich. Where is thy power then, to beat
    him back?
Where be thy tenants, and thy followers?
Are they not now upon the western shore,
Safe-conducting the rebels from their ships?
    Stan. No, my good lord, my friends are in the
    north.
    K. Rich. Cold friends to me: What do they
    in the north,
When they should serve their sovereign in the west?
    Stan. They have not been commanded, mighty
    king:
Pleaseth your majesty to give me leave,
I'll muster up my friends; and meet your grace,
Where, and what time, your majesty shall please.
    K. Rich. Ay, ay, thou wouldst be gone to join
    with Richmond:
I will not trust you, sir.
    Stan.   Most mighty sovereign,
You have no cause to hold my friendship doubtful;
I never was, nor never will be false.
    K. Rich. Well, go, muster men. But, hear
    you, leave behind

Your son, George Stanley; look your heart be
    firm,
Or else his head's assurance is but frail.
    Stan. So deal with him, as I prove true to
    you.   [*Exit* STAN.

Enter a Messenger.

    Mess. My gracious sovereign, now in Devon-
    shire,
As I by friends am well advertised,
Sir Edward Courtney, and the haughty prelate,
Bishop of Exeter, his elder brother,
With many more confederates, are in arms.

Enter another Messenger.

    2nd Mess. In Kent, my liege, the Guildfords
    are in arms;
And every hour more competitors
Flock to the rebels, and their power grows strong.

Enter another Messenger.

    3rd Mess. My lord, the army of great Bucking-
    ham—
    K. Rich. Out on ye, owls! nothing but songs
    of death?   [*He strikes him.*
There, take thou that, till thou bring better news.
    3rd Mess. The news I have to tell your majesty,
Is,—that, by sudden floods and fall of waters,
Buckingham's army is dispers'd and scatter'd;
And he himself wander'd away alone,
No man knows whither.
    K. Rich.   O, I cry you mercy:
There is my purse, to cure that blow of thine.
Hath any well-advised friend proclaim'd
Reward to him that brings the traitor in?
    3rd Mess. Such proclamation hath been made,
    my liege.

Enter another Messenger.

    4th Mess. Sir Thomas Lovel, and lord marquis
    Dorset,
'T is said, my liege, in Yorkshire are in arms.
But this good comfort bring I to your highness,—
The Bretagne navy is dispers'd by tempest:
Richmond, in Dorsetshire, sent out a boat
Unto the shore, to ask those on the banks,
If they were his assistants, yea, or no;
Who answer'd him, they came from Buckingham
Upon his party: he, mistrusting them,
Hois'd sail, and made his course again for Bretagne.
    K. Rich. March on, march on, since we are up
    in arms;

If not to fight with foreign enemies,
Yet to beat down these rebels here at home.

Enter CATESBY.

Cate. My liege, the duke of Buckingham is
taken,
That is the best news: That the earl of Rich-
mond
Is with a mighty power landed at Milford,"
Is colder news, but yet they must be told.

K. Rich. Away towards Salisbury; while we
reason here,
A royal battle might be won and lost :—
Some one take order, Buckingham be brought
To Salisbury ;—the rest march on with me.
[*Exeunt.*

SCENE V.—*A Room in Lord Stanley's House.*

Enter STANLEY *and* SIR CHRISTOPHER URSWICK.

Stan. Sir Christopher, tell Richmond this from
me :—

That, in the sty of this most bloody boar,
My son George Stanley is frank'd up in hold :
If I revolt, off goes young George's head ;
The fear of that withholds my present aid.
But, tell me, where is princely Richmond now ?

Chris. At Pembroke, or at Ha'rford-west, in
Wales.

Stan. What men of name resort to him ?

Chris. Sir Walter Herbert, a renowned soldier ;
Sir Gilbert Talbot, sir William Stanley ;
Oxford, redoubted Pembroke, sir James Blunt
And Rice ap Thomas, with a valiant crew ;
And many other of great fame and worth :
And towards London do they bend their course,
If by the way they be not fought withal.

Stan. Well, hie thee to thy lord ; commend
me to him ;
Tell him, the queen hath heartily consented
He shall espouse Elizabeth her daughter.
These letters will resolve him of my mind.
Farewell. [*Gives Papers to* CHRIS.]
[*Exeunt*

ACT V.

SCENE I.—Salisbury. *An open Place.*

Enter the SHERIFF, *and Guard, with* BUCKING-
HAM, *led to Execution.*

Buck. Will not king Richard let me speak with
him ?

Sher. No, my good lord ; therefore be patient.

Buck. Hastings, and Edward's children, Rivers,
Grey,
Holy king Henry, and thy fair son Edward,
Vaughan, and all that have miscarried
By underhand corrupted foul injustice ;
If that your moody discontented souls
Do through the clouds behold this present hour,
Even for revenge mock my destruction !—
This is All-Souls' day, fellows, is it not ?

Sher. It is, my lord.

Buck. Why, then All-Souls' day is my body's
doomsday.
This is the day, which, in king Edward's time,
I wish'd might fall on me, when I was found
False to his children, or his wife's allies :
This is the day, wherein I wish'd to fall

By the false faith of him whom most I trusted ;
This, this All-Souls' day to my fearful soul,
Is the determin'd respite of my wrongs.
That high All-seer which I dallied with,
Hath turned my feigned prayer on my head,
And given in earnest what I begg'd in jest.
Thus doth he force the swords of wicked men
To turn their own points on their masters' bosoms :
Thus Margaret's curse falls heavy on my neck,—
" When he," quoth she, " shall split thy heart
with sorrow,
Remember Margaret was a prophetess "—
Come, sirs, convey me to the block of shame ;
Wrong hath but wrong, and blame the due of
blame. [*Exeunt* BUCK., *&c.*

SCENE II.—*Plain near Tamworth.*

Enter, with Drum and Colours, RICHMOND, OX-
FORD, SIR JAMES BLUNT, SIR WALTER HER-
BERT, *and Others, with Forces, marching.*

Richm. Fellows in arms, and my most loving
friends,

Bruis'd underneath the yoke of tyranny,
Thus far into the bowels of the land
Have we march'd on without impediment;
And here receive we from our father Stanley
Lines of fair comfort and encouragement.
The reckless, bloody, and usurping boar,
That spoil'd your summer fields, and fruitful vines,
Swills your warm blood like wash, and makes his
　　　trough
In your embowell'd bosoms, this foul swine
Lies now even in the centre of this isle,
Near to the town of Leicester, as we learn:
From Tamworth thither, is but one day's march.
In God's name, cheerly on, courageous friends,
To reap the harvest of perpetual peace
By this one bloody trial of sharp war.

Oxf. Every man's conscience is a thousand
　　　swords,
To fight against that bloody homicide.

Herb. I doubt not, but his friends will turn to us.

Blunt. He hath no friends, but who are friends
　　　for fear;
Which, in his dearest need, will fly from him.

Richm. All for our vantage. Then, in God's
　　　name, march:
True hope is swift, and flies with swallow's wings,
Kings it makes gods, and meaner creatures kings.
　　　　　　　　　　　　　　　　[*Exeunt.*

SCENE III.—*Bosworth Field.*

Enter KING RICHARD, *and Forces; the* DUKE OF
　　NORFOLK, EARL OF SURREY, *and Others.*

K. Rich. Here pitch our tents, even here in
　　　Bosworth field.—
My lord of Surrey, why look you so sad?

Sur. My heart is ten times lighter than my
　　　looks.

K. Rich. My lord of Norfolk,——

Nor. 　　　　Here, most gracious liege.

K. Rich. Norfolk, we must have knocks: Ha!
　　　must we not?

Nor. We must both give and take, my loving
　　　lord.

K. Rich. Up with my tent: Here will I lie
　　　to-night;
　　　[*Soldiers begin to set up the King's Tent.*
But where, to-morrow?—Well, all's one for that.—
Who hath descried the number of the traitors?

Nor. Six or seven thousand is their utmost power.

K. Rich. Why, our battalia trebles that ac-
　　　count:
1042

Besides, the king's name is a tower of strength
Which they upon the adverse faction want.
Up with the tent.—Come, noble gentlemen.
Let us survey the vantage of the ground;—
Call for some men of sound direction:—
Let's want no discipline, make no delay;
For, lords, to-morrow is a busy day.　　[*Exeunt.*

Enter, on the other side of the Field, RICHMOND,
　　SIR WILLIAM BRANDON, OXFORD, *and other*
　　Lords. *Some of the Soldiers pitch* RICHMOND'S
　　Tent.

Richm. The weary sun hath made a golden set,
And, by the bright track of his fiery car,
Gives token of a goodly day to-morrow.—
Sir William Brandon, you shall bear my stand-
　　　ard.—
Give me some ink and paper in my tent:—
I'll draw the form and model of our battle,
Limit each leader to his several charge,
And part in just proportion our small power.
My lord of Oxford,—you, sir William Brandon,—
And you, sir Walter Herbert, stay with me:
The earl of Pembroke keeps his regiment;—
Good captain Blunt, bear my good night to him,
And by the second hour in the morning
Desire the earl to see me in my tent:—
Yet one thing more, good captain, do for me;
Where is lord Stanley quarter'd, do you know?

Blunt. Unless I have mista'en his colours much,
(Which, well I am assur'd, I have not done,)
His regiment lies half-a-mile at least
South from the mighty power of the king.

Richm. If without peril it be possible,
Sweet Blunt, make some good means to speak
　　　with him,
And give him from me this most needful note.

Blunt. Upon my life, my lord, I'll undertake it;
And so, God give you quiet rest to-night!

Richm. Good night, good captain Blunt. Come,
　　　gentlemen,
Let us consult upon to-morrow's business;
In to my tent, the air is raw and cold.
　　　　　　[*They withdraw into the Tent.*

Enter, to his Tent, KING RICHARD, NORFOLK,
　　RATCLIFF, *and* CATESBY.

K. Rich. What is't o'clock?

Cate. 　　　　It's supper time, my lord.
It's nine o'clock.

K. Rich. 　　　　I will not sup to-night.—
Give me some ink and paper.—

What, is my beaver easier than it was?—
And all my armour laid into my tent?

Cate. It is, my liege; and all things are in
readiness.

K. Rich. Good Norfolk, hie thee to thy charge;
Use careful watch, choose trusty sentinels.

Nor. I go, my lord.

K. Rich. Stir with the lark to-morrow, gentle
Norfolk.

Nor. I warrant you, my lord.   [*Exit.*

K. Rich. Ratcliff,——

Rat. My lord?

K. Rich.   Send out a pursuivant at arms
To Stanley's regiment; bid him bring his power
Before sun-rising, lest his son George fall
Into the blind cave of eternal night.—
Fill me a bowl of wine.—Give me a watch;
        [*To* Cate.
Saddle white Surrey for the field to-morrow.—
Look that my staves be sound, and not too
heavy.

Ratcliff,——

Rat. My lord?

K. Rich. Saw'st thou the melancholy lord
Northumberland?

Rat. Thomas the earl of Surrey, and himself,
Much about cock-shut time, from troop to troop,
Went through the army, cheering up the soldiers.

K. Rich. I am satisfied. Give me a bowl of
wine.
I have not that alacrity of spirit,
Nor cheer of mind, that I was wont to have.—
So, set it down.—Is ink and paper ready?

Rat. It is, my lord.

K. Rich. Bid my guard watch; leave me.
About the mid of night, come to my tent
And help to arm me.—Leave me, I say.
        [*K.* Rich. *retires into his Tent. Exeunt* Rat.
and Cate.

Richmond's *Tent opens, and discovers him and
his Officers, &c.*

Enter Stanley.

Stan. Fortune and victory sit on thy helm!

Richm. All comfort that the dark night can
afford,
Be to thy person, noble father-in-law!
Tell me, how fares our loving mother?

Stan. I, by attorney, bless thee from thy mother,
Who prays continually for Richmond's good:
So much for that.—The silent hours steal on

And flaky darkness breaks within the east.
In brief, for so the season bids us be,
Prepare thy battle early in the morning;
And put thy fortune to the arbitrement
Of bloody strokes, and mortal-staring war.
I, as I may, (that which I would, I cannot,)
With best advantage will deceive the time,
And aid thee in this doubtful shock of arms:
But on thy side I may not be too forward,
Lest, being seen, thy brother tender George
Be executed in his father's sight.
Farewell; The leisure and the fearful time
Cuts off the ceremonious vows of love,
And ample interchange of sweet discourse,
Which so long sunder'd friends should dwell
upon;
God give us leisure for these rites of love!
Once more, adieu:—Be valiant, and speed well!

Richm. Good lords, conduct him to his regi-
ment:
I'll strive, with troubled thoughts, to take a nap
Lest leaden slumber peise me down to-morrow,
When I should mount with wings of victory:
Once more, good night, kind lords and gentle-
men.   [*Exeunt Lords, &c., with* Stan.
O Thou! whose captain I account myself,
Look on my forces with a gracious eye;
Put in their hands thy bruising irons of wrath,
That they may crush down with a heavy fall
The usurping helmets of our adversaries!
Make us thy ministers of chastisement,
That we may praise thee in thy victory!
To thee I do commend my watchful soul,
Ere I let fall the windows of mine eyes;
Sleeping, and waking, O, defend me still! [*Sleeps.*

The Ghost of Prince Edward, *Son to* Henry *the
Sixth, rises between the two Tents.*

Ghost. Let me sit heavy on thy soul to-morrow!
        [*To* K. Rich.
Think, how thou stab'dst me in my prime of
youth
At Tewkesbury: Despair therefore, and die!—
Be cheerful, Richmond; for the wronged souls
Of butcher'd princes fight in thy behalf:
King Henry's issue, Richmond, comforts thee.

The Ghost of King Henry the Sixth *rises.*

Ghost. When I was mortal, my anointed body
        [*To* K. Rich.
By thee was punched full of deadly holes:
Think on the Tower, and me: Despair, and die;

Harry the Sixth bids thee despair and die.—
Virtuous and holy, be thou conqueror!
[*To* RICHM.
Harry, that prophesy'd thou should'st be king,
Doth comfort thee in sleep: Live thou, and flourish!

The Ghost of Clarence rises.

Ghost. Let me sit heavy on thy soul to-morrow!
[*To* K. RICH.
I, that was wash'd to death with fulsome wine,
Poor Clarence, by thy guile betray'd to death!
To-morrow in the battle think on me,
And fall thy edgeless sword: Despair, and die!
Thou offspring of the house of Lancaster,
[*To* RICHM.
The wronged heirs of York do pray for thee;
Good angels guard thy battle! Live, and flourish!

The Ghosts of Rivers, Grey, and Vaughan, rise.

Riv. Let me sit heavy on thy soul to-morrow,
[*To* K. RICH.
Rivers, that died at Pomfret! Despair, and die!
Grey. Think upon Grey, and let thy soul despair!
[*To* K. RICH.
Vaugh. Think upon Vaughan; and, with guilty fear,
Let fall thy lance! Despair, and die!—
[*To* K. RICH.
All. Awake; and think, our wrongs in Richard's bosom
[*To* RICHM.
Will conquer him;—awake, and win the day!

The Ghost of Hastings rises.

Ghost. Bloody and guilty, guiltily awake;
[*To* K. RICH.
And in a bloody battle end thy days!
Think on lord Hastings; and despair, and die!—
Quiet untroubled soul, awake, awake!
[*To* RICHM.
Arm, fight, and conquer, for fair England's sake!

The Ghosts of the two young Princes rise.

Ghosts. Dream on thy cousins smother'd in the Tower:
Let us be lead within thy bosom, Richard,
And weigh thee down to ruin, shame, and death!
Thy nephews' souls bid thee despair, and die.—
Sleep, Richmond, sleep in peace, and wake in joy;
Good angels guard thee from the boar's annoy!
Live, and beget a happy race of kings!
Edward's unhappy sons do bid thee flourish.
1044

The Ghost of Queen Anne rises.

Ghost. Richard, thy wife, that wretched Anne thy wife,
That never slept a quiet hour with thee,
Now fills thy sleep with perturbations:
To-morrow in the battle think on me,
And fall thy edgeless sword: Despair, and die!—
Thou, quiet soul, sleep thou a quiet sleep;
[*To* RICHM.
Dream of success and happy victory!
Thy adversary's wife doth pray for thee.

The Ghost of Buckingham rises.

Ghost. The first was I, that help'd thee to the crown;
[*To* K. RICH
The last was I that felt thy tyranny:
O, in the battle think on Buckingham,
And die in terror of thy guiltiness!
Dream on, dream on, of bloody deeds and death;
Fainting, despair; despairing, yield thy breath!—
I died for hope, ere I could lend thee aid:
[*To* RICHM.
But cheer thy heart, and be thou not dismay'd:
God, and good angels fight on Richmond's side;
And Richard falls in height of all his pride.
[*The Ghosts vanish. K.* RICH. *starts out of his dream.*

K. Rich. Give me another horse,—bind up my wounds,—
Have mercy, Jesu!—Soft; I did but dream.—
O coward conscience, how dost thou afflict me!—
The lights burn blue.—It is now dead midnight.
Cold fearful drops stand on my trembling flesh.
What do I fear? myself? there's none else by:
Richard loves Richard; that is, I am I.
Is there a murderer here? No;—Yes; I am:
Then fly,—What, from myself? Great reason
Why?
Lest I revenge. What? Myself on myself?
I love myself. Wherefore? for any good,
That I myself have done unto myself?
O, no: alas, I rather hate myself,
For hateful deeds committed by myself.
I am a villain: Yet I lie, I am not.
Fool, of thyself speak well:—Fool, do not flatter
My conscience hath a thousand several tongues,
And every tongue brings in a several tale,
And every tale condemns me for a villain.
Perjury, perjury, in the high'st degree,
Murder, stern murder, in the dir'st degree;
All several sins, all us'd in each degree,

Throng to the bar, crying all,—Guilty! guilty!
I shall despair.—There is no creature loves me;
And, if I die, no soul will pity me:—
Nay, wherefore should they? since that I myself
Find in myself no pity to myself.
Methought, the souls of all that I had murder'd
Came to my tent: and every one did threat
To-morrow's vengeance on the head of Richard.

Enter RATCLIFF.

Rat. My lord,——
K. Rich. Who 's there?
Rat. Ratcliff, my lord; 't is I. The early vil-
lage cock
Hath twice done salutation to the morn;
Your friends are up, and buckle on their armour.
K. Rich. O, Ratcliff, I have dream'd a fearful
dream!—
What thinkest thou? will our friends prove all
true?
Rat. No doubt, my lord.
K. Rich.   Ratcliff, I fear, I fear,—
Rat. Nay, good my lord, be not afraid of
shadows.
K. Rich. By the apostle Paul, shadows to-night
Have struck more terror to the soul of Richard,
Than can the substance of ten thousand soldiers,
Armed in proof, and led by shallow Richmond.
It is not yet near day. Come, go with me;
Under our tents I 'll play the eaves-dropper,
To hear, if any mean to shrink from me.
        [*Exeunt* K. RICH. *and* RAT.

RICHMOND *wakes.   Enter* OXFORD *and Others.*

Lords. Good morrow, Richmond.
Richm. 'Cry mercy, lords, and watchful gen-
tlemen,
That you have ta'en a tardy sluggard here.
Lords. How have you slept, my lord?
Richm. The sweetest sleep, and fairest-boding
dreams,
That ever enter'd in a drowsy head,
Have I since your departure had, my lords.
Methought, their souls, whose bodies Richard
murder'd,
Came to my tent, and cried—On! victory!
I promise you, my heart is very jocund
In the remembrance of so fair a dream.
How far into the morning is it, lords?
Lords. Upon the stroke of four.
Richm. Why, then 't is time to arm, and give
direction.— [*He advances to the Troops.*

More than I have said, loving countrymen,
The leisure and enforcement of the time
Forbids to dwell on: Yet remember this,—
God, and our good cause, fight upon our side;
The prayers of holy saints, and wronged souls,
Like high-rear'd bulwarks, stand before our faces
Richard except, those, whom we fight against,
Had rather have us win, than him they follow.
For what is he they follow? truly, gentlemen,
A bloody tyrant, and a homicide
One rais'd in blood, and one in blood establish'd
One that made means to come by what he hath,
And slaughter'd those that were the means to
help him;
A base foul stone, made precious by the foil
Of England's chair, where he is falsely set;
One that hath ever been God's enemy:
Then, if you fight against God's enemy,
God will, in justice, ward you as his soldiers,
If you do sweat to put a tyrant down,
You sleep in peace, the tyrant being slain;
If you do fight against your country's foes,
Your country's fat shall pay your pains the hire;
If you do fight in safeguard of your wives,
Your wives shall welcome home the conquerors;
If you do free your children from the sword,
Your children's children quit it in your age.
Then, in the name of God, and all these rights,
Advance your standards, draw your willing swords:
For me, the ransom of my bold attempt
Shall be this cold corpse on the earth's cold face;
But if I thrive, the gain of my attempt
The least of you shall share his part thereof.
Sound, drums and trumpets, boldly and cheer-
fully;
God, and Saint George! Richmond, and victory!
        [*Exeunt.*

Re-enter KING RICHARD, RATCLIFF, *Attendants,
and Forces.*

K. Rich. What said Northumberland, as touch-
ing Richmond?
Rat. That he was never trained up in arms.
K. Rich. He said the truth: And what said
Surrey then?
Rat. He smil'd and said, the better for our
purpose.
K. Rich. He was i' the right; and so, indeed,
it is.   [*Clock strikes.*
Tell the clock there.—Give me a calendar.—
Who saw the sun to-day?
Rat.   Not I, my lord.

1045

K. Rich. Then he disdains to shine; for, by
the book,
He should have brav'd the east an hour ago:
A black day will it be to somebody.—
Ratcliff,——
Rat. My lord?
K. Rich.   The sun will not be seen to-day;
The sky doth frown and lour upon our army.
I would, these dewy tears were from the ground.
Not shine to-day! Why, what is that to me,
More than to Richmond? for the self-same heaven,
That frowns on me, looks sadly upon him.

Enter NORFOLK.

Nor. Arm, arm, my lord; the foe vaunts in
the field.
K. Rich. Come, bustle, bustle;—Caparison my
horse;—
Call up lord Stanley, bid him bring his power:—
I will lead forth my soldiers to the plain,
And thus my battle shall be ordered.
My foreward shall be drawn out all in length,
Consisting equally of horse and foot;
Our archers shall be placed in the midst;
John duke of Norfolk, Thomas earl of Surrey,
Shall have the leading of this foot and horse.
They thus directed, we ourself will follow
In the main battle; whose puissance on either
side
Shall be well winged with our chiefest horse.
This, and Saint George to boot!" What think'st
thou, Norfolk?
Nor. A good direction, warlike sovereign,—
This found I on my tent this morning.
                              [*Giving a Scroll.*
K. Rich. "Jocky of Norfolk, be not too bold,
                              [*Reads.*
.   For Dickon thy master is bought and
sold."
A thing devised by the enemy.—
Go, gentlemen, every man unto his charge:
Let not our babbling dreams affright our souls;
Conscience is but a word that cowards use,
Devis'd at first to keep the strong in awe;
Our strong arms be our conscience, swords our
law.
March on, join bravely, let us to 't pell-mell;
If not to heaven, then hand in hand to hell.——
     What shall I say more than I have infer'd?
Remember whom you are to cope withal;—
A sort of vagabonds, rascals, and run-aways,
A scum of Bretagnes, and base lackey peasants,
1916

Whom their o'er-cloyed country vomits forth
To desperate ventures and assur'd destruction.
You sleeping safe, they bring you to unrest;
You having lands, and bless'd with beauteous
wives,
They would restrain the one, distain the other.
And who doth lead them, but a paltry fellow,
Long kept in Bretagne at our mother's cost?
A milk-sop, one that never in his life
Felt so much cold as over shoes in snow?
Let 's whip these stragglers o'er the seas again;
Lash hence these over-weening rags of France,
These famish'd beggars, weary of their lives;
Who, but for dreaming on this fond exploit,
For want of means, poor rats, had hang'd them-
selves:
If we be conquer'd, let men conquer us,
And not these bastard Bretagnes; whom our
fathers
Have in their own land beaten, bobb'd, and
thump'd,
And, on record, left them the heirs of shame.
Shall these enjoy our lands? lie with our wives?
Ravish our daughters?—Hark, I hear their drum.
                              [*Drum afar off*
Fight, gentlemen of England! fight, bold yeo-
men!
Draw, archers, draw your arrows to the head;
Spur your proud horses hard, and ride in blood;
Amaze the welkin with your broken staves!

Enter a Messenger.

What says lord Stanley? will he bring his power?
Mess. My lord, he doth deny to come.
K. Rich. Off instantly with his son George's
head.
Nor. My lord, the enemy is pass'd the marsh;
After the battle let George Stanley die.
K. Rich. A thousand hearts are great within
my bosom:
Advance our standards, set upon our foes;
Our ancient word of courage, fair Saint George,
Inspire us with the spleen of fiery dragons!
Upon them! Victory sits on our helms. [*Exeunt.*

SCENE IV.—*Another Part of the Field.*

Alarum: Excursions. Enter NORFOLK, *and*
Forces; to him CATESBY.

Cate. Rescue, my lord of Norfolk, rescue,
rescue!
The king enacts more wonders than a man,

Paring an opposite to every danger;
His horse is slain, and all on foot he fights,
Seeking for Richmond in the throat of death:
Rescue, fair lord, or else the day is lost!

Alarum. Enter KING RICHARD.

K. Rich. A horse! a horse! my kingdom for
a horse!

Cate. Withdraw, my lord, I'll help you to a
horse.

K. Rich. Slave, I have set my life upon a cast,
And I will stand the hazard of the die:
I think, there be six Richmonds in the field;
Five have I slain to-day, instead of him :—
A horse! a horse! my kingdom for a horse!
[*Exeunt.*

Alarums. Enter KING RICHARD *and* RICHMOND;
*and exeunt, fighting. Retreat, and flourish.
Then enter* RICHMOND, STANLEY, *bearing the
Crown, with divers other* Lords, *and* Forces.

Richm. God, and your arms, be prais'd, victorious friends;
The day is ours, the bloody dog is dead.

Stan. Courageous Richmond, well hast thou
acquit thee!
Lo, here, this long-usurped royalty,
From the dead temples of this bloody wretch
Have I pluck'd off, to grace thy brows withal;
Wear it, enjoy it, and make much of it.

Richm. Great God of heaven, say, amen, to
all !—
But, tell me first, is young George Stanley living?

Stan. He is, my lord, and safe in Leicester
town;
Whither, if it please you, we may now withdraw us.

Richm. What men of name are slain on either
side?

Stan. John duke of Norfolk, Walter lord Fer-
rers,
Sir Robert Brakenbury, and sir William Brandon.

Richm. Inter their bodies as becomes their
births.
Proclaim a pardon to the soldiers fled,
That in submission will return to us;
And then, as we have ta'en the sacrament,⁵⁴
We will unite the white rose with the red :—
Smile heaven upon this fair conjunction,
That long hath frown'd upon their enmity !—
What traitor hears me, and says not,—amen?
England hath long been mad, and scarr'd herself;
The brother blindly shed the brother's blood,
The father rashly slaughter'd his own son,
The son, compell'd, been butcher to the sire;
All this divided York and Lancaster,
Divided, in their dire division.—
O, now, let Richmond and Elizabeth,
The true succeeders of each royal house,
By God's fair ordinance conjoin together!
And let their heirs, (God, if thy will be so,)
Enrich the time to come with smooth-fac'd peace,
With smiling plenty, and fair prosperous days!
Abate the edge of traitors, gracious Lord,
That would reduce⁵⁵ these bloody days again,
And make poor England weep in streams of
blood !
Let them not live to taste this land's increase,
That would with treason wound this fair land's
peace !
Now civil wounds are stopp'd, peace lives again;
That she may long live here, God say—Amen !
[*Exeunt*

1847

NOTES TO KING RICHARD THE THIRD.

¹ *Made glorious summer by this sun of York.*

Edward the Fourth adopted a blazing sun as his cognizance, in memory of the *three suns* which are said to have appeared to him at Mortimer's Cross, before his victory at Towton. See Henry the Sixth, Part III., act ii., sc. 1. So in Drayton's *Miseries of Queen Margaret*—

Three *suns* were seen that instant to appear,
  Which soon again shut themselves up in one ;
Ready to buckle as the armies were,
  Which this brave duke took to himself alone, &c.

According to tradition, such phenomena frequently heralded in remarkable events.

² *Toys,* i. e., fancies, freaks of imagination.

³ *We are the queen's abjects.*

That is, not only her subjects, but her creatures, her slaves ; beings of no regard in her eyes.

⁴ *Or else lie for you,* i. e., be imprisoned in your stead.

⁵ *O, he hath kept an evil diet long.*

Edward's death was supposed to be hastened by his excessive passion at the treachery of the French king ; but his constitution was undermined by long indulgence in dissipation, and he died after an illness of a few weeks, on the 9th of April, 1483, in the twenty-first year of his reign, and the forty-first or forty-second of his age.

⁶ *Poor key-cold figure of a holy king !*

Key-cold is synonymous with a word at present in use, *stone-cold.* A key, on account of the coldness of the metal of which it is made, is frequently employed to stop a slight bleeding.

⁷ *To his unhappiness.*

His unhappy disposition, natural tendency to mischief.

⁸ *O, gentlemen, see, see! dead Henry's wounds*
  Open their congeal'd mouths, and bleed afresh !

This alludes to a superstition once universally believed, that the wounds of a murdered man opened and bled afresh at the touch or sight of the murderer ; as though heaven endowed the dead with power to indicate the assassin. Numerous allusions to this idle but not unnatural fancy are to be found in our old writers. Thus, in *Arden of Feversham*—

The more I sound his name, the more he bleeds :
This blood condemns me, and in gushing forth
Speaks as it falls, and asks me why I did it.

⁹ *And fall somewhat into a slower method.*

By our old authors, *quick* was often used for *lively*, and *slower* for *serious*.

¹⁰ *Repair to Crosby-place.*

Crosby-place is now Crosby-square, in Bishopsgate-street. The house in which Richard there resided was built in 1466 by Sir John Crosby, an alderman of London. Stow describes it as "very large and beautiful, and the highest at that time in London." The ancient hall of this building is still existing ; and, after having been put to various uses—converted at one time into a dissenting chapel, and at another into a warehouse—it has lately been restored in imitation of its ancient splendour, and now serves as a concert and lecture-hall.

¹¹ *Stabb'd in my angry mood at Tewkesbury.*

"Here," says Mr. Malone, "we have the exact time of this scene ascertained, namely, August, 1471. King Edward, however, is in the second act introduced dying. That king died in April, 1483 ; so there is an interval between this and the next act of almost twelve years. Clarence, who is represented in the preceding scene as committed to the Tower before the burial of King Henry the Sixth, was in fact not confined or put to death till seven years afterwards, March, 1477-8."

¹² *A beggarly denier,* i. e., the twelfth part of a French sous.

¹³ *The Countess Richmond.*

The mother of the earl of Richmond, afterwards Henry the Seventh, on the death of her first husband, Edmund Tudor, was married to Lord Stanley.

¹⁴ *Ah, gentle villain,* i. e., high born villain, of gentle blood.

" Wert thou not banished on pain of death?

After the battle of Tewkesbury, in May, 1471, Queen Margaret was confined in the Tower, from whence she was ransomed by her father Reignier, in 1475; she returned to France, and died there in 1482. The present scene is in 1477 or 1478, and her introduction is an historical anachronism.

" Could all but answer for that peevish brat!

Mr. M. Mason would read—could all not, &c., an emendation which seems essential to the sense of the passage.

" Thou elvish-mark'd, abortive, rooting hog!

Richard's arms bore the device of a boar; Margaret, in allusion to this, contemptuously calls him hog, and adds the epithet rooting to signify his destructive nature.

" With that grim ferryman.

Charon, who is fabled to have rowed the souls of the dead over the rivers Styx and Acheron to the infernal regions. He was represented as a robust old man, extremely ugly, having piercing eyes, and a long white beard. As he demanded an obolus for his trouble, it became a custom among the ancients to place a piece of money under the tongue of a corpse to satisfy the wishes of its grim guide.

" The costard, i. e., the head.

" Before I be convict by course of law.

In attributing the death of Clarence to Richard, Shakespeare followed the current reports of his own time. But Clarence was not put to death without trial or condemnation; he was tried and found guilty by his peers, and received sentence on the 7th of February. On the 18th of the same month, or, according to other authorities, on the 11th of March, it was reported that the duke had died in the Tower. A rumour ran that he had been murdered, and suspicion fell upon the duke of Gloster, but no evidence exists to prove him the criminal.

" The forfeit, sovereign, of my servant's life.

He means the remission of the forfeit.

" Enter the Duchess of York.

Cecily, daughter of Ralph Nevile, first Earl of Westmoreland, and widow of Richard Duke of York, who was killed at the battle of Wakefield, in 1460. She survived her husband thirty-five years.

" Forthwith from Ludlow the young prince be fetch'd.

At the death of King Edward, the young prince, then a boy of thirteen, was living at Ludlow Castle, under the care of his maternal uncle the Earl of Rivers. He had been sent there by the king to see justice done in the marches; and by the authority of his presence, to restrain the outrages and savage conduct of the Welshmen.

" Last night, I heard, they lay at Stony-Stratford;
And at Northampton they do rest to-night.

Stony-Stratford is nearer to London than Northampton;

but Richard, who was in the marches of Scotland when he heard of Edward's death, hastened to London, and arrived at Northampton the day that his nephew reached Stony Stratford, from which place he carried the young king back to Northampton, where he treacherously seized Rivers, Grey, Vaughan, and Hawes.

" I say, without characters fame lives long.
Thus, like the formal vice, iniquity, [Aside.
I moralize two meanings in one word.

The prince having heard part of the former line, asks Richard what he says?—who, to deceive him preserves in his reply the latter words of the line, but substitutes others at the beginning of it, of a different import from those he had uttered. He then adds to himself, " I moralize," that is, refine upon what I have uttered; convey two meanings in one word or sentence. The formal vice was the buffoon or jester of the old English interludes, who was probably an equivocator, hiding profane or obscene remarks under a mock air of morality.

" For we to-morrow hold divided councils.

That is, we hold a private consultation, separate from the known and public council. The latter was held in the Tower, but a private council of Richard's friends met constantly at his residence in Crosby-place.

" To-night the boar had rased off his helm.

By the boar is meant Gloster, from his having a boar for his cognizance. The word rased, or rached, was used to describe the injuries done by a boar, such as tearing and mangling with his tusks.

" Enter Ratcliff, with a guard, conducting Rivers, Grey, &c.

The Earl of Rivers was the Queen's brother; Sir Richard Grey, her son; she has been deservedly pitied for losing her children, but the deaths of her other kindred appear to have been forgotten in the general slaughters and troubles of the time.

" And wants but nomination.

That is, the only thing wanting, is the appointment of a particular day for the ceremony.

" Three times to-day my foot-cloth horse did stumble.

For a horse to stumble was anciently esteemed an omen of evil to the rider. So, in The Honest Lawyer:—" And just at the threshold Master Bromley stumbled. Signs! signs!"

" Enter Gloster and Buckingham, in rusty armour, marvellous ill-favoured.

Why Gloster and Buckingham should enter in this singular apparel, does not readily appear from the play, but the reason is thus clearly given in Holinshed, who was Shakespeare's historical authority:—" The Protector, immediately after dinner, intending to set some colour upon the matter, sent in all haste for many substantial men out of the citie into the Tower; and at their coming, himselfe, with the Duke of Buckingham, stood harnessed in old ill-faring brigandiers, such as no man should weene that they would vouchsafe to have put upon their backes, except that some sudden necessitie had constreined them."

" I mean his conversation with Shore's wife.

That is, familiar intercourse. The phrase, *criminal conversation*, is still in use.

" Only for saying—he would make his son Heir to the crown.

This is an historical fact; the object of this shameful tyranny was one Walker, a substantial citizen and grocer, at the Crown, in Cheapside, whom Edward caused to be hanged for his innocent quibble.

" To leave the brats of Clarence out of sight.

The children of Clarence were two, Edward and Margaret; Edward, Earl of Warwick, was confined by Richard in Sheriff-hutton Castle, and afterwards beheaded by Henry the Seventh, on account of his superior title to the throne. Margaret was married to Sir Richard de la Pole; she was created Countess of Salisbury by Henry the Eighth, and finally condemned to the scaffold at the age of seventy, by that regal murderer, from motives of a jealous policy. She refused to submit to the sentence, and with her grey hair streaming down her shoulders, ran wildly about the scaffold, followed by the executioner, who struck at her several times with his axe, and at length succeeded in severing her head from her body. She was the last member of the house of Lancaster.

" I did; with his contract with Lady Lucy.

This lady was not the wife, but the mistress of Edward; but Comines, a contemporary historian, says that Edward, previous to his marriage with Lady Grey, was married by the Bishop of Bath to Lady Eleanor Butler, widow of Lord Butler of Sudeley, and daughter to the great Earl of Shrewsbury. On this ground the children of Edward were declared illegitimate by the only parliament assembled by Richard the Third.

" God defend, his grace should say us nay!

This obsequious mayor was Edmund Shaw, brother to Doctor Shaw, whom Richard had employed to prove his title to the crown from the pulpit at Saint Paul's Cross.

" Were red-hot steel to sear me to the brain!

She alludes to the ancient mode of punishing a regicide or other notorious criminal, by placing a crown of iron, heated red-hot, upon his head. In some of the monkish accounts of a place of future torment, a burning crown is appropriated to those who have deprived any lawful monarch of his kingdom.

" With a week of teen, i. e., of sorrow.

" The boy is foolish.

The son of Clarence, from long confinement and a total neglect of his education, became idiotic.

" To Brecknock.

To the Castle of Brecknock, in Wales, where Buckingham's estate lay.

" The Bretagne Richmond.

He thus scornfully alludes to Richmond, because that

prince resided for a length of time in a kind of honourable custody at the court of Francis the Second, Duke of Bretagne.

" Decline all this, i. e., run through all this from first to last.

" Faith, none, but Humphrey Hour.

Many conjectures have been penned respecting the party here alluded to. Malone says, "I believe nothing more than a quibble was meant. In our poet's twentieth sonnet we find a similar conceit; a quibble between *hues* (colours) and *Hughes* (formerly spelt *Hewes*), the person addressed."

" Relenting fool, and shallow, changing woman.

"Such," says Steevens, "was the real character of the queen-dowager, who would have married her daughter to King Richard, and did all in her power to alienate the Marquis of Dorset, her son, from the Earl of Richmond."

" Is with a mighty power landed at Milford.

Richmond landed at Milford Haven with an army not exceeding five thousand men, and of these, not above two thousand were English.

" Keeps his regiment, i. e., remains with it.

" It's nine o'clock.

The quarto reads,—it is *six* of the clock; full supper time. This was more in accordance with the customs of the period, when, indeed, to sup at nine would have been a remarkable incident. At this time breakfast was usually taken at seven o'clock in the morning, dinner at ten, and supper at four in the afternoon. A fourth meal, entitled liveries, consisting of a cold collation, was taken in bed about eight or nine in the evening.

" Give me a watch.

Richard may request either an instrument to tell the time, a guard for his tent, or a watch-light or candle to burn by him. Mr. Steevens inclines to the latter interpretation, and thinks a particular kind of candle, marked out into sections, was here meant. As each portion of this kind of candle occupied a certain time in burning, it supplied the place of the more modern instrument by which we measure the hours.

" Look that my staves be sound.

Staves are the wood of the lances. As it was usual to carry several of them into the field, the lightness of them was a matter of great consequence.

" Saw'st thou the melancholy Lord Northumberland!

Richard suspected Northumberland, and calls him melancholy because he seemed apathetic in his cause. He had good reason for his doubts, for Northumberland stood aloof from the contest, and afterwards joined the victor.

" Cock-shut time, i. e., twilight.

" *So thee was punched full of deadly holes.*

The inelegant expression, *punched*, appears not to have been so common in our poet's time as at present, as it is also employed by Chapman in his version of the sixth *Iliad :—*

— · With a goad he *punch'd* each furious dame.

" *This and Saint George to boot.*

That is, this is the order of our battle, which promises success; and beyond this is the protection of our patron saint.

" *And then as we have ta'en the sacrament.*

So, in Holinshed :—" The earle himselfe first tooke a corporall oth on his honor, promising that incontinent after he shuld be possessed of the crowne and dignitie of the realme of England, he would be conjoined in matrimonie with the ladie Elizabeth, daughter to King Edward the Fourth."

" *Abate the edge of traitors, gracious Lord,*
That would reduce——

To *abate*, is to lower, depress, subdue. *Reduce*, is to bring back, an obsolete sense of the word.

1061

King Henry the Eighth.

THIS drama commences in the twelfth year of Henry's reign, with the arrest of the duke of Buckingham, in April, 1521, and terminates with the birth of the Princess Elizabeth, on the 7th of September, 1533; thus including a period of twelve years. Queen Katharine lived until 1536, three years after the birth of Elizabeth; but, for the sake of dramatic effect, the poet anticipates her death.

Anne Bullen had been bred in the gay court of France, and when she attracted the notice of Henry, was in her twentieth year. Beautiful, accomplished, graceful, and vivacious, the amorous monarch would have made her his mistress, but to this the young lady would not submit; and it is supposed that her resolution in this respect was probably strengthened by a statement that Henry had seduced her sister, and then abandoned her for the embraces of another. But in encouraging the addresses of Henry, and in listening to proposals which she knew could only be fulfilled by the degradation of the queen, her mistress, Anne was guilty of a greater crime than she would have committed in becoming the paramour of the tyrant. But the punishment of her ingratitude hung trembling over her devoted head—her career of triumph was but a brief one. Not four months after the death of Katharine, Anne Bullen was doomed. Henry's libidinous gaze was fascinated by one of her maids of honour, and he accused the queen of adultery, a crime of which it is most probable that she was innocent—but the freedom and gaiety of her manners were twisted into evidence against her, and the royal profligate signed the warrant for her death. The beautiful neck which he had embraced was mangled on the scaffold, and the luxuriant tresses which had been his delight and admiration dabbled in blood. Anne had been a queen but three years; on the day after her execution, or rather murder, the pampered ruffian married Jane Seymour.

The two most finished characters in this play are Queen Katharine and the Cardinal Wolsey. Shakespeare robes the former with great dignity, both of mind and person. She is a perfect model of a noble matron; patient towards her sovereign and oppressor, yet jealous of her own dignity, and in her deepest dejection relying upon eternal justice—

> Heaven is above all yet; there sits a Judge,
> That no king can corrupt.

Her death-scene is exceedingly affecting; her generous care for her dependents, touching and womanly; the poet endeavours to compensate for her trials and sufferings here, by showing her, through the means of a dream, at the very portals of paradise. Wolsey is a singular compound of opposing qualities, grasping, yet profusely liberal; supercilious and haughty, yet parasitical and mean; courageous and capable in prosperity, yet timid and helpless in adversity. His talent for magnificence amounts to genius; he gives way to pleasure, is gay and cheerful; he covers his craftiness with an air of blunt frankness. The avarice of the king urged Wolsey to impose unprecedented taxes on the people, and paved the way for his fall. Then he is at once crushed, and grovels in the earth—the proud cardinal, with his princely palaces and his kingly retinue, sinks instantly into the abject and supplicating priest. Then follows his compelled and questionable repentance, and in the anguish of his spirit he utters that memorable sentence which Shakespeare, recognising as earnest and passionate poetry which no art could exalt, took from the lips of the fallen statesman, "Had I but served my God as diligently as I have served the king, he would not have given me over in my grey hairs." The noble advice which Wolsey, after his fall, gives to Cromwell, had not been the guide of his own conduct, but it is natural in a declining statesman to preach lofty principles, and even to persuade himself that he had practised them. The two opposite estimates of his character by Queen Katharine and her attendant Griffith, after the cardinal's death, are profound analyzations of a remarkable mind, and show what opposing portraits of the same object may be taken from different points of view. After praise and blame cometh the truth, and Shakespeare has given us a singularly accurate picture of the luxurious and powerful cardinal. Whatever were Wolsey's faults, it is probable that he restrained the tyranny of the king, for Henry did not plunge into his revolting cruelties until after the death of his great minister.

One thing which strikes the reader of this drama is the slavish meanness of the nobility, in comparison with their turbulent defiance of the crown during the reign of the peaceful Henry the Sixth. Indeed this play has a far more modern air and appearance than its predecessors; at the period to which it refers, society was in a transition state; the iron barons of the old age had passed away, and the birth of our intellectual era was rapidly approaching.

I cannot conclude this notice without directing attention to the exquisite adulation to Queen Elizabeth, with which it terminates; a piece of flattery which may be excused on account of its elegance and appropriateness. The few lines introduced into it, in eulogy of James the First, are supposed to be the work of Ben Jonson.

Malone attributes the production of this play to the year 1601—two years previous to the death of the poet's patron, Elizabeth.

1014

PERSONS REPRESENTED.

KING HENRY THE EIGHTH.
Appears, Act I. sc. 2; sc. 4. Act II. sc. 2; sc. 4. Act III. sc. 2. Act V. sc. 1; sc. 2; sc. 4.

CARDINAL WOLSEY.
Appears, Act I. sc. 1; sc. 2; sc. 4. Act II. sc. 2; sc. 4. Act III. sc. 1; sc. 2.

CARDINAL CAMPEIUS.
Appears, Act II. sc. 2; sc. 4. Act III. sc. 1.

CAPUCIUS, *Ambassador to the Emperor Charles.*
Appears, Act IV. sc. 2.

CRANMER, *an Agent of the King, afterwards Archbishop of Canterbury.*
Appears, Act V. sc. 1; sc. 2; sc. 4.

DUKE OF NORFOLK.
Appears, Act I. sc. 1. Act II. sc. 2. Act III. sc. 2. Act IV. sc. 1. Act V. sc. 4.

DUKE OF BUCKINGHAM.
Appears, Act I. sc. 1. Act II. sc. 1.

DUKE OF SUFFOLK.
Appears, Act I. sc. 2. Act II. sc. 2. Act III. sc. 2. Act IV. sc. 1. Act V. sc. 1; sc. 2; sc. 4.

EARL OF SURREY.
Appears, Act III. sc. 2. Act IV. sc. 1. Act V. sc. 2.

GARDINER, *a Creature of Wolsey's, afterwards Bishop of Winchester.*
Appears, Act II. sc. 2. Act IV. sc. 1. Act V. sc. 1; sc. 2.

BISHOP OF LINCOLN.
Appears, Act II. sc. 4.

LORD ABERGAVENNY.
Appears, Act I. sc. 1.

LORD SANDS.
Appears, Act I. sc. 3; sc. 4. Act II. sc. 1.

SIR HENRY GUILDFORD.
Appears, Act I. sc. 4.

SIR THOMAS LOVELL.
Appears, Act I. sc. 3; sc. 3; sc. 4. Act II. sc. 1. Act III. sc. 2. Act V. sc. 1.

SIR ANTONY DENNY.
Appears, Act V. sc. 1.

SIR NICHOLAS VAUX.
Appears, Act II. sc. 1.

CROMWELL, *an Attendant on Wolsey.*
Appears, Act III. sc. 2. Act V. sc. 2.

LORD CHAMBERLAIN.
Appears, Act I. sc. 3; sc. 4. Act II. sc. 2; sc. 3. Act III. sc. 2. Act V. sc. 2.

LORD CHANCELLOR.
Appears, Act IV. sc. 1. Act V. sc. 2.

GRIFFITH, *Gentleman-Usher to Queen Katharine.*
Appears, Act II. sc. 4. Act IV. sc. 2.

OTHER GENTLEMEN.
Appear, Act II. sc. 1. Act IV. sc. 1.

SECRETARIES *to* WOLSEY.
Appear, Act I. sc. 1.

DOCTOR BUTTS, *Physician to the King.*
Appears, Act V. sc. 2.

GARTER KING-AT-ARMS.
Appears, Act IV. sc. 1. Act V. sc. 4.

SURVEYOR *to the Duke of Buckingham.*
Appears, Act I. sc. 2.

BRANDON *and a* SERGEANT-AT-ARMS.
Appear, Act I. sc. 1.

DOOR-KEEPER *of the Council-chamber.*
Appears, Act V. sc. 2.

PORTER *and his* MAN.
Appear, Act V. sc. 2.

A CRIER.
Appears, Act II. sc. 4.

PAGE *to the Bishop of Winchester.*
Appears, Act V. sc. 1.

QUEEN KATHARINE, *Wife to King Henry, afterwards divorced.*
Appears, Act I. sc. 2. Act II. sc. 4. Act III. sc. 1. Act IV. sc. 2.

ANNE BULLEN, *her Maid of Honour, afterwards Queen.*
Appears, Act I. sc. 4. Act II. sc. 3. Act IV. sc. 1.

AN OLD LADY, *Friend to Anne Bullen.*
Appears, Act II. sc. 3. Act V. sc. 1.

PATIENCE, *an Attendant on Queen Katharine.*
Appears, Act III. sc. 1. Act IV. sc. 2.

Several Lords and Ladies, Women attending upon the Queen, Spirits which appear to her, Scribes, Officers, Guards, and other Attendants.

SCENE,—*Chiefly in* LONDON *and* WESTMINSTER *once at* KIMBOLTON.

King Henry the Eighth.

PROLOGUE.

I come no more to make you laugh; things now,
That bear a weighty and a serious brow,
Sad, high, and working, full of state and woe,
Such noble scenes as draw the eye to flow,
We now present. Those that can pity, here
May, if they think it well, let fall a tear;
The subject will deserve it. Such, as give
Their money out of hope they may believe,
May here find truth too. Those, that come to see
Only a show or two, and so agree,
The play may pass; if they be still, and willing,
I 'll undertake, may see away their shilling
Richly in two short hours. Only they,
That come to hear a merry, bawdy play,
A noise of targets; or to see a fellow
In a long motely coat, guarded with yellow,'
Will be deceiv'd: for, gentle hearers, know
To rank our chosen truth with such a show
As fool and fight is, beside forfeiting
Our own brains, and the opinion that we bring,
(To make that only true we now intend,)
Will leave us never an understanding friend.
Therefore, for goodness' sake, and as you are known
The first and happiest hearers of the town,
Be sad, as we would make ye: Think, ye see
The very persons of our noble story,
As they were living; think, you see them great
And follow'd with the general throng, and sweat,
Of thousand friends; then, in a moment, see
How soon this mightiness meets misery!
And, if you can be merry then, I 'll say,
A man may weep upon his wedding day.

ACT I.

SCENE I.—London. *An Ante-chamber in the Palace.*

Enter the Duke of Norfolk, *at one Door; at the other, the* Duke of Buckingham, *and the Lord* Abergavenny.

Buck. Good morrow, and well met. How have you done,
Since last we saw in France?

Nor.   I thank your grace:
Healthful; and ever since a fresh admirer
Of what I saw there.

Buck.   An untimely ague

Stay'd me a prisoner in my chamber, when
Those suns of glory, those two lights of men,
Met in the vale of Arde.

Nor.   'Twixt Guynes and Arde:
I was then present, saw them salute on horseback;
Beheld them, when they lighted, how they clung
In their embracement, as they grew together:
Which had they, what four thron'd ones could
have weigh'd
Such a compounded one?

Buck.   All the whole time
I was my chamber's prisoner.

Nor.   Then you lost

The view of earthly glory : Men might say,
Till this time, pomp was single ; but now married
To one above itself.' Each following day
Became the next day's master, till the last,
Made former wonders it's : To-day, the French,
All clinquant,' all in gold, like heathen gods,
Shone down the English ; and, to-morrow, they
Made Britain, India : every man, that stood,
Show'd like a mine. Their dwarfish pages were
As cherubims, all gilt : the madams too,
Not us'd to toil, did almost sweat to bear
The pride upon them, that their very labour
Was to them as a painting : now this mask
Was cry'd incomparable ; and the ensuing night
Made it a fool, and beggar. The two kings,
Equal in lustre, were now best, now worst,
As presence did present them ; him in eye,
Still him in praise : and, being present both,
'T was said, they saw but one ; and no discerner
Durst wag his tongue in censure. When these
          suns
(For so they phrase them,) by their heralds chal-
          leng'd
The noble spirits to arms, they did perform
Beyond thought's compass ; that former fabulous
          story,
Being now seen possible enough, got credit,
That Bevis was believ'd.⁵
      Buck.   O, you go far.
      Nor. As I belong to worship, and affect
In honour honesty, the tract of every thing
Would by a good discourser lose some life,
Which action's self was tongue to. All was royal ;
To the disposing of it nought rebell'd,
Order gave each thing view ; the office did
Distinctly his full function.
      Buck.   Who did guide,
I mean, who set the body and the limbs
Of this great sport together, as you guess?
      Nor. One, certes, that promises no element⁶
In such a business.
      Buck.   I pray you, who, my lord?
      Nor. All this was order'd by the good dis-
          cretion
Of the right reverend cardinal of York.
      Buck. The devil speed him ! no man's pie is
          free'd
From his ambitious finger. What had he
To do in these fierce vanities? I wonder,
That such a keech can with his very bulk
Take up the rays o' the beneficial sun,
And keep it from the earth.

      Nor.   Surely, sir,
There 's in him stuff that puts him to these
          ends :
For, being not propp'd by ancestry, (whose grace
Chalks successors their way,) nor call'd upon
For high feats done to the crown ; neither allied
To eminent assistants, but, spider-like,
Out of his self-drawing web, he gives us note,
The force of his own merit makes his way ;
A gift that heaven gives for him, which buys
A place next to the king.
      Aber.   I cannot tell
What heaven hath given him, let some graver
          eye
Pierce into that ; but I can see his pride
Peep through each part of him : Whence has he
          that?
If not from hell, the devil is a niggard ;
Or has given all before, and he begins
A new hell in himself.
      Buck.   Why the devil,
Upon this French going-out, took he upon him,
Without the privity o' the king, to appoint
Who should attend on him? He makes up the file
Of all the gentry ; for the most part such
Too, whom as great a charge as little honour
He meant to lay upon : and his own letter,
The honourable board of council out,
Must fetch him in he papers.'
      Aber.   I do know
Kinsmen of mine, three at the least, that have
By this so sicken'd their estates, that never
They shall abound as formerly.
      Buck.   O, many
Have broke their backs with laying manors on
          them
For this great journey. What did this vanity,
But minister communication of
A most poor issue?
      Nor.   Grievingly I think,
The peace between the French and us not values
The cost that did conclude it.
      Buck.   Every man,
After the hideous storm that follow'd,⁸ was
A thing inspir'd ; and, not consulting, broke
Into a general prophecy,—That this tempest,
Dashing the garment of this peace, aboded
The sudden breach on 't.
      Nor.   Which is budded out,
For France hath flaw'd the league, and hath at-
          tach'd
Our merchants' goods at Bourdeaux.

Aber.   Is it therefore
The ambassador is silenc'd?

Nor.   Marry, is 't.

Aber. A proper title of a peace; and purchas'd
At a superfluous rate!

Buck.   Why, all this business
Our reverend cardinal carried.

Nor.   'Like it your grace,
The state takes notice of the private difference
Betwixt you and the cardinal. I advise you,
(And take it from a heart that wishes towards
        you
Honour and plenteous safety,) that you read
The cardinal's malice and his potency
Together: to consider further, that
What his high hatred would effect, wants not
A minister in his power: You know his nature,
That he 's revengeful; and I know, his sword
Hath a sharp edge: it 's long, and, it may be said,
It reaches far; and where 't will not extend,
Thither he darts it. Bosom up my counsel,
You 'll find it wholesome. Lo, where comes that
        rock,
That I advise your shunning.

Enter CARDINAL WOLSEY, (*the Purse borne before
him,*) *certain of the Guard, and two Secretaries
with Papers. The Cardinal in his Passage
fixeth his Eye on Buckingham, and Buckingham on him, both full of disdain.*

Wol. The duke of Buckingham's surveyor! ha!
Where 's his examination?

1st Secr.   Here, so please you.

Wol. Is he in person ready?

1st Secr.   Ay, please your grace.

Wol. Well, we shall then know more; and
        Buckingham
Shall lessen this big look.

                    [*Exeunt* WOL. *and Train.*

Buck. This butcher's cur is venom-mouth'd,
        and I
Have not the power to muzzle him; therefore,
        best
Not wake him in his slumber. A beggar's book
Out-worths a noble's blood?

Nor.   What, are you chaf'd?
Ask God for temperance; that 's the appliance
        only,
Which your disease requires.

Buck.   I read in his looks
Matter against me; and his eye revil'd
Me, as his abject object; at this instant
        he

He bores me with some trick: He 's gone to the
        king;
I 'll follow, and out-stare him.

Nor.   Stay, my lord,
And let your reason with your choler question
What 't is you go about: To climb steep hills,
Requires slow pace at first: Anger is like
A full-hot horse; who being allow'd his way,
Self-mettle tires him. Not a man in England
Can advise me like you: be to yourself
As you would to your friend.

Buck.   I 'll to the king;
And from a mouth of honour quite cry down
This Ipswich fellow's insolence; or proclaim,
There 's difference in no persons.

Nor.   Be advis'd;
Heat not a furnace for your foe so hot
That it do singe yourself: We may outrun,
By violent swiftness, that which we run at,
And lose by over-running. Know you not,
The fire, that mounts the liquor till it run o'er,
In seeming to augment it, wastes it? Be advis'd
I say again, there is no English soul
More stronger to direct you than yourself;
If with the sap of reason you would quench,
Or but allay, the fire of passion.

Buck.   Sir,
I am thankful to you; and I 'll go along
By your prescription:—but this top-proud fellow
(Whom from the flow of gall I name not, but
From sincere motions,) by intelligence,
And proofs as clear as founts in July, when
We see each grain of gravel, I do know
To be corrupt and treasonous.

Nor.   Say not, treasonous.

Buck. To the king I 'll say 't; and make my
        vouch as strong
As shore of rock. Attend. This holy fox,
Or wolf, or both, (for he is equal ravenous,
As he is subtle; and as prone to mischief,
As able to perform it: his mind and place
Infecting one another, yea, reciprocally,)
Only to show his pomp as well in France
As here at home, suggests the king our master
To this last costly treaty, the interview,
That swallow'd so much treasure, and like a glass
Did break i' the rinsing.

Nor.   'Faith, and so it did.

Buck. Pray, give me favour, sir. This cunning
        cardinal
The articles o' the combination drew,
As himself pleas'd; and they were ratified.

As he cried, Thus let be: to as much end,
As give a crutch to the dead: But our count-
cardinal
Has done this, and 't is well; for worthy Wolsey,
Who cannot err, he did it. Now this follows,
(Which, as I take it, is a kind of puppy
To the old dam, treason,)—Charles the emperor,
Under pretence to see the queen his aunt,
(For 't was, indeed, his colour; but he came
To whisper Wolsey,) here makes visitation:
His fears were, that the interview, betwixt
England and France, might, through their amity,
Breed him some prejudice; for from this league
Peep'd harms that menac'd him: He privily
Deals with our cardinal; and, as I trow,—
Which I do well; for, I am sure, the emperor
Paid ere he promis'd; whereby his suit was
granted,
Ere it was ask'd;—but when the way was made,
And pav'd with gold, the emperor thus desir'd;—
That he would please to alter the king's course,
And break the foresaid peace. Let the king
know,
(As soon he shall by me,) that thus the cardinal
Does buy and sell his honour as he pleases,
And for his own advantage.

Nor.   I am sorry
To hear this of him; and could wish, he were
Something mistaken in 't.

Buck.   No, not a syllable;
I do pronounce him in that very shape,
He shall appear in proof.

Enter BRANDON; *a Sergeant-at-Arms before him,
and two or three of the Guard.*

Bran. Your office, sergeant; execute it.
Serg.   Sir,
My lord the duke of Buckingham, and earl
Of Hereford, Stafford, and Northampton, I
Arrest thee of high treason, in the name
Of our most sovereign king.

Buck.   Lo you, my lord,
The net has fall'n upon me; I shall perish
Under device and practice.

Bran.   I am sorry
To see you ta'en from liberty, to look on
The business present: 'T is his highness' pleasure,
You shall to the Tower.

Buck.   It will help me nothing,
To plead mine innocence; for that die is on me,
Which makes my whitest part black. The will of
heaven

Be done in this and all things!—I obey.—
O my lord Aberga'ny, fare you well.

Bran. Nay, he must bear you company:—The
king   [*To* ABER.
Is pleas'd, you shall to the Tower, till you know
How he determines further.

Aber.   As the duke said,
The will of heaven be done, and the king's pleasure
By me obey'd.

Bran.   Here is a warrant from
The king, to attach lord Montacute; and the bodies
Of the duke's confessor, John de la Court,
One Gilbert Peck, his chancellor,—

Buck.   So, so;
These are the limbs of the plot: No more, I hope.

Bran. A monk o' the Chartreux.

Buck.   O, Nicholas Hopkins?

Bran.   He

Buck. My surveyor is false; the o'er-great car-
dinal
Hath show'd him gold: my life is spann'd already
I am the shadow of poor Buckingham;
Whose figure even this instant cloud puts on,
By dark'ning my clear sun.—My lord, farewell.
                                    [*Exeunt.*

SCENE II.—*The Council-Chamber.*

Cornets. Enter KING HENRY, CARDINAL WOLSEY,
the Lords of the Council, SIR THOMAS LOVELL,
*Officers, and Attendants. The King enters
leaning on the Cardinal's Shoulder.*

K. Hen. My life itself, and the best heart of it,
Thanks you for this great care: I stood i' the level
Of a full-charg'd confederacy, and give thanks
To you that chok'd it.—Let be call'd before us
That gentleman of Buckingham's: in person
I 'll hear him his confessions justify;
And point by point the treasons of his master
He shall again relate.

    [*The* KING *takes his State. The Lords of the
    Council take their several Places. The*
    CARD. *places himself under the* KING's
    Feet on his right Side.

*A Noise within, crying, "Room for the Queen."
Enter the* QUEEN, *ushered by the* DUKES OF
NORFOLK *and* SUFFOLK: *she kneels. The* KING
*riseth from his State, takes her up, kisses, and
placeth her by him.*

Q. Kath. Nay, we must longer kneel; I am a
suitor.

1059

K. Hen. Arise, and take place by us :—Half
    your suit
Never name to us; you have half our power :
The other moiety, ere you ask, is given ;
Repeat your will, and take it.
    Q. Kath.   Thank your majesty.
That you would love yourself ; and, in that love,
Not unconsider'd leave your honour, nor
The dignity of your office, is the point
Of my petition.
    K. Hen.   Lady mine, proceed.
    Q. Kath. I am solicited, not by a few,
And those of true condition, that your subjects
Are in great grievance : there have been com-
    missions
Sent down among them, which hath flaw'd the
    heart
Of all their loyalties :—wherein, although,
My good lord cardinal, they vent reproaches
Most bitterly on you, as putter-on
Of these exactions, yet the king our master,
(Whose honour heaven shield from soil !) even he
    escapes not
Language unmannerly, yea, such which breaks
The ties of loyalty, and almost appears
In loud rebellion.
    Nor.   Not almost appears,
It doth appear : for, upon these taxations,
The clothiers all, not able to maintain
The many to them 'longing, have put off
The spinsters, carders, fullers, weavers, who,
Unfit for other life, compell'd by hunger
And lack of other means, in desperate manner
Daring the event to the teeth, are all in uproar,
And Danger serves among them.
    K. Hen.   Taxation !
Wherein ? and what taxation ?—My lord cardinal,
You that are blam'd for it alike with us,
Know you of this taxation ?
    Wol.   Please you, sir,
I know but of a single part, in aught
Pertains to the state ; and front but in that file
Where others tell steps with me.
    Q. Kath.   No, my lord,
You know no more than others : but you frame
Things, that are known alike ; which are not
    wholesome
To those which would not know them, and yet
    must
Perforce be their acquaintance. These exactions,
Whereof my sovereign would have note, they are
Most pestilent to the hearing ; and, to bear them,
1000

The back is sacrifice to the load. They say,
They are devis'd by you : or else you suffer
Too hard an exclamation.
    K. Hen.   Still exaction !
The nature of it ? In what kind, let 's know,
Is this exaction ?
    Q. Kath.   I am much too venturous
In tempting of your patience ; but am bolden'd
Under your promis'd pardon. The subject's grief
Comes through commissions, which compel from
    each
The sixth part of his substance, to be levied
Without delay ; and the pretence for this
Is nam'd, your wars in France : This makes bold
    mouths :
Tongues spit their duties out, and cold hearts
    freeze
Allegiance in them ; their curses now,
Live where their prayers did ; and it 's come to
    pass,
That tractable obedience is a slave
To each incensed will. I would, your highness
Would give it quick consideration, for
There is no primer business.
    K. Hen.   By my life,
This is against our pleasure.
    Wol.   And for me,
I have no further gone in this, than by
A single voice ; and that not pass'd me, but
By learned approbation of the judges.
If I am traduc'd by tongues, which neither know
My faculties, nor person, yet will be
The chronicles of my doing,—let me say,
'T is but the fate of place, and the rough brake
That virtue must go through. We must not stint
Our necessary actions, in the fear
To cope malicious censurers ; which ever,
As ravenous fishes, do a vessel follow
That is new trimm'd ; but benefit no further
Than vainly longing. What we oft do best,
By sick interpreters, once weak ones, is
Not ours, or not allow'd ; what worst, as oft,
Hitting a grosser quality, is cried up
For our best act. If we shall stand still,
In fear our motion will be mock'd or carp'd at,
We should take root here where we sit, or sit
State statues only.
    K. Hen.   Things done well,
And with a care, exempt themselves from fear ;
Things done without example, in their issue
Are to be fear'd. Have you a precedent
Of this commission ! I believe, not any.

We must not rend our subjects from our laws,
And stick them in our will. Sixth part of each?
A trembling contribution. Why, we take,
From every tree, lop, bark, and part o' the timber;
And, though we leave it with a root, thus hack'd,
The air will drink the sap. To every county,
Where this is question'd, send our letters, with
Free pardon to each man that has denied
The force of this commission: Pray, look to 't;
I put it to your care.
  Wol.   A word with you.
                    [*To the* Secretary.
Let there be letters writ to every shire,
Of the king's grace and pardon. The griev'd
    commons
Hardly conceive of me; let it be nois'd,
That, through our intercession, this revokement
And pardon comes: I shall anon advise you
Further in the proceeding   [*Exit Secretary.*

        Enter Surveyor.

  Q. Kath. I am sorry, that the duke of Buck-
    ingham
Is run in your displeasure.
  K. Hen.   It grieves many:
The gentleman is learn'd, and a most rare speaker,
To nature none more bound; his training such,
That he may furnish and instruct great teachers,
And never seek for aid out of himself.
Yet see •
When these so noble benefits shall prove
Not well dispos'd, the mind growing once corrupt,
They turn to vicious forms, ten times more ugly
Than ever they were fair. This man so complete,
Who was enroll'd 'mongst wonders, and when we,
Almost with ravish'd list'ning, could not find
His hour of speech a minute; he, my lady,
Hath into monstrous habits put the graces
That once were his, and is become as black
As if besmear'd in hell. Sit by us; you shall hear
(This was his gentleman in trust,) of him
Things to strike honour sad.—Bid him recount
The fore-recited practices; whereof
We cannot feel too little, hear too much.
  Wol. Stand forth; and with bold spirit relate
    what you,
Most like a careful subject, have collected
Out of the duke of Buckingham.
  K. Hen.   Speak freely.
  Surv. First, it was usual with him, every day
It would infect his speech, That if the king
Should without issue die, he'd carry it so

To make the sceptre his: These very words
I have heard him utter to his son-in-law,
Lord Aberga'ny; to whom by oath he menac'd
Revenge upon the cardinal.
  Wol.   Please your highness, note
This dangerous conception in this point.
Not friended by his wish, to your high person
His will is most malignant; and it stretches
Beyond you, to your friends.
  Q. Kath.   My learn'd lord cardinal,
Deliver all with charity.
  K. Hen.   Speak on:
How grounded he his title to the crown,
Upon our fail? to this point hast thou heard him
At any time speak aught?
  Surv.   He was brought to this
By a vain prophecy of Nicholas Hopkins.
  K. Hen. What was that Hopkins?
  Surv.   Sir, a Chartreux friar,
His confessor; who fed him every minute
With words of sovereignty.
  K. Hen.   How know'st thou this?
  Surv. Not long before your highness sped to
    France,
The duke being at the Rose, within the parish
Saint Lawrence Poultney, did of me demand
What was the speech amongst the Londoners
Concerning the French journey: I replied,
Men fear'd, the French would prove perfidious,
To the king's danger. Presently the duke
Said, 'T was the fear, indeed; and that he doubted,
'T would prove the verity of certain words
Spoke by a holy monk; "that oft," says he,
"Hath sent to me, wishing me to permit
John de la Court, my chaplain, a choice hour
To hear from him a matter of some moment:
Whom after under the confession's seal
He solemnly had sworn, that, what he spoke,
My chaplain to no creature living, but
To me, should utter, with demure confidence
This pausingly ensu'd,—Neither the king, nor his
    heirs,
(Tell you the duke) shall prosper: bid him strive
To gain the love of the commonalty; the duke
Shall govern England."
  Q. Kath.   If I know you well,
You were the duke's surveyor, and lost your office
On the complaint o' the tenants: Take good
    heed,
You charge not in your spleen a noble person,
And spoil your nobler soul! I say, take heed;
Yes, heartily beseech you.

K. Hen.   Let him on :—
Go forward.
    Surv.   On my soul, I 'll speak but truth.
I told my lord the duke, By the devil's illusions
The monk might be deceiv'd ; and that 't was
                    dang'rous for him,
To ruminate on this so far, until
It forg'd him some design, which, being believ'd,
It was much like to do : He answer'd, " Tush !
It can do me no damage :" adding further,
That, had the king in his last sickness fail'd,
The cardinal's and sir Thomas Lovell's heads
Should have gone off.
    K. Hen.   Ha ! what, so rank ? Ah, ha !
There 's mischief in this man :——Canst thou say
                    further ?
    Surv. I can, my liege.
    K. Hen.   Proceed.
    Surv.   Being at Greenwich,
After your highness had reprov'd the duke
About sir William Blomer,—
    K. Hen.   I remember,
Of such a time :—Being my servant sworn,
The duke retain'd him his.——But on : What
                    hence ?
    Surv. " If," quoth he, " I for this had been
                    committed,
As, to the Tower, I thought,—I would have play'd
The part my father meant to act upon
The usurper Richard ;" who, being at Salisbury,
Made suit to come in his presence ; which, if
                    granted,
As he made semblance of his duty, would
Have put his knife into him."
    K. Hen.   A giant traitor !
    Wol. Now, madam, may his highness live in
                    freedom,
And this man out of prison ?
    Q. Kath.   God mend all !
    K. Hen. There 's something more would out of
                    thee : What say'st ?
    Surv. After—" the duke his father,"—with
" the knife,"—
He stretch'd him, and, with one hand on his
                    dagger,
Another spread on his breast, mounting his eyes,
He did discharge a horrible oath ; whose tenor
Was,—Were he evil us'd, he would out-go
His father, by as much as a performance
Does an irresolute purpose.
    K. Hen.   There 's his period,
To sheath his knife in us.   He is attach'd ;

Call him to present trial : if he may
Find mercy in the law, 't is his ; if none,
Let him not seek 't of us : By day and night,
He 's traitor to the height.   [*Exeunt.*

SCENE III.—*A Room in the Palace.*

Enter the Lord Chamberlain *and* Lord Sands.

    Cham. Is it possible, the spells of France should
                    juggle
Men into such strange mysteries ?
    Sands.   New customs,
Though they be never so ridiculous,
Nay, let them be unmanly, yet are follow'd.
    Cham. As far as I see, all the good our English
Have got by the late voyage, is but merely
A fit or two o' the face ;" but they are shrewd
                    ones ;
For when they hold them, you would swear
                    directly,
Their very noses had been counsellors
To Pepin, or Clotharius, they keep state so.
    Sands. They have all new legs, and lame ones ;
                    one would take it,
That never saw them pace before, the spavin,
A springhalt reign'd among them.
    Cham.   Death ! my lord,
Their clothes are after such a pagan cut too,
That, sure, they have worn out Christendom.
                    How now ?
What news, sir Thomas Lovell ?

    Enter Sir Thomas Lovell.

    Lov.   'Faith, my lord,
I hear of none, but the new proclamation
That 's clapp'd upon the court-gate.
    Cham.   What is 't for ?
    Lov. The reformation of our travell'd gallants,
That fill the court with quarrels, talk, and tailors.
    Cham. I am glad, 't is there ; now I would pray
                    our monsieurs
To think an English courtier may be wise,
And never see the Louvre.
    Lov.   They must either
(For so run the conditions,) leave these remnants
Of fool, and feather, that they got in France,
With all their honourable points of ignorance,
Pertaining thereunto, (as fights, and fireworks ;
Abusing better men than they can be,
Out of a foreign wisdom,) renouncing clean
The faith they have in tennis, and tall stockings,
Short blister'd breeches, and those types of travel,

And understand again like honest men;
Or pack to their old playfellows: there, I take it,
They may *cum privilegio*, wear away
The lag end of their lewdness, and be laugh'd at.
　Sands. 'T is time to give them physic, their
　　diseases
Are grown so catching.
　Cham.　　　　　　What a loss our ladies
Will have of these trim vanities!
　Lov.　　　　　　　Ay, marry,
There will be woe indeed, lords; the sly whoresons
Have got a speeding trick to lay down ladies;
A French song, and a fiddle, has no fellow.
　Sands. The devil fiddle them! I am glad, they're
　　going;
(For, sure, there 's no converting of them;) now
An honest country lord, as I am, beaten
A long time out of play, may bring his plain-song,
And have an hour of hearing; and, by'r-lady,
Held current music too.
　Cham.　　　　Well said, lord Sands;
Your colt's tooth is not cast yet.
　Sands.　　　　　No, my lord;
Nor shall not, while I have a stump.
　Cham.　　　　　　Sir Thomas,
Whither were you a going?
　Lov.　　　　To the cardinal's;
Your lordship is a guest too.
　Cham.　　　　　O, 't is true:
This night he makes a supper, and a great one,
To many lords and ladies; there will be
The beauty of this kingdom, I 'll assure you.
　Lov. That churchman bears a bounteous mind
　　indeed,
A hand as fruitful as the land that feeds us;
His dews fall every where.
　Cham.　　　　No doubt, he 's noble;
He had a black mouth, that said other of him.
　Sands. He may, my lord, he has wherewithal;
　　in him,
Sparing would show a worse sin than ill doctrine:
Men of his way should be most liberal,
They are set here for examples.
　Cham.　　　　True, they are so;
But few now give so great ones. My barge stays;
Your lordship shall along:—Come, good sir
　　Thomas,
We shall be late else: which I would not be,
For I was spoke to, with sir Henry Guildford,
This night to be comptrollers.
　Sands.　　.　　I am your lordship's.
　　　　　　　　　　　　　　　[*Exeunt*

SCENE IV.—*The Presence-Chamber in York
　　Place.*

*Hautboys.　A small Table under a State for the
Cardinal, a longer Table for the Guests.　Enter
at one Door* ANNE BULLEN, *and divers Lords,
Ladies, and Gentlewomen, as Guests; at another Door, enter Sir* HENRY GUILDFORD.

　Guild. Ladies, a general welcome from his
　　grace
Salutes ye all: This night he dedicates
To fair content, and you: none here, he hopes,
In all this noble bevy, has brought with her
One care abroad; he would have all as merry
As first-good company, good wine, good welcome
Can make good people.——O, my lord, you are
　　tardy;

Enter Lord CHAMBERLAIN, *Lord* SANDS, *and*
　　Sir THOMAS LOVELL.

The very thought of this fair company
Clapp'd wings to me.
　Cham.　You are young, sir Harry Guildford.
　Sands. Sir Thomas Lovell, had the cardinal
But half my lay-thoughts in him, some of these
Should find a running banquet ere they rested,
I think, would better please them: By my life,
They are a sweet society of fair ones.
　Lov. O, that your lordship were but now con-
　　fessor
To one or two of these!
　Sands.　　　　I would, I were;
They should find easy penance.
　Lov.　　　　　'Faith, how easy!
　Sands. As easy as a down-bed would afford it.
　Cham. Sweet ladies, will it please you sit? Sir
　　Harry,
Place you that side, I 'll take the charge of this:
His grace is ent'ring.—Nay, you must not freeze;
Two women plac'd together makes cold weather:—
My lord Sands, you are one will keep them waking;
Pray, sit between these ladies.
　Sands.　　　　By my faith,
And thank your lordship.—By your leave, sweet
　　ladies:
　　[*Seats himself between* ANNE BULLEN *and
　　　　another Lady.*
If I chance to talk a little wild, forgive me;
I had it from my father.
　Anne.　　　　Was he mad, sir?
　Sands. O, very mad, exceeding mad, in love too:

But he would bite none; just as I do now,
He would kiss you twenty with a breath.
                              [*Kisses her.*
Cham.   Well said, my lord.—
So, now you are fairly seated :—Gentlemen,
The penance lies on you, if these fair ladies
Pass away frowning.
Sands.   For my little cure,
Let me alone.

Hautboys. Enter CARDINAL WOLSEY, *attended ;
and takes his State.*

  Wol. You are welcome, my fair guests ; that
    noble lady,
Or gentleman, that is not freely merry,
Is not my friend : This, to confirm my welcome ;
And to you all good health.   [*Drinks.*
Sands.   Your grace is noble :—
Let me have such a bowl may hold my thanks,
And save me so much talking.
Wol.   My lord Sands,
I am beholden to you : cheer your neighbours.—
Ladies, you are not merry ;—Gentlemen,
Whose fault is this ?
Sands.   The red wine first must rise
In their fair cheeks, my lord ; then we shall have
    them
Talk us to silence.
Anne.   You are a merry gamester,
My lord Sands.
Sands.   Yes, if I make my play.
Here's to your ladyship : and pledge it, madam,
For 't is to such a thing,—
Anne.   You cannot show me.
Sands. I told your grace, they would talk anon.
      [*Drum and Trumpets within: Chambers
            discharged.*
Wol.   What 's that ?
Cham. Look out there, some of you.
                              [*Exit a Servant.*
Wol.   What warlike voice ?
And to what end is this ?—Nay, ladies, fear not ;
By all the laws of war you are privileg'd.

Re-enter Servant.

Cham. How now ! what is 't ?
Serv.   A noble troop of strangers ;
For so they seem : they have left their barge, and
    landed ;
And hither make, as great ambassadors
From foreign princes.
Wol.   Good lord chamberlain,
1064

Go, give them welcome, you can speak the French
    tongue :
And, pray, receive them nobly, and conduct them
Into our presence, where this heaven of beauty
Shall shine at full upon them :—Some attend
    him.—
    [*Exit* CHAM., *attended. All arise, and Tables
        removed.*
You have now a broken banquet ; but we 'll mend
    it.
A good digestion to you all : and, once more,
I shower a welcome on you ;—Welcome all.

Hautboys. Enter the KING, *and twelve Others,
as Maskers, habited like Shepherds, with sixteen
Torch-bearers ; ushered by the* LORD CHAMBER-
LAIN. *They pass directly before the Cardinal,
and gracefully salute him.*

A noble company ! what are their pleasures ?
Cham. Because they speak no English, thus
    they pray'd
To tell your grace ;—That, having heard by fame
Of this so noble and so fair assembly
This night to meet here, they could do no less,
Out of the great respect they bear to beauty,
But leave their flocks ; and, under your fair conduct,
Crave leave to view these ladies, and entreat
An hour of revels with them.
Wol.   Say, lord chamberlain,
They have done my poor house grace ; for which
    I pay them
A thousand thanks, and pray them take their
    pleasures.
    [*Ladies chosen for the Dance. The* KING
        chooses ANNE BULLEN.
K. Hen. The fairest hand I ever touch'd ! O
    beauty,
Till now I never knew thee.   [*Music. Dance.*
Wol. My lord,——
Cham.   Your grace ?
Wol.   Pray, tell them thus much from me
There should be one amongst them, by his person,
More worthy this place than myself ; to whom,
If I but knew him, with my love and duty
I would surrender it.
Cham.   I will, my lord.
    [CHAM. *goes to the Company, and returns.*
Wol. What say they ?
Cham.   Such a one, they all confess,
There is, indeed ; which they would have your
    grace
Find out, and he will take it.

Wol.   Let me see then.—
       [*Comes from his State.*
By all your good leaves, gentlemen ;—Here I 'll
    make
My royal choice.
    K. Hen.   You have found him, cardinal ;"
       [*Unmasking.*
You hold a fair assembly ; you do well, lord :
You are a churchman, or, I 'll tell you, cardinal,
I should judge now unhappily.
    Wol.   I am glad,
Your grace is grown so pleasant.
    K. Hen.   My lord chamberlain,
Pr'ythee, come hither : What fair lady 's that?
    Cham. An 't please your grace, sir Thomas
      Bullen's daughter,
The viscount Rochford, one of her highness' wo-
    men.
    K. Hen. By heaven, she is a dainty one.—
      Sweetheart,

I were unmannerly, to take you out,
And not to kiss you."—A health, gentlemen,
Let it go round.
    Wol. Sir Thomas Lovell, is the banquet ready
I' the privy chamber?
    Lov.   Yes, my lord.
    Wol.   Your grace,
I fear, with dancing is a little heated."
    K. Hen. I fear, too much.
    Wol.   There 's fresher air, my lord,
In the next chamber.
    K. Hen. Lead in your ladies, every one.—Sweet
    partner,
I must not yet forsake you :—Let 's be merry ;—
Good my lord cardinal, I have half a dozen
    healths
To drink to these fair ladies, and a measure
To lead them once again ; and then let 's dream
Who 's best in favour.—Let the music knock it.
       [*Exeunt, with Trumpets.*

ACT II.

SCENE I.—*A Street.*

Enter Two Gentlemen, meeting.

1st Gent. Whither away so fast?
    2nd Gent.   O,—God save you!
Even to the hall, to hear what shall become
Of the great duke of Buckingham.
    1st Gent.   I 'll save you
That labour, sir. All 's now done, but the cere-
    mony
Of bringing back the prisoner.
    2nd Gent.   Were you there ?
    1st Gent. Yes, indeed, was I.
    2nd Gent.   Pray, speak, what has happen'd ?
    1st Gent. You may guess quickly what.
    2nd Gent.   Is he found guilty?
    1st Gent. Yes, truly is he, and condemn'd upon
    it.
    2nd Gent. I am sorry for 't.
    1st Gent.   So are a number more.
    2nd Gent. But, pray, how pass'd it ?
    1st Gent. I 'll tell you in a little. The great
    duke
Came to the bar ; where, to his accusations,
He pleaded still, not guilty, and alleg'd

Many sharp reasons to defeat the law.
The king's attorney, on the contrary,
Urg'd on the examinations, proofs, confessions
Of divers witnesses ; which the duke desir'd
To him brought, *vivâ voce,* to his face :
At which appear'd against him, his surveyor ;
Sir Gilbert Peck his chancellor ; and John Court,
Confessor to him ; with that devil-monk,
Hopkins, that made this mischief.
    2nd Gent.   That was he,
That fed him with his prophecies ?
    1st Gent.   The same.
All these accus'd him strongly ; which he fain
Would have flung from him, but, indeed, he could
    not :
And so his peers, upon this evidence,
Have found him guilty of high treason. Much
He spoke, and learnedly, for life ; but all
Was either pitied in him, or forgotten.
    2nd Gent. After all this, how did he bear him-
    self ?
    1st Gent. When he was brought again to the
    bar,—to hear
His knell rung out, his judgment,—he was stirr'd
With such an agony, he sweat extremely,

And something spoke in choler, ill, and hasty:
But he fell to himself again, and, sweetly,
In all the rest show'd a most noble patience.
  2nd Gent. I do not think, he fears death.
  1st Gent.   Sure, he does not,
He never was so womanish; the cause
He may a little grieve at.
  2nd Gent.   Certainly,
The cardinal is the end of this.
  1st Gent.   'T is likely,
By all conjectures: First, Kildare's attainder,
Then deputy of Ireland; who remov'd,
Earl Surrey was sent thither, and in haste too,
Lest he should help his father.
  2nd Gent.   That trick of state
Was a deep envious one.
  1st Gent.   At his return,
No doubt, he will requite it. This is noted,
And generally; whoever the king favours,
The cardinal instantly will find employment,
And far enough from court too.
  2nd Gent.   All the commons
Hate him perniciously, and, o' my conscience.
Wish him ten fathom deep: this duke as much
They love and dote on; call him, bounteous
        Buckingham,
The mirror of all courtesy;—
  1st Gent.   Stay there, sir,
And see the noble ruin'd man you speak of.

Enter BUCKINGHAM *from his Arraignment; Tip-
staves before him; the Axe with the Edge towards him; Halberds on each side; with him,
SIR THOMAS LOVELL, SIR NICHOLAS VAUX, SIR
WILLIAM SANDS, and common People.*

  2nd Gent. Let's stand close, and behold him.
  Buck.   All good people,
You that thus far have come to pity me,
Hear what I say, and then go home and lose me.
I have this day receiv'd a traitor's judgment,
And by that name must die: Yet, heaven bear
        witness,
And, if I have a conscience, let it sink me,
Even as the axe falls, if I be not faithful!
The law I bear no malice for my death,
It has done, upon the premises, but justice:
But those, that sought it, I could wish more chris-
      tians:
Be what they will, I heartily forgive them:
Yet let them look they glory not in mischief,
Nor build their evils on the graves of great men;
For then my guiltless blood must cry against them.
  1066

For further life in this world I ne'er hope,
Nor will I sue, although the king have mercies
More than I dare make faults. You few that
      lov'd me,
And dare be bold to weep for Buckingham,
His noble friends, and fellows, whom to leave
Is only bitter to him, only dying,
Go with me, like good angels, to my end:
And, as the long divorce of steel falls on me,
Make of your prayers one sweet sacrifice,
And lift my soul to heaven.—Lead on, o' God's
      name.
  Lov. I do beseech your grace for charity,
If ever any malice in your heart
Were hid against me, now to forgive me frankly.
  Buck. Sir Thomas Lovell, I as free forgive you,
As I would be forgiven: I forgive all;
There cannot be those numberless offences
'Gainst me, I can't take peace with: no black envy
Shall make my grave.—Commend me to his grace;
And, if he speak of Buckingham, pray, tell him.
You met him half in heaven: my vows and prayers
Yet are the king's; and, till my soul forsake me,
Shall cry for blessings on him: May he live
Longer than I have time to tell his years!
Ever belov'd, and loving, may his rule be!
And, when old time shall lead him to his end,
Goodness and he fill up one monument!
  Lov. To the water side I must conduct your
    grace;
Then give my charge up to sir Nicholas Vaux,
Who undertakes you to your end.
  Vaux.   Prepare there,
The duke is coming: see, the barge be ready;
And fit it with such furniture, as suits
The greatness of his person.
  Buck.   Nay, sir Nicholas,
Let it alone; my state now will but mock me.
When I came hither, I was lord high constable,
And duke of Buckingham; now, poor Edward
    Bohun:
Yet I am richer than my base accusers,
That never knew what truth meant: I now seal it
And with that blood will make them one day
    groan for 't.
My noble father, Henry of Buckingham.
Who first rais'd head against usurping Richard,
Flying for succour to his servant Banister,
Being distress'd, was by that wretch betray'd,
And without trial fell; God's peace be with him
Henry the Seventh succeeding, truly pitying
My father's loss, like a most royal prince,

Restor'd me to my honours, and, out of ruins,
Made my name once more noble. Now his son,
Henry the Eighth, life, honour, name, and all
That made me happy, at one stroke has taken
For ever from the world. I had my trial,
And, must needs say, a noble one: which makes
                                                    me
A little happier than my wretched father:
Yet thus far we are one in fortunes,—Both
Fell by our servants, by those men we lov'd most;
A most unnatural and faithless service!
Heaven has an end in all: Yet, you that hear me,
This from a dying man receive as certain:
Where you are liberal of your loves, and counsels,
Be sure, you be not loose; for those you make
                                                    friends,
And give your hearts to, when they once perceive
The least rub in your fortunes, fall away
Like water from ye, never found again
But where they mean to sink ye. All good people,
Pray for me! I must now forsake ye; the last
                                                    hour
Of my long weary life is come upon me.
Farewell:
And when you would say something that is sad,
Speak how I fell.—I have done; and God forgive
       me!   [*Exeunt* Buck. *and* Train.
    1st Gent. O, this is full of pity!—Sir, it calls,
I fear, too many curses on their heads,
That were the authors.
    2nd Gent.   If the duke be guiltless,
'T is full of woe: yet I can give you inkling
Of an ensuing evil, if it fall,
Greater than this.
    1st Gent.   Good angels keep it from us!
Where may it be? You do not doubt my faith,
                                                    sir?
    2nd Gent. This secret is so weighty, 't will re-
                                                    quire
A strong faith to conceal it.
    1st Gent.   Let me have it;
I do not talk much.
    2nd Gent.   I am confident;
You shall, sir: Did you not of late days hear
A buzzing, of a separation
Between the king and Katharine?
    1st Gent.   Yes, but it held not:
For when the king once heard it, out of anger
He sent command to the lord mayor, straight
To stop the rumour, and allay those tongues
That durst disperse it.
    2nd Gent.   But that slander, sir,

Is found a truth now: for it grows again
Fresher than e'er it was; and held for certain,
The king will venture at it. Either the cardinal,
Or some about him near, have, out of malice
To the good queen, possessed him with a scruple
That will undo her: To confirm this too,
Cardinal Campeius is arriv'd, and lately;
As all think, for this business.
    1st Gent.   'T is the cardinal;
And merely to revenge him on the emperor,
For not bestowing on him, at his asking,
The archbishopric of Toledo, this is purpos'd.
    2nd Gent. I think, you have hit the mark: But
                                         is 't not cruel,
That she should feel the smart of this? The car-
                                                    dinal
Will have his will, and she must fall.
    1st Gent.   'T is woful.
We are too open here to argue this;
Let 's think in private more.   [*Exeunt*

SCENE II.—*An Ante-chamber in the Palace.*

Enter the Lord Chamberlain, *reading a Letter.*

    Cham. My lord,—The horses your lordship sent for,
with all the care I had, I saw well chosen, ridden, and furnished. They were young, and handsome; and of the best
breed in the north. When they were ready to set out for
London, a man of my lord cardinal's, by commission, and
main power, took 'em from me; with this reason,—His
master would be served before a subject, if not before
the king: which stopped our mouths, sir.

I fear, he will, indeed: Well, let him have them:
He will have all, I think.

Enter the Dukes of Norfolk *and* Suffolk.

    Nor.   Well met, my good
Lord Chamberlain.
    Cham.   Good day to both your graces.
    Suf. How is the king employ'd?
    Cham.   I left him private,
Full of sad thoughts and troubles.
    Nor.   What 's the cause?
    Cham. It seems, the marriage with his brother's
                                                    wife
Has crept too near his conscience.
    Suf.   No, his conscience
Has crept too near another lady.
    Nor.   'T is so;
This is the cardinal's doing, the king-cardinal:
That blind priest, like the eldest son of fortune,
Turns what he lists. The king will know him one
                                                    day.

Suf. Pray God, he do! he 'll never know himself else.

Nor. How holily he works in all his business!
And with what zeal! For, now he has crack'd the
    league
Between us and the emperor, the queen's great
    nephew,
He dives into the king's soul; and there scatters
Dangers, doubts, wringing of the conscience,
Fears, and despairs, and all these for his marriage:
And, out of all these to restore the king,
He counsels a divorce: a loss of her,
That, like a jewel, has hung twenty years
About his neck, yet never lost her lustre;
Of her, that loves him with that excellence
That angels love good men with; even of her
That, when the greatest stroke of fortune fails,
Will bless the king: And is not this course pious?
    Cham. Heaven keep me from such counsel!
        'T is most true,
These news are every where; every tongue speaks
    them,
And every true heart weeps for 't: All, that dare
Look into these affairs, see this main end,—
The French king's sister. Heaven will one day open
The king's eyes, that so long have slept upon
This bold bad man.
    Suf.   And free us from his slavery.
    Nor. We had need pray,
And heartily, for our deliverance;
Or this imperious man will work us all
From princes into pages:" all men's honours
Lie in one lump before him, to be fashion'd
Into what pitch he please.
    Suf.   For me, my lords,
I love him not, nor fear him; there 's my creed:
As I am made without him, so I 'll stand,
If the king please; his curses and his blessings
Touch me alike, they are breath I not believe in.
I knew him, and I know him; so I leave him
To him, that made him proud, the Pope.
    Nor.   Let 's in;
And, with some other business, put the king
From these sad thoughts, that work too much
    upon him :—
My lord, you 'll bear us company?
    Cham.   Excuse me;
The king hath sent me other-where: besides,
You 'll find a most unfit time to disturb him:
Health to your lordships.
    Nor.   Thanks, my good lord chamberlain.
                                [*Exit* CHAM.

1068

NORFOLK *opens a folding-door. The* KING *is discovered sitting, and reading pensively.*

Suf. How sad he looks! sure, he is much afflicted.

K. Hen. Who is there? ha?

Nor.   'Pray God, he be not angry.

K. Hen. Who 's there, I say? How dare you
    thrust yourselves
Into my private meditations?
Who am I? ha?

Nor. A gracious king, that pardons all offences
Malice ne'er meant: our breach of duty, this way,
Is business of estate; in which, we come
To know your royal pleasure.

K. Hen.   You are too bold;
Go to; I 'll make ye know your times of business:
Is this an hour for temporal affairs? ha?

Enter WOLSEY *and* CAMPEIUS.

Who 's there? my good lord cardinal?—O my
    Wolsey,
The quiet of my wounded conscience,
Thou art a cure fit for a king.—You 're welcome,
                                [*To* CAM.
Most learned reverend sir, into our kingdom;
Use us, and it :—My good lord, have great care
I be not found a talker."   [*To* WOL.
    Wol.   Sir, you cannot.
I would, your grace would give us but an hour
Of private conference.
    K. Hen.   We are busy; go.
                                [*To* NOR. *and* SUF.
    Nor. This priest has no pride in him? ⎫
    Suf.   Not to speak of; ⎪
I would not be so sick though, for his place: ⎬ *Aside.*
But this cannot continue.   ⎪
    Nor.   If it do,   ⎪
I 'll venture one heave at him.   ⎪
    Suf.   I another.   ⎭
                            [*Exeunt* NOR. *and* SUF.

Wol. Your grace has given a precedent of
    wisdom
Above all princes, in committing freely
Your scruple to the voice of Christendom:
Who can be angry now? what envy reach you?
The Spaniard, tied by blood and favour to her,
Must now confess, if they have any goodness,
The trial just and noble. All the clerks,
I mean, the learned ones, in christian kingdoms,
Have their free voices; Rome, the nurse of judgment,

Invited by your noble self, hath sent
One general tongue unto us, this good man,
This just and learned priest, cardinal Campeius;
Whom, once more, I present unto your highness.

   K. Hen. And, once more, in mine arms I bid
      him welcome,
And thank the holy conclave for their loves;
They have sent me such a man I would have
      wish'd for.

   Cam. Your grace must needs deserve all stran-
      gers' loves,
You are so noble: To your highness' hand
I tender my commission; by whose virtue,
(The court of Rome commanding,)—you, my lord
Cardinal of York, are join'd with me their servant,
In the unpartial judging of this business.

   K. Hen. Two equal men. The queen shall be
      acquainted
Forthwith, for what you come:—Where's Gar-
      diner?

   Wol. I know, your majesty has always lov'd
      her
So dear in heart, not to deny her that
A woman of less place might ask by law,
Scholars, allow'd freely to argue for her.

   K. Hen. Ay, and the best, she shall have; and
      my favour
To him that does best; God forbid else. Cardinal,
Pr'ythee, call Gardiner to me, my new secretary;
I find him a fit fellow.   [*Exit* WOL.

      Re-enter WOLSEY, *with* GARDINER.

   Wol. Give me your hand: much joy and fa-
      vour to you;
You are the king's now.

   Gard.   But to be commanded
For ever by your grace, whose hand has rais'd
      me.   [*Aside.*

   K. Hen. Come hither, Gardiner.
                [*They converse apart.*

   Cam. My lord of York, was not one doctor Pace
In this man's place before him?

   Wol.   Yes, he was.

   Cam. Was he not held a learned man?

   Wol.   Yes, surely.

   Cam. Believe me, there's an ill opinion spread
      then
Even of yourself, lord cardinal.

   Wol.   How! of me?

   Cam. They will not stick to say, you envied
      him;
And, fearing he would rise, he was so virtuous,

Kept him a foreign man still; which so griev'd
      him,
That he ran mad, and died.

   Wol.   Heaven's peace be with him!
That's christian care enough: for living mur-
      murers,
There's places of rebuke. He was a fool;
For he would needs be virtuous: That good
      fellow,
If I command him, follows my appointment;
I will have none so near else. Learn this, brother,
We live not to be grip'd by meaner persons.

   K. Hen. Deliver this with modesty to the
      queen.   [*Exit* GARD.
The most convenient place that I can think of,
For such receipt of learning, is Black-Friars;
There ye shall meet about this weighty business:—
My Wolsey, see it furnish'd.—O my lord,
Would it not grieve an able man, to leave
So sweet a bedfellow? But conscience, con-
      science,—
O, 't is a tender place, and I must leave her.
                [*Exeunt.*

SCENE III.—*An Ante-chamber in the Queen's
      Apartments.*

     Enter ANNE BULLEN, *and an old* Lady.

   Anne. Not for that neither;—Here's the pang
      that pinches:
His highness having liv'd so long with her: and
      she
So good a lady, that no tongue could ever
Pronounce dishonour of her,—by my life,
She never knew harm-doing;—O now, after
So many courses of the sun enthron'd,
Still growing in a majesty and pomp,—the which
To leave is a thousand-fold more bitter, than
'T is sweet at first to acquire,—after this process,
To give her the avaunt! it is a pity
Would move a monster.

   Old L.   Hearts of most hard temper
Melt and lament for her.

   Anne.   O, God's will! much better
She ne'er had known pomp: though it be tem-
      poral,
Yet, if that cruel fortune do divorce
It from the bearer, 't is a sufferance, panging
As soul and body's severing.

   Old L.   Alas, poor lady!
She's a stranger now again.

   Anne.   So much the more

Must pity drop upon her. Verily,
I swear, 't is better to be lowly born,
And range with humble livers in content,
Than to be perk'd up in a glistering grief,
And wear a golden sorrow.

    Old L.   Our content
Is our best having.

    Anne.   By my troth, and maidenhead,
I would not be a queen.

    Old L.   Beshrew me, I would,
And venture maidenhead for 't; and so would you,
For all this spice of your hypocrisy:
You, that have so fair parts of woman on you,
Have too a woman's heart; which ever yet
Affected eminence, wealth, sovereignty;
Which, to say sooth, are blessings; and which
         gifts
(Saving your mincing) the capacity
Of your soft cheveril conscience[22] would receive,
If you might please to stretch it.

    Anne.   Nay, good troth,——

    Old L. Yes, troth, and troth,—You would not
      be a queen?

    Anne. No, not for all the riches under heaven.

    Old L. 'T is strange; a three-pence bowed
      would hire me,
Old as I am, to queen it: But, I pray you,
What think you of a duchess? have you limbs
To bear that load of title?

    Anne.   No, in truth.

    Old L. Then you are weakly made: Pluck off
      a little;
I would not be a young count in your way,
For more than blushing comes to: if your back
Cannot vouchsafe this burden, 't is too weak
Ever to get a boy.

    Anne.   How you do talk!
I swear again, I would not be a queen
For all the world.

    Old L.   In faith, for little England
You 'd venture an embailing?[21] I myself
Would for Carnarvonshire, although there 'long'd
No more to the crown but that. Lo, who comes
      here?

        Enter the LORD CHAMBERLAIN.

    Cham. Good morrow, ladies. What wer't worth
to know
The secret of your conference?

    Anne.   My good lord,
Not your demand; it values not your asking:
Our mistress' sorrows we were pitying.

    Cham. It was a gentle business, and becoming
The action of good women: there is hope,
All will be well.

    Anne.   Now I pray God, amen!

    Cham. You bear a gentle mind, and heavenly
      blessings
Follow such creatures. That you may, fair lady,
Perceive I speak sincerely, and high note 's
Ta'en of your many virtues, the king's majesty
Commends his good opinion to you, and
Does purpose honour to you no less flowing
Than marchioness of Pembroke; to which title
A thousand pounds a year, annual support,
Out of his grace he adds.

    Anne.   I do not know,
What kind of my obedience I should tender;
More than my all is nothing: nor my prayers
Are not words duly hallow'd, nor my wishes
More worth than empty vanities; yet prayers,
      and wishes,
Are all I can return. 'Beseech your lordship,
Vouchsafe to speak my thanks, and my obedience,
As from a blushing handmaid, to his highness;
Whose health, and royalty, I pray for.

    Cham.   Lady,
I shall not fail to approve the fair conceit,
The king hath of you.—I have perus'd her well;
         [*Aside.*
Beauty and honour in her are so mingled,
That they have caught the king: and who knows
      yet,
But from this lady may proceed a gem,
To lighten all this isle?—I 'll to the king,
And say, I spoke with you.

    Anne.   My honour'd lord.
         [*Exit* CHAM.

    Old L. Why, this it is: see, see!
I have been begging sixteen years in court,
(Am yet a courtier beggarly,) nor could
Come pat betwixt too early and too late,
For any suit of pounds: and you, (O fate!)
A very fresh-fish here, (fie, fie upon
This compell'd fortune!) have your mouth fill'd up,
Before you open it.

    Anne.   This is strange to me.

    Old L. How tastes it? is it bitter? forty
      pence, no.[24]
There was a lady once, ('t is an old story,)
That would not be a queen, that would she not,
For all the mud in Egypt:—Have you heard it?

    Anne. Come, you are pleasant.

    Old L.   With your theme, I could

O'ermount the lark. The marchioness of Pem-
broke!
A thousand pounds a year! for pure respect;
No other obligation: By my life,
That promises more thousands: Honour's train
Is longer than his foreskirt.   By this time,
I know, your back will bear a duchess:—Say,
Are you not stronger than you were?

Anne.   Good lady,
Make yourself mirth with your particular fancy,
And leave me out on 't.   'Would I had no being,
If this elate my blood a jot; it faints me,
To think what follows.
The queen is comfortless, and we forgetful
In our long absence: Pray, do not deliver
What here you have heard, to her.

Old L.   What do you think me?
                                   [*Exeunt.*

SCENE IV.—*A Hall in* Blackfriars.

*Trumpets, Sennet, and Cornets. Enter two
Vergers, with short Silver Wands; next them,
two Scribes, in the Habits of Doctors; after
them, the* ARCHBISHOP OF CANTERBURY *alone;
after him, the* BISHOPS OF LINCOLN, ELY, RO-
CHESTER, *and* SAINT ASAPH; *next them, with
some small distance, follows a Gentleman bearing the Purse, with the Great Seal, and a Cardinal's Hat; then two Priests, bearing each a
Silver Cross; then a Gentleman-Usher bare-
headed, accompanied with a Serjeant-at-Arms,
bearing a Silver Mace; then two Gentlemen,
bearing two great Silver Pillars;* [26] *after them,
side by side, the two Cardinals* WOLSEY *and*
CAMPEIUS; *two Noblemen, with the Sword
and Mace.   Then enter the* KING *and* QUEEN,
*and their Trains.   The King takes place under
the cloth of state; the two Cardinals sit under
him as judges.   The Queen takes place at some
distance from the King.   The Bishops place
themselves on each side the court, in manner of
a consistory; between them, the Scribes.   The
Lords sit next the Bishops.   The Crier and the
rest of the Attendants stand in convenient order
about the stage.*

Wol. Whilst our commission from Rome is read,
Let silence be commanded.

K. Hen.   What's the need?
It hath already publicly been read,
And on all sides the authority allow'd;
You may then spare that time.

Wol.   Be 't so:—Proceed.
Scribe. Say, Henry king of England, come into
the court.
Crier. Henry king of England, &c.
K. Hen. Here.
Scribe. Say, Katharine queen of England, come
into court.
Crier. Katharine, queen of England, &c.

[*The* QUEEN *makes no answer, rises out of
her chair, goes about the court,* [27] *comes
to the* KING, *and kneels at his feet; then
speaks.*]

Q. Kath. Sir, I desire you, do me right and
justice;
And to bestow your pity on me: for
I am a most poor woman, and a stranger,
Born out of your dominions; having here
No judge indifferent, nor no more assurance
Of equal friendship and proceeding.   Alas, sir,
In what have I offended you? what cause
Hath my behaviour given to your displeasure,
That thus you should proceed to put me off,
And take your good grace from me?   Heaven
witness,
I have been to you a true and humble wife,
At all times to your will conformable:
Ever in fear to kindle your dislike,
Yea, subject to your countenance; glad, or sorry
As I saw it inclin'd.   When was the hour,
I ever contradicted your desire,
Or made it not mine too?   Or which of your
friends
Have I not strove to love, although I knew
He were mine enemy? what friend of mine
That had to him deriv'd your anger, did I
Continue in my liking? nay, gave notice
He was from thence discharg'd?   Sir, call to mind
That I have been your wife, in this obedience,
Upward of twenty years, and have been blest
With many children by you: If, in the course
And process of this time, you can report,
And prove it too, against mine honour aught,
My bond to wedlock, or my love and duty,
Against your sacred person, in God's name,
Turn me away; and let the foul'st contempt
Shut door upon me, and so give me up
To the sharpest kind of justice.   Please you, sir
The king, your father, was reputed for
A prince most prudent, of an excellent
And unmatch'd wit and judgment: Ferdinand,
My father, king of Spain, was reckon'd one

The wisest prince, that there had reign'd by
    many
A year before: It is not to be question'd
That they had gather'd a wise council to them
Of every realm, that did debate this business,
Who deem'd our marriage lawful: Wherefore I
    humbly
Beseech you, sir, to spare me, till I may
Be by my friends in Spain advis'd; whose counsel
I will implore: if not, i' the name of God,
Your pleasure be fulfill'd!

    Wol.   You have here, lady,
(And of your choice,) these reverend fathers; men
Of singular integrity and learning,
Yea, the elect of the land, who are assembled
To plead your cause: It shall be therefore bootless,
That longer you desire the court; as well
For your own quiet, as to rectify
What is unsettled in the king.

    Cam.   His grace
Hath spoken well, and justly: Therefore, madam,
It's fit this royal session do proceed;
And that, without delay, their arguments
Be now produc'd, and heard.

    Q. Kath.   Lord cardinal,—
To you I speak.

    Wol.   Your pleasure, madam?

    Q. Kath.   Sir,
I am about to weep; but, thinking that
We are a queen, (or long have dream'd so,)
    certain,
The daughter of a king, my drops of tears
I'll turn to sparks of fire.

    Wol.   Be patient yet.

    Q. Kath. I will, when you are humble; nay,
    before,
Or God will punish me. I do believe,
Induc'd by potent circumstances, that
You are mine enemy; and make my challenge,
You shall not be my judge: for it is you
Have blown this coal betwixt my lord and me,—
Which God's dew quench!—Therefore, I say again,
I utterly abhor, yea, from my soul,
Refuse you for my judge; whom, yet once more,
I hold my most malicious foe, and think not
At all a friend to truth.

    Wol.   I do profess,
You speak not like yourself; who ever yet
Have stood to charity, and display'd the effects
Of disposition gentle, and of wisdom
O'ertopping woman's power. Madam, you do me
    wrong:

470

I have no spleen against you; nor injustice
For you, or any: how far I have proceeded,
Or how far further shall, is warranted
By a commission from the consistory,
Yea, the whole consistory of Rome. You charge
    me,
That I have blown this coal: I do deny it:
The king is present: if it be known to him,
That I gainsay my deed, how may he wound,
And worthily, my falsehood? yea, as much
As you have done my truth. But if he know
That I am free of your report, he knows,
I am not of your wrong. Therefore in him
It lies, to cure me: and the cure is, to
Remove these thoughts from you: The which
    before
His highness shall speak in, I do beseech
You, gracious madam, to unthink your speaking,
And to say no more.

    Q. Kath.   My lord, my lord,
I am a simple woman, much too weak
To oppose your cunning. You are meek, and
    humble-mouth'd;
You sign your place and calling, in full seeming,
With meekness and humility: but your heart
Is cramm'd with arrogancy, spleen, and pride.
You have, by fortune, and his highness' favours,
Gone slightly o'er low steps; and now are mounted
Where powers are your retainers: and your
    words,
Domestics to you, serve your will, as 't please
Yourself pronounce their office. I must tell you,
You tender more your person's honour, than
Your high profession spiritual: That again
I do refuse you for my judge; and here
Before you all, appeal unto the pope,
To bring my whole cause 'fore his holiness,
And to be judg'd by him.

    [*She curt'sies to the KING, and offers to depart.*
    Cam.   The queen is obstinate,
Stubborn to justice, apt to accuse it, and
Disdainful to be try'd by it; 't is not well.
She's going away.

    K. Hen. Call her again.

    Crier. Katharine, queen of England, come into
    the court.

    Grif. Madam, you are call'd back.

    Q. Kath. What need you note it? pray you,
    keep your way:
When you are call'd, return.—Now the Lord help,
They vex me past my patience!—pray you, pass
    on:

I will not tarry: no, nor ever more,
Upon this business, my appearance make
In any of their courts.
[*Exeunt* QUEEN, GRIF., *and her other Attendants.*
K. Hen. Go thy ways, Kate:
That man i' the world, who shall report he has
A better wife, let him in nought be trusted,
For speaking false in that; Thou art, alone,
(If thy rare qualities, sweet gentleness,
Thy meekness saint-like, wife-like government,—
Obeying in commanding,—and thy parts
Sovereign and pious else, could speak thee out,)
The queen of earthly queens:—She's noble born;
And, like her true nobility, she has
Carried herself towards me.
Wol. Most gracious sir,
In humblest manner I require your highness,
That it shall please you to declare, in hearing
Of all these ears, (for where I am robb'd and
bound,
There must I be unloos'd; although not there
At once and fully satisfied,) whether ever I
Did broach this business to your highness; or
Laid any scruple in your way, which might
Induce you to the question on 't? or ever
Have to you,—but with thanks to God for such
A royal lady,—spoke one the least word, might
Be to the prejudice of her present state,
Or touch her of good person?
K. Hen. My lord cardinal,
I do excuse you; yea, upon mine honour,
I free you from 't. You are not to be taught
That you have many enemies, that know not
Why they are so, but, like to village curs,
Bark when their fellows do: by some of these
The queen is put in anger. You are excus'd:
But will you be more justified? you ever
Have wish'd the sleeping of this business; never
Desir'd it to be stirr'd; but oft have hinder'd; oft
The passages made toward it:—on my honour,
I speak my good lord cardinal to this point,
And thus far clear him. Now, what moved me
to 't,—
I will be bold with time, and your attention:—
Then mark the inducement. Thus it came;—give
heed to 't:—
My conscience first receiv'd a tenderness,
Scruple, and prick, on certain speeches uter'd
By the bishop of Bayonne, then French ambassa-
dor;
Who had been hither sent on the debating
A marriage, 'twixt the duke of Orleans and

Our daughter Mary: I' the progress of this busi-
ness,
Ere a determinate resolution, he
(I mean, the bishop) did require a respite;
Wherein he might the king his lord advertise
Whether our daughter were legitimate,
Respecting this our marriage with the dowager,
Sometime our brother's wife. This respite shook
The bosom of my conscience, enter'd me,
Yea, with a splitting power, and made to tremble
The region of my breast; which forc'd such way
That many maz'd considerings did throng,
And press'd in with this caution. First, methought,
I stood not in the smile of heaven; who had
Commanded nature, that my lady's womb,
If it conceiv'd a male child by me, should
Do no more offices of life to 't, than
The grave does to the dead: for her male issue
Or died where they were made, or shortly after
This world had air'd them: Hence I took a thought,
This was a judgment on me; that my kingdom,
Well worthy the best heir o' the world, should
not
Be gladded in 't by me: Then follows, that
I weigh'd the danger which my realms stood in
By this my issue's fail; and that gave to me
Many a groaning throe. Thus hulling in
The wild sea of my conscience, I did steer
Toward this remedy, whereupon we are
Now present here together; that 's to say,
I meant to rectify my conscience,—which
I then did feel full sick, and yet not well,—
By all the reverend fathers of the land,
And doctors learn'd.—First, I began in private
With you, my lord of Lincoln; you remember
How under my oppression I did reek,
When I first mov'd you.
Lin. Very well, my liege.
K. Hen. I have spoke long; be pleas'd your
self to say,
How far you satisfied me.
Lin. So please your highness,
The question did at first so stagger me,—
Bearing a state of mighty moment in 't,
And consequence of dread—that I committed
The daring'st counsel which I had, to doubt;
And did entreat your highness to this course,
Which you are running here.
K. Hen. I then mov'd you,
My lord of Canterbury; and got your leave
To make this present summons:—Unsolicited
I left no reverend person in this court;

But by particular consent proceeded,
Under your hands and seals. Therefore, go on:
For no dislike i' the world against the person
Of the good queen, but the sharp thorny points
Of my alleged reasons, drive this forward:
Prove but our marriage lawful, by my life,
And kingly dignity, we are contented
To wear our mortal state to come, with her,
Katharine our queen, before the primest crea-
　　　ture
That's paragon'd o' the world.

　　Cam.　　　　　　So please your highness,

The queen being absent, 't is a needful fitness
That we adjourn this court till further day:
Meanwhile must be an earnest motion
Made to the queen, to call back her appeal
She intends unto his holiness. [*They rise to depart.*
　　K. Hen.　　　　I may perceive, [*Aside.*
These cardinals trifle with me: I abhor
This dilatory sloth, and tricks of Rome.
My learn'd and well-beloved servant, Cranmer,
Pr'ythee return! with thy approach, I know,
My comfort comes along. Break up the court,
I say, set on. [*Exeunt, in manner as they entered.*

ACT III.

SCENE I.—*Palace at* Bridewell. *A Room in the
Queen's Apartment.*

The QUEEN, *and some of her Women, at work.*

　Q. Kath. Take thy lute, wench: my soul grows
　　　sad with troubles;
Sing, and disperse them, if thou canst: leave
　　working.

SONG

　Orpheus with his lute made trees,
　And the mountain-tops, that freeze,
　　Bow themselves, when he did sing:
　To his music, plants, and flowers,
　Ever sprung; as sun, and showers,
　　There had been a lasting spring.

　Every thing that heard him play,
　Even the billows of the sea,
　　Hung their heads, and then lay by.
　In sweet music is such art,
　Killing care, and grief of heart,
　　Fall asleep, or, hearing, die.

Enter a Gentleman.

　Q. Kath. How now?
　Gent. An't please your grace, the two great
　　　cardinals
Wait in the presence.

　Q. Kath.　　　　Would they speak with me?
　Gent. They will'd me say so, madam.
　Q. Kath.　　　　　　Pray their graces
To come near. [*Exit Gent.*] What can be their
　　　business

With me, a poor weak woman, fallen from favour?
I do not like their coming, now I think on 't.
They should be good men; their affairs as right-
　　eous;
But all hoods make not monks.

Enter WOLSEY *and* CAMPEIUS.

　Wol.　　　　　Peace to your highness!
　Q. Kath. Your graces find me here part of a
　　　housewife;
I would be all, against the worst may happen.
What are your pleasures with me, reverend lords?
　Wol. May it please you, noble madam, to with-
　　　draw
Into your private chamber, we shall give you
The full cause of our coming.

　Q. Kath.　　　　　Speak it here;
There 's nothing I have done yet, o' my conscience,
Deserves a corner: 'Would, all other women
Could speak this with as free a soul as I do!
My lords, I care not, (so much I am happy
Above a number,) if my actions
Were tried by every tongue, every eye saw them,
Envy and base opinion set against them,
I know my life so even: If your business
Seek me out, and that way I am wife in,
Out with it boldly: Truth loves open dealing.
　*Wol. Tanta est erga te mentis integritas, regina
　　serenissima,—*
　Q. Kath. O, good my lord, no Latin;
I am not such a truant since my coming,
As not to know the language I have liv'd in.

A strange tongue makes my cause more strange,
    suspicious;
Pray, speak in English: here are some will thank
    you,
If you speak truth, for their poor mistress' sake;
Believe me, she has had much wrong: Lord car-
    dinal,
The willing'st sin I ever yet committed,
May be absolv'd in English.

Wol.   Noble lady,
I am sorry, my integrity should breed,
(And service to his majesty and you,)
So deep suspicion, where all faith was meant.
We come not by the way of accusation,
To taint that honour every good tongue blesses;
Nor to betray you any way to sorrow;
You have too much, good lady: but to know
How you stand minded in the weighty difference
Between the king and you; and to deliver,
Like free and honest men, our just opinions,
And comforts to your cause.

Cam.   Most honour'd madam,
My lord of York,—out of his noble nature,
Zeal and obedience he still bore your grace;
Forgetting, like a good man, your late censure
Both of his truth and him, (which was too far,)—
Offers, as I do, in a sign of peace,
His service and his counsel.

Q. Kath.   To betray me. [*Aside.*
My lords, I thank you both for your good wills,
Ye speak like honest men, (pray God, ye prove so?)
But how to make you suddenly an answer,
In such a point of weight, so near mine honour,
(More near my life, I fear,) with my weak wit,
And to such men of gravity and learning,
In truth, I know not. I was set at work
Among my maids; full little, God knows, looking
Either for such men, or such business.
For her sake that I have been, (for I feel
The last fit of my greatness,) good your graces,
Let me have time, and counsel, for my cause;
Alas! I am a woman, friendless, hopeless.

Wol. Madam, you wrong the king's love with
    these fears;
Your hopes and friends are infinite.

Q. Kath.   In England,
But little for my profit: Can you think, lords,
That any Englishman dare give me counsel?
Or be a known friend, 'gainst his highness'
    pleasure,
(Though he be grown so desperate to be honest,)
And live a subject? Nay, forsooth, my friends,

They that most weigh out my afflictions,
They that my trust must grow to, live not here;
They are, as all my other comforts, far hence,
In mine own country, lords.

Cam.   I would, your grace
Would leave your griefs, and take my counsel.

Q. Kath.   How, sir?

Cam. Put your main cause into the king's pro-
    tection;
He's loving, and most gracious; 't will be much
Both for your honour better, and your cause;
For, if the trial of the law o'ertake you,
You 'll part away disgrac'd.

Wol.   He tells you rightly.

Q. Kath. Ye tell me what ye wish for both, my
    ruin:
Is this your christian counsel? out upon ye!
Heaven is above all yet; there sits a Judge,
That no king can corrupt.

Cam.   Your rage mistakes us.

Q. Kath. The more shame for ye; holy men
    I thought ye,
Upon my soul, two reverend cardinal virtues;
But cardinal sins, and hollow hearts, I fear ye:
Mend them for shame, my lords. Is this your
    comfort?
The cordial that ye bring a wretched lady?
A woman lost among ye, laugh'd at, scorn'd?
I will not wish ye half my miseries,
I have more charity: But say, I warn'd ye;
Take heed, for heaven's sake, take heed, lest at
    once
The burden of my sorrows fall upon ye.

Wol. Madam, this is a mere distraction;
You turn the good we offer into envy.

Q. Kath. Ye turn me into nothing: Woe
    upon ye,
And all such false professors! Would ye have me
(If you have any justice, any pity;
If ye be any thing but churchmen's habits,)
Put my sick cause into his hands that hates me?
Alas! he has banish'd me his bed already;
His love, too long ago; I am old, my lords,
And all the fellowship I hold now with him
Is only my obedience. What can happen
To me, above this wretchedness? all your studies
Make me a curse like this.

Cam.   Your fears are worse.

Q. Kath. Have I liv'd thus long—(let me speak
    myself,
Since virtue finds no friends,)—a wife, a true one?
A woman (I dare say, without vain-glory,)

Never yet branded with suspicion?
Have I with all my full affections
Still met the king? lov'd him next heaven? obey'd
    him?
Been, out of fondness, superstitious to him?
Almost forgot my prayers to content him?
And am I thus rewarded? 't is not well, lords.
Bring me a constant woman to her husband,
One that ne'er dream'd a joy beyond his pleasure;
And to that woman, when she has done most,
Yet will I add an honour,—a great patience.

   Wol. Madam, you wander from the good we
     aim at.

   Q. Kath. My lord, I dare not make myself so
     guilty
To give up willingly that noble title
Your master wed me to: nothing but death
Shall e'er divorce my dignities.

   Wol.   'Pray, hear me.

   Q. Kath. 'Would I had never trod this English
     earth,
Or felt the flatteries that grow upon it!
Ye have angels' faces, but heaven knows your
    hearts.
What will become of me now, wretched lady?
I am the most unhappy woman living.—
Alas! poor wenches, where are now your for-
    tunes?   [*To her Women.*
Shipwreck'd upon a kingdom, where no pity,
No friends, no hope; no kindred weep for me,
Almost, no grave allow'd me:—Like the lily,
That once was mistress of the field, and flourish'd,
I 'll hang my head, and perish.

   Wol.   If your grace
Could but be brought to know, our ends are honest,
You 'd feel more comfort: why should we, good
    lady,
Upon what cause, wrong you? alas! our places,
The way of our profession is against it;
We are to cure such sorrows, not to sow them.
For goodness' sake, consider what you do;
How you may hurt yourself, ay, utterly
Grow from the king's acquaintance, by this carriage.
The hearts of princes kiss obedience,
So much they love it; but, to stubborn spirits,
They swell, and grow as terrible as storms.
I know, you have a gentle, noble temper,
A soul as even as a calm: I pray, think us
Those we profess, peace-makers, friends, and ser-
    vants.

   Cam. Madam, you 'll find it so. You wrong
     your virtues
     1676

With these weak women's fears. A noble spirit,
As yours was put into you, ever casts
Such doubts, as false coin, from it. The king
    loves you;
Beware, you lose it not: For us, if you please
To trust us in your business, we are ready
To use our utmost studies in your service.

   Q. Kath. Do what ye will, my lords: And,
     pray, forgive me,
If I have us'd myself unmannerly;
You know, I am a woman, lacking wit
To make a seemly answer to such persons.
Pray, do my service to his majesty:
He has my heart yet; and shall have my prayers,
While I shall have my life. Come, reverend
    fathers,
Bestow your counsels on me: she now begs,
That little thought, when she set footing here,
She should have bought her dignities so dear.
                       [*Exeunt.*

SCENE II.—*Ante-chamber to the King's Apartment.*

Enter the DUKE OF NORFOLK, *the* DUKE OF SUF-
FOLK, *the* EARL OF SURREY, *and the* LORD
CHAMBERLAIN.

   Nor. If you will now unite in your complaints
And force them with a constancy, the cardinal
Cannot stand under them: If you omit
The offer of this time, I cannot promise,
But that you shall sustain more new disgraces,
With these you bear already.

   Sur.   I am joyful
To meet the least occasion, that may give me
Remembrance of my father-in-law, the duke,
To be reveng'd on him.

   Suf.   Which of the peers
Have uncontemn'd gone by him, or at least
Strangely neglected? when did he regard
The stamp of nobleness in any person,
Out of himself?

   Cham.   My lords, you speak your pleasures:
What he deserves of you and me, I know;
What we can do to him, (though now the time
Gives way to us,) I much fear. If you cannot
Bar his access to the king, never attempt
Any thing on him; for he hath a witchcraft
Over the king in his tongue.

   Nor.   O, fear him not;
His spell in that is out: the king hath found
Matter against him, that for ever mars

The honey of his language. No, he's settled,
Not to come off, in his displeasure.
  Sur.   Sir,
I should be glad to hear such news as this
Once every hour.
  Nor.   Believe it, this is true
In the divorce, his contrary proceedings
Are all unfolded; wherein he appears,
As I could wish mine enemy.
  Sur.   How came
His practices to light?
  Suf.   Most strangely.
  Sur.   O, how, how?
  Suf. The cardinal's letter to the pope miscarried,
And came to the eye o' the king; wherein was read,
How that the cardinal did entreat his holiness
To stay the judgment o' the divorce: For if
It did take place, "I do," quoth he, "perceive,
My king is tangled in affection to
A creature of the queen's, lady Anne Bullen."
  Sur. Has the king this?
  Suf.   Believe it.
  Sur.   Will this work?
  Cham. The king in this perceives him, how he
                                          coasts,
And hedges, his own way. But in this point
All his tricks founder, and he brings his physic
After his patient's death; the king already
Hath married the fair lady.
  Sur.   'Would he had!
  Suf. May you be happy in your wish, my lord!
For, I profess, you have it.
  Sur.   Now may all joy
Trace the conjunction!
  Suf.   My amen to 't!
  Nor.   All men's.
  Suf. There's order given for her coronation:
Marry, this is yet but young, and may be left
To some ears unrecounted.—But, my lords,
She is a gallant creature, and complete
In mind and feature: I persuade me, from her
Will fall some blessing to this land, which shall
In it be memoriz'd.
  Sur.   But, will the king
Digest this letter of the cardinal's?
The Lord forbid!
  Nor.   Marry, amen!
  Suf.   No, no;
There be more wasps that buzz about his nose,
Will make this sting the sooner. Cardinal Campeius
Is stolen away to Rome; hath ta'en no leave;

Has left the cause o' the king unhandled; and
Is posted, as the agent of our cardinal,
To second all his plot. I do assure you
The king cry'd ha! at this.
  Cham.   Now, God increase him
And let him cry ha, louder!
  Nor.   But, my lord,
When returns Cranmer?
  Suf. He is return'd, in his opinions; which
Have satisfied the king for his divorce,
Together with all famous colleges
Almost in Christendom: shortly, I believe,
His second marriage shall be publish'd, and
Her coronation. Katharine no more
Shall be call'd, queen; but princess dowager,
And widow to prince Arthur.
  Nor.   This same Cranmer's
A worthy fellow, and hath ta'en much pain
In the king's business.
  Suf.   He has; and we shall see him
For it, an archbishop.
  Nor.   So I hear.
  Suf.   'T is so.
The cardinal—

        Enter WOLSEY *and* CROMWELL.

  Nor.   Observe, observe, he's moody.
  Wol. The packet, Cromwell, gave it you the
                                          king?
  Crom. To his own hand, in his bedchamber.
  Wol. Look'd he o' the inside of the paper?
  Crom.   Presently
He did unseal them: and the first he view'd,
He did it with a serious mind; a heed
Was in his countenance: You, he bade
Attend him here this morning.
  Wol.   Is he ready
To come abroad?
  Crom.   I think, by this he is.
  Wol. Leave me a while.—   [*Exit* CROM.
It shall be to the duchess of Alençon,
The French king's sister: he shall marry her.—
Anne Bullen? No; I'll no Anne Bullens for him:
There is more in it than fair visage.—Bullen!
No, we'll no Bullens.—Speedily I wish
To hear from Rome.—The marchioness of Pembroke!
  Nor. He's discontented.
  Suf.   May be, he hears the king
Does whet his anger to him.
  Sur.   Sharp enough,
Lord, for thy justice!

                                          1077

Wol. The late queen's gentlewoman; a knight's
                     daughter,
To be her mistress' mistress! the queen's queen!—
This candle burns not clear: 't is I must snuff it:
Then, out it goes.—What though I know her vir-
                     tuous,
And well-deserving? yet I know her for
A spleeny Lutheran; and not wholesome to
Our cause, that she should lie i' the bosom of
Our hard-rul'd king. Again, there is sprung up
An heretic, an arch one, Cranmer; one
Hath crawl'd into the favour of the king,
And is his oracle.

    Nor.   He is vex'd at something.

    Suf. I would, 't were something that would
            fret the string,
The master-cord of his heart!

    Enter the KING, *reading a Schedule;*[31] *and*
                 LOVELL.

    Suf.   The king, the king.

    K. Hen. What piles of wealth hath he accu-
            mulated
To his own portion! and what expense by the hour
Seems to flow from him! How, i' the name of
                 thrift,
Does he rake this together!—Now, my lords;
Saw you the cardinal?

    Nor.   My lord, we have
Stood here observing him: Some strange commo-
              tion
Is in his brain: he bites his lip, and starts;
Stops on a sudden, looks upon the ground,
Then, lays his finger on his temple; straight,
Springs out into fast gate; then, stops again,
Strikes his breast hard; and anon, he casts
His eye against the moon: in most strange postures
We have seen him set himself.

    K. Hen.   It may well be;
There is a mutiny in his mind. This morning
Papers of state he sent me to peruse,
As I requir'd: And, wot you, what I found
There; on my conscience, put unwittingly?
Forsooth, an inventory, thus importing,—
The several parcels of his plate, his treasure,
Rich stuffs, and ornaments of household; which
I find at such proud rate, that it out-speaks
Possession of a subject.

    Nor.   It's heaven's will;
Some spirit put this paper in the packet,
To bless your eye withal.

    K. Hen.   If we did think

His contemplation were above the earth,
And fix'd on spiritual object, he should still
Dwell in his musings: but, I am afraid,
His thinkings are below the moon, not worth
His serious considering.

    [*He takes his seat, and whispers* Lov., *who
             goes to* WOL.

    Wol.   Heaven forgive me!
Ever God bless your highness!

    K. Hen.   Good my lord,
You are full of heavenly stuff, and bear the in-
            ventory
Of your best graces in your mind; the which
You were now running o'er; you have scarce time
To steal from spiritual leisure a brief span,
To keep your earthly audit: Sure, in that
I deem you an ill husband; and am glad
To have you therein my companion.

    Wol.   Sir,
For holy offices I have a time; a time
To think upon the part of business, which
I bear i' the state; and nature does require
Her times of preservation, which, perforce,
I her frail son, amongst my brethren mortal,
Must give my tendance to.

    K. Hen.   You have said well.

    Wol. And ever may your highness yoke to-
            gether,
As I will lend you cause, my doing well
With my well saying!

    K. Hen.   'T is well said again;
And 't is a kind of good deed, to say well:
And yet words are no deeds. My father lov'd you:
He said, he did; and with his deed did crown
His word upon you. Since I had mine office,
I have kept you next my heart; have not alone
Employ'd you where high profits might come
            home,
But par'd my present havings, to bestow
My bounties upon you.

    Wol.   What should this mean!

    Sur. The Lord increase this business! [*Aside.*

    K. Hen.   Have I not made you
The prime man of the state? I pray you, tell me,
If what I now pronounce, you have found true:
And, if you may confess it, say withal,
If you are bound to us, or no. What say you?

    Wol. My sovereign, I confess, your royal graces
Shower'd on me daily, have been more than could
My studied purposes require; which went
Beyond all man's endeavours:—my endeavours
Have ever come too short of my desires,

Yet, fill'd with my abilities: Mine own ends
Have been mine so, that evermore they pointed
To the good of your most sacred person, and
The profit of the state. For your great graces
Heap'd upon me, poor undeserver, I
Can nothing render but allegiant thanks;
My prayers to heaven for you; my loyalty,
Which ever has, and ever shall be growing,
Till death, that winter, kill it.

K. Hen.   Fairly answer'd;
A loyal and obedient subject is
Therein illustrated: The honour of it
Does pay the act of it; as, i' the contrary,
The foulness is the punishment. I presume,
That, as my hand has open'd bounty to you,
My heart dropp'd love, my power rain'd honour
            more
On you, than any; so your hand, and heart,
Your brain, and every function of your power,
Should, notwithstanding that your bond of duty,
As 't were in love's particular, be more
To me, your friend, than any.

Wol.   I do profess,
That for your highness' good I ever labour'd
More than mine own; that am, have, and will be.
Though all the world should crack their duty to
            you,
And throw it from their soul; though perils did
Abound, as thick as thought could make them, and
Appear in forms more horrid; yet my duty,
As doth a rock against the chiding flood,
Should the approach of this wild river break,
And stand unshaken yours.

K. Hen.   'T is nobly spoken:
Take notice, lords, he has a loyal breast,
For you have seen him open 't.—Read o'er this:
            [*Giving him Papers.*
And, after, this: and then to breakfast, with
What appetite you have.
            [*Exit* KING, *frowning upon* WOLSEY: *the
            Nobles throng after him, smiling and
            whispering.*

Wol.   What should this mean?
What sudden anger 's this? how have I reap'd it?
He parted frowning from me, as if ruin
Leap'd from his eyes: So looks the chafed lion
Upon the daring huntsman that has gall'd him;
Then makes him nothing. I must read this paper;
I fear the story of his anger.—'T is so:
This paper has undone me:—'T is the account
Of all that world of wealth I have drawn together
For mine own ends; indeed, to gain the popedom,

And fee my friends in Rome. O negligence,
Fit for a fool to fall by! What cross devil
Made me put this main secret in the packet
I sent the king? Is there no way to cure this?
No new device to beat this from his brains?
I know, 't will stir him strongly: Yet I know
A way, if it take right, in spite of fortune
Will bring me off again. What 's this—"To the
            Pope?"
The letter, as I live, with all the business
I writ to his holiness. Nay then, farewell!
I have touch'd the highest point of all my great-
            ness;
And, from that full meridian of my glory,
I haste now to my setting: I shall fall
Like a bright exhalation in the evening,
And no man see me more.

Re-enter the DUKES OF NORFOLK *and* SUFFOLK,
the EARL OF SURREY, *and the* LORD CHAMBER-
LAIN.

Nor. Hear the king's pleasure, cardinal: who
            commands you
To render up the great seal presently
Into our hands; and to confine yourself
To Asher-house, my lord of Winchester's,
Till you hear further from his highness.

Wol.   Stay,
Where 's your commission, lords? words cannot
            carry
Authority so weighty.

Suf.   Who dare cross them?
Bearing the king's will from his mouth expressly?

Wol. Till I find more than will, or words, to
            do it,
(I mean, your malice,) know, officious lords,
I dare, and must deny it. Now I feel
Of what coarse metal ye are moulded,—envy.
How eagerly ye follow my disgraces,
As if it fed ye! and how sleek and wanton
Ye appear in every thing may bring my ruin!
Follow your envious courses, men of malice:
You have christian warrant for them, and, no
            doubt,
In time will find their fit rewards. That seal,
You ask with such a violence, the king,
(Mine, and your master,) with his own hand gave
            me:
Bade me enjoy it, with the place and honours,
During my life; and, to confirm his goodness,
Tied it by letters patents: Now, who 'll take it?

Sur. The king, that gave it.

1079

Wol.   It must be himself then.
Sur. Thou art a proud traitor, priest.
Wol.   Proud lord, thou liest;
Within these forty hours Surrey durst better
Have burnt that tongue, than said so.
     Sur.   Thy ambition,
Thou scarlet sin, robb'd this bewailing land
Of noble Buckingham, my father-in-law :
The heads of all thy brother cardinals,
(With thee, and all thy best parts bound together,)
Weigh'd not a hair of his. Plague of your policy !
You sent me deputy for Ireland;
Far from his succour, from the king, from all
That might have mercy on the fault thou gav'st
     him ;
Whilst your great goodness, out of holy pity,
Absolv'd him with an axe.
     Wol.   This, and all else
This talking lord can lay upon my credit,
I answer, is most false. The duke by law
Found his deserts : how innocent I was
From any private malice in his end,
His noble jury and foul cause can witness.
If I lov'd many words, lord, I should tell you,
You have as little honesty as honour ;
That I, in the way of loyalty and truth,
Toward the king, my ever royal master,
Dare mate a sounder man than Surrey can be,
And all that love his follies.
     Sur.   By my soul,
Your long coat, priest, protects you ; thou should'st
     feel
My sword i' the life-blood of thee else.—My lords,
Can ye endure to hear this arrogance ?
And from this fellow ? If we live thus tamely,
To be thus jaded by a piece of scarlet,
Farewell nobility ; let his grace go forward,
And dare us with his cap, like larks.
     Wol.   All goodness
Is poison to thy stomach.
     Sur.   Yes, that goodness
Of gleaning all the land's wealth into one,
Into your own hands, cardinal, by extortion ;
The goodness of your intercepted packets,
You writ to the pope, against the king : your
     goodness,
Since you provoke me, shall be most notorious.—
My lord of Norfolk,—as you are truly noble,
As you respect the common good, the state
Of our despis'd nobility, our issues,
Who, if he live, will scarce be gentlemen,—
Produce the grand sum of his sins, the articles
     1080

Collected from his life :—I 'll startle you
Worse than the sacring bell, when the brown
     wench"
Lay kissing in your arms, lord cardinal.
     Wol. How much, methinks, I could despise this
     man,
But that I am bound in charity against it !
     Nor. Those articles, my lord, are in the king's
     hand :
But, thus much, they are foul ones.
     Wol.   So much fairer,
And spotless, shall mine innocence arise,
When the king knows my truth.
     Sur.   This cannot save you :
I thank my memory, I yet remember
Some of these articles ; and out they shall.
Now, if you can blush, and cry guilty, cardinal,
You 'll show a little honesty.
     Wol.   Speak on, sir ;
I dare your worst objections : if I blush,
It is, to see a nobleman want manners.
     Sur. I 'd rather want those, than my head.
Have at you.
First, that, without the king's assent, or knowledge,
You wrought to be a legate ; by which power
You maim'd the jurisdiction of all bishops.
     Nor. Then, that in all you writ to Rome, or
     else
To foreign princes, *Ego et Rex meus*
Was still inscrib'd ; in which you brought the king
To be your servant.
     Suf.   Then, that, without the knowledge
Either of king or council, when you went
Ambassador to the emperor, you made bold
To carry into Flanders the great seal.
     Sur. Item, you sent a large commission
To Gregory de Cassalis, to conclude,
Without the king's will, or the state's allowance,
A league between his highness and Ferrara.
     Suf. That, out of mere ambition, you have
     caus'd
Your holy hat to be stamp'd on the king's coin.
     Sur. Then, that you have sent innumerable
     substance,
(By what means got, I leave to your own con-
     science,)
To furnish Rome, and to prepare the ways
You have for dignities : to the mere undoing
Of all the kingdom. Many more there are ;
Which, since they are of you, and odious,
I will not taint my mouth with.
     Cham.   O my lord,

Press not a falling man too far; 't is virtue:
His faults lie open to the laws; let them,
Not you, correct him. My heart weeps to see
　　him
So little of his great self.
　Sur.　　　　I forgive him.
　Suf. Lord cardinal, the king's further pleasure
　is,—
Because all those things, you have done of late
By your power legatine within this kingdom,
Fall into the compass of a *præmunire*,—
That therefore such a writ be sued against you;
To forfeit all your goods, lands, tenements,
Chattels, and whatsoever, and to be
Out of the king's protection:—This is my charge.
　Nor. And so we 'll leave you to your medita-
　　tions
How to live better. For your stubborn answer,
About the giving back the great seal to us,
The king shall know it, and, no doubt, shall thank
　　you.
So fare you well, my little good lord cardinal.
　　　　　　　　　[*Exeunt all but* Wol.
　Wol. So farewell to the little good you bear me.
Farewell, a long farewell, to all my greatness!
This is the state of man: To-day he puts forth
The tender leaves of hope, to-morrow blossoms,
And bears his blushing honours thick upon him:
The third day, comes a frost, a killing frost;
And,—when he thinks, good easy man, full surely
His greatness is a ripening,—nips his root,
And then he falls, as I do. I have ventur'd,
Like little wanton boys that swim on bladders,
This many summers in a sea of glory;
But far beyond my depth: my high-blown pride
At length broke under me; and now has left me,
Weary, and old with service, to the mercy
Of a rude stream, that must for ever hide me.
Vain pomp, and glory of this world, I hate ye;
I feel my heart new open'd: O, how wretched
Is that poor man, that hangs on princes' favours!
There is, betwixt that smile we would aspire to,
That sweet aspéct of princes, and their ruin,
More pangs and fears than wars or women have;
And when he falls, he falls like Lucifer,
Never to hope again.—

Enter Cromwell, *amazedly.*
　　　　　　　Why, how now, Cromwell?
　Crom. I have no power to speak, sir.
　Wol.　　　　　　　What, amaz'd
At my misfortunes? can thy spirit wonder,

A great man should decline? Nay, an you weep,
I am fallen indeed.
　Crom.　　　　How does your grace?
　Wol.　　　　　　　Why, well;
Never so truly happy, my good Cromwell.
I know myself now; and I feel within me
A peace above all earthly dignities,
A still and quiet conscience. The king has cur'd
　me,
I humbly thank his grace; and from these
　shoulders,
These ruin'd pillars, out of pity, taken
A load would sink a navy, too much honour:
O, 't is a burden, Cromwell, 't is a burden,
Too heavy for a man that hopes for heaven.
　Crom. I am glad, your grace has made that
　　right use of it.
　Wol. I hope, I have: I am able now, methinks,
(Out of a fortitude of soul I feel,)
To endure more miseries, and greater far,
Than my weak-hearted enemies dare offer.
What news abroad?
　Crom.　　　　The heaviest, and the worst,
Is your displeasure with the king.
　Wol.　　　　　　　God bless him!
　Crom. The next is, that sir Thomas More is
　　chosen
Lord chancellor in your place.
　Wol.　　　　That 's somewhat sudden:
But he 's a learned man. May he continue
Long in his highness' favour, and do justice
For truth's sake, and his conscience; that his
　　bones,
When he has run his course, and sleeps in bless-
　　ings,
May have a tomb of orphans' tears wept on 'em!
What more?
　Crom. That Cranmer is return'd with welcome,
Install'd lord archbishop of Canterbury.
　Wol. That 's news indeed.
　Crom.　　　Last, that the lady Anne,
Whom the king hath in secrecy long married,
This day was view'd in open, as his queen,
Going to chapel; and the voice is now
Only about her coronation.
　Wol. There was the weight that pull'd me
　　down. O Cromwell,
The king has gone beyond me, all my glories
In that one woman I have lost for ever:
No sun shall ever usher forth mine honours,
Or gild again the noble troops that waited
Upon my smiles. Go, get thee from me, Cromwell;

I am a poor fallen man, unworthy now
To be thy lord and master: Seek the king;
That sun I pray, may never set! I have told him
What, and how true thou art: he will advance
thee;
Some little memory of me will stir him,
(I know his noble nature,) not to let
Thy hopeful service perish too: Good Cromwell,
Neglect him not; make use now, and provide
For thine own future safety.
   Crom.   O my lord,
Must I then leave you? must I needs forego
So good, so noble, and so true a master?
Bear witness, all that have not hearts of iron,
With what a sorrow Cromwell leaves his lord.—
The king shall have my service; but my prayers,
For ever, and for ever, shall be yours.
   Wol. Cromwell, I did not think to shed a tear
In all my miseries; but thou hast forc'd me
Out of thy honest truth to play the woman.
Let's dry our eyes: and thus far hear me, Crom-
well;
And,—when I am forgotten, as I shall be;
And sleep in dull cold marble, where no mention
Of me more must be heard of,—say, I taught thee,
Say, Wolsey,—that once trod the ways of glory,
And sounded all the depths and shoals of honour,
Found thee a way, out of his wreck, to rise in;

A sure and safe one, though thy master miss'd it
Mark but my fall, and that that ruin'd me.
Cromwell, I charge thee, fling away ambition;
By that sin fell the angels; how can man then,
The image of his Maker, hope to win by 't?
Love thyself last: cherish those hearts that hate
thee;
Corruption wins not more than honesty.
Still in thy right hand carry gentle peace,
To silence envious tongues. Be just, and fear
not:
Let all the ends thou aim'st at be thy country's,
Thy God's, and truth's; then if thou fall'st, O
Cromwell,
Thou fall'st a blessed martyr. Serve the king,
And,—Pr'ythee, lead me in:
There take an inventory of all I have,
To the last penny; 't is the king's: my robe,
And my integrity to heaven, is all
I dare now call mine own. O Cromwell, Crom-
well,
Had I but serv'd my God with half the zeal
I serv'd my king, he would not in mine age
Have left me naked to mine enemies.
   Crom. Good sir, have patience.
   Wol.   So I have. Farewell
The hopes of court! my hopes in heaven do dwell.
       [*Exeunt.*

ACT IV.

SCENE I.—*A Street in* Westminster.

Enter Two Gentlemen, *meeting.*

   1st Gent. You are well met once again.
   2nd Gent.   And so are you.
   1st Gent. You come to take your stand here,
and behold
The lady Anne pass from her coronation?
   2nd Gent. 'T is all my business. At our last
encounter,
The duke of Buckingham came from his trial.
   1st Gent. 'T is very true: but that time offer'd
sorrow;
This, general joy.
   2nd Gent.   'T is well: The citizens,
1082

I am sure, have shown at full their royal minds;
As, let them have their rights, they are ever forward
In celebration of this day with shows,
Pageants, and sights of honour.
   1st Gent.   Never greater,
Nor, I 'll assure you, better taken, sir.
   2nd Gent. May I be bold to ask what that con-
tains,
That paper in your hand?
   1st Gent.   Yes; 't is the list
Of those, that claim their offices this day.
By custom of the coronation.
The duke of Suffolk is the first, and claims
To be high steward; next, the duke of Norfolk,
He to be earl marshal; you may read the rest.

2nd Gent. I thank you, sir; had I not known
    those customs,
I should have been beholden to your paper.
But, I beseech you, what 's become of Katharine,
The princess dowager? how goes her business?
    1st Gent. That I can tell you too. The arch-
      bishop
Of Canterbury, accompanied with other
Learned and reverend fathers of his order,
Held a late court at Dunstable, six miles off
From Ampthill, where the princess lay; to which
She oft was cited by them, but appear'd not:
And, to be short, for not appearance, and
The king's late scruple, by the main assent
Of all these learned men she was divorc'd,
And the late marriage made of none effect:
Since which, she was removed to Kimbolton,
Where she remains now, sick.
    2nd Gent.   Alas, good lady!—
                     [*Trumpets.*
The trumpets sound: stand close, the queen is
    coming

THE ORDER OF THE PROCESSION.

A lively flourish of Trumpets; then enter

1. Two Judges.
2. Lord Chancellor, with the purse and mace before him.
3. Choristers singing.   [*Music.*
4. Mayor of London bearing the mace. Then Garter, in his coat of arms, and on his head, a gilt copper crown.
5. Marquis Dorset, bearing a sceptre of gold, on his head a demi-coronal of gold. With him, the Earl of Surrey, bearing the rod of silver with the dove, crowned with an earl's coronet. Collars of SS.
6. Duke of Suffolk, in his robe of estate, his coronet on his head, bearing a long white wand, as high-steward. With him, the Duke of Norfolk, with the rod of marshalship, a coronet on his head. Collars of SS.
7. A canopy borne by four of the Cinque-ports; under it, the Queen in her robe; her hair richly adorned with pearl, crowned. On each side of her, the Bishops of London and Winchester.
8. The old Duchess of Norfolk, in a coronal of gold, wrought with flowers, bearing the Queen's train.
9. Certain Ladies or Countesses, with plain circlets of gold without flowers.

    2nd Gent. A royal train, believe me.—These I
know;—
Who 's that, that bears the sceptre?
    1st Gent.   Marquis Dorset:
And that the earl of Surrey, with the rod.
    2nd Gent. A bold brave gentleman: And that
should be
The duke of Suffolk.
    1st Gent.   'T is the same; high-steward.

    2nd Gent. And that my lord of Norfolk?
    1st Gent.   Yes.
    2nd Gent.   Heaven bless thee
                   [*Looking on the* QUEEN.
Thou hast the sweetest face I ever look'd on.—
Sir, as I have a soul, she is an angel;
Our king has all the Indies in his arms,
And more, and richer, when he strains that lady:
I cannot blame his conscience.
    1st Gent.   They, that bear
The cloth of honour over her, are four barons
Of the Cinque-ports.
    2nd Gent. Those men are happy; and so are
all, are near her.
I take it, she that carries up the train,
Is that old noble lady, duchess of Norfolk.
    1st Gent. It is; and all the rest are countesses.
    2nd Gent. Their coronets say so. These are
stars, indeed;
And, sometimes, falling ones.
    1st Gent.   No more of that.
         [*Exit Procession, with a great flourish of
               Trumpets.*

Enter a Third Gentleman.

God save you, sir! Where have you been broil-
    ing?
    3rd Gent. Among the crowd i' the abbey,
    where a finger
Could not be wedg'd in more; and I am stifled
With the mere rankness of their joy.
    2nd Gent.   You saw
The ceremony?
    3rd Gent.   That I did.
    1st Gent.   How was it?
    3rd Gent. Well worth the seeing.
    2nd Gent.   Good sir, speak it to us?
    3rd Gent. As well as I am able. The rich stream
Of lords, and ladies, having brought the queen
To a prepar'd place in the choir, fell off
A distance from her; while her grace sat down
To rest a while, some half an hour, or so,
In a rich chair of state, opposing freely
The beauty of her person to the people.
Believe me, sir, she is the goodliest woman
That ever lay by man: which when the people
Had the full view of, such a noise arose
As the shrouds make at sea in a stiff tempest,
As loud, and to as many tunes: hats, cloaks,
(Doublets, I think,) flew up; and had their faces
Been loose, this day they had been lost. Such joy
I never saw before. Great-bellied women,

That had not half a week to go, like rams
In the old time of war, would shake the press,
And make them reel before them. No man living
Could say, "This is my wife," there; all were
    woven
So strangely in one piece.
    2nd Gent.   But, 'pray, what follow'd?
    3rd Gent. At length her grace rose, and with
        modest paces
Came to the altar; where she kneel'd, and, saint-
    like,
Cast her fair eyes to heaven, and pray'd devoutly.
Then rose again, and bow'd her to the people:
When by the archbishop of Canterbury
She had all the royal makings of a queen;
As holy oil, Edward Confessor's crown,
The rod, and bird of peace, and all such emblems
Laid nobly on her: which perform'd, the choir
With all the choicest music of the kingdom,
Together sung *Te Deum*. So she parted,
And with the same full state pac'd back again
To York-place, where the feast is held.
    1st Gent.   Sir, you
Must no more call it York-place, that is past:
For, since the cardinal fell, that title 's lost;
'T is now the king's, and call'd—Whitehall.
    3rd Gent.   I know it;
But 't is so lately alter'd, that the old name
Is fresh about me.
    2nd Gent.   What two reverend bishops
Were those that went on each side of the queen?
    3rd Gent. Stokesly and Gardiner; the one, of
        Winchester,
(Newly prefer'd from the king's secretary,)
The other, London.
    2nd Gent.   He of Winchester
Is held no great good lover of the archbishop's,
The virtuous Cranmer.
    3rd Gent.   All the land knows that:
However, yet there 's no great breach; when it
    comes,
Cranmer will find a friend will not shrink from him.
    2nd Gent. Who may that be, I pray you?
    3rd Gent.   Thomas Cromwell;
A man in much esteem with the king, and truly
A worthy friend.—The king
Has made him master o' the jewel-house,
And one, already, of the privy-council.
    2nd Gent. He will deserve more.
    3rd Gent.   Yes, without all doubt.
Come, gentlemen, ye shall go my way, which
Is to the court, and there ye shall be my guests;

Something I can command. As I walk thither
I 'll tell ye more.
    Both.   You may command us, sir
                           [*Exeunt.*

SCENE II.—Kimbolton.

Enter KATHARINE, *Dowager, sick; led between* GRIFFITH *and* PATIENCE.

    Grif. How does your grace?
    Kath.   O, Griffith, sick to death:
My legs, like loaden branches, bow to the earth,
Willing to leave their burden: Reach a chair;—
So,—now, methinks, I feel a little ease.
Didst thou not tell me, Griffith, as thou led'st me,
That the great child of honour, cardinal Wolsey,
Was dead?
    Grif. Yes, madam: but, I think, your grace,
Out of the pain you suffer'd, gave no ear to 't.
    Kath. Pr'ythee, good Griffith, tell me how he
        died:
If well, he stepp'd before me, happily,
For my example.
    Grif.   Well, the voice goes, madam:
For after the stout earl Northumberland
Arrested him at York, and brought him forward
(As a man sorely tainted,) to his answer,
He fell sick suddenly, and grew so ill,
He could not sit his mule.
    Kath.   Alas, poor man.
    Grif. At last, with easy roads, he came to
    Leicester,
Lodg'd in the abbey; where the reverend abbot,
With all his convent, honourably receiv'd him;
To whom he gave these words,—" O father abbot,
An old man, broken with the storms of state,
Is come to lay his weary bones among ye;
Give him a little earth for charity!"
So went to bed: where eagerly his sickness
Pursu'd him still; and, three nights after this,
About the hour of eight, (which he himself
Foretold, should be his last,) full of repentance,
Continual meditations, tears, and sorrows,
He gave his honours to the world again,
His blessed part to heaven, and slept in peace.
    Kath. So may he rest; his faults lie gently on
    him!
Yet thus far, Griffith, give me leave to speak him,
And yet with charity,—He was a man
Of an unbounded stomach, ever ranking
Himself with princes; one, that by suggestion
Ty'd all the kingdom: simony was fair play

His own opinion was his law: I' the presence
He would say untruths; and be ever double,
Both in his words and meaning: He was never,
But where he meant to ruin, pitiful;
His promises were, as he then was, mighty;
But his performance, as he is now, nothing.
Of his own body he was ill, and gave
The clergy ill example.

   Grif.   Noble madam,
Men's evil manners live in brass; their virtues
We write in water. May it please your highness
To hear me speak his good now?

   Kath.   Yes, good Griffith;
I were malicious else.

   Grif.   This cardinal,
Though from an humble stock, undoubtedly
Was fashion'd to much honour from his cradle.
He was a scholar, and a ripe, and good one;
Exceeding wise, fair spoken, and persuading:
Lofty, and sour, to them that lov'd him not;
But, to those men that sought him, sweet as
   summer.
And though he were unsatisfied in getting,
(Which was a sin,) yet in bestowing, madam,
He was most princely: Ever witness for him
Those twins of learning, that he rais'd in you,
Ipswich and Oxford! one of which fell with him,
Unwilling to outlive the good that did it;
The other, though unfinish'd, yet so famous,
So excellent in art, and still so rising,
That Christendom shall ever speak his virtue.
His overthrow heap'd happiness upon him;
For then, and not till then, he felt himself,
And found the blessedness of being little:
And, to add greater honours to his age
Than man could give him, he died, fearing God.

   Kath. After my death I wish no other herald,
No other speaker of my living actions,
To keep mine honour from corruption,
But such an honest chronicler as Griffith.
Whom I most hated living, thou hast made me,
With thy religious truth, and modesty,
Now in his ashes honour: Peace be with him!—
Patience, be near me still; and set me lower:
I have not long to trouble thee.—Good Griffith,
Cause the musicians play me that sad note
I nam'd my knell, whilst I sit meditating
On that celestial harmony I go to.
                  [*Sad and solemn music.*

   Grif. She is asleep: Good wench, let 's sit
   down quiet,
For fear we wake her;—Softly, gentle Patience.

The Vision. Enter, solemnly tripping one after another, six Personages, clad in white robes, wearing on their heads garlands of bays, and golden vizards on their faces; branches of bays, or palm, in their hands. They first congee unto her, then dance; and, at certain changes, the first two hold a spare garland over her head; at which the other four make reverend court'sies; then the two that held the garland, deliver the same to the other next two, who observe the same order in their changes, and holding the garland over her head: which done, they deliver the same garland to the last two, who likewise observe the same order: at which, (as it were by inspiration,) she makes in her sleep signs of rejoicing, and holdeth up her hands to heaven: and so in their dancing they vanish, carrying the garland with them. The music continues.

   Kath. Spirits of peace, where are ye? Are ye
   all gone?
And leave me here in wretchedness behind ye?

   Grif. Madam, we are here.

   Kath.   It is not you I call for:
Saw ye none enter, since I slept?

   Grif.   None, madam.

   Kath. No? Saw you not, even now, a blessed
   troop
Invite me to a banquet; whose bright faces
Cast thousand beams upon me, like the sun?
They promis'd me eternal happiness;
And brought me garlands, Griffith, which I feel
I am not worthy yet to wear: I shall,
Assuredly.

   Grif. I am most joyful, madam, such good
   dreams
Possess your fancy.

   Kath.   Bid the music leave,
They are harsh and heavy to me. [*Music ceases.*

   Pat.   Do you note,
How much her grace is alter'd on the sudden?
How long her face is drawn? How pale she
   looks,
And of an earthly coldness? Mark her eyes!

   Grif. She is going, wench; pray, pray.

   Pat.   Heaven comfort her!

Enter a Messenger.

   Mess. An 't like your grace,—

   Kath.   You are a saucy fellow
Deserve we no more reverence?

   Grif.   You are to blame,

Knowing she will not lose her wonted greatness,
To use so rude behaviour: go to, kneel.

  Mess. I humbly do entreat your highness'
    pardon;
My haste made me unmannerly: There is staying
A gentleman, sent from the king, to see you.

  Kath. Admit him entrance, Griffith: But this
    fellow
Let me ne'er see again. [*Exeunt* GRIF. *and* MESS.

    Re-enter GRIFFITH, *with* CAPUCIUS.

              If my sight fail not,
You should be lord ambassador from the emperor,
My royal nephew, and your name Capucius.

  Cap. Madam, the same, your servant.

  Kath.   O my lord,
The times, and titles, now are alter'd strangely
With me, since first you knew me. But, I pray
    you,
What is your pleasure with me?

  Cap.   Noble lady,
First, mine own service to your grace; the next,
The king's request that I would visit you;
Who grieves much for your weakness, and by me
Sends you his princely commendations,
And heartily entreats you take good comfort.

  Kath. O my good lord, that comfort comes too
    late;
'T is like a pardon after execution:
That gentle physic, given in time, had cur'd me;
But now I am past all comforts here, but prayers.
How does his highness?

  Cap.   Madam, in good health.

  Kath. So may he ever do! and ever flourish,
When I shall dwell with worms, and my poor
    name
Banish'd the kingdom!—Patience, is that letter,
I caus'd you write, yet sent away?

  Pat.   No, madam. [*Giving it to* KATH.

  Kath. Sir, I most humbly pray you to deliver
This to my lord the king.

  Cap.   Most willing, madam.

  Kath. In which I have commended to his
    goodness
The model of our chaste loves, his young daugh-
    ter:—
The dews of heaven fall thick in blessings on her!—

1085

Beseeching him, to give her virtuous breeding;
(She is young, and of a noble modest nature;
I hope, she will deserve well;) and a little
To love her for her mother's sake, that lov'd him
Heaven knows how dearly. My next poor petition
Is, that his noble grace would have some pity
Upon my wretched women, that so long,
Have follow'd both my fortunes faithfully:
Of which there is not one, I dare avow,
(And now I should not lie,) but will deserve
For virtue, and true beauty of the soul,
For honesty, and decent carriage,
A right good husband, let him be a noble:
And, sure, those men are happy that shall have
    them.
The last is, for my men;—they are the poorest,
But poverty could never draw them from me;—
That they may have their wages duly paid them,
And something over to remember me by;
If heaven had pleased to have given me longer
    life,
And able means, we had not parted thus.
These are the whole contents:—And, good my
    lord,
By that you love the dearest in this world,
As you wish Christian peace to souls departed,
Stand these poor people's friend, and urge the
    king
To do me this last right.

  Cap.   By heaven, I will;
Or let me lose the fashion of a man!

  Kath. I thank you, honest lord. Remember me
In all humility unto his highness:
Say, his long trouble now is passing
Out of this world; tell him, in death I bless'd
    him,
For so I will.—Mine eyes grow dim.—Farewell,
My lord.—Griffith, farewell.—Nay, Patience,
You must not leave me yet. I must to bed;
Call in more women.—When I am dead, good
    wench,
Let me be us'd with honour; strew me over
With maiden flowers, that all the world may know
I was a chaste wife to my grave: embalm me,
Then lay me forth; although unqueen'd, yet like
A queen, and daughter to a king, inter me.
I can no more.—— [*Exeunt*, *leading* KATH.

ACT V.

SCENE I.—*A Gallery in the Palace.*

Enter GARDINER *Bishop of Winchester, a Page
with a Torch before him, met by* SIR THOMAS
LOVELL.

Gar. It 's one o'clock, boy, is 't not ?

Boy. It hath struck.

Gar. These should be hours for necessities,
Not for delights ; times to repair our nature
With comforting repose, and not for us
To waste these times.—Good hour of night, sir
     Thomas !
Whither so late ?

Lov.   Came you from the king. my lord ?

Gar. I did, sir Thomas ; and left him at
     primero
With the duke of Suffolk.

Lov.   I must to him too,
Before he go to bed. I 'll take my leave.

Gar. Not yet, sir Thomas Lovell. What 's the
     matter ?
It seems, you are in haste ; and if there be
No great offence belongs to 't, give your friend
Some touch of your late business : Affairs, that
     walk
(As, they say, spirits do,) at midnight, have
In them a wilder nature, than the business
That seeks despatch by day.

Lov.   My lord, I love you ;
And durst commend a secret to your ear
Much weightier than this work. The queen 's in
     labour,
They say, in great extremity ; and fear'd,
She 'll with the labour end.

Gar.   The fruit, she goes with,
I pray for heartily ; that it may find
Good time, and live : but for the stock, sir Thomas,
I wish it grubb'd up now.

Lov.   Methinks, I could
Cry the amen ; and yet my conscience says
She 's a good creature, and, sweet lady, does
Deserve our better wishes.

Gar.   But, sir, sir,—
Hear me, sir Thomas : You are a gentleman
Of mine own way ; I know you wise, religious ;

And, let me tell you, it will ne'er be well,—
'T will not, sir Thomas Lovell, take 't of me,
Till Cranmer, Cromwell, her two hands, and she
Sleep in their graves.

Lov.   Now, sir, you speak of two
The most remark'd i' the kingdom. As for Crom-
     well,—
Beside that of the jewel-house, he 's made master
O' the rolls, and the king's secretary ; further, sir,
Stands in the gap and trade of more preferments,
With which the time will load him : The arch-
     bishop
Is the king's hand, and tongue : And who dare
     speak
One syllable against him ?

Gar.   Yes, yes, sir Thomas,
There are that dare ; and I myself have ventur'd
To speak my mind of him : and, indeed, this day,
Sir, (I may tell it you,) I think, I have
Incens'd the lords o' the council, that he is
(For so I know he is, they know he is,)
A most arch heretic, a pestilence
That does infect the land : with which they moved,
Have broken with the king ; who hath so far
Given ear to our complaint, (of his great grace
And princely care ; foreseeing those fell mischiefs
Our reasons laid before him,) he hath commanded,
To-morrow morning to the council-board
He be convented. He 's a rank weed, sir Thomas,
And we must root him out. From your affairs
I hinder you too long : good night, sir Thomas.

Lov. Many good nights, my lord ; I rest your
     servant.   [*Exeunt* GAR. *and Page.*

As LOVELL *is going out, enter the* KING, *and the*
DUKE OF SUFFOLK.

K. Hen. Charles, I will play no more to-night ;
My mind 's not on 't, you are too hard for me.

Suf. Sir, I never did win of you before.

K. Hen. But little, Charles ;
Nor shall not, when my fancy 's on my play.—
Now, Lovell, from the queen what is the news ?

Lov. I could not personally deliver to her
What you commanded me, but by her woman
I sent your message ; who return'd her thanks

1987

In the greatest humbleness, and desir'd your highness
Most heartily to pray for her.

K. Hen.   What say'st thou? ha!
To pray for her? what, is she crying out?

Lov. So said her woman; and that her sufferance made
Almost each pang a death.

K. Hen.   Alas, good lady!

Suf. God safely quit her of her burden, and
With gentle travail, to the gladding of
Your highness with an heir!

K. Hen.   'T is midnight, Charles;
Pr'ythee, to bed; and in thy prayers remember
The estate of my poor queen. Leave me alone;
For I must think of that, which company
Will not be friendly to.

Suf.   I wish your highness
A quiet night, and my good mistress will
Remember in my prayers.

H. Hen.   Charles, good night.— [*Exit* Suf.

     Enter Sir Anthony Denny.

Well, sir, what follows?

Den. Sir, I have brought my lord the archbishop,
As you commanded me.

K. Hen.   Ha! Canterbury?

Den. Ay, my good lord.

K. Hen.   'T is true: Where is he, Denny?

Den. He attends your highness' pleasure.

K. Hen.   Bring him to us. [*Exit* Den.

Lov. This is about that which the bishop
spake;
I am happily come hither.   [*Aside.*

     Re-enter Denny, *with* Cranmer.

K. Hen.   Avoid the gallery.
          [Lov. *seems to stay.*
Ha!—I have said.—Be gone.
What!—   [*Exeunt* Lov. *and* Den.

Cran. I am fearful:—Wherefore frowns he
thus?
'T is his aspect of terror. All 's not well.

K. Hen. How now, my lord? You do desire
to know
Wherefore I sent for you.

Cran.   It is my duty,
To attend your highness' pleasure.

K. Hen.   'Pray you, arise,
My good and gracious lord of Canterbury.
Come, you and I must walk a turn together;
108*

I have news to tell you: Come, come, give me
your hand
Ah, my good lord, I grieve at what I speak,
And am right sorry to repeat what follows:
I have, and most unwillingly, of late
Heard many grievous, I do say, my lord,
Grievous complaints of you; which, being con-
sider'd,
Have mov'd us and our council, that you shall
This morning come before us; where, I know,
You cannot with such freedom purge yourself,
But that, till further trial, in those charges
Which will require your answer, you must take
Your patience to you, and be well contented
To make your house our Tower: You a brother
of us,
It fits we thus proceed, or else no witness
Would come against you.

Cran.   I humbly thank your highness;
And am right glad to catch this good occasion
Most throughly to be winnow'd, where my chaff
And corn shall fly asunder: for, I know,
There 's none stands under more calumnious
tongues,
Than I myself, poor man.

K. Hen.   Stand up, good Canterbury
Thy truth, and thy integrity, is rooted
In us, thy friend: Give me thy hand, stand up;
Pr'ythee, let 's walk. Now, by my holy-dame,
What manner of man are you? My lord, I look'd
You would have given me your petition, that
I should have ta'en some pains to bring together
Yourself and your accusers; and to have heard
you
Without indurance, further.

Cran.   Most dread liege,
The good I stand on is my truth, and honesty;
If they shall fail, I, with mine enemies,
Will triumph o'er my person; which I weigh not,
Being of those virtues vacant. I fear nothing
What can be said against me.

K. Hen.   Know you not how
Your state stands i' the world, with the whole
world?
Your enemies
Are many, and not small; their practices
Must bear the same proportion; and not ever
The justice and the truth o' the question carries
The due o' the verdict with it: At what ease
Might corrupt minds procure knaves as corrupt
To swear against you? such things have been done
You are potently oppos'd; and with a malice

Of as great size. Ween you of better luck,
I mean, in perjur'd witness, than your Master,
Whose minister you are, whiles here he liv'd
Upon this naughty earth? Go to, go to;
You take a precipice for no leap of danger,
And woo your own destruction.

   Cran.   God, and your majesty,
Protect mine innocence, or I fall into
The trap is laid for me!

   K. Hen.   Be of good cheer;
They shall no more prevail, than we give way to.
Keep comfort to you; and this morning see
You do appear before them; if they shall chance,
In charging you with matters, to commit you,
The best persuasions to the contrary
Fail not to use, and with what vehemency
The occasion shall instruct you: if entreaties
Will render you no remedy, this ring
Deliver them, and your appeal to us
There make before them.—Look, the good man
weeps!
He's honest, on mine honour. God's blest mother!
I swear, he is true-hearted; and a soul
None better in my kingdom.—Get you gone,
And do as I have bid you.—[*Exit* Cran.] He
has strangled
His language in his tears.

           Enter an old Lady.

   Gent. [*Within.*] Come back: What mean you?
   Lady. I'll not come back; the tidings that I
bring
Will make my boldness manners.—Now, good
angels
Fly o'er thy royal head, and shade thy person
Under their blessed wings!

   K. Hen.   Now, by thy looks
I guess thy message. Is the queen deliver'd?
Say, ay; and of a boy.

   Lady.   Ay, ay, my liege;
And of a lovely boy: The God of heaven
Both now and ever bless her!—'t is a girl,
Promises boys hereafter. Sir, your queen
Desires your visitation, and to be
Acquainted with this stranger; 't is as like you,
As cherry is to cherry.

   K. Hen.   Lovell,—

           Enter LOVELL.

   Lov.   Sir.
   K. Hen. Give her an hundred marks. I'll to
the queen.   [*Exit* King.

   Lady. An hundred marks! By this light, I'll
have more.
An ordinary groom is for such payment.
I will have more, or scold it out of him.
Said I for this, the girl is like to him?
I will have more, or else unsay 't; and now
While it is hot, I'll put it to the issue. [*Exeunt.*

SCENE II.—*Lobby before the Council-Chamber.*

Enter CRANMER; Servants, Door-Keeper, &c.,
attending.

   Cran. I hope, I am not too late; and yet the
gentleman,
That was sent to me from the council, pray'd me
To make great haste. All fast? what means
this?—Hoa!
Who waits there?—Sure, you know me?
   D. Keep.   Yes, my lord;
But yet I cannot help you.
   Cran.   Why?
   D. Keep. Your grace must wait, till you be
call'd for.

           Enter DOCTOR BUTTS.

   Cran.   So
   Butts. This is a piece of malice. I am glad,
I came this way so happily: The king
Shall understand it presently.   [*Exit* Butts.
   Cran. [*Aside.*]   'T is Butts,
The king's physician: As he pass'd along,
How earnestly he cast his eyes upon me!
Pray heaven, he found not my disgrace! For cer-
tain,
This is of purpose laid, by some that hate me,
(God turn their hearts! I never sought their mal-
ice,)
To quench mine honour: they would shame to
make me
Wait else at door; a fellow counsellor,
Among boys, grooms, and lacqueys. But their
pleasures
Must be fulfill'd, and I attend with patience.

Enter, at a window above, the KING *and* BUTTS.

   Butts. I'll show your grace the strangest
sight,—
   K. Hen.   What's that, Butts?
   Butts. I think, your highness saw this many a
day.
   K. Hen. Body o' me, where is it?
   Butts.   There, my lord:

The high promotion of his grace of Canterbury;
Who holds his state at door, 'mongst pursuivants,
Pages, and footboys.

K. Hen. Ha! 'T is he, indeed:
Is this the honour they do one another?
'T is well, there 's one above them yet. I had
thought,
They had parted so much honesty among them,
(At least, good manners,) as not thus to suffer
A man of his place, and so near our favour,
To dance attendance on their lordships' pleasures,
And at the door too, like a post with packets.
By holy Mary, Butts, there 's knavery:
Let them alone, and draw the curtain close;
We shall hear more anon.— [*Exeunt.*

THE COUNCIL-CHAMBER.

Enter the LORD CHANCELLOR, *the* DUKE OF SUF-
FOLK, EARL OF SURREY, LORD CHAMBERLAIN,
GARDINER, *and* CROMWELL. *The Chancellor
places himself at the upper end of the table, on
the left hand; a seat being left void above him,
as for the Archbishop of Canterbury. The rest
seat themselves in order on each side.* CROM-
WELL *at the lower end, as Secretary.*

Chan. Speak to the business, master secretary:
Why are we met in council?

Crom. Please your honours,
The chief cause concerns his grace of Canterbury.

Gar. Has he had knowledge of it?

Crom. Yes.

Nor. Who waits there?

D. Keep. Without, my noble lords?

Gar. Yes.

D. Keep. My lord archbishop:
And has done half an hour, to know your pleasures.

Chan. Let him come in.

D. Keep. Your grace may enter now.
[CRANMER *approaches the Council-table.*

Chan. My good lord archbishop, I am very
sorry
To sit here at this present, and behold
That chair stand empty: But we all are men,
In our natures frail; and capable
Of our flesh, few are angels:* out of which frailty,
And want of wisdom, you, that best should teach
us,
Have misdemean'd yourself, and not a little,
Toward the king first, then his laws, in filling
The whole realm, by your teaching, and your
chaplains,

1090

(For so we are inform'd,) with new opinions.
Divers, and dangerous; which are heresies,
And, not reform'd, may prove pernicious.

Gar. Which reformation must be sudden too,
My noble lords: for those, that tame wild horses,
Pace them not in their hands to make them gen
tle;
But stop their mouths with stubborn bits, and
spur them,
Till they obey the manage. If we suffer
(Out of our easiness, and childish pity
To one man's honour) this contagious sickness,
Farewell all physic: And what follows then?
Commotions, uproars, with a general taint
Of the whole state: as, of late days, our neigh
bours,
The upper Germany, can dearly witness,
Yet freshly pitied in our memories.

Cran. My good lords, hitherto, in all the pro
gress
Both of my life and office, I have labour'd,
And with no little study, that my teaching,
And the strong course of my authority,
Might go one way, and safely; and the end
Was ever, to do well: nor is there living
(I speak it with a single heart, my lords,)
A man, that more detests, more stirs against,
Both in his private conscience, and his place,
Defacers of a public peace, than I do.
'Pray heaven, the king may never find a heart
With less allegiance in it! Men, that make
Envy, and crooked malice, nourishment,
Dare bite the best. I do beseech your lordships,
That, in this case of justice, my accusers,
Be what they will, may stand forth face to face,
And freely urge against me.

Suf. Nay, my lord,
That cannot be; you are a counsellor,
And, by that virtue, no man dare accuse you.

Gar. My lord, because we have business of
more moment,
We will be short with you. 'T is his highness'
pleasure,
And our consent, for better trial of you.
From hence you be committed to the Tower;
Where, being but a private man again,
You shall know many dare accuse you boldly,
More than, I fear, you are provided for.

Cran. Ah, my good lord of Winchester, I thank
you,
You are always my good friend; if your will pass,
I shall both find your lordship judge and juror,

You are so merciful: I see your end,
'T is my undoing: Love, and meekness, lord,
Become a churchman better than ambition;
Win straying souls with modesty again,
Cast none away. That I shall clear myself,
Lay all the weight ye can upon my patience.
I make as little doubt, as you do conscience,
In doing daily wrongs. I could say more,
But reverence to your calling makes me modest.

Gar. My lord, my lord, you are a sectary,
That 's the plain truth; your painted gloss discovers,
To men that understand you, words, and weakness.

Crom. My lord of Winchester, you are a little,
By your good favour, too sharp; men so noble,
However faulty, yet should find respect
For what they have been: 't is a cruelty,
To load a falling man.

Gar.   Good master secretary,
I cry your honour mercy; you may, worst
Of all this table, say so.

Crom.   Why, my lord?

Gar. Do not I know you for a favourer
Of this new sect? ye are not sound.

Crom.   Not sound?

Gar. Not sound, I say.

Crom.   'Would you were half so honest!
Men's prayers then would seek you, not their fears.

Gar. I shall remember this bold language.

Crom.   Do.
Remember your bold life too.

Cham.   This is too much;
Forbear, for shame, my lords.

Gar.   I have done.

Crom.   And I.

Cham. Then thus for you, my lord,—It stands agreed,
I take it, by all voices, that forthwith
You be convey'd to the Tower a prisoner;
There to remain, till the king's further pleasure
Be known unto us: Are you all agreed, lords?

All. We are.

Cram.   Is there no other way of mercy,
But I must needs to the Tower, my lords?

Gar.   What other
Would you expect? You are strangely troublesome.
Let some o' the guard be ready there.

           Enter Guard.

Cran.   For me?
Must I go like a traitor thither?

Gar.   Receive him,
And see him safe i' the Tower.

Cran.   Stay, good my lords,
I have a little yet to say. Look there, my lords
By virtue of that ring, I take my cause
Out of the gripes of cruel men, and give it
To a most noble judge, the king my master.

Cham. This is the king's ring.

Sur.   'T is no counterfeit.

Suf. 'T is the right ring, by heaven: I told ye all,
When we first put this dangerous stone a rolling,
T would fall upon ourselves.

Nor.   Do you think, my lords,
The king will suffer but the little finger
Of this man to be vex'd?

Cham.   'T is now too certain.
How much more is his life in value with him?
'Would I were fairly out on 't.

Crom.   My mind gave me,
In seeking tales, and informations,
Against this man, (whose honesty the devil
And his disciples only envy at,)
Ye blew the fire that burns ye: Now have at ye.

     Enter KING, *frowning on them; takes his seat.*

Gar. Dread sovereign, how much are we bound
       to heaven,
In daily thanks, that gave us such a prince;
Not only good and wise, but most religious:
One that, in all obedience, makes the church
The chief aim of his honour; and, to strengthen
That holy duty, out of dear respect,
His royal self in judgment comes to hear
The cause betwixt her and this great offender.

K. Hen. You were ever good at sudden commendations,
Bishop of Winchester. But know, I come not
To hear such flattery now, and in my presence;
They are too thin and bare to hide offences.
To me you cannot reach, you play the spaniel,
And think with wagging of your tongue to win
       me:
But, whatsoe'er thou tak'st me for, I am sure,
Thou hast a cruel nature, and a bloody.—
Good man, [*To* Cran.] sit down. Now let me
see the proudest
He, that dares most, but wag his finger at thee:
By all that 's holy, he had better starve,
Than but once think this place becomes thee not.

Sur. May it please your grace,——

K. Hen.   No, sir, it does not please me

I had thought I had had men of some under-
    standing
And wisdom, of my council; but I find none.
Was it discretion, lords, to let this man,
This good man, (few of you deserve that title,)
This honest man, wait like a lousy footboy
At chamber door? and one as great as you are?
Why, what a shame was this! Did my com-
    mission
Bid ye so far forget yourselves? I gave ye
Power as he was a counsellor to try him,
Not as a groom: There's some of ye, I see,
More out of malice than integrity,
Would try him to the utmost, had ye mean;
Which ye shall never have, while I live.
    Chan.   Thus far,
My most dread sovereign, may it like your grace
To let my tongue excuse all. What was purpos'd
Concerning his imprisonment, was rather
(If there be faith in men,) meant for his trial,
And fair purgation to the world, than malice;
I am sure, in me.
    K. Hen.   Well, well, my lords, respect him;
Take him, and use him well, he's worthy of it.
I will say thus much for him, If a prince
May be beholden to a subject, I
Am, for his love and service, so to him.
Make me no more ado, but all embrace him;
Be friends, for shame, my lords.—My lord of Can-
    terbury,
I have a suit which you must not deny me:
That is, a fair young maid that yet wants baptism,
You must be godfather, and answer for her.
    Cran. The greatest monarch now alive may glory
In such an honour: How may I deserve it,
That am a poor and humble subject to you?
    K. Hen. Come, come, my lord, you'd spare
       your spoons? you shall have
Two noble partners with you; the old duchess of
    Norfolk,
And lady marquis Dorset: Will these please you?
Once more, my lord of Winchester, I charge you,
Embrace, and love this man.
    Gar.   With a true heart,
And brother-love, I do it.
    Cran.   And let heaven
Witness, how dear I hold this confirmation.
    K. Hen. Good man, those joyful tears show thy
    true heart.
The common voice, I see, is verified
Of thee, which says thus, "Do my lord of Can-
    terbury
100?

A shrewd turn, and he is your friend for ever."—
Come, lords, we trifle time away; I long
To have this young one made a christian.
As I have made ye one, lords, one remain;
So I grow stronger, you more honour gain.
                    [*Exeunt*

SCENE III.—*The Palace Yard.*

Noise and Tumult within.   Enter Porter *and his
Man.*

    Port. You'll leave your noise anon, ye rascals:
Do you take the court for Paris-garden? ye rude
slaves, leave your gaping.
    [*Within.*] Good master porter, I belong to the
larder.
    Port. Belong to the gallows, and be hanged,
you rogue: Is this a place to roar in?—Fetch me
a dozen crab-tree slaves, and strong ones; these
are but switches to them.—I'll scratch your
heads: You must be seeing christenings? Do
you look for ale and cakes here, you rude rascals?
    Man. Pray, sir, be patient; 'tis as much im-
possible
(Unless we sweep them from the door with cannons,)
To scatter them, as 'tis to make them sleep
On May-day morning; which will never be:
We may as well push against Paul's, as stir them.
    Port. How got they in, and be hang'd?
    Man. Alas, I know not: How gets the tide
in?
As much as one sound cudgel of four foot
(You see the poor remainder) could distribute,
I made no spare, sir.
    Port.   You did nothing, sir.
    Man. I am not Sampson, nor sir Guy, nor Col-
brand, to mow them down before me: but, if I
spared any, that had a head to hit, either young
or old, he or she, cuckold or cuckold-maker, let me
never hope to see a queen again; and that I would
not for a crown, God save her.
    [*Within.*] Do you hear, master Porter?
    Port. I shall be with you presently, good mas-
ter puppy.—Keep the door close, sirrah.
    Man. What would you have me do?
    Port. What should you do, but knock them
down by the dozens? Is this Moorfields to muster
in? or have we some strange Indian with the
great tool come to court, the women so besiege
us? Bless me, what a fry of fornication is at
door! On my christian conscience, this one chris-

tening will beget a thousand; here will be father,
godfather, and all together.

Man. The spoons will be the bigger, sir. There
is a fellow somewhat near the door, he should be
a brazier by his face, for, o' my conscience, twenty
of the dog-days now reign in 's nose; all that
stand about him are under the line, they need no
other penance: That fire-drake" did I hit three
times on the head, and three times was his nose
discharged against me; he stands there, like a
mortar piece, to blow us. There was a haber-
dasher's wife of small wit near him, that railed
upon me till her pink'd porringer fell off her head,
for kindling such a combustion in the state. I
miss'd the meteor once, and bit that woman, who
cried out, "clubs!" when I might see from far
some forty truncheoneers draw to her succour,
which were the hope of the Strand, where she was
quartered. They fell on; I made good my place;
at length they came to the broomstaff with me, I
defied them still; when suddenly a file of boys
behind them, loose shot, delivered such a shower
of pebbles, that I was fain to draw mine honour
in, and let them win the work: The devil was
amongst them, I think, surely.

Port. These are the youths that thunder at a
play-house, and fight for bitten apples; that no
audience, but the Tribulation of Tower-hill, or the
limbs of Limehouse, their dear brothers, are able
to endure. I have some of them in *Limbo Patrum*,
and there they are like to dance these three days;
besides the running banquet of two beadles, that
is to come.

Enter the LORD CHAMBERLAIN.

Cham. Mercy o' me, what a multitude are here!
They grow still to, from all parts they are coming,
As if we kept a fair here! Where are these
porters,
These lazy knaves?—Ye have made a fine hand,
fellows.
There 's a trim rabble let in: Are all these
Your faithful friends o' the suburbs? We shall
have
Great store of room, no doubt, left for the ladies,
When they pass back from the christening.

Port. An 't please your honour
We are but men; and what so many may do,
Not being torn a pieces, we have done:
An army cannot rule them.

Cham. As I live,
If the king blame me for 't, I 'll lay ye all

By the heels, and suddenly; and on your heads
Clap round fines, for neglect: You are lazy
knaves:
And here ye lie baiting of bombards, when
Ye should do service. Hark, the trumpets sound
They 're come already from the christening:
Go, break among the press, and find a way out
To let the troop pass fairly; or I 'll find
A Marshalsea, shall hold you play these two
months.

Port. Make way there for the princess.

Man. You great fellow, stand close up, or I 'll
make your head ache.

Port. You i' the camblet, get up o' the rail; I 'll
pick you o'er the pales else.   [*Exeunt*

SCENE IV.—*The Palace.*

Enter Trumpets, sounding; then two Aldermen,
LORD MAYOR, GARTER, CRANMER, DUKE OF NOR-
FOLK, *with his Marshal's Staff,* DUKE OF SUF-
FOLK, *two Noblemen bearing great standing-
bowls for the christening gifts; then four
Noblemen bearing a canopy, under which the*
DUCHESS OF NORFOLK, *Godmother, bearing the
Child richly habited in a mantle, &c. Train
borne by a Lady; then follow the* MARCHIONESS
OF DORSET, *the other Godmother, and Ladies.
The Troop pass once about the stage, and
Garter speaks.*

Gart. Heaven, from thy endless goodness, send
prosperous life, long, and ever happy, to the high
and mighty princess of England, Elizabeth!

Flourish.—Enter KING, *and Train.*

Cran. [*Kneeling.*] And to your royal grace,
and the good queen,
My noble partners, and myself, thus pray:—
All comfort, joy, in this most gracious lady,
Heaven ever laid up to make parents happy,
May hourly fall upon ye!

K. Hen. Thank you, good lord archbishop;
What is her name?

Cran. Elizabeth.

K. Hen. Stand up, lord.—
         [*The* KING *kisses the Child.*
With this kiss take my blessing: God protect
thee!
Into whose hands I give thy life.

Cran. Amen.

K. Hen. My noble gossips, ye have been too
prodigal

I thank ye heartily; so shall this lady,
When she has so much English.
    Cran.   Let me speak, sir,
For heaven now bids me; and the words I utter
Let none think flattery, for they 'll find them
    truth.
This royal infant, (heaven still move about her!)
Though in her cradle, yet now promises
Upon this land a thousand thousand blessings,
Which time shall bring to ripeness: She shall be
(But few now living can behold that goodness,)
A pattern to all princes living with her,
And all that shall succeed: Sheba was never
More covetous of wisdom, and fair virtue,
Than this pure soul shall be: all princely graces,
That mould up such a mighty piece as this is,
With all the virtues that attend the good,
Shall still be doubled on her: truth shall nurse her,
Holy and heavenly thoughts still counsel her:
She shall be lov'd, and fear'd: Her own shall
    bless her;
Her foes shake like a field of beaten corn,
And hang their heads with sorrow: Good grows
    with her:
In her days, every man shall eat in safety
Under his own vine, what he plants; and sing
The merry songs of peace to all his neighbours:
God shall be truly known; and those about her
From her shall read the perfect ways of honour,
And by those claim their greatness, not by blood.
Nor shall this peace sleep with her: But as when
The bird of wonder dies, the maiden phœnix,
Her ashes new create another heir,
As great in admiration as herself;
So shall she leave her blessedness to one,
(When heaven shall call her from this cloud of
    darkness,)

Who, from the sacred ashes of her honour,
Shall star-like rise, as great in fame as she was,
And so stand fix'd: Peace, plenty, love, truth
    terror,
That were the servants to this chosen infant,
Shall then be his, and like a vine grow to him;
Wherever the bright sun of heaven shall shine,
His honour and the greatness of his name
Shall be, and make new nations: He shall flourish,
And, like a mountain cedar, reach his branches
To all the plains about him:—Our children's
    children
Shall see this, and bless heaven.
    K. Hen.   Thou speakest wonders.
    Cran. She shall be, to the happiness of England,
An aged princess; many days shall see her,
And yet no day without a deed to crown it.
'Would I had known no more! but she must die,
(She must, the saints must have her;) yet a virgin,
A most unspotted lily shall she pass
To the ground, and all the world shall mourn her
    K. Hen. O lord archbishop,
Thou hast made me now a man; never, before
This happy child, did I get any thing:
This oracle of comfort has so pleas'd me,
That, when I am in heaven, I shall desire
To see what this child does, and praise my
    Maker.—
I thank ye all,—To you, my good lord mayor,
And your good brethren, I am much beholden;
I have receiv'd much honour by your presence,
And ye shall find me thankful. Lead the way,
    lords;—
Ye must all see the queen, and she must thank ye,
She will be sick else. This day, no man think
He has business at his house; for all shall stay,
This little one shall make it holiday. [*Exeunt*

EPILOGUE.

'T is ten to one, this play can never please
All that are here: Some come to take their ease,
And sleep an act or two; but those, we fear,
We have frighted with our trumpets; so, 't is clear,
They 'll say, 't is naught: others, to hear the city
Abus'd extremely, and to cry,—' that 's witty!"
Which we have not done neither that, I fear
1054

All the expected good we are like to hear
For this play at this time, is only in
The merciful construction of good women;
For such a one we show'd 'em: If they smile,
And say, 't will do, I know, within a while
All the best men are ours; for 't is ill hap,
If they hold, when their ladies bid them clap.

NOTES TO KING HENRY THE EIGHTH.

¹ In a long motley coat, guarded with yellow.

An allusion to the fools or buffoons who played so great
part in the Interludes which held possession of the stage
before Shakespeare's time, and whom he has so frequently
introduced into his own works.

² And if you can be merry then, I'll say,
A man may weep upon his wedding day.

Dr. Johnson says—" Though it is very difficult to decide
whether short pieces be genuine or spurious, yet I cannot
restrain myself from expressing my suspicion that neither
the Prologus nor Epilogue to this play is the work of Shakespeare; non color, non color. It appears to me very likely
that they were supplied by the friendship or officiousness
of Jonson, whose manner they will be perhaps found exactly to resemble. There is yet another supposition possible: the Prologue and Epilogue may have been written after
Shakespeare's departure from the stage, upon some accidental revival of the play, and there will then be reason for
imagining that the writer, whoever he was, intended no
great kindness to him, this play being recommended by a
subtle and covert censure of his other works. There is, in
Shakespeare, so much of *fool and fight*——

——The fellow
In a long motley coat, guarded with yellow—

appears so often in his drama, that I think it is not very
likely that he would have animadverted so severely on
himself. All this, however, is very dubious, since we know
not the exact date of this or the other plays, and cannot tell
how our author might have changed his practice or opinions." Of the correctness of this conjecture of Dr. Johnson, no one acquainted with the dramas of the famous Ben
can entertain any doubt ; the Prologue and Epilogue unquestionably proceeded from his pen. Malone, Farmer,
and Steevens also coincide in this opinion. The latter
says—"I think I now and then perceive his hand (Jonson's) in the dialogue."

Till this time, pomp was single ; but now married to one
above itself.

Before this time all pompous shows were exhibited by
one prince only, but on this occasion the monarchs of
England and France vied with each other. Norfolk is
describing the meeting of Henry the Eighth and Francis

the First in a plain between Guisnes and Ardres, which
plain was afterwards called "the Field of the Cloth of
Gold."

⁴ All clinquant, i. e., glittering, shining.

⁵ That Bevis was believ'd.

That is, the old romance of Bevis was no longer held
to be incredible, because men had seen such wonders done
in their own days. This Bevis (or Beavois) was a Saxon
knight, who, for his heroism, was, by William the Conqueror, created Earl of Southampton.

⁶ One, certes, that promises no element.

That is, no initiation ; one that had not been practised
in the conducting of pageantries.

⁷ Must fetch him in he papers.

He papers, i. e., he sets down on paper. The meaning
is, that those persons whom Wolsey, even without the
concurrence of the council, nominated to any duty, were
compelled to perform it.

⁸ After the hideous storm that follow'd.

Holinshed mentions a "hideous storme" of wind and
rain which followed the meeting of Henry and Francis,
and induced many men to believe that it prognosticated
trouble and hatred between those princes.

⁹ ——A beggar's book
Outworths a noble's blood.

A contemptuous allusion to Wolsey's learning, which
Buckingham considered was more regarded than his own
hereditary rank.

¹⁰ The part my father meant to act upon
The usurper Richard.

That is, Richard the Third. Buckingham, the lord of
that tyrant, on being led to execution, begged to see his
sovereign, as it was supposed, to move his compassion to
entreaties, but as we here learn to be revenged by some
trusting him.

11 *A fit or two of the face.*

A fit of the face seems to be what we now call a *grimace*, an artificial cast of the countenance.

12 *A springhalt reign'd among them.*

The *springhalt*, or, properly, *stringhalt*, is a disease incident to horses, which gives them a convulsive motion in their paces.

13 *Of fool and feather.*

This alludes to an effeminate fashion of the young courtiers, that of carrying fans of feathers in their hands. It is spoken of in Greene's *Farewell to Folly*, 1617—"we strive to be counted womanish, by keeping of beauty, by curling the hair, *by wearing plumes of feathers in our hands*, which in wars, our ancestors wore on their heads."

14 *As fights, and fireworks.*

Some very extraordinary fireworks were let off on the last evening of the interview of Henry and Francis at the Field of the Cloth of Gold. The young nobility who appear to have been vain of imitating all the pageantry of that occasion, might have there acquired their fondness for the pyrotechnic art.

15 *Short blister'd breeches.*

Breeches puffed or swelled out like blisters.

16 *Chambers discharged.*

Chambers are guns which stand erect upon their breech; these are called chambers because they are merely cavities to lodge powder in, and are not used for offensive purposes, but merely on holiday occasions. To this they are well suited, as they make a report more than proportioned to their size.

17 *You have found him, Cardinal.*

Holinshed says the cardinal mistook, and pitched upon Sir Edward Neville; upon which the king laughed, and pulled off both his own mask and Sir Edward's.

18 *I were unmannerly, to take you out,*
And not to kiss you.

At this period, and for some time after, to kiss a lady was an act of courtesy, not of familiarity; in dancing it was the customary fee of a lady's partner. So, in *A Dialogue between Custom and Veritie, concerning the use and abuse of Dauncing and Minstrelsie*—

But some reply, what foole would daunce,
If that when daunce is doon,
He may not have at ladyes lips
That which in daunce he woon.

19 *I fear with dancing is a little heated.*

In Cavendish's *Life of Wolsey* we are told that the king, on being discovered and desired by Wolsey to take his place, said he would "first go and shift him; and thereupon, went into the cardinal's bed-chamber, where was a great fire prepared for him, and there he new apparreled himselfe with rich and princely garments. And in the king's absence the dishes of the banquet were cleane taken away, and the tables covered with new and perfumed clothes. Then the king took his seat under the clouth of estate, com-

manding every person to sit still as before; and then came in a new banquet before his majestie of two hundred dishes, and so they passed the night in banqueting and dancing until morning."

20 *Now, poor Edward Bohun.*

The Duke of Buckingham's name was Stafford. Shakespeare was led into the mistake by Holinshed.

21 *From princes into pages.*

Alluding to the retinue of the Cardinal, who had several of the nobility among his personal attendants.

22 —— *My good lord, have great care*
I be not found a talker.

That is, see that my welcome of this prelate be not found to be mere words; do not let my profession of hospitality prove mere talk.

23 *Of your soft cheveril conscience.*

That is, flexible conscience; cheveril is soft kid leather.

24 —— *In faith, for little England,*
You'd venture an embolling.

This is a difficult expression; Dr. Johnson interprets it thus:—"You would venture to be distinguished by the *ball*, the ensign of royalty." Malone reads, *empalling*, i. e., being invested with the *pall* or robes of state; and Whalley asks, might we not read—an embalming, i. e., an anointing with the balm or oil of consecration.

25 *Is it bitter? forty pence, no.*

Forty pence is half a noble, or the sixth part of a pound; it was the proverbial expression of a small wager or a small sum.

26 *Bearing two great silver pillars.*

Two pillars or crosses of silver were usually borne before the Cardinal; the one denoted his being legate, the other was carried before him as cardinal or archbishop.

27 *Goes about the court.*

"Because (says Cavendish) she could not come to the king directlie, for the distance between severed them."

28 *My learn'd and well-beloved servant, Cranmer,*
Pr'ythee return.

This is an apostrophe to the absent bishop. Cranmer was then abroad, collecting the opinions of the various colleges on the subject of the king's divorce. This would not have been worth noticing, had not some editors been led into the supposition that the lines were addressed to Cranmer, and inserted a marginal direction to that effect.

29 *Wait in the presence,* i. e., in the presence-chamber.

30 *And that way I am wif'. in.*

That is, if you come to examine the title by which I am the king's wife; or, if you wish to know how I have behaved as a wife. Some editors read *wise* for *wife*, i. e., if your business relates to me, or to any thing of which I have any knowledge.

¹¹ *Enter the King, reading a schedule.*

That the Cardinal gave the King an inventory of his own private wealth, by mistake, and thereby ruined himself, is a known variation from the truth of history. Wolsey's fall was brought about by several circumstances, but chiefly by the part which he was compelled to take in delaying the King's divorce from Katharine, and by the dislike entertained towards him by Anne Boleyn.

¹² *To Asher-house, my Lord of Winchester's.*

Fox, Bishop of Winchester, died September 14, 1528, and Wolsey held this see *in commendam.* Esher, therefore, was his own house.

¹³ —— *I'll startle you*
Worse than the sacring bell, when the brown wench, &c.

The *sacring* or *consecration* bell, is the bell which is rung to give notice of the approach of the Host when it is carried in procession. The Cardinal's amorous propensities are alluded to in some satires of the period.

¹⁴ —— *One, that by suggestion*
Ty'd all the kingdom.

By *suggestions* to the King and Pope, Wolsey *ty'd*, that is, limited, circumscribed, and set bounds to the liberties and properties of all persons in the kingdom.

¹⁵ *Enter, at a window above.*

"The suspicious vigilance (says Steevens) of our ancestors contrived windows which overlooked the insides of chapels, halls, kitchens, passages, &c. Some of these convenient peep-holes may still be found in colleges, and such ancient houses as have not suffered from the reformations of modern architecture. Without a previous knowledge of this custom, Shakespeare's scenery, in the present instance, would be obscure."

¹⁶ —— *But we all are men,*
In our own natures frail, and capable
Of our flesh, few are angels.

There is evidently some corruption in this sentence, for as it stands it has no meaning. Mr. Malone's emendation appears the most reasonable. He reads—

In our own natures frail, incapable
Of our flesh, few are angels, &c.

Mr. M. Mason reads—

In our own natures frail and *culpable*, &c.

¹⁷ *You'd spare your spoons.*

It was the custom for the sponsors at christenings to offer gilt spoons as a present to the child. These spoons were called *apostle spoons*, because the figures of the apostles were carved on the tops of the handles.

¹⁸ *Paris-garden.*

A celebrated bear-garden on the Bankside, so called from Robert de Paris, who had a house and garden there in the time of Richard the Second.

¹⁹ *That fire-drake.*

That is, that *Will o' the Wisp*, or *ignis fatuus*, in allusion to his flaming nose.

www.ingramcontent.com/pod-product-compliance
Lightning Source LLC
Chambersburg PA
CBHW031347290326
41932CB00044B/355